Commercial Law

2001

GOLD BOOK

BENDER PAMPHLET EDITION

New York
Uniform Commercial Code
With New York Annotations
and Official Uniform Comments
General Obligations Law

As amended by the 2000 Regular Legislative Session through June 23, 2000.

LOCATIONS FOR LOCAL FILINGS
INTEGRATED INDEX

For forms and further discussion, see:

BENDER'S FORMS FOR THE CONSOLIDATED LAWS
BENDER'S UNIFORM COMMERCIAL CODE SERVICE

LEXIS Publishing™

LEXIS®-NEXIS® • MARTINDALE-HUBBELL®
MATTHEW BENDER® • MICHIE™ • SHEPARD'S®

QUESTIONS ABOUT THIS PUBLICATION?

For questions about the **Editorial Content** appearing in these volumes or reprint permission, please call:

Mia Smith, J.D., at .... 1-800-252-9257 Ext. 2268
Deirdre E. Schmidel, at .... 1-800-252-9257 Ext. 2265

Outside the United States and Canada please call .... (212) 448-2000

For assistance with replacement pages, shipments, billing or other customer service matters, please call:

Customer Services Department at .... (800) 833-9844
Outside the United States and Canada, please call .... (518) 487-3000
Fax number .... (518) 487-3584

For information on other Matthew Bender publications, please call
Your account manager or .... (800) 223-1940
Outside the United States and Canada, please call .... (518) 487-3000

ISBN 0-8205-4812-X

The 1990 Official Text and prior Official Texts and/or Comments of the Uniform Commercial Code as amended, printed in this publication have been reproduced with permission of National Conference of Commisioners on Uniform State Laws and the American Law Institute.

This publication is designed to provide accurate and authoritative information in regard to the subject matter covered. It is sold with the understanding that the publisher is not engaged in rendering legal, accounting, or other professional services. If legal advice or other expert assistance is required, the services of a competent professional should be sought.

Editorial Offices
2 Park Avenue, New York, NY 10016-5675 (212) 448-2000
201 Mission St., San Francisco, CA 94105-1831 (415) 908-3200
www.lexis.com

TABLE OF CONTENTS

NEW YORK

OVERVIEW OF U. C. C. REVISED ARTICLE 8

By Richard B. Smith*

Paul M. Shupack**

I. Background.

The prior uniform version of Article 8, last amended in 1978 to cover uncertificated securities and enacted in New York in 1982, left uncertainty concerning the law for holding, transfer and pledging securities held through intermediaries (that is, what has become the bulk of publicly held securities). Revised Article 8, enacted in 1997, makes its greatest contribution by providing clear and certain rules for the holding, transferring and pledging of securities held in securities accounts with brokers and banks, which, in turn, often hold them through other intermediaries including clearing corporations. This mode of holding securities is known as the "indirect holding system." During the 1980's, New York's version of Article 8 had become increasingly non–uniform as the legislature added amendments addressing aspects of indirect holding. Thus, New York's statute had already moved toward Revised Article 8. Nonetheless, adoption of Revised Article 8 represents a significant change in New York law, because it codifies the law governing indirect holding without using analogies drawn from the "direct holding system" in which the investor is the registered owner on the books of the issuer or its transfer agent. Accompanying Revised Article 8 are conforming amendments to Article 9, which return to Article 9 all provisions governing security interests in investment securities as well as providing clearer rules for pledging securities within the indirect holding system.

The statute that follows this overview reprints the text enacted in New York. Because of publishing time constraints, it does not include the Official Comments that accompany the Uniform Act or any New York annotations. For a detailed section–by–section comparison of the prior New York version of Article

* Mr. Smith is a retired partner and now senior counsel of Davis Polk & Wardwell in New York City. He is a former SEC Commissioner, is currently a Uniform Law Commissioner for New York, and was a member of the NCCUSL/ALI Drafting Committee for the revision of U.C.C. Article 8.

** Mr. Shupack is a professor of law at Cardozo Law School in New York City. He was chairman of the working group that prepared the Report on Revised Article 8 for the New York legislature by the Association of the Bar of the City of New York.

8 to the Uniform text of Revised Article 8, as well as an explanation for the non-uniform provisions, see the Report on *Proposed Revisions to Article 8 of the New York Uniform Commercial Code, with Conforming and Miscellaneous Amendments to Articles 1, 5, 9 and 13 Thereof as well as Conforming and Miscellaneous Amendments to Other Statutes*, prepared by and obtainable from The Association of the Bar of the City of New York. For an exposition by the Reporter of the policies underlying and the meaning of the provisions of Uniform Revised Article 8, see the Reporter's Prefatory Note to the Uniform text and James Steven Rogers, *Policy Perspectives on Revised Article 8, 43 UCLA L. Rev 1431 (1997)*. For an overview of Uniform Revised Article 8 designed to aid the practicing lawyer, see THE ABCS OF THE UCC, ARTICLE 8: INVESTMENT SECURITIES, published by and obtainable from the Chicago office of the Section of Business Law of the American Bar Association.

At this writing, 40 States in addition to New York, the District of Columbia and Puerto Rico have enacted Revised Article 8. The U. S. Treasury has also, in effect, adopted Revised Article 8 to apply to U.S. Government securities (see 31 C.F.R. Part 306, Subpart O as revised August 23, 1996) and the Federal Agencies have done the same with respect to their securities.

II. Principal Changes in New York Law Accomplished by Revised Article 8.

a. Adoption of Part 5 of Article 8, which creates a new type of property called a "security entitlement," and which provides a complete system of rules for the ownership and transfer of securities held indirectly.

b. Simultaneous adoption of amendments to Article 9 (and particularly the new §§ 9-115 and 9-116), providing for the perfection of security interests in investment property by taking control or by filing, and the assurance of priority to those who take control.

c. Repeal of the Statute of Frauds for contracts for the sale or purchase of securities, except for contracts for purchase or sale of shares in cooperative apartment corporations (§ 8-113).

d. Revision of the choice of laws rules to allow issuers, investors and securities intermediaries to determine in advance the applicable substantive law that will govern their rights and obligations in connection with the issuance, ownership, transfer and pledging of securities and the acquisition, pledging and termination of security entitlements (§ 8–110).

III. Substantive Differences Between New and Prior Article 8 Part by Part.

Article 8 deals with a type of property — investment securities. The prior version of Article 8 contained four parts. Revised Article 8 contains five parts. While each of the first four parts of Revised Article 8 have the same names as the corresponding parts of prior Article 8, the substance contained in each of these parts has, to some extent, been modified. The truly new part of Revised Article 8 is contained within Part 5, which has no analog in prior Article 8.

Part 1 deals with definitions and general matters. Contained within this part are some of the important substantive changes made by Revised Article 8.

Section 8–102 adds new definitions to Article 8 for terms principally used in Part 5. These terms (security entitlement, entitlement holder, entitlement order, financial asset, and securities intermediary) were created to deal with the *sui generis* form of property interest in a securities account. In addition, certain defined terms that appeared in prior Article 8 have been redefined, changing the substantive law by changing the meaning of a defined term. Two of the more important changes in this respect are "adverse claim" (§ 8–102(a)(1)) and "good faith" (§ 8-102(a)(10)). Adverse claim is now defined so as to reject the holding of *Fallon v. Wall Street Clearing Corp., 182 A.D.2d 245, 586 N.Y.S.2d 953 (1st Dep't. 1992)*. This change in meaning must be read in conjunction with § 8-105 (Notice of Adverse Claim), § 8–112 (Creditor's Legal Process, which makes clear, as prior law did not, that its provisions are the exclusive means by which a creditor may reach a debtor's interest in a financial asset) and § 8–403 (Demand that Issuer Not Register Transfer, discussed below). Good faith is now defined to mean "honesty in fact and the observance of reasonable commercial standards of fair dealing" instead of simple "honesty in fact." This change in definition will have little effect in answering whether a purchaser took free of an adverse claim, as the requirement of good faith has been eliminated as an element of qualifying as a "protected purchaser" (see § 8-303, discussed below).

Section 8-103 responds to questions concerning scope left unanswered under prior Article 8 by setting forth rules for determining whether certain obligations and interests (such as investment company shares, limited partnership interests, commodity contracts and negotiable instruments) are or are not a "security" covered by all of revised Article 8 or a "financial asset," a broader term defined in § 8–102(a)(9) to include any property held in a securities account which is expressly agreed to be subject to Part 5 (only) of revised Article 8. The term "security entitlement," key to Part 5, relates to the broader term "financial asset." (See discussion in Section IV below for use of the even broader term "investment property" in the amendments to Article 9.)

Section 8–106 introduces a key concept in Revised Article 8 — the concept of control. The concept of control performs two functions within Article 8 and the related amendments to Article 9. The first function is to describe those acts that signal the completion of a transfer within the direct and indirect holding systems. The second function aids in determining perfection and priority of a secured lender. Obtaining control will, in the usual case, give the secured party with control rights superior to other claimants to a security or a security entitlement. The concept applies both to the direct and indirect holding systems, but the mechanics by which control is achieved depend upon the holding system in which the security is held. Subsections (a) and (b) set forth the means of obtaining control over certificated securities. Subsection (c) does the same for uncertificated securities, and subsection (d) describes how to take control of security entitlements. Subsection (e) provides for automatic control in certain circumstances, including cases where a customer grants a security interest in its securities entitlement to secure a margin loan. Subsection (f) provides for special rules concerning control by agreement — a species of control appropriate for uncertificated securities and security entitlements. It states that control is not lost if the registered owner or entitlement holder retains the right to make substitution or otherwise to deal with the financial assets subject to a control agreement. Subsection (g) protects issuers and securities intermediaries by allowing them to decline from entering into control agreements. See Section IV below for a discussion of "control" as it relates to security interests in investment property.

Section 8–108 sets forth the warranties given by a transferor within the direct holding system, while § 8–109 sets forth the warranties given by a person who originates an entitlement order within the indirect holding system. Section 8–108 makes no substantial change in the warranties on transfer provided by prior § 8–306. Section 8–109 is new and is one of the provisions providing for rules for indirect holding of securities.

Section 8–110 contains the basic applicable law provisions for Article 8. It separates two sets of issues. The first set addresses what jurisdiction's law governs the validity of a security, the rights and duties of the issuer with respect to registration of transfer of a certificated or uncertificated security, and the effectiveness of registration of transfer of a certificated or uncertificated security by the issuer. Subsections (a) and (c) apply the local law (but not the conflict of laws rules) of the issuer's jurisdiction to these subjects and codify the common–law rule with respect to the ownership and transfer of bearer or registered security certificates. Subsection (d) defines the issuer's jurisdiction. If permitted by that jurisdiction, the issuer may specify the law of any other jurisdiction except as to the validity of a security, which must be determined under the law of the jurisdiction of the issuer's organization.

The second set of issues addresses what jurisdiction's law is applicable to the relationship between securities intermediaries and entitlement holders. Questions arising out of the acquisition of a security entitlement from the securities intermediary, the rights and duties of the intermediary and entitlement holder arising out of a security entitlement and questions concerning adverse claims to a security entitlement are all determined by the law of the securities intermediary's jurisdiction. Section 8–110(e) sets forth rules to determine what that jurisdiction is, and § 8–110(f) makes clear that physical location of financial assets or of computer facilities has no relevance to the determination of the securities intermediary's jurisdiction. The securities intermediary's jurisdiction is the one specified in an agreement between the securities intermediary and the entitlement holder, or, in the absence of agreement, the jurisdiction where the securities account is maintained or the jurisdiction in which is located the office identified in an account statement. Failing any of these, the jurisdiction is that in which the chief executive office of the securities intermediary is located. See § 8–110(e)(2)–(4).

Section 8–111 provides that a rule adopted by a clearing corporation is effective as to its participants and third parties, even though the rule may conflict with Revised Article 8. Any such rule, of course, would require approval by the Securities and Exchange Commission. This section evidences the reality that, with respect to security entititlements, Revised Article 8 is intended to operate within a context of regulated entities.

Part 2 of Article 8 deals with the relationship between issuers and securities holders. Revised Article 8 makes no material changes to the rules of Part 2 under the prior version, except for the elimination of provisions relating to initial transaction statements for uncertificated securities (see discussion of Part 4 below).

Part 3 deals with the transfer of certificated and uncertificated securities. Certificated securities (which are tangible) and uncertificated securities (which are not) are the two forms of securities evidencing a direct relationship between the issuer and a securities holder. Part 3 describes the methods of transfer of each of these forms of securities, and rules determining the consequences of transfer. New York's prior version of Part 3 dealt not only with these two types of property, but also, as a consequence of the 1982 enactment, contained two provisions (§§ 8-313 and 8-321) that dealt with indirectly held securities. Revised Article 8 treats indirectly held securities separately in its Part 5.

With respect to certificated and uncertificated securities, the rules under Part 3 of Revised Article 8 differ from its predecessor in two notable ways. First, Revised Article 8 eliminates the obligation of issuers of uncertificated securities to issue transaction statements. These have been found to be largely irrelevant in actual practice. Second, Revised Article 8 replaces the term "bona fide purchaser" with the term "protected purchaser." As defined in § 8-303, protected purchaser no longer contains the element that the transferee take in good faith. Instead, it requires, in addition to the element of value, simply that the transferee does not have "notice of any adverse claim" (a term defined in § 8–105). This change in statute makes little change in New York law, as New York courts have equated good faith with lack of notice. *See, e.g. Benjamin Ctr. v Hampton Affiliates, Inc., 106 A.D.2d 422, 428 (N.Y. App. Div. 1984), aff'd as modified, 66 N.Y.2d 782 (1985).*

Part 4 deals with registration. It describes the duties an issuer owes to the holder, the transferor or the transferee of a certificated or uncertificated security. Most of the changes from the prior version of Article 8 result from the elimination of all statutory requirements relating to transaction statements upon registration of transfer of uncertificated securities. The one apparently significant change that affects both certificated and uncertificated securities appears in § 8-403. The prior version of this section imposed on an issuer a duty of inquiry into adverse claims upon receipt of a written notification of the adverse claim. Revised Article 8 recognizes two different categories of adverse claimants. The registered owner (usually asserting a claim based on theft or loss of the security) may prevent transfer (for a limited period) by a simple notice given to the issuer. Other adverse claimants must obtain legal process in order to interfere with a registered owner's right to have the issuer honor requests for registration of transfer.

Part 5 is new and novel. It provides a systematic set of rules governing the holding of securities through intermediaries. It builds on two fundamental propositions. First, as specified in §§ 8-504 through 8-508, a security entitlement consists of rights that an entitlement holder has against a securities intermediary and the correlative duties of the intermediary. These rights and duties may be varied by agreement, subject to the underlying obligation of good faith imposed by Article 1 on all transactions governed by the U.C.C. As discussed above, Revised Article 8 defines "good faith" in a way different from the Article 1 definition to include "the observance of reasonable commercial standards of fair dealing" (§ 8-102(a)(10)). By reason of § 8-509(a), the rights and duties of a securities intermediary may be satisfied by the intermediary's acting in conformity with any overlapping requirements of regulatory statutes (principally rules of the Securities and Exchange Commission under federal securities law).

Second, the entitlement holder does not have a traceable property interest in a *specific financial asset*, but does own a property interest, called the "security entitlement." Section 8–503 provides that, with respect to a specific financial asset, the entitlement holder has a pro-rata property interest in all interests in that financial asset held by the securities intermediary. Section 8–511 makes clear that security entitlements (and the financial assets to which they relate) are not the property of the intermediary and not subject to claims of creditors of the intermediary unless the the creditor has taken control.

Subsection 8–503(e) prohibits an entitlement holder from asserting a property interest with respect to a particular financial asset against the purchaser of the financial asset or interest in the financial asset, even if the property were traceable to the purchaser. That rule has one exception. If the purchaser acts in collusion with the securities intermediary violating its obligations to the entitlement holder, then the entitlement holder may act against the purchaser. Collusion is a term not defined by Revised Article 8. The New York Legislature, in a statement of legislative intent, discusses types of conduct that could or would not constitute "collusion," but this statement does not disturb the uniform text. Both the Legislature in its declaration (Laws 1997, Chapter 566, § 1) and the Governor in his signing memorandum have emphasized the importance of uniformity of law among jurisdictions in the essentially trans-state indirect holding system.

IV. Perfecting Security Interests in Investment Property.

The provisions governing perfection of security interests in "investment property" are to be found primarily in § 9-115. Investment property is a broader term than financial asset (the overarching term in Part 5 of Article 8) because investment property includes "commodity contracts" (which are not subject to Revised Article 8). The definition of "proceeds" in § 9-306 has been amended to include payments or distributions made with respect to investment property. Assuming that a security interest in investment property has attached, the method of perfection depends on the form the investment property takes and the nature of the secured party.

No matter what the form of investment property, perfection can be achieved by the secured party's having taken control or by the secured party having filed against the debtor, unless the debtor is a broker or a securities or commodity intermediary. In the case of a securities or commodity intermediary, the security interest is perfected automatically upon attachment (§ 9-116), and filing has no effect (§ 9-115(c) and (d)). The method for taking control of investment property depends on the form taken by the investment property.

In the case of security certificates, delivery of the certificate to a secured party pursuant to agreement will perfect the security interest, but unless the delivery is accompanied by an endorsement to the secured party or an endorsement in blank, the perfected secured party will not have control and, hence, not have priority. In the case of uncertificated securities, a secured party can take control by having the securities registered in the name of the secured party, or by having the issuer agree that it will comply with the secured party's instructions without the registered owner's further consent. In the case of security entitlements, control requires either the creation of a security entitlement in the name of the secured party or an agreement with the securities intermediary that it will comply with the secured party's instructions without the entitlement holder's further consent. Security interests in certificated securities can also be perfected temporarily for 21 days under the provisions of §§ 9-304(4) and 9-304(5). As noted above in the discussion of § 8-106, control over uncertificated securities or security entitlements is not lost if the registered owner or entitlement holder, respectively, retains the right to make substitution or otherwise to deal with the financial assets subject to the control agreement.

With one exception, a purchaser who has taken control will have priority over the person who has perfected only by filing (§ 9-115(5)(a)). The exception concerns shares in cooperative apartment corporations.

V. Special Provisions for Cooperative Apartment Corporation Shares.

Revised Article 8 and the amendments to Article 9 contain special provisions for cooperative apartment corporation shares. Despite the general abolition of a Statute of Frauds for securities, § 8–113 requires that a contract for the sale of shares in a cooperative corporation must be in writing. Section 9–115(7) removes this type of property from its priority rules based on control. For shares in cooperative apartment corporations, the secured lender must perfect by filing;

taking control of this sort of property will not perfect a security interest. Section 9–304(7) requires that such a filing "identify the real estate . . . with a description sufficient for its identification."

VI. Transition Provisions.

Revised Article 8 provides that it becomes effective 30 days after its enactment. That day was October 10, 1997. Section 8-602 provides that security interests in investment property perfected as of that date remain perfected for a period of one year, even though Revised Article 8 requires a method of perfection differing from that used to perfect under prior Article 8.

UNIFORM COMMERCIAL CODE

UCC

(*Except for Articles 2–A and 4–A, all Articles of the U.C.C. set forth below are enacted by Laws of 1962, Ch. 553, eff. Sept. 27, 1964, as amended by the 1994 Regular Legislative Session through August 16, 1994. Article 2-A was enacted by Laws of 1994, Ch. 114, eff. June 30, 1995. Article 4-A was enacted by Laws of 1990, Ch. 208, eff. Jan. 1, 1991. Article 11 was enacted by Laws of 1977, Ch. 866, eff. July 2, 1978. "New York Annotations," included after each section of Articles 1, 2, 3, 4, 5, 6, 7, 8, 9, and 13, were prepared by Professors William E. Hogan and Norman Penney of Cornell Law School for the New York State Commission on Uniform State Laws.*)

TABLE OF CONTENTS

ARTICLE 1

GENERAL PROVISIONS

PART 1

SHORT TITLE, CONSTRUCTION, APPLICATION AND SUBJECT MATTER OF THE ACT

PART 2

GENERAL DEFINITIONS AND PRINCIPLES OF INTERPRETATION

ARTICLE 2

SALES

PART 1

SHORT TITLE, GENERAL CONSTRUCTION AND SUBJECT MATTER

PART 2

FORM, FORMATION AND READJUSTMENT OF CONTRACT

PART 3

GENERAL OBLIGATION AND CONSTRUCTION OF CONTRACT

PART 4

TITLE, CREDITORS AND GOOD FAITH PURCHASERS

PART 5

PERFORMANCE

PART 6

BREACH, REPUDIATION AND EXCUSE

PART 7

REMEDIES

ARTICLE 2A

LEASES

PART 1

GENERAL PROVISIONS

UCC

PART 2

FORMATION AND CONSTRUCTION OF LEASE CONTRACT

PART 3

EFFECT OF LEASE CONTRACT

PART 4

PERFORMANCE OF LEASE CONTRACT: REPUDIATED, SUBSTITUTED AND EXCUSED

PART 5

DEFAULT

A. IN GENERAL

B. DEFAULT BY LESSOR

UCC

C. DEFAULT BY LESSEE

ARTICLE 3

COMMERCIAL PAPER

PART 1

SHORT TITLE, FORM AND INTERPRETATION

PART 2

TRANSFER AND NEGOTIATION

PART 3

RIGHTS OF A HOLDER

PART 4

LIABILITY OF PARTIES

PART 5

PRESENTMENT, NOTICE OF DISHONOR AND PROTEST

PART 6

DISCHARGE

PART 7

ADVICE OF INTERNATIONAL SIGHT DRAFT

PART 8

MISCELLANEOUS

ARTICLE 4

BANK DEPOSITS AND COLLECTIONS

PART 1

GENERAL PROVISIONS AND DEFINITIONS

PART 2

COLLECTION OF ITEMS: DEPOSITARY AND COLLECTING BANKS

PART 3

COLLECTION OF ITEMS: PAYOR BANKS

PART 4

RELATIONSHIP BETWEEN PAYOR BANK AND ITS CUSTOMER

PART 5

COLLECTION OF DOCUMENTARY DRAFTS

ARTICLE 4A

FUNDS TRANSFERS

PART 1

SUBJECT MATTER AND DEFINITIONS

PART 2

ISSUE AND ACCEPTANCE OF PAYMENT ORDER

PART 3

EXECUTION OF SENDER'S PAYMENT ORDER BY RECEIVING BANK

PART 4

PAYMENT

PART 5

MISCELLANEOUS PROVISIONS

ARTICLE 5

LETTERS OF CREDIT

ARTICLE 6

BULK TRANSFERS

ARTICLE 7

WAREHOUSE RECEIPTS, BILLS OF LADING AND OTHER DOCUMENTS OF TITLE

PART 1

GENERAL

PART 2

WAREHOUSE RECEIPTS: SPECIAL PROVISIONS

PART 3

BILLS OF LADING: SPECIAL PROVISIONS

PART 4

WAREHOUSE RECEIPTS AND BILLS OF LADING: GENERAL OBLIGATIONS

PART 5

WAREHOUSE RECEIPTS AND BILLS OF LADING: NEGOTIATION AND TRANSFER

PART 6

WAREHOUSE RECEIPTS AND BILLS OF LADING: MISCELLANEOUS PROVISIONS

ARTICLE 8

INVESTMENT SECURITIES

PART 1

SHORT TITLE AND GENERAL MATTERS

PART 2

ISSUE AND ISSUER

UCC

PART 3

TRANSFER OF CERTIFICATED AND UNCERTIFICATED SECURITIES

PART 4

REGISTRATION

PART 5

SECURITY ENTITLEMENTS

PART 6

TRANSITION PROVISIONS FOR REVISED ARTICLE 8 AND FOR THE CONFORMING AMENDMENTS TO ARTICLES 1, 5, 9 AND 13

ARTICLE 9

SECURED TRANSACTIONS, SALES OF ACCOUNTS, CONTRACT RIGHTS AND CHATTEL PAPER

PART 1

SHORT TITLE, APPLICABILITY AND DEFINITIONS

PART 2

VALIDITY OF SECURITY AGREEMENT AND RIGHTS OF PARTIES THERETO

PART 3

RIGHTS OF THIRD PARTIES; PERFECTED AND UNPERFECTED SECURITY INTERESTS; RULES OF PRIORITY

PART 4

FILING

PART 5

DEFAULT

ARTICLE 10

[Renumbered 13]

ARTICLE 11

PROVISIONS FOR TRANSITION FROM ORIGINAL ARTICLE 9 TO REVISED ARTICLE 9

UCC

ARTICLE 12

[No article 12 has been enacted]

ARTICLE 13

EFFECTIVE DATE AND REPEALER

UCC

ARTICLE 1
GENERAL PROVISIONS

PART 1

SHORT TITLE, CONSTRUCTION, APPLICATION AND SUBJECT MATTER OF THE ACT

PART 2

GENERAL DEFINITIONS AND PRINCIPLES OF INTERPRETATION

PART 1

SHORT TITLE, CONSTRUCTION, APPLICATION AND SUBJECT MATTER OF THE ACT

Section 1–101. Short Title.

This Act shall be known and may be cited as Uniform Commercial Code.

New York Annotations

Each article of the Code must be considered in light of the generally applicable definitions and rules specified in Article 1. However, care must be taken to examine the provisions of each article to ascertain whether the more general provision or definition has been modified to meet the needs of a particular situation. Although the New York Law Revision Commission stated no general conclusion about Article 1, ten of the article's seventeen sections were revised either during or after the Commission's hearings. In Section 1–201, sixteen of the forty-six definitions were modified. Here, as elsewhere, the great majority of the Commission's recommendations were followed.

Official Uniform Comment

Each Article of the Code (except this Article and Article 10) may also be cited by its own short title. See Sections 2–101, 3–101, 4–101, 5–101, 6–101, 7–101, 8–101 and 9–101.

Section 1–102. Purposes; Rules of Construction; Variation by Agreement.

(1) This Act shall be liberally construed and applied to promote its underlying purposes and policies.

(2) Underlying purposes and policies of this Act are

(a) to simplify, clarify and modernize the law governing commercial transactions;

(b) to permit the continued expansion of commercial practices through custom, usage and agreement of the parties;

(c) to make uniform the law among the various jurisdictions.

(3) The effect of provisions of this Act may be varied by agreement, except as otherwise provided in this Act and except that the obligations of good faith, diligence, reasonableness, and care prescribed by this Act may not be disclaimed by agreement but the parties may by agreement determine the standards by which the performance of such obligations is to be measured if such standards are not manifestly unreasonable.

(4) The presence in certain provisions of this Act of the words "unless otherwise agreed" or words of similar import does not imply that the effect of other provisions may not be varied by agreement under subsection (3).

(5) In this Act unless the context otherwise requires

(a) words in the singular number include the plural, and in the plural include the singular;

(b) words of the masculine gender include the feminine and the neuter, and when the sense so indicates words of the neuter gender may refer to any gender.

UCC

New York Annotations

(1) and (2) *Purposes and policies.* The admonition in subsection (1) that the Code shall be "liberally construed" is not expressly stated in any of the present Uniform Acts adopted in New York. However, a similar expression is found in the last paragraph of the Factor's Lien Act, Personal Property Law, § 45, and in Lien Law, § 23, dealing with mechanic's liens. The construction and application of the Code to "promote its underlying purposes and policies" is a requirement found in existing laws at least in regard to the policy of uniformity, e.g., Personal Property Law, § 58–j (trust receipts); Personal Property Law, § 30–i (conditional sales); Personal Property Law, § 180 (stock transfers); Personal Property Law, § 238 (bills of lading); General Business Law, § 141 (warehouse receipts); and even where New York did not adopt such language explicitly the courts have implied such a term. Agar v. Orda, 264 N.Y. 248, 190 N.E. 479 (1934) (sales); Brown v. Brown (Rowan), 91 Misc. 220, 154 N.Y.S. 1098 (1915) (negotiable instruments). Subsection (c) is thus clearly a restatement of existing law. On the other hand, subsections (2)(a) and (b) state broader and more ambitious purposes and policies than those contained in the present Uniform Acts. The underlying purposes and policies of the Code are to simplify, clarify, and modernize the law governing commercial transactions, and to permit the continued expansion of such practices through custom, usage, and agreement of the parties.

(3) and (4) *Variation by agreement.* Subject to the explicit exceptions in subsection (3), this provision permits the parties to vary the effect of the Code provisions. Thus the Code generally espouses freedom of contract except for certain specific rules, such as the rights given to debtors in default under security agreements (Section 9–501 and also see Section 1–105(2), 1–208, 2–302, 2–719, 5–116(2), and 9–318(4)), and except for "obligations" such as "good faith, diligence, reasonableness and care" prescribed by the Code.

In form this section is new but it has many analogous provisions in the present law, e.g., Personal Property Law, § 152, permitting variation of implied obligations by agreement. On the other hand, Comment 2 indicates that subsection (3) is designed to prevent the limiting effect of cases like Manhattan Co. v. Morgan, 242 N.Y. 38, 150 N.E. 594 (1926) (negotiability by contract), at least as to giving legal consequence to the parties' agreement. Compare, Alexander Enoch v. Brandon, 249 N.Y. 263, 164 N.E. 45 (1928). On the inability of the parties to avoid the "good faith" obligation, the Code seems to be in accord with Matter of Kiamie, 309 N.Y. 325, 130 N.E. 2d 745 (1955), and Restatement, Contracts, § 265 and New York Annotations.

It must be noted that only those obligations of reasonableness and care that are "prescribed by this Act" cannot be disclaimed. This is analogous to the provisions of Personal Property Law, § 189 (bills of lading). See Section 7–309. See Restatement, Contracts, § 574 and New York Annotations.

Finally, the provision permitting the parties to establish the standards by which performance of these obligations is to be measured is new, but is in a sense consistent with Restatement, Contracts, §§ 574, 575 and New York Annotations.

(5) *Accord.* General Construction Law, §§ 22 and 35.

Historical Note: Former subsection (2) was criticized in the hearings of the Law Revision Commission as cumbersome and partly self-contradictory; the changes simplify and clarify. Subsection (3) was revised in Supplement No. 1 to state affirmatively, and at the outset, that freedom of contract is a principle of the Code; former paragraph (c), forbidding disclaimer of "general obligations" and giving examples of such obligations, was revised at the same time to state categorically the obligations not subject to disclaimer and thus to avoid loose coverage of an unduly wide range of Code provisions.

The Law Revision Commission recommended that paragraphs (a), (b), (f), and (g), of former subsection (3) be deleted. Paragraphs (3)(a) and (b), dealing with the effect of agreements on Code definitions and the rights of third parties, were deleted as unnecessary; paragraph (3)(f), on the effect of Comments, was deleted because the old Comments were clearly out of date and it was not known when new ones could be prepared; and paragraph (3)(g), prohibiting the use of prior drafts to ascertain legislative intent, was deleted because the changes from the text enacted in Pennsylvania in 1953 are clearly legitimate legislative history.

New subsection (5) is modelled on 1 U.S.C. § 1 and N.Y. General Construction Law, §§ 22 and 35. (1956 Recommendations, p. 2.)

Official Uniform Comment

Prior Uniform Statutory Provision: Section 74, Uniform Sales Act; Section 57, Uniform Warehouse Receipts Act; Section 52, Uniform Bills of Lading Act; Section 19, Uniform Stock Transfer Act; Section 18, Uniform Trust Receipts Act.

Changes: Rephrased and new material added.

Purposes of Changes:

1. Subsections (1) and (2) are intended to make it clear that:

This Act is drawn to provide flexibility so that, since it is intended to be a semi-permanent piece of legislation, it will provide its own machinery for expansion of commercial practices. It is intended to make it possible for the law embodied in this Act to be developed by the courts in the light of unforeseen and new circumstances and practices. However, the proper construction of the Act requires that its interpretation and application be limited to its reason.

Courts have been careful to keep broad acts from being hampered in their effects by later acts of limited scope. Pacific Wool Growers v. Draper & Co., 158 Or. 1, 73 P.2d 1391 (1937), and compare Section 1–104. They have recognized the policies embodied in an act as applicable in reason to subject matter which was not expressly included in the language of the act, Commercial Nat. Bank of New Orleans v. Canal-Louisiana Bank & Trust Co., 239 U.S. 520, 36 S.Ct. 194, 60 L.Ed. 417 (1916) (bona fide purchase policy of Uniform Warehouse Receipts Act extended to case not covered but of equivalent nature). They have done the same where reason and policy so required, even where the subject-matter had been intentionally excluded from the act in general. Agar v. Orda, 264 N.Y. 248, 190 N.E. 479 (1934) (Uniform Sales Act change in seller's remedies applied to contract for sale of choses in action even though the general coverage of that Act was intentionally limited to goods "other than things in action".) They have implemented a statutory policy with liberal and useful remedies not provided in the statutory text. They have disregarded a statutory limitation of remedy where the reason of the limitation did not apply. Fiterman v. J.N. Johnson & Co., 156 Minn. 201, 194 N.W. 399 (1923) (requirement of return of the goods as a condition to rescission for breach of warranty; also, partial rescission allowed). Nothing in this Act stands in the way of the continuance of such action by the courts.

The Act should be construed in accordance with its underlying purposes and policies. The text of each section should be read in the light of the purpose and policy of the rule or principle in question, as also of the Act as a whole, and the application of the language should be construed narrowly or broadly, as the case may be, in conformity with the purposes and policies involved.

2. Subsection (3) states affirmatively at the outset that freedom of contract is a principle of the Code: "the effect" of its provisions may be varied by "agreement." The meaning of the statute itself must be found in its text, including its definitions, and in appropriate extrinsic aids; it cannot be varied by agreement. But the Code seeks to avoid the type of interference with evolutionary growth found in Manhattan Co. v. Morgan, 242 N.Y. 38, 150 N.E. 594 (1926). Thus private parties cannot make

an instrument negotiable within the meaning of Article 3 except as provided in Section 3–104; nor can they change the meaning of such terms as "bona fide purchaser," "holder in due course," or "due negotiation," as used in this Act. But an agreement can change the legal consequences which would otherwise flow from the provisions of the Act. "Agreement" here includes the effect given to course of dealing, usage of trade and course of performance by Sections 1–201, 1–205 and 2–208; the effect of an agreement on the rights of third parties is left to specific provisions of this Act and to supplementary principles applicable under the next section. The rights of third parties under Section 9–301 when a security interest is unperfected, for example, cannot be destroyed by a clause in the security agreement.

This principle of freedom of contract is subject to specific exceptions found elsewhere in the Act and to the general exception stated here. The specific exceptions vary in explicitness: the statute of frauds found in Section 2–201, for example, does not explicitly preclude oral waiver of the requirement of a writing, but a fair reading denies enforcement to such a waiver as part of the "contract" made unenforceable; Section 9–501(3), on the other hand, is quite explicit. Under the exception for "the obligations of good faith, diligence, reasonableness and care prescribed by this Act," provisions of the Act prescribing such obligations are not to be disclaimed. However, the section also recognizes the prevailing practice of having agreements set forth standards by which due diligence is measured and explicitly provides that, in the absence of a showing that the standards manifestly are unreasonable, the agreement controls. In this connection, Section 1–205 incorporating into the agreement prior course of dealing and usages of trade is of particular importance.

3. Subsection (4) is intended to make it clear that, as a matter of drafting, words such as "unless otherwise agreed" have been used to avoid controversy as to whether the subject matter of a particular section does or does not fall within the exceptions to subsection (3), but absence of such words contains no negative implication since under subsection (3) the general and residual rule is that the effect of all provisions of the Act may be varied by agreement.

4. Subsection (5) is modelled on 1 U.S.C. Section 1 and New York General Construction Law Sections 22 and 35.

Section 1–103. Supplementary General Principles of Law Applicable.

Unless displaced by the particular provisions of this Act, the principles of law and equity, including the law merchant and the law relative to capacity to contract, principal and agent, estoppel, fraud, misrepresentation, duress, coercion, mistake, bankruptcy, or other validating or invalidating cause shall supplement its provisions.

New York Annotations

In principle this section is identical to Personal Property Law, § 58–i (trust receipts); § 80–h (conditional sales); § 154 (sales); § 179 (stock transfer); § 237 (bills of lading); General Business Law, § 140 (warehouse receipts); and N.I.L., § 7. The section is somewhat more explicit than the existing provisions (e.g., validating causes are included), but it seems to be consistent with the local case law. Schnitzer v. Fruehauf Trailer Co., 283 App. Div. 421, 128 N.Y.S.2d 242, aff'd, 307 N.Y. 876, 122 N.E.2d 754 (1954). Thus, except for the greater explicitness and the underlying intent expressed in the Comment that the listing is merely illustrative, this section will not change New York law.

Official Uniform Comment

Prior Uniform Statutory Provision: Sections 2 and 73, Uniform Sales Act; Section 196, Uniform Negotiable Instruments Act; Section 56, Uniform Warehouse Receipts Act; Section 51, Uniform Bills of Lading Act; Section 18, Uniform Stock Transfer Act; Section 17, Uniform Trust Receipts Act.

Changes: Rephrased, the reference to "estoppel" and "validating" being new.

Purposes of Changes:

1. While this section indicates the continued applicability to commercial contracts of all supplemental bodies of law except insofar as they are explicitly displaced by this Act, the principle has been stated in more detail and the phrasing enlarged to make it clear that the "validating", as well as the "invalidating" causes referred to in the prior uniform statutory provisions, are included here. "Validating" as used here in conjunction with "invalidating" is not intended as a narrow word confined to original validation, but extends to cover any factor which at any time or in any manner renders or helps to render valid any right or transaction.

2. The general law of capacity is continued by express mention to make clear that section 2 of the old Uniform Sales Act (omitted in this Act as stating no matter not contained in the general law) is also consolidated in the present section. Hence, where a statute limits the capacity of a non-complying corporation to sue, this is equally applicable to contracts of sale to which such corporation is a party.

3. The listing given in this section is merely illustrative; no listing could be exhaustive. Nor is the fact that in some sections particular circumstances have led to express reference to other fields of law intended at any time to suggest the negation of the general application of the principles of this section.

Section 1–104. Construction Against Implicit Repeal.

This Act being a general act intended as a unified coverage of its subject matter, no part of it shall be deemed to be impliedly repealed by subsequent legislation if such construction can reasonably be avoided.

New York Annotations

Accord: Matter of Tiffany, 179 N.Y. 455, 72 N.E. 512 (1904). See Penal Law, § 2500, and General Construction Law, § 100.

Official Uniform Comment

Prior Uniform Statutory Provision: None.

Purposes:

To express the policy that no Act which bears evidence of carefully considered permanent regulative intention should lightly be regarded as impliedly repealed by subsequent legislation. This Act, carefully integrated and intended as a uniform codification of permanent character covering an entire "field" of law, is to be regarded as particularly resistant to implied repeal. See Pacific Wool Growers v. Draper & Co., 158 Or. 1, 73 P.2d 1391 (1937).

Section 1–105. Territorial Application of the Act; Parties' Power to Choose Applicable Law.

(1) Except as provided hereafter in this section, when a transaction bears a reasonable relation to this state and also to another state or nation the parties may agree that the law either of this state or of such other state or nation shall govern their rights and duties. Failing such agreement this Act applies to transactions bearing an appropriate relation to this state.

(2) Where one of the following provisions of this Act specifies the applicable law, that provision governs and a contrary agreement is effective only to the extent permitted by the law (including the conflict of laws rules) so specified:

Rights of creditors against sold goods.	Section 2–402.
Applicability of the Article on leases.	Sections 2A–105 and 2A–106.
Applicability of the Article on Bank Deposits and Collections.	Section 4–102.
Governing Law in the Article on Fund Transfers.	Section 4A–507.
Letters of credit.	Section 5–116.
Bulk transfers subject to the Article on Bulk Transfers.	Section 6–102.
Applicability of the Article on Investment Securities.	Section 8–110.
Perfection provisions of the Article on Secured Transactions.	Section 9–103.

Amended by L. 1977, Ch. 866, eff. July 2, 1978; L. 1990, Ch. 208, eff. Jan. 1, 1991; L. 1997, Ch. 566, eff. Oct. 10, 1997; L. 2000, Ch. 471, eff. Nov. 1, 2000.

New York Annotations

(1) Subject to the explicit exception in subsection (2), the Code adopts the view that the parties may agree that their rights and duties are to be governed by the law of any state having a reasonable relation to the transaction. This is new, although it is supported by dictum in Swift & Co. v. Bankers Trust Co., 280 N.Y. 135, 19 N.E.2d 992 (1939), and by the weight given to the parties' presumed intent in Youssoupoff v. Widener, 246 N.Y. 174, 158 N.E. 64 (1927). Where no such agreement has been made and subsection (2) is not applicable, the Code applies to any transaction "bearing an appropriate relation" to the enacting state. Comment 3 suggests that the Code adopts the significant contacts test of Auten v. Auten, 308 N.Y. 155, 124 N.E.2d 99 (1954), which has cast doubt upon the choice of law rules made under the earlier somewhat more rigid tests, such as place of the making of the contract, or the place of performance, Smith Co., Ltd. v. Moscahlades, 193 App. Div. 126, 183 N.Y.S. 500 (1920), or the location of the goods sold, Youssoupoff v. Widener, *supra.* See Haag v. Barnes, 9 N.Y.2d 554, 175, N.E.2d 441 (1961).

(2) Here five specific areas are excluded from the agreement of the parties as to choice of law. See the annotations to the enumerated sections and note that most of these areas affect third parties at least potentially.

Historical Note: The former attempt in this section to state in some detail the territorial application of the Act did not meet with general acceptance. The New York Law Revision Commission proposed that the section be deleted altogether and the

UCC

subject left wholly to the common law. That recommendation could not be accepted completely. The parties' right to choose the applicable law should be affirmatively stated, and if that is done the limits on that right must also be set out. Such limits are essential: especially in Article 9, parties taking a security interest or asked to extend credit which may be subject to a security interest must have sure ways to find out whether and where to file and where to look for possible existing filings.

As revised, this section is subject to the firm rules in the sections listed and provides affirmatively for freedom of contract as to the applicable law in all other multi-state transactions. Where there is no agreement, the revised section requests the court to apply the Act to multi-state transactions having an "appropriate" relation to any state which has enacted it, whether or not the forum state has enacted it. This removes all the "horrible examples" of the application of the old section and goes a long way toward adopting the recommendation of the Law Revision Commission that the question be left to the law outside of the Code.

What is an "appropriate" relation to the enacting state, justifying application of the Act, is left to judicial decision, and the court is not strictly bound by common-law conflict-of-laws rules developed in other contexts. Thus a conflicts decision refusing to apply a purely local statute or rule of law to a particular multi-state transaction may not be a valid precedent for refusal to apply the Code in an analogous situation; application of the Code in such circumstances may be justified by its comprehensiveness, by the policy of uniformity, and by the fact that it is in large part a reformulation and restatement of the law merchant and of the understanding of a business community which transcends state and even national boundaries. Cases where a relation to the enacting state is not "appropriate" include, for example, those where the parties have clearly contracted on the basis of some other law, as where the law of the place of contracting and the law of the place of performance are the same and are contrary to the law under the Code. (1956 Recommendations, p. 5; Excerpts, p. 358.)

Official Uniform Comment

Prior Uniform Statutory Provision: None.

Purposes:

1. Subsection (1) states affirmatively the right of the parties to a multi-state transaction or a transaction involving foreign trade to choose their own law. That right is subject to the firm rules stated in the five sections listed in subsection (2), and is limited to jurisdictions to which the transaction bears a "reasonable relation." In general, the test of "reasonable relation" is similar to that laid down by the Supreme Court in Seeman v. Philadelphia Warehouse Co., 274 U.S. 403, 47 S.Ct. 626, 71 L.Ed. 1123 (1927). Ordinarily the law chosen must be that of a jurisdiction where a significant enough portion of the making or performance of the contract is to occur or occurs. But an agreement as to choice of law may sometimes take effect as a shorthand expression of the intent of the parties as to matters governed by their agreement, even though the transaction has no significant contact with the jurisdiction chosen.

2. Where there is no agreement as to the governing law, the Act is applicable to any transaction having an "appropriate" relation to any state which enacts it. Of course, the Act applies to any transaction which takes place in its entirety in a state which has enacted the Act. But the mere fact that suit is brought in a state does not make it appropriate to apply the substantive law of that state. Cases where a relation to the enacting state is not "appropriate" include, for example, those where the parties have clearly contracted on the basis of some other law, as where the law of the place of contracting and the law of the place of contemplated performance are the same and are contrary to the law under the Code.

3. Where a transaction has significant contacts with a state which has enacted the Act and also with other jurisdictions, the question what relation is "appropriate" is left to judicial decision. In deciding that question, the court is not strictly bound by precedents established in other contexts. Thus a conflict-of-laws decision refusing to apply a purely local statute or rule of law to a particular multi-state transaction may not be valid precedent for refusal to apply the Code in an analogous situation. Application of the Code in such circumstances may be justified by its comprehensiveness, by the policy of uniformity, and by the fact that it is in large part a reformulation and restatement of the law merchant and of the understanding of a business community which transcends state and even national boundaries. Compare Global Commerce Corp. v. Clark-Babbitt Industries, Inc., 239 F.2d 716, 719 (2d Cir. 1956). In particular, where a transaction is governed in large part by the Code, application of another law to some detail of performance because of an accident of geography may violate the commercial understanding of the parties.

4. The Act does not attempt to prescribe choice-of-law rules for states which do not enact it, but this section does not prevent application of the Act in a court of such a state. Common-law choice of law often rests on policies of giving effect to agreements and of uniformity of result regardless of where suit is brought. To the extent that such policies prevail, the relevant considerations are similar in such a court to those outlined above.

5. Subsection (2) spells out essential limitations on the parties' right to choose the applicable law. Especially in Article 9 parties taking a security interest or asked to extend credit which may be subject to a security interest must have sure ways to find out whether and where to file and where to look for possible existing filings.

6. Section 9–103 should be consulted as to the rules for perfection of security interests and the effects of perfection and non–perfection.

Section 1–106. Remedies to Be Liberally Administered.

(1) The remedies provided by this Act shall be liberally administered to the end that the aggrieved party may be put in as good a position as if the other party had fully performed but neither consequential or special nor penal damages may be had except as specifically provided in this Act or by other rule of law.

(2) Any right or obligation declared by this Act is enforceable by action unless the provision declaring it specifies a different and limited effect.

New York Annotations

The rule of this section that remedies are to be liberally administered has no counterpart in the present commercial statutes of New York. But see Civil Practice Act, §§ 3 and 275 [now CPLR §§ 104, 3026]. Subsection (2) is substantially the same as Personal Property Law, § 153 (sales).

Historical Note: The reference to "special" damages was added for clarification, as suggested on behalf of the Pennsylvania State Chamber of Commerce. (1956 Recommendations, p. 7.)

Official Uniform Comment

Prior Uniform Statutory Provision: Subsection (1)–none; Subsection (2)–Section 72, Uniform Sales Act.

Changes: Reworded.

Purposes of Changes and New Matter:

Subsection(1) is intended to effect three things:

1. First, to negate the unduly narrow or technical interpretation of some remedial provisions of prior legislation by providing that the remedies in this Act are to be liberally administered to the end stated in the section. Second, to make it clear that compensatory damages are limited to compensation. They do not include consequential or special damages, or penal damages; and the Act elsewhere makes it clear that damages must be minimized. Cf. Sections 1–203, 2–706(1), and 2–712(2). The third purpose of subsection (1) is to reject any doctrine that damages must be calculable with mathematical accuracy. Compensatory damages are often at best approximate: they have to be proved with whatever definiteness and accuracy the facts permit, but no more. Cf. Section 2–204(3).

2. Under subsection (2) any right or obligation described in this Act is enforceable by court action, even though no remedy may be expressly provided, unless a particular provision specifies a different and limited effect. Whether specific performance or other equitable relief is available is determined not by this section but by specific provisions and by supplementary principles. Cf. Sections 1–103, 2–716.

3."Consequential" or "special" damages and "penal" damages are not defined in terms in the Code, but are used in the sense given them by the leading cases on the subject.

Cross References:

Sections 1–103, 1–203, 2–204(3), 2–701, 2–706(1), 2–712(2) and 2–716.

Definitional Cross References:

"Action". Section 1–201.
"Aggrieved party". Section 1–201.
"Party". Section 1–201.
"Remedy". Section 1–201.
"Rights". Section 1–201.

Section 1–107. Waiver or Renunciation of Claim or Right After Breach.

Any claim or right arising out of an alleged breach can be discharged in whole or in part without consideration by a written waiver or renunciation signed and delivered by the aggrieved party.

New York Annotations

This section is in general accord with N.I.L., §§ 200(3), 201(2), and 203. See also Section 3–605. As to non-negotiable contractual obligations, the section seems to be in general accord with Personal Property Law, § 33(2), and Debtor and Creditor Law, § 243. The latter two statutes apply to discharge of rights even before breach, while the heading of this section limits its application to discharge after breach. See Section 2–209.

Historical Note: The revision made it clear that this section does not give effect to an undelivered renunciation, in accordance with a recommendation of the Law Revision Commission. (1956 Recommendations, p. 7; Excerpts, p. 358.)

Official Uniform Comment

Prior Uniform Statutory Provision: Compare Section 1, Uniform Written Obligations Act; Sections 119(3), 120(2) and 122, Uniform Negotiable Instruments Law.

Purposes:

This section makes consideration unnecessary to the effective renunciation or waiver of rights or claims arising out of an alleged breach of a commercial contract where such renunciation is in writing and signed and delivered by the aggrieved party. Its provisions, however, must be read in conjunction with the section imposing an obligation of good faith. (Section 1–203). There may, of course, also be an oral renunciation or waiver sustained by consideration but subject to Statute of Frauds provisions and to the section of Article 2 on Sales dealing with the modification of signed writings (Section 2–209). As is made express in the latter section this Act fully recognizes the effectiveness of waiver and estoppel.

Cross References:

Sections 1–203, 2–201 and 2–209. And see Section 2–719.

Definitional Cross References:

"Aggrieved party". Section 1–201.
"Rights". Section 1–201.
"Signed". Section 1–201.
"Written". Section 1–201.

Section 1–108. Severability.

If any provision or clause of this Act or application thereof to any person or circumstances is held invalid, such invalidity shall not affect other provisions or applications of the Act which can be given effect without the invalid provision or application, and to this end the provisions of this Act are declared to be severable.

New York Annotations

This provision is identical to that provided in Personal Property Law, § 58–k (trust receipts).

Official Uniform Comment

This is the model severability section recommended by the National Conference of Commissioners on Uniform State Laws for inclusion in all acts of extensive scope.

Definitional Cross Reference:

"Person". Section 1–201.

Section 1–109. Section Captions.

Section captions are parts of this Act.

New York Annotations

This provision is new to the statutes. Compare General Construction Law, § 81. In People v. Molyneux, 40 N.Y. 113 (1869), there is language in accord with this provision. See also Matter of Blake, 208 Misc. 22, 141 N.Y.S.2d 194 (1955). On the other hand, some cases have indicated that the heading or caption of the statute, like the title, may not be used to vary the plain legislative language. Squadrito v. Griebsch, 1 N.Y.2d 471, 136 N.E.2d 504 (1956). People v. O'Neil, 280 App.Div. 145, 112 N.Y.S.2d 756 (1952). This section will make it clear that the section captions are relevant in all cases governed by the Code.

Official Uniform Comment

Prior Uniform Statutory Provision: None.

Purposes:

To make explicit in all jurisdictions that section captions are a part of the text of this Act and not mere surplusage.

PART 2

GENERAL DEFINITIONS AND PRINCIPLES OF INTERPRETATION

Section 1–201. General Definitions.

Subject to additional definitions contained in the subsequent Articles of this Act which are applicable to specific Articles or Parts thereof, and unless the context otherwise requires, in this Act:

(1) "Action" in the sense of a judicial proceeding includes recoupment, counterclaim, set-off, suit in equity and any other proceedings in which rights are determined.

(2) "Aggrieved party" means a party entitled to resort to a remedy.

(3) "Agreement" means the bargain of the parties in fact as found in their language or by implication from other circumstances including course of dealing or usage of trade or course of performance as provided in this Act (Sections 1–205 and 2–208). Whether an agreement has legal consequences is determined by the provisions of this Act, if applicable; otherwise by the law of contracts (Section 1–103). (Compare "Contract".)

(4) "Bank" means any person engaged in the business of banking.

(5) "Bearer" means the person in possession of an instrument, document of title, or certificated security payable to bearer or indorsed in blank.

(6) "Bill of lading" means a document evidencing the receipt of goods for shipment issued by a person engaged in the business of transporting or forwarding goods, and includes an airbill. "Airbill" means a document serving for air transportation as a bill of lading does for marine or rail transportation, and includes an air consignment note or air waybill.

(7) “Branch” includes a separately incorporated foreign branch of a bank.

(8) “Burden of establishing” a fact means the burden of persuading the triers of fact that the existence of the fact is more probable than its non-existence.

(9) “Buyer in ordinary course of business” means a person who in good faith and without knowledge that the sale to him is in violation of the ownership rights or security interest of a third party in the goods buys in ordinary course from a person in the business of selling goods of that kind but does not include a collateral loan broker. All persons who sell minerals or the like (including oil and gas) at wellhead or minehead shall be deemed to be persons in the business of selling goods of that kind. “Buying” may be for cash or by exchange of other property or on secured or unsecured credit and includes receiving goods or documents of title under a pre-existing contract for sale but does not include a transfer in bulk or as security for or in total or partial satisfaction of a money debt.

(10) “Conspicuous”: A term or clause is conspicuous when it is so written that a reasonable person against whom it is to operate ought to have noticed it. A printed heading in capitals (as: NON-NEGOTIABLE BILL OF LADING) is conspicuous. Language in the body of a form is “conspicuous” if it is in larger or other contrasting type or color. But in a telegram any stated term is “conspicuous”. Whether a term or clause is “conspicuous” or not is for decision by the court.

(11) “Contract” means the total legal obligation which results from the parties' agreement as affected by this Act and any other applicable rules of law. (Compare “Agreement”.)

(12) “Creditor” includes a general creditor, a secured creditor, a lien creditor and any representative of creditors, including an assignee for the benefit of creditors, a trustee in bankruptcy, a receiver in equity and an executor or administrator of an insolvent debtor's or assignor's estate.

(13) “Defendant” includes a person in the position of defendant in a cross-action or counterclaim.

(14) “Delivery” with respect to instruments, documents of title, chattel paper or certificated securities means voluntary transfer of possession.

(15) “Document of title” includes bill of lading, dock warrant, dock receipt, warehouse receipt or order for the delivery of goods, and also any other document which in the regular course of business or financing is treated as adequately evidencing that the person in possession of it is entitled to receive, hold and dispose of the document and the goods it covers. To be a document of title a document must purport to be issued by or addressed to a bailee and purport to cover goods in the bailee's possession which are either identified or are fungible portions of an identified mass.

(16) “Fault” means wrongful act, omission or breach.

(17) "Fungible" with respect to goods or securities means goods or securities of which any unit is, by nature or usage of trade, the equivalent of any other like unit. Goods which are not fungible shall be deemed fungible for the purposes of this Act to the extent that under a particular agreement or document unlike units are treated as equivalents.

(18) "Genuine" means free of forgery or counterfeiting.

(19) "Good faith" means honesty in fact in the conduct or transaction concerned.

(20) "Holder" means a person who is in possession of a document of title or an instrument or an investment certificated security drawn, issued or indorsed to him or to his order or to bearer or in blank.

(21) To "honor" is to pay or to accept and pay, or where a credit so engages to purchase or discount a draft complying with the terms of the credit.

(22) "Insolvency proceedings" includes any assignment for the benefit of creditors or other proceedings intended to liquidate or rehabilitate the estate of the person involved.

(23) A person is "insolvent" who either has ceased to pay his debts in the ordinary course of business or cannot pay his debts as they become due or is insolvent within the meaning of the federal bankruptcy law.

(24) "Money" means a medium of exchange authorized or adopted by a domestic or foreign government as a part of its currency except that it does not include rare or unusual coins used for numismatic purposes. Such rare or unusual coins shall be considered goods; provided, however, that nothing in this subsection shall be deemed to impair or alter the obligation of an insurer to an insured under a contract of insurance heretofore or hereafter issued or delivered in this state covering loss of or damage to property.

(25) A person has "notice" of a fact when

(a) he has actual knowledge of it; or

(b) he has received a notice or notification of it; or

(c) from all the facts and circumstances known to him at the time in question he has reason to know that it exists.

A person "knows" or has "knowledge" of a fact when he has actual knowledge of it. "Discover" or "learn" or a word or phrase of similar import refers to knowledge rather than to reason to know. The time and circumstances under which a notice or notification may cease to be effective are not determined by this Act.

(26) A person "notifies" or "gives" a notice or notification to another by taking such steps as may be reasonably required to inform the other in ordinary course whether or not such other actually comes to know of it. A person "receives" a notice or notification when

(a) it comes to his attention; or

(b) it is duly delivered at the place of business through which the contract was made or at any other place held out by him as the place for receipt of such communications.

(27) Notice, knowledge or a notice or notification received by an organization is effective for a particular transaction from the time when it is brought to the attention of the individual conducting that transaction, and in any event from the time when it would have been brought to his attention if the organization had exercised due diligence. An organization exercises due diligence if it maintains reasonable routines for communicating significant information to the person conducting the transaction and there is reasonable compliance with the routines. Due diligence does not require an individual acting for the organization to communicate information unless such communication is part of his regular duties or unless he has reason to know of the transaction and that the transaction would be materially affected by the information.

(28) "Organization" includes a corporation, government or governmental subdivision or agency, business trust, estate, trust, partnership or association, two or more persons having a joint or common interest, or any other legal or commercial entity.

(29) "Party", as distinct from "third party", means a person who has engaged in a transaction or made an agreement within this Act.

(30) "Person" includes an individual or an organization. (See Section 1–102).

(31) "Presumption" or "presumed" means that the trier of fact must find the existence of the fact presumed unless and until evidence is introduced which would support a finding of its non-existence.

(32) "Purchase" includes taking by sale, discount, negotiation, mortgage, pledge, lien, issue or re-issue, gift or any other voluntary transaction creating an interest in property.

(33) "Purchaser" means a person who takes by purchase.

(34) "Remedy" means any remedial right to which an aggrieved party is entitled with or without resort to a tribunal.

(35) "Representative" includes an agent, an officer of a corporation or association, and a trustee, executor or administrator of an estate, or any other person empowered to act for another.

(36) "Rights" includes remedies.

[Editor's note: the following subsection is effective until and including June 29, 1995.]

(37) "Security interest" means an interest in personal property or fixtures which secures payment or performance of an obligation. The retention or reservation of title by a seller of goods notwithstanding shipment or delivery to the buyer (Section 2–401) is limited in effect to a reservation of a "security

interest". The term also includes any interest of a buyer of accounts or chattel paper which is subject to Article 9. The special property interest of a buyer of goods on identification of such goods to a contract for sale under Section 2–401 is not a "security interest", but a buyer may also acquire a "security interest" by complying with Article 9. Unless a lease or consignment is intended as security, reservation of title thereunder is not a "security interest" but a consignment is in any event subject to the provisions on consignment sales (Section 2–326). Whether a lease is intended as security is to be determined by the facts of each case; however, (a) the inclusion of an option to purchase does not of itself make the lease one intended for security, and (b) an agreement that upon compliance with the terms of the lease the lessee shall become or has the option to become the owner of the property for no additional consideration or for a nominal consideration does make the lease one intended for security.

[Editor's note: the following subsection is effective June 30, 1995.]

(37) "Security interest" means an interest in personal property or fixtures which secures payment or performance of an obligation. The retention or reservation of title by a seller of goods notwithstanding shipment or delivery to the buyer (Section 2-401) is limited in effect to a reservation of a "security interest". The term also includes any interest of a buyer of accounts or chattel paper which is subject to Article 9. The special property interest of a buyer of goods on identification of such goods to a contract for sale under Section 2-401 is not a "security interest", but a buyer may also acquire a "security interest" by complying with Article 9. Unless a lease or consignment is intended as security, reservation of title thereunder is not a "security interest", but a consignment is in any event subject to the provisions on consignment sales (Section 2-326). Whether a transaction creates a lease or security interest is determined by the facts of each case; however, a transaction creates a security interest if the consideration the lessee is to pay the lessor for the right to possession and use of the goods is an obligation for the term of the lease not subject to termination by the lessee, and

(a) the original term of the lease is equal to or greater than the remaining economic life of the goods,

(b) the lessee is bound to renew the lease for the remaining economic life of the goods or is bound to become the owner of the goods,

(c) the lessee has an option to renew the lease for the remaining economic life of the goods for no additional consideration or nominal additional consideration upon compliance with the lease agreement, or

(d) the lessee has an option to become the owner of the goods for no additional consideration or nominal additional consideration upon compliance with the lease agreement.

A transaction does not create a security interest merely because it provides that:

(a) the present value of the consideration the lessee is obligated to pay the lessor for the right to possession and use of the goods is substantially equal to or is greater than the fair market value of the goods at the time the lease is entered into,

(b) the lessee assumes risk of loss of the goods, or agrees to pay taxes, insurance, filing, recording, or registration fees, or service or maintenance costs with respect to the goods,

(c) the lessee has an option to renew the lease or to become the owner of the goods,

(d) the lessee has an option to renew the lease for a fixed rent that is equal to or greater than the reasonably predictable fair market rent for the use of the goods for the term of the renewal at the time the option is to be performed, or

(e) the lessee has an option to become the owner of the goods for a fixed price that is equal to or greater than the reasonably predictable fair market value of the goods at the time the option is to be performed.

For purposes of this subsection (37):

(a) Additional consideration is not nominal if (i) when the option to renew the lease is granted to the lessee the rent is stated to be the fair market rent for the use of the goods for the term of the renewal determined at the time the option is to be performed, or (ii) when the option to become the owner of the goods is granted to the lessee the price is stated to be the fair market value of the goods determined at the time the option is to be performed. Additional consideration is nominal if it is less than the lessee's reasonably predictable cost of performing under the lease agreement if the option is not exercised;

(b) "Reasonably predictable" and "remaining economic life of the goods" are to be determined with reference to the facts and circumstances at the time the transaction is entered into; and

(c) "Present value" means the amount as of a date certain of one or more sums payable in the future, discounted to the date certain. The discount is determined by the interest rate specified by the parties if the rate is not manifestly unreasonable at the time the transaction is entered into; otherwise, the discount is determined by a commercially reasonable rate that takes into account the facts and circumstances of each case at the time the transaction was entered into.

(38) "Send" in connection with any writing or notice means to deposit in the mail or deliver for transmission by any other usual means of communication with postage or cost of transmission provided for and properly addressed and in the case of an instrument to an address specified thereon or otherwise agreed, or if there be none to any address reasonable under the circumstances. The receipt

of any writing or notice within the time at which it would have arrived if properly sent has the effect of a proper sending.

(39) "Signed" includes any symbol executed or adopted by a party with present intention to authenticate a writing. Without limiting the generality of the preceding sentence, any financing or other statement or security agreement filed pursuant to Part 4 of Article 9 which contains a copy, however made, of the signature of a secured party or his representative, or of a debtor or his representative, is "signed" by the secured party or the debtor, as the case may be.

(40) "Surety" includes guarantor.

(41) "Telegram" includes a message transmitted by radio, tele-type, cable, any mechanical method of transmission, or the like.

(42) "Term" means that portion of an agreement which relates to a particular matter.

(43) "Unauthorized" signature or indorsement means one made without actual, implied or apparent authority and includes a forgery.

(44) "Value". Except as otherwise provided with respect to negotiable instruments and bank collections (Sections 3–303, 4–208 and 4–209) a person gives "value" for rights if he acquires them

(a) in return for a binding commitment to extend credit or for the extension of immediately available credit whether or not drawn upon and whether or not a charge-back is provided for in the event of difficulties in collection; or

(b) as security for or in total or partial satisfaction of a pre-existing claim; or

(c) by accepting delivery pursuant to a pre-existing contract for purchase; or

(d) generally, in return for any consideration sufficient to support a simple contract.

(45) "Warehouse receipt" means a receipt issued by a person engaged in the business of storing goods for hire.

(46) "Written" or "writing" includes printing, typewriting or any other intentional reduction to tangible form.

Amended by Laws 1963, Ch. 1003, eff. Sept. 27, 1963; Laws 1981, Ch. 686, eff. July 21, 1981; Laws 1982, Ch. 928, eff. Dec. 21, 1982 and deemed to have been in full force and effect on and after Sept. 1, 1982: L. 1983, Ch. 321, eff. June 21, 1983.

1977 Amendment

Subsections (9) and (37) of Section 1–201 were amended by L. 1977, ch. 866, effective July 2, 1978. The following sentence was added to 1–201(9):

"All persons who sell minerals or the like (including oil and gas) at wellhead or minehead shall be deemed to be persons in the business of selling goods of that kind."

The amendment to Section 1–201(37) deleted the words "contract rights."

New York Annotations

The definitions appearing in this section are designed to be used throughout the Code. It is important to note the fact that for policy reasons these terms may be varied by specific provisions in the substantive rules of the various articles, e.g., "buyer in ordinary course" is defined in Section 1–201(9), but the buyer group, protected against pre-existing security interests in Section 9–307(1), is enlarged by the explicit provision in the latter section that the buyer is sheltered even though the buyer knows of the existence of the outstanding security interest.

(1) "Action". This definition is consistent with, but, by adding "any other proceeding by which rights are determined," the Code term is somewhat broader in scope than the definitions in Personal Property Law, §§ 156 (sales), and 239 (bills of lading), and in General Business Law, § 142 (warehouse receipts). See also N.I.L., § 2 (equity not referenced), and General Construction Law, §§ 11–a and 46–a.

(2) "Aggrieved party." No comment appears to be required.

(3) "Agreement." To the extent that the term is neutral on the question of whether or not legal consequences flow from the "agreement," it is consistent with New York cases, e.g., Peirce v. Cornell, 117 App.Div. 66, 102 N.Y.S. 102 (1907). See Restatement, Contracts, § 3. The Code adds consideration of usages of trade, course of dealing, course of performance, and course of surrounding circumstances.

(4) "Bank." Substantially the same definition is now contained in N.I.L., § 2. In N.I.L., § 350(a), dealing with bank collections, a somewhat different definition turns on being "in the business of receiving and paying deposits of money within this state."

(5) "Bearer." In N.I.L., § 2, this term is defined so as to be limited to monetary negotiable instruments, whereas the Code definition seems broad enough to include the possessor of documents of title or investment securities. See §§ 7–501(3) and 3–204.

(6) "Bill of lading." Personal Property Law, § 187 (Uniform Bills of Lading Act, § 1), provides that bills of lading issued by a common carrier shall be subject to that Act. The Code is not so limited and will extend the definition to include bills issued by freight forwarders as well as air carriers. "Air bill" is new.

(7) "Branch." In bank collection matters, Section 4–106 must be consulted.

(8) "Burden of establishing." No comment appears necessary.

(9) "Buyer in ordinary course of business." This subparagraph gives a single meaning to a term now employed in three separate New York statutes. In Personal Property Law, § 58–a, where a trustee under a trust receipt transaction has liberty of sale, he has the power to transfer ownership to "a buyer in the ordinary course of trade." In Personal Property Law, § 69, a "buyer for value in the ordinary course of business" from the conditional buyer is protected if the original seller consented to resale. See, Rand's Discount Co. v. Universal C. I. T. Credit Corp., 9 N.Y.2d 454, 174 N.E.2d 599 (1961). The most completely developed statement of the term is in Lien Law, § 230–c. There a "buyer in the ordinary course of trade," purchasing from a dealer any goods covered by a dealer's chattel mortgage, is protected against the dealer's mortgagee. Unlike the Code, that subparagraph requires "new value", and explicitly permits another dealer to fall within the protected group except where the goods are within § 301(1) of the Personal Property Law. The Code, like the dealer's chattel mortgage provision, excludes other secured parties from the protected group, leaving their rights to ordinary priority rules. (See Section 9–312.) The Code's exclusion of pawnbrokers is new. Both the trust receipts and the dealer's chattel mortgage provisions make it clear that the buyer must take delivery. See on this point Sections 2–403(2), 7–205(1), 7–503, and 9–307(1). "Ordinary course" is also used as a test in the Bulk Sales Act, see Personal Property Law, § 44, and Sternberg v. Rubenstein, 305 N.Y. 235, 112 N.E.2d 210 (1953).

(10) "Conspicuous." It is important to note that it is for the court to decide whether attention can reasonably be expected to be called to the term or clause. The policy principle of this subparagraph is not unlike that of Personal Property Law, §§ 302 and 402, requiring specific type size in the disclosures called for in the installment sales legislation. Boldface type on a "confirmation" which referred to an arbitration clause on the reverse side has been held to be significant on the issue of the effect of the clause. Application of Central States Paper & Bag Co., 132 N.Y.S.2d 69, aff'd 284 App. Div. 841, 134 N.Y.S.2d 271, app. den. 307 N.Y. 943, 122 N.E.2d 336 (1954).

(11) "Contract." This definition is consistent with Personal Property Law, §§ 33 and 152. By distinguishing between "agreement" and "contract" the Code removes a source of ambiguity noted in Restatement, Contracts, § 1, Comment c.

(12) "Creditor." This definition expands upon Debtor and Creditor Law, § 270. (Uniform Fraudulent Conveyance Act, § 1.) Note that the Uniform Fraudulent Conveyance Act is not affected by the Code.

(13) "Defendant." This subparagraph rephrases Personal Property Law, § 156, and adds a reference to "cross action."

(14) "Delivery." This definition corresponds to that contained in Personal Property Law, §§ 183 (stock transfer) and 156 (sales); and in General Business Law, § 142 (warehouse receipts). Unlike N.I.L., § 2, the Code omits any reference to "actual or constructive" possession.

(15) "Document of title." The Code definition is consistent with Personal Property Law, § 156 (sales), but the scope is broadened by general language to include newly developing practices. Further, the Code adds a specific requirement that the document be issued by or addressed to a bailee. See Comment 15.

(16) "Fault." This is consistent with Personal Property Law, § 156 (sales).

(17) "Fungible." This definition is consistent with Personal Property Law, § 156 (sales), and General Business Law, § 142 (warehouse receipts); however, the second sentence is new in explicitly permitting parties to agree that certain goods are to be treated as fungible.

(18) "Genuine." The term has been given a broader meaning in one case involving the warranty of an indorser of a warehouse receipt under General Business Law, §§ 91 and 128, where "genuine" was held to mean a "truthful statement of the transaction." Stanford Seed Co. v. Balfour, Guthrie G. Co. Ltd., 27 Misc.2d 147, 208 N.Y.S.2d 996 (1960). See Section 7–507 and Section 1–203.

(19) "Good faith." This use of the term is the same as in Personal Property Law, § 156(2) (sales), § 183 (stock transfers), § 239(2) (bills of lading), and in General Business Law, § 142 (warehouse receipts). For some purposes the definition is expanded by other sections of the Code, e.g., Section 2–103(1)(b).

(20) "Holder." Generally this definition is in accord with N.I.L., § 2, Personal Property Law, § 239 (bills of lading), and General Business Law, § 142 (warehouse receipts). The Code term is broader than the latter two sections since it omits the requirement that the alleged "holder" have a "right of property" in the document of title. The subparagraph also is new in that it extends to investment securities.

(21) "Honor." New and appears to require no comment.

(22) "Insolvency proceedings." New and appears to require no comment.

(23) "Insolvent." This definition is consistent with but broader than that in § 156 of the Personal Property Law (sales). The Code adds the third alternative, "insolvent within the meaning of the federal bankruptcy law."

(24) "Money." See annotation to Sections 3–103, 3–107, and 8–102(1)(b).

(25) "Notice." This is a new provision. N.I.L., § 95, includes (a) and (b) but not (c) of this subparagraph. Note that Comment 25 states that the last sentence leaves to the common law the question of "forgotten notice". See First Nat'l Bank of Odessa v. Fazzari, 22 Misc.2d 351, 193 N.Y.S.2d 367 (1959), rev'd 13 A.D.2d 582, 212 N.Y.S.2d 380, mod. 10 N.Y.2d 394, 179 N.E.2d 493, 223 N.Y.S.2d 483 (1961).

(26) "Notifies." The first sentence of this subparagraph appears to be consistent with N.I.L., § 176, which provides that when "notice of dishonor is duly addressed and deposited in the post-office, the sender is deemed to have given due notice, notwithstanding any miscarriage in the mails." To some extent, the subparagraph is also consistent with the rule on formation of ordinary contracts. See, Wester v. Casein Company of America, 206 N.Y. 506, 100 N.E. 488 (1912). The second sentence is supported by Restatement, Contracts, § 69.

(27) "Receipt of notice by an organization." This subparagraph, though broader in scope, seems consistent with the last paragraph of Personal Property Law, § 219. A carrier has not received notification within the meaning of the last cited section unless "an officer or agent of the carrier, the actual or apparent scope of whose duties includes action upon such notification, has been notified; and no notification shall be effective until the officer or agent to whom it is given has had time with the exercise of reasonable diligence to communicate with the agent or agents having actual possession or control of the goods." Cf. General Construction Law, § 33, on notice to a board or a body. As to the last two sentences, Cf. Restatement (Second), Agency §§ 268, 272, 278 (1958).

(28) "Organization." This subparagraph covers every kind of legal entity other than a single individual and is much broader than the definitions of "persons" in the existing commercial statutes. In N.I.L., § 2, "persons" includes a body of persons whether incorporated or not. However, in Personal Property Law, § 239 (bills of lading); § 183 (stock transfers); § 61 (conditional sales); and in General Business Law, § 142 (warehouse receipts), "person" includes a corporation or partnership or two or more persons having a joint or common interest. The trust receipts definition is more complete: "an individual, trustee, receiver, or other fiduciary, partnership, corporation, business trust, or other association, and two or more persons having a joint or common interest." (Personal Property Law, § 51(8).) As to government and governmental subdivisions, see General Construction Law, § 37.

(29) "Party." No annotation appears necessary. See Comment 29.

(30) "Person." See annotation to "Organization," *supra.* The Comment 30 points out that the reference to Section 1–102 is to subsection (5) of that section.

(31) "Presumption." Although this term is not clearly defined in present New York law, the Code definition appears consistent with some existing case law. People v. Richetti, 302 N.Y. 290, 97 N.E.2d 908 (1951) (presumption of regularity of judgment of conviction exists only until contrary substantial evidence appears).

(32) "Purchase," and (33) "Purchaser." These definitions are broader than Personal Property Law, § 156 (sales), § 61 (conditional sales), § 156 (bills of lading), and § 183 (stock transfers); and General Business Law, § 142 (warehouse receipts), where "purchase" includes taking as a mortgagee and pledgee. In those sections "purchaser" is defined as including a mortgagee or pledgee. In relation to trust receipts, "purchase" is said to mean "taking by sale, conditional sale, lease, mortgage or pledge, legal or equitable," and "purchaser" is any person taking by purchase. "A pledgee, mortgagee or other claimant of a security interest created by contract is, in so far as concerns his specific security, a purchaser and not a creditor." (Personal Property Law, § 51.) The Code adds to these definitions several clarifying phrases including "gift". Note that usually the Code section, where the word "purchaser" is used, also contains a requirement that "value" be given, e.g., Section 2–403(1). Compare Sections 7–210(5) and 7–308(4).

(34) "Remedy." No annotation seems necessary except to note that self-help is included herein, e.g., Section 2–711.

(35) "Representative." No annotation seems necessary, but note that the definition does not provide tests for determining whether or not a person is empowered to act for another, such tests would continue to be provided under the law of agency. See Section 1–103.

(36) "Rights." See comment to "Remedy."

(37) "Security interest." This definition is patterned after that contained in Personal Property Law, § 51(12) (trust receipts). As to that portion of the definition dealing with "reservation of the property by the seller or consignor" see Personal Property Law, § 101(1) (sales) and § 226 (bills of lading). As to the use of the term "security interest" in Articles 2, 4, and 7, see Sections 9–113, 4–208, and 7–209. Obviously the context shows that the term draws on these notions of security for a debt rather than the concept of investment securities in Article 8. See Section 8–102(1)(a). That portion of the definition which includes outright purchase of certain intangible collateral is new. See annotation to Section 9–102.

(38) "Send." See N.I.L., § 179, which would be replaced by this provision. The definition is new to the commercial statutes. The requirement of "proper address" is similar to N.I.L., § 176, on notice of protest when "duly addressed."

(39) "Signed." This definition is much like that contained in General Construction Law, § 46, except that the Code definition does not expressly state that the symbol must be on the writing. Comment 39 seems to state such a requirement.

(40) "Surety." This is new to the statutes but is in accord with Restatement, Security, § 82, Comment g. The question is not clear under the cases. Compare Pink v. Investors Syndicate Title & Guaranty Co., 246 App.Div. 172, 285 N.Y.S. 155, aff'd 273 N.Y. 483, 6 N.E.2d 414 (1936), and Bank of Italy v. Merchants Nat'l Bank, 197 App.Div. 150, 188 N.Y.S. 183 (1921).

(41) "Telegram," and (42) "Term." No annotation required.

(43) "Unauthorized signature." The commercial statutes do not presently define or use this term. N.I.L., § 42, does provide the same legal consequences when a signature is "forged or made without authority."

(44) "Value." This definition has its closest counterpart in the present trust receipts law. Personal Property Law, § 51(15). However, clause (c) has no counterpart in existing statutes. The inclusion of bank credit as value in clause (a), even though such credit is not drawn upon, accords with the special Code rule in bank collections (Sections 4–208(1)(b) and 4–209), but not with the general rule for negotiable instruments (Section 3–303). In documentary transactions this rule will apparently change New York law. First National Bank of Blanchester v. Stengel, 169 N.Y.S. 217 (1918), aff'd, 185 App.Div. 906, 171 N.Y.S. 1085, aff'd, 227 N.Y. 659, 126 N.E. 906 (1920). Clauses (a) and (d) are otherwise in accord with the definition in present statutes, Personal Property Law, § 156(1) (sales), § 183 (stock transfers), § 239 (bills of lading), and § 51(15) (trust receipts), N.I.L., § 2, and General Business Law, § 142 (warehouse receipts). Clause (b) is clearly analogous to all previously cited statutes, except N.I.L., § 2. Personal Property Law, §§ 60–81 (conditional sales) contain no definition of value.

(45) "Warehouse receipt." General Business Law, §§ 90 and 142(1) state respectively that a warehouse receipt may be issued by any warehouseman and that a warehouseman is a person lawfully engaged in the business of storing goods for profit. The Code omits the requirement of lawfulness to subject the bailee to liability under Article 1 even though he does business illegally. See annotation to Section 7–102(h).

(46) "Written" or "writing." N.I.L., § 2, provides that "written" or "writing" includes "printed" or "printing." General Construction Law, § 56, now provides that "writing" and "written" include every legible representation of letters upon a material substance, except when applied to the signature of an instrument.

Historical Note: (3) "Agreement." The changes leave the effect of course of dealing and the like to other provisions such as Section 1–205, and meet suggestions of the Law Revision Commission.

(9) "Buyer in ordinary course of business." The reference to "good faith" was added on the recommendation of the Law Revision Commission to make it clear that one

who buys dishonestly is not within the definition. The "without knowledge" addition spells out one important type of dishonesty. The reference to an exchange of property was added for clarification, and the reference to "securities" before "or documents" was deleted as inappropriate. The exception for buyers from farmers was replaced by an exception in Section 9–307 to meet the suggestion of the Law Revision Commission that the exception was inappropriate in Section 2–403.

(11) "Contract." The change to "legal obligation" was for clarification in response to criticism by the Law Revision Commission.

(12) "Creditor." The change, made in Supp. No. 1, widens the definition to include all classes of creditors and all representatives of creditors.

(15) "Document of title." "Regular" was substituted for "current" to conform to a change made in Section 7–501, and meets a suggestion of the Law Revision Commission.

(25) "Notice." The changes in subparagraphs (25), (26), and (27) were made for clarification in response to criticism by the Law Revision Commission. Based on a study of all the provisions of the Code relating to knowledge, notice, and notification, the changes make it clear that the Code employs four distinct concepts: (1) to notify or to give or send a notice or notification, (2) to receive a notice or notification, (3) to have notice or reason to know, and (4) to know, discover, or learn. The last sentence in subparagraph (25) makes it clear that the Code does not undertake to state all the variations in the law of effective duration of a notice or notification received.

(26) "Notifies." See subparagraph (25).

(27) "Receipt of notice by an organization." See subparagraph (25).

(29) "Party." The change makes the definition applicable to parties to a bargain without regard to the legal obligation resulting from the bargain and meets a Law Revision Commission suggestion.

(30) "Person." The cross-reference is inserted to direct attention to new subparagraph (5) of Section 1–102.

(32) "Purchase." The reference to "negotiation" was added for clarification.

(37) "Security interest." Supp. No. 1 changed the definition to make it clear that in the Code, and particularly in Article 9, "Security interest" is limited to personal property and fixtures, and except for fixtures does not apply to real estate. Other changes make it clear that a true consignment or lease is not a secured transaction subject to all the filing, priority, and enforcement provisions of Article 9, and eliminated the undefined concept of a "financing" buyer of accounts, chattel paper, or contract rights. The exclusion provisions of Article 9 satisfactorily specify types of transactions in accounts, chattel paper, and contract rights not subject to the article. Further revision modified the second and fourth sentences to conform to changes made in Section 2–401 and to new Section 9–113. Those changes were made in response to the suggestion of the Law Revision Commission that there was need for clarification of the application of Article 9 to "security interests" arising in a sale of goods. The sixth sentence clarifies what is meant by a lease "intended as security" in the fifth sentence.

(39) "Signed." The change, substituting all the language after "any" for "authentication", was recommended by the Law Revision Commission for clarification.

(43) "Unauthorized." The change expressly covers indorsements as recommended by the Law Revision Commission.

(44) "Value." To meet published criticism noted by the Law Revision Commission, a uniform definition in Article 1 was substituted for the separate definitions previously appearing in Sections 7–102(1)(g), 8–303, and 9–108(1). See also the former cross-references in Sections 2–103(3) and 8–102(4). The new definition was modelled on former Section 9–108(1), with clarifying changes. The separate definitions of "value" for Articles 3 and 4 are preserved.

(45) "Warehouse receipt." The definition was conformed to the definition of "warehouseman" in Section 7–102(1)(h), as suggested by the Law Revision Commission.

(1956 Recommendations, pp. 13–15; Excerpts, pp. 359–363.)

Official Uniform Comment

Prior Uniform Statutory Provision, Changes and New Matter:

1. "Action". See similar definitions in Section 191, Uniform Negotiable Instruments Law; Section 76, Uniform Sales Act; Section 58, Uniform Warehouse Receipts Act; Section 53, Uniform Bills of Lading Act. The definition has been rephrased and enlarged.

2. "Aggrieved party". New.

3. "Agreement". New. As used in this Act the word is intended to include full recognition of usage of trade, course of dealing, course of performance and the surrounding circumstances as effective parts thereof, and of any agreement permitted under the provisions of this Act to displace a stated rule of law.

4. "Bank". See Section 191, Uniform Negotiable Instruments Law.

5. "Bearer". From Section 191, Uniform Negotiable Instruments Law. The prior definition has been broadened.

6. "Bill of Lading". See similar definitions in Section 1, Uniform Bills of Lading Act. The definition has been enlarged to include freight forwarders' bills and bills issued by contract carriers as well as those issued by common carriers. The definition of airbill is new.

7. "Branch". New.

8. "Burden of establishing a fact". New.

9. "Buyer in ordinary course of business". From Section 1, Uniform Trust Receipts Act. The definition has been expanded to make clear the type of person protected. Its major significance lies in Section 2–403 and in the Article on Secured Transactions (Article 9).

The reference to minerals and the like makes clear that a buyer in ordinary course buying minerals under the circumstances described takes free of a prior mortgage created by the sellers. See Comment to Section 9–103.

A pawnbroker cannot be a buyer in ordinary course of business because the person from whom he buys goods (or acquires ownership after foreclosing an initial pledge) is typically an ordinary user and not a person engaged in selling goods of that kind.

10. "Conspicuous". New. This is intended to indicate some of the methods of making a term attention-calling. But the test is whether attention can reasonably be expected to be called to it.

11. "Contract". New. But see Sections 3 and 71, Uniform Sales Act.

12. "Creditor". New.

13. "Defendant". From Section 76, Uniform Sales Act. Rephrased.

14. "Delivery". Section 76, Uniform Sales Act, Section 191, Uniform Negotiable Instruments Law, Section 58, Uniform Warehouse Receipts Act and Section 53, Uniform Bills of Lading Act.

15. "Document of title". From Section 76, Uniform Sales Act, but rephrased to eliminate certain ambiguities. Thus, by making it explicit that the obligation or designation of a third party as "bailee" is essential to a document of title, this definition clearly rejects any such result as obtained in Hixson v. Ward, 254 Ill. App. 505 (1929), which treated a conditional sales contract as a document of title. Also the definition is left open so that new types of documents may be included. It is unforeseeable what documents may one day serve the essential purpose now filled by warehouse receipts and bills of lading. Truck transport has already opened up problems which do not fit the patterns of practice resting upon the assumption that a draft can move through

banking channels faster than the goods themselves can reach their destination. There lie ahead air transport and such probabilities as teletype transmission of what may some day be regarded commercially as "Documents of Title". The definition is stated in terms of the function of the documents with the intention that any document which gains commercial recognition as accomplishing the desired result shall be included within its scope. Fungible goods are adequately identified within the language of the definition by identification of the mass of which they are a part.

Dock warrants were within the Sales Act definition of document of title apparently for the purpose of recognizing a valid tender by means of such paper. In current commercial practice a dock warrant or receipt is a kind of interim certificate issued by steamship companies upon delivery of the goods at the dock, entitling a designated person to have issued to him at the company's office a bill of lading. The receipt itself is invariable nonnegotiable in form although it may indicate that a negotiable bill is to be forthcoming. Such a document is not within the general compass of the definition, although trade usage may in some cases entitle such paper to be treated as a document of title. If the dock receipt actually represents a storage obligation undertaken by the shipping company, then it is a warehouse receipt within this Section regardless of the name given to the instrument.

The goods must be "described", but the description may be by marks or labels and may be qualified in such a way as to disclaim personal knowledge of the issuer regarding contents or condition. However, baggage and parcel checks and similar "tokens" of storage which identify stored goods only as those received in exchange for the token are not covered by this Article.

The definition is broad enough to include an airway bill.

16. "Fault". From Section 76, Uniform Sales Act.

17. "Fungible". See Sections 5, 6 and 76, Uniform Sales Act; Section 58, Uniform Warehouse Receipts Act. Fungibility of goods "by agreement" has been added for clarity and accuracy. As to securities, see Section 8–107 and Comment.

18. "Genuine". New.

19. "Good faith". See Section 76(2), Uniform Sales Act; Section 58(2), Uniform Warehouse Receipts Act; Section 53(2), Uniform Bills of Lading Act; Section 22(2), Uniform Stock Transfer Act. "Good faith", whenever it is used in the Code, means at least what is here stated. In certain Articles, by specific provision, additional requirements are made applicable. See, e.g., Secs. 2–103(1)(b), 7–404. To illustrate, in the Article on Sales, Section 2–103, good faith is expressly defined as including in the case of a merchant observance of reasonable commercial standards of fair dealing in the trade, so that throughout that Article wherever a merchant appears in the case an inquiry into his observance of such standards is necessary to determine his good faith.

20. "Holder". See similar definitions in Section 191, Uniform Negotiable Instruments Law; Section 58, Uniform Warehouse Receipts Act; Section 53, Uniform Bills of Lading Act.

21. "Honor". New.

22. "Insolvency proceedings". New.

23. "Insolvent". Section 76(3), Uniform Sales Act. The three tests of insolvency–"ceased to pay his debts in the ordinary course of business," "cannot pay his debts as they become due," and "insolvent within the meaning of the federal bankruptcy law"–are expressly set up as alternative tests and must be approached from a commercial standpoint.

24. "Money". Section 6(5), Uniform Negotiable Instruments Law. The test adopted is that of sanction of government, whether by authorization before issue or adoption afterward, which recognizes the circulating medium as a part of the official currency of that government. The narrow view that money is limited to legal tender is rejected.

25. "Notice". New. Compare N.I.L. Sec. 56. Under the definition a person has notice when he has received a notification of the fact in question. But by the last sentence

the act leaves open the time and circumstances under which notice or notification may cease to be effective. Therefore such cases as Graham v. White-Phillips Co., 296 U.S. 27, 56 S.Ct. 21, 80 L.Ed. 20(1935), are not overruled.

26. "Notifies". New. This is the word used when the essential fact is the proper dispatch of the notice, not its receipt. Compare "Send". When the essential fact is the other party's receipt of the notice, that is stated. The second sentence states when a notification is received.

27. New. This makes clear that reason to know, knowledge, or a notification, although "received" for instance by a clerk in Department A of an organization, is effective for a transaction conducted in Department B only from the time when it was or should have been communicated to the individual conducting that transaction.

28. "Organization". This is the definition of every type of entity or association, excluding an individual, acting as such. Definitions of "person" were included in Section 191, Uniform Negotiable Instruments Law; Section 76, Uniform Sales Act; Section 58, Uniform Warehouse Receipts Act; Section 53, Uniform Bills of Lading Act; Section 22, Uniform Stock Transfer Act; Section 1, Uniform Trust Receipts Act. The definition of "organization" given here includes a number of entities or associations not specifically mentioned in prior definition of "person", namely, government, governmental subdivision or agency, business trust, trust and estate.

29. "Party". New. Mention of a party includes, of course, a person acting through an agent. However, where an agent comes into opposition or contrast to his principal, particular account is taken of that situation.

30. "Person". See Comment to definition of "Organization". The reference to Section 1–102 is to subsection (5) of that section.

31. "Presumption". New.

32. "Purchase". Section 58, Uniform Warehouse Receipts Act; Section 76, Uniform Sales Act; Section 53, Uniform Bills of Lading Act; Section 22, Uniform Stock Transfer Act; Section 1, Uniform Trust Receipts Act. Rephrased.

33. "Purchaser". Section 58, Uniform Warehouse Receipts Act; Section 76, Uniform Sales Act; Section 53, Uniform Bills of Lading Act; Section 22, Uniform Stock Transfer Act; Section 1, Uniform Trust Receipts Act. Rephrased.

34. "Remedy". New. The purpose is to make it clear that both remedy and rights (as defined) include those remedial rights of "self help" which are among the most important bodies of rights under this Act, remedial rights being those to which an aggrieved party can resort on his own motion.

35. "Representative". New.

36. "Rights". New. See Comment to "Remedy".

37. "Security Interest". See Section 1, Uniform Trust Receipts Act. The present definition is elaborated, in view especially of the complete coverage of the subject in Article 9. Notice that in view of the Article the term includes the interest of certain outright buyers of certain kinds of property. The last two sentences give guidance on the question whether reservation of title under a particular lease of personal property is or is not a security interest.

38. "Send". New. Compare "notifies".

39. "Signed". New. The inclusion of authentication in the definition of "signed" is to make clear that as the term is used in this Act a complete signature is not necessary. Authentication may be printed, stamped or written; it may be by initials or by thumbprint. It may be on any part of the document and in appropriate cases may be found in a billhead or letterhead. No catalog of possible authentications can be complete and the court must use common sense and commercial experience passing upon these matters. The question always is whether the symbol was executed or adopted by the party with present intention to authenticate the writing.

40. "Surety". New.

41. "Telegram". New.

42. "Term". New.

43. "Unauthorized". New.

44. "Value". See Sections 25, 26, 27, 191, Uniform Negotiable Instruments Law; Section 76, Uniform Sales Act; Section 53, Uniform Bills of Lading Act; Section 58, Uniform Warehouse Receipts Act; Section 22(1), Uniform Stock Transfer Act; Section 1, Uniform Trust Receipts Act. All the Uniform Acts in the commercial law field (except the Uniform Conditional Sales Act) have carried definitions of "value". All those definitions provided that value was any consideration sufficient to support a simple contract, including the taking of property in satisfaction of or as security for a pre-existing claim. Subsections (a), (b) and (d) in substance continue the definitions of "value" in the earlier acts. Subsection (c) makes explicit that "value" is also given in a third situation: where a buyer by taking delivery under a pre-existing contract converts a contingent into a fixed obligation.

This definition is not applicable to Articles 3 and 4, but the express inclusion of immediately available credit as value follows the separate definitions in those Articles. See Sections 4–208, 4–209, 3–303. A bank or other financing agency which in good faith makes advances against property held as collateral becomes a bona fide purchaser of that property even though provision may be made for chargeback in case of trouble. Checking credit is "immediately available" within the meaning of this section if the bank would be subject to an action for slander of credit in case checks drawn against the credit were dishonored, and when a chargeback is not discretionary with the bank, but may only be made when difficulties in collection arise in connection with the specific transaction involved.

45. "Warehouse receipt". See Section 76(1), Uniform Sales Act; Section 1, Uniform Warehouse Receipts Act. Receipts issued by a field warehouse are included provided the warehouseman and the depositor of the goods are different persons.

46. "Written" or "writing". This is a broadening of the definition contained in Section 191 of the Uniform Negotiable Instruments Law.

Section 1–202. Prima Facie Evidence by Third Party Documents.

A document in due form purporting to be a bill of lading, policy or certificate of insurance, official weigher's or inspector's certificate, consular invoice, or any other document authorized or required by the contract to be issued by a third party shall be prima facie evidence of its own authenticity and genuineness and of the facts stated in the document by the third party.

New York Annotations

This section is new and would expand the usefulness of such documents. Note that the rules of this section apply only to documents authorized or required by the contract to be issued by third parties.

In order to measure adequately the effect of this section, the term "prima facie evidence" must first be defined. No definition appears in the Code (see Section 1–201(31) for presumption). The Court of Appeals has used the term in various ways and the interpretation seems to depend upon the precise issue being raised in a particular factual context. Sometimes the term is used in connection with a holding that the particular evidence is rebuttable and disappears when contrary evidence appears. Castorina v. Rosen, 290 N.Y. 445, 447, 49 N.E.2d 521 (1943); Matter of Seigle, 289 N.Y. 300, 303, 45 N.E.2d 809 (1942). The term has also been used when the Court applied a presumption of receipt of notice notwithstanding denial of receipt by the addressee. Trusts & Guarantee Co., Ltd. v. Barnhardt, 270 N.Y. 350, 354, 1 N.E.2d 459 (1936). When used in a statute as in Civil Practice Act, § 375 [now

CPLR rule 4528], making certain weather reports "prima facie evidence", the effect given such evidence has apparently remained in the case despite rebutting testimony. Schleede v. State, 5 Misc.2d 785, 160 N.Y.S.2d 686 (1957).

Other provisions of the Civil Practice Act using the term include § 375–b [now CPLR rule 4529] (U.S. Dept. of Agriculture certificates); § 356 (surveyor's chain certificate).

The problem of proving the genuineness of such documents could now be met in part by Civil Practice Act, § 322 [now CPLR § 3123], dealing with a notice to admit facts.

The exception that this section makes to the hearsay evidence rule is in a sense an extension of Civil Practice Act, § 374–a [now CPLR rule 4518], on the admissibility of certain written records made in the regular course of business.

Official Uniform Comment

Prior Uniform Statutory Provision: None.

Purposes:

1. This section is designed to supply judicial recognition for documents which have traditionally been relied upon as trustworthy by commercial men.

2. This section is concerned only with documents which have been given a preferred status by the parties themselves who have required their procurement in the agreement and for this reason the applicability of the section is limited to actions arising out of the contract which authorized or required the document. The documents listed are intended to be illustrative and not all inclusive.

3. The provisions of this section go no further than establishing the documents in question as prima facie evidence and leave to the court the ultimate determination of the facts where the accuracy or authenticity of the documents is questioned. In this connection the section calls for a commercially reasonable interpretation.

Definitional Cross References:

"Bill of lading". Section 1–201.
"Contract". Section 1–201.
"Genuine". Section 1–201.

Section 1–203. Obligation of Good Faith.

Every contract or duty within this Act imposes an obligation of good faith in its performance or enforcement.

New York Annotations

The Court of Appeals has frequently said, "Every contract implies good faith and fair dealing between the parties." M. O'Neil Supply Co. v. Petroleum Heat & Power Co., Inc., 280 N.Y. 50, 10 N.E.2d 676 (1939); Wigand v. Bachman-Bechtel Brewing Co., 222 N.Y. 272, 118 N.E. 618 (1918). Note that the Comment points out more specific applications of this concept in other sections of the Code. For Article 2, Section 2–103 defines good faith in the case of a merchant as including the observance of reasonable commercial standards of fair dealing in the trade. The result called for by this section has been accomplished occasionally under existing law by the implication of promises, e.g., Simon v. Etgon, 212 N.Y. 589, 107 N.E. 1066 (1915); Norcross v. Wills, 198 N.Y. 336, 91 N.E. 803 (1910).

Historical Note: The words "or duty" were added to make it clear that third parties as well as parties to a contract have an obligation of good faith. (1956 Recommendations, p. 15.)

Official Uniform Comment

Prior Uniform Statutory Provision: None.

Purposes:

This section sets forth a basic principle running throughout this Act. The principle involved is that in commercial transactions good faith is required in the performance and enforcement of all agreements or duties. Particular applications of this general principle appear in specific provisions of the Act such as the option to accelerate at will (Section 1–208), the right to cure a defective delivery of goods (Section 2–508), the duty of a merchant buyer who has rejected goods to effect salvage operations (Section 2–603), substituted performance (Section 2–614), and failure of presupposed conditions (Section 2–615). The concept, however, is broader than any of these illustrations and applies generally, as stated in this section, to the performance or enforcement of every contract or duty within this Act. It is further implemented by Section 1–205 on course of dealing and usage of trade.

It is to be noted that under the Sales Article definition of good faith (Section 2–103), contracts made by a merchant have incorporated in them the explicit standard not only of honesty in fact (Section 1–201), but also of observance by the merchant of reasonable commercial standards of fair dealing in the trade.

Cross References:

Sections 1–201; 1–205; 1–208; 2–103; 2–508; 2–603; 2–614; 2–615.

Definitional Cross References:

"Contract". Section 1–201.
"Good faith". Section 1–201; 2–103.

Section 1–204. Time; Reasonable Time; "Seasonably".

(1) Whenever this Act requires any action to be taken within a reasonable time, any time which is not manifestly unreasonable may be fixed by agreement.

(2) What is a reasonable time for taking any action depends on the nature, purpose and circumstances of such action.

(3) An action is taken "seasonably" when it is taken at or within the time agreed or if no time is agreed at or within a reasonable time.

New York Annotations

Except for the reference to fixing the time by agreement, subsections (2) and (3) appear to be consistent with N.I.L., § 4. Commercial Nat'l Bank v. Zimmerman, 185 N.Y. 210, 77 N.E. 1020 (1906). Further the term "seasonably" is new. The limitation that the time for action set by an agreement must not be manifestly unreasonable conforms to Section 1–102(3) on the establishment of standards for an obligation of "reasonableness". Note Section 1–102(4) in this connection.

Historical Note: The change in subsection (1) makes it clear, as recommended by the Law Revision Commission, that an agreement fixing a reasonable time may be subsequent to the main agreement. (1956 Recommendations, p. 16; Excerpts, p. 363.)

Official Uniform Comment

Prior Uniform Statutory Provision: None.

Purposes:

1. Subsection (1) recognizes that nothing is stronger evidence of a reasonable time than the fixing of such time by a fair agreement between the parties. However, provision is made for disregarding a clause which whether by inadvertence or overreaching fixes a time so unreasonable that it amounts to eliminating all remedy under the contract. The parties are not required to fix the most reasonable time but may fix any time which is not obviously unfair as judged by the time of contracting.

2. Under the section, the agreement which fixes the time need not be part of the main agreement, but may occur separately. Notice also that under the definition of "agreement" (Section 1–201) the circumstances of the transaction, including course of dealing or usages of trade or course of performance may be material. On the question what is a reasonable time these matters will often be important.

Definitional Cross Reference:

"Agreement". Section 1–201.

Section 1–205. Course of Dealing and Usage of Trade.

(1) A course of dealing is a sequence of previous conduct between the parties to a particular transaction which is fairly to be regarded as establishing a common basis of understanding for interpreting their expressions and other conduct.

(2) A usage of trade is any practice or method of dealing having such regularity of observance in a place, vocation or trade as to justify an expectation that it will be observed with respect to the transaction in question. The existence and scope of such a usage are to be proved as facts. If it is established that such a usage is embodied in a written trade code or similar writing the interpretation of the writing is for the court.

(3) A course of dealing between parties and any usage of trade in the vocation or trade in which they are engaged or of which they are or should be aware give particular meaning to and supplement or qualify terms of an agreement.

(4) The express terms of an agreement and an applicable course of dealing or usage of trade shall be construed wherever reasonable as consistent with each other; but when such construction is unreasonable express terms control both course of dealing and usage of trade and course of dealing controls usage of trade.

(5) An applicable usage of trade in the place where any part of performance is to occur shall be used in interpreting the agreement as to that part of the performance.

(6) Evidence of a relevant usage of trade offered by one party is not admissible unless and until he has given the other party such notice as the court finds sufficient to prevent unfair surprise to the latter.

New York Annotations

(1) "Course of dealing" is referred to in Personal Property Law, §§ 90(1) and 152 (sales). No further definition of the term has been found in the statutes. The Code provision would give such course of dealing greater effect in clarifying and supplementing express terms. The subsection seems consistent with Sinkwich v. E.F. Drew & Co., Inc., 9 A.D.2d 42, 189 N.Y.S.2d 630 (1959), where a continued interpretation of the contract bound the parties. The Code Definition would prevent one party from imposing his practice on another, as was apparently done (through Personal Property Law, § 152) in Matthes v. Benn, 107 Misc. 633, 176 N.Y.S. 770 (1919) (see discussion, *infra,* subsection (2)).

(2) Personal Property Law, § 152, also refers to custom "in varying obligations" that arise by "implication of law." The Code's requirement that the usages of trade have the specified "regularity of observance" is consistent with New York case law, Walls v. Bailey, 49 N.Y. 464 (1872). It may be that the Code will permit the use of the most recently developed usages where present law would require a notorious and long general practice. See Frye v. State, 192 Misc. 260, 78 N.Y.S.2d 342 (1948).

(3) This subsection seems to be in accord with the New York cases which permit parol evidence of trade usage to explain the meaning of a term of an agreement, Fox Film Corp. v. Springer, 273 N.Y. 434, 8 N.E.2d 23 (1937); Franklin Sugar Refining Co. v. Lipowicz, 247 N.Y. 465, 160 N.E. 916 (1928); Newhall v. Appleton, 114 N.Y. 140, 21 N.E. 105 (1889), or to supplement such terms, De Carlton v. Glaser, 172 App. Div. 132, 158 N.Y.S. 271 (1916), aff'd 225 N.Y. 687, 122 N.E. 878 (1919).

(4) The provision that express terms of the agreement shall control both course of dealing and usage of the trade is consistent with the New York case law that rejects usage where it contradicts the agreement. Gravenhorst v. Zimmerman, 236 N.Y. 22, 139 N.E. 766 (1923). Some New York authority suggests that usage will not be permitted to accomplish an unfair or immoral purpose, e.g., Fuller v. Robinson, 86 N.Y. 306 (1881) (rejected usage that a principal did not rely on broker's representation).

The provision establishing course of dealing over usage of the trade is new. In Matthes v. Benn, supra, subsection (1), both concepts pointed to the same result.

(5) *Accord:* Deveso v. Chandler, 210 App. Div. 684, 206 N.Y.S. 604 (1924); Smith Co., Ltd. v. Moscahlades, 193 App.Div. 126, 183 N.Y.S. 500 (1920).

(6) This is new to the statutes. Presently, in order to obtain rebutting evidence, a party may obtain an adjournment, Clifton Shirting Co., Inc. v. Bronne Shirt Co., Inc., 213 App.Div. 239, 209 N.Y.S. 709 (1925).

Historical Note: This section was entirely rewritten and most of the changes followed recommendations of the Law Revision Commission for clarification. The elimination of former subsection(3), binding parties engaged in a particular vocation to its usages, meets an objection made on behalf of the American Bankers Association. (1956 Recommendations, p. 17; Excerpts, pp. 363–4.)

Official Uniform Comment

Prior Uniform Statutory Provision: No such general provision but see Sections 9(1), 15(5), 18(2), and 71, Uniform Sales Act.

Purposes:

This section makes it clear that:

1. This Act rejects both the "lay-dictionary" and the "conveyancer's" reading of a commercial agreement. Instead the meaning of the agreement of the parties is to be determined by the language used by them and by their action, read and interpreted

UCC

in the light of commercial practices and other surrounding circumstances. The measure and background for interpretation are set by the commercial context, which may explain and supplement even the language of a formal or final writing.

2. Course of dealing under subsection (1) is restricted, literally, to a sequence of conduct between the parties previous to the agreement. However, the provisions of the Act on course of performance make it clear that a sequence of conduct after or under the agreement may have equivalent meaning. (Section 2–208.)

3. "Course of dealing" may enter the agreement either by explicit provisions of the agreement or by tacit recognition.

4. This Act deals with "usage of trade" as a factor in reaching the commercial meaning of the agreement which the parties have made. The language used is to be interpreted as meaning what it may fairly be expected to mean to parties involved in the particular commercial transaction in a given locality or in a given vocation or trade. By adopting in this context the term "usage of trade" this Act expresses its intent to reject those cases which see evidence of "custom" as representing an effort to displace or negate "established rules of law". A distinction is to be drawn between mandatory rules of law such as the Statute of Frauds provisions of Article 2 on Sales whose very office is to control and restrict the actions of the parties, and which cannot be abrogated by agreement, or by a usage of trade, and those rules of law (such as those in Part 3 of Article 2 on Sales) which fill in points which the parties have not considered and in fact agreed upon. The latter rules hold "unless otherwise agreed" but yield to the contrary agreement of the parties. Part of the agreement of the parties to which such rules yield is to be sought for in the usages of trade which furnish the background and give particular meaning to the language used, and are the framework of common understanding controlling any general rules of law which hold only when there is no such understanding.

5. A usage of trade under subsection (2) must have the "regularity of observance" specified. The ancient English tests for "custom" are abandoned in this connection. Therefore, it is not required that a usage of trade be "ancient or immemorial", "universal" or the like. Under the requirement of subsection (2) full recognition is thus available for new usages and for usages currently observed by the great majority of decent dealers, even though dissidents ready to cut corners do not agree. There is room also for proper recognition of usage agreed upon by merchants in trade codes.

6. The policy of this Act controlling explicit unconscionable contracts and clauses (Sections 1–203, 2–302) applies to implicit clauses which rest on usage of trade and carries forward the policy underlying the ancient requirement that a custom or usage must be "reasonable". However, the emphasis is shifted. The very fact of commercial acceptance makes out a prima facie case that the usage is reasonable, and the burden is no longer on the usage to establish itself as being reasonable. But the anciently established policing of usage by the courts is continued to the extent necessary to cope with the situation arising if an unconscionable or dishonest practice should become standard.

7. Subsection (3), giving the prescribed effect to usages of which the parties "are or should be aware", reinforces the provision of subsection (2) requiring not universality but only the described "regularity of observance" of the practice or method. This subsection also reinforces the point of subsection (2) that such usages may be either general to trade or particular to a special branch of trade.

8. Although the terms in which this Act defines "agreement" include the elements of course of dealing and usage of trade, the fact that express reference is made in some sections to those elements is not to be construed as carrying a contrary intent or implication elsewhere. Compare Section 1–102(4).

9. In cases of a well established line of usage varying from the general rules of this Act where the precise amount of the variation has not been worked out into a single standard, the party relying on the usage is entitled, in any event, to the minimum

variation demonstrated. The whole is not to be disregarded because no particular line of detail has been established. In case a dominant pattern has been fairly evidenced, the party relying on the usage is entitled under this section to go to the trier of fact on the question of whether such dominant pattern has been incorporated into the agreement.

10. Subsection (6) is intended to insure that this Act's liberal recognition of the needs of commerce in regard to usage of trade shall not be made into an instrument of abuse.

Cross References:

Point 2: Section 2–208.
Point 4: Section 2–201 and Part 3 of Article 2.
Point 6: Sections 1–203 and 2–302.
Point 8: Sections 1–102 and 1–201.
Point 9: Section 2–204(3).

Definitional Cross References:

"Agreement". Section 1–201.
"Contract". Section 1–201.
"Party". Section 1–201.
"Term". Section 1–201.

Section 1–206. Statute of Frauds for Kinds of Personal Property Not Otherwise Covered.

(1) Except in the cases described in subsection (2) of this section a contract for the sale of personal property is not enforceable by way of action or defense beyond five thousand dollars in amount or value of remedy unless there is some writing which indicates that a contract for sale has been made between the parties at a defined or stated price, reasonably identifies the subject matter, and is signed by the party against whom enforcement is sought or by his authorized agent.

(2) Subsection (1) of this section does not apply to contracts for the sale of goods (Section 2–201) nor of securities (Section 8–113) nor to security agreements (Section 9–203).

(3) Subsection one of this section does not apply to a qualified financial contract as that term is defined in paragraph two of subdivision b of section 5-701 of the general obligations law if either (a) there is, as provided in paragraph three of subdivision b of section 5-701 of such law, sufficient evidence to indicate that a contract has been made or (b) the parties thereto, by means of a prior or subsequent written contract, have agreed to be bound by the terms of such qualified financial contract from the time they reach agreement (by telephone, by exchange of electronic messages, or otherwise) on those terms.

Added by Laws 1994, Ch. 467, § 2, eff. Sept. 18, 1994.

Amended by Laws 1997, Ch. 566, § 3, eff. Oct. 10, 1997.

New York Annotations

Prior to 1960 the statute of frauds provision of Personal Property Law, § 85 (sales), applied to the sale of "any goods or choses in action." In 1960 this provision was substantially revised by Laws 1960, c. 287, eff. Sept. 1, 1960, and a separate statute of frauds for the sale of choses in action was enacted in Personal Property Law, § 85–a. The dollar limitation for choses in action was retained at fifty dollars, and exceptions were retained for those cases where the buyer accepted and received part of the choses in action or gave something in earnest or part payment. (See the annotation to Section 2–201 for the treatment of goods.

In the Code most sales of choses in action will be governed by the provisions of Section 8–319 (securities) and Section 9–203 (secured transactions). Since the sales article (Section 2–201) does not cover other choses in action, this section was developed. The Code here makes no exceptions to the requirement of a writing but raises the dollar limitation to five thousand dollars and changes the elements that must be in the writing.

Historical Note: Former Section 1–206, Right to Signed Receipt for Goods or Payment, was deleted on the recommendation of the Law Revision Commission. The Commission feared that the section might encourage the use of receipt forms containing clauses impairing the rights of the person to whom tender is made. Compare former Section 3–802(3). Section 1–205 adequately provides for situations where a signed receipt is customary. See also Section 3–505(1)(d).

The new section fills a gap in the Code provisions requiring writings, which was pointed out by the Law Revision Commission. (1956 Recommendations, p. 18; Excerpts, pp. 364 and 368.)

Official Uniform Comment

Prior Uniform Statutory Provision: Section 4, Uniform Sales Act (which was based on Section 17 of the Statute of 29 Charles II).

Changes: Completely rewritten by this and other sections.

Purposes:

To fill the gap left by the Statute of Frauds provisions for goods (Section 2–201), securities (Section 8–319), and security interests (Section 9–203). The Uniform Sales Act covered the sale of "choses in action"; the principal gap relates to sale of the "general intangibles" defined in Article 9 (Section 9–106) and to transactions excluded from Article 9 by Section 9–104. Typical are the sale of bilateral contracts, royalty rights or the like. The informality normal to such transactions is recognized by lifting the limit for oral transactions to $5,000. In such transactions there is often no standard of practice by which to judge, and values can rise or drop without warning; troubling abuses are avoided when the dollar limit is exceeded by requiring that the subject-matter be reasonably identified in a signed writing which indicates that a contract for sale has been made at a defined or stated price.

Definitional Cross References:

"Action". Section 1–201.
"Agreement". Section 1–201.
"Contract". Section 1–201.
"Contract for sale". Section 2–106.
"Goods". Section 2–105.
"Party". Section 1–201.
"Sale". Section 2–106.
"Signed". Section 1–201.
"Writing". Section 1–201.

Section 1–207. Performance or Acceptance Under Reservation of Rights.

A party who with explicit reservation of rights performs or promises performance or assents to performance in a manner demanded or offered by the other party does not thereby prejudice the rights reserved. Such words as "without prejudice", "under protest" or the like are sufficient.

New York Annotations

This section permits a party involved in a Code-covered transaction to accept whatever he can get by way of payment, performance, etc., without losing his rights to demand the remainder of the goods, to set-off a failure of quality, or to sue for the balance of the payment, so long as he explicitly reserves his rights.

The only existing statute analogous to this provision is Personal Property Law, § 130 (sales), which provides that the buyer's acceptance of the goods shall not bar any suit by the buyer for damages or other legal remedy so long as the buyer gives notice of the claimed breach within a reasonable time. Comment 2 makes it clear that this section does not alter the similar notice required by Code Sections 2–607 and 2–608.

Case law involving the issues dealt with in this section deal with the problem in terms of the doctrine of consideration. Thus a distinction is drawn between liquidated and unliquidated claims. In Nassoiy v. Tomlinson, 148 N.Y. 326, 42 N.E. 715 (1896), the debtor paid no more than the exact amount he claimed was due. The court held that the conditional payment was payment of an unliquidated claim if any part was disputed, and that the acceptance of the payment discharged the entire debt. Compare Schuttinger v. Woodruff, 259 N.Y. 212, 181 N.E. 361 (1932), and Leidy v. Proctor, 226 App.Div. 322, 235 N.Y.S. 101 (1929). The Code rule would permit, in Code-covered transactions, the acceptance of a part performance or payment tendered in full settlement without requiring the acceptor to gamble with his legal right to demand the balance of the performance or payment.

Official Uniform Comment

Prior Uniform Statutory Provision: None.

Purposes:

1. This section provides machinery for the continuation of performance along the lines contemplated by the contract despite a pending dispute, by adopting the mercantile device of going ahead with delivery, acceptance, or Payment "without prejudice," "under protest," "under reserve," "with reservation of all our rights," and the like. All of these phrases completely reserve all rights within the meaning of this section. The section therefore contemplates that limited as well as general reservations and acceptance by a party may be made "subject to satisfaction of our purchaser," "subject to acceptance by our customers," or the like.

2. This section does not add any new requirement of language of reservation where not already required by law, but merely provides a specific measure on which a party can rely as he makes or concurs in any interim adjustment in the course of performance. It does not affect or impair the provisions of this Act such as those under which the buyer's remedies for defect survive acceptance without being expressly claimed if notice of the defects is given within a reasonable time. Nor does it disturb the policy of those cases which restrict the effect of a waiver of a defect

to reasonable limits under the circumstances, even though no such reservation is expressed.

The section is not addressed to the creation or loss of remedies in the ordinary course of performance but rather to a method of procedure where one party is claiming as of right something which the other feels to be unwarranted.

Cross Reference:

Section 2–607.

Definitional Cross References:

"Party". Section 1–201.
"Rights". Section 1–201.

Section 1–208. Option to Accelerate at Will.

A term providing that one party or his successor in interest may accelerate payment or performance or require collateral or additional collateral "at will" or "when he deems himself insecure" or in words of similar import shall be construed to mean that he shall have power to do so only if he in good faith believes that the prospect of payment or performance is impaired. The burden of establishing lack of good faith is on the party against whom the power has been exercised.

New York Annotations

This section is an application of Section 1–203 which imposes a general obligation of good faith upon the parties in performing or enforcing obligations. The issue raised by this section has apparently not been treated by the Court of Appeals. But see, Jenkins v. Blackstone Motor Co., Inc., 216 App.Div. 583, 215 N.Y.S. 694, aff'd, 243 N.Y. 651, 154 N.E. 643 (1926). Early dicta in New York cases indicated an absolute right in a mortgagee to take possession under such a clause. Hyer v. Sutton, 59 Hun 40, 12 N.Y.S. 378 (1891); Allen v. Vose, 34 Hun 57 (1884). The present rule seems to require that the mortgagee must at least act in good faith in accelerating the obligation. Nuccio v. O'Connor, 202 App.Div. 108, 195 N.Y.S. 593 (1922); Oppenheimer v. Moore, 107 App.Div. 301, 95 N.Y.S. 138 (1905). The last cited cases seem to accord with the Code rule in placing the burden of establishing lack of good faith. However, there has also been an indication that the mortgagee must show reasonable grounds for feeling insecure. Carter v. Phillips, 127 Misc. 903, 217 N.Y.S. 621 (1926); Hawver v. Bell, 64 Hun 636. 19 N.Y.S. 612 (1892), aff'd, 141 N.Y. 140, 36 N.E. 6 (1894). The Code's enactment would remove the ambiguity. In Personal Property Law, § 413 (10), clauses permitting the holder to accelerate, in the absence of default, arbitrarily and without reasonable cause, are prohibited in retail installment sales. Personal Property Law, § 302(13), makes such a clause unenforceable in motor vehicle retail installment sales.

Historical Note: Various changes in language recommended by the Law Revision Commission were for clarification. (1956 Recommendations, p. 18; Excerpts, p. 365.)

Official Uniform Comment

Prior Uniform Statutory Provision: None.

Purposes:

The increased use of acceleration clauses either in the case of sales on credit or in time paper or in security transactions has led to some confusion in the cases as to the effect to be given to a clause which seemingly grants the power of an acceleration at the whim and caprice of one party. This Section is intended to make clear that despite language which can be so construed and which further might be held to make the agreement void as against public policy or to make the contract illusory or too indefinite for enforcement, the clause means that the option is to be exercised only in the good faith belief that the prospect of payment or performance is impaired.

Obviously this section has no application to demand instruments or obligations whose very nature permits call at any time with or without reason. This section applies only to an agreement or to paper which in the first instance is payable at a future date.

Definitional Cross References:

"Burden of establishing". Section 1–201.
"Good faith". Section 1–201.
"Party". Section 1–201.
"Term". Section 1–201.

Section 1–209. Subordinated Obligations.

An obligation may be issued as subordinated to payment of another obligation of the person obligated, or a creditor may subordinate his right to payment of an obligation by agreement with either the person obligated or another creditor of the person obligated. Such a subordination does not create a security interest as against either the common debtor or a subordinated creditor. This section shall be construed as declaring the law as it existed prior to the enactment of this section and not as modifying it.

Added by Laws 1966, Ch. 416, eff. May 23, 1966.

Official Uniform Comment

Source: New York.

Prior Uniform Statutory Provision: None.

Reason for Change: The drafting history of Article 9 makes it clear that there was no intention to cover agreements by which the rights of one unsecured creditor are subordinated to the rights of another unsecured creditor of a common debtor. Nevertheless, since in insolvency proceedings dividends otherwise payable to a subordinated creditor are turned over to the superior creditor, fears have been expressed that a subordination agreement might be treated as a "security agreement" creating a "security interest" in property of the subordinated creditor, and that inappropriate provisions of Article 9 might be applied. This optional section is intended to allay such fears by making an explicit declaration that a subordination agreement does not of itself create a security interest. Nothing in this section prevents the creation of a security interest in such a case when the parties to the agreement so intend.

Purposes:

1. Billions of dollars of subordinated debt are held by the public and by institutional investors. Commonly, the subordinated debt is subordinated on issue or acquisition and is evidenced by an investment security or by a negotiable or non-negotiable note. Debt is also sometimes subordinated after it arises, either by agreement between the

subordinating creditor and the debtor, by agreement between two creditors of the same debtor, or by agreement of all three parties. The subordinated creditor may be a stockholder or other "insider" interested in the common debtor; the subordinated debt may consist of accounts or other rights to payment not evidenced by any instrument. All such cases are included in the terms "subordinated obligation," "subordination," and "subordinated creditor."

2. Subordination agreements are enforceable between the parties as contracts; and in the bankruptcy of the common debtor dividends otherwise payable to the subordinated creditor are turned over to the superior creditor. This "turn-over" practice has on occasion been explained in terms of "equitable lien," "equitable assignment," or "constructive trust," but whatever the label the practice is essentially an equitable remedy and does not mean that there is a transaction "intended to create a security interest," a "sale of accounts, contract rights or chattel paper," or a "security interest created by contract," within the meaning of Section 9–102. On the other hand, nothing in this section prevents one creditor from assigning his rights to another creditor of the same debtor in such a way as to create a security interest within Article 9, where the parties so intend.

3. The last sentence of this section is intended to negate any implication that the section changes the law. It is intended to be declaratory of pre-existing law. Both the history and the text of Article 9 make it clear that it was not intended to cover subordination agreements. The provisions of Section 9–203 for signature by the "debtor" would be entirely unworkable if read to require signature by public holders of subordinated investment securities. The priorities, filing provisions and remedies on default provided by Article 9 would also be largely inappropriate in many situations. The precautionary language of Section 9–316 preserving subordination of priority by agreement between secured parties points to the conclusion that similar arrangements among unsecured lenders are not covered unless otherwise within the scope of the Article.

4. The enforcement of subordination agreements is largely left to supplementary principles under Section 1–103. If the subordinated debt is evidenced by an investment security, Section 8–202(1) authorizes enforcement against purchasers on terms stated or referred to on the security. If the fact of subordination is noted on a negotiable instrument, a holder under Sections 3–302 and 3–306 is subject to the term because notice precludes him from taking free of the subordination. Sections 3–302(3)(a), 3–306 and 8–317 severely limit the rights of levying creditors of a subordinated creditor in such cases.

Definitional Cross References:

"Agreement". Section 1–201.
"Creditor". Section 1–201.
"Debtor". Section 9–105.
"Person". Section 1–201.
"Rights". Section 1–201.
"Security interest". Section 1–201.

ARTICLE 2

SALES

PART 1

SHORT TITLE, GENERAL CONSTRUCTION AND SUBJECT MATTER

PART 2

FORM, FORMATION AND READJUSTMENT OF CONTRACT

PART 3

GENERAL OBLIGATION AND CONSTRUCTION OF CONTRACT

PART 4

TITLE, CREDITORS AND GOOD FAITH PURCHASERS

PART 5

PERFORMANCE

PART 6

BREACH, REPUDIATION AND EXCUSE

PART 7

REMEDIES

PART 1

SHORT TITLE, GENERAL CONSTRUCTION AND SUBJECT MATTER

Section 2–101. Short Title.

This Article shall be known and may be cited as Uniform Commercial Code—Sales.

New York Annotations

Article 2 of the Code is designed to replace the Uniform Sales Act adopted in New York in 1911, Personal Property Law, §§ 82–158 and the several modifications of that Act subsequently adopted by New York alone, i.e., the 1948 amendment to Personal Property Law, § 150, allowing damages to a rescinding buyer; the 1952 addition of Personal Property Law, § 145–a, providing a limited restitutionary right to a defaulting buyer; the 1958 amendment, relating to open price terms in Personal Property Law, § 91; the 1960 changes in the statute of frauds in Personal Property Law, §§ 85 and 85–a; and the 1960 addition of Personal Property Law, § 84–a, relating to offer and acceptance.

Some of these non-uniform amendments are reflected in the Code (Sections 2–711, 2–718) and others were patterned upon Code provisions (Sections 2–201 and 2–207). Another example of a correspondence between the Code rule and the developing New York law lies in the close similarity between Section 2–318 and the recent decision of the Court of Appeals on the privity requirement in warranty litigation. Greenberg v. Lorenz, 9 N.Y.2d 195, 173 N.E.2d 773.

It is thus clear that in the majority of sales cases the results under the Code will be the same as under the existing law even though the form of expression of the rules has been changed.

The most notable change in approach lies in the Code statement of more specific rules in contrast to the broadly stated provisions of the Sales Act. For example, the Code places much less weight on "property in the goods" in determining the outcome of sales controversies. Although this Article does establish the same kind of general rules for governing the passage of "property" or title (Section 2–401), particular disputes over such matters as risk of loss or the remedies of the parties are governed by separate and more particular provisions drafted in light of the specific problem involved (see, for example, Sections 2–509 and 2–709).

Moreover Article 2, unlike the Uniform Sales Act, restates some aspects of contract law. The Code provides rules for such matters as offer and acceptance (Sections 2–206 and 2–207), delegation and assignment (Section 2–210), and definiteness (Sections 2–305, 2–306, and 2–310). Definitions are provided for the first time for a number of frequently used contract terms, such as F.O.B., F.A.S., C.I.F., and C.F. in Sections 2–319 through 2–325.

Where Article 2 does change present law the most significant provisions seem to be in the development of special rules for "merchants" (e.g., Sections 2–201 and 2–207); the invalidation of "unconscionable" contract terms (Section 2–302), the limitations upon disclaimer provisions (Section 2–316); the expanded protection given to certain bona fide purchasers (Section 2–403); the placing of risk of loss in many cases upon the possessor rather than the owner (Sections 2–509 and 2–510); the alterations in the rights of the buyer to obtain the specific goods (Sections 2–502 and 2–716); the seller's right to the price (Section 2–709); and the limitations upon the buyer's right of rejection (Sections 2–508, 2–612, and 2–614).

Present provisions of the Sales Act dealing with documents of title (Personal Property Law, §§ 108-121) are covered in Article 7 rather than in Article 2 of the Code.

A textual treatment of Article 2 may be found in Hawkland, Sales and Bulk Sales (Under the UCC). (1958)

Historical Note: The Law Revision Commission reported that the Code innovations as to "title", the exclusion of technical objections to judicial recognition of the existence of a contract, and the liberalization of remedies were approved in principle. The Commission did state a number of objections as to the statement of particular sales rules in the earlier drafts of the Code; but, during or after its study, 65 of the Article's 124 sections were revised. (1956 Report, pp. 35-37.)

Official Uniform Comment

This Article is a complete revision and modernization of the Uniform Sales Act which was promulgated by the National Conference of Commissioners on Uniform State Laws in 1906 and has been adopted in 34 states and Alaska, the District of Columbia and Hawaii.

The coverage of the present Article is much more extensive than that of the old Sales Act and extends to the various bodies of case law which have been developed both outside of and under the latter.

The arrangement of the present Article is in terms of contract for sale and the various steps of its performance. The legal consequences are stated as following directly from the contract and action taken under it without resorting to the idea of when property or title passed or was to pass as being the determining factor. The purpose is to avoid making practical issues between practical men turn upon the location of an intangible something, the passing of which no man can prove by evidence and to substitute for such abstractions proof of words and actions of a tangible character.

Section 2–102. Scope; Certain Security and Other Transactions Excluded From This Article.

Unless the context otherwise requires, this Article applies to transactions in goods; it does not apply to any transaction which although in the form of an unconditional contract to sell or present sale is intended to operate only as a security transaction nor does this Article impair or repeal any statute regulating sales to consumers, farmers or other specified classes of buyers.

New York Annotations

Accord: Personal Property Law, § 155. This Article, like the Sales Act, does apply to the general sales aspects of such transactions as conditional sales. Peuser v. March, 218 N.Y. 505, 113 N.E. 494 (1916). This section preserves the effect of such regulatory statutes as the Motor Vehicle Retail Installment Sales Act, Personal Property Law, §§ 301–312; and the Retail Installment Sales Act, Personal Property Law, §§ 401–419.

Historical Note: The opening provision was inserted by Supp. No. 1 to eliminate any ambiguity as to the application of Article 2 to contracts not related to the sale of goods. (1956 Recommendations, p. 19.)

Official Uniform Comment

Prior Uniform Statutory Provision: Section 75, Uniform Sales Act.

Changes: Section 75 has been rephrased.

Purposes of Changes and New Matter: To make it clear that:

The Article leaves substantially unaffected the law relating to purchase money security such as conditional sale or chattel mortgage though it regulates the general sales aspects of such transactions. "Security transaction" is used in the same sense as in the Article on Secured Transactions (Article 9).

Cross Reference:

Article 9.

Definitional Cross References:

"Contract". Section 1–201.
"Contract for sale". Section 2–106.
"Present sale". Section 2–106.
"Sale". Section 2–106.

Section 2–103. Definitions and Index of Definitions.

(1) In this Article unless the context otherwise requires

(a) "Buyer" means a person who buys or contracts to buy goods.

(b) "Good faith" in the case of a merchant means honesty in fact and the observance of reasonable commercial standards of fair dealing in the trade.

(c) "Receipt" of goods means taking physical possession of them.

(d) "Seller" means a person who sells or contracts to sell goods.

(2) Other definitions applying to this Article or to specified Parts thereof, and the sections in which they appear are:

"Acceptance". Section 2–606.

"Banker's credit". Section 2–325.

"Between merchants". Section 2–104.

"Cancellation". Section 2–106(4).

"Commercial unit". Section 2–105.

"Confirmed credit". Section 2–325.

"Conforming to contract". Section 2–106.

"Contract for sale". Section 2–106.

"Cover". Section 2–712.

"Entrusting". Section 2–403.

"Financing agency". Section 2–104.

"Future goods". Section 2–105.

"Goods". Section 2–105.

"Identification". Section 2–501.

"Installment contract". Section 2–612.

"Letter of Credit". Section 2–325.

"Lot". Section 2–105.

"Merchant". Section 2–104.

"Overseas". Section 2–323.

"Person in position of seller". Section 2–707.

"Present sale". Section 2–106.

"Sale". Section 2–106.

"Sale on approval". Section 2–326.

"Sale or return". Section 2–326.

"Termination". Section 2–106.

(3) The following definitions in other Articles apply to this Article:

"Check". Section 3–104.

"Consignee". Section 7–102.

"Consignor". Section 7–102.

"Consumer goods". Section 9–109.

"Dishonor". Section 3–507.

"Draft". Section 3–104.

(4) In addition Article 1 contains general definitions and principles of construction and interpretation applicable throughout this Article.

New York Annotations

(1)(a) and (d) The phrase "or any legal successor in interest of such person" is omitted from the definitions of "buyer" and "seller." Compare Personal Property Law, § 156. Section 2–210 makes it clear that successors in interest do not always succeed to all rights and duties.

(1)(b) "Good faith" requires honesty as under the New York law (Personal Property Law, § 156(2); Code Section 1–201(19)). The requirement of the "observance of reasonable commercial standards of fair dealing in the trade" in the case of a merchant is new. For the definition of "merchant", see Section 2–104.

(1)(c) "Receipt" is not defined in the New York Sales Act. Compare the definition of "delivery" (Personal Property Law, § 156).

Historical Note: The reference to "fair dealing" in the definition of "good faith" was added to subsection (1)(b) at the suggestion of the Law Revision Commission to eliminate the possibility that the definition might be read as imposing on merchants a general standard of due care. The added cross-references to Sections 2–606, 2–501, and 9–109, follow suggestions of the Law Revision Commission without change in intended meaning. (1956 Recommendations, p. 21; Excerpts, pp. 364–5.)

Official Uniform Comment

Prior Uniform Statutory Provision: Subsection (1): Section 76, Uniform Sales Act.

Changes:

The definitions of "buyer" and "seller" have been slightly rephrased, the reference in Section 76 of the prior Act to "any legal successor in interest of such person" being omitted. The definition of "receipt" is new.

Purposes of Changes and New Matter:

1. The phrase "any legal successor in interest of such person" has been eliminated since Section 2–210 of this Article, which limits some types of delegation of performance on assignment of a sales contract, makes it clear that not every such successor can be safely included in the definition. In every ordinary case, however, such successors are as of course included.

2. "Receipt" must be distinguished from delivery particularly in regard to the problems arising out of shipment of goods, whether or not the contract calls for making delivery by way of documents of title, since the seller may frequently fulfill his obligations to "deliver" even though the buyer may never "receive" the goods. Delivery with respect to documents of title is defined in Article 1 and requires transfer of physical delivery. Otherwise the many divergent incidents of delivery are handled incident by incident.

Cross References:

Point 1: See Section 2–210 and Comment thereon.
Point 2: Section 1–201.

Definitional Cross Reference:

"Person". Section 1–201.

Section 2–104. Definitions: "Merchant"; "Between Merchants"; "Financing Agency".

(1) "Merchant" means a person who deals in goods of the kind or otherwise by his occupation holds himself out as having knowledge or skill peculiar to the practices or goods involved in the transaction or to whom such knowledge or skill may be attributed by his employment of an agent or broker or other intermediary who by his occupation holds himself out as having such knowledge or skill.

(2) "Financing agency" means a bank, finance company or other person who in the ordinary course of business makes advances against goods or documents of title or who by arrangement with either the seller or the buyer intervenes in ordinary course to make or collect payment due or claimed under the contract for sale, as by purchasing or paying the seller's draft or making advances against it or by merely taking it for collection whether or not documents of title accompany the draft. "Financing agency" includes also a bank or other person who similarly intervenes between persons who are in the position of seller and buyer in respect to the goods (Sections 2–707).

(3) "Between merchants" means in any transaction with respect to which both parties are chargeable with the knowledge or skill of merchants.

New York Annotations

In (1) and (3) The Code goes beyond New York law in setting forth special rules for merchants. However, implied warranties are imposed on a seller "who deals" in the goods. Personal Property Law, § 96. Compare provisions as to custom and usage and usages of the trade in Personal Property Law, §§ 99 and 152.

(2) On "financing agency" see Sections 2–506, 2–512(1)(b).

Official Uniform Comment

Prior Uniform Statutory Provision: None. But see Sections 15(2), (5), 16(c), 45(2) and 71, Uniform Sales Act, and Sections 35 and 37, Uniform Bills of Lading Act for examples of the policy expressly provided for in this Article.

Purposes:

1. This Article assumes that transactions between professionals in a given field require special and clear rules which may not apply to a casual or inexperienced seller or buyer. It thus adopts a policy of expressly stating rules applicable "between merchants" and "as against a merchant", wherever they are needed instead of making them depend upon the circumstances of each case as in the statutes cited above. This section lays the foundation of this policy by defining those who are to be regarded as professionals or "merchants" and by stating when a transaction is deemed to be "between merchants".

2. The term "merchant" as defined here roots in the "law merchant" concept of a professional in business. The professional status under the definition may be based upon specialized knowledge as to the goods, specialized knowledge as to business practices, or specialized knowledge as to both and which kind of specialized

knowledge may be sufficient to establish the merchant status is indicated by the nature of the provisions.

The special provisions as to merchants appear only in this Article and they are of three kinds. Sections 2–201(2), 2–205, 2–207 and 2–209 dealing with the statute of frauds, firm offers, confirmatory memoranda and modification rest on normal business practices which are or ought to by typical of and familiar to any person in business. For purposes of these sections almost every person in business would, therefore, be deemed to be a "merchant" under the language "who . . . by his occupation holds himself out as having knowledge or skill peculiar to the practices . . . involved in the transaction . . ." since the practices involved in the transaction are non-specialized business practices such as answering mail. In this type of provision, banks or even universities, for example, well may be "merchants." But even these sections only apply to a merchant in his mercantile capacity; a lawyer or bank president buying fishing tackle for his own use is not a merchant.

On the other hand, in Section 2–314 on the warranty of merchantability, such warranty is implied only "if the seller is a merchant with respect to goods of that kind." Obviously this qualification restricts the implied warranty to a much smaller group than everyone who is engaged in business and requires a professional status as to particular kinds of goods. The exception in Section 2–402 (2) for retention of possession by a merchant-seller falls in the same class; as does Section 2–403(2) on entrusting of possession to a merchant "who deals in goods of that kind".

A third group of sections includes 2–103(1)(b), which provides that in the case of a merchant "good faith" includes observance of reasonable commercial standards of fair dealing in the trade; 2–327(1)(c), 2–603 and 2–605, dealing with responsibilities of merchant buyers to follow seller's instructions, etc.; 2–509 on risk of loss, and 2–609 on adequate assurance of performance. This group of sections applies to persons who are merchants under either the "practices" of the "goods" aspect of the definition of merchant.

3. The "or to whom such knowledge or skill may be attributed by his employment of an agent or broker . . ." clause of the definition of merchant means that even persons such as universities, for example, can come within the definition of merchant if they have regular purchasing departments or business personnel who are familiar with business practices and who are equipped to take any action required.

Cross References:

Point 1: See Sections 1–102 and 1–203.

Point 2: See Sections 2–314, 2–315 and 2–320 to 2–325, of this Article, and Article 9.

Definitional Cross References:

"Bank". Section 1–201.
"Buyer". Section 2–103.
"Contract for sale". Section 2–106.
"Document of title". Section 1–201.
"Draft". Section 3–104.
"Goods". Section 2–105.
"Person". Section 1–201.
"Purchase". Section 1–201.
"Seller". Section 2–103.

Section 2–105. Definitions: Transferability; "Goods"; "Future" Goods; "Lot"; "Commercial Unit".

(1) "Goods" means all things (including specially manufactured goods) which are movable at the time of identification to the contract for sale other than the

money in which the price is to be paid, investment securities (Article 8) and things in action. "Goods" also includes the unborn young of animals and growing crops and other identified things attached to realty as described in the section on goods to be severed from realty (Section 2–107).

(2) Goods must be both existing and identified before any interest in them can pass. Goods which are not both existing and identified are "future" goods. A purported present sale of future goods or of any interest therein operates as a contract to sell.

(3) There may be a sale of a part interest in existing identified goods.

(4) An undivided share in an identified bulk of fungible goods is sufficiently identified to be sold although the quantity of the bulk is not determined. Any agreed proportion of such a bulk or any quantity thereof agreed upon by number, weight or other measure may to the extent of the seller's interest in the bulk be sold to the buyer who then becomes an owner in common.

(5) "Lot" means a parcel or a single article which is the subject matter of a separate sale or delivery, whether or not it is sufficient to perform the contract.

(6) "Commercial unit" means such a unit of goods as by commercial usage is a single whole for purposes of sale and division of which materially impairs its character or value on the market or in use. A commercial unit may be a single article (as a machine) or a set of articles (as a suite of furniture or an assortment of sizes) or a quantity (as a bale, gross, or carload) or any other unit treated in use or in the relevant market as a single whole.

UCC

New York Annotations

(1) "Goods." This definition, which fixes the coverage of most of Article 2, follows the Sales Act in general (Personal Property Law, § 156). Thus choses in action are excluded, but the Code excludes "money" only when it is a medium of payment, not when treated as a commodity, as in a sale of rare coins. Compare, Melzer v. Zimmerman, 118 Misc. 407, 194 N.Y.S. 222, aff'd 205 App.Div. 886, 198 N.Y.S. 932 (1923) (recovery for breach of contract to deliver Austrian kronen measured by Personal Property Law, § 148). Growing crops such as fruit or hay, whether or not "industrial", are goods under the Code, as are the unborn young of animals. Compare Section 2–501 on insurable interest in growing crops. See also annotations to Section 2–201 and Section 2–107.

(2) "Future" goods. As under present law, there can be no present sale of unidentified goods. Personal Property Law § 86.

(3) and (4) *Accord,* Personal Property Law, § 87.

(5) and (6) "Lot"; "Commercial unit". These are new.

Historical Note: Subsection (1) was revised at the suggestion of the Law Revision Commission to leave the effect of material harm to realty entirely to Section 2–107. (1956 Recommendations, p. 22; Excerpts, p. 366.)

Official Uniform Comment

Prior Uniform Statutory Provision: Subsections (1), (2), (3) and (4)–Sections 5, 6 and 76, Uniform Sales Act; Subsections (5) and (6)–none.

Changes: Rewritten.

Purposes of Changes and New Matter:

1. Subsection (1) on "goods": The phraseology of the prior uniform statutory provision has been changed so that:

The definition of goods is based on the concept of movability and the term "chattels personal" is not used. It is not intended to deal with things which are not fairly identifiable as movables before the contract is performed.

Growing crops are included within the definition of goods since they are frequently intended for sale. The concept of "industrial" growing crops has been abandoned, for under modern practices fruit, perennial hay, nursery stock and the like must be brought within the scope of this Article. The young of animals are also included expressly in this definition since they, too, are frequently intended for sale and may be contracted for before birth. The period of gestation of domestic animals is such that the provisions of the section on identification can apply as in the case of crops to be planted. The reason of this definition also leads to the inclusion of a wool crop or the like as "goods" subject to identification under this Article.

The exclusion of "money in which the price is to be paid" from the definition of goods does not mean that foreign currency which is included in the definition of money may not be the subject matter of a sales transaction. Goods is intended to cover the sale of money when money is being treated as a commodity but not to include it when money is the medium of payment.

As to contracts to sell timber, minerals, or structures to be removed from the land Section 2–107(1) (Goods to be severed from Realty: recording) controls.

The use of the word "fixtures" is avoided in view of the diversity of definitions of that term. This Article in including within its scope "things attached to realty" adds the further test that they must be capable of severance without material harm thereto. As between the parties any identified things which fall within that definition become "goods" upon the making of the contract for sale.

"Investment securities" are expressly excluded from the coverage of this Article. It is not intended by this exclusion, however, to prevent the application of a particular section of this Article by analogy to securities (as was done with the Original Sales Act in Agar v. Orda, 264 N.Y. 248, 190 N.E. 479, 99 A.L.R. 269(1934) when the reason of that section makes such application sensible and the situation involved is not covered by the Article of this Act dealing specifically with such securities (Article 8).

2. References to the fact that a contract for sale can extend to future or contingent goods and that ownership in common follows the sale of a part interest have been omitted here as obvious without need for expression; hence no inference to negate these principles should be drawn from their omission.

3. Subsection (4) does not touch the question of how far an appropriation of a bulk of fungible goods may or may not satisfy the contract for sale.

4. Subsections (5) and (6) on "lot" and "commercial unit" are introduced to aid in the phrasing of later sections.

5. The question of when an identification of goods takes place is determined by the provisions of Section 2–501 and all that this section says is what kinds of goods may be the subject of a sale.

Cross References:

Point 1: Sections 2–107, 2–201, 2–501 and Article 8.
Point 5: Section 2–501.
See also Section 1–201.

Definitional Cross References:

"Buyer". Section 2–103.
"Contract". Section 1–201.
"Contract for sale". Section 2–106.
"Fungible". Section 1–201.
"Money". Section 1–201.
"Present sale". Section 2–106.
"Sale". Section 2–106.
"Seller". Section 2–103.

Section 2–106. Definitions: "Contract"; "Agreement"; "Contract for Sale"; "Sale"; "Present Sale"; "Conforming" to Contract; "Termination"; "Cancellation".

(1) In this Article unless the context otherwise requires "contract" and "agreement" are limited to those relating to the present or future sale of goods. "Contract for sale" includes both a present sale of goods and a contract to sell goods at a future time. A "sale" consists in the passing of title from the seller to the buyer for a price (Section 2–401). A "present sale" means a sale which is accomplished by the making of the contract.

(2) Goods or conduct including any part of a performance are "conforming" or conform to the contract when they are in accordance with the obligations under the contract.

(3) "Termination" occurs when either party pursuant to a power created by agreement or law puts an end to the contract otherwise than for its breach. On "termination" all obligations which are still executory on both sides are discharged but any right based on prior breach or performance survives.

(4) "Cancellation" occurs when either party puts an end to the contract for breach by the other and its effect is the same as that of "termination" except that the cancelling party also retains any remedy for breach of the whole contract or any unperformed balance.

New York Annotations

These definitions articulate specific sections of the Code and do not require separate treatment. The definition of "contract for sale" and "sale" carry forward Personal Property Law, § 82, but the Code makes it clear that "contract for sale" includes a present sale.

Historical Note: Subsection (1) was revised in Supp. No. 1 to clarify the application of sections of Article 2 which refer to "contracts" and "agreements." In particular it defines the scope of Sections 2–202, 2–206, 2–207, 2–209(2), 2–210 and 2–302. "Term" is already defined in Section 1–201(42) by reference to "agreement." (1956 Recommendations, p. 23.)

Official Uniform Comment

Prior Uniform Statutory Provision: Subsection (1)–Section 1 (1) and (2), Uniform Sales Act; Subsection (2)–none, but subsection generally continues policy of Sections 11, 44 and 69, Uniform Sales Act; Subsections (3) and (4)–none.

Changes: Completely rewritten.

Purposes of Changes and New Matter:

1. Subsection (1): "Contract for sale" is used as a general concept throughout this Article, but the rights of the parties do not vary according to whether the transaction is a present sale or a contract to sell unless the Article expressly so provides.

2. Subsection (2): It is in general intended to continue the policy of requiring exact performance by the seller of his obligations as a condition to his right to require acceptance. However, the seller is in part safeguarded against surprise as a result of sudden technicality on the buyer's part by the provisions of Section 2–508 on seller's cure of improper tender of delivery. Moreover usage of trade frequently permits commercial leeways in performance and the language of the agreement itself must be read in the light of such custom or usage and also, prior course of dealing, and in a long term contract, the course of performance.

3. Subsections (3) and (4): These subsections are intended to make clear the distinction carried forward throughout this Article between termination and cancellation.

Cross References:

Point 2: Sections 1–203, 1–205, 2–208 and 2–508.

Definitional Cross References:

"Agreement". Section 1–201.
"Buyer". Section 2–103.
"Contract". Section 1–201.
"Goods". Section 2–105.
"Party". Section 1–201.
"Remedy". Section 1–201.
"Rights". Section 1–201.
"Seller". Section 2–103.

Section 2–107. Goods to Be Severed From Realty: Recording.

(1) A contract for the sale of minerals or the like (including oil and gas) or a structure or its materials to be removed from realty is a contract for the sale of goods within this Article if they are to be severed by the seller but until severance a purported present sale thereof which is not effective as a transfer of an interest in land is effective only as a contract to sell.

(2) A contract for the sale apart from the land of growing crops or other things attached to realty and capable of severance without material harm thereto but not described in subsection (1) or of timber to be cut is a contract for the sale of goods within this Article whether the subject matter is to be severed by the buyer or by the seller even though it forms part of the realty at the time of contracting, and the parties can by identification effect a present sale before severance.

(3) The provisions of this section are subject to any third party rights provided by the law relating to realty records, and the contract for sale may be executed and recorded as a document transferring an interest in land and shall then constitute notice to third parties of the buyer's rights under the contract for sale.

1977 Amendment

UCC Section 2–107 was amended by L. 1978, ch. 866, effective July 2, 1978, deleting the word "timber" from the first sentence and adding "(including oil and gas)". The words "or of timber to be cut" were added to subsection (2).

New York Annotations

Under subsection (1) a sale of timber, minerals or the like or a structure or its materials, to be severed by the seller, is considered a sale of "goods," which is defined in Section 2–105(1) to include "identified things attached to realty" as described in this section. If severance is to be effected by the buyer, however, the Code purports to treat this as a sale of realty. See Comment 1. Section 156 of the New York Personal Property Law does not distinguish between severance by the buyer and severance by the seller. Thus, a sale of a building removed by the buyer was said to be a sale of personal property. See Cervadoro v. First Nat. Bank & Trust Co. of Hudson, 267 App. Div. 314, 45 N.Y.S.2d 738 (1944); Utica Carting, Storage & Contracting Co. v. World Fire & Marine Ins. Co., 277 App. Div. 483, 100 N.Y.S.2d 941, 36 A.L.R.2d 500, reargument and appeal denied, 278 App. Div. 629, 102 N.Y.S.2d 637 (1951).

Subsection (2) covers "growing" crops and other things outside subsection (1) which are "attached to realty and capable of severance without material harm thereto." A contract for the sale of a thing which, when removed, would cause material harm to the realty would not, therefore, constitute a sale of "goods." Under New York Personal Property Law, § 156, however, damage to the realty does not remove the contract from the Act.

No provision equivalent to subsection (3) exists in the New York statutes. While § 291 of the Real Property Law covers recordation of a conveyance of "real property," which is defined in § 290 as "lands, tenements and hereditaments and chattels real, except a lease for a term not exceeding three years," § 291 has been held not to contemplate or require that a transfer of personal property be filed. Nat'l Hudson River Bank v. Chaskin, 28 App. Div. 311, 51 N.Y.S. 64 (1898). Nor do the cases indicate that property described in this section may properly be recorded under § 291.

Historical Note: Suggestions of the Law Revision Commission were followed in revising subsection (1) to make it clear that a purported present sale can take effect as a contract to sell under Section 2–105(2); in substituting "present sale before severance" for "constructive severance" in subsection (2); and in separating as subsection (3) the provisions on third party rights. The provisions of subsection (3) are made applicable to the entire section, rather than to subsection (2) alone. (1956 Recommendations, p. 24; Excerpts, p. 367.)

Official Uniform Comment

Prior Uniform Statutory Provision: See Section 76, Uniform Sales Act on prior policy; Section 7, Uniform Conditional Sales Act.

Purposes:

1. Subsection (1). Notice that this subsection applies only if the minerals or structures "are to be severed by the seller". If the buyer is to sever, such transactions are considered contracts affecting land and all problems of the Statute of Frauds and of the recording of land rights apply to them. Therefore, the Statute of Frauds section of this Article does not apply to such contracts though they must conform to the Statute of Frauds affecting the transfer of interests in land.

2. Subsection (2). "Things attached" to the realty which can be severed without material harm are goods within this Article regardless of who is to effect the severance. The word "fixtures" has been avoided because of the diverse definitions of this term, the test of "severance without material harm" being substituted.

The provision in subsection (3) for recording such contracts is within the purview of this Article since it is a means of preserving the buyer's rights under the contract of sale.

3. The security phases of things attached to or to become attached to realty are dealt with in the Article on Secured Transactions (Article 9) and it is to be noted that the definition of goods in that Article differs from the definition of goods in this Article.

However, both Articles treat as goods growing crops and also timber to be cut under a contract of severance.

Cross References:

Point 1: Section 2–201.
Point 2: Section 2–105.
Point 3: Articles 9 and 9–105.

Definitional Cross References:

"Buyer". Section 2–103.
"Contract". Section 1–201.
"Contract for sale". Section 2–106.
"Goods". Section 2–105.
"Party". Section 1–201.
"Present sale". Section 2–106.
"Rights". Section 1–201.
"Seller". Section 2–103.

PART 2

FORM, FORMATION AND READJUSTMENT OF CONTRACT

Section 2–201. Formal Requirements; Statute of Frauds.

(1) Except as otherwise provided in this section a contract for the sale of goods for the price of $500 or more is not enforceable by way of action or defense unless there is some writing sufficient to indicate that a contract for sale has been made between the parties and signed by the party against whom enforcement is sought or by his authorized agent or broker. A writing is not insufficient because it omits or incorrectly states a term agreed upon but the contract is not enforceable under this paragraph beyond the quantity of goods shown in such writing.

(2) Between merchants if within a reasonable time a writing in confirmation of the contract and sufficient against the sender is received and the party receiving it has reason to know its contents, it satisfies the requirements of subsection (1) against such party unless written notice of objection to its contents is given within ten days after it is received.

(3) A contract which does not satisfy the requirements of subsection (1) but which is valid in other respects is enforceable

(a) if the goods are to be specially manufactured for the buyer and are not suitable for sale to others in the ordinary course of the seller's business and the seller, before notice of repudiation is received and under circumstances which reasonably indicate that the goods are for the buyer, has made either a substantial beginning of their manufacture or commitments for their procurement; or

(b) if the party against whom enforcement is sought admits in his pleading, testimony or otherwise in court that a contract for sale was made, but the contract is not enforceable under this provision beyond the quantity of goods admitted; or

(c) with respect to goods for which payment has been made and accepted or which have been received and accepted (Section 2–606).

(4) Subsection one does not apply to a qualified financial contract as that term is defined in paragraph two of subdivision b of section 5-701 of the general obligations law if either (a) there is, as provided in paragraph three of subdivision b of section 5-701 of such law, sufficient evidence to indicate that a contract has been made or (b) the parties thereto, by means of a prior or subsequent written contract, have agreed to be bound by the terms of such qualified financial contract from the time they reach agreement (by telephone, by exchange of electronic messages, or otherwise) on those terms.

Added by Laws 1994, ch. 467, § 3, eff. Sept. 18, 1994.

New York Annotations

Upon enactment of the Uniform Sales Act in New York the dollar limitation upon the applicability of the statute of frauds was changed from five hundred to fifty dollars. In 1960 the section was amended to make the dollar limitation as to goods five hundred dollars. L.1960, c. 287, eff. Sept. 1, 1960, Personal Property Law, § 85. The Code also contains the five hundred dollar limitation as to goods.

(1) Subject matter

(a) *Choses in action.* The Uniform Sales Act originally embraced "goods or choses in action," but the recent New York amendment treated choses in action separately. Personal Property Law, § 85–a. This Code section excludes things in action by the definition of goods in Section 2–105. Securities, as defined in Section 8–102(1) (a), are subject to a separate statute of frauds in Section 8–319. Compare, Agar v. Orda, 144 Misc. 149, 258 N.Y.S. 274, aff'd 239 App. Div. 827, 264 N.Y.S. 939, aff'd, 264 N.Y. 248, 190 N.E. 479 (1934) (shares of stock covered by Personal Property Law sales rules). Some sales of accounts receivable are subject to the formal requisites of Sections 9–203 and 9–302. See Section 9–102(1) (b) and Section 9–302, Comment 5. Contracts to sell other choses in action are controlled by Section 1–206, which contains significantly different requirements.

(b) *Specially manufactured goods.* The exception contained in the 1960 revision of Personal Property Law, § 85, is apparently patterned after subsection 3(a) of this section. Neither is limited, as was the prior statute, to special manufacture by the "seller." The case law in New York is ambiguous on this point. Compare E. G. Young Lumber Co. v. New York Bondstone Corp., 15 Misc.2d 985, 179 N.Y.S.2d 45 (1958), and Rosette Pennington, Inc. v. Hayes, 10 Misc.2d 999, 170 N.Y.S.2d 216 (1957). The Code newly limits the exception to cases where the seller has made a "substantial beginning" of manufacture or has made "commitments for their procurement."

(2) The memorandum

(a) *Sufficiency.* The Uniform Sales Act demand for "some note or memorandum in writing of the contract of sale" was construed to require that all material terms of agreement be in the writing. Donald Friedman & Co., Inc. v. Newmann, 255 N.Y. 340, 174 N.E. 703 (1931) (price incorrectly stated); Carter, Macy Co., Inc. v. Matthews, 220 App. Div. 679, 222 N.Y.S. 472, aff'd, 247 N.Y. 532, 161 N.E. 171 (1928). The Code, like the 1960 New York amendment, requires only that the memorandum "indicate that a contract for sale has been made between the parties." Both the Code and the 1960 New York amendment introduce the new limitation that the contract is not enforceable beyond the quantity shown in the writing; but both provide that a writing is not insufficient because it omits or incorrectly states an agreed-upon term.

(b) *Special rule for merchants.* Subsection (2) makes a new provision that the statute is satisfied between merchants if written confirmation is received and not objected to within ten days. But the confirmation must be sufficient to bind the sender. Compare, Carter, Macy Co., Inc. v. Matthews, 220 App. Div. 679, 222 N.Y.S. 472, aff'd, 247 N.Y. 532, 161 N.E. 171 (1928).

(3) *Admissions in court.* Subsection 3(b) gives effect to admissions in court. Neither the Sales Act nor the 1960 amendment of Personal Property Law, § 85, has such a provision, but the result is consistent with some case law, Martocci v. Greater New York Brewery, Inc., 301 N.Y. 57, 92 N.E.2d 887 (1950) (memo made sufficient by pleadings). To the extent that the Code prevents a party from pleading the statute of frauds after admitting the oral contract in his pleadings, it changes New York law. Donald Friedman & Co., Inc. v. Newman, 255 N.Y. 340, 174 N.E. 703 (1931) and Harris v. Knickerbacker, 5 Wend. 638, 643 (1830). Note that this exception operates only to the extent of the quantity admitted. It is unlikely that a party can be forced to admit the contract in his testimony. Smith v. Muss, 203 Misc. 356, 117 N.Y.S.2d 501 (1952), app. den. 281 App.Div. 957 (1953).

(4) *Payment and receipt.* Under the Sales Act and the 1960 New York amendment the entire contract may be enforced if the buyer accepts and receives the goods or makes part payment. Helen Whiting, Inc. v. Trojan Textile Corp., 307 N.Y. 360, 121 N.E.2d 367 (1954) (15 yards of goods delivered; contract for 83,000 yards); John Thallon & Co., Inc. v. Edsil Trading Corp., 302 N.Y. 390, 98 N.E.2d 572 (1951). Subsection 3(c) allows the exception only to the extent of the partial receipt or payment. This provision thus limits the enforcement of oral contracts more than the present law, but expresses the same policy as the limitation of enforcement under subsection (1) to the quantity stated in the memorandum and the similar limitation on the effect of an admission in court under subsection 3(b).

Historical Note: Subsection (3) (b) was revised to meet suggestions of the Law Revision Commission that its application to admissions on cross-examination should be clarified, and that it should be subject to a limitation similar to that imposed by the second sentence of subsection (1). A further suggestion that choses in action should be covered was met by the insertion of a new Section 1–206. (1956 Recommendations, p. 25; Excerpts, p 367.)

Official Uniform Comment

Prior Uniform Statutory Provision: Section 4, Uniform Sales Act (which was based on Section 17 of the Statute of 29 Charles II).

Changes: Completely rephrased; restricted to sale of goods. See also Sections 1–206, 8–319 and 9–203.

Purposes of Changes: The changed phraseology of this section is intended to make it clear that:

1. The required writing need not contain all the material terms of the contract and such material terms as are stated need not be precisely stated. All that is required is that the writing afford a basis for believing that the offered oral evidence rests on a real transaction. It may be written in lead pencil on a scratch pad. It need not indicate which party is the buyer and which the seller. The only term which must appear is the quantity term which need not be accurately stated but recovery is limited to the amount stated. The price, time and place of payment or delivery, the general quality of the goods, or any particular warranties may all be omitted.

Special emphasis must be placed on the permissibility of omitting the price term in view of the insistence of some courts on the express inclusion of this term even where the parties have contracted on the basis of a published price list. In many valid contracts for sale the parties do not mention the price in express terms, the buyer being bound to pay and the seller to accept a reasonable price which the trier of the fact may well be trusted to determine. Again, frequently the price is not mentioned since the parties have based their agreement on a price list or catalogue known to both of them and this list serves as an efficient safeguard against perjury. Finally, "market" prices and valuations that are current in the vicinity constitute a similar check. Thus if the price is not stated in the memorandum it can normally be supplied without danger of fraud. Of course if the "price" consists of goods rather than money the quantity of goods must be stated.

Only three definite and invariable requirements as to the memorandum are made by this subsection. First, it must evidence a contract for the sale of goods; second, it must be "signed", a word which includes any authentication which identifies the party to be charged; and third, it must specify a quantity.

2."Partial performance" as a substitute for the required memorandum can validate the contract only for the goods which have been accepted or for which payment has been made and accepted.

Receipt and acceptance either of goods or of the price constitutes an unambiguous overt admission by both parties that a contract actually exists. If the court can make a just apportionment, therefore, the agreed price of any goods actually delivered can be recovered without a writing or, if the price has been paid, the seller can be forced to deliver an apportionable part of the goods. The overt actions of the parties make admissible evidence of the other terms of the contract necessary to a just apportionment. This is true even though the actions of the parties are not in themselves inconsistent with a different transaction such as a consignment for resale or a mere loan of money.

Part performance by the buyer requires the delivery of something by him that is accepted by the seller as such performance. Thus, part payment may be made by money or check, accepted by the seller. If the agreed price consists of goods or services, then they must also have been delivered and accepted.

3. Between merchants, failure to answer a written confirmation of a contract within ten days of receipt is tantamount to a writing under subsection (2) and is sufficient against both parties under subsection (1). The only effect, however, is to take away from the party who fails to answer the defense of the Statute of Frauds; the burden of persuading the trier of fact that a contract was in fact made orally prior to the written confirmation is unaffected. Compare the effect of a failure to reply under Section 2–207.

4. Failure to satisfy the requirements of this section does not render the contract void for all purposes, but merely prevents it from being judicially enforced in favor of a party to the contract. For example, a buyer who takes possession of goods as provided in an oral contract which the seller has not meanwhile repudiated, is not a trespasser. Nor would the Statute of Frauds provisions of this section be a defense to a third person who wrongfully induces a party to refuse to perform an oral contract, even though the injured party cannot maintain an action for damages against the party so refusing to perform.

UCC

5. The requirement of "signing" is discussed in the comment to Section 1–201.

6. It is not necessary that the writing be delivered to anybody. It need not be signed or authenticated by both parties but it is, of course, not sufficient against one who has not signed it. Prior to a dispute no one can determine which party's signing of the memorandum may be necessary but from the time of contracting each party should be aware that to him it is signing by the other which is important.

7. If the making of a contract is admitted in court, either in a written pleading, by stipulation or by oral statement before the court, no additional writing is necessary for protection against fraud. Under this section it is no longer possible to admit the contract in court and still treat the Statute as a defense. However, the contract is not thus conclusively established. The admission so made by a party is itself evidential against him of the truth of the facts so admitted and of nothing more; as against the other party, it is not evidential at all.

Cross References:

See Sections 1–201, 2–202, 2–207, 2–209 and 2–304.

Definitional Cross References:

"Action". Section 1–201.
"Between merchants". Section 2–104.
"Buyer". Section 2–103
"Contract". Section 1–201.
"Contract for sale". Section 2–106.
"Goods". Section 2–105.
"Notice". Section 1–201.
"Party". Section 1–201.
"Reasonable time". Section 1–204.
"Sale". Section 2–106.
"Seller". Section 2–103.

Section 2–202. Final Written Expression: Parol or Extrinsic Evidence.

Terms with respect to which the confirmatory memoranda of the parties agree or which are otherwise set forth in a writing intended by the parties as a final expression of their agreement with respect to such terms as are included therein may not be contradicted by evidence of any prior agreement or of a contemporaneous oral arrangement but may be explained or supplemented

(a) by course of dealing or usage of trade (Section 1–205) or by course of performance (Section 2–208); and

(b) by evidence of consistent additional terms unless the court finds the writing to have been intended also as a complete and exclusive statement of the terms of the agreement.

New York Annotations

General contract rules now govern parol evidence in New York.

(1) *Writings protected.* Writings which are a complete "integration" of the parties' agreement may not be supplemented, contradicted, or varied by parol evidence under the Code and the New York cases. Thomas v. Scutt, 127 N.Y. 133, 27 N.E. 961 (1891); Engelhorn v. Reitlinger, 122 N.Y. 76, 25 N.E. 297 (1890). See also Restatement, Contracts, §§ 228, 237, and New York Annotations.

(2) *Course of dealing, usage of trade, and course of performance.* This subsection would change the rule in New York that evidence of course of performance is inadmissible unless the contract is ambiguous. City of New York v. N.Y. City Ry. Co., 193 N.Y. 543, 86 N.E. 565 (1908); Porter v. Pennsylvania Railroad Co., 217 App.Div. 49, 215 N.Y.S. 727 (1926). Also Restatement, Contracts, § 235(e). The Code allows such evidence where the meaning of the words or other manifestations is not ambiguous or uncertain. Evidence of trade usage and course of dealing, inadmissible in New York where the contract is unambiguous, could also be brought in under this section where no ambiguity in the contract exists. See Dana v. Fiedler, 12 N.Y. 40, 62 Am.Dec. 130 (1854); Reback v. Story Productions, Inc., 15 Misc.2d 681, 181 N.Y.S.2d 980, aff'd, 9 A.D.2d 880, 193 N.Y.S.2d 520, appeal dismissed conditionally, 9 A.D.2d 606, 193 N.Y.S.2d 611 (1959).

(3) *Consistent additional terms.* This subsection follows New York law in allowing evidence of consistent additional terms if the writing is not the final expression of the parties' agreement. Routledge v. Worthington Co., 119 N.Y. 592, 23 N.E. 1111, 1112 (1890). But whereas New York admits such evidence only where the writing upon inspection does not appear to state the complete contract, this provision allows it unless the court affirmatively finds the writing to have been intended as a total integration of the terms of the agreement. See Mitchill v. Lath, 247 N.Y. 377, 160 N.E. 646 (1928), the leading case in New York. The Code's approach to the determination of integration might result in the admission of evidence which would be excluded under the New York rule. This subsection and New York agree, however, that when an instrument is a partial integration of an agreement the additional terms must supplement and cannot contradict or vary the terms. Thomas v. Scutt, 127 N.Y. 133, 27 N.E. 961 (1891). It also seems likely that the partial integration concept of this Code provision would succumb to a "merger clause" ("this writing contains the entire agreement between buyer and seller and no warranties have been made other than those stated herein").

Historical Note: The words "of the agreement" were substituted for "agreed upon" at the end of the section, at the suggestion of the Law Revision Commission to make it clear that the provision is not limited to express terms. See Section 1–201. (1956 Recommendations, p. 26; Excerpts, p. 368.)

Official Uniform Comment

Prior Uniform Statutory Provision: None.

Purposes:

1. This section definitely rejects:

(a) Any assumption that because a writing has been worked out which is final on some matters, it is to be taken as including all the matters agreed upon;

(b) The premise that the language used has the meaning attributable to such language by rules of construction existing in the law rather than the meaning which arises out of the commercial context in which it was used; and

(c) The requirement that a condition precedent to the admissibility of the type of evidence specified in paragraph (a) is an original determination by the court that the language used is ambiguous.

2. Paragraph (a) makes admissible evidence of course of dealing, usage of trade and course of performance to explain or supplement the terms of any writing stating the agreement of the parties in order that the true understanding of the parties as to the agreement may be reached. Such writings are to be read on the assumption that the course of prior dealings between the parties and the usages of trade were taken for granted when the document was phrased. Unless carefully negated they have

become an element of the meaning of the words used. Similarly, the course of actual performance by the parties is considered the best indication of what they intended the writing to mean.

3. Under paragraph (b) consistent additional terms, not reduced to writing, may be proved unless the court finds that the writing was intended by both parties as a complete and exclusive statement of all the terms. If the additional terms are such that, if agreed upon, they would certainly have been included in the document in the view of the court, then evidence of their alleged making must be kept from the trier of fact.

Cross References:

Point 3: Sections 1–205, 2–207, 2–302 and 2–316.

Definitional Cross References:

"Agreed" and "agreement". Section 1–201.
"Course of dealing". Section 1–205.
"Parties". Section 1–201.
"Term". Section 1–201.
"Usage of trade". Section 1–205.
"Written" and "writing". Section 1–201.

Section 2–203. Seals Inoperative.

The affixing of a seal to a writing evidencing a contract for sale or an offer to buy or sell goods does not constitute the writing a sealed instrument and the law with respect to sealed instruments does not apply to such a contract or offer.

New York Annotations

Accord: Civil Practice Act, § 342 [now General Construction Law, § 44–a]. See, also Personal Property Law, § 84.

Official Uniform Comment

Prior Uniform Statutory Provision: Section 3, Uniform Sales Act.
Changes: Portion pertaining to "seals" rewritten.

Purposes of Changes:

1. This section makes it clear that every effect of the seal which relates to "sealed instruments" as such is wiped out insofar as contracts for sale are concerned. However, the substantial effects of a seal, except extension of the period of limitations, may be had by appropriate drafting as in the case of firm offers (see Section 2–205).

2. This section leaves untouched any aspects of a seal which relate merely to signatures or to authentication of execution and the like. Thus, a statute providing that a purported signature gives prima facie evidence of its own authenticity or that a signature gives prima facie evidence of consideration is still applicable to sales transactions even though a seal may be held to be a signature within the meaning of such a statute. Similarly, the authorized affixing of a corporate seal bearing the corporate name to a contractual writing purporting to be made by the corporation may have effect as a signature without any reference to the law of sealed instruments.

Cross References:

Point 1: Section 2–205.

Definitional Cross References:

"Contract for sale". Section 2–106.
"Goods". Section 2–105.
"Writing". Section 1–201.

Section 2–204. Formation in General.

(1) A contract for sale of goods may be made in any manner sufficient to show agreement, including conduct by both parties which recognizes the existence of such a contract.

(2) An agreement sufficient to constitute a contract for sale may be found even though the moment of its making is undetermined.

(3) Even though one or more terms are left open a contract for sale does not fail for indefiniteness if the parties have intended to make a contract and there is a reasonably certain basis for giving an appropriate remedy.

New York Annotations

(1) *Manner of formation. Accord* with subsection (1): Personal Property Law, § 84.

(2) *Time of formation.* No New York authority has been found which indicates that a finding of the exact time of the formation of the contract is essential to a determination that a contract has been formed, and Personal Property Law, § 84, is consistent with this view when it states that a contract "may be inferred from the conduct of the parties."

(3) *Omitted terms; indefiniteness.* See annotation to Section 2–305, Open Price Term; Section 2–311, Options and Cooperation Respecting Performance. Compare, Restatement, Contracts, §§ 32, 33 and New York Annotations.

Historical Note: The change in subsection (1), adding a reference to conduct of the parties, was recommended for clarification on behalf of the Pennsylvania State Chamber of Commerce. Subsection (2) was rephrased for clarity as suggested by the New York Law Revision Commission. (1956 Recommendations, p. 26; Excerpts, p. 369.)

Official Uniform Comment

Prior Uniform Statutory Provision: Sections 1 and 3, Uniform Sales Act.

Changes: Completely rewritten by this and other sections of this Article.

Purposes of Changes:

Subsection (1) continues without change the basic policy of recognizing any manner of expression of agreement, oral, written or otherwise. The legal effect of such an agreement is, of course, qualified by other provisions of this Article.

Under subsection (1) appropriate conduct by the parties may be sufficient to establish an agreement. Subsection (2) is directed primarily to the situation where the interchanged correspondence does not disclose the exact point at which the deal was closed, but the actions of the parties indicate that a binding obligation has been undertaken.

Subsection (3) states the principle as to "open terms" underlying later sections of the Article. If the parties intend to enter into a binding agreement, this subsection recognizes that agreement as valid in law, despite missing terms, if there is any reasonably certain basis for granting a remedy. The test is not certainty as to what the parties were to do nor as to the exact amount of damages due the plaintiff. Nor is the fact that one or more terms are left to be agreed upon enough of itself to defeat an otherwise adequate agreement. Rather, commercial standards on the point of "indefiniteness" are intended to be applied, this Act making provision elsewhere for missing terms needed for performance, open price, remedies and the like.

The more terms the parties leave open, the less likely it is that they have intended to conclude a binding agreement, but their actions may be frequently conclusive on the matter despite the omissions.

Cross References:

Subsection (1): Sections 1–103, 2–201 and 2–302.
Subsection (2): Sections 2–205 through 2–209.
Subsection (3): See Part 3.

Definitional Cross References

"Agreement". Section 1–201.
"Contract". Section 1–201.
"Contract for sale". Section 2–106.
"Goods". Section 2–105.
"Party". Section 1–201.
"Remedy". Section 1–201.
"Term". Section 1–201.

Section 2–205. Firm Offers.

An offer by a merchant to buy or sell goods in a signed writing which by its terms gives assurance that it will be held open is not revocable, for lack of consideration, during the time stated or if no time is stated for a reasonable time, but in no event may such period of irrevocability exceed three months; but any such term of assurance on a form supplied by the offeree must be separately signed by the offeror.

New York Annotations

This section is substantially the same as Personal Property Law, § 33(5), the New York "firm offer" statute. The Code adds a time limit of three months on irrevocability without consideration, and limits the effect of printed forms supplied by the offeree containing words of irrevocability.

Historical Note: The section was redrawn at the suggestion of the Law Revision Commission in the interest of clarity, without change in meaning. (1956 Recommendations, p. 27; Excerpts, p. 369.)

Official Uniform Comment

Prior Uniform Statutory Provision: Sections 1 and 3, Uniform Sales Act.

Changes: Completely rewritten by this and other sections of this Article.

Purposes of Changes:

1. This section is intended to modify the former rule which required that "firm offers" be sustained by consideration in order to bind, and to require instead that they must merely be characterized as such and expressed in signed writings.

2. The primary purpose of this section is to give effect to the deliberate intention of a merchant to make a current firm offer binding. The deliberation is shown in the case of an individualized document by the merchant's signature to the offer, and in the case of an offer included on a form supplied by the other party to the transaction by the separate signing of the particular clause which contains the offer. "Signed" here also includes authentication but the reasonableness of the authentication herein allowed must be determined in the light of the purpose of the section. The circumstances surrounding the signing may justify something less than a formal signature or initialing but typically the kind of authentication involved here would consist of a minimum of initialing of the clause involved. A handwritten memorandum on the writer's letterhead purporting in its terms to "confirm" a firm offer already made would be enough to satisfy this section, although not subscribed, since under the circumstances it could not be considered a memorandum of mere negotiation and it would adequately show its own authenticity. Similarly, an authorized telegram will suffice, and this is true even though the original draft contained only a typewritten signature. However, despite settled courses of dealing or usages of the trade whereby firm offers are made by oral communication and relied upon without more evidence, such offers remain revocable under this Article since authentication by a writing is the essence of this section.

3. This section is intended to apply to current "firm" offers and not to long term options, and an outside time limit of three months during which such offers remain irrevocable has been set. The three month period during which firm offers remain irrevocable under this section need not be stated by days or by date. If the offer states that it is "guaranteed" or "firm" until the happening of a contingency which will occur within the three month period, it will remain irrevocable until that event. A promise made for a longer period will operate under this section to bind the offeror only for the first three months of the period but may of course be renewed. If supported by consideration it may continue for as long as the parties specify. This section deals only with the offer which is not supported by consideration.

4. Protection is afforded against the inadvertent signing of a firm offer when contained in a form prepared by the offeree by requiring that such a clause be separately authenticated. If the offer clause is called to the offeror's attention and he separately authenticates it, he will be bound; Section 2–302 may operate, however, to prevent an unconscionable result which otherwise would flow from other terms appearing in the form.

5. Safeguards are provided to offer relief in the case of material mistake by virtue of the requirement of good faith and the general law of mistake.

Cross References:

Point 1: Section 1–102.
Point 2: Section 1–102.
Point 3: Section 2–201.
Point 5: Section 2–302.

Definitional Cross References:

"Goods". Section 2–105.
"Merchant". Section 2–104.
"Signed". Section 1–201.
"Writing". Section 1–201.

Section 2–206. Offer and Acceptance in Formation of Contract.

(1) Unless otherwise unambiguously indicated by the language or circumstances

(a) an offer to make a contract shall be construed as inviting acceptance in any manner and by any medium reasonable in the circumstances;

(b) an order or other offer to buy goods for prompt or current shipment shall be construed as inviting acceptance either by a prompt promise to ship or by the prompt or current shipment of conforming or non-conforming goods, but such a shipment of non-conforming goods does not constitute an acceptance if the seller seasonably notifies the buyer that the shipment is offered only as an accommodation to the buyer.

(2) Where the beginning of a requested performance is a reasonable mode of acceptance an offeror who is not notified of acceptance within a reasonable time may treat the offer as having lapsed before acceptance.

New York Annotations

(1) (a) *Manner and medium of acceptance.* This subsection would change New York law to the extent that the subsection allows any kind of reasonable acceptance where the offer is ambiguous. "Reasonableness" is not the test in New York. Rather, the question of whether there has been an acceptance is determined by the meaning of the terms of the offer. Petterson v. Pattberg, 248 N.Y. 86, 161 N.E. 428 (1928); Fisk v. Batterson, 165 App.Div. 952, 150 N.Y.S. 242, aff'd *per curiam,* 221 N.Y. 693, 117 N.E. 1067 (1915); Restatement, Contracts, § 64, and New York Annotations thereto. Barber-Greene Co., Inc. v. Dollard, Jr., Inc., 239 App.Div. 655, 269 N.Y.S. 211, aff'd per curiam, 267 N.Y. 545, 196 N.E. 571 (1935).

(b) *Acceptance by shipment.* Subsection (1) (b) would change the rule in New York by giving the offeree the option of accepting an offer to buy goods for prompt or current shipment either by shipping the goods or by promising to ship the goods. New York is in accord with the general rule that an order indicating that prompt delivery is expected, authorizes and invites prompt shipment as sufficient acceptance of the offer. Quick v. Wheeler, 78 N.Y. 300 (1879); Moore v. Scott Stamp & Coin Co., 178 F.2d 3 (2d Cir. 1949). But there is no authority for the proposition that shipment cuts off the power of revocation. Neither is there case support for the view that a promise cannot be an acceptance of an order contemplating prompt shipment of goods.

(2) *Non-conforming shipments.* A shipment of non-conforming goods would not in New York constitute an acceptance unless there were some communication, other than the shipment of non-conforming goods, that the seller had accepted the offer, in which case there would be a promissory acceptance. Consequently subsection (1) (b) is contrary to New York law insofar as it makes shipment of non-conforming goods an acceptance unless the seller communicates to the buyer that the non-conforming goods are offered only as an accommodation to the latter. Hind v. Willich, 127 Misc. 355, 216 N.Y.S. 155, aff'd, 221 App.Div. 857, 224 N.Y.S. 819 (1927); Staiger v. Soht, 116 App.Div. 874, 102 N.Y.S. 342, aff'd *per curiam,* 191 N.Y. 527, 84 N.E. 1120 (1908).

(3) *Beginning of performance.* Beginning a requested performance can in New York be an acceptance which obligates the offeree to complete the performance. Quick v. Wheeler, 78 N.Y. 300 (1879); Mendell v. Willyoung, 42 Misc. 210, 85 N.Y.S.

647 (1903). But see Sonino v. Magrini, 225 App.Div. 536, 234 N.Y.S. 63 (1929). Subsection (2) would add the requirement that the offeror be notified of such acceptance in order to cut off his power of revocation.

Historical Note: Former subsection (2) was revised and incorporated in subsection (1) (b) to meet criticism by the Law Revision Commission. The revised language, recommended on behalf of the Pennsylvania State Chamber of Commerce, makes it clear that the seller can avoid ambiguity by seasonable notification. Other changes in the section were made at the suggestion of the Law Revision Commission in the interest of clarity, without change of meaning. (1956 Recommendations, p. 27; Excerpts, p. 370.)

Official Uniform Comment

Prior Uniform Statutory Provision: Sections 1 and 3, Uniform Sales Act.

Changes: Completely rewritten in this and other sections of this Article.

Purposes of Changes: To make it clear that:

1. Any reasonable manner of acceptance is intended to be regarded as available unless the offeror has made quite clear that it will not be acceptable. Former technical rules as to acceptance, such as requiring that telegraphic offers be accepted by telegraphed acceptance, etc., are rejected and a criterion that the acceptance be "in any manner and by any medium reasonable under the circumstances," is substituted. This section is intended to remain flexible and its applicability to be enlarged as new media of communication develop or as the more time-saving present day media come into general use.

2. Either shipment or a prompt promise to ship is made a proper means of acceptance of an offer looking to current shipment. In accordance with ordinary commercial understanding the section interprets an order looking to current shipment as allowing acceptance either by actual shipment or by a prompt promise to ship and rejects the artificial theory that only a single mode of acceptance is normally envisaged by an offer. This is true even though the language of the offer happens to be "ship at once" or the like. "Shipment" is here used in the same sense as in Section 2–504; it does not include the beginning of delivery by the seller's own truck or by messenger. But loading on the seller's own truck might be a bargaining or performance under subsection (2).

3. The beginning of performance by an offeree can be effective as acceptance so as to bind the offeror only if followed within a reasonable time by notice to the offeror. Such a beginning of performance must unambiguously express the offeree's intention to engage himself. For the protection of both parties it is essential that notice follow in due course to constitute acceptance. Nothing in this section however bars the possibility that under the common law performance begun may have an intermediate effect of temporarily barring revocation of the offer, or at the offeror's option, final effect in constituting acceptance.

4. Subsection (1) (b) deals with the situation where a shipment made following an order is shown by a notification of shipment to be referable to that order but has a defect. Such a non-conforming shipment is normally to be understood as intended to close the bargain, even though it proves to have been at the same time a breach. However, the seller by stating that the shipment is non-conforming and is offered only as an accommodation to the buyer keeps the shipment or notification from operating as an acceptance.

Definitional Cross References:

"Buyer". Section 2–103.

"Conforming". Section 2–106.

"Contract". Section 1–201.
"Goods". Section 2–105.
"Notifies". Section 1–201.
"Reasonable time". Section 1–204.

Section 2–207. Additional Terms in Acceptance or Confirmation.

(1) A definite and seasonable expression of acceptance or a written confirmation which is sent within a reasonable time operates as an acceptance even though it states terms additional to or different from those offered or agreed upon, unless acceptance is expressly made conditional on assent to the additional or different terms.

(2) The additional terms are to be construed as proposals for addition to the contract. Between merchants such terms become part of the contract unless:

(a) the offer expressly limits acceptance to the terms of the offer;

(b) they materially alter it; or

(c) notification of objection to them has already been given or is given within a reasonable time after notice of them is received.

(3) Conduct by both parties which recognizes the existence of a contract is sufficient to establish a contract for sale although the writings of the parties do not otherwise establish a contract. In such case the terms of the particular contract consist of those terms on which the writings of the parties agree, together with any supplementary terms incorporated under any other provisions of this Act.

New York Annotations

In 1960, upon the recommendation of the Law Revision Commission, Personal Property Law, § 84–a, was added to the sales law of New York. This section of the Code appears to be the progenitor of that revision. However, significant differences still remain, and these are pointed out below.

(1) *Validity of acceptance.* Prior to the 1960 addition, New York adopted and usually applied the rule of exact acceptance, i.e., that the acceptance must be unqualified and must not vary from the terms of the offer, e.g., F. W. Berk & Co., Inc. v. Derecktor, 301 N.Y. 110, 92 N.E.2d 914 (1950); Gram v. Mutual Life Insurance Co. of N.Y., 300 N.Y. 375, 91 N.E.2d 307 (1950); Poel v. Brunswick-Balke-Collender Co., 216 N.Y. 310, 110 N.E. 619 (1915). Occasionally the courts construed the communication to avoid the problem, e.g., Valashinas v. Koniuto, 308 N.Y. 233, 124 N.E.2d 300 (1954); Matter of arbitration between Wachusett Spinning Mills, Inc. and Blue Bird Silk Mfg. Co., Inc., 7 A.D.2d 382, 183 N.Y.S.2d 601, aff'd, 6 N.Y.2d 948, 161 N.E.2d 222 (1959); Propstra v. Dyer, 189 F.2d 810 (2d Cir. 1951); Washington Electric Cooperative, Inc. V. Norry Electric Corp., 193 F.2d 412 (2d Cir. 1951); Glickstein & Terner, Inc. v. Sheffield Glass Bottle Co., 214 App.Div. 626, 212 N.Y.S. 444 (1925). The 1960 statute introduced a test of materiality of the variation and placed a burden upon the acceptor to make his acceptance expressly conditional upon the additional or different terms. The Code goes one step beyond this approach and makes the acceptance effective regardless of materiality unless the acceptor expressly conditions his assent.

(2) *Incorporation of additional terms.* If a contract is formed, both the 1960 New York statute and the Code treat the varying terms as proposals for addition to the

contract. The Code adds a means whereby in a limited class of cases these proposals become part of the contract. At this point a materiality test is employed by the Code. See the analogous provision in Restatement, Contracts, § 72 (acceptance by silence), and New York Annotations. This section was helpfully discussed in Application of Doughboy Industries. 17 A.D.2d 216, 233 N.Y.S.2d 488 (1962).

(3) *Conduct recognizing existence.* On the establishment of a contract by conduct, see annotation to Section 2–204.

Historical Note: The section was entirely rewritten in Supp. No. 1, and was later redrawn in a special supplement to express more clearly what was intended. (1956 Recommendations, p. 28.)

Official Uniform Comment

Prior Uniform Statutory Provision: Sections 1 and 3, Uniform Sales Act.

Changes: Completely rewritten by this and other sections of this Article.

Purposes of Changes:

1. This section is intended to deal with two typical situations. The one is the written confirmation, where an agreement has been reached either orally or by informal correspondence between the parties and is followed by one or both of the parties sending formal memoranda embodying the terms so far as agreed upon and adding terms not discussed. The other situation is offer and acceptance, in which a wire or letter expressed and intended as an acceptance or the closing of an agreement adds further minor suggestions or proposals such as "ship by Tuesday," "rush", "ship draft against bill of lading inspection allowed," or the like. A frequent example of the second situation is the exchange of printed purchase order and acceptance (sometimes called "acknowledgment") forms. Because the forms are oriented to the thinking of the respective drafting parties, the terms contained in them often do not correspond. Often the seller's form contains terms different from or additional to those set forth in the buyer's form. Nevertheless, the parties proceed with the transaction. [Comment 1 was amended in 1966.]

2. Under this Article a proposed deal which in commercial understanding has in fact been closed is recognized as a contract. Therefore, any additional matter contained in the confirmation or in the acceptance falls within subsection (2) and must be regarded as a proposal for an added term unless the acceptance is made conditional on the acceptance of the additional or different terms. [Comment 2 was amended in 1966.]

3. Whether or not additional or different terms will become part of the agreement depends upon the provisions of subsection (2). If they are such as materially to alter the original bargain, they will not be included unless expressly agreed to by the other party. If, however, they are terms which would not so change the bargain they will be incorporated unless notice of objection to them has already been given or is given within a reasonable time.

4. Examples of typical clauses which would normally "materially alter" the contract and so result in surprise or hardship if incorporated without express awareness by the other party are: a clause negating such standard warranties as that of merchantability or fitness for a particular purpose in circumstances in which either warranty normally attaches; a clause requiring a guaranty of 90% or 100% deliveries in a case such as a contract by cannery, where the usage of the trade allows greater quantity leeways; a clause reserving to the seller the power to cancel upon the buyer's failure to meet any invoice when due; a clause requiring that complaints be made in a time materially shorter than customary or reasonable.

5. Examples of clauses which involve no element of unreasonable surprise and which therefore are to be incorporated in the contract unless notice of objection is

seasonably given are: a clause setting forth and perhaps enlarging slightly upon the seller's exemption due to supervening causes beyond his control, similar to those covered by the provision of this Article on merchant's excuse by failure of presupposed conditions or a clause fixing in advance any reasonable formula of proration under such circumstances; a clause fixing a reasonable time for complaints within customary limits, or in the case of a purchase for sub-sale, providing for inspection by the sub-purchaser; a clause providing for interest on overdue invoices or fixing the seller's standard credit terms where they are within the range of trade practice and do not limit any credit bargained for; a clause limiting the right of rejection for defects which fall within the customary trade tolerances for acceptance "with adjustment" or otherwise limiting remedy in a reasonable manner (see Sections 2–718 and 2–719).

6. If no answer is received within a reasonable time after additional terms are proposed, it is both fair and commercially sound to assume that their inclusion has been assented to. Where clauses on confirming forms sent by both parties conflict each party must be assumed to object to a clause of the other conflicting with one on the confirmation sent by himself. As a result the requirement that there be notice of objection which is found in subsection (2) is satisfied and the conflicting terms do not become a part of the contract. The contract then consists of the terms originally expressly agreed to terms on which the confirmations agree, and terms supplied by this Act, including subsection (2). The written confirmation is also subject to Section 2–201. Under that section a failure to respond permits enforcement of a prior oral agreement: under this section a failure to respond permits additional terms to become part of the agreement. [Comment 6 was amended in 1966.]

7. In many cases, as where goods are shipped, accepted and paid for before any dispute arises, there is no question whether a contract has been made. In such cases, where the writings of the parties do not establish a contract, it is not necessary to determine which act or document constituted the offer and which the acceptance. See Section 2–204. The only question is what terms are included in the contract, and subsection (3) furnishes the governing rule. [Comment 7 was added in 1966.]

Cross References:

See generally Section 2–302.

Point 5: Sections 2–513, 2–602, 2–607, 2–609, 2–612, 2–614, 2–615, 2–616, 2–718 and 2–719.

Point 6: Sections 1–102 and 2–104.

Definitional Cross References:

"Between merchants". Section 2–104.
"Contract". Section 1–201.
"Notification". Section 1–201.
"Reasonable time". Section 1–204.
"Seasonably". Section 1–204.
"Send". Section 1–201.
"Term". Section 1–201.
"Written". Section 1–201.

Section 2–208. Course of Performance or Practical Construction.

(1) Where the contract for sale involves repeated occasions for performance by either party with knowledge of the nature of the performance and opportunity for objection to it by the other, any course of performance accepted or acquiesced in without objection shall be relevant to determine the meaning of the agreement.

(2) The express terms of the agreement and any such course of performance, as well as any course of dealing and usage of trade, shall be construed whenever reasonable as consistent with each other; but when such construction is unreasonable, express terms shall control course of performance and course of performance shall control both course of dealing and usage of trade (Section 1–205).

(3) Subject to the provisions of the next section on modification and waiver, such course of performance shall be relevant to show a waiver or modification of any term inconsistent with such course of performance.

New York Annotations

On rendering failure to object to a course of performance "relevant" but not controlling to determine the meaning of an agreement, see, *accord:* Personal Property Law § 84 (contract "may be inferred from the conduct of the parties"); Personal Property Law, § 152 (implied terms may be negatived or varied "by the course of dealing"); Carthage Tissue Paper Mills v. Village of Carthage, 200 N.Y. 1, 93 N.E. 60 (1910); City of New York v. New York City Ry. Co., 193 N.Y. 543, 86 N.E. 565 (1908). But compare Brainard v. New York Central R. R. Co., 242 N.Y. 125, 151 N.E. 152 (1926).

The various rules of precedence established in subsection (2) are consistent with Section 1–205. As to waiver by failure to object, see, *accord:* Personal Property Law, § 130 (failure to give notice of breach of warranty); Restatement, Contracts, §§ 298, 411–413 and New York Annotations.

Historical Note: At the suggestion of the Law Revision Commission, the section was divided into three subsections: the reference to acquiescence was inserted in subsection (1); new subsection (2) was modelled on provisions in Section 1–205; and the cross-reference to the following section was added to subsection (3). (1956 Recommendations, p. 29; Excerpts, p. 371.)

Official Uniform Comment

Prior Uniform Statutory Provision: No such general provision but concept of this section recognized by terms such as "course of dealing", "the circumstances of the case," "the conduct of the parties," etc., in Uniform Sales Act.

Purposes:

1. The parties themselves know best what they have meant by their words of agreement and their action under that agreement is the best indication of what that meaning was. This section thus rounds out the set of factors which determines the meaning of the "agreement" and therefore also of the "unless otherwise agreed" qualification to various provisions of this Article.

2. Under this section a course of performance is always relevant to determine the meaning of the agreement. Express mention of course of performance elsewhere in this Article carries no contrary implication when there is a failure to refer to it in other sections.

3. Where it is difficult to determine whether a particular act merely sheds light on the meaning of the agreement or represents a waiver of a term of the agreement, the preference is in favor of "waiver" whenever such construction, plus the application of the provisions on the reinstatement of rights waived (see Section 2–209), is needed

to preserve the flexible character of commercial contracts and to prevent surprise or other hardship.

4. A single occasion of conduct does not fall within the language of this section but other sections such as the ones on silence after acceptance and failure to specify particular defects can affect the parties' rights on a single occasion (see Sections 2–605 and 2–607).

Cross References:

Point 1: Section 1–201.
Point 2: Section 2–202.
Point 3: Sections 2–209, 2–601 and 2–607.
Point 4: Sections 2–605 and 2–607.

Section 2–209. Modification, Rescission and Waiver.

(1) An agreement modifying a contract within this Article needs no consideration to be binding.

(2) A signed agreement which excludes modification or rescission except by a signed writing cannot be otherwise modified or rescinded, but except as between merchants such a requirement on a form supplied by the merchant must be separately signed by the other party.

(3) The requirements of the statute of frauds section of this Article (Section 2–201) must be satisfied if the contract as modified is within its provisions.

(4) Although an attempt at modification or rescission does not satisfy the requirements of subsection (2) or (3) it can operate as a waiver.

(5) A party who has made a waiver affecting an executory portion of the contract may retract the waiver by reasonable notification received by the other party that strict performance will be required of any term waived, unless the retraction would be unjust in view of a material change of position in reliance on the waiver.

New York Annotations

(1) *Modification without consideration.* Subsection (1) abolishes the requirement of consideration in agreements modifying sales contracts. Such modification can be validly accomplished under New York law by a written agreement signed by the party against whom it is sought to enforce the modification. Personal Property Law, § 33(2). Whether a modification of a contract is effective under the established doctrines of consideration is often a very difficult problem. Compare, McKenzie v. Harrison, 120 N.Y. 260, 24 N.E. 458 (1890), and Mance v. Hossington, 205 N.Y. 33,98 N.E. 203 (1912).

(2) *Signed agreement excluding modification or rescission.* Subsection (2) is consistent with and in part based on Personal Property Law, § 33–c. The provision as to merchants is new and is designed to avoid surprise to a consumer. Comment 3 indicates that the words "modification or rescission" include abandonment or other change by mutual consent, contrary to Green v. Doniger, 300 N.Y. 238, 90 N.E.2d 56 (1949). Thus the Code is consistent with present Personal Property Law, § 33–c, which was amended to avoid that decision.

Under subsections (4) and (5) an ineffective attempt at modification or rescission can operate as a waiver, but the waiver can be withdrawn if a material change of position has not resulted from reliance on the waiver. *Accord:* Restatement, Contracts §§ 88(2), 297, and New York Annotations.

(3) *Effect of the statute of frauds.* The present law, like the Code, requires a signed writing if the contract as modified or rescinded is within the statute of frauds. Lieberman v. Templar Motor Co., 236 N.Y. 139, 140 N.E. 222 (1923). Subsection (4) permitting an invalid modification or rescission to operate as a waiver does not seem to go beyond New York law, e.g., Van Iderstine Co. v. Barnet Leather Co., 242 N.Y. 425, 152 N.E. 250 (1926).

Historical Note: References to "rescission" were added to subsections (2) and (4) for clarification by Supp. No. 1. Subsection (5) was revised to meet suggestions of the Law Revision Commission for clarification. (1956 Recommendations, p. 30; Excerpts, pp. 371–2.)

Official Uniform Comment

Prior Uniform Statutory Provision: Subsection (1)–Compare Section 1, Uniform Written Obligations Act; Subsections (2) to (5)–none.

Purposes of Changes and New Matter:

1. This section seeks to protect and make effective all necessary and desirable modifications of sales contracts without regard to the technicalities which at present hamper such adjustments.

2. Subsection (1) provides that an agreement modifying a sales contract needs no consideration to be binding.

However, modifications made thereunder must meet the test of good faith imposed by this act. The effective use of bad faith to escape performance on the original contract terms is barred, and the extortion of a "modification" without legitimate commercial reason is ineffective as a violation of the duty of good faith. Nor can a mere technical consideration support a modification made in bad faith.

The test of "good faith" between merchants or as against merchants includes "observance of reasonable commercial standards of fair dealing in the trade" (Section 2–103), and may in some situations require an objectively demonstrable reason for seeking a modification. But such matters as a market shift which makes performance come to involve a loss may provide such a reason even though there is no such unforeseen difficulty as would make out a legal excuse from performance under Sections 2–615 and 2 616.

3. Subsections (2) and (3) are intended to protect against false allegations of oral modifications. "Modification or rescission" includes abandonment or other change by mutual consent, contrary to the decision in Green v. Doniger, 300 N.Y. 238, 90 N.E. 2d 56 (1949); it does not include unilateral "termination" or "cancellation" as defined in Section 2–106.

The Statute of Frauds provisions of this Article are expressly applied to modifications by subsection (3). Under those provisions the "delivery and acceptance" test is limited to the goods which have been accepted, that is, to the past. "Modification" for the future cannot therefore be conjured up by oral testimony if the price involved is $500.00 or more since such modification must be shown at least by an authenticated memo. And since a memo is limited in its effect to the quantity of goods set forth in it there is safeguard against oral evidence.

Subsection (2) permits the parties in effect to make their own Statute of Frauds as regards any future modification of the contract by giving effect to a clause in a signed agreement which expressly requires any modification to be by signed writing.

But note that if a consumer is to be held to such a clause on a form supplied by a merchant it must be separately signed.

4. Subsection (4) is intended, despite the provisions of subsections (2) and (3), to prevent contractual provisions excluding modification except by a signed writing from limiting in other respects the legal effect of the parties' actual later conduct. The effect of such conduct as a waiver is further regulated in subsection (5).

Cross References:

Point 1: Section 1–203.
Point 2: Sections 1–201, 1–203, 2–615 and 2–616.
Point 3: Sections 2–106, 2–201 and 2–202.
Point 4: Sections 2–202 and 2–208.

Definitional Cross References:

"Agreement". Section 1–201.
"Between merchants". Section 2–104.
"Contract". Section 1–201.
"Notification". Section 1–201.
"Signed". Section 1–201.
"Term". Section 1–201.
"Writing". Section 1–201.

Section 2–210. Delegation of Performance; Assignment of Rights.

(1) A party may perform his duty through a delegate unless otherwise agreed or unless the other party has a substantial interest in having his original promisor perform or control the acts required by the contract. No delegation of performance relieves the party delegating of any duty to perform or any liability for breach.

(2) Unless otherwise agreed all rights of either seller or buyer can be assigned except where the assignment would materially change the duty of the other party, or increase materially the burden or risk imposed on him by his contract, or impair materially his chance of obtaining return performance. A right to damages for breach of the whole contract or a right arising out of the assignor's due performance of his entire obligation can be assigned despite agreement otherwise.

(3) Unless the circumstances indicate the contrary a prohibition of assignment of "the contract" is to be construed as barring only the delegation to the assignee of the assignor's performance.

(4) An assignment of "the contract" or of "all my rights under the contract" or an assignment in similar general terms is an assignment of rights and unless the language or the circumstances (as in an assignment for security) indicate the contrary, it is a delegation of performance of the duties of the assignor and its acceptance by the assignee constitutes a promise by him to perform those duties. This promise is enforceable by either the assignor or the other party to the original contract.

(5) The other party may treat any assignment which delegates performance as creating reasonable grounds for insecurity and may without prejudice to his rights against the assignor demand assurances from the assignee (Section 2–609).

New York Annotations

(1) *Delegation. Accord:* Devlin v. The Mayor, et al., 63 N.Y. 8 (1875); see Restatement, Contracts, §§ 151 and 161, and New York Annotations.

(2) *Assignment.* The first sentence is in *accord* with New York law, Restatement, Contracts, §§ 151 and 161, and New York Annotations. Note that Section 9–318 (4) makes ineffective a term prohibiting the assignment of a "contract right" or "account" as defined in Sections 9–102, 9–104 and 9–106. Together with the second sentence of this section, Section 9–318(4) is contrary to the New York position sustaining the effectiveness of an explicitly worded contractual prohibition on assignment. Allhusen v. Caristo Construction Corp., 303 N.Y. 446, 103 N.E.2d 891 (1952). See also Section 5–116. No conflict will arise between the Code and Personal Property Law, § 41, which explicitly permits other statutes to control. [NOTE: Personal Property Law § 41 was repealed by Laws 1964, Ch. 664, eff. Sept. 27, 1964 and is now covered by General Obligations Law §§ 1–203, 13–101, 13–103, 13–105 and 13–107]

(3) *Interpretation.* For strict construction of clauses broadly prohibiting assignments, see Snyder v. City of New York, 74 App. Div. 421, 77 N.Y.S. 637 (1902).

Historical Note: Changes suggested by the Law Revision Commission were made for clarification, without change of meaning. (1956 Recommendations, p. 31; Excerpts, pp. 372–3.)

Official Uniform Comment

Prior Uniform Statutory Provision: None.

Purposes:

1. Generally, this section recognizes both delegation of performance and assignability as normal and permissible incidents of a contract for the sale of goods.

2. Delegation of performance, either in conjunction with an assignment or otherwise, is provided for by subsection (1) where no substantial reason can be shown as to why the delegated performance will not be as satisfactory as personal performance.

3. Under subsection (2) rights which are no longer executory such as a right to damages for breach or a right to payment of an "account" as defined in the Article on Secured Transactions (Article 9) may be assigned although the agreement prohibits assignment. In such cases no question of delegation of any performance is involved. The assignment of a "contract right" as defined in the Article on Secured Transactions (Article 9) is not covered by this subsection.

4. The nature of the contract or the circumstances of the case, however, may bar assignment of the contract even where delegation of performance is not involved. This Article and this section are intended to clarify this problem, particularly in cases dealing with output requirement and exclusive dealing contracts. In the first place the section on requirements and exclusive dealing removes from the construction of the original contract most of the "personal discretion" element by substituting the reasonably objective standard of good faith operation of the plant or business to be supplied. Secondly, the section on insecurity and assurances, which is specifically referred to in subsection (5) of this section, frees the other party from the doubts

and uncertainty which may afflict him under an assignment of the character in question by permitting him to demand adequate assurance of due performance without which he may suspend his own performance. Subsection (5) is not in any way intended to limit the effect of the section on insecurity and assurances and the word "performance" includes the giving of orders under a requirements contract. Of course, in any case where a material personal discretion is sought to be transferred, effective assignment is barred by subsection (2).

5. Subsection (4) lays down a general rule of construction distinguishing between a normal commercial assignment, which substitutes the assignee for the assignor both as to rights and duties, and a financing assignment in which only the assignor's rights are transferred.

This Article takes no position on the possibility of extending some recognition or power to the original parties to work out normal commercial readjustments of the contract in the case of financing assignments even after the original obligor has been notified of the assignment. This question is dealt with in the Article on Secured Transactions (Article 9).

6. Subsection (5) recognizes that the non-assigning original party has a stake in the reliability of the person with whom he has closed the original contract, and is, therefore, entitled to due assurance that any delegated performance will be properly forthcoming.

7. This section is not intended as a complete statement of the law of delegation and assignment but is limited to clarifying a few points doubtful under the case law. Particularly, neither this section nor this Article touches directly on such questions as the need or effect of notice of the assignment, the rights of successive assignees, or any question of the form of an assignment, either as between the parties or as against any third parties. Some of these questions are dealt with in Article 9.

Cross References:

Point 3: Articles 5 and 9.
Point 4: Sections 2–306 and 2–609.
Point 5: Article 9, Sections 9–317 and 9–318.
Point 7: Article 9.

Definitional Cross References:

"Agreement". Section 1–201.
"Buyer". Section 2–103.
"Contract". Section 1–201.
"Party". Section 1–201.
"Rights". Section 1–201.
"Seller". Section 2–103.
"Term". Section 1–201.

PART 3

GENERAL OBLIGATION AND CONSTRUCTION OF CONTRACT

Section 2–301. General Obligations of Parties.

The obligation of the seller is to transfer and deliver and that of the buyer is to accept and pay in accordance with the contract.

New York Annotations

Accord: Personal Property Law, § 122.

Official Uniform Comment

Prior Uniform Statutory Provision: Sections 11 and 41, Uniform Sales Act.
Changes: Rewritten.

Purposes of Changes:

This section uses the term "obligation" in contrast to the term "duty" in order to provide for the "condition" aspects of delivery and payment insofar as they are not modified by other sections of this Article such as those on cure of tender. It thus replaces not only the general provisions of the Uniform Sales Act on the parties' duties, but also the general provisions of that Act on the effect of conditions. In order to determine what is "in accordance with the contract" under this Article usage of trade, course of dealing and performance, and the general background of circumstances must be given due consideration in conjunction with the lay meaning of the words used to define the scope of the conditions and duties.

Cross References:

Section 1–106. See also Sections 1–205, 2–208, 2–209, 2–508 and 2–612.

Definitional Cross References:

"Buyer". Section 2–103.
"Contract". Section 1–201.
"Party". Section 1–201.
"Seller". Section 2–103.

Section 2–302. Unconscionable Contract or Clause.

(1) If the court as a matter of law finds the contract or any clause of the contract to have been unconscionable at the time it was made the court may refuse to enforce the contract, or it may enforce the remainder of the contract without the unconscionable clause, or it may so limit the application of any unconscionable clause as to avoid any unconscionable result.

(2) When it is claimed or appears to the court that the contract or any clause thereof may be unconscionable the parties shall be afforded a reasonable opportunity to present evidence as to its commercial setting, purpose and effect to aid the court in making the determination.

New York Annotations

This section states a theory new to sales law and is apparently designed to carry equity practice into the sales field. See Restatement, Contracts, § 367 and New York Annotations. The Comment, citing cases from other states, concludes that the results intended under this section have been accomplished by indirection by interpretation of language and the like. Compare the analogous law relating to liquidated damages and penalties. Restatement, Contracts, § 339 and New York Annotations; or to express conditions involving forfeiture, Restatement, Contracts, § 302 and New York Annotations; or to interpreting contracts in light of a "good faith requirement", Price v. Spielman Motor Sales Co., Inc., 261 App.Div. 626, 26 N.Y.S.2d 836 (1941); M. O'Neil Supply Co., Inc. v. Petroleum Heat & Power Co., Inc., 280 N.Y. 50, 19 N.E.2d 676 (1939); or to substantial performance of a building contract, Jacob & Youngs, Inc. v. Kent, 230 N.Y. 239, 129 N.E. 889 (1921).

Historical Note: Subsection (1) was revised in Supp. No. 1 to make it clear that unconscionability is a question of law to be decided by the court and that the court in making such a decision is not to apply hindsight but is rather to consider the question of unconscionability as of the date of formation of the contract. Subsection (2) was changed in Supp. No. 1 to show clearly that the parties have a right to a reasonable opportunity to present evidence going to the question of unconscionability. Subsection (1) was further revised at the suggestion of the Law Revision Commission in the interest of clarity, without change of meaning. (1956 Recommendations, p. 31; Excerpts. pp. 373–4.)

Official Uniform Comment

Prior Uniform Statutory Provision: None.

Purposes:

1. This section is intended to make it possible for the courts to police explicitly against the contracts or clauses which they find to be unconscionable. In the past such policing has been accomplished by adverse construction of language, by manipulation of the rules of offer and acceptance or by determinations that the clause is contrary to public policy or to the dominant purpose of the contract. This section is intended to allow the court to pass directly on the unconscionability of the contract or particular clause therein and to make a conclusion of law as to its unconscionability. The basic test is whether, in the light of the general commercial background and the commercial needs of the particular trade or case, the clauses involved are so one-sided as to be unconscionable under the circumstances existing at the time of the making of the contract. Subsection (2) makes it clear that it is proper for the court to hear evidence upon these questions. The principle is one of the prevention of oppression and unfair surprise (Cf. Campbell Soup Co. v. Wentz, 172 F.2d 80, 3d Cir. 1948) and not of disturbance of allocation of risks because of superior bargaining power. The underlying basis of this section is illustrated by the results in cases such as the following:

Kansas City Wholesale Grocery Co. v. Weber Packing Corporation, 93 Utah 414, 73 P.2d 1272 (1937), where a clause limiting time for complaints was held inapplicable to latent defects in a shipment of catsup which could be discovered only by microscopic analysis; Hardy v. General Motors Acceptance Corporation, 38 Ga. App. 463, 144 S.E. 327 (1928), holding that a disclaimer of warranty clause applied only to express warranties, thus letting in a fair implied warranty; Andrews Bros. v. Singer & Co. (1934 CA) 1 K.B. 17, holding that where a car with substantial mileage was delivered instead of a "new" car, a disclaimer of warranties, including those "implied," left unaffected an "express obligation" on the description, even though the Sale of Goods Act called such an implied warranty; New Prague Flouring Mill Co. v. G.A. Spears, 194 Iowa 417, 189 N.W. 815 (1922), holding that a clause permitting the seller, upon the buyer's failure to supply shipping instructions, to cancel, ship, or allow delivery date to be indefinitely postponed 30 days at a time by the inaction, does not indefinitely postpone the date of measuring damages for the buyer's breach, to the seller's advantage; and Kansas Flour Mills Co. v. Dirks, 100 Kan. 376, 164 P. 273 (1917), where under a similar clause in a rising market the court permitted the buyer to measure his damages for non-delivery at the end of only one 30 day postponement; Green v. Arcos, Ltd. (1931 CA) 47 T.L.R. 336, where a blanket clause prohibiting rejection of shipments by the buyer was restricted to apply to shipments where discrepancies represented merely mercantile variations; Meyer v. Packard Cleveland Motor Co., 106 Ohio St. 328, 140 N.E. 118 (1922), in which the court held that a "waiver" of all agreements not specified did not preclude implied warranty of fitness of a rebuilt dump truck for ordinary use as a dump truck; Austin Co. v. J. H. Tillman Col., 104 Or. 541, 209 P. 131 (1922), where a clause limiting the buyer's remedy to return was held to be applicable only if the seller had delivered a machine needed for a construction job which reasonably met the contract description; Bekkevold v. Potts, 173 Minn. 87, 216 N.W. 790, 59 A.L.R. 1164 (1927), refusing to allow warranty of fitness for purpose imposed by law to be negated by clause excluding all warranties "made" by the seller; Robert A. Munroe & Co. v. Meyer (1930) 2 K.B. 312, holding that the warranty of description overrides a clause reading "with all faults and defects" where adulterated meat not up to the contract description was delivered.

2. Under this section the court, in its discretion, may refuse to enforce the contract as a whole if it is permeated by the unconscionability, or it may strike any single clause or group of clauses which are so tainted or which are contrary to the essential purpose of the agreement, or it may simply limit unconscionable clauses so as to avoid unconscionable results.

3. The present section is addressed to the court, and the decision is to be made by it. The commercial evidence referred to in subsection (2) is for the court's consideration, not the jury's. Only the agreement which results from the court's action on these matters is to be submitted to the general triers of the facts.

Definitional Cross Reference:

"Contract". Section 1–201.

Section 2–303. Allocation or Division of Risks.

Where this Article allocates a risk or a burden as between the parties "unless otherwise agreed", the agreement may not only shift the allocation but may also divide the risk or burden.

New York Annotations

Accord: Personal Property Law, § 152. See annotation to Section 2–719; compare Personal Property Law, § 103 (rules on risk "unless otherwise agreed").

Official Uniform Comment

Prior Uniform Statutory Provision: None.

Purposes:

1. This section is intended to make it clear that the parties may modify or allocate "unless otherwise agreed" risks or burdens imposed by this Article as they desire, always subject, of course, to the provisions on unconscionability.

Compare Section 1–102(4).

2. The risk or burden may be divided by the express terms of the agreement or by the attending circumstances, since under the definition of "agreement" in this Act the circumstances surrounding the transaction as well as the express language used by the parties enter into the meaning and substance of the agreement.

Cross References:

Point 1: Sections 1–102, 2–302.

Point 2: Section 1–201

Definitional Cross References:

"Party". Section 1–201.

"Agreement". Section 1–201.

Section 2–304. Price Payable in Money, Goods, Realty, or Otherwise.

(1) The price can be made payable in money or otherwise. If it is payable in whole or in part in goods each party is a seller of the goods which he is to transfer.

(2) Even though all or part of the price is payable in an interest in realty the transfer of the goods and the seller's obligations with reference to them are subject to this Article, but not the transfer of the interest in realty or the transferor's obligations in connection therewith.

New York Annotations

This section expands Personal Property Law, § 90(2), to cover cases, excluded by Personal Property Law, § 90(3), where the consideration for a transfer of property in goods includes real property. In such cases the Code covers the transfer of the goods and the seller's obligations with reference to them, but not the transfer of the realty. Contracts of barter of goods are covered both by the Sales Act and this section. The section also eliminates the possibility that the exchange of goods for services will be outside the Article. See, Young v. Gerosa, 11 A.D.2d 67, 202 N.Y.S2d 470 (1960); Haag v. Klee, 162 Misc. 250, 293 N.Y.S. 266 (1936).

Official Uniform Comment

Prior Uniform Statutory Provision: Subsections (2) and (3) of Section 9, Uniform Sales Act.

Changes: Rewritten.

Purposes of Changes:

1. This section corrects the phrasing of the Uniform Sales Act so as to avoid misconstruction and produce greater accuracy in commercial result. While it continues the essential intent and purpose of the Uniform Sales Act it rejects any purely verbalistic construction in disregard of the underlying reason of the provisions.

2. Under subsection (1) the provisions of this Article are applicable to transactions where the "price" of goods is payable in something other than money. This does not mean, however, that this whole Article applies automatically and in its entirety simply because an agreed transfer of title to goods is not a gift. The basic purposes and reasons of the Article must always be considered in determining the applicability of any of its provisions.

3. Subsection (2) lays down the general principle that when goods are to be exchanged for realty, the provisions of this Article apply only to those aspects of the transaction which concern the transfer of title to goods but do not affect the transfer of the realty since the detailed regulation of various particular contracts which fall outside the scope of this Article is left to the courts and other legislation. However, the complexities of these situations may be such that each must be analyzed in the light of the underlying reasons in order to determine the applicable principles. Local statutes dealing with realty are not to be lightly disregarded or altered by language of this Article. In contrast, this Article declares definite policies in regard to certain

matters legitimately within its scope though concerned with real property situations, and in those instances the provisions of this Article control.

Cross References:

Point 1: Section 1–102.
Point 3: Sections 1–102, 1–103, 1–104 and 2–107.

Definitional Cross References:

"Goods". Section 2–105.
"Money". Section 1–201.
"Party". Section 1–201.
"Seller". Section 2–103.

Section 2–305. Open Price Term.

(1) The parties if they so intend can conclude a contract for sale even though the price is not settled. In such a case the price is a reasonable price at the time for delivery if

(a) nothing is said as to price; or

(b) the price is left to be agreed by the parties and they fail to agree; or

(c) the price is to be fixed in terms of some agreed market or other standard as set or recorded by a third person or agency and it is not so set or recorded.

(2) A price to be fixed by the seller or by the buyer means a price for him to fix in good faith.

(3) When a price left to be fixed otherwise than by agreement of the parties fails to be fixed through fault of one party the other may at his option treat the contract as cancelled or himself fix a reasonable price.

(4) Where, however, the parties intend not to be bound unless the price be fixed or agreed and it is not fixed or agreed there is no contract. In such a case the buyer must return any goods already received or if unable so to do must pay their reasonable value at the time of delivery and the seller must return any portion of the price paid on account.

New York Annotations

The first sentence of subsection (1) is in *accord* with Personal Property Law, § 90(1), and the New York case law. Similarly the provision for a reasonable price where nothing is said as to price has support in the New York cases enforcing such agreements at "current rates," or at the "market." Shields v. Pettie, 4 N.Y. 122 (1850), Konitzky v. Meyer, 49 N.Y. 571 (1872); Huron Milling Co. v. Hedges, 257 F.2d 258 (2d Cir: (1958); as well as in Personal Property Law, § 90(4). But compare, Lambert v. Hays, 136 App.Div. 574, 121 N.Y.S. 80 (1910). Contrary to subsection (1)(b) the New York cases seem to conclude that an agreement to sell goods at a price to be agreed upon in the future is itself unenforceable. See Sun Printing & Publishing Ass'n v. Remington Paper & Power Co., Inc., 235 N.Y. 338, 139 N.E. 470 (1923); Varney v. Ditmars, 217 N.Y. 223, 111 N.E. 822 (1916); United Press v. N.Y. Press Co., Ltd., 164 N.Y. 406, 58 N.E. 527 (1900); but, compare Saul v.

Arthur Rosenberg Co., Inc., 109 N.Y.S.2d 589 (1951), with Becher v. Nat'l Cloak & Suit Co., 128 App.Div. 423, 112 N.Y.S 839 (1908). Where an external standard is supplied as in subsection (1)(c) the contract has been enforced in New York as sufficiently definite, e.g., Boret v. L. Vogelstein & Co., Inc., 188 App.Div. 605, 177 N.Y.S. 402, aff'd mem., 230 N.Y. 573, 130 N.E. 898 (1920).

Subsection (3) is new, but in permitting the offended party to fix the price the subsection adopts an approach similar to Personal Property Law, § 91(2), permitting arbitration. This subsection of the Code leaves the matter to the offended party.

Subsection (4) is new.

Official Uniform Comment

Prior Uniform Statutory Provision: Sections 9 and 10, Uniform Sales Act.

Changes: Completely rewritten.

Purposes of Changes:

1. This section applies when the price term is left open on the making of an agreement which is nevertheless intended by the parties to be a binding agreement. This Article rejects in these instances the formula that "an agreement to agree is unenforceable" if the case falls within subsection (1) of this section, and rejects also defeating such agreements on the ground of "indefiniteness". Instead this Article recognizes the dominant intention of the parties to have the deal continue to be binding upon both. As to future performance, since this Article recognizes remedies such as cover (Section 2–712), resale (Section 2–706) and specific performance (Section 2–716) which go beyond any mere arithmetic as between contract price and market price, there is usually a "reasonably certain basis for granting an appropriate remedy for breach" so that the contract need not fail for indefiniteness.

2. Under some circumstances the postponement of agreement on price will mean that no deal has really been concluded, and this is made express in the preamble of subsection (1) ("The parties if they so intend") and in subsection (4). Whether or not this is so is, in most cases, a question to be determined by the trier of fact.

3. Subsection (2), dealing with the situation where the price is to be fixed by one party rejects the uncommercial idea that an agreement that the seller may fix the price means that he may fix any price he may wish by the express qualification that the price so fixed must be fixed in good faith. Good faith includes observance of reasonable commercial standards of fair dealing in the trade if the party is a merchant. (Section 2–103). But in the normal case a "posted price" or a future seller's or buyer's "given price," "price in effect," "market price," or the like satisfies the good faith requirement.

4. The section recognizes that there may be cases in which a particular person's judgment is not chosen merely as a barometer or index of a fair price but is an essential condition to the parties' intent to make any contract at all. For example, the case where a known and trusted expert is to "value" a particular painting for which there is no market standard differs sharply from the situation where a named expert is to determine the grade of cotton, and the difference would support a finding that in the one the parties did not intend to make a binding agreement if that expert were unavailable whereas in the other they did so intend. Other circumstances would of course affect the validity of such a finding.

5. Under subsection (3), wrongful interference by one party with any agreed machinery for price fixing in the contract may be treated by the other party as a repudiation justifying cancellation, or merely as a failure to take cooperative action thus shifting to the aggrieved party the reasonable leeway in fixing the price.

6. Throughout the entire section, the purpose is to give effect to the agreement which has been made. That effect, however, is always conditioned by the requirement

of good faith action which is made an inherent part of all contracts within this Act. (Section 1–203).

Cross References:

Point 1: Sections 2–204(3), 2–706, 2–712 and 2–716.
Point 3: Section 2–103.
Point 5: Sections 2–311 and 2–610.
Point 6: Section 1–203.

Definitional Cross References:

"Agreement". Section 1–201.
"Burden of establishing". Section 1–201.
"Buyer". Section 2–103.
"Cancellation". Section 2–106.
"Contract". Section 1–201.
"Contract for sale". Section 2–106.
"Fault". Section 1–201.
"Goods". Section 2–105.
"Party". Section 1–201.
"Receipt of goods". Section 2–103.
"Seller". Section 2–103.
"Term". Section 1–201.

Section 2–306. Output, Requirements and Exclusive Dealings.

(1) A term which measures the quantity by the output of the seller or the requirements of the buyer means such actual output or requirements as may occur in good faith, except that no quantity unreasonably disproportionate to any stated estimate or in the absence of a stated estimate to any normal or otherwise comparable prior output or requirements may be tendered or demanded.

(2) A lawful agreement by either the seller or the buyer for exclusive dealing in the kind of goods concerned imposes unless otherwise agreed an obligation by the seller to use best efforts to supply the goods and by the buyer to use best efforts to promote their sale.

New York Annotations

Subsection (1) is new to the statutes. Output and requirements contracts are enforced in New York. Matter of McNutt Co. v. Eckert, 257 N.Y. 100, 177 N.E. 386 (1931); Edison Electric Illuminating Co. v. Thacher, 229 N.Y. 172, 128 N.E. 124 (1921); Ehronworth v. George F. Stuhmer & Co., 229 N.Y. 210, 128 N.E. 108 (1920). Restatement, Contracts, §§ 32, 77–80 and New York Annotations. Compare Schlegal Mfg. Co. v. Peter Cooper's Glue Factory, 231 N.Y. 459, 132 N.E. 148 (1921) (no mutuality since jobber-buyer not obligated in any way; market price nearly tripled). See, 26 A.L.R.2d 1139. In New York Central Iron Works Co. v. United States Radiator Co., 174 N.Y. 331, 66 N.E. 967 (1903), the contract was enforced, but dictum calls for "good faith" and fair dealing and prohibits speculative as distinguished from business use of the contract. See also Mar-Bond Beverage Corp. v. Dublin Distributors, Inc., 9 A.D.2d 730, 195 N.Y.S.2d 730 (1959) (mutuality from performance).

Subsection (2) is apparently based upon Wood v. Lucy, Lady Duff-Gordon, 222 N.Y. 88, 18 N.E. 214 (1917) (dealer under exclusive dealing contract must use reasonable efforts to sell the goods). Compare Smith v. Diem, 223 App.Div. 572, 229 N.Y.S. 56, aff'd, 249 N.Y. 590, 164 N.E. 595 (1928).

Historical Note: Subsection (2) was rewritten at the suggestion of the Law Revision Commission to make it clear that disclaimer of the obligation is permitted. The substitution of the phrase "to use best efforts" for "due diligence" was recommended on behalf of the Pennsylvania State Chamber of Commerce to avoid conflict with Section 1–102(3) and to use language normally used in business. (1956 Recommendations, p. 33; Excerpts, p. 374.)

Official Uniform Comment

Prior Uniform Statutory Provision: None.

Purposes:

1. Subsection (1) of this section, in regard to output and requirements, applies to this specific problem the general approach of this Act which requires the reading of commercial background and intent into the language of any agreement and demands good faith in the performance of that agreement. It applies to such contracts of nonproducing establishments such as dealers or distributors as well as to manufacturing concerns.

2. Under this Article, a contract for output or requirements is not too indefinite since it is held to mean the actual good faith output or requirements of the particular party. Nor does such a contract lack mutuality of obligation since, under this section, the party who will determine quantity is required to operate his plant or conduct his business in good faith and according to commercial standards of fair dealing in the trade so that his output or requirements will approximate a reasonably foreseeable figure. Reasonable elasticity in the requirements is expressly envisaged by this section and good faith variations from prior requirements are permitted even when the variation may be such as to result in discontinuance. A shutdown by a requirements buyer for lack of orders might be permissible when a shut-down merely to curtail losses would not. The essential test is whether the party is acting in good faith. Similarly, a sudden expansion of the plant by which requirements are to be measured would not be included within the scope of the contract as made but normal expansion undertaken in good faith would be within the scope of this section. One of the factors in an expansion situation would be whether the market price had risen greatly in a case in which the requirements contract contained a fixed price. Reasonable variation of an extreme sort is exemplified in Southwest Natural Gas Co. v. Oklahoma Portland Cement Co., 102 F.2d 630 (C.C.A. 10, 1939). This Article takes no position as to whether a requirements contract is a provable claim in bankruptcy.

3. If an estimate of output or requirements is included in the agreement, no quantity unreasonably disproportionate to it may be tendered or demanded. Any minimum or maximum set by the agreement shows a clear limit on the intended elasticity. In similar fashion, the agreed estimate is to be regarded as a center around which the parties intend the variation to occur.

4. When an enterprise is sold, the question may arise whether the buyer is bound by an existing output or requirements contract. That question is outside the scope of this Article, and is to be determined on other principles of law. Assuming that the contract continues, the output or requirements in the hands of the new owner continue to be measured by the actual good faith output or requirements under the normal operation of the enterprise prior to sale. The sale itself is not grounds for sudden expansion or decrease.

5. Subsection (2), on exclusive dealing, makes explicit the commercial rule embodied in this Act under which the parties to such contracts are held to have impliedly, even when not expressly, bound themselves to use reasonable diligence as well as good faith in their performance of the contract. Under such contracts the exclusive agent is required, although no express commitment has been made, to use reasonable effort and due diligence in the expansion of the market or the promotion of the product, as the case may be. The principal is expected under such a contract to refrain from supplying any other dealer or agent within the exclusive territory. An exclusive dealing agreement brings into play all of the good faith aspects of the output and requirement problems of subsection (1). It also raises questions of insecurity and right to adequate assurance under this Article.

Cross References:

Point 4: Section 2–210.
Point 5: Sections 1–203 and 2–609.

Definitional Cross References:

"Agreement". Sections 1–201.
"Buyer". Section 2–103.
"Contract for sale". Section 2–106.
"Good Faith". Section 1–201.
"Goods". Section 2–105.
"Party". Section 1–201.
"Term". Section 1–201.
"Seller". Section 2–103.

Section 2–307. Delivery in Single Lot or Several Lots.

Unless otherwise agreed all goods called for by a contract for sale must be tendered in a single delivery and payment is due only on such tender but where the circumstances give either party the right to make or demand delivery in lots the price if it can be apportioned may be demanded for each lot.

New York Annotations

Accord: Personal Property Law, §§ 123, 126(1); see Equitable Trading Co. v. Stoneman, 131 App.Div. 376, 115 N.Y.S. 285 (1909). See Section 2–511.

Official Uniform Comment

Prior Uniform Statutory Provision: Section 45 (1), Uniform Sales Act.
Changes: Rewritten and expanded.

Purposes of Changes:

1. This section applies where the parties have not specifically agreed whether delivery and payment are to be by lots and generally continues the essential intent of original Act, Section 45(1) by assuming that the parties intended delivery to be in a single lot.

2. Where the actual agreement or the circumstances do not indicate otherwise, delivery in lots is not permitted under this section and the buyer is properly entitled to reject for a deficiency in the tender, subject to any privilege in the seller to cure the tender.

3. The "but" clause of this section goes to the case in which it is not commercially feasible to deliver or to receive the goods in a single lot as for example, where a contract calls for the shipment of ten carloads of coal and only three cars are available at a given time. Similarly, in a contract involving brick necessary to build a building the buyer's storage space may be limited so that it would be impossible to receive the entire amount of brick at once, or it may be necessary to assemble the goods as in the case of cattle on the range, or to mine them.

In such cases, a partial delivery is not subject to rejection for the defect in quantity alone, if the circumstances do not indicate a repudiation or default by the seller as to the expected balance or do not give the buyer ground for suspending his performance because of insecurity under the provisions of Section 2–609. However, in such cases the undelivered balance of goods under the contract must be forthcoming within a reasonable time and in a reasonable manner according to the policy of Section 2–503 on manner of tender of delivery. This is reinforced by the express provisions of Section 2–608 that if a lot has been accepted on the reasonable assumption that its nonconformity will be cured, the acceptance may be revoked if the cure does not seasonably occur. The section rejects the rule of Kelly Construction Co. v. Hackensack Brick Co., 91 N.J.L. 585, 103 A. 417, 2 A.L.R. 685 (1918) and approves the result in Lynn M. Ranger, Inc. v. Gildersleeve, 106 Conn. 372, 138 A. 142 (1927) in which a contract was made for six carloads of coal then rolling from the mines and consigned to the seller but the seller agreed to divert the carloads to the buyer as soon as the car numbers became known to him. He arranged a diversion of two cars and then notified the buyer who then repudiated the contract. The seller was held to be entitled to his full remedy for the two cars diverted because simultaneous delivery of all of the cars was not contemplated by either party.

4. Where the circumstances indicate that a party has a right to delivery in lots, the price may be demanded for each lot if it is apportionable.

Cross References:

Point 1: Section 1–201.
Point 2: Sections 2–508 and 2–601.
Point 3: Sections 2–503, 2–608 and 2–609.

Definitional Cross References:

"Contract for sale". Section 2–106.
"Goods". Section 2–105.
"Lot". Section 2–105.
"Party". Section 1–201.
"Rights". Section 1–201.

Section 2–308. Absence of Specified Place for Delivery.

Unless otherwise agreed

(a) the place for delivery of goods is the seller's place of business or if he has none his residence; but

(b) in a contract for sale of identified goods which to the knowledge of the parties at the time of contracting are in some other place, that place is the place for their delivery; and

(c) documents of title may be delivered through customary banking channels.

New York Annotations

Paragraphs (a) and (b) are in *accord* with Personal Property Law, § 124(1). Paragraph (c) is new, but is in accord with prevailing business practice.

Official Uniform Comment

Prior Uniform Statutory Provision: Paragraphs (a) and (b)–Section 43(1), Uniform Sales Act; Paragraph (c)–none.

Changes: Slight modification in language.

Purposes of Changes and New Matter:

1. Paragraphs (a) and (b) provide for those noncommercial sales and for those occasional commercial sales where no place or means of delivery has been agreed upon by the parties. Where a delivery by carrier is "required or authorized by the agreement", the seller's duties as to delivery of the goods are governed not by this section but by Section 2–504.

2. Under paragraph (b) when the identified goods contracted for are known to both parties to be in some location other than the seller's place of business or residence, the parties are presumed to have intended that place to be the place of delivery. This paragraph also applies (unless, as would be normal, the circumstances show that delivery by way of documents is intended) to a bulk of goods in the possession of a bailee. In such a case, however, the seller has the additional obligation to procure the acknowledgement by the bailee of the buyer's right to possession.

3. Where "customary banking channels" call only for due notification by the banker that the documents are on hand, leaving the buyer himself to see to the physical receipt of the goods, tender at the buyer's address is not required under paragraph (c). But that paragraph merely eliminates the possibility of a default by the seller if "customary banking channels" have been properly used in giving notice to the buyer. Where the bank has purchased a draft accompanied by documents or has undertaken its collection on behalf of the seller, Part 5 of Article 4 spells out its duties and relations to its customer. Where the documents move forward under a letter of credit the Article on Letters of Credit spells out the duties and relations between the bank, the seller and the buyer.

4. The rules of this section apply only "unless otherwise agreed." The surrounding circumstances, usage of trade, course of dealing and course of performance, as well as the express language of the parties, may constitute an "otherwise agreement".

Cross References:

Point 1: Sections 2–504 and 2–505.
Point 2: Section 2–503.
Point 3: Section 2–512, Articles 4, Part 5, and 5.

Definitional Cross References:

"Contract for sale". Section 2–106.
"Delivery". Section 1–201.
"Document of title". Section 1–201.
"Goods". Section 2–105.
"Party". Section 1–201.
"Seller". Section 2–103.

Section 2–309. Absence of Specific Time Provisions; Notice of Termination.

(1) The time for shipment or delivery or any other action under a contract if not provided in this Article or agreed upon shall be a reasonable time.

(2) Where the contract provides for successive performances but is indefinite in duration it is valid for a reasonable time but unless otherwise agreed may be terminated at any time by either party.

(3) Termination of a contract by one party except on the happening of an agreed event requires that reasonable notification be received by the other party and an agreement dispensing with notification is invalid if its operation would be unconscionable.

New York Annotations

(1) *Performance within a reasonable time. Accord.* Personal Property Law, § 124(2); A. B. Murray Co., Inc. v. Lidgerwood Mfg. Co., 241 N.Y. 455, 150 N.E. 514 (1926); John F. Trainor Co. v. G. Amsinck Co., Inc., 236 N.Y. 392, 140 N.E. 931 (1923). Subsection (1) extends the Sales Act provision to "any other action under a contract" as well as to shipment. Accord: The Lamport Co., Inc. v. Fisher Bookbinding Co., Inc., 277 App.Div. 870, 98 N.Y.S.2d 410 (1950) (unreasonable delay in inspecting).

(2) *Indefinite duration.* That agreements which state no time of termination may be terminated by notice is in accord with Watson v. Gugino, 204 N.Y. 535, 98 N.E. 18 (1912), and Martin v. New York Life Ins. Co., 148 N.Y. 117, 42 N.E. 416 (1895) (employment contracts). See Restatement, Contracts, §§ 32, 33, 44 and New York Annotations.

(3) *Notice of termination.* In Bailey v. S. S. Stafford, Inc., 178 App.Div. 811, 166 N.Y.S. 79 (1917), a six months' notice was held to be adequate to terminate such a contract; but in Cronk v. Vogt's Ice Cream, Inc., 15 N.Y.S.2d 649 (1939), it is indicated that in some circumstances no notice is necessary. The provision invalidating "unconscionable" agreements dispensing with notification is new.

Official Uniform Comment

Prior Uniform Statutory Provision: Subsection (1)–see Sections 43(2), 45(2), 47(1) and 48, Uniform Sales Act, for policy continued under this Article; Subsection (2)–none; Subsection (3)–none.

Changes: Completely different in scope.

Purposes of Changes and New Matter:

1. Subsection (1) requires that all actions taken under a sales contract must be taken within a reasonable time where no time has been agreed upon. The reasonable time under this provision turns on the criteria as to "reasonable time" and on good faith and commercial standards set forth in Sections 1–203, 1–204 and 2–103. It thus depends upon what constitutes acceptable commercial conduct in view of the nature, purpose and circumstances of the action to be taken. Agreement as to a definite time, however, may be found in a term implied from the contractual circumstances, usage of trade or course of dealing or performance as well as in an express term. Such cases fall outside of this subsection since in them the time for action is "agreed" by usage.

2. The time for payment, where not agreed upon, is related to the time for delivery; the particular problems which arise in connection with determining the appropriate time of payment and the time for any inspection before payment which is both allowed by law and demanded by the buyer are covered in Section 2–513.

3. The facts in regard to shipment and delivery differ so widely as to make detailed provision for them in the text of this Article impracticable. The applicable principles, however, make it clear that surprise is to be avoided, good faith judgment is to be protected, and notice or negotiation to reduce the uncertainty to certainty is to be favored.

4. When the time for delivery is left open, unreasonable early offers of or demands for delivery are intended to be read under this Article as expressions of desire or intention, requesting the assent or acquiescence of the other party, not as final positions which may amount without more to breach or to create breach by the other side. See Sections 2–207 and 2–609.

5. The obligation of good faith under this Act requires reasonable notification before a contract may be treated as breached because a reasonable time for delivery or demand has expired. This operates both in the case of a contract originally indefinite as to time and of one subsequently made indefinite by waiver.

When both parties let an originally reasonable time go by in silence, the course of conduct under the contract may be viewed as enlarging the reasonable time for tender or demand of performance. The contract may be terminated by abandonment.

6. Parties to a contract are not required in giving reasonable notification to fix, at peril of breach, a time which is in fact reasonable in the unforeseeable judgment of a later trier of fact. Effective communication of a proposed time limit calls for a response, so that failure to reply will make out acquiescence. Where objection is made, however, or if the demand is merely for information as to when goods will be delivered or will be ordered out, demand for assurances on the ground of insecurity may be made under this Article pending further negotiations. Only when a party insists on undue delay or on rejection of the other party's reasonable proposal is there a question of flat breach under the present section.

7. Subsection (2) applies a commercially reasonable view to resolve the conflict which has arisen in the cases as to contracts of indefinite duration. The "reasonable time" of duration appropriate to a given arrangement is limited by the circumstances. When the arrangement has been carried on by the parties over the years, the "reasonable time" can continue indefinitely and the contract will not terminate until notice.

8. Subsection (3) recognizes that the application of principles of good faith and sound commercial practice normally call for such notification of the termination of a going contract relationship as will give the other party reasonable time to seek a substitute arrangement. An agreement dispensing with notification or limiting the time for the seeking of a substitute arrangement is, of course, valid under this subsection unless the results of putting it into operation would be the creation of an unconscionable state of affairs.

9. Justifiable cancellation for breach is a remedy for breach and is not the kind of termination covered by the present subsection.

10. The requirement of notification is dispensed with where the contract provides for termination on the happening of an "agreed event." "Event" is a term chosen here to contrast with "option" or the like.

Cross References:

Point 1: Sections 1–203, 1–204 and 2–103.

Point 2: Sections 2–320, 2–321, 2–504, and 2–511 through 2–514.

Point 5: Section 1–203.

Point 6: Section 2–609.

UCC

Point 7: Section 2–204.
Point 9: Sections 2–106, 2–318, 2–610 and 2–703.

Definitional Cross References:

"Agreement". Section 1–201.
"Contract". Section 1–201.
"Notification". Section 1–201.
"Party". Section 1–201.
"Reasonable time". Section 1–204.
"Termination". Section 2–106.

Section 2–310. Open Time for Payment or Running of Credit; Authority to Ship Under Reservation.

Unless otherwise agreed

(a) payment is due at the time and place at which the buyer is to receive the goods even though the place of shipment is the place of delivery; and

(b) if the seller is authorized to send the goods he may ship them under reservation, and may tender the documents of title, but the buyer may inspect the goods after their arrival before payment is due unless such inspection is inconsistent with the terms of the contract (Section 2–513); and

(c) if delivery is authorized and made by way of documents of title otherwise then by subsection (b) then payment is due at the time and place at which the buyer is to receive the documents regardless of where the goods are to be received; and

(d) where the seller is required or authorized to ship the goods on credit the credit period runs from the time of shipment but post-dating the invoice or delaying its dispatch will correspondingly delay the starting of the credit period.

New York Annotations

(a) *Time of payment.* Paragraph (a) follows Personal Property Law, § 123, in establishing a presumption against the extension of credit. It also clears up a source of ambiguity in the present law by providing that payment under a shipment contract is due on arrival at destination. Compare Personal Property Law, §§ 123 and 127(1), with Deveso v. Chandler, 210 App.Div. 684, 206 N.Y.S. 604 (1924), aff'd 241 N.Y. 559, 150 N.E. 554 (1925), and Imperial Products Co., Inc. v. Capitol Chemical Co., 187 App.Div. 599, 176 N.Y.S. 49, aff'd 228 N.Y. 528, 126 N.E. 911 (1920).

(b) and (c) *Shipment under reservation; inspection.* Shipment by the seller with a reservation is authorized by Personal Property Law, § 101. But the Sales Act contains no provision authorizing shipment under reservation and the demand of payment against documents when a shipment contract is silent. Such authority and the right to inspect are matters which may be determined by usage of the trade. Compare Imperial Products Co., Inc. v. Capitol Chemical Co., 187 App.Div. 599, 176 N.Y.S. 49, aff'd 228 N.Y. 528, 126 N.E. 911 (1919), and Deveso v. Chandler, 210 App. Div. 684, 206 N.Y.S. 604, aff'd 241 N.Y. 559, 150 N.E. 554 (1925). Paragraph (c) follows Personal Property Law, § 128(3), in requiring payment before inspection where that right has been contracted away as in a C. O. D. contract. See Sections 2–321 and 2–513. Accord: Brown v. Raritan Chemical Works, Inc., 188

App.Div. 578, 177 N.Y.S. 309 (1919) (net cash against delivery order); Plumb v. J. W. Haliauer & Sons Co., 145 App.Div. 20, 130 N.Y.S. 147 (1911).

(d) *Sale on credit; the credit period.* Although this rule is new, it is described in the Comment as "common commercial understanding", and is reflected in Grabfelder v. Vosburgh, 90 App.Div. 307,85 N.Y.S. 633 (1904).

Historical Note: Subparagraphs (b) and (c) were changed at the suggestion of the Law Revision Commission for clarification and to avoid possible inconsistency with Sections 2–321 and 2–513. The "unless" clause in paragraph (b) was recommended on behalf of the Pennsylvania State Chamber of Commerce. (1956 Recommendations, p. 35; Excerpts, p. 375.)

Official Uniform Comment

Prior Uniform Statutory Provision; Sections 42 and 47(2), Uniform Sales Act.

Changes: Completely rewritten in this and other sections.

Purposes of Changes: This section is drawn to reflect modern business methods of dealing at a distance rather than face to face. Thus:

1. Paragraph (a) provides that payment is due at the time and place "the buyer is to receive the goods" rather than at the point of delivery except in documentary shipment cases (paragraph (c)). This grants an opportunity for the exercise by the buyer of his preliminary right to inspection before paying even though under the delivery term the risk of loss may have previously passed to him or the running of the credit period has already started.

2. Paragraph (b) while providing for inspection by the buyer before he pays, protects the seller. He is not required to give up possession of the goods until he has received payment, where no credit has been contemplated by the parties. The seller may collect through a bank by a sight draft against an order bill of lading 'hold until arrival; inspection allowed." The obligations of the bank under such a provision are set forth in Part 5 of Article 4. In the absence of a credit term, the seller is permitted to ship under reservation and if he does payment is then due where and when the buyer is to receive the documents.

3. Unless otherwise agreed, the place for the receipt of the documents and payment is the buyer's city but the time for payment is only after arrival of the goods, since under paragraph (b), and Sections 2–512 and 2–513 the buyer is under no duty to pay prior to inspection.

4. Where the mode of shipment is such that goods must be unloaded immediately upon arrival, too rapidly to permit adequate inspection before receipt, the seller must be guided by the provisions of this Article on inspection which provide that if the seller wishes to demand payment before inspection, he must put an appropriate term into the contract. Even requiring payment against documents will not of itself have this desired result it the documents are to be held until the arrival of the goods. But under (b) and (c) if the terms are C.I.F., C.O.D., or cash against documents payment may be due before inspection.

5. Paragraph (d) states the common commercial understanding that an agreed credit period runs from the time of shipment or from that dating of the invoice which is commonly recognized as a representation of the time of shipment. The provision concerning any delay in sending forth the invoice is included because such conduct results in depriving the buyer of his full notice and warning as to when he must be prepared to pay.

Cross References:

Generally: Part 5.
Point 1: Section 2–509.

Point 2: Sections 2–505, 2–511, 2–512, 2–513 and Article 4.
Point 3: Sections 2–308(b), 2–512 and 2–513.
Point 4: Section 2–513(3)(b).

Definitional Cross References:

"Buyer". Section 2–103.
"Delivery". Section 1–201.
"Document of title". Section 1–201.
"Goods". Section 2–105.
"Receipt of goods". Section 2–103.
"Send". Section 1–201.
"Term". Section 1–201.

Section 2–311. Options and Cooperation Respecting Performance.

(1) An agreement for sale which is otherwise sufficiently definite (subsection (3) of Section 2–204) to be a contract is not made invalid by the fact that it leaves particulars of performance to be specified by one of the parties. Any such specification must be made in good faith and within limits set by commercial reasonableness.

(2) Unless otherwise agreed specifications relating to assortment of the goods are at the buyer's option and except as otherwise provided in subsections (1)(c) and (3) of Section 2–319 specifications or arrangements relating to shipment are at the seller's option.

(3) Where such specification would materially affect the other party's performance but is not seasonably made or where one party's cooperation is necessary to the agreed performance of the other but is not seasonably forthcoming, the other party in addition to all other remedies

(a) is excused for any resulting delay in his own performance; and

(b) may also either proceed to perform in any reasonable manner or after the time for a material part of his own performance treat the failure to specify or to cooperate as a breach by failure to deliver or accept the goods.

New York Annotations

(1) *Definiteness.* Accord: James Talcott, Inc. v. Marshall Field & Co., 15 N.Y.S.2d 846, aff'd 258 App.Div. 1045, 17 N.Y.S.2d 1020 (1940); Storm v. Rosenthal, 156 App.Div. 544, 141 N.Y.S. 339 (1913). The limit of "commercial reasonableness" is new but is supported by reliance on usage in James Talcott, Inc. v. Marshall Field & Co., supra.

(2) *Specifications.* This provision is new but it is described in the Comment as a "standard commercial interpretation."

(3) *Lack of cooperation.* The Sales Act did not deal with this problem. See a similar contractual provision in Elias Sayour & Co., Inc. v. J.P. Stevens & Co., Inc., 205 Misc. 807, 130 N.Y.S.2d 492 (1954).

Historical Note. Clarifying changes, including the clear adoption of standards in subsection (1), were made at the suggestion of the Law Revision Commission, without change of policy. (1956 Recommendations, p. 36; Excerpts, p. 375.)

Official Uniform Comment

Prior Uniform Statutory Provision: None.

Purposes:

1. Subsection (1) permits the parties to leave certain detailed particulars of performance to be filled in by either of them without running the risk of having the contract invalidated for indefiniteness. The party to whom the agreement gives power to specify the missing details is required to exercise good faith and to act in accordance with commercial standards so that there is no surprise and the range of permissible variation is limited by what is commercially reasonable. The "agreement" which permits one party so to specify may be found as well in a course of dealing, usage of trade, or implication from circumstances as in explicit language used by the parties.

2. Options as to assortment of goods or shipping arrangements are specifically reserved to the buyer and seller respectively under subsection (2) where no other arrangement has been made. This section rejects the test which mechanically and without regard to usage or the purpose of the option gave the option to the party "first under a duty to move" and applies instead a standard commercial interpretation to these circumstances. The "Unless otherwise agreed" provision of this subsection covers not only express terms but the background and circumstances which enter into the agreement.

3. Subsection (3) applies when the exercise of an option or cooperation by one party is necessary to or materially affects the other party's performance, but it is not seasonably forthcoming; the subsection relieves the other party from the necessity for performance or excuses his delay in performance as the case may be. The contract-keeping party may at his option under this subsection proceed to perform in any commercially reasonable manner rather than wait. In addition to the special remedies provided, this subscription also reserves "all other remedies". The remedy of particular importance in this connection is that provided for insecurity. Request may also be made pursuant to the obligation of good faith for a reasonable indication of the time and manner of performance for which a party is to hold himself ready.

4. The remedy provided in subsection (3) is one which does not operate in the situation which falls within the scope of Section 2–614 on substituted performance. Where the failure to cooperate results from circumstances set forth in that Section, the other party is under a duty to proffer or demand (as the case may be) substitute performance as a condition to claiming rights against the noncooperating party.

Cross References:

Point 1: Section 1–201, 2–204 and 1–203.
Point 3: Sections 1–203 and 2–609.
Point 4: Section 2–614.

Definitional Cross References:

"Agreement". Section 1–201.
"Buyer". Section 2–103.
"Contract for sale". Section 2–106.
"Goods". Section 2–105.
"Party". Section 1–201.
"Seasonably". Section 1–204.
"Seller". Section 2–103.

UCC

Section 2–312. Warranty of Title and Against Infringement; Buyer's Obligation Against Infringement.

(1) Subject to subsection (2) there is in a contract for sale a warranty by the seller that

(a) the title conveyed shall be good, and its transfer rightful; and

(b) the goods shall be delivered free from any security interest or other lien or encumbrance of which the buyer at the time of contracting has no knowledge.

(2) A warranty under subsection (1) will be excluded or modified only by specific language or by circumstances which give the buyer reason to know that the person selling does not claim title in himself or that he is purporting to sell only such right or title as he or a third person may have.

(3) Unless otherwise agreed a seller who is a merchant regularly dealing in goods of the kind warrants that the goods shall be delivered free of the rightful claim of any third person by way of infringement or the like but a buyer who furnishes specifications to the seller must hold the seller harmless against any such claim which arises out of compliance with the specifications.

New York Annotations

(1)(a) *Title.* The implied warranty of title of subsection (1)(a) is comparable to that of Personal Property Law, § 94(1). Pinney v. Geraghty, 209 App.Div. 630, 205 N.Y.S. 645 (1924).

(b) *Freedom from liens and encumbrances.* The warranty of freedom from liens and encumbrances is comparable to that of Personal Property Law, §§ 94(1) and (2). The Comment indicates that the abolished warranty of quiet possession is absorbed in the warranty of title.

(2) *Exception where title not claimed by seller.* As under Personal Property Law, § 94(4), the seller is free of liability under the implied warranty of title if he does not purport to have title or to be able to convey it. The requirement of specific language for other modification or an exclusion of liability is more stringent than Personal Property Law, § 152; see Wilson v. Manhasset Ford, Inc., 27 Misc.2d 154, 209 N.Y.S.2d 210 (1960) (disclaimer of warranty of title to automobile against public policy). Compare Section 2–316.

(3) *Claims of infringement.* This is new to the statute.

Historical Note. Supp. No. 1 deleted the portion of former subsection (1)(b) dealing with infringement and inserted new subsection (3) to cover the subject matter. The changes limit to merchant sellers the warranty against infringement and make express provision for goods manufactured to a buyer's specifications. The changes meet criticisms made by the New York Patent Law Association and adopted by the Patent Law Committee of the National Association of Manufacturers and by the Commercial Code Committee of the Pennsylvania State Chamber of Commerce. See also Section 2–607. The changes in subsection (2), recommended on behalf of the Pennsylvania State Chamber of Commerce to conform to the policy of Section 2–316, also meet criticism by the New York Law Revision Commission. (1956 Recommendations, p. 36; Excerpts, p. 376.)

Official Uniform Comment

Prior Uniform Statutory Provision: Section 13, Uniform Sales Act.

Changes: Completely rewritten, the provisions concerning infringement being new.

Purposes of Changes:

1. Subsection (1) makes provision for a buyer's basic needs in respect to a title which he in good faith expects to acquire by his purchase, namely, that he receive a good, clean title transferred to him also in a rightful manner so that he will not be exposed to a lawsuit in order to protect it.

The warranty extends to a buyer whether or not the seller was in possession of the goods at the time the sale or contract to sell was made.

The warranty of quiet possession is abolished. Disturbance of quiet possession, although not mentioned specifically, is one way, among many, in which the breach of the warranty of title may be established.

The "knowledge" referred to in subsection 1(b) is actual knowledge as distinct from notice.

2. The provisions of this Article requiring notification to the seller within a reasonable time after the buyer's discovery of a breach apply to notice of a breach of the warranty of title, where the seller's breach was innocent. However, if the seller's breach was in bad faith he cannot be permitted to claim that he has been misled or prejudiced by the delay in giving notice. In such case the "reasonable" time for notice should receive a very liberal interpretation. Whether the breach by the seller is in good faith or bad faith Section 2–725 provides that the cause of action accrues when the breach occurs. Under the provisions of that section the breach of the warranty of good title occurs when tender of delivery is made since the warranty is not one which extends to "future performance of the goods."

3. When the goods are part of the seller's normal stock and are sold in his normal course of business, it is his duty to see that no claim of infringement of a patent or trademark by a third party will mar the buyer's title. A sale by a person other than a dealer, however, raises no implication in its circumstances of such a warranty. Nor is there such an implication when the buyer orders goods to be assembled, prepared or manufactured on his own specification. If, in such a case, the resulting product infringes a patent or trademark, the liability will run from buyer to seller. There is, under such circumstances, a tacit representation on the part of the buyer that the seller will be safe in manufacturing according to the specifications, and the buyer is under an obligation in good faith to indemnify him for any loss suffered.

4. This section rejects the cases which recognize the principle that infringements violate the warranty of title but deny the buyer a remedy unless he has been expressly prevented from using the goods. Under this Article "eviction" is not a necessary condition to the buyer's remedy since the buyer's remedy arises immediately upon receipt of notice of infringement; it is merely one way of establishing the fact of breach.

5. Subsection (2) recognizes that sales by sheriffs, executors, foreclosing lienors and persons similarly situated are so out of the ordinary commercial course that their peculiar character is immediately apparent to the buyer and therefore no personal obligation is imposed upon the seller who is purporting to sell only an unknown or limited right. This subsection does not touch upon and leaves open all questions of restitution arising in such cases, when a unique article so sold is reclaimed by a third party as the rightful owner.

6. The warranty of subsection (1) is not designated as an "implied" warranty, and hence is not subject to Section 2–316(3). Disclaimer of the warranty of title is governed instead by subsection (2), which requires either specific language or the described circumstances.

Cross References:

Point 1: Section 2–403.

Point 2: Sections 2–607 and 2–725.
Point 3: Section 1–203.
Point 4: Sections 2–609 and 2–725.
Point 6: Section 2–316.

Definitional Cross References:

"Buyer". Section 2–103.
"Contract for sale". Section 2–106.
"Goods". Section 2–105.
"Person". Section 1–201.
"Right". Section 1–201.
"Seller". Section 2–103.

Section 2–313. Express Warranties by Affirmation, Promise, Description, Sample.

(1) Express warranties by the seller are created as follows:

(a) Any affirmation of fact or promise made by the seller to the buyer which relates to the goods and becomes part of the basis of the bargain creates an express warranty that the goods shall conform to the affirmation or promise.

(b) Any description of the goods which is made part of the basis of the bargain creates an express warranty that the goods shall conform to the description.

(c) Any sample or model which is made part of the basis of the bargain creates an express warranty that the whole of the goods shall conform to the sample or model.

(2) It is not necessary to the creation of an express warranty that the seller use formal words such as "warrant" or "guarantee" or that he have a specific intention to make a warranty, but an affirmation merely of the value of the goods or a statement purporting to be merely the seller's opinion or commendation of the goods does not create a warranty.

New York Annotations

(1) *Express warranties: Scope and terminology.* The Code treats descriptions and the use of samples or models, as well as affirmations and promises, as "express" warranties rather than implied warranties as under Personal Property Law, §§ 95 and 97.

(a) Affirmations of fact and promises are express warranties under subsection (1)(a), as under Personal Property Law, § 93.

(b) Subsection (1)(b) establishes an express warranty based on a description equivalent to the implied warranty of Personal Property Law, § 95. Some confusion has been created by the prior law's characterization of such liability as implied rather than express. Alaska Pacific Salmon Co. v. Reynolds Metals Co., 163 F.2d 643 (2d Cir. 1947) (applying New York law).

(c) Subsection (1)(c) is comparable to the implied warranty in a sale by sample under Personal Property Law, § 97. Compare Henry & Co., Ltd. v. Talcott, 175 N.Y. 385, 67 N.E. 617 (1903) (sale by sample creates express warranty at common law). See, Alper Blouse Co., Inc., v. E. E. Connor & Co., Inc., 2 N.Y.2d 281, 140 N.E.2d 358 (1957); 309 N.Y. 67, 127 N.E.2d 813 (1955).

Materiality. The requirement that affirmations, etc., become a part of the basis of the bargain in order to establish a warranty is much the same as the "reliance" requirement of Personal Property Law, § 93. See Comment 3.

(2) *Formal words not necessary. Accord:* Personal Property Law, § 93, and Hawkins v. Pemberton, 51 N.Y. 198 (1872).

Statements of value or opinion. Accord: Personal Property Law, § 93. The word "commendation" is new. Harburger v. Stern Bros., 189 N.Y.S. 74 (1921) (clothes will "wear like iron" opinion). Compare, Valente, Inc. v. Mascitti, 163 Misc. 287, 295 N.Y.S. 330 (1937) (radio could "get" Rome clearly is warranty).

Historical Note: The Law Revision Commission criticized the limitation of subsection (1) to language, a sample, or a model which becomes or is made "a basis of the bargain" on the ground that "basis" might have the same connotation as "basic" and thus might drastically restrict the scope of express warranties. To avoid this unintended connotation, the phrase "part of the basis of the bargain" was substituted. (1956 Recommendations, p. 37; Excerpts, p. 376.).

UCC

Official Uniform Comment

Prior Uniform Statutory Provision: Sections 12, 14 and 16, Uniform Sales Act.

Changes: Rewritten.

Purposes of Changes: To consolidate and systematize basic principles with the result that:

1. "Express" warranties rest on "dickered" aspects of the individual bargain, and go so clearly to the essence of that bargain that words of disclaimer in a form are repugnant to the basic dickered terms. "Implied" warranties rest so clearly on a common factual situation or set of conditions that no particular language or action is necessary to evidence them and they will arise in such a situation unless unmistakably negated.

2. This section reverts to the older case law insofar as the warranties of description and sample are designated "express" rather than "implied".

Although this section is limited in its scope and direct purpose to warranties made by the seller to the buyer as part of a contract for sale, the warranty sections of this Article are not designed in any way to disturb those lines of case law growth which have recognized that warranties need not be confined either to sales contracts or to the direct parties to such a contract. They may arise in other appropriate circumstances such as in the case of bailments for hire, whether such bailment is itself the main contract or is merely a supplying of containers under a contract for the sale of their contents. The provisions of Section 2–318 on third party beneficiaries expressly recognize this case law development within one particular area. Beyond that, the matter is left to the case law with the intention that the policies of this Act may offer useful guidance in dealing with further cases as they arise.

3. The present section deals with affirmations of fact by the seller, descriptions of the goods or exhibitions of samples, exactly as any other part of a negotiation which ends in a contract is dealt with. No specific intention to make a warranty is necessary if any of these factors is made part of the basis of the bargain. In actual practice affirmations of fact made by the seller about the goods during a bargain are regarded as part of the description of those goods; hence no particular reliance on such statements need be shown in order to weave them into the fabric of the agreement. Rather, any fact which is to take such affirmations, once made, out of the agreement requires clear affirmative proof. The issue normally is one of fact.

4. In view of the principle that the whole purpose of the law of warranty is to determine what it is that the seller has in essence agreed to sell, the policy is adopted of those cases which refuse except in unusual circumstances to recognize a material deletion of the seller's obligation. Thus, a contract is normally a contract for a sale

of something describable and described. A clause generally disclaiming "all warranties, express or implied" cannot reduce the seller's obligation with respect to such description and therefore cannot be given literal effect under Section 2–316.

This is not intended to mean that the parties, if they consciously desire, cannot make their own bargain as they wish. But in determining what they have agreed upon good faith is a factor and consideration should be given to the fact that the probability is small that a real price is intended to be exchanged for a pseudo-obligation.

5. Paragraph (1)(b) makes specific some of the principles set forth above when a description of the goods is given by the seller.

A description need not be by words. Technical specifications, blueprints and the like can afford more exact description than mere language and if made part of the basis of the bargain goods must conform with them. Past deliveries may set the description of quality, either expressly or impliedly by course of dealing. Of course, all descriptions by merchants must be read against the applicable trade usages with the general rules as to merchantability resolving any doubts.

6. The basic situation as to statements affecting the true essence of the bargain is no different when a sample or model is involved in the transaction. This section includes both a "sample" actually drawn from the bulk of goods which is the subject matter of the sale, and a "model" which is offered for inspection when the subject matter is not at hand and which has not been drawn from the bulk of the goods.

Although the underlying principles are unchanged, the facts are often ambiguous when something is shown as illustrative, rather than as a straight sample. In general, the presumption is that any sample or model just as any affirmation fact is intended to become a basis of the bargain. But there is no escape from the question of fact. When the seller exhibits a sample purporting to be drawn from an existing bulk, good faith of course requires that the sample be fairly drawn. But in mercantile experience the mere exhibition of a "sample" does not to itself show whether it is merely intended to "suggest" or to "be" the character of the subject-matter of the contract. The question is whether the seller has so acted with reference to the sample as to make him responsible that the whole shall have at least the values shown by it. The circumstances aid in answering this question. If the sample has been drawn from an existing bulk, it must be regarded as describing values of the goods contracted for unless it is accompanied by an unmistakable denial of such responsibility. If, on the other hand, a model of merchandise not on hand is offered, the mercantile presumption that it has become a literal description of the subject matter is not so strong, and particularly so if modification on the buyer's initiative impairs any feature of the model.

7. The precise time when words of description or affirmation are made or samples are shown is not material. The sole question is whether the language or samples or models are fairly to be regarded as part of the contract. If language is used after the closing of the deal (as when the buyer when taking delivery asks and receives an additional assurance), the warranty becomes a modification, and need not be supported by consideration if it is otherwise reasonable and in order (Section 2–209).

8. Concerning affirmations of value or a seller's opinion or commendation under subsection (2), the basic question remains the same: What statements of the seller have in the circumstances and in objective judgment become part of the basis of the bargain? As indicated above, all of the statements of the seller do so unless good reason is shown to the contrary. The provisions of subsection (2) are included, however, since common experience discloses that some statements or predictions cannot fairly be viewed as entering into the bargain. Even as to false statements of value, however, the possibility is left open that a remedy may be provided by the law relating to fraud or misrepresentation.

Cross References:

Point 1: Section 2–316

Point 2: Sections 1–102(3) and 2–318.
Point 3: Section 2–316(2)(b).
Point 4: Section 2–316.
Point 5: Sections 1–205(4) and 2–314.
Point 6: Section 2–316.
Point 7: Section 2–209.
Point 8: Section 1–103.

Definitional Cross References:

"Buyer". Section 2–103.
"Conforming". Section 2–106.
"Goods". Section 2–105.
"Seller". Section 2–103.

Section 2–314. Implied Warranty: Merchantability; Usage of Trade.

(1) Unless excluded or modified (Section 2–316), a warranty that the goods shall be merchantable is implied in a contract for their sale if the seller is a merchant with respect to goods of that kind. Under this section the serving for value of food or drink to be consumed either on the premises or elsewhere is a sale.

(2) Goods to be merchantable must be at least such as

(a) pass without objection in the trade under the contract description; and

(b) in the case of fungible goods, are of fair average quality within the description; and

(c) are fit for the ordinary purposes for which such goods are used; and

(d) run, within the variations permitted by the agreement, of even kind, quality and quantity within each unit and among all units involved; and

(e) are adequately contained, packaged, and labeled as the agreement may require; and

(f) conform to the promises or affirmations of fact made on the container or label if any.

(3) Unless excluded or modified (Section 2–316), other implied warranties may arise from course of dealing or usage of trade.

New York Annotations

(1)(a) *Sales by merchant.* The warranty imposed on merchants by subsection (1) is the same as that imposed in the case of goods bought by description "from a seller who deals in goods of that description", under Personal Property Law, § 96(2). However, the scope of this warranty is broadened by the Code's elimination of the requirement that the sale be by description.

(b) *Service of food or drink.* This is new to the statute, but the New York case law is consistent with the Code. Temple v. Keeler, 238 N.Y. 344, 144 N.E. 635 (1924). Cases like Perlmutter v. Beth David Hospital, 308 N.Y. 100, 123 N.E.2d 792 (1954) (hospital did not "sell" blood to patient), would be unaffected by the Code.

(2) *Definition of merchantable quality.* The Code tests are new statutory law and are standards of minimal quality. Similar tests have been suggested in the previous case law, e.g., Mcneil & Higgins Co. v. Czarnikow-Rienda Co., 274 Fed. 397 (S.D.N.Y.1921) ("pass generally under that description after free examination"); Ryan v. Progressive Grocery Stores, Inc., 255 N.Y. 388, 175 N.E. 105 (1931) (loaf of bread with pin not merchantable); Cooper v. Newman, 11 N.Y.S.2d 319 (1939) (exploding syphon [sic]); Silverstein v. R. H. Macy & Co., Inc., 266 App.Div. 5, 40 N.Y.S.2d 916 (1943) (express warranty from maker's pamphlets).

(3) *Warranty by usage of trade.* Subsection (3) is comparable to Personal Property Law, § 96(5). See, Silverstein v. R. H. Macy & Co., Inc., 266 App.Div. 5, 40 N.Y.S.2d 916 (1943) (authority of agent to warrant from usage).

Historical Note: As suggested by the Law Revision Commission, the former minimum statutory definition of "guarantee" was deleted. Subsection (2)(b) was limited to fungible goods to meet criticism of the Commission. (1956 Recommendations, p. 38; Excerpts, p. 377.)

Official Uniform Comment

Prior Uniform Statutory Provision: Section 15(2), Uniform Sales Act.

Changes: Completely rewritten.

Purposes of Changes: This section, drawn in view of the steadily developing case law on the subject, is intended to make it clear that:

1. The seller's obligation applies to present sales as well as to contracts to sell subject to the effects of any examination of specific goods. (Subsection (2) of Section 2–316). Also, the warranty of merchantability applies to sales for use as well as to sales for resale.

2. The question when the warranty is imposed turns basically on the meaning of the terms of the agreement as recognized in the trade. Goods delivered under an agreement made by a merchant in a given line of trade must be of a quality comparable to that generally acceptable in that line of trade under the description or other designation of the goods used in the agreement. The responsibility imposed rests on any merchant-seller, and the absence of the words "grower or manufacturer or not" which appeared in Section 15(2) of the Uniform Sales Act does not restrict the applicability of this section.

3. A specific designation of goods by the buyer does not exclude the seller's obligation that they be fit for the general purposes appropriate to such goods. A contract for the sale of second-hand goods, however, involves only such obligation as is appropriate to such goods for that is their contract description. A person making an isolated sale of goods is not a "merchant" within the meaning of the full scope of this section and, thus, no warranty of merchantability would apply. His knowledge of any defects not apparent on inspection would, however, without need for express agreement and in keeping with the underlying reason of the present section and the provisions on good faith, impose an obligation that known material but hidden defects be fully disclosed.

4. Although a seller may not be a "merchant" as to the goods in question, if he states generally that they are "guaranteed" the provisions of this section may furnish a guide to the content of the resulting express warranty. This has particular significance in the case of second-hand sales, and has further significance in limiting the effect of fine-print disclaimer clauses where their effect would be inconsistent with large-print assertions of "guarantee".

5. The second sentence of subsection (1) covers the warranty with respect to food and drink. Serving food or drink for value is a sale, whether to be consumed on the premises or elsewhere. Cases to the contrary are rejected. The principal warranty is that stated in subsections (1) and (2)(c) or this section.

6. Subsection (2) does not purport to exhaust the meaning of "merchantable" nor to negate any of its attributes not specifically mentioned in the text of the statute, but arising by usage of trade or through case law. The language used is "must be at least such as . . .," and the intention is to leave open other possible attributes of merchantability.

7. Paragraphs (a) and (b) of subsection (2) are to be read together. Both refer, as indicated above, to the standards of that line of the trade which fits the transaction and the seller's business. "Fair average" is a term directly appropriate to agricultural bulk products and means goods centering around the middle belt of quality, not the least or the worst that can be understood in the particular trade by the designation, but such as can pass "without objection." Of course a fair percentage of the least is permissible but the goods are not "fair average" if they are all of the least or worst quality possible under the description. In cases of doubt as to what quality is intended, the price at which a merchant closes a contract is an excellent index of the nature and scope of his obligation under the present section.

8. Fitness for the ordinary purposes for which goods of the type are used is a fundamental concept of the present section and is covered in paragraph (c). As stated above, merchantability is also a part of the obligation owing to the purchaser for use. Correspondingly, protection, under this aspect of the warranty, of the person buying for resale to the ultimate consumer is equally necessary, and merchantable goods must therefore be "honestly" resalable in the normal course of business because they are what they purport to be.

9. Paragraph (d) on evenness of kind, quality and quantity follows case law. But precautionary language has been added as a reminder of the frequent usages of trade which permit substantial variations both with and without an allowance or an obligation to replace the varying units.

10. Paragraph (e) applies only where the nature of the goods and of the transactions require a certain type of container, package or label. Paragraph (f) applies, on the other hand, wherever there is a label or container on which representations are made, even though the original contract, either by express terms or usage of trade, may not have required either the labelling or the representation. This follows from the general obligation of good faith which requires that a buyer should not be placed in the position of reselling or using goods delivered under false representations appearing on the package or container. No problem of extra consideration arises in this connection since, under this Article, an obligation is imposed by the original contract not to deliver mislabeled articles, and the obligation is imposed where mercantile good faith so requires and without reference to the doctrine of consideration.

11. Exclusion or modification of the warranty of merchantability, or of any part of it, is dealt with in the section to which the text of the present section makes explicit precautionary references. That section must be read with particular reference to its subsection (4) on limitation of remedies. The warranty of merchantability, wherever it is normal, is so commonly taken for granted that its exclusion from the contract is a matter threatening surprise and therefore requiring special precaution.

12. Subsection (3) is to make explicit that usage of trade and course of dealing can create warranties and that they are implied rather than express warranties and thus subject to exclusion or modification under Section 2–316. A typical instance would be the obligation to provide pedigree papers to evidence conformity of the animal to the contract in the case of a pedigreed dog or blooded bull.

13. In an action based on breach of warranty, it is of course necessary to show not only the existence of the warranty but the fact that the warranty was broken and that the breach of the warranty was the proximate cause of the loss sustained. In such an action an affirmative showing by the seller that the loss resulted from some action or event following his own delivery of the goods can operate as a defense. Equally, evidence indicating that the seller exercised care in the manufacture, processing or

selection of the goods is relevant to the issue of whether the warranty was in fact broken. Action by the buyer following an examination of the goods which ought to have indicated the defect complained of can be shown as matter bearing on whether the breach itself was the cause of the injury.

Cross References:

Point 1: Section 2–316.
Point 3: Sections 1–203 and 2–104.
Point 5: Section 2–315.
Point 11: Section 2–316.
Point 12: Section 1–201, 1–205 and 2–316.

Definitional Cross References:

"Agreement". Section 1–201.
"Contract". Section 1–201.
"Contract for sale". Section 2–106.
"Goods". Section 2–105.
"Merchant". Section 2–104.
"Seller". Section 2–103.

Section 2–315. Implied Warranty: Fitness for Particular Purpose.

Where the seller at the time of contracting has reason to know any particular purpose for which the goods are required and that the buyer is relying on the seller's skill or judgment to select or furnish suitable goods, there is unless excluded or modified under the next section an implied warranty that the goods shall be fit for such purpose.

New York Annotations

This section derives its provisions from Personal Property Law, § 96(1). In addition it elaborates and strengthens the provisions of present law in several respects: (1) the skill or judgment upon which the buyer must rely is defined as skill or judgment "to select" or "to furnish" suitable goods; (2) it is enough that the seller "has reason to know" a buyer's purpose as compared with a buyer having to "make known his purpose" under the Uniform Sales Act. However, the New York cases seem to be in accord with the Code; the courts have not insisted upon a verbal statement of the buyer's purpose but have imposed the warranty if the seller had reason to know that purpose. See, e. g., Temple v. Keeler, 238 N.Y. 344, 144 N.E. 635 (1924) (food served in restaurant); Rinaldi v. Mohican Co., 225 N.Y. 70, 121 N.E. 471 (1918) (pork sold by butcher); Compare, Canavan v. Mechanicville, 229 N.Y. 473, 128 N.E. 882 (1920) (waterworks makes no warranty of fitness for human consumption since purpose not made known.

Sale under patent or trade name. The Code contains no provision comparable to Personal Property Law, § 96(4), under which an implied warranty of fitness for a particular purpose is made inapplicable to sales of a specified article under its patent or other trade name. The New York cases have frequently held the implied warranty of fitness for a particular purpose inapplicable to a sale by patent or trade name by virtue of this section. Bareham & McFarland, Inc. v. Kane, 228 App.Div. 396, 240 N.Y.S. 123 (1930) ("No. 52 Therm-Oil Heating Equipment"; contract also indicated disclaimer); Ellen v. Heacock, 247 App.Div. 476, 286 N.Y.S. 740 (1936) ("Delco" oil burner); Aldock v. Wnuk, 198 Misc. 474, 98 N.Y.S.2d 964 (1950) ("Plumb" hammer; complaint held to state cause of action for breach of warranty of merchantable quality); Empire Cream Separator Co. v. Quinn, 184 App.Div. 302, 171 N.Y.S. 413 (1918) ("Empire Mechanical Milker"; defendant the manufacturer); Sure Seal Co. v. Loeber, 171 App.Div. 225, 157 N.Y.S. 327 (1916) ("Sure Cap Seals"; court also was convinced by evidence that the goods were fit). Cf. Shampine v. Fleming, 280 App.Div. 558, 115 N.Y.S.2d 702, appeal granted, 280 App.Div. 1027, 117 N.Y.S.2d 663 (1952) ("Rototiller Tractor"; neither pleaded nor proven that buyer relied on seller's skill and judgment; no record of further disposition of case). Randy Knitware, Inc. v. American Cyanamid Co., 7 A.D.2d 116, 180 N.Y.S.2d 471 (1958), rev'd on other grounds, 7 N.Y.2d 791, 163 N.E.2d 349 (1959). Eaton v. Massey–Harris-Ferguson, Inc., 161 F.Supp. 853 (W.D.N.Y. 1957). On the other hand, in certain cases the seller's reliance on the trade name rule of the Sales Act has been unsuccessful because the name used was not a trade name. Sturn v. Williams Oven Mfg. Co., 201 App.Div. 113, 193 N.Y.S. 852 (1922) (No. 40 oven without piping).

The omission of the trade name qualification from the Code makes it clear that a sale under a patent or trade name is merely one factor to be considered in determining whether the buyer actually relied on the seller. This omission, however, seems to clarify the present law rather than change it, since the presence of a trade name has not been held to be decisive where other factors show reliance by the buyer on the seller's skill and judgment. Foley v. Liggett & Myers Tobacco Co., Inc., 136 Misc. 468, 241 N.Y.S. 233, aff'd 232 App.Div. 822, 249 N.Y.S. 924 (1931).

Official Uniform Comment

Prior Uniform Statutory Provision: Section 15(1), (4), (5), Uniform Sales Act.
Changes: Rewritten.

Purposes of Changes:

1. Whether or not this warranty arises in any individual case is basically a question of fact to be determined by the circumstances of the contracting. Under this section the buyer need not bring home to the seller actual knowledge of the particular purpose for which the goods are intended or of his reliance on the seller's skill and judgment, if the circumstances are such that the seller has reason to realize the purpose intended or that the reliance exists. The buyer, of course, must actually be relying on the seller.

2. A "particular purpose" differs from the ordinary purpose for which the goods are used in that it envisages a specific use by the buyer which is peculiar to the nature of his business whereas the ordinary purposes for which goods are used are those envisaged in the concept of merchantability and go to uses which are customarily made of the goods in question. For example, shoes are generally used for the purpose of walking upon ordinary ground, but a seller may know that a particular pair was selected to be used for climbing mountains.

A contract may of course include both a warranty of merchantability and one of fitness for a particular purpose.

The provisions of this Article on the cumulation and conflict of express and implied warranties must be considered on the question of inconsistency between or among warranties. In such a case any question of fact as to which warranty was intended by the parties to apply must be resolved in favor of the warranty of fitness for particular purpose as against all other warranties except where the buyer has taken upon himself the responsibility of furnishing the technical specifications.

3. In connection with the warranty of fitness for a particular purpose the provisions of this Article on the allocation or division of risks are particularly applicable in any transaction in which the purpose for which the goods are to be used combines requirements both as to the quality of the goods themselves and compliance with

certain laws or regulations. How the risks are divided is a question of fact to be determined, where not expressly contained in the agreement, from the circumstances of contracting, usage or trade, course of performance and the like, matters which may constitute the "otherwise agreement" of the parties by which they may divide the risk or burden.

4. The absence from this section of the language used in the Uniform Sales Act in referring to the seller, "whether he be the grower or manufacturer or not," is not intended to impose any requirement that the seller be a grower or manufacturer. Although normally the warranty will arise only where the seller is a merchant with the appropriate "skill or judgment," it can arise as to nonmerchants where this is justified by the particular circumstances.

5. The elimination of the "patent or other trade name" exception constitutes the major extension of the warranty of fitness which has been made by the cases and continued in this Article. Under the present section the existence of a patent or other trade name and the designation of the article by that name, or indeed in any other definite manner, is only one of the facts to be considered on the question of whether the buyer actually relied on the seller, but it is not of itself decisive of the issue. If the buyer himself is insisting on a particular brand he is not relying on the seller's skill and judgment and so no warranty results. But the mere fact that the article purchased has a particular patent or trade name is not sufficient to indicate nonreliance if the article has been recommended by the seller as adequate for the buyer's purposes.

6. The specific reference forward in the present section to the following section on exclusion or modification of warranties is to call attention to the possibility of eliminating the warranty in any given case. However, it must be noted that under the following section the warranty of fitness for a particular purpose must be excluded or modified by a conspicuous writing.

Cross References:

Point 2: Sections 2–314 and 2–317.
Point 3: Section 2–303.
Point 6: Section 2–316.

Definitional Cross References:

"Buyer". Section 2–103.
"Goods". Section 2–105.
"Seller". Section 2–103.

Section 2–316. Exclusion or Modification of Warranties.

(1) Words or conduct relevant to the creation of an express warranty and words or conduct tending to negate or limit warranty shall be construed wherever reasonable as consistent with each other; but subject to the provisions of this Article on parol or extrinsic evidence (Section 2–202) negation or limitation is inoperative to the extent that such construction is unreasonable.

(2) Subject to subsection (3), to exclude or modify the implied warranty of merchantability or any part of it the language must mention merchantability and in case of a writing must be conspicuous, and to exclude or modify any implied warranty of fitness the exclusion must be by a writing and conspicuous. Language to exclude all implied warranties of fitness is sufficient if it states, for example, that "There are no warranties which extend beyond the description on the face hereof."

(3) Notwithstanding subsection (2)

(a) unless the circumstances indicate otherwise, all implied warranties are excluded by expressions like "as is", "with all faults" or other language which in common understanding calls the buyer's attention to the exclusion of warranties and makes plain that there is no implied warranty; and

(b) when the buyer before entering into the contract has examined the goods or the sample or model as fully as he desired or has refused to examine the goods there is no implied warranty with regard to defects which an examination ought in the circumstances to have revealed to him; and

(c) an implied warranty can also be excluded or modified by course of dealing or course of performance or usage of trade.

(4) Remedies for breach of warranty can be limited in accordance with the provisions of this Article on liquidation or limitation of damages and on contractual modification of remedy (Sections 2–718 and 2–719).

New York Annotations

(1) *Construction of disclaimer in light of express warranty.* Subsection (1) seems consistent with the general principle of law that a contract must be read as a whole to give effect, if possible, to each provision, and that specific provisions govern more general language. Restatement, Contracts, §§ 235, 236 and New York Annotations. However, it would appear that the Code would alter the result in cases under Personal Property Law, § 152, Lumbrazo v. Woodruff, 256 N.Y. 92, 175 N.E. 525 (1931), and Railroad Waterproofing Corp. v. Memphis Supply, Inc., 303 N.Y. 849, 104 N.E.2d 486 (1952), where controlling effect was given to the language of the disclaimer rather than to the language of warranty. The Code calls for results similar to that reached in Morris Run Coal Co., Inc. v. Carthage Sulphite Pulp & Paper Co., Inc., 210 App.Div. 678, 206 N.Y.S. 676, aff'd 242 N.Y. 567, 152 N.E. 430 (1926). Note that oral express warranties continue to be barred by the parol evidence rule in appropriate cases. See Section 2–202.

(2) *Disclaimer of implied warranty of merchantability or fitness must be specific.* The requirement of conspicuous, written, and somewhat specific language to disclaim the implied warranties of fitness and merchantability goes beyond New York law under which a general disclaimer of all warranties has been given full effect. Freemantle v. United States Hoffman Machinery Corp., 2 A.D.2d 634, 151 N.Y.S.2d 856 (1956); Shampine v. Fleming; 280 App.Div. 558, 115 N.Y.S.2d 702 (1952); Sayeg v. Gloria Light Co., 236 App.Div. 761, 259 N.Y.S. 492 (1932). Compare, Marino v. Maytag Atlantic Co., 141 N.Y.S.2d 432 (1955) (effect of maker's disclaimer on retailer's liability), and Moore v. Schlossman's, Inc., 5 Misc.2d 693, 161 N.Y.S.2d 213 (1957) (buyer must be given reasonable notice of intended exclusion). See, Alaska Pacific Salmon Co. v. Reynolds Metals Co., 163 F.2d 643 (2d Cir. 1947).

(3) *Exceptions.* The exceptions in paragraphs (a), (b), and (c) of subsection (3) are situations in which the Code deems the circumstances sufficient in themselves to call the buyer's attention to the exclusion of the implied warranties and thus equivalent to a specific exclusion.

(a) This is new to the statute but the effect given to such words as "as is" is consistent with ordinary commercial usage. See 1 Williston, Sales, Sec. 239 (1948); Bronx County Appliance Corp. v. Beecher, 113 N.Y.S.2d 622 (1952).

(b) Subsection (3)(b) incorporates Personal Property Law, § 96(3), which excludes warranties only where the buyer has examined the goods, while the Code extends the rule to cases where the buyer "refuses" to examine the goods. Cf. American Waste Co., Inc. v. Joseph St. Mary, 210 App. Div. 383, 206 N.Y.S. 316 (1924).

(c) This is in accord with Personal Property Law, § 152. See Annotation to Section 1–205, *supra.*

(4) *Limitation on remedies.* See Annotations to Sections 2–718 and 2–719, *infra.*

Historical Note: Former subsection (2) was rewritten and divided into subsections (2) and (3) in Supp. No. 1 to relieve the seller from the requirement of disclaiming the warranty of fitness in specific language and yet afford the buyer an adequate warning of such disclaimer. Subsequently subsection (1) was rewritten and subsections (3)(a) and (3)(b) were changed for clarification and to meet criticism by the Law Revision Commission. (1956 Recommendations, p. 40; Excerpts, pp. 377–8.)

Official Uniform Comment

Prior Uniform Statutory Provision: None. See Sections 15 and 71, Uniform Sales Act.

Purposes:

1. This section is designed principally to deal with those frequent clauses in sales contracts which seek to exclude "all warranties, express or implied." It seeks to protect a buyer from unexpected and unbargained language of disclaimer by denying effect to such language when inconsistent with language of express warranty and permitting the exclusion of implied warranties only by conspicuous language or other circumstances which protect the buyer from surprise.

2. The seller is protected under this Article against false allegations of oral warranties by its provisions on parol and extrinsic evidence and against unauthorized representations by the customary "lack of authority" clauses. This Article treats the limitations or avoidance of consequential damages as a matter of limiting remedies for breach, separate from the matter of creation of liability under a warranty. If no warranty exists, there is of course no problem of limiting remedies for breach of warranty. Under subsection (4) the question of limitation of remedy is governed by the sections referred to rather than by this section.

3. Disclaimer of the implied warranty of merchantability is permitted under subsection (2), but with the safeguard that such disclaimers must mention merchantability and in case of a writing must be conspicuous.

4. Unlike the implied warranty of merchantability, implied warranties of fitness for a particular purpose may be excluded by general language, but only if it is in writing and conspicuous.

5. Subsection (2) presupposes that the implied warranty in question exists unless excluded or modified. Whether or not language of disclaimer satisfies the requirements of this section, such language may be relevant under other sections to the question whether the warranty was ever in fact created. Thus, unless the provisions of this Article on parol and extrinsic evidence prevent, oral language of disclaimer may raise issues of fact as to whether reliance by the buyer occurred and whether the seller had "reason to know" under the section on implied warranty of fitness for a particular purpose.

6. The exceptions to the general rule set forth in paragraphs (a), (b) and (c) of subsection (3) are common factual situations in which the circumstances surrounding the transactions are in themselves sufficient to call the buyer's attention to the fact that no implied warranties are made or that a certain implied warranty is being excluded.

7. Paragraph (a) of subsection (3) deals with general terms such as "as is," "as they stand," "with all faults," and the like. Such terms in ordinary commercial usage

are understood to mean that the buyer takes the entire risk as to the quality of the goods involved. The terms covered by paragraph (a) are in fact merely a particularization of paragraph (c) which provides for exclusion or modification of implied warranties by usage of trade.

8. Under paragraph (b) of subsection (3) warranties may be excluded or modified by the circumstances where the buyer examines the goods or a sample or model of them before entering into the contract. "Examination" as used in this paragraph is not synonymous with inspection before acceptance or at any other time after the contract has been made. It goes rather to the nature of the responsibility assumed by the seller at the time of the making of the contract. Of course if the buyer discovers the defect and uses the goods anyway, or if he unreasonably fails to examine the goods before he uses them, resulting injuries may be found to result from his own action rather than proximately from a breach of warranty. See Sections 2–314 and 2–715 and comments thereto.

In order to bring the transaction within the scope of "refused to examine" in paragraph (b), it is not sufficient that the goods are available for inspection. There must in addition be a demand by the seller that the buyer examine the goods fully. The seller by the demand puts the buyer on notice that he is assuming the risk of defects which the examination ought to reveal. The language "refused to examine" in this paragraph is intended to make clear the necessity for such demand.

Application of the doctrine of "caveat emptor" in all cases where the buyer examines the goods regardless of statements made by the seller is, however, rejected by this Article. Thus, if the offer of examination is accompanied by words as to their merchantability or specific attributes and the buyer indicates clearly that he is relying on those words rather than on his examination, they give rise to an "express" warranty. In such cases the question is one of fact as to whether a warranty of merchantability has been expressly incorporated in the agreement. Disclaimer of such an express warranty is governed by subsection (1) of the present section.

The particular buyer's skill and the normal method of examining goods in the circumstances determine what defects are excluded by the examination. A failure to notice defects which are obvious cannot excuse the buyer. However, an examination under circumstances which do not permit chemical or other testing of the goods would not exclude defects which could be ascertained only by such testing. Nor can latent defects be excluded by a simple examination. A professional buyer examining a product in his field will be held to have assumed the risk as to all defects which a professional in the field ought to observe, while a nonprofessional buyer will be held to have assumed the risk only for such defects as a layman might be expected to observe.

9. The situation in which the buyer gives precise and complete specifications to the seller is not explicitly covered in this section, but this is a frequent circumstance by which the implied warranties may be excluded. The warranty of fitness for a particular purpose would not normally arise since in such a situation there is usually no reliance on the seller by the buyer. The warranty of merchantability in such a transaction, however, must be considered in connection with the next section on the cumulation and conflict of warranties. Under paragraph (c) of that section in case of such an inconsistency the implied warranty of merchantability is displaced by the express warranty that the goods will comply with the specifications. Thus, where the buyer gives detailed specifications as to the goods, neither of the implied warranties as to quality will normally apply to the transaction unless consistent with the specifications.

Cross References:

Point 2: Sections 2–202, 2–718 and 2–719.

Point 7: Sections 1–205 and 2–208.

UCC

Definitional Cross References:

"Agreement". Section 1–201.
"Buyer". Section 2–103.
"Contract". Section 1–201.
"Course of dealing". Section 1–205.
"Goods". Section 2–105.
"Remedy". Section 1–201.
"Seller". Section 2–103.
"Usage of trade". Section 1–205.

Section 2–317. Cumulation and Conflict of Warranties Express or Implied.

Warranties whether express or implied shall be construed as consistent with each other and as cumulative, but if such construction is unreasonable the intention of the parties shall determine which warranty is dominant. In ascertaining that intention the following rules apply:

(a) Exact or technical specifications displace an inconsistent sample or model or general language of description.

(b) A sample from an existing bulk displaces inconsistent general language of description.

(c) Express warranties displace inconsistent implied warranties other than an implied warranty of fitness for a particular purpose.

New York Annotations

This section incorporates the narrower rule of Personal Property Law, § 96(6), to the effect that an express warranty does not negate an implied warranty unless inconsistent therewith.

Official Uniform Comment

Prior Uniform Statutory Provision: On cumulation of warranties see Sections 14, 15, and 16, Uniform Sales Act.

Changes: Completely rewritten into one section.

Purposes of Changes:

1. The present section rests on the basic policy of this Article that no warranty is created except by some conduct (either affirmative action or failure to disclose) on the part of the seller. Therefore, all warranties are made cumulative unless this construction of the contract is impossible or unreasonable.

This Article thus follows the general policy of the Uniform Sales Act except that in case of the sale of an article by its patent or trade name the elimination of the warranty of fitness depends solely on whether the buyer has relied on the seller's skill and judgment; the use of the patent or trade name is but one factor in making this determination.

2. The rules of this section are designed to aid in determining the intention of the parties as to which of inconsistent warranties which have arisen from the circumstances of their transaction shall prevail. These rules of intention are to be applied

only where factors making for an equitable estoppel of the seller do not exist and where he has in perfect good faith made warranties which later turn out to be inconsistent. To the extent that the seller has led the buyer to believe that all of the warranties can be performed, he is estopped from setting up any essential inconsistency as a defense.

3. The rules in subsections (a), (b) and (c) are designed to ascertain the intention of the parties by reference to the factor which probably claimed the attention of the parties in the first instance. These rules are not absolute but may be changed by evidence showing that the conditions which existed at the time of contracting make the construction called for by the section inconsistent or unreasonable.

Cross Reference:

Point 1: Section 2–315.

Definitional Cross Reference:

"Party". Section 1–201.

Section 2–318. Third Party Beneficiaries of Warranties Express or Implied.

A seller's warranty whether express or implied extends to any natural person if it is reasonable to expect that such person may use, consume or be affected by the goods and who is injured in person by breach of the warranty. A seller may not exclude or limit the operation of this section.

Amended by Laws 1975, Ch. 774, eff. Sept. 1, 1975.

New York Annotations

The present statutory law does not specify, as does this section, that the seller's warranty runs to certain persons other than the immediate purchaser. Until 1961 recovery upon warranty has been generally restricted to plaintiffs "in privity" with the defendant seller. Chysky v. Drake Bros. Co., Inc., 235 N.Y. 468, 139 N.E. 576 (1923); Campo v. Scofield, 301 N.Y. 468, 95 N.E.2d 802 (1950); Gimenez v. The Great Atlantic and Pacific Tea Co., 264 N.Y. 390, 191 N.E. 27 (1934); Turner v. Edison Storage Battery Co., 248 N.Y. 73, 161 N.E. 423 (1928); Redmond v. Borden's Farm Prods. Co., Inc., 245 N.Y. 512, 157 N.E. 838 (1927). However, at least in the food cases, an injured plaintiff who did not make the purchase could have recovered if it could be presumed or shown that the buyer acted as his agent. Mouren v. The Great Atlantic and Pacific Tea Co., 1 N.Y.2d 884, 136 N.E.2d 715 (1956) (husband agent for wife); Bowman v. The Great Atlantic and Pacific Tea Co., 308 N.Y. 780, 125 N.E.2d 165 (1955) (one sister agent for another when purchasing with common funds); Ryan v. Progressive Grocery Stores, Inc., 255 N.Y. 388, 175 N.E. 105 (1931) (wife agent for husband). Cf. Gimenez v. The Great Atlantic and Pacific Tea Co., 264 N.Y. 390, 191 N.E. 27 (1934).

Infants injured by food purchased by parents were less successful, at least in the appellate courts, until the recent case of Greenberg v. Lorenz, 9 N.Y.2d 195, 173 N.E.2d 773 (1961), where an infant was permitted to recover for injuries sustained from canned salmon containing sharp metal even though the food was purchased by her father. The court cited this section of the Code and said that as to food and household goods the presumption should be that the purchase was made for all members of the household.

Some other means of ameliorating the strictness of the rule have been suggested, Conklin v. Hotel Waldorf Astoria Corp., 5 Misc.2d 496, 161 N.Y.S.2d 205 (1957) (third party beneficiary); Parish v. The Great Atlantic and Pacific Tea Co., 13 Misc.2d 33, 177 N.Y.S.2d 7 (1958) (reject privity test). As to food, no privity is required in a tort action based on Agriculture and Markets Law, §§ 199, 199–a, and 200. Catalanello v. Cudahy Packing Co., 264 App.Div. 723, 34 N.Y.S.2d 37 (1942).

Greenberg v. Lorenz, supra, comes close to the Code rule by extending coverage of the seller's warranty to the buyer's family and household members so long as it is reasonable to expect that such person may be affected. The Code is silent on the question of the liability of manufacturers or wholesalers to the ultimate consumers. In short, the Code enlarges the number of prospective plaintiffs in a warranty action but it does not increase the number of potential defendants. In no way is the Code intended to limit the extension of warranty protection by the courts to a greater number of plaintiffs or the expansion of the manufacturer's liability as in Randy Knitwear v. American Cyanamid Co., 11 N.Y.2d 5, 181 N.E.2d 399 (1962) and Goldberg v. Kollsman Instrument Corp., 12 N.Y.2d 432, 191 N.E.2d 432 (1963), Cf. Official Comment to Section 2–313.

Official Uniform Comment

Prior Uniform Statutory Provision: None.

Purposes:

1. The last sentence of this section does not mean that a seller is precluded from excluding or disclaiming a warranty which might otherwise arise in connection with the sale provided such exclusion or modification is permitted by Section 2–316. Nor does that sentence preclude the seller from limiting the remedies of his own buyer and of any beneficiaries, in any manner provided in Sections 2–718 or 2–719. To the extent that the contract of sale contains provisions under which warranties are excluded or modified, or remedies for breach are limited, such provisions are equally operative against beneficiaries of warranties under this section. What this last sentence forbids is exclusion of liability by the seller to the persons to whom the warranties which he has made to his buyer would extend under this section.

2. The purpose of this section is to give certain beneficiaries the benefit of the same warranty which the buyer received in the contract of sale, thereby freeing any such beneficiaries from any technical rules as to "privity." It seeks to accomplish this purpose without any derogation of any right or remedy resting on negligence. It rests primarily upon the merchant-seller's warranty under this Article that the goods sold are merchantable and fit for the ordinary purposes for which such goods are used rather than the warranty of fitness for a particular purpose. Implicit in the section is that any beneficiary of a warranty may bring a direct action for breach of warranty against the seller whose warranty extends to him [As amended in 1966].

3. The first alternative expressly includes as beneficiaries within its provisions the family, household and guests of the purchaser. Beyond this, the section in this form is neutral and is not intended to enlarge or restrict the developing case law on whether the seller's warranties, given to his buyer who resells, extend to other persons in the distributive chain. The second alternative is designed for states where the case law has already developed further and for those that desire to expand the class of beneficiaries. The third alternative goes further, following the trend of modern decisions as indicated by Restatement of Torts 2d § 402A [Tentative Draft No. 10, 1965] in extending the rule beyond injuries to the person [As amended in 1966].

Cross References:

Point 1: Section 2–316,2–718 and 2–719.

Point 2: Section 2–314.

Definitional Cross References:

"Buyer". Section 2–103.
"Goods". Section 2–105.
"Seller". Section 2–103.

Section 2–319. F.O.B. and F.A.S. Terms.

(1) Unless otherwise agreed the term F.O.B. (which means "free on board") at a named place, even though used only in connection with the stated price, is a delivery term under which

(a) when the term is F.O.B. the place of shipment, the seller must at that place ship the goods in the manner provided in this Article (Section 2–504) and bear the expense and risk of putting them into the possession of the carrier; or

(b) when the term is F.O.B. the place of destination, the seller must at his own expense and risk transport the goods to that place and there tender delivery of them in the manner provided in this Article (Section 2–503);

(c) when under either (a) or (b) the term is also F.O.B. vessel, car or other vehicle, the seller must in addition at his own expense and risk load the goods on board. If the term is F.O.B. vessel the buyer must name the vessel and in an appropriate case the seller must comply with the provisions of this Article on the form of bill of lading (Section 2–323).

(2) Unless otherwise agreed the term F.A.S. vessel (which means "free alongside") at a named port, even though used only in connection with the stated price, is a delivery term under which the seller must

(a) at his own expense and risk deliver the goods alongside the vessel in the manner usual in that port or on a dock designated and provided by the buyer; and

(b) obtain and tender a receipt for the goods in exchange for which the carrier is under a duty to issue a bill of lading.

(3) Unless otherwise agreed in any case falling within subsection (1)(a) or (c) or subsection (2) the buyer must seasonably give any needed instructions for making delivery, including when the term is F.A.S or F.O.B. the loading berth of the vessel and in an appropriate case its name and sailing date. The seller may treat the failure of needed instructions as a failure of cooperation under this Article (Section 2–311). He may also at his option move the goods in any reasonable manner preparatory to delivery or shipment.

(4) Under the term F.O.B. vessel or F.A.S. unless otherwise agreed the buyer must make payment against tender of the required documents and the seller may not tender nor the buyer demand delivery of the goods in substitution for the documents.

New York Annotations

(1) *F.O.B.* The Uniform Sales Act does not define shipping terms such as F.O.B. This section of the Code, however, states commercial understanding that the term defines the point to which the seller has responsibility for transportation of the goods free of transportation expense to the buyer. See American Foreign Trade Definitions (Chamber of Commerce, 1941) II–A, II–B; 2 Williston Sales, Sec. 280 (1948).

Risk. By placing the risk on the seller until the F.O.B. point, the Code calls for results comparable to those reached under Personal Property Law, §§ 100 (Rules 4 and 5), 103, and 127; e.g., Vogt v. Chase Brothers Co., 235 N.Y. 206, 139 N.E. 242 (1923); Standard Casing Co., Inc. v. California Casing Co., Inc., 233 N.Y. 413, 135 N.E. 834 (1922). Any question as to when the risk passes to the buyer can be avoided by use of the appropriate F.O.B. term. Under Section 2–319(1)(b) the risk is on the seller until the destination is reached where the F.O.B. place of destination term is employed, but the result in the former case is not clear. See Section 2–509, *infra.*

(2) *F.A.S.* The Code's definition in subsection (2) expresses commercial understanding of the term. 2 Williston, Sales, Sec. 280–h (1948); American Foreign Trade Definitions (Chamber of Commerce, 1941) III.

(3) *Buyer's instructions.* The rule of subsection (3) imposing a duty to give needed instruction is consistent both with commercial understanding, American Foreign Trade Definitions (Chamber of Commerce 1941) II–e, III, and with the case law. Partola Mfg. Co. v. General Chemical Co., 234 N.Y. 320, 137 N.E. 603 (1922).

(4) *Payment against documents.* Subsection (4) is new. Compare Section 2–513.

Historical Note: Subsection (2) was developed in its present form to meet suggestions of the Law Revision Commission and to conform to the Revised American Foreign Trade Definitions–1941. (1956 Recommendations, p. 42; Excerpts, p. 378.)

Official Uniform Comment

Prior Uniform Statutory Provision: None.

Purposes:

1. This section is intended to negate the uncommercial line of decision which treats an "F.O.B." term as "merely a price term." The distinctions taken in subsection (1) handle most of the issues which have on occasion led to the unfortunate judicial language just referred to. Other matters which have led to sound results being based on unhappy language in regard to F.O.B. clauses are dealt with in this Act by Section 2–311(2) (seller's option re arrangements relating to shipment) and Sections 2–614 and 615 (substituted performance and seller's excuse).

2. Subsection (1)(c) not only specifies the duties of a seller who engages to deliver "F.O.B. vessel," or the like, but ought to make clear that no agreement is soundly drawn when it looks to reshipment from San Francisco or New York, but speaks merely of "F.O.B." the place.

3. The buyer's obligations stated in subsection (1)(c) and subsection (3) are, as shown in the text, obligations of cooperation. The last sentence of subsection (3) expressly, though perhaps unnecessarily, authorizes the seller, pending instructions, to go ahead with such preparatory moves as shipment from the interior to the named point of delivery. The sentence presupposes the usual case in which instructions "fail"; a prior repudiation by the buyer, giving notice that breach was intended, would remove the reason for the sentence, and would normally bring into play, instead, the second sentence of Section 2–704, which duly calls for lessening damages.

4. The treatment of "F.O.B. vessel" in conjunction with F.A.S. fits, in regard to the need for payment against documents, with standard practice and case law; but

"F.O.B. vessel" is a term which by its very language makes express the need for an "on board" document. In this respect, that term is stricter than the ordinary overseas "shipment" contract (C.I.F., etc., Section 2–320).

Cross References:

Sections 2–311(3), 2–323, 2–503 and 2–504.

Definitional Cross References:

"Agreed". Section 1–201.
"Bill of lading". Section 1–201.
"Buyer". Section 2–103.
"Goods". Section 2–105.
"Seasonably". Section 1–204.
"Seller". Section 2–103.
"Term". Section 1–201.

Section 2–320. C.I.F. and C. & F. Terms.

(1) The term C.I.F. means that the price includes in a lump sum the cost of the goods and the insurance and freight to the named destination. The term C. & F. or C.F. means that the price so includes cost and freight to the named destination.

(2) Unless otherwise agreed and even though used only in connection with the stated price and destination, the term C.I.F. destination or its equivalent requires the seller at his own expense and risk to

(a) put the goods into the possession of a carrier at the port for shipment and obtain a negotiable bill or bills of lading covering the entire transportation to the named destination; and

(b) load the goods and obtain a receipt from the carrier (which may be contained in the bill of lading) showing that the freight has been paid or provided for; and

(c) obtain a policy or certificate of insurance, including any war risk insurance, of a kind and on terms then current at the port of shipment, in the usual amount, in the currency of the contract, shown to cover the same goods covered by the bill of lading and providing for payment of loss to the order of the buyer or for the account of whom it may concern; but the seller may add to the price the amount of the premium for any such war risk insurance; and

(d) prepare an invoice of the goods and procure any other documents required to effect shipment or to comply with the contract; and

(e) forward and tender with commercial promptness all the documents in due form and with any indorsement necessary to perfect the buyer's rights.

(3) Unless otherwise agreed the term C. & F. or its equivalent has the same effect and imposes upon the seller the same obligations and risks as a C.I.F. term except the obligation as to insurance.

(4) Under the term C.I.F. or C. & F. unless otherwise agreed the buyer must make payment against tender of the required documents and the seller may not tender nor the buyer demand delivery of the goods in substitution for the documents.

Amended by Laws 1964, Ch. 476, eff. May 23, 1964.

New York Annotations

(1) *Definitions.* The Uniform Sales Act does not specify the effect to be given these shipping terms. The Code's definition of C.I.F. states commercial understanding that the price quoted by the seller under this term includes the cost of goods, the insurance, and the freight. See 2 Williston, Sales, Sec. 280–c (1948); American Foreign Trade Definitions (Chamber of Commerce, 1941) V; Seaver v. Lindsay Light Co., 233 N.Y. 273, 135 N.E. 329 (1922); Smith Co. v. Moscahlades, 103 App.Div. 126, 183 N.Y.S. 500 (1920). The Code similarly states commercial understanding in defining C. & F. as meaning that the price quoted includes cost and freight to the named destination. See 2 Williston, Sales, Sec. 280–h (1948); American Foreign Trade Definitions (Chamber of Commerce, 1941) IV.

(2) *Seller's obligations and risks under C.I.F. contract.* The detailed obligations listed in subsection (2) are for the most part consistent with New York case law, see Smith Co. v. Moscahlades, *supra,* and reflect commercial understanding. See 2 Williston, Sales, Sec. 280–c (1948); American Foreign Trade Definitions (Chamber of Commerce, 1941) V. In placing the risk on the buyer the Code accords with commercial understanding. See 2 Williston, Sales, Sec. 280–c (1948); American Foreign Trade Definitions (Chamber of Commerce, 1941) V. Such commercial understanding has been held to be sufficient to override the presumption of Rule 5 of Personal Property Law, § 100, arising from the seller's obligation to pay the freight. Smith v. Moscahlades, *supra.* The balance of the provisions of subsection (2) appear to be in accord with Cundill v. Millhauser Corp., 257 N.Y. 416, 178 N.E. 680 (1931) (Comment 14); Seaver v. Lindsay Light Co., *supra,* and Dwane v. Weil, 199 App.Div. 719, 192 N.Y.S. 393, aff'd 235 N.Y. 527, 139 N.E. 720 (1923). But cf., Dixon, Irmaos & Cia, Ltda. v. Chase Nat'l Bank, 144 F.2d 759 (2d Cir. 1944), cert. denied, 324 U.S. 850, 65 S.Ct. 687 (1945), with subsection (2)(b). The provision as to war risk insurance is new. See Comment 7.

(3) *Seller's obligations and risks under C. & F. contracts.* The Code is in this instance in accord with the Trade Definitions, *supra,* IV and V. See, 2 Williston, Sales, Sec. 280–h (1948), pointing out that the question is not free from doubt under present law.

(4) *Payments against and tender of documents rather than goods.* Accords with usage, see 2 Williston, Sales, Sec. 280–c (1948), and with Harper v. Hochstim, 278 Fed. 102 (2d Cir. 1921).

Official Uniform Comment

Prior Uniform Statutory Provision: None.

Purposes: To make it clear that:

1. The C.I.F. contract is not a destination but a shipment contract with risk of subsequent loss or damage to the goods passing to the buyer upon shipment if the seller has properly performed all his obligations with respect to the goods. Delivery to the carrier is delivery to the buyer for purposes of risk and "title". Delivery of possession of the goods is accomplished by delivery of the bill of lading, and upon

tender of the required documents the buyer must pay the agreed price without awaiting the arrival of the goods and if they have been lost or damaged after proper shipment he must seek his remedy against the carrier or insurer. The buyer has no right of inspection prior to payment or acceptance of the documents.

2. The seller's obligations remain the same even though the C.I.F. term is "used only in connection with the stated price and destination".

3. The insurance stipulated by the C.I.F. term is for the buyer's benefit, to protect him against the risk of loss or damage to the goods in transit. A clause in a C.I.F. contract "insurance-for the account of sellers" should be viewed in its ordinary mercantile meaning that the sellers must pay for the insurance and not that it is intended to run to the seller's benefit.

4. A bill of lading covering the entire transportation from the port of shipment is explicitly required but the provision on this point must be read in the light of its reason to assure the buyer of as full protection as the conditions of shipment reasonably permit, remembering always that this type of contract is designed to move the goods in the channels commercially available. To enable the buyer to deal with the goods while they are afloat the bill of lading must be one that covers only the quantity of goods called for by the contract. The buyer is not required to accept his part of the goods without a bill of lading because the latter covers a larger quantity, nor is he required to accept a bill of lading for the whole quantity under a stipulation to hold the excess for the owner. Although the buyer is not compelled to accept either goods or documents under such circumstances he may of course claim his rights in any goods which have been identified to his contract.

5. The seller is given the option of paying or providing for the payment of freight. He has no option to ship "freight collect" unless the agreement so provides. The rule of the common law that the buyer need not pay the freight if the goods do not arrive is preserved.

Unless the shipment has been sent "freight collect" the buyer is entitled to receive documentary evidence that he is not obligated to pay the freight; the seller is therefore required to obtain a receipt "showing that the freight has been paid or provided for." The usual notation in the appropriate space on the bill of lading that the freight has been prepaid is a sufficient receipt, as at common law. The phrase "provided for" is intended to cover the frequent situation in which the carrier extends credit to a shipper for the freight on successive shipments and receives periodical payments of the accrued freight charges from him.

6. The requirement that unless otherwise agreed the seller must procure insurance "of a kind and on terms then current at the port for shipment in the usual amount, in the currency of the contract, sufficiently shown to cover the same goods covered by the bill of lading", applies to both marine and war risk insurance. As applied to marine insurance, it means such insurance as is usual or customary at the port for shipment with reference to the particular kind of goods involved, the character and equipment of the vessel, the route of the voyage, the port of destination and any other considerations that affect the risk. It is the substantial equivalent of the ordinary insurance in the particular trade and on the particular voyage and is subject to agreed specifications of type or extent of coverage. The language does not mean that the insurance must be adequate to cover all risks to which the goods may be subject in transit. There are some types of loss or damage that are not covered by the usual marine insurance and are excepted in bills of lading or in applicable statutes from the causes of loss or damage for which the carrier or the vessel is liable. Such risks must be borne by the buyer under this Article.

Insurance secured in compliance with a C.I.F. term must cover the entire transportation of the goods to the named destination.

7. An additional obligation is imposed upon the seller in requiring him to procure customary war risk insurance at the buyer's expense. This changes the common law

on the point. The seller is not required to assume the risk of including the C.I.F. price the cost of such insurance, since it often fluctuates rapidly, but is required to treat it simply as a necessary for the buyer's account. What war risk insurance is "current" or usual turns on the standard forms of policy or rider in common use.

8. The C.I.F. contract calls for insurance covering the value of the goods at the time and place of shipment and does not include any increase in market value during transit or any anticipated profit to the buyer on a sale by him.

The contract contemplates that before the goods arrive at their destination they may be sold again and again on C.I.F. terms and that the original policy of insurance and bill of lading will run with the interest in the goods by being transferred to each successive buyer. A buyer who becomes the seller in such an intermediate contract for sale does not thereby, if his sub-buyer knows the circumstances, undertake to insure the goods again at an increased price fixed in the new contract or to cover the increase in price by additional insurance, and his buyer may not reject the documents on the ground that the original policy does not cover such higher price. If such a sub-buyer desires additional insurance he must procure it for himself.

Where the seller exercises an option to ship "freight collect" and to credit the buyer with the freight against the C.I.F. price, the insurance need not cover the freight since the freight is not at the buyer's risk. On the other hand, where the seller prepays the freight upon shipping under a bill of lading requiring prepayment and providing that the freight shall be deemed earned and shall be retained by the carrier "ship and/or cargo lost or not lost," or using words of similar import, he must procure insurance that will cover the freight, because notwithstanding that the goods are lost in transit the buyer is bound to pay the freight as part of the C.I.F. price and will be unable to recover it back from the carrier.

9. Insurance "for the account of whom it may concern" is usual and sufficient. However, for a valid tender the policy of insurance must be one which can be disposed of together with the bill of lading and so must be "sufficiently shown to cover the same goods covered by the bill of lading". It must cover separately the quantity of goods called for by the buyer's contract and not merely insure his goods as part of a larger quantity in which others are interested, a case provided for in American mercantile practice by the use of negotiable certificates of insurance which are expressly authorized by this section. By usage these certificates are treated as the equivalent of separate policies and are good tender under C.I.F. contracts. The term "certificate of insurance", however, does not of itself include certificates or "cover notes" issued by the insurance broker and stating that the goods are covered by a policy. Their sufficiency as substitutes for policies will depend upon proof of an established usage or course of dealing. The present section rejects the English rule that not only broker' certificates and "cover notes" but also certain forms of American insurance certificates are not the equivalent of policies and are not good tender under a C.I.F. contract.

The seller's failure to tender a proper insurance document is waived if the buyer refuses to make payment on other and untenable grounds at a time when proper insurance could have been obtained and tendered by the seller if timely objection had been made. Even a failure to insure on shipment may be cured by seasonable tender of a policy retroactive in effect; e.g., one insuring the goods "lost or not lost." The provisions of this Article on cure of improper tender and on waiver of buyer's objections by silence are applicable to insurance tenders under a C.I.F. term. Where there is no waiver by the buyer as described above, however, the fact that the goods arrive safely does not cure the seller's breach of his obligations to insure them and tender to the buyer a proper insurance document.

10. The seller's invoice of the goods shipped under a C.I.F. contract is regarded as a usual and necessary document upon which reliance may properly be placed. It is the document which evidences points of description, quality and the like which

do not readily appear in other documents. This Article rejects those statements to the effect that the invoice is a usual but not a necessary document under a C.I.F. term.

11. The buyer needs all of the documents required under a C.I.F. contract, in due form and with necessary endorsements, so that before the goods arrive he may deal with them by negotiating the documents or may obtain prompt possession of the goods after their arrival. If the goods are lost or damaged in transit the documents are necessary to enable him promptly to assert his remedy against the carrier or insurer. The seller is therefore obligated to do what is mercantilely reasonable in the circumstances and should make every reasonable exertion to send forward the documents as soon as possible after the shipment. The requirement that the documents be forwarded with "commercial promptness" expresses a more urgent need for action than that suggested by the phrase "reasonable time."

12. Under a C.I.F. contract the buyer, as under the common law, must pay the price upon tender of the required documents without first inspecting the goods, but his payment in these circumstances does not constitute an acceptance of the goods nor does it impair his right of subsequent inspection or his options and remedies in the case of improper delivery. All remedies and rights for the seller's breach are reserved to him. The buyer must pay before inspection and assert his remedy against the seller afterward unless the nonconformity of the goods amounts to a real failure of consideration, since the purpose of choosing this form of contract is to give the seller protection against the buyer's unjustifiable refection of the goods at a distant port of destination which would necessitate taking possession of the goods and suing the buyer there.

13. A valid C.I.F. contract may be made which requires part of the transportation to be made on land and part on the sea, as where the goods are to be brought by rail from an inland point to a seaport and thence transported by vessel to the named destination under a "through" or combination bill of lading issued by the railroad company. In such a case shipment by rail from the inland point within the contract period is a timely shipment notwithstanding that the loading of the goods on the vessel is delayed by causes beyond the seller's control.

14. Although subsection (2) stating the legal effects of the C.I.F. term is an "unless otherwise agreed" provision, the express language used in an agreement is frequently a precautionary, fuller statement of the normal C.I.F. terms and hence not intended as a departure or variation from them. Moreover, the dominant outlines of the C.I.F. term are so well understood commercially that any variation should, whenever reasonably possible, be read as falling within those dominant outlines rather than as destroying the whole meaning of a term which essentially indicates a contract for proper shipment rather than one for delivery at destination. Particularly careful consideration is necessary before a printed form or clause is construed to mean agreement otherwise and where a C.I.F. contract is prepared on a printed form designed for some other type of contract, the C.I.F. terms must prevail over printed clauses repugnant to them.

15. Under subsection (4) the fact that the seller knows at the time of the tender of the documents that the goods have been lost in transit does not affect his rights if he has performed his contractual obligations. Similarly, the seller cannot perform under a C.I.F. term by purchasing and tendering landed goods.

16. Under the C. & F. term, as under the C.I.F. term, title and risk of loss are intended to pass to the buyer on shipment. A stipulation in a C. & F. contract that the seller shall effect insurance on the goods and charge the buyer with the premium (in effect that he shall act as the buyer's agent for that purpose) is entirely in keeping with the pattern. On the other hand, it often happens that the buyer is in a more advantageous position than the seller to effect insurance on the goods or that he has in force an "open" or "floating" policy covering all shipments made by him or to

him, in either of which events the C. & F. term is adequate without mention of insurance.

17. It is to be remembered that in a French contract the term "C.A.F." does not mean "Cost and Freight" but has exactly the same meaning as the term "C.I.F." since it is merely the French equivalent of that term. The "A" does not stand for "and" but for "assurance" which means insurance.

Cross References:

Point 4: Section 2–323.
Point 6: Section 2–509(1)(a).
Point 9: Sections 2–508 and 2–605(1)(a).
Point 12: Sections 2–321(3), 2–512 and 2–513(3) and Article 5.

Definitional Cross References:

"Bill of lading". Section 1–201.
"Buyer". Section 2–103.
"Contract". Section 1–201.
"Goods". Section 2–105.
"Rights". Section 1–201.
"Seller". Section 2–103.
"Term". Section 1–201.

Section 2–321. C.I.F. or C. & F.: "Net Landed Weights"; "Payment on Arrival"; Warranty of Condition on Arrival.

Under a contract containing a term C.I.F. or C. & F.

(1) Where the price is based on or is to be adjusted according to "net landed weights", "delivered weights", "out turn" quantity or quality or the like, unless otherwise agreed the seller must reasonably estimate the price. The payment due on tender of the documents called for by the contract is the amount so estimated, but after final adjustment of the price a settlement must be made with commercial promptness.

(2) An agreement described in subsection (1) or any warranty of quality or condition of the goods on arrival places upon the seller the risk of ordinary deterioration, shrinkage and the like in transportation but has no effect on the place or time of identification to the contract for sale or delivery or on the passing of the risk of loss.

(3) Unless otherwise agreed where the contract provides for payment on or after arrival of the goods the seller must before payment allow such preliminary inspection as is feasible; but if the goods are lost delivery of the documents and payment are due when the goods should have arrived.

New York Annotations

(1) Neither the Uniform Sales Act nor the American Foreign Trade Definitions (Chamber of Commerce, 1941) provide for the issues raised by this subsection.

(2) Subsection (2) is in *accord* with Dwane v. Weil, 199 App.Div. 719, 192 N.Y.S. 393, aff'd 235 N.Y. 527, 139 N.E. 720 (1923), in not shifting all risk of loss to the seller where there is an agreement as to "shrinkage".

(3) See Section 2–513 on inspection.

Official Uniform Comment

Prior Uniform Statutory Provision: None.

Purposes:

This section deals with two variations of the C.I.F. contract which have evolved in mercantile practice but are entirely consistent with the basic C.I.F. pattern. Subsections (1) and (2), which provide for a shift to the seller of the risk of quality and weight deterioration during shipment, are designed to conform the law to the best mercantile practice and usage without changing the legal consequences of the C.I.F. or C. & F. term as to the passing of marine risks to the buyer at the point of shipment. Subsection (3) provides that where under the contract documents are to be presented for payment after arrival of the goods, this amounts merely to a postponement of the payment under the C.I.F. contract and is not to be confused with the "no arrival, no sale" contract. If the goods are lost, delivery of the documents and payment against them are due when the goods should have arrived. The clause for payment on or after arrival is not to be construed as such a condition precedent to payment that if the goods are lost in transit the buyer need never pay and the seller must bear the loss.

Cross References:

Section 2–324.

Definitional Cross References:

"Agreement". Section 1–201.
"Contract". Section 1–201.
"Delivery". Section 1–201.
"Goods". Section 2–105.
"Seller". Section 2–103.
"Term". Section 1–201.

Section 2–322. Delivery "Ex-Ship".

(1) Unless otherwise agreed a term for delivery of goods "ex-ship" (which means from the carrying vessel) or in equivalent language is not restricted to a particular ship and requires delivery from a ship which has reached a place at the named port of destination where goods of the kind are usually discharged.

(2) Under such a term unless otherwise agreed

(a) the seller must discharge all liens arising out of the carriage and furnish the buyer with a direction which puts the carrier under a duty to deliver the goods; and

(b) the risk of loss does not pass to the buyer until the goods leave the ship's tackle or are otherwise properly unloaded.

New York Annotations

The Uniform Sales Act does not treat the effect to be given this term. The American Foreign Trade Definitions (Chamber of Commerce, 1941) deal only with "ex dock" and "ex factory". The Code definition seems to accord with dicta in Jules Maes & Co. v. W. R. Grace & Co., 239 N.Y. 519, 147 N.E. 177 (1924), which quoted British authority in accord with the Code rules.

Official Uniform Comment

Prior Uniform Statutory Provision: None.

Purposes:

1. The delivery term, "ex-ship", as between seller and buyer, is the reverse of the F.A.S. term covered.

2. Delivery need not be made from any particular vessel under a clause calling for delivery "ex-ship", even though a vessel on which shipment is to be made originally is named in the contract, unless the agreement by appropriate language, restricts the clause to delivery from a named vessel.

3. The appropriate place and manner of unloading at the port of destination depend upon the nature of the goods and the facilities and usages of the port.

4. A contract fixing a price "ex-ship" with payment "cash against documents" calls only for such documents as are appropriate to the contract. Tender of a delivery order and of a receipt for the freight after the arrival of the carrying vessel is adequate. The seller is not required to tender a bill of lading as a document of title nor is he required to insure the goods for the buyer's benefit, as the goods are not at the buyer's risk during the voyage.

Cross Reference:

Point 1: Section 2–319(2).

Definitional Cross References:

"Buyer". Section 2–103.
"Goods". Section 2–105.
"Seller". Section 2–103.
"Term". Section 1–201.

Section 2–323. Form of Bill of Lading Required in Overseas Shipment; "Overseas".

(1) Where the contract contemplates overseas shipment and contains a term C.I.F. or C. & F. or F.O.B. vessel, the seller unless otherwise agreed must obtain a negotiable bill of lading stating that the goods have been loaded on board or, in the case of a term C.I.F. or C. & F., received for shipment.

(2) Where in a case within subsection (1) a bill of lading has been issued in a set of parts, unless otherwise agreed if the documents are not to be sent from abroad the buyer may demand tender of the full set; otherwise only one part of the bill of lading need be tendered. Even if the agreement expressly requires a full set

(a) due tender of a single part is acceptable within the provisions of this Article on cure of improper delivery (subsection (1) of Section 2–508); and

(b) even though the full set is demanded, if the documents are sent from abroad the person tendering an incomplete set may nevertheless require payment upon furnishing an indemnity which the buyer in good faith deems adequate.

(3) A shipment by water or by air or a contract contemplating such shipment is "overseas" insofar as by usage of trade or agreement it is subject to the commercial, financing or shipping practices characteristic of international deep water commerce.

New York Annotations

(1) *Type of bill of lading.* The Uniform Sales Act does not deal with this problem. Commercial practice is not uniform. See American Foreign Trade Definitions (Chamber of Commerce, 1941) II–A, II–B, II–C, and II–D, II–E, IV and V. Cf. Uniform Customs and Practice for Commercial Documentary Credits (International Chamber of Commerce, 1951) Art. 19(a). In Vietor v. Nat'l City Bank, 200 App.Div. 557, 193 N.Y.S. 868, aff'd 237 N.Y. 538, 143 N.E. 733 (1923), a custom of traders was effective to make it unnecessary actually to load the goods on board prior to issuance of the bill of lading.

Subsection (2), in allowing tender of an incomplete set of documents with an indemnity bond against loss where a bill of lading has been issued in parts, appears to codify the practice in Dixon, Irmaos & Cia, Ltda. v. Chase Nat'l Bank, 144 F.2d 759 (2d Cir. 1944), cert. denied, 324 U.S. 850, 65 S.Ct. 687 (1945). A full set of sea or ocean bills of lading is required under Uniform Customs and Practice for Commercial Documentary Credits (International Chamber of Commerce, 1951) Art. 15(a).

Historical Note: Supp. No. 1 revised subsection (1) to make clear in the text, what was previously stated in Comment 4 to Section 2–319, that "F.O.B. vessel" calls for an "on board" bill of lading. A further change was based on a suggestion of the Law Revision Commission for clarification of subsection (2)(b) by substituting "an incomplete set" for "a single part" and by inserting "part or" before "parts as are then available". (1956 Recommendations, p. 45; Excerpts, p. 379.)

Official Uniform Comment

Prior Uniform Statutory Provision: None.

Purposes:

1. Subsection (1) follows the "American" rule that a regular bill of lading indicating delivery of the goods at the dock for shipment is sufficient, except under a term "F.O.B. vessel." See Section 2–319 and comment thereto.

2. Subsection (2) deals with the problem of bills of lading covering deep water shipments, issued not as a single bill of lading but in a set of parts, each part referring to the other parts and the entire set constituting in commercial practice and at law a single bill of lading. Commercial practice in international commerce is to accept and pay against presentation of the first part of a set if the part is sent from overseas even though the contract of the buyer requires presentation of a full set of bills of lading provided adequate indemnity for the missing parts is forthcoming.

This subsection codifies that practice as between buyer and seller. Article 5 (Section 5–113) authorizes banks presenting drafts under letters of credit to give indemnities against the missing parts, and this subsection means that the buyer must accept and act on such indemnities if he in good faith deems them adequate. But neither this subsection nor Article 5 decides whether a bank which has issued a letter of credit is similarly bound. The issuing bank's obligation under a letter of credit is independent and depends on its own terms. See Article 5.

Cross References:

Sections 2–508(2), 5–113.

Definitional Cross References:

"Bill of lading". Section 1–201.
"Buyer". Section 2–103.
"Contract". Section 1–201.
"Delivery". Section 1–201.
"Financing agency". Section 2–104.
"Person". Section 1–201.
"Seller". Section 2–103.
"Send". Section 1–201.
"Term". Section 1–201.

Section 2–324. "No Arrival, No Sale" Term.

Under a term "no arrival, no sale" or terms of like meaning, unless otherwise agreed,

(a) the seller must properly ship conforming goods and if they arrive by any means he must tender them on arrival but he assumes no obligation that the goods will arrive unless he has caused the non-arrival; and

(b) where without fault of the seller the goods are in part lost or have so deteriorated as no longer to conform to the contract or arrive after the contract time, the buyer may proceed as if there had been casualty to identified goods (Section 2–613).

New York Annotations

The Uniform Sales Act contains no provision dealing with this term. When "no arrival, no sale" or a similar term is used, the Code obligates the seller to ship the goods and to tender them; it gives the buyer the choice of accepting or rejecting any goods that do arrive if there is a casualty in transit, but in that event the seller is relieved of all other liability. Except for the buyer's option to take the goods that arrive, the Code seems to accord with New York case law, e.g., Abe Stein Co. v. Robertson, 167 N.Y. 101, 60 N.E. 329 (1901); Salmon v. Berg, 37 N.Y.S.2d 985, aff'd 266 App.Div. 951, 44 N.Y.S.2d 341 (1943); Haber v. S. A. Jacobson Co., 185 App.Div. 650, 173 N.Y.S. 524 (1918). On the buyer's option, Shields v. Pettie, 4 N.Y. 122 (1850), indicates that safe arrival is a condition precedent to any liability of the seller. This case has been modified by the later opinions, *supra.* See, 1 Williston, Sales, Sec. 188–b (1948).

Historical Note: At the suggestion of the Law Revision Commission, reference to a "to arrive" term was deleted because of the statement in Comment 4 that such a term does not always have the full meaning given it by this section. To accord with a change in Section 2–613, "identified goods" was substituted for "unique goods" in paragraph (b). (1956 Recommendations, p. 45; Excerpts, p. 379.)

Official Uniform Comment

Prior Uniform Statutory Provision: None.

Purposes:

1. The "no arrival, no sale" term in a "destination" overseas contract leaves risk of loss on the seller but gives him an exemption from liability for non-delivery. Both the nature of the case and the duty of good faith require that the seller must not interfere with the arrival of the goods in any way. If the circumstances impose upon him the responsibility for making or arranging the shipment, he must have a shipment made despite the exemption clause. Further, the shipment made must be a conforming one, for the exemption under a "no arrival, no sale" term applies only to the hazards of transportation and the goods must be proper in all other respects.

The reason of this section is that where the seller is reselling goods bought by him as shipped by another and this fact is known to the buyer, so that the seller is not under any obligation to make the shipment himself, the seller is entitled under the "no arrival, no sale" clause to exemption from payment of damages for non-delivery if the goods do not arrive or if the goods which actually arrive are non-conforming. This does not extend to sellers who arrange shipment by their own agents, in which case the clause is limited to casualty due to marine hazards. But sellers who make known that they are contracting only with respect to what will be delivered to them by parties over whom they assume no control are entitled to the full quantum of the exemption.

2. The provisions of this Article on identification must be read together with the present section in order to bring the exemption into application. Until there is some designation of the goods in a particular shipment or on a particular ship as being those to which the contract refers there can be no application of an exemption for their non-arrival.

3. The seller's duty to tender the agreed or declared goods if they do arrive is not impaired because of their delay in arrival or by their arrival after transshipment.

4. The phrase "to arrive" is often employed in the same sense as "no arrival, no sale" and may then be given the same effect. But a "to arrive" term, added to a C.I.F. or C. & F. contract, does not have the full meaning given by this section to "no arrival, no sale". Such a "to arrive" term is usually intended to operate only to the extent that the risks are not covered by the agreed insurance and the loss or casualty is due to such uncovered hazards. In some instances the "to arrive" term may be regarded as a time of payment term, or, in the case of the reselling seller discussed in point 1 above, as negating responsibility for conformity of the goods, if they arrive, to any description which was based on his good faith belief of the quality. Whether this is the intention of the parties is a question of fact based on all the circumstances surrounding the resale and in case of ambiguity the rules of Sections 2–316 and 2–317 apply to preclude dishonor.

5. Paragraph (b) applies where goods arrive impaired by damage or partial loss during transportation and makes the policy of this Article on casualty to identified goods applicable to such a situation. For the term cannot be regarded as intending to give the seller an unforeseen profit through casualty; it is intended only to protect him from loss due to causes beyond his control.

Cross References:

Point 1: Section 1–203.
Point 2: Section 2–501(a) and (c).
Point 5: Section 2–613.

Definitional Cross References:

"Buyer". Section 2–103.
"Conforming". Section 2–106.
"Contract". Section 1–201.

"Fault". Section 1–201.
"Goods". Section 2–105.
"Sale". Section 2–106.
"Seller". Section 2–103.
"Term". Section 1–201.

Section 2–325. "Letter of Credit" Term; "Confirmed Credit".

(1) Failure of the buyer seasonably to furnish an agreed letter of credit is a breach of the contract for sale.

(2) The delivery to seller of a proper letter of credit suspends the buyer's obligation to pay. If the letter of credit is dishonored, the seller may on seasonable notification to the buyer require payment directly from him.

(3) Unless otherwise agreed the term "letter of credit" or "banker's credit" in a contract for sale means an irrevocable credit issued by a financing agency of good repute and, where the shipment is overseas, of good international repute. The term "confirmed credit" means that the credit must also carry the direct obligation of such an agency which does business in the seller's financial market.

New York Annotations

Irrevocable letter of credit required. Subsection (3) seems to be in accord with commercial practice in requiring an irrevocable letter of credit where a letter of credit is agreed upon in a sales contract. 2 Williston, Sales, Sec. 469–e (1948). Note that this section deals only with the sales contract and does not revive former Section 5–105, which dealt with the bank's contract and which presumptively made all credits revocable in the absence of express stipulation. On "confirmed credit" note must be taken of Comment 3.

Historical Note: The changes adopted a suggestion of the Law Revision Commission that subsection (2) should follow more explicitly the analogous policy of Section 3–802 by requiring dishonor. Compare Comment 1. (1956 Recommendations, p. 46; Excerpts, p. 379.)

Official Uniform Comment

Prior Uniform Statutory Provision: None.

Purposes: To express the established commercial and banking understanding as to the meaning and effects of terms calling for "letters of credit" or "confirmed credit":

1. Subsection (2) follows the general policy of this Article and Article 3 (Section 3–802) on conditional payment, under which payment by check or other short-term instrument is not ordinarily final as between the parties if the recipient duly presents the instrument and honor is refused. Thus the furnishing of a letter of credit does not substitute the financing agency's obligation for the buyer's, but the seller must first give the buyer reasonable notice of his intention to demand direct payment from him.

2. Subsection (3) requires that the credit be irrevocable and be a prime credit as determined by the standing of the issuer. It is not necessary, unless otherwise agreed, that the credit be a negotiation credit; the seller can finance himself by an assignment of the proceeds under Section 5–116(2).

3. The definition of "confirmed credit" is drawn on the supposition that the credit is issued by a bank which is not doing direct business in the seller's financial market; there is no intention to require the obligation of two banks both local to the seller.

Cross References:

Section 2–403, 2–511(3) and 3–802 and Article 5.

Definitional Cross References:

"Buyer". Section 2–103.
"Contract for sale". Section 2–106.
"Draft". Section 3–104.
"Financing agency". Section 2–104.
"Notifies". Section 1–201.
"Overseas". Section 2–323.
"Purchaser". Section 1–201.
"Seasonably". Section 1–204.
"Seller". Section 2–103.
"Term". Section 1–201.

Section 2–326. Sale on Approval and Sale or Return; Consignment Sales and Rights of Creditors.

(1) Unless otherwise agreed, if delivered goods may be returned by the buyer even though they conform to the contract, the transaction is

(a) a "sale on approval" if the goods are delivered primarily for use, and

(b) a "sale or return" if the goods are delivered primarily for resale.

(2) Except as provided in subsection (3), goods held on approval are not subject to the claims of the buyer's creditors until acceptance; goods held on sale or return are subject to such claims while in the buyer's possession.

(3) Where goods are delivered to a person for sale and such person maintains a place of business at which he deals in goods of the kind involved, under a name other than the name of the person making delivery, then with respect to claims of creditors of the person conducting the business the goods are deemed to be on sale or return. The provisions of this subsection are applicable even though an agreement purports to reserve title to the person making delivery until payment or resale or uses such words as "on consignment" or "on memorandum". However, this subsection is not applicable if the person making delivery

(a) complies with an applicable law providing for a consignor's interest or the like to be evidenced by a sign, or

(b) establishes that the person conducting the business is generally known by his creditors to be substantially engaged in selling the goods of others, or

(c) complies with the filing provisions of the Article on Secured Transactions (Article 9).

(4) Any "or return" term of a contract for sale is to be treated as a separate contract for sale within the statute of frauds section of this Article (Section 2–201) and as contradicting the sale aspect of the contract within the provisions of this Article on parol or extrinsic evidence (Section 2–202).

New York Annotations

(1) *Transactions distinguished.* Subsection (1) provides a new distinction for testing whether the arrangement is a "sale or return" or a "sale on approval", i.e. whether the goods are delivered primarily for resale or for use. Present law states the distinction in terms of whether or not property in the goods has passed. Personal Property Law, § 100, Rules 3(1) and (2). In the following cases the sale or return rule has been applied: Bernadette, Joseph & Co. v. Van Buren, 212 App.Div. 702, 209 N.Y.S. 559 (1925); Atlas Shoe Co. v. Lewis, 202 App.Div. 244, 195 N.Y.S. 618 (1922); Cronk & Carrier Mfg. Co. v. Galbraith Milling Co., 17 App.Div. 568, 188 N.Y.S. 484 (1921); Columbia Weighing Machine Co. v. Kleckner, 130 Misc. 861, 225 N.Y.S. 167 (1927). In the following case the sale on approval rule was applied: Brown & Lowe Co. v. Potolski, 221 App.Div. 299, 223 N.Y.S. 71 (1927).

(2) *Claims of buyer's creditors.* Under present law, once the arrangement between seller and buyer is classified as a "sale on approval", the Code result is followed even as against the buyer's trustee in bankruptcy, Ginsberg v. Martin, 122 Misc. 468, 203 N.Y.S. 110 (1924). See Section 1–201(12) for the broad definition of "creditor"

(3) *Consignment.* Subsection (3) provides that where a person has a place of business at which he deals in goods of the kind involved in a particular transaction under a name other than the person making delivery, words such as "on consignment" or "on memorandum" will not prevent the transaction from being a sale or return, thus subjecting the goods to the claims of the creditors of the person taking delivery. Consequently, doubts as to the nature of the deal are resolved in favor of such creditors, and the possibility of using the bailment form to conceal what is in fact a sale is reduced. See In re Carpenter, 125 Fed. 831 (N.D.N.Y. 1903). Under present law, difficult fact questions as to the nature of the transaction have arisen. 2 Williston, Sales, Sec. 338 (1948). The person making the delivery is protected where there is adequate notoriety, i. e. where there is filing under Article 9, or compliance with a sign-posting law (New York has none), or where the person in possession is generally known by his creditors to be substantially engaged in selling the goods of others. Thus the Code gives creditors protection comparable to that presently given to bona fide purchasers from agents, consignees, and factors entrusted with merchandise and authority to sell. See annotation to Section 2–403(2), *infra.* One should also note that sometimes the form of "consignment" is used for security purposes (Section 1–201(37)) and in such cases Article 9 will govern this aspect of the transaction completely.

(4) *Statute of Frauds.* The rule of subsection (4) is new and the first sentence may change present law. Fitzpatrick v. Associated Gas & Electric Co., 148 Misc. 538, 266 N.Y.S. 116 (1933). In respect of the parol evidence rule present law is not clear. Homix Products, Inc. v. Henry Pape, Inc., 274 App.Div. 648, 86 N.Y.S.2d 648, aff'd 299 N.Y. 773, 87 N.E.2d 678 (1949); but the Code rule seems to be consistent with authority elsewhere. See 3 Williston, Contracts, Sec, 641 (1936).

Historical Note: At the suggestion of the Law Revision Commission, former subsections (1) and (2) were completely rewritten as subsections (1), (2), and (3). New subsection (1) makes the distinction between "sale on approval" and "sale or return" depend on whether goods are delivered for use or for resale, rather than on the title test previously stated. New subsection (2) makes explicit the implications of the previous text in respect of the rights of the buyer's creditors. The second sentence of former subsection (2) is rewritten as subsection (3), with references to "buyer and "seller" deleted. Former subsection (3) is renumbered subsection (4). (1956 Recommendations, p. 47; Excerpts, pp. 379–380.)

Official Uniform Comment

Prior Uniform Statutory Provision: Section 19(3), Uniform Sales Act.

Changes: Completely rewritten in this and the succeeding section.

Purposes of Changes: To make it clear that:

1. A "sale on approval" or "sale or return" is distinct from other types of transactions with which they have frequently been confused. The type of "sale on approval", "on trial" or "on satisfaction" dealt with involves a contract under which the seller undertakes a particular business risk to satisfy his prospective buyer with the appearance or performance of the goods in question. The goods are delivered to the proposed purchaser but they remain the property of the seller until the buyer accepts them. The price has already been agreed. The buyer's willingness to receive and test the goods is the consideration for the seller's engagement to deliver and sell. The type of "sale or return" involved herein is a sale to a merchant whose unwillingness to buy is overcome only by the seller's engagement to take back the goods (or any commercial unit of goods) in lieu of payment if they fail to be resold. These two transactions are so strongly delineated in practice and in general understanding that every presumption runs against a delivery to a consumer being a "sale or return" and against a delivery to a merchant for resale being a "sale on approval."

The right to return the goods for failure to conform to the contract does not make the transaction a "sale on approval" or "sale or return" and has nothing to do with this and the following section. The present section is not concerned with remedies for breach of contract. It deals instead with a power given by the contract to turn back the goods even though they are wholly as warranted.

This section nevertheless presupposes that a contract for sale is contemplated by the parties although that contract may be of the peculiar character here described.

Where the buyer's obligation as a buyer is conditioned not on his personal approval but on the article's passing a described objective test, the risk of loss by casualty pending the test is properly the seller's and proper return is at his expense. On the point of "satisfaction" as meaning "reasonable satisfaction" where an industrial machine is involved, this Article takes no position.

2. Pursuant to the general policies of this Act which require good faith not only between the parties to the sales contract, but as against interested third parties, subsection (3) resolves all reasonable doubts as to the nature of the transaction in favor of the general creditors of the buyer. As against such creditors words such as "on consignment" or "on memorandum", with or without words of reservation of title in the seller, are disregarded when the buyer has a place of business at which he deals in goods of the kind involved. A necessary exception is made where the buyer is known to be engaged primarily in selling the goods of others or is selling under a relevant sign law, or the seller complies with the filing provisions of Article 9 as if his interest were a security interest. However, there is no intent in this Section to narrow the protection afforded to third parties in any jurisdiction which has a selling Factors Act. The purpose of the exception is merely to limit the effect of the present subsection itself, in the absence of any such Factors Act, to cases in which creditors of the buyer may reasonably be deemed to have been misled by the conflict in the pre-existing case law by recognition that an "or return" provision is so definitely at odds with any ordinary contract for sale of goods that where written agreements are involved it must be contained in a written memorandum. The "or return" aspect of a sales contract must be treated as a separate contract under the Statute of Frauds section and as contradicting the sale insofar as questions of parol or extrinsic evidence are concerned.

Cross References:

Point 2: Article 9.

Point 3: Sections 2–201 and 2–202.

Definitional Cross References:

"Between merchants". Section 2–104.
"Conform". Section 2–103.
"Contract for sale". Section 2–106.
"Creditor". Section 1–201.
"Goods". Section 2–105.
"Sale". Section 2–106.
"Seller". Section 2–103.

Section 2–327. Special Incidents of Sale on Approval and Sale or Return.

(1) Under a sale on approval unless otherwise agreed

(a) although the goods are identified to the contract the risk of loss and the title do not pass to the buyer until acceptance; and

(b) use of the goods consistent with the purpose of trial is not acceptance but failure seasonably to notify the seller of election to return the goods is acceptance, and if the goods conform to the contract acceptance of any part is acceptance of the whole; and

(c) after due notification of election to return, the return is at the seller's risk and expense but a merchant buyer must follow any reasonable instructions.

(2) Under a sale or return unless otherwise agreed

(a) the option to return extends to the whole or any commercial unit of the goods while in substantially their original condition, but must be exercised seasonably; and

(b) the return is at the buyer's risk and expense.

New York Annotations

(1) *Sale on approval.* (a) *Risks.* In providing that risk of loss and title do not pass to the buyer until acceptance, this subsection is consistent with Personal Property Law, § 100, Rule 3(2)(a), and § 103. See Section 2–606 and subsection (b) of this section for the meaning of "acceptance".

(b) *Acceptance.* In providing that a failure seasonably to notify the seller of the election to return constitutes acceptance, this subsection accords with Personal Property Law, § 100, Rule 3(2)(b). See Brown & Lowe Co. v. Potolski, 221 App.Div. 299, 223 N.Y.S. 71 (1927); Fox v. Proctor, 160 App. Div. 712, 145 N.Y.S. 709, aff'd 217 N.Y. 711, 112 N.E. 470 (1916); Gerstenblith v. Meyer, 191 N.Y.S. 1 (1921). The Code adds the new provision that acceptance of any part equals acceptance of the whole.

(c) *Rights after notice of return.* There is no direct counterpart to this subsection in the present statutes. Since property would rest in the seller, the rights of the parties are probably stated in the Code. An analogous provision that a rejecting buyer need not return the goods to the seller now exists in Personal Property Law, § 131. The requirement of "due notification" and the special rule for merchant buyers are new.

(2) *Sale or return.* (a) *Option to return and seasonable return.* The Code's provision for return of any commercial unit, as well as the whole, of the goods has no counterpart in the existing statute. The rule is consistent with the case law. Greacen v. Poehlman,

191 N.Y. 493, 84 N.E. 390 (1908). The requirement that the return be exercised seasonably is generally in accord with Personal Property Law, § 100, Rule 3(1).

(b) *Risk and expense of return.* No comparable provision is presently contained in the New York statutes. However, in the analogous case of rescission of an ordinary sales contract the buyer must "return or offer to return" the goods. Personal Property Law, § 150(3).

Official Uniform Comment

Prior Uniform Statutory Provision: Section 19(3), Uniform Sales Act.

Changes: Completely rewritten in preceding and this section.

Purposes of Changes: To make it clear that:

1. In the case of a sale on approval:

If all of the goods involved conform to the contract, the buyer's acceptance of part of the goods constitutes acceptance of the whole. Acceptance of part falls outside the normal intent of the parties in the "on approval" situation and the policy of this Article allowing partial acceptance of a defective delivery has no application here. A case where a buyer takes home two dresses to select one commonly involves two distinct contracts; if not, it is covered by the words "unless otherwise agreed".

2. In the case of a sale or return, the return of any unsold unit merely because it is unsold is the normal intent of the "sale or return" provision, and therefore the right to return for this reason alone is independent of any other action under the contract which would turn on wholly different considerations. On the other hand, where the return of goods is for breach, including return of items resold by the buyer and returned by the ultimate purchasers because of defects, the return procedure is governed not by the present section but by the provisions on the effects and revocation of acceptance.

3. In the case of a sale on approval the risk rests on the seller until acceptance of the goods by the buyer, while in a sale or return the risk remains throughout on the buyer.

4. Notice of election to return given by the buyer in a sale on approval is sufficient to relieve him of any further liability. Actual return by the buyer to the seller is required in the case of a sale or return contract. What constitutes due "giving" of notice, as required in "on approval" sales is governed by the provisions on good faith and notice. "Seasonable" is used here as defined in Section 1–204. Nevertheless, the provisions of both this Article and of the contract on this point must be read with commercial reason and with full attention to good faith.

Cross References:

Point 1: Sections 2–501, 2–601 and 2–603.
Point 2: Sections 2–607 and 2–608.
Point 4: Sections 1–201 and 1–204.

Definitional Cross References:

"Agreed". Section 1–201.
"Buyer". Section 2–103.
"Commercial unit". Section 2–105.
"Conform". Section 2–106.
"Contract". Section 1–201.
"Goods". Section 2–105.
"Merchant". Section 2–104.
"Notification". Section 1–201.
"Notifies". Section 1–201.

"Sale on approval". Section 2–326.
"Sale or return". Section 2–326.
"Seasonably". Section 1–204.
"Seller". Section 2–103.

Section 2–328. Sale by Auction.

(1) In a sale by auction if goods are put up in lots each lot is the subject of a separate sale.

(2) A sale by auction is complete when the auctioneer so announces by the fall of the hammer or in other customary manner. Where a bid is made while the hammer is falling in acceptance of a prior bid the auctioneer may in his discretion reopen the bidding or declare the goods sold under the bid on which the hammer was falling.

(3) Such a sale is with reserve unless the goods are in explicit terms put up without reserve. In an auction with reserve the auctioneer may withdraw the goods at any time until he announces completion of the sale. In an auction without reserve, after the auctioneer calls for bids on an article or lot, that article or lot cannot be withdrawn unless no bid is made within a reasonable time. In either case a bidder may retract his bid until the auctioneer's announcement of completion of the sale, but a bidder's retraction does not revive any previous bid.

(4) If the auctioneer knowingly receives a bid on the seller's behalf or the seller makes or procures such a bid, and notice has not been given that liberty for such bidding is reserved, the buyer may at his option avoid the sale or take the goods at the price of the last good faith bid prior to the completion of the sale. This subsection shall not apply to any bid at a forced sale.

New York Annotations

(1) *Sale in lots. Accord* with Personal Property Law, § 102(1).

(2) *When sale complete.* The first sentence of this subsection follows Personal Property Law, § 102(2). The provision made in the second sentence in connection with bids made while the hammer is falling is new, and no cases were found on the point.

(3) *"With reserve".* Subsection (3) also follows Personal Property Law, § 102(2) in presuming that auction sales are "with reserve" unless explicitly announced to be without reserve". Comment 2 indicates that the "crucial point" is the "putting up" of the goods, and this accords with Benjamin v. First Citizens Bank & Trust Co. of Utica, 248 App.Div. 610, 287 N.Y.S. 947 (1936) (goods may be withdrawn before bidding even where sale advertised as "without reserve"). The rule on the bidder's power to retract his bid even in an auction "without reserve" also follows Personal Property Law, § 102(2).

(4) *Bids by seller.* Subsection (4) follows Personal Property Law, § 102(4); in permitting the buyer to avoid an auction sale at which the seller or his agent bid and where no notice of such a right to bid was given at the sale. Cf., United Industrial Syndicate, Inc. v. Aetna Industrial Corp., 99 N.Y.S.2d 375 (1950) (although no "announcement" was made, sale was not voidable since failure to state right was

inadvertent and everyone present knew that owners were bidding). The Code adds a new right in the buyer at such a sale to take the goods at the last good faith bid prior to the completion of the sale. Note that the Code also newly excepts from the entire subsection bids at a "forced sale," which is not otherwise defined. See Drew v. John Deere, 19 A.D.2d 308, 241 N.Y.S. 2d 267 (1963).

Historical Note: Subsections (3) and (4) were revised at the suggestion of the Law Revision Commission. The changes in subsection (3) incorporate the rule stated in Comment 2, that the seller may withdraw the goods even after announcing an auction without reserve until the goods are "put up"; they also restore the rule of the Uniform Sales Act that a bidder may retract his bid before the hammer falls even in an auction without reserve. The changes in subsection (4) clarified the prohibition on seller bidding. (1956 Recommendations, p. 49; Excerpts, p. 380.)

Official Uniform Comment

Prior Uniform Statutory Provision: Section 21, Uniform Sales Act.

Changes: Completely rewritten.

Purposes of Changes: To make it clear that:

1. The auctioneer may in his discretion either reopen the bidding or close the sale on the bid on which the hammer was falling when a bid is made at that moment. The recognition of a bid of this kind by the auctioneer in his discretion does not mean a closing in favor of such a bidder, but only that the bid has been accepted as a continuation of the bidding. If recognized, such a bid discharges the bid on which the hammer was falling when it was made.

2. An auction "with reserve" is the normal procedure. The crucial point, however, for determining the nature of an auction is the "putting up" of the goods. This Article accepts the view that the goods may be withdrawn before they are actually "put up," regardless of whether the auction is advertized as one without reserve, without liability on the part of the auction announcer to persons who are present. This is subject to any peculiar facts which might bring the case within the "firm offer" principle of this Article, but an offer to persons generally would require unmistakable language in order to fall within that section. The prior announcement of the nature of the auction either as with reserve or without reserve will, however, enter as an "explicit term" in the "putting up" of the goods and conduct thereafter must be governed accordingly. The present section continues the prior rule permitting withdrawal of bids in auctions both with and without reserve; and the rule is made explicit that the retraction of a bid does not revive a prior bid.

Cross Reference:

Point 2: Section 2–205.

Definitional Cross References:

"Buyer". Section 2–103.
"Good faith". Section 1–201.
"Goods". Section 2–105.
"Lot". Section 2–105.
"Notice". Section 1–201.
"Sale". Section 2–106.
"Seller". Section 2–103.

PART 4

TITLE, CREDITORS AND GOOD FAITH PURCHASERS

Section 2–401. Passing of Title; Reservation for Security; Limited Application of This Section.

Each provision of this Article with regard to the rights, obligations and remedies of the seller, the buyer, purchasers or other third parties applies irrespective of title to the goods except where the provision refers to such title. Insofar as situations are not covered by the other provisions of this Article and matters concerning title become material the following rules apply:

(1) Title to goods cannot pass under a contract for sale prior to their identification to the contract (Section 2–501), and unless otherwise explicitly agreed the buyer acquires by their identification a special property as limited by this Act. Any retention or reservation by the seller of the title (property) in goods shipped or delivered to the buyer is limited in effect to a reservation of a security interest. Subject to these provisions and to the provisions of the Article on Secured Transactions (Article 9), title to goods passes from the seller to the buyer in any manner and on any conditions explicitly agreed on by the parties.

(2) Unless otherwise explicitly agreed title passes to the buyer at the time and place at which the seller completes his performance with reference to the physical delivery of the goods, despite any reservation of a security interest and even though a document of title is to be delivered at a different time or place; and in particular and despite any reservation of a security interest by the bill of lading

(a) if the contract requires or authorizes the seller to send the goods to the buyer but does not require him to deliver them at destination, title passes to the buyer at the time and place of shipment; but

(b) if the contract requires delivery at destination, title passes on tender there.

(3) Unless otherwise explicitly agreed where delivery is to be made without moving the goods,

(a) if the seller is to deliver a document of title, title passes at the time when and the place where he delivers such documents; or

(b) if the goods are at the time of contracting already identified and no documents are to be delivered, title passes at the time and place of contracting.

(4) A rejection or other refusal by the buyer to receive or retain the goods, whether or not justified, or a justified revocation of acceptance revests title to the goods in the seller. Such revesting occurs by operation of law and is not a "sale".

New York Annotations

Specific provision, without reference to "title," is made in the Code for most of the rights, obligations, and remedies of the seller, buyer, and third parties in connection with risk of loss, action for the price, and the effect of the sale on the rights of third persons. Any such specific provision dealing with a specific problem will override any implication to be drawn from the location of title. For this reason, "title" is material only in situations not covered by such provisions and is therefore less important in determining the rights of parties than it is under the Uniform Sales Act.

(1) *Time at which title passes–explicit agreement.* The rule of subsection (1) that title cannot pass prior to "identification" of the goods to the contract is comparable to that of Personal Property Law, § 98, that no property passes until the goods are "ascertained." The further provision that, subject to the foregoing limitation, title passes in the manner and on the conditions "explicitly agreed on" by the parties is consistent with Personal Property Law, § 99(1). However, where the Code requires explicit agreement to vary the Code's rules governing passage of title, Personal Property Law, § 99(2), provides that intent may be implied on the basis of the terms of the contract, conduct and usage of the parties, usage of the trade, and the circumstances. Mitchell v. Gilmour, 256 App.Div. 893, 9 N.Y.S.2d 45 (1939); Socony Mobil Oil Co. v. Wayne County Produce Co., Inc., 24 Misc.2d 519, 196 N.Y.S.2d 729 (1959); DeLanoy, Kipp & Swan, Inc. v. New Amsterdam Cas. Co., 171 Misc. 342, 11 N.Y.S.2d 625, aff'd 289 N.Y. 823, 47 N.E.2d 433 (1943).

(a) *Effect of reservation of title.* The rule in subsection (1) that a reservation of title after shipment or delivery is limited to a security interest is consistent with Personal Property Law, § 101 (2), where title passes on shipment although a bill of lading is made out to seller or his order for security. Personal Property Law, § 103, is also analogous to the Code provision in that risk of loss shifts to the buyer where the seller has retained a property interest in order to secure performance. See Sections 2–505 and 2–509. The broader rule of subsection (1) extends to all cases where title is determinative. The applicability of Article 9 to the security interest reserved by the seller is governed by Section 9–113.

(b) *Buyer's special property.* Part 7 of Article 2 governs the incidents of the "special property" in the goods which the buyer acquires upon identification in the absence of an explicit agreement to the contrary. See Section 2–703 and Section 2–711. "Identification" of the goods is governed by Section 2–501. This special property interest is not a security interest within Article 9. See Section 1–201(37) and Section 9 113.

(2) *No explicit agreement–delivery requiring moving of goods.* The rule of subsection (2) is that in the absence of explicit agreement title passes when the seller "completes his performance with reference to the physical delivery of the goods." Although this rule is phrased differently, it seems consistent with Rules 4(2) and 5 of § 100 of the Personal Property Law, which draw a distinction between cases where the contract requires delivery to a destination (Rule 5) and where the contract merely requires the sending of the goods to the buyer (Rule 4(2)). Some of the New York case law presently interprets Rule 5 as requiring "acceptance" by the buyer when the goods reach the destination. Korde Corp. v. Casino Classics, Inc., 280 App.Div. 740, 116 N.Y.S.2d 908 (1952), and cases cited therein. The Code contains no such requirement.

(3) *No explicit agreement–delivery without moving the goods.*

(a) *Seller is to deliver document.* The provision is new, but is consistent with implications drawn from Personal Property Law, §§ 115 and 129. See, Bank of Italy v. Merchants' Nat'l Bank, 113 Misc. 314, 185 N.Y.S. 43, aff'd 197 App.Div. 150, 188 N.Y.S. 183 (1920).

(b) *Goods identified when contract made and no document to be delivered.* Subsection (3)(b) is similar to the passage of title rule of Personal Property Law, § 100(1), and the common law–namely, that title passes when the contract is made in the case of an unconditional contract to sell specific goods in a deliverable state. Groat v. Gile, 51 N.Y. 431 (1873) (common law); Sanitary Carpet Cleaner v. Reed

Mfg. Co., 159 App.Div. 587, 145 N.Y.S. 218 (1913); Doyle's Main Motors, Inc. v. Davis, 118 N.Y.S.2d 867 (1953). However, unlike the present law, it seems that the Code rule applies only where the delivery is to be made without moving the goods.

(4) *Rejection or refusal of goods by the buyer.* The rule of subsection (4) is new.

Historical Note: Changes in subsection (1) and related changes in other sections were made to conform to other provisions and to clarify the application of Article 9 to "security interests" arising in a sale of goods, as suggested by the Law Revision Commission. The principal substantive change in this section is the revision of former subsection (1)(a) so that the seller's interest after identification and before delivery is no longer limited to a security interest. This change conforms to subsection (2) under which the seller normally retains title under delivery, and to Section 2–501, under which identification may be postponed by agreement and the seller may in some circumstances substitute other goods even after identification. Section 1–201(37), defining "security interest", was revised to conform.

The revision also introduced the term "special property" to refer to the buyer's rights after identification. At the same time, Section 1–201(37) was revised to exclude the buyer's special property from the definition of "security interest", and former Section 9–204(6) was deleted. The incidents of the buyer's special property are defined in the remedy provisions of Article 2, and the new term was introduced into Section 2–502 and 2–722. No. change in Section 2–716 was required in this respect.

As part of the revision a new Section 9–113 was added, exempting from certain provisions of Article 9 "security interests" arising under Article 2 before the buyer lawfully obtains possession of the goods. In addition to the seller's rights of resale and stoppage under Section 2–703, 2–705, and 2–706, the new section applies to rights under such Section as 2–506, 2–707, and 2–711.

Also as part of the revision, the subject-matter of former subsection (1)(b) was covered by revisions of Sections 2–402 and 2–403. (1956 Recommendations, p. 50; Excerpts, pp. 381–2.)

Official Uniform Comment

Prior Uniform Statutory Provision: See generally, Sections 17, 18, 19 and 20, Uniform Sales Act.

Purposes: To make it clear that:

1. This Article deals with the issues between seller and buyer in terms of step by step performance or non-performance under the contract for sale and not in terms of whether or not "title" to the goods has passed. That the rules of this section in no way alter the rights of either the buyer, seller or third parties declared elsewhere in the Article is made clear by the preamble of this section. This section, however, in no way intends to indicate which line of interpretation would be followed in cases where the applicability of "public" regulation depends upon a "sale" or upon location of "title" without further definition. The basic policy of this Article that known purpose and reason should govern interpretation cannot extend beyond the scope of its own provisions. It is therefore necessary to state what a "sale" is and when title passes under this Article in case the courts deem any public regulation to incorporate the defined term of the "private" law.

2. "Future" goods cannot be the subject of a present sale. Before title can pass the goods must be identified in the manner set forth in Section 2–501. The parties, however, have full liberty to arrange by specific terms for the passing of title to goods which are existing.

3. The "special property" of the buyer in goods identified to the contract is excluded from the definition of "security interest"; its incidents are defined in provisions of this Article such as those on the rights of the seller's creditors, on good faith purchase, on the buyer's right to goods on the seller's right to specific performance or replevin.

4. The factual situations in subsections (2) and (3) upon which passage of title turn actually base the test upon the time when the seller has finally committed himself in regard to specific goods. Thus in a "shipment" contract he commits himself by the act of making the shipment. If shipment is not contemplated subsection (3) turns on the seller's final commitment, i.e. the delivery of documents or the making of the contract.

Cross References:

Point 2: Sections 2–102, 2–501 and 2–502.
Point 3: Sections 1–201, 2–402, 2–403, 2–502 and 2–716.

Definitional Cross References:

"Agreement". Section 1–201.
"Bill of lading". Section 1–201.
"Buyer". Section 2–103.
"Contract". Section 1–201.
"Contract for sale". Section 2–106.
"Delivery". Section 1–201.
"Document of title". Section 1–201.
"Good faith". Section 2–103.
"Goods". Section 2–105.
"Party". Section 1–201.
"Purchaser". Section 1–201.
"Receipt" of goods. Section 2–103.
"Remedy". Section 1–201.
"Rights". Section 1–201.
"Sale". Section 2–106.
"Security interest". Section 1–201.
"Seller". Section 2–103.
"Send". Section 1–201.

Section 2–402. Rights of Seller's Creditors Against Sold Goods.

(1) Except as provided in subsections (2) and (3), rights of unsecured creditors of the seller with respect to goods which have been identified to a contract for sale are subject to the buyer's rights to recover the goods under this Article (Sections 2–502 and 2–716).

(2) A creditor of the seller may treat a sale or an identification of goods to a contract for sale as void if as against him a retention of possession by the seller as fraudulent under any rule of law of the state where the goods are situated, except that retention of possession in good faith and current course of trade by a merchant-seller for a commercially reasonable time after a sale or identification is not fraudulent.

(3) Nothing in this Article shall be deemed to impair the rights of creditors of the seller

(a) under the provisions of the Article on Secured Transactions (Article 9); or

(b) where identification to the contract or delivery is made not in current course of trade but in satisfaction of or as security for a pre-existing claim for money, security or the like and is made under circumstances which under any rule of law of the state where the goods are situated would apart from this Article constitute the transaction a fraudulent transfer or voidable preference.

New York Annotations

(1) *Sold goods in seller's possession.* Subsection 3 contains the general rule of Section 26 of the Uniform Sales Act (Personal Property Law, § 107), whereby the rules of local law on transactions in fraud of creditors are preserved. The exception in subsection (2), however, under which the buyer's interest in goods left with a merchant-seller in the "current course of trade" and "for a commercially reasonable time after a sale or identification" is protected, is not included in the present statute. Since in New York the seller's retention of possession is presumptively rather than conclusively fraudulent, the section works no major change. Holley v. A. W. Haile Motor Co., 188 App.Div. 798, 177 N.Y.S. 429 (1919); Kimball v. Cash, 107 Misc. 363, 176 N.Y.S. 541 (1919). See generally 2 Williston, Sales, Secs. 351–404 (1948).

(2) *Creditors' rights from other sources.* Subsection (3) is designed to recognize explicitly any rights the creditors of the seller may have under Article 9 or under the state law governing preferential identification or fraudulent transfers.

(3) *Buyer's rights to identified goods.* Subsection (1), in transactions not affected by subsections (2) and (3), subordinates the claims of the seller's creditors to the buyer's right to recover identified goods.

Historical Note: At the suggestion of the Law Revision Commission, a new subsection (1) was inserted to subordinate the rights of the seller's creditors to the buyer's possessory remedies. The new subsection preserves an important consequence of the rules formerly stated in Section 2–401(1)(a) and (b), now deleted. For clarification, former subsection (2), renumbered (3), is changed by the insertion of a cross-reference to Article 9 and of a conflict-of-laws provision similar to that in former subsection (1), renumbered (2). (1956 Recommendations, p. 52; Excerpts, p. 382.)

Official Uniform Comment

Prior Uniform Statutory Provision: Subsection (2)–Section 26, Uniform Sales Act; Subsections (1) and (3)–none.

Changes: Rephrased.

Purposes of Changes and New Matter: To avoid confusion on ordinary issues between current sellers and buyers and issues in the filed of preference and hindrance by making it clear that:

1. Local law on questions of hindrance of creditors by the seller's retention of possession of the goods are outside the scope of this Article, but retention of possession in the current course of trade is legitimate. Transactions which fall within the law's policy against improper preferences are reserved from the protection of this Article.

2. The retention of possession of the goods by a merchant seller for a commercially reasonable time after a sale or identification in current course is exempted from attack as fraudulent. Similarly, the provisions of subsection (3) have no application to identification or delivery made in the current course of trade, as measured against general commercial understanding of what a "current" transaction is.

Definitional Cross References:

"Contract for sale". Section 2–106.

"Creditor". Section 1–201.
"Good faith". Section 2–103.
"Goods". Section 2–105.
"Merchant". Section 2–104.
"Money". Section 1–201.
"Reasonable time". Section 1–204.
"Rights". Section 1–201.
"Sale". Section 2–106.
"Seller". Section 2–103.

Section 2–403. Power to Transfer; Good Faith Purchase of Goods; "Entrusting".

(1) A purchaser of goods acquires all title which his transferor had or had power to transfer except that a purchaser of a limited interest acquires rights only to the extent of the interest. A person with voidable title has power to transfer a good title to a good faith purchaser for value. When goods have been delivered under a transaction of purchase the purchaser has such power even though

(a) the transferor was deceived as to the identity of the purchaser, or

(b) the delivery was in exchange for a check which is later dishonored, or

(c) it was agreed that the transaction was to be a "cash sale", or

(d) the delivery was procured through fraud punishable as larcenous under the criminal law.

(2) Any entrusting of possession of goods to a merchant who deals in goods of that kind gives him power to transfer all rights of the entruster to a buyer in ordinary course of business.

(3) "Entrusting" includes any delivery and any acquiescence in retention of possession regardless of any condition expressed between the parties to the delivery or acquiescence and regardless of whether the procurement of the entrusting or the possessor's disposition of the goods has been such as to be larcenous under the criminal law.

(4) The rights of other purchasers of goods and of lien creditors are governed by the Articles on Secured Transactions (Article 9), Bulk Transfers (Article 6) and Documents of Title (Article 7).

New York Annotations

(1) *Power to transfer.* Subsection (1), in giving a purchaser all title his transferor "had power to transfer", appears consistent with the principles of agency and estoppel. Personal Property Law, § 104. Island Trading Co., Inc. v. Berg Bros., Inc., 239 N.Y. 229, 146 N.E. 345 (1924).

Bona fide purchaser. The provision of subsection (1), giving title to a good faith purchaser for value from one who has a voidable title, repeats the principle of Personal Property Law, § 105. See Casey v. Kastel, 237 N.Y. 305, 142 N.E. 671 (1924) (shares of stock by infant). The protection is extended under the specific provision of the

Code to a bona fide purchaser from one who obtained delivery of the goods by common-law larceny. See Phelps v. McQuade, 220 N.Y. 232, 115 N.E. 441 (1917); Amols v. Bernstein, 214 App.Div. 469, 212 N.Y.S. 518 (1925). Compare Stanton Motor Corp. v. Rosetti, 11 A.D.2d 296, 203 N.Y.S.2d 273 (1960), and Damis v. Barcia, 266 App.Div. 698, 40 N.Y.S.2d 107 (1943).

(2) *Entrusting to a merchant who deals.* The provisions of subsection (2) go beyond present law; protection is afforded to one who purchases in the ordinary course of business from a merchant, to whom the goods have been entrusted, even though the merchant was given no authority to deal with the goods by the entruster. No New York case has gone this far in safeguarding the rights of an innocent purchaser. Cf. Zendman v. Harry Winston, Inc., 305 N.Y. 180, 111 N.E.2d 871 (1953) (N.J. Uniform Sales Act); Utica Trust & Deposit Co. v. Decker, 244 N.Y. 340, 155 N.E. 665 (1927), and Factor's Act, Personal Property Law, § 43.

The protection of subsection (2) is limited to a "buyer in the ordinary course of business." This term is defined in Section 1–201(9) and is more restrictive than "good faith purchaser for value." The Code definition excludes transfers in bulk or as security for or in satisfaction of a debt. The definition is approximately the same as that of "buyer in the ordinary course of trade" in Sec. 1 of the Uniform Trust Receipts Act (Personal Property Law, § 51(1)) and "buyer for value in the ordinary course of business" under Sec. 9 of the Uniform Conditional Sales Act (Personal Property Law, § 69). The Code definition also excludes pawnbrokers.

(3) *Definition of "Entrusting".* Subsection (3) defines the term "entrusting" as including any delivery or acquiescence in retention of possession. Thus the protection given purchasers from a seller in possession by Personal Property Law, § 106, is continued. Gorman v. La Bella, 146 Misc. 408, 262 N.Y.S. 345 (1933). However, unlike the present law, under the Code the seller in possession must be a "merchant." See Section 2–104. Furthermore, the definition of "buyer in the ordinary course of business" excludes a subsequent mortgagee.

Historical Note: Following suggestions of the Law Revision Commission, a third sentence was inserted in subsection (1) to clarify the application of the second sentence to four specific cases of voidable title, including the case of a "cash sale", formerly covered by Section 2–401(1)(b).

Official Uniform Comment

Prior Uniform Statutory Provision: Sections 20(4), 23, 24, 25, Uniform Sales Act; Section 9, especially 9(2), Uniform Trust Receipts Act; Section 9, Uniform Conditional Sales Act.

Changes: Consolidated and rewritten.

Purposes of Changes. To gather together a series of prior uniform statutory provisions and the case-law thereunder and to state a unified and simplified policy on good faith purchase of goods.

1. The basic policy of our law allowing transfer of such title as the transferor has is generally continued and expanded under subsection (1). In this respect the provisions of the section are applicable to a person taking by any form of "purchase" as defined by this Act. Moreover the policy of this Act expressly providing for the application of supplementary general principles of law to sales transactions wherever appropriate joins with the present section to continue unimpaired all rights acquired under the law of agency or of apparent agency or ownership or other estoppel, whether based on statutory provisions or on case law principles. The section also leaves unimpaired the powers given to selling factors under the earlier Factors Acts. In addition subsection (1) provides specifically for the protection of the good faith purchaser for value in a number of specific situations which have been troublesome under prior law.

On the other hand, the contract of purchase is of course limited by its own terms as in a case of pledge for a limited amount or of sale of a fractional interest in goods.

2. The many particular situations in which a buyer in ordinary course of business from a dealer has been protected against reservation of property or other hidden interest are gathered by subsections (2)–(4) into a single principle protecting persons who buy in ordinary course out of inventory. Consignors have no reason to complain, nor have lenders who hold a security interest in the inventory, since the very purpose of goods in inventory is to be turned into cash by sale.

The principle is extended in subsection (3) to fit with the abolition of the old law of "cash sale" by subsection (1)(c). It is also freed from any technicalities depending on the extended law of larceny; such extension of the concept of theft to include trick, particular types of fraud, and the like is for the purpose of helping conviction of the offender; it has no proper application to the long-standing policy of civil protection of buyers from persons guilty of such trick or fraud. Finally, the policy is extended, in the interest of simplicity and sense, to any entrusting by a bailor; this is in consonance with the explicit provisions of Section 7–205 on the powers of a warehouseman who is also in the business of buying and selling fungible goods of the kind he warehouses. As to entrusting by a secured party, subsection (2) is limited by the more specific provisions of Section 9–307(1), which deny protection to a person buying farm products from a person engaged in farming operations.

3. The definition of "buyer in ordinary course of business" (Section 1–201) is effective here and preserves the essence of the healthy limitations engrafted by the case-law on the older statutes. The older loose concept of good faith and wide definition of value combined to create apparent good faith purchasers in many situations in which the result outraged common sense; the court's solution was to protect the original title especially by use of "cash sale" or of over technical construction of the enabling clauses of the statutes. But such rulings then turned into limitations on the proper protection of buyers in the ordinary market. Section 1–201(9) cuts down the category of buyer in ordinary course in such fashion as to take care of the results of the cases, but with no price either in confusion or in injustice to proper dealings in the normal market.

4. Except as provided in subsection (1), the rights of purchasers other than buyers in ordinary course are left to the Articles on Secured Transactions, Documents of Title, and Bulk Sales.

Cross References:

Point 1: Sections 1–103 and 1–201.
Point 2: Sections 1–201, 2–402, 7–205 and 9–307(1).
Points 3 and 4: Sections 1–102, 1–201, 2–104, 2–707 and Articles 6, 7 and 9.

Definitional Cross References:

"Buyer in ordinary course of business". Section 1–201.
"Good faith". Sections 1–201 and 2–103.
"Goods". Section 2–105.
"Person". Section 1–201.
"Purchaser". Section 1–201.
"Signed". Section 1–201.
"Term". Section 1–201.
"Value". Section 1–201.

PART 5

PERFORMANCE

Section 2–501. Insurable Interest in Goods; Manner of Identification of Goods.

(1) The buyer obtains a special property and an insurable interest in goods by identification of existing goods as goods to which the contract refers even though the goods so identified are nonconforming and he has an option to return or reject them. Such identification can be made at any time and in any manner explicitly agreed to by the parties. In the absence of explicit agreement identification occurs

(a) when the contract is made if it is for the sale of goods already existing and identified;

(b) if the contract is for the sale of future goods other than those described in paragraph (c), when goods are shipped, marked or otherwise designated by the seller as goods to which the contract refers;

(c) when the crops are planted or otherwise become growing crops or the young are conceived if the contract is for the sale of unborn young to be born within twelve months after contracting or for the sale of crops to be harvested within twelve months or the next normal harvest season after contracting, whichever is longer.

(2) The seller retains an insurable interest in goods so long as title to or any security interest in the goods remains in him and where the identification is by the seller alone he may until default or insolvency or notification to the buyer that the identification is final substitute other goods for those identified.

(3) Nothing in this section impairs any insurable interest recognized under any other statute or rule of law.

New York Annotations

Insurability of interest. The rules of this section governing the buyer's or the seller's "insurable interest" are by subsection (3) effective only if existing law would negate insurability. Presently § 148 of the Insurance Law expresses the test in terms of lawful and substantial economic interest in the safety or preservation of property from loss, destruction or pecuniary damage."

Identification. A new concept under the Code comparable to "appropriation" as used in Personal Property Law, § 100, Rule 4, "identification" is significant since it affects not only the buyer's insurable interest but also his "special property in the goods". See Section 2–401. Under existing law, "appropriation" defines when property passes to unascertained or future goods. Personal Property Law, § 100, Rule 4. Geo. Boiko & Co. v. Atlantic Woolen Mills, Inc., 195 App.Div. 207, 186 N.Y.S. 624, aff'd 234 N.Y. 583, 138 N.E. 455 (1922); Proctor & Gamble Co. v. Peters, White & Co., 233 N.Y. 97, 134 N.E. 849 (1922).

Crops; unborn young. This provision is new. As to fungible goods, see Section 2–105(4).

Historical Note: Supp. No. 1 inserted new subsection (3) to eliminate any possibility that this section might impair the insurability of contract interests or of the seller's interests as a mere bailee. A reference to the buyer's special property" was inserted in subsection (1) to conform to changes in Section 1–201(37) and 2–401. (1956 Recommendations, p. 54.)

Official Uniform Comment

Prior Uniform Statutory Provision: See Sections 17 and 19, Uniform Sales Act.

Purposes:

1. The present section deals with the manner of identifying goods to the contract so that an insurable interest in the buyer and the rights set forth in the next section will accrue. Generally speaking, identification may be made in any manner "explicitly agreed to" by the parties. The rules of paragraphs (a), (b) and (c) apply only in the absence of such "explicit agreement".

2. In the ordinary case identification of particular existing goods as goods to which the contract refers is unambiguous and may occur in one of many ways. It is possible, however, for the identification to be tentative or contingent. In view of the limited effect given to identification by this Article, the general policy is to resolve all doubts in favor of identification.

3. The provision of this section as to "explicit agreement" clarifies the present confusion in the law of sales which has arisen from the fact that under prior uniform legislation all rules of presumption with reference to the passing of title or to appropriation (which in turn depended upon identification) were regarded as subject to the contrary intention of the parties or of the party appropriating. Such uncertainty is reduced to a minimum under this section by requiring "explicit agreement" of the parties before the rules of paragraphs (a), (b) and (c) are displaced-as they would be by a term giving the buyer power to select the goods. An "explicit" agreement, however, need not necessarily be found in the terms used in the particular transaction. Thus, where a usage of the trade has previously been made explicit by reduction to a standard set of "rules and regulations" currently incorporated by reference into the contracts of the parties, a relevant provision of those "rules and regulations" is "explicit" within the meaning of this section.

4. In view of the limited function of identification there is no requirement in this section that the goods be in deliverable state or that all of the seller's duties with respect to the processing of the goods be completed in order that identification occur. For example, despite identification the risk of loss remains on the seller under the risk of loss provisions until completion of his duties as to the goods and all of his remedies remain dependent upon his not defaulting under the contract.

5. Undivided shares in an identified fungible bulk, such as grain in an elevator or oil in a storage tank, can be sold. The mere making of the contract with reference to an undivided share in an identified fungible bulk is enough under subsection (a) to effect an identification if there is no explicit agreement otherwise. The seller's duty, however, to segregate and deliver according to the contract is not affected by such an identification but is controlled by other provisions of this Article.

6. Identification of crops under paragraph (c) is made upon planting only if they are to be harvested within the year or within the next normal harvest season. The phrase "next normal harvest season" fairly includes nursery stock raised for normally quick "harvest," but plainly excludes a "timber" crop to which the concept of a harvest "season" is inapplicable.

Paragraph (c) is also applicable to a crop of wool or the young of animals to be born within twelve months after contracting. The product of a lumbering, mining or fishing operation, though seasonal, is not within the concept of "growing". Identification under a contract for all or part of the output of such an operation can be effected early in the operation.

Cross References:

Point 1: Section 2–502.
Point 4: Sections 2–509, 2–510 and 2–703.
Point 5: Sections 2–105, 2–308, 2–503 and 2–509.
Point 6: Sections 2–105(1), 2–107(1) and 2–402.

Definitional Cross References:

"Agreement". Section 1–201.
"Contract". Section 1–201.
"Contract for sale". Section 2–106.
"Future goods". Section 2–105.
"Goods". Section 2–105.
"Notification". Section 1–201.
"Party". Section 1–201.
"Sale". Section 2–106.
"Security interest". Section 1–201.
"Seller". Section 2–103.

Section 2–502. Buyer's Right to Goods on Seller's Insolvency.

(1) Subject to subsection (2) and even though the goods have not been shipped a buyer who has paid a part or all of the price of goods in which he has a special property under the provisions of the immediately preceding section may on making and keeping good a tender of any unpaid portion of their price recover them from the seller if the seller becomes insolvent within ten days after receipt of the first installment on their price.

(2) If the identification creating his special property has been made by the buyer he acquires the right to recover the goods only if they conform to the contract for sale.

New York Annotations

The buyer's remedy upon the seller's insolvency is new. Compare Personal Property Law, § 147, basing buyer's right to obtain the goods on title, and § 149, basing specific performance on "specific or ascertained goods." This remedy corresponds to the seller's rights under Section 2–702 and the present law. Mann v. Pusrin, 158 N.Y.S. 906 (1916). The fact that the buyer must have a "special property" in the goods means that the buyer's remedy is not a "security interest" under Article 9. See Sections 1–201(37) and 9–113.

Historical Note: The changes deleted reference to the buyer's "insurable interest" and substituted reference to his "special property" for clarification and conformity with changes in Sections 1–201(37), 2–401, and 2–501. (1956 Recommendations, p. 55; Excerpts, p. 384.)

Official Uniform Comment

Prior Uniform Statutory Provision: Compare Sections 17, 18 and 19, Uniform Sales Act.

Purposes:

1. This section gives an additional right to the buyer as a result of identification of the goods to the contract in the manner provided in Section 2–501. The buyer is given a right to the goods on the seller's insolvency occurring within 10 days after he receives the first installment on their price.

2. The question of whether the buyer also acquires a security interest in identified goods and has rights to the goods when insolvency takes place after the ten-day period provided in this section depends upon compliance with the provisions of the Article on Secured Transactions (Article 9).

3. Subsection (2) is included to preclude the possibility of unjust enrichment which exists if the buyer were permitted to recover goods even though they were greatly superior in quality or quantity to that called for by the contract for sale.

Cross References:

Point 1: Section 1–201 and 2–702.
Point 2: Article 9.

Definitional Cross References:

"Buyer". Section 2–103.
"Conform". Section 2–106.
"Contract for sale". Section 2–106.
"Goods". Section 2–105.
"Insolvent". Section 1–201.
"Right". Section 1–201.
"Seller". Section 2–103.

Section 2–503. Manner of Seller's Tender of Delivery.

(1) Tender of delivery requires that the seller put and hold conforming goods at the buyer's disposition and give the buyer any notification reasonably necessary to enable him to take delivery. The manner, time and place for tender are determined by the agreement and this Article, and in particular

(a) tender must be at a reasonable hour, and if it is of goods they must be kept available for the period reasonably necessary to enable the buyer to take possession; but

(b) unless otherwise agreed the buyer must furnish facilities reasonably suited to the receipt of the goods.

(2) Where the case is within the next section respecting shipment tender requires that the seller comply with its provisions.

(3) Where the seller is required to deliver at a particular destination tender requires that he comply with subsection (1) and also in any appropriate case tender documents as described in subsections (4) and (5) of this section.

(4) Where goods are in the possession of a bailee and are to be delivered without being moved

(a) tender requires that the seller either tender a negotiable document of title covering such goods or procure acknowledgement by the bailee of the buyer's right to possession of the goods; but

(b) tender to the buyer of a non-negotiable document of title or of a written direction to the bailee to deliver is sufficient tender unless the buyer seasonably objects, and receipt by the bailee of notification of the buyer's rights fixes those rights as against the bailee and all third persons; but risk of loss of the goods and of any failure by the bailee to honor the non-negotiable document of title or to obey the direction remains on the seller until the buyer has had a reasonable time to present the document or direction, and a refusal by the bailee to honor the document or to obey the direction defeats the tender.

(5) Where the contract requires the seller to deliver documents

(a) he must tender all such documents in correct form, except as provided in this Article with respect to bills of lading in a set (subsection (2) of Section 2–323); and

(b) tender through customary banking channels is sufficient and dishonor of a draft accompanying the documents constitutes non-acceptance or rejection.

New York Annotations

In general this section follows the results under the existing law. The express requirement of notice to the buyer is new. Compare, on the issue of reasonable time, Personal Property Law, § 124(4).

Subsection (3) of this section is designed to change the rule as to what is a destination contract. Compare Personal Property Law, § 100(5). Terms calling for the seller to pay the cost of transportation no longer operate as an agreement to deliver to the buyer or at an agreed destination. See Comment 5. Compare Personal Property Law, § 100, Rule 5.

Subsection (4) on goods in possession of a bailee is generally in *accord* with Personal Property Law, § 124(3).

Subsection (5) *Accord:* Personal Property Law, § 101(4).

Historical Note: Subsection (4) was revised at the suggestion of the Law Revision Commission for clarification. (1956 Recommendations, p. 56; Excerpts, p. 384.)

Official Uniform Comment

Prior Uniform Statutory Provision: See Sections 11, 19, 20, 43 (3) and (4), 46 and 51, Uniform Sales Act

Changes: The general policy of the above sections is continued and supplemented but subsection (3) changes the rule of prior section 19(5) as to what constitutes a "destination" contract and subsection (4) incorporates a minor correction as to tender of delivery of goods in the possession of a bailee.

Purposes of Changes:

1. The major general rules governing the manner of proper or due tender of delivery are gathered in this section. The term "tender" is used in this Article in two different senses. In one sense it refers to "due tender" which contemplates an offer coupled with a present ability to fulfill all the conditions resting on the tendering party and must be followed by actual performance if the other party shows himself ready to proceed. Unless the context unmistakably indicates otherwise this is the meaning of "tender" in this Article and the occasional addition of the word "due" is only for clarity and emphasis. At other times it is used to refer to an offer of goods or

documents under a contract as if in fulfillment of its conditions even though there is a defect when measured against the contract obligation. Used in either sense, however, "tender" connotes such performance by the tendering party as puts the other party in default if he fails to proceed in some manner.

2. The seller's general duty to tender and deliver is laid down in Section 2–301 and more particularly in Section 2–507. The seller's right to a receipt if he demands one and receipts are customary is governed by Section 1–205. Subsection (1) of the present section proceeds to set forth two primary requirements of tender: first, that the seller "put and hold conforming goods at the buyer's disposition" and, second, that he "give the buyer any notice reasonably necessary to enable him to take delivery."

In cases in which payment is due and demanded upon delivery the "buyer's disposition" is qualified by the seller's right to retain control of the goods until payment by the provision of this Article on delivery on condition. However, where the seller is demanding payment on delivery he must first allow the buyer to inspect the goods in order to avoid impairing his tender unless the contract for sale is on C.I.F., C.O.D., cash against documents or similar terms negating the privilege of inspection before payment.

In the case of contracts involving documents the seller can "put and hold conforming goods at the buyer's disposition" under subsection (1) by tendering documents which give the buyer complete control of the goods under the provisions of Article 7 on due negotiation.

3. Under paragraph (a) of subsection (1) usage of the trade and the circumstances of the particular case determine what is a reasonable hour for tender and what constitutes a reasonable period of holding the goods available.

4. The buyer must furnish reasonable facilities for the receipt of the goods tendered by the seller under subsection (1), paragraph (b). This obligation of the buyer is no part of the seller's tender.

5. For the purposes of subsections (2) and (3) there is omitted from this Article the rule under prior uniform legislation that a term requiring the seller to pay the freight or cost of transportation to the buyer is equivalent to an agreement by the seller to deliver to the buyer or at an agreed destination. This omission is with the specific intention of negating the rule, for under this Article the "shipment" contract is regarded as the normal one and the "destination" contract as the variant type. The seller is not obligated to deliver at a named destination and bear the concurrent risk of loss until arrival, unless he has specifically agreed so to deliver or the commercial understanding of the terms used by the parties contemplates such delivery.

6. Paragraph (a) of subsection (4) continues the rule of the prior uniform legislation as to acknowledgment by the bailee. Paragraph (b) of subsection (4) adopts the rule that between the buyer and the seller the risk of loss remains on the seller during a period reasonable for securing acknowledgment of the transfer from the bailee, while as against all other parties the buyer's rights are fixed as of the time the bailee receives notice of the transfer.

7. Under subsection (5) documents are never "required" except where there is an express contract term or it is plainly implicit in the peculiar circumstances of the case or in a usage of trade. Documents may, of course, be "authorized" although not required, but such cases are not within the scope of this subsection. When documents are required, there are three main requirements of this subsection: (1) "All": each required document is essential to a proper tender; (2) "Such": the documents must be the ones actually required by the contract in terms of source and substance; (3) "Correct form": All documents must be in correct form.

When a prescribed document cannot be procured, a question of fact arises under the provision of this Article on substituted performance as to whether the agreed manner of delivery is actually commercially impracticable and whether the substitute is commercially reasonable.

Cross References:

Point 2: Sections 1–205, 2–301, 2–310, 2–507 and 2–513 and Article 7.
Point 5: Sections 2–308, 2–310 and 2–509.
Point 7: Section 2–614(1).
Specific matters involving tender are covered in many additional sections of this Article. See Sections 1–205, 2–301, 2–306 to 2–319, 2–321(3), 2–504, 2–507(2), 2–511(1), 2–513, 2–612 and 2–614.

Definitional Cross References:

"Agreement". Section 1–201.
"Bill of lading". Section 1–201.
"Buyer". Section 2–103.
"Conforming". Section 2–106.
"Contract". Section 1–201.
"Delivery". Section 1–201.
"Dishonor". Section 3–508.
"Document of title". Section 1–201.
"Draft". Section 3–104.
"Goods". Section 2–105.
"Notification". Section 1–201.
"Reasonable time". Section 1–204.
"Receipt of goods". Section 2–103.
"Rights". Section 1–201.
"Seasonably". Section 1–204.
"Seller". Section 2–103.
"Written". Section 1–201.

Section 2–504. Shipment by Seller.

Where the seller is required or authorized to send the goods to the buyer and the contract does not require him to deliver them at a particular destination, then unless otherwise agreed he must

(a) put the goods in the possession of such a carrier and make such a contract for their transportation as may be reasonable having regard to the nature of the goods and other circumstances of the case; and

(b) obtain and promptly deliver or tender in due form any document necessary to enable the buyer to obtain possession of the goods or otherwise required by the agreement or by usage of trade; and

(c) promptly notify the buyer of the shipment.

Failure to notify the buyer under paragraph (c) or to make a proper contract under paragraph (a) is a ground for rejection only if material delay or loss ensues.

New York Annotations

This section is generally in *accord* with Personal Property Law, § 127. Even where risk has passed, the seller has been held responsible for adequate delivery to the carrier, Madeirense DaBrasil, S/A v. Stulman-Emrick Lumber Co., 147 F.2d 399 (2d Cir. 1945), or for failure to make an adequate declaration of value to the carrier, Miller v. Harvey, 221 N.Y. 54, 116 N.E. 781 (1917); Lopez v. Isaacs, Inc., 210 App.Div.

601, 206 N.Y.S.405 (1924). Similarly the tender of necessary documents has been held to be the seller's responsibility, Cundill v. A. W. Millhauser Corp., 257 N.Y. 416, 178 N.E. 680 (1931). The express requirement of notice to the buyer in subsection (c) is broader than Personal Property Law, § 127(3), requiring notice only where the seller knows it is usual to insure.

Historical Note: Subparagraph (a) was revised at the suggestion of the Law Revision Commission to make it clear that the seller's duty includes selection of an appropriate carrier. (1956 Recommendations, p. 57; Excerpts, p. 384.)

Official Uniform Comment

Prior Uniform Statutory Provision: Section 46, Uniform Sales Act.

Changes: Rewritten.

Purposes of Changes: To continue the general policy of the prior uniform statutory provision while incorporating certain modifications with respect to the requirement that the contract with the carrier be made expressly on behalf of the buyer and as to the necessity of giving notice of the shipment to the buyer, so that:

1. The section is limited to "shipment" contracts as contrasted with "destination" contracts or contracts for delivery at the place where the goods are located. The general principles embodied in this section cover the special cases of F.O.B. point of shipment contracts and C.I.F. and C. & F. contracts. Under the preceding section on manner of tender of delivery, due tender by the seller requires that he comply with the requirements of this section in appropriate cases.

2. The contract to be made with the carrier under paragraph (a) must conform to all express terms of the agreement, subject to any substitution necessary because of failure of agreed facilities as provided in the later provision on substituted performance. However, under the policies of this Article on good faith and commercial standards and on buyer's rights on improper delivery, the requirements of explicit provisions must be read in terms of their commercial and not their literal meaning. This policy is made express with respect to bills of lading in a set in the provision of this Article on form of bills of lading required in overseas shipment.

3. In the absence of agreement, the provision of this Article on options and cooperation respecting performance gives the seller the choice of any reasonable carrier, routing and other arrangements. Whether or not the shipment is at the buyer's expense the seller must see to any arrangements, reasonable in the circumstances, such as refrigeration, watering of live stock, protection against cold, the sending along of any necessary help, selection of specialized cars and the like for paragraph (a) is intended to cover all necessary arrangements whether made by contract with the carrier or otherwise. There is, however, a proper relaxation of such requirements if the buyer is himself in a position to make the appropriate arrangements and the seller gives him reasonable notice of the need to do so. It is an improper contract under paragraph (a) for the seller to agree with the carrier to a limited valuation below the true value and thus cut off the buyer's opportunity to recover from the carrier in the event of loss, when the risk of shipment is placed on the buyer by his contract with the seller.

4. Both the language of paragraph (b) and the nature of the situation it concerns indicate that the requirement that the seller must obtain and deliver promptly to the buyer in due form any document necessary to enable him to obtain possession of the goods is intended to cumulate with the other duties of the seller such as those covered in paragraph (a).

In this connection, in the case of pool car shipments a delivery order furnished by the seller on the pool car consignee, or on the carrier for delivery out of a larger quantity, satisfies the requirements of paragraph (b) unless the contract requires some other form of document.

5. This Article, unlike the prior uniform statutory provision, makes it the seller's duty to notify the buyer of shipment in all cases. The consequences of his failure to do so, however, are limited in that the buyer may reject on this ground only where material delay or loss ensues.

A standard and acceptable manner of notification in open credit shipments is the sending of an invoice and in the case of documentary contracts is the prompt forwarding of the documents as under paragraph (b) of this section. It is also usual to send on a straight bill of lading but this is not necessary to the required notification. However, should such a document prove necessary or convenient to the buyer, as in the case of loss and claim against the carrier, good faith would require the seller to send it on request.

Frequently the agreement expressly requires prompt notification as by wire or cable. Such a term may be of the essence and the final clause of paragraph (c) does not prevent the parties from making this a particular ground for rejection. To have this vital and irreparable effect upon the seller's duties, such a term should be part of the "dickered" terms written in any "form," or should otherwise be called seasonably and sharply to the seller's attention.

6. Generally, under the final sentence of the section, rejection by the buyer is justified only when the seller's dereliction as to any of the requirements of this section in fact is followed by material delay or damage. It rests on the seller, so far as concerns matters not within the peculiar knowledge of the buyer, to establish that his error has not been followed by events which justify rejection.

Cross References:

Point 1: Sections 2–319, 2–320 and 2–503(2).
Point 2: Sections 1–203, 2–323(2), 2–601 and 2–614(1).
Point 3: Section 2–311(2).
Point 5: Section 1–203.

Definitional Cross References:

"Agreement". Section 1–201.
"Buyer". Section 2–103.
"Contract". Section 1–201.
"Delivery". Section 1–201.
"Goods". Section 2–105.
"Notifies". Section 1–201.
"Seller". Section 2–103.
"Send". Section 1–201.
"Usage of trade". Section 1–205.

Section 2–505. Seller's Shipment Under Reservation.

(1) Where the seller has identified goods to the contract by or before shipment:

(a) his procurement of a negotiable bill of lading to his own order or otherwise reserves in him a security interest in the goods. His procurement of the bill to the order of a financing agency or of the buyer indicates in addition only the seller's expectation of transferring that interest to the person named.

(b) a non-negotiable bill of lading to himself or his nominee reserves possession of the goods as security but except in a case of conditional delivery (subsection (2) of Section 2–507) a non-negotiable bill of lading naming the buyer as consignee reserves no security interest even though the seller retains possession of the bill of lading.

(2) When shipment by the seller with reservation of a security interest is in violation of the contract for sale it constitutes an improper contract for transportation within the preceding section but impairs neither the rights given to the buyer by shipment and identification of the goods to the contract nor the seller's powers as a holder of a negotiable document.

New York Annotations

(1) *Security interest.* The existing statutory policy found in the Bills of Lading Act, Personal Property Law, § 226, and in Personal Property Law, § 101(2) and (3) is continued with the change in emphasis from the phraseology of title and property to that of interest and possession.

(2) *Improper shipment.* This subsection is new; but compare Personal Property Law, § 100, Rule 4(2), requiring shipment "in pursuance of a contract."

Historical Note: The words "but no more" were deleted from subsection (1)(a) after "in the goods", at the suggestion of the Law Revision Commission to conform to subsection (1)(b). The purpose was clarification without change of meaning. The limiting effect of the deleted words is adequately accomplished by Sections 1–201(37) and 2–401(1). (1956 Recommendations, p. 57; Excerpts, p. 385.)

Official Uniform Comment

Prior Uniform Statutory Provision: Section 20(2), (3), (4), Uniform Sales Act.

Changes: Completely rephrased, the "powers" of the parties in cases of reservation being emphasized primarily rather than the "rightfulness" of reservation.

Purposes of Changes: To continue in general the policy of the prior uniform statutory provision with certain modification of emphasis and language, so that:

1. The security interest reserved to the seller under subsection (1) is restricted to securing payment or performance by the buyer and the seller is strictly limited in his disposition and control of the goods as against the buyer and third parties. Under this Article, the provision as to the passing of interest expressly applies "despite any reservation of security title" and also provides that the "rights, obligations and remedies" of the parties are not altered by the incidence of title generally. The security interest, therefore, must be regarded as a means given to the seller to enforce his rights against the buyer which is unaffected by and in turn does not affect the location of title generally. The rules set forth in subsection (1) are not to be altered by any apparent "contrary intent" of the parties as to passing of title, since the rights and remedies of the parties to the contract of sale, as defined in this Article, rest on the contract and its performance or breach and not on stereotyped presumptions as to the location of title.

This Article does not attempt to regulate local procedure in regard to the effective maintenance of the seller's security interest when the action is in replevin by the buyer against the carrier.

2. Every shipment of identified goods under a negotiable bill of lading reserves a security interest in the seller under subsection (1) paragraph (a).

It is frequently convenient for the seller to make the bill of lading to the order of a nominee such as his agent at destination, the financing agency to which he expects to negotiate the document or the bank issuing a credit to him. In many instances, also, the buyer is made the order party. This Article does not deal directly with the question as to whether a bill of lading made out by the seller to the order of a nominee gives the carrier notice of any rights which the nominee may have so as to limit its freedom or obligation to honor the bill of lading in the hands of the seller as the original shipper if the expected negotiation fails. This is dealt with in the Article on Documents of Title (Article 7).

3. A non-negotiable bill of lading taken to a party other than the buyer under subsection (1) paragraph (b) reserves possession of the goods as security in the seller but if he seeks to withhold the goods improperly the buyer can tender payment and recover them.

4. In the case of a shipment by non-negotiable bill of lading taken to a buyer, the seller, under subsection (1) retains no security interest or possession as against the buyer and by the shipment he *de facto* loses control as against the carrier except where he rightfully and effectively stops delivery in transit. In cases in which the contract gives the seller the right to payment against delivery, the seller, by making an immediate demand for payment, can show that his delivery is conditional, but this does not prevent the buyer's power to transfer full title to a sub-buyer in ordinary course or other purchaser under Section 2–103.

5. Under subsection (2) an improper reservation by the seller which would constitute a breach in no way impairs such of the buyer's rights as result from identification of the goods. The security title reserved by the seller under subsection (1) does not protect his holding of the document or the goods for the purpose of exacting more than is due him under the contract.

Cross References:

Point 1: Section 1–201.
Point 2: Article 7.
Point 3: Sections 2–501(2) and 2–504.
Point 4: Sections 2–403, 2–507(2) and 2–705.
Point 5: Sections 2–310, 2–319(4), 2–320(4), 2–501 and 2–502 and Article 7.

Definitional Cross References:

"Bill of lading". Section 1–201.
"Buyer". Section 2–103.
"Consignee". Section 7–102.
"Contract". Section 1–201.
"Contract for sale". Section 2–106.
"Delivery". Section 1–201.
"Financing agency". Section 2–104.
"Goods". Section 2–105.
"Holder". Section 1–201.
"Person". Section 1–201.
"Security interest". Section 1–201.
"Seller". Section 2–103.

Section 2–506. Rights of Financing Agency.

(1) A financing agency by paying or purchasing for value a draft which relates to a shipment of goods acquires to the extent of the payment or purchase and in addition to its own rights under the draft and any document of title securing it any rights of the shipper in the goods including the right to stop delivery and the shipper's right to have the draft honored by the buyer.

(2) The right to reimbursement of a financing agency which has in good faith honored or purchased the draft under commitment to or authority from the buyer is not impaired by subsequent discovery of defects with reference to any relevant document which was apparently regular on its face.

New York Annotations

This section is new to the statutes. To the extent that the financing agency acquires the security interest of a seller in the goods care must be taken to determine whether filing is required under Article 9. See Section 1–201(37) and Section 9–113. See Section 4–208(3) as to the rights in the document. Similarly to the extent that the financing agency by reason of this section obtains the shipper's right to the price, where it pays a straight bill of lading attached to the draft, the financing agency may lose that right as against seller's creditors or subsequent assignees unless a filing is made under Article 9. The Code result as between seller, buyer, and financing agency would be the same as in George F. Hinrichs, Inc. v. Standard T. & S. Bank, 279 Fed. 382 (2d Cir. 1922).

Historical Note: Subsection (1) was revised at the suggestion of the Law Revision Commission for clarification without change of meaning. Subsection (2) was changed at the same time to conform to Section 5–109 requiring care to ascertain whether a document is apparently regular on its face. (1956 Recommendations, p. 58; Excerpts, p. 385.)

Official Uniform Comment

Prior Uniform Statutory Provision: None.

Purposes:

1. "Financing agency" is broadly defined in this Article to cover every normal instance in which a party aids or intervenes in the financing of a sales transaction. The term as used in subsection (1) is not in any sense intended as a limitation and covers any other appropriate situation which may arise outside the scope of the definition.

2. "Paying" as used in subsection (1) is typified by the letter of credit, or "authority to pay" situation in which a banker, by arrangement with the buyer or other consignee, pays on his behalf for the price of the goods. It is immaterial whether the draft is formally drawn on the party paying or his principal, whether it is a sight draft paid in cash or a time draft "paid" in the first instance by acceptance, or whether the payment is viewed as absolute or conditional. All of these cases constitute "payment" under this subsection. Similarly, "purchasing for value" is used to indicate the whole area of financing by the seller's banker, and the principle of subsection (1) is applicable without any niceties of distinction between "purchase", "discount," "advance against collection" or the like. But it is important to notice that the only right to have the draft honored that is acquired is that *against the buyer;* if any right against any one else is claimed it will have to be under some separate obligation of that other person. A letter of credit does not necessarily protect *purchasers* of drafts. See Article 5. And for the relations of the parties to documentary drafts see Part 5 of Article 4.

3. Subsection (1) is made applicable to payments or advances against a draft which "relates to" a shipment of goods and this has been chosen as a term of maximum breadth. In particular the term is intended to cover the case of a draft against an invoice or against a delivery order. Further, it is unnecessary that there be an explicit

assignment of the invoice attached to the draft to bring the transaction within the reason of this subsection.

4. After shipment, "the rights of the shipper in the goods" are merely security rights and are subject to the buyer's right to force delivery upon tender of the price. The rights acquired by the financing agency are similarly limited and, moreover, if the agency fails to procure any outstanding negotiable document of title, it may find its exercise of these rights hampered or even defeated by the seller's disposition of the document to a third party. This section does not attempt to create any new rights in the financing agency against the carrier which would force the latter to honor a stop order from the agency, a stranger to the shipment, or any new rights against a holder to whom a document of title has been duly negotiated under Article 7.

Cross References:

Point 1: Section 2–104(2) and Article 4.
Point 2: Part 5 of Article 4, and Article 5.
Point 4: Sections 2–501 and 2–502(1) and Article 7.

Definitional Cross References:

"Buyer". Section 2–103.
"Document of title". Section 1–201.
"Draft". Section 3–104.
"Financing agency". Section 2–104.
"Good faith". Section 2–103.
"Goods". Section 2–105.
"Honor". Section 1–201.
"Purchase". Section 1–201.
"Rights". Section 1–201.
"Value". Section 1–201.

Section 2–507. Effect of Seller's Tender; Delivery on Condition.

(1) Tender of delivery is a condition to the buyer's duty to accept the goods and, unless otherwise agreed, to his duty to pay for them. Tender entitles the seller to acceptance of the goods and to payment according to the contract.

(2) Where payment is due and demanded on the delivery to the buyer of goods or documents of title, his right as against the seller to retain or dispose of them is conditional upon his making the payment due.

New York Annotations

This section conforms to the principles established in existing law. As to tender, see §§ 123 and 124 of the Personal Property Law, and British Aluminum Co., Ltd. v. Trefts, 163 App.Div. 184, 148 N.Y.S. 144 (1914). As to the phrases "unless otherwise agreed," and "according to the terms of the contract," see Personal Property Law, §§ 90, 122, and 150.

Official Uniform Comment

Prior Uniform Statutory Provision: See Sections 11, 41, 42 and 69, Uniform Sales Act.

Purposes:

1. Subsection (1) continues the policies of the prior uniform statutory provisions with respect to tender and delivery by the seller. Under this Article the same rules in these matters are applied to present sales and to contracts for sale. But the provisions of this subsection must be read within the framework of the other sections of this Article which bear upon the question of delivery and payment.

2. The "unless otherwise agreed" provision of subsection (1) is directed primarily to cases in which payment in advance has been promised or a letter of credit term has been included. Payment "according to the contract" contemplates immediate payment, payment at the end of an agreed credit term, payment by a time acceptance or the like. Under this Act, "contract" means the total obligation in law which results from the parties' agreement including the effect of this Article. In this context, therefore, there must be considered the effect in law of such provisions as those on means and manner of payment and on failure of agreed means and manner of payment.

3. Subsection (2) deals with the effect of a conditional delivery by the seller and in such a situation makes the buyer's "right as against the seller" conditional upon payment. These words are used as words in limitation to conform with the policy set forth in the bona fide purchase sections of this Article. Should the seller after making such a conditional delivery fail to follow up his rights, the condition is waived. The provision of this Article for a ten day limit within which the seller may reclaim goods delivered on credit to an insolvent buyer is also applicable here.

Cross References:

Point 1: Sections 2–310, 2–503, 2–511, 2–601 and 2–711 to 2–713.
Point 2: Sections 1–201, 2–511 and 2–614.
Point 3: Sections 2–401, 2–403, and 2–702(1)(b).

Definitional Cross References:

"Buyer". Section 2–103.
"Contract". Section 1–201.
"Delivery". Section 1–201.
"Document of title". Section 1–201.
"Goods". Section 2–105.
"Rights". Section 1–201.
"Seller". Section 2–103.

Section 2–508. Cure by Seller of Improper Tender or Delivery; Replacement.

(1) Where any tender or delivery by the seller is rejected because non-conforming and the time for performance has not yet expired, the seller may seasonably notify the buyer of his intention to cure and may then within the contract time make a conforming delivery.

(2) Where the buyer rejects a non-conforming tender which the seller had reasonable grounds to believe would be acceptable with or without money allowance the seller may if he seasonably notifies the buyer have a further reasonable time to substitute a conforming tender.

New York Annotations

No similar statutory rule exists in the present New York Law.

UCC

(1) A power to cure within contract period as specified in subsection (1) is consistent with present case law. Lowinson v. Newman, 201 App.Div. 266, 194 N.Y.S. 253 (1922).

(2) Some New York cases allow the seller to cure even after the time of performance in the light of buyer's postponement of delivery or prior oral agreement permitting such replacement. Mutual Chemical Co. of America v. Marden, Orth & Hastings Co., Inc., 235 N.Y. 145, 139 N.E. 221 (1923); Van Iderstine Co., Inc. v. Barnet Leather Co., Inc., 242 N.Y. 425, 152 N.E. 250 (1926). See also Restatement, Contracts, § 276.

Official Uniform Comment

Prior Uniform Statutory Provision: None.

Purposes:

1. Subsection (1) permits a seller who has made a non-confirming tender in any case to make a conforming delivery within the contract time upon seasonable notification to the buyer. It applies even where the seller has taken back the non-conforming goods and refunded the purchase price. He may still make a good tender within the contract period. The closer, however, it is to the contract date, the greater is the necessity for extreme promptness on the seller's part in notifying of his intention to cure, if such notification is to be "seasonable" under this subsection.

The rule of this subsection moreover, is qualified by its underlying reasons. Thus if, after contracting for June delivery, a buyer later makes known to the seller his need for shipment early in the month and the seller ships accordingly, the "contract time" has been cut down by the supervening modification and the time for cure of tender must be referred to this modified time term.

2. Subsection (2) seeks to avoid injustice to the seller by reason of a surprise rejection by the buyer. However, the seller is not protected unless he had "reasonable grounds to believe" that the tender would be acceptable. Such reasonable grounds can lie in prior course of dealing, course of performance or usage of trade as well as in the particular circumstances surrounding the making of the contract. The seller is charged with commercial knowledge of any factors in a particular sales situation which require him to comply strictly with his obligations under the contract as, for example, strict conformity of documents in an overseas shipment or the sale of precision parts or chemicals for use in manufacture. Further, if the buyer gives notice either implicitly, as by a prior course of dealing involving rigorous inspections, or expressly, as by the deliberate inclusion of a "no replacement" clause in the contract, the seller is to be held to rigid compliance. If the clause appears in a "form" contract evidence that it is out of line with trade usage or the prior course of dealing and was not called to the seller's attention may be sufficient to show that the seller had reasonable grounds to believe that the tender would be acceptable.

3. The words "a further reasonable time to substitute a conforming tender" are intended as words of limitation to protect the buyer. What is a "reasonable time" depends upon the attending circumstances. Compare Section 2–511 on the comparable case of a seller's surprise demand for legal tender.

4. Existing trade usages permitting variations without rejection but with price allowance enter into the agreement itself as contractual limitations of remedy and are not covered by this section.

Cross References:

Point 2: Section 2–302.
Point 3: Section 2–511.
Point 4: Sections 1–205 and 2–721.

Definitional Cross References:

"Buyer". Section 2–103.
"Conforming". Section 2–106.
"Contract". Section 1–201.
"Money". Section 1–201.
"Notifies". Section 1–201.
"Reasonable time". Section 1–204.
"Seasonably". Section 1–204.
"Seller". Section 2–103.

Section 2–509. Risk of Loss in the Absence of Breach.

(1) Where the contract requires or authorizes the seller to ship the goods by carrier

(a) if it does not require him to deliver them at a particular destination, the risk of loss passes to the buyer when the goods are duly delivered to the carrier even though the shipment is under reservation (Section 2–505); but

(b) if it does require him to deliver them at a particular destination and the goods are there duly tendered while in the possession of the carrier, the risk of loss passes to the buyer when the goods are there duly so tendered as to enable the buyer to take delivery.

(2) Where the goods are held by a bailee to be delivered without being moved, the risk of loss passes to the buyer

(a) on his receipt of a negotiable document of title covering the goods; or

(b) on acknowledgment by the bailee of the buyer's right to possession of the goods; or

(c) after his receipt of a non-negotiable document of title or other written direction to deliver, as provided in subsection (4)(b) of Section 2–503.

(3) In any case not within subsection (1) or (2), the risk of loss passes to the buyer on his receipt of the goods if the seller is a merchant; otherwise the risk passes to thc buyer on tender of delivery.

(4) The provisions of this section are subject to contrary agreement of the parties and to the provisions of this Article on sale on approval (Section 2–327) and on effect of breach on risk of loss (Section 2–510).

New York Annotations

Where existing law gears its general provisions concerning risk of loss to the passage of property (Personal Property Law, §§ 100 and 103), the Code tests risk of loss allocation by reference to objective facts such as delivery to the carrier, tender and receipt of the goods. The results are not radically changed, however. The rule of subsection (1)(a), transferring risk to the buyer under a shipment contract on delivery to a carrier, corresponds to Personal Property Law, § 100, Rules 4(2) and (5), read together with § 103, e.g., Badhwar v. Colorado Fuel & Iron Corp., 138 F.Supp. 595, aff'd, 245 F.2d 903 (2d Cir. 1957). Note, however, that the Code rejects the notion that the seller's payment of freight charges creates a destination contract. Section 2–503 and Comment 5.

Subsection (1)(b) conforms to Personal Property Law, § 100, Rule 5.

Subsection (2) conforms to Section 2–503(4) on tender of delivery.

Subsection (3) alters existing law as expressed in Personal Property Law, § 100, Rules 1 and 4 (1). Risk here is transferred only on actual receipt by the buyer where the seller is a merchant, and on tender of delivery in other cases. See Section 2–104(1) for the definition of "merchant."

Historical Note: In response to criticism by the Law Revision Commission, the section was revised for clarification. Subsection (1) was revised to make clear that it does not apply to "shipment" in the seller's own trucks, and to eliminate the post-amble regarding risk of loss in documentary transaction which had produced misunderstanding. Subsection (2) was inserted to spell out the rules governing risk of loss in cases covered by Section 2–503 (4). Former subsection (2) and (3) were renumbered (3) and (4), and a cross-reference to the following section was inserted in (4). (1956 Recommendations, p. 59; Excerpts, p. 386.)

Official Uniform Comment

Prior Uniform Statutory Provision: Section 22, Uniform Sales Act.

Changes: Rewritten, subsection (3) of this section modifying prior law.

Purposes of Changes: To make it clear that:

1. The underlying theory of these sections on risk of loss is the adoption of the contractual approach rather than an arbitrary shifting of the risk with the "property" in the goods. The scope of the present section, therefore, is limited strictly to those cases where there has been no breach by the seller. Where for any reason his delivery or tender fails to conform to the contract, the present section does not apply and the situation is governed by the provisions on effect of breach on risk of loss.

2. The provisions of subsection (1) apply where the contract "requires or authorizes" shipment of the goods. This language is intended to be construed parallel to comparable language in the section on shipment by seller. In order that the goods be "duly delivered to the carrier" under paragraph (a) a contract must be entered into with the carrier which will satisfy the requirements of the section on shipment by the seller and the delivery must be made under circumstances which will enable the seller to take any further steps necessary to a due tender. The underlying reason for this subsection does not require that the shipment be made after contracting, but where, for example, the seller buys the goods afloat and later diverts the shipment to the buyer, he must identify the goods to the contract before the risk of loss can pass. To transfer the risk it is enough that a proper shipment and a proper identification come to apply to the same goods although, aside from special agreement, the risk will not pass retroactively to the time of shipment in such a case.

3. Whether the contract involves delivery at the seller's place of business or at the situs of the goods, a merchant seller cannot transfer risk of loss and it remains upon him until actual receipt by the buyer, even though full payment has been made and the buyer has been notified that the goods are at his disposal. Protection is afforded him, in the event of breach by the buyer, under the next section.

The underlying theory of this rule is that a merchant who is to make physical delivery at his own place continues meanwhile to control the goods and can be expected to insure his interest in them. The buyer, on the other hand, has no control of the goods and it is extremely unlikely that he will carry insurance on goods not yet in his possession.

4. Where the agreement provides for delivery of the goods as between the buyer and seller without removal from the physical possession of a bailee, the provisions on manner of tender of delivery apply on the point of transfer of risk. Due delivery

of a negotiable document of title covering the goods or acknowledgment by the bailee that he holds for the buyer completes the "delivery" and passes the risk.

5. The provisions of this section are made subject by subsection (4) to the "contrary agreement" of the parties. This language is intended as the equivalent of the phrase "unless otherwise agreed" used more frequently throughout this Act. "Contrary" is in no way used as a word of limitation and the buyer and seller are left free to readjust their rights and risks as declared by this section in any manner agreeable to them. Contrary agreement can also be found in the circumstances of the case, a trade usage or practice, or a course of dealing or performance.

Cross References:

Point 1: Section 2–510(1).
Point 2: Sections 2–503 and 2–504.
Point 3: Sections 2–104, 2–503 and 2–510.
Point 4: Section 2–503(4).
Point 5: Section 1–201.

Definitional Cross References:

"Agreement". Section 1–201.
"Buyer". Section 2–103.
"Contract". Section 1–201.
"Delivery". Section 1–201.
"Document of title". Section 1–201.
"Goods". Section 2–105.
"Merchant". Section 2–104.
"Party". Section 1–201.
"Receipt" of goods. Section 2–103.
"Sale on approval". Section 2–326.
"Seller". Section 2–103.

Section 2–510. Effect of Breach on Risk of Loss.

(1) Where a tender or delivery of goods so fails to conform to the contract as to give a right of rejection the risk of their loss remains on the seller until cure of acceptance.

(2) Where the buyer rightfully revokes acceptance he may to the extent of any deficiency in his effective insurance coverage treat the risk of loss as having rested on the seller from the beginning.

(3) Where the buyer as to conforming goods already identified to the contract for sale repudiates or is otherwise in breach before risk of their loss has passed to him, the seller may to the extent of any deficiency in his effective insurance coverage treat the risk of loss as resting on the buyer for a commercially reasonable time.

New York Annotations

Subsection (1) is new to the statutes, but probably conforms to the present law. Under Personal Property Law, § 100, Rule 4(2), property to unascertained or future goods passes by appropriation by delivery to a carrier "in pursuance of a contract to sell." The Code rule is also comparable to Rule 4(1) of § 100 of the Personal

Property Law, since title is there said to remain in the seller until he puts the goods in a deliverable state. Compare Triway Co. v. Teper, 194 Misc. 996, 88 N.Y.S.2d 50 (1949), and Karash v. Klein, 118 Misc. 751, 194 N.Y.S.611 (1922).

Subsections (2) and (3) are new, particularly as to the effect given to insurance. Otherwise the provision governing risk upon revocation of acceptance is similar to the placing of risk on the seller after rescission by the buyer in the present law. Personal Property Law, § 150(5). Further compare Personal Property Law, § 103(b) (risk of loss for delay in delivery).

Historical Note: In response to criticism by the Law Revision Commission, the section was revised for clarification. The changes limit subsection (1) to cases where the breach is such as to give a right of rejection, conform subsection (2) to Section 2–608, and limit the buyers' risk under subsection (3) to a "commercially reasonable time" so that the aggrieved seller cannot hold the goods indefinitely at the buyer's risk. On the last point, compare Sections 1–203, 2–610, 2–704, and 2–706. (1956 Recommendations, p. 60; Excerpts, p. 387).

Official Uniform Comment

Prior Uniform Statutory Provision: None.

Purposes: To make clear that:

1. Under subsection (1) the seller by his individual action cannot shift the risk of loss to the buyer unless his action conforms with all the conditions resting on him under the contract.

2. The "cure" of defective tenders contemplated by subsection (1) applies only to those situations in which the seller makes changes in goods already tendered, such as repair, partial substitution, sorting out from an improper mixture and the like since "cure" by repossession and new tender has no effect on the risk of loss of the goods originally tendered. The seller's privilege of cure does not shift the risk, however, until the cure is completed.

Where defective documents are involved a cure of the defect by the seller or a waiver of the defects by the buyer will operate to shift the risk under this section. However, if the goods have been destroyed prior to the cure or the buyer is unaware of their destruction at the time he waives the defect in the documents, the risk of the loss must still be borne by the seller, for the risk shifts only at the time of cure, waiver of documentary defects or acceptance of the goods.

3. In cases where there has been a breach of the contract, if the one in control of the goods is the aggrieved party, whatever loss or damage may prove to be uncovered by his insurance falls upon the contract breaker under subsections (2) and (3) rather than upon him. The word "effective" as applied to insurance coverage in those subsections is used to meet the case of supervening insolvency of the insurer. The "deficiency" referred to in the text means such deficiency in the insurance coverage as exists without subrogation. This section merely distributes the risk of loss as stated and is not intended to be disturbed by any subrogation of an insurer.

Cross Reference:

Section 2–509.

Definitional Cross References:

"Buyer". Section 2–103.
"Conform". Section 2–106.
"Contract for sale". Section 2–106.
"Goods". Section 2–105.
"Seller". Section 2–103.

Section 2–511. Tender of Payment by Buyer; Payment by Check.

(1) Unless otherwise agreed tender of payment is a condition to the seller's duty to tender and complete any delivery.

(2) Tender of payment is sufficient when made by any means or in any manner current in the ordinary course of business unless the seller demands payment in legal tender and gives any extension of time reasonably necessary to procure it.

(3) Subject to the provisions of this Act on the effect of an instrument on an obligation (Section 3–802), payment by check is conditional and is defeated as between the parties by dishonor of the check on due presentment.

New York Annotations

(1) Subsection (1) follows the presumption of present law that payment and tender of delivery are concurrent conditions. Personal Property Law, § 123.

(2) Subsection (2) is new to the statutes, but seems to be in accord with New York case law. Bass v. White, 65 N.Y. 565 (1875); Manners & Co., Inc. v. Hirshenhorn & Sons, 280 App. Div. 711, 116 N.Y.S.2d 532 (1952).

(3) Subsection (3), making payment by check conditional as between the parties, is also new to the statutes. More complete treatment of this question is afforded in Section 3–802. For the rights of subsequent purchasers see Section 2–403(1).

Historical Note: The "subject to" clause was inserted in subsection (3) to meet the suggestion of the Law Revision Commission that Section 3–802 provided a different rule in some cases of payment by an instrument such as a cashier's check. (1956 Recommendations, p. 60; Excerpts, p. 387.)

Official Uniform Comment

Prior Uniform Statutory Provision: Section 42, Uniform Sales Act.

Changes: Rewritten by this section and Section 2–507.

Purposes of Changes:

1. The requirement of payment against delivery in subsection (1) is applicable to non-commercial sales generally and to ordinary sales at retail although it has no application to the great body of commercial contracts which carry credit terms. Subsection (1) applies also to documentary contracts in general and to contracts which look to shipment by the seller but contain no term on time and manner of payment, in which situations the payment may, in proper case, be demanded against delivery of appropriate documents.

In the case of specific transactions such as C.O.D. sales or agreements providing for payment against documents, the provisions of this subsection must be considered in conjunction with the special sections of the Article dealing with such terms. The provision that tender of payment is a condition to the seller's duty to tender and complete "any delivery" integrates this section with the language and policy of the section on delivery in several lots which call for separate payment. Finally, attention should be directed to the provision on right to adequate assurance of performance which recognizes, even before the time for tender, an obligation on the buyer not to impair the seller's expectation of receiving payment in due course.

2. Unless there is agreement otherwise the concurrence of the conditions as to tender of payment and tender of delivery requires their performance at a single place or

time. This Article determines that place and time by determining in various other sections the place and time for tender of delivery under various circumstances and in particular types of transactions. The sections dealing with time and place of delivery together with the section on right to inspection of goods answer the subsidiary question as to when payment may be demanded before inspection by the buyer.

3. The essence of the principle involved in subsection (2) is avoidance of commercial surprise at the time of performance. The section on substituted performance covers the peculiar case in which legal tender is not available to the commercial community.

4. Subsection (3) is concerned with the rights and obligations as between the parties to a sales transaction when payment is made by check. This Article recognizes that the taking of a seemingly solvent party's check is commercially normal and proper and, if due diligence is exercised in collection, is not to be penalized in any way. The conditional character of the payment under this section refers only to the effect of the transaction "as between the parties" thereto and does not purport to cut into the law of "absolute" and "conditional" payment as applied to such other problems as the discharge of sureties or the responsibilities of a drawee bank which is at the same time an agent for collection.

The phrase "by check" includes not only the buyer's own but any check which does not effect a discharge under Article 3 (Section 3–802). Similarly the reason of this subsection should apply and the same result should be reached where the buyer "pays" by sight draft on a commercial firm which is financing him.

5. Under subsection (3) payment by check is defeated if it is not honored upon due presentment. This corresponds to the provisions of article on Commercial Paper. (Section 3–802). But if the seller procures certification of the check instead of cashing it, the buyer is discharged. (Section 3–411).

6. Where the instrument offered by the buyer is not a payment but a credit instrument such as a note or a check postdated by even one day, the seller's acceptance of the instrument insofar as third parties are concerned, amounts to a delivery on credit and his remedies are set forth in the section on buyer's insolvency. As between the buyer and the seller, however, the matter turns on the present subsection and the section on conditional delivery and subsequent dishonor of the instrument gives the seller rights on it as well as for breach of the contract for sale.

Cross References:

Point 1: Sections 2–307, 2–310, 2–320, 2–325, 2–503, 2–513 and 2–609.
Point 2: Sections 2–307, 2–310, 2–319, 2–322, 2–503, 2–504 and 2–513.
Point 3: Section 2–614.
Point 5: Article 3, esp. Sections 3–802 and 3–411.
Point 6: Sections 2–507, 2–702, and Article 3.

Definitional Cross References:

"Buyer". Section 2–103.
"Check". Section 3–104.
"Dishonor". Section 3–508.
"Party". Section 1–201.
"Reasonable time". Section 1–204.
"Seller". Section 2–103.

Section 2–512. Payment by Buyer Before Inspection.

(1) Where the contract requires payment before inspection nonconformity of the goods does not excuse the buyer from so making payment unless

(a) the non-conformity appears without inspection; or

(b) despite tender of the required documents the circumstances would justify injunction against honor under this Code (Section 5–109(b)).

(2) Payment pursuant to subsection (1) does not constitute an acceptance of goods or impair the buyer's right to inspect or any of his remedies.

Amended by Laws 2000, Ch. 471, eff. Nov. 1, 2000.

New York Annotations

(1) There is no present counterpart to the provision requiring the buyer to pay the price before inspection where the contract requires such payment.

(2) The preservation of the buyer's rights and remedies in spite of payment before inspection is consistent with the policy of Personal Property Law, § 130.

Official Uniform Comment

Prior Uniform Statutory Provision: None, but see Sections 47 and 49, Uniform Sales Act.

Purposes:

1. Subsection (1) of the present section recognizes that the essence of a contract providing for payment before inspection is the intention of the parties to shift to the buyer the risks which would usually rest upon the seller. The basic nature of the transaction is thus preserved and the buyer is in most cases required to pay first and litigate as to any defects later.

2. "Inspection" under this section is an inspection in a manner reasonable for detecting defects in goods whose surface appearance is satisfactory.

3. Clause (a) of this subsection states an exception to the general rule based on common sense and normal commercial practice. The apparent nonconformity referred to is one which is evident in the mere process of taking delivery.

4. Clause (b) is concerned with contracts for payment against documents and incorporates the general clarification and modification of the case law contained in the section on excuse of a financing agency. Section 5–114.

5. Subsection (2) makes explicit the general policy of the Uniform Sales Act that the payment required before inspection in no way impairs the buyer's remedies or rights in the event of a default by the seller. The remedies preserved to the buyer are all of his remedies, which include as a matter of reason the remedy for total non-delivery after payment in advance.

The provision on performance or acceptance under reservation of rights does not apply to the situations contemplated here in which payment is made in due course under the contract and the buyer need not pay "under protest" or the like in order to preserve his rights as to defects discovered upon inspection.

6. This section applies to cases in which the contract requires payment before inspection either by the express agreement of the parties or by reason of the effect in law of that contract. The present section must therefore be considered in conjunction with the provision on right to inspection of goods which sets forth the instances in which the buyer is not entitled to inspection before payment.

Cross References:

Point 4: Article 5.

Point 5: Section 1–207.
Point 6: Section 2–513(3).

Definitional Cross References:

"Buyer". Section 2–103.
"Conform". Section 2–106.
"Contract". Section 1–201.
"Financing agency". Section 2–104.
"Goods". Section 2–105.
"Remedy". Section 1–201.
"Rights". Section 1–201.

Section 2–513. Buyer's Right to Inspection of Goods.

(1) Unless otherwise agreed and subject to subsection (3), where goods are tendered or delivered or identified to the contract for sale, the buyer has a right before payment or acceptance to inspect them at any reasonable place and time and in any reasonable manner. When the seller is required or authorized to send the goods to the buyer, the inspection may be after their arrival.

(2) Expenses of inspection must be borne by the buyer but may be recovered from the seller if the goods do not conform and are rejected.

(3) Unless otherwise agreed and subject to the provisions of this Article on C.I.F. contracts (subsection (3) of Section 2–321), the buyer is not entitled to inspect the goods before payment of the price when the contract provides

(a) for delivery "C.O.D." or on other like terms; or

(b) for payment against documents of title, except where such payment is due only after the goods are to become available for inspection.

(4) A place or method of inspection fixed by the parties is presumed to be exclusive but unless otherwise expressly agreed it does not postpone identification or shift the place for delivery or for passing the risk of loss. If compliance becomes impossible, inspection shall be as provided in this section unless the place or method fixed was clearly intended as an indispensable condition failure of which avoids the contract.

New York Annotations

Subsections (1) and (3) follow the law set forth in Personal Property Law, § 128(2) and (3). Inspection at destination is clearly authorized as in the New York cases, e.g., Deveso v. Chandler, 210 App. Div. 684, 206 N.Y.S. 604, aff'd 241 N.Y. 559, 150 N.E. 554 (1924).

Subsection (2) is new.

Subsection (4) is new.

Historical Note: Subsection (1) was revised at the suggestion of the Law Revision Commission by deleting the limitation of the right of inspection to cases "where the buyer has not previously examined the goods". Thus the buyer may be entitled to a second inspection where "reasonable" to identify the goods or to discover change of condition during shipment. Other changes were for clarification. (1956 Recommendations, p. 62; Excerpts, p. 387.)

Official Uniform Comment

Prior Uniform Statutory Provision: Section 47(2), (3), Uniform Sales Act.

Changes: Rewritten, Subsections (2) and (3) being new.

Purposes of Changes and New Matter: To correspond in substance with the prior uniform statutory provision and to incorporate in addition some of the results of the better case law so that:

1. The buyer is entitled to inspect goods as provided in subsection (1) unless it has been otherwise agreed by the parties. The phrase "unless otherwise agreed" is intended principally to cover such situations as those outlined in subsections (3) and (4) and those in which the agreement of the parties negates inspection before tender of delivery. However, no agreement by the parties can displace the entire right of inspection except where the contract is simply for the sale of "this thing." Even in a sale of boxed goods "as is" inspection is a right of the buyer, since if the boxes prove to contain some other merchandise altogether the price can be recovered back; nor do the limitations of the provision on effect of acceptance apply in such a case.

2. The buyer's right of inspection is available to him upon tender, delivery or appropriation of the goods with notice to him. Since inspection is available to him on tender, where payment is due against delivery he may, unless otherwise agreed, make his inspection before payment of the price. It is also available to him after receipt of the goods and so may be postponed after receipt for a reasonable time. Failure to inspect before payment does not impair the right to inspect after receipt of the goods unless the case falls within subsection (4) on agreed and exclusive inspection provisions. The right to inspect goods which have been appropriated with notice to the buyer holds whether or not the sale was by sample.

3. The buyer may exercise his right of inspection at any reasonable time or place and in any reasonable manner. It is not necessary that he select the most appropriate time, place or manner to inspect or that his selection be the customary one in the trade or locality. Any reasonable time, place or manner is available to him and the reasonableness will be determined by trade usages, past practices between the parties and the other circumstances of the case.

The last sentence of subsection (1) makes it clear that the place of arrival of shipped goods is a reasonable place for their inspection.

4. Expenses of an inspection made to satisfy the buyer of the seller's performance must be assumed by the buyer in the first instance. Since the rule provides merely for an allocation of expense there is no policy to prevent the parties from providing otherwise in the agreement. Where the buyer would normally bear the expenses of the inspection but the goods are rightly rejected because of what the inspection reveals, demonstrable and reasonable costs of the inspection are part of his incidental damage caused by the seller's breach.

5. In the case of payment against documents, subsection (3) requires payment before inspection, since shipping documents against which payment is to be made will commonly arrive and be tendered while the goods are still in transit. This Article recognizes no exception in any peculiar case in which the goods happen to arrive before the documents. However, where by the agreement payment is to await the arrival of the goods, inspection before payment becomes proper since the goods are then "available for inspection."

Where by the agreement the documents are to be held until arrival the buyer is entitled to inspect before payment since the goods are then "available for inspection." Proof of usage is not necessary to establish this right, but if inspection before payment is disputed the contrary must be established by usage or by an explicit contract term to that effect.

For the same reason, that the goods are available for inspection, a term calling for payment against storage documents or a delivery order does not normally bar the buyer's right to inspection before payment under subsection (3)(b). This result is reinforced by the buyer's right under subsection (1) to inspect goods which have been appropriated with notice to him.

6. Under subsection (4) an agreed place or method in inspection is generally held to be intended as exclusive. However, where compliance with such an agreed inspection term becomes impossible, the question is basically one of intention. If the parties clearly intend that the method of inspection named is to be a necessary condition without which the entire deal is to fail, the contract is at an end if that method becomes impossible. On the other hand, if the parties merely seek to indicate a convenient and reliable method but do not intend to give up the deal in the event of its failure, any reasonable method of inspection may be substituted under this Article.

Since the purpose of an agreed place of inspection is only to make sure at that point whether or not the goods will be thrown back, the "exclusive" feature of the named place is satisfied under this Article if the buyer's failure to inspect there is held to be an acceptance with the knowledge of such defects as inspection would have revealed within the section on waiver of buyer's objections by failure to particularize. Revocation of the acceptance is limited to the situations stated in the section pertaining to that subject. The reasonable time within which to give notice of defects within the section on notice of breach begins to run from the point of the "acceptance."

7. Clauses on time of inspection are commonly clauses which limit the time in which the buyer must inspect and give notice of defects. Such clauses are therefore governed by the section of this Article which requires that such a time limitation must be reasonable.

8. Inspection under this Article is not to be regarded as a "condition precedent to the passing of title" so that risk until inspection remains on the seller. Under subsection (4) such an approach cannot be sustained. Issues between the buyer and seller are settled in this Article almost wholly by special provisions and not by the technical determination of the locus of the title. Thus "inspection as a condition to the passing of title" becomes a concept almost without meaning. However, in peculiar circumstances inspection may still have some of the consequences hitherto sought and obtained under that concept.

9. "Inspection" under this section has to do with the buyer's check-up on whether the seller's performance is in accordance with a contract previously made and is not to be confused with the "examination" of the goods or of a sample or model of them at the time of contracting which may affect the warranties involved in the contract.

Cross References:

Generally: Sections 2–310 (b), 2–321(3) and 2–606(1)(b).
Point 1: Section 2–607.
Point 2: Sections 2–501 and 2–502.
Point 4: Section 2–715.
Point 5: Section 2–321(3).
Point 6: Sections 2–606 to 2–608.
Point 7: Section 1–204.
Point 8: Comment to Section 2–401.
Point 9: Section 2–316(3)(b).

Definitional Cross References:

"Buyer". Section 2–103.
"Conform". Section 2–106.
"Contract". Section 1–201.

"Contract for sale". Section 2–106.
"Document of title". Section 1–201.
"Goods". Section 2–105.
"Party". Section 1–201.
"Presumed". Section 1–201.
"Reasonable time". Section 1–204.
"Rights". Section 1–201.
"Seller". Section 2–103.
"Send". Section 1–201.
"Term". Section 1–201.

Section 2–514. When Documents Deliverable on Acceptance; When on Payment.

Unless otherwise agreed documents against which a draft is drawn are to be delivered to the drawee on acceptance of the draft if it is payable more than three days after presentment; otherwise, only on payment.

New York Annotations

This section is derived from the Uniform Bills of Lading Act, Sec. 41 (Personal Property Law, § 227), but is broader in scope since is covers any "document" regardless of its form. See Sections 1–503 and 5–112.

Official Uniform Comment

Prior Uniform Statutory Provision: Section 41, Uniform Bills of Lading Act.

Changes: Rewritten.

Purposes of Changes: To make the provision one of general application so that:

1. It covers any document against which a draft may be drawn, whatever may be the form of the document, and applies to interpret the action of a seller or consignor insofar as it may affect the rights and duties of any buyer, consigned or financing agency concerned with the paper. Supplementary or corresponding provisions are found in Sections 4–503 and 5–112.

2. An "arrival" draft is a sight draft within the purpose of this section.

Cross References:

Point 1: See Sections 2–502, 2–505(2), 2–507(2), 2–512, 2–513, 2–607 concerning protection of rights of buyer and seller, and 4–503 and 5–112 on delivery of documents.

Definitional Cross References:

"Delivery". Section 1–201.
"Draft". Section 3–104.

Section 2–515. Preserving Evidence of Goods in Dispute.

In furtherance of the adjustment of any claim or dispute

(a) either party on reasonable notification to the other and for the purpose of ascertaining the facts and preserving evidence has the right to inspect, test and sample the goods including such of them as may be in the possession or control of the other; and

(b) the parties may agree to a third party inspection or survey to determine the conformity or condition of the goods and may agree that the findings shall be binding upon them in any subsequent litigation or adjustment.

New York Annotations

This section is new to sales law, but paragraph (b) conforms to the policy favorable toward the settlement of disputes by arbitrators. See Civil Practice Act, § 1448 et seq. [now CPLR § 7501 et seq.]

Official Uniform Comment

Prior Uniform Statutory Provision: None.

Purposes:

1. To meet certain serious problems which arise when there is a dispute as to the quality of the goods and thereby perhaps to aid the parties in reaching a settlement, and to further the use of devices which will promote certainty as to the condition of the goods, or at least aid in preserving evidence of their condition.

2. Under paragraph (a), to afford either party an opportunity for preserving evidence, whether or not agreement has been reached, and thereby to reduce uncertainty in any litigation and, in turn perhaps, to promote agreement.

Paragraph (a) does not conflict with the provisions on the seller's right to resell rejected goods or the buyer's similar right. Apparent conflict between these provisions which will be suggested in certain circumstances is to be resolved by requiring prompt action by the parties. Nor does paragraph (a) impair the effect of a term for payment before inspection. Short of such defects as amount to fraud or substantial failure of consideration, nonconformity is neither an excuse nor a defense to an action for non-acceptance of documents. Normally, therefore, until the buyer has made payment, inspected and rejected the goods, there is no occasion or use for the rights under paragraph (a).

3. Under paragraph (b), to provide for third party inspection upon the agreement of the parties, thereby opening the door to amicable adjustment based upon the findings of such third parties.

The use of the phrase "conformity or condition" makes it clear that the parties' agreement may range from a complete settlement of all aspects of the dispute by a third party to the use of a third party merely to determine and record the condition of the goods so that they can be resold or used to reduce the stake in controversy. "Conformity", at one end of the scale of possible issues, includes the whole question of interpretation of the agreement and its legal effect, the state of the goods in regard to quality and condition, whether any defects are due to factors which operate at the risk of the buyer, and the degree of non-conformity where that may be material. "Condition", at the other end of the scale, includes nothing but the degree of damage or deterioration which the goods show. Paragraph (b) is intended to reach any point in the gamut which the parties may agree upon.

The principle of the section on reservation of rights reinforces this paragraph in simplifying such adjustments as the parties wish to make in partial settlement while reserving their rights as to any further points. Paragraph (b) also suggests the use of arbitration, where desired, of any points left open, but nothing in this section is intended to repeal or amend any statute governing arbitration. Where any question arises as to the extent of the parties' agreement under the paragraph, the presumption should be that it was meant to extend only to the relation between the contract description and the goods as delivered, since that is what a craftsman in the trade would normally be expected to report upon. Finally, a written and authenticated report of inspection or tests by a third party, whether or not sampling has been practicable, is entitled to be admitted as evidence under this Act, for it is a third party document.

Cross References:

Point 2: Sections 2–513(3), 2–706 and 2–711(2) and Article 5.
Point 3: Sections 1–202 and 1–207.

Definitional Cross References:

"Conform". Section 2–106.
"Goods". Section 2–105.
"Notification". Section 1–201.
"Party". Section 1–201.

PART 6

BREACH, REPUDIATION AND EXCUSE

Section 2–601. Buyer's Rights on Improper Delivery.

Subject to the provisions of this Article on breach in installment contracts (Section 2–612) and unless otherwise agreed under the sections on contractual limitations of remedy (Sections 2–718 and 2–719), if the goods or the tender of delivery fail in any respect to conform to the contract, the buyer may

(a) reject the whole; or

(b) accept the whole; or

(c) accept any commercial unit or units and reject the rest.

New York Annotations

(a) *Performance by seller; rejection of whole.* The general rule of subparagraph (a) allowing rejection is in accord with Personal Property Law, § 150(1)(c). The right of rejection is, however, limited in other sections of the Code. See, e.g., Sections 2–508 (cure) and 2–612 (installment contracts). The Code abandons the distinction between "rejection" and "recission" under Personal Property Law, § 150(1)(c) and (d), and the limitation of rejection to cases where "the property therein has not passed." Roughly comparable to "recission" under the present law is revocation of acceptance under Section 2–608.

(b) *Acceptance. Accord:* Personal Property Law, §§ 150(1)(a), (b), and 130.

(c) *Partial acceptance.* The Uniform Sales Act provides for partial acceptance only in limited situations. Personal Property Law, § 125(2) and (3). Portfolio & Co. v. Rubin, 233 N.Y. 439, 135 N.E. 439, 135 N.E. 843 (1922).

Official Uniform Comment

Prior Uniform Statutory Provision: No one general equivalent provision but numerous provisions, dealing with situations of non-conformity where buyer may accept or reject, including Sections 11, 44 and 69(1), Uniform Sales Act.

Changes: Partial acceptance in good faith is recognized and the buyer's remedies on the contract for breach of warranty and the like, where the buyer has returned the goods after transfer of title, are no longer barred.

Purposes of Changes: To make it clear that:

1. A buyer accepting a nonconforming tender is not penalized by the loss of any remedy otherwise open to him. This policy extends to cover and regulate the acceptance of a part of any lot improperly tendered in any case where the price can reasonably be apportioned. Partial acceptance is permitted whether the part of the goods accepted conforms or not. The only limitation on partial acceptance is that good faith and commercial reasonableness must be used to avoid undue impairment of the value of the remaining portion of the goods. This is the reason for the insistence on the "commercial unit" in paragraph (c). In this respect, the test is not only what unit has been the basis of contract, but whether the partial acceptance produces so materially adverse an effect on the remainder as to constitute bad faith.

2. Acceptance made with the knowledge of the other party is final. An original refusal to accept may be withdrawn by a later acceptance if the seller has indicated that he is holding the tender open. However, if the buyer attempts to accept, either in whole or in part, after his original rejection has caused the seller to arrange for other disposition of the goods, the buyer must answer for any ensuing damage since the next section provides that any exercise of ownership after rejection is wrongful as against the seller. Further, he is liable even though the seller may choose to treat his action as acceptance rather than conversion, since the damage flows from the misleading notice. Such arrangements for resale or other disposition of the goods by the seller must be viewed as within the normal contemplation of a buyer who has given notice of rejection. However, the buyer's attempts in good faith to dispose of defective goods where the seller has failed to give instructions within a reasonable time are not to be regarded as an acceptance.

Cross References:

Sections 2–602(2)(a), 2–612, 2–718 and 2–719.

Definitional Cross References:

"Buyer". Section 2–103.
"Commercial unit". Section 2–105.
"Conform". Section 2–106.
"Contract". Section 1–201.
"Goods". Section 2–105.
"Installment contract". Section 2–612.
"Rights". Section 1–201.

Section 2–602. Manner and Effect of Rightful Rejection.

(1) Rejection of goods must be within a reasonable time after their delivery or tender. It is ineffective unless the buyer seasonably notifies the seller.

(2) Subject to the provisions of the two following sections on rejected goods (Sections 2–603 and 2–604),

(a) after rejection any exercise of ownership by the buyer with respect to any commercial unit is wrongful as against the seller; and

(b) if the buyer has before rejection taken physical possession of goods in which he does not have a security interest under the provisions of this Article (subsection (3) of Section 2–711), he is under a duty after rejection to hold them with reasonable care at the seller's disposition for a time sufficient to permit the seller to remove them; but

(c) the buyer has no further obligations with regard to goods rightfully rejected.

(3) The seller's rights with respect to goods wrongfully rejected are governed by the provisions of this Article on seller's remedies in general (Section 2–703).

New York Annotations

(1) *Rejection within reasonable time; notice.* Subsection (1) is in accord with Personal Property Law, § 129, under which the buyer is deemed to have accepted if he keeps the goods an unreasonable time without notice of rejection. Compare Personal Property Law, § 150(3), cutting off a buyer's right to rescission under such circumstances.

(2)*Exercise of ownership after rejection; duty of buyer to hold with reasonable care.* The rule of subsection (2) (a) is in accord with Personal Property Law, § 129. However, subsection (2) (b) seems to impose a broader responsibility than the parallel § 131 of the Personal Property Law which provides only that "it is sufficient if he notifies the seller that he refuses to accept them." See Section 2–603. But compare Personal Property Law, § 150(3), which provides that in case of a rescission the buyer must "offer to return the goods to the seller in substantially as good condition as they were in at the time the property was transferred to the buyer."

Official Uniform Comment

Prior Uniform Statutory Provision: Section 50, Uniform Sales Act.

Changes: Rewritten.

Purposes of Changes: To make it clear that:

1. A tender or delivery of goods made pursuant to a contract of sale, even though wholly non-conforming, requires affirmative action by the buyer to avoid acceptance. Under subsection (1), therefore, the buyer is given a reasonable time to notify the seller of his rejection, but without such seasonable notification his rejection is ineffective. The sections of this Article dealing with inspection of goods must be read in connection with the buyer's reasonable time for action under this subsection. Contract provisions limiting the time for rejection fall within the rule of the section on "Time" and are effective if the time set gives the buyer a reasonable time for discovery of defects. What constitutes a due "notifying" of rejection by the buyer to the seller is defined in Section 1–201.

2. Subsection (2) lays down the normal duties of the buyer upon rejection, which flow from the relationship of the parties. Beyond his duty to hold the goods with reasonable care for the buyer's [seller's] disposition, this section continues the policy of prior uniform legislation in generally relieving the buyer from any duties with respect to them, except when the circumstances impose the limited obligation of salvage upon him under the next section.

3. The present section applies only to rightful rejection by the buyer. If the seller has made a tender which in all respects conforms to the contract, the buyer has a positive duty to accept and his failure to do so constitutes a "wrongful rejection" which gives the seller immediate remedies for breach. Subsection (3) is included here to emphasize the sharp distinction between the rejection of an improper tender and the non-acceptance which is a breach by the buyer.

4. The provisions of this section are to be appropriately limited or modified when a negotiation is in process.

Cross References:

Point 1: Sections 1–201, 1–204(1) and (3), 2–512(2), 2–513(1) and 2–606(1)(b).
Point 2: Section 2–603(1).
Point 3: Section 2–703.

Definitional Cross References:

"Buyer". Section 2–103.
"Commercial unit". Section 2–105.
"Goods". Section 2–105.
"Merchant". Section 2–104.
"Notifies". Section 1–201.
"Reasonable time". Section 1–204.
"Remedy". Section 1–201.
"Rights". Section 1–201.
"Seasonably". Section 1–204.
"Security interest". Section 1–201.
"Seller". Section 2–103.

Section 2–603. Merchant Buyer's Duties as to Rightfully Rejected Goods.

(1) Subject to any security interest in the buyer (subsection (3) of Section 2–711), when the seller has no agent or place of business at the market of rejection a merchant buyer is under a duty after rejection of goods in his possession or control to follow any reasonable instructions received from the seller with respect to the goods and in the absence of such instructions to make reasonable efforts to sell them for the seller's account if they are perishable or threaten to decline in value speedily. Instructions are not reasonable if on demand indemnity for expenses is not forthcoming.

(2) When the buyer sells goods under subsection (1), he is entitled to reimbursement from the seller or out of the proceeds for reasonable expenses of caring for and selling them, and if the expenses include no selling commission then to such commission as is usual in the trade or if there is none to a reasonable sum not exceeding ten per cent on the gross proceeds.

(3) In complying with this section the buyer is held only to good faith and good faith conduct hereunder is neither acceptance nor conversion nor the basis of an action for damages.

New York Annotations

(1) *Duty to follow instructions and make reasonable efforts to sell.* The Sales Act does not specifically impose any duty upon the merchant buyer who rightfully rejects. Under Personal Property Law, § 131, where the buyer rejects the goods, it is sufficient "if he notifies the seller that he refuses to accept them." On the other hand, where rescission is involved, Personal Property Law, § 150(3), requires the buyer to return or offer to return the goods but not otherwise to deal with them.

Insofar as this section imposes a duty on the merchant buyer to resell, it apparently changes existing law. It is comparable, however, to the obligation imposed by the Perishable Agricultural Commodities Act, 7 U.S.C. § 499(b) (3), as to goods shipped in interstate commerce, which makes it unlawful for any commission merchant to discard, dump, or destroy such goods without reasonable cause.

The obligation is also roughly comparable to the buyer's duty as bailee and his power of resale under Personal Property Law, §§ 150 (5) and 141. See dictum, White v. Schweitzer, 221 N.Y. 461, 117 N.E. 941 (1917).

(2) *Buyer's reimbursement for expenses.* This is new, although the buyer is entitled under present law to recover any damages resulting from a breach of warranty. Gotham Nat. Bank v. Sharood Co., 23 F.2d 567 (2d Cir. 1928). Subsection (3) immunizes the buyer who in good faith exercises the power conferred by this section.

Official Uniform Comment

Prior Uniform Statutory Provision: None.

Purposes:

1. This section recognizes the duty imposed upon the merchant buyer by good faith and commercial practice to follow any reasonable instructions of the seller as to reshipping, storing, delivery to a third party, reselling or the like. Subsection (1) goes further and extends the duty to include the making of reasonable efforts to effect a salvage sale where the value of the goods is threatened and the seller's instructions do not arrive in time to prevent serious loss.

2. The limitations on the buyer's duty to resell under this section arises from commercial necessity and thus is present only when the seller has "no agent or place of business at the market of rejection". A financing agency which is acting in behalf of the seller in handling the documents rejected by the buyer is sufficiently the seller's agent to lift the burden of salvage resale from the buyer. (See provisions of Sections 4–503 and 5–112 on bank's duties with respect to rejected documents.) The buyer's duty to resell is extended only to goods in his "possession or control", but these are intended as words of wide, rather than narrow, import. In effect, the measure of the buyer's "control" is whether he can practicably effect control without undue commercial burden.

3. The explicit provisions for reimbursement and compensation to the buyer in subsection (2) are applicable and necessary only where he is not acting under instructions from the seller. As provided in subsection (1) the seller's instructions to be "reasonable" must on demand of the buyer include indemnity for expenses.

4. Since this section makes the resale of perishable goods an affirmative duty in contrast to a mere right to sell as under the case law, subsection (3) makes it clear that the buyer is liable only for the exercise of good faith in determining whether the value of the goods is sufficiently threatened to justify a quick resale or whether he has waited a sufficient length of time for instructions, or what a reasonable means and place of resale is.

5. A buyer who fails to make a salvage sale when his duty to do so under this section has arisen is subject to damages pursuant to the section on liberal administration of remedies.

Cross References:

Point 2: Sections 4–503 and 5–112.
Point 5: Section 1–106. Compare generally section 2–706.

Definitional Cross References:

"Buyer". Section 2–103.
"Good faith". Section 1–201.
"Goods". Section 2–105.
"Merchant". Section 2–104.
"Security interest". Section 1–201.
"Seller". Section 2–103.

Section 2–604. Buyer's Options as to Salvage of Rightfully Rejected Goods.

Subject to the provisions of the immediately preceding section on perishables if the seller gives no instructions within a reasonable time after notification of rejection the buyer may store the rejected goods for the seller's account or reship them to him or resell them for the seller's account with reimbursement as provided in the preceding section. Such action is not acceptance or conversion.

New York Annotations

The Sales Act contains no comparable provision, but Personal Property Law, § 150, gives the rescinding buyer a power of resale where he has a lien to secure repayment. Under some circumstances a change may be effected since under Personal Property Law, § 129, a buyer is deemed to have accepted goods by any act in relation to the goods which is inconsistent with the ownership of the seller; see, e.g., White v. Schweitzer, 221 N.Y. 461, 117 N.E. 941 (1917) (resale). The Code provision encourages salvage by buyers who have rightfully rejected, without the danger of incurring liability for the price by acceptance.

Official Uniform Comment

Prior Uniform Statutory Provision: None.

Purposes:

The basic purpose of this section is twofold: on the one hand it aims at reducing the stake in dispute and on the other at avoiding the pinning of a technical "acceptance" on a buyer who has taken steps towards realization on or preservation of the goods in good faith. This section is essentially a salvage section and the buyer's right to act under it is conditioned upon (1) non-conformity of the goods, (2) due notification of rejection to the seller under the section on manner of rejection, and (3) the absence of any instructions from the seller which the merchant-buyer has a duty to follow under the preceding section.

This section is designed to accord all reasonable leeway to a rightfully rejecting buyer acting in good faith. The listing of what the buyer may do in the absence of instructions from the seller is intended to be not exhaustive but merely illustrative. This is not a "merchant's" section and the options are pure options given to merchant and non-merchant buyers alike. The merchant-buyer, however, may in some instances be under a duty rather than an option to resell under the provisions of the preceding section.

Cross References:

Sections 2–602(1) and 2–603(1) and 2–706.

Definitional Cross References:

"Buyer". Section 2–103.
"Notification". Section 1–201.
"Reasonable time". Section 1–204.
"Seller". Section 2–103.

Section 2–605. Waiver of Buyer's Objections by Failure to Particularize.

(1) The buyer's failure to state in connection with rejection a particular defect which is ascertainable by reasonable inspection precludes him from relying on the unstated defect to justify rejection or to establish breach

(a) where the seller could have cured it if stated seasonably; or

(b) between merchants when the seller has after rejection made a request in writing for a full and final written statement of all defects on which the buyer proposes to rely.

(2) Payment against documents made without reservation of rights precludes recovery of the payment for defects apparent on the face of the documents.

New York Annotations

(1) *Failure to state particular defect in connection with rejection.* The Sales Act has no such provision, but a similar rule is recognized as a matter of contract law at least in those cases where the buyer specifies some grounds and then seeks to rely on others. See, Restatement, Contract, § 304 and New York Annotations. Compare Personal Property Law, § 130, dealing with cases other than rejection and requiring notice to the seller of the breach of warranty. The provision in subsection (1) (b) for a written statement upon request by the seller in a transaction "between merchants" is new.

(2) *Payment against documents:* This subsection seems to establish waiver as a matter of law as to defects apparent on the face of the documents. Compare Personal Property Law, § 150(3), denying recission after acceptance of the goods with knowledge of a defect.

Official Uniform Comment

Prior Uniform Statutory Provision: None.

Purposes:

1. The present section rests upon a policy of permitting the buyer to give a quick and informal notice of defects in a tender without penalizing him for omissions in

his statement, while at the same time protecting a seller who is reasonably misled by the buyer's failure to state curable defects.

2. Where the defect in a tender is one which could have been cured by the seller, a buyer who merely rejects the delivery without stating his objections to it is probably acting in commercial bad faith and seeking to get out of a deal which has become unprofitable. Subsection (1)(a), following the general policy of this Article which looks to preserving the deal wherever possible, therefore insists that the seller's right to correct his tender in such circumstances be protected.

3. When the time for cure is past, subsection (1)(b) makes it plain that a seller is entitled upon request to a final statement of objections upon which he can rely. What is needed is that he make clear to the buyer exactly what is being sought. A formal demand under paragraph (b) will be sufficient in the case of a merchant-buyer.

4. Subsection (2) applies to the particular case of documents the same principle which the section on effects of acceptance applies to the case of goods. The matter is dealt with in this section in terms of "waiver" of objections rather than of right to revoke acceptance, partly to avoid any confusion with the problems of acceptance of goods and partly because defects in documents which are not taken as grounds for rejection are generally minor ones. The only defects concerned in the present subsection are defects in the documents which are apparent on their face. Where payment is required against the documents they must be inspected before payment, and the payment then constitutes acceptance of the documents. Under the section dealing with this problem, such acceptance of the documents does not constitute an acceptance of the goods or impair any option or remedies of the buyer for their improper delivery.

Where the documents are delivered without requiring such contemporary action as payment from the buyer, the reason of the next section on what constitutes acceptance of goods, applies. Their acceptance by non-objection is therefore postponed until after a reasonable time for their inspection. In either situation, however, the buyer "waives" only what is apparent on the face of the documents.

Cross References:

Point 2: Section 2–508.
Point 4: Sections 2–512(2), 2–606(1)(b), 2–607(2).

Definitional Cross References:

"Between merchants". Section 2–104.
"Buyer". Section 2–103.
"Seasonably". Section 1–204.
"Seller". Section 2–103.
"Writing" and "written". Section 1–201.

Section 2–606. What Constitutes Acceptance of Goods.

(1) Acceptance of goods occurs when the buyer

(a) after a reasonable opportunity to inspect the goods signifies to the seller that the goods are conforming or that he will take or retain them in spite of their non-conformity; or

(b) fails to make an effective rejection (subsection (1) of Section 2– 602), but such acceptance does not occur until the buyer has had a reasonable opportunity to inspect them; or

(c) does any act inconsistent with the seller's ownership; but if such act is wrongful as against the seller it is an acceptance only if ratified by him.

(2) Acceptance of a part of any commercial unit is acceptance of that entire unit.

New York Annotations

(1) *General rule. Accord:* Personal Property Law, §§ 128(1) and 129. Note, however, that Sections 2–603 and 2–604 permit the buyer to take action from which the present law might infer "acceptance."

(2) *Partial acceptance.* Subsection (2) applies to a "commercial unit" the rule now applied to cases where the price can be apportioned. Portfolio v. Rubin, 233 N.Y. 439, 135 N.E. 843 (1922). See Sections 2–105 and 2–327 (1) (b).

Historical Note: Subsection (1) (a), which formerly read "signifies his acceptance to the seller", was changed for clarification on the suggestion of the Law Revision Commission. (1956 Recommendations, p. 65; Excerpts, p. 391.)

Official Uniform Comment

Prior Uniform Statutory Provision: Section 48, Uniform Sales Act.

Changes: Rewritten, the qualification in paragraph (c) and subsection (2) being new; otherwise the general policy of the prior legislation is continued.

Purposes of Changes and New Matter: To make it clear that:

1. Under this Article "acceptance" as applied to goods means that the buyer, pursuant to the contract, takes particular goods which have been appropriated to the contract as his own, whether or not he is obligated to do so, and whether he does so by words, action, or silence when it is time to speak. If the goods conform to the contract, acceptance amounts only to the performance by the buyer of one part of his legal obligation.

2. Under this Article acceptance of goods is always acceptance of identified goods which have been appropriated to the contract or are appropriated by the contract. There is no provision for "acceptance of title" apart from acceptance in general, since acceptance of title is not material under this Article to the detailed rights and duties of the parties. (See Section 2–401). The refinements of the older law between acceptance of goods and of title become unnecessary in view of the provisions of the sections on effect and revocation of acceptance, on effects of identification and on risk of loss, and those sections which free the seller's and buyer's remedies from the complications and confusions caused by the question of whether title has or has not passed to the buyer before breach.

3. Under paragraph (a), payment made after tender is always one circumstance tending to signify acceptance of the goods but in itself it can never be more than one circumstance and is not conclusive. Also, a conditional communication of acceptance always remains subject to its expressed conditions.

4. Under paragraph (c), any action taken by the buyer, which is inconsistent with his claim that he has rejected the goods, constitutes an acceptance. However, the provisions of paragraph (c) are subject to the sections dealing with rejection by the buyer which permit the buyer to take certain actions with respect to the goods pursuant to his options and duties imposed by those sections, without effecting an acceptance of the goods. The second clause of paragraph (c) modifies some of the prior case law and makes it clear that "acceptance" in law based on the wrongful act of the acceptor is acceptance only as against the wrongdoer and then only at the option of the party wronged.

In the same manner in which a buyer can bind himself, despite his insistence that he is rejecting or has rejected the goods, by an act inconsistent with the seller's ownership under paragraph (c), he can obligate himself by a communication of acceptance despite a prior rejection under paragraph (a). However, the sections on buyer's rights on improper delivery and on the effect of rightful rejection, make it clear that after he once rejects a tender, paragraph (a) does not operate in favor of the buyer unless the seller has re-tendered the goods or has taken affirmative action indicating that he is holding the tender open. See also Comment 2 to Section 2–601.

5. Subsection (2) supplements the policy of the section on buyer's rights on improper delivery, recognizing the validity of a partial acceptance but insisting that the buyer exercise this right only as to whole commercial units.

Cross References:

Point 2: Sections 2–401, 2–509, 2–510, 2–607, 2–608 and Part 7.
Point 4: Sections 2–601 through 2–604.
Point 5: Section 2–601.

Definitional Cross References:

"Buyer". Section 2–103.
"Commercial unit". Section 2–105.
"Goods". Section 2–105.
"Seller". Section 2–103.

Section 2–607. Effect of Acceptance; Notice of Breach; Burden of Establishing Breach After Acceptance; Notice of Claim or Litigation to Person Answerable Over.

(1) The buyer must pay at the contract rate for any goods accepted.

(2) Acceptance of goods by the buyer precludes rejection of the goods accepted and if made with knowledge of a non-conformity cannot be revoked because of it unless the acceptance was on the reasonable assumption that the non-conformity would be seasonably cured but acceptance does not of itself impair any other remedy provided by this Article for non-conformity.

(3) Where a tender has been accepted

(a) the buyer must within a reasonable time after he discovers or should have discovered any breach notify the seller of breach or be barred from any remedy; and

(b) if the claim is one for infringement or the like (subsection (3) of Section 2–312) and the buyer is sued as a result of such a breach he must so notify the seller within a reasonable time after he receives notice of the litigation or be barred from any remedy over for liability established by the litigation.

(4) The burden is on the buyer to establish any breach with respect to the goods accepted.

(5) Where the buyer is sued for breach of a warranty or other obligation for which his seller is answerable over

(a) he may give his seller written notice of the litigation. If the notice states that the seller may come in and defend and that if the seller does not do so he will be bound in any action against him by his buyer by any determination of fact common to the two litigations, then unless the seller after seasonable receipt of the notice does come in and defend he is so bound.

(b) if the claim is one for infringement or the like (subsection (3) of Section 2–312) the original seller may demand in writing that his buyer turn over to him control of the litigation including settlement or else be barred from any remedy over and if he also agrees to bear all expense and to satisfy any adverse judgment, then unless the buyer after seasonable receipt of the demand does turn over control the buyer is so barred.

(6) The provisions of subsections (3), (4) and (5) apply to any obligation of a buyer to hold the seller harmless against infringement or the like (subsection (3) of Section 2–312).

New York Annotations

(1) *Payment at contract rate.* Under Personal Property Law, § 144, liability for payment of the price turned on passage of property in the goods; acceptance as a primary test is new. See Section 2–709, infra. This change narrows the seller's right to recover the full price.

(2) *Effect as to rejection.* Insofar as this section precludes revocation of acceptance if buyer accepted goods with knowledge of their nonconformity, it is in *accord* with Personal Property Law, § 150(3), which precludes rescission by the buyer where he "knew of the breach of warranty when he accepted the goods." Insofar as the buyer's right to reject is preserved until acceptance, this section changes the law which ended the power to reject upon passage of title. Personal Property Law, § 150(1) (c). The provision as to "cure" is new. See Sections 2–508 and 2–608. The preservation of other remedies after acceptance is in *accord* with Personal Property Law, § 130

(3) *Remedy lost by failure to give notice. Accord:* Personal Property Law, § 130. There is some New York case law holding that the Sales Act notice requirement does not apply to goods purchased "for immediate use" or "for immediate human consumption." Silverstein v. R.H. Macy & Co., Inc., 266 App.Div. 5, 40 N.Y.S.2d 916 (1943); Kennedy v. Woolworth Co., 205 App.Div. 648, 200 N.Y.S. 121 (1923). It should be observed that the notice here required demands less of the buyer than that called for by Section 2–605, dealing with rejection. The provision as to notice of litigation of a claim of infringement in subsection (3) (b) is new.

(4) *Burden of proof.* New.

(5) *"Vouching in."* This is new to the statutes. Compare Section 3–803. The common-law doctrine of "vouching in" is recognized in New York. Hartford Accident and Indemnity Co. v. First Nat. Bank & Trust Co., 281 N.Y. 162, 22 N.E.2d 324 (1939); Cohen v. Bass, Inc., 246 N.Y. 270, 158 N.E.618 (1927); Prescott v. Le Conte, 83 App.Div. 482, 82 N.Y.S. 411, aff'd 178 N.Y. 585, 70 N.E. 1108 (1904). Where personal service can be had, Civil Practice Act, § 193–a [now CPLR §§ 1007, 1008], provides for impleader. See 3 Williston, Sales, Sec. 614(a) (1948).

Historical Note: Subsections (3)(b), (5), and (6) were added by Supp. No. 1 to meet criticisms made by the New York Patent Law Association. See also Section 2–312. New subsections (3)(b) and (5)(b) give a warrantor against infringement an opportunity to defend or compromise third-party claims or be relieved of his liability. New subsection (5)(a) codifies for all warranties the practice of voucher to defend. Compare Section 3–803. New subsection (6) makes these provisions applicable to the buyer's liability for infringement under the changes in Section 2–312. (1956 Recommendations, p. 66.)

Official Uniform Comment

Prior Uniform Statutory Provision: Subsection (1)–Section 41, Uniform Sales Act; Subsections (2) and (3)–Sections 49 and 69, Uniform Sales Act.

Changes: Rewritten.

Purposes of Changes: To continue the prior basic policies with respect to acceptance of goods while making a number of minor though material changes in the interest of simplicity and commercial convenience so that:

1. Under subsection (1), once the buyer accepts a tender the seller acquires a right to its price on the contract terms. In cases of partial acceptance, the price of any part accepted is, if possible, to be reasonably apportioned, using the type of apportionment familiar to the courts in quantum valebant cases, to be determined in terms of "the contract rate," which is the rate determined from the bargain in fact (the agreement) after the rules and policies of this Article have been brought to bear.

2. Under subsection (2) acceptance of goods precludes their subsequent rejection. Any return of the goods thereafter must be by way of revocation of acceptance under the next section. Revocation is unavailable for a non-conformity known to the buyer at the time of acceptance, except where the buyer has accepted on the reasonable assumption that the non-conformity would be seasonably cured.

3. All other remedies of the buyer remain unimpaired under subsection (2). This is intended to include the buyer's full rights with respect to future installments despite his acceptance of any earlier non-conforming installment.

4. The time of notification is to be determined by applying commercial standards to a merchant buyer. "A reasonable time" for notification from a retail consumer is to be judged by different standards so that in his case it will be extended, for the rule of requiring notification is designed to defeat commercial bad faith, not to deprive a good faith consumer of his remedy.

The content of the notification need merely be sufficient to let the seller know that the transaction is still troublesome and must be watched. There is no reason to require that the notification which saves the buyer's rights under this section must include a clear statement of all the objections that will be relied on by the buyer, as under the section covering statements of defects upon rejection (Section 2–605). Nor is there reason for requiring the notification to be a claim for damages or of any threatened litigation or other resort to a remedy. The notification which saves the buyer's rights under this Article need only be such as informs the seller that the transaction is claimed to involve a breach, and thus opens the way for normal settlement through negotiation.

5. Under this Article various beneficiaries are given rights for injuries sustained by them because of the seller's breach of warranty. Such a beneficiary does not fall within the reason of the present section in regard to discovery of defects and the giving of notice within a reasonable time after acceptance, since he has nothing to do with acceptance. However, the reason of this section does extend to requiring the beneficiary to notify the seller that an injury has occurred. What is said above, with regard to the extended time for reasonable notification from the lay consumer after the injury is also applicable here; but even a beneficiary can be properly held to the use of good faith in notifying, once he has had time to become aware of the legal situation.

6. Subsection (4) unambiguously places the burden of proof to establish breach on the buyer after acceptance. However, this rule becomes one purely of procedure when the tender accepted was non-conforming and the buyer has given the seller notice of breach under subsection (3). For subsection (2) makes it clear that acceptance leaves unimpaired the buyer's right to be made whole, and that right can be exercised by the buyer not only by way of cross-claim for damages, but also by way of recoupment in diminution or extinction of the price.

7. Subsections (3) (b) and (5) (b) give a warrantor against infringement an opportunity to defend or compromise third-party claims or be relieved of his liability. Subsection (5) (a) codifies for all warranties the practice of voucher to defend. Compare Section 3–803. Subsection (6) makes these provisions applicable to the buyer's liability for infringement under Section 2–312.

8. All of the provisions of the present section are subject to any explicit reservation of rights.

Cross References:

Point 1: Section 1–201.
Point 2: Section 2–608.
Point 4: Sections 1–204 and 2–605.
Point 5: Section 2–318.
Point 6: Section 2–717.
Point 7: Sections 2–312 and 3–803.
Point 8: Section 1–207.

Definitional Cross References:

"Burden of establishing". Section 1–201.
"Buyer". Section 2–103.
"Conform". Section 2–106.
"Contract". Section 1–201.
"Goods". Section 2–105.
"Notifies". Section 1–201.
"Reasonable time". Section 1–204.
"Remedy". Section 1–201.
"Seasonably". Section 1–204.

Section 2–608. Revocation of Acceptance in Whole or in Part.

(1) The buyer may revoke his acceptance of a lot or commercial unit whose non-conformity substantially impairs its value to him if he has accepted it

(a) on the reasonable assumption that its non-conformity would be cured and it has not been seasonably cured; or

(b) without discovery of such non-conformity if his acceptance was reasonably induced either by the difficulty of discovery before acceptance or by the seller's assurances.

(2) Revocation of acceptance must occur within a reasonable time after the buyer discovers or should have discovered the ground for it and before any substantial change in condition of the goods which is not caused by their own defects. It is not effective until the buyer notifies the caused by their own defects. It is not effective until the buyer notifies the seller of it.

(3) A buyer who so revokes has the same rights and duties with regard to the goods involved as if he had rejected them.

New York Annotations

The buyer's power under the Code to revoke acceptance performs the same general function as rescission under Personal Property Law, § 150(1) (d). But since the Code does not limit rejection to cases where the property has not passed, this power is important only after acceptance. The Code also permits partial revocation of acceptance which is consistent with Portfolio v. Rubin, 233 N.Y. 439, 135 N.E. 843 (1922), allowing partial rejection. Revocation of acceptance is extended to cases where the buyer knew of the breach but has assurances that it would be cured; the power to revoke is denied when lack of knowledge is not excused. See Section 2–607. Under Personal Property Law, § 150(3), the right to rescission turns on knowledge without such qualification. For the meaning of "assurances," see Comment 3.

(1) *Substantial impairment of value necessary.* Under Personal Property Law, § 150(1) (d), the buyer's power to rescind arises where there is a breach of warranty by the seller. The Code limits revocation of acceptance to cases where the "non-conformity substantially impairs its value to him." The right to reject is not so limited either in Personal Property Law, § 150(1) (c) or in Section 2–601.

(2) *Revocation within a reasonable time; notice. Accord:* Personal Property Law, § 150(3).

(3) *Buyer's rights and duties on revocation.* Personal Property Law, § 150(3), imposes a duty on the buyer to return or offer to return the goods upon rescission. By Personal Property Law, § 131, the buyer who rejects has no such duty. This is changed by the Code which imposes the same duties in both cases. See Sections 2–602 and 2–603. This means that the buyer who revokes acceptance is not limited to recovery of payments made but may also recover damages. See Section 2–711. Unlike the Uniform Sales Act, the New York law permits a similar recovery. Personal Property Law, § 150(1) (d).

Official Uniform Comment

Prior Uniform Statutory Provision: Section 69(1) (d), (3), (4) and (5), Uniform Sales Act.

Changes: Rewritten.

Purposes of Changes: To make it clear that:

1. Although the prior basic policy is continued, the buyer is no longer required to elect between revocation of acceptance and recovery of damages for breach. Both are now available to him. The non-alternative character of the two remedies is stressed by the terms used in the present section. The section no longer speaks of "rescission," a term capable of ambiguous application either to transfer of title to the goods or to the contract of sale and susceptible also of confusion with cancellation for cause of an executed or executory portion of the contract. The remedy under this section is instead referred to simply as "revocation of acceptance" of goods tendered under a contract for sale and involves no suggestion of "election" of any sort.

2. Revocation of acceptance is possible only where the nonconformity substantially impairs the value of the goods to the buyer. For this purpose the test is not what the seller had reason to know at the time of contracting; the question is whether the non-conformity is such as will in fact cause a substantial impairment of value to the buyer though the seller had no advance knowledge as to the buyer's particular circumstances.

3. "Assurances" by the seller under paragraph (b) of subsection (1) can rest as well in the circumstances or in the contract as in explicit language used at the time of delivery. The reason for recognizing such assurances is that they induce the buyer to delay discovery. These are the only assurances involved in paragraph (b). Explicit assurances may be made either in good faith or bad faith. In either case any remedy accorded by this Article is available to the buyer under the section on remedies for fraud.

4. Subsection (2) requires notification of revocation of acceptance within a reasonable time after discovery of the grounds for such revocation. Since this remedy

will be generally resorted to only after attempts at adjustment have failed, the reasonable time period should extend in most cases beyond the time in which notification of breach must be given, beyond the time for discovery of non-conformity after acceptance and beyond the time for rejection after tender. The parties may by their agreement limit the time for notification under this section, but the same sanctions and considerations apply to such agreements as are discussed in the comment on manner and effect of rightful rejection.

5. The content of the notice under subsection (2) is to be determined in this case as in others by considerations of good faith, prevention of surprise, and reasonable adjustment. More will generally be necessary than the mere notification of breach required under the preceding section. On the other hand the requirements of the section on waiver of buyer's objections do not apply here. The fact that quick notification of trouble is desirable affords good ground for being slow to bind a buyer by his first statement. Following the general policy of this Article, the requirements of the content of notification are less stringent in the case of a non-merchant buyer.

6. Under subsection (2) the prior policy is continued of seeking substantial justice in regard to the condition of goods restored to the seller. Thus the buyer may not revoke his acceptance if the goods have materially deteriorated except by reason of their own defects. Worthless goods, however, need not be offered back and minor defects in the articles reoffered are to be disregarded.

7. The policy of the section allowing partial acceptance is carried over into the present section and the buyer may revoke his acceptance, in appropriate cases, as to the entire lot or any commercial unit thereof.

Cross References:

Point 3: Section 2–721.
Point 4: Sections 1–204, 2–602 and 2–607.
Point 5: Sections 2–605 and 2–607.
Point 7: Section 2–601.

Definitional Cross References:

"Buyer". Section 2–103.
"Commercial unit". Section 2–105.
"Conform". Section 2–106.
"Goods". Section 2–105.
"Lot". Section 2–105.
"Notifies". Section 1–201.
"Reasonable time". Section 1–204.
"Rights". Section 1–201.
"Seasonably". Section 1–204.
"Seller". Section 2–103.

Section 2–609. Right to Adequate Assurance of Performance.

(1) A contract for sale imposes an obligation on each party that the other's expectation of receiving due performance will not be impaired. When reasonable grounds for insecurity arise with respect to the performance of either party the other may in writing demand adequate assurance of due performance and until he receives such assurance may if commercially reasonable suspend any performance for which he has not already received the agreed return.

(2) Between merchants the reasonableness of grounds for insecurity and the adequacy of any assurance offered shall be determined according to commercial standards.

(3) Acceptance of any improper delivery or payment does not prejudice the aggrieved party's right to demand adequate assurance of future performance.

(4) After receipt of a justified demand failure to provide within a reasonable time not exceeding thirty days such assurance of due performance as is adequate under the circumstances of the particular case is a repudiation of the contract.

New York Annotations

This section broadens the right of the aggrieved party to suspend performance when the other party manifests inability to perform or intention not to perform. Personal Property Law, §§ 144(2) and 146. See Hanna v. Florence Iron Co., 222 N.Y. 290, 118 N.E. 629 (1918), and Restatement, Contracts, §§ 280, 287, 306, 323 and New York Annotations. The provision for "adequate assurance" is new.

Official Uniform Comment

Prior Uniform Statutory Provision: Sections 53, 54(1) (b), 55 and 63(2), Uniform Sales Act.

Purposes:

1. The section rests on the recognition of the fact that the essential purpose of a contract between commercial men is actual performance and they do not bargain merely for a promise, or for a promise plus the right to win a lawsuit and that a continuing sense of reliance and security that the promised performance will be forthcoming when due, is an important feature of the bargain. If either the willingness or the ability of a party to perform declines materially between the time of contracting and the time for performance, the other party is threatened with the loss of a substantial part of what he has bargained for. A seller needs protection not merely against having to deliver on credit to a shaky buyer, but also against having to procure and manufacture the goods, perhaps turning down other customers. Once he has been given reason to believe that the buyer's performance has become uncertain, it is an undue hardship to force him to continue his own performance. Similarly, a buyer who believes that the seller's deliveries have become uncertain cannot safely wait for the due date of performance when he has been buying to assure himself of materials for his current manufacturing or to replenish his stock of merchandise.

2. Three measures have been adopted to meet the needs of commercial men in such situations. First, the aggrieved party is permitted to suspend his own performance and any preparation therefor, with excuse for any resulting necessary delay, until the situation has been clarified. "Suspend performance" under this section means to hold up performance pending the outcome of the demand, and includes also the holding up of any preparatory action. This is the same principle which governs the ancient law of stoppage and seller's lien, and also of excuse of a buyer from prepayment if the seller's actions manifest that he cannot or will not perform. (Original Act, Section 63 (2).)

Secondly, the aggrieved party is given the right to require adequate assurance that the other party's performance will be duly forthcoming. This principle is reflected in the familiar clauses permitting the seller to curtail deliveries if the buyer's credit becomes impaired, which when held within the limits of reasonableness and good faith actually express no more than the fair business meaning of any commercial contract.

Third, and finally, this section provides the means by which the aggrieved party may treat the contract as broken if his reasonable grounds for insecurity are not cleared up within a reasonable time. This is the principle underlying the law of anticipatory breach, whether by way of defective part performance or by repudiation. The present section merges these three principles of law and commercial practice into a single theory of general application to all sales agreements looking to future performance.

3. Subsection (2) of the present section requires that "reasonable" grounds and "adequate" assurance as used in subsection (1) be defined by commercial rather than legal standards. The express reference to commercial standards carries no connotation that the obligation of good faith is not equally applicable here.

Under commercial standards and in accord with commercial practice, a ground for insecurity need not arise from or be directly related to the contract in question. The law as to "dependence" or "independence" of promises within a single contract does not control the application of the present section.

Thus a buyer who falls behind in "his account" with the seller, even though the items involved have to do with separate and legally distinct contracts, impairs the seller's expectation of due performance. Again, under the same test, a buyer who requires precision parts which he intends to use immediately upon delivery, may have reasonable grounds for insecurity if he discovers that his seller is making defective deliveries of such parts to other buyers with similar needs. Thus, too, in a situation such as arose in Jay Dreher Corporation v. Delco Appliance Corporation, 93 F.2d 275 (C.C.A.2, 1937), where a manufacturer gave a dealer an exclusive franchise for the sale of his product but on two or three occasions breached the exclusive dealing clause, although there was no default in orders, deliveries or payments under the separate sales contract between the parties, the aggrieved dealer would be entitled to suspend his performance of the contract for sale under the present section and to demand assurance that the exclusive dealing contract would be lived up to. There is no need for an explicit clause tying the exclusive franchise into the contract for the sale of goods since the situation itself ties the agreements together.

The nature of the sales contract enters also into the question of reasonableness. For example, a report from an apparently trustworthy source that the seller had shipped defective goods or was planning to ship them would normally give the buyer reasonable grounds for insecurity. But when the buyer has assumed the risk of payment before inspection of the goods, as in a sales contract on C.I.F. or similar cash against documents terms, that risk is not to be evaded by a demand for assurance. Therefore no ground for insecurity would exist under this section unless the report went to a ground which would excuse payment by the buyer.

4. What constitutes "adequate" assurance of due performance is subject to the same test of factual conditions. For example, where the buyer can make use of a defective delivery, a mere promise by a seller of good repute that he is giving the matter his attention and that the defect will not be repeated, is normally sufficient. Under the same circumstances, however, a similar statement by a known corner-cutter might will be considered insufficient without the posting of a guaranty or, if so demanded by the buyer, a speedy replacement of the delivery involved. By the same token where a delivery has defects, even though easily curable, which interfere with easy use by the buyer, no verbal assurance can be deemed adequate which is not accompanied by replacement, repair, money-allowance, or other commercially reasonable cure.

A fact situation such as arose in Corn Products Refining Co. v. Fasola, 94 N.J.L. 181, 109 A. 505 (1920) offers illustration both of reasonable grounds for insecurity and "adequate" assurance. In that case a contract for the sale of oils on 30 days' credit, 2% off for payment within 10 days, provided that credit was to be extended to the buyer only if his financial responsibility was satisfactory to the seller. The buyer had been in the habit of taking advantage of the discount but at the same time that he failed to make his customary 10 day payment, the seller heard rumors, in fact false, that the buyer's financial condition was shaky. Thereupon, the seller demanded cash before shipment or security satisfactory to him. The buyer sent a good credit report from his banker, expressed willingness to make payments when due on the 30 day terms and insisted on further deliveries under the contract. Under this Article the rumors, although false, were enough to make the buyer's financial condition "unsatisfactory" to the seller under the contract clause. Moreover, the buyer's practice of taking the cash discounts is enough, apart from the contract clause, to lay a commercial foundation for suspicion when the practice is suddenly stopped. These matters, however, go only to the justification of the seller's demand for security, or his "reasonable grounds for insecurity".

The adequacy of the assurance given is not measured as in the type of "satisfaction" situation affected with intangibles, such as in personal service cases, cases involving a third party's judgment as final, or cases in which the whole contract is dependent on one party's satisfaction, as in a sale on approval. Here, the seller must exercise good faith and observe commercial standards. This Article thus approves the statement of the court in James B. Berry's Sons Co. of Illinois v. Monark Gasoline Oil Co., Inc. 32 F.2d 74 (C.C.A.8, 1929), that the seller's satisfaction under such a clause must be based upon reason and must not be arbitrary or capricious; and rejects the purely personal "good faith" test of the Corn Products Refining Co. case, which held that in the seller's sole judgment, if for *any* reason he was dissatisfied, he was entitled to revoke the credit. In the absence of the buyer's failure to take the 2% discount as was his custom, the banker's report given in that case would have been "adequate" assurance under this Act, regardless of the language of the "satisfaction" clause. However, the seller is reasonably entitled to feel insecure at a sudden expansion of the buyer's use of a credit term, and should be entitled either to security or to a satisfactory explanation.

The entire foregoing discussion as to adequacy of assurance by way of explanation is subject to qualification when repeated occasions for the application of this section arise. This Act recognizes that repeated delinquencies must be viewed as cumulative. On the other hand, commercial sense also requires that if repeated claims for assurance are made under this section, the basis for these claims must be increasingly obvious.

5. A failure to provide adequate assurance of performance and thereby to re-establish the security of expectation, results in a breach only "by repudiation" under subsection (4). Therefore, the possibility is continued of retraction of the repudiation under the section dealing with that problem, unless the aggrieved party has acted on the breach in some manner.

The thirty day limit on the time to provide assurance is laid down to free the question of reasonable time from uncertainty in later litigation.

6. Clauses seeking to give the protected party exceedingly wide powers to cancel or readjust the contract when ground for insecurity arises must be read against the fact that good faith is a part of the obligation of the contract and not subject to modification by agreement and includes, in the case of a merchant, the reasonable observance of commercial standards of fair dealing in the trade. Such clauses can thus be effective to enlarge the protection given by the present section to a certain extent, to fix the reasonable time within which requested assurance must be given, or to define adequacy of the assurance in any commercially reasonable fashion. But any clause seeking to set up arbitrary standards for action is ineffective under this Article. Acceleration clauses are treated similarly in the Articles on Commercial Paper and Secured Transactions.

Cross References:

Point 3: Section 1–203.
Point 5: Section 2–611.
Point 6: Sections 1–203 and 1–208 and Articles 3 and 9.

Definitional Cross References:

"Aggrieved party". Section 1–201.
"Between merchants". Section 2–104.
"Contract". Section 1–201.
"Contract for sale". Section 2–106.
"Party". Section 1–201.
"Reasonable time". Section 1–204.
"Rights". Section 1–201.
"Writing". Section 1–201.

Section 2–610. Anticipatory Repudiation.

When either party repudiates the contract with respect to a performance not yet due the loss of which will substantially impair the value of the contract to the other, the aggrieved party may

(a) for a commercially reasonable time await performance by the repudiating party; or

(b) resort to any remedy for breach (Section 2–703 or Section 2–711), even though he has notified the repudiating party that he would await the latter's performance and has urged retraction; and

(c) in either case suspend his own performance or proceed in accordance with the provisions of this Article on the seller's right to identify goods to the contract notwithstanding breach or to salvage unfinished goods (Section 2–704).

New York Annotations

This section is consistent with the New York cases recognizing the doctrine of anticipatory repudiation. Burtis v. Thompson, 42 N.Y. 246 (1870); Howard v. Daly, 61 N.Y. 362 (1875); Windmuller v. Pope, 107 N.Y 674, 14 N.E. 436 (1887); Nichols v. Scranton Steel Co., 137 N.Y. 471, 33 N.E. 561 (1893). There is some confusion as to the scope of the doctrine in connection with promises to pay money. Compare Hall v. Nassau Consumers' Ice Co., 260 N.Y. 417, 183 N.E. 903 (1933) with Kelly v. Security Mutual Life Ins. Co., 186 N.Y. 16, 78 N.E. 584 (1906), and McCready v. Lindenborn, 172 N.Y. 400, 65 N.E. 208 (1902). The right of the aggrieved party to suspend performance is supported by DeForest Radio T. & T. Co. v. Triangle Radio S. Co., 243 N.Y. 283, 153 N.E. 75 (1926). Dictum in the latter case also relies on an election theory rejected by subparagraph (b). The Sales Act contains no comparable provision. See Restatement, Contracts, § 318 and New York Annotation.

Historical Note: Supp. No. 1 limited the aggrieved party's right to await performance to a "commercially reasonable time", preventing interpretation to permit indefinite delay and recovery of avoidable damages. At the suggestion of the Law Revision Commission, further changes were made for clarification, limiting the section to repudiation in respect of "not yet due", making it clear that awaiting performance does not bar remedy for breach, and inserting a cross-reference to Section 2–704. (1956 Recommendations, p. 68; Excerpts, p. 392.)

Official Uniform Comment

Prior Uniform Statutory Provision: See Sections 63(2) and 65, Uniform Sales Act.

Purposes: To make it clear that:

1. With the problem of insecurity taken care of by the preceding section and with provision being made in this Article as to the effect of a defective delivery under an installment contract, anticipatory repudiation centers upon an overt communication of intention or an action which renders performance impossible or demonstrates a clear determination not to continue with performance.

Under the present section when such a repudiation substantially impairs the value of the contract, the aggrieved party may at any time resort to his remedies for breach, or he may suspend his own performance while he negotiates with, or awaits performance by, the other party. But if he awaits performance beyond a commercially reasonable time he cannot recover resulting damages which he should have avoided.

2. It is not necessary for repudiation that performance be made literally and utterly impossible. Repudiation can result from action which reasonably indicates a rejection of the continuing obligation. And, a repudiation automatically results under the preceding section on insecurity when a party fails to provide adequate assurance of due future performance within thirty days after a justifiable demand therefore has been made. Under the language of this section, a demand by one or both parties for more than the contract calls for in the way of counter-performance is not in itself a repudiation nor does it invalidate a plain expression of desire for future performance. However, when under a fair reading it amounts to a statement of intention not to perform except on conditions which go beyond the contract, it becomes a repudiation.

3. The test chosen to justify an aggrieved party's action under this section is the same as that in the section on breach in installment contracts-namely the substantial value of the contract. The most useful test of substantial value is to determine whether material inconvenience or injustice will result if the aggrieved party is forced to wait and receive an ultimate tender minus the part or aspect repudiated.

4. After repudiation, the aggrieved party may immediately resort to any remedy he chooses provided he moves in good faith (see Section 1–203). Inaction and silence by the aggrieved party may leave the matter open but it cannot be regarded as misleading the repudiating party. Therefore the aggrieved party is left free to proceed at any time with his options under this section, unless he has taken some positive action which in good faith requires notification to the other party before the remedy is pursued.

Cross References:

Point 1: Section 2–609 and 2–612.
Point 2: Section 2–609.
Point 3: Section 2–612.
Point 4: Section 1–203.

Definitional Cross References:

"Aggrieved party". Section 1–201.
"Contract". Section 1–201.
"Party". Section 1–201.
"Remedy". Section 1–201.

Section 2–611. Retraction of Anticipatory Repudiation.

(1) Until the repudiating party's next performance is due he can retract his repudiation unless the aggrieved party has since the repudiation cancelled or materially changed his position or otherwise indicated that he considers the repudiation final.

(2) Retraction may be by any method which clearly indicates to the aggrieved party that the repudiating party intends to perform, but must include any assurance justifiably demanded under the provisions of this Article (Section 2–609).

(3) Retraction reinstates the repudiating party's rights under the contract with the due excuse and allowance to the aggrieved party for any delay occasioned by the repudiation.

New York Annotations

The repudiator's power of retraction as limited by this section is recognized in the New York case law. Windmuller v. Pope, 107 N.Y. 674, 14 N.E. 436 (1887); DeForest Radio T. & T. Co. v. Triangle Radio S. Co., 243 N.Y. 283, 153 N.E. 75 (1926). Cf. Perlman v. M. Israel & Sons, Inc., 306 N.Y. 254, 117 N.E.2d 352 (1954).

Historical Note: The change in the caption adding "Anticipatory" was inserted to meet criticism by the Law Revision Commission, and makes it clear that this section, like the preceding section, applies only to repudiation in respect of a performance not yet due. (1956 Recommendations, p. 68; Excerpts, p. 393.)

Official Uniform Comment

Prior Uniform Statutory Provision: None.

Purposes: To make it clear that:

1. The repudiating party's right to reinstate the contract is entirely dependent upon the action taken by the aggrieved party. If the latter has cancelled the contract or materially changed his position at any time after the repudiation, there can be no retraction under this section.

2. Under subsection (2) an effective retraction must be accompanied by any assurances demanded under the section dealing with right to adequate assurance. A repudiation is of course sufficient to give reasonable ground for insecurity and to warrant a request for assurance as an essential condition of the retraction. However, after a timely and unambiguous expression of retraction, a reasonable time for the assurance to be worked out should be allowed by the aggrieved party before cancellation.

Cross References:

Point 2: Section 2–609.

Definitional Cross References:

"Aggrieved party". Section 1–201.
"Cancellation". Section 2–106.
"Contract". Section 1–201.
"Party". Section 1–201.
"Rights". Section 1–201.

Section 2–612. "Installment Contract"; Breach.

(1) An "installment contract" is one which requires or authorizes the delivery of goods in separate lots to be separately accepted, even though the contract contains a clause "each delivery is a separate contract" or its equivalent.

(2) The buyer may reject any installment which is non-conforming if the non-conformity substantially impairs the value of that installment and cannot be cured or if the non-conformity is a defect in the required documents; but if the non-conformity does not fall within subsection (3) and the seller gives adequate assurance of its cure the buyer must accept that installment.

(3) Whenever non-conformity or default with respect to one or more installments substantially impairs the value of the whole contract there is a breach of the whole. But the aggrieved party reinstates the contract if he accepts a non-conforming installment without seasonably notifying of cancellation or if he brings an action with respect only to past installments or demands performance as to future installments.

New York Annotations

(1) *Definition.* The provision is broader than that of Personal Property Law, § 126(2). The Code does not require that the separate lots be "separately paid for". Further, the Code definition covers cases where the installment delivery is "authorized" even "tacitly", as well as cases where it is "required". See Comments 1 and 2; compare DeVivo v. Gallerani, 105 Misc. 606, 174 N.Y.S. 13 (1919). As to the effect of contract clauses that "each delivery is a separate contract", see, *accord,* Koppel v. St. Regis Paper Co., 47 N.Y.S.2d 443, rev'd on other grounds, 56 N.Y.S.2d 790 (1944).

(2) *Rejection of installments.* The Sales Act does not separately provide for the rejection of installments, but the matter is dealt with under Personal Property Law, § 150, which does not limit rejection, as this section does, to cases where non-conformity "substantially impairs the value and cannot be cured." Baxter v. Savoy Shirt Co., 238 N.Y. 106, 143 N.E. 807 (1924). The Code seems to preserve the unqualified right of rejection for defects in required documents, as it does for contracts other than installment contracts. See Section 2–601.

(3) *Breach of whole contract. Accord* in different terms: Personal Property Law, § 126. Helgar Corp. v. Warner's Features, Inc., 222 N.Y. 449, 119 N.E. 113 (1918); Hershey Farms v. State of N.Y., 202 Misc. 105, 110 N.Y.S.2d 324 (1952). On loss of right to cancel, see William C. Atwater & Co., Inc. v. Panama R. Co., 255 N.Y. 496, 175 N.E. 189 (1931).

Historical Note: Subsection (1) was changed on the recommendation of the Law Revision Commission to eliminate the requirement of separate payment. (1956 Recommendations, p. 69; Excerpts, p. 393.)

Official Uniform Comment

Prior Uniform Statutory Provision: Section 45(2), Uniform Sales Act.

Changes: Rewritten.

Purposes of Changes: To continue prior law but to make explicit the more mercantile interpretation of many of the rules involved, so that:

1. The definition of an installment contract is phrased more broadly in this Article so as to cover installment deliveries tacitly authorized by the circumstances or by the option of either party.

2. In regard to the apportionment of the price for separate payment this Article applies the more liberal test of what can be apportioned rather than the test of what is clearly apportioned by the agreement. This article also recognizes approximate calculation or apportionment of price subject to subsequent adjustment. A provision

for separate payment for each lot delivered ordinarily means that the price is at least roughly calculable by units of quantity, but such a provision is not essential to an "installment contract". If separate acceptance of separate deliveries is contemplated, no generalized contrast between wholly "entire" and wholly "divisible" contracts has any standing under this Article.

3. This Article rejects any approach which gives clauses such as "each delivery is a separate contract" their legalistically literal effect. Such contracts nonetheless call for installment deliveries. Even where a clause speaks of "a separate contract for all purposes", a commercial reading of the language under the section on good faith and commercial standards requires that the singleness of the document and the negotiation, together with the sense of the situation, prevail over any uncommercial and legalistic interpretation.

4. One of the requirements for rejection under subsection (2) is non-conformity substantially impairing the value of the installment in question. However, an installment agreement may require accurate conformity in quality as a condition to the right to acceptance if the need for such conformity is made clear either by express provision or by the circumstances. In such a case the effect of the agreement is to define explicitly what amounts to substantial impairment of value impossible to cure. A clause requiring accurate compliance as a condition to the right to acceptance must, however, have some basis in reason, must avoid imposing hardship by surprise and is subject to waiver or to displacement by practical construction.

Substantial impairment of the value of an installment can turn not only on the quality of the goods but also on such factors as time, quantity, assortment, and the like. It must be judged in terms of the normal or specifically known purposes of the contract. The defect in required documents refers to such matters as the absence of insurance documents under a C.I.F. contract, falsity of a bill of lading, or one failing to show shipment within the contract period or to the contract destination. Even in such cases, however, the provisions on cure of tender apply if appropriate documents are readily procurable.

5. Under subsection (2) an installment delivery must be accepted if the non-conformity is curable and the seller gives adequate assurance of cure. Cure of non-conformity of an installment in the first instance can usually be afforded by an allowance against the price, or in the case of reasonable discrepancies in quantity either by a further delivery or a partial rejection. This Article requires reasonable action by a buyer in regard to discrepant delivery and good faith requires that the buyer make any reasonable minor outlay of time or money necessary to cure an overshipment by severing out an acceptable percentage thereof. The seller must take over a cure which involves any material burden; the buyer's obligation reaches only to cooperation. Adequate assurance for purposes of subsection (2) is measured by the same standards as under the section on right to adequate assurance of performance.

6. Subsection (3) is designed to further the continuance of the contract in the absence of an overt cancellation. The question arising when an action is brought as to a single installment only is resolved by making such action waive the right of cancellation. This involves merely a defect in one or more installments, as contrasted with the situation where there is a true repudiation within the section on anticipatory repudiation. Whether the non-conformity in any given installment justifies cancellation as to the future depends, not on whether such non-conformity indicates an intent or likelihood that the future deliveries will also be defective, but whether the non-conformity substantially impairs the value of the whole contract. If only the seller's security in regard to future installments is impaired, he has the right to demand adequate assurances of proper future performance but has not an immediate right to cancel the entire contract. It is clear under this Article, however, that defects in prior installments are cumulative in effect, so that acceptance does not wash out the defect "waived". Prior policy is continued, putting the rule as to buyer's default on the same footing as that in regard to seller's default.

7. Under the requirement of seasonable notification of cancellation under subsection (3), a buyer who accepts a non-conforming installment which substantially impairs the value of the entire contract should properly be permitted to withhold his decision as to whether or not to cancel pending a response from the seller as to his claim for cure or adjustment. Similarly, a seller may withhold a delivery pending payment for prior ones, at the same time delaying his decision as to cancellation. A reasonable time for notifying a cancellation, judged by commercial standards under the section on good faith, extends of course to include the time covered by any reasonable negotiation in good faith. However, during this period the defaulting party is entitled, on request, to know whether the contract is still in effect, before he can be required to perform further.

Cross References:

Point 2: Sections 2–307 and 2–607.
Point 3: Section 1–203.
Point 5: Sections 2–208 and 2–609.
Point 6: Section 2–610.

Definitional Cross References:

"Action". Section 1–201.
"Aggrieved party". Section 1–201.
"Buyer". Section 2–103.
"Cancellation". Section 2–106.
"Conform". Section 2–106.
"Contract". Section 1–201.
"Lot". Section 2–105.
"Notifies". Section 1–201.
"Seasonably". Section 1–204.
"Seller". Section 2–103.

Section 2–613. Casualty to Identified Goods.

Where the contract requires for its performance goods identified when the contract is made, and the goods suffer casualty without fault of either party before the risk of loss passes to the buyer, or in a proper case under a "no arrival, no sale" term (Section 2–324) then

(a) if the loss is total the contract is avoided; and

(b) if the loss is partial or the goods have so deteriorated as no longer to conform to the contract the buyer may nevertheless demand inspection and at his option either treat the contract as avoided or accept the goods with due allowance from the contract price for the deterioration or the deficiency in quantity but without further right against the seller.

New York Annotations

This section deals with the problems treated separately in Personal Property Law, §§ 88 and 89. The Code uses the phrase "goods identified when the contract is made" instead of the phrase "specific goods".

Moreover, under the Sales Act the buyer was given the choice of avoiding the contract or receiving the goods remaining after partial loss only on payment of the contract price for all or a divisible part of the goods. Under the Code the buyer may accept the goods and receive due allowance from the contract price for deterioration or deficiency. There has been little litigation of this problem since World War I. Compare Restatement, Contracts, §§ 456, 457, 460 and New York Annotations.

Historical Note: On the recommendation of the Law Revision Commission the preamble was revised to make the section applicable to contracts for "goods identified when the contract is made", rather than to contracts for "irreplaceable" or "unique" goods, and to conform to a change in Section 2–324. (1956 Recommendations, p. 70; Excerpts, p. 394.)

UCC

Official Uniform Comment

Prior Uniform Statutory Provision: Sections 7 and 8, Uniform Sales Act.

Changes: Rewritten, the basic policy being continued but the test of a "divisible" or "indivisible" sale or contract being abandoned in favor of adjustment in business terms.

Purposes of Changes:

1. Where goods whose continued existence is presupposed by the agreement are destroyed without fault of either party, the buyer is relieved from his obligation but may at his option take the surviving goods at a fair adjustment. "Fault" is intended to include negligence and not merely wilful wrong. The buyer is expressly given the right to inspect the goods in order to determine whether he wishes to avoid the contract entirely or to take the goods with a price adjustment.

2. The section applies whether the goods already destroyed at the time of contracting without the knowledge of either party or whether they are destroyed subsequently but before the risk of loss passes to the buyer. Where under the agreement, including of course usage of trade, the risk has passed to the buyer before the casualty, the section has no application. Beyond this, the essential question in determining whether the rules of this section are to be applied is whether the seller has or has not undertaken the responsibility for the continued existence of the goods in proper condition through the time of agreed or expected delivery.

3. The section on the term "no arrival, no sale" makes clear that delay in arrival, quite as much as physical change in the goods, gives the buyer the options set forth in this section.

Cross Reference:

Point 3: Section 2–324.

Definitional Cross References:

"Buyer". Section 2–103.
"Conform". Section 2–106
"Contract". Section 1–201.
"Fault". Section 1–201.
"Goods". Section 2–105.
"Party". Section 1–201.
"Rights". Section 1–201.
"Seller". Section 2–103.

Section 2–614. Substituted Performance.

(1) Where without fault of either party the agreed berthing, loading, or unloading facilities fail or an agreed type of carrier becomes unavailable or the

agreed manner of delivery otherwise becomes commercially impracticable but a commercially reasonable substitute is available, such substitute performance must be tendered and accepted.

(2) If the agreed means or manner of payment fails because of domestic or foreign governmental regulation, the seller may withhold or stop delivery unless the buyer provides a means or manner of payment which is commercially a substantial equivalent. If delivery has already been taken, payment by the means or in the manner provided by the regulation discharges the buyer's obligation unless the regulation is discriminatory, oppressive or predatory.

New York Annotations

The Sales Act does not specifically deal with the problem of this section. Personal Property Law, § 150, on breach of warranty, would seem to require strict compliance with the terms of the contract and thus preclude the possibility of substituted performance. However, a result substantially similar to that required under subsection (1) was reached on common-law principles in Iasigi v. Rosenstein, 141 N.Y. 414, 36 N.E. 509 (1894). See, however, Miller & Sons Co. v. E. M. Sergeant Co., 191 App.Div. 814, 182 N.Y.S. 382 (1920). See Restatement, Contracts, §§ 462, 463, and New York Annotations.

Official Uniform Comment

Prior Uniform Statutory Provision: None.

Purposes:

1. Subsection (1) requires the tender of a commercially reasonable substituted performance where agreed to facilities have failed or become commercially impracticable. Under this Article, in the absence of specific agreement, the normal or usual facilities enter into the agreement either through the circumstances, usage of trade or prior course of dealing.

This section appears between Section 2–613 on casualty to identified goods and the next section on excuse by failure to presupposed conditions, both of which deal with excuse and complete avoidance of the contract where the occurrence or non-occurrence of a contingency which was a basic assumption of the contract makes the expected performance impossible. The distinction between the present section and those sections lies in whether the failure or impossibility of performance arises in connection with an incidental matter or goes to the very heart of the agreement. The differing lines of solution are contrasted in a comparison of International Paper Co. v. Rockefeller, 161 App. Div. 180, 146 N.Y.S. 371 (1914) and Meyer v. Sullivan, 40 Cal. App. 723, 181 P. 847 (1919). In the former case a contract for the sale of spruce to be cut from a particular tract of land was involved. When a fire destroyed the trees growing on that tract the seller was held excused since performance was impossible. In the latter case the contract called for delivery of wheat "f.o.b. Kosmos Steamer at Seattle." The war led to cancellation of that line's sailing schedule after space had been duly engaged and the buyer was held entitled to demand substituted delivery at the warehouse on the line's loading dock. Under this Article, of course, the seller would also be entitled, had the market gone the other way, to make a substituted tender in that manner.

There must, however, be a true commercial impracticability to excuse the agreed to performance and justify a substituted performance. When this is the case a reasonable substituted performance tendered by either party should excuse him from strict compliance with contract terms which do not go to the essence of the agreement.

2. The substitution provided in this section as between buyer and seller does not carry over into the obligation of a financing agency under a letter of credit, since such an agency is entitled to performance which is plainly adequate on its face and without need to look into commercial evidence outside of the documents. See Article 5, especially Sections 5–102, 5–103, 5–109, 5–110, 5–114.

3. Under subsection (2) where the contract is still executory on both sides, the seller is permitted to withdraw unless the buyer can provide him with a commercially equivalent return despite the governmental regulation. Where, however, only the debt for the price remains, a larger leeway is permitted. The buyer may pay in the manner provided by the regulation even though this may not be commercially equivalent provided that the regulation is not "discriminatory, oppressive or predatory."

Cross Reference:

Point 2: Article 5.

Definitional Cross:

"Buyer". Section 2–103.
"Fault". Section 1–201.
"Party". Section 1–201.
"Seller". Section 2–103.

Section 2–615. Excuse by Failure of Presupposed Conditions.

Except so far as a seller may have assumed a greater obligation and subject to the preceding section on substituted performance:

(a) Delay in delivery or non-delivery in whole or in part by a seller who complies with paragraphs (b) and (c) is not a breach of his duty under a contract for sale if performance as agreed has been made impracticable by the occurrence of a contingency the non-occurrence of which was a basic assumption on which the contract was made or by compliance in good faith with any applicable foreign or domestic governmental regulation or order whether or not it later proves to be invalid.

(b) Where the causes mentioned in paragraph (a) affect only a part of the seller's capacity to perform, he must allocate production and deliveries among his customers but may at his option include regular customers not then under contract as well as his own requirements for further manufacture. He may so allocate in any manner which is fair and reasonable.

(c) The seller must notify the buyer seasonably that there will be delay or non-delivery and, when allocation is required under paragraph (b), of the estimated quota thus made available for the buyer.

New York Annotations

The Sales Act has no comparable provision. The rules of this section of the Code deal with the general contract rules governing impossibility and frustration which are incorporated into the Sales Act by Personal Property Law, § 154.

(a) *Failure of basic assumption. Accord:* Restatement, Contracts, §§ 454–461 and New York Annotations. Excuse based on valid domestic or foreign governmental regulations goes beyond Restatement, Contracts, § 458.

(b) *Failure of part; allocation. Accord:* Restatement, Contracts, § 464(1) and New York Annotations.

(c) *Notice of excuse.* Subparagraph (c) is new.

Historical Note: Subparagraph (b) was revised in Supp. No. 1 to make it clear that the seller may include his own manufacturing requirements when forced to allocate. (1956 Recommendations, p. 71.)

Official Uniform Comment

Prior Uniform Statutory Provision: None

Purposes:

1. This section excuses a seller from timely delivery of goods contracted for, where his performance has become commercially impracticable because of unforeseen supervening circumstances not within the contemplation of the parties at the time of contracting. The destruction of specific goods and the problem of the use of substituted performance on points other than delay or quantity, treated elsewhere in this Article, must be distinguished from the matter covered by this section.

2. The present section deliberately refrains from any effort at an exhaustive expression of contingencies and is to be interpreted in all cases sought to be brought within its scope in terms of its underlying reason and purpose.

3. The first test for excuse under this Article in terms of basic assumption is a familiar one. The additional test of commercial impracticability (as contrasted with "impossibility", "frustration of performance" or "frustration of the venture") has been adopted in order to call attention to the commercial character of the criterion chosen by this Article.

4. Increased cost alone does not excuse performance unless the rise in cost is due to some unforseen contingency which alters the essential nature of the performance. Neither is a rise or a collapse in the market in itself a justification, for that is exactly the type of business risk which business contracts made at fixed prices are intended to cover. But a severe shortage of raw materials or of supplies due to a contingency such as war, embargo, local crop failure, unforeseen shutdown of major sources of supply or the like, which either causes a marked increase in cost or altogether prevents the seller from securing supplies necessary to his performance, is within the contemplation of this section. (See Ford & Sons, Ltd., v. Henry Leetham & Sons, Ltd., 21 Com. Cas. 55 (1915, K.B.D.).)

5. Where a particular source of supply is exclusive under the agreement and fails through casualty, the present section applies rather than the provision on destruction or deterioration of specific goods. The same holds true where a particular source of supply is shown by the circumstances to have been contemplated or assumed by the parties at the time of contracting. (See Davis Co. v. Hoffmann-LaRoche Chemical Works, 178 App. Div. 855, 166 N.Y.S. 179 (1917) and International Paper Co. v. Rockefeller, 161 App.Div. 180, 146 N.Y.S. 371 (1914).) There is no excuse under this section, however, unless the seller has employed all due measures to assure himself that his source will not fail. (See Canadian Industrial Alcohol Co., Ltd., v. Dunbar Molasses Co., 258 N.Y. 194, 179 N.E. 383, 80 A.L.R. 1173 (1932) and Washington Mfg. Co. v. Midland Lumber Co., 113 Wash. 593, 194 P. 777 (1921).)

In the case of failure of production by an agreed source for causes beyond the seller's control, the seller should, if possible, be excused since production by an agreed source is without more a basic assumption of the contract. Such excuse should not result in relieving the defaulting supplier from liability nor in dropping into the seller's lap an unearned bonus of damages over. The flexible adjustment machinery of this Article provides the solution under the provision on the obligation of good faith. A condition to his making good the claim of excuse is the turning over to the buyer of his rights against the defaulting source of supply to the extent of the buyer's contract in relation to which excuse is being claimed.

6. In situations in which neither sense nor justice is served by either answer when the issue is posed in flat terms of "excuse" or "no excuse," adjustment under the various provisions of this Article is necessary, especially the sections on good faith, on insecurity and assurance and on the reading of all provisions in the light of their purposes, and the general policy of this Act to use equitable principles in furtherance of commercial standards and good faith.

7. The failure of conditions which go to convenience or collateral values rather than to the commercial practicability of the main performance does not amount to a complete excuse. However, good faith and the reason of the present section and of the preceding one may properly be held to justify and even to require any needed delay involved in a good faith inquiry seeking a readjustment of the contract terms to meet the new conditions.

8. The provisions of this section are made subject to assumption of greater liability by agreement and such agreement is to be found not only in the expressed terms of the contract but in the circumstances surrounding the contracting, in trade usage and the like. Thus the exemptions of this section do not apply when the contingency in question is sufficiently foreshadowed at the time of contracting to be included among the business risks which are fairly to be regarded as part of the dickered terms, either consciously or as a matter of reasonable, commercial interpretation from the circumstances. (See Madeirense Do Brasil, S.A. v. Stulman-Emrick Lumber Co., 147 F.2d 399 (C.C.A., 2 Cir., 1945).) The exemption otherwise present through usage of trade under the present section may also be expressly negated by the language of the agreement. Generally, express agreements as to exemptions designed to enlarge upon or supplant the provisions of this section are to be read in the light of mercantile sense and reason, for this section itself sets up the commercial standard for normal and reasonable interpretation and provides a minimum beyond which agreement may not go.

Agreement can also be made in regard to the consequences of exemption as laid down in paragraphs (b) and (c) and the next section on procedure on notice claiming excuse.

9. The case of a farmer who has contracted to sell crops to be grown on designated land may be regarded as falling either within the section on casualty to identified goods or this section, and he may be excused, when there is a failure of the specific crop, either on the basis of the destruction of identified goods or because of the failure of a basic assumption of the contract.

Exemption of the buyer in the case of a "requirements" contract is covered by the "Output and Requirements" section both as to assumption and allocation of the relevant risks. But when a contract by a manufacturer to buy fuel or raw material makes no specific reference to a particular venture and no such reference may be drawn from the circumstances, commercial understanding views it as a general deal in the general market and not conditioned on any assumption of the continuing operation of the buyer's plant. Even when notice is given by the buyer that the supplies are needed to fill a specific contract of a normal commercial kind, commercial understanding does not see such a supply contract as conditioned on the continuance of the buyer's further contract for outlet. On the other hand, where the buyer's contract is in reasonable commercial understanding conditioned on a definite and specific venture or assumption as, for instance, a war procurement subcontract known to be based on a prime contract which is subject to termination, or a supply contract for a particular construction venture, the reason of the present section may well apply and entitle the buyer to the exemption.

10. Following its basic policy of using commercial practicability as a test for excuse, this section recognizes as of equal significance either a foreign or domestic regulation and disregards any technical distinctions between "law", "regulation", "order" and the like. Nor does it make the present action of the seller depend upon the eventual judicial determination of the legality of the particular governmental action. The seller's good faith belief in the validity of the regulation is the test under this Article and the best evidence of his good faith is the general commercial acceptance of the regulation. However, governmental interference cannot excuse unless it truly "supervenes" in such a manner as to be beyond the seller's assumption of risk. And any action by the party claiming excuse which causes or colludes in inducing the governmental action preventing his performance would be in breach of good faith and would destroy his exemption.

11. An excused seller must fulfill his contract to the extent which the supervening contingency permits, and if the situation is such that his customers are generally affected he must take account of all in supplying one. Subsections (a) and (b), therefore, explicitly permit in any proration a fair and reasonable attention to the needs of regular customers who are probably relying on spot order for supplies. Customers at different stages of the manufacturing process may be fairly treated by including the seller's manufacturing requirements. A fortiori, the seller may also take account of contracts later in date than the one in question. The fact that such spot orders may be closed at an advanced price causes no difficulty, since any allocation which exceeds normal past requirements will not be reasonable. However, good faith requires, when prices have advanced, that the seller exercise real care in making his allocations, and in case of doubt his contract customers should be favored and supplies prorated evenly among them regardless of price. Save for the extra care thus required by changes in the market, this section seeks to leave every reasonable business leeway to the seller.

Cross References:

Point 1: Sections 2–613 and 2–614.
Point 2: Section 1–102.
Point 5: Sections 1–203 and 2–613.
Point 6: Sections 1–102, 1–203 and 2–609.
Point 7: Section 2–614.
Point 8: Sections 1–201, 2–302 and 2–616.
Point 9: Sections 1–102, 2–306 and 2–613.

Definitional Cross References:

"Between merchants". Section 2–104.
"Buyer". Section 2–103.
"Contract". Section 1–201.
"Contract for sale". Section 2–106.
"Good faith". Section 1–201.
"Merchant". Section 2–104.
"Notifies". Section 1–201.
"Seasonably". Section 1–204.
"Seller". Section 2–103.

Section 2–616. Procedure on Notice Claiming Excuse.

(1) Where the buyer receives notification of a material or indefinite delay or an allocation justified under the preceding section he may by written

notification to the seller as to any delivery concerned, and where the prospective deficiency substantially impairs the value of the whole contract under the provisions of this Article relating to breach of installment contracts (Section 2–612), then also as to the whole,

(a) terminate and thereby discharge any unexecuted portion of the contract; or

(b) modify the contract by agreeing to take his available quota in substitution.

(2) If after receipt of such notification from the seller the buyer fails so to modify the contract within a reasonable time not exceeding thirty days the contract lapses with respect to any deliveries affected.

(3) The provisions of this section may not be negated by agreement except in so far as the seller has assumed a greater obligation under the preceding section.

New York Annotations

The procedures established by this section implement the rules established under Sections 2–614 and 2–615. No comparable provisions are in the Sales Act and the rules appear to be new. As to the buyer's option to cancel when the seller's failure of performance is excused, see, *accord:* Restatement, Contracts, §§ 274–276.

Official Uniform Comment

Prior Uniform Statutory Provision: None.

Purposes:

This section seeks to establish simple and workable machinery for providing certainty as to when a supervening and excusing contingency "excuses" the delay, "discharges" the contract, or may result in a waiver of the delay by the buyer. When the seller notifies, in accordance with the preceding section, claiming excuse, the buyer may acquiesce, in which case the contract is so modified. No consideration is necessary in a case of this kind to support such a modification. If the buyer does not elect so to modify the contract, he may terminate it and under subsection (2) his silence after receiving the seller's claim of excuse operates as such a termination. Subsection (3) denies effect to any contract clause made in advance of trouble which would require the buyer to stand ready to take delivery by unforeseen circumstances.

Cross References:

Point 1: Sections 2–209 and 2–615.

Definitional Cross References:

"Buyer". Section 2–103.
"Contract". Section 1–201.
"Installment contract". Section 2–612.
"Notification". Section 1–201.
"Reasonable time". Section 1–204.
"Seller". Section 2–103.
"Termination". Section 2–106.

"Written". Section 1–201.

PART 7

REMEDIES

Section 2–701. Remedies for Breach of Collateral Contracts Not Impaired.

Remedies for breach of any obligation or promise collateral or ancillary to a contract for sale are not impaired by the provisions of this Article.

New York Annotations

This section appears to limit the scope of the Sales Article to parts of a contract related to the sale of goods, and requires no annotation. See Section 2–102, *supra.*

Official Uniform Comment

Prior Uniform Statutory Provision: None.

Purposes:

Whether a claim for breach of an obligation collateral to the contract for sale requires separate trial to avoid confusion of issues is beyond the scope of this Article; but contractual arrangements which as a business matter enter vitally into the contract should be considered a part thereof in so far as cross-claims or defenses are concerned.

Definitional Cross References:

"Contract for sale". Section 2–106.
"Remedy". Section 1–201.

Section 2–702. Seller's Remedies on Discovery of Buyer's Insolvency.

(1) Where the seller discovers the buyer to be insolvent he may refuse delivery except for cash including payment for all goods theretofore delivered under the contract, and stop delivery under this Article (Section 2–705).

(2) Where the seller discovers that the buyer has received goods on credit while insolvent he may reclaim the goods upon demand made within ten days after the receipt, but if misrepresentation of solvency has been made to the particular seller in writing within three months before delivery the ten day limitation does not apply. Except as provided in this subsection the seller may not base a right to reclaim goods on the buyer's fraudulent or innocent misrepresentation of solvency or of intent to pay.

(3) The seller's right to reclaim under subsection (2) is subject to the rights of a buyer in ordinary course or other good faith purchaser under this Article (Section 2–403). Successful reclamation of goods excludes all other remedies with respect to them.

N.Y. Commission Comments

The 1958 and 1962 Official Texts of Section 2–702(3) include the phrase "or lien creditor" following "purchaser" in the first sentence of subsection (3). Subsection (3) as enacted in New York in 1962 omitted that phrase for the reason stated in the Commission's 1962 Report:

"The omission in the first sentence of subsection (3) of 'or lien creditor' follows the Code as enacted in Illinois and is designed to prevent the frustration of the seller's rights to reclaim the goods when the buyer becomes bankrupt as in In re Kravitz, 278 F.2d 820 (3rd Cir. 1960)."

New York Annotations

(1) *Refusal of delivery.* The right on insolvency to refuse delivery except for cash, even though credit was agreed upon, follows Personal Property Law, § 135(1)(c). The right to insist on payment for past deliveries as well as for the current delivery is new. On stoppage, see Section 2–705, *infra.* "Insolvent" is defined in Section 1–201(23).

(2) *Reclamation.* Where goods are delivered on credit, the present law gives the seller a power to rescind and recover the goods when the buyer fraudulently misrepresents his credit status or his intent to pay. Baldwin v. Childs, 249 N.Y. 212, 163 N.E. 737 (1928); Whitten v. Fitzwater, 129 N.Y. 626, 29 N.E. 298 (1891); Hotchkin v. Third Nat. Bank, 127 N.Y. 329, 27 N.E. 1050 (1891); Mann v. Pusrin, 158 N.Y.S. 906 (1916); In re Meiselman, 105 F.2d 995 (2d Cir. 1939). Restatement, Contracts, §473 and New York Annotations. The Code adds (1) automatic reclamation on proof of insolvency within ten days, and (2) a limitation of ten days or a requirement of a written representation of solvency made within three months prior to delivery. Reclamation under the Code is an exclusive remedy because it prefers the seller to other creditors. Although there is recognition in bankruptcy of the seller's right to rescind in cases of actual fraud, e.g. In re Meiselman, *supra,* doubt has been cast upon the bankruptcy status of the Code remedy for both actual and presumed fraud. See In re Kravitz, 278 F.2d 820 (3rd Cir. 1960), and Note, 45 Cornell L.Q. 566 (1960). See Section 9–113, *infra.*

Historical Note: At the suggestion of the Law Revision Commission, former subsection (1)(b) was rewritten as subsections (2) and (3). The changes make it clear that demand within ten days after receipt may be sufficient even though repossession cannot be accomplished until later, that the section applies to innocent as well as fraudulent misrepresentation of solvency or intent to pay, and that it excludes any other reclamation for such misrepresentation but not for misrepresentation of other facts. (1956 Recommendations, p. 72; Excerpts, p. 395.)

Official Uniform Comment

Prior Uniform Statutory Provision: Subsection (1)–Sections 53(1)(b), 54(1)(c) and 57, Uniform Sales Act; Subsection (2)–none; Subsection (3)–Section 76(3), Uniform Sales Act.

Changes: Rewritten, the protection given to a seller who has sold on credit and has delivered goods to the buyer immediately preceding his insolvency being extended.

Purposes of Changes and New Matter: To make it clear that:

1. The seller's right to withhold the goods or to stop delivery except for cash when he discovers the buyer's insolvency is made explicit in subsection (1) regardless of the passage of title, and the concept of stoppage has been extended to include goods in the possession of any bailee who has not yet attorned to the buyer.

2. Subsection (2) takes as its base line the proposition that any receipt of goods on credit by an insolvent buyer amounts to a tacit business misrepresentation of solvency and therefore is fraudulent as against the particular seller. This Article makes discovery of the buyer's insolvency and demand within a ten day period a condition of the right to reclaim goods on this ground. The ten day limitation period operates from the time of receipt of the goods.

An exception to this time limitation is made when a written misrepresentation of solvency has been made to the particular seller within three months prior to the delivery. To fall within the exception the statement of solvency must be in writing, addressed to the particular seller and dated within three months of the delivery.

3. Because the right of the seller to reclaim goods under this section constitutes preferential treatment as against the buyer's other creditors, subsection (3) provides that such reclamation bars all his other remedies as to the goods involved. As amended 1966.

Cross References:

Point 1: Section 2–401 and 2–705.
Compare Section 2–502.

Definitional Cross References:

"Buyer". Section 2–103.
"Buyer in ordinary course of business". Section 1–201.
"Contract". Section 1–201.
"Good faith". Section 2–105.
"Goods". Section 2–105.
"Insolvent". Section 1–201.
"Person". Section 1–201.
"Purchaser". Section 1–201.
"Receipt of goods". Section 2–103.
"Remedy". Section 1–201.
"Rights". Section 1–201.
"Seller". Section 2–103.
"Writing". Section 1–201.

Section 2–703. Seller's Remedies in General.

Where the buyer wrongfully rejects or revokes acceptance of goods or fails to make a payment due on or before delivery or repudiates with respect to a part or the whole, then with respect to any goods directly affected and, if the breach is of the whole contract (Section 2–612), then also with respect to the whole undelivered balance, the aggrieved seller may

(a) withhold delivery of such goods;

(b) stop delivery by any bailee as hereafter provided (Section 2–705);

(c) proceed under the next section respecting goods still unidentified to the contract;

(d) resell and recover damages as hereafter provided (Section 2–706);

(e) recover damages for non-acceptance (Section 2–708) or in a proper case the price (Section 2–709);

(f) cancel.

New York Annotations

The section collects the remedies of the seller under other sections, and requires no annotation. "Cancellation" is defined in Section 2–106(4).

Historical Note: At the suggestion of the Law Revision Commission, subsection (e) was changed to make it clear that the aggrieved seller is not required to elect between damages under Section 2–706 and damages under Section 2–708. See Comment 1 to this section and Comment 2 to Section 2–706. (1956 Recommendations, p. 73; Excerpts, p. 396.)

Official Uniform Comment

Prior Uniform Statutory Provision: No comparable index section. See Section 53, Uniform Sales Act.

Purposes:

1. This section is an index section which gathers together in one convenient place all of the various remedies open to a seller for any breach by the buyer. This Article rejects any doctrine of election of remedy as a fundamental policy and thus the remedies are essentially cumulative in nature and include all of the available remedies for breach. Whether the pursuit of one remedy bars another depends entirely on the facts of the individual case.

2. The buyer's breach which occasions the use of the remedies under this section may involve only one lot or delivery of goods, or may involve all of the goods which are the subject matter of the particular contract. The right of the seller to pursue a remedy as to all the goods when the breach is as to only one or more lots is covered by the section on breach in installment contracts. The present section deals only with the remedies available after the goods involved in the breach have been determined by that section.

3. In addition to the typical ease of refusal to pay or default in payment, the language in the preamble, "fails to make a payment due", is intended to cover the dishonor of a check on due presentment, or the non-acceptance of a draft, and the failure to furnish an agreed letter of credit.

4. It should also be noted that this Act requires its remedies to be liberally administered and provides that any right or obligation which it declares is enforceable by action unless a different effect is specifically prescribed (Section 1–106).

Cross References:

Point 2: Section 2–612.
Point 3: Section 3: Section 2–325.
Point 4: Section 1–106.

Definitional Cross References:

"Aggrieved party". Section 1–201.
"Buyer". Section 2–103.
"Cancellation". Section 2–106.
"Contract". Section 1–201.
"Goods". Section 2–105.
"Remedy". Section 1–201.
"Seller". Section 2–103.

Section 2–704. Seller's Right to Identify Goods to the Contract Notwithstanding Breach or to Salvage Unfinished Goods.

(1) An aggrieved seller under the preceding section may

(a) identify to the contract conforming goods not already identified if at the time he learned of the breach they are in his possession or control;

(b) treat as the subject of resale goods which have demonstrably been intended for the particular contract even though those goods are unfinished.

(2) Where the goods are unfinished an aggrieved seller may in the exercise of reasonable commercial judgment for the purposes of avoiding loss and of effective realization either complete the manufacture and wholly identify the goods to the contract or cease manufacture and resell for scrap or salvage value or proceed in any other reasonable manner.

New York Annotations

This section is preliminary to later provisions giving the seller the right to fix the buyer's damages by resale (Section 2–706) and, in special circumstances, to sue for the price (Section 2–709). Identification of the goods is important also in relation to insurability of the interest of the buyer (Section 2–501) and in shifting risk of loss to a party guilty of a breach (Section 2–510).

Historical Note: Supp. No. 1 changed the section to make it clear that the seller may resell unfinished goods for scrap or salvage value, and accomplishes the same result which the Commercial Code Committee of the Pennsylvania Chamber of Commerce had proposed by amending Section 2–709(2). (1956 Recommendations, p.74.)

Official Uniform Comment

Prior Uniform Statutory Provision: Sections 63(3) and 64(4), Uniform Sales Act.

Changes: Rewritten, the seller's rights being broadened.

Purposes of Changes:

1. This section gives an aggrieved seller the right at the time of breach to identify to the contract any conforming finished goods, regardless of their resalability, and to use reasonable judgment as to completing unfinished goods. It thus makes the goods available for resale under the resale section, the seller's primary remedy, and in the special case in which resale is not practicable, allows the action for the price which would then be necessary to give the seller the value of his contract.

2. Under this Article the seller is given express power to complete manufacture or procurement of goods for the contract unless the exercise of reasonable commercial judgment as to the facts as they appear at the time he learns of the breach makes it clear that such action will result in a material increase in damages. The burden is on the buyer to show the commercially unreasonable nature of the seller's action in completing manufacture.

Cross References:

Section 2–703 and 2–706.

Definitional Cross References:

"Aggrieved party". Section 1–201.
"Conforming". Section 2–106.
"Contract". Section 1–201.
"Goods". Section 2–105.
"Rights". Section 1–201.
"Seller". Section 2–103.

Section 2–705. Seller's Stoppage of Delivery in Transit or Otherwise.

(1) The seller may stop delivery of goods in the possession of a carrier or other bailee when he discovers the buyer to be insolvent (Section 2–702) and may stop delivery of carload, truckload, planeload or larger shipments of express or freight when the buyer repudiates or fails to make a payment due before delivery or if for any other reason the seller has a right to withhold or reclaim the goods.

(2) As against such buyer the seller may stop delivery, until

(a) receipt of the goods by the buyer; or

(b) acknowledgment to the buyer by any bailee of the goods except a carrier that the bailee holds the goods for the buyer; or

(c) such acknowledgment to the buyer by a carrier by reshipment or as warehouseman; or

(d) negotiation to the buyer of any negotiable document of title covering the goods.

(3)(a) To stop delivery the seller must so notify as to enable the bailee by reasonable diligence to prevent delivery of the goods.

(b) After such notification the bailee must hold and deliver the goods according to the directions of the seller but the seller is liable to the bailee for any ensuing charges or damages.

(c) If a negotiable document of title has been issued for goods the bailee is not obliged to obey a notification to stop until surrender of the document.

(d) A carrier who has issued a non-negotiable bill of lading is not obliged to obey a notification to stop received from a person other than the consignor.

New York Annotations

(1) *Right of stoppage.* The right to resume possession of goods in transit conferred by Personal Property Law, §§ 138 and 139, is continued under the Code and applied to other bailees as well as carriers. Rummel v. Blanchard, 216 N.Y. 348, 110 N.E. 765 (1915). As to carload shipments the right is expanded to operate in cases where the buyer repudiates or fails to make a down payment, or in any case where the seller would have a right to withhold or reclaim (e.g. fraud by buyer). Where there is a less than carload shipment the right is limited as under present law to cases of insolvency. Hunter v. Payne, 113 Misc. 385, 184 N.Y.S. 433, aff'd 197 App.Div. 919, 188 N.Y.S. 926 (1920). "Insolvent" is defined in Section 1–201(23).

(2) *Termination of right.* Under Personal Property Law, § 139(1)(a) and (2)(a), the right of stoppage is lost on delivery, while under Section 2–705(2)(a) the test is receipt of the goods. Subsection (2)(b) and (c) on "acknowledgement" by a bailee or carrier are more specific than Personal Property Law, § 139(2)(b). Compare Rummell v. Blanchard, *supra.* and Buss v. Long Island Storage Warehouse Co., 64 F.2d 338 (2d Cir. 1933). In the case of carriers the right of stoppage is prolonged beyond notification of arrival until a separate contact is made with the buyer (Comment 3). Comment 2 indicates that the right may be terminated by shipment to a subpurchaser. See In re Charles T. Stork & Co., 271 F. 279 (2d Cir. 1921).

Documents of title. Subsections (2)(d) and (3)(c) continue the rule of Personal Property Law, § 140(2), so that a negotiable bill of lading overrides the right of stoppage. Section 7–303 makes a substantial change in the law of stoppage since a carrier is made immune from liability for honoring instructions from the consignor of a non-negotiable bill even where the instruction is an improper stop order. Subsection (3)(d) follows this principle. The buyer's rights, against the seller, in such a case remain unimpaired.

Historical Note: The changes adopted recommendations of the Law Revision Commission that the word "wrongfully" be deleted as unnecessary from subsection (1) and that a new subsection (3)(d) be added. The change in subsection (1) conforms to the usage in Sections 2–610 and 2–703. The new subsection (3)(d) transfers to the text the rule previously stated in Comment 2 to this section, that strangers to the contract of carriage have no right of stoppage as against the carrier. (1956 Recommendations, p. 75; Excerpts, pp. 396–7.)

Official Uniform Comment

Prior Uniform Statutory Provision: Sections 57–59, Uniform Sales Act; see also Sections 12, 14 and 42, Uniform Bills of Lading Act and Sections 9, 11 and 49, Uniform Warehouse Receipts Act.

Changes: This section continues and develops the above sections of the Uniform Sales Act in the light of the other uniform statutory provisions noted.

Purposes: To make it clear that:

1. Subsection (1) applies the stoppage principle to other bailees as well as carriers. It also expands the remedy to cover the situations, in addition to buyer's insolvency, specified in the subsection. But since stoppage is a burden in any case to carriers, and might be a very heavy burden to them if it covered all small shipments in all these situations, the right to stop for reasons other than insolvency is limited to carload, truckload, planeload or larger shipments. The seller shipping to a buyer of doubtful credit can protect himself by shipping C.O.D.

Where stoppage occurs for insecurity it is merely a suspension of performance, and if assurances are duly forthcoming from the buyer the seller is not entitled to resell or divert.

Improper stoppage is a breach by the seller if it effectively interferes with the buyer's right to due tender under the section on manner of tender of delivery. However, if the bailee obeys an unjustified order to stop he may also be liable to the buyer. The measure of his obligation is dependent on the provisions of the Documents of Title Article (Section 7–303). Subsection 3(b) therefore gives him a right of indemnity as against the seller in such a case.

2. "Receipt by the buyer" includes receipt by the buyer's designated representative, the subpurchaser, when shipment is made direct to him and the buyer himself never receives the goods. It is entirely proper under this Article that the seller, by making such direct shipment to the subpurchaser, be regarded as acquiescing in the latter's purchase and as thus barred from stoppage of the goods as against him.

As between the buyer and the seller, the latter's right to stop the goods at any time until they reach the place of final delivery is recognized by this section.

Under subsection 3(c) and (d), the carrier is under no duty to recognize the stop order of a person who is a stranger to the carrier's contract. But the seller's right as against the buyer to stop delivery remains, whether or not the carrier is obligated to recognize the stop order. If the carrier does obey it, the buyer cannot complain merely because of that circumstance; and the seller becomes obligated under subsection 3(b) to pay the carrier any ensuing damages or charges.

3. A diversion of a shipment is not a "reshipment" under subsection 2(c) when it is merely an incident to the original contract of transportation. Nor is the procurement of "exchange bills" of lading which change only the name of the consignee to that of the buyer's local agent but do not alter the destination of a reshipment.

Acknowledgement by the carrier as a "warehouseman" within the meaning of this Article requires a contract of a truly different character from the original shipment, a contract not in extension of transit but as a warehouseman.

4. Subsection (3)(c) makes the bailee's obedience of a notification to stop conditional upon the surrender of any outstanding negotiable document.

5. Any charges or losses incurred by the carrier in following the seller's orders, whether or not he was obligated to do so, fall to the seller's charge.

6. After an effective stoppage under this section the seller's rights in the goods are the same as if he had never made a delivery.

Cross References:

Sections 2–702 and 2–703.
Point 1: Sections 2–503 and 2–609, and Article 7.
Point 2: Section 2–103 and Article 7.

Definitional Cross References:

"Buyer". Section 2–103.
"Contract for sale". Section 2–106.
"Document of title". Section 1 201.
"Goods". Section 2–105.
"Insolvent". Section 1–201.
"Notification". Section 1–201.
"Receipt of goods". Section 2–103.
"Rights". Section 1–201.
"Seller". Section 2–103.

Section 2–706. Seller's Resale Including Contract for Resale.

(1) Under the conditions stated in Section 2–703 on seller's remedies, the seller may resell the goods concerned or the undelivered balance thereof. Where the resale is made in good faith and in a commercially reasonable manner the seller may recover the difference between the resale price and the contract price together with any incidental damages allowed under the provisions of this Article (Section 2–710), but less expenses saved in consequence of the buyer's breach.

(2) Except as otherwise provided in subsection (3) or unless otherwise agreed resale may be at public or private sale including sale by way of one or more contracts to sell or of identification to an existing contract of the seller. Sale may be as a unit or in parcels and at any time and place and on any terms but

every aspect of the sale including the method, manner, time, place and terms must be commercially reasonable. The resale must be reasonably identified as referring to the broken contract, but it is not necessary that the goods be in existence or that any or all of them have been identified to the contract before the breach.

(3) Where the resale is at private sale the seller must give the buyer reasonable notification of his intention to resell.

(4) Where the resale is at public sale

(a) only identified goods can be sold except where there is a recognized market for a public sale of futures in goods of the kind; and

(b) it must be made at a usual place or market for public sale if one is reasonably available and except in the case of goods which are perishable or threaten to decline in value speedily the seller must give the buyer reasonable notice of the time and place of the resale; and

(c) if the goods are not to be within the view of those attending the sale the notification of sale must state the place where the goods are located and provide for their reasonable inspection by prospective bidders; and

(d) the seller may buy.

(5) A purchaser who buys in good faith at a resale takes the goods free of any rights of the original buyer even though the seller fails to comply with one or more of the requirements of this section.

(6) The seller is not accountable to the buyer for any profit made on any resale. A person in the position of a seller (Section 2–707) or a buyer who has rightfully rejected or justifiably revoked acceptance must account for any excess over the amount of his security interest, as hereinafter defined (subsection (3) of Section 2–711).

New York Annotations

(1) *Right of resale to fix damages.* Subsection (1) allows the seller to act promptly to resell if buyer defaults; under Personal Property Law, § 141, the right arises only if the goods are perishable, or the right of resale is expressly reserved, or the buyer has been in default "an unreasonable time".

Unlike the Sales Act, the Code explicitly provides that the resale fixes the value of the goods for the purpose of measuring damages. The New York case law seems to be in accord: D'Aprile v. Turner-Looker Co., 239 N.Y. 427, 147 N.E. 15 (1925); Anness v. Seaboard Trading Co. 230 App.Div. 69, 243 N.Y.S. 27 (1930); Taylor v. Kurzrok, 214 App.Div. 308, 212 N.Y.S. 133 (1925). *Contra,* Duncan v. Wohl, South & Co., 201 App.Div. 737, 195 N.Y.S. 381 (1922). See Higgins v. California Prune & Apricot Growers, Inc., 16 F.2d 190 (2d Cir. 1926).

(2) *Conduct of sale.* The requirement that the resale be "commercially reasonable" may give the seller more latitude than the requirement of "reasonable care and judgment" in Personal Property Law, § 141 (5).

(3) *Notice.* The Code in subsections (3) and (4)(b) requires notice in some cases where the present law does not. Personal Property Law, § 141(3) and (4) makes notice

relevant to the question whether the seller sold prematurely. Under the Code a seller who fails to give the required notice could still recover damages based on market price rather than the resale price. (Section 2–708.)

(4) *Public sales.* Subsection (4) establishes new standards for public sales. Compare Personal Property Law, § 141(5).

(5) Subsection (5) gives to good faith purchasers greater protection than Personal Property Law, § 141(2), which apparently requires a resale, "as authorized in this section."

(6) *Accord as to seller:* Personal Property Law, § 141(1). The provision making other parties accountable for profits on resale changes the law. As to a person in the position of a seller, see Personal Property Law, §§ 133 (2), 141(1), and 156 (definition of seller). As to a rescinding buyer, see Personal Property Law, § 150(5).

Historical Note: "Expenses" was substituted for "any expense" in subsection (1) and in Sections 2–708(1), 2–712(2), and 2–713(1) to avoid the possibility that proof of damages might fail because of a speculative possibility that some expense might have been saved. (1956 Recommendations, p. 75.)

Official Uniform Comment

Prior Uniform Statutory Provision: Section 60, Uniform Sales Act.

Changes: Rewritten.

Purposes of Changes: To simplify the prior statutory provision and to make it clear that:

1. The only condition precedent to the seller's right of resale under subsection (1) is a breach by the buyer within the section on the seller's remedies in general or insolvency. Other meticulous conditions and restrictions of the prior uniform statutory provision are disapproved by this Article and are replaced by standards of commercial reasonableness. Under this section the seller may resell the goods after any breach by the buyer. Thus, an anticipatory repudiation by the buyer gives rise to any of the seller's remedies for breach, and to the right of resale. This principle is supplemented by subsection (2) which authorizes a resale of goods which are not identified to the contract before the breach.

2. In order to recover the damages prescribed in subsection (1) the seller must act "in good faith and in a commercially reasonable manner" in making the resale. This standard is intended to be more comprehensive than that of "reasonable care and judgment" established by the prior uniform statutory provision. Failure to act properly under this section deprives the seller of the measure of damages here provided and relegates him to that provided in Section 2–708.

Under this Article the seller resells by authority of law, in his own behalf, for his own benefit and for the purpose of fixing his damages. The theory of a seller's agency is thus rejected.

3. If the seller complies with the prescribed standard of duty in making the resale, he may recover from the buyer the damages provided for in subsection (1). Evidence of market or current prices at any particular time or place is relevant only on the question of whether the seller acted in a commercially reasonable manner in making the resale.

The distinction drawn by some courts between cases where the title had not passed to the buyer and the seller had resold as owner, and cases where the title had passed and the seller had resold by virtue of his lien on the goods, is rejected.

4. Subsection (2) frees the remedy of resale from legalistic restrictions and enables the seller to resell in accordance with reasonable commercial practices so as to realize as high a price as possible in the circumstances. By "public" sale is meant a sale by auction. A "private" sale may be effected by solicitation and negotiation conducted either directly or through a broker. In choosing between a public and private sale

the character of the goods must be considered and relevant trade practices and usages must be observed.

5. Subsection (2) merely clarifies the common law rule that the time for resale is a reasonable time after the buyer's breach by using the language "commercially reasonable". What is such a reasonable time depends upon the nature of the goods, the condition of the market and the other circumstances of the case; its length cannot be measured by any legal yardstick or divided into degrees. Where a seller contemplating resale receives a demand from the buyer for inspection under the section of preserving evidence of goods in dispute, the time for resale may be appropriately lengthened.

On the question of the place for resale, subsection (2) goes to the ultimate test, the commercial reasonableness of the seller's choice as to the place for an advantageous resale. This Article rejects the theory that the seller is required to resell at the agreed place for delivery and that a resale elsewhere can be permitted only in exceptional cases.

6. The purpose of subsection (2) being to enable the seller to dispose of the goods to the best advantage, he is permitted in making the resale to depart from the terms and conditions of the original contract for sale to any extent "commercially reasonable" in the circumstances.

7. The provision of subsection (2) that the goods need not be in existence to be resold applies when the buyer is guilty of anticipatory repudiation of a contract for future goods, before the goods or some of them have come into existence. In such a case the seller may exercise the right of resale and fix his damages by "one or more contracts to sell" the quantity of conforming future goods affected by the repudiation. The companion provision of subsection (2) that resale may be made although the goods were not identified to the contract prior to the buyer's breach, likewise contemplates an anticipatory repudiation by the buyer not occurring after the goods are in existence. If the goods so identified conform to the contract, their resale will fix the seller's damages quite as satisfactorily as if they had been identified before the breach.

8. Where the resale is to be by private sale, subsection (3) requires that reasonable notification of the seller's intention to resell must be given to the buyer. The length of notification of a private sale depends upon the urgency of the matter. Notification of the time and place of this type of sale is not required.

Subsection (4)(b) requires that the seller give the buyer reasonable notice of the time and place of a public resale so that he may have an opportunity to bid or to secure the attendance of other bidders. An exception is made in the case of goods "which are perishable or threaten to decline speedily in value."

9. Since there would be no reasonable prospect of competitive bidding elsewhere, subsection (4) requires that a public resale "must be made at a usual place or market for public sale if one is reasonably available;" i.e., a place or market which prospective bidders may reasonably be expected to attend. Such a market may still be "reasonably available" under this subsection, though at a considerable distance from the place where the goods are located. In such a case the expense of transporting the goods for resale is recoverable from the buyer as part of the seller's incidental damages under subsection (1). However, the question of availability is one of commercial reasonableness in the circumstances and if such "usual" place or market is not reasonably available, a duly advertised public resale may be held at another place if it is one which prospective bidders may reasonably be expected to attend, as distinguished from a place where there is no demand whatsoever for goods of the kind.

Paragraph (a) of subsection (4) qualifies the last sentence of subsection (2) with respect to resales of unidentified and future goods at public sale. If conforming goods are in existence the seller may identify them to the contract after the buyer's breach and then resell them at public sale. If the goods have not been identified, however, he may resell them at public sale only as "future" goods and only where there is a recognized market for public sale of futures in goods of the kind.

The provisions of paragraph (c) of subsection (4) are intended to permit intelligent bidding.

The provision of paragraph (d) of subsection (4) permitting the seller to bid and, of course, to become the purchaser, benefits the original buyer by tending to increase the resale price and thus decreasing the damages he will have to pay.

10. This Article departs in subsection (5) from the prior uniform statutory provision in permitting a good faith purchaser at resale to take a good title as against the buyer even though the seller fails to comply with the requirements of this section.

11. Under subsection (6), the seller retains profit, if any, without distinction based on whether or not he had a lien since this Article divorces the question of passage of title to the buyer from the seller's right of resale or the consequences of its exercise. On the other hand, where "a person in the position of a seller" or a buyer acting under the present section he does so only for the limited purpose of obtaining cash for his "security interest" in the goods. Once that purpose has been accomplished any excess in the resale price belongs to the seller to whom an accounting must be made as provided in the last sentence of subsection (6).

Cross References:

Point 1: Sections 2–610, 2–702 and 2–703.
Point 2: Section 1–201.
Point 3: Sections 2–708 and 2–710.
Point 4: Section 2–328.
Point 8: Section 2–104.
Point 9: Section 2–710.
Point 11: Sections 2–401, 2–707 and 2–711(3).

Definitional Cross References:

"Buyer". Section 2–103.
"Contract". Section 1–201.
"Contract for sale". Section 2–106.
"Good faith". Section 2–103.
"Goods". Section 2–105.
"Merchant". Section 2–104.
"Notification". Section 1–201.
"Person in position of seller". Section 2–707.
"Purchase". Section 1–201.
"Rights". Section 1–201.
"Sale". Section 2–106.
"Security interest". Section 1–201.
"Seller". Section 2–103.

Section 2–707. "Person in the Position of a Seller".

(1) A "person in the position of a seller" includes as against a principal an agent who has paid or become responsible for the price of goods on behalf of his principal or anyone who otherwise holds a security interest or other right in goods similar to that of a seller.

(2) A person in the position of a seller may as provided in this Article withhold or stop delivery (Section 2–705) and resell (Section 2–706) and recover incidental damages (Section 2–710).

New York Annotations

This section expands Personal Property Law, § 133(2), to include a financing agency with a security interest. Note that under Section 2–706 a person in the position of a seller must account to the buyer for any profit on a resale, and under Section 2–705(3)(d) the carrier need not honor directions to stop from one not the "consignor."

Historical Note: The section was revised at the suggestion of the Law Revision Commission for clarification without change of meaning. (1956 Recommendations, p. 76; Excerpts, p. 397.)

Official Uniform Comment

Prior Uniform Statutory Provision: Section 52(2), Uniform Sales Act.

Changes: Rewritten.

Purposes of Changes: To make it clear that:

In addition to following in general the prior uniform statutory provision, the case of a financing agency which has acquired documents by honoring a letter of credit for the buyer or by discounting a draft for the seller has been included in the term "a person in the position of a seller."

Cross Reference:

Article 5, Section 2–506.

Definitional Cross References:

"Consignee". Section 7–102.
"Consignor". Section 7–102.
"Goods". Section 2–105.
"Security interest". Section 1–201.
"Seller". Section 2–103.

Section 2–708. Seller's Damages for Non-Acceptance or Repudiation.

(1) Subject to subsection (2) and to the provisions of this Article with respect to proof of market price (Section 2–723), the measure of damages for non-acceptance or repudiation by the buyer is the difference between the market price at the time and place for tender and the unpaid contract price together with any incidental damages provided in this Article (Section 2–710), but less expenses saved in consequence of the buyer's breach.

(2) If the measure of damages provided in subsection (1) is inadequate to put the seller in as good a position as performance would have done then the measure of damages is the profit (including reasonable overhead) which the seller would have made from full performance by the buyer together with any incidental damages provided in this Article (Section 2–710), due allowance for costs reasonably incurred and due credit for payments or proceeds of resale.

New York Annotations

The fundamental rule of measuring damages approximates that of Personal Property Law, § 145. But the limitations imposed by present New York law on the right to recover profits are omitted. See, e.g., A. Lenobel Inc. v. Senif, 252 App.Div.533, 300 N.Y.S. 226 (1937) (profit not recovered by dealer in fixed price articles). As to seller's damages for anticipatory repudiation, see Section 2–723.

Historical Note: The section was revised in Supp. No. 1 to extend the rule clearly to cases of repudiation and to clarify the privilege of the seller to realize junk value when it is manifestly useless to complete the operation of manufacture. Further changes, made for clarification to meet criticisms of the Law Revision Commission, divided the section into two subsections, inserted cross-references to Sections 2–710 and 2–723, substituted "market" for "current" price, and inserted the provision for credit for payments in new subsection (2). As to "expenses", see Section 2–706. (1956 Recommendations, p. 77; Excerpts, p. 397.)

Official Uniform Comment

Prior Uniform Statutory Provision: Section 64, Uniform Sales Act.

Changes: Rewritten.

Purposes of Changes: To make it clear that:

1. The prior uniform statutory provision is followed generally in setting the current market price at the time and place for tender as the standard by which damages for non-acceptance are to be determined. The time and place of tender is determined by reference to the section on manner of tender of delivery, and to the sections on the effect of such terms as FOB, FAS, CIF, C & F, Ex Ship and No Arrival, No Sale.

In the event that there is no evidence available of the current market price at the time and place of tender, proof of a substitute market may be made under the section on determination and proof of market price. Furthermore, the section on the admissibility of market quotations is intended to ease materially the problem of providing competent evidence.

2. The provision of this section permitting recovery of expected profit including reasonable overhead where the standard measure of damages is inadequate, together with the new requirement that price actions may be sustained only where resale is impractical, are designed to eliminate the unfair and economically wasteful results arising under the older law when fixed price articles were involved. This section permits the recovery of lost profits in all appropriate cases, which would include all standard priced goods. The normal measure there would be list price less cost to the dealer or list price less manufacturing cost to the manufacturer. It is not necessary to a recovery of "profit" to show a history of earnings, especially if a new venture is involved.

3. In all cases the seller may recover incidental damages.

Cross References:

Point 1: Sections 2–319 through 2–324, 2–503, 2–723 and 2–724.
Point 2: Section 2–709.
Point 3: Section 2–710.

Definitional Cross References:

"Buyer". Section 2–103.
"Contract". Section 1–201.
"Seller". Section 2–103.

Section 2–709. Action for the Price.

(1) When the buyer fails to pay the price as it becomes due the seller may recover, together with any incidental damages under the next section, the price

(a) of goods accepted or of conforming goods lost or damaged within a commercially reasonable time after risk of their loss has passed to the buyer; and

(b) of goods identified to the contract if the seller is unable after reasonable effort to resell them at a reasonable price or the circumstances reasonably indicate that such effort will be unavailing.

(2) Where the seller sues for the price he must hold for the buyer any goods which have been identified to the contract and are still in his control except that if resale becomes possible he may resell them at any time prior to the collection of the judgment. The net proceeds of any such resale must be credited to the buyer, and payment of the judgment entitles him to any goods not resold.

(3) After the buyer has wrongfully rejected or revoked acceptance of the goods or has failed to make a payment due or has repudiated (Section 2–610), a seller who is held not entitled to the price under this section shall nevertheless be awarded damages for non-acceptance under the preceding section.

New York Annotations

(1)(a) The Code restricts the seller's action for the price, making the action for damages the primary remedy. Liability for the price initially hinges upon acceptance rather than upon title as under existing law. See Section 2–606; Personal Property Law, § 144. As under Personal Property Law, § 128(1), the buyer's acceptance is delayed until he has had a reasonable opportunity to inspect the goods.

The most significant change from present law deals with goods loaded on a carrier by the seller where buyer is responsible for the freight. Under Personal Property Law, §§ 100, Rule 4(2), and 144(1), title passes on loading and buyer becomes responsible for the full price regardless of damage in transit or resalability. Under this subsection and Section 2–509 the Code preserves this result for goods lost or damaged in transit. However, under the Code the buyer is not liable for the full price for unaccepted conforming goods which are readily resalable. The Code also omits the provision of Personal Property Law, § 144, for enforcement of a contract term for advance payment. See Comment 6.

(1)(b) This subsection, in giving an action for the price where the goods cannot readily be resold, is comparable to Personal Property Law, § 144(3). See Standard Fabrics Corp. v. Hob Mfg. Co., 199 App.Div. 508, 191 N.Y.S. 821 (1922). The seller is no longer required to "notify the buyer that the goods are thereafter held by the seller as bailee for the buyer."

(2) *Accord:* Personal Property Law, § 144(3). D'Aprile v. Turner-Looker Co., 239 N.Y. 427, 147 N.E. 15 (1925).

(3) This subsection expresses a policy consistent with Civil Practice Act, § 258 (now CPLR § 601) (joinder of inconsistent causes of action) and the "clean up" principle of equity jurisdiction.

Historical Note: The change adding "commercially reasonable time" to subsection (1)(a) meets the point made by the Law Revision Commission that the seller should not be able to hold the goods at the buyer's risk indefinitely. Compare Sections 2–610(a), 2–706(2), 2–708, and 2–710. (1956 Recommendations, p.78; Excerpts, p. 398.)

Official Uniform Comment

Prior Uniform Statutory Provision: Section 63, Uniform Sales Act.

Changes: Rewritten, important commercially needed changes being incorporated.

Purposes of Changes: To make it clear that:

1. Neither the passing of title to the goods nor the appointment of a day certain for payment is now material to a price action.

2. The action for the price is now generally limited to those cases where resale of the goods is impracticable except where the buyer has accepted the goods or where they have been destroyed after risk of loss has passed to the buyer.

3. This section substitutes an objective test by action for the former "not readily resalable" standard. An action for the price under subsection (1)(b) can be sustained only after a "reasonable effort to resell" the goods "at reasonable price" has actually been made or where the circumstances "reasonably indicate" that such an effort will be unavailing.

4. If a buyer is in default not with respect to the price, but on an obligation to make an advance, the seller should recover not under this section for the price as such, but for the default in the collateral (though coincident) obligation to finance the seller. If the agreement between the parties contemplates that the buyer will acquire, on making the advance, a security interest in the goods, the buyer on making the advance has such an interest as soon as the seller has rights in the agreed collateral. See Section 9–204.

5."Goods accepted" by the buyer under subsection (1)(a) include only goods as to which there has been no justified revocation of acceptance, for such a revocation means that there has been a default by the seller which bars his rights under this section. "Goods lost or damaged" are covered by the section on risk of loss. "Goods identified to the contract" under subsection (1)(b) are covered by the section on identification and the section on identification notwithstanding breach.

6. This section is intended to be exhaustive in its enumeration of cases where an action for the price lies.

7. If the action for the price fails, the seller may nonetheless have proved a case entitling him to damages for non-acceptance. In such a situation, subsection (3) permits recovery of those damages in the same action.

Cross References:

Point 4: Section 1–106.
Point 5: Sections 2–501, 2–509, 2–510 and 2–704.
Point 7: Section 2–708.

Definitional Cross References:

"Action". Section 1–201.
"Buyer". Section 2–103.
"Conforming". Section 2–106.
"Contract". Section 1–201.
"Goods". Section 2–105.
"Seller". Section 2–103.

Section 2–710. Seller's Incidental Damages.

Incidental damages to an aggrieved seller include any commercially reasonable charges, expenses or commissions incurred in stopping delivery, in the transportation, care and custody of goods after the buyer's breach, in connection with return or resale of the goods or otherwise resulting from the breach.

UCC

New York Annotations

Accord: Personal Property Law §§ 132, 145, 151; Ackerman v. Rubens, 167 N.Y. 405, 60 N.E. 750 (1901); Sawyer v. Dean, 114 N.Y. 469, 21 N.E. 1012 (1889); Derami, Inc. v. John B. Cabot, Inc., 277 App.Div 852, 98 N.Y.S.2d 34 (1950). Note Section 1–106(1), which provides that neither consequential nor penal damages may be recovered unless specifically provided in the Code or by other rule of law.

Official Uniform Comment

Prior Uniform Statutory Provision: See Sections 64 and 70, Uniform Sales Act.

Purposes: To authorize reimbursement of the seller for expenses reasonably incurred by him as a result of the buyer's breach. The section sets forth the principal normal and necessary additional elements of damage flowing from the breach but intends to allow all commercially reasonable expenditures made by the seller.

Definitional Cross References:

"Aggrieved party". Section 1–201.
"Buyer". Section 2–103.
"Goods". Section 2–105.
"Seller". Section 2–103.

Section 2–711. Buyer's Remedies in General; Buyer's Security Interest in Rejected Goods.

(1) Where the seller fails to make delivery or repudiates or the buyer rightfully rejects or justifiably revokes acceptance then with respect to any goods involved, and with respect to the whole if the breach goes to the whole contract (Section 2–612), the buyer may cancel and whether or not he has done so may in addition to recovering so much of the price as has been paid

(a) "cover" and have damages under the next section as to all the goods affected whether or not they have been identified to the contract; or

(b) recover damages for non-delivery as provided in this Article (Section 2–713).

(2) Where the seller fails to deliver or repudiates the buyer may also

(a) if the goods have been identified recover them as provided in this Article (Section 2–502); or

(b) in a proper case obtain specific performance or replevy the goods as provided in this Article (Section 2–716).

(3) On rightful rejection or justifiable revocation of acceptance a buyer has a security interest in goods in his possession or control for any payments made on their price and any expenses reasonably incurred in their inspection, receipt, transportation, care and custody and may hold such goods and resell them in like manner as an aggrieved seller (Section 2–706).

New York Annotations

This section, like Section 2–703, supra, sums up remedies conferred in other sections. Subsection (1), permitting the buyer to revoke acceptance and recover damages, is an important innovation outside New York, but is in accord with Personal Property Law, § 150(1)(d). Compare Uniform Sales Act, Section 69(1)(d). Subsection (3) giving the buyer a lien extends Personal Property Law, § 150(5), to rejection. See Jones v. Healy, 237 App.Div. 264, 261 N.Y.S. 464 (1932).

Historical Note: Subsection (3) was revised in accordance with suggestions of Law Revision Commission to extend the buyer's security interest for expenses to cases where none of the price has been paid, and to leave requirements of notification to Sections 2–602, 2–608, and 2–706. (1956 Recommendations, p. 79; Excerpts, p. 399.)

Official Uniform Comment

Prior Uniform Statutory Provision: No comparable index section; Subsection (3)–Section 69(5), Uniform Sales Act.

Changes: The prior uniform statutory provision is generally continued and expanded in Subsection (3).

Purposes of Changes and New Matter:

1. To index in this section the buyer's remedies, subsection (1) covering those remedies permitting the recovery of money damages, and subsection (2) covering those which permit reaching the goods themselves. The remedies listed here are those available to a buyer who has not accepted the goods or who has justifiably revoked his acceptance. The remedies available to a buyer with regard to goods finally accepted appear in the section dealing with breach in regard to accepted goods. The buyer's right to proceed as to all goods when the breach is as to only some of the goods is determined by the section on breach in installment contracts and by the section on partial acceptance.

Despite the seller's breach, proper retender of delivery under the section on cure of improper tender or replacement can effectively preclude the buyer's remedies under this section, except for any delay involved.

2. To make it clear in subsection (3) that the buyer may hold and resell rejected goods if he has paid a part of the price or incurred expenses of the type specified. "Paid" as used here includes acceptance of a draft or other time negotiable instrument or the signing of a resale is coextensive with that of a seller under this Article except that the buyer may not keep any profit resulting from the resale and is limited to retaining only the amount of the price paid and the costs involved in the inspection and handling of the goods. The buyer's security interest in the goods is intended to be limited to the items listed in subsection (3), and the buyer is not permitted to retain such funds as he might believe adequate for his damages. The buyer's right to cover, or to have damages for non-delivery, is not impaired by his exercise of his right of resale.

3. It should also be noted that this Act requires its remedies to be liberally administered and provides that any right or obligation which it declares is enforceable by action unless a different effect is specifically prescribed (Section 1–106).

Cross References:

Point 1: Sections 2–508, 2–601(c), 2–608, 2–612 and 2–714.
Point 2: Section 2–706.
Point 3: Section 1–106.

Definitional Cross References:

"Aggrieved party". Section 1–201.
"Buyer". Section 2–103.
"Cancellation". Section 2–106.
"Contract". Section 1–201.
"Cover". Section 2–712.
"Goods". Section 2–105.
"Notifies". Section 1–201.
"Receipt of goods". Section 2–103.
"Remedy". Section 1–201.
"Security interest". Section 1–201.
"Seller". Section 2–103.

Section 2–712. "Cover"; Buyer's Procurement of Substitute Goods.

(1) After a breach within the preceding section the buyer may "cover" by making in good faith and without unreasonable delay any reasonable purchase of or contract to purchase goods in substitution for those due from the seller.

(2) The buyer may recover from the seller as damages the difference between the cost of cover and the contract price together with any incidental or consequential damages as hereinafter defined (Section 2–715), but less expenses saved in consequence of the seller's breach.

(3) Failure of the buyer to effect cover within this section does not bar him from any other remedy.

New York Annotations

This section gives more conclusive weight than the present law to the price paid for substitute goods in fixing the buyer's damages. Compare Section 2–706, supra, on the seller's damages. Note that the alternative of damages based on market price remains available to the buyer. Compare Section 2–713, and Personal Property Law, § 148; Rosenthal v. Empire Brick & Supply Co., 123 App.Div. 503, 108 N.Y.S. 347 (1908) (repurchase within a reasonable time not conclusive).

Historical Note: As to "expenses", see Historical Note to Section 2–706. (1956 Recommendations, p. 79.)

Official Uniform Comment

Prior Uniform Statutory Provision: None.

Purposes:

1. This section provides the buyer with a remedy aimed at enabling him to obtain the goods he needs thus meeting his essential need. This remedy is the buyer's equivalent of the seller's right to resell.

2. The definition of "cover" under subsection (1) envisages a series of contracts or sales, as well as a single contract or sale; goods not identical with those involved but commercially usable as reasonable substitutes under the circumstances of the particular case; and contracts on credit or delivery terms differing from the contract in breach, but again reasonable under the circumstances. The test of proper cover is whether at the time and place the buyer acted in good faith and in a reasonable

manner, and it is immaterial that hindsight may later prove that the method of cover used was not the cheapest or most effective.

The requirement that the buyer must cover "without unreasonable delay" is not intended to limit the time necessary for him to look around and decide as to how he may best effect cover. The test here is similar to that generally used in this Article as to reasonable time and seasonable action.

3. Subsection (3) expresses the policy that cover is not a mandatory remedy for the buyer. The buyer is always free to choose between cover and damages for non-delivery under the next section.

However, this subsection must be read in conjunction with the section which limits the recovery of consequential damages to such as could not have been obviated by cover. Moreover, the operation of the section on specific performance of contracts for "unique" goods must be considered in this connection for availability of the goods to the particular buyer for his particular needs is the test for that remedy and inability to cover is made an express condition to the right of the buyer to replevy the goods.

4. This section does not limit cover to merchants, in the first instance. It is the vital and important remedy for the consumer buyer as well. Both are free to use cover: the domestic or non-merchant consumer is required only to act in normal good faith while the merchant buyer must also observe all reasonable commercial standards of fair dealing in the trade, since this falls within the definition of good faith on his part.

Cross References:

Point 1: Section 2–706.
Point 2: Section 1–204.
Point 3: Section 2–713, 2–715 and 2–716.
Point 4: Section 1–203.

Definitional Cross References:

"Buyer". Section 2–103.
"Contract". Section 1–201.
"Good faith". Section 2–103.
"Goods". Section 2–105.
"Purchase". Section 1–201.
"Remedy". Section 1–201.
"Seller". Section 2–103.

Section 2–713. Buyer's Damages for Non-Delivery or Repudiation.

(1) Subject to the provisions of this Article with respect to proof of market price (Section 2–723), the measure of damages for non-delivery or repudiation by the seller is the difference between the market price at the time when the buyer learned of the breach and the contract price together with any incidental and consequential damages provided in this Article (Section 2–715), but less expenses saved in consequence of the seller's breach.

(2) Market price is to be determined as of the place for tender or, in cases of rejection after arrival or revocation of acceptance, as of the place of arrival.

New York Annotations

(1) In general, subsection (1) follows Personal Property Law, § 148(3). The fact that damages are measured at the time the buyer learned of the breach is consistent

with some New York case law. Perkins v. Minford, 235 N.Y. 301, 139 N.E. 276 (1923); Boyd v. Quinn, 18 Misc. 169, 41 N.Y.S. 391 (1896). Compare Rosenthal v. Empire Brick & Supply Co., 123 App.Div. 503, 108 N.Y.S. 437 (1908). The same requirement may work a change in the time for measuring the market value in cases involving anticipatory repudiation under Section 2–610. Segall v. Finlay, 245 N.Y. 61, 156 N.E. 97 (1927). See Section 2–703.

(2) Market value is determined under the Code at the place for tender (Section 2–503), or in cases of rejection or revocation of acceptance, at the place of arrival. The first test is consistent with New York case law, e.g., Standard Casing Co. v. California Casing Co., 233 N.Y. 413, 135 N.E. 834 (1922) (no goods shipped; buyer's recovery tested at shipping point). One New York case supports measuring market value at place of arrival for rejected goods. Taylor v. Saxe, 134 N.Y.67, 31 N.E. 258 (1892). See Section 2–723.

Historical Note: The section was revised for clarification to meet criticism of the Law Revision Commission. The changes, conforming to the style of changes in Section 2–708, insert a cross-reference to Section 2–723, substitute "market" for "current" price, cover repudiation expressly, and substitute "expenses" for "any expense". As to the last change, see Historical Note to Section 2–706. (1956 Recommendations, p. 80, Excerpts, p. 399.)

Official Uniform Comment

Prior Uniform Statutory Provision: Section 67(3), Uniform Sales Act.

Changes: Rewritten.

Purposes of Changes: To clarify the former rule so that:

1. The general baseline adopted in this section uses as a yardstick the market in which the buyer would have obtained cover had he sought that relief. So the place for measuring damages is the place of tender (or the place of arrival if the goods are rejected or their acceptance is revoked after reaching their destination) and the crucial time is the time at which the buyer learns of the breach.

2. The market or current price to be used in comparison with the contract price under this section is the price for goods of the same kind and in the same branch of trade.

3. When the current market price under this section is difficult to prove the section on determination and proof of market price is available to permit a showing of a comparable market price or, where no market price is available, evidence of spot sale prices is proper. Where the unavailability of a market price is caused by a scarcity of goods of the type involved, a good case is normally made for specific performance under this Article. Such scarcity conditions, moreover, indicate that the price has risen and under the section providing for liberal administration of remedies, opinion evidence as to the value of the goods would be admissible in the absence of a market price and a liberal construction of allowable consequential damages should also result.

4. This section carries forward the standard rule that the buyer must deduct from his damages any expenses saved as a result of the breach.

5. The present section provides a remedy which is completely alternative to cover under the preceding section and applies only when and to the extent that the buyer has not covered.

Cross References:

Point 3: Sections 1–106, 2–716 and 2–723.
Point 5: Section 2–712.

Definitional Cross References:

"Buyer". Section 2–103.

"Contract". Section 1–201.
"Seller". Section 2–103.

Section 2–714. Buyer's Damages for Breach in Regard to Accepted Goods.

(1) Where the buyer has accepted goods and given notification (subsection (3) of Section 2–607) he may recover as damages for any non-conformity of tender the loss resulting in the ordinary course of events from the seller's breach as determined in any manner which is reasonable.

(2) The measure of damages for breach of warranty is the difference at the time and place of acceptance between the value of the goods accepted and the value they would have had if they had been as warranted, unless special circumstances show proximate damages of a different amount.

(3) In a proper case any incidental and consequential damages under the next section may also be recovered.

New York Annotations

(1) *Accord:* Personal Property Law, §§ 130 (warranty or promise) and 150(1)(a) and (b).

(2) Subsection (2) is, in principle, in *accord* with Personal Property Law, § 150(6) and (7). The provision that market value is to be tested at the place of acceptance may change the New York law, since Personal Property Law, § 150(7), refers the time of testing market value to the time of delivery and this may inferentially determine place.

Official Uniform Comment

Prior Uniform Statutory Provision: Section 69(6) and (7), Uniform Sales Act.
Changes: Rewritten.

Purposes of Changes:

1. This section deals with the remedies available to the buyer after the goods have been accepted and the time for revocation of acceptance has gone by. In general this section adopts the rule of the prior uniform statutory provision for measuring damages where there has been a breach of warranty as to goods accepted, but goes further to lay down an explicit provision as to the time and place for determining the loss.

The section on deduction of damages from price provides an additional remedy for a buyer who still owes part of the purchase price, and frequently the two remedies will be available concurrently. The buyer's failure to notify of his claim under the section on effects of acceptance, however, operates to bar his remedies under either that section or the present section.

2. The "non-conformity" referred to in subsection (1) includes not only breaches of warranties but also any failure of the seller to perform according to his obligations under the contract. In the case of such non-conformity, the buyer is permitted to recover for his loss "in any manner which is reasonable."

3. Subsection (2) describes the usual, standard and reasonable method of ascertaining damages in the case of breach of warranty but it is not intended as an exclusive measure. It departs from the measure of damages for non-delivery in

utilizing the place of acceptance rather than the place of tender. In some cases the two may coincide, as where the buyer signifies his acceptance upon the tender. If, however, the non-conformity is such as would justify revocation of acceptance, the time and place of acceptance under this section is determined as of the buyer's decision not to revoke.

4. The incidental and consequential damages referred to in subsection (3), which will usually accompany an action brought under this section, are discussed in detail in the comment on the next section.

Cross References:

Point 1: Compare Section 2–711; Sections 2–607 and 2–717.
Point 2: Section 2–106.
Point 3: Sections 2–608 and 2–713.
Point 4: Section 2–715.

Definitional Cross References:

"Buyer". Section 2–103.
"Conform". Section 2–106.
"Goods". Section 1–201.
"Notification". Section 1–201.
"Seller". Section 2–103.

Section 2–715. Buyer's Incidental and Consequential Damages.

(1) Incidental damages resulting from the seller's breach include expenses reasonably incurred in inspection, receipt, transportation and care and custody of goods rightfully rejected, any commercially reasonable charges, expenses or commissions in connection with effecting cover and any other reasonable expense incident to the delay or other breach.

(2) Consequential damages resulting from the seller's breach include

(a) any loss resulting from general or particular requirements and needs of which the seller at the time of contracting had reason to know and which could not reasonably be prevented by cover or otherwise; and

(b) injury to person or property proximately resulting from any breach of warranty.

New York Annotations

(1) *Incidental damages.* The Code creates a new statutory enumeration of items of expense recoverable by the buyer. Insofar as the section allows recovery of the expenses of repurchase, storage, and transportation costs, it is in accord with New York law. Taylor v. Saxe, 134 N.Y. 67, 31 N.E. 258 (1892) (storage and freight); Messmore v. The N.Y. Shot and Lead Co., 40 N.Y. 422 (1869) (freight); Martin Ross Mfg. Corp. v. Ulius, 181 Misc. 995, 48 N.Y.S.2d 756 (1944).

(2) *Consequential damages.* Compare, Personal Property Law, §§ 148(3) and 150.

(a) *Loss resulting from buyer's needs.* This subsection is new to the statutes but the test permitting recovery of such damages where the seller had reason to know of the buyer's needs or requirements does little more than liberalize the "contemplation of the parties" test of the New York cases. Czarnikow-Rionda Co. v. Federal Sugar

Refining Co., 255 N.Y. 33, 173 N.E. 913 (1930); Griffin v. Colver, 16 N.Y. 489 (1858); Cramerton Mills, Inc v. Nathan & Cohen Co., Inc., 231 App.Div. 28, 246 N.Y.S. 259 (1930); Raymore Realty Co. v. Pfotenhauer-Nesbit Co., 145 App.Div. 163, 129 N.Y.s. 1002 (1911).

(b) *Injury to person or property. Accord:* Ryan v. Progressive Grocery Stores, Inc., 255 N.Y. 388, 175 N.E. 105 (1931) (personal injuries); Swain v. Schieffelin, 134 N.Y. 471, 31 N.E. 1025 (1892) (property); Ellen v. Heacock, 247 App.Div. 476, 286 N.Y.S. 740 (1936).

Historical Note: At the suggestion of the Law Revision Commission, subsection (1) was changed to avoid a possible interpretation that damages from delay are necessarily "incidental" rather than "consequential", and the preamble of subsection (2) was conformed to the opening language of subsection (1). (1956 Recommendations, p. 81; Excerpts, pp. 399–400.)

Official Uniform Comment

Prior Uniform Statutory Provisions: Subsection (2)(b)–Sections 69(7) and 70, Uniform Sales Act.

Changes: Rewritten.

Purposes of Changes and New Matter:

1. Subsection (1) is intended to provide reimbursement for the buyer who incurs reasonable expenses in connection with the handling of rightfully rejected goods or goods whose acceptance may be justifiably revoked, or in connection with effecting cover where the breach of the contract lies in non-conformity or non-delivery of the goods. The incidental damages listed are not intended to be exhaustive but are merely illustrative of the typical kinds of incidental damage.

2. Subsection (2) operates to allow the buyer, in an appropriate case, any consequential damages which are the result of the seller's breach. The "tacit agreement" test for the recovery of consequential damages is rejected. Although the older rule at common law which made the seller liable for all consequential damages of which he had "reason to know" in advance is followed, the liberality of that rule is modified by refusing to permit recovery unless the buyer could not reasonably have prevented the loss by cover or otherwise. Subparagraph (2) carries forward the provisions of the prior uniform statutory provision as to consequential damages resulting from breach of warranty, but modifies the rule by requiring first that the buyer attempt to minimize his damages in good faith, either by cover or otherwise.

3. In the absence of excuse under the section on merchant's excuse by failure of presupposed conditions, the seller is liable for consequential damages in all cases where he had reason to know of the buyer's general or particular requirements at the time of contracting. It is not necessary that there be a conscious acceptance of an insurer's liability on the seller's part, nor is his obligation for consequential damages limited to cases in which he fails to use due effort in good faith.

Particular needs of the buyer must generally be made known to the seller while general needs must rarely be made known to charge the seller with knowledge.

Any seller who does not wish to take the risk of consequential damages has available the section on contractual limitation of remedy.

4. The burden of proving the extent of loss incurred by way of consequential damage is on the buyer, but the section on liberal administration of remedies rejects any doctrine of certainty which requires almost mathematical precision in the proof of loss. Loss may be determined in any manner which is reasonable under the circumstances.

5. Subsection (2)(b) states the usual rule as to breach of warranty, allowing recovery for injuries "proximately" resulting from the breach. Where the injury involved

follows the use of goods without discovery of the defect causing the damage, the question of "proximate" cause turns on whether it was reasonable for the buyer to use the goods without such inspection as would have revealed the defects. If it was not reasonable for him to do so, or if he did in fact discover the defect prior to his use, the injury would not proximately result from the breach of warranty.

6. In the case of sale of wares to one in the business of reselling them, resale is one of the requirements of which the seller has reason to know within the meaning of subsection (2)(a).

Cross References:

Point 1: Section 2–608.
Point 3: Sections 1–203, 2–615 and 2–719.
Point 4: Section 1–106.

Definitional Cross References:

"Cover". Section 2–712.
"Goods". Section 1–201.
"Person". Section 1–201.
"Receipt of goods". Section 2–103.
"Seller". Section 2–103.

Section 2–716. Buyer's Right to Specific Performance or Replevin.

(1) Specific performance may be decreed where the goods are unique or in other proper circumstances.

(2) The decree for specific performance may include such terms and conditions as to payment of the price, damages, or other relief as the court may deem just.

(3) The buyer has a right of replevin for goods identified to the contract if after reasonable effort he is unable to effect cover for such goods or the circumstances reasonably indicate that such effort will be unavailing or if the goods have been shipped under reservation and satisfaction of the security interest in them has been made or tendered.

New York Annotations

Specific performance: Subsection (1) broadens the rule of Personal Property Law, § 149. The Code eliminates the test that the goods must be "specific or ascertained," a technical requirement cited by some lower courts in denying relief. Goodman v. Henry Caplan, Inc., 188 Misc. 242, 65 N.Y.S.2d 576 (1946); Cohen v. Rosenstock Motors Inc., 188 Misc. 426, 65 N.Y.S.2d 481 (1946); Gellis v. Falcon Buick Co., 191 Misc. 566, 76 N.Y.S.2d 94 (1947); Kalieski v. Grole Motors, Inc., 69 N.Y.S.2d 645 (1946); Blake v. Tyson Radio Hempstead Corp., 103 N.Y.S.2d 872 (1951). Compare, Doyle's Main Motors, Inc. v. Davis, 118 N.Y.S.2d 867 (1953). Comment 2 indicates that the use of the term "unique goods" is not intended to revive the common-law tests of equity jurisdiction and is not the sole test for relief. See Glick v. Beer, 263 App.Div. 599, 33 N.Y.S.2d 833 (1942).

Replevin. Subsection (3) abandons the rule that uses the property concept to determine the availability of replevin. Austin, Nichols & Co. v. Heermance Refrigerating Co., 199 App.Div. 626, 192 N.Y.S 71 (1922). In some cases the Code will narrow the right of replevin as where title passes to goods available on the market. On the other hand, where title to goods is deemed to remain in the seller, replevin may still be available if substitute goods are unobtainable. Cf. Civil Practice Act, §§ 1089–1131 (now CPLR § 7101 et seq.). Note should also be taken to reach the buyer's independent right to reach the goods under Section 2–502.

Official Uniform Comment

Prior Uniform Statutory Provision: Section 68, Uniform Sales Act.

Changes: Rephrased.

Purposes of Changes: To make it clear that:

1. The present section continues in general prior policy as to specific performance and injunction against breach. However, without intending to impair in any way the exercise of the court's sound discretion in the matter, this Article seeks to further a more liberal attitude than some courts have shown in connection with the specific performance of contracts of sale.

2. In view of this Article's emphasis on the commercial feasibility of replacement, a new concept of what are "unique" goods is introduced under this section. Specific performance is no longer limited to goods which are already specific or ascertained at the time of contracting. The test of uniqueness under this section must be made in terms of the total situation which characterizes the contract. Output and requirements contracts involving a particular or peculiarly available source or market present today the typical commercial specific performance situation, as contrasted with contracts for the sale of heirlooms or priceless works of art which were usually involved in the older cases. However, uniqueness is not the sole basis of the remedy under this section for the relief may also be granted "in other proper circumstances" and inability to cover is strong evidence of "other proper circumstances".

3. The legal remedy of replevin is given the buyer in cases in which cover is reasonably unavailable and goods have been identified to the contract. This is in addition to the buyer's right to recover identified goods on the seller's insolvency (Section 2–502).

4. This section is intended to give the buyer rights to the goods comparable to the seller's rights to the price.

5. If a negotiable document of title is outstanding, the buyer's right of replevin relates of course to the document not directly to the goods. See Article 7, especially Section 7–602.

Cross References:

Point 3: Section 2–502.
Point 4: Section 2–709.
Point 5: Article 7.

Definitional Cross References:

"Buyer". Section 2–103.
"Goods". Section 1–201.
"Rights". Section 1–201.

Section 2–717. Deduction of Damages From the Price.

The buyer on notifying the seller of his intention to do so may deduct all or any part of the damages resulting from any breach of the contract from any part of the price still due under the same contract.

New York Annotations

This section expands so as to cover any breach of contract the provision of the Sales Act allowing recoupment in diminution or extinction of the price where there has been a breach of warranty. Personal Property Law, § 150(1)(a). Peuser v. Marsh, 218 N.Y. 505, 113 N.E. 494 (1916) (installment contract). The requirement of notice is new and, although it seems that the two notices could be combined, this section requires more than the notice of breach called for by Section 2–607.

Historical Note: At the suggestion of the Law Revision Commission the section was revised to state explicitly, as previously stated in the Comment, that this section only applies to breach and price under the same contract. (1956 Recommendations, p. 81; Excerpts, p. 400.)

Official Uniform Comment

Prior Uniform Statutory Provision: See Section 69(1)(a), Uniform Sales Act.

Purposes:

1. This section permits the buyer to deduct from the price damages resulting from any breach by the seller and does not limit the relief to cases of breach of warranty as did the prior uniform statutory provision. To bring this provision into application the breach involved must be of the same contract under which the price in question is claimed to have been earned.

2. The buyer, however, must give notice of his intention to withhold all or part of the price if he wishes to avoid a default within the meaning of the section on insecurity and right to assurances. In conformity with the general policies of this Article, no formality of notice is required and any language which reasonably indicates the buyer's reason for holding up his payment is sufficient.

Cross Reference:

Point 2: Section 2–609.

Definitional Cross References:

"Buyer". Section 2–103.
"Notifies". Section 1–201.

Section 2–718. Liquidation or Limitation of Damages; Deposits.

(1) Damages for breach by either party may be liquidated in the agreement but only at an amount which is reasonable in the light of the anticipated or actual harm caused by the breach, the difficulties of proof of loss, and the inconvenience or nonfeasibility of otherwise obtaining an adequate remedy. A term fixing unreasonably large liquidated damages is void as a penalty.

(2) Where the seller justifiably withholds delivery of goods because of the buyer's breach, the buyer is entitled to restitution of any amount by which the sum of his payments exceeds

(a) the amount to which the seller is entitled by virtue of terms liquidating the seller's damages in accordance with subsection (1), or

(b) in the absence of such terms, twenty per cent of the value of the total performance for which the buyer is obligated under the contract or $500, whichever is smaller.

(3) The buyer's right to restitution under subsection (2) is subject to offset to the extent that the seller establishes

(a) a right to recover damages under the provisions of this Article other than subsection (1), and

(b) the amount or value of any benefits received by the buyer directly or indirectly by reason of the contract.

(4) Where a seller has received payment in goods their reasonable value or the proceeds of their resale shall be treated as payments for the purposes of subsection (2); but if the seller has notice of the buyer's breach before reselling goods received in part performance, his resale is subject to the conditions laid down in this Article on resale by an aggrieved seller (Section 2–706).

New York Annotations

(1) *Liquidated damages.* There is now no statutory provision. However, to the extent that the Code permits enforcement of such contractual provisions, it is consistent with Personal Property Law, § 152, permitting variation by agreement. In general, the tests here proposed are similar to those set forth in Restatement, Contracts, § 339 and New York Annotations. On the burden of showing reasonable basis for the provision, see Weatherproof Improvement Contracting Corp v. Kramer, 12 Misc.2d 100, 172 N.Y.S.2d 688(1956).

(2) *Deposits.* This subsection serves the same function as the 1952 New York modification of the Uniform Sales Act, Personal Property Law, § 145–a, and is designed to prevent unjust enrichment to the seller where the buyer has made a substantial deposit before receiving the goods and then defaults in paying the balance due. See Bisner v. Mantell, 197 Misc. 807, 95 N.Y.S.2d 793 (1950). The Code differs from the present New York statute in that it provides for the retention by the seller in all cases of $500 or 20% of the price, whichever is smaller, while Personal Property Law, § 145–a, calls for the retention of 20% of the price. Further, the Code calls for the application of Section 2–706 on the conduct of a resale by a seller who was partially paid in goods and learns of the buyer's breach prior to disposing of such goods.

Historical Note: To meet criticism by the Law Revision Commission, former subsection (2)was entirely rewritten as subsections (2), (3), and (4). The revision, based in part on New York Personal Property Law, § 145–a, makes it clear that a defaulting buyer may be entitled to restitution under the section, that the section is not limited to cases of explicit agreement for forfeiture, and that the buyer's right to restitution is subject to offset in the cases set forth in new subsection (3). (1956 Recommendations, p. 82; Excerpts, pp. 400–1.)

Official Uniform Comment

Prior Uniform Statutory Provision: None.

Purposes:

1. Under subsection (1) liquidated damage clauses are allowed where the amount involved is reasonable in the light of the circumstances of the case. The subsection

sets forth explicitly the elements to be considered in determining the reasonableness of a liquidated damage clause. A term fixing unreasonably large liquidated damages is expressly made void as a penalty. An unreasonably small amount would be subject to similar criticism and might be stricken under the section on unconscionable contracts or clauses.

2. Subsection (2) refuses to recognize a forfeiture unless the amount of the payment so forfeited represents a reasonable liquidation of damages as determined under subsection (1). A special exception is made in the case of small amounts (20% of the price of $500, whichever is smaller) deposited as security. No distinction is made between cases in which the payment is to be applied on the price and those in which it is intended as security for performance. Subsection (2) is applicable to any deposit of down or part payment. In the case of a deposit or turn in of goods resold before the breach, the amount actually received on the resale is to be viewed as the deposit rather than the amount allowed the buyer for the trade in. However, if the seller knows of the breach prior to the resale of the goods turned in, he must make reasonable efforts to realize their true value, and this is assured by requiring him to comply with the conditions laid down in the section on resale by an aggrieved seller.

Cross References:

Point 1: Section 2–302.
Point 2: Section 2–706.

Definitional Cross References:

"Aggrieved party". Section 1–201.
"Agreement". Section 1–201.
"Buyer". Section 2–103.
"Goods". Section 2–105.
"Notice". Section 1–201.
"Party". Section 1–201.
"Remedy". Section 1–201.
"Seller". Section 2–103.
"Term". Section 1–201.

Section 2–719. Contractual Modification or Limitation of Remedy.

(1) Subject to the provisions of subsection (2) and (3) of this section and of the preceding section on liquidation and limitation of damages,

(a) the agreement may provide for remedies in addition to or in substitution for those provided in this Article and may limit or alter the measure of damages recoverable under this Article, as by limiting the buyer's remedies to return of the goods and repayment of the price or to repair and replacement of non-conforming goods or parts; and

(b) resort to a remedy as provided is optional unless the remedy is expressly agreed to be exclusive, in which case it is the sole remedy.

(2) Where circumstances cause an exclusive or limited remedy to fail of its essential purpose, remedy may be had as provided in this Act.

(3) Consequential damages may be limited or excluded unless the limitation or exclusion is unconscionable. Limitation of consequential damages for injury

to the person in the case of consumer goods is prima facie unconscionable but limitation of damages where the loss is commercial is not.

New York Annotations

(1) The rule of subsection (1)(a) that remedies may be modified is consistent with the general rule of the Sales Act, Personal Property Law, § 152. See, *accord,* Plimpton v. Brown Bros., 224 N.Y. 724, 121 N.E. 886 (1918), affirming per curiam, 172 App.Div. 936, 156 N.Y.S. 1141; Lee v. Industrial Laundry Mach. Co., 261 App.Div. 741, 27 N.Y.S.2d 202 (1941). Subsection (1)(b) is new, although it is consistent with the rule of construction of resolving ambiguities against the draftsman. See Section 2–316. The contractual modification cannot be unconscionable, Section 2–302. See Randy Knitwear, Inc. v. American Cyanamid Co., 7 N.Y.2d 791, 163 N.E.2d 349 (1959) (reasonableness of time limit on claim is a fact question).

(2) Subsection (2) is new, but see Moore v. Schlossman's, Inc., 5 Misc.2d 693, 161 N.Y.S.2d 213 (1957) (limitation on remedy to repair or exchange not effective on facts to bar rescission).

(3) The permission to limit or exclude consequential damages is in *accord* with Associated Spinners v. Massachusetts Textile Co., 75 N.Y.S.2d 263 (1947). The requirement that such limitation must not be unconscionable is new, and is a specific application of Section 2–302. "Consumer goods" are defined in Section 9–109(1), as goods "used or bought for use primarily for personal, family or household purposes", and that definition is incorporated in Article 2. See Section 2–103(3).

Official Uniform Comment

Prior Uniform Statutory Provision: None.

Purposes:

1. Under this section parties are left free to shape their remedies to their particular requirements and reasonable agreements limiting or modifying remedies are to be given effect.

However, it is of the very essence of a sales contract that at least minimum adequate remedies be available. If the parties intend to conclude a contract for sale within this Article they must accept the legal consequence that there be at least a fair quantum of remedy for breach of the obligations or duties outlined in the contract. Thus any clause purporting to modify or limit the remedial provisions of this Article in an unconscionable manner is subject to deletion and in that event the remedies made available by this Article are applicable as if the stricken clause had never existed. Similarly, under subsection (2), where an apparently fair and reasonable clause because of circumstances fails in its purpose or operates to deprive either party of the substantial value of the bargain, it must give way to the general remedy provisions of this Article.

2. Subsection (1)(b) creates a presumption that clauses prescribing remedies are cumulative rather than exclusive. If the parties intend the term to describe the sole remedy under the contract, this must be clearly expressed.

3. Subsection (3) recognizes the validity of clauses limiting or excluding consequential damages but makes it clear that they may not operate in an unconscionable manner. Actually such terms are merely an allocation of unknown or undeterminable risks. The seller in all cases is free to disclaim warranties in the manner provided in Section 2–316.

Cross References:

Point 1: Section 2–302.
Point 3: Section 2–316.

Definitional Cross References:

"Agreement". Section 1–201.
"Buyer". Section 2–103.
"Conforming". Section 2–106.
"Contract". Section 1–201.
"Goods". Section 2–105.
"Remedy". Section 1–201.
"Seller". Section 2–103.

Section 2–720. Effect of "Cancellation" or "Rescission" on Claims for Antecedent Breach.

Unless the contrary intention clearly appears, expressions of "cancellation" or "rescission" of the contract or the like shall not be construed as a renunciation or discharge of any claim in damages for an antecedent breach.

New York Annotations

The section is consistent with the New York alteration of Uniform Sales Act, Section 69(1)(d), permitting "rescission", return of the goods and a suit for damages. Personal Property Law, § 150(1)(d). The section also accords with the conclusion that a seller's offer to replace that part of a delivery containing allegedly defective goods did not amount to an intent to cancel the contract by returning the parties to "their positions before the contract" was made. Keller Tailors Trimmings Co. v. Burke Rugby, Inc., 308 N.Y. 441, 126 N.E.2d 551 (1955).

Official Uniform Comment

Prior Uniform Statutory Provision: None.

Purpose:

This section is designed to safeguard a person holding a right of action from any unintentional loss of rights by the ill-advised use of such terms as "cancellation", "rescission", or the like. Once a party's rights have accrued they are not to be lightly impaired by concessions made in business decency and without intention to forego them. Therefore, unless the cancellation of a contract expressly declares that it is "without reservation of rights", or the like, it cannot be considered to be a renunciation under this section.

Cross Reference:

Section 1–107.

Definitional Cross References:

"Cancellation". Section 2–106.
"Contract". Section 1–201.

Section 2–721. Remedies for Fraud.

Remedies for material misrepresentation or fraud include all remedies available under this Article for non-fraudulent breach. Neither rescission or a claim for rescission of the contract for sale nor rejection or return of the goods shall bar or be deemed inconsistent with a claim for damages or other remedy.

New York Annotations

This section, like Civil Practice Act, § 112-e [now CPLR § 3002], and Personal Property Law, § 150(1)(d), abolishes the doctrine of election of remedies for fraud or innocent misrepresentation. It assumes that an action based on fraud is not restricted to the common-law rules, but is governed by rules at least as liberal as those applicable where fraud is present. Note that Section 2–702(2) contains an express limitation on the seller's right to rescind for fraudulent misrepresentation of credit by the buyer.

Historical note: Clarifying changes were made to meet criticisms of the Law Revision Commission. The reference to claims "for" rescission follows the usage of New York Civil Practice Act, § 112-e. (1956 Recommendations, p. 84; Excerpts, pp. 401-2.)

Official Uniform Comment

Prior Uniform Statutory Provision: None.

Purposes: To correct the situation by which remedies for fraud have been more circumscribed than the more modern and mercantile remedies for breach of warranty. Thus the remedies for fraud are extended by this section to coincide in scope with those for non-fraudulent breach. This section thus makes it clear that neither rescission of the contract for fraud nor rejection of the goods bars other remedies unless the circumstances of the case make the remedies incompatible.

Definitional Cross References:

"Contract for sale". Section 2–106.
"Goods". Section 1–201.
"Remedy". Section 1–201.

Section 2–722. Who Can Sue Third Parties for Injury to Goods.

Where a third party so deals with goods which have been identified to a contract for sale as to cause actionable injury to a party to that contract

(a) a right of action against the third party is in either party to the contract for sale who has title to or a security interest or a special property or an insurable interest in the goods; and if the goods have been destroyed or converted a right of action is also in the party who either bore the risk of loss under the contract for sale or has since the injury assumed that risk as against the other;

(b) if at the time of the injury the party plaintiff did not bear the risk of loss as against the other party to the contract for sale and there is no arrangement between them for disposition of the recovery, his suit or settlement is, subject to his own interest, as a fiduciary for the other party to the contract;

(c) either party may with the consent of the other sue for the benefit of whom it may concern.

New York Annotations

There is no provision in the existing commercial statutes comparable to this section, defining who may sue third parties for injury to the goods. Only [former] Civil Practice Act, § 210, the real party in interest statute, now controls such matters. [Former] § 210 expressly defines the real party in interest as including a person "authorized by statute" to sue, and would therefore not conflict with the Code.

Historical Note: At the suggestion of the Law Revision Commission former subsection (a), testing buyer's exclusive standing to sue by acceptance, was deleted as inappropriate to cases where seller remains in possession or otherwise retains an interest after acceptance. Reference to the buyer's "special property" was inserted to conform to the revision of Section 2–401. (1956 Recommendations, p. 85; Excerpts, p. 402.)

Official Uniform Comment

Prior Uniform Statutory Provision: None.

Purposes: To adopt and extend somewhat the principle of the statutes which provide for suit by the real party in interest. The provisions of this section apply only after identification of the goods. Prior to that time only the seller has a right of action. During the period between identification and final acceptance (except in the case of revocation of acceptance) it is possible for both parties to have the right of action. Even after final acceptance both parties may have the right of action if the seller retains possession or otherwise retains an interest.

Definitional Cross References:

"Action". Section 1–201.
"Buyer". Section 2–103.
"Contract for sale". Section 2–106.
"Goods". Section 2–105.
"Party". Section 1–201.
"Rights". Section 1–201.
"Security interest". Section 1–201.

Section 2–723. Proof of Market Price: Time and Place.

(1) If an action based on anticipatory repudiation comes to trial before the time for performance with respect to some or all of the goods, any damages based on market price (Section 2–708 or Section 2–713) shall be determined according to the price of such goods prevailing at the time when the aggrieved party learned of the repudiation.

(2) If evidence of a price prevailing at the times or places described in this Article is not readily available the price prevailing within any reasonable time before or after the time described or at any other place which in commercial judgment or under usage of trade would serve as a reasonable substitute for the one described may be used, making any proper allowance for the cost of transporting the goods to or from such other place.

(3) Evidence of a relevant price prevailing at a time or place other than the one described in this Article offered by one party is not admissible unless and until he has given the other party such notice as the court finds sufficient to prevent unfair surprise.

New York Annotations

(1) *Anticipatory repudiation.* Present law provides no solution for the problem of measuring recovery where an action, based on anticipatory repudiation, is brought before the date due for performance. It is not clear that this section has an independent significance when the seller repudiates, since Section 2–713 provides for measuring recovery when the buyer "learns of the breach." On the other hand, where the buyer repudiates, this section does have independent effect, since it makes the time the seller learned of the breach the crucial point. Existing law would call for measuring recovery at the time performance was due. See annotations to Sections 2–713 and 2–708.

(2) *Substitute market.* Where evidence of the market price required by the Code is not readily available, the substituted price of an adjacent market as to time or place is permitted. There is support for this approach in the case law. Parrott v. Allison, 145 F.2d 415 (2d Cir. 1944); Rice v. Manley, 66 N.Y. 82 (1876) (nearest available market); Lyles v. Hagy, 28 Hun 240 (1882) (adjustment for transportation). The notice requirement is new and is designed to prevent unfair surprise.

Historical Note: Subsection (1) was revised at the suggestion of the Law Revision Commission to make clear that it has no application to actions for damages based on resale or cover. The last sentence, renumbered subsection (3), was revised to conform to Section 1–205(6). (1956 Recommendations, p. 85; Excerpts, p. 402).

Official Uniform Comment

Prior Uniform Statutory Provision: None.

Purposes: To eliminate the most obvious difficulties arising in connection with the determination of market price, when that is stipulated as a measure of damages by some provision of this Article. Where the appropriate market price is not readily available the court is here granted reasonable leeway in receiving evidence of prices current in other comparable markets or at other times comparable to the one in question. In accordance with the general principle of this Article against surprise, however, a party intending to offer evidence of such a substitute price must give suitable notice to the other party.

This section is not intended to exclude the use of any other reasonable method of determining market price or of measuring damages if the circumstances of the case make this necessary.

Definitional Cross References:

"Action". Section 1–201.
"Aggrieved party". Section 1–201.
"Goods". Section 2–105.
"Notifies". Section 1–201.
"Party". Section 1–201.
"Reasonable time". Section 1–204.
"Usage of trade". Section 1–205.

Section 2–724. Admissibility of Market Quotations.

Whenever the prevailing price or value or any goods regularly bought and sold in any established commodity market is in issue, reports in official publications or trade journals or in newspapers or periodicals of general circulation published as the reports of such market shall be admissible in evidence. The circumstances of the preparation of such a report may be shown to affect its weight but not its admissibility.

New York Annotations

Civil Practice Act, § 375–a [now CPLR 4533], is in accord with this section, except that the Code makes admissible reports "in official publications or trade journals" in addition to those in newspapers or periodicals and limits the effect of the section to goods sold in a "commodity market" rather than "regularly organized stock or commodity market."

Official Uniform Comment

Prior Uniform Statutory Provision: None.

Purposes: To make market quotations admissible in evidence while providing for a challenge of the material by showing the circumstances of its preparation.

No explicit provision as to the weight to be given to market quotations is contained in this section, but such quotations, in the absence of compelling challenge, offer an adequate basis for a verdict.

Market quotations are made admissible when the price or value of goods traded "in any established market" is in issue. The reason of the section does not require that the market be closely organized in the manner of a produce exchange. It is sufficient if transactions in the commodity are frequent and open enough to make a market established by usage in which one price can be expected to affect another and in which an informed report of the range and trend of prices can be assumed to be reasonably accurate.

This section does not in any way intend to limit or negate the application of similar rules of admissibility to other material, whether by action of the courts or by statute. The purpose of the present section is to assure a minimum of mercantile administration in this important situation and not to limit any liberalizing trend in modern law.

Definitional Cross Reference:

"Goods". Section 2–105.

Section 2–725. Statute of Limitations in Contracts for Sale.

(1) An action for breach of any contract for sale must be commenced within four years after the cause of action has accrued. By the original agreement the parties may reduce the period of limitation to not less than one year but may not extend it.

(2) A cause of action accrues when the breach occurs, regardless of the aggrieved party's lack of knowledge of the breach. A breach of warranty occurs when tender of delivery is made, except that where a warranty explicitly extends to future performance of the goods and discovery of the breach must await the time of such performance the cause of action accrues when the breach is or should have been discovered.

(3) Where an action commenced within the time limited by subsection (1) is so terminated as to leave available a remedy by another action for the same

breach such other action may be commenced after the expiration of the time limited and within six months after the termination of the first action unless the termination resulted from voluntary discontinuance or from dismissal for failure or neglect to prosecute.

(4) This section does not alter the law on tolling of the statute of limitations nor does it apply to causes of action which have accrued before this Act becomes effective.

New York Annotations

(1) *Statutory period.* The four-year period under the Code would change present law which now provides a six-year period of limitation on simple contract actions, Civil Practice Act, § 48 [now CPLR § 213]. This six-year limitation on contract actions, rather than the three-year limit on personal injuries resulting for negligence (Civil Practice Act, § 49(6)) [now CPLR § 214], has been held to apply to a claim for personal injuries arising from a breach of implied warranty. Blessington v. McCrory Stores Corp., 305 N.Y. 140, 111 N.E.2d 421 (1953). Compare the shorter periods in Court of Claims Act, § 10, which probably would take precedence over the Code rule.

(2) *Modification by contract.* Insofar as the Code only permits the parties to reduce the period of limitation, it is in accord with Civil Practice Act, § 10(1) [now CPLR § 201]. The requirement of a minimum period of one year is new. Compare Sapinkopf v. Cunard S.S. Co., 254 N.Y. 111, 172 N.E. 259 (1930) (denying a carrier's power to reduce the period by agreement to a time unreasonably short).

(3) *Accrual of the cause of action.* Under New York law ignorance or concealment of facts will not prevent the running of the statutory period, unless a special statute provides otherwise. Brick v. Cohn-Hall-Marx Co., 276 N.Y. 259, 11 N.E.2d 902 (1937). Similarly, the rule as to a breach of warranty is in accord with the New York law. Moore v. Maddock, 251 N.Y. 420, 167 N.E. 572 (1929) and Citizens Utilities Co. v. American Locomotive Co., 11 N.Y.2d 409, 230 N.Y.S.2d 194, 184 N.E.2d 171 (1962). The exception made under the Sales Act by the implied warranty of quiet possession is not continued. Personal Property Law, § 94, Code Section 2–312 and Comment.

(4) *Saving clause.* Subsection (3) is consistent with Civil Practice Act, § 23 [now CPLR § 205] except that the Code permits an additional six months rather than one year.

Official Uniform Comment

Prior Uniform Statutory Provision: None.

Purposes: To introduce a uniform statute of limitations for sales contracts, thus eliminating the jurisdictional variations and providing needed relief for concerns doing business on a nationwide scale whose contracts have heretofore been governed by several different periods of limitation depending upon the state in which the transaction occurred. This Article takes sales contracts out of the general laws limiting the time for commencing contractual actions and selects a four year period as the most appropriate to modern business practice. This is within the normal commercial record keeping period.

Subsection (1) permits the parties to reduce the period of limitation. The minimum period is set at one year. The parties may not, however, extend the statutory period.

Subsection (2), providing that the cause of action accrues when the breach occurs, states an exception where the warranty extends to future performance.

Subsection (3) states the saving provision included in many state statutes and permits an additional short period for bringing new actions, where suits begun within the four year period have been terminated so as to leave a remedy still available for the same breach.

Subsection (4) makes it clear that this Article does not purport to alter or modify in any respect the law on tolling of the Statute of Limitations as it now prevails in the various jurisdictions.

Definitional Cross References:

"Action". Section 1–201.
"Aggrieved party". Section 1–201.
"Agreement". Section 1–201.
"Contract for sale". Section 2–106.
"Goods". Section 2–105.
"Party". Section 1–201.
"Remedy". Section 1–201.
"Term". Section 1–201.
"Termination". Section 2–106.

ARTICLE 2A

LEASES

[Editor's note: Article 2a takes effect June 30, 1995.]

PART 1

GENERAL PROVISIONS

PART 2

FORMATION AND CONSTRUCTION OF LEASE CONTRACT

UCC

PART 3

EFFECT OF LEASE CONTRACT

PART 4

PERFORMANCE OF LEASE CONTRACT: REPUDIATED, SUBSTITUTED AND EXCUSED

PART 5

DEFAULT

A. IN GENERAL

B. DEFAULT BY LESSOR

C. DEFAULT BY LESSEE

PART 1

GENERAL PROVISIONS

Section 2A–101. Short Title.

This Article shall be known and may be cited as the Uniform Commercial Code—Leases.

OFFICIAL COMMENT

Rationale for Codification:

There are several reasons for codifying the law with respect to leases of goods. An analysis of the case law as it applies to leases of goods suggests at least three significant issues to be resolved by codification. First, what is a lease? It is necessary to define lease to determine whether a transaction creates a lease or a security interest disguised as a lease. If the transaction creates a security interest disguised as a lease, the lessor will be required to file a financing statement or take other action to perfect its interest in the goods against third parties. There is no such requirement with respect to leases. Yet the distinction between a lease and a security interest disguised as a lease is not clear. Second, will the lessor be deemed to have made warranties to the lessee? If the transaction is a sale the express and implied warranties of Article 2 of the Uniform Commercial Code apply. However, the warranty law with respect to leases is uncertain. Third, what remedies are available to the lessor upon the lessee's default? If the transaction is a security interest disguised as a lease, the answer is stated in Part 5 of the Article on Secured Transactions (Article 9). There is no clear answer with respect to leases.

There are reasons to codify the law with respect to leases of goods in addition to those suggested by a review of the reported cases. The answer to this important question should not be limited to the issues raised in these cases. Is it not also proper to determine the remedies available to the lessee upon the lessor's default? It is, but that issue is not reached through a review of the reported cases. This is only one of the many issues presented in structuring, negotiating and documenting a lease of goods.

Statutory Analogue:

After it was decided to proceed with the codification project, the drafting committee of the National Conference of Commissioners on Uniform State Laws looked for a statutory analogue, gradually narrowing the focus to the Article on Sales (Article 2) and the Article on Secured Transactions (Article 9). A review of the literature with respect to the sale of goods reveals that Article 2 is predicated upon certain assumptions: Parties to the sales transaction frequently are without counsel; the agreement of the parties often is oral or evidenced by scant writings; obligations between the parties are bilateral; applicable law is influenced by the need to preserve freedom of contract. A review of the literature with respect to personal property security law reveals that Article 9 is predicated upon very different assumptions: Parties to a secured transaction regularly are represented by counsel; the agreement of the parties frequently is reduced to a writing, extensive in scope; the obligations between the parties are essentially unilateral; and applicable law seriously limits freedom of contract.

The lease is closer in spirit and form to the sale of goods than to the creation of a security interest. While parties to a lease are sometimes represented by counsel and their agreement is often reduced to a writing, the obligations of the parties are bilateral and the common law of leasing is dominated by the need to preserve freedom of contract. Thus the drafting committee concluded that Article 2 was the appropriate statutory analogue.

Issues:

The drafting committee then identified and resolved several issues critical to codification:

Scope: The scope of the Article was limited to leases (Section 2A–102). There was no need to include leases intended as security, i.e., security interests disguised as leases, as they are adequately treated in Article 9. Further, even if leases intended as security were included, the need to preserve the distinction would remain, as policy suggests treatment significantly different from that accorded leases.

Definition of Lease: Lease was defined to exclude leases intended as security (Section 2A–101(1)(j)). Given the litigation to date a revised definition of security interest was suggested for inclusion in the Act. (Section 1–201(37)). This revision sharpens the distinction between leases and security interests disguised as leases.

Filing: The lessor was not required to file a financing statement against the lessee or take any other action to protect the lessor's interest in the goods (Section 2A–301). The refined definition of security interest will more clearly signal the need to file to potential lessors of goods. Those lessors who are concerned will file a protective financing statement (Section 9–408).

Warranties: All of the express and implied warranties of the Article on Sales (Article 2) were included (Sections 2A–210 through 2A–216), revised to reflect differences in lease transactions. The lease of goods is sufficiently similar to the sale of goods to justify this decision. Further, many courts have reached the same decision.

Certificate of Title Laws: Many leasing transactions involve goods subject to certificate of title statutes. To avoid conflict with those statutes, this Article is subject to them (Section 2A–104(1)(a)).

Consumer Leases: Many leasing transactions involve parties subject to consumer protection statutes or decisions. To avoid conflict with those laws this Article is subject to them to the extent provided in Section 2A–104(1)(c) and (2)). Further, certain consumer protections have been incorporated in the Article.

Finance Leases: Certain leasing transactions substitute the supplier of the goods for the lessor as the party responsible to the lessee with respect to warranties and the like. The definition of finance lease (Section 2A–103(1)(g)) was developed to describe these transactions. Various sections of the Article implement the substitution of the supplier for the lessor, including Sections 2A–209 and 2A–407. No attempt was made to fashion a special rule where the finance lessor is an affiliate of the supplier of goods; this is to be developed by the courts, case by case.

Sale and Leaseback: Sale and leaseback transactions are becoming increasingly common. A number of state statutes treat transactions where possession is retained by the seller as fraudulent per se or prima facie fraudulent. That position is not in accord with modern practice and thus is changed by the Article "if the buyer bought for value and in good faith" (Section 2A–308(3)).

Remedies: The Article has not only provided for lessor's remedies upon default by the lessee (Sections 2A–523 through 2A–531), but also for lessee's remedies upon default by the lessor (Sections 2A–508 through 2A–522). This is a significant departure from Article 9 which provides remedies only for the secured party upon default by the debtor. This difference is compelled by the bilateral nature of the obligations between the parties to a lease.

Damages: Many leasing transactions are predicated on the parties' ability to stipulate an appropriate measure of damages in the event of default. The rule with respect to sales of goods (Section 2–718) is not sufficiently flexible to accommodate this practice. Consistent with the common law emphasis upon freedom to contract, the Article has created a revised rule that allows greater flexibility with respect to leases of goods (Section 2A–504(1)).

History:

This Article is a revision of the Uniform Personal Property Leasing Act, which was approved by the National Conference of Commissioners on Uniform State Laws in August, 1985. However, it was believed that the subject matter of the Uniform Personal Property Leasing Act would be better treated as an article of this Act. Thus, although the Conference promulgated the Uniform Personal Property Leasing Act as a Uniform Law, activity was held in abeyance to allow time to restate the Uniform Personal Property Leasing Act as Article 2A.

UCC

In August, 1986 the Conference approved and recommended this Article (including conforming amendments to Article 1 and Article 9) for promulgation as an amendment to this Act. In December, 1986 the Council of the American Law Institute approved and recommended this Article (including conforming amendments to Article 1 and Article 9), with official comments, for promulgation as an amendment to this Act. In March, 1987 the Permanent Editorial Board for the Uniform Commercial Code approved and recommended this Article (including conforming amendments to Article 1 and Article 9), with official comments, for promulgation as an amendment to this Act. In May, 1987 the American Law Institute approved and recommended this Article (including conforming amendments to Article 1 and Article 9), with official comments, for promulgation as an amendment to this Act. In August, 1987 the Conference confirmed its approval of the final text of this Article.

Upon its initial promulgation, Article 2A was rapidly enacted in several states, was introduced in a number of other states, and underwent bar association, law revision commission and legislative study in still further states. In that process debate emerged, principally sparked by the study of Article 2A by the California Bar Association, California's nonuniform amendments to Article 2A, and articles appearing in a symposium on Article 2A published after its promulgation in the Alabama Law Review. The debate chiefly centered on whether Article 2A had struck the proper balance or was clear enough concerning the ability of a lessor to grant a security interest in its leasehold interest and in the residual, priority between a secured party and the lessee, and the lessor's remedy structure under Article 2A.

This debate over issues on which reasonable minds could and did differ began to affect the enactment effort for Article 2A in a deleterious manner. Consequently, the Standby Committee for Article 2A, composed predominantly of the former members of the drafting committee, reviewed the legislative actions and studies in the various states, and opened a dialogue with the principal proponents of the nonuniform amendments. Negotiations were conducted in conjunction with, and were facilitated by, a study of the uniform Article and the nonuniform Amendments by the New York Law Revision Commission. Ultimately, a consensus was reached, which has been approved by the membership of the Conference, the Permanent Editorial Board, and the Council of the Institute. Rapid and uniform enactment of Article 2A is expected as a result of the completed amendments. The Article 2A experience reaffirms the essential viability of the procedures of the Conference and the Institute for creating and updating uniform state law in the commercial law area.

Relationship of Article 2A to Other Articles:

The Article on Sales provided a useful point of reference for codifying the law of leases. Many of the provisions of that Article were carried over, changed to reflect differences in style, leasing terminology or leasing practices. Thus, the official comments to those sections of Article 2 whose provisions were carried over are incorporated by reference in Article 2A, as well; further, any case law interpreting those provisions should be viewed as persuasive but not binding on a court when deciding a similar issue with respect to leases. Any change in the sequence that has been made when carrying over a provision from Article 2 should be viewed as a matter of style, not substance. This is not to suggest that in other instances Article 2A did not also incorporate substantially revised provisions of Article 2, Article 9 or otherwise where the revision was driven by a concern over the substance; but for the lack of a mandate, the drafting committee might well have made the same or a similar change in the statutory analogue. Those sections in Article 2A include Sections 2A–104, 2A–105, 2A–106, 2A–108(2) and (4), 2A–109(2), 2A–208, 2A–214(2) and (3)(a), 2A–216, 2A–303, 2A–306, 2A–503, 2A–504(3)(b), 2A–506(2), and 2A–515. For lack of relevance or significance not all of the provisions of Article 2 were incorporated in Article 2A.

This codification was greatly influenced by the fundamental tenet of the common law as it has developed with respect to leases of goods: freedom of the parties to contract. Note that, like all other Articles of this Act, the principles of construction and interpretation contained in Article 1 are applicable throughout Article 2A (Section 2A–103(4)). These principles include the ability of the parties to vary the effect of the provisions of Article 2A, subject to certain limitations including those that relate to the obligations of good faith, diligence, reasonableness and care (Section 1–102(3)). Consistent with those principles no negative inference is to be drawn by the episodic use of the phrase "unless otherwise agreed" in certain provisions of Article 2A. Section 1–102(4). Indeed, the contrary is true, as the general rule in the Act, including this Article, is that the effect of the Act's provisions may be varied by agreement. Section 1–102(3). This conclusion follows even where the statutory analogue contains the phrase and the correlative provision in Article 2A does not.

Section 2A–102. Scope.

This Article applies to any transaction, regardless of form, that creates a lease.

OFFICIAL COMMENT

Uniform Statutory Source: Section 9–102(1). Throughout this Article, unless otherwise stated, references to "Section" are to other sections of this Act.

Changes: Substantially revised.

Purposes:

This Article governs transactions as diverse as the lease of a hand tool to an individual for a few hours and the leveraged lease of a complex line of industrial equipment to a multinational organization for a number of years.

To achieve that end it was necessary to provide that this Article applies to any transaction, regardless of form, that creates a lease. Since lease is defined as a transfer of an interest in goods (Section 2A–103(1)(j)) and goods is defined to include fixtures (Section 2A–103(1)(h)), application is limited to the extent the transaction relates to goods, including fixtures. Further, since the definition of lease does not include a sale (Section 2–106(1)) or retention or creation of a security interest (Section 1–201(37)), application is further limited; sales and security interests are governed by other Articles of this Act.

Finally, in recognition of the diversity of the transactions to be governed, the sophistication of many of the parties to these transactions, and the common law tradition as it applies to the bailment for hire or lease, freedom of contract has been preserved. DeKoven, Proceedings After Default by the Lessee Under a True Lease of Equipment, in 1C P. Coogan, W. Hogan, D. Vagts, Security Transactions Under the Uniform Commercial Code, § 29B.02[2] (1986). *[Editor's Note: Please note that this chapter has been removed from Vol. 1C of Secured Transactions Under the Uniform Commercial Code]*Thus, despite the extensive regulatory scheme established by this Article, the parties to a lease will be able to create private rules to govern their transaction. Sections 2A–103(4) and 1–102(3). However, there are special rules in this Article governing consumer leases, as well as other state and federal statutes, that may further limit freedom of contract with respect to consumer leases.

A court may apply this Article by analogy to any transaction, regardless of form, that creates a lease of personal property other than goods, taking into account the expressed intentions of the parties to the transaction and any differences between a lease of goods and a lease of other property. Such application has precedent as the provisions of the Article on Sales (Article 2) have been applied by analogy to leases of goods. E.g., Hawkland, The Impact of the Uniform Commercial Code on Equipment Leasing, 1972 Ill. L.F. 446; Murray, Under the Spreading Analogy of

Article 2 of the Uniform Commercial Code, 39 Fordham L. Rev. 447 (1971). Whether such application would be appropriate for other bailments of personal property, gratuitous or for hire, should be determined by the facts of each case. See Mieske v. Bartell Drug Co., 92 Wash. 2d 40, 46–48, 593 P.2d 1308, 1312 (1979).

Further, parties to a transaction creating a lease of personal property other than goods, or a bailment of personal property may provide by agreement that this Article applies. Upholding the parties' choice is consistent with the spirit of this Article.

Cross References:

Sections 1–102(3), 1–201(37), Article 2, esp. Section 2–106(1), and Sections 2A–103(1)(h), 2A–103(1)(j) and 2A–103(4).

Definitional Cross Reference:

"Lease". Section 2A–103(1)(j).

Section 2A–103. Definitions and Index of Definitions.

(1) In this Article unless the context otherwise requires:

(a) "Buyer in ordinary course of business" means a person who in good faith and without knowledge that the sale to him or her is in violation of the ownership rights or security interest or leasehold interest of a third party in the goods, buys in ordinary course from a person in the business of selling goods of that kind but does not include a pawnbroker. "Buying" may be for cash or by exchange of other property or on secured or unsecured credit and includes receiving goods or documents of title under a preexisting contract for sale but does not include a transfer in bulk or as security for or in total or partial satisfaction of a money debt.

(b) "Cancellation" occurs when either party puts an end to the lease contract for default by the other party.

(c) "Commercial unit" means such a unit of goods as by commercial usage is a single whole for purposes of lease and division of which materially impairs its character or value on the market or in use. A commercial unit may be a single article, as a machine, or a set of articles, as a suite of furniture, or a line of machinery, or a quantity, as a gross or carload, or any other unit treated in use or in the relevant market as a single whole.

(d) "Conforming goods or performance under a lease contract" means goods or performance that are in accordance with the obligations under the lease contract.

(e) "Consumer lease" means a lease that a lessor regularly engaged in the business of leasing or selling makes to a lessee who is an individual and who takes under the lease primarily for personal, family, or household purposes.

(f) "Fault" means wrongful act, omission, breach, or default.

(g) "Finance lease" means a lease with respect to which: (i) the lessor does not select, manufacture, or supply the goods; (ii) the lessor acquires the goods or the right to possession and use of the goods in connection with the lease;

and (iii) one of the following occurs: (A) the lessee receives a copy of the contract by which the lessor acquired the goods or the right to possession and use of the goods before signing the lease contract; (B) the lessee's approval of the contract by which the lessor acquired the goods or the right to possession and use of the goods is a condition to effectiveness of the lease contract; (C) the lessee, before signing the lease contract, receives an accurate and complete statement designating the promises and warranties, and any disclaimers of warranties, limitations or modifications of remedies, or liquidated damages, including those of any third party, such as the manufacturer of the goods, provided to the lessor by the person supplying the goods in connection with or as part of the contract by which the lessor acquired the goods or the right to possession and use of the goods; or (D) if the lease is not a consumer lease, the lessor, before the lessee signs the lease contract, informs the lessee in writing (a) of the identity of the person supplying the goods to the lessor, unless the lessee has selected that person and directed the lessor to acquire the goods or the right to possession and use of the goods from that person, (b) that the lessee is entitled under this Article to the promises and warranties, including those of any third party, provided to the lessor by the person supplying the goods in connection with or as part of the contract by which the lessor acquired the goods or the right to possession and use of the goods, and (c) that the lessee may communicate with the person supplying the goods to the lessor and receive an accurate and complete statement of those promises and warranties, including any disclaimers and limitations of them or of remedies.

(h) "Goods" means all things that are movable at the time of identification to the lease contract, or are fixtures (Section 2A–309), but the term does not include money, documents, instruments, accounts, chattel paper, general intangibles, or minerals or the like, including oil and gas, before extraction. The term also includes the unborn young of animals.

(i) "Installment lease contract" means a lease contract that authorizes or requires the delivery of goods in separate lots to be separately accepted, even though the lease contract contains a clause "each delivery is a separate lease" or its equivalent.

(j) "Lease" means a transfer of the right to possession and use of goods for a term in return for consideration, but a sale, including a sale on approval or a sale or return, or retention or creation of a security interest is not a lease. Unless the context clearly indicates otherwise, the term includes a sublease.

(k) "Lease agreement" means the bargain, with respect to the lease, of the lessor and the lessee in fact as found in their language or by implication from other circumstances including course of dealing or usage of trade or course of performance as provided in this Article. Unless the context clearly indicates otherwise, the term includes a sublease agreement.

(l) "Lease contract" means the total legal obligation that results from the lease agreement as affected by this Article and any other applicable rules of law.

Unless the context clearly indicates otherwise, the term includes a sublease contract.

(m) "Leasehold interest" means the interest of the lessor or the lessee under a lease contract.

(n) "Lessee" means a person who acquires the right to possession and use of goods under a lease. Unless the context clearly indicates otherwise, the term includes a sublessee.

(o) "Lessee in ordinary course of business" means a person who in good faith and without knowledge that the lease to him or her is in violation of the ownership rights or security interest or leasehold interest of a third party in the goods leases in ordinary course from a person in the business of selling or leasing goods of that kind but does not include a pawnbroker. "Leasing" may be for cash or by exchange of other property or on secured or unsecured credit and includes receiving goods or documents of title under a preexisting lease contract but does not include a transfer in bulk or as security for or in total or partial satisfaction of a money debt.

(p) "Lessor" means a person who transfers the right to possession and use of goods under a lease. Unless the context clearly indicates otherwise, the term includes a sublessor.

(q) "Lessor's residual interest" means the lessor's interest in the goods after expiration, termination, or cancellation of the lease contract.

(r) "Lien" means a charge against or interest in goods to secure payment of a debt or performance of an obligation, but the term does not include a security interest.

(s) "Lot" means a parcel or a single article that is the subject matter of a separate lease or delivery, whether or not it is sufficient to perform the lease contract.

(t) "Merchant lessee" means a lessee that is a merchant with respect to goods of the kind subject to the lease.

(u) "Present value" means the amount as of a date certain of one or more sums payable in the future, discounted to the date certain. The discount is determined by the interest rate specified by the parties if the rate was not manifestly unreasonable at the time the transaction was entered into; otherwise, the discount is determined by a commercially reasonable rate that takes into account the facts and circumstances of each case at the time the transaction was entered into.

(v) "Purchase" includes taking by sale, lease, mortgage, security interest, pledge, gift, or any other voluntary transaction creating an interest in goods.

(w) "Sublease" means a lease of goods the right to possession and use of which was acquired by the lessor as a lessee under an existing lease.

(x) "Supplier" means a person from whom a lessor buys or leases goods to be leased under a finance lease.

(y) "Supply contract" means a contract under which a lessor buys or leases goods to be leased.

(z) "Termination" occurs when either party pursuant to a power created by agreement or law puts an end to the lease contract otherwise than for default.

(2) Other definitions applying to this Article and the sections in which they appear are:

"Accessions". Section 2A–310(1).

"Construction mortgage". Section 2A–309(1)(d).

"Encumbrance". Section 2A–309(1)(e).

"Fixtures". Section 2A–309(1)(a).

"Fixture filing". Section 2A–309(1)(b).

"Purchase money lease". Section 2A–309(1)(c).

(3) The following definitions in other articles apply to this Article:

"Account". Section 9-106.

"Between merchants". Section 2-104(3).

"Buyer". Section 2-103(1)(a).

"Chattel paper". Section 9-105(1)(b).

"Consumer goods". Section 9-109(1).

"Document". Section 9-105(1)(f).

"Entrusting". Section 2-403(3).

"General intangibles". Section 9-106.

"Good faith". Section 2-103(1)(b).

"Instrument". Section 9-105(1)(i).

"Merchant". Section 2-104(1).

"Mortgage". Section 9-105(1)(j).

"Pursuant to commitment". Section 9-105(1)(k).

"Receipt". Section 2-103(1)(c).

"Sale". Section 2-106(1).

"Sale on approval". Section 2-326.

"Sale or return". Section 2-326.

"Seller". Section 2-103(1)(d).

(4) In addition, Article 1 contains general definitions and principles of construction and interpretation applicable throughout this Article.

OFFICIAL COMMENT

(a) "Buyer in ordinary course of business". Section 1–201(9).

UCC

(b) "Cancellation". Section 2–106(4). The effect of a cancellation is provided in Section 2A-505(1).

(c) "Commercial unit". Section 2–105(6).

(d) "Conforming". Section 2–106(2).

(e) "Consumer lease". New. This Article includes a subset of rules that applies only to consumer leases. Sections 2A–106, 2A–108(2), 2A–108(4), 2A–109(2), 2A–221, 2A–309, 2A–406, 2A–407, 2A–504(3)(b), and 2A–516(3)(b).

For a transaction to qualify as a consumer lease it must first qualify as a lease. Section 2A–103(1)(j). Note that this Article regulates the transactional elements of a lease, including a consumer lease; consumer protection statutes–present and future–and existing consumer protection decisions are unaffected by this Article. Section 2A–104(1)(c) and (2). Of course, Article 2A as state law also is subject to federal consumer protection law.

This definition is modeled after the definition of consumer lease in the Consumer Leasing Act, 15 U.S.C. § 1667 (1982), and in the Unif. Consumer Credit Code § 1.301(14), 7A U.L.A. 43 (1974). However, this definition of consumer lease differs from its models in several respects: the lessor can be a person regularly engaged either in the business of leasing or of selling goods, the lease need not be for a term exceeding four months, a lease primarily for an agricultural purpose is not covered and whether there should be a limitation by dollar amount and its amount is left up to the individual states.

This definition focuses on the parties as well as the transaction. If a lease is within this definition, the lessor must be regularly engaged in the business of leasing or selling, and the lessee must be an individual not an organization; note that a lease to two or more individuals having a common interest through marriage or the like is not excluded as a lease to an organization under Section 1–201(28). The lessee must take the interest primarily for a personal, family or household purpose. If required by the enacting state, total payments under the lease contract, excluding payments for options to renew or buy, cannot exceed the figure designated.

(f) "Fault". Section 1–201(16).

(g) "Finance Lease". New. This Article includes a subset of rules that applies only to finance leases. Sections 2A–209, 2A–211(2), 2A–212(1), 2A–213, 2A–219(1), 2A–220(1)(a), 2A–221, 2A–405(c), 2A–407, 2A–516(2) and 2A–517(1)(a) and (2).

For a transaction to qualify as a finance lease it must first qualify as a lease. Section 2A–103(1)(j). Unless the lessor is comfortable that the transaction will qualify as a finance lease, the lease agreement should include provisions giving the lessor the benefits created by the subset of rules applicable to the transaction that qualifies as a finance lease under this Article.

A finance lease is the product of a three party transaction. The supplier manufactures or supplies the goods pursuant to the lessee's specification, perhaps even pursuant to a purchase order, sales agreement or lease agreement between the supplier and the lessee. After the prospective finance lease is negotiated, a purchase order, sales agreement, or lease agreement is entered into by the lessor (as buyer or prime lessee) or an existing order, agreement or lease is assigned by the lessee to the lessor, and the lessor and the lessee then enter into a lease or sublease of the goods. Due to the limited function usually performed by the lessor, the lessee looks almost entirely to the supplier for representations, covenants and warranties. If a manufacturer's warranty carries through, the lessee may also look to that. Yet, this definition does not restrict the lessor's function solely to the supply of funds; if the lessor undertakes or performs other functions, express warranties, covenants and the common law will protect the lessee.

This definition focuses on the transaction, not the status of the parties; to avoid confusion it is important to note that in other contexts, e.g., tax and accounting, the term finance lease has been used to connote different types of lease transactions, including leases that are disguised secured transactions. M. Rice, Equipment Financing, 62–71 (1981). A lessor who is a merchant with respect to goods of the kind subject to the lease may be a lessor under a finance lease. Many leases that are leases back to the seller of goods (Section 2A–308(3)) will be finance leases. This conclusion is easily demonstrated by a hypothetical. Assume that B has bought goods from C pursuant to a sales contract. After delivery to and acceptance of the goods by B, B negotiates to sell the goods to A and simultaneously to lease the goods back from A, on terms and conditions that, we assume, will qualify the transaction as a lease. Section 2A–103(1)(j). In documenting the sale and lease back, B assigns the original sales contract between B, as buyer, and C, as seller, to A. A review of these facts leads to the conclusion that the lease from A to B qualifies as a finance lease, as all three conditions of the definition are satisfied. Subparagraph (i) is satisfied as A, the lessor, had nothing to do with the selection, manufacture, or supply of the equipment. Subparagraph (ii) is satisfied as A, the lessor, bought the equipment at the same time that A leased the equipment to B, which certainly is in connection with the lease. Finally, subparagraph (iii) (A) is satisfied as A entered into the sales contract with B at the same time that A leased the equipment back to B. B, the lessee, will have received a copy of the sales contract in a timely fashion.

Subsection (i) requires the lessor to remain outside the selection, manufacture and supply of the goods; that is the rationale for releasing the lessor from most of its traditional liability. The lessor is not prohibited from possession, maintenance or operation of the goods, as policy does not require such prohibition. To insure the lessee's reliance on the supplier, and not on the lessor, subsection (ii) requires that the goods (where the lessor is the buyer of the goods) or that the right to possession and use of the goods (where the lessor is the prime lessee and the sublessor of the goods) be acquired in connection with the lease (or sublease) to qualify as a finance lease. The scope of the phrase "in connection with" is to be developed by the courts, case by case. Finally, as the lessee generally relies almost entirely upon the supplier for representations–and covenants, and upon the supplier or a manufacturer, or both, for warranties with respect to the goods, subsection (iii) requires that one of the following occur: (A) the lessee receive a copy of the supply contract before signing the lease contract; (B) the lessee's approval of the supply contract is a condition to the effectiveness of the lease contract; (C) the lessee receives a statement describing the promises and warranties and any limitations relevant to the lessee before signing the lease contract; or (D) before signing the lease contract and except in a consumer lease, the lessee receive a writing identifying the supplier (unless the supplier was selected and required by the lessee) and the rights of the lessee under Section 2A–209, and advising the lessee a statement of promises and warranties is available from the supplier. Thus, even where oral supply orders or computer placed supply orders are compelled by custom and usage the transaction may still qualify as a finance lease if the lessee approves the supply contract before the lease contract is effective and such approval was a condition to the effectiveness of the lease contract. Moreover, where the lessor does not want the lessee to see the entire supply contract, including price information, the lessee may be provided with a separate statement of the terms of the supply contract relevant to the lessee; promises between the supplier and the lessor that do not affect the lessee need not be included. The statement can be a restatement of those terms or a copy of portions of the supply contract with the relevant terms clearly designated. Any implied warranties need not be designated, but a disclaimer or modification of remedy must be designated. A copy of any manufacturer's warranty is sufficient if that is the warranty provided. However, a copy of any Regulation M disclosure given pursuant to 12 C.F.R. § 213.4(g) concerning warranties in itself is not sufficient since those disclosures need only briefly identify express warranties and need not include any disclaimer of warranty.

If a transaction does not qualify as a finance lease, the parties may achieve the same result by agreement; no negative implications are to be drawn if the transaction does not qualify. Further, absent the application of special rules (fraud, duress, and the like), a lease that qualifies as a finance lease and is assigned by the lessor or the lessee to a third party does not lose its status as a finance lease under this Article. Finally, this Article creates no special rule where the lessor is an affiliate of the supplier; whether the transaction qualifies as a finance lease will be determined by the facts of each case.

(h) "Goods". Section 9–105(1)(h). See Section 2A–103(3) for reference to the definition of "Account", "Chattel paper", "Document", "General intangibles" and "Instrument". See Section 2A–217 for determination of the time and manner of identification.

(i) "Installment lease contract". Section 2–612(1).

(j) "Lease". New. There are several reasons to codify the law with respect to leases of goods. An analysis of the case law as it applies to leases of goods suggests at least several significant issues to be resolved by codification. First and foremost is the definition of a lease. It is necessary to define lease to determine whether a transaction creates a lease or a security interest disguised as a lease. If the transaction creates a security interest disguised as a lease, the transaction will be governed by the Article on Secured Transactions (Article 9) and the lessor will be required to file a financing statement or take other action to perfect its interest in the goods against third parties. There is no such requirement with respect to leases under the common law and, except with respect to leases of fixtures (Section 2A–309), this Article imposes no such requirement. Yet the distinction between a lease and a security interest disguised as a lease is not clear from the case law at the time of the promulgation of this Article. DeKoven, *Leases of Equipment: Puritan Leasing Company v. August, A Dangerous Decision,* 12 U.S.F. L. Rev. 257 (1978).

At common law a lease of personal property is a bailment for hire. While there are several definitions of bailment for hire, all require a thing to be let and a price for the letting. Thus, in modern terms and as provided in this definition, a lease is created when the lessee agrees to furnish consideration for the right to the possession and use of goods over a specified period of time. Mooney, *Personal Property Leasing: A Challenge,* 36 Bus. Law. 1605, 1607 (1981). Further, a lease is neither a sale (Section 2–106(1)) nor a retention or creation of a security interest (Section 1–201(37)). Due to extensive litigation to distinguish true leases from security interests, an amendment to Section 1–201(37) has been promulgated with this Article to create a sharper distinction.

This section as well as Section 1–201(37) must be examined to determine whether the transaction in question creates a lease or a security interest. The following hypotheticals indicate the perimeters of the issue. Assume that A has purchased a number of copying machines, new, for $1,000 each; the machines have an estimated useful economic life of three years. A advertises that the machines are available to rent for a minimum of one month and that the monthly rental is $100.00. A intends to enter into leases where A provides all maintenance without charge to the lessee. Further, the lessee will rent the machine, month to month, with no obligation to renew. At the end of the lease term the lessee will be obligated to return the machine to A's place of business. This transaction qualifies as a lease under the first half of the definition, for the transaction includes a transfer by A to a prospective lessee of possession and use of the machine for a stated term, month to month. The machines are goods (Section 2A–103(1)(h)). The lessee is obligated to pay consideration in return, $100.00 for each month of the term.

However, the second half of the definition provides that a sale or a security interest is not a lease. Since there is no passing of title, there is no sale. Sections 2A–103(3) and 2–106(1). Under pre-Act security law this transaction would have created a bailment for hire or a true lease and not a conditional sale. Da Rocha v. Macomber, 330 Mass. 611, 614–15, 116 N.E.2d 139, 142 (1953). Under Section 1–201(37), as amended with the promulgation of this Article, the same result would follow. While the lessee is obligated to pay rent for the one month term of the lease, one of the other four conditions of the second paragraph of Section 1–201(37) must be met and none is. The term of the lease is one month and the economic life of the machine is 36 months; thus, subparagraph (a) of Section 1–201(37) is not now satisfied. Considering the amount of the monthly rent, absent economic duress or coercion, the lessee is not bound either to renew the lease for the remaining economic life of the goods or to become the owner. If the lessee did lease the machine for 36 months, the lessee would have paid the lessor $3,600 for a machine that could have been purchased for $1,000; thus, subparagraph (b) of Section 1–201(37) is not satisfied. Finally, there are no options; thus, subparagraphs (c) and (d) of Section 1–201(37) are not satisfied. This transaction creates a lease, not a security interest. However, with each renewal of the lease the facts and circumstances at the time of each renewal must be examined to determine if that conclusion remains accurate, as it is possible that a transaction that first creates a lease, later creates a security interest.

Assume that the facts are changed and that A requires each lessee to lease the goods for 36 months, with no right to terminate. Under pre-Act security law this transaction would have created a conditional sale, and not a bailment for hire or true lease. Hervey v. Rhode Island Locomotive Works, 93 U.S. 664, 672–73 (1876). Under this subsection, and Section 1–201(37), as amended with the inclusion of this Article in the Act, the same result would follow. The lessee's obligation for the term is not subject to termination by the lessee and the term is equal to the economic life of the machine.

Between these extremes there are many transactions that can be created. Some of the transactions have not been properly categorized by the courts in applying the 1978 and earlier Official Texts of Section 1–201(37). This subsection, together with Section 1–201(37), as amended with the promulgation of this Article, draws a brighter line, which should create a clearer signal to the professional lessor and lessee.

(k) "Lease agreement". This definition is derived from the first sentence of Section 1–201(3). Because the definition of lease is broad enough to cover future transfers, lease agreement includes an agreement contemplating a current or subsequent transfer. Thus it was not necessary to make an express reference to an agreement for the future lease of goods (Section 2–106(1)). This concept is also incorporated in the definition of lease contract. Note that the definition of lease does not include transactions in ordinary building materials that are incorporated into an improvement on land. Section 2A–309(2).

The provisions of this Article, if applicable, determine whether a lease agreement has legal consequences; otherwise the law of bailments and other applicable law determine the same. Sections 2A–103(4) and 1–103.

(l) "Lease contract". This definition is derived from the definition of contract in Section 1 201(11). Note that a lease contract may be for the future lease of goods, since this notion is included in the definition of lease.

(m) "Leasehold interest". New.

(n) "Lessee". New.

(o) "Lessee in ordinary course of business". Section 1–201(9).

(p) "Lessor". New.

(q) "Lessor's residual interest". New.

(r) "Lien". New. This term is used in Section 2A–307 (Priority of Liens Arising by Attachment or Levy on, Security Interests in, and Other Claims to Goods).

(s) "Lot". Section 2–105(5).

(t) "Merchant lessee". New. This term is used in Section 2A–511 (Merchant Lessee's Duties as to Rightfully Rejected Goods). A person may satisfy the requirement of dealing in goods of the kind subject to the lease as lessor, lessee, seller, or buyer.

(u) "Present value". New. Authorities agree that present value should be used to determine fairly the damages payable by the lessor or the lessee on default. E.g., Taylor v. Commercial Credit Equip. Corp., 170 Ga. App. 322, 316 S.E.2d 788 (Ct. App. 1984). Present value is defined to mean an amount that represents the discounted value as of a date certain of one or more sums payable in the future. This is a function of the economic principle that a dollar today is more valuable to the holder than a dollar payable in two years. While there is no question as to the principle, reasonable people would differ as to the rate of discount to apply in determining the value of that future dollar today. To minimize litigation, this Article allows the parties to specify the discount or interest rate, if the rate was not manifestly unreasonable at the time the transaction was entered into. In all other cases, the interest rate will be a commercially reasonable rate that takes into account the facts and circumstances of each case, as of the time the transaction was entered into.

(v) "Purchase". Section 1–201(32). This definition omits the reference to lien contained in the definition of purchase in Article 1 (Section 1–201(32)). This should not be construed to exclude consensual liens from the definition of purchase in this Article; the exclusion was mandated by the scope of the definition of lien in Section 2A–103(1)(r). Further, the definition of purchaser in this Article adds a reference to lease; as purchase is defined in Section 1–201(32) to include any other voluntary transaction creating an interest in property, this addition is not substantive.

(w) "Sublease". New.

(x) "Supplier". New.

(y) "Supply contract". New.

(z) "Termination". Section 2–106(3). The effect of a termination is provided in Section 2A–505(2).

Section 2A–104. Leases Subject to Other Law.

(1) A lease, although subject to this Article, is also subject to any applicable:

(a) certificate of title statute of this state;

(b) certificate of title statute of another jurisdiction (Section 2A–105); or

(c) consumer protection law of this state, both decisional and statutory.

(2) In case of conflict between this Article, other than Sections 2A–105, 2A–304(3), and 2A–305(3), and a statute referred to in subsection (1), the statute controls. Decisional consumer protection law may supplement the application of provisions of this Article.

(3) Failure to comply with an applicable law has only the effect specified therein.

OFFICIAL COMMENT

Uniform Statutory Source: Sections 9–203(4) and 9–302(3)(b) and (c).
Changes: Substantially revised.

Purposes:

1. This Article creates a comprehensive scheme for the regulation of transactions that create leases. Section 2A–102. Thus, the Article supersedes all prior legislation dealing with leases, except to the extent set forth in this Section.

2. Subsection (1) states the general rule that a lease, although governed by the scheme of this Article, also may be governed by certain other applicable laws. This

may occur in the case of a consumer lease. Section 2A-103(1)(e). Those laws may be state statutes existing prior to enactment of Article 2A or passed afterward. In this case, it is desirable for this Article to specify which statute controls. Or the law may be a preexisting consumer protection decision. This Article preserves such decisions. Or the law may be a statute of the United States. Such a law controls without any statement in this Article under applicable principles of preemption.

An illustration of a statute of the United States that governs consumer leases is the Consumer Leasing Act, 15 U.S.C. §§ 1667-1667(e) (1982) and its implementing regulation, Regulation M, 12 C.F.R. § 213 (1986); the statute mandates disclosures of certain lease terms, delimits the liability of a lessee in leasing personal property, and regulates the advertising of lease terms. An illustration of a state statute that governs consumer leases and which if adopted in the enacting state prevails over this Article is the Unif. Consumer Credit Code, which includes many provisions similar to those of the Consumer Leasing Act, e.g., Unif. Consumer Credit Code §§ 3.202, 3.209, 3.401, 7A U.L.A. 108–09, 115, 125 (1974), as well as provisions in addition to those of the Consumer Leasing Act, e.g., Unif. Consumer Credit Code §§ 5.109–.111, 7A U.L.A. 1-71–76 (1974) (the right to cure a default). Such statutes may define consumer lease so as to govern transactions within and without the definition of consumer lease under this Article.

3. Under subsection (2), subject to certain limited exclusions, in case of conflict a statute or a decision described in subsection (1) prevails over this Article. For example, a provision like Unif. Consumer Credit Code § 5.112, 7A U.L.A. 176 (1974), limiting self-help repossession, prevails over Section 2A-525(3). A consumer protection decision rendered after the effective date of this Article may supplement its provisions. For example, in relation to Article 9 a court might conclude that an acceleration clause may not be enforced against an individual debtor after late payments have been accepted unless a prior notice of default is given. To the extent the decision establishes a general principle applicable to transactions other than secured transactions, it may supplement Section 2A-502.

4. Consumer protection in lease transactions is primarily left to other law. However, several provisions of this Article do contain special rules that may not be varied by agreement in the case of a consumer lease. E.g., Sections 2A–106, 2A–108, and 2A–109(2). Were that not so, the ability of the parties to govern their relationship by agreement together with the position of the lessor in a consumer lease too often could result in a one-sided lease agreement.

5. In construing this provision the reference to statute should be deemed to include applicable regulations. A consumer protection decision is "final" on the effective date of this Article if it is not subject to appeal on that date or, if subject to appeal, is not later reversed on appeal. Of course, such a decision can be overruled by a later decision or superseded by a later statute.

Cross References:

Sections 2A–103(1)(e), 2A–106, 2A–108, 2A–109(2) and 2A–525(3).

Definitional Cross Reference:

"Lease". Section 2A–103(1)(j).

Section 2A–105. Territorial Application of Article to Goods Covered by Certificate of Title.

Subject to the provisions of Sections 2A–304(3) and 2A–305(3), with respect to goods covered by a certificate of title issued under a statute of this state or of another jurisdiction, compliance and the effect of compliance or noncompliance with a certificate of title statute are governed by the law (including the conflict of laws rules) of the jurisdiction issuing the certificate until the earlier of (a) surrender of the certificate, or (b) four months after the goods are removed from that jurisdiction and thereafter until a new certificate of title is issued by another jurisdiction.

OFFICIAL COMMENT

Uniform Statutory Source: Section 9–103(2)(a) and (b).

Changes: Substantially revised. The provisions of the last sentence of Section 9–103(2)(b) have not been incorporated as it is superfluous in this context. The provisions of Section 9–103(2)(d) have not been incorporated because the problems dealt with are adequately addressed by this section and Sections 2A–304(3) and 305(3).

Purposes:

The new certificate referred to in (b) must be permanent, not temporary. Generally, the lessor or creditor whose interest is indicated on the most recently issued certificate of title will prevail over interests indicated on certificates issued previously by other jurisdictions. This provision reflects a policy that it is reasonable to require holders of interests in goods covered by a certificate of title to police the goods or risk losing their interests when a new certificate of title is issued by another jurisdiction.

Cross References:

Sections 2A–304(3), 2A–305(3), 9–103(2)(b) and 9–103(2)(d).

Definitional Cross Reference:

"Goods". Section 2A–103(1)(h).

Section 2A–106. Limitation on Power of Parties to Consumer Lease to Choose Applicable Law and Judicial Forum.

(1) If the law chosen by the parties to a consumer lease is that of a jurisdiction other than a jurisdiction in which the lessee resides at the time the lease agreement becomes enforceable or within thirty days thereafter or in which the goods are to be used, the choice is not enforceable.

(2) If the judicial forum chosen by the parties to a consumer lease is a forum that would not otherwise have jurisdiction over the lessee, the choice is not enforceable.

OFFICIAL COMMENT

Uniform Statutory Source: Unif. Consumer Credit Code § 1.201(8), 7A U.L.A. 36 (1974).

Changes: Substantially revised.

Purposes:

There is a real danger that a lessor may induce a consumer lessee to agree that the applicable law will be a jurisdiction that has little effective consumer protection, or to agree that the applicable forum will be a forum that is inconvenient for the lessee in the event of litigation. As a result, this section invalidates these choice of law or forum clauses, except where the law chosen is that of the state of the consumer's residence or where the goods will be kept, or the forum chosen is one that otherwise would have jurisdiction over the lessee.

Subsection (1) limits potentially abusive choice of law clauses in consumer leases. The 30-day rule in subsection (1) was suggested by Section 9–103(1)(c). This section has no effect on choice of law clauses in leases that are not consumer leases. Such clauses would be governed by other law.

Subsection (2) prevents enforcement of potentially abusive jurisdictional consent clauses in consumer leases. By using the term judicial forum, this section does not limit selection of a nonjudicial forum, such as arbitration. This section has no effect on choice of forum clauses in leases that are not consumer leases; such clauses are, as a matter of current law, "prima facie valid". The Bremen v. Zapata Off-Shore Co., 407 U.S. 1, 10 (1972). Such clauses would be governed by other law, including the Model Choice of Forum Act (1968).

Cross Reference:

Section 9–103(1)(c).

Definitional Cross References:

"Consumer lease". Section 2A–103(1)(e).
"Lease agreement". Section 2A–103(1)(k).
"Lessee". Section 2A–103(1)(n).
"Goods". Section 2A–103(1)(h).
"Party". Section 1–201(29).

Section 2A–107. Waiver or Renunciation of Claim or Right After Default.

Any claim or right arising out of an alleged default or breach of warranty may be discharged in whole or in part without consideration by a written waiver or renunciation signed and delivered by the aggrieved party.

OFFICIAL COMMENT

Uniform Statutory Source: Section 1-107.

Changes: Revised to reflect leasing practices and terminology. This clause is used throughout the official comments to this Article to indicate the scope of change in the provisions of the Uniform Statutory Source included in the section; these changes range from one extreme, e.g., a significant difference in practice (a warranty as to merchantability is not implied in a finance lease (Section 2A-212)) to the other extreme, e.g., a modest difference in style or terminology (the transaction governed is a lease not a sale (Section 2A-203)).

Cross References:

Sections 2A-203 and 2A-212.

Definitional Cross References:

"Aggrieved party". Section 1-201(2).
"Delivery". Section 1-201(14).

UCC

"Rights". Section 1-201(36).
"Signed". Section 1-201(39).
"Written". Section 1-201(46).

Section 2A-108. Unconscionability.

(1) If the court as a matter of law finds a lease contract or any clause of a lease contract to have been unconscionable at the time it was made the court may refuse to enforce the lease contract, or it may enforce the remainder of the lease contract without the unconscionable clause, or it may so limit the application of any unconscionable clause as to avoid any unconscionable result.

(2) With respect to a consumer lease, if the court as a matter of law finds that a lease contract or any clause of a lease contract has been induced by unconscionable conduct or that unconscionable conduct has occurred in the collection of a claim arising from a lease contract, the court may grant appropriate relief.

(3) Before making a finding of unconscionability under subsection (1) or (2), the court, on its own motion or that of a party, shall afford the parties a reasonable opportunity to present evidence as to the setting, purpose, and effect of the lease contract or clause thereof, or of the conduct.

(4) In an action in which the lessee claims unconscionability with respect to a consumer lease:

(a) if the court finds unconscionability under subsection (1) or (2), the court shall award reasonable attorney's fees to the lessee.

(b) in determining attorney's fees, the amount of recovery on behalf of the claimant under subsections (1) and (2) is not controlling.

OFFICIAL COMMENT

Uniform Statutory Source: Section 2–302 and Unif. Consumer Credit Code § 5.108, 7A U.L.A. 167–69 (1974).

Changes: Subsection (1) is taken almost verbatim from the provisions of Section 2–302(1). Subsection (2) is suggested by the provisions of Unif. Consumer Credit Code § 5.108(1), (2), 7A U.L.A. 167 (1974). Subsection (3), taken from the provisions of Section 2–302(2), has been expanded to cover unconscionable conduct. Unif. Consumer Credit Code § 5.108(3), 7A U.L.A. 167 (1974). The provision for the award of attorney's fees to consumers, subsection (4), covers unconscionability under subsection (1) as well as (2). Subsection (4) is modeled on the provisions of Unif. Consumer Credit Code § 5.108(6), 7A U.L.A. 169 (1974).

Purposes:

Subsections (1) and (3) of this section apply the concept of unconscionability reflected in the provisions of Section 2–302 to leases. See Dillman & Assocs. v. Capitol Leasing Co., 110 Ill. App. 3d 335, 342, 442 N.E.2d 311, 316 (App. Ct. 1982). Subsection (3) omits the adjective "commercial" found in subsection 2–302(2) because subsection (3) is concerned with all leases and the relevant standard of conduct is determined by the context.

The balance of the section is modeled on the provisions of Unif. Consumer Credit Code § 5.108, 7A U.L.A. 167–69 (1974). Thus subsection (2) recognizes that a consumer lease or a clause in a consumer lease may not itself be unconscionable but that the agreement would never have been entered into if unconscionable means had not been employed to induce the consumer to agree. To make a statement to induce the consumer to lease the goods, in the expectation of invoking an integration clause in the lease to exclude the statement's admissibility in a subsequent dispute, may be unconscionable. Subsection (2) also provides a consumer remedy for unconscionable conduct, such as using or threatening to use force or violence, in the collection of a claim arising from a lease contract. These provisions are not exclusive. The remedies of this section are in addition to remedies otherwise available for the same conduct under other law, for example, an action in tort for abusive debt collection or under another statute of this State for such conduct. The reference to appropriate relief in subsection (2) is intended to foster liberal administration of this remedy. Sections 2A–103(4) and 1–106(1).

Subsection (4) authorizes an award of reasonable attorney's fees if the court finds unconscionability with respect to a consumer lease under subsections (1) or (2). Provision is also made for recovery by the party against whom the claim was made if the court does not find unconscionability and does find that the consumer knew the action to be groundless. Further, subsection (4)(b) is independent of, and thus will not override, a term in the lease agreement that provides for the payment of attorney's fees.

Cross References:

Sections 1–106(1), 2–302 and 2A–103(4).

Definitional Cross References:

"Action". Section 1–201(1).
"Consumer lease". Section 2A–103 (1)(e).
"Lease contract". Section 2A–103 (1)(l).
"Lessee". Section 2A–103(1)(n).
"Party". Section 1–201(29).

Section 2A–109. Option to Accelerate at Will.

(1) A term providing that one party or his or her successor in interest may accelerate payment or performance or require collateral or additional collateral "at will" or "when he or she deems himself or herself insecure" or in words of similar import must be construed to mean that he or she has power to do so only if he or she in good faith believes that the prospect of payment or performance is impaired.

(2) With respect to a consumer lease, the burden of establishing good faith under subsection (1) is on the party who exercised the power; otherwise the burden of establishing lack of good faith is on the party against whom the power has been exercised.

OFFICIAL COMMENT

Uniform Statutory Source: Section 1-208 and Unif. Consumer Credit Code § 5.109(2), 7A U.L.A. 171 (1974).

Purposes:

Subsection (1) reflects modest changes in style to the provisions of the first sentence of Section 1–208.

Subsection (2), however, reflects a significant change in the provisions of the second sentence of Section 1–208 by creating a new rule with respect to a consumer lease. A lease provision allowing acceleration at the will of the lessor or when the lessor deems itself insecure is of critical importance to the lessee. In a consumer lease it is a provision that is not usually agreed to by the parties but is usually mandated by the lessor. Therefore, where its invocation depends not on specific criteria but on the discretion of the lessor, its use should be regulated to prevent abuse. Subsection (1) imposes a duty of good faith upon its exercise. Subsection (2) shifts the burden of establishing good faith to the lessor in the case of a consumer lease, but not otherwise.

Cross Reference:

Section 1–208.

Definitional Cross References:

"Burden of establishing". Section 1–201(8).
"Consumer lease". Section 2A–103(1)(e).
"Good faith". Sections 1–201(19) and 2–103(1)(b).
"Party". Section 1–201(29).
'Term'. Section 1–201(42).

PART 2

FORMATION AND CONSTRUCTION OF LEASE CONTRACT

Section 2A–201. Statute of Frauds.

(1) A lease contract is not enforceable by way of action or defense unless:

(a) the total payments to be made under the lease contract, excluding payments for options to renew or buy, are less than $1,000; or

(b) there is a writing, signed by the party against whom enforcement is sought or by that party's authorized agent, sufficient to indicate that a lease contract has been made between the parties and to describe the goods leased and the lease term.

(2) Any description of leased goods or of the lease term is sufficient and satisfies subsection (1)(b), whether or not it is specific, if it reasonably identifies what is described.

(3) A writing is not insufficient because it omits or incorrectly states a term agreed upon, but the lease contract is not enforceable under subsection (1)(b) beyond the lease term and the quantity of goods shown in the writing.

(4) A lease contract that does not satisfy the requirements of subsection (1), but which is valid in other respects, is enforceable:

(a) if the goods are to be specially manufactured or obtained for the lessee and are not suitable for lease or sale to others in the ordinary course of the lessor's business, and the lessor, before notice of repudiation is received and under circumstances that reasonably indicate that the goods are for the lessee, has made either a substantial beginning of their manufacture or commitments for their procurement;

(b) if the party against whom enforcement is sought admits in that party's pleading, testimony, or otherwise in court that a lease contract was made, but the lease contract is not enforceable under this provision beyond the quantity of goods admitted; or

(c) with respect to goods that have been received and accepted by the lessee.

(5) The lease term under a lease contract referred to in subsection (4) is:

(a) if there is a writing signed by the party against whom enforcement is sought or by that party's authorized agent specifying the lease term, the term so specified;

(b) if the party against whom enforcement is sought admits in that party's pleading, testimony, or otherwise in court a lease term, the term so admitted; or

(c) a reasonable lease term.

(6) A lease contract enforceable under this section shall not be rendered unenforceable by the operation of New York General Obligations Law Section 5-701.

OFFICIAL COMMENT

Uniform Statutory Source: Sections 2–201, 9–203(1) and 9–110.

Changes: This section is modeled on Section 2–201, with changes to reflect the differences between a lease contract and a contract for the sale of goods. In particular, subsection (1)(b) adds a requirement that the writing "describe the goods leased and the lease term", borrowing that concept, with revisions, from the provisions of Section 9–203(1)(a). Subsection (2), relying on the statutory analogue in Section 9–110, sets forth the minimum criterion for satisfying that requirement.

Purposes:

The changes in this section conform the provisions of Section 2–201 to custom and usage in lease transactions. Section 2–201(2), stating a special rule between merchants, was not included in this section as the number of such transactions involving leases, as opposed to sales, was thought to be modest. Subsection (4) creates no exception for transactions where payment has been made and accepted. This represents a departure from the analogue, Section 2–201(3)(c). The rationale for the departure is grounded in the distinction between sales and leases. Unlike a buyer in a sales transaction, the lessee does not tender payment in full for goods delivered, but only payment of rent for one or more months. It was decided that, as a matter of policy, this act of payment is not a sufficient substitute for the required memorandum. Subsection (5) was needed to establish the criteria for supplying the lease term if it is omitted, as the lease contract may still be enforceable under subsection (4).

Cross References:

Sections 2–201, 9–110 and 9–203(1)(a).

Definitional Cross References:

"Action". Section 1–201(1).
"Agreed". Section 1–201(3).
"Buying". Section 2A–103(1)(a).
"Goods". Section 2A–103(1)(h).
"Lease". Section 2A–103(1)(j).
"Lease contract". Section 2A–103(1)(l).
"Lessee". Section 2A–103(1)(n).
"Lessor". Section 2A–103(1)(p).
"Notice". Section 1–201(25).
"Party". Section 1–201(29).
"Sale". Section 2–106(1).
"Signed". Section 1–201(39).
"Term". Section 1–201(42).
"Writing". Section 1–201(46).

Section 2A–202. Final Written Expression: Parol or Extrinsic Evidence.

Terms with respect to which the confirmatory memoranda of the parties agree or which are otherwise set forth in a writing intended by the parties as a final expression of their agreement with respect to such terms as are included therein may not be contradicted by evidence of any prior agreement or of a contemporaneous oral agreement but may be explained or supplemented:

(a) by course of dealing or usage of trade or by course of performance; and

(b) by evidence of consistent additional terms unless the court finds the writing to have been intended also as a complete and exclusive statement of the terms of the agreement.

OFFICIAL COMMENT

Uniform Statutory Source: Section 2–202.

Definitional Cross References:

"Agreement". Section 1–201(3).
"Course of dealing". Section 1–205.
"Party". Section 1–201(29).
"Term". Section 1–201(42).
"Usage of trade". Section 1–205.
"Writing". Section 1–201(46).

Section 2A–203. Seals Inoperative.

The affixing of a seal to a writing evidencing a lease contract or an offer to enter into a lease contract does not render the writing a sealed instrument and the law with respect to sealed instruments does not apply to the lease contract or offer.

OFFICIAL COMMENT

Uniform Statutory Source: Section 2-203.
Changes: Revised to reflect leasing practices and terminology.

Definitional Cross References:

"Lease contract". Section 2A-103(1)(1).
"Writing". Section 1-201(46).

Section 2A–204. Formation in General.

(1) A lease contract may be made in any manner sufficient to show agreement, including conduct by both parties which recognizes the existence of a lease contract.

(2) An agreement sufficient to constitute a lease contract may be found although the moment of its making is undetermined.

(3) Although one or more terms are left open, a lease contract does not fail for indefiniteness if the parties have intended to make a lease contract and there is a reasonably certain basis for giving an appropriate remedy.

OFFICIAL COMMENT

Uniform Statutory Source: Section 2-204.
Changes: Revised to reflect leasing practices and terminology.

Definitional Cross References:

"Agreement". Section 1-201(3).
"Lease contract". Section 2A-103(1)(1).
"Party". Section 1-201(29).
"Remedy". Section 1-201(34).
"Term". Section 1-201(42).

Section 2A–205. Firm Offers.

An offer by a merchant to lease goods to or from another person in a signed writing that by its terms gives assurance it will be held open is not revocable, for lack of consideration, during the time stated or, if no time is stated, for a reasonable time, but in no event may the period of irrevocability exceed three months. Any such term of assurance on a form supplied by the offeree must be separately signed by the offeror.

OFFICIAL COMMENT

Uniform Statutory Source: Section 2–205.
Changes: Revised to reflect leasing practices and terminology.

Definitional Cross References:

"Goods". Section 2A–103(1)(h).
"Lease". Section 2A–103(1)(j).

"Merchant". Section 2-104(1).
"Person". Section 1-201(30).
"Reasonable time". Section 1-204(1) and (2).
"Signed". Section 1-201(39).
"Term". Section 1-201(42).
"Writing". Section 1-201(46).

Section 2A-206. Offer and Acceptance in Formation of Lease Contract.

(1) Unless otherwise unambiguously indicated by the language or circumstances, an offer to make a lease contract must be construed as inviting acceptance in any manner and by any medium reasonable in the circumstances.

(2) If the beginning of a requested performance is a reasonable mode of acceptance, an offeror who is not notified of acceptance within a reasonable time may treat the offer as having lapsed before acceptance.

OFFICIAL COMMENT

Uniform Statutory Source: Section 2-206(1)(a) and (2).
Changes: Revised to reflect leasing practices and terminology.

Definitional Cross References:

"Lease contract". Section 2A-103(1)(l).
"Notifies". Section 1-201(26).
"Reasonable time". Section 1-204(1) and (2).

Section 2A-207. Course of Performance or Practical Construction.

(1) If a lease contract involves repeated occasions for performance by either party with knowledge of the nature of the performance and opportunity for objection to it by the other, any course of performance accepted or acquiesced in without objection is relevant to determine the meaning of the lease agreement.

(2) The express terms of a lease agreement and any course of performance, as well as any course of dealing and usage of trade, must be construed whenever reasonable as consistent with each other; but if that construction is unreasonable, express terms control course of performance, course of performance controls both course of dealing and usage of trade, and course of dealing controls usage of trade.

(3) Subject to the provisions of Section 2A-208 on modification and waiver, course of performance is relevant to show a waiver or modification of any term inconsistent with the course of performance.

OFFICIAL COMMENT

Uniform Statutory Source: Sections 2-208 and 1-205(4).
Changes: Revised to reflect leasing practices and terminology, except that subsection (2) was further revised to make the subsection parallel the provisions of Section 1-205(4) by adding that course of dealing controls usage of trade.

Purposes:

The section should be read in conjunction with Section 2A–208. In particular, although a specific term may control over course of performance as a matter of lease construction under subsection (2), subsection (3) allows the same course of dealing to show a waiver or modification, if Section 2A–208 is satisfied.

Cross References:

Sections 1–205(4), 2–208 and 2A–208.

Definitional Cross References:

"Course of dealing". Section 1–205.
"Knowledge". Section 1–201(25).
"Lease agreement". Section 2A–103(1)(k).
"Lease contract". Section 2A–103(1)(l).
"Party". Section 1–201(29).
"Term". Section 1–201(42).
"Usage of trade". Section 1–205.

Section 2A–208. Modification, Rescission and Waiver.

(1) An agreement modifying a lease contract needs no consideration to be binding.

(2) A signed lease agreement that excludes modification or rescission except by a signed writing may not be otherwise modified or rescinded, but, except as between merchants, such a requirement on a form supplied by a merchant must be separately signed by the other party.

(3) Although an attempt at modification or rescission does not satisfy the requirements of subsection (2), it may operate as a waiver.

(4) A party who has made a waiver affecting an executory portion of a lease contract may retract the waiver by reasonable notification received by the other party that strict performance will be required of any term waived, unless the retraction would be unjust in view of a material change of position in reliance on the waiver.

OFFICIAL COMMENT

Uniform Statutory Source: Section 2–209.

Changes: Revised to reflect leasing practices and terminology, except that the provisions of subsection 2–209(3) were omitted.

Purposes:

Section 2–209(3) provides that "the requirements of the statute of frauds section of this Article (Section 2–201) must be satisfied if the contract as modified is within its provisions." This provision was not incorporated as it is unfair to allow an oral modification to make the entire lease contract unenforceable, e.g. if the modification takes it a few dollars over the dollar limit. At the same time, the problem could not be solved by providing that the lease contract would still be enforceable in its pre-modification state (if it then satisfied the statute of frauds) since in some cases that might be worse than no enforcement at all. Resolution of the issue is left to the courts based on the facts of each case.

Cross References:

Sections 2–201 and 2–209.

Definitional Cross References:

"Agreement". Section 1–201(3).
"Between merchants". Section 2–104(3).
"Lease agreement". Section 2A–103(1)(k).
"Lease contract". Section 2A–103(1)(l).
"Merchant". Section 2–104(1).
"Notification". Section 1–201(26).
"Party". Section 1–201(29).
"Signed". Section 1–201(39).
"Term". Section 1–201(42).
"Writing". Section 1–201(46).

Section 2A–209. Lessee Under Finance Lease as Beneficiary of Supply Contract.

(1) The benefit of a supplier's promises to the lessor under the supply contract and of all warranties, whether express or implied, including those of any third party provided in connection with or as part of the supply contract, extends to the lessee to the extent of the lessee's leasehold interest under a finance lease related to the supply contract, but is subject to the terms of the warranty and of the supply contract and all defenses or claims arising therefrom.

(2) The extension of the benefit of a supplier's promises and of warranties to the lessee under subsection (1) does not: (i) modify the rights and obligations of the parties to the supply contract, whether arising therefrom or otherwise, or (ii) impose any duty or liability under the supply contract on the lessee.

(3) Any modification or rescission of the supply contract by the supplier and lessor is effective between the supplier and the lessee unless, before the modification or rescission, the supplier has received notice that the lessee has entered into a finance lease related to the supply contract. If the modification or rescission is effective between the supplier and the lessee, the lessor is deemed to have assumed, in addition to the obligations of the lessor to the lessee under the lease contract, promises of the supplier to the lessor and warranties that were so modified or rescinded as they existed and were available to the lessee before modification or rescission.

(4) In addition to the extension of the benefit of the supplier's promises and of warranties to the lessee under subsection (1), the lessee retains all rights which the lessee may have against the supplier that arise from any agreement between the lessee and supplier or under other law.

OFFICIAL COMMENT

Uniform Statutory Source: None.

Changes: This section is modeled on Section 9–318, the Restatement (Second) of Contracts §§ 302–315 (1981), and leasing practices. *See* Earman Oil Co. v. Burroughs Corp., 625 F.2d 1291, 1296–97 (5th Cir. 1980).

Purposes:

1. The function performed by the lessor in a finance lease is extremely limited. Section 2A–103(1)(g). The lessee looks to the supplier of the goods for warranties and the like or, in some cases as to warranties, to the manufacturer if a warranty made by that person is passed on. That expectation is reflected in subsection (1), which is self-executing. As a matter of policy, the operation of this provision may not be excluded, modified or limited; however, an exclusion, modification, or limitation of any term of the supply contract or warranty, including any with respect to rights and remedies, and any defense or claim such as a statute of limitations, effective against the lessor as the acquiring party under the supply contract, is also effective against the lessee as the beneficiary designated under this provision. For example, the supplier is not precluded from excluding or modifying an express or implied warranty under a supply contract. Sections 2–312(2) and 2–316, or Section 2A–214. Further, the supplier is not precluded from limiting the rights and remedies of the lessor and from liquidating damages. Sections 2–718 and 2–719 or Sections 2A–503 and 2A–504. If the supply contract excludes or modifies warranties, limits remedies, or liquidates damages with respect to the lessor, such provisions are enforceable against the lessee as beneficiary. Thus, only selective discrimination against the beneficiaries designated under this section is precluded, *i.e.*, exclusion of the supplier's liability to the lessee with respect to warranties made to the lessor. This section does not affect the development of other law with respect to products liability.

2. Enforcement of this benefit is by action. Sections 2A–103(4) and 1–106(2).

3. The benefit extended by these provisions is not without a price, as this Article also provides in the case of a finance lease that is not a consumer lease that the lessee's promises to the lessor under the lease contract become irrevocable and independent upon the lessee's acceptance of the goods. Section 2A–407.

4. Subsection (2) limits the effect of subsection (1) on the supplier and the lessor by preserving, notwithstanding the transfer of the benefits of the supply contract to the lessee, all of the supplier's and the lessor's rights and obligations with respect to each other and others; it further absolves the lessee of any duties with respect to the supply contract that might have been inferred from the extension of the benefits thereof.

5. Subsections (2) and (3) also deal with difficult issues related to modification or rescission of the supply contract. Subsection (2) states a rule that determines the impact of the statutory extension of benefit contained in subsection (1) upon the relationship of the parties to the supply contract and, in a limited respect, upon the lessee. This statutory extension of benefit, like that contained in Sections 2A–216 and 2–318, is not a modification of the supply contract by the parties. Thus, subsection (3) states the rules that apply to a modification or rescission of the supply contract by the parties. Subsection (3) provides that a modification or rescission is not effective between the supplier and the lessee if, before the modification or rescission occurs, the supplier received notice that the lessee has entered into the finance lease. On the other hand, if the modification or rescission is effective, then to the extent of the modification or rescission of the benefit or warranty, the lessor by statutory dictate assumes an obligation to provide to the lessee that which the lessee would otherwise lose. For example, assume a reduction in an express warranty from four years to one year. No prejudice to the lessee may occur if the goods perform as agreed. If, however, there is a breach of the express warranty after one year and before four years pass, the lessor is liable. A remedy for any prejudice to the lessee because of the bifurcation

of the lessee's recourse resulting from the action of the supplier and the lessor is left to resolution by the courts based on the facts of each case.

6. Subsection (4) makes it clear that the rights granted to the lessee by this section do not displace any rights the lessee otherwise may have against the supplier.

Cross References:

Sections 2A–103(1)(g), 2A–407 and 9–318.

Definitional Cross References:

"Action". Section 1–201(1).
"Finance lease". Section 2A–103(1)(g).
"Leasehold interest". Section 2A–103(1)(m).
"Lessee". Section 2A–103(1)(n).
"Lessor". Section 2A–103(1)(p).
"Notice". Section 1–201(25).
"Party". Section 1–201(29).
"Rights". Section 1–201(36).
"Supplier". Section 2A–103(1)(x).
"Supply contract". Section 2A–103(1)(y).
"Term". Section 1–201(42).

Section 2A–210. Express Warranties.

(1) Express warranties by the lessor are created as follows:

(a) any affirmation of fact or promise made by the lessor to the lessee which relates to the goods and becomes part of the basis of the bargain creates an express warranty that the goods will conform to the affirmation or promise.

(b) any description of the goods which is made part of the basis of the bargain creates an express warranty that the goods will conform to the description.

(c) any sample or model that is made part of the basis of the bargain creates an express warranty that the whole of the goods will conform to the sample or model.

(2) It is not necessary to the creation of an express warranty that the lessor use formal words, such as "warrant" or "guarantee," or that the lessor have a specific intention to make a warranty, but an affirmation merely of the value of the goods or a statement purporting to be merely the lessor's opinion or commendation of the goods does not create a warranty.

OFFICIAL COMMENT

Uniform Statutory Source: Section 2-313.
Changes: Revised to reflect leasing practices and terminology.

Purposes:

All of the express and implied warranties of the Article on Sales (Article 2) are included in this Article, revised to reflect the differences between a sale of goods and a lease of goods. Sections 2A-210 through 2A-216. The lease of goods is sufficiently similar to the sale of goods to justify this decision. Hawkland, *The Impact of the Uniform Commercial Code on Equipment Leasing,* 1972 Ill. L.F. 446, 459-60. Many state and federal courts have reached the same conclusion.

Value of the goods, as used in subsection (2), includes rental value.

Cross References:

Article 2, esp. Section 2-313, and Sections 2A-210 through 2A-216.

Definitional Cross References:

"Conforming". Section 2A-103(1)(d).
"Goods". Section 2A-103(1)(h).
"Lessee". Section 2A-103(1)(n).
"Lessor". Section 2A-103(1)(p).
"Value". Section 1-201(44).

Section 2A–211. Warranties Against Interference and Against Infringement; Lessee's Obligation Against Infringement.

(1) There is in a lease contract a warranty that for the lease term no person holds a claim to or interest in the goods that arose from an act or omission of the lessor, other than a claim by way of infringement or the like, which will interfere with the lessee's enjoyment of its leasehold interest.

(2) Except in a finance lease there is in a lease contract by a lessor who is a merchant regularly dealing in goods of the kind a warranty that the goods are delivered free of the rightful claim of any person by way of infringement or the like.

(3) A lessee who furnishes specifications to a lessor or a supplier shall hold the lessor and the supplier harmless against any claim by way of infringement or the like that arises out of compliance with the specifications.

OFFICIAL COMMENT

Uniform Statutory Source: Section 2-312.

Changes: This section is modeled on the provisions of Section 2-312, with modifications to reflect the limited interest transferred by a lease contract and the total interest transferred by a sale. Section 2-312(2), which is omitted here, is incorporated in Section 2A-214. The warranty of quiet possession was abolished with respect to sales of goods. Section 2-312 official comment 1. Section 2A-211(1) reinstates the warranty of quiet possession with respect to leases. Inherent in the nature of the limited interest transferred by the lease–the right to possession and use of the goods–is the need of the lessee for protection greater than that afforded to the buyer. Since the scope of the protection is limited to claims or interests that arose from acts or omissions of the lessor, the lessor will be in position to evaluate the potential cost, certainly a far better position than that enjoyed by the lessee. Further, to the extent the market will allow, the lessor can attempt to pass on the anticipated additional cost to the lessee in the guise of higher rent.

Purposes:

General language was chosen for subsection (1) that expresses the essence of the lessee's expectation: with an exception for infringement and the like, no person holding a claim or interest that arose from an act or omission of the lessor will be able to interfere with the lessee's use and enjoyment of the goods for the lease term. Subsection (2), like other similar provisions in later sections, excludes the finance lessor from extending this warranty; with few exceptions (Sections 2A-210 and 2A-211(1)), the lessee under a finance lease is to look to the supplier for warranties and the like or, in some cases as to warranties, to the manufacturer if a warranty made by that person is passed on. Subsections (2) and (3) are derived from Section 2-312(3). These subsections, as well as the analogue, should be construed so that applicable principles of law and equity supplement their provisions. Sections 2A-103(4) and 1-103.

Cross References:

Sections 2-312, 2-312(1), 2-312(2), 2-312 official comment 1, 2A-210, 2A-211(1) and 2A-214.

Definitional Cross References:

"Delivery". Section 1-201(14).
"Finance lease". Section 2A-103(1)(g).
"Goods". Section 2A-103(1)(h).
"Lease". Section 2A-103(1)(j).
"Lease contract". Section 2A-103(1)(l).
"Leasehold interest". Section 2A-103(1)(m).
"Lessee". Section 2A-103(1)(n).
"Lessor". Section 2A-103(1)(p).
"Merchant". Section 2-104(1).
"Person". Section 1-201(30).
"Supplier". Section 2A-103(1)(x).

Section 2A–212. Implied Warranty of Merchantability.

(1) Except in a finance lease, a warranty that the goods will be merchantable is implied in a lease contract if the lessor is a merchant with respect to goods of that kind.

(2) Goods to be merchantable must be at least such as:

(a) pass without objection in the trade under the description in the lease agreement;

(b) in the case of fungible goods, are of fair average quality within the description;

(c) are fit for the ordinary purposes for which goods of that type are used;

(d) run, within the variation permitted by the lease agreement, of even kind, quality, and quantity within each unit and among all units involved;

(e) are adequately contained, packaged, and labeled as the lease agreement may require; and

(f) conform to any promises or affirmations of fact made on the container or label.

(3) Other implied warranties may arise from course of dealing or usage of trade.

OFFICIAL COMMENT

Uniform Statutory Source: Section 2–314.

Changes: Revised to reflect leasing practices and terminology. *E.g.,* Glenn Dick Equip. Co. v. Galey Constr., Inc., 97 Idaho 216, 225, 541 P.2d 1184, 1193 (1975) (implied warranty of merchantability (Article 2) extends to lease transactions).

Definitional Cross References:

"Conforming". Section 2A–103(1)(d).
"Course of dealing". Section 1–205.
"Finance lease". Section 2A–103(1)(g).
"Fungible". Section 1–201(17).
"Goods". Section 2A–103(1)(h).
"Lease agreement". Section 2A–103(1)(k).
"Lease contract". Section 2A–103(1)(l).
"Lessor". Section 2A–103(1)(p).
"Merchant". Section 2–104(1).
"Usage of trade". Section 1–205.

Section 2A–213. Implied Warranty of Fitness for Particular Purpose.

Except in a finance lease, if the lessor at the time the lease contract is made has reason to know of any particular purpose for which the goods are required and that the lessee is relying on the lessor's skill or judgment to select or furnish suitable goods, there is in the lease contract an implied warranty that the goods will be fit for that purpose.

OFFICIAL COMMENT

Uniform Statutory Source: Section 2–315.

Changes: Revised to reflect leasing practices and terminology. *E.g.,* All-States Leasing Co. v. Bass, 96 Idaho 873, 879, 538 P.2d 1177, 1183 (1975) (implied warranty of fitness for a particular purpose (Article 2) extends to lease transactions).

Definitional Cross References:

"Finance lease". Section 2A–103(1)(g).
"Goods". Section 2A–103(1)(h).
"Knows". Section 1–201(25).
"Lease contract". Section 2A–103(1)(l).
"Lessee". Section 2A–103(1)(n).
"Lessor". Section 2A–103(1)(p).

Section 2A–214. Exclusion or Modification of Warranties.

(1) Words or conduct relevant to the creation of an express warranty and words or conduct tending to negate or limit a warranty must be construed wherever reasonable as consistent with each other; but, subject to the provisions of section 2A–202 on parol or extrinsic evidence, negation or limitation is inoperative to the extent that the construction is unreasonable.

(2) Subject to subsection (3), to exclude or modify the implied warranty of merchantability or any part of it the language must mention "merchantability",

be by a writing, and be conspicuous. Subject to subsection (3), to exclude or modify any implied warranty of fitness the exclusion must be by a writing and be conspicuous. Language to exclude all implied warranties of fitness is sufficient if it is in writing, is conspicuous and states, for example, "there is no warranty that the goods will be fit for a particular purpose".

(3) Notwithstanding subsection (2), but subject to subsection (4),

(a) unless the circumstances indicate otherwise, all implied warranties are excluded by expressions like "as is," or "with all faults," or by other language that in common understanding calls the lessee's attention to the exclusion of warranties and makes plain that there is no implied warranty, if in writing and conspicuous;

(b) if the lessee before entering into the lease contract has examined the goods or the sample or model as fully as desired or has refused to examine the goods, there is no implied warranty with regard to defects that an examination ought in the circumstances to have revealed; and

(c) an implied warranty may also be excluded or modified by course of dealing, course of performance, or usage of trade.

(4) To exclude or modify a warranty against interference or against infringement (Section 2A–211) or any part of it, the language must be specific, be by a writing, and be conspicuous, unless the circumstances, including course of performance, course of dealing, or usage of trade, give the lessee reason to know that the goods are being leased subject to a claim or interest of any person.

OFFICIAL COMMENT

Uniform Statutory Source: Sections 2–316 and 2–312(2).

Changes: Subsection (2) requires that a disclaimer of the warranty of merchantability be conspicuous and in writing as is the case for a disclaimer of the warranty of fitness; this is contrary to the rule stated in Section 2–316(2) with respect to the disclaimer of the warranty of merchantability. This section also provides that to exclude or modify the implied warranty of merchantability, fitness or against interference or infringement the language must be in writing and conspicuous. There are, however, exceptions to the rule. E.g., course of dealing, course of performance, or usage of trade may exclude or modify an implied warranty. Section 2A–214(3)(c). The analogue of Section 2–312(2) has been moved to subsection (4) of this section for a more unified treatment of disclaimers; there is no policy with respect to leases of goods that would justify continuing certain distinctions found in the Article on Sales (Article 2) regarding the treatment of the disclaimer of various warranties. Compare Sections 2–312(2) and 2–316(2). Finally, the example of the disclaimer of the implied warranty of fitness stated in subsection (2) differs from the analogue stated in Section 2–316(2); this example should promote a better understanding of the effect of the disclaimer.

Purposes:

These changes were made to reflect leasing practices. *E.g.,* FMC Finance Corp. v. Murphree, 632 F.2d 413, 418 (5th Cir. 1980) (disclaimer of implied warranty under lease transactions must be conspicuous and in writing). The omission of the provisions of Section 2–316(4) was not substantive. Sections 2A–503 and 2A–504.

Cross References:

Article 2, esp. Sections 2–312(2) and 2–316, and Sections 2A–503 and 2A–504.

Definitional Cross References:

"Conspicuous". Section 1–201(10).
"Course of dealing". Section 1–205.
"Fault". Section 2A–103(1)(f).
"Goods". Section 2A–103(1)(h).
"Knows". Section 1–201(25).
"Lease". Section 2A–103(1)(j).
"Lease contract". Section 2A–103(1)(l).
"Lessee". Section 2A–103(1)(n).
"Person". Section 1–201(30).
"Usage of trade". Section 1–205.
"Writing". Section 1–201(46).

Section 2A–215. Cumulation and Conflict of Warranties Express or Implied.

Warranties, whether express or implied, must be construed as consistent with each other and as cumulative, but if that construction is unreasonable, the intention of the parties determines which warranty is dominant. In ascertaining that intention the following rules apply:

(1) exact or technical specifications displace an inconsistent sample or model or general language of description.

(2) a sample from an existing bulk displaces inconsistent general language of description.

(3) express warranties displace inconsistent implied warranties other than an implied warranty of fitness for a particular purpose.

OFFICIAL COMMENT

Uniform Statutory Source: Section 2–317.

Definitional Cross Reference:

"Party". Section 1–201(29).

Section 2A–216. Third-Party Beneficiaries of Express or Implied Warranties.

A warranty to or for the benefit of a lessee under this Article, whether express or implied, extends to any natural person if it is reasonable to expect that such person may use, consume, or be affected by the goods and who is injured in person by breach of the warranty. This section does not displace principles of law and equity that extend a warranty to or for the benefit of a lessee to other persons. The operation of this section may not be excluded, modified, or limited, but an exclusion, modification, or limitation of the warranty, including any with respect to rights and remedies, effective against the lessee is also effective against the beneficiary designated under this section.

OFFICIAL COMMENT

Uniform Statutory Source: Section 2–318.

Changes: The provisions of Section 2–318 have been included in this section, modified in two respects: first, to reflect leasing practice, including the special practices of the lessor under a finance lease; second, to reflect and thus codify elements of the official comment to Section 2–318 with respect to the effect of disclaimers and limitations of remedies against third parties.

Purposes:

Alternative A is based on the 1962 version of Section 2–318 and is least favorable to the injured person as the doctrine of privity imposed by other law is abrogated to only a limited extent. Alternatives B and C are based on later additions to Section 2–318 and are more favorable to the injured person. In determining which alternative to select, the state legislature should consider making its choice parallel to the choice it made with respect to Section 2–318, as interpreted by the courts.

The last sentence of each of Alternatives A, B and C does not preclude the lessor from excluding or modifying an express or implied warranty under a lease. Section 2A–214. Further, that sentence does not preclude the lessor from limiting the rights and remedies of the lessee and from liquidating damages. Sections 2A–503 and 2A–504. If the lease excludes or modifies warranties, limits remedies for breach, or liquidates damages with respect to the lessee, such provisions are enforceable against the beneficiaries designated under this section. However, this last sentence forbids selective discrimination against the beneficiaries designated under this section, i.e., exclusion of the lessor's liability to the beneficiaries with respect to warranties made by the lessor to the lessee.

Other law, including the Article on Sales (Article 2), may apply in determining the extent to which a warranty to or for the benefit of the lessor extends to the lessee and third parties. This is in part a function of whether the lessor has bought or leased the goods.

This Article does not purport to change the development of the relationship of the common law, with respect to products liability, including strict liability in tort (as restated in Restatement (Second) of Torts, § 402A (1965)), to the provisions of this Act. *Compare* Cline v. Prowler Indus. of Maryland, 418 A.2d 968 (Del. 1980) and Hawkins Constr. Co. v. Matthews Co., 190 Neb. 546, 209 N.W.2d 643 (1973) *with* Dippel v. Sciano, 37 Wis 2d 443, 155 N.W.2d 55 (1967).

Cross References:

Article 2, esp. Section 2–318, and Sections 2A–214, 2A–503 and 2A–504.

Definitional Cross References:

"Goods". Section 2A–103(1)(h).
"Lessee". Section 2A–103(1)(n).
"Person". Section 1–201(30).
"Remedy". Section 1–201(34).
"Rights". Section 1–201(36).

Section 2A–217. Identification.

Identification of goods as goods to which a lease contract refers may be made at any time and in any manner explicitly agreed to by the parties. In the absence of explicit agreement, identification occurs:

(1) when the lease contract is made if the lease contract is for a lease of goods that are existing and identified;

(2) when the goods are shipped, marked, or otherwise designated by the lessor as goods to which the lease contract refers, if the lease contract is for a lease of goods that are not existing and identified; or

(3) when the young are conceived, if the lease contract is for a lease of unborn young of animals.

OFFICIAL COMMENT

Uniform Statutory Source: Section 2–501.

Changes: This section, together with Section 2A–218, is derived from the provisions of Section 2–501, with changes to reflect lease terminology; however, this section omits as irrelevant to leasing practice the treatment of special property.

Purposes:

With respect to subsection (b) there is a certain amount of ambiguity in the reference to when goods are designated, e.g., when the lessor is both selling and leasing goods to the same lessee/buyer and has marked goods for delivery but has not distinguished between those related to the lease contract and those related to the sales contract. As in Section 2–501(1)(b), this issue has been left to be resolved by the courts, case by case.

Cross References:

Sections 2–501 and 2A–218.

Definitional Cross References:

"Agreement". Section 1–201(3).
"Goods". Section 2A–103(1)(h).
"Lease". Section 2A–103(1)(j).
"Lease contract". Section 2A–103(1)(l).
"Lessor". Section 2A–103(1)(p).
"Party". Section 1–201(29).

Section 2A–218. Insurance and Proceeds.

(1) A lessee obtains an insurable interest when existing goods are identified to the lease contract even though the goods identified are nonconforming and the lessee has an option to reject them.

(2) If a lessee has an insurable interest only by reason of the lessor's identification of the goods, the lessor, until default or insolvency or notification to the lessee that identification is final, may substitute other goods for those identified.

(3) Notwithstanding a lessee's insurable interest under subsections (1) and (2), the lessor retains an insurable interest until an option to buy has been exercised by the lessee and risk of loss has passed to the lessee.

(4) Nothing in this section impairs any insurable interest recognized under any other statute or rule of law.

(5) The parties by agreement may determine that one or more parties have an obligation to obtain and pay for insurance covering the goods and by agreement may determine the beneficiary of the proceeds of the insurance.

OFFICIAL COMMENT

Uniform Statutory Source: Section 2–501.

Changes: This section, together with Section 2A–217, is derived from the provisions of Section 2–501, with changes and additions to reflect leasing practices and terminology.

Purposes:

Subsection (2) states a rule allowing substitution of goods by the lessor under certain circumstances, until default or insolvency of the lessor, or until notification to the lessee that identification is final. Subsection (3) states a rule regarding the lessor's insurable interest that, by virtue of the difference between a sale and a lease, necessarily is different from the rule stated in Section 2–501(2) regarding the seller's insurable interest. For this purpose the option to buy shall be deemed to have been exercised by the lessee when the resulting sale is closed, not when the lessee gives notice to the lessor. Further, subsection (5) is new and reflects the common practice of shifting the responsibility and cost of insuring the goods between the parties to the lease transaction.

Cross References:

Sections 2–501, 20501(2) and 2A–217.

Definitional Cross References:

"Agreement". Section 1–201(3).
"Buying". Section 2A–103(1)(a).
"Conforming". Section 2A–103(1)(d).
"Goods". Section 2A–103(1)(h).
"Insolvent". Section 1–201(23).
"Lease contract". Section 2A–103(1)(l).
"Lessee". Section 2A–103(1)(n).
"Lessor". Section 2A–103(1)(p).
"Notification". Section 1–201(26).
"Party". Section 1–201(29).

Section 2A–219. Risk of Loss.

(1) Except in the case of a finance lease, risk of loss is retained by the lessor and does not pass to the lessee. In the case of a finance lease, risk of loss passes to the lessee.

(2) Subject to the provisions of this Article on the effect of default on risk of loss (Section 2A–220), if risk of loss is to pass to the lessee and the time of passage is not stated, the following rules apply:

(a) if the lease contract requires or authorizes the goods to be shipped by carrier:

(i) and it does not require delivery at a particular destination, the risk of loss passes to the lessee when the goods are duly delivered to the carrier; but

(ii) if it does require delivery at a particular destination and the goods are there duly tendered while in the possession of the carrier, the risk of loss passes to the lessee when the goods are there duly so tendered as to enable the lessee to take delivery.

(b) if the goods are held by a bailee to be delivered without being moved, the risk of loss passes to the lessee on acknowledgment by the bailee of the lessee's right to possession of the goods.

(c) in any case not within paragraph (a) or (b), the risk of loss passes to the lessee on the lessee's receipt of the goods if the lessor, or, in the case of a finance lease, the supplier, is a merchant; otherwise the risk passes to the lessee on tender of delivery.

OFFICIAL COMMENT

Uniform Statutory Source: Section 2–509(1) through (3).

Changes: Subsection (1) is new. The introduction to subsection (2) is new, but subparagraph (a) incorporates the provisions of Section 2–509(1); subparagraph (b) incorporates the provisions of Section 2–509(2) only in part, reflecting current practice in lease transactions.

Purposes:

Subsection (1) states rules related to retention or passage of risk of loss consistent with current practice in lease transactions. The provisions of subsection (4) of Section 2–509 are not incorporated as they are not necessary. This section does not deal with responsibility for loss caused by the wrongful act of either the lessor or the lessee.

Cross References:

Sections 2–509(1), 2–509(2) and 2–509(4).

Definitional Cross References:

"Delivery". Section 1–201(14).
"Finance lease". Section 2A–103(1)(g).
"Goods". Section 2A–103(1)(h).
"Lease contract". Section 2A–103(1)(l).
"Lessee". Section 2A–103(1)(n).
"Lessor". Section 2A–103(1)(p).
"Merchant". Section 2–104(1).
"Receipt". Section 2–103(1)(c).
"Rights". Section 1–201(36).
"Supplier". Section 2A–103(1)(x).

Section 2A–220. Effect of Default on Risk of Loss.

(1) Where risk of loss is to pass to the lessee and the time of passage is not stated:

(a) if a tender or delivery of goods so fails to conform to the lease contract as to give a right of rejection, the risk of their loss remains with the lessor, or, in the case of a finance lease, the supplier, until cure or acceptance.

(b) if the lessee rightfully revokes acceptance, he or she, to the extent of any deficiency in his or her effective insurance coverage, may treat the risk of loss as having remained with the lessor from the beginning.

(2) Whether or not risk of loss is to pass to the lessee, if the lessee as to conforming goods already identified to a lease contract repudiates or is otherwise in default under the lease contract, the lessor, or, in the case of a finance lease, the supplier, to the extent of any deficiency in his or her effective insurance coverage may treat the risk of loss as resting on the lessee for a commercially reasonable time.

OFFICIAL COMMENT

Uniform Statutory Source: Section 2–510.

Changes: Revised to reflect leasing practices and terminology. The rule in Section (1)(b) does not allow the lessee under a finance lease to treat the risk of loss as having remained with the supplier from the beginning. This is appropriate given the limited circumstances under which the lessee under a finance lease is allowed to revoke acceptance. Section 2A–517 and Section 2A–516 official comment.

Definitional Cross References:

"Conforming". Section 2A–103(1)(d).
"Delivery". Section 1–201(14).
"Finance lease". Section 2A–103(1)(g).
"Goods". Section 2A–103(1)(h).
"Lease contract". Section 2A–103(1)(l).
"Lessee". Section 2A–103(1)(n).
"Lessor". Section 2A–103(1)(p).
"Reasonable time". Section 1–204(1) and (2).
"Rights". Section 1–201(36).
"Supplier". Section 2A–103(1)(x).

Section 2A–221. Casualty to Identified Goods.

If a lease contract requires goods identified when the lease contract is made, and the goods suffer casualty without fault of the lessee, the lessor or the supplier before delivery, or the goods suffer casualty before risk of loss passes to the lessee pursuant to the lease agreement or Section 2A–219, then:

(1) if the loss is total, the lease contract is avoided; and

(2) if the loss is partial or the goods have so deteriorated as to no longer conform to the lease contract, the lessee may nevertheless demand inspection

and at his or her option either treat the lease contract as avoided or, except in a finance lease that is not a consumer lease, accept the goods with due allowance from the rent payable for the balance of the lease term for the deterioration or the deficiency in quantity but without further right against the lessor.

OFFICIAL COMMENT

Uniform Statutory Source: Section 2–613.

Changes: Revised to reflect leasing practices and terminology.

Purpose:

Due to the vagaries of determining the amount of due allowance (Section 2–613(b)), no attempt was made in subsection (b) to treat a problem unique to lease contracts and installment sales contracts: determining how to recapture the allowance, e.g., application to the first or last rent payments or allocation, pro rata, to all rent payments.

Cross References:

Section 2–613.

Definitional Cross References:

"Conforming". Section 2A–103(1)(d).
"Consumer lease". Section 2A–103 (1)(e).
"Delivery". Section 1–201(14).
"Fault". Section 2A–103(1)(f).
"Finance lease". Section 2A–103(1)(g).
"Goods". Section 2A–103(1)(h).
"Lease". Section 2A–103(1)(j).
"Lease agreement". Section 2A–103 (1)(k).
"Lease contract". Section 2A–103 (1)(l).
"Lessee". Section 2A–103(1)(n).
"Lessor". Section 2A–103(1)(p).
"Rights". Section 1–201(36).
"Supplier". Section 2A–103(1)(x).

PART 3

EFFECT OF LEASE CONTRACT

Section 2A–301. Enforceability of Lease Contract.

Except as otherwise provided in this Article, a lease contract is effective and enforceable according to its terms between the parties, against purchasers of the goods, and against creditors of the parties.

OFFICIAL COMMENT

Uniform Statutory Source: Section 9–201.

Changes: The first sentence of Section 9–201 was incorporated, modified to reflect leasing terminology. The section sentence of Section 9–201 was eliminated as not relevant to leasing practices.

Purposes:

1. This section establishes a general rule regarding the validity and enforceability of a lease contract. The lease contract is effective and enforceable between the parties and against third parties. Exceptions to this general rule arise where there is a specific rule to the contrary in this Article. Enforceability is, thus, dependent upon the lease contract meeting the requirements of the Statute of Frauds provisions of Section 2A–201. Enforceability is also a function of the lease contract conforming to the principles of construction and interpretation contained in the Article on General Provisions (Article 1). Section 2A–103(4).

2. The effectiveness or enforceability of the lease contract is not dependent upon the lease contract or any financing statement or the like being filed or recorded; however, the priority of the interest of a lessor of fixtures with respect to the interests of certain third parties in such fixtures is subject to the provisions of the Article on Secured Transactions (Article 9). Section 2A–309. Prior to the adoption of this Article filing or recording was not required with respect to leases, only leases intended as security. The definition of security interest, as amended concurrently with the adoption of this Article, more clearly delineates leases and leases intended as security and thus signals the need to file. Section 1–201(37). Those lessors who are concerned about whether the transaction creates a lease or a security interest will continue to file a protective financing statement. Section 9–408. Coogan, Leasing and the Uniform Commercial Code, in Equipment Leasing-Leveraged Leasing, 681, 744–46 (2d ed. 1980).

3. *Hypothetical:*

(a) In construing this section it is important to recognize its relationship to other sections in this Article. This is best demonstrated by reference to a hypothetical. Assume that on February 1 A, a manufacturer of combines and other farm equipment, leased a fleet of six combines to B, a corporation engaged in the business of farming, for a 12 month term. Under the lease agreement between A and B, A agreed to defer B's payment of the first two months' rent to April 1. On March 1 B recognized that it would need only four combines and thus subleased two combines to C for an 11 month term.

(b) This hypothetical raises a number of issues that are answered by the sections contained in this part. Since lease is defined to include sublease (Section 2A–103(1)(j) and (w)), this section provides that the prime lease between A and B and the sublease between B and C are enforceable in accordance with their terms, except as otherwise provided in this Article; that exception, in this case, is one of considerable scope.

(c) The separation of ownership, which is in A, and possession, which is in B with respect to four combines and which is in C with respect to two combines, is not relevant. Section 2A–302. A's interest in the six combines cannot be challenged simply because A parted with possession to B, who in turn parted with possession of some of the combines to C. Yet it is important to note that by the terms of Section 2A–302 this conclusion is subject to change if otherwise provided in this Article.

(d) B's entering the sublease with C raises an issue that is treated by this part. In a dispute over the leased combines A may challenge B's right to sublease. The rule is permissive as to transfers of interests under a lease contract, including subleases. Section 2A–303(2). However, the rule has two significant qualifications. If the prime lease contract between A and B prohibits B from subleasing the combines, or makes such a sublease an event of default, Section 2A–303(2) applies; thus, while B's interest under the prime lease may be transferred under the sublease to C, A may have a remedy pursuant to Section 2A–303(5). Absent a prohibition or default provision in the prime lease contract A might be able to argue that the sublease to C materially increases A's risk; thus, while B's interest under the prime lease may be transferred under the sublease to C, A may have a remedy pursuant to Section 2A–303(5). Section 2A–303(5)(b)(ii).

(e) Resolution of this issue is also a function of the section dealing with the sublease of goods by a prime lessee (Section 2A–305). Subsection (1) of Section 2A–305, which is subject to the rules of Section 2A–303 stated above, provides that C takes subject to the interest of A under the prime lease between A and B. However, there are two exceptions. First, if B is a merchant (Sections 2A–103(3) and 2–104(1)) dealing in goods of that kind and C is a sublessee in the ordinary course of business (Sections 2A–103(1)(o) and 2A–103(1)(n)), C takes free of the prime lease between A and B. Second, if B has rejected the six combines under the prime lease with A, and B disposes of the goods by sublease to C, C takes free of the prime lease if C can establish good faith. Section 2A–511(4).

(f) If the facts of this hypothetical are expanded and we assume that the prime lease obligated B to maintain the combines, an additional issue may be presented. Prior to entering the sublease, B, in satisfaction of its maintenance covenant, brought the two combines that it desired to sublease to a local independent dealer of A's. The dealer did the requested work for B. C inspected the combines on the dealer's lot after the work was completed. C signed the sublease with B two days later. C, however, was prevented from taking delivery of the two combines as B refused to pay the dealer's invoice for the repairs. The dealer furnished the repair service to B in the ordinary course of the dealer's business. If under applicable law the dealer has a lien on repaired goods in the dealer's possession, the dealer's lien will take priority over B's and C's interests, and also should take priority over A's interest, depending upon the terms of the lease contract and the applicable law. Section 2A–306.

(g) Now assume that C is in financial straits and one of C's creditors obtains a judgment against C. If the creditor levies on C's subleasehold interest in the two combines, who will prevail? Unless the levying creditor also holds a lien covered by Section 2A–306, discussed above, the judgment creditor will take its interest subject to B's rights under the sublease and A's rights under the prime lease. Section 2A–307(1). The hypothetical becomes more complicated if we assume that B is in financial straits and B's creditor holds the judgment. Here the judgment creditor takes subject to the sublease unless the lien attached to the two combines before the sublease contract became enforceable. Section 2A–307(2)(a). However, B's judgment creditor cannot prime A's interest in the goods because, with respect to A, the judgment creditor is a creditor of B in its capacity as lessee under the prime lease between A and B. Thus, here the judgment creditor's interest is subject to the lease between A and B. Section 2A–307(1).

(h) Finally, assume that on April 1 B is unable to pay A the deferred rent then due under the prime lease, but that C is current in its payments under the sublease from B. What effect will B's default under the prime lease between A and B have on C's rights under the sublease between B and C? Section 2A–301 provides that a lease contract is effective against the creditors of either party. Since a lease contract includes a sublease contract (Section 2A–103(1)(l)), the sublease contract between B and C arguably could be enforceable against A, a prime lessor who has extended unsecured credit to B, the prime lessee/sublessor, if the sublease contract meets the requirements of Section 2A–201. However, the rule stated in Section 2A–301 is subject to other provisions in this Article. Under Section 2A–305, C, as sublessee, would take subject to the prime lease contract in most cases. Thus, B's default under the prime lease will in most cases lead to A's recovery of the goods from C. Section 2A–523. A and C could provide otherwise by agreement. Section 2A–311. C's recourse will be to assert a claim for damages against B. Sections 2A–211(1) and 2A–508.

4. *Relationship Between Sections:*

(a) As the analysis of the hypothetical demonstrates, Part 3 of the Article focuses on issues that relate to the enforceability of the lease contract (Sections 2A–301, 2A–302 and 2A–303) and to the priority of various claims to the goods subject to the lease contract (Sections 2A-304, 2A-305, 2A-306, 2A-307, 2A-308, 2A-309, 2A-310, and 2A-311).

(b) This section states a general rule of enforceability, which is subject to specific rules to the contrary stated elsewhere in the Article. Section 2A-302 negates any notion that the separation of title and possession is fraudulent as a rule of law. Finally, Section 2A-303 states rules with respect to the transfer of the lessor's interest (as well as the residual interest in the goods) or the lessee's interest under the lease contract. Qualifications are imposed as a function of various issues, including whether the transfer is the creation or enforcement of a security interest or one that is material to the other party to the lease contract. In addition, a system of rules is created to deal with the rights and duties among assignor, assignee and the other party to the lease contract.

(c) Sections 2A-304 and 2A-305 are twins that deal with good faith transferees of goods subject to the lease contract. Section 2A-304 creates a set of rules with respect to transfers by the lessor of goods subject to a lease contract; the transferee considered is a subsequent lessee of the goods. The priority dispute covered here is between the subsequent lessee and the original lessee of the goods (or persons claiming through the original lessee). Section 2A-305 creates a set of rules with respect to transfers by the lessee of goods subject to a lease contract; the transferees considered are buyers of the goods or sublessees of the goods. The priority dispute covered here is between the transferee and the lessor of the goods (or persons claiming through the lessor).

(d) Section 2A-306 creates a rule with respect to priority disputes between holders of liens for services or materials furnished with respect to goods subject to a lease contract and the lessor or the lessee under that contract. Section 2A-307 creates a rule with respect to priority disputes between the lessee and creditors of the lessor and priority disputes between the lessor and creditors of the lessee.

(e) Section 2A-308 creates a series of rules relating to allegedly fraudulent transfers and preferences. The most significant rule is that set forth in subsection (3) which validates sale-leaseback transactions if the buyer-lessor can establish that he or she bought for value and in good faith.

(f) Sections 2A-309 and 2A-310 create a series of rules with respect to priority disputes between various third parties and a lessor of fixtures or accessions, respectively, with respect thereto.

(g) Finally, Section 2A-311 allows parties to alter the statutory priorities by agreement.

Cross References:

Article 1, especially Section 1-201(37), and Sections 2-104(1), 2A-103(1)(j), 2A-103(1)(l), 2A-103(1)(n), 2A-103(1)(o) and 2A-103(1)(w), 2A-103(3), 2A-103(4), 1A-201, 2A-301 through 2A-303, 2A-303(2), 2A-303(5), 2A-304 through 2A-307, 2A-307(1), 2A-307(2)(a), 2A-308 through 2A-311, 2A-508, 2A-511(4), 2A-523, Article 9, especially Sections 9-201 and 9-408.

Definitional Cross References:

"Creditor". Section 1-201(12).
"Goods". Section 2A-103(1)(h).
"Lease contract". Section 2A-103(1)(l).
"Party". Section 1-201(29).
"Purchaser". Section 1-201(33).
"Term". Section 1-201(42).

Section 2A–302. Title to and Possession of Goods.

Except as otherwise provided in this Article, each provision of this Article applies whether the lessor or a third party has title to the goods, and whether the lessor, the lessee, or a third party has possession of the goods, notwithstanding any statute or rule of law that possession or the absence of possession is fraudulent.

OFFICIAL COMMENT

Uniform Statutory Source: Section 9–202.

Changes: Section 9–202 was modified to reflect leasing terminology and to clarify the law of leases with respect to fraudulent conveyances or transfers.

Purposes:

The separation of ownership and possession of goods between the lessor and the lessee (or a third party) has created problems under certain fraudulent conveyance statutes. *See, e.g., In re* Ludlum Enters., 510 F.2d 996 (5th Cir. 1975); Suburbia Fed. Sav. & Loan Ass'n v. Bel-Air Conditioning Co., 385 So. 2d 1151 (Fla. Dist. Ct. App. 1980). This section provides, among other things, that separation of ownership and possession per se does not affect the enforceability of the lease contract. Sections 2A–301 and 2A–308.

Cross References:

Sections 2A–301, 2A–308 and 9–202.

Definitional Cross References:

"Goods". Section 2A–103(1)(h).
"Lessee". Section 2A–103(1)(n).
"Lessor". Section 2A–103(1)(p).

Section 2A–303. Alienability of Party's Interest Under Lease Contract or of Lessor's Residual Interest in Goods; Delegation of Performance; Transfer of Rights.

(1) As used in this section, "creation of a security interest" includes the sale of a lease contract that is subject to Article 9, secured transactions, by reason of Section 9-102(1)(b).

(2) Except as provided in subsections (3) and (4), a provision in a lease agreement which (i) prohibits the voluntary or involuntary transfer, including a transfer by sale, sublease, creation or enforcement of a security interest, or attachment, levy, or other judicial process, of an interest of a party under the lease contract or of the lessor's residual interest in the goods, or (ii) makes such a transfer an event of default, gives rise to the rights and remedies provided in subsection (5), but a transfer that is prohibited or is an event of default under the lease agreement is otherwise effective.

(3) A provision in a lease agreement which (i) prohibits the creation or enforcement of a security interest in an interest of party under the lease contract

or in the lessor's residual interest in the goods, or (ii) makes such a transfer an event of default, is not enforceable unless, and then only to the extent that, there is an actual transfer by the lessee of the lessee's right of possession or use of the goods in violation of the provision or an actual delegation of a material performance of either party to the lease contract in violation of the provision. Neither the granting nor the enforcement of a security interest in (i) the lessor's interest under the lease contract or (ii) the lessor's residual interest in the goods is a transfer that materially impairs the prospect of obtaining return performance by, materially changes the duty of, or materially increases the burden or risk imposed on, the lessee within the purview of subsection (5) unless, and then only to the extent that, there is an actual delegation of a material performance of the lessor.

(4) A provision in a lease agreement which (i) prohibits a transfer of a right to damages for default with respect to the whole lease contract or of a right to payment arising out of the transferor's due performance of the transferor's entire obligation, or (ii) makes such a transfer an event of default, is not enforceable, and such a transfer is not a transfer that materially impairs the prospect of obtaining return performance by, materially changes the duty of, or materially increases the burden or risk imposed on, the other party to the lease contract within the purview of subsection (5).

(5) Subject to subsections (3) and (4):

(a) if a transfer is made which is made an event of default under the lease agreement, the party to the lease contract not making the transfer, unless that party waives the default or otherwise agrees, has the rights and remedies described in Section 2A–501(2);

(b) if paragraph (a) is not applicable and if a transfer is made that (i) is prohibited under a lease agreement or (ii) materially impairs the prospect of obtaining return performance by, materially changes the duty of, or materially increases the burden or risk imposed on, the other party to the lease contract, unless the party not making the transfer agrees at any time to the transfer in the lease contract or otherwise, then, except as limited by contract, (i) the transferor is liable to the party not making the transfer for damages caused by the transfer to the extent that the damages could not reasonably be prevented by the party not making the transfer and (ii) a court having jurisdiction may grant other appropriate relief, including cancellation of the lease contract or an injunction against the transfer.

(6) A transfer of "the lease" or of "all my rights under the lease," or a transfer in similar general terms, is a transfer of rights and, unless the language or the circumstances, as in a transfer for security, indicate the contrary, the transfer is a delegation of duties by the transferor to the transferee. Acceptance by the transferee constitutes a promise by the transferee to perform those duties. The promise is enforceable by either the transferor or the other party to the lease contract.

(7) Unless otherwise agreed by the lessor and the lessee, a delegation of performance does not relieve the transferor as against the other party of any duty to perform or of any liability for default.

(8) In a consumer lease, to prohibit the transfer of an interest of a party under the lease contract or to make a transfer an event of default, the language must be specific, by a writing, and conspicuous.

OFFICIAL COMMENT

Uniform Statutory Source: Sections 2–210 and 9–311.

Changes: The provisions of Sections 2–210 and 9–311 were incorporated in this section, with substantial modifications to reflect leasing terminology and practice and to harmonize the principles of the respective provisions, i.e. limitations on delegation of performance on the one hand and alienability of rights on the other. In addition, unlike Section 2–210 which deals only with voluntary transfers, this section deals with involuntary as well as voluntary transfers. Moreover, the principle of Section 9–318(4) denying effectiveness to contractual terms prohibiting assignments of receivables due and to become due also is implemented.

Purposes: 1. Subsection (2) states a rule, consistent with Section 9–311, that voluntary and involuntary transfers of an interest of a party under the lease contract or of the lessor's residual interest, including by way of the creation or enforcement of a security interest, are effective, notwithstanding a provision in the lease agreement prohibiting the transfer or making the transfer an event of default. Although the transfers are effective, the provision in the lease agreement is nevertheless enforceable, but only as provided in subsection (5). Under subsection (5) the prejudiced party is limited to the remedies on "default under the lease contract" in this Article and, except as limited by this Article, as provided in the lease agreement, if the transfer has been made an event of default. Section 2A–501(2). Usually, there will be a specific provision to this effect or a general provision making a breach of a covenant an event of default. In those cases where the transfer is prohibited, but not made an event of default, the prejudiced party may recover damages; or, if the damage remedy would be ineffective adequately to protect that party, the court can order cancellation of the lease contract or enjoin the transfer. This rule that such provisions generally are enforceable is subject to subsections (3) and (4), which make such provisions unenforceable in certain instances.

2. The first such instance is described in subsection (3). A provision in a lease agreement which prohibits the creation or enforcement of a security interest, including sales of lease contracts subject to Article 9 (Sections 9–102(1)(b) and 9–104(f)), or makes it an event of default is generally not enforceable, reflecting the policy of Section 9–318(4). However, that policy gives way to the doctrine stated in Section 2–210(2), which gives one party to a contract the right to protect itself against an actual delegation (but not just a provision under which delegation might later occur) of a material performance by the other party. Accordingly, such provision in a lease agreement is enforceable when the transfer delegates a material performance. Generally, as expressly provided in subsection (6), a transfer for security is not a delegation of duties. However, inasmuch as the creation of a security interest includes the sale of a lease contract, if there are then unperformed duties on the part of the lessor/seller, there could be a delegation of duties in the sale, and, if such a delegation actually takes place and is of a material performance, a provision in a lease agreement prohibiting it or making it an event of default would be enforceable, giving rise to the rights and remedies stated in subsection (5). The statute does not define "material." The parties may set standards to determine its meaning. The term is intended to

exclude delegations of matters such as accounting to a professional accountant and the performance of, as opposed to the responsibility for maintenance duties to a person in the maintenance service industry.

3. For similar reasons, the lessor is entitled to protect its residual interest in the goods by prohibiting anyone but the lessee from possessing or using them. Accordingly, under subsection (3) if there is an actual transfer by the lessee of its right of possession or use of the goods in violation of a provision in the lease agreement, such a provision likewise is enforceable, giving rise to the rights and remedies stated in subsection (5). A transfer of the lessee's right of possession or use of the goods resulting from the enforcement of a security interest granted by the lessee in its leasehold interest is a "transfer by the lessee" under this subsection.

4. Finally, subsection (3) protects against a claim that the creation or enforcement of a security interest in the lessor's interest under the lease contract or in the residual interest is a transfer that materially impairs the prospect of obtaining return performance by, materially changed the duty of, or materially increases the burden or risk imposed on the lessee so as to give rise to the rights and remedies stated in subsection (5), unless the transfer involves an actual delegation of a material performance of the lessor.

5. While it is not likely that a transfer by the lessor of its right to payment under the lease contract would impair at a future time the ability of the lessee to obtain the performance due the lessee under the lease contract from the lessor, if under the circumstances reasonable grounds for insecurity as to receiving that performance arise, the lessee may employ the provision of this Article for demanding adequate assurance of due performance and has the remedy provided in that circumstance. Section 2A–401.

6. Sections 9–206 and 9–318(1) through (3) also are relevant. Section 9–206 sanctions an agreement by a lessee not to assert certain types of claims or defenses against the lessor's assignee. Section 9–318(1) through (3) deal with, among other things, the other party's rights against the assignee where Section 9–206(1) does not apply. Since the definition of contract under Section 1–201(11) includes a lease agreement, the definition of account debtor under Section 9–105(1)(a) includes a lessee of goods. As a result, Section 9–206 applies to lease agreements, and there is not need to restate those sections in this Article. The reference to "defenses or claims arising out of a sale" in Section 9–318(1) should be interpreted broadly to include defenses or claims arising out of a lease inasmuch as that section codifies the common law rule with respect to contracts, including lease contracts.

7. Subsection (4) is based upon Section 2–210(2) and Section 9–318(4). It makes unenforceable a prohibition against transfers of certain rights to payment or a provision making the transfer an event of default. It also provides that such transfers do not materially impair the prospect of obtaining return performance by, materially change the duty of, or materially increase the burden or risk imposed on, the other party to the lease contract so as to give rise to the rights and remedies stated in subsection (5). Accordingly, a transfer of a right to payment cannot be prohibited or made an event of default, or be one that materially impairs performance, changes duties or increases risk, if the right is already due or will become due without further performance being required by the party to receive payment. Thus, a lessor can transfer the right to future payments under the lease contract, including by way of a grant of a security interest, and the transfer will not give rise to the rights and remedies stated in subsection (5) if the lessor has no remaining performance under the lease contract. The mere fact that the lessor is obligated to allow the lessee to remain in possession and to use the goods as long as the lessee is not in default does not mean that there is "remaining performance" on the part of the lessor. Likewise, the fact that the lessor has potential liability under a "nonoperating" lease contract for breaches of warranty does not mean that there is "remaining performance." In contrast, the

lessor would have "remaining performance" under a lease contract requiring the lessor to regularly maintain and service the goods or to provide "upgrades" of the equipment on a periodic basis in order to avoid obsolescence. The basic distinction is between a mere potential duty to respond which is not "remaining performance," and an affirmative duty to render stipulated performance. Although the distinction may be difficult to draw in some cases, it is instructive to focus on the difference betwen "operating" and "nonoperating" leases as generally understood in the marketplace. Even if there is "remaining performance" under a lease contract, a transfer for security of a right to payment that is made an event of a default or that is in violation of a prohibition against transfer does not give rise to the rights and remedies under subsection (5) if it does not constitute an actual delegation of a material performance under subsection (3).

8. The application of either the rule of subsection (3) or the rule of subsection (4) to the grant by the lessor of a security interest in the lessor's right to future payment under the lease contract may produce the same result. Both subsections generally protect security transfers by the lessor in particular because the creation by the lessor of a security interest or the enforcement of that interest generally will not prejudice the lessee's rights if it does not result in a delegation of the lessor's duties. To the contrary, the receipt of loan proceeds or relief from the enforcement of an antecedent debt normally should enhance the lessor's ability to perform its duties under the lease contract. Nevertheless, there are circumstances where relief might be justified. For example, if ownership of the goods is transferred pursuant to enforcement of a security interest to a party whose ownership would prevent the lessee from continuing to possess the goods, relief might be warranted. See 49 U.S.C. § 1401(1) and (b) which places limitations on the operation of aircraft in the United States based on the citizenship or corporate qualification of the registrant.

9. Relief on the ground of material prejudice when the lease agreement does not prohibit the transfer or make it an event of default should be afforded only in extreme circumstances, considering the fact that the party asserting material prejudice did not insist upon a provision in the lease agreement that would protect against such a transfer.

10. Subsection (5) implements the rule of subsection (2). Subsection (2) provides that, even though a transfer is effective, a provision in the lease agreement prohibiting it or making it an event of default may be enforceable as provided in subsection (5). *See* Brummond v. First National Bank of Clovis, 656 P.2d 884, 35 U.C.C. Rep. Serv. (Callaghan) 1311 (N. Mex. 1983), stating the analogous rule for Section 9–311. If the transfer prohibited by the lease agreement is made an event of default, then, under subsection 5(a), unless the default is waived or there is an agreement otherwise; the aggrieved party has the rights and remedies referred to in Section 2A 501(2), viz. those in this Article and, except as limited in the Article, those provided in the lease agreement. In the unlikely circumstance that the lease agreement prohibits the transfer without making a violation of the prohibition an event of default or, even if there is no prohibition against the transfer, and the transfer is one that materially impairs performance, changes duties, or increases risk (for example, a sublease or assignment to a party using the goods improperly or for an illegal purpose), then subsection 5(b) is applicable. In that circumstance, unless the party aggrieved by the transfer has otherwise agreed in the lease contract, such as by assenting to a particular transfer or to transfers in general, or agrees in some other manner, the aggrieved party has the right to recover damages from the transferor and a court may, in appropriate circumstances, grant other relief, such as cancellation of the lease contract or an injunction against the transfer.

11. If a transfer gives rise to the rights and remedies provided in subsection (5), the transferee as an alternative may propose, and the other party may accept, adequate cure or compensation for past defaults and adequate assurance of future due

performance under the lease contract. Subsection (5) does not preclude any other relief that may be available to a party to the lease contract aggrieved by a transfer subject to an enforceable prohibition, such as an action for interference with contractual relations.

12. Subsection (8) requires that a provision in a consumer lease prohibiting a transfer, or making it an event of default, must be specific, written and conspicuous. See Section 1–201(1). This assists in protecting a consumer lessee against surprise assertions of default.

13. Subsection (6) is taken almost verbatim from the provisions of Section 2–210(4). The subsection states a rule of construction that distinguishes a commercial assignment, which substitutes the assignee for the assignor as to rights and duties, and an assignment for security or financing assignment, which substitutes the assignee for the assignor only as to rights. Note that the assignment for security or financing assignment is a subset of all security interests. Security interest is defined to include "any interest of a buyer of . . . chattel paper". Section 1–201(37). Chattel paper is defined to include a lease. Section 9–105(1)(b). Thus, a buyer of leases is the holder of security interest in the leases. That conclusion should not influence this issue, as the policy is quite different. Whether a buyer of leases is the holder of a commercial assignment, or an assignment for security or financing assignment should be determined by the language of the assignment or the circumstances of the assignment.

Cross References:

Section 1–201(11), 1–201(37), 2–210, 2A–401, 9–102(1)(b), 9–104(f), 9–105(1)(a), 9–206, and 9–318.

Definitional Cross References:

"Agreed" and "Agreement". Section 1–201(3).
"Conspicuous". Section 1–201(10).
"Goods". Section 2A–103(1)(h).
"Lease". Section 2A–103(1)(j).
"Lease contract". Section 2A–103 (1)(l).
"Lessee". Section 2A–103(1)(n).
"Lessor". Section 2A–103(1)(p).
"Lessor's residual interest". Section 2A–103(1)(q).
"Notice". Section 1–201(25).
"Party". Section 1–201(29).
"Person". Section 1–201(30).
"Reasonable time". Section 1–204(1) and (2).
"Rights". Section 1–201(36).
"Term". Section 1–201(42).
"Writing". Section 1–201(46).

Section 2A–304. Subsequent Lease of Goods by Lessor.

(1) Subject to Section 2A–303, a subsequent lessee from a lessor of goods under an existing lease contract obtains, to the extent of the leasehold interest transferred, the leasehold interest in the goods that the lessor had or had power to transfer, and, except as provided in subsection (2) and Section 2A–527(4), takes subject to the existing lease contract. A lessor with voidable title has power to transfer a good leasehold interest to a good faith subsequent lessee for value, but only to the extent set forth in the preceding sentence. If goods have been delivered under a transaction of purchase, the lessor has that power even though:

(a) the lessor's transferor was deceived as to the identity of the lessor;

(b) the delivery was in exchange for a check which is later dishonored;

(c) it was agreed that the transaction was to be a "cash sale"; or

(d) the delivery was procured through fraud punishable as larcenous under the criminal law.

(2) A subsequent lessee in the ordinary course of business from a lessor who is a merchant dealing in goods of that kind to whom the goods were entrusted by a prior lessee before the interest of the subsequent lessee became enforceable against that lessor obtains, to the extent of the leasehold interest transferred, all of that lessor's and the prior lessee's rights to the goods and takes free of the existing lease contract.

(3) A subsequent lessee from the lessor of goods that are subject to an existing lease contract and are covered by a certificate of title issued under a statute of this state or of another jurisdiction takes no greater rights than those provided both by this section and by the certificate of title statute.

OFFICIAL COMMENT

Uniform Statutory Source: Section 2–403.

Changes: While Section 2–403 was used as a model for this section, the provisions of Section 2–403 were significantly revised to reflect leasing practices and to integrate this Article with certificate of the statutes.

Purposes:

1. This section must be read in conjunction with, as it is subject to, the provisions of Section 2A–303, which govern voluntary and involuntary transfers of rights and duties under a lease contract, including the lessor's residual interest in the goods.

2. This section must also be read in conjunction with Section 2–403. This section and Section 2A–305 are derived from Section 2–403, which states a unified policy on good faith purchases of goods. Given the scope of the definition of purchaser (Section 1–201(33)), a person who bought goods to lease as well as a person who bought goods subject to an existing lease from a lessor will take pursuant to Section 2–403. Further, a person who leases such goods from the person who bought them should also be protected under Section 2–403, first because the lessee's rights are derivative and second because the definition of purchaser should be interpreted to include one who takes by lease; no negative implication should be drawn from the inclusion of lease in the definition of purchase in this Article. Section 2A–103(1)(v).

3. There are hypotheticals that relate to an entrustee's unauthorized lease of entrusted goods to a third party that are outside the provisions of Section 2–403, 2A–304 and 2A–305. Consider a sale of goods by M, a merchant, to B, a buyer. After paying for the goods B allows M to retain possession of the goods as B is short of storage. Before B calls for the goods M leases the goods to L, a lessee. This transaction is not governed by the ordinary course of business. Section 1–201(9). Further, this transaction is not governed by Section 2A–304(2) as B is not an existing lessee. Finally, this transaction is not governed by Section 2A–305(2) as B is not M's lessor. Section 2A–307(2) resolves the potential dispute between B, M and L. By virtue of B's entrustment of the goods to M and M's lease of goods to L, B has a cause of action against M under the common law. Section 2A–103(4) and 1–103. See, e.g.,

Restatement (Second) of Torts §§ 222A–243. Thus, B is a creditor of M. Section 2A–103(4) and 1–201(12). Section 2A–307(2) provides that B, as M's creditor, takes subject to M's lease to L. Thus, if L does not default under the lease, L's enjoyment and possession of the goods should be undisturbed. However, B is not without recourse. B's action should result in a judgment against M providing, among other things, a turnover of all proceeds arising from M's lease to L, as well as a transfer of all of M's right, title and interest as lessor under M's lease to L, including M's residual interest in the goods. Section 2A–103(1)(q).

4. Subsection (1) states a rule with respect to the leasehold interest obtained by a subsequent lessee from a lessor of goods under an existing lease contract. The interest will include such leasehold interest as the lessor has in the goods as well as the leasehold interest that the lessor had the power to transfer. Thus, the subsequent lessee obtains unimpaired all rights acquired under the law of agency, apparent agency, ownership or other estoppel, whether based upon statutory provisions or upon case law principles. Section 2A–103(4) and 1–103. In general, the subsequent lessee takes subject to the existing lease contract, including the existing lessee's rights thereunder. Furthermore, the subsequent lease contract is, of course, limited by its own terms, and the subsequent lessee takes only to the extent of the leasehold interest transferred thereunder.

5. Subsection (1) further provides that a lessor with voidable title has power to transfer a good leasehold interest to a good faith subsequent lessee for value. In addition, subsections (1)(a) through (d) provide specifically for the protection of the good faith subsequent lessee for value in a number of specific situations which have been troublesome under prior law.

6. The position of an existing lessee who entrusts leased goods to its lessor is not distinguished from the position of other entrusters. Thus, subsection (2) provides that the subsequent lessee in the ordinary course of business takes free of the existing lease contract between the lessor entrustee and the lessee entruster, if the lessor is a merchant dealing in goods of that kind. Further, the subsequent lessee obtains all of the lessor entrustee's and the lessee entruster's rights to the goods, but only to the extent of the leasehold interest transferred by the lessor entrustee. Thus, the lessor entrustee retains the residual interest in the goods. Section 2A–103(1)(q). However, entrustment by the existing lessee must have occurred before the interest of the subsequent lessee became enforceable against the lessor. Entrusting is defined in Section 2–403(3) and that definition applies here. Section 2A–103(3).

7. Subsection (3) takes a rule with respect to a transfer of goods from a lessor to a subsequent lessee where the goods are subject to an existing lease and covered by a certificate of title. The subsequent lessee's rights are no greater than those provided by this section and the applicable certificate of title statute, including any applicable case law construing such statute. Where the relationship between the certificate of title statute and Section 2–403, the statutory analogue to this section, has been construed by a court, that construction is incorporated here. Section 2A–103(4) and 1–102(1) and (2). The better rule is that the certificate of title statutes are in harmony with Section 2–403 and thus would be in harmony with this section. *E.g.,* Atwood Chevrolet–Olds v. Aberdeen Mun. School Dist., 431 So.2d 926, 928 (Miss. 1983); Godfrey v. Gilsdorf, 476 P.2d 3, 6, 86 Nev. 714, 718 (1970); Martin v. Nager, 192 N.J. Super. 189, 197–98, 469 A.2d 519, 523 (Super. Ct. Ch. Div. 1983). Where the certificate of title statute is silent on the issue of transfer, this section will control.

Cross References:

Section 1–102, 1–103, 1–201(33), 2–403, 2A–103(1)(v), 2A–103(3), 2A–103(4), 2A–303 and 2A–305.

Definitional Cross References:

"Agreed". Section 1–201(3).
"Delivery". Section 1–201(14).
"Entrusting". Section 2–403(3).
"Good faith". Sections 1–201(19) and 2–103(1)(b).
"Goods". Section 2A–103(1)(h).
"Lease". Section 2A–103(1)(j).
"Lease contract". Section 2A–103(1)(l).
"Leasehold interest". Section 2A–103(1)(m).
"Lessee". Section 2A–103(1)(n).
"Lessee in the ordinary course of business". Section 2A–103(1)(o).
"Lessor". Section 2A–103(1)(p).
"Merchant". Section 2–104(1).
"Purchase". Section 2A–103(1)(v).
"Rights". Section 2–201(36).
"Value". Section 1–201(44).

Section 2A–305. Sale or Sublease of Goods by Lessee.

(1) Subject to the provisions of Section 2A–303, a buyer or sublessee from the lessee of goods under an existing lease contract obtains, to the extent of the interest transferred, the leasehold interest in the goods that the lessee had or had power to transfer, and except as provided in subsection (2) and Section 2A–511(4), takes subject to the existing lease contract. A lessee with a voidable leasehold interest has power to transfer a good leasehold interest to a good faith buyer for value or a good faith sublessee for value, but only to the extent set forth in the preceding sentence. When goods have been delivered under a transaction of lease the lessee has that power even though:

(a) the lessor was deceived as to the identity of the lessee;

(b) the delivery was in exchange for a check which is later dishonored; or

(c) the delivery was procured through fraud punishable as larcenous under the criminal law.

(2) A buyer in the ordinary course of business or a sublessee in the ordinary course of business from a lessee who is a merchant dealing in goods of that kind to whom the goods were entrusted by the lessor obtains, to the extent of the interest transferred, all of the lessor's and lessee's rights to the goods, and takes free of the existing lease contract.

(3) A buyer or sublessee from the lessee of goods that are subject to an existing lease contract and are covered by a certificate of title issued under a statute of this state or of another jurisdiction takes no greater rights than those provided both by this section and by the certificate of title statute.

OFFICIAL COMMENT

Uniform Statutory Source: Section 2-403.

Changes: While Section 2-403 was used as a model for this section, the provisions of Section 2-403 were significantly revised to reflect leasing practice and to integrate this Article with certificate of title statutes.

UCC

Purposes:

This section, a companion to Section 2A-304, states the rule with respect to the leasehold interest obtained by a buyer or sublessee from a lessee of goods under an existing lease contract. Cf. Section 2A-304 official comment. Note that this provision is consistent with existing case law, which prohibits the bailee's transfer of title to a good faith purchaser for value under Section 2-403(1). Rohweder v. Aberdeen Product. Credit Ass'n 765 F.2d 109 (8th Cir. 1985).

Subsection (2) is also consistent with existing case law. American Standard Credit, Inc. v. National Cement Co., 643 F.2d 248, 269-70 (5th Cir. 1981); *but cf.* Exxon Co., U.S.A. v. TLW Computer Indus., 37 U.C.C. Rep. Serv. (Callaghan) 1052, 1057-58 (D. Mass. 1983). Unlike Section 2A-304(2), this subsection does not contain any requirement with respect to the time that the goods were entrusted to the merchant. In Section 2A-304(2) the competition is between two customers of the merchant lessor; the time of entrusting was added as a criterion to create additional protection to the customer who was first in time: the existing lessee. In subsection (2) the equities between the competing interests were viewed as balanced.

There appears to be some overlap between Section 2-403(2) and Section 2A-305(2) with respect to a buyer in the ordinary course of business. However, an examination of this Article's definition of buyer in the ordinary course of business (Section 2A-103(1)(a)) makes clear that this reference was necessary to treat entrusting in the context of a lease.

Subsection (3) states a rule of construction with respect to a transfer of goods from a lessee to a buyer or sublessee, where the goods are subject to an existing lease and covered by a certificate of title. *Cf.* Section 2A-304 official comment.

Cross References:

Sections 2-403, 2A-103(1)(a), 2A-304 and 2A-305(2).

Definitional Cross References:

"Buyer". Section 2-103(1)(a).
"Buyer in the ordinary course of business". Section 2A-103(1)(a).
"Delivery". Section 1-201(14).
"Entrusting". Section 2-403(3).
"Good faith". Sections 1-201(19) and 2-103(1)(b).
"Goods". Section 2A-103(1)(h).
"Lease". Section 2A-103(1)(j).
"Lease contract". Section 2A-103(1)(l).
"Leasehold interest." Section 2A-103(1)(m).
"Lessee". Section 2A-103(1)(n).
"Lessee in the ordinary course of business". Section 2A-103(1)(o).
"Lessor". Section 2A-103(1)(p).
"Merchant". Section 2-104(1).
"Rights". Section 1-201(36).
"Sale". Section 2-106(1).
"Sublease". Section 2A-103(1)(w).
"Value". Section 1-201(44).

Section 2A-306. Priority of Certain Liens Arising by Operation of Law.

If a person in the ordinary course of his or her business furnishes services or materials with respect to goods subject to a lease contract, a lien upon those goods in the possession of that person given by statute or rule of law for those materials or services takes priority over any interest of the lessor or lessee under the lease contract or this Article unless the lien is created by statute and the statute provides otherwise or unless the lien is created by rule of law and the rule of law provides otherwise.

OFFICIAL COMMENT

Uniform Statutory Source: Section 9-310.

Changes: The approach reflected in the provisions of Section 9-310 was included, but revised to conform to leasing terminology and to expand the exception to the special priority granted to protected liens to cover liens created by rule of law as well as those created by statute.

Purposes:

This section should be interpreted to allow a qualified lessor or a qualified lessee to be the competing lienholder if the statute or rule of law so provides. The reference to statute includes applicable regulations and cases; these sources must be reviewed in resolving a priority dispute under this section.

Cross Reference:

Section 9-310.

Definitional Cross References:

"Goods". Section 2A-103(1)(h).
"Lease Contract". Section 2A-103(1)(l).
"Lessee". Section 2A-103(1)(n).
"Lessor". Section 2A-103(1)(p).
"Lien". Section 2A-103(1)(r).
"Person". Section 1-201(30).

Section 2A–307. Priority of Liens Arising by Attachment or Levy on, Security Interests in, and Other Claims to Goods.

(1) Except as otherwise provided in Section 2A–306, a creditor of a lessee takes subject to the lease contract.

(2) Except as otherwise provided in subsections (3) and (4) and in Sections 2A–306 and 2A–308, a creditor of a lessor takes subject to the lease contract unless:

(a) the creditor holds a lien that attached to the goods before the lease contract became enforceable;

(b) the creditor holds a security interest in the goods and the lessee did not give value and receive delivery of the goods without knowledge of the security interest; or

(c) the creditor holds a security interest in the goods that was perfected (Section 9-303) before the lease contract became enforceable.

(3) A lessee in the ordinary course of business takes the leasehold interest free of a security interest in the goods created by the lessor even though the

security interest is perfected (Section 9-303) and the lessee knows of its existence.

(4) A lessee other than a lessee in the ordinary course of business takes the leasehold interest free of a security interest to the extent that it secures future advances made after the secured party acquires knowledge of the lease or more than forty-five days after the lease contract becomes enforceable, whichever first occurs, unless the future advances are made pursuant to a commitment entered into without knowledge of the lease and before the expiration of the forty-five day period.

OFFICIAL COMMENT

Uniform Statutory Source: None for subsection (1). Subsection (2) is derived from Section 9–301, and subsections (3) and (4) are derived from Section 9–307(1) and (3), respectively.

Changes: The provisions of Sections 9–301 and 9–307(1) and (3) were incorporated, and modified to reflect leasing terminology and the basic concepts reflected in this Article.

Purposes:

1. Subsection (1) states a general rule of priority that a creditor of the lessee takes subject to the lease contract. The term lessee (Section 2A–103(1)(n)) includes sublessee. Therefore, this subsection not only covers disputes between the prime lessor and a creditor of the prime lessee but also disputes between the prime lessor, or the sublessor, and a creditor of the sublessee. Section 2A–301 official comment 3(g). Further, by using the term creditor (Section 1–201(12)), this subsection will cover disputes with general creditor, a secured creditor, a lien creditor and any representative of creditors. Section 2A–103(4).

2. Subsection (2) states a general rule of priority that a creditor of a lessor takes subject to the lease contract. Note the discussion above with regard to the scope of these rules. Section 2A–301 official comment 3(g). Thus, the section will not only cover disputes between the prime lessee and a creditor of the prime lessor but also disputes between the prime lessee, or the sublessee, and a creditor of the sublessor.

3. To take priority over the lease contract, and the interests derived therefrom, the creditor must come within one of three exceptions stated within the rule. First, subsection (2)(a) provides that where the creditor holds a lien (Section 2A–103(1)(r)) that attached before the lease contract became enforceable (Section 2A–301), the creditor does not take subject to the lease. Second, subsection (2)(b) provides that when the creditor holds a security interest (Section 1–201(37)), whether or not perfected, the creditor has priority over a lessee who did not give value (Section 1–201(44)) and receive delivery of the goods without knowledge (Section 1–201(25)) of the security interest. As to other lessees, under subsection (2)(c) a secured creditor holding a perfected security interest before the time the lease contract became enforceable (Section 2A–301) does not take subject to the lease. With respect to this provision, the lessee in these circumstances is treated like a buyer so that perfection of a purchase money security interest does not relate back (Section 9–301).

4. The rules of this section operate in favor of whichever party to the lease contract may enforce it, even if one party perhaps may not, e.g., under Section 2A–201(1)(b).

5. The rules stated in subsections (2)(b) and (c), and the rule in subsection (3), are best understood by reviewing a hypothetical. Assume that a merchant engaged in the business of selling and leasing musical instruments obtained possessions of

a truck load of musical instruments on deferred payment terms from a supplier of musical instruments on January 6. To secure payment of such credit the merchant granted the supplier a security interest in the instruments; the security interest was perfected by filing on January 15. The merchant, as lessor, entered into a lease to an individual of one of the musical instruments supplied by the supplier; the lease became enforceable on January 10. Under subsection (2)(b) the lessee will prevail (assuming the lessee qualifies thereunder) unless subsection (c) provides otherwise. Under the rule stated in subsection (2)(c) a priority dispute between the supplier, as the lessor's secured creditor, and the lessee would be determined by ascertaining on January 10 (the day the lease became enforceable) the validity and perfected status of the security interest in the musical instrument and the enforceability of the lease contract by the lessee. Nothing more appearing, under the rule stated in subsection (2)(c), the supplier's security interest in the musical instrument would not have priority over the lease contract. Moreover, subsection (2) states that its rules are subject to the rules of subsections (3) and (4). Under this hypothetical the lessee should qualify as a "lessee in the ordinary course of business". Section 2A-103(1)(o). Subsection (3) also makes clear that the lessee in the ordinary course of business will win even if he or she knows of the existence of the supplier's security interest.

6. Subsection (3) and (4), which are modeled on the provisions of Section 9-307(1) and (3), respectively, state two exceptions to the priority rule stated in subsection (2) with respect to a creditor who holds a security interest. The lessee in the ordinary course of business will be treated in the same fashion as the buyer in the ordinary course of business, given a priority dispute with a secured creditor over goods subject to a lease contract.

Cross References:

Sections 1-201(12), 1-201(25), 1-201(37), 1-201(44), 2A-103(1)(n), 2A-103(1)(o), 2A-103(1)(r), 2A-103(4), 2A-201(1)(b), 2A-301 official comment 3(g), Article 9, especially Section 9-301, 9-307(1), and 9-307(3).

Definitional Cross References:

"Creditor". Section 1-201(12).
"Goods". Section 2A-103(1)(h).
"Knowledge" and "Knows". Section 1-201(25).
"Lease". Section 2A-103(1)(j).
"Lease contract". Section 2A-103(1)(l).
"Leasehold interest". Section 2A-103(1)(m).
"Lessee". Section 2A-103(1)(n).
"Lessee in the ordinary course of business". Section 2A-103(1)(o).
"Lessor". Section 2A-103(1)(p).
"Lien". Section 2A-103(1)(r).
"Party". Section 1-201(29).
"Pursuant to commitment". Section 2A-103(3).
"Security interest". Section 1-201(37).

Section 2A-308. Special Rights of Creditors.

(1) A creditor of a lessor in possession of goods subject to a lease contract may treat the lease contract as void if as against the creditor retention of possession by the lessor is fraudulent under any statute or rule of law, but retention of possession in good faith and current course of trade by the lessor for a commercially reasonable time after the lease contract becomes enforceable is not fraudulent.

UCC

(2) Nothing in this Article impairs the rights of creditors of a lessor if the lease contract (a) becomes enforceable, not in current course of trade but in satisfaction of or as security for a preexisting claim for money, security, or the like, and (b) is made under circumstances which under any statute or rule of law apart from this Article would constitute the transaction a fraudulent transfer or voidable preference.

(3) A creditor of a seller may treat a sale or an identification of goods to a contract for sale as void if as against the creditor retention of possession by the seller is fraudulent under any statute or rule of law, but retention of possession of the goods pursuant to a lease contract entered into by the seller as lessee and the buyer as lessor in connection with the sale or identification of the goods is not fraudulent if the buyer bought for value and in good faith.

OFFICIAL COMMENT

Uniform Statutory Source: Section 2–402(2) and (3)(b).

Changes: Rephrased and new material added to conform to leasing terminology and practice.

Purposes:

Subsection (1) states a general rule of avoidance where the lessor has retained possession of goods if such retention is fraudulent under any statute or rule of law. However, the subsection creates an exception under certain circumstances for retention of possession of goods for a commercially reasonable time after the lease contract becomes enforceable.

Subsection (2) also preserves the possibility of an attack on the lease by creditors of the lessor if the lease was made in satisfaction of or as security for a preexisting claim, and would constitute a fraudulent transfer or voidable preference under other law.

Finally, subsection (3) states a new rule with respect to sale-leaseback transactions, i.e., transactions where the seller sells goods to a buyer but possession of the goods is retained by the seller pursuant to a lease contract between the buyer as lessor and the seller as lessee. Notwithstanding any statute or rule of law that would treat such retention as fraud, whether per se, prima facie, or otherwise, the retention is not fraudulent if the buyer bought for value (Section 1–201(44)) and in good faith (Sections 1–201(19) and 2–103(1)(b)). Section 2A–103(3) and (4). This provision overrides Section 2–402(2) to the extent it would otherwise apply to a sale-leaseback transaction.

Cross References:

Sections 1–201(19), 1–201(44), 2–402(2) and 2A–103(4).

Definitional Cross References:

"Buyer". Section 2–103(1)(a).
"Contract". Section 1–201(11).
"Creditor". Section 1–201(12).
"Good faith". Sections 1–201(19) and 2–103(1)(b).
"Goods". Section 2A–103(1)(h).
"Lease contract". Section 2A–103(1)(l).
"Lessee". Section 2A–103(1)(n).

"Lessor". Section 2A–103(1)(p).
"Money". Section 1–201(24).
"Reasonable time". Section 1–204(1) and (2).
"Rights". Section 1–201(36).
"Sale". Section 2–106(1).
"Seller". Section 2–103(1)(d).
"Value". Section 1–201(44).

Section 2A–309. Lessor's and Lessee's Rights When Goods Become Fixtures.

(1) In this section:

(a) Goods are "fixtures" when they become so related to particular real estate that an interest in them arises under real estate law;

(b) A "fixture filing" is the filing, in the office where a mortgage on the real estate would be filed or recorded, of a financing statement covering goods that are or are to become fixtures and conforming to the requirements of Section 9-402(5);

(c) A lease is a "purchase money lease" unless the lessee has possession or use of the goods or the right to possession or use of the goods before the lease agreement is enforceable;

(d) A mortgage is a "construction mortgage" to the extent it secures an obligation incurred for the construction of an improvement on land including the acquisition cost of the land, if the recorded writing so indicates; and

(e) "Encumbrance" includes real estate mortgages and other liens on real estate and all other rights in real estate that are not ownership interests.

(2) Under this Article a lease may be of goods that are fixtures or may continue in goods that become fixtures, but no lease exists under this Article of ordinary building materials incorporated into an improvement on land.

(3) This Article does not prevent creation of a lease of fixtures pursuant to real estate law.

(4) The perfected interest of a lessor of fixtures has priority over a conflicting interest of an encumbrancer or owner of the real estate if:

(a) the lease is a purchase money lease, the conflicting interest of the encumbrancer or owner arises before the goods become fixtures, the interest of the lessor is perfected by a fixture filing before the goods become fixtures or within ten days thereafter, and the lessee has an interest of record in the real estate or is in possession of the real estate; or

(b) the interest of the lessor is perfected by a fixture filing before the interest of the encumbrancer or owner is of record, the lessor's interest has priority over any conflicting interest of a predecessor in title of the encumbrancer or owner, and the lessee has an interest of record in the real estate or is in possession of the real estate.

(5) The interest of a lessor of fixtures, whether or not perfected, has priority over the conflicting interest of an encumbrancer or owner of the real estate if:

(a) the fixtures are readily removable factory or office machines, readily removable equipment that is not primarily used or leased for use in the operation of the real estate, or readily removable replacement of domestic appliances that are goods subject to a consumer lease, and before the goods become fixtures the lease contract is enforceable; or

(b) the conflicting interest is a lien on the real estate obtained by legal or equitable proceedings after the lease contract is enforceable; or

(c) the encumbrancer or owner has consented in writing to the lease or has disclaimed an interest in the goods as fixtures; or

(d) the lessee has a right to remove the goods as against the encumbrancer or owner. If the lessee's right to remove terminates, the priority of the interest of the lessor continues for a reasonable time.

(6) Notwithstanding subsection (4)(a) but otherwise subject to subsections (4) and (5), the interest of a lessor of fixtures, including the lessor's residual interest, is subordinate to the conflicting interest of an encumbrancer of the real estate under a construction mortgage recorded before the goods become fixtures if the goods become fixtures before the completion of the construction. To the extent given to refinance a construction mortgage, the conflicting interest of an encumbrancer of the real estate under a mortgage has this priority to the same extent as the encumbrancer of the real estate under the construction mortgage.

(7) In cases not within the preceding subsections, priority between the interest of a lessor of fixtures, including the lessor's residual interest, and the conflicting interest of an encumbrancer or owner of the real estate who is not the lessee is determined by the priority rules governing conflicting interests in real estate.

(8) If the interest of a lessor of fixtures, including the lessor's residual interest, has priority over all conflicting interests of all owners and encumbrancers of the real estate, the lessor or the lessee may (i) on default, expiration, termination, or cancellation of the lease agreement but subject to the lease agreement and this Article, or (ii) if necessary to enforce other rights and remedies of the lessor or the lessee under this Article, remove the goods from the real estate, free and clear of all conflicting interests of all owners and encumbrancers of the real estate, but the lessor or the lessee must reimburse any encumbrancer or owner of the real estate who is not the lessee and who has not otherwise agreed for the cost of repair of any physical injury, but not for any diminution in value of the real estate caused by the absence of the goods removed or by any necessity of replacing them. A person entitled to reimbursement may refuse permission to remove until the party seeking removal gives adequate security for the performance of this obligation.

(9) Even though the lease agreement does not create a security interest, the interest of a lessor of fixtures, including the lessor's residual interest, is perfected

by filing a financing statement as a fixture filing for leased goods that are or are to become fixtures in accordance with the relevant provisions of the article on secured transactions (Article 9).

OFFICIAL COMMENT

Uniform Statutory Source: Section 9–313.
Changes: Revised to reflect leasing terminology and to add new material.

Purposes:

1. While Section 9–313 provided a model for this section, certain provisions were substantially revised.

2. Section 2A–309(1)(c), which is new, defines purchase money lease to exclude leases where the lessee had possession or use of the goods or the right thereof before the lease agreement became enforceable. This term is used in subsection (4)(a) as one of the conditions that must be satisfied to obtain priority over the conflicting interest of an encumbrancer or owner of the real estate.

3. Section 2A–309(4), which states one of several priority rules found in this section, deletes reference to office machines and the like (Section 9–313(4)(c)) as well as certain liens (Section 9–313(4)(d)). However, these items are included in subsection (5), another priority rule that is more permissive than the rule found in subsection (4) as it applies whether or not the interest of the lessor is perfected. In addition, subsection (5)(a) expands the scope of the provisions of Section 9–313(4)(c) to include readily removable equipment not primarily used or leased for use in the operation of real estate; the qualifier is intended to exclude from the expanded rule equipment integral to the operation of real estate, *e.g.,* heating and air conditioning equipment.

4. The rule stated in subsection (7) is more liberal than the rule stated in Section 9–313(7) in that issues of priority not otherwise resolved in this subsection are left for resolution by the priority rules governing conflicting interests in real estate, as opposed to the Section 9–313(7) automatic subordination of the security interest in fixtures. Note that, for the purpose of this section, where the interest of an encumbrancer or owner of the real estate is paramount to the interest of the lessor, the latter term includes the residual interest of the lessor.

5. The rule stated in subsection (8) is more liberal than the rule stated in Section 9–313(8) in that the right of removal is extended to both the lessor and the lessee and the occasion for removal includes expiration, termination or cancellation of the lease agreement, and enforcement of rights and remedies under this Article, as well as default. The new language also provides that upon removal the goods are free and clear of conflicting interests of owners and encumbrancers of the real estate.

6. Finally, subsection (9) provides a mechanism for the lessor of fixtures to perfect its interest by filing a financing statement under the provisions of the Article on Secured Transactions (Article 9), even though the lease agreement does not create a security interest. Section 1–201(37). The relevant provisions of Article 9 must be interpreted permissively to give effect to this mechanism as it implicitly expands the scope of Article 9 so that its filing provisions apply to transactions that create a lease of fixtures, even though the lease agreement does not create a security interest. This mechanism is similar to that provided in Section 2–326(3)(c) for the seller of goods on consignment, even though the consignment is not "intended as security." Section 1–201(37). Given the lack of litigation with respect to the mechanism created for consignment sales, this new mechanism should prove effective.

Cross References:

Sections 1–201(37), 2A–309(1)(c), 2A–309(4), Article 9, especially Sections 9–313, 9–313(4)(c), 9–313(4)(d), 9–313(7), 9–313(8) and 9–408.

Definitional Cross References:

"Agreed". Section 1–201(3).
"Cancellation". Section 2A–103(1)(b).
"Conforming". Section 2A–103(1)(d).
"Consumer lease". Section 2A–103(1)(e).
"Goods". Section 2A–103(1)(h).
"Lease". Section 2A–103(1)(j).
"Lease agreement". Section 2A–103(1)(k).
"Lease contract". Section 2A–103(1)(l).
"Lessee". Section 2A–103(1)(n).
"Lessor". Section 2A–103(1)(p).
"Lien". Section 2A–103(1)(r).
"Mortgage". Section 9–105(1)(j).
"Party". Section 1–201(29).
"Person". Section 1–201(30).
"Reasonable time". Section 1–204(1) and (2).
"Remedy". Section 1–201(34).
"Rights". Section 1–201(36).
"Security interest". Section 1–201(37).
"Termination". Section 2A–103(1)(z).
"Value". Section 1–201(44).
"Writing". Section 1–201(46).

Section 2A–310. Lessor's and Lessee's Rights When Goods Become Accessions.

(1) Goods are "accessions" when they are installed in or affixed to other goods.

(2) The interest of a lessor or a lessee under a lease contract entered into before the goods became accessions is superior to all interests in the whole except as stated in subsection (4).

(3) The interest of a lessor or a lessee under a lease contract entered into at the time or after the goods became accessions is superior to all subsequently acquired interests in the whole except as stated in subsection (4) but is subordinate to interests in the whole existing at the time the lease contract was made unless the holders of such interests in the whole have in writing consented to the lease or disclaimed an interest in the goods as part of the whole.

(4) The interest of a lessor or a lessee under a lease contract described in subsection (2) or (3) is subordinate to the interest of:

(a) a buyer in the ordinary course of business or a lessee in the ordinary course of business of any interest in the whole acquired after the goods became accessions; or

(b) a creditor with a security interest in the whole perfected before the lease contract was made to the extent that the creditor makes subsequent advances without knowledge of the lease contract.

(5) When under subsections (2) or (3) and (4) a lessor or a lessee of accessions holds an interest that is superior to all interests in the whole, the lessor or the lessee may (a) on default, expiration, termination, or cancellation of the lease contract by the other party but subject to the provisions of the lease contract and this Article, or (b) if necessary to enforce his or her other rights and remedies under this Article, remove the goods from the whole, free and clear of all interests in the whole, but he or she must reimburse any holder of an interest in the whole who is not the lessee and who has not otherwise agreed for the cost of repair of any physical injury but not for any diminution in value of the whole caused by the absence of the goods removed or by any necessity for replacing them. A person entitled to reimbursement may refuse permission to remove until the party seeking removal gives adequate security for the performance of this obligation.

OFFICIAL COMMENT

Uniform Statutory Source: Section 9–314.

Changes: Revised to reflect leasing terminology and to add new material.

Purposes:

Subsections (1) and (2) restate the provisions of subsection (1) of Section 9–314 to clarify the definition of accession and to add leasing terminology to the priority rule that applies when the lease is entered into before the goods become accessions. Subsection (3) restates the provisions of subsection (2) of Section 9–314 to add leasing terminology to the priority rule that applies when the lease is entered into on or after the goods become accessions. Unlike the rule with respect to security interests, the lease is merely subordinate, not invalid.

Subsection (4) creates two exceptions to the priority rules stated in subsections (2) and (3). Subsection (4) deletes the special priority rule found in the provisions of Section 9–314(3)(b) as the interests of the lessor and lessee are entitled to greater protection.

Finally, subsection (5) is modeled on the provisions of Section 9–314(4) with respect to removal of accessions, restated to reflect the parallel changes in Section 2A–309(8).

Neither this section nor Section 9–314 governs where the accession to the goods is not subject to the interest of a lessor or a lessee under a lease contract and is not subject to the interest of a secured party under a security agreement. This issue is to be resolved by the courts, case by case.

Cross References:

Sections 2A–309(8), 9–314(1), 9–314(2), 9–314(3)(b), 9–314(4).

Definitional Cross References:

"Agreed". Section 1–201(3).
"Buyer in the ordinary course of business". Section 2A–103(1)(a).
"Cancellation". Section 2A–103(1)(b).
"Creditor". Section 1–201(12)."Goods". Section 2A–103(1)(h).
"Holder". Section 1–201(20).
"Knowledge". Section 1–201(25).
"Lease". Section 2A–103(1)(j).

"Lease contract". Section 2A–103(1)(l).
"Lessee". Section 2A–103(1)(n).
"Lessee in the ordinary course of business". Section 2A–103(1)(o).
"Lessor". Section 2A–103(1)(p).
"Party". Section 1–201(29).
"Person". Section 1–201(30).
"Remedy". Section 1–201(34).
"Rights". Section 1–201(36).
"Security interest". Section 1–201(37).
"Termination". Section 2A–103(1)(z).
"Value". Section 1–201(44).
"Writing". Section 1–201(46).

Section 2A–311. Priority Subject to Subordination.

Nothing in this Article prevents subordination by agreement by any person entitled to priority.

OFFICIAL COMMENT

Uniform Statutory Source: Section 2–609.

Changes: Revised to reflect leasing practices and terminology. Note that in the analogue to subsection (3) (Section 2–609(4)), the adjective "justified" modifies demand. The adjective was deleted here as unnecessary, implying no substantive change.

Definitional Cross References:

"Aggrieved party". Section 1–201(2).
"Agreed". Section 1–201(3).
"Between merchants". Section 2–104(3).
"Conforming". Section 2A–103(1)(d).
"Delivery". Section 1–201(14).
"Lease contract". Section 2A–103(1)(l).
"Party". Section 1–201(29).
"Reasonable time". Section 1–204(1) and (2).
"Receipt". Section 2–103(1)(c).
"Rights". Section 1–201(36).
"Writing". Section 1–201(46).

PART 4

PERFORMANCE OF LEASE CONTRACT: REPUDIATED, SUBSTITUTED AND EXCUSED

Section 2A–401. Insecurity: Adequate Assurance of Performance.

(1) A lease contract imposes an obligation on each party that the other's expectation of receiving due performance will not be impaired.

(2) If reasonable grounds for insecurity arise with respect to the performance of either party, the insecure party may demand in writing adequate assurance of due performance. Until the insecure party receives that assurance, if

commercially reasonable the insecure party may suspend any performance for which he or she has not already received the agreed return.

(3) A repudiation of the lease contract occurs if assurance of due performance adequate under the circumstances of the particular case is not provided to the insecure party within a reasonable time, not to exceed thirty days after receipt of a demand by the other party.

(4) Between merchants, the reasonableness of grounds for insecurity and the adequacy of any assurance offered must be determined according to commercial standards.

(5) Acceptance of any nonconforming delivery or payment does not prejudice the aggrieved party's right to demand adequate assurance of future performance.

Official Comment

Uniform Statutory Source: Section 2-609.

Changes: Revised to reflect leasing practices and terminology. Note that in the analogue to subsection (3) (Section 2-609(4)), the adjective "justified" modifies demand. The adjective was deleted here as unnecessary, implying no substantive change.

Definitional Cross References:

"Aggrieved party". Section 1–201(2).
"Agreed". Section 1–201(3).
"Between merchants". Section 2–104(3).
"Conforming". Section 2A–103(1)(d).
"Delivery". Section 1–201(14).
"Lease contract". Section 2A–103(1)(l).
"Party". Section 1–201(29).
"Reasonable time". Section 1–204(1) and (2).
"Receipt". Section 2–103(1)(c).
"Rights". Section 1–201(36).
"Writing". Section 1–201(46).

Section 2A–402. Anticipatory Repudiation.

If either party repudiates a lease contract with respect to a performance not yet due under the lease contract, the loss of which performance will substantially impair the value of the lease contract to the other, the aggrieved party may:

(1) for a commercially reasonable time, await retraction of repudiation and performance by the repudiating party;

(2) make demand pursuant to Section 2A–401 and await assurance of future performance adequate under the circumstances of the particular case; or

(3) resort to any right or remedy upon default under the lease contract or this Article, even though the aggrieved party has notified the repudiating party that the aggrieved party would await the repudiating party's performance and assurance and has urged retraction. In addition, whether or not the aggrieved party is pursuing one of the foregoing remedies, the aggrieved party may suspend

performance or, if the aggrieved party is the lessor, proceed in accordance with the provisions of this Article on the lessor's right to identify goods to the lease contract notwithstanding default or to salvage unfinished goods (Section 2A–524).

OFFICIAL COMMENT

Uniform Statutory Source: Section 2–610.

Changes: Revised to reflect leasing practices and terminology.

Definitional Cross References:

"Aggrieved party". Section 1–201(2).
"Goods". Section 2A–103(1)(h).
"Lease contract". Section 2A–103(1)(l).
"Lessor". Section 2A–103(1)(p).
"Notifies". Section 1–201(26).
"Party". Section 1–201(29).
"Reasonable time". Section 1–204(1) and (2).
"Remedy". Section 1–201(34).
"Rights". Section 1–201(36).
"Value". Section 1–201(44).

Section 2A–403. Retraction of Anticipatory Repudiation.

(1) Until the repudiating party's next performance is due, the repudiating party can retract the repudiation unless, since the repudiation, the aggrieved party has canceled the lease contract or materially changed the aggrieved party's position or otherwise indicated that the aggrieved party considers the repudiation final.

(2) Retraction may be by any method that clearly indicates to the aggrieved party that the repudiating party intends to perform under the lease contract and includes any assurance demanded under Section 2A–401.

(3) Retraction reinstates a repudiating party's rights under a lease contract with due excuse and allowance to the aggrieved party for any delay occasioned by the repudiation.

OFFICIAL COMMENT

Uniform Statutory Source: Section 2–611.

Changes: Revised to reflect leasing practices and terminology. Note that in the analogue to subsection (2) (Section 2–611(2)) the adjective "justifiably" modifies demanded. The adjective was deleted here (as it was in Section 2A–401) as unnecessary, implying no substantive change.

Definitional Cross References:

"Aggrieved party". Section 1–201(2).
"Cancellation". Section 2A–103(1)(b).
"Lease contract". Section 2A–103(1)(l).
"Party". Section 1–201(29).
"Rights". Section 1–201(36).

Section 2A–404. Substituted Performance.

(1) If without fault of the lessee, the lessor and the supplier, the agreed berthing, loading, or unloading facilities fail or the agreed type of carrier becomes unavailable or the agreed manner of delivery otherwise becomes commercially impracticable, but a commercially reasonable substitute is available, the substitute performance must be tendered and accepted.

(2) If the agreed means or manner of payment fails because of domestic or foreign governmental regulation:

(a) the lessor may withhold or stop delivery or cause the supplier to withhold or stop delivery unless the lessee provides a means or manner of payment that is commercially a substantial equivalent; and

(b) if delivery has already been taken, payment by the means or in the manner provided by the regulation discharges the lessee's obligation unless the regulation is discriminatory, oppressive, or predatory.

OFFICIAL COMMENT

Uniform Statutory Source: Section 2–614.
Changes: Revised to reflect leasing practices and terminology.

Definitional Cross References:

"Agreed". Section 1–201(3).
"Delivery". Section 1–201(14).
"Fault". Section 2A–103(1)(f).
"Lessee". Section 2A–103(1)(n).
"Lessor". Section 2A–103(1)(p).
"Supplier". Section 2A–103(1)(x).

Section 2A–405. Excused Performance.

(1) Subject to Section 2A–404 on substituted performance, the following rules apply:

(a) delay in delivery or nondelivery in whole or in part by a lessor or a supplier who complies with paragraph (b) and subsection (2) is not a default under the lease contract if performance as agreed has been made impracticable by the occurrence of a contingency the nonoccurrence of which was a basic assumption on which the lease contract was made or by compliance in good faith with any applicable foreign or domestic governmental regulation or order, whether or not the regulation or order later proves to be invalid.

(b) if the causes mentioned in paragraph (a) affect only part of the lessor's or the supplier's capacity to perform, he or she shall allocate production and deliveries among his or her customers but at his or her option may include regular customers not then under contract for sale or lease as well as his or her own requirements for further manufacture. He or she may so allocate in any manner that is fair and reasonable.

(2) The lessor seasonably shall notify the lessee and in the case of a finance lease the supplier seasonably shall notify the lessor and the lessee, if known, that there will be delay or nondelivery and, if allocation is required under subsection (1) (b), of the estimated quota thus made available for the lessee.

OFFICIAL COMMENT

Uniform Statutory Source: Section 2–615.
Changes: Revised to reflect leasing practices and terminology.

Definitional Cross References:

"Agreed". Section 1–201(3).
"Contract". Section 1–201(11).
"Delivery". Section 1–201(14).
"Finance lease". Section 2A–103(1)(g).
"Good faith". Sections 1–201(19) and 2–103(1)(b).
"Knows". Section 1–201(25).
"Lease". Section 2A–103(1)(j).
"Lease contract". Section 2A–103(1)(l).
"Lessee". Section 2A–103(1)(n).
"Lessor". Section 2A–103(1)(p).
"Notifies". Section 1–201(26).
"Sale". Section 2–106(1).
"Seasonably". Section 1–204(3).
"Supplier". Section 2A–103(1)(x).

Section 2A–406. Procedure on Excused Performance.

(1) If the lessee receives notification of a material or indefinite delay or an allocation justified under Section 2A–405, the lessee may by written notification to the lessor as to any goods involved, and with respect to all of the goods if under an installment lease contract the value of the whole lease contract is substantially impaired (Section 2A–510):

(a) terminate the lease contract (Section 2A–505(2)); or

(b) except in a finance lease that is not a consumer lease, modify the lease contract by accepting the available quota in substitution, with due allowance from the rent payable for the balance of the lease term for the deficiency but without further right against the lessor.

(2) If, after receipt of a notification from the lessor under Section 2A–405, the lessee fails so to modify the lease agreement within a reasonable time not exceeding thirty days, the lease contract lapses with respect to any deliveries affected.

OFFICIAL COMMENT

Uniform Statutory Source: Section 2–616(1) and (2).

Changes: Revised to reflect leasing practices and terminology. Note that subsection 1(a) allows the lessee under a lease, including a finance lease, the right to terminate the lease for excused performance (Sections 2A–404 and 2A–405). However, subsection 1(b), which allows the lessee the right to modify the lease for excused performance, excludes a finance lease that is not a consumer lease. This exclusion is compelled by the same policy that led to codification of provisions with respect to irrevocable promises. Section 2A–407.

Definitional Cross References:

"Consumer lease". Section 2A–103(1)(e).
"Delivery". Section 1–201(14).
"Finance lease". Section 2A–103(1)(g).
"Goods". Section 2A–103(1)(h).
"Installment lease contract". Section 2A–103(1)(i).
"Lease agreement". Section 2A–103(1)(k).
"Lease contract". Section 2A–103(1)(l).
"Lessee". Section 2A–103(1)(n).
"Lessor". Section 2A–103(1)(p).
"Notice". Section 1–201(25).
"Reasonable time". Section 1–204 (1) and (2).
"Receipt". Section 2–103(1)(c).
"Rights". Section 1–201(36).
"Termination". Section 2A–103(1)(z).
"Value". Section 1–201(44).
"Written". Section 1–201(46).

Section 2A–407. Irrevocable Promises: Finance Leases.

(1) In the case of a finance lease that is not a consumer lease the lessee's promises under the lease contract become irrevocable and independent upon the lessee's acceptance of the goods.

(2) A promise that has become irrevocable and independent under subsection (1):

(a) is effective and enforceable between the parties, and by or against third parties including assignees of the parties; and

(b) is not subject to cancellation, termination, modification, repudiation, excuse, or substitution without the consent of the party to whom the promise runs.

(3) This section does not affect the validity under any other law of a covenant in any lease contract making the lessee's promises irrevocable and independent upon the lessee's acceptance of the goods.

OFFICIAL COMMENT

Uniform Statutory Source: None.

Purposes:

1. This section extends the benefits of the classic "hell or high water" clause to a finance lease that is not a consumer lease. This section is self-executing; no special provision need be added to the contract. This section makes covenants in a finance lease irrevocable and independent due to the function of the finance lessor in a three

party relationship: the lessee is looking to the supplier to perform the essential covenants and warranties. Section 2A–209. Thus, upon the lessee's acceptance of the goods the lessee's promises to the lessor under the lease contract become irrevocable and independent. The provisions of this section remain subject to the obligation of good faith (Sections 2A–103(4) and 1–203), and the lessee's revocation of acceptance (Section 2A–517).

2. The section requires the lessee to perform even if the lessor's performance after the lessee's acceptance is not in accordance with the lease contract; the lessee may, however, have and pursue a cause of action against the lessor, e.g., breach of certain limited warranties (Sections 2A–210 and 2A–211(1)). This is appropriate because the benefit of the supplier's promises and warranties to the lessor under the supply contract and, in some cases, the warranty of a manufacturer who is not the supplier, is extended to the lessee under the finance lease. Section 2A–209. Despite this balance, this section excludes a finance lease that is a consumer lease. That a consumer be obligated to pay notwithstanding defective goods or the like is a principle that is not tenable under case law (Unico v. Owen, 50 N.J. 101, 232 A.2d 405 (1967)), state statute (Unif. Consumer Credit Code §§ 3.403–.405, 7A U.L.A. 126–31 (1974), or federal statute (15 U.S.C. § 1666i (1982)).

3. The relationship of the three parties to a transaction that qualifies as a finance lease is best demonstrated by a hypothetical. A, the potential lessor, has been contacted by B, the potential lessee, to discuss the lease of an expensive line of equipment that B has recently placed an order for with C, the manufacturer of such goods. The negotiation is completed and A, as lessor, and B, as lessee, sign a lease of the line of equipment for a 60–month term. B, as buyer, assigns the purchase order C to A. If this transaction creates a lease (Section 2A–103(1)(j)), this transaction should qualify as a finance lease. Section 2A–103(1)(g).

4. The line of equipment is delivered by C to B's place of business. After installation by C and testing by B, B accepts the goods by signing a certificate of delivery and acceptance, a copy of which is sent by B to A and C. One year later the line of equipment malfunctions and B falls behind in its manufacturing schedule.

5. Under this Article, because the lease is a finance lease, no warranty of fitness or merchantability is extended by A to B. Sections 2A–212(1) and 2A–213. Absent an express provision in the lease agreement, application of Section 2A–210 or Section 2A–211(1), or application of the principles of law and equity, including the law with respect to fraud, duress, or the like (Sections 2A–103(4) and 1–103), B has no claim against A. B's obligation to pay rent to A continues as the obligation became irrevocable and independent when B accepted the line of equipment (Section 2A–407(1)). B has no right of set-off with respect to any part of the rent still due under the lease. Section 2A–508(6). However, B may have another remedy. Despite the lack of privity between B and C (the purchase order with C having been assigned by B to A), B may have a claim against C. Section 2A–209(1).

6. This section does not address whether a "hell or high water" clause, *i.e.*, a clause that is to the effect of this section, is enforceable if included in a finance lease that is a consumer lease or a lease that is not a finance lease. That issue will continue to be determined by the facts of each case and other law which this section does not affect. Sections 2A–104, 2A–103(4), 9–206 and 9–318. However, with respect to finance leases that are not consumer leases courts have enforced "hell or high water" clauses. In re O.P.M. Leasing Servs., 21 Bankr. 993, 1006 (Bankr. S.D.N.Y. 1982).

7. Subsection (2) further provides that a promise that has become irrevocable and independent under subsection (1) is enforceable not only between the parties but also against third parties. Thus, the finance lease can be transferred or assigned without disturbing enforceability. Further, subsection (2) also provides that the promise cannot, among other things, be cancelled or terminated without the consent of the lessor.

Cross References:

Sections 1–103, 1–203, 2A–103(1)(g), 2A–103(1)(j), 2A–103(4), 2A–104, 2A–209, 2A–209(1), 2A–210, 2A–211(1), 2A–212(1), 2A–213, 2A–517(1)(b), 9–206 and 9–318.

Definitional Cross References:

"Cancellation". Section 2A–103(1)(b).
"Consumer lease". Section 2A–103(1)(e).
"Finance lease". Section 2A–103(1)(g).
"Goods". Section 2A–103(1)(h).
"Lease contract". Section 2A–103(1)(l).
"Lessee". Section 2A–103(1)(n).
"Party". Section 1–201(29).
"Termination". Section 2A–103(1)(z).

PART 5

DEFAULT

A. In General

Section 2A–501. Default: Procedure.

(1) Whether the lessor or the lessee is in default under a lease contract is determined by the lease agreement and this Article.

(2) If the lessor or the lessee is in default under the lease contract, the party seeking enforcement has rights and remedies as provided in this Article and, except as limited by this Article, as provided in the lease agreement.

(3) If the lessor or the lessee is in default under the lease contract, the party seeking enforcement may reduce the party's claim to judgment, or otherwise enforce the lease contract by self-help or any available judicial procedure or nonjudicial procedure, including administrative proceeding, arbitration, or the like, in accordance with this Article.

(4) Except as otherwise provided in Section 1-106(1) or this Article or the lease agreement, the rights and remedies referred to in subsections (2) and (3) are cumulative.

(5) If the lease agreement covers both real property and goods, the party seeking enforcement may proceed under this part as to the goods, or under other applicable law as to both the real property and the goods in accordance with that party's rights and remedies in respect of the real property, in which case this part does not apply.

OFFICIAL COMMENT

Uniform Statutory Source: Section 9–501.
Changes: Substantially revised.

Purposes:

1. Subsection (1) is new and represents a departure from the Article on Secured Transactions (Article 9) as the subsection makes clear that whether a party to the lease agreement is in default is determined by this Article as well as the agreement. Sections 2A–508 and 2A–523. It further departs from Article 9 in recognizing the potential default of either party, a function of the bilateral nature of the obligations between the parties to the lease contract.

2. Subsection (2) is a version of the first sentence of Section 9–501(1), revised to reflect leasing terminology.

3. Subsection (3), an expansive version of the second sentence of Section 9–501(1), lists the procedures that may be followed by the party seeking enforcement; in effect, the scope of the procedures listed in subsection (3) is consistent with the scope of the procedures available to the foreclosing secured party.

4. Subsection (4) establishes that the parties' rights and remedies are cumulative. DeKoven, *Leases of Equipment: Puritan Leasing Company v. August, A Dangerous Decision,* 12 U.S.F. L. Rev. 257, 276–80 (1978). Cumulation, and largely unrestricted selection, of remedies is allowed in furtherance of the general policy of the Commercial Code, stated in Section 1–106, that remedies be liberally administered to put the aggrieved party in as good a position as if the other party had fully performed. Therefore, cumulation of, or selection among, remedies is available to the extent necessary to put the aggrieved party in as good a position as it would have been in had there been full performance. However, cumulation of, or selection among, remedies is not available to the extent that the cumulation or selection would put the aggrieved party in a better position than it would have been in had there been full performance by the other party.

5. Section 9–501(3), which, among other things, states that certain rules, to the extent they give rights to the debtor and impose duties on the secured party, may not be waived or varied, was not incorporated in this Article. Given the significance of freedom of contract in the development of the common law as it applies to bailments for hire and the lessee's lack of an equity of redemption, there was no reason to impose that restraint.

Cross References:

Sections 1–106, 2A–508, 2A–523, Article 9, especially Sections 9–501(1) and 9–501(3).

Definitional Cross References:

"Goods". Section 2A–103(1)(h).
"Lease agreement". Section 2A–103 (1)(k).
"Lease contract". Section 2A–103 (1)(l).
"Lessee". Section 2A–103(1)(n).
"Lessor". Section 2A–103(1)(p)."Party". Section 1–201(29).
"Remedy". Section 1–201(34).
"Rights". Section 1–201(36).

Section 2A–502. Notice After Default.

Except as otherwise provided in this Article or the lease agreement, the lessor or lessee in default under the lease contract is not entitled to notice of default or notice of enforcement from the other party to the lease agreement.

OFFICIAL COMMENT

Uniform Statutory Source: None.

Purposes:

This section makes clear that absent agreement to the contrary or provision in this Article to the contrary, e.g., Section 2A–516(3)(a), the party in default is not entitled to notice of default or enforcement. While a review of Part 5 of Article 9 leads to the same conclusion with respect to giving notice of default to the debtor, it is never stated. Although Article 9 requires notice of disposition and strict foreclosure, the different scheme of lessors' and lessees' rights and remedies developed under the common law, and codified by this Article, generally does not require notice of enforcement; furthermore, such notice is not mandated by due process requirements. However, certain sections of this Article do require notice. E.g., Section 2A–517(4).

Cross References:

Sections 2A–516(3)(a), 2A–517(4), and Article 9, esp. Part 5.

Definitional Cross References:

"Lease agreement". Section 2A–103(1)(k).
"Lease contract". Section 2A–103(1)(l).
"Lessee". Section 2A–103(1)(n).
"Lessor". Section 2A–103(1)(p).
"Notice". Section 1–201(25).
"Party". Section 1–201(29).

Section 2A–503. Modification or Impairment of Rights and Remedies.

(1) Except as otherwise provided in this Article, the lease agreement may include rights and remedies for default in addition to or in substitution for those provided in this Article and may limit or alter the measure of damages recoverable under this Article.

(2) Resort to a remedy provided under this Article or in the lease agreement is optional unless the remedy is expressly agreed to be exclusive. If circumstances cause an exclusive or limited remedy to fail of its essential purpose, or provision for an exclusive remedy is unconscionable, remedy may be had as provided in this Article.

(3) Consequential damages may be liquidated under Section 2A–504, or may otherwise be limited, altered, or excluded unless the limitation, alteration, or exclusion is unconscionable. Limitation, alteration, or exclusion of consequential damages for injury to the person in the case of consumer goods is prima facie unconscionable but limitation, alteration, or exclusion of damages where the loss is commercial is not prima facie unconscionable.

(4) Rights and remedies on default by the lessor or the lessee with respect to any obligation or promise collateral or ancillary to the lease contract are not impaired by this Article.

OFFICIAL COMMENT

Uniform Statutory Source: Sections 2–719 and 2–701.

Changes: Rewritten to reflect lease terminology and to clarify the relationship between this section and Section 2A–504.

Purposes:

1. A significant purpose of this Part is to provide rights and remedies for those parties to a lease who fail to provide them by agreement or whose rights and remedies fail of their essential purpose or are unenforceable. However, it is important to note that this implies no restriction on freedom to contract. Section 2A–103(4) and 1–102(3). Thus, subsection (1), a revised version of the provisions of Section 2–719(1), allows the parties to the lease agreement freedom to provide for rights and remedies in addition to or in substitution for those provided in this Article and to alter or limit the measure of damages recoverable under this Article. Except to the extent otherwise provided in this Article (*e.g.,* Sections 2A–105, 106 and 108(1) and (2)), this Part shall be construed neither to restrict the parties' ability to provide for rights and remedies or to limit or alter the measure of damages by agreement, nor to imply disapproval of rights and remedy schemes other than those set forth in this Part.

2. Subsection (2) makes explicit with respect to this Article what is implicit in Section 2–719 with respect to the Article on Sales (Article 2): if an exclusive remedy is held to be unconscionable, remedies under this Article are available. Section 2–719 official comment 1.

3. Subsection (3), a revision of Section 2–719(3), makes clear that consequential damages may also be liquidated. Section 2A–504(1).

4. Subsection (4) is a revision of the provisions of Section 2–701. This subsection leaves the treatment of default with respect to obligations or promises collateral or ancillary to the lease contract to other law. Sections 2A–103(4) and 1–103. An example of such an obligation would be that of the lessor to the secured creditor which has provided the funds to leverage the lessor's lease transaction; an example of such a promise would be that of the lessee, as seller, to the lessor, as buyer, in a sale–leaseback transaction.

Cross References:

Sections 1–102(3), 1–103, Article 2, especially Sections 2–701, 2–719, 2–719(1), 2–719(3), 2–719 official comment 1, and Sections 2A–103(4), 2A–105, 2A–106, 2A–108(1), 2A–108(2), and 2A–504.

Definitional Cross References:

"Agreed". Section 1–201(3).
"Consumer goods". Section 9–109(1).
"Lease agreement". Section 2A–103(1)(k).
"Lease contract". Section 2A–103(1)(l).
"Lessee". Section 2A–103(1)(n).
"Lessor". Section 2A–103(1)(p).
"Person". Section 1–201(3).
"Remedy". Section 1–201(34).
"Rights". Section 1–201(36).

Section 2A–504. Liquidation of Damages.

(1) Damages payable by either party for default, or any other act or omission, including indemnity for loss or diminution of anticipated tax benefits or loss

or damage to lessor's residual interest, may be liquidated in the lease agreement but only at an amount or by a formula that is reasonable in light of the then anticipated harm caused by the default or other act or omission.

(2) If the lease agreement provides for liquidation of damages, and such provision does not comply with subsection (1), or such provision is an exclusive or limited remedy that circumstances cause to fail of its essential purpose, remedy may be had as provided in this Article.

(3) If the lessor justifiably withholds or stops delivery of goods because of the lessee's default or insolvency (Section 2A–525 or 2A–526), the lessee is entitled to restitution of any amount by which the sum of his or her payment exceeds:

(a) the amount to which the lessor is entitled by virtue of terms liquidating the lessor's damages in accordance with subsection (1); or

(b) in the absence of those terms, 20 percent of the then present value of the total rent the lessee was obligated to pay for the balance of the lease term, or, in the case of a consumer lease, the lesser of such amount or $500.

(4) A lessee's right to restitution under subsection (3) is subject to offset to the extent the lessor establishes:

(a) a right to recover damages under the provisions of this Article other than subsection (1); and

(b) the amount or value of any benefits received by the lessee directly or indirectly by reason of the lease contract.

OFFICIAL COMMENT

Uniform Statutory Source: Sections 2-718(1), (2), (3) and 2-719(2).
Changes: Substantially rewritten.

Purposes:

Many leasing transactions are predicated on the parties' ability to agree to an appropriate amount of damages or formula for damages in the event of default or other act or omission. The rule with respect to sales of goods (Section 2-718) may not be sufficiently flexible to accommodate this practice. Thus, consistent with the common law emphasis upon freedom to contract with respect to bailments for hire, this section has created a revised rule that allows greater flexibility with respect to leases of goods.

Subsection (1), a significantly modified version of the provisions of Section 2-718(1), provides for liquidation of damages in the lease agreement at an amount or by a formula. Section 2-718(1) does not by its express terms include liquidation by a formula; this change was compelled by modern leasing practice. Subsection (1), in a further expansion of Section 2-718(1), provides for liquidation of damages for default as well as any other act or omission.

A liquidated damages formula that is common in leasing practice provides that the sum of lease payments past due, accelerated future lease payments, and the lessor's estimated residual interest, less the net proceeds of disposition (whether by sale or re-lease) of the leased goods is the lessor's damages. Tax indemnities, costs, interest and attorney's fees are also added to determine the lessor's damages. Another common liquidated damages formula utilizes a periodic depreciation allocation as a credit to the aforesaid amount in mitigation of a lessor's damages. A third formula provides for a fixed number of periodic payments as a means of liquidating damages. Stipulated loss or stipulated damage schedules are also common. Whether these formulae are enforceable will be determined in the context of each case by applying a standard of reasonableness in light of the harm anticipated when the formula was agreed to. Whether the inclusion of these formulae will affect the classification of the transaction as a lease or a security interest is to be determined by the facts of each case. Section 1-201(37). *E.g., In re* Noack, 44 Bankr. 172, 174-75 (Bankr. E.D. Wis. 1984).

This section does not incorporate two other tests that under sales law determine enforceability of liquidated damages, i.e., difficulties of proof of loss and inconvenience or nonfeasibility of otherwise obtaining an adequate remedy. The ability to liquidate damages is critical to modern leasing practice; given the parties' freedom to contract at common law, the policy behind retaining these two additional requirements here was thought to be outweighed. Further, given the expansion of subsection (1) to enable the parties to liquidate the amount payable with respect to an indemnity for loss or diminution of anticipated tax benefits resulted in another change: the last sentence of Section 2-718(1), providing that a term fixing unreasonably large liquidated damages is void as a penalty, was also not incorporated. The impact of local, state and federal tax laws on a leasing transaction can result in an amount payable with respect to the tax indemnity many times greater than the original purchase price of the goods. By deleting the references to unreasonably large liquidated damages the parties are free to negotiate a formula, restrained by the rule of reasonableness in this section. These changes should invite the parties to liquidate damages. Peters, *Remedies for Breach of Contracts Relating to the Sale of Goods Under the Uniform Commercial Code: A Roadmap for Article Two,* 73 Yale L.J. 199, 278 (1963).

Subsection (2), a revised version of Section 1-719(2), provides that if the liquidated damages provision is not enforceable or fails of its essential purpose, remedy may be had as provided in this Article.

Subsection (3)(b) of this section differs from subsection (2)(b) of Section 2-718; in the absence of a valid liquidated damages amount or formula the lessor is permitted to retain 20 percent of the present value of the total rent payable under the lease. The alternative limitation of $500 contained in Section 2-718 is deleted as unrealistically low with respect to a lease other than a consumer lease.

Cross References:

Sections 1-201(37), 2-718, 2-718(1), 2-718(2)(b) and 2-719(2).

Definitional Cross References:

"Consumer lease". Section 2A-103(1)(e).
"Delivery". Section 1-201(14).
"Goods". Section 2A-103(1)(h).
"Insolvent". Section 1-201(23).
"Lease agreement". Section 2A-103(1)(k).
"Lease contract".Section 2A-103(1)(l).
"Lessee". Section 2A-103(1)(n).
"Lessor". Section 2A-103(1)(p).
"Lessor's residual interest". Section 2A-103(1)(q).
"Party". Section 1-201(29).
"Present value". Section 2A-103(1)(u).
"Remedy". Section 1-201(34).

"Rights". Section 1-201(36).
"Term". Section 1-201(42).
"Value". Section 1-201(44).

Section 2A–505. Cancellation and Termination and Effect of Cancellation, Termination, Rescission, or Fraud on Rights and Remedies.

(1) On cancellation of the lease contract, all obligations that are still executory on both sides are discharged, but any right based on prior default or performance survives, and the cancelling party also retains any remedy for default of the whole lease contract or any unperformed balance.

(2) On termination of the lease contract, all obligations that are still executory on both sides are discharged but any right based on prior default or performance survives.

(3) Unless the contrary intention clearly appears, expressions of "cancellation," "rescission," or the like of the lease contract may not be construed as a renunciation or discharge of any claim in damages for an antecedent default.

(4) Rights and remedies for material misrepresentation or fraud include all rights and remedies available under this Article for default.

(5) Neither rescission nor a claim for rescission of the lease contract nor rejection or return of the goods may bar or be deemed inconsistent with a claim for damages or other right or remedy.

OFFICIAL COMMENT

Uniform Statutory Source: Sections 2–106(3) and (4), 2–720 and 2–721.
Changes: Revised to reflect leasing practices and terminology.

Definitional Cross References:

"Cancellation". Section 2A–103(1)(b).
"Goods". Section 2A–103(1)(h).
"Lease contract". Section 2A–103(1)(l).
"Party". Section 1–201(29).
"Remedy". Section 1–201(34).
"Rights". Section 1–201(36).
"Termination". Section 2A–103(1)(z).

Section 2A–506. Statute of Limitations.

(1) An action for default under a lease contract, including breach of warranty or indemnity, must be commenced within four years after the cause of action accrued. In a lease contract that is not a consumer lease, by the original lease contract the parties may reduce the period of limitation to not less than one year.

(2) A cause of action for default accrues when the act or omission on which the default or breach of warranty is based is or should have been discovered by the aggrieved party, or when the default occurs, whichever is later. A cause

of action for indemnity accrues when the act or omission on which the claim for indemnity is based is or should have been discovered by the indemnified party, whichever is later.

(3) If an action commenced within the time limited by subsection (1) is so terminated as to leave available a remedy by another action for the same default or breach of warranty or indemnity, the other action may be commenced after the expiration of the time limited and within six months after the termination of the first action unless the termination resulted from voluntary discontinuance or from dismissal for failure or neglect to prosecute.

(4) This section does not alter the law on tolling of the statute of limitations nor does it apply to causes of action that have accrued before this Article becomes effective.

OFFICIAL COMMENT

Uniform Statutory Source: Section 2–725.
Changes: Substantially rewritten.

Purposes:

Subsection (1) does not incorporate the limitation found in Section 2–725(1) prohibiting the parties from extending the period of limitation. Breach of warranty and indemnity claims often arise in a lease transaction; with the passage of time such claims often diminish or are eliminated. To encourage the parties to commence litigation under these circumstances makes little sense.

Subsection (2) states two rules for determining when a cause of action accrues. With respect to default, the rule of Section 2–725(2) is not incorporated in favor of a more liberal rule of the later of the date when the default occurs or when the act or omission on which it is based is or should have been discovered. With respect to indemnity, a similarly liberal rule is adopted.

Cross References:

Sections 2–725(1) and 2–725(2).

Definitional Cross References:

"Action". Section 1–201(1).
"Aggrieved party". Section 1–201(2).
"Lease contract". Section 2A–103(1)(l).
"Party". Section 1–201(29).
"Remedy". Section 1–201(34).
"Termination". Section 2A–103(1)(z).

Section 2A–507. Proof of Market Rent: Time and Place.

(1) Damages based on market rent (Section 2A–519 or 2A–528) are determined according to the rent for the use of the goods concerned for a lease term identical to the remaining lease term of the original lease agreement and prevailing at the times specified in sections 2A–519 and 2A–528.

(2) If evidence of rent for the use of the goods concerned for a lease term identical to the remaining lease term of the original lease agreement and

prevailing at the times or places described in this Article is not readily available, the rent prevailing within any reasonable time before or after the time described or at any other place or for a different lease term which in commercial judgment or under usage of trade would serve as a reasonable substitute for the one described may be used, making any proper allowance for the difference, including the cost of transporting the goods to or from the other place.

(3) Evidence of a relevant rent prevailing at a time or place or for a lease term other than the one described in this Article offered by one party is not admissible unless and until he or she has given the other party notice the court finds sufficient to prevent unfair surprise.

(4) If the prevailing rent or value of any goods regularly leased in any established market is in issue, reports in official publications of trade journals or in newspapers or periodicals of general circulation published as the reports of that market are admissible in evidence. The circumstances of the preparation of the report may be shown to affect its weight but not its admissibility.

OFFICIAL COMMENT

Uniform Statutory Source: Sections 2–723 and 2–724.
Changes: Revised to reflect leasing practices and terminology. Section 2A–519 and 2A–528 specify the times as of which market rent is to be determined.

Definitional Cross References:

"Goods". Section 2A–103(1)(h).
"Lease". Section 2A–103(1)(j).
"Lease agreement". Section 2A–103(1)(k).
"Notice". Section 1–201(25).
"Party". Section 1–201(29).
"Reasonable time". Section 1–204(1) and (2).
"Usage of trade". Section 1–205.
"Value". Section 1–201(44).

B. DEFAULT BY LESSOR

Section 2A–508. Lessee's Remedies.

(1) If a lessor fails to deliver the goods in conformity to the lease contract (Section 2A–509) or repudiates the lease contract (Section 2A–402), or a lessee rightfully rejects the goods (Section 2A–509) or justifiably revokes acceptance of the goods (Section 2A–517), then with respect to any goods involved, and with respect to all of the goods if under an installment lease contract the value of the whole lease contract is substantially impaired (Section 2A–510), the lessor is in default under the lease contract and the lessee may:

(a) cancel the lease contract (Section 2A–505 (1));

(b) recover so much of the rent and security as has been paid and is just under the circumstances;

(c) cover and recover damages as to all goods affected whether or not they have been identified to the lease contract (Sections 2A–518 and 2A–520), or recover damages for nondelivery (Sections 2A–519 and 2A–520);

(d) exercise any other rights or pursue any other remedies provided in the lease contract.

(2) If a lessor fails to deliver the goods in conformity to the lease contract or repudiates the lease contract, the lessee may also:

(a) if the goods have been identified, recover them (Section 2A–522); or

(b) in a proper case, obtain specific performance or replevy the goods (Section 2A–521).

(3) If a lessor is otherwise in default under a lease contract, the lessee may exercise the rights and pursue the remedies provided in the lease contract, which may include a right to cancel the lease, and in Section 2A–519(3).

(4) If a lessor has breached a warranty, whether express or implied, the lessee may recover damages (Section 2A–519(4)).

(5) On rightful rejection or justifiable revocation of acceptance, a lessee has a security interest in goods in the lessee's possession or control for any rent and security interest that has been paid and any expenses reasonably incurred in their inspection, receipt, transportation, and care and custody and may hold those goods and dispose of them in good faith and in a commercially reasonable manner, subject to Section 2A–527(5).

(6) Subject to the provisions of Section 2A–407, a lessee, on notifying the lessor of the lessee's intention to do so, may deduct all or any part of the damages resulting from any default under the lease contract from any part of the rent still due under the same lease contract.

OFFICIAL COMMENT

Uniform Statutory Source: Sections 2–711 and 2–717.
Changes: Substantially rewritten.

Purposes:

1. This section is an index to Sections 2A–509 through 522 which set out the lessee's rights and remedies after the lessor's default. The lessor and the lessee can agree to modify the rights and remedies available under this Article; they can, among other things, provide that for defaults other than those specified in subsection (1) the lessee can exercise the rights and remedies referred to in subsection (1); and they can create a new scheme of rights and remedies triggered by the occurrence of the default. Sections 2A–103(4) and 1–102(3).

2. Subsection (1), a substantially rewritten version of the provisions of Section 2–711(1), lists three cumulative remedies of the lessee where the lessor has failed to deliver c conforming goods or has repudiated the contract, or the lessee has rightfully rejected or justifiably revoked. Sections 2A–501(2) and (4). Subsection (1) also allows the lessee to exercise any contractual remedy. This Article rejects any general doctrine of election of remedy. To determine if one remedy bars another in a particular case

is a function of whether the lessee has been put in as good a position as if the lessor had fully performed the lease agreement. Use of multiple remedies is barred only if the effect is to put the lessee in a better position that it would have been in had the lessor fully performed under the lease. Sections 2A–103(4), 2A–501(4), and 1–106(1). Subsection (1)(b), in recognition that no bright line can be created that would operate fairly in all installment lease cases and in recognition of the fact that a lessee may be able to cancel the lease (revoke acceptance of the goods) after the goods have been in use for some period of time, does not require that all lease payments made by the lessee under the lease be returned upon cancellation. Rather, only such portion as is just of the rent and security payments made may be recovered. If a defect in the goods is discovered immediately upon tender to the lessee and the goods are rejected immediately, then the lessee should recover all payments made. If, however, for example, a 36-month equipment lease is terminated in the 12th month because the lessor has materially breached the contract by failing to perform its maintenance obligations, it may be just to return only a small part or none of the rental payments already made.

3. Subsection (2), a version of the provisions of Section 2–711(2) revised to reflect leasing terminology, lists two alternative remedies for the recovery of the goods by the lessee; however, each of these remedies is cumulative with respect to those listed in subsection (1).

4. Subsection (3) is new. It covers defaults which do not deprive the lessee of the goods and which are not so serious as to justify rejection or revocation of acceptance under subsection (1). It also covers defaults for which the lessee could have rejected or revoked acceptance of the goods but elects not to do so and retains the goods. In either case, a lessee which retains the goods is entitled to recover damages as stated in Section 2A–519(3). That measures of damages is "the loss resulting in the ordinary course of events from the lessor's default as determined in any manner that is reasonable together with incidental and consequential damages, less expenses saved in consequence of the lessor's breach."

5. Subsection (1)(d) and subsection (3) recognize that the lease agreement may provide rights and remedies in addition to or different from those which Article 2A provides. In particular, subsection (3) provides that the lease agreement may give the remedy of cancellation of the lease for defaults by the lessor that would not otherwise be material defaults which would justify cancellation under subsection (1). If there is a right to cancel, there is, of course, a right to reject or revoke acceptance of the goods.

6. Subsection (4) is new and merely adds to the completeness of the index by including a reference to the lessee's recovery of damages upon the lessor's breach of warranty; such breach may not rise to the level of a default by the lessor justifying revocation of acceptance. If the lessee properly rejects or revokes acceptance of the goods because of a breach of warranty, the rights and remedies are those provided in subsection (1) rather than those in Section 2A-519(4).

7. Subsection (5), a revised version of the provisions of Section 2–711(3), recognizes, on rightful rejection or justifiable revocation, the lessee's security interest in goods in its possession and control. Section 9–113, which recognized security interest arising under the Article on Sales (Article 2), was amended with the adoption of this Article to reflect the security interests arising under this Article. Pursuant to Section 2A–511(4), a purchaser who purchases goods from the lessee in good faith takes free of any rights of the lessor, or in the case of a finance lease the supplier. Such goods, however, must have been rightfully rejected and disposed of pursuant to Section 2A–511 or 2A–512. However, Section 2A–517(5) provides that the lessee will have the same rights and duties with respect to goods where acceptance has been revoked as with respect to goods rejected. Thus, Section 2A–511(4) will apply to the lessee's disposition of such goods.

8. Pursuant to Section 2A–527(5), the lessee must account to the lessor for the excess proceeds of such disposition, after satisfaction of the claim secured by the lessee's security interest.

9. Subsection (6), a slightly revised version of the provisions of Section 2–717, sanctions a right of set–off by the lessee, subject to the rule of Section 2A–407 with respect to the irrevocable promises in a finance lease that is not a consumer lease, and further subject to an enforceable "hell or high water" clause in the lease agreement. Section 2A–407 official comment. No attempt is made to state how the set–off should occur; this is to be determined by the facts of each case.

10. There is no special treatment of the finance lease in this section. Absent supplemental principles of law and equity to the contrary, in the case of most finance leases, following the lessee's acceptance of the goods the lessee will have no rights or remedies against the lessor, because the lessor's obligations to the lessee are minimal. Sections 2A–210 and 2A–211(1). Since the lessee will look to the supplier for performance, this is appropriate. Section 2A–209.

Cross References:

Sections 1–102(3), 1–103, 1–106(1), Article 2, especially Sections 2–711, 2–717 and Sections 2A–103(4), 2A–209, 2A–210, 2A–211(1), 2A–407, 2A–501(2), 2A–501(4), 2A–509 through 2A–522, 2A–511(3), 2A–517(5), 2A–527(5) and Section 9–113.

Definitional Cross References:

"Conforming". Section 2A–103(1)(d).
"Delivery". Section 1–201(14).
"Good faith". Sections 1–201(19) and 2–103(1)(b).
"Goods". Section 2A–103(1)(h).
"Installment lease contract". Section 2A–103(1)(i).
"Lease contract". Section 2A–103(1)(l).
"Lessee". Section 2A–103(1)(n).
"Lessor". Section 2A–103(1)(p).
"Notifies". Section 1–201(26).
"Receipt". Section 2–103(1)(c).
"Remedy". Section 1–201(34).
"Rights". Section 1–201(36).
"Security interest". Section 1–201(37).
"Value". Section 1–201(44).

Section 2A–509. Lessee's Rights on Improper Delivery: Rightful Rejection.

(1) Subject to the provisions of Section 2A–510 on default in installment lease contracts, if the goods or the tender or delivery fail in any respect to conform to the lease contract, the lessee may reject or accept the goods or accept any commercial unit or units and reject the rest of the goods.

(2) Rejection of goods is ineffective unless it is within a reasonable time after tender or delivery of the goods and the lessee seasonably notifies the lessor.

OFFICIAL COMMENT

Uniform Statutory Source: Sections 2–601 and 2–602(1).

Changes: Revised to reflect leasing practices and terminology.

Definitional Cross References:

"Commercial unit". Section 2A–103(1)(c).
"Conforming". Section 2A–103(1)(d).
"Delivery". Section 1–201(14).
"Goods". Section 2A–103(1)(h).
"Installment lease contract". Section 2A–103(1)(i).
"Lease contract". Section 2A–103(1)(l).
"Lessee". Section 2A–103(1)(n).
"Lessor". Section 2A–103(1)(p).
"Notifies". Section 1–201(26).
"Reasonable time". Section 1–204(1) and (2).
"Rights". Section 1–201(36).
"Seasonably". Section 1–204(3).

Section 2A–510. Installment Lease Contracts: Rejection and Default.

(1) Under an installment lease contract a lessee may reject any delivery that is nonconforming if the nonconformity substantially impairs the value of that delivery and cannot be cured or the nonconformity is a defect in the required documents; but if the nonconformity does not fall within subsection (2) and the lessor or the supplier gives adequate assurance of its cure, the lessee must accept that delivery.

(2) Whenever nonconformity or default with respect to one or more deliveries substantially impairs the value of the installment lease contract as a whole there is a default with respect to the whole. But, the aggrieved party reinstates the installment lease contract as a whole if the aggrieved party accepts a nonconforming delivery without seasonably notifying of cancellation or brings an action with respect only to past deliveries or demands performance as to future deliveries.

OFFICIAL COMMENT

Uniform Statutory Source: Section 2–612.
Changes: Revised to reflect leasing practices and terminology.

Definitional Cross References:

"Action". Section 1–201(1).
"Aggrieved party". Section 1–201(2).
"Cancellation". Section 2A–103(1)(b).
"Conforming". Section 2A–103(1)(d).
"Delivery". Section 1–201(14).
"Installment lease contract". Section 2A–103(1)(i).
"Lessee". Section 2A–103(1)(n).
"Lessor". Section 2A–103(1)(p).
"Notifies". Section 1–201(26).
"Seasonably". Section 1–204(3).
"Supplier". Section 2A–103(1)(x).
"Value". Section 1–201(44).

Section 2A–511. Merchant Lessee's Duties as to Rightfully Rejected Goods.

(1) Subject to any security interest of a lessee (Section 2A–508(5)), if a lessor or a supplier has no agent or place of business at the market of rejection, a merchant lessee, after rejection of goods in his or her possession or control, shall follow any reasonable instructions received from the lessor or the supplier with respect to the goods. In the absence of those instructions, a merchant lessee shall make reasonable efforts to sell, lease, or otherwise dispose of the goods for the lessor's account if they threaten to decline in value speedily. Instructions are not reasonable if on demand indemnity for expenses is not forthcoming.

(2) If a merchant lessee (subsection (1)) or any other lessee (Section 2A–512) disposes of goods, he or she is entitled to reimbursement either from the lessor or the supplier or out of the proceeds for reasonable expenses of caring for and disposing of the goods and, if the expenses include no disposition commission, to such commission as is usual in the trade, or if there is none, to a reasonable sum not exceeding 10 percent of the gross proceeds.

(3) In complying with this section or Section 2A–512, the lessee is held only to good faith. Good faith conduct hereunder is neither acceptance or conversion nor the basis of an action for damages.

(4) A purchaser who purchases in good faith from a lessee pursuant to this section or Section 2A–512 takes the goods free of any rights of the lessor and the supplier even though the lessee fails to comply with one or more of the requirements of this Article.

OFFICIAL COMMENT

Uniform Statutory Source: Sections 2-603 and 2-706(5).

Changes: Revised to reflect leasing practices and terminology. This section, by its terms, applies to merchants as well as others. Thus, in construing the section it is important to note that under this Act the term good faith is defined differently for merchants (Section 2–103(1)(b)) than for others (Section 1–201(19)). Section 2A–103(3) and (4).

Definitional Cross References:

"Action". Section 1–201(1).
"Good faith". Sections 1–201(19) and 2–103(1)(b).
"Goods". Section 2A–103(1)(h).
"Lease". Section 2A–103(1)(j).
"Lessee". Section 2A–103(1)(n).
"Lessor". Section 2A–103(1)(p).
"Merchant lessee". Section 2A–103(1)(t).
"Purchaser". Section 1–201(33).
"Rights". Section 1–201(36).
"Security interest". Section 1–201(37).
"Supplier". Section 2A–103(1)(x).
"Value". Section 1–201(44).

Section 2A–512. Lessee's Duties as to Rightfully Rejected Goods.

(1) Except as otherwise provided with respect to goods that threaten to decline in value speedily (Section 2A–511) and subject to any security interest of a lessee (Section 2A–508(5)):

(a) the lessee, after rejection of goods in the lessee's possession, shall hold them with reasonable care at the lessor's or the supplier's disposition for a reasonable time after the lessee's seasonable notification of rejection;

(b) if the lessor or the supplier gives no instructions within a reasonable time after notification of rejection, the lessee may store the rejected goods for the lessor's or the supplier's account or ship them to the lessor or the supplier or dispose of them for the lessor's or the supplier's account with reimbursement in the manner provided in Section 2A–511; but

(c) the lessee has no further obligations with regard to goods rightfully rejected.

(2) Action by the lessee pursuant to subsection (1) is not acceptance or conversion.

OFFICIAL COMMENT

Uniform Statutory Source: Sections 2–602(2)(b) and (c) and 2–604.
Changes: Substantially rewritten.

Purposes:

The introduction to subsection (1) references goods that threaten to decline in value speedily and not perishables, the reference in Section 2–604, the statutory analogue. This is a change in style, not substance, as the first phrase includes the second. Subparagraphs (a) and (c) are revised versions of the provisions of Section 2–602(2)(b) and (c). Subparagraph (a) states the rule with respect to the lessee's treatment of goods in its possession following rejection; subparagraph (b) states the rule regarding such goods if the lessor or supplier then fails to give instructions to the lessee. If the lessee performs in a fashion consistent with subparagraphs (a) and (b), subparagraph (c) exonerates the lessee.

Cross References:

Sections 2–602(2)(b), 2–602(2)(c) and 2–604.

Definitional Cross References:

"Action". Section 1–201(1).
"Goods". Section 2A–103(1)(h).
"Lessee". Section 2A–103(1)(n).
"Lessor". Section 2A–103(1)(p).
"Notification". Section 1–201(26).
"Reasonable time". Section 1–204(1) and (2).
"Seasonably". Section 1–204(3).
"Security interest". Section 1–201(37).
"Supplier". Section 2A–103(1)(x).
"Value". Section 1–201(44).

Section 2A–513. Cure by Lessor of Improper Tender or Delivery; Replacement.

(1) If any tender or delivery by the lessor or the supplier is rejected because nonconforming and the time for performance has not yet expired, the lessor or the supplier may seasonably notify the lessee of the lessor's or the supplier's intention to cure and may then make a conforming delivery within the time provided in the lease contract.

(2) If the lessee rejects a nonconforming tender that the lessor or the supplier had reasonable grounds to believe would be acceptable with or without money allowance, the lessor or the supplier may have a further reasonable time to substitute a conforming tender if he or she seasonably notifies the lessee.

OFFICIAL COMMENT

Uniform Statutory Source: Section 2–508.

Changes: Revised to reflect leasing practices and terminology.

Definitional Cross References:

"Conforming". Section 2A–103(1)(d).
"Delivery". Section 1–201(14).
"Lease contract". Section 2A–103(1)(l).
"Lessee". Section 2A–103(1)(n).
"Lessor". Section 2A–103(1)(p).
"Money". Section 1–201(24).
"Notifies". Section 1–201(26).
"Reasonable time". Section 1–204(1) and (2).
"Seasonably". Section 1–204(3).
"Supplier". Section 2A–103(1)(x).

Section 2A–514. Waiver of Lessee's Objections.

(1) In rejecting goods, a lessee's failure to state a particular defect that is ascertainable by reasonable inspection precludes the lessee from relying on the defect to justify rejection or to establish default:

(a) if, stated seasonably, the lessor or the supplier could have cured it (Section 2A–513); or

(b) between merchants if the lessor or the supplier after rejection has made a request in writing for a full and final written statement of all defects on which the lessee proposes to rely.

(2) A lessee's failure to reserve rights when paying rent or other consideration against documents precludes recovery of the payment for defects apparent on the face of the documents.

OFFICIAL COMMENT

Uniform Statutory Source: Section 2–605.

Changes: Revised to reflect leasing practices and terminology.

Purposes:

The principles applicable to the commercial practice of payment against documents (subsection 2) are explained in official comment 4 to Section 2–605, the statutory analogue to this section.

Cross Reference:

Section 2–605 official comment 4.

Definitional Cross References:

"Between merchants". Section 2–104(3).
"Goods". Section 2A–103(1)(h).
"Lessee". Section 2A–103(1)(n).
"Lessor". Section 2A–103(1)(p).
"Rights". Section 1–201(36).
"Seasonably". Section 1–204(3).
"Supplier". Section 2A–103(1)(x).
"Writing". Section 1–201(46).

Section 2A–515. Acceptance of Goods.

(1) Acceptance of goods occurs after the lessee has had a reasonable opportunity to inspect the goods and

(a) the lessee signifies or acts with respect to the goods in a manner that signifies to the lessor or the supplier that the goods are conforming or that the lessee will take or retain them in spite of their nonconformity; or

(b) the lessee fails to make an effective rejection of the goods (Section 2A–509 (2)).

(2) Acceptance of a part of any commercial unit is acceptance of that entire unit.

OFFICIAL COMMENT

Uniform Statutory Source. Section 2–606.

Changes: The provisions of Section 2–606(1)(a) were substantially rewritten to provide that the lessee's conduct may signify acceptance. Further, the provisions of Section 2–606(1)(c) were not incorporated as irrelevant given the lessee's possession and use of the leased goods.

Cross References:

Sections 2–606(1)(a) and 2–606(1)(c).

Definitional Cross References:

"Commercial unit". Section 2A–103(1)(c).
"Conforming". Section 2A–103(1)(d).
"Goods". Section 2A–103(1)(h).
"Lessee". Section 2A–103(1)(n).
"Lessor". Section 2A–103(1)(p).

"Supplier". Section 2A–103(1)(x).

Section 2A–516. Effect of Acceptance of Goods; Notice of Default; Burden of Establishing Default After Acceptance; Notice of Claim or Litigation to Person Answerable Over.

(1) A lessee must pay rent for any goods accepted in accordance with the lease contract, with due allowance for goods rightfully rejected or not delivered.

(2) A lessee's acceptance of goods precludes rejection of the goods accepted. In the case of a finance lease, other than a consumer lease in which the supplier assisted in the preparation of the lease contract or participated in negotiating the terms of the lease contract with the lessor, if made with knowledge of a nonconformity, acceptance cannot be revoked because of it. In any other case, if made with knowledge of a nonconformity, acceptance cannot be revoked because of it unless the acceptance was on the reasonable assumption that the nonconformity would be seasonably cured. Acceptance does not of itself impair any other remedy provided by this Article or the lease agreement for nonconformity.

(3) If a tender has been accepted:

(a) within a reasonable time after the lessee discovers or should have discovered any default, the lessee shall notify the lessor and the supplier, if any, or be barred from any remedy against the party not notified;

(b) except in the case of a consumer lease, within a reasonable time after the lessee receives notice of litigation for infringement or the like (Section 2A–211) the lessee shall notify the lessor or be barred from any remedy over for liability established by the litigation; and

(c) the burden is on the lessee to establish any default.

(4) If a lessee is sued for breach of a warranty or other obligation for which a lessor or a supplier is answerable over the following apply:

(a) the lessee may give the lessor or the supplier, or both, written notice of the litigation. If the notice states that the person notified may come in and defend and that if the person notified does not do so that person will be bound in any action against that person by the lessee by any determination of fact common to the two litigations, then unless the person notified after seasonable receipt of the notice does come in and defend that person is so bound; and

(b) the lessor or the supplier may demand in writing that the lessee turn over control of the litigation including settlement if the claim is one for infringement or the like (Section 2A–211) or else be barred from any remedy over. If the demand states that the lessor or the supplier agrees to bear all expense and to satisfy any adverse judgment, then unless the lessee after seasonable receipt of the demand does turn over control the lessee is so barred.

(5) Subsections (3) and (4) apply to any obligation of a lessee to hold the lessor or the supplier harmless against infringement or the like (Section 2A–211).

OFFICIAL COMMENT

Uniform Statutory Source: Section 2-607.
Changes: Substantially revised.

Purposes:

1. Subsection (2) creates a special rule for finance leases, precluding revocation if acceptance is made with knowledge of nonconformity with respect to the lease agreement, as opposed to the supply agreement; this is not inequitable as the lessee has a direct claim against the supplier. Section 2A-209(1). Revocation of acceptance of a finance lease is permitted if the lessee's acceptance was without discovery of the nonconformity (with respect to the lease agreement, not the supply agreement) and was reasonably induced by the lessor's assurances. Section 2A-517(1)(b). Absent exclusion or modification, the lessor under a finance lease makes certain warranties to the lessee. Sections 2A-210 and 2A-211(1). Revocation of acceptance is not prohibited even after the lessee's promise has become irrevocable and independent. Section 2A-407 official comment. Where the finance lease creates a security interest, the rule may be to the contrary. General Elec. Credit Corp. of Tennessee v. Ger-Beck Mach. Co., 806 F.2d 1207 (3rd Cir. 1986).

2. Subsection (3)(a) requires the lessee to give notice of default, within a reasonable time after the lessee discovered or should have discovered the default. In a finance lease, notice may be given either to the supplier, the lessor, or both, but remedy is barred against the party not notified. In a finance lease, the lessor is usually not liable for defects in the goods and the essential notice is to the supplier. While notice to the finance lessor will often not give any additional rights to the lessee, it would be good practice to give the notice since the finance lessor has an interest in the goods. Subsection (3)(a) does not use the term finance lease, but the definition of supplier is a person from whom a lessor buys or leases goods to be leased under a finance lease. Section 2A-103(1)(x). Therefore, there can be a "supplier" only in a finance lease. Subsection (4) applies similar notice rules as to lessors and suppliers if a lessee is sued for a breach of warranty or other obligation for which a lessor or supplier is answerable over.

3. Subsection (3)(b) requires the lessee to give the lessor notice of litigation for infringement or the like. There is an exception created in the case of a consumer lease. While such an exception was considered for a finance lease, it was not created because it was not necessary–the lessor in a finance lease does not give a warranty against infringement. Section 2A-211(2). Even though not required under subsection (3)(b), the lessee who takes under a finance lease should consider giving notice of litigation for infringement or the like to the supplier, because the lessee obtains the benefit of the suppliers' promises subject to the suppliers' defenses or claims. Sections 2A-209(1) and 2-607(3)(b).

Cross References:

Sections 2-607(3)(b), 2A-103(1)(x), 2A-209(1), 2A-210, 2A-211(1), 2A-211(2), 2A-407 official comment and 2A-517(1)(b).

Definitional Cross References:

"Action". Section 1-201(1).
"Agreement". Section 1-201(3).

UCC

"Burden of establishing". Section 1-201(8).
"Conforming". Section 2A-103(1)(d).
"Consumer lease". Section 2A-103(1)(e).
"Delivery". Section 1-201(14).
"Discover". Section 1-201(25).
"Finance lease". Section 2A-103(1)(g).
"Goods". Section 2A-103(1)(h).
"Knowledge". Section 1-201(25).
"Lease agreement". Section 2A-103(1)(k).
"Lease contract". Section 2A-103(1)(l).
"Lessee". Section 2A-103(1)(n).
"Lessor". Section 2A-103(1)(p).
"Notice". Section 1-201(25).
"Notifies". Section 1-201(26).
"Person". Section 1-201(30).
"Reasonable time". Section 1-204(1) and (2).
"Receipt". Section 2-103(1)(c).
"Remedy". Section 1-201(34).
"Seasonably". Section 1-204(3).
"Supplier". Section 2A-103(1)(x).
"Written". Section 1-201(46).

Section 2A–517. Revocation of Acceptance of Goods.

(1) A lessee may revoke acceptance of a lot or commercial unit whose nonconformity substantially impairs its value to the lessee if the lessee has accepted it:

(a) except in the case of a finance lease, on the reasonable assumption that its nonconformity would be cured and it has not been seasonably cured; or

(b) without discovery of the nonconformity if the lessee's acceptance was reasonably induced either by the lessor's assurances or, except in the case of a finance lease, by the difficulty of discovery before acceptance.

(2) Except in the case of a finance lease that is not a consumer lease, a lessee may revoke acceptance of a lot or commercial unit if the lessor defaults under the lease contract and the default substantially impairs the value of that lot or commercial unit to the lessee.

(3) If the lease agreement so provides, the lessee may revoke acceptance of a lot or commercial unit because of other defaults by the lessor.

(4) Revocation of acceptance must occur within a reasonable time after the lessee discovers or should have discovered the ground for it and before any substantial change in condition of the goods which is not caused by the nonconformity. Revocation is not effective until the lessee notifies the lessor.

(5) A lessee who so revokes has the same right and duties with regard to the goods involved as if the lessee had rejected them.

OFFICIAL COMMENT

Uniform Statutory Source: Section 2–608.

Changes: Revised to reflect leasing practices and terminology. Note that in the case of a finance lease the lessee retains a limited right to revoke acceptance. Sections 2A–517(1)(b) and 2A–516 official comment. New subsections (2) and (3) added.

Purposes:

1. The section states the situations under-which the lessee may retain the goods to the lessor and cancel the lease. Subsection (2) recognizes that the lessor may have continuing obligations under the lease and that a default as to those obligations may be sufficiently material to justify revocation of acceptance of the leased items and cancellation of the lease by the lessee. For example, a failure by the lessor to fulfill its obligation to maintain leased equipment or to supply other goods which are necessary for the operation of the leased equipment may justify revocation of acceptance and cancellation of the lease.

2. Subsection (3) specifically provides that the lease agreement may provide that the lessee can revoke acceptance for defaults by the lessor which in the absence of such an agreement might not be considered sufficiently serious to justify revocation. That is, the parties are free to contract on the question of what defaults are so material that the lessee can cancel the lease.

Cross References:

Section 2A–516 official comment.

Definitional Cross References:

"Commercial unit". Section 2A–103(1)(c).
"Conforming". Section 2A–103(1)(d).
"Discover". Section 1–201(25).
"Finance lease". Section 2A–103(1)(g).
"Goods". Section 2A–103(1)(h).
"Lessee". Section 2A–103(1)(n).
"Lessor". Section 2A–103(1)(p).
"Lot". Section 2A–103(1)(s).
"Notifies". Section 1–201(26).
"Reasonable time". Section 1–204(1) and (2).
"Rights". Section 1–201(36).
"Seasonably". Section 1–204(3).
"Value". Section 1–201(44).

Section 2A–518. Cover; Substitute Goods.

(1) After a default by a lessor under the lease contract of the type described in Section 2A–508(1) or, if agreed, after other default by the lessor, the lessee may cover by making any purchase or lease of or contract to purchase or lease goods in substitution for those due from the lessor.

(2) Except as otherwise provided with respect to damages liquidated in the lease agreement (Section 2A–504) or otherwise determined pursuant to agreement of the parties (Sections 1-102(3) and 2A–503), if a lessee's cover is by a lease agreement substantially similar to the original lease agreement and the new lease agreement is made in good faith and in a commercially reasonable manner, the lessee may recover from the lessor as damages (a) the present value, as of the date of the commencement of the term of the new lease agreement,

UCC

of the rent under the new lease agreement applicable to that period of the new lease term which is comparable to the then remaining term of the original lease agreement minus the present value as of the same date of the total rent for the then remaining lease term of the original lease agreement, and (b) any incidental or consequential damages, less expenses saved in consequence of the lessor's default.

(3) If the lessee's cover is by lease agreement that qualifies for treatment under subsection (2), the lessee may elect to proceed under subsection (2) or Section 2A–519. If a lessee's cover is by lease agreement that for any reason does not qualify for treatment under subsection (2), or is by purchase or otherwise, the lessee may recover from the lessor as if the lessee had elected not to cover.

OFFICIAL COMMENT

Uniform Statutory Source: Section 2-712.
Changes: Substantially revised.

Purposes:

1. Subsection (1) allows the lessee to take action to fix its damages after default by the lessor. Such action may consist of the lease of goods. The decision to cover is a function of commercial judgment, not a statutory mandate replete with sanctions for failure to comply. *Cf.* Section 9-507.

2. Subsection (2) states a rule for determining the amount of lessee's damages provided that there is no agreement to the contrary. The lessee's damages will be established using the new lease agreement as a measure if the following three criteria are met: (i) the lessee's cover is by lease agreement, (ii) the lease agreement is substantially similar to the original lease agreement, and (iii) such cover was effected in good faith, and in a commercially reasonable manner. Thus, the lessee will be entitled to recover from the lessor the present value, as of the date of commencement of the term of the new lease agreement, of the rent under the new lease agreement applicable to that period which is comparable to the then remaining term of the original lease agreement less the present value of the rent reserved for the remaining term under the original lease, together with incidental or consequential damages less expenses saved in consequence of the lessor's default. Consequential damages may include loss suffered by the lessee because of deprivation of the use of the goods during the period between the default and the acquisition of the goods under the new lease agreement. If the lessee's cover does not satisfy the criteria of subsection (2), Section 2A-519 governs.

3. Two of the three criteria to be met by the lessee are familiar, but the concept of the new lease agreement being substantially similar to the original lease agreement is not. Given the many variables facing a party who intends to lease goods and the rapidity of change in the market place, the policy decision was made not to draft with specificity. It was thought unwise to seek to establish certainty at the cost of fairness. Thus, the decision of whether the new lease agreement is substantially similar to the original will be determined case by case.

4. While the section does not draw a bright line, it is possible to describe some of the factors that should be considered in finding that a new lease agreement is substantially similar to the original. First, the goods subject to the new lease agreement should be examined. For example, in a lease of computer equipment the new lease might be for more modern equipment. However, it may be that at the time of the

lessor's breach it was not possible to obtain the same type of goods in the market place. Because the lessee's remedy under Section 2A-519 is intended to place the lessee in essentially the same position as if he had covered, if goods similar to those to have been delivered under the original lease are not available, then the computer equipment in this hypothetical should qualify as a commercially reasonable substitute. *See* Section 2-712(1).

5. Second, the various elements of the new lease agreement should also be examined. Those elements include the presence or absence of options to purchase or release; the lessor's representations, warranties and covenants to the lessee, as well as those to be provided by the lessee to the lessor; and the services, if any, to be provided by the lessor or by the lessee. All of these factors allocate cost and risk between the lessor and the lessee and thus affect the amount of rent to be paid. If the differences between the original lease and the new lease can be easily valued, it would be appropriate for a court to adjust the difference in rental to take account of the difference between the two leases, find that the new lease is substantially similar to the old lease, and award cover damages under this section. If, for example, the new lease requires the lessor to insure the goods in the hands of the lessee, while the original lease required the lessee to insure, the usual cost of such insurance could be deducted from the rent due under the new lease before determining the difference in rental between the two leases.

6. Having examined the goods and the agreement, the test to be applied is whether, in light of these comparisons, the new lease agreement is substantially similar to the original lease agreement. These findings should not be made with scientific precision, as they are a function of economics, nor should they be made independently with respect to the goods and each element of the agreement, as it is important that a sense of commercial judgment pervade the finding. To establish the new lease as a proper measure of damage under subsection (2), these factors, taken as a whole, must result in a finding that the new lease agreement is substantially similar to the original.

7. A new lease can be substantially similar to the original lease even though its term extends beyond the remaining term of the original lease, so long as both (a) the lease terms are commercially comparable (e.g., it is highly unlikely that a one-month rental and a five-year lease would reflect similar commercial realities), and (b) the court can fairly apportion a part of the rental payments under the new lease to that part of the term of the new lease which is comparable to the remaining lease term under the original lease. Also, the lease term of the new lease may be comparable to the term of the original lease even though the beginning and ending dates of the two leases are not the same. For example, a two-month lease of agricultural equipment for the months of August and September may be comparable to a two-month lease running from the 15th of August to the 15th of October if in the particular location two-month leases beginning on August 15th are basically interchangeable with two-month leases beginning August 1st. Similarly, the term of a one-year truck lease beginning on the 15th of January may be comparable to the term of a one-year truck lease beginning January 2d. If the lease terms are found to be comparable, the court may base cover damages on the entire difference between the costs under the two leases.

Cross References:

Sections 2-712(1), 2A-519 and 9-507.

Definitional Cross References:

"Agreement". Section 1-201(3).
"Contract". Section 1-201(11).
"Good faith". Sections 1-201(19) and 2-103(1)(b).

UCC

"Goods". Section 2A-103(1)(h).
"Lease". Section 2-103(1)(j).
"Lease agreement". Section 2A-103(1)(k).
"Lease contract". Section 2A-103(1)(l).
"Lessee". Section 2A-103(1)(n).
"Lessor". Section 2A-103(1)(p).
"Party". Section 1-201(29).
"Present value". Section 2A-103(1)(u).
"Purchase". Section 2A-103(1)(v).

Section 2A–519. Lessee's Damages for Nondelivery, Repudiation, Default, and Breach of Warranty in Regard to Accepted Goods.

(1) Except as otherwise provided with respect to damages liquidated in the lease agreement (Section 2A–504) or otherwise determined pursuant to agreement of the parties (Section 1-102(3) and 2A–503), if a lessee elects not to cover or a lessee elects to cover and the cover is by lease agreement, whether or not the lease agreement qualifies for treatment under Section 2A–518(2), or is by purchase or otherwise, the measure of damages for non-delivery or repudiation by the lessor or for rejection or revocation of acceptance by the lessee is the present value, as of the date of the default, of the then market rent minus the present value as of the same date of the original rent, computed for the remaining lease term of the original lease agreement, together with incidental and consequential damages, less expenses saved in consequence of the lessor's default.

(2) Market rent is to be determined as of the place for tender or, in cases of rejection after arrival or revocation of acceptance, as of the place of arrival.

(3) Except as otherwise agreed, if the lessee has accepted goods and given notification (Section 2A–516(3)), the measure of damages for nonconforming tender or delivery or other default by a lessor is the loss resulting in the ordinary course of events from the lessor's default as determined in any manner that is reasonable together with incidental and consequential damages, less expenses saved in consequence of the lessor's default.

(4) Except as otherwise agreed, the measure of damages for breach of warranty is the present value at the time and place of acceptance of the difference between the value of the use of the goods accepted and the value if they had been as warranted for the lease term, unless special circumstances show proximate damages of a different amount, together with incidental and consequential damages, less expenses saved in consequence of the lessor's default or breach of warranty.

OFFICIAL COMMENT

Uniform Statutory Source: Sections 2–713 and 2–714.
Changes: Substantially revised.

Purposes:

1. Subsection (1), a revised version of the provisions of Section 2–713(1), states the basic rule governing the measure of lessee's damages for non-delivery or repudiation by the lessor or for rightful rejection or revocation of acceptance by the lessee. This measure will apply, absent agreement to the contrary, if the lessee does not cover or if the cover does not qualify under Section 2A–518. There is no sanction for cover that does not qualify.

2. The measure of damage is the present value, as of the date of default, of the market rent for the remaining term of the lease less the present value of the original rent for the remaining term of the lease, plus incidental and consequential damages less expenses saved in consequence of the default. Note that the reference in Section 2A–519(1) is to the date of default not to the date of an event of default. An event of default under a lease agreement becomes a default under a lease agreement only after the expiration of any relevant period of grace and compliance with any notice requirements under this Article and the lease agreement. American Bar Foundation, *Commentaries on Indentures*, § 5–1, at 216–217 (1971). Section 2A–501(1). This conclusion is also a function of whether, as a matter of fact or law, the event of default has been waived, suspended or cured. Sections 2A–103(4) and 1–103.

3. Subsection (2), a revised version of the provisions of Section 2–713(2), states the rule with respect to determining market rent.

4. Subsection (3), a revised version of the provisions of Section 2–714(1) and (3), states the measure of damages where goods have been accepted and acceptance is not revoked. The subsection applies both to defaults which occur at the inception of the lease and to defaults which occur subsequently, such as failure to comply with an obligation to maintain the leased goods. The measure in essence is the loss, in the ordinary course of events, flowing from the default.

5. Subsection (4), a revised version of the provisions of Section 2–714(2), states the measure of damages for breach of warranty. The measure in essence is the present value of the difference between the value of the .goods accepted and of the goods if they had been as warranted.

6. Subsections (1), (3) and (4) specifically state that the parties may by contract vary the damages rules stated in those subsections.

Cross References:

Sections 2–713(1), 2–713(2), 2–714 and Section 2A–518.

Definitional Cross References:

"Conformity". Section 2A–103(1)(d).
"Delivery". Section 1–201(14).
"Goods". Section 2A–103(1)(h).
"Lease". Section 2A–103(1)(j).
"Lease agreement". Section 2A–103(1)(k).
"Lessee". Section 2A–103(1)(n).
"Lessor". Section 2A–103(1)(p).
"Notification". Section 1–201(26).
"Present value". Section 2A–103(1)(u).
"Value". Section 1–201(44).

Section 2A–520. Lessee's Incidental and Consequential Damages.

(1) Incidental damages resulting from a lessor's default include expenses reasonably incurred in inspection, receipt, transportation, and care and custody

of goods rightfully rejected or goods the acceptance of which is justifiably revoked, any commercially reasonable charges, expenses or commissions in connection with effecting cover, and any other reasonable expense incident to the default.

(2) Consequential damages resulting from a lessor's default include:

(a) any loss resulting from general or particular requirements and needs of which the lessor at the time of contracting had reason to know and which could not reasonably be prevented by cover or otherwise; and

(b) injury to person or property proximately resulting from any breach of warranty.

OFFICIAL COMMENT

Uniform Statutory Source: Section 2–715.

Changes: Revised to reflect leasing terminology and practices.

Purposes:

Subsection (1), a revised version of the provisions of Section 2–715(1), lists some examples of incidental damages resulting from a lessor's default; the list is not exhaustive. Subsection (1) makes clear that it applies not only to rightful rejection, but also to justifiable revocation.

Subsection (2), a revised version of the provisions of Section 2–715(2), lists some examples of consequential damages resulting from a lessor's default; the list is not exhaustive.

Cross Reference:

Section 2–715.

Definitional Cross References:

"Goods". Section 2A–103(1)(h).
"Knows". Section 1–201(25).
"Lessee". Section 2A–103(1)(n).
"Lessor". Section 2A–103(1)(p).
"Person". Section 1–201(30).
"Receipt". Section 2–103(1)(c).

Section 2A–521. Lessee's Right to Specific Performance or Replevin.

(1) Specific performance may be decreed if the goods are unique or in other proper circumstances.

(2) A decree for specific performance may include any terms and conditions as to payment of the rent, damages, or other relief that the court deems just.

(3) A lessee has a right of replevin, detinue, sequestration, claim and delivery, or the like for goods identified to the lease contract if after reasonable effort the lessee is unable to effect cover for those goods or the circumstances reasonably indicate that the effort will be unavailing.

OFFICIAL COMMENT

Uniform Statutory Source: Section 2–716.

Changes: Revised to reflect leasing practices and terminology, and to expand the reference to the right of replevin in subsection (3) to include other similar rights of the lessee.

Definitional Cross References:

"Delivery". Section 1–201(14).
"Goods". Section 2A–103(1)(h).
"Lease contract". Section 2A–103(1)(l).
"Lessee". Section 2A–103(1)(n).
"Rights". Section 1–201(36).
"Term". Section 1–201(42).

Section 2A–522. Lessee's Right to Goods on Lessor's Insolvency.

(1) Subject to subsection (2) and even though the goods have not been shipped, a lessee who has paid a part or all of the rent and security for goods identified to a lease contract (Section 2A–217) on making and keeping good a tender of any unpaid portion of the rent and security due under the lease contract may recover the goods identified from the lessor if the lessor becomes insolvent within ten days after receipt of the first installment of rent and security.

(2) A lessee acquires the right to recover goods identified to a lease contract only if they conform to the lease contract.

OFFICIAL COMMENT

Uniform Statutory Source: Section 2–502.

Changes: Revised to reflect leasing practices and terminology.

Definitional Cross References:

"Conforming". Section 2A–103(1)(d).
"Goods". Section 2A–103(1)(h).
"Insolvent". Section 1–201(23).
"Lease contract". Section 2A–103(1)(l).
"Lessee". Section 2A–103(1)(n).
"Lessor". Section 2A–103(1)(p).
"Receipt". Section 2–103(1)(c).
"Rights". Section 1–201(36).

C. DEFAULT BY LESSEE

Section 2A–523. Lessor's Remedies.

(1) If a lessee wrongfully rejects or revokes acceptance of goods or fails to make a payment when due or repudiates with respect to a part or the whole, then, with respect to any goods involved, and with respect to all of the goods if under an installment lease contract the value of the whole lease contract is substantially impaired (Section 2A–510), the lessee is in default under the lease contract and the lessor may:

(a) cancel the lease contract (Section 2A–505 (1));

(b) proceed respecting goods not identified to the lease contract (Section 2A–524);

(c) withhold delivery of the goods and take possession of goods previously delivered (Section 2A–525);

(d) stop delivery of the goods by any bailee (Section 2A–526);

(e) dispose of the goods and recover damages (Section 2A–527), or retain the goods and recover damages (Section 2A–528), or in a proper case recover rent (Section 2A–529);

(f) exercise any other rights or pursue any other remedies provided in the lease contract.

(2) If a lessor does not fully exercise a right or obtain a remedy to which the lessor is entitled under subsection (1), the lessor may recover the loss resulting in the ordinary course of events from the lessee's default as determined in any reasonable manner, together with incidental damages, less expenses saved in consequence of the lessee's default.

(3) If a lessee is otherwise in default under a lease contract, the lessor may exercise the rights and pursue the remedies provided in the lease contract, which may include a right to cancel the lease. In addition, unless otherwise provided in the lease contract:

(a) if the default substantially impairs the value of the lease contract to the lessor, the lessor may exercise the rights and pursue the remedies provided under subsection (1) or (2); or

(b) if the default does not substantially impair the value of the lease contract to the lessor, the lessor may recover as provided in subsection (2).

OFFICIAL COMMENT

Uniform Statutory Source: Section 2-703.
Changes: Substantially revised.

Purposes:

1. Subsection (1) is an index to Sections 2A-524 through 2A-531 and states that the remedies provided in those sections are available for the defaults referred to in subsection (1): wrongful rejection or revocation of acceptance, failure to make a payment when due, or repudiation. In addition, remedies provided in the lease contract are available. Subsection (2) sets out a remedy if the lessor does not pursue to completion a right or actually obtain a remedy available under subsection (1), and subsection (3) sets out statutory remedies for defaults not specifically referred to in subsection (1). Subsection (3) provides that, if any default by the lessee other than those specifically referred to in subsection (1) is material, the lessor can exercise the remedies provided in subsection (1) or (2); otherwise the available remedy is as provided in subsection (3). A lessor who has brought an action seeking or has nonjudicially pursued one or more of the remedies available under subsection (1) may amend so as to claim or may nonjudicially pursue a remedy under subsection

(2) unless the right or remedy first chosen has been pursued to an extent actually inconsistent with the new course of action. The intent of the provision is to reject the doctrine of election of remedies and to permit an alteration of course by the lessor unless such alteration would actually have an effect on the lessee that would be unreasonable under the circumstances. Further, the lessor may pursue remedies under both subsections (1) and (2) unless doing so would put the lessor in a better position than it would have been in had the lessee fully performed.

2. The lessor and the lessee can agree to modify the rights and remedies available under the Article; they can, among other things, provide that for defaults other than those specified in subsection (1) the lessor can exercise the rights and remedies referred to in subsection (1), whether or not the default would otherwise be held to substantially impair the value of the lease contract to the lessor; they can also create a new scheme of rights and remedies triggered by the occurrence of the default. Sections 2A-103(4) and 1-102(3).

3. Subsection (1), a substantially rewritten version of Section 2-703, lists various cumulative remedies of the lessor where the lessee wrongfully rejects or revokes acceptance, fails to make a payment when due, or repudiates. Section 2A-501(2) and (4). The subsection also allows the lessor to exercise any contractual remedy.

4. This Article rejects any general doctrine of election of remedy. Whether, in a particular case, one remedy bars another, is a function of whether lessor has been put in as good a position as if the lessee had fully performed the lease contract. Multiple remedies are barred only if the effect is to put the lessor in a better position than it would have been in had the lessee fully performed under the lease. Sections 2A-103(4), 2A-501(4), and 1-106(1).

5. Hypothetical: To better understand the application of subparagraphs (a) through (e), it is useful to review a hypothetical. Assume that A is a merchant in the business of selling and leasing new bicycles of various types. B is about to engage in the business of subleasing bicycles to summer residents of and visitors to an island resort. A, as lessor, has agreed to lease 60 bicycles to B. While there is one master lease, deliveries and terms are staggered. 20 bicycles are to be delivered by A to B's island location on June 1; the term of the lease of these bicycles is four months. 20 bicycles are to be delivered by A to B's island location on July 1; the term of the lease of these bicycles is three months. Finally, 20 bicycles are to be delivered by A to B's island location on August 1; the term of the lease of these bicycles is two months. B is obligated to pay rent to A on the 15th day of each month during the term for the lease. Rent is $50 per month, per bicycle. B has no option to purchase or release and must return the bicycles to A at the end of the term, in good condition, reasonable wear and tear excepted. Since the retail price of each bicycle is $400 and bicycles used in the retail rental business have a useful economic life of 36 months, this transaction creates a lease. Sections 2A-103(1)(j) and 1-201(37).

6. A's current inventory of bicycles is not large. Thus, upon signing the lease with B in February, A agreed to purchase 60 new bicycles from A's principal manufacturer, with special instructions to drop ship the bicycles to B's island location in accordance with the delivery schedule set forth in the lease.

7. The first shipment of 20 bicycles was received by B on May 21. B inspected the bicycles, accepted the same as conforming to the lease and signed a receipt of delivery and acceptance. However, due to poor weather that summer, business was terrible and B was unable to pay the rent due on June 15. Pursuant to the lease A sent B notice of default and proceeded to enforce his rights and remedies against B.

8. A's counsel first advised A that under Section 2A-510(2) and the terms of the lease B's failure to pay was a default with respect to the whole. Thus, to minimize A's continued exposure, A was advised to take possession of the bicycles. If A had possession of the goods A could refuse to deliver. Section 2A-525(1). However, the

UCC

facts here are different. With respect to the bicycles in B's possession, A has the right to take possession of the bicycles, without breach of the peace. Section 22A-525(2). If B refuses to allow A access to the bicycles, A can proceed by action, including replevin or injunctive relief.

9. With respect to the 40 bicycles that have not been delivered, this Article provides various alternatives. First, assume that 20 of the remaining 40 bicycles have been manufactured and delivered by the manufacturer to a carrier for shipment to B. Given the size of the shipment, the carrier was using a small truck for the delivery and the truck had not yet reached the island ferry when the manufacturer (at the request of A) instructed the carrier to divert the shipment to A's place of business. A's right to stop delivery is recognized under these circumstances. Section 2A-526(1). Second, assume that the 20 remaining bicycles were in the process of manufacture when B defaulted. A retains the right (as between A as lessor and B as lessee) to exercise reasonable commercial judgment whether to complete manufacture or to dispose of the unfinished goods for scrap. Since A is not the manufacturer and A has a binding contract to buy the bicycles, A elected to allow the manufacturer to complete the manufacture of the bicycles, but instructed the manufacturer to deliver the completed bicycles to A's place of business. Section 2A-524(2).

10. Thus, so far A has elected to exercise the remedies referred to in subparagraphs (b) through (d) in subsection (1). None of these remedies bars any of the others because A's election and enforcement merely resulted in A's possession of the bicycles. Had B performed A would have recovered possession of the bicycles. Thus A is in the process of obtaining the benefit of his bargain. Note that A could exercise any other rights or pursue any other remedies provided in the lease contract (Section 2A-523(1)(f)), or elect to recover his loss due to the lessee's default under Section 2A-523(2).

11. A's counsel next would determine what action, if any, should be taken with respect to the goods. As stated in subparagraph (e) and as discussed fully in Section 2A-527(1) the lessor may, but has no obligation to, dispose of the goods by a substantially similar lease (indeed, the lessor has no obligation whatsoever to dispose of the goods at all) and recover damages based on that action, but lessor will not be able to recover damages which put it in a better position than performance would have done, nor will it be able to recover damages for losses which it could have reasonably avoided. In this case, since A is in the business of leasing and selling bicycles, A will probably inventory the 60 bicycles for its retail trade.

12. A's counsel then will determine which of the various means of ascertaining A's damages against B are available. Subparagraph (e) catalogues each relevant section. First, under Section 2A-527(2) the amount of A's claim is computed by comparing the original lease between A and B with any subsequent lease of the bicycles but only if the subsequent lease is substantially similar to the original lease contract. While the section does not define this term, the official comment does establish some parameters. If, however, A elects to lease the bicycles to his retail trade, it is unlikely that the resulting lease will be substantially similar to the original, as leases to retail customers are considerably different from leases to wholesale customers like B. If, however, the leases were substantially similar, the damage claim is for accrued and unpaid rent to the beginning of the new lease, plus the present value as of the same date, of the rent reserved under the original lease for the balance of its term less the present value as of the same date of the rent reserved under the replacement lease for a term comparable to the balance of the term of the original lease, together with incidental damages less expenses saved in consequence of the lessee's default.

13. If the new lease is not substantially similar or if A elects to sell the bicycles or to hold the bicycles, damages are computed under Section 2A-528 or 2A-529.

14. If A elects to pursue his claim under Section 2A-528(1), the damage rule is the same as that stated in Section 2A-527(2) except that damages are measured from

default if the lessee never took possession of the goods or from the time when the lessor did or could have regained possession and that the standard of comparison is not the rent reserved under a substantially similar lease entered into by the lessor but a market rent, as defined in Section 2A-507. Further, if the facts of this hypothetical were more elaborate A may be able to establish that the measure of damage under subsection (1) is inadequate to put him in the same position that B's performance would have, in which case A can claim the present value of his lost profits.

15. Yet another alternative for computing A's damage claim against B which will be available in some situations is recovery of the present value, as of entry of judgment, of the rent for the then remaining lease term under Section 2A-529. However, this formation is not available if the goods have been repossessed or tendered back to A. For the 20 bicycles repossessed and the remaining 40 bicycles, A will be able to recover the present value of the rent only if A is unable to dispose of them, or circumstances indicate the effort will be unavailing. If A has prevailed in an action for the rent, at any time up to collection of a judgment by A against B, A might dispose of the bicycles. In such case A's claim for damages against B is governed by Section 2A-527 or 2A-528. Section 2A 529(3). The resulting recalculation of claim should reduce the amount recoverable by A against B and the lessor is required to cause an appropriate credit to be entered against the earlier judgment. However, the nature of the post-judgment proceedings to resolve this issue, and the sanctions for a failure to comply, if any, will be determined by other law.

16. Finally, if the lease agreement had so provided pursuant to subparagraph (f), A's claim against B would not be determined under any of these statutory formulae, but pursuant to a liquidated damages clause. Section 2A-504(1).

17. These various methods of computing A's damage claim against B are alternatives subject to Section 2A-501(4). However, the pursuit of any one of these alternatives is not a bar to, nor has it been barred by, A's earlier action to obtain possession of the 60 bicycles. These formulae, which vary as a function of an overt or implied mitigation of damage theory, focus on allowing A a recovery of the benefit of his bargain with B. Had B performed, A would have received the rent as well as the return of the 60 bicycles at the end of the term.

18. Finally, A's counsel should also advise A of his right to cancel the lease contract under subparagraph (a). Section 2A-505(1). Cancellation will discharge all existing obligations but preserve A's rights and remedies.

19. Subsection (2) recognizes that a lessor who is entitled to exercise the rights or to obtain a remedy granted by subsection (1) may choose not to do so. In such cases, the lessor can recover damages as provided in subsection (2). For example, for non-payment of rent, the lessor may decide not to take possession of the goods and cancel the lease, but rather to merely sue for the unpaid rent as it comes due plus lost interest or other damages "determined in any reasonable manner." Subsection (2) also negates any loss of alternative rights and remedies by reason of having invoked or commenced the exercise or pursuit of any one or more rights or remedies.

20. Subsection (3) allows the lessor access to a remedy scheme provided in this Article as well as that contained in the lease contract if the lessee is in default for reasons other than those stated in subsection (1). Note that the reference to this Article includes supplementary principles of law and equity, *e.g.*, fraud, misrepresentation and duress. Sections 2A-103(4) and 1-103.

21. There is no special treatment of the finance lease in this section. Absent supplementary principles of law to the contrary, in most cases the supplier will have no rights or remedies against the defaulting lessee. Section 2A-209(2)(ii). Given that the supplier will look to the lessor for payment, this is appropriate. However, there is a specific exception to this rule with respect to the right to identify goods to the lease contract. Section 2A-524(2). The parties are free to create a different result in a particular case. Sections 2A-103(4) and 1-102(3).

Cross References:

Sections 1-102(3), 1-103, 1-106(1), 1-201(37), 2-703, 2A-103(1)(j), 2A-103(4), 2A-209(2)(ii), 2A-501(4), 2A-504(1), 2A-505(1), 2A-507, 2A-510(2), 2A-524 through 2A-531, 2A-524(2), 2A-525(1), 2A-525(2), 2A-526(1), 2A-527(1), 2A-527(2), 2A-528(1) and 2A-529(3).

Definitional Cross References:

"Delivery". Section 1-201(14).
"Goods". Section 2A-103(1)(h).
"Installment lease contract". Section 2A-103(1)(i).
"Lease contract". Section 2A-103(1)(l).
"Lessee". Section 2A-103(1)(n).
"Lessor". Section 2A-103(1)(p).
"Remedy". Section 1-201(34).
"Rights". Section 1-201(36).
"Value". Section 1-201(44).

Section 2A–524. Lessor's Right to Identify Goods to Lease Contract.

(1) After default by the lessee under the lease contract of the type described in Section 2A–523 (1) or Section 2A–523 (3)(a) or, if agreed, after other default by the lessee, the lessor may:

(a) identify to the lease contract conforming goods not already identified if at the time the lessor learned of the default they were in the lessor's or the supplier's possession or control; and

(b) dispose of goods (Section 2A–527(1)) that demonstrably have been intended for the particular lease contract even though those goods are unfinished.

(2) If the goods are unfinished, in the exercise of reasonable commercial judgment for the purposes of avoiding loss and of effective realization, an aggrieved lessor or the supplier may either complete manufacture and wholly identify the goods to the lease contract or cease manufacture and lease, sell, or otherwise dispose of the goods for scrap or salvage value or proceed in any other reasonable manner.

OFFICIAL COMMENT

Uniform Statutory Source: Section 2–704.
Changes: Revised to reflect leasing practices and terminology.

Purposes:

The remedies provided by this section are available to the lessor (i) if there has been a default by the lessee which falls within Section 2A–523(1) or 2A–523(3)(a), or (ii) if there has been any other default for which the lease contract gives the lessor the remedies provided by this section. Under "(ii)", the lease contract may give the lessor the remedies of identification and disposition provided by this section in various ways. For example, a lease provision might specifically refer to the remedies of identification and disposition, or it might refer to this section by number (i.e., 2A–524), or it might do so by a more general reference such as "all rights and remedies provided by Article 2A for default by the lessee."

Definitional Cross References:

"Aggrieved party". Section 1–201(2).

"Conforming". Section 2A–103(1)(d).
"Goods". Section 2A–103(1)(h).
"Learn". Section 1–201(25).
"Lease". Section 2A–103(1)(j).
"Lease contract". Section 2A–103(1)(l).
"Lessor". Section 2A–103(1)(p).
"Rights". Section 1–201(36).
"Supplier". Section 2A–103(1)(x).
"Value". Section 1–201(44).

Section 2A–525. Lessor's Right to Possession of Goods.

(1) If a lessor discovers the lessee to be insolvent, the lessor may refuse to deliver the goods.

(2) After a default by the lessee under the lease contract of the type described in Section 2A–523(1) or 2A–523(3)(a) or, if agreed, after other default by the lessee, the lessor has the right to take possession of the goods. If the lease contract so provides, the lessor may require the lessee to assemble the goods and make them available to the lessor at a place to be designated by the lessor which is reasonably convenient to both parties. Without removal, the lessor may render unusable any goods employed in trade or business, and may dispose of goods on the lessee's premises (Section 2A–527).

(3) The lessor may proceed under subsection (2) without judicial process if it can be done without breach of the peace or the lessor may proceed by action.

OFFICIAL COMMENT

Uniform Statutory Source: Sections 2–702(1) and 9–503.
Changes: Substantially revised.

Purposes:

1. Subsection (1), a revised version of the provisions of Section 2–702(1), allows the lessor to refuse to deliver goods if the lessee is insolvent. Note that the provisions of Section 2–702(2), granting the unpaid seller certain rights of reclamation, were not incorporated in this section. Subsection (2) made this unnecessary.

2. Subsection (2), a revised version of the provisions of Section 9–503, allows the lessor, on a Section 2A–523(1) or 2A–523(3)(a) default by the lessee, the right to take possession of or reclaim the goods. Also, the lessor can contract for the right to take possession of the goods for other defaults by the lessee. Therefore, since the lessee's insolvency is an event of default in a standard lease agreement, subsection (2) is the functional equivalent of Section 2–702(2). Further, subsection (2) sanctions the classic crate and delivery clause obligating the lessee to assemble the goods and to make them available to the lessor. Finally, the lessor may leave the goods in place, render them unusable (if they are goods employed in trade or business), and dispose of them on the lessee's premises.

3. Subsection (3), a revised version of the provisions of Section 9–503, allows the lessor to proceed under subsection (2) without judicial process, absent breach of the peace, or by action. Sections 2A–501(3), 2A–103(4) and 1–201(1). In the appropriate case action includes injunctive relief. Clark Equip. Co. v. Armstrong Equip. Co., 431 F.2d 54 (5th Cir. 1970), *cert. denied*, 402 U.S. 909 (1971). This Section, as well

as a number of other Sections in this Part, are included in the Article to codify the lessor's common law right to protect the lessor's reversionary interest in the goods. Section 2A–103(1)(q). These Sanctions are intended to supplement and not displace principles of law and equity with respect to the protection of such interest. Sections 2A–103(4) and 1–103. Such principles apply in many instances, *e.g.*, loss or damage to goods if risk of loss passes to the lessee, failure of the lessee to return goods to the lessor in the condition stipulated in the lease, and refusal of the lessee to return goods to the lessor after termination or cancellation of the lease. *See also* Section 2A-532.

Cross References:

Sections 1–106(2), 2–702(1), 2–702(2), 2A–103(4), 2A–501(3), 2A–532 and 9–503.

Definitional Cross References:

"Action". Section 1–201(1).
"Delivery". Section 1–201(14).
"Discover". Section 1–201(25).
"Goods". Section 2A–103(1)(h).
"Insolvent". Section 1–201(23).
"Lease contract". Section 2A–103(1)(l).
"Lessee". Section 2A–103(1)(n).
"Lessor". Section 2A–103(1)(p).
"Party". Section 1–201(29).
"Rights". Section 1–201(36).

Section 2A–526. Lessor's Stoppage of Delivery in Transit or Otherwise.

(1) A lessor may stop delivery of goods in the possession of a carrier or other bailee if the lessor discovers the lessee to be insolvent and may stop delivery of carload, truckload, planeload, or larger shipments of express or freight if the lessee repudiates or fails to make a payment due before delivery, whether for rent, security or otherwise under the lease contract, or for any other reason the lessor has a right to withhold or take possession of the goods.

(2) In pursuing its remedies under subsection (1), the lessor may stop delivery until:

(a) receipt of the goods by the lessee;

(b) acknowledgment to the lessee by any bailee of the goods, except a carrier, that the bailee holds the goods for the lessee; or

(c) such an acknowledgment to the lessee by a carrier via reshipment or as warehouseman.

(3)(a) To stop delivery, a lessor shall so notify as to enable the bailee by reasonable diligence to prevent delivery of the goods.

(b) After notification, the bailee shall hold and deliver the goods according to the directions of the lessor, but the lessor is liable to the bailee for any ensuing charges or damages.

(c) A carrier who has issued a nonnegotiable bill of lading is not obliged to obey a notification to stop received from a person other than the consignor.

OFFICIAL COMMENT

Uniform Statutory Source: Section 2–705.
Changes: Revised to reflect leasing practices and terminology.

Definitional Cross References:

"Bill of lading". Section 1–201(6).
"Delivery". Section 1–201(14).
"Discover". Section 1–201(25).
"Goods". Section 2A–103(1)(h).
"Insolvent". Section 1–201(23).
"Lease contract". Section 2A–103(1)(l).
"Lessee". Section 2A–103(1)(n).
"Lessor". Section 2A–103(1)(p).
"Notifies" and "Notification". Section 1–201(26).
"Person". Section 1–201(30).
"Receipt". Section 2–103(1)(c).
"Remedy". Section 1–201(34).
"Rights". Section 1–201(36).

Section 2A–527. Lessor's Rights to Dispose of Goods.

(1) After a default by a lessee under the lease contract of the type described in Section 2A–523(1) or 2A–523(3)(a) or after the lessor refuses to deliver or takes possession of goods (Section 2A–525 or 2A–526), or, if agreed, after other default by a lessee, the lessor may dispose of the goods concerned or the undelivered balance thereof by lease, sale, or otherwise.

(2) Except as otherwise provided with respect to damages liquidated in the lease agreement (Section 2A–504) or otherwise determined pursuant to agreement of the parties (Sections 1-102(3) and 2A–503), if the disposition is by lease agreement substantially similar to the original lease agreement and the new lease agreement is made in good faith and in a commercially reasonable manner, the lessor may recover from the lessee as damages (a) accrued and unpaid rent as of the date of the commencement of the term of the new lease agreement, (b) the present value, as of the same date, of the total rent for the then remaining lease term of the original lease agreement minus the present value, as of the same date, of the rent under the new lease agreement applicable to that period of the new lease term which is comparable to the then remaining lease term of the original lease agreement, and (c) any incidental damages allowed under Section 2A–530, less expenses saved in consequence of the lessee's default.

(3) If the lessor's disposition is by lease agreement that qualifies for treatment under subsection (2), the lessor may elect to proceed under subsection (2) or Section 2A–528. If the lessor's disposition is by lease agreement that for any reason does not qualify for treatment under subsection (2), or is by sale or

otherwise, the lessor may recover from the lessee as if the lessor had elected not to dispose of the goods.

(4) A subsequent buyer or lessee who buys or leases from the lessor in good faith for value as a result of a disposition under this section takes the goods free of the original lease contract and any rights of the original lessee even though the lessor fails to comply with one or more of the requirements of this Article.

(5) The lessor is not accountable to the lessee for any profit made on any disposition. A lessee who has rightfully rejected or justifiably revoked acceptance shall account to the lessor for any excess over the amount of the lessee's security interest (Section 2A–508(5)).

OFFICIAL COMMENT

Uniform Statutory Source: Sections 2–706(1), (5) and (6).
Changes: Substantially revised.

Purposes:

1. Subsection (1), a revised version of the first sentence of subsection 2-706(1), allows the lessor the right to dispose of goods after a statutory or other material default by the lessee (even if the goods remain in the lessee's possession–Section 2A-525(2)), after the lessor refuses to deliver or takes possession of the goods, or, if agreed, after other contractual default. The lessor's decision to exercise this right is a function of a commercial judgment, not a statutory mandate replete with sanctions for failure to comply. *Cf.* Section 9-507. As the owner of the goods, in the case of a lessor, or as the prime lessee of the goods, in the case of a sublessor, compulsory disposition of the goods is inconsistent with the nature of the interest held by the lessor or the subleasor and is not necessary because the interest held by the lessee or the sublessee is not protected by a right of redemption under the common law or this Article. Subsection 2A-527(5).

2. The rule for determining the measure of damages recoverable by the lessor against the lessee is a function of severable variables. If the lessor has elected to effect disposition under subsection (1) and such disposition is by lease that qualifies under subsection (2), the measure of damages set forth in subsection (2) will apply, absent agreement to the contrary. Sections 2A-504, 2A-103(4) and 1-102(3).

3. The lessor's damages will be established using the new lease agreement as a measure if the following three criteria are satisfied: (i) the lessor disposed of the goods by lease, (ii) the lease agreement is substantially similar to the original lease agreement, and (iii) such disposition was in good faith, and in a commercially reasonable manner. Thus, the lessor will be entitled to recover from the lessee the accrued and unpaid rent as of the date of commencement of the term of the new lease, and the present value, as of the same date, of the rent under the original lease for the then remaining term less the present value as of the same date of the rent under the new lease agreement applicable to the period of the new lease comparable to the remaining term under the original lease, together with incidental damages less expenses saved in consequence of the lessee's default. If the lessor's disposition does not satisfy the criteria of subsection (2), the lessor may calculate its claim against the lessee pursuant to Section 2A-528. Section 2A-523(1)(e).

4. Two of the three criteria to be met by the lessor are familiar, but the concept of the new lease agreement that is substantially similar to the original lease agreement

is not. Given the many variables facing a party who intends to lease goods and the rapidity of change in the market place, the policy decision was made not to draft with specificity. It was thought unwise to seek to establish certainty at the cost of fairness. The decision of whether the new lease agreement is substantially similar to the original will be determined case by case.

5. While the section does not draw a bright line, it is possible to describe some of the factors that should be considered in a finding that a new lease agreement is substantially similar to the original. The various elements of the new lease agreement should be examined. Those elements include the options to purchase or release; the lessor's representations, warranties and covenants to the lessee as well as those to be provided by the lessee to the lessor; and the services, if any, to be provided by the lessor or by the lessee. All of these factors allocate cost and risk between the lessor and the lessee and thus affect the amount of rent to be paid. These findings should not be made with scientific precision, as they are a function of economics, nor should they be made independently, as it is important that a sense of commercial judgment pervade the finding. *See* Section 2A-507(2). To establish the new lease as a proper measure of damage under subsection (2), these various factors, taken as a whole, must result in a finding that the new lease agreement is substantially similar to the original. If the differences between the original lease and the new lease can be easily valued, it would be appropriate for a court to find that the new lease is substantially similar to the old lease, adjust the difference in the rent between the two leases to take account of the differences, and award damages under this section. If, for example, the new lease requires the lessor to insure the goods in the hands of the lessee, while the original lease required the lessee to insure, the usual cost of such insurance could be deducted from rent due under the new lease before the difference in rental between the two leases is determined.

6. The following hypothetical illustrates the difficulty of providing a bright line. Assume that A buys a jumbo tractor for $1 million and then leases the tractor to B for a term of 36 months. The tractor is delivered to and is accepted by B on May 1. On June 1 B fails to pay the monthly rent to A. B returns the tractor to A, who immediately releases the tractor to C for a term identical to the term remaining under the lease between A and B. All terms and conditions under the lease between A and C are identical to those under the original lease between A and B, except that C does not provide any property damage or other insurance coverage, and B agreed to provide complete coverage. Coverage is expensive and difficult to obtain. It is a question of fact whether it is so difficult to adjust the recovery to take account of the difference between the two leases as to insurance that the second lease is not substantially similar to the original.

7. A new lease can be substantially similar to the original lease even though its term extends beyond the remaining term of the original lease, so long as both (a) the lease terms are commercially comparable (e.g., it is highly unlikely that a one-month rental and a five-year lease would reflect similar realities), and (b) the court can fairly apportion a part of the rental payments under the new lease to that part of the term of the new lease which is comparable to the remaining lease term under the original lease. Also, the lease term of the new lease may be comparable to the remaining term of the original lease even though the beginning and ending dates of the two leases are not the same. For example, a two-month lease of agricultural equipment for the months of August and September may be comparable to a two-month lease running from the 15th of August to the 15th of October if in the particular location two-month leases beginning on August 15th are basically interchangeable with two-month leases beginning August 1st. Similarly, the term of a one-year truck lease beginning on the 15th of January may be comparable to the term of a one-year truck lease beginning January 2d. If the lease terms are found to be comparable, the court may base cover damages on the entire difference between the costs under the two leases.

8. Subsection (3), which is new, provides that if the lessor's disposition is by lease that does not qualify under subsection (2), or is by sale or otherwise, Section 2A-528 governs.

9. Subsection (4), a revised version of subsection 2-706(5), applies to protect a subsequent buyer or lessee who buys or leases from the lessor in good faith and for value, pursuant to a disposition under this section. Note that by its terms, the rule in subsection 2A-304(1), which provides that the subsequent lessee takes subject to the original lease contract, is controlled by the rule stated in this subsection.

10. Subsection (5), a revised version of subsection 2-706(6), provides that the lessor is not accountable to the lessee for any profit made by the lessor on a disposition. This rule follows from the fundamental premise of the bailment for hire that the lessee under a lease of goods has no equity of redemption to protect.

Cross References:

Sections 1–102(3), 2–706(1), 2–706(5), 2–706(6), 2A–103(4), 2A–304(1), 2A–504, 2A–507(2), 2A–523(1)(e), 2A–525(2), 2A–527(5), 2A–528 and 9–507.

Definitional Cross References:

"Buyer" and "Buying". Section 2–103(1)(a).
"Delivery". Section 1–201(14).
"Good faith". Sections 1–201(19) and 2–103(1)(b).
"Goods". Section 2A–103(1)(h).
"Lease". Section 2A–103(1)(j).
"Lease contract". Section 2A–103(1)(l).
"Lessee". Section 2A–103(1)(n).
"Lessor". Section 2A–103(1)(p).
"Present value". Section 2A–103(1)(u).
"Rights". Section 1–201(36).
"Sale". Section 2–106(1).
"Security interest". Section 1–201(37).
"Value". Section 1–201(44).

Section 2A–528. Lessor's Damages for Nonacceptance, Failure to Pay, Repudiation, or Other Default.

(1) Except as otherwise provided with respect to damages liquidated in the lease agreement (Section 2A–504) or otherwise determined pursuant to agreement of the parties (Sections 1-102(3) and 2A–503), if a lessor elects to retain the goods or a lessor elects to dispose of the goods and the disposition is by lease agreement whether or not the lease agreement qualifies for treatment under Section 2A–527(2), or is by sale or otherwise, the lessor may recover from the lessee as damages for a default of the type described in Section 2A–523(1) or 2A–523 (3)(a), or, if agreed, for other default of the lessee, (a) accrued and unpaid rent as of the date of default if the lessee has never taken possession of the goods, or, if the lessee has taken possession of the goods, as of the date the lessor repossesses the goods or an earlier date on which the lessee makes a tender of the goods to the lessor, (b) the present value as of the date determined under clause (a) of the total rent for the then remaining lease term of the original lease agreement minus the present value as of the same date of the market rent at the place where the goods are located computed for the same lease term, and

(c) any incidental damages allowed under Section 2A–530, less expenses saved in consequence of the lessee's default.

(2) If the measure of damages provided in subsection (1) is inadequate to put a lessor in as good a position as performance would have, the measure of damages is the present value of the profit, including reasonable overhead, the lessor would have made from full performance by the lessee, together with any incidental damages allowed under Section 2A–530, due allowance for costs reasonably incurred and due credit for payments or proceeds of disposition.

OFFICIAL COMMENT

Uniform Statutory Source: Section 2–708.
Changes: Substantially revised.

Purposes:

1. Subsection (1), a substantially revised version of Section 2–708(1), states the basic rule governing the measure of lessor's damages for a default described in Section 2A–523(1) or (3)(a), and, if agreed, for a contractual default. This measure will apply if the lessor elects to retain the goods (whether undelivered, returned by the lessee, or repossessed by the lessor after acceptance and default by the lessee) or if the lessor's disposition does not qualify under subsection 2A–527(2). Section 2A–527(3). Note that under some of these conditions, the lessor may recover damages from the lessee pursuant to the rule set forth in Section 2A–529. There is no sanction for disposition that does not qualify under subsection 2A–527(2). Application of the rule set forth in this section is subject to agreement to the contrary. Sections 2A–504, 2A–103(4) and 1–102(3).

2. If the lessee has never taken possession of the goods, the measure of damage is the accrued and unpaid rent as of the date of default together with the present value, as of the date of default, of the original rent for the remaining term of the lease less the present value as of the same date of market rent, and incidental damages, less expenses saved in consequence of the default. Note that the reference in Section 2A–528(1)(i) and (ii) is to the date of default not to the date of an event of default. An event of default under a lease agreement becomes a default under a lease agreement only after the expiration of any relevant period of grace and compliance with any notice requirements under this Article and the lease agreement. American Bar Foundation, *Commentaries on Indentures*, § 5–1, at 216–217 (1971). Section 2A–501(1). This conclusion is also a function of whether, as a matter of fact or law, the event of default has been waived, suspended or cured. Sections 2A–103(4) and 1–103. If the lessee has taken possession of the goods, the measure of damages is the accrued and unpaid rent as of the earlier of the time the lessor repossesses the goods or the time the lessee tenders the goods to the lessor plus the difference between the present value, as of the same time, of the rent under the lease for the remaining lease term and the present value, as of the same time, of the market rent.

3. Market rent will be computed pursuant to Section 2A-507.

4. Subsection (2), a somewhat revised version of the provisions of subsection 2–708(2), states a measure of damages which applies if the measure of damages in subsection (1) is inadequate to put the lessor in as good a position as performance would have. The measure of damage is the lessor's profit, including overhead, together with incidental damages, with allowance for costs reasonably incurred and credit for payments or proceeds of disposition. In determining the amount of due credit with respect to proceeds of disposition a proper value should be attributed to the lessor's residual interest in the goods. Sections 2A–103(1)(q) and 2A–507(4).

5. In calculating profit, a court should include any expected appreciation of the goods, *e.g.* the foal of a leased brood mare. Because this subsection is intended to give the lessor the benefit of the bargain, a court should consider any reasonable benefit or profit expected by the lessor from the performance of the lease agreement. *See* Honeywell, Inc. v. Lithonia Lighting, Inc., 317 F. Supp. 406, 413 (N.D. Ga. 1970); Locks v. Wade, 36 N.J. Super. 128, 131, 114 A.2d 875, 877 (Super. Ct. App. Div. 1955). Further, in calculating profit the concept of present value must be given effect. Taylor v. Commercial Credit Equip. Corp., 170 Ga. App. 322, 316 S.E.2d 788 (Ct. App. 1984). *See generally* Section 2A–103(1)(u).

Cross References:

Sections 1–102(3), 2–708, 2A–103(1)(u), 2A–402, 2A–504, 2A–507, 2A–527(2) and 2A–529.

Definitional Cross References:

"Agreement". Section 1–201(3).
"Goods". Section 2A–103(1)(h).
"Lease". Section 2A–103(1)(j).
"Lease agreement". Section 2A–103(l)(k).
"Lessee". Section 2A–103(1)(n).
"Lessor". Section 2A–103(1)(p).
"Party". Section 1–201(29).
"Present value". Section 2A–103(1)(u).
"Sale". Section 2–106(1).

Section 2A–529. Lessor's Action for the Rent.

(1) After default by the lessee under the lease contract of the type described in Section 2A–523(1) or 2A–523(3)(a) or, if agreed, after other default by the lessee, if the lessor complies with subsection (2), the lessor may recover from the lessee as damages:

(a) for goods accepted by the lessee and not repossessed by or tendered to the lessor, and for conforming goods lost or damaged within a commercially reasonable time after risk of loss passes to the lessee (Section 2A–219), (i) accrued and unpaid rent as of the date of entry of judgment in favor of the lessor, (ii) the present value as of the same date of the rent for the then remaining lease term of the lease agreement, and (iii) any incidental damages allowed under Section 2A–530, less expenses saved in consequence of the lessee's default; and

(b) for goods identified to the lease contract, if the lessor is unable after reasonable effort to dispose of them at a reasonable price or the circumstances reasonably indicate that effort will be unavailing, (i) accrued and unpaid rent as of the date of entry of judgment in favor of the lessor, (ii) the present value as of the same date of the rent for the then remaining lease term of the lease agreement, and (iii) any incidental damages allowed under Section 2A–530, less expenses saved in consequence of the lessee's default.

(2) Except as provided in subsection (3), the lessor shall hold for the lessee for the remaining lease term of the lease agreement any goods that have been identified to the lease contract and are in the lessor's control.

(3) The lessor may dispose of the goods at any time before collection of the judgment for damages obtained pursuant to subsection (1). If the disposition is before the end of the remaining lease term of the lease agreement, the lessor's recovery against the lessee for damages is governed by Section 2A–527 or Section 2A–528, and the lessor will cause an appropriate credit to be provided against a judgment for damages to the extent that the amount of the judgment exceeds the recovery available pursuant to Section 2A–527 or Section 2A–528.

(4) Payment of the judgment for damages obtained pursuant to subsection (1) entitles the lessee to the use and possession of the goods not then disposed of for the remaining lease term of and in accordance with the lease agreement.

(5) After default by the lessee under the lease contract of the type described in Section 2A–523 (1) or Section 2A–523 (3)(a) or, if agreed, after other default by the lessee, a lessor who is held not entitled to rent under this section must nevertheless be awarded damages for non-acceptance under Section 2A–527 or 2A–528.

OFFICIAL COMMENT

Uniform Statutory Source: Section 2–709.

Changes: Substantially revised.

Purposes:

1. Absent a lease contract provision to the contrary, an action for the full unpaid rent (discounted to present value as of the time of entry of judgment as to rent due after that time) is available as to goods not lost or damaged only if the lessee retains possession of the goods or the lessor is or apparently will be unable to dispose of them at a reasonable price after reasonable effort. There is no general right in a lessor to recover the full rent from the lessee upon holding the goods for the lessee. If the lessee tenders goods back to the lessor, and the lessor refuses to accept the tender, the lessor will be limited to the damages it would have suffered had it taken back the goods. The rule in Article 2 that the seller can recover the price of accepted goods is rejected here. In a lease, the lessor always has a residual interest in the goods which the lessor usually realizes upon at the end of a lease term by either sale or a new lease. Therefore, it is not a substantial imposition on the lessor to require it to take back and dispose of the goods if the lessee chooses to tender them back before the end of the lease term: the lessor will merely do earlier what it would have done anyway, sell or relet the goods. Further, the lessee will frequently encounter substantial difficulties if the lessee attempts to sublet the goods for the remainder of the lease term. In contrast to the buyer who owns the entire interest in goods and can easily dispose of them, the lessee is selling only the right to use the goods under the terms of the lease and the sublessee must assume a relationship with the lessor. In that situation, it is usually more efficient to eliminate the original lessee as a middleman by allowing the lessee to return the goods to the lessor who can then redispose of them.

2. In some situations even where possession of the goods is reacquired, a lessor will be able to recover as damages the present value of the full rent due, not under this section, but under 2A–528(2) which allows a lost profit recovery if necessary to put the lessor in the position it would have been in had the lessee performed. Following is an example of such a case. A is a lessor of construction equipment and maintains a substantial inventory. B leases from A a backhoe for a period of two

weeks at a rental of $1,000. After three days, B returns the backhoe and refuses to pay the rent. A has five backhoes in inventory, including the one returned by B. During the next 11 days after the return by B of the backhoe, A rents no more than three backhoes at any one time and, therefore, always has two on hand. If B had kept the backhoe for the full rental period, A would have earned the full rental on that backhoe, plus the rental on the other backhoes it actually did rent during that period. Getting this backhoe back before the end of the lease term did not enable A to make any leases it would not otherwise have made. The only way to put A in the position it would have been in had the lessee fully performed is to give the lessor the full rentals. A realized no savings at all because the backhoe was returned early and might even have incurred additional expense if it was paying for parking space for equipment in inventory. A has no obligation to relet the backhoe for the benefit of B rather than leasing that backhoe or any other in inventory for its own benefit. Further, it is probably not reasonable to expect A to dispose of the backhoe by sale when it is returned in an effort to reduce damages suffered by B. Ordinarily, the loss of a two-week rental would not require A to reduce the size of its backhoe inventory. Whether A would similarly be entitled to full rentals as lost profit in a one-year lease of a backhoe is a question of fact: in any event the lessor, subject to mitigation of damages rules, is entitled o be put in as good a position as it would have been had the lessee fully performed the lease contract.

3. Under subsection (2) a lessor who is able and elects to sue for the rent due under a lease must hold goods not lost or damaged for the lessee. Subsection (3) creates an exception to the subsection (2) requirement. If the lessor disposes of those goods prior to collection of the judgment (whether as a matter of law or agreement), the lessor's recovery is governed by the measure of damages in Section 2A–527 if the disposition is by lease that is substantially similar to the original lease, or otherwise by the measure of damages in Section 2A–528. Section 2A–523 official comment.

4. Subsection (4), which is new, further reinforces the requisites of Subsection (2). In the event the judgment for damages obtained by the lessor against the lessee pursuant to subsection (1) is satisfied, the lessee regains the right to use and possession of the remaining goods for the balance of the original lease term; a partial satisfaction of the judgment creates no right in the lessee to use and possession of the goods.

5. The relationship between subsections (2) and (4) is important to understand. Subsection (2) requires the lessor to hold for the lessee identified goods in the lessor's possession. Absent agreement to the contrary, whether in the lease or otherwise, under most circumstances the requirement that the lessor hold the goods for the lessee for the term will mean that the lessor is not allowed to use them. Sections 2A–103(4) and 1–203. Further, the lessor's use of the goods could be viewed as a disposition of the goods that would bar the lessor from recovery under this section, remitting the lessor to the two preceding sections for a determination of the lessor's claim for damages against the lessee.

6. Subsection (5), the analogue of subsection 2–709(3), further reinforces the thrust of subsection (3) by stating that a lessor who is held not entitled to rent under this section has not elected a remedy; the lessor must be awarded damages under Sections 2A–527 and 2A–528. This is a function of two significant policies of this Article–that resort to a remedy is optional, unless expressly agreed to be exclusive (Section 2A–503(2)) and that rights and remedies provided in this Article generally are cumulative. (Section 2A–501(2) and (4)).

Cross References:

Sections 1–203, 2–709, 2–709(3), 2A–103(4), 2A–501(2), 2A–501(4), 2A–503(2), 2A–504, 2A–523(1)(e), 2A–525(2), 2A–527, 2A–528 and 2A–529(2).

Definitional Cross References:

"Action". Section 1–201(1).
"Conforming". Section 2A–103(1)(d).
"Goods". Section 2A–103(1)(h).
"Lease". Section 2A–103(1)(j).
"Lease agreement". Section 2A–103(1)(k).
"Lease contract". Section 2A–103(1)(l).
"Lessee". Section 2A–103(1)(n).
"Lessor". Section 2A–103(1)(p).
"Present value". Section 2A–103(1)(u).
"Reasonable time". Section 1–204(1) and (2).

Section 2A–530. Lessor's Incidental Damages.

Incidental damages to an aggrieved lessor include any commercially reasonable charges, expenses, or commissions incurred in stopping delivery, in the transportation, care and custody of goods after the lessee's default, in connection with return or disposition of the goods, or otherwise resulting from the default.

OFFICIAL COMMENT

Uniform Statutory Source: Section 2–710.
Changes: Revised to reflect leasing practices and terminology.

Definitional Cross References:

"Aggrieved party". Section 1–201(2).
"Delivery". Section 1–201(14).
"Goods". Section 2A–103(1)(h).
"Lessee". Section 2A–103(1)(n).
"Lessor". Section 2A–103(1)(p).

Section 2A–531. Standing to Sue Third Parties for Injury to Goods.

(1) If a third party so deals with goods that have been identified to a lease contract as to cause actionable injury to a party to the lease contract (a) the lessor has a right of action against the third party, and (b) the lessee also has a right of action against the third party if the lessee:

(i) has a security interest in the goods;

(ii) has an insurable interest in the goods; or

(iii) bears the risk of loss under the lease contract or has since the injury assumed that risk as against the lessor and the goods have been converted or destroyed.

(2) If at the time of the injury the party plaintiff did not bear the risk of loss as against the other party to the lease contract and there is no arrangement between them for disposition of the recovery, his or her suit or settlement, subject to his or her own interest, is as a fiduciary for the other party to the lease contract.

(3) Either party with the consent of the other may sue for the benefit of whom it may concern.

OFFICIAL COMMENT

Uniform Statutory Source: Section 2–722.
Changes: Revised to reflect leasing practices and terminology.

Definitional Cross References:

"Action". Section 1–201(1).
"Goods". Section 2A–103(1)(h).
"Lease contract". Section 2A–103(1)(l).
"Lessee". Section 2A–103(1)(n).
"Lessor". Section 2A–103(1)(p).
"Party". Section 1–201(29).
"Rights". Section 1–201(36).
"Security interest". Section 1–201(37).

Section 2A–532. Lessor's Rights to Residual Interest.

In addition to any other recovery permitted by this Article or other law, the lessor may recover from the lessee an amount that will fully compensate the lessor for any loss of or damage to the lessor's residual interest in the goods caused by the default of the lessee.

OFFICIAL COMMENT

Uniform Statutory Source: None.

Purposes:

This section recognizes the right of the lessor to recover under this Article (as well as under other law) from the lessee for failure to comply with the lease obligations as to the condition of leased goods when returned to the lessor, for failure to return the goods at the end of the lease, or for any other default which causes loss or injury to the lessor's residual interest in the goods.

ARTICLE 3

COMMERCIAL PAPER

PART 1

SHORT TITLE, FORM AND INTERPRETATION

PART 2

TRANSFER AND NEGOTIATION

PART 3

RIGHTS OF A HOLDER

PART 4

LIABILITY OF PARTIES

PART 5

PRESENTMENT, NOTICE OF DISHONOR AND PROTEST

PART 6

DISCHARGE

PART 7

ADVICE OF INTERNATIONAL SIGHT DRAFT

PART 8

MISCELLANEOUS

PART 1

SHORT TITLE, FORM AND INTERPRETATION

Section 3–101. Short Title.

This Article shall be known and may be cited as Uniform Commercial Code–Commercial Paper.

New York Annotations

See also N.Y.N.I.L., § 1. (All references to the Negotiable Instruments Law are to the New York statute unless otherwise stated.)

Article 3, dealing with commercial paper, is largely a revision of the New York Negotiable Instruments Law. Some new matters are dealt with in this Article and several subjects previously covered by the N.I.L. are treated separately and elsewhere in the Code. Bank deposits and collections are the subject of Article 4; letters of credit are governed by Article 5; negotiable instruments involved in secured transactions are frequently governed by Article 9, and most significantly corporate bonds, heretofore generally controlled by the N.I.L. when in bearer form, are treated in Article 8, as are all "investment securities".

There are relatively few major changes made by the Code in the New York law of commercial paper, most changes being of a technical character. Several of the more notable innovations bear mention, however. First, the many provisions concerning presentment, notice of dishonor and protest, scattered through 67 sections of the N.I.L., are assembled, pared down, and simplified in Part 5 of Article 3. Second, the provisions as to restrictive endorsements are changed to give the restrictively endorsed paper full negotiability in the bank collection process after the first bank taker. See Sections 3–102, 3–205, 3–206, 3–304, 3–419, 3–603, 4–203, and 4–205. Contra: Soma v. Handrulis, 277 N.Y. 223, 14 N.E.2d 46 (1938). Third, the rule making paper, originally made payable to bearer, always bearer paper, is changed by Section 3–204. The latest indorsement (blank or special) will control. Fourth, Section 3–406 makes a drawer, whose negligence contributes to an alteration, liable to a holder in due course. Fifth, the risk of loss as to an incomplete undelivered instrument is shifted by Section 3–115. Sixth, the indorser's warranties are, in general, extended to payors (Section 3–417). Seventh, the concept of "payment in due course" as discharge is abandoned in favor of a new scheme permitting discharge of a party paying, even with knowledge of an outstanding claim. If certain conditions are met. (Section 3–603). Eighth, the Code extends the application of suretyship principles to accommodation makers and drawers as well as indorsers. (Section 3–606.)

In summary, this article is designed to clear up conflicting interpretations arising under the present law, and to "Streamline" and modify the present law in order to eliminate a number of archaic provisions which have rarely been used. In some few instances there have been policy changes involving a reallocation of the risk between the parties to the instrument.

A textual treatment of Article 3 may be found in Hawkland, Commercial (Negotiable Instruments–Under the UCC) (1959).

Historical Note: Of the 79 sections found in the 1957 draft of Article 3, 40 were carried forward from the 1952 draft and were approved by the Law Revision Commission as they were there set forth. Criticisms and suggestions were made with reference to the remaining 39 sections, resulting in 25 of the sections being revised to adopt the Law Revision Commission's suggestions or to meet its criticisms. Five sections were revised so as to adopt the suggestions in part, four sections were revised for other reasons and in the case of only five sections were the suggestions not adopted.

Official Uniform Comment

This Article represents a complete revision and modernization of the Uniform Negotiable Instruments Law.

The Comments which follow will point out the respects in which this Article changes the Negotiable Instruments Law, which was promulgated by the National Conference of Commissioners on Uniform State Laws in 1896, and was subsequently enacted in every American jurisdiction. Needless to say, in the 50 odd years of the history of that statute, there have been vast changes in commercial practices relating to the handling of negotiable instruments. The need for revision of this important statute was felt for some years before the present project was undertaken.

It should be noted especially that this Article does not apply in any way to the handling of securities. Article 8 deals with that subject. See Sec. 3–103.

Section 3–102. Definitions and Index of Definitions.

(1) In this Article unless the context otherwise requires

(a) "Issue" means the first delivery of an instrument to a holder or a remitter.

(b) An "order" is a direction to pay and must be more than an authorization or request. It must identify the person to pay with reasonable certainty. It may be addressed to one or more such persons jointly or in the alternative but not in succession.

(c) A "promise" is an undertaking to pay and must be more than an acknowledgment of an obligation.

(d) "Secondary party" means a drawer or endorser

(e) "Instrument" means a negotiable instrument.

(2) Other definitions applying to this Article and the sections in which they appear are:

"Acceptance". Section 3–410.

"Accommodation party". Section 3–415.

"Alteration". Section 3–407.

"Certificate of Deposit". Section 3–104.

"Certification". Section 3–411.

"Check". Section 3–104.

"Definite time". Section 3–109.

"Dishonor". Section 3–507.

"Draft". Section 3–104.

"Holder in due course". Section 3–302.

"Negotiation". Section 3–202.

"Note". Section 3–104.

"Notice of dishonor". Section 3–508.

"On demand". Section 3–108.

"Presentment". Section 3–504.

"Protest". Section 3–509.

"Restrictive Indorsement". Section 3–205.

"Signature". Section 3–401.

(3) The following definitions in other Articles apply to this Article:

"Account". Section 4–104.

"Banking Day". Section 4–104.

"Clearing house". Section 4–104.

"Collecting bank". Section 4–105.

"Customer". Section 4–104.

"Depositary Bank". Section 4–105.

"Documentary Draft". Section 4–104.

"Intermediary Bank". Section 4–105.

"Item". Section 4–104.

"Midnight deadline". Section 4–104.

"Payor bank". Section 4–105.

(4) In addition Article 1 contains general definitions and principles of construction and interpretation applicable throughout this Article.

New York Annotations

(1)(a) This paragraph *accords* with the definition of "issue" found in N.I.L., § 2, with two exceptions. The phrase "complete in form", found in N.I.L., § 2, is omitted to provide consistency with present law relating to incomplete instruments (N.I.L., §§ 33 and 34) and would effect no substantive change. Second, the inclusion of delivery "to a remitter" in the definition of issuance is new.

(b) This is new in that there is no statutory definition of an "order". The definition accords with general law (See Britton, Bills and Notes, 43–44 (1943)), but there are no New York cases on point. The Code's allowance of alternative drawees is new and effects a change in present law. N.I.L., § 212.

(c) This is new in that there is no statutory definition of a "promise." As the Comment suggests, the definition probably reflects general law, but would seem to run counter to a series of cases (mostly pre-N.I.L.) that spell out a promise from an acknowledgement of an obligation. See Hegeman v. Moon, 131 N.Y. 462, 30 N.E. 487, (1892); Hoag v. Garden City Bank & Trust Co., 257 App.Div. 30, 12 N.Y.S.2d 610 (1939); Shimel v. Williams, 136 Misc. 464, 240 N.Y.S. 161 (1930); Matter of Nellis, 126 Misc. 638, 214 N.Y.S. 378 (1926); Didato v. Coniglio, 50 Misc. 280, 100 N.Y.S. 466 (1906).

(d) Although this is new, in that there is no present statutory definition of the term "secondary party," the definition accords generally with N.I.L., § 3, and case law. Anglo & London-Paris Nat. Bank v. S.A.Jacobson Co., 196 App.Div. 51, 187 N.Y.S. 508 (1921), and Clarke v. Stumpf, 190 App. Div. 538, 180 N.Y.S. 125 (1920).

(e) *Accord:* N.I.L., § 2.

(2) (3) (4) See annotations and comments to sections cited.

Historical Note: A definition of the term "Intermediary Bank" (by cross-reference to Article 4) was inserted as necessary in Article 3 because the term has been introduced in Section 3–205 and other sections of that article. The addition of "Restrictive Indorsement" in subsection (2) was made to provide an appropriate cross-reference; see Sections 3–205, 3–206, 3–304, 3–306, 3–419, 3–603, 4–203, and 4–205. (1956 Recommendations, p. 88.)

Official Uniform Comment

Prior Uniform Statutory Provision: Sections 1(5), 128 and 191, Uniform Negotiable Instruments Law.

Changes: See below.

Purposes of Changes:

1. The definition of "issue" in Section 191 of the original act has been clarified in two respects. The Section 191 definition required that the instrument delivered

by "complete in form" inconsistently with the provisions of Sections 14 and 15 (relating to incomplete instruments) of the original act. The "complete in form" language has therefore been deleted. Furthermore the Section 191 definition required that the delivery be "to a person who takes as a holder", thus raising difficulties in the case of the remitter (see Comment 3 to Sec. 3–302) who may not be a party to the instrument and thus not a holder. The definition in subsection (1) (a) of this Section thus provides that the delivery may be to a holder or to a remitter.

2. The definitions of "order" [subsection (b)] and "promise" [subsection (c)] are new, but state principles clearly recognized by the courts. In the case of orders the dividing line between "a direction to pay" and "an authorization or request" may not be self-evident in the occasional unusual, and therefore non-commercial, case. The prefixing of words of courtesy to the direction–as "please pay" or "kindly pay"–should not lead to a holding that the direction has degenerated into a mere request. On the other hand informal language–such as "I wish you would pay"–would not qualify as an order and such an instrument would be non-negotiable. The definition of "promise" is intended to make it clear that a mere I.O.U. is not a negotiable instrument, and to change the result in occasional cases which have held that "Due Currier & Barker seventeen dollars and fourteen cents, value received." and "I borrowed from P. Shemonia the sum of five hundred dollars with four per cent interest; the borrowed money ought to be paid within four months from the above date" were promises sufficient to make the instruments into notes.

3. The last sentence of subsection (1) (b) ("order") permits the order to be addressed to one or more persons (as drawees) in the alternative, recognizing the practice of corporations issuing dividend checks and of other drawers who for commercial convenience name a number of drawees, usually in different parts of the country. The section on presentment provides that presentment may be made to any one of such drawees. Drawees in succession are not permitted because the holder should not be required to make more than one presentment, and upon the first dishonor should have his recourse against the drawer and indorsers.

4. Comments on the definitions indexed follow the sections in which the definitions are contained.

Cross Reference:

Point 3: Section 3–504(3) (a).

Definitional Cross References:

"Bank". Section 1–201.
"Delivery". Section 1–201.
"Holder". Section 1–201.
"Money". Section 1–201.
"Person". Section 1–201.

Section 3–103. Limitations on Scope of Article.

(1) This Article does not apply to money, documents of title or investment securities.

(2) The provisions of this Article are subject to the provisions of the Article on Bank Deposits and Collections (Article 4) and Secured Transactions (Article 9).

New York Annotations

(1) This provision is new and is less extensive in its coverage than the N.I.L. While domestic currency is governed by federal legal tender statutes (31 U.S.C. §§ 463 and 821 (1950) so that as to such currency the section would effect no change, foreign currency has been held to be within the ambit of the N.I.L. Brown v. Perera, 176 N.Y.S. 215 (1918). In the case of foreign currency, therefore, the section would appear to change the law. The exclusion of documents of title from the coverage of the statute regulating negotiable instruments generally, accords with New York law. The exclusion of investment securities from the operation of Article 3 represents a distinct departure from comparable present law since certain types of such securities have been held to be negotiable instruments. Enoch v. Brandon, 249 N.Y. 263, 164 N.E. 45 (1928); Hibbs v. Brown, 190 N.Y. 167, 82 N.E. 1108 (1907).

Official Uniform Comment

Prior Uniform Statutory Provision: None.

Purposes:

1. This Article is restricted to commercial paper–that is to say, to drafts, checks, certificates of deposit and notes as defined in Section 3–104(2). Subsection (1) expressly excludes any money, as defined in this Act (Section 1–201), even though the money may be in the form of a bank note which meets all the requirements of Section 3–104(1). Money is of course negotiable at common law or under separate statutes, but no provision of this Article is applicable to it. Subsection (1) also expressly excludes documents of title and investment securities which fall within Articles 7 and 8, respectively. To this extent the section follows decisions which held that interim certificates calling for the delivery of securities were not negotiable instruments under the original statute. Such paper is now covered under Article 8, but is not within any section of this Article. Likewise, bills of lading, warehouse receipts and other documents of title which fall within Article 7 may be negotiable under the provision of that Article, but are not covered by any section of this Article.

2. Instruments which fall within the scope of this Article may also be subject to other Articles of the Code. Many items in course of bank collection will of course be negotiable instruments, and the same may be true of collateral pledged as security for a debt. In such cases this Article, which is general, is, in case of conflicting provisions, subject to the Articles which deal specifically with the type of transaction or instrument involved: Article 4 (Bank Deposits and Collections) and Article 9 (Secured Transactions). In the case of a negotiable instrument which is subject to Article 4 because it is in course of collection or to Article 9 because it is used as collateral, the provisions of this Article continue to be applicable except insofar as there may be conflicting provisions in the Bank Collection or Secured Transactions Article.

An instrument which qualifies as "negotiable" under this Article may also qualify as a "security" under Article 8. It will be noted that the formal requisites of negotiability (Section 3–104) go to matters of form exclusively; the definition of "security" on the other hand (Section 8–102) looks principally to the manner in which an instrument is used ("commonly dealt in upon securities exchanges . . . or commonly recognized . . . as a medium for investment"). If an instrument negotiable in form under Section 3–104 is, because of the manner of its use, a "security" under Section 8–102, Article 8 and not this Article applies. See subsection (1) of this Section and Section 8–102(1)(b).

Cross References:

Point 1: Articles 7 and 8; Section 1–201, 3–104(1) and (2), 3–107.
Point 2: Articles 4 and 9; Sections 3–104 and 8–102

Definitional Cross References:

"Document of title". Section 1–201.
"Money". Section 1–201.

Section 3–104. Form of Negotiable Instruments; "Draft"; "Check"; "Certificate of Deposit"; "Note".

(1) Any writing to be a negotiable instrument within this Article must

(a) be signed by the maker or drawer; and

(b) contain an unconditional promise or order to pay a sum certain in money and no other promise, order, obligation or power given by the maker or drawer except as authorized by this Article; and

(c) be payable on demand or at a definite time; and

(d) be payable to order or to bearer.

(2) A writing which complies with the requirements of this section is

(a) a "draft" ("bill of exchange") if it is an order;

(b) a "check" if it is a draft drawn on a bank and payable on demand;

(c) a "certificate of deposit" if it is an acknowledgment by a bank of receipt of money with an engagement to repay it;

(d) a "note" if it is a promise other than a certificate of deposit.

(3) As used in other Articles of this Act, and as the context may require, the terms "draft", "check", "certificate of deposit" and "note" may refer to instruments which are not negotiable within this Article as well as to instruments which are so negotiable.

New York Annotations

(1)(a) *Accord:* N.I.L., § 20(1).

(b) *Accord:* N.I.L., § 20(2). This subsection adds the limitation that the writing must not contain any "other promise, order, obligation or power given by the maker or drawer except as authorized by this chapter." The comparable provision in N.I.L., § 24, is followed by a list of specified additional provisions which are stated as not affecting negotiability. This list has been considered illustrative rather than exhaustive. First National Bank of Bridgeport v. Blackman, 249 N.Y. 322, 164 N.E. 113 (1928) (probably making present law more liberal than the Code provision). In view of the separate treatment of investment securities in Article 8, it is doubtful if this narrower approach is of any practical importance.

(c) In *accord:* N.I.L., § 20(3), except that the Code provision "at a definite time" is in substitution for the N.I.L. "at a fixed or determinable future time", because of the Code's disqualification of an instrument payable on the occurrence of an event certain to happen but uncertain as to time. See Section 3–109(2) and the annotation thereto.

(d) In *accord:* N.I.L., § 20(4).

(2)(a) Substantially in *accord:* N.I.L., § 210.

(b) Substantially in *accord:* N.I.L., § 321.

(c) This is new. There is no statutory definition of a certificate of deposit, but the Code is substantially in *accord* with the definition found in Gerard v. Bank of New York Trust Co., 265 N.Y. 336, 193 N.E. 165 (1934).

(d) Substantially in *accord:* N.I.L., § 320.

(3) See Section 3–805.

Historical Note: Subsection (3) was inserted to make clear the same policy as in Section 3–805. (1956 Recommendations, p. 89.)

Official Uniform Comment

Prior Uniform Statutory Provision: Sections 1, 5, 10, 126, 184 and 185, Uniform Negotiable Instruments Law.

Changes: Parts of original sections combined and reworded; new provisions; original Section 10 omitted.

Purposes of Changes and New Matter: The changes are intended to bring together in one section related provisions and definitions formerly widely separated.

1. Under subsection (1)(b) and writing, to be a negotiable instrument within this Article, must be payable in money. In a few states there are special statutes, enacted at an early date when currency was less sound and barter was prevalent, which make promises to pay in commodities negotiable. Even under these statutes commodity notes are now little used and have no general circulation. This Article makes no attempt to provide for such paper, as it is a matter of purely local concern. Even if retention of the old statutes is regarded in any state as important, amendment of this section may not be necessary, since "within this Article" in subsection (1) leaves open the possibility that some writings may be made negotiable by other statutes or by judicial decision. The same is true as to any new type of paper which commercial practice may develop in the future.

2. While a writing cannot be made a negotiable instrument within this Article by contract or by conduct, nothing in this section is intended to mean that in a particular case a court may not arrive at a result similar to that of negotiability by finding that the obligor is estopped by his conduct from asserting a defense against a bona fide purchaser. Such an estoppel rests upon ordinary principles of the law of simple contract; it does not depend upon negotiability, and it does not make the writing negotiable for any other purpose. But a contract to build a house or to employ a workman, or equally a security agreement does not become a negotiable instrument by the mere insertion of a clause agreeing that it shall be one.

3. The words "no other promise, order, obligation or power" in subsection (1)(b) are an expansion of the first sentence of the original Section 5. Section 3–112 permits an instrument to carry certain limited obligations or powers in addition to the simple promise or order to pay money. Subsection (1) of this Section is intended to say that it cannot carry others.

4. Any writing which meets the requirements of subsection (1) and is not excluded under Section 3–103 is a negotiable instrument, and all sections of this Article apply to it, even though it may contain additional language beyond that contemplated by this section. Such an instrument is a draft, a check, a certificate of deposit or a note as defined in subsection (2). Traveler's checks in the usual form, for instance, are negotiable instruments under this Article when they have been completed by the identifying signature.

5. This Article omits the original Section 10, which provided that the instrument need not follow the language of the act if it "clearly indicates an intention to conform" to it. The provision has served no useful purpose, and it has been an encouragement

to bad drafting and to liberality in holding questionable paper to be negotiable. The omission is not intended to mean that the instrument must follow the language of this section, or that one term may not be recognized as clearly the equivalent of another, as in the case of "I undertake" instead of "I promise," or "Pay to holder" instead of "Pay to bearer." It does not mean that either the language of the section or a clear equivalent must be found, and that in doubtful cases the decision should be against negotiability.

6. Subsection (3) is intended to make clear the same policy expressed in Section 3–805.

Cross References:

Sections 3–105 through 3–112, 3–401, 3–402 and 3–403.
Point 1: Section 3–107.
Point 3: Section 3–112.
Point 4: Sections 3–103 and 3–805.
Point 6: Section 3–805.

Definitional Cross References:

"Bank". Section 1–201.
"Bearer". Section 1–201.
"Definite time". Section 3–109.
"Money". Section 1–201.
"On demand". Section 3–108.
"Order". Section 3–102.
"Promise". Section 3–102.
"Signed". Section 1–201.
"Term". Section 1–201.
"Writing". Section 1–201.

Section 3–105. When Promise or Order Unconditional.

(1) A promise or order otherwise unconditional is not made conditional by the fact that the instrument

(a) is subject to implied or constructive conditions; or

(b) states its consideration, whether performed or promised, or the transaction which gave rise to the instrument, or that the promise or order is made or the instrument matures in accordance with or "as per" such transaction; or

(c) refers to or states that it arises out of a separate agreement or refers to a separate agreement for rights as to prepayment or acceleration; or

(d) states that it is drawn under a letter of credit; or

(e) states that it is secured, whether by mortgage, reservation of title or otherwise; or

(f) indicates a particular account to be debited or any other fund or source from which reimbursement is expected; or

(g) is limited to payment out of a particular fund or the proceeds of a particular source, if the instrument is issued by a government or governmental agency or unit; or

(h) is limited to payment out of the entire assets of a partnership, unincorporated association, trust or estate by or on behalf of which the instrument is issued.

(2) A promise or order is not unconditional if the instrument

(a) states that it is subject to or governed by any other agreement; or

(b) states that it is to be paid only out of a particular fund or source except as provided in this section.

New York Annotations

(1) (a) New. No New York cases have been found.

(b) *Accords* with New York rule that recital of executed consideration does not condition a promise, Atterbury v. Bank of Washington Heights, 241 N.Y. 231, 149 N.E. 841 (1925), but may change New York law by providing the same result for recital of promised consideration. Chase v. Kellogg, 13 N.Y.S. 351, aff'd mem. 129 N.Y. 668 (1892). The second clause of paragraph (b) is substantially the same as N.I.L., § 22(2). The third and final clause of paragraph (b), although not found in the N.I.L., seems to reflect existing New York law. Pub. Nat. Bank & Trust Co. of New York v. Garcia Sugars Corp., 173 Misc. 364, 16 N.Y.S.2d 914, aff'd, 259 App.Div. 878, 20 N.Y.S.2d 1015, appeal denied, 259 App.Div. 1001, 21 N.Y.S.2d 395, aff'd 285 N.Y. 661, 33 N.E.2d 867 (1941).

(c) *Accords* with New York decisional law. Enoch v. Brandon, 249 N.Y. 263, 164 N.E. 45 (1928).

(d) New, and no New York cases were found on this point; but seems merely an elaboration of (c) above.

(e) *Accords* with New York decisional law as to recitals of security by way of a mortgage, Enoch v. Brandon, 249 N.Y. 263, 164 N.E. 45 (1928), or reservation of title, Third National Bank of Buffalo v. Bowman-Spring, 50 App.Div. 66, 63 N.Y.S. 410 (1900).

(f) *Accord:* N.I.L., § 22(1); Schmittler v. Simon, 101 N.Y. 554, 5 N.E. 452 (1886).

(g) This special treatment accorded to governmental paper represents new law, not found in the N.I.L., and a change in decisional law. See Bull v. Sims, 23 N.Y. 570 (1861). It *accords,* however, with statutes declaring that, under certain conditions, obligations of certain municipal corporations, so conditioned, are negotiable. See, e.g., Local Finance Law, § 161.00; Public Authorities Law, §§ 561(1), 661(1), 1010, 1056(1), 1057, 1080(1), 1098(1), 1126(1), 1127, 1156(1), 1157, 1256(1), 1257, 1317(1), 1318, 1349–m, 1363, 1388(1), 1408(1), 1433(1), 1458(1), 1483(1), 1508(1), 1533(1), 1553(1), 1558(1) (Endicott Parking Authority), 1569–i(1), 1595–i(1), 1657, 1682(1), 1710(1), 1730(1), 1731, 1771(1), and 1805(5). Many of these instruments, as investment securities, would be within Article 8 of the Code rather than Article 3.

(h) This is new. In *accord* as to instruments payable only out of the assets of an unincorporated association is Hibbs v. Brown, 190 N.Y. 167, 82 N.E. 1108 (1907). Permitting payment to be limited to the assets of a partnership, trust, or estate may change the law of New York. See Hibbs v. Brown, *supra,* 190 N.Y. at 178 and 180, 82 N.E. at 1111 and 1112, distinguishing partnerships from unincorporated associations, and see Schmittler v. Simon, 101 N.Y. 554, 5 N.E. 452 (1886), which implies that a draft payable only out of the assets of an estate is non-negotiable.

(2) (a) This is new but *accords* with decisional law. Old Colony Trust Co. v. Stumpel, 247 N.Y. 538, 161 N.E. 173 (1928).

(b) *Accord:* N.I.L., § 22.

Official Uniform Comment

Prior Uniform Statutory Provision: Section 3, Uniform Negotiable Instruments Law.

Changes: Completely revised.

Purposes of Changes: The section is intended to make it clear that, so far as negotiability is affected, the conditional or unconditional character of the promise or order is to be determined by what is expressed in the instrument itself; and to permit certain specific limitations upon the terms of payment.

1. Paragraph (a) of subsection (1) rejects the theory of decisions which have held that a recital in an instrument that it is given in return for an executory promise gives rise to an implied condition that the instrument is not to be paid if the promise is not performed, and that this condition destroys negotiability. Nothing in the section is intended to imply that language may not be fairly construed to mean what it says, but implications, whether of law or fact, are not to be considered in determining negotiability.

2. Paragraph (b) of subsection (1) is an amplification of Section 3(2) of the original act. The final clause is intended to resolve a conflict in the decisions over the effect of such language as "This note is given for payment as per contract for the purchase of goods of even date, maturity being in conformity with the terms of such contract." It adopts the general commercial understanding that such language is intended as a mere recital of the origin of the instrument and a reference to the transaction for information, but is not meant to condition payment according to the terms of any other agreement.

3. Paragraph (c) of subsection (1) likewise is intended to resolve a conflict, and to reject cases in which a reference to a separate agreement was held to mean that payment of the instrument must be limited in accordance with the terms of the agreement, and hence was conditioned by it. Such a reference normally is inserted for the purpose of making a record or giving information to anyone who may be interested, and in the absence of any express statement to that effect is not intended to limit the terms of payment. Inasmuch as rights as to prepayment or acceleration has to do with a "speed-up" in payment and since notes frequently refer to separate agreements for a statement of these rights, such reference does not destroy negotiability even though it has mild aspects of incorporation by reference. The general reasoning with respect to subparagraph (c) also applies to a draft which on its face states that it is drawn under a letter of credit (subparagraph (d)). Paragraphs (c) and (d) therefore adopt the position that negotiability is not affected. If the reference goes further and provides that payment must be made according to the terms of the agreement, it falls under paragraph (a) of subsection (2) [As amended 1962].

4. Paragraph (e) of subsection (1) is intended to settle another conflict in the decisions, over the effect of "title security notes" and other instruments which recite the security given. It rejects cases which have held that the mere statement that the instrument is secured, by reservation of title or otherwise, carries the implied condition that payment is to be made only if the security agreement is fully performed. Again such a recital normally is included only for the purpose of making a record or giving information, and is not intended to condition payment in any way. The provision adopts the position of the great majority of the courts.

5. Paragraph (f) of subsection (1) is a rewording of Section 3(1) of the original act.

6. Paragraph (g) of subsection (1) is new. It is intended to permit municipal corporations or other governments or governmental agencies to draw checks or to issue other short-term commercial paper in which payment is limited to a particular fund or to the proceeds of particular taxes or other sources of revenue. The provision will permit some municipal warrants to be negotiable if they are in proper form.

Normally such warrants lack the words "order" or "bearer," or are marked "Not Negotiable," or are payable only in serial order, which makes them conditional.

7. Paragraph (h) of subsection (1) is new. It adopts the policy of decisions holding that an instrument issued by an unincorporated association is negotiable although its payment is expressly limited to the assets of the association, excluding the liability of individual members; and recognizing as negotiable an instrument issued by a trust estate without personal liability of the trustee. The policy is extended to a partnership and to any estate. The provision affects only the negotiability of the instrument, and is not intended to change the law of any state as to the liability of a partner, trustee, executor, administrator, or any other person on such an instrument.

8. Paragraph (a) of subsection (2) retains the generally accepted rule that where an instrument contains such language as "subject to terms of contract between maker and payee of this date," its payment is conditioned according to the terms of the agreement and the instrument is not negotiable. The distinction is between a mere recital of the existence of the separate agreement or a reference to it for information, which under paragraph (c) of subsection (1) will not affect negotiability, and any language which, fairly construed, requires the holder to look to the other agreement for the terms of payment. The intent of the provision is that an instrument is not negotiable unless the holder can ascertain all of its essential terms from its face. In the specific instance of rights as to prepayment or acceleration, however, there may be a reference to a separate agreement without destroying negotiability [As amended 1962].

9. Paragraph (b) of subsection (2) restates the last sentence of Section 3 of the original act. As noted above, exceptions are made by paragraphs (g) and (h) of subsection (1) in favor of instruments issued by governments or governmental agencies, or by a partnership, unincorporated association, trust or estate.

Cross Reference:

Section 3–104.

Definitional Cross References:

"Account". Section 4–104.
"Agreement". Section 1–201.
"Instrument". Section 3–102.
"Issue". Section 3–102.
"Order". Section 3–102.
"Promise". Section 3–102.

Section 3–106. Sum Certain.

(1) The sum payable is a sum certain even though it is to be paid

(a) with a stated rate of interest or by stated installments; or

(b) with stated different rates of interest before and after default or a specified date; or

(c) with a stated discount or addition if paid before or after the date fixed for payment; or

(d) with exchange or less exchange, whether at a fixed rate or at the current rate; or

(e) with costs of collection or an attorney's fee or both upon default.

(2) For the purposes of subsection one of this section, "a stated rate of interest" shall also include a rate of interest that cannot be calculated by looking only to the instrument but which is readily ascertainable by a reference in the instrument to a published statute, regulation, rule of court, generally accepted commercial or financial index, compendium of interest rates, or announced rate of a named financial institution.

(3) Nothing in this section shall validate any term which is otherwise illegal.

Amended by Laws 1988, Ch. 225, eff. July 8, 1988.

New York Annotations

(1) (a) *Accord:* N.I.L., § 21 (1) and (2).

(b) This is new but seems to reflect New York decisional law. Lessen v. Lindsey, 238 App.Div. 262, 264 N.Y.S. 391 (1933).

(c) This is new. No New York cases were found on this point. Elsewhere the authorities are divided. Compare Commercial Credit Co. v. Nissen, 49 S.D. 303, 207 N.W. 61, 51 A.L.R. 287 (1926), and Waterhouse v. Chouinard, 128 Me. 505, 149 Atl. 21 (1930).

(d) *Accords* with N.I.L., § 21(4), except the Code adds "or less exchange." No change would seem to result from this addition.

(e) Substantially in *accord* with N.I.L., § 21(5).

Official Uniform Comment

Prior Uniform Statutory Provision: Sections 2 and 6(5), Uniform Negotiable Instruments Law.

Changes: Reworded.

Purposes of Changes: The new language is intended to clarify doubts arising under the original section as to interest, discounts or additions, exchanges, costs and attorney's fees, and acceleration or extension.

1. The section rejects decisions which have denied negotiability to a note with a term providing for a discount for early payment on the ground that at the time of issue the amount payable was not certain. It is sufficient that at any time of payment the holder is able to determine the amount then payable from the instrument itself with any necessary computation. Thus a demand note bearing interest at six per cent is negotiable. A stated discount or addition for early or late payment does not affect the certainty of the sum so long as the computation can be made, nor do different rates of interest before and after default or a specified date. The computation must be one which can be made from the instrument itself without reference to any outside source, and this section does not make negotiable a note payable with interest "at the current rate."

2. Paragraph (d) recognizes the occasional practice of making the instrument payable with exchange deducted rather than added.

3. In paragraph (e) "upon default" is substituted for the language of the original Section 2(5) in order to include any default in payment of interest or installments.

4. The section contains no specific language relating to the effect of acceleration clauses on the certainty of the sum payable. Section 2(3) of the original act contained a saving clause for provisions accelerating principal on default in payment of an installment or of interest, which led to doubt as to the effect of other accelerating provisions. This Article (Section 3–109, Definite Time) broadly validates acceleration clauses; it is not necessary to state the matter in this section as well. The disappearance

of the language referred to in old Section 2(3) means merely that it was regarded as surplusage.

5. Most states have usury laws prohibiting excessive rates of interest. In some states there are statutes or rules of law invalidating a term providing for increased interest after maturity, or for costs and attorney's fees. Subsection (2) is intended to make it clear that this section is concerned only with the effect of such terms upon negotiability, and is not meant to change the law of any state as to the validity of the term itself.

Cross References:

Section 3–104.
Point 4: Section 3–109.

Definitional Cross Reference:

"Term". Section 1–201.

Section 3–107. Money.

(1) An instrument is payable in money if the medium of exchange in which it is payable is money at the time the instrument is made. An instrument payable in "currency" or "current funds" is payable in money.

(2) A promise or order to pay a sum stated in a foreign currency is for a sum certain in money and may be satisfied by payment of that number of dollars which the stated foreign currency will purchase at the buying sight rate for that currency on the day on which the instrument is payable, or, if payable on demand, on the day of demand.

New York Annotations

(1) The N.I.L. contains no definition of money. Money is defined in the Code as "a medium of exchange authorized or adopted by a domestic or foreign government as a part of its currency" (Section 1–201(24)). As to foreign currency, see annotation to subsection (2) below. The Code definition requirement of governmental backing seems to accord with New York decisional law. Reisfeld v. Jacobs, 107 Misc. 1, 176 N.Y.S. 223 (1919). The second sentence of subsection (1) seems to accord with decisional law. Merchants' Nat. Bank v. Santa Maria Sugar Co., 162 App.Div. 248, 147 N.Y.S. 498, aff'd mem. 220 N.Y. 732, 116 N.E. 1061 (1917).

(2) This is new. Although New York decisional law has treated instruments payable in foreign money and to be payable in that foreign country as payable in money and therefore negotiable, Hebblethwaite v. Flint, 185 App.Div. 249, 173 N.Y.S. 81 (1919); Brown v. Perera, 176 N.Y.S. 215 (1918), there is some pre-N.I.L. authority for treating an instrument payable in foreign money and to be paid in the United States as not payable in money and therefore non-negotiable. Thompson v. Sloan, 23 Wend. 71 (1840). There are no New York cases on the Code presumption that an instrument payable in foreign currency may be satisfied by equivalent American money at the current rate. See, however, Incitti v. Ferrante, 12 N.J.Misc. 840, 175 Atl. 908 (1933). The Code provision that the amount payable is to be determined on the day the instrument is payable, or on the day demand is made, seems to accord with New York decisional law. Parker v. Hoppe, 257 N.Y. 333, 178 N.E. 550(1931); Kantor v. Aristo Hosiery Co., 222 App.Div. 502, 226 N.Y.S. 582 (1928).

Official Uniform Comment

Prior Uniform Statutory Provision: Section 6(5), Uniform Negotiable Instruments Law.

Changes: Completely rewritten.

Purposes of Changes and New Matter: To make clear when an instrument is payable in money and to state rules applicable to instruments drawn payable in a foreign currency.

1. The term "money" is defined in Section 1–201 as "a medium of exchange authorized or adopted by a domestic or foreign government as a part of its currency". That definition rejects the narrow view of some early cases that "money" is limited to legal tender. Legal tender acts do no more than designate a particular kind of money which the obligee will be required to accept in discharge of an obligation. It rejects also the contention sometimes advanced that "money" includes any medium of exchange current and accepted in the particular community, whether it be gold dust, beaver pelts, or cigarettes in occupied Germany. Such unusual "currency" is necessarily of uncertain and fluctuating value, and an instrument intended to pass generally in commerce as negotiable may not be made payable therein.

The test adopted is that of the sanction of government, which recognizes the circulating medium as a part of the official currency of that government. In particular the provision adopts the position that an instrument expressing the amount to be paid in sterling, francs, lire or other recognized currency of a foreign government is negotiable even though payable in the United States.

2. The provision on "currency" or "current funds" accepts the view of the great majority of the decisions, that "currency" or "current funds" means that the instrument is payable in money.

3. Either the amount to be paid or the medium of payment may be expressed in terms of a particular kind of money. A draft passing between Toronto and Buffalo may, according to the desire and convenience of the parties, call for payment of 100 United States dollars or of 100 Canadian dollars; and it may require either sum to be paid in either currency. Under this section an instrument in any of these forms is negotiable, whether payable in Toronto or in Buffalo.

4. As stated in the preceding paragraph the intention of the parties in making an instrument payable in a foreign currency may be that the medium of payment shall be either dollars measured by the foreign currency or the foreign currency in which the instrument is drawn. Under subsection (2) the presumption is, unless the instrument otherwise specifies, that the obligation may be satisfied by payment in dollars in an amount determined by the buying sight rate for the foreign currency on the day the instrument becomes payable. Inasmuch as the buying sight rate will fluctuate from day to day, it might be argued that an instrument expressed in a foreign currency but actually payable in dollars is not for a "sum certain". Subsection (2) makes it clear that for the purposes of negotiability under this Article such an instrument, despite exchange fluctuations, is for a sum certain.

Cross References:

Section 3–104.
Point 1: Section 1–201.
Point 4: Section 4–212(6).

Definitional Cross References:

"Instrument". Section 3–102.
"Money". Section 1–201.
"Order". Section 3–102.

"Promise". Section 3–102.
"Purchase". Section 1–201.

Section 3–108. Payable on Demand.

Instruments payable on demand include those payable at sight or on presentation and those in which no time for payment is stated.

New York Annotations

Accord: N.I.L., § 26. However, the last sentence of § 26, making overdue instruments payable on demand in certain circumstances, is omitted.

Official Uniform Comment

Prior Uniform Statutory Provision: Section 7, Uniform Negotiable Instruments Law.

Changes: Reworded, final sentence of original section omitted.

Purposes of Changes: Except for the omission of the final sentence this section restates the substance of original Section 7. The final sentence dealt with the status of a person issuing, accepting or indorsing an instrument after maturity and provided that as to such a person the instrument was payable on demand. That language implied that the ordinary rules relating to demand instruments as to due course, holding, presentment, notice of dishonor and so on were applicable. This Article abandons that concept which served no special purpose except to trap the unwary. Under Section 3–302 (Holder in Due Course) and in view of the deletion from this section of the final sentence of original Section 7 there is no longer the possibility that one taking time paper after maturity may acquire due course rights against a post-maturity indorser. Section 3–501(4), however, provides that the indorser after maturity is not entitled to presentment, notice of dishonor or protest.

Cross References:

Sections 3–104, 3–302 and 3–501(4).

Definitional Cross Reference:

"Instrument". Section 3–102.

Section 3–109. Definite Time.

(1) An instrument is payable at a definite time if by its terms it is payable

(a) on or before a stated date or at a fixed period after a stated date; or

(b) at a fixed period after sight; or

(c) at a definite time subject to any acceleration; or

(d) at a definite time subject to extension at the option of the holder, or to extension to a further definite time at the option of the maker or acceptor or automatically upon or after a specified act or event.

(2) An instrument which by its terms is otherwise payable only upon an act or event uncertain as to time of occurrence is not payable at a definite time even though the act or event has occurred.

New York Annotations

(1)(a) *Accord:* N.I.L., § 23(1)(2).

(b) *Accord:* N.I.L., § 23(1).

(c) This provision of the Code, as limited by Section 1–208, would seem to *accord* with present New York law. N.I.L., § 23(1) (2) (3); Higgins v. Hocking Valley R. Co., 188 App.Div. 684, 177 N.Y.S. 444 (1919); Glide v. Sheridan, 173 Misc. 542, 18 N.Y.S.2d 339 (1939); Lincoln Nat. Bank & Trust Co. v. Marsh, 24 N.Y.S.2d 281 (1940). But see, Old Colony Trust Co. v. Stumpel, 126 Misc. 375, 379, 213 N.Y.S. 536, 539–540, aff'd 219 App.Div. 771, 220 N.Y.S. 893 aff'd (on other grounds) 247 N.Y. 538, 161 N.E. 173 (1928) (that an instrument accelerable upon the holder's deeming himself insecure is non-negotiable). See generally, Britton, Bills and Notes, 107 (1943).

(d) This is new. It is said to reflect existing law but no New York cases were found. See generally, Britton, Bills and Notes, 113–115 (1943).

(2) This probably changes the statutory and case law rule in New York which countenances, as negotiable, notes made payable at death or at a fixed period after death (or some other event certain to happen): N.I.L., § 23(3); Carnwright v. Gray, 127 N.Y. 92, 27 N.E. 835 (1891); Hegeman v. Moon, 131 N.Y. 462, 30 N.E. 487 (1892). See, however, dictum in Kerr v. Smith, 156 App.Div. 807, 142 N.Y.S. 57 (1913).

Historical Note: The reference to acceleration at the option of the acceptor in (1)(d) was inserted in response to a suggestion made by the Law Revision Commission. It is intended to make clear that an acceptor as well as a maker may be given an option to demand an extension. (1956 Recommendations, p. 91; Excerpts, p. 404.)

Official Uniform Comment

Prior Uniform Statutory Provision: Sections 4 and 17(3), Uniform Negotiable Instruments Law.

Changes: Reworded; new provisions; rule of original Section 4(3) reversed.

Purposes of Changes and New Matter: To remove uncertainties arising under the original section, and to eliminate commercially unacceptable instruments.

1. Subsection (2) reverses the rule of the original Section 4(3) as to instruments payable after events certain to happen but uncertain as to time. Almost the only use of such instruments has been in the anticipation of inheritance or future interests by borrowing on post-obituary notes. These have been much more common in England than in the United States. They are at best questionable paper, not acceptable in general commerce, with no good reason for according them free circulation as negotiable instruments. As in the case of the occasional note payable "one year after the war" or at a similar uncertain date, they are likely to be made under unusual circumstances suggesting good reason for preserving defenses of the maker. They are accordingly eliminated.

2. With this change "definite time" is substituted for "fixed or determinable future time." The time of payment is definite if it can be determined from the face of the instrument.

3. An undated instrument payable "thirty days after date" is not payable at a definite time, since the time of payment cannot be determined on its face. It is, however, an incomplete instrument within the provisions of Section 3–115 dealing with such instruments and may be completed by dating it. It is then payable at a definite time.

4. Paragraph (c) of subsection (1) resolves a conflict in the decisions on the negotiability of instruments containing acceleration clauses as to the meaning and effect of "on or before a fixed or determinable future time" in the original Section

4(2). (Instruments expressly stated to be payable "on or before" a given date are dealt with in subsection (1)(a)). So far as certainty of time of payment is concerned a note payable at a definite time but subject to acceleration is no less certain than a note payable on demand, whose negotiability never has been questioned. It is in fact more certain, since it at least states a definite time beyond which the instrument cannot run. Objections to the acceleration clause must be based rather on the possibility of abuse by the holder, which has nothing to do with negotiability and is not limited to negotiable instruments. That problem is now covered by Section 1–208.

Subsection (1) (c) is intended to mean that the certainty of time of payment or the negotiability of the instrument is not affected by any acceleration clause, whether acceleration be at the option of the maker or the holder, or automatic upon the occurrence of some event, and whether it be conditional or unrestricted. If the acceleration term itself is uncertain it may fail on ordinary contract principles, but the instrument then remains negotiable and is payable at the definite time.

The effect of acceleration clauses upon a holder in due course is covered by the new definition of the holder in due course (Section 3–302) and by the section on notice to purchaser (subsection (3) of Section 3–304). If the purchaser is not aware of any acceleration, his delay in making presentment may be excused under the section dealing with excused presentment (subsection (1) of Section 3–511).

5. Paragraph (d) of subsection (1) is new. It adopts the generally accepted rule that a clause providing for extension at the option of the holder, even without a time limit, does not affect negotiability since the holder is given only a right which he would have without the clause. If the extension is to be at the option of the maker or acceptor or is to be automatic, a definite time limit must be stated or the time of payment remains uncertain and the instrument is not negotiable. Where such a limit is stated, the effect upon certainty of time of payment is the same as if the instrument were made payable at the ultimate date with a term providing for acceleration.

The construction and effect of extension clauses is covered by paragraph (f) of Section 3–118 on ambiguous terms and rules of construction, to which reference should be made.

Cross References:

Section 3–104.
Point 3: Section 3–115.
Point 4: Sections 1–208, 3–118(f), 3–304(3), and 3–511(1).
Point 5: Section 3–118(f).

Definitional Cross References:

"Holder". Section 1–201.
"Instrument". Section 3–102.
"Term". Section 1–201.

Section 3–110. Payable to Order.

(1) An instrument is payable to order when by its terms it is payable to the order or assigns of any person therein specified with reasonable certainty, or to him or his order, or when it is conspicuously designated on its face as "exchange" or the like and names a payee. It may be payable to the order of

(a) the maker or drawer; or

(b) the drawee; or

(c) a payee who is not maker, drawer or drawee; or

(d) two or more payees together or in the alternative; or

(e) an estate, trust or fund, in which case it is payable to the order of the representative of such estate, trust or fund or his successors; or

(f) an office, or an officer by his title as such in which case it is payable to the principal but the incumbent of the office or his successors may act as if he or they were the holder; or

(g) a partnership or unincorporated association, in which case it is payable to the partnership or association and may be indorsed or transferred by any person thereto authorized.

(2) An instrument not payable to order is not made so payable by such words as "payable upon return of this instrument properly indorsed."

(3) An instrument made payable both to order and to bearer is payable to order unless the bearer words are handwritten or typewritten.

New York Annotations

(1) *Accord:* N.I.L., § 27, except for the Code's addition of the last clause dealing with "exchange" paper and the express reference to "assigns" (as equivalent to order), both of which are new. The express reference to "assigns" probably *accords* with New York case law. Brainerd v. N.Y. & H. R. Co., 25 N.Y. 496 (1862); Zander v. N.Y. Security & T. Co., 178 N.Y. 208, 211, 70 N.E. 449,451 (1940) (dictum). Exchange paper is recognized by the Geneva Convention on international usage.

(a) *Accord:* N.I.L., § 27(2).

(b) *Accord:* N.I.L., § 27(3).

(c) *Accord:* N.I.L., § 27(1).

(d) Substantially the same as N.I.L., § 27(4) (5), except for changes in terminology explained in Comment 1.

(e) This is new and probably changes the New York rule. There is early case law holding an instrument payable to an estate to be payable to a fictitious person, and hence payable to bearer. Lewinsohn v. Kent & Stanley Co., 87 Hun 257, 33 N.Y.S. 826 (1895); Scott v. Parker, 25 N.Y.St.R. 865, 5 N.Y.S. 753 (1889).

(f) Similar to N.I.L., § 27(6), but probably changes the rule treating instruments payable to persons as fiduciaries payable to such persons individually, the rest being surplusage. Litchfield v. Flint, 104 N.Y. 543, 11 N.E. 58 (1887); Davis v. Garr, 6 N.Y. 124 (1851); Britton, Bills and Notes, 176–184 (1943). See N.I.L., § 72, making instruments payable to a person as cashier or other fiscal officer of a bank or corporation payable to the bank or corporation.

(g) This is new. No New York authority has been found.

(2) This is new and probably changes New York law. Nelson v. Citizens Bank, 191 App.Div. 19, 180 N.Y.S. 747, aff'd mem. 232 N.Y. 581, 134 N.E. 580 (1922) (words "payable on return of this certificate of deposit properly indorsed" held words of negotiability). Compare State Bank v. Central Mercantile Bank, 248 N.Y. 428, 162 N.E. 475 (1928) (where payable "only" to depositor on return of the certificate, etc., held not negotiable).

(3) This is new. No New York cases were found on this point. A New York case, by way of dictum, approves the following rule: "If the bill or note be payable to the bearer A, it is the same as if simply payable to A, and is not negotiable. But

if payable to A or bearer, it is the same as if payable to bearer, it is the same as if payable to bearer, and so is payable to A or holder." Bloomingdale v. National Butchers' and Drovers' Bank, 33 Misc. 594, 595, 68 N.Y.S. 35, 36 (1901). That written provisions prevail over printed provisions is the present statutory rule of construction, N.I.L., § 36(4), and is also found in decisional law. Miller v. Hannibal & St. Jo. R. R. Co., 90 N.Y. 430 (1882).

Historical Note: In (1) (f) the words "by his title" were inserted and the last portion of the subsection was revised to read "the principal but the incumbent of the office or his successors may act as if he or they were the holder" to accord with Section 3–117(a), in response to suggestions made by the Law Revision Commission. (1956 Recommendations, p. 92; Excerpts, p.404.)

Official Uniform Comment

Prior Uniform Statutory Provision: Section 8, Uniform Negotiable Instruments Law.

Changes: Reworded, new provisions.

Purposes of Changes and New Matter: The changes are intended to remove uncertainties arising under the original section.

1. Paragraph (d) of subsection (1) replaces the original subsections (4) and (5). It eliminates the word "jointly," which has carried a possible implication of a right of survivorship. Normally an instrument payable to "A and B" is intended to be payable to the two parties as tenants in common, and there is no survivorship in the absence of express language to that effect. The instrument may be payable to "A or B," in which case it is payable to either A or B individually. It may even be made payable to "A and/or B," in which case it is payable either to A or to B singly, or to the two together. The negotiation, enforcement and discharge of the instrument in all such cases are covered by the section on instruments payable to two or more persons (Sec. 3–116).

2. Paragraph (e) of subsection (1) is intended to change the result of decisions which have held that an instrument payable to the order of the estate of a decedent was payable to bearer, on the ground that the name of the payee did not purport to be that of any person. The intent in such cases is obviously not to make the instrument payable to bearer, but to the order of the representative of the estate. The provision extends the same principle to an instrument payable to the order of "Tilden Trust," or "Community Fund". So long as the payee can be identified, it is not necessary that it be a legal entity; and in each case the instrument is treated as payable to the order of the appropriate representative or his successor.

3. Under paragraph (f) of subsection (1) an instrument may be made payable to the office itself ("Swedish Consulate") or to the officer by his title as such ("Treasurer of City Club"). In either case it runs to the incumbent of the office and his successors. The effect of instruments in such a form is covered by the section on instruments payable with words of description (Sec. 3–117).

4. Vestigial theories relating to the lack of "legal entity" of partnerships and various forms of unincorporated associations-such as labor unions and business trusts-make it the part of wisdom to specify that instruments made payable to such groups are order paper payable as designated and not bearer paper (subsection (1)(g)). As in the case of incorporated associations, any person having authority from the partnership or association to whose order the instrument is payable may indorse or otherwise deal with the instrument.

5. Subsection (2) is intended to change the result of cases holding that "payable upon return of this certificate properly indorsed" indicated an intention to make the instrument payable to any indorsee and so must be construed as the equivalent of "Pay to order." Ordinarily the purpose of such language is only to insure return of

the instrument with indorsement in lieu of a receipt, and the word "order" is omitted with the intention that the instrument shall not be negotiable.

6. Subsection (3) is directed at occasional instruments reading "Pay to the order of John Doe or bearer." Such language usually is found only where the drawer has filled in the name of the payee on a printed form, without intending the ambiguity or noticing the word "bearer." Under such circumstances the name of the specified payee indicates an intent that the order words shall control. If the word "bearer" is handwritten or typewritten, there is sufficient indication of an intent that the instrument shall be payable to bearer. Instruments payable to "order of bearer" are covered not by this section but by the following Section 3–111.

Cross References:

Sections 3–104 and 3–111.
Point 1: Section 3–116.
Points 2, 3 and 4: Section 3–117.

Definitional Cross References:

"Bearer". Section 1–201.
"Conspicuous". Section 1–201.
"Instrument". Section 3–102.
"Negotiation". Section 3–202.
"Person". Section 1–201.
"Term". Section 1–201.

Section 3–111. Payable to Bearer.

An instrument is payable to bearer when by its terms it is payable to

(a) bearer or the order of bearer; or

(b) a specified person or bearer; or

(c) "cash" or the order of "cash", or any other indication which does not purport to designate a specific payee.

New York Annotations

(a) *Accord* as to instruments payable to "bearer", N.I.L., § 28(1). As to instruments payable to "the order of bearer" being bearer paper, no New York cases were found directly on point. See generally, Britton, Bills and Notes, 39 (1943). In U.S. v. White, 2 Hill 59 (1849), the court somewhat perplexed, called an instrument payable to "the order of the person who should thereafter endorse" both a limited form of bearer note and an enlarged form of order note, saying "If it could have effect in no other way, we should hold it payable to bearer generally."

(b) *Accord:* N.I.L., § 28(2).

(c) Corresponds with N.I.L., § 28(4), except for the use of the illustrative example of payable to "cash". See Bacal v. Nat. City Bank, 146 Misc. 732, 733, 262 N.Y.S. 839 (1933) (check drawn "to the order of cash" payable to bearer). Official Comment 2, pointing out that instruments drawn "pay to the order of . . . ." are not payable to bearer, but rather are incomplete instruments, accords with New York decisional law. Nicholaras v. Stewart, 25 N.Y.S.2d 157 (1941).

Official Uniform Comment

Prior Uniform Statutory Provision: Section 9, Uniform Negotiable instruments Law.

Changes: Reworded; original subsections (3) and (5) omitted here but covered by Sections on impostors and signature in name of payee (Section 3–405) and on special and blank indorsements (Section 3–204).

Purposes of Changes: The rewording is intended to remove uncertainties.

1. Language such as "order of bearer" usually results when a printed form is used and the word "bearer" is filled in. Subsection (a) rejects the view that the instrument is payable to order, and adopts the position that "bearer" is the unusual word and should control. Compare Comment 6 to Section 3–110.

2. Paragraph (c) is reworded to remove any possible implication that "Pay to the order of . . ." makes the instrument payable to bearer. It is an incomplete order instrument, and falls under Section 3–115. Likewise "Pay Treasurer of X Corporation" does not mean pay bearer, even though there may be no such officer. Instruments payable to the order of an estate, trust, fund, partnership, unincorporated association or office are covered by the preceding section. This subsection applies only to such language as "Pay Cash," "Pay to the order of cash", "Pay bills payable," "Pay to the order of one keg of nails," or other words which do not purport to designate any specific payee.

3. Under Section 40 of the original Act an instrument payable to bearer on its face remained bearer paper negotiable by delivery although subsequently specially indorsed. It should be noted that Section 3–204 on special indorsement reverses this rule and allows the special indorsement to control.

Cross References:

Sections 3–104, 3–405 and 3–204.
Point 2: Sections 3–110(1) (a) and (f) and 3–115.
Point 3: Section 3–204.

Definitional Cross References:

"Bearer". Section Section 1–201.
"Instrument". Section 3–102.
"Person". Section 1–201.
"Term". Section 1–201.

Section 3–112. Terms and Omissions Not Affecting Negotiability.

(1) The negotiability of an instrument is not affected by

(a) the omission of a statement of any consideration or of the place where the instrument is drawn or payable; or

(b) a statement that collateral has been given to secure obligations either on the instrument or otherwise of an obligor on the instrument or that in the case of default on those obligations the holder may realize on or dispose of the collateral; or

(c) a promise or power to maintain or protect collateral or to give additional collateral; or

(d) a term authorizing a confession of judgment on the instrument if it is not paid when due; or

(e) a term purporting to waive the benefit of any law intended for the advantage or protection of any obligor; or

(f) a term in a draft providing that the payee by indorsing or cashing it acknowledges full satisfaction of an obligation of the drawer; or

(g) a statement in a draft drawn in a set of parts (Section 3–801) to the effect that the other is effective only if no other part has been honored.

(2) Nothing in this section shall validate any term which is otherwise illegal.

Amended by Laws 1963, ch. 1003, eff. Sept. 27, 1964.

New York Annotations

(1) (a) *Accord:* N.I.L., § 25 (2) (3).

(b) Similar to N.I.L., § 24(1), except the Code provision is not limited to default at maturity and refers to "collateral" rather than "collateral securities." No New York authority has been found on the question whether authorization to sell collateral on default prior to maturity affects negotiability. Recitals of collateral have been held not to destroy negotiability. Arnold v. Rock River Valley Union R. Co., 5 Duer 207 (1856); Continental Casualty Co. v. Aetna Casualty & Surety Co., 251 App. Div. 467, 296 N.Y.S. 833 (1937).

(c) This is new but reflects New York decisional law. First Nat. Bank of Bridgeport v. Blackman, 249 N.Y. 322, 164 N.E. 113 (1928).

(d) *Accord:* N.I.L., § 24(2).

(e) *Accord:* N.I.L., § 24(3).

(f) This is new but probably such a term would be permitted under N.I.L., § 22(2) (statement of the transaction).

(g) This is new. No New York authority directly in point was found, except that in Kerr S. S. Co. v. Chartered Bank of India, Australia and China, 292 N.Y. 253, 263, 54 N.E.2d 813, 820 (1944), a draft issued in first and second of exchange and reciting "On Demand Pay This First of Exchange (Second being unpaid)" was treated as a negotiable instrument without discussion of the negotiable question.

(2) *Accord:* N.I.L., § 24.

Historical Note: Section 3–112(1)(c) was rewritten in order that clauses customarily included in many instruments may not be taken to impair negotiability. Subparagraph (g) was added to subsection (1), in response to a suggestion of the Law Revision Commission, to insure that the condition in a question will not adversely affect negotiability. (1956 Recommendations, p. 93.)

Official Uniform Comment

Prior Uniform Statutory Provision: Sections 5 and 6, Uniform Negotiable Instruments Law.

Changes: Reworded; new provisions; Subsection (4) of original Section 5 omitted. Subsection (4) of the original Section 6 is now covered by Section 3–113, and Subsection (5) by Section 3–107.

Purposes of Changes and New Matter: The changes are intended to remove uncertainties arising under the original sections. Subsection (4) of the original Section 5 is omitted because it has been important only in connection with bonds and other investment securities now covered by Article 8 of this Act. An option to require something to be done in lieu of payment of money is uncommon and not desirable in commercial paper.

This section permits the insertion of certain obligations and powers in addition to the simple promise or order to pay money. Under section 3–104, dealing with form of negotiable instruments, the instrument may not contain any other promise, order, obligation or power.

1. Paragraph (b) of subsection (1) permits a clause authorizing the sale or disposition of collateral given to secure obligations either on the instrument or otherwise of an obligor on the instrument upon any default in those obligations, including a default in payment of an installment or of interest. It is not limited, as was the original Section 5(1), to default at maturity. The reference to obligations of an obligor on the instrument is intended to recognize so-called cross collateral provisions that appear in collateral note forms used by banks and others throughout the United States and to permit the use of these provisions without destroying negotiability. Paragraph (c) is new. It permits a clause, apparently now within the original section, containing a promise or power to maintain or protect collateral or to give additional collateral, whether on demand or on some other condition. Such terms frequently are accompanied by a provision for acceleration if the collateral is not given, which is now permitted by the section on what constitutes a definite time. Section 1–208 should be consulted as to the construction to be given such clauses under this Act.

2. As under the original Section 5(2), paragraph (d) is intended to mean that a confession of judgment may be authorized only if the instrument is not paid when due, and that otherwise negotiability is affected. The use of judgment notes is confirmed to two or three states, and in others the judgment clauses are made illegal or ineffective either by special statutes or by decisions. Subsection (2) is intended to say that any such local rule remains unchanged, and that the clause itself may be invalid, although the negotiability of the instrument is not affected.

3. As in the case of the original Section 5(3), paragraph (e) applies not only to any waiver of the benefits of this Article, such as presentment, notice of dishonor or protest, but also to a waiver of the benefits of any other law such as a homestead exemption. Again subsection (2) is intended to mean that any rule which invalidates the waiver itself is not changed, and that while negotiability is not affected, a waiver of the statute of limitations contained in an instrument may be invalid.

This paragraph is to be read together with subsection (1) of Section 3–104 on form of negotiable instruments. A waiver cannot make the instrument negotiable within this Article where it does not comply with the requirements of that section.

4. Paragraph (f) is new. The effect of a clause of acknowledgment of satisfaction upon negotiability has been uncertain under the original section.

5. Paragraph (g) is intended to insure that a condition arising from the statement in question will not adversely affect negotiability.

Cross References:

Sections 3–104 and 3–105.
Point 1: Sections 1–208 and 3–109(1)(c).
Point 3: Section 3–104.

Definitional Cross References:

"Draft". Section 3–104.
"Instrument". Section 3–102.
"On demand". Section 3–108.
"Promise". Section 3–102.
"Term". Section 1–201.

Section 3–113. Seal.

An instrument otherwise negotiable is within this Article even though it is under a seal.

New York Annotations

Similar to N.I.L., § 25(4). See also Civil Practice Act, § 342 [now General Construction Law, § 44–a], nullifying the effect of the seal.

Official Uniform Comment

Prior Uniform Statutory Provision: Section 6(4), Uniform Negotiable Instruments Law.

Changes: Reworded.

Purposes of Changes: The revised wording is intended to change the result of decisions holding that while a seal does not affect the negotiability of an instrument it may affect it in other respects falling within the statute, such as the conclusiveness of consideration. The section is intended to place sealed instruments on the same footing as any other instruments so far as all sections of this Article are concerned. It does not affect any other statutes or rules of law relating to sealed instruments except insofar as, in the case of negotiable instruments, they are inconsistent with this Article. Thus a sealed instrument which is within this Article may still be subject to a longer statute of limitations than negotiable instruments not under seal, or to such local rules of procedures as that it may be enforced by an action of special assumpsit.

Cross Reference:

Section 3–104.

Definitional Cross Reference:

"Instrument". Section 3–102.

Section 3–114. Date, Antedating, Postdating.

(1) The negotiability of an instrument is not affected by the fact that it is undated, antedated or postdated.

(2) Where an instrument is antedated or postdated the time when it is payable is determined by the stated date if the instrument is payable on demand or at a fixed period after date.

(3) Where the instrument or any signature thereon is dated, the date is presumed to be correct.

New York Annotations

(1) Similar to N.I.L., §§ 25(1) (undated instrument negotiable) and 31 (antedated and postdated instruments "not invalid"). Holding post-dated checks negotiable: Kuflik v. Vaccaro, 103 Misc. 239, 170 N.Y.S. 13 (1918); Marra v. Warren, 192 Misc. 296, 80 N.Y.S.2d 412 (1947). No New York cases involving antedated instruments were found.

(2) This is new but *accords* with New York decisional law. Mohawk Bank v. Broderick & Powell, 10 Wend. 304, aff'd 13 Wend. 133 (1834).

(3) Extends N.I.L., § 30, to apply to any signature on the instrument and uses the term "presumed," defined in Section 1–201, in lieu of the term "deemed prima facie."

UCC

Official Uniform Comment

Prior Uniform Statutory Provision: Sections 6(1), 11, 12 and 17(3), Uniform Negotiable Instruments Law.

Changes: Reworded; new provision; parts of original section 12 omitted.

Purposes of Changes and New Matter: The rewording is intended to remove uncertainties arising under the original sections.

1. The reference to an "illegal of fraudulent purpose" in the original Section 12 is omitted as inaccurate and misleading. Any fraud or illegality connected with the date of an instrument does not affect its negotiability, but is merely a defense under Sections 3–306 and 3–307 to the same extent as any other fraud or illegality. The provision in the same section as to acquisition of title upon delivery is also omitted, as obvious and unnecessary.

2. Subsection (2) is new. An undated instrument payable "thirty days after date" is uncertain as to time of payment, and does not fall within Section 3–109(1)(a) on definite time. It is, however, an incomplete instrument, and the date may be inserted as provided in the section dealing with such instruments (Section 3–115). When the instrument has been dated, this subsection follows decisions under the original Act in providing that the time of payment is to be determined from the stated date, even though the instrument is antedated or postdated. An antedated instrument may thus be due before it is issued. As to the liability of indorsers in such a case, see Section 3–501(4), on indorsement after maturity.

3. Subsection (3) extends the original Section 11 to any signature on an instrument. As to the meaning of "presumed", see Section 1–201.

Cross References:

Point 1: Sections 3–306 and 3–307.
Point 2: Sections 3–109(1)(a), 3–115 and 3–501(4).
Point 3: Section 1–201.

Definitional Cross References:

"Instrument". Section 3–102.
"Issue". Section 3–102.
"On demand". Section 3–108.
"Presumed". Section 1–201.
"Signature". Section 3–401.

Section 3–115. Incomplete Instruments.

(1) When a paper whose contents at the time of signing show that it is intended to become an instrument is signed while still incomplete in any necessary respect it cannot be enforced until completed, but when it is completed in accordance with authority given it is effective as completed.

(2) If the completion is unauthorized the rules as to material alteration apply (Section 3–407), even though the paper was not delivered by the maker or drawer; but the burden of establishing that any completion is unauthorized is on the party so asserting.

New York Annotations

This section condenses, rewords, and revises the rules relating to "incomplete instruments."

(1) Similar to first sentence of N.I.L., § 33. Omitted are N.I.L., § 32, and the second and third sentences of N.I.L., § 33. See *Points 1 and 3* of the Comment.

(2) *Contra* and holding that non–delivery and unauthorized completion together constitute a real defense are N.I.L., § 34; Holzman Cohen & Co. v. Teague, 172 App.Div. 75, 158 N.Y.S. 211 (1916); Linick v. A.J. Nutting & Co. 140 App.Div. 265, 125 N.Y.S. 93 (1910).

Official Uniform Comment

Prior Uniform Statutory Provision: Sections 13, 14 and 15, Uniform Negotiable Instruments Law.

Changes: Condensed and reworded; original Section 13 and parts of Section 14 omitted; rule of Section 15 reversed.

Purposes of Changes:

1. The original sections were lengthy and confusing. Section 13 is eliminated because it has suggested some uncertain distinction between undated instruments and those incomplete in other respects, and has carried the inference that only a holder may fill in the date. An instrument lacking in an essential date is merely one kind of incomplete instrument, to be treated like any other. The third sentence of Section 14, providing that the instrument must be filled up strictly in accordance with the authority given and within a reasonable time, is eliminated as entirely superfluous, since any authority must always be exercised in accordance with its limitations, and expires within a reasonable time unless a time limit is fixed.

2. The language "signed while still incomplete in any necessary respect" in subsection (1) is substituted for "wanting in any material particular" in the original Section 14, in order to make it entirely clear that a complete writing which lacks an essential element of an instrument and contains no blanks or spaces or anything else to indicate that what is missing is to be supplied, does not fall within the section. "Necessary" means necessary to a complete instrument. It will always include the promise or order, the designation of the payee, and the amount payable. It may include the time of payment where a blank is left for that time to be filled in; but where it is clear that no time is intended to be stated the instrument is complete, and is payable on demand under Section 3–108. It does not include the date of issue, which under Section 3–114 (1) is not essential, unless the instrument is made payable at a fixed period after that date.

3. This section omits the second sentence of the original Section 14, providing that "a signature on a blank paper delivered by the person making the signature in order that the paper may be converted into a negotiable instrument operates as a prima facie authority to fill it up as such for any amount." This had utility only in connection with the ancient practice of signing blank paper to be filled in later as an acceptance, at a time when communications were slow and difficult. The practice has been obsolete for nearly a century. It affords obvious opportunity for fraud, and should not be encouraged by express sanction in the statute. The omission is not intended, however, to mean that any person may not be authorized to write in an instrument over a signature either before or after delivery.

4. Subsection (2) states the rule generally recognized by the courts, that any unauthorized completion is an alteration of the instrument which stands on the same footing as any other alteration. Reference is therefore made to Section 3–407 where the effect of alteration is stated. Subsection (3) of that section provides that a subsection holder in due course may in all cases enforce the instrument as completed, and replaces the final sentence of the original Section 14.

5. The language "even though the paper was not delivered" reverses the rule of the original Section 15, which provides that where an incomplete instrument has not

been delivered it will not, if completed, be a valid contract in the hands of any holder as against any person whose signature was placed thereon before delivery. Since under this Article (Sections 3–305 and 3–407) neither non-delivery nor unauthorized completion is a defense against a holder in due course, it has always been illogical that the two together should invalidate the instrument in his hands. A holder in due course sees and takes the same paper, whether it was complete when stolen or completed afterward by the thief, and in each case he relies in good faith on the maker's signature. The loss should fall upon the party whose conduct in signing blank paper has made the fraud possible, rather than upon the innocent purchaser. The result is consistent with the theory of decisions holding the drawer of a check stolen and afterwards filled in to be estopped from setting up the non-delivery against an innocent party.

A similar provision protecting a depositary bank which pays an item in good faith is contained in Section 4–401. The policy of that Section should apply in favor of drawees other than banks.

6. The language on burden of establishing unauthorized completion is substituted for the "prima facie authority" of the original section 14. It follows the generally accepted rule that the full burden of proof by a preponderance of the evidence is upon the party attacking the completed instrument. "Burden of establishing" is defined in Section 1–201.

Cross References:

Point 2: Section 3–108 and 3–114(1).
Point 4: Section 3–407.
Point 5: Sections: 3–305(2), 3–407(3) and 4–401.
Point 6: Section 1–201.

Definitional Cross References:

"Alteration". Section 3–407.
"Burden of establishing". Section 1–201.
"Delivery". Section 1–201.
"Instrument". Section 3–102.
"Party". Section 1–201.
"Signed". Section 1–201.

Section 3–116. Instrument Payable to Two or More Persons.

An instrument payable to the order of two or more persons

(a) if in the alternative is payable to any one of them and may be negotiated, discharged or enforced by any of them who has possession of it;

(b) if not in the alternative is payable to all of them and may be negotiated, discharged or enforced only by all of them.

New York Annotations

(a) U.N.I.L., § 41 (N.I.L., § 71), is said by Britton to be inapplicable to alternative payees, being applicable to joint payees only. (Bills and Notes, p. 185 (1943).) No New York cases involving negotiation or discharge by less than all alternative payees have been found. Moreover, Passut v. Heubner, 81 Misc. 249, 142 N.Y.S. 546 (1913), involving enforcement, stated that "A promissory note payable to two persons in the alternative creates a joint interest in the payees"

(b) Generally in *accord* with N.I.L., § 71. But note that partners are no longer expressly excepted, and that this section is not limited to endorsement but includes negotiation, discharge, and enforcement. On negotiation, see First Nat. Bank of Brooklyn v. Gridley, 112 App. Div. 398, 98 N.Y.S. 445 (1906); Allen v. Corn Exchange Bank, 87 App. Div. 335, 84 N.Y.S. 1001 (1903). The last section of the Official Comment says an instrument payable to "A and/or B" is payable alternatively or jointly, which is an accord with Glens Falls Indemnity Co. v. Chase Nat'l Bank, 257 N.Y. 441, 178 N.E. 751 (1931).

Official Uniform Comment

Prior Uniform Statutory Provision: Section 41, Uniform Negotiable Instruments Law.

Changes: Revised in wording and substance.

Purposes of Changes: The changes are intended to make clear the distinction between an instrument payable to "A or B" and one payable to "A and B". The first names either A or B as payee, so that either of them who is in possession becomes a holder as that term is defined in Section 1-201 and may negotiate, enforce or discharge the instrument. The second is payable only to A and B together, and as provided in the original section both must indorse in order to negotiate the instrument, although one may of course be authorized to sign for the other. Likewise both must join in any action to enforce the instrument, and the rights of one are not discharged without his consent by the act of the other.

If the instrument is payable to "A and/or B," it is payable in the alternative to A, or to B, or to A and B together, and it may be negotiated, enforced or discharged accordingly.

Cross Reference:

Section 1-201.

Definitional Cross References:

"Instrument". Section 3-102.

"Person". Section 1 201.

Section 3-117. Instruments Payable With Words of Description.

An instrument made payable to a named person with the addition of words describing him

(a) as agent or officer of a specified person is payable to his principal but the agent or officer may act as if he were the holder;

(b) as any other fiduciary for a specified person or purpose is payable to the payee and may be negotiated, discharged or enforced by him;

(c) in any other manner is payable to the payee unconditionally and the additional words are without effect on subsequent parties.

New York Annotations

(a) Similar to but broader than N.I.L., § 72, in that it extends the rule, not limited to cashiers and other fiscal officers of banks or corporations, to all officers and agents of all "persons" (defined in Section 1-201(30)). As extended, this rule may change the law of New York. See Davis v. Garr, 6 N.Y. 124, 133 (1851) (instrument payable to named persons, trustees of specified association or their successors, held payable to such persons individually, the designation being surplusage.)

(b) Probably *accords* with New York decisional law. Litchfield v. Flint, 104 N.Y.543, 11 N.E.58, (1887); Reznor v. Webb., 36 How. Pr. 353 (1867); Davis v. Garr, *supra.*

(c) No New York cases were found on this point other than those cited in the annotation to subparagraph (b) above.

Official Uniform Comment

Prior Uniform Statutory Provision: Section 42, Uniform Negotiable Instruments Law.

Changes: Revised and extended.

Purposes of Changes:

1. Subsection (a) extends the policy of the original Section 42, which covered only cashiers and fiscal officers of banks and corporations, to any case where a payee is named with words describing him as agent or officer of another named person. The intent is to include all such descriptions as "John Doe, Treasurer of Town of Framingham," "John Doe, President Home Telephone Co.," "John Doe, Secretary of City Club," or "John Doe, agent of Richard Doe." In all such cases it is commercial understanding that the description is not added for mere identification but for the purpose of making the instrument payable to the principal, and that the agent or officer is named as payee only for convenience in enabling him to cash the check.

2. Subsection (b) covers such descriptions as "John Doe, Trustee of Smithers Trust," "John Doe, Administrator of the Estate of Richard Roe," or "John Doe, Executor under Will of Richard Roe." In such cases the instrument is payable to the individual named, and he may negotiate it, enforce it or discharge it, but he remains subject to any liability for breach of his obligation as a fiduciary. Any subsequent holder of the instrument is put on notice of the fiduciary position, and under the section on notice to purchaser (Section 3–304) is not a holder in due course if he takes with notice that John Doe has negotiated the instrument in payment of or as security for his own debt or in any transaction for his own benefit, or otherwise in breach of duty.

3. Any other words of description, such as "John Doe, 1121 Main Street," "John Doe, Attorney," or "Jane Doe, unremarried widow", are to be treated as mere identification, and not in any respect as a condition of payment. The same is true of any description of the payee as "Treasurer," "President," "Agent," "Trustee," "Executor," or "Administrator," which does not name the principal or beneficiary. In all such cases the person named may negotiate, enforce or discharge the instrument if he is otherwise identified, even though he does not meet the description. Any subsequent party dealing with the instrument may disregard the description and treat the paper as payable unconditionally to the individual, and is fully protected in the absence of independent notice of other facts sufficient to affect his position.

Cross Reference:

Point 2: Section 3–304(2).

Definitional Cross References:

"Holder". Section 1–201.
"Instrument". Section 3–102.
"Party". Section 1–201.

"Person". Section 1-201.

Section 3-118. Ambiguous Terms and Rules of Construction.

The following rules apply to every instrument:

(a) Where there is doubt whether the instrument is a draft or a note the holder may treat it as either. A draft on the drawer is effective as a note.

(b) Handwritten terms control typewritten and printed terms, and typewritten control printed.

(c) Words control figures except that if the words are ambiguous figures control.

(d) Unless otherwise specified a provision for interest means interest at the judgment rate at the place of payment from the date of the instrument, or if it is undated from the date of issue.

(e) Unless the instrument otherwise specifies two or more persons who sign as maker, acceptor or drawer or indorser and as a part of the same transaction are jointly and severally liable even though the instrument contains such words as "I promise to pay."

(f) Unless otherwise specified consent to extension authorizes a single extension for not longer than the original period. A consent to extension, expressed in the instrument, is binding on secondary parties and accommodation makers. A holder may not exercise his option to extend an instrument over the objection of a maker or acceptor or other party who in accordance with Section 3-604 tenders full payment when the instrument is due.

New York Annotations

(a) The first sentence is substantially in accord with N.I.L., § 36(5). See also Didato v. Coniglio, 50 Misc. 280, 100 N.Y.S. 466 (1906). Except for the present option in the holder to treat the draft (bill of exchange) as such, rather than as a note, the concluding sentence of this Code subparagraph and N.I.L., § 214, are substantially the same. Pavenstedt v. New York Life Ins. Co., 203 N.Y. 91, 96 N.E. 104 (1911).

(b) *Accord:* N.I.L., § 36(4), with the addition that handwritten terms control typewritten, and typewritten terms control printed.

(c) *Accords,* in simplified form, with N.I.L., § 36(1). See also Kasnowitz v. Manufacturers Trust Co., 171 Misc. 545, 13 N.Y.S.2d 211 (1939).

(d) *Accord:* N.I.L., § 36(2), with the addition that unless otherwise specified the rate of interest shall be "the judgment rate at the place of payment." That where a note is payable "with interest", its rate being unspecified, the rate shall be the "judgment rate" ("legal rate" or "statutory rate") seems to accord with New York decisional law. O'Brien v. Young, 95 N.Y. 428 (1884); Chelsea Exchange Bank v. Warner, 202 App.Div. 499, 195 N.Y.S. 419 (1922). As to the law of the place of payment fixing the interest rate, no New York authority precisely in point has been found.

(e) *Accord;* N.I.L., § 36(7), and last sentence of N.I.L., § 118.

(f) This is new. The first sentence changes the case law rule in New York that where the duration of the extension is not provided, a reasonable time will be implied,

UCC

varying according to the circumstances. Traders Nat. Bank v. Parker. 130 N.Y. 415, 29 N.E. 1094 (1892).

Historical Note: The second and third sentences of subparagraph (f) were added at the suggestion of the Law Revision Commission to make clear that the extension binds secondary parties, and that the holder may not force an extension on a maker or acceptor who makes due tender. (1956 Recommendations, p. 95; Excerpts, p. 404.)

Official Uniform Comment

Prior Uniform Statutory Provision: Sections 17 and 68, Uniform Negotiable Instruments Law.

Changes: Reworded; new provisions; original subsections (3) and (6) of Section 17 omitted. The original Section 17(3) is covered, so far as the question can arise, by Sections 3–109(1)(a) and 3–114 of this Article. The original Section 17(6) is now covered by Section 3–402.

Purposes of Changes and New Matter:

1. The purpose of this section is to protect holders and to encourage the free circulation of negotiable paper by stating rules of law which will preclude a resort to parol evidence for any purpose except reformation of the instrument. Except as to such reformation, these rules cannot be varied by an proof that any party intended the contrary.

2. Subsection (a): The language of the original Section 17(5) is changed to make it clear that the provision is not limited to ambiguities of phrasing, but extends to any case where the form of the instrument leaves its character as a draft or a note in doubt.

3. Subsection (b): The original Section 17(4) is revised to cover typewriting because of its frequent use in instruments, particularly in promissory notes.

4. Subsection (c): The rewording of the original Section 17(1) is intended to make it clear that figures control only where the words are ambiguous and the figures are not.

5. Subsection (d): The revision of the original Section 17(2) is intended to make it clear that where the instrument provides for payment "with interest" without specifying the rate, the judgment rate of interest of the place of payment is to be taken as intended.

6. Subsection (e): This subsection combines and revises the original Section 17(7) and the last sentence of the original Section 68. The rule applies to any two or more persons who sign in the same capacity, whether as makers, drawers, acceptors or indorsers. It applies only where such parties sign as a part of the same transaction; successive indorsers are, of course, liable severally but not jointly.

7. Subsection (f): This provision is new. It has reference to such clauses as "The makers and indorsers of this note consent that it may be extended without notice to them." Such terms usually are inserted to obtain the consent of the indorsers and any accommodation maker to extension which might otherwise discharge them under Section 3–606 dealing with impairment of recourse or collateral. An extension in accord with these terms binds secondary parties. The holder may not force an extension on a maker or acceptor who makes due tender; the holder is not free to refuse payment and keep interest running on a good note or other instrument by extending it over the objection of a maker or acceptor or other party who in accordance with Section 3–604 tenders full payment when the instrument is due. Where consent to extension has been given, the subsection provides that unless otherwise specified the consent is to be construed as authorizing only one extension for not longer than the original period of the note.

Cross References:

Sections 3–109, 3–114, 3–402 and 3–606.
Point 7: Sections 3–604 and 3–606.

Definitional Cross References:

"Draft". Section 3–104.
"Holder". Section 1–201.
"Instrument". Section 3–102.
"Issue". Section 3–102.
"Note". Section 3–104.
"Person". Section 1–201.
"Promise". Section 3–102.
"Signed". Section 1–201.
"Term". Section 1–201.

Section 3–119. Other Writings Affecting Instrument.

(1) As between the obligor and his immediate obligee or any transferee the terms of an instrument may be modified or affected by any other written agreement executed as a part of the same transaction, except that a holder in due course is not affected by any limitation of his rights arising out of the separate written agreement if he had no notice of the limitation when he took the instrument.

(2) A separate agreement does not affect the negotiability of an instrument.

New York Annotations

(1) The first part of this subsection, as to the effect of a separate writing on commercial paper when executed as part of the same transaction on a person other than a holder in due course, accords with existing decisional law. Title Guarantee & Trust Co. v. Pam, 232 N.Y. 441, 134 N.E. 525 (1922); Kelso & Co. v. Ellis, 224 N.Y. 528, 121 N.E. 364 (1918). The limited exception as to holders in due course in the second part of the subsection would appear to clarify conflicting case law authority in New York. One line of authority holds that knowledge of the terms of a separate agreement does not bind a holder in due course to those terms. National Bank of Watervliet v. Martin, 203 App.Div. 390, 196 N.Y.S. 714, aff'd mem. 235 N.Y. 611, 139 N.E. 755 (1923); Petroleum Acceptance Corp. v. Queen Anne Laundry Service, Inc., 265 App.Div. 692, 40 N.Y.S.2d 495 (1943); Credit Alliance Corp. v. Buffalo Linen Supply Co., 238 App.Div. 18, 263 N.Y.S. 39 (1933). A contrary view is represented by Federal Credit Bureau, Inc. v. Zelkor Dining Car Corp., 238 App.Div. 379, 264 N.Y.S. 723 (1933).

The Code would reject the rule of National Bank of Watervliet v. Martin, *supra,* in that, although the holder would qualify as a holder in due course notwithstanding his knowledge of the separate agreement, the holder would be bound by any limitation of which he had knowledge at the time of taking. See also United States v. Novsam Realty Corp., 125 F. 2d 456 (2d Cir. 1942) (*contra* to Zelkor case), and Palmer, "Negotiable Instruments Under the Uniform Commercial Code," 48 Mich. L.Rev. 255, 267-268 (1950).

(2) *Accords* with New York decisional law. Old Colony Trust Co. v. Stumpel, 126 Misc. 375, 213 N.Y.S. 536, aff'd without opinion, 219 App. Div. 771, 220 N.Y.S. 893, aff'd on other grounds, 247 N.Y. 538, 161 N.E. 173 (1928); Merchants Nat.

Bank v. Santa Maria Sugar Co., 162 App.Div. 248, 147 N.Y.S. 498, aff'd mem. 220 N.Y. 732, 116 N.E. 1061 (1917).

Official Uniform Comment

Prior Uniform Statutory Provision: None.

Purposes: This section is new. It is intended to resolve conflicts as to the effect of a separate writing upon a negotiable instrument.

1. This Article does not attempt to state general rules as to when an instrument may be varied or affected by parol evidence, except to the extent indicated by the comment to the preceding section. This section is limited to the effect of a separate written executed as a part of the same transaction. The separate writing is most commonly an agreement creating or providing for a security interest such as a mortgage, chattel mortgage, conditional sale or pledge. It may, however, be any type of contract, including an agreement that upon certain conditions the instrument shall be discharged or is not to be paid, or even an agreement that it is a sham and not to be enforced at all. Nothing in this section is intended to validate any such agreement which is fraudulent or void as against public policy, as in the case of a note given to deceive a bank examiner.

2. Other parties, such as an accommodation indorser, are not affected by the separate writing unless they were also parties to it as a part of the transaction by which they became bound on the instrument.

3. The section applies to negotiable instruments the ordinary rule that writings executed as a part of the same transaction are to be read together as a single agreement. As between the immediate parties a negotiable instrument is merely a contract, and is no exception to the principle that the courts will look to the entire contract in writing. Accordingly a note may be affected by an acceleration clause, a clause providing for discharge under certain conditions, or any other relevant term in the separate writing. "May be modified or affected" does not mean that the separate agreement must necessarily be given effect. There is still room for construction of the writing as not intended to affect the instrument at all, or as intended to affect it only for a limited purpose such as foreclosure or other realization of collateral. If there is outright contradiction between the two, as where the note is for $1,000 but the accompanying mortgage recites that it is for $2,000, the note may be held to stand on its own feet and not to be affected by the contradiction.

4. Under this Article a purchaser of the instrument may become a holder in due course although he takes it with knowledge that it was accompanied by a separate agreement, if he has no notice of any defense or claim arising from the terms of the agreement. If any limitation in the separate writing in itself amounts to a defense or claim, as in the case of an agreement that the note is a sham and cannot be enforced, a purchaser with notice of it cannot be a holder in due course. The section also covers limitations which do not in themselves give notice of any present defense or claim, such as conditions providing that under certain conditions the note shall be extended for one year. A purchaser with notice of such limitations may be a holder in due course, but he takes the instrument subject to the limitation. If he is without such notice, he is not affected by such a limiting clause in the separate writing.

5. Subsection (2) rejects decisions which have carried the rule that contemporaneous writings must be read together to the length of holding that a clause in a mortgage affecting a note destroyed the negotiability of an instrument is always to be determined by what appears on the face of the instrument alone, and if it is negotiable in itself a purchaser without notice of a separate writing is in no way affected by it. If the instrument itself states that it is subject to or governed by any other agreement, it is not negotiable under this Article; but if it merely refers to a separate agreement or states that it arises out of such an agreement, it is negotiable.

Cross References:

Point 1: Section 3–119.
Point 4: Section 3–304(4)(b).
Point 5: Section 3–105(2)(a) and (1)(c).

Definitional Cross References:

"Agreement". Section 1–201.
"Holder in due course". Section 3–302
"Instrument". Section 3–102.
"Notice". Section 1–201.
"Rights". Section 1–201.
"Term". Section 1–201.
"Written" and "writing". Section 1–201.

Section 3–120. Instruments "Payable Through" Bank.

An instrument which states that it is "payable through" a bank or the like designates that bank as a collecting bank to make presentment but does not of itself authorize the bank to pay the instrument.

New York Annotations

This is entirely new and no New York cases were found on this point.

Official Uniform Comment

Prior Uniform Statutory Provision: None.

Purposes: Insurance, dividend or payroll checks, and occasionally other types of instruments, are sometimes made payable "through" a particular bank. This section states the commercial understanding as to the effect of such language. The bank is not named as drawee, and it is not ordered or even authorized to pay the instrument out of the drawer's account or any other funds of the drawer in its hands. Neither is it required to take the instrument for collection in the absence of special agreement to that effect. It is merely designated as a collecting bank through which presentment is properly made to the drawee.

Definition Cross References:

"Bank". Section 1–201.
"Collecting bank". Section 4–105.
"Instrument". Section 3–102.
"Presentment". Section 3–504.

Section 3–121. Instruments Payable at Bank.

A note or acceptance which states that it is payable at a bank is the equivalent of a draft drawn on the bank payable when it falls due out of any funds of the maker or acceptor in current account or otherwise available for such payment.

New York Annotations

This section is Alternative A of the 1958 Official Text, is in accord with N.Y.N.I.L., § 147, and codifies current New York commercial and banking practice. Heinrich

v. Middletown First Nat. Bank, 219 N.Y. 1, 113 N.E. 531 (1916); Baldwin's Bank v. Smith, 215 N.Y. 76, 109 N.E. 138 (1915).

Official Uniform Comment

Prior Uniform Statutory Provision: Section 87, Uniform Negotiable Instruments Law.

Changes: Alternative sections offered.

Purposes of Changes: The original section 87 has been amended so extensively that no uniformity has been achieved, and in many parts of the country it has been consistently disregarded in practice.

The original section represents the commercial and banking practice of New York and the surrounding states, according to which a note or acceptance made payable at a bank is treated as the equivalent of a draft drawn on the bank. The bank is not only authorized but ordered to make payment out of the account of the maker or acceptor when the instrument falls due, and it is expected to do so without consulting him. In the western and southern states a contrary understanding prevails. The note or acceptance payable at a bank is treated as merely designating a place of payment, as if the instrument were made payable at the office of an attorney. The bank's only function is to notify the maker or acceptor that the instrument has been presented and to ask for his instructions; and in the absence of specific instructions it is not regarded as required or even authorized to pay. Notwithstanding the original section western and southern banks have consistently followed the practice of asking for instructions and treating a direction not to pay as a revocation, equivalent to a direction to stop payment.

Both practices are well established, and the division is along geographical lines. A change in either practice might lead to undesirable consequences for holders, banks or depositors. The instruments involved are chiefly promissory notes, which frequently cross state lines. There is no great need for uniformity. This section therefore offers alternative provisions, the first of which states the New York commercial understanding, and the second that of the south and west.

Cross Reference:

Section 3–502.

Definitional Cross References:

"Acceptance". Section 3–410.
"Account". Section 4–104.
"Bank". Section 1–201.
"Draft". Section 3–104.
"Instrument". Section 3–102.
"Note". Section 3–104.
"Order". Section 3–102.

Section 3–122. Accrual of Cause of Action.

(1) A cause of action against a maker or an acceptor accrues

(a) in the case of a time instrument on the day after maturity;

(b) in the case of a demand instrument upon its date or, if no date is stated, on the date of issue.

(2) A cause of action against the obligor of a demand or time certificate of deposit accrues upon demand, but demand on a time certificate may not be made until on or after the date of maturity.

(3) A cause of action against a drawer of a draft or an indorser of any instrument accrues upon demand following dishonor of the instrument. Notice of dishonor is a demand.

(4) Unless an instrument provides otherwise, interest runs at the rate provided by law for a judgment

(a) in the case of a maker, acceptor or other primary obligor of a demand instrument, from the date of demand;

(b) in all other cases from the date of accrual of the cause of action.

New York Annotations

(1) (a) *Accords* with N.I.L., § 130, that no demand is necessary to charge a maker or acceptor. Accords with Osborn v. Moncure, 3 Wend. 170 (1829), insofar as this subsection may be taken to mean that action is premature until the day following the maturity date of a time instrument notwithstanding demand and refusal on the maturity date.

(b) *Accords* with decisional law. Mills v. Davis, 113 N.Y. 243, 21 N.E. 68 (1889) (statute of limitations begins to run on date of demand note); Sheldon v. Heaton, 88 Hun 535, 34 N.Y.S. 856 (1895) (action maintainable at once on "due bill").

(2) *Accords* with decisional law as to accrual of cause of action on demand deposits. Sokoloff v. National City Bank, 250 N.Y. 69, 164 N.E. 745 (1928); Payne V. Gardiner, 29 N.Y. 146 (1864); Sheldon v. Heaton, *supra.* See also Civil Practice Act, § 15(2) [now CPLR § 206(a)].

(3) This would change New York law as to when the statute of limitations begins to run. Under the Civil Practice Act, § 15 [now CPLR § 206(a),] the cause of action against drawer or indorser is computed from dishonor ("the time when the right to make the demand is complete"), not from notice of dishonor or other demand.

(4) This subsection seems to accord with decisional law that interest after demand or maturity runs at the legal rate even thought the instrument expresses a different rate. Metropolitan Savings Bank v. Tuttle, 290 N.Y. 497, 49 N.E.2d 983 (1943); O'Brien v. Young, 95 N.Y. 428 (1844). The exception in the subsection, "unless an instrument provides otherwise," seems to have reference to a provision for an increased rate after default, and, if so, accords with decisional law. Union Estates Co. v. Adlon Construction Co., 221 N.Y. 183, 116 N.E. 984 (1917).

Official Uniform Comment

Prior Uniform Statutory Provision: None.

Purpose:

1. This section is new. It follows the generally accepted rule that action may be brought on a demand note immediately upon issue, without demand, since presentment is not required to charge the maker under the original Act or under this Article. An exception is made in the case of certificates of deposit for the reason that banking custom and expectation is that demand will be made before any liability is incurred by the bank, and the additional reason that such certificates are issued with the

understanding that they will be held for a considerable length of time, which in many instances exceeds the period of the statute of limitations. As to makers and acceptors of time instruments generally, the cause of actions accrues on the day after maturity. As to drawers of drafts (including checks) and all indorsers, the cause of action accrues, in conformity with their underlying contract on the instrument (Sections 3–413 and 3–414), only upon demand made, typically in the form of a notice of dishonor, after the instrument has been presented to and dishonored by the person designated on the instrument to pay it.

2. Closely related to the accrual of a cause of action is the question of when interest begins to run where the instrument is blank on the point. A term in the instrument providing for interest controls. (See Section 3–118(d) for the construction of term which provides for interest but does not specify the rate or the time from which it runs.) In the absence of such a term and except in the case of a maker, acceptor or other primary obligor of a demand instrument subsection (4) states the rule that interest at the judgment rate runs from the date the cause of action accrues. In the case of a primary obligor of a demand instrument, interest runs from the date of demand although the cause of action (subsection (1)(a)) accrues on the stated date of the instrument or on issue. There has been a conflict in the decisions as to when "legal" interest begins to run on the demand note. Such courts have taken the view that, since the note is due when issued without demand, it should follow that interest runs from the same date. On the other hand it is clear that there is no default until after demand by the holder and thus no reason for the imposition of the penalty on the maker. Subsection (4), therefore, adopts the position of the majority of the courts that on a demand note interest runs only from demand. This same rule is applied to acceptors and other primary obligors on a demand instrument.

Cross References:

Point 1: Sections 3–501, 3–413 and 3–414.
Point 2: Section 3–118(d).

Definitional Cross References:

"Action". Section 1–201.
"Certificate of deposit". Section 3–102.
"Dishonor". Section 3–507.
"Draft". Section 3–104.
"Instrument". Section 3–102.
"Note". Section 3–104.
"Notice of dishonor". Section 3–508.
"On demand". Section 3–108.

PART 2

TRANSFER AND NEGOTIATION

Section 3–201. Transfer: Right to Indorsement.

(1) Transfer of an instrument vests in the transferee such rights as the transferor has therein, except that a transferee who has himself been a party to any fraud or illegality affecting the instrument or who as a prior holder had notice of a defense or claim against it cannot improve his position by taking from a later holder in due course.

(2) A transfer of a security interest in an instrument vests the foregoing rights in the transferee to the extent of the interest transferred.

(3) Unless otherwise agreed any transfer for the value of an instrument not then payable to bearer gives the transferee the specifically enforceable right to have the unqualified indorsement of the transferor. Negotiation takes effect only when the indorsement is made and until that time there is no presumption that the transferee is the owner.

New York Annotations

(1) The first part of the subsection accords generally with N.I.L., LL., § 79, but by its terms is not confined to transfers "for value." This does not, however, change existing law. A negotiable instrument may be the subject of a gift although payable to order and not indorsed. Matter of Hall, 16 Misc. 174, 179, 38 N.Y.S. 1135, 1138, aff'd 20 App.Div, 624, 46 N.Y.S. 1093 (1897).

The second part of the subsection is generally in accord with N.I.L., § 97, and case law, but may serve to settle a conflict of authorities as to one situation. In addition to the case of participants 1n the fraud, clearly covered by N.I.L., § 97, cases have extended the rule to prevent a reacquiring payee, who had knowledge of the fraud originally, from acquiring the rights of a later holder in due course, even though he was not a participant. Gruntal v. National Surety Co., 254 N.Y. 468, 173 N.E. 682 (1930). Where the reacquirer, an indorsee with knowledge of the fraud, negotiates to a holder in due course and later reacquires, the Second Department has held such reacquirer to be a holder in due course, Horan v. Mason, 141 App.Div. 89, 125 N.Y.S. 668 (1910), while the Fourth Department has reached a contrary result, Harter v. People's Bank of Buffalo, 221 App.Div. 122, 223 N.Y.S. 118 (1927). The Code would reject the rule of the Horan case.

(2) *Accords* with N.I.L., § 53, and present decisional law. Nat. Bank v. Albers, 244 App.Div. 127, 278 N.Y.S. 381 (1935); Pearce and Miller Engineering Co. v. Brouwer, 10 Misc 502, 31 N.Y.S. 195 (1894).

(3) *Accords* generally with N.I.L., § 79, except that the Code specifies that a transferee is presumptively entitled to an unqualified indorsement. Although no New York cases were found on this latter point, it seems to accord with general law. Britton, Bills and Notes, 292–294 (1943). Goshen Nat. Bank v. Bingham, 118 N.Y. 349, 23 N.E. 180 (1890), supports the last sentence by stating that a subsequent indorsement of a check does not relate back to the time when the check was transferred without indorsement. See also Manufacturers' Commercial Co. v. Blitz, 131 App.Div. 17, 115 N.Y.S. 402 (1909).

Official Uniform Comment

Prior Uniform Statutory Provision: Section 27, 49 and 58, Uniform Negotiable Instruments Law.

Changes: Combined and reworded; new provisions.

Purposes of Changes and New Matter: To make it clear that:

1. The section applies to any transfer, whether by a holder or not. Any person who transfers an instrument transfers whatever rights he has in it. The transferee acquires those rights even though they do not amount to "title."

2. The transfer of rights is not limited to transfers for value. An instrument may be transferred as a gift, and the donee acquires whatever rights the donor had.

3. A holder in due course may transfer his rights as such. The "shelter" provision of the last sentence of the original Section 58 is merely one illustration of the rule

that anyone may transfer what he has. Its policy is to assure the holder in due course a freemarket for the paper, and that policy is continued in this section. The provision is not intended and should not be used to permit any holder who has himself been a party to any fraud or illegality affecting the instrument, or who has received notice of any defense or claim against it, to wash the paper clean by passing it into the hands of a holder in due course and then repurchasing it. The operation of the provision is illustrated by the following examples:

(a) A induces M by fraud to make an instrument payable to A, A negotiates it to B, who takes as a holder in due course. After the instruments is overdue B gives it to C, who has notice of the fraud. C succeeds to B's rights as a holder in due course, cutting off the defense.

(b) A induces M by fraud to make an instrument payable to A, A negotiates it to B, who takes as a holder in due course. A then repurchases the instrument from B. A does not succeed to B's rights as a holder in due course, and remains subject to the defense of fraud.

(c) A induces M by fraud to make an instrument payable to A, A negotiates it to B, who takes with notice of the fraud. B negotiates it to C, a holder in due course, and then repurchases the instrument from C. B does not succeed to C's rights as a holder in due course, and remains subject to the defense of fraud.

(d) The same facts as (c), except that B had no notice of the fraud when he first acquired the instrument, but learned of it while he was a holder and with such knowledge negotiated to C. B does not succeed to C's rights as a holder in due course, and his position is not improved by the negotiation and repurchase.

4. The rights of a transferee with respect to collateral for the instrument are determined by Article 9 (Secured Transactions).

5. Subsection (2) restates original Section 27 and is intended to make it clear that a transfer of a limited interest in the instrument passes the rights of the transfer to the extent of the interest given. Thus a transferee for security acquires all such rights subject of course to the provisions of Article 9 (Secured Transactions).

6. Subsection (3) applies only to the transfer for value of an instrument payable to order or specially indorsed. It has no application to a gift, or to an instrument payable or indorsed to bearer or indorsed in blank. The transferee acquires, in the absence of any agreement to the contrary, the right to have the indorsement of the transferor. The right is now made enforceable by an action for specific performances. Unless otherwise agreed, it is a right to the general indorsement of the transferor with full liability as indorser, rather than to an indorsement without recourse. The question commonly arises where the purchaser has paid in advance and the indorsement is omitted fraudulently or through oversight; a transferor who is willing to indorse only without recourse or unwilling to indorse at all should make his intentions clear. The agreement for the transferee to take less than an unqualified indorsement need not be an express one, and the understanding may be implied from conduct, from past practice, or from the circumstances of the transaction.

7. Subsection (3) follows the second sentence of the original Section 49 in providing that there is no effective negotiation until the indorsement is made. Until that time the purchaser does not become a holder, and if he receives earlier notice of defense against or claim to the instrument he does not qualify as a holder in due course under Section 3–202 (1)(c).

8. The final clause of subsection (3), which is new, is intended to make it clear that the transferee without indorsement of an order instrument is not a holder and so is not aided by the presumption that he is entitled to recover on the instrument provided in Section 3–307(2). The terms of the obligation do not run to him, and he must account for his possession of the unindorsed paper by proving the transaction through which he acquired it. Proof of a transfer to him by a holder is proof that he has acquired the rights of a holder and that he is entitled to the presumption.

Cross References:

Section 3–202 and 3–416.
Point 5: Article 9.
Point 7: Section 3–302(1)(c).
Point 8: Section 3–307(2).

Definitional Cross References:

"Bearer". Section 1–201.
"Holder". Section 1–201.
"Holder in due course". Section 3–302.
"Instrument". Section 3–102.
"Negotiation". Section 3–202.
"Notice". Section 1–201.
"Party". Section 1–201.
"Presumption". Section 1–201.
"Right". Section 1–201.
"Security interest". Section 1–201.

Section 3–202. Negotiation.

(1) Negotiation is the transfer of an instrument in such form that the transferee becomes a holder. If the instrument is payable to order it is negotiated by delivery with any necessary indorsement; if payable to bearer it is negotiated by delivery.

(2) An indorsement must be written by or on behalf of the holder and on the instrument or on a paper so firmly affixed thereto as to become a part thereof.

(3) An indorsement is effective for negotiation only when it conveys the entire instrument or any unpaid residue. If it purports to be of less it operates only as a partial assignment.

(4) Words of assignment, condition, waiver, guaranty, limitation or disclaimer of liability and the like accompanying an indorsement do not affect its character as an indorsement.

New York Annotations

(1) *Accord:* N.I.L., § 60.

(2) *Accord:* N.I.L., § 61, except for "by or on behalf of the holder", which is in accord with N.I.L., §§ 42 and 60. The new subsection deletes the phrase "without additional words."

(3) *Accord:* N.I.L., § 62. Under present law the obligation on a bill or note is indivisible and an action at law cannot be maintained on a partial indorsement. King v. King, 7 App.Div. 547, 77 N.Y.S. 40, appeal dismissed, 172 N.Y. 604, 64 N.E. 1122 (1902); Barkley v. Muller, 164 App.Div. 351, 149 N.Y.S. 620 (1914). Blake v. Weiden, 291 N.Y. 134, 51 N.E.2d 677 (1942), seems generally to support the last sentence of the subsection in that the opinion apparently treats a partial indorsement as being, in effect, a partial assignment which is enforceable in equity, at least where all parties are before the court.

(4) This is new although decisional law seems generally in accord. As to words of assignment, see in *accord:* Fay v. Witte, 262 N.Y. 215, 186 N.E. 678 (1933). Words of guaranty: the New York decisions are prior to the N.I.L. and in conflict. Signature

to a guaranty is not an indorsement: Lamourieux v. Hewitt, 5 Wend. 307 (1830); Brown v. Curtiss, 2 N.Y. 225 (1849); contra, Leggett v. Raymond, 6 Hill 639 (1844). No New York cases have been found as to the effect of words of condition, waiver, limitation, or disclaimer of liability upon an indorsement. See, however N.I.L., §§ 67, 68, 69, and 115.

Official Uniform Comment

Prior Uniform Statutory Provision: Sections 30, 31 and 32, Uniform Negotiable Instruments Law.

Changes: Combined and reworded; new provisions.

Purposes of Changes and New Matter: To make it clear that:

1. Negotiation is merely a special form of transfer, the importance of which lies entirely in the fact that it makes the transferee a holder as defined in Section 1–201. Any negotiation carries a transfer of rights as provided in the section on transfer (subsections (1) and (2) of Section 3–201).

2. Any instrument which has been specially indorsed can be negotiated only with the indorsement of the special indorse as provided in Section 3–204 on special indorsement. An instrument indorsed in blank may be negotiated by delivery alone, provided that it bears the indorsement of all prior special indorsees.

3. Subsection (2) follows decisions holding that a purported indorsement on a mortgage or other separate paper pinned or clipped to an instrument is not sufficient for negotiation. The indorsement must be on the instrument itself or on a paper intended for the purpose which is so firmly affixed to the instrument as to become an extension or part of it. Such a paper is called an allonge.

4. The cause of action on an instrument cannot be split. Any indorsement which purports to convey to any party less than the entire amount of the instrument is not effective for negotiation. This is true of either "Pay A one-half," or "Pay A two-thirds and B one-third," and neither A nor B becomes a holder. On the other hand an indorsement reading merely "Pay A and B" is effective, since it transfers the entire cause of action to A and B as tenants in common.

The partial indorsement does, however, operate as a partial assignment of the cause of action. The provision makes no attempt to state the legal effect of such an assignment, which is left to the local law. In a jurisdiction in which a partial assignee had any rights, either a law or inequity, the partial indorsee had such rights; and in any jurisdiction where a partial assignee has no rights the partial indorsee has none.

5. Subsection (4) is intended to reject decisions holding that the addition of such words as "I hereby assign all my right, title and interest in the within note" prevents the signature from operating as an indorsement. Such words usually are added by laymen out of an excess of caution and a desire to indicate formally that the instrument is conveyed, rather than with any intent to limit the effect of the signature.

6. Subsection (4) is also intended to reject decisions which have held that the addition of "I guarantee payment" indicates an intention not to indorse but merely to guarantee. Any signature with such added words is an indorsement, and if it is made by a holder is effective for negotiation; but the liability of the indorser may be affected by the words of guarantee as provided in the section on the contract of guarantor. (Section 3–416.)

Cross References:

Section 3–417.
Point 1: Sections 1–201 and 3–201(1) and (2).
Point 2: Section 3–204.
Point 6: Section 3–416.

Definitional Cross References:

"Bearer". Section 1–201.
"Delivery". Section 1–201.
"Holder". Section 1–201.
"Instrument". Section 3–102.
"Written". Section 1–201.

Section 3–203. Wrong or Misspelled Name.

Where an instrument is made payable to a person under a misspelled name or one other than his own he may indorse in that name or his own or both; but signature in both names may be required by a person paying or giving value for the instrument.

New York Annotations

Accord: N.I.L., § 73. The final clause is new and may change present law in giving the drawee the right to demand an indorsement, which under the N.I.L. the payee or indorsee apparently need not add unless he "think fit."

Official Uniform Comment

Prior Uniform Statutory Provisions: Section 43, Uniform Negotiable Instruments Law.

Changes: Reworded.

Purposes of Changes: To make it clear that:

1. The party whose name is wrongly designated or misspelled may make an indorsement effective for negotiation by signing in his true name only. This is not commercially satisfactory, since any subsequent purchaser may be left in doubt as to the state of the title; but whether it is done intentionally or through oversight, the party transfers his right and is liable on his indorsement, and there is a negotiation if identity exists.

2. He may make an effective indorsement in the wrongly designated or misspelled name only. This again is not commercially satisfactory, since his liability as an indorser may require proof of identity.

3. He may indorse in both names. This is the proper and desirable form of indorsement, and any person called upon to pay in instrument or under contract to purchase it may protect his interest by demanding indorsement in both names, and is not in default if such demand is refused.

Cross Reference:

Section 3–401(2).

Definitional Cross References:

"Instrument". Section 3–102.
"Person". Section 1–201.
"Signature". Section 3–401.

Section 3–204. Special Indorsement; Blank Indorsement.

(1) A special indorsement specifies the person to whom or to whose order it makes the instrument payable. Any instrument specially indorsed becomes

payable to the order of the special indorsee and may be further negotiated only by his indorsement.

(2) An indorsement in blank specifies no particular indorsee and may consist of a mere signature. An instrument payable to order and indorsed in blank becomes payable to bearer and may be negotiated by delivery only until specially indorsed.

(3) The holder may convert a blank indorsement into a special indorsement by writing over the signature of the indorser in blank any contract consistent with the character of the indorsement.

New York Annotations

(1) *Accord,* generally: N.I.L., § 64; *contra* to N.I.L., § 70. The rule "once bearer [on its face], always bearer" is rejected. Under the Code the nature of the last indorsement controls on "any" instrument.

(2) *Accord:* N.I.L., §§ 28(5), 64

(3) *Accord:* N.I.L., § 65.

Historical Notes: Subsection (3), consisting of the terms, without change, of the present U.N.I.L., § 35 (N.I.L., § 65), was added to carry forward the relevant policy of the Uniform Act. The last sentence of subsection (2) was revised to correct an erroneous statement of law. A note drawn payable to "Peter Payee or order," indorsed "For collection, Peter Payee", is restrictively indorsed but has bearer characteristics. (1956 Recommendations, p. 98; Excerpts, p. 405.)

Official Uniform Comment

Prior Uniform Statutory Provisions: Sections 9(5), 33, 34, 35, 36, and 40, Uniform Negotiable Instruments Law.

Changes: Combined and reworded; rule of Section 40 reversed.

Purposes of Changes:

The last sentence of subsection (1) reverses the rule of the original Section, under which an instrument drawn payable to bearer and specially indorsed could be further negotiated by delivery alone. The principle here adopted is that the special indorser, as the owner even of a bearer instrument, has the right to direct the payment and to require the indorsement of his indorsee as evidence of the satisfaction of his own obligation. The special indorsee may of course make it payable to bearer again by himself indorsing in blank.

Cross Reference:

Section 3–202.

Definitional Cross References:

"Bearer". Section 1–201.
"Delivery". Section 1–201.
"Instrument". Section 3–102.
"Person". Section 1–201.
"Signature". Section 3–3–401.

Section 3–205. Restrictive Indorsements.

An indorsement is restrictive which either

(a) is conditional; or

(b) purports to prohibit further transfer of the instrument; or

(c) includes the words "for collection", "for deposit", "pay any bank", or like terms signifying a purpose of deposit or collection; or

(d) otherwise states that it is for the benefit or use of the indorser or of another person.

New York Annotations

(a) This is new law. However, the comments to the section indicate that it is the purpose of the section to include in its definition the types of indorsement described in N.I.L., § 69 (conditional indorsements).

(b) Similar to N.I.L., §§ 66(1) and (2), except that the N.I.L. is limited to "negotiation" while the Code speaks of "transfer."

(c) Similar to N.I.L., § 66(2), except that the Code is more limited since it applies to "deposit or collection."

(d) Similar to N.I.L., § 66(3).

Historical Note: Section 3–205 was completely rewritten, in the light of Law Revision Commission criticism, to provide a definition of restrictive indorsements which included the varieties of indorsement described in U.N. I.L., §§ 36 and 39 (N.I.L., § 66 and 69), as was done in Supp. No. 1, Section 3–206(2). Here, however, the separate mention of conditional indorsements, those prohibiting transfer, indorsements in the bank deposit or collection process, and other indorsements to a fiduciary, permits separate treatment in subsequent sections where policy so requires.

This was part of a series of changes affecting Sections 3–102, 3–205, 3–206, 3–304, 3–419, and 3–603 and 4–205. The purpose of the changes was to require a taker or payor under restrictive indorsement to apply or pay value given consistently with the indorsements, with certain exceptions applying to banks in the collection process (other than depository banks), and to some other tankers and payors. (1956 Recommendations, p. 99.)

Official Uniform Comment

Prior Uniform Statutory Provisions: Sections 36 and 39, Uniform Negotiable Instruments Law.

Changes: Combined and reworded; new provisions.

Purposes of Changes and New Matter:

1. This section is intended to provide a definition of restrictive indorsements which will include the varieties of indorsement described in original Sections 36 and 39. The separate mention of conditional indorsements, those prohibiting transfer, indorsements in the bank deposit or collection process, and other indorsements to a fiduciary, permits separate treatment in subsequent sections where policy so requires.

2. This is part of a series of changes of the prior uniform statutory provisions effected by Sections 3–102, 3–205, 3–206, 3–304, 3–419, 3–603, and in Article 4, Sections 4–203 and 4–205. The purpose of the changes is generally to require a taker or payor under restrictive indorsement to apply or pay value given consistently with

the indorsement, but to provide certain exceptions applying to banks in the collection process (other than depositary banks), and to some other takers and payors.

Cross References:

Section 3–102, 3–202(2), 3–205, 3–206, 3–304, 3–419, 3–603, 4–203 and 4–205.

Definitional Cross References:

"Instrument". Section 3–102.
"Person". Section 1–201.

Section 3–206. Effect of Restrictive Indorsement.

(1) No restrictive indorsement prevents further transfer or negotiation of the instrument.

(2) An intermediary bank, or a payor bank which is not the depositary bank, is neither given notice nor otherwise affected by a restrictive indorsement of any person except the bank's immediate transferor or the person presenting for payment.

(3) Except for an intermediary bank, any transferee under an indorsement which is conditional or includes the words "for collection", "for deposit", "pay any bank", or like terms (sub-paragraphs (a) and (c) of Section 3–205) must pay or apply any value given by him for or on the security of the instrument consistently with the indorsement and to the extent that he does so he becomes a holder for value. In addition such transferee is a holder in due course if he otherwise complies with the requirements of Section 3–302 on what constitutes a holder in due course.

(4) The first taker under an indorsement for the benefit of the indorser or another person (subparagraph (d) of Section 3–205) must pay or apply any value given by him for or on the security of the instrument consistently with the indorsement and to the extent that he does so he becomes a holder for value. In addition such taker is a holder in due course if he otherwise complies with the requirement of Section 3–302 on what constitutes a holder in due course. A later holder for value is neither given notice nor other affected by such restrictive indorsement unless he has knowledge that a fiduciary or other person has negotiated the instrument in any transaction for his own benefit or otherwise in breach of duty (subsection (2) of Section 3–304).

New York Annotations

(1) *Contra:* N.I.L., § 77. Under this provision a restrictive indorsement would no longer terminate negotiability of the instrument.

(2) *Contra:* N.I.L., §§ 67 and 77. N.I.L., § 67, limits the title of subsequent indorsees to that of the first restrictive indorsee. The limitation would now be applicable only to the first bank-taker under a restrictive indorsement. *Contra:* Soma v. Handrulis, 277 N.Y. 223, 14 N.E.2d 46 (1938).

(3) Alters N.I.L., § 69, and is contrary to N.I.L., § 77, by permitting any transferee under a conditional or "collection" indorsement, other than an intermediate bank, to become, under the stated conditions, a holder in due course.

(4) Changes the rule of N.I.L., § 77, for the same reason as subsection (3), but in a more limited manner.

Historical Note: Section 3–206, in the light of Law Revision Commission criticism, was completely rewritten to treat separately paper indorsed for bank-collection, and that indorsed in trust; to provide that an indorsement "for deposit," or the like, has the effect it now has under U.N.I.L., §§ 37 and 47 (N.I.L., §§ 67 and 77) (with an exception, however, which provides holder-in-due-course status for an intermediary bank and discharges a payor band not a depositary bank). See Historical Note to Section 3–205. There was a further purpose– to permit one to whom an instrument is endorsed in trust to negotiate the instrument, and to make his transferee a holder in due course. (1956 Recommendations, p. 101; Excerpts, p. 406.)

Official Uniform Comment

Prior Uniform Statutory Provision: Sections 36, 37, 39 and 47, Uniform Negotiable Instruments Law.

Changes: Completely revised.

Purposes of Changes:

1. Subsections (1) and (2) apply to all four classes of restrictive indorsements defined in Section 3–205. Conditional indorsements and indorsements for deposit or collection, defined in paragraphs (a) and (c) of Section 3–205, are also subject to subsection (3); and trust indorsements as defined in paragraph (d) of Section 3–205 are subject to subsection (4). This section negated the implication which has sometimes been found in the original Sections 37 and 47, that under a restrictive indorsement neither the indorsee nor any subsequent taker from him could become a holder in due course. By omitting the original Section 47, this Article also avoids any implication that a discharge is effective against a holder in due course. See Section 3–602.

2. Under subsection (1) an indorsement reading "Pay A only," or any other indorsement purporting to prohibit further transfer, is without effect for that purpose. Such indorsements have rarely appeared in reported American cases. Ordinarily further negotiation will be contemplated by the indorser, if only for bank collection. The indorsee becomes a holder, and the indorsement does not of itself give notice to subsequent parties of any defense or claim of the indorser. Hence this section gives such an indorsement the same effect as an unrestricted indorsement.

3. Subsection (2) permits an intermediary bank (Sections 3–102(3) and 4–105) or a payor bank which is not a depositary bank (Sections 3–102(3) and 4–105) to disregard any restrictive indorsement except that of the bank's immediate transferor. Such banks ordinarily handle instruments, especially checks, in bulk and have no practicable opportunity to consider the effect of restrictive indorsements. Subsection (2) does not affect the rights of the restrictive indorser against parties outside the bank collection process or against the first bank in the collection process; such rights are governed by subsections (3) and (4) and Section 3–603.

4. Conditional indorsements are treated by this section like indorsements for deposit or collection. Under subsection (3) any transferee under such an indorsement except an intermediary bank becomes a holder for value to the extent that he acts consistently with the indorsement in paying or applying any value given by him for or on the security of the instrument. Contrary to the original Section 39, subsection (3) permits a transferee under a conditional indorsement to become a holder in due course free of the conditional indorser's claim.

5. Of the indorsements covered by this section those "for collection", "for deposit" and "pay any bank" are overwhelmingly the most frequent. Indorsements "for

collection" or "for deposit" may be either special or blank; indorsements "pay any bank" are governed by Section 4–201(2). Instruments so indorsed are almost invariably destined to be lodged in a blank for collection. Subsection (3) requires any transferee other than an intermediary bank to act consistently with the purpose of collection, and Section 3–603 lays down a similar rule for payors not covered by subsection (2).

6. Subsection (4), applying to trust indorsements other than those for deposit or collection (paragraph (d) of Section 3–205) is similar to subsection (3); but in subsection (4) the duty to act consistently with the indorsement is limited to the first taker under it. If an instrument is indorsed "Pay T in trust for B" or "Pay T for B" or "Pay T for account of B" or "Pay T as agent for B", whether B is the indorser or a third person, T is of course subject to liability for any breach of his obligation as fiduciary. But trustees commonly and legitimately sell trust assets in transactions entirely outside the bank collection process; the trustee therefore has power to negotiate the instrument and make his transferee a holder in due course. Whether transferees from T have notice of a breach of trust such as to deny them the status of holders in due course is governed by the section on notice to purchasers (Section 3–304); the trust indorsement does not of itself give such notice. Payors are immunized either by subsection (2) of this section or by Section 3–603: payment to the trustee or to a purchaser from the trustee is "consistent with the terms" of the trust indorsement under Section 3–603(1)(b).

7. Several sections of Article 3 and Article 4 are explicitly made subject to the rules stated in this section. See Sections 3–306, 3–419, 4–203 and 4–205.

Cross References:

Point 1: Section 3–205 and 3–602.
Point 2: Section 3–205(b).
Point 3: Section 3–102(3), 3–419(4), 3–603, 4–105, 4–205(2).
Point 4: Section 3–205(a).
Point 5: Sections 3–205, 3–603 and 4–201.
Point 6: Sections 3–205, 3–304 and 3–603.
Point 7: Sections 3–306, 3–419, 4–203 and 4–205.

Definitional Cross References:

"Bank". Section 1–201.
"Depositary bank". Sections 3–102(3) and 4–105.
"Holder in due course". Section 3–302.
"Intermediary bank". Sections 3–102(3) and 4–105.
"Negotiation". Sections 3–102(2) and 3–202.
"Payor bank". Sections 3–102(3) and 4–105.
"Restrictive indorsement". Section 3–205.
"Transfer". Section 3–201.

Section 3–207. Negotiation Effective Although It May Be Rescinded.

(1) Negotiation is effective to transfer the instrument although the negotiation is

(a) made by an infant, a corporation exceeding its powers, or any other person without capacity; or

(b) obtained by fraud, duress or mistake of any kind; or

(c) part of an illegal transaction; or

(d) made in breach of duty.

(2) Except as against a subsequent holder in due course such negotiation is in an appropriate case subject to recission, the declaration of a constructive trust or any other remedy permitted by law.

New York Annotations

(1)(a) Similar to but broader than N.I.L., § 41, in that the Code includes negotiations by "any other person without capacity."

(b) *Accord:* Fraud: Sullivan v. Bonesteel, 79 N.Y. 631 (1880); Duress: Fidelity Int'l T. Co. v. Conalizo, 211 App.Div. 325, 207 N.Y.S. 422 (1925).

(c) This subsection may change what appears to be the New York rule that the negotiation of an instrument in gambling transaction is void, except as to holder in due course, and that even a party other than the loser can resist liability. Hurley v. Union T. Co. of Rochester, 244 App.Div. 590, 280 N.Y.S. 474 (1935); Bernstein v. Fuerth, 132 Misc. 343, 229 N.Y.S. 791 (1928); Singer v. Union Table and Spring Co., 151 Misc. 909, 271 N.Y.S. 349 (1934).

(d) See City Bank of New Haven v. Perkins, 29 N.Y. 554 (1864).

While subsection (1) is generally in accord with N.I.L., §§ 91 and 98, the status of a taker of an instrument by unlawful means (as provided in (a), (b), (c), and (d)) is now changed from a party whose title is "defective" (with its consequences under the foregoing sections of the N.I.L.) to that of a holder subject to divestment by the rightful owner.

(2) Allows all remedies now afforded to recover an instrument. These remedies are only cut off by a holder in due course.

Historical Note: Pursuant to a Law Revision Commission suggestion the words "in a appropriate case" were added in subsection (2) to make it clear that Section 3–207 does not give a blanket substantive right where it would not otherwise exist. (1956 Recommendations, p. 101; Excerpts, p. 406.)

Official Uniform Comment

Prior Uniform Statutory Provision: Sections 22, 58 and 59, Uniform Negotiable Instruments Law.

Changes: Completely revised.

Purposes of Changes: To make it clear that:

1. The original Section 22, which covered negotiation by an infant or a corporation, is extended by this section to include other negotiations which may be rescinded. The provision applies even though the party's lack of capacity, or the illegality, is of a character which goes to the essence of the transaction and makes it entirely void, is entitled to recover the instrument and have his indorsement cancelled.

2. It is inherent in the character of negotiable paper that any person in possession of an instrument which by its terms runs to him is a holder, and that anyone may deal with him as a holder. The principle finds its most extreme application in the due course may take the paper even from a thief and be protected against the claim of the rightful owner. Where there is actual negotiation, even in an entirely void transaction, it is no less effective. The policy of this provision, as well as of the last sentence of the original Section 59, is that any person to whom an instrument is negotiated is a holder until the instrument has been recovered from his possession; and that any person who negotiates an instrument thereby parts with all his rights in it until such recovery. The remedy of any such claimant is to recover the paper by replevin or otherwise; to impound it or to enjoin its enforcement, collection or

negotiation; to recover its proceeds from the holder; or to intervene in any action brought by the holder against the obligor. As provided in the section on the rights of one not a holder in due course (Section 3–306) his claim is not a defense to the obligor unless he himself defends the action.

3. Negotiation under this Article always includes delivery. (Section 3–202, and see Section 1–201(14)). Acquisition of possession by a thief can therefore never be negotiation under this section. But delivery by the thief to another person may be.

4. Nothing in this section is intended to impose any liability on the party negotiating. He may assert any defense available to him under Sections 3–305, 3–306, and 3–307.

5. A holder in due course takes the instrument free from all claims to it on the part of any person (Section 3–305(1)). Against him there can be no recission or other remedy, even though the prior negotiation may have been fraudulent or illegal in its essence and entirely void. As against any other party the claimant may have any remedy permitted by law. This section is not intended to specify what that remedy may be, or to prevent any court from imposing conditions or limitations such as prompt action or return of the consideration received. All such questions are left to the law of the particular jurisdiction. Subsection (2) of Section 3–207 gives no right where it would not otherwise exist. The section is intended to mean that any remedies afforded by the local law are cut off only by a holder in due course, and that other parties, such as bona fide purchaser with notice that the instrument is overdue, take it subject to the claim as provided in paragraph (a) of the section on the rights of one not a holder in due course (Section 3–306).

Cross References:

Point 2: Sections 1–201 and 3–306(d).
Point 3: Sections 1–201 and 3–202
Point 4: Sections 3–305, 3–306 and 3–307.
Point 5: Sections 3–305(1) and 3–306(a).

Definitional Cross References:

"Holder in due course". Section 3–302.
"Instrument". Section 3–102.
"Negotiation". Section 3–202.
"Person". Section 1–201.
"Remedy". Section 1–201.

Section 3–208. Reacquisition.

Where an instrument is returned to or reacquired by a prior party he may cancel any indorsement which is not necessary to his title and reissue or further negotiate the instrument, but any intervening party is discharged as against the reacquiring party and subsequent holders not in due course and if his indorsement has been cancelled is discharged as against subsequent holders in due course as well.

New York Annotations

This is a combination and rephrasing of N.I.L., §§ 78, 80, and 202, with "no change in the substance of the law intended." The words "returned to or reacquired" are substituted for the words "negotiating back in N.I.L., § 80, to cover the case where an indorsee returns an instrument without indorsing it.

Official Uniform Comment

Prior Uniform Statutory Provision: Sections 48, 50 and 121, Uniform Negotiable Instruments Law.

Changes: Parts of original sections combined and rephrased.

Purposes of Changes: No change in the substance of the law is intended. "Returned to or reacquired by" is substituted for "negotiated back to" in the original Section 50 in order to make it clear that the section applies to a return by an indorsee who does not himself indorse. "Discharged" is substituted for the original language to make it clear that the discharge of the intervening party is included within the rule of the section on effect of discharge against a holder in due course (Section 3–602) and is not effective against a subsequent holder in due course who takes without notice of it.

The reacquirer may keep the instrument himself or he may further negotiate it. On further negotiation he may or may not cancel intervening indorsements. In any case intervening indorsers are discharged as to the reacquirer, since if he attempted to enforce it against them they would have an action back against him. Where the reacquirer negotiates without cancelling the intervening indorsements, the section provides that such indorsers are discharged except against subsequent holders in due course. The intervening indorser whose indorsements is stricken is, in conformity with Section 3–605, discharged even as against subsequent holders in due course.

Cross References:

Sections 3–602, 3–603(2) and 3–605.

Definitional Cross References:

"Holder in due course". Section 3–302.
"Instrument". Section 3–102.
"Party". Section 1–201.

PART 3

RIGHTS OF A HOLDER

Section 3–301. Rights of a Holder.

The holder of an instrument whether or not he is the owner may transfer or negotiate it and, except as otherwise provided in Section 3–603 on payment or satisfaction, discharge it or enforce payment in his own name.

New York Annotations

Accord: N.I.L., §§ 2, 60 (first clause), and 90 (second clause).

Official Uniform Comment

Prior Uniform Statutory Provision: Section 51, Uniform Negotiable Instruments Law.

Changes: Reworded. The provision in the original Section 51 as to discharge by payment is now covered by Section 3–603(1).

Purposes of Changes: The section is revised to state in one provision all the rights of a holder, and to make it clear that every holder has such rights. The only limitations

UCC

are those found in Section 3-603 on payment or satisfaction. That section provides (with stated exceptions) that payment to a holder discharges the liability of the party paying even though made with knowledge of a claim of another person to the instrument, unless the adverse claimant posts indemnity or procures the issuance of appropriate legal process restraining the payment. Thus payment to a holder in adverse claim situation would not give discharge if the adverse claimant had followed either of the procedures provided for in the "unless" clause of Section 3-603; nor would a discharge result from payment in two other specific situations described in Section 3-603.

Cross References:

Sections 1-201, 3-307 and 3-603(1).

Definitional Cross References:

"Holder". Section 1-201.
"Instrument". Section 3-102.
"Rights". Section 1-201.

Section 3-302. Holder in Due Course.

(1) A holder in due course is a holder who takes the instrument

(a) for value; and

(b) in good faith; and

(c) without notice that it is overdue or has been dishonored or of any defense against or claim to it on the part of any person.

(2) A payee may be a holder in due course.

(3) A holder does not become a holder in due course of an instrument:

(a) by purchase of it at judicial sale or by taking it under legal process; or

(b) by acquiring it in taking over an estate; or

(c) by purchasing it as part of a bulk transaction not in regular course of business of the transferor.

(4) A purchaser of a limited interest can be a holder in due course only to the extent of the interest purchased.

New York Annotations

(1) (a) and (b) *Accord.* N.I.L., § 91(3). As to what is "value", see Section 3-303 and the annotations thereto. As to "good faith" and the absence of "bad faith" [section 3-304(7)], see Hall v. Bank of Blasdell, 306 N.Y. 336, 118 N.E.2d 464 (1954) and Gersetta Corporation v. Wessex-Campbell Silk Co., 3 F.2d 236 (3nd Cir. 1924).

(c) N.I.L. § 91(2), by its terms requires that a holder in fact take before maturity, without regard to notice. No New York case found seems to deal with the problem of notice, but the cases do speak of taking before maturity. Pan-American Securities Corporation v. Fried Krupp Aktiengesellschaft, 169 Misc. 445, 6 N.Y.S.2d 993, aff'd 256 App.Div. 955, 10 N.Y.S. 205 (1939). This provision seems intended to cover cases where the holder takes an instrument which may or may not have been accelerated. See Northampton National Bank v. Kidder 106 N.Y. 221, 12 N.E. 577 (1887).

(2) Although the court of Appeals has not passed directly on this point, the Code provision seems to accord with the weight of lower court authority. First National Bank & Trust Co. of Elmira v. Conzo, 169 Misc. 268, 7 N.Y.S.2d 334 (1938); Yokohama Speice Bank v. Milbert Importing Corp., 182 Misc. 281, 44 N.Y.S.2d 71 (1943); South Shore Securities Co. v. Goode, 7 Misc. 2d 215, 159 N.Y.S.2d 743 (1956), 5 Misc. 2d 972, 162 N.Y.S.2d 962 (1957); Zanitti v. Malanga, 19 Misc.2d 862, 190 N.Y.S.2d 185 (1959); *contra:* Alpert v. City Motor Sales, 194 Misc. 909, 90 N.Y.S.2d 479 (1949).

(3) (a) *Accord:* Briggs v. Merrill, 58 Barb. 389 (1870) (receiver acquiring "title by legal process").

(b) (c) No New York cases directly on point were found, but this entire subsection appears to contain a few applications of the common law requirement that the holder must take "in the usual course of business."

(4) *Accord:* N.I.L., § 53, as to security interests. Jones v. Schreyer, 49 N.Y. 674 (1872); In re Levines`Estate, 156 Misc. 836, 282 N.Y.S. 769 (1935); Pearce & Miller Engineering Co. v. Brouwer, 10 Misc. 502, 31 N.Y.S. 195 (1894).

Historical Note: Subsection (1)(b) was rewritten in Supplement No. 1 to strike out a reference to reasonable commercial standards. The omission is intended to make clear that the doctrine of an objective standard of good faith, exemplified by the case of Gill v. Cubitt, 3 B & C. 466 (1824), is not intended to be incorporated in Article 3. (1956) Recommendations, p. 103.)

Official Uniform Comment

Prior Uniform Statutory Provision: Section 52, Uniform Negotiable Instruments Law.

Changes: Reworded; new provisions.

Purposes of Changes and New Matter: The changes are intended to remove uncertainties arising under the original section.

1. The language "without notice that is overdue" is substituted for that of the original subsection (2) in order to make it clear that the purchaser of an instrument which is in fact overdue may be a holder in due course if he takes it without notice that it is overdue. Such notice is covered by the section on notice to purchaser (Section 3–304.).

2. Subsection (2) is intended to settle the long continued conflict over the status of the payee as a holder in due course. This conflict has turned very largely upon the word "negotiated" in the original Section 52(4), which is now eliminated. The position here taken is that the payee may become a holder in due course to the same extent and under the same circumstances as any other holder. This is true whether he takes the instrument by purchase from a third person or directly from the obligor. All that is necessary is that the payee meet the requirements of this section. In the following cases, among others, the payee is a holder in due course:

a. A remitter, purchasing goods from P, obtains a bank draft payable to P and forwards it to P, who takes it for value, in good faith and without notice as required by this section.

b. The remitter buys the bank draft payable to P, but is forwarded by the bank directly to P, who takes it in good faith and without notice in payment of the remitter's obligation to him.

c. A and B sign a note as co-makers. A induces B to sign by fraud, and without authority from B delivers the note to P, who takes it for value, in good faith and without notice.

d. A defrauds the maker into signing an instrument payable to P. P pays A for it good faith and without notice, and the maker delivers the instrument directly to P.

e. D draws a check payable to P and gives it to his agent to be delivered to P in payment of D's debt. The agent delivers it to P, who takes it in good faith and without notice in payment to the agent's debt to P. But as to this case see Section 3–304(2), which may apply.

f. D draws a check payable to P but blank as to the amount, and gives it to his agent to be delivered to P. The agent fills in the check with an excessive amount, and P takes it for value, in good faith and without notice.

g. D draws a check blank as to the name of the payee, and gives it to his agent to be filled in with the name of A and delivered to A. The agent fills in the name of P, and P takes the check in good faith, for value and without notice.

3. Subsection (3) is intended to state existing case law. It covers a few situations in which the purchaser takes the instrument under unusual circumstances which indicate that he is merely a successor in interest to the prior holder and can acquire no better rights. (If such prior holder was himself a holder in due course, the purchaser succeeds to that status under Section 3–201 on Transfer). The provision applies to a purchaser at an execution sale, a sale in bankruptcy or a sale by a state bank commissioner of the assets of an insolvent bank. It applies equally to an attaching creditor or any other person who acquires the instrument by legal process, even under an antecedent claim; and equally to a representative, such as an executor, administrator, receiver or assignee for the benefit of creditors, who takes over the instrument as part of an estate, even though he is representing antecedent creditors.

Subsection (3)(c) applies to bulk purchases lying outside of the ordinary course of business of the seller. It applies, for example, when a new partnership takes over for value all of the assets of an old or consolidated corporation taking over in bulk the assets of a predecessor. It has particular application to the purchase by one bank of a substantial part of the paper held by another bank which is threatened with insolvency and seeking to liquidate its assets.

4. A purchaser of a limited interest–as a pledge in a security transaction–may become a holder in due course, but he may enforce the instrument over defenses only to the extent of his interest, and defenses good against the pledgor remain available insofar as the pledgor retains an equity in the instrument. This is merely a special application of the general rule (Section 1–201) that a purchaser of a limited interest acquires rights only to the extent of the interest purchases. Section 27 of the original Act contained a similar provision.

Cross References:

Sections 1–201, 3–303, 3–305 and 3–306.
Point 1: Section 3–304(5).
Point 3: Section 3–201.
Point 4: Section 1–201.

Definitional Cross References:

"Good faith". Section 1–201.
"Holder". Section 1–201.
"Instrument". Section 3–102.
"Notice". Section 1–201.
"Notice of dishonor". Section 3–508.
"Person". Section 1–201.
"Purchase". Section 1–201.
"Purchaser". Section 1–201.

"Value". Section 3–303.

Section 3–303. Taking for Value.

A holder takes the instrument for value

(a) to the extent that the agreed consideration has been performed or that he acquires a security interest in or a lien on the instrument otherwise than by legal process; or

(b) when he takes the instrument in payment of or as security for an antecedent claim against any person whether or not the claim is due; or

(c) when he gives a negotiable instrument for it or makes an irrevocable commitment to a third person.

New York Annotations

(a) Adopts the rule of N.I.L., § 93, that the consideration shall have been actually given, and eliminates the language of N.I.L., § 51, that value is "any consideration sufficient to support a simple contact." The subparagraph resolves the apparent conflict between N.I.L., § 93, and the first sentence of N.I.L., § 51, by requiring that the agreed consideration shall actually have been given. This accords with decisional law differentiating between consideration and value. An executory promise is sufficient to support the obligations embodied in the instrument. Finberg v. DeGoode, 199 App.Div. 177, 191 N.Y.S. 390 (1926). But an executory promise does not constitute value so as to qualify a transferee as a holder in due course. Citizens State Bank v. Cowles, 180 N.Y. 346, 73 N.E. 33 (1905) (bank receiving deposit and giving revocable credit not a holder in due course); Bankers Trust Co. v. Nagler, 16 A.D.2d 477, 229 N.Y.S.2d 142 (1962), citing Official Comment 3 to Section 3–303. See however, Section 4–209 for the special rule applicable to bank collections. The last part of the paragraph accords with N.I.L., § 53, but limits lienholders as takers for value to those who take other than by legal process.

(b) "As payment." *Accord:* N.I.L., § 51. American Exch. Nat. Bank v. New York Belting, etc., Co., 148 N.Y. 698, 43 N.E. 168 (1896); Kelso & Co. v. Ellis, 224 N.Y. 528, 121 N.E. 364 (1918).

"As security." The pre-N.I.L. rule was that a note given for security did not constitute value, Coddington v. Bay, 20 Johns 637, 11 Am.Dec. 342 (1822), and New York, at first, adhered to the rule even after the adoption of the N.I.L. Sutherland v. Mead, 80 App.Div. 103, 80 N.Y.S. 504 (1903). Later, however, the Court of Appeals, by way of strong dictum, appeared to adopt the contrary and majority view in the interest of uniformity under the N.I.L. Kelso & Co. v. Ellis, *supra.* See also A.E. McBee v. Shoemaker, 174 App.Div. 291, 160 N.Y.S. 251 (1916); King v. Bowling Green Trust Co., 145 App.Div. 398, 129 N.Y.S. 977 (1911). This latter view, treating a note given for security as given for value, is in accord with the Code.

(c) Although no case has been found directly so holding, it has been stated that New York is among those jurisdictions which do not regard the giving of a negotiable instrument in exchange for another as the giving of value so as to constitute either party to the exchange a holder in due course. It is further stated that where, however, the instrument passes into the hands of a bona fide holder or is paid, the holder of the other instrument will be recognized as a holder in due course. See Annot., 69 A.L.R. 408, 412, citing Mayer v. Heidelbach, 123 N.Y. 332, 25 N.E. 416 (1890); Bacon v. Holloway, 2 E.D. Smith 159 (1853); Baruch v. Buckley, 167 App.Div. 113, 151 N.Y.S. 853 (1915). These and other cases examined, however, all appear to be distinguishable on the point at issue. If, however, the New York rule does require transfer to a bona fide holder or payment, this subparagraph will change the rule by removing this requirement.

Illustrating "irrevocable commitment," see Freeport Bank v. Viemeister, 227 App.Div. 457, 238 N.Y.S. 169 (1929).

Official Uniform Comment

Prior Uniform Statutory Provision: Sections 25, 26, 27 and 54, Uniform Negotiable Instruments Law.

Changes: Combined and reworded; original Section 26 omitted.

Purposes of Changes: The changes are intended to remove uncertainties arising under the original Act.

1. The original Section 26 which had reference to the liability of accommodation parties is omitted as erroneous and misleading, since a holder who does not himself give value cannot qualify as a holder in due course in his own right merely because value has previously been given for the instrument.

2. In this Article value is divorced from consideration (Section 3-408). The latter is important only on the question of whether the obligation of a party can be enforced against him; while value is important only on the question of whether the holder who has acquired that obligation qualifies as a particular kind of holder.

3. Paragraph (a) resolves an apparent conflict between the original Section 54 and the first sentence of the original Section 25, by requiring that the agreed consideration shall actually have been given. An executory promise to give value is not itself value, except as provided in paragraph (c). The underlying reason of policy is that when the purchaser learns of a defense against the instrument or of a defect in the title he is not required to enforce the instrument, but is free to rescind the transaction for breach of the transferor's warranty (Section 3-417). There is thus not the same necessity for giving him the status of a holder in due course, cutting off claims and defenses, as where he has actually paid value. A common illustration is the bank credit not drawn upon, which a claim or defense appears.

4. Paragraph (a) limits the language of the original Section 27, eliminating the attaching creditor or any other person who acquires alien by legal process. Any such lienor has been uniformly held not be a holder in due course.

5. Paragraph (b) restates the last sentence of the original Section 25. It adopts the generally accepted rule that the holder takes for value when he takes the instrument as security for an antecedent debt, even though there is no extension of time or other concession, and whether or not the debt is due. The provision extends the same rule to any claim against any person; there is no requirement that the claim arise out of contract. In particular the provision is intended to apply to an instrument given in payment of or as security for the debt of a third person, even though no concession is made in return.

6. Paragraph (c) is new, but states generally recognized exceptions to the rule that an executory promise is not value. A negotiable instrument is value because it carries the possibility of negotiation to a holder in due course, after which the party who gives it cannot refuse to pay. The same reasoning applies to any irrevocable commitment to a third person, such as a letter of credit issued when an instrument is taken.

Cross References:

Sections 3-302 and 3-415.
Point 1: Section 3-415.
Point 2: Section 3-408.

Point 3: Section 3–417.

Definitional Cross References:

"Holder". Section 1–201.
"Instrument". Section 3–102.
"Person". Section 1–201.
"Security interest". Section 1–201.

Section 3–304. Notice to Purchaser.

(1) The purchaser has notice of a claim or defense if

(a) the instrument is so incomplete, bears such visible evidence of forgery or alteration, or is otherwise so irregular as to call into question its validity, terms or ownership or to create an ambiguity as to the party to pay; or

(b) the purchaser has notice that the obligation of any party is voidable in whole or in part or that all parties have been discharged.

(2) The purchaser has notice of a claim against the instrument when he has knowledge that a fiduciary has negotiated the instrument in payment or or as security for his own debt or in any transaction for his own benefit or otherwise in breach of duty.

(3) The purchaser has notice that an instrument is overdue if he has reason to know.

(a) that any part of the principal amount is overdue or that there is an uncured default in payment of another instrument of the same series; or

(b) that acceleration of the instrument has been made; or

(c) that he is taking a demand instrument after demand has been made or more than a reasonable length of time after its issue. A reasonable time for a check drawn and payable within the states and territories of the United States and the District of Columbia is presumed to be thirty days.

(4) Knowledge of the following facts does not of itself give the purchaser notice of a defense or claim

(a) that the instrument is antedated or postdated;

(b) that it was issued or negotiated in return for an executory promise or accompanied by a separate agreement, unless the purchaser has notice that a defense or claim has arisen from the terms thereof;

(c) that any party has signed for accommodation;

(d) that an incomplete instrument has been completed, unless the purchaser has notice of any improper completion;

(e) that any person negotiating the instrument is or was a fiduciary;

(f) that there has been default in payment of interest on the instrument or in payment of any other instrument, except one of the same series.

(5) The filing or recording of a document does not of itself constitute notice within the provisions of this Article to a person who would otherwise be a holder in due course.

(6) To be effective notice must be received at such time and in such manner as to give a reasonable opportunity to act on it.

(7) In any event, to constitute notice of a claim or defense, the purchaser must have knowledge of the claim or defense or knowledge of such facts that his action in taking the instrument amounts to bad faith.

N.Y. Commission Comments

The Code as enacted in New York in 1962, added to Section 3–304 as it appears in the 1958 and 1962 Official Texts, a new subsection (7) for the reason stated in the Commission's 1962 Report:

"The * * * added subsection carries forward the present language of the Uniform Negotiable Instruments Law § 56, N.Y.N.I.L. § 95, and the standards which the New York courts have followed in determining the qualification of a holder as a holder in due course.

"The remainder of N.Y.N.I.L. § 95, insofar as it relates to checks drawn by an officer or agent of a corporation against the account of the corporation to himself as payee, or the endorsement of a check in the name of a corporation to an officer or agent of the corporation as endorsee, or the deposit of any such check to the personal account of the officer or agent, has been transferred to § 9 of the Banking Law * * *"

New York Annotations

(1)(a) The terminology is more narrow than that found in the present N.I.L., § 91(1), under which a holder in due course must take an instrument "complete and regular upon its face." Compare New Rochelle Securities Co. v. International Thrift Society, 270 N.Y. 52, 200 N.E. 71 (1936) (altered date) (see Comment 2), and Elias v. Whitney, 50 Misc. 326, 98 N.Y.S. 667 (1906).

(b) This subparagraph is apparently intended to include the same defenses denominated "defect[s] in title" under N.I.L., § 94. Reference to voidable obligation, according to the Comments, is to make clear that notice of a right of set off or recoupment does not prevent a holder from being a holder in due course. Since defenses which render an instrument a nullity are good even against a holder in due course (Section 3–305(2) (b)), there was no need to include defenses other than those rendering the instrument voidable.

(2) *Accord:* Ward v. City Trust Co., 192 N.Y. 61, 84 N.E. 585 (1909); Wilson v. Metropolitan El. R. Co., 120 N.Y. 145, 24 N.E. 384 (1890); Wen Kroy R. Co. v. Public Nat. Bank & Trust Co., 260 N.Y. 84, 183 N.E. 73 (1932). See also Soma v. Handrulis, 277 N.Y. 223, 14 N.E.2d 46 (1938), and N.I.L., § 95.

(3)(a) and (b) Compare N.I.L., § 91(2). Overdueness which prevents holding in due course is not overdueness in fact but reason to know that the instrument is overdue either as to any part of the principal or by reason of acceleration. Under decisional law, a purchaser after maturity may not be a holder in due course, and an instrument is overdue when acceleration has occurred. Northampton Nat. Bank v. Kidder, 106 N.Y. 221, 12 N.E. 577 (1886).

(c) Under present law, if a demand instrument is negotiated an unreasonable length of time after issue, the holder is not in due course. N.I.L. § 92. The first part of the subparagraph as to taking a "demand instrument after demand" is new and no authorities have been found. As to the presumption created in the Code, compare Springer v. Erdman, 125 Misc. 112, 210 N.Y.S. 224 (1925) (no inference of bad faith from fact eleven days elapsed from date of check before it was cashed).

(4) (a) Seems to *accord* with cases holding that an indorsee is not put upon inquiry merely because negotiation is prior to the date of the instrument. Kuflik v. Vaccaro, 103 Misc. 239, 170 N.Y.S. 13 (1918); Albert v. Hoffman, 64 Misc. 87, 117 N.Y.S. 1043 (1909). See also N.I.L., § 31.

(b) There is some authority that a purchaser who knows the terms and nature of an executory agreement pursuant to which the instrument is given is charged with notice of a defense which has already arisen at the time of the negotiation, when he could have ascertained the existence of the defense by inquiry. Securities Investment Co. v. Maxwell, 131 Misc. 160, 226 N.Y.S. 273, aff'd mem. 224 App.Div. 872, 230 N.Y.S. 907 (1928); Colonial Discount Co., Inc. v. Rumens, 249 App.Div. 736, 291 N.Y.S. 676, aff'd mem. 274 N.Y. 612, 10 N.E.2d 376 (1937). See, however, Davis v. MacCready, 17 N.Y. 230 (1858), holding that even where a claim or defense is in existence, actual knowledge of it, or knowledge of such facts that the action of the purchaser amounts to bad faith, must be shown. There is much authority that a purchaser is not charged with notice of a defense which has not yet arisen by virtue of his knowledge of the executory character of the consideration in the accompanying agreement. Tradesmen's Bank v. Curtis, 167 N.Y. 194, 60 N.E. 429 (1901); Commercial Investment Co. v. Pearson, 236 App.Div. 772, 259 N.Y.S. 963 (1932); Credit Alliance Corp. v. Buffalo Linen Supply Co., 238 App.Div. 18, 263 N.Y.S. 39 (1933).

(c) *Accord:* N.I.L., § 55; Packard v. Windholz, 88 App.Div. 365, 84 N.Y.S. 666, aff'd 180 N.Y. 549, 73 N.E. 1129 (1905).

(d) This subparagraph would reverse the rule that when a purchaser knows that an instrument was incomplete when delivered, he is put on inquiry to ascertain the extent of the authority to complete it. Dumbrow v. Gelb, 72 Misc. 400, 130 N.Y.S. 182 (1911). It would also limit N.I.L., § 59.

(e) This states a proposition preliminary to paragraph (b) of subsection (2) as to when a purchaser has notice.

(f) *Accord:* Citizens Sav. Bank v. Couse, 68 Misc. 153, 124 N.Y.S. 79 (1910); Newell v. Gregg, 51 Barb. 263 (1868).

(5) No New York cases have been found although there is authority for the proposition that the rights of a purchaser of negotiable paper are not affected by constructive notice. Manufacturers & Traders Trust Co. v. Sapowitch, 296 N.Y. 226, 230, 72 N.E.2d 166, 168–169 (1947) (not involving record notice).

(6) This is new law and no New York authority has been found.

(7) *Accord:* N.I.L., § 95. Cf. Section 1–201(25), (26) and (27).

Historical Note: Pursuant to Law Revision Commission comment, language was deleted in subsection (2) concerning preferences in bankruptcy; this change was made because notice of a claim against the instrument need not logically or naturally flow from notice of a preference. Further revision, after a general study of the entire subject of notice in the Code and a specific reexamination of this section, substituted "knowledge" for "reasonable cause to believe" in subsection (2) and substituted "reason to know" for the same phrase in subsection (3). These changes conform to the definitions in Section 1–201 (25) and to the usage in the rest of the Code. The revision also, in *accord* with the revision concerning restrictive indorsement (see Section 3–205), deleted former subsection (3), renumbered the succeeding subsections, and deleted reference to restrictive indorsements from subsection (4) (e). (1956 Recommendations, p. 105; Excerpts, p. 407.)

Official Uniform Comment

Prior Uniform Statutory Provision: Section 45, 52, 53, 55 and 56, Uniform Negotiable Instruments Law.

Changes: Combined and reworded; new provisions.

Purposes of Changes and New Matter: The original sections are expanded with the addition of specific provisions intended to remove uncertainties in the existing law.

1. "Notice" is defined in Section 1–201.

2. Paragraph (a) of subsection (1) replaces the provision in the original Section 52(1) requiring that the instrument be "complete and regular on its face." An instrument may be blank as to some unnecessary particular, may contain minor erasures, or even have an obvious change in the date, as where "January 2, 1948" is changed to "January 2, 1949", without even exciting suspicion. Irregularity is properly a question of notice to the purchaser of something wrong, and is so treated here.

3. "Voidable" obligation in paragraph (b) of subsection (1) is intended to limit the provision to notice of defense which will permit any party to avoid his original obligation on the instrument, as distinguished from a set-off or counterclaim.

4. Notice that one party has been discharged is not notice to the purchaser of an infirmity in the obligation of other parties who remain liable on the instrument. A purchaser with notice that an indorser is discharged takes subject to that discharge as provided in the section on effect of discharge against a holder in due course (Section 3–602) but is not prevented from taking the obligation of the maker in due course. If he has notice that all parties are discharged he cannot be a holder in due course.

5. Subsection (2) follows the policy of Section 6 of the Uniform Fiduciaries Act, and specifies the same elements as notice of improper conduct of a fiduciary. Under paragraph (e) of subsection (4) mere notice of the existence of the fiduciary relation is not enough in itself to prevent the holder from taking in due course, and he is free to take the instrument on the assumption that the fiduciary is acting properly. The purchaser may pay cash into the hands of the fiduciary without notice of any breach of the obligation. Section 3–206 should be consulted for the effect of a restrictive indorsement.

6. Subsection (3) removes an uncertainty in the original Act by providing that reason to know of an overdue installment or other part of the principal amount is notice that the instrument is overdue and thus prevents the purchaser from taking in due course. On the other hand subsection (4)(f) makes notice that interest is overdue insufficient, on the basis of banking and commercial practice, the decisions under the original Act, and the frequency with which interest payments are in fact delayed. Notice of default in payment of any other instrument, except an uncured default in another instrument of the same series, is likewise insufficient.

7. Subsection (3) departs from the original Section 52(2) by providing that the purchaser may take accelerated paper, or a demand instrument on which demand has in fact been made, as a holder in due course if he takes without notice of the acceleration or demand. With this change the original Section 45 is eliminated, as the presumption that any negotiation has taken place before the instrument was in fact overdue is of importance only in aid of a holder in due course. Under this section it is not conclusive that the instrument was in fact overdue when it was negotiated, if the holder takes without notice of that fact.

The "reasonable time after issue" is retained from the original Section 53, but paragraph (c) adds a presumption, as that term is defined in this act (Section 1–201), that a domestic check is stale after thirty days.

8. Paragraph (a) of subsection (4) rejects decisions holding that an instrument known to be antedated or postdated is not "regular." Such knowledge does not prevent a holder from taking in due course.

9. Paragraph (b) of subsection (4) is to be read together with the provisions of this Article as to when a promise or order is unconditioned and as to other writings affecting the instrument (Sections 3–105 and 3–119). Mere notice of the existence

of an executory promise or a separate agreement does not prevent the holder from taking in due course, and such notice may even appear in the instrument itself. If the purchaser has notice of any default in the promise or agreement which gives rise to a defense or claim against the instrument, he is on notice to the same extent as in the case of any other information as to the existence of a defense or claim.

10. Paragraph (d) of subsection (4) follows the policy of the original Section 14, under which any person in possession of an instrument has prima facie authority to fill blanks. It is intended to mean that the holder may take in due course even though a blank is filled in his presence, if he is without notice that the filling is improper. Section 3–407 on alteration should be consulted as to the rights of subsequent holders following such an alteration.

11. Subsection (5) is new. It removes an uncertainty arising under the original Act as to the effect of "constructive notice" through public filing or recording.

12. Subsection (6) is new. It means that notice must be received with a sufficient margin of time to afford a reasonable opportunity to act on it, and that a notice received by the president of a bank one minute before the banks`teller cashes a check is not effective to prevent the bank from becoming a holder in due course. See in this connection the provision on notice to an organization, Sec. 1–201(27).

Cross References:

Sections 3–201 and 3–302.
Point 1: Section 1–201.
Point 4: Section 3–602.
Point 5: Section 3–206.
Point 7: Section 1–201.
Point 9: Sections 3–105(1)(b) and (c) and 3–119.
Point 10: Section 3–407.
Point 12: Section 1–201.

Definitional Cross References:

"Accommodation party". Section 3–415.
"Agreement". Section 1–201.
"Alteration". Section 3–407.
"Bank". Section 1–201.
"Check". Section 3–104.
"Holder in due course". Section 3–302.
"Instrument". Section 3–102.
"Issue". Section 3–102.
"Negotiation". Section 3–202.
"Notice". Section 1–201.
"Party". Section 1–201.
"Person". Section 1–201.
"Presumed". Section 1–201.
"Promise". Section 3–102.
"Purchaser". Section 1–201.
"Reasonable time". Section 1–204.
"Signed". Section 1–201.
"Term". Section 1–201.

Section 3–305. Rights of a Holder in Due Course.

To the extent that a holder is a holder in due course he takes the instrument free from

(1) all claims to it on the part of any person; and

(2) all defenses of any party to the instrument with whom the holder has not dealt except

(a) infancy, to the extent that it is a defense to a simple contract; and

(b) such other incapacity, or duress, or illegality of the transaction, as renders the obligation of the party a nullity; and

(c) such misrepresentation as has induced the party to sign the instrument with neither knowledge nor reasonable opportunity to obtain knowledge of its character or its essential terms; and

(d) discharge in insolvency proceedings; and

(e) any other discharge of which the holder has notice when he takes the instrument.

New York Annotations

(1) *Accords* generally with N.I.L. § 96. "Takes" is substituted for "holds" to make clear that defenses may arise against the holder after the transfer, and "claims to it on the part of any person" is substituted for "defect of title of prior parties," to make explicit that a holder in due course takes free not only from any claim of legal title but also from all liens, equities, or claims of any other kind. See Comments 1 and 2. The practical result would seem to be no real change in New York law.

(2) *Accord:* N.I.L., § 96. As to undelivered instruments, compare N.I.L., §§ 34–35. The rule of § 34 is reversed by this subsection. § 35 achieves the same result as this subsection in a different fashion. Compare Sections 3–306 and 3–307. Abandoned Property Law, § 1404, may create an additional exception.

(a) Under present law, although infancy is not a defect in title, since an infant can pass title (N.I.L., § 41), it is a defense against liability and seems to be a real defense. Darlington v. Hamilton Bank, 63 Misc. 289, 116 N.Y.S. 678 (1909). This subparagraph applies only to defenses. The right of rescission of a transfer of an instrument is cut off. See Section 3–207.

(b) Probably *accords* with New York law. The only case found holding incapacity to be a real defense was Loomis v. Ruck, 56 N.Y. 462 (1874), involving coverture, now governed by Domestic Relations Law, § 51. No cases involving insanity or intoxication were found. Duress is generally deemed a personal defense unless aggravated, in which case it may be a real defense. See Loomis v. Ruck, *supra.* Under present case law such illegality as renders the transaction void constitutes a real defense. Sabine v. Paine, 223 N.Y. 401, 119 N.E. 849 (1918) (usury); Larschen v. Lantzes, 115 Misc. 616, 189 N.Y.S. 137 (1921) (gambling); Penal Law, § 992 (wager contracts void); General Business Law, § 373 (usurious contracts void).

(c) *Accord:* First National Bank of Odessa v. Fazzari, 22 Misc. 2d 351, 193 N.Y.S.2d 367, rev'd on other ground, 13 A.D.2d 582, 212 N.Y.S.2d 380, mod. 10 N.Y.2d 394, 223 N.Y.S.2d 483, 179 N.E.2d 493 (1961.) See also Hutkoff v. Moje, 20 Misc. 632, 46 N.Y.S. 905 (1897), and National Exchange Bank v. Veneman, 43 Hun 241 (1887) on fraud in the factum as a real defense, and Chapman v. Rose, 56 N.Y. 137 (1874), and Munnich v. Jaffe, 164 App.Div. 30, 149 N.Y.S. 338 (1914), on negligence as affecting this defense.

(d) Restates the rule under the federal Bankruptcy Act, 11 U.S.C. § 35, See also Debtor and Creditor Law, § 83.

(e) Enlarges N.I.L., § 203, to include a holder in due course with notice of any discharge. Under the notice to purchaser, Section 3-304(1), (b), notice of any discharge which leaves other parties liable on the instrument does not prevent the purchaser from becoming a holder in due course. A holder in due course is not bound by any discharge of which he has no notice. Section 3-602.

Official Uniform Comment

Prior Uniform Statutory Provision: Sections 15, 16, and 57, Uniform Negotiable Instruments Law.

Changes: Combined and recorded; new provisions; rule of original Section 15 reversed.

Purposes of Changes and New Matter:

1. The section applies to any person who is himself a holder in due course, and equally to any transferee who acquires the rights of one (Section 3-201). "Takes" is substituted for "Holds" in the original Section 57 because a holder in due course may still be subject to any claims or defenses which arise against him after he has taken the instrument.

2. The language "all claims to it on the part of any person" is substituted for "any defect of title of prior parties" in the original Section the instrument free not only from any claim of legal title but also from all liens, equities or claims of any other kind. This includes any claim for rescission of a prior negotiation, in accordance with the provisions of the section on reacquisition (Section 3-208).

3. "All defenses" includes nondelivery, conditional delivery or delivery for a special purpose. Under this Article such nondelivery or qualified delivery is a defense (Sections 3-306 and 3-307) and the defendant has the full burden of establishing it. Accordingly the "conclusive presumption" of the third sentence of the original Section 16 is abrogated in favor of a rule of law cutting off the defense.

The effect of this section, together with the sections dealing with incomplete instruments (Section 3-115) and alteration (Section 3-407) is to cut off the defense of nondelivery of an incomplete instrument against a holder in due course, and to change the rule of the original Section 15.

4. Paragraph (a) of subsection (2) is new. It follows the decisions under the original Act in providing that the defense of infancy may be asserted against a holder in due course, even though its effect is to render the instrument voidable but not void. The policy is one of protection of the infant against those who take advantage of him even at the expense of occasional loss to an innocent purchaser. No attempt is made to state when infancy is available as a defense or the conditions under which it may be asserted. In some jurisdictions it is held that an infant cannot rescind the transaction or set up the defense unless he restores the holder to his former position, which in the case of a holder in due course is normally impossible. In other states an infant who has misrepresented his age may be estopped to assert his infancy. Such questions are left to the local law, as an integral part of the policy of each state as to the protection of infants.

5. Paragraph (b) of subsection (2) is new. It covers mental incompetence, guardianship, ultra vires acts or lack of corporate capacity to do business, any remaining incapacity or married women, or any other incapacity apart from infancy. Such incapacity is largely statutory. Its existence and effect is left to the law of each state. If under the local law the effect is to render the obligation of the instrument entirely null and void, the defense may be asserted against a holder in due course. If the effect is merely to render the obligation voidable at the election of the obligor, the defense is cut off.

6. Duress is a matter of degree. An instrument signed at the point of a gun is void, even in the hands of a holder in due course. One signed under threat to prosecute the son of the maker for theft may be merely voidable, so that the defense is cut off. Illegality is most frequently a matter of gambling or usury, but may arise in many other forms under a great variety of statutes. The statutes differ greatly in their provisions and the interpretations given them. They are primarily a matter of local concern and local policy. All such matters are therefore left to the local law. If under that law the effect of the duress or the illegality is to make the obligation entirely null and void, the defense may be asserted against a holder in due course. Otherwise it is cut off.

7. Paragraph (c) of subsection (2) is new. It follows the great majority of the decisions under the original Act in recognizing the defense of "real" or "essential" fraud, sometimes called fraud in the essence or fraud in the factum, as effective against a holder in due course. The common illustration is that of the maker who is tricked into signing a note in the belief that it is merely a receipt or some other document. The theory of the defense is that his signature on the instrument is ineffective because he did not intend to sign such an instrument at all. Under this provision the defense extends to an instrument signed with knowledge that it is a negotiable instrument, but without knowledge of its essential terms.

The test of the defense here stated is that of excusable ignorance of the contents of the writing signed. The party must not only have been in ignorance, but must also have had no reasonable opportunity to obtain knowledge. In determining what is a reasonable opportunity all relevant factors are to be taken into account, including the age and sex of the party, his intelligence, education and business experience; his ability to read or to understand English, the representations made to him and his reason to rely on them or to have confidence in the person making them; the presence or absence of any third person who might read or explain the instrument to him, or any other possibility of obtaining independent information; and the apparent necessity, or lack of it, for acting without delay.

Unless the misrepresentation meets this test, the defense is cut off by a holder in due course.

8. Paragraph (d) is also new. It is inserted to make it clear that any discharge in bankruptcy or other insolvency proceedings, as defined in this Article, is not cut off when the instrument is purchased by a holder in due course.

9. Paragraph (e) of subsection (2) is also new. Under the notice to purchaser section of this Article (Section 3-304), notice of any discharge which leaves other parties liable on the instrument does not prevent the purchaser from becoming a holder in due course. The obvious case is that of the cancellation of an indorsement, which leaves the maker and prior indorsers liable. As to such parties the purchaser may be a holder in due course, but he takes the instrument subject to the discharge of which he has notice. If he is without notice, the discharge is not effective against him (Section 3-602).

Cross References:

Point 1: Section 3-201(1).
Point 2: Section 3-208.
Point 3: Sections 3-115(2), 3-306(c), 3-307(2) and 3-407(3).
Point 9: Sections 3-304(1)(b) and 3-602.

Definitional Cross References:

"Contract". Section 1-201.
"Holder in due course". Section 3-302.
"Insolvency proceedings". Section 1-201.

"Instrument". Section 3–102.
"Notice". Section 1–201.
"Party". Section 1–201.
"Person". Section 1–201.
"Term". Section 1–201.

Section 3–306. Rights of One Not Holder in Due Course.

Unless he has the rights of a holder in due course any person takes the instrument subject to

(a) all valid claims to it on the part of any person; and

(b) all defenses of any party which would be available in an action on a simple contract; and

(c) the defenses of want or failure of consideration, nonperformance of any condition precedent, non delivery, or delivery for a special purpose (Section 3–408); and

(d) the defense that he or a person through whom he holds the instrument acquired it by theft, or that payment or satisfaction to such holder would be inconsistent with the terms of a restrictive indorsement. The claim of any third person to the instrument is not otherwise available as a defense to any party liable thereon unless the third person himself defends the action for such party.

New York Annotations

(a) and (b) *Accord* generally with N.I.L., § 97. There is some authority, however, for the view that a purchaser of overdue paper takes subject only to defenses to liability and not to claims of title. Matter of Clover, 154 N.Y. 443, 48 N.E. 892 (1897).

(c) *Accord:* N.I.L., §§ 35, 54.

(d) *Accords* generally with N.I.L., §§ 66, 67, and the last sentence of § 98 (which prevents the right of a third party from being set up as a defense, but makes no exception in the case of theft). The Code's recognition of the defense of *jus tertii* in the case of theft accords with New York decisional law, Hays v. Hathorn, 74 N.Y. 486 (1878), but the elimination of the *jus tertii* defense in the case of illegal transactions probably changes New York law. Hurley v. Union Trust Co., 244 App.Div. 590, 280 N.Y.S. 474 (1935); Singer v. Union Table & Spring Co., 151 Misc. 909, 271 N.Y.S. 349 (1934); Penal Law, §§ 991-993. As to the possibility of such a defense in the finder situation, see dictum in Hurley v. Union Trust Co., 244 App.Div. at 592, 280 N.Y.S. at 477.

Historical Note: Pursuant to the Law Revision Commission suggestions, a reference to Section 3–408 was added to subparagraph (c), and subparagraph (d) was rewritten to achieve consistency with Section 3–603 and related sections. (1956 Recommendations, p. 106; Excerpts, pp. 407–408.)

Official Uniform Comment

Prior Uniform Statutory Provision: Sections 16, 28, 58 and 59, Uniform Negotiable Instruments Law.

Changes: Combined, condensed and reworded.

Purposes of Changes: The changes are intended to remove the following uncertainties arising under the original sections:

1. Any transferee who acquires the rights of a holder in due course under the transfer section of this Article (Section 3–201) is included within the provisions of the preceding Section 305. This section covers any person who neither qualifies in his own right as a holder in due course nor has acquired the rights of one by transfer. In particular the section applies to a bona fide purchaser with notice that the instrument is overdue.

2. "All valid claims to it on the part of any person" includes not only claims of legal title, but all liens, equities, or other claims of right against the instrument or its proceeds. It includes claims to rescind a prior negotiation and to recover the instrument or its process.

3. Paragraph (b) restates the first sentence of the original Section 58.

4. Paragraph (c) condenses the original Sections 16 and 28. Want or failure of consideration is specifically mentioned, as in the original Section 28, in order to make it clear that either is a defense which the defendant has the burden of establishing under the following section of this Article. The language as to an "ascertained or liquidated amount or otherwise" in the original Section 28 is omitted because it is believed to be superfluous. The third sentence of Section 16 is now covered by the preceding section. The fourth sentence is omitted in favor of the rule stated in the following section, which places the full burden of establishing the defense of nondelivery, conditional delivery or delivery for a special purpose upon the defendant, and makes any presumption unnecessary.

5. Paragraph (d) is substituted for the last sentence of the original Section 59, as a more detailed and explicit statement of the same policy, which is also found in the original Section 22. The contract of the obligor is to pay the holder of the instrument, and the claims of other persons against the holder are generally not his concern. He is not required to set up such a claim as a defense, since he usually will have no satisfactory evidence of his own on the issue; and the provision that he may not do so is intended as much for his protection as for that of the holder. The claimant who has lost possession of an instrument so payable or indorsed that another may become a holder has lost his rights on the instrument, which by its terms no longer runs to him. The provision includes all claims for rescission of a negotiation, whether bases in incapacity, fraud, duress, mistake, illegality, breach of trust or duty or any other reason. It includes claims based on conditional delivery or delivery for a special purpose. It includes claims of legal title, lien constructive trust or other equity against the instrument or its proceeds. The exception made in the case of theft is based on the policy which refuses to aid a proved thief to recover, and refuses to aid him indirectly by permitting his transferee to recover unless the transferee is a holder in due course. The exception concerning restrictive indorsements is intended to achieve consistency with Section 3–603 and related sections.

Nothing in this section is intended to prevent the claimant from intervening in the holder's action against the obligor or defending the action for the latter, and asserting his claim in the course of such intervention or defense. Nothing here stated is intended to prevent any interpleader, deposit in or other available procedure under which the defendant may bring the claimant into court or be discharged without himself litigating the claim as a defense. Compare Section 3–803 on vouching in other parties alleged to be liable.

Cross References:

Section 3–302.
Point 1: Sections 3–201(1) and 3–305.
Point 2: Section 3–207.
Point 3: Section 3–307(2).
Point 4: Sections 3–305 and 3–307(2).
Point 5: Section 3–803.

Definitional Cross References:

"Action". Section 1–201.
"Contract". Section 1–201.
"Delivery". Section 1–201.
"Holder in due course". Section 3–302.
"Instrument". Section 3–102.
"Party". Section 1–201.
"Person". Section 1–201.
"Rights". Section 1–201.

Section 3–307. Burden of Establishing Signatures, Defenses and Due Course.

(1) Unless specifically denied in the pleadings each signature on an instrument is admitted. When the effectiveness of a signature is put in issue

(a) the burden of establishing it is on the party claiming under the signature; but

(b) the signature is presumed to be genuine or authorized except where the action is to enforce the obligation of a purported signer who has died or become incompetent before proof is required.

(2) When signatures are admitted or established, production of the instrument entitles a holder to recover on it unless the defendant establishes a defense.

(3) After it is shown that a defense exists a person claiming the rights of a holder in due course has the burden of establishing that he or some person under whom he claims is in all respects a holder in due course.

New York Annotations

(1) The first sentence of this subsection would appear to change New York law. It was held in Hoffstaedter v. Lichtenstein, 203 App.Div. 494, 196 N.Y.S. 577 (1922), that under a general denial the defendant could offer evidence as to the circumstances attending his alleged making of the note sued upon. Compare N.Y. City Municipal Court Code, § 92 [now CCA § 1102(b)].

(a) *Accord:* Prensky v. Bruno, 194 N.Y.S. 75 (1922). See also Matter of Pirie, 198 N.Y. 209, 91 N.E. 587 (1910); Tommasone v. Giaquinto, 153 N.Y.S. 953 (1915).

(b) No authority recognizing such a presumption has been found. There is authority denying any presumption of genuineness of indorsements from the fact of possession and requiring the holder to show such genuineness to make a prima facie case. Donahue v. Bank of America, 161 N.Y.S. 232 (1916).

(2) In substitution for first clause of N.I.L., § 98. Accords generally with Bedell v. Carll, 33 N.Y. 581 (1865); Hays v. Hathorn, 74 N.Y. 486 (1878); General Investment Co. v. Interborough Rapid Transit Co., 235 N.Y. 133, 139 N.E. 216 (1923).

(3) *Accord:* N.I.L. § 98, but any defense now shifts the burden. This would change the rule of Mitchell v. Baldwin, 88 App.Div. 265, 84 N.Y.S. 1043 (1903), where it was held that proof of want of consideration does not shift the burden. It appears that under the present law the burden of proving an affirmative defense is on the defendant. New York Bankers, Inc. v. Duncan, 257 N.Y. 160, 165, 177 N.E. 407, 408 (1931). This is equally true under the Code provision that "after it is shown that

a defense exists," a person claiming the rights of a holder in due course must establish such holdership.

Historical Note: The phrase "it is shown that a defense exists" was inserted in subsection (3), in accordance with a suggestion of the American Bankers Association Committee, to restore the expression "it is shown that," which occurs in U.N.I.L., § 59 (N.I.L., § 98), in order to make clear that no change in the quantum of evidence is here intended. (1956 Recommendations, p. 107.)

Official Uniform Comment

Prior Uniform Statutory Provision: Section 59, Uniform Negotiable Instruments Law.

Changes: Reworded; new provisions.

Purposes of Changes and New Matter:

1. Subsection (1) is new, although similar provisions are found in a number of states. The purpose of the requirement of a specific denial in the pleadings is to give the plaintiff notice that he must meet a claim of forgery or lack of authority as to the particular signature, and to afford him an opportunity to investigate and obtain evidence. Where local rules of pleading permit, the denial may be on information and belief, or it may be a denial of knowledge sufficient to form a belief. It need not be under oath unless the local statutes or rules require verification. In the absence of such specific denial the signature stands admitted, and is not in issue. Nothing in this section is intended, however, to prevent amendment of the pleading in a proper case.

The question of the burden of establishing the signature arises only when it has been put in issue by specific denial. "Burden of establishing" is defined in the definitions section of this Act(Section 1–201). The burden is on the party claiming under the signature, but he is aided by the presumption that it is genuine or authorized [as] stated in paragraph (b). "Presumption" is also defined in this Act (Section 1–201). It means that until some evidence is introduced which would support a finding that the signature is forged or unauthorized the plaintiff is not required to prove that it is authentic. The presumption rests upon the fact that in ordinary experience forged or unauthorized signatures are very uncommon, and normally any evidence is within the control of the defendant or more accessible to him. He is therefore required to make some sufficient showing of the grounds for his denial before the plaintiff is put to his proof. His evidence need not be sufficient to require a directed verdict in his favor, but it must be enough to support his denial by permitting a finding in his favor. Until he introduces such evidence the presumption requires a finding for the plaintiff. Once such evidence is introduced the burden of establishing the signature by a preponderance of the total evidence is on the plaintiff.

Under paragraph (b) this presumption does not arise where the action is to enforce the obligation of a purported signer who has died or become incompetent before the evidence is required, and so is disabled from obtaining or introducing it. "Action" of course includes a claim asserted against the estate of a deceased or an incompetent.

2. Subsection (2) is substituted for the first clause of the original Section 59. Once signatures are proved or admitted, a holder makes out his case by mere production of the instrument, and is entitled to recover in the absence of any further evidence. The defendant has the burden of establishing any and all defenses, not only in the first instance but by a preponderance of the total evidence. The provision applies only to a holder, as defined in this Act (Section 1–201). Any other person in possession of an instrument must prove his right to it and account for the absence of any necessary indorsement. If he establishes a transfer which gives him the rights of holder (Section

3–201), this provision becomes applicable, and he is then entitled to recover unless the defendant establishes a defense.

3. Subsection (3) rephrases the last clause of the original Section 59. Until it is shown that a defense exists the issue as to whether the holder is a holder in due course does not arise. In the absence of a defense any holder is entitled to recover and there is no occasion to say that he is deemed prima facie to be a holder in due course. When it is shown that a defense exists the plaintiff may, if he so elects, seek to cut off the defense by establishing that he is himself a holder in due course, or that he has acquired the rights of a prior holder in due course (Section 3–201). On this issue he has the full burden of proof by a preponderance of the total evidence. "In all respects" means that he must sustain this burden by affirmative proof that the instrument was taken for value, that it was taken in good faith, and that it was taken without notice (Section 3–302).

Nothing in this section is intended to say that the plaintiff must necessarily prove that he is the holder in due course. He may elect to introduce no further evidence, in which case a verdict may be directed for the plaintiff or the defendant, or the issue of the defense may be left to the jury, according to weight and sufficiency of the defendant's evidence. He may elect to rebut the defense itself by proof to the contrary, in which case again a verdict may be directed for either party or the issue may be for the jury. This subsection means only that if the plaintiff claims the rights of a holder in due course against the defense he has the burden of proof upon that issue.

Cross References:

Sections 3–305, 3–306, 3–401, 3–403 and 3–404.
Point 1: Section 1–201.
Point 2: Sections 1–201 and 3–201(1).
Point 3: Sections 3–201(1) and 3–302.

Definitional Cross References:

"Action". Section 1–201.
"Burden of establishing". Section 1–201.
"Defendant". Section 1–201.
"Genuine". Section 1–201.
"Holder". Section 1–201.
"Holder in due course". Section 3–302.
"Instrument". Section 3–102.
"Party". Section 1–201.
"Person". Section 1–201.
"Presumed". Section 1–201.
"Rights". Section 1–201.
"Signature". Section 3–401.

PART 4

LIABILITY OF PARTIES

Section 3–401. Signature.

(1) No person is liable on an instrument unless his signature appears thereon.

(2) A signature is made by use of any name, including any trade or assumed name, upon an instrument, or by any word or mark used in lieu of a written signature.

UCC

New York Annotations

(1) Generally in *accord:* N.I.L., § 37; Manufacturer's and Traders Bank v. Love, 13 App.Div. 561, 564, 43 N.Y.S. 812, 814 (1897). See also Ranger v. Thalmann, 84 App.Div. 341, 82 N.Y.S. 846, aff'd on opinion below, 178 N.Y. 574, 70 N.E. 1108 (1904).

In *accord:* N.I.L., § 37 (second sentence); Dewitt v. Walton, 9 N.Y. 571, 574 (1854) (dicta in concurring opinion of Parker, J.)

Official Uniform Comment

Prior Uniform Statutory Provision: Section 18, Uniform Negotiable Instruments Law.

Changes: Reworded.

Purposes of Changes: To make it clear that:

1. No one is liable on an instrument unless and until he has signed it. The chief application of the rule has been in cases holding that a principle whose name does not appear on an instrument signed by his agent is not liable on the instrument even though the payee knew when it was issued that it was intended to be the obligation of one who did not sign. The exceptions made as to collateral and virtual acceptances by the original Sections 134 and 135 are now abrogated by the definition of an acceptance and the rules governing its operation. An allonge is part of the instrument to which it is affixed. Section 3–202(2).

Nothing in this section is intended to prevent any liability arising apart from the instrument itself. The party who does not sign may still be liable on the original obligation for which the instrument was given, or for breach of any agreement to sign, or in tort for misrepresentation, or even on an oral guaranty of payment where the statute of frauds is satisfied. He may of course be liable under any separate writing. The provision is not intended to prevent an estoppel to deny that the party has signed, as where the instrument is purchased in good faith reliance upon his assurance that a forged signature is genuine.

2. A signature may be handwritten, typed, printed or made in any other manner. It need not be subscribed, and may appear in the body of the instrument, as in the case of "I, John Doe, promise to pay–" without any other signature. It may be made by mark, or even by thumbprint. It may be made in any name, including any trade name or assumed name, however false and fictitious, which is adopted for the purpose. Parol evidence is admissable to identify the signer, and when he is identified the signature is effective.

This section is not intended to affect any local statute or rule of law requiring a signature by mark to be witnessed, or any signature to be otherwise authenticated, or requiring any form of proof. It is to be read together with the provision under which a person paying or giving value for the instrument may require indorsement in both the right name and the wrong one; and with the provision that the absence of an indorsement in the right name may make an instrument so irregular as to call its ownership into question and put a purchaser upon notice which will prevent his taking as a holder in due course.

Cross References:

Sections 3–202(2), 3–402 through 3–406.
Point 1: Section 3–410.
Point 2: Section 3–203.

Definitional Cross References:

"Person". Section 1–201.

"Instrument". Section 3–102.
"Signed". Section 1–201.
"Written". Section 1–201.

Section 3–402. Signature in Ambiguous Capacity.

Unless the instrument clearly indicates that a signature is made in some other capacity it is an indorsement.

New York Annotations

In general *accord:* N.I.L., §§ 36(6) and 113; Fay v. Witte, 262 N.Y. 215, 186 N.E. 678 (1933).

Official Uniform Comment

Prior Uniform Statutory Provision: Sections 17(6) and 63, Uniform Negotiable Instruments Law.

Changes: Combined and Reworded.

Purposes of Changes: The revised language is intended to say that any ambiguity as to the capacity in which a signature is made must be resolved by a rule of law that it is an indorsement. Parol evidence is not admissable to show any other capacity, except for the purpose of reformation of the instrument as it may be permitted under the rules of the particular jurisdiction. The question is to be determined from the face of the instrument alone, and unless the instrument itself makes clear that he has signed in some other capacity the signor must be treated as an indorser.

The indication that the signature is made in another capacity must be clear without reference to anything but the instrument. It may be found in the language used. Thus if John Doe signs after "I, John Doe, promise to pay," he is clearly a maker; and "John Doe, witness" is not liable at all. The capacity may be found in any clearly evidenced purpose of the signature, as where a drawee signing in an unusual place on the paper has no visible reason to sign at all unless he is an acceptor. It may be found in usage or custom. Thus by long established practice judicially noticed or otherwise established a signature in the lower right hand corner of an instrument indicates an intent to sign as the maker of a note or the drawer of a draft. Any similar clear indication of an intent to sign in some other capacity may be enough to remove the signature from the application of this section.

Cross Reference:

Section 3–401.

Definitional Cross References:

"Instrument". Section 3–102.
"Signature". Section 3–401.

Section 3–403. Signature by Authorized Representative.

(1) A signature may be made by an agent or other representative, and his authority to make it may be established as in other cases of representation. No particular form of appointment is necessary to establish such authority.

(2) An authorized representative who signs his own name to an instrument

UCC

(a) is personally obligated if the instrument neither names the person represented nor shows that the representative signed in a representative capacity;

(b) except as otherwise established between the immediate parties, is personally obligated if the instrument names the person represented but does not show that the representative signed in a representative capacity, or if the instrument does not name the person represented but does show that the representative signed in a representative capacity.

(3) Except as otherwise established the name of an organization preceded or followed by the name and office of an authorized individual is a signature made in a representative capacity.

New York Annotations

(1) Generally *accords* with N.I.L., § 38, except that the Code adds "or other representative" capacity. This would not seem to change New York law, in view of the many cases including all kinds of representatives within the meaning of the term agent. See, for example, Megowan v. Peterson, 173 N.Y. 1, 65 N.E. 738 (1902) ("trustee" for creditors); Hellawell v. Garrett Busch & Son, Inc., 157 Misc. 805, 285 N.Y.S. 717, modified, 248 App.Div. 737, 290 N.Y.S. 143 (1936) (executrix). See also N.I.L., § 39, referring to the consequences of signing "for or on behalf of a principal, or in a representative capacity".

(2) (a) *Accord:* N.I.L., § 39. Where an agent or other representative signs merely his own name, alone, both the fact of representation and the name of the person being represented being omitted, decisional law appears to accord with the Code in prohibiting parol evidence to exonerate the representative, even as between parties with full notice. Purgold v. J.L. Hachtmann & Co., Inc., 201 N.Y.S. 76 aff'd without opinion, 204 App.Div. 864, 197 N.Y.S. 942 (1922); contra, in admitting parol evidence as against a payee with notice, Azzarello v. Richards, 198 Misc. 723, 99 N.Y.S.2d 597 (1950).

(b) *Accord:* Hoffstaedter v. Lichtenstein, 203 App.Div. 494, 196 N.Y.S. 577 (1922); Central Bank of Rochester v. Gleason (Northway Trailer Car Co.), 206 App.Div. 28, 200 N.Y.S. 384 (1923), as to the situation where name of person represented is disclosed but the fact of representation is not, and Megowan v. Peterson, 173 N.Y. 1, 5, 65 N.E. 738, 739 (1902), as to the situation where the fact of representation is disclosed but the name of the person represented is not.

(3) *Accord:* Chelsea Exchange Bank v. First United Presbyterian Church, 89 Misc. 616, 152 N.Y.S. 201 (1915); Thompson v. Tioga R. Co., 36 Barb. 79 (1861).

Historical Note: The present Code provision in Section 3–403 (2), reflecting a reversal of the rule prescribed in the 1952 draft, was adopted in response to criticism made by the Law Revision Commission. (1956 Recommendations, p. 108; Excerpts, p. 408.)

Official Uniform Comment

Prior Uniform Statutory Provision: Sections 19, 20 and 21, Uniform Negotiable Instruments Law.

Changes: Combined and reworded; original section 21 omitted.

Purpose of Changes:

1. The definition of "representative" in this Act (Section 1–201) includes an officer of a corporation, a trustee, an executor or administrator of an estate, or any other

person empowered to act for another. It is not intended to mean that a trust or an estate is necessarily a legal entity with the capacity to issue negotiable instruments, but merely that if it can issue them they may be signed by the representative.

The power to sign for another may be an express authority, or it may be implied in law or in fact, or it may rest merely upon apparent authority. It may be established as in other cases of representation, and when relevant parol evidence is admissable to prove or deny it.

2. Subsection (2) applies only to the signature of a representative whose authority to sign for another is established. If he is not authorized his signature has the effect of an unauthorized signature (Section 3–404). Even though he is authorized the principle is not liable on the instrument, under the provisions (Section 3–401) relating to signatures, unless the instrument names him and clearly shows that the signature is made on his behalf.

3. Assuming that Peter Pringle is a principal and Arthur Adams is his agent, an instrument for example, bear the following signatures affixed by the agent–

(a) "Peter Pringle", or
(b) "Arthur Adams", or
(c) "Peter Pringle by Arthur Adams, Agent", or
(d) "Arthur Adams, Agent", or
(e) "Peter Pringle Arthur Adams".

A signature in form (a) does not bind Adams if authorized (Sections 3–401 and 3–404).

A signature as in (b) personally obliges the agent and parol evidence is inadmissable under subsection (2) (a) to disestablish his obligation.

The unambiguous way to make the representation clear is to sign as in (c). Any other definite indication is sufficient, as where the instrument reads "Peter Pringle promises to pay" and it is signed "Arthur Adams, Agent." Adams is not bound if he is authorized (Section 3–404).

Subsection 2(b) adopts the New York (minority) rule of Megowan v. Peterson, 173 N.Y.1 (1902), in such a case as (d); and adopts the majority rule in such a case as (e). In both cases the section admits parol evidence in litigation between the immediate parties to prove signature by the agent in his representative capacity. [Paragraph 3 was amended in 1966].

4. The original Section 21, covering signatures by "procuration," is omitted. It was based on English practice under which the words "per procuration" added to any signature are understood to mean that the signer is acting under a power of attorney which the holder is free to examine. The holder is thus put on notice of the limited authority, and there can be no apparent authority extending beyond the power of attorney. This meaning of "per procuration" is almost unknown in the United States, and the words are understood by the ordinary banker or attorney to be merely the equivalent of "by." The omission is not intended to suggest that a signature "by procuration" can no longer have the effect which it had under the original Section 21, in any case where a party chooses to use the expression.

Cross References:

Point 1: Section 1–201.
Point 2: Sections 3–401(1), 3–404 and 3–405.

Definitional Cross References:

"Instrument". Section 3–102.
"Person". Section 1–201.
"Representative". Section 1–201.
"Signature". Section 3–401.

UCC

Section 3–404. Unauthorized Signatures.

(1) Any unauthorized signature is wholly inoperative as that of the person whose name is signed unless he ratifies it or is precluded from denying it; but it operates as the signature of the unauthorized signer in favor of any person who in good faith pays the instrument or takes it for value.

(2) Any unauthorized signature may be ratified for all purposes of this Article. Such ratification does not of itself affect any rights of the person ratifying against the actual signer.

New York Annotations

(1) The first clause is in accord with N.I.L., § 42, although the term "forgery" is not used since it is included under the definition of an "unauthorized signature". See Section 1–201(43). The second clause holding the "unauthorized signer" is new, and is in accord with New Georgia National Bank v. J. & G. Lippmann, 249 N.Y. 307, 164 N.E. 108 (1928), except that the Code provision would seem to extend the rule of that case to cover the forgery situation as well.

(2) This is new law and there appear to be no New York cases on the question whether a forgery is capable of being ratified. Cases in other jurisdictions are collected in Annot., 150 A.L.R. 978 (1944). Britton, Bills and Notes 558–560 (1943).

Official Uniform Comment

Prior Uniform Statutory Provision: Section 23, Uniform Negotiable Instruments Law.

Changes: Reworded; new provisions.

Purposes of Changes and New Matter: The changes are intended to remove uncertainties arising under the original section:

1. "Unauthorized signature" is a defined term (Section 1–201). It includes both a forgery and a signature made by an agent exceeding his actual or apparent authority.

2. The final clause of subsection (1) is new. It states the generally accepted rule that the unauthorized signature, while it is wholly inoperative as that of the person whose name is signed, is effective to impose liability upon the actual signer or to transfer any rights that he may have in the instrument. His liability is not in damages for breach of a warranty of his authority, but is full liability on the instrument in the capacity in which he has signed. It is, however, limited to the parties who take or pay the instrument in good faith; and one who knows that the signature is unauthorized cannot recover from the signer on the instrument.

3. Subsection (2) is new. It settles the conflict which has existed in the decisions as to whether a forgery may be ratified. A forged signature may at least be adopted; and the word "ratified" is used in order to make it clear that the adoption is retroactive, and that it may be found from conduct as well as from express statements. Thus it may be found from the retention of benefits received in the transaction with knowledge of the unauthorized signature; and although the forger is not an agent, the ratification is governed by the same rules and principles as if he were.

This provision makes ratification effective only for the purposes of this Article. The unauthorized signature becomes valid so far as its effect as a signature is concerned. The ratification relieves the actual signer from liability on the signature. It does not of itself relive him from liability to the person whose name is signed. It does not in any way affect the criminal law. No policy of the criminal law requires that the person whose name is forged shall not assume liability to others on the instrument; but he cannot affect the rights of the state. While ratification may be taken into account with other relevant facts in determining punishment, it does not relieve the signer of criminal liability.

4. The words "or is precluded from denying it" are retained in subsection (1) to recognize the possibility of an estoppel against the person whose name is signed, as where he expressly or tacitly represents to an innocent purchaser that the signature is genuine; and to recognize the negligence which precludes a denial of the signature.

Cross References:

Sections 3–307, 3–401, 3–403 and 3–405.
Point 1: Section 1–201.
Point 4: Section 3–406.

Definitional Cross References:

"Good faith". Section 1–201.
"Instrument". Section 3–102.
"Person". Section 1–201.
"Rights". Section 1–201.
"Signature". Section 3–401.
"Signed". Section 1–201.
"Unauthorized signature". Section 1–201.
"Value". Section 3–303.

Section 3–405. Impostors; Signature in Name of Payee.

(1) An indorsement by any person in the name of a named payee is effective if

(a) an impostor by use of the mails or otherwise has induced the maker or drawer to issue the instrument to him or his confederate in the name of the payee; or

(b) a person signing as or on behalf of a maker or drawer intends the payee to have no interest in the instrument; or

(c) an agent or employee of the maker or drawer has supplied him with the name of the payee intending the latter to have no such interest.

(2) Nothing in this section shall affect the criminal or civil liability of the person so indorsing.

Amended by Laws 1964, ch. 476, eff. Sept. 27, 1964.

New York Annotations

(1)(a) This is new law and would result in several changes in New York law. Rather than treat the instrument as bearer in form, the instrument is regarded as payable to the impostor. No distinction is made as to imposture through the mails. This would change what appears to be the New York rule requiring face to face dealings. See American Surety Co. v. Empire Trust Co., 262 N.Y. 181, 186 N.E. 436 (1933); Mercantile National Bank v. Silverman, 148 App.Div. 1, 132 N.Y.S. 1017, affirmed on opinion below, 210 N.Y. 567, 104 N.E. 1134 (1914); International Aircraft Trading Co. v. Manufacturers Trust Co., 297 N.Y. 285, 291, 79 N.E.2d 249, 251 (1948) (dicta);

Halsey v. Bank of New York & Trust Co., 270 N.Y. 134, 139, 200 N.E. 671, 673 (1936). Also abandoned is the New York rule requiring a prior course of dealings for the purpose of identifying the imposter as the object of the transferor's dominant intent. Cohen v. Lincoln Savings Bank, 275 N.Y. 399, 407–412, 10 N.E.2d 457, 461–463 (1937).

(b) and (c) *Accord:* N.I.L., § 28(3) as amended in 1960, ("Fictitious Payee Act"), the only change being the Code's requirement of an indorsement, not necessary under the N.I.L., treatment of such paper as "bearer paper."

(2) This is new, but would appear to make no change in existing law.

Historical Note: At the suggestion of the Law Revision Commission, subsections (1) (b) and (1) (c) were amended by the addition of the words "maker or" in each to make the provision applicable to notes as well as drafts. (1956 Recommendations, p. 109; Excerpts, p. 409.)

Official Uniform Comment

Prior Uniform Statutory Provision: Section 9(3), Uniform Negotiable Instruments Law.

Changes: Reworded; new provisions.

Purposes of Changes and New Matter:

1. This section enlarges the original subsection to include additional situations which it has not been held to cover. The words "fictitious or nonexisting person" have been eliminated as misleading, since the existence or nonexistence of the named payee is not decisive and is important only as it may bear on the intent that he shall have no interest in the instrument. The instrument is not made payable to bearer and indorsements are still necessary to negotiation. The section however recognizes as effective indorsement of the types of paper covered no matter by whom made. This solution is thought preferable to making such instruments bearer paper; on the face of things they are payable to order and a subsequent taker should require what purports to be a regular chain of indorsements. On the other hand it is thought to be unduly restrictive to require that the actual indorsement be made by the imposter or other fraudulent actor. In most cases the person whose fraud procured the instrument to be issued will himself indorse; when some other third person indorses it will most probably be a case of theft or a second independent fraud superimposed upon the original fraud. In neither case does there seem to be sufficient reason to reverse the rule of the section. To recapitulate: the instrument does not become bearer paper, a purportedly regular chain in indorsements is required, but any person–first thief, second imposter or third murderer–can effectively indorse in the name of the payee.

2. Subsection (1)(a) is new. It rejects decisions which distinguish between face-to-face imposture and imposture by mail and hold that where the parties deal by mail the dominant intent of the drawer to is to deal with the name rather than with the person so that the resulting instrument may be negotiated only by indorsement of the payee whose name has been taken in vain. The result of the distinction has been under some prior law, to throw the loss in the mail imposture forward to a subsequent holder or to the drawee. Since the maker or drawer believes the two to be one and the same, the two intentions cannot be and the "dominant intent" is a fiction. The position here taken is that the loss, regardless of the type of fraud which the particular imposter has committed, should fall upon the maker or drawer.

"Imposter" refers to an impersonation, and does not extend to a false representation that the party is the authorized agent of the payee. The maker or drawer who takes the precaution of making the instrument payable to the principal is entitled to have his indorsement.

3. Subsection (1)(b) restates the substance of the original subsection 9(3). The test stated is not whether the named payee is "fictitious," but whether the signer intends that he shall have no interest in the instrument. The following situations illustrate the application of the subsection.

a. The drawer of a check, for his own reasons, makes it payable to P knowing that P does not exist.

b. The drawer makes the check payable in the name of P. A person named P exists, but the drawer does not know it.

c. The drawer makes the check payable to P, an existing person whom he knows, intending to receive the money himself and that P shall have no interest in the check.

d. The treasurer of a corporation draws its check payable to P, who to the knowledge of the treasurer does not exist.

e. The treasurer of a corporation draws its check payable to P. P exists but the treasurer has fraudulently added his name to the payroll intending that he shall not receive the check.

f. The president and the treasurer of a corporation both sign a check payable to P. P does not exist. The treasurer knows it but the president does not.

g. The same facts as f, except that P exists and the treasurer knows it, but intends that P shall have no interest in the check.

In all the cases stated an indorsement by any person in the name of P is effective.

4. Paragraph (c) is new. It extends the rule of the original subsection 9(3) to include the padded payroll cases, where the drawer's agent or employee prepares the check for signature or otherwise furnishes the signing officer with the name of the payee. The principal followed is that the loss should fall upon the employer as a risk of his business enterprise rather than upon the subsequent holder or drawee. The reasons are that the employer is normally in a better position to prevent such forgeries by reasonable care in the selection or supervision of his employees, or, if he is not, is at least in a better position to cover the loss by fidelity insurance; and that the cost of such insurance is properly an expense of his business rather than of the business of the holder or drawee.

The provision applies only to the agent or employee of the drawer, and only to the agent or employee who supplies him with the name of the payee. The following situations illustrate its application.

a. An employee of a corporation prepares a padded payroll for its treasurer, which includes the name of P. P does not exist, and the employee knows it, but the treasurer does not. The treasurer draws the corporation's check payable to P.

b. The same facts as a, except that P exists and the employee knows it but intends him to have no interest in the check. In both cases an indorsement by any person in the name of P is effective and the loss falls on the corporation.

5. The section is not intended to affect the criminal liability for forgery or any other crime, or civil liability to the drawer or to any other person. It is to be read together with the section under which an unauthorized signer is personally liable on the signature to any person who takes the instrument in good faith (3–404(1)).

Cross References:

Sections 3–401, 3–403, 3–404 and 3–406.
Point 5: Section 3–404(1).

Definitional Cross References:

"Instrument". Section 3–102.
"Issue". Section 3–102.
"Person". Section 1–201.
"Signature". Section 3–401.

Section 3–406. Negligence Contributing to Alteration or Unauthorized Signature.

Any person who by his negligence substantially contributes to a material alteration of the instrument or to the making of an unauthorized signature is precluded from asserting the alteration or lack of authority against a holder in due course or against a drawee or other payor who pays the instrument in good faith and in accordance with the reasonable commercial standards of the drawee's or payor's business.

New York Annotations

Accord as to drawee, but *contra* as to holder in due course and other payor. National Exchange Bank v. Lester, 194 N.Y. 461, 87 N.E. 779 (1909); Young v. Grote, 4 Bing. 253, 130 Eng. Rep. 764 (1827). See also Slattery & Co. v. National City Bank, 114 Misc. 48, 186 N.Y.S. 679 (1920) (plaintiff, drawer, estopped by negligent mailing).

Historical Note: The reasonable commercial standards" clause was included at the suggestion of the Law Revision Commission which recommended that contributory negligence should defeat rights under the section. (1956 Recommendations, p. 109; Excerpts, p. 409.)

Official Uniform Comment

Prior Uniform Statutory Provision: None.

Purposes:

1. This section is new. It adopts the doctrine of Young v. Grote, 4 Bing. 253 (1827), which held that a drawer who so negligently draws an instrument as to facilitate its material alteration is liable to a drawee who pays the altered instrument in good faith. It should be noted that the rule as stated in the section requires that the negligence "substantially" contribute to the alteration.

2. The section extends the above principle to the protection of a holder in due course and of payors who may not technically be drawees. It rejects decisions which have held that the maker of a note owes no duty of care to the holder because at the time the instrument is drawn there is no contract between them. By drawing the instrument and "setting it afloat upon a sea of strangers" the maker or drawer voluntarily enters into a relation with later holders which justifies his responsibility. In this respect an instrument so negligently drawn as to facilitate alteration does not differ in principle from and instrument containing blanks which may be filled.

The holder in due course under the rules governing alteration (Section 3–407) may enforce the altered instrument according to its original tenor. Where negligence of the obligor has substantially contributed to the alteration, this section gives the holder the alternative right to enforce the instrument as altered.

3. No attempt is made to define negligence which will contribute to an alteration. The question is left to the court or the jury upon the circumstances of the particular cases. Negligence usually has been found where spaces are left in the body of the instrument in which words or figures may be inserted. No unusual precautions are required, and the section is not intended to change decisions holding that the drawer of a bill is under no duty to use sensitized paper, indelible ink or a protectograph; or that it is not negligence to leave spaces between the lines or at the end of the instrument in which a provision for interest or the like can be written.

4. The section applies only where negligence contributes to the alteration. It must afford an opportunity of which advantage is in fact taken. The section approves decisions which have refused to hold the drawer responsible where he has left spaces in a check but the payee erased all the writing with chemicals and wrote in an entirely new check.

5. This section does not make the negligent party liable in tort for damages resulting from the alteration. Instead it estops him from asserting it against the holder in due course or drawee. The reason is that in the usual case the extent of loss, which involves the possibility of ultimate recovery from the wrongdoer, cannot be determined at the time of litigation, and the decision would have to be made on the unsatisfactory basis of burden of proof. The holder or drawee is protected by an estoppel, and the task of pursuing the wrongdoer is left to the negligent party. Any amount in fact recovered from the wrongdoer must be held for the benefit of the negligent party under the ordinary principles of equity.

6. The section protects parties who act not only in good faith. (Section 1–201) but also in observance of the reasonable standards of their business. Thus any bank which takes or pays an altered check which ordinary banking standards would require it to refuse cannot take advantage of the estoppel.

7. The section applies the same rule to negligence which contributes to forgery or other unauthorized signature, as defined in this Act (Section 1–201). The most obvious case is that of a drawer who makes use of a signature stamp or other automatic signing device and is negligent in looking after it. The section extends, however, to cases where the party has notices that forgeries of his signature have occurred and is negligent in failing to prevent further forgeries by the same person. It extends to negligence which contributes to a forgery of the signature of another, as in the case where a check is negligently mailed to the wrong person having the same name as the payee. As in the case of alteration, no attempt is made to specify what is negligence, and the question is one for the court or the jury on the facts of the particular case.

Cross References:

Sections 3–401 and 3–404.
Point 2: Section 3–407(3).
Point 6: Section 1–201.
Point 7: Section 1–201.

Definitional Cross References:

"Alteration". Section 3–407.
"Good Faith". Section 1–201.
"Holder in due course". Section 3–302.
"Instrument". Section 3–102.
"Person". Section 1–201.
"Unauthorized signature". Section 1–201.

Section 3–407. Alteration.

(1) Any alteration of an instrument is material which changes the contract of any party thereto in any respect, including any such change in

(a) the number or relations of the parties; or

(b) an incomplete instrument, by completing it otherwise than as authorized; or

(c) the writing as signed, by adding to it or by removing any part of it.

(2) As against any person other than a subsequent holder in due course

(a) alteration by the holder which is both fraudulent and material discharges any party whose contract is thereby changed unless that party assents or is precluded from asserting the defense;

(b) no other alteration discharges any party and the instrument may be enforced according to its original tenor, or as to incomplete instruments according to the authority given.

(3) A subsequent holder in due course may in all cases enforce the instrument according to its original tenor, and when an incomplete instrument has been completed, he may enforce it as completed.

New York Annotations

(1) *Accord:* N.I.L., § 206; Booth v. Powers, 56 N.Y. 22, 29 (1874).

(2) *Accord:* N.I.L., § 205, except that alteration must be by the holder, the alteration must be for a fraudulent purpose as well as material, the defense must be raised by the party whose contract is changed by the alteration, and, if the above are not applicable, the instrument may be enforced according to its original tenor. In accord as to alteration by a stranger, see Gleason v. Hamilton, 138 N.Y. 353, 34 N.E. 283 (1893) (alteration of mortgage). As to "fraudulent" alteration see Booth v. Powers, 56 N.Y. 22, 29–30 (1874), and Oltarsh v. Turf Broadway, Inc., 12 Misc.2d 984, 986, 175 N.Y.S.2d 714, 717 (1958).

(3) *Accord:* N.I.L., §§ 33 and 205. The separate rule in N.I.L., § 34, as to incomplete undelivered instruments is reversed. See also, Linick v. A. J. Nutting & Co., 140 App.Div. 265, 125 N.Y.S. 93 (1910). and Holzman, Cohen & Co. v. Teague, 172 App.Div. 75, 158 N.Y.S. 211 (1916).

Official Uniform Comment

Prior Uniform Statutory Provision: Sections 14, 15, 124 and 125, Uniform Negotiable Instruments Law.

Changes: Combined and reworded; new provisions; rule of original Section 15 reversed.

Purposes of Changes and New Matter: The changes are intended to remove uncertainties arising under the original sections, and to modify the rules as to discharge.

1. Subsection (1) substitutes a general definition for the list of illustrations in the original Section 125. Any alteration is material only as it may change the contract of a party to the instrument; and the addition or deletion of words which do not in any way affect the contract of any previous signer is not material. But any change in the contract of a party, however slight, is a material alteration; and the addition of one cent to the amount payable, or an advance of one day in the date of payment, will operate as a discharge if it is fraudulent.

Specific mention is made of a change in the number or relations of the parties in order to make it clear that any such change is material only if it changes the contract of one who has signed. The addition of a co-maker or a surety does not change in most jurisdictions the contract of one who has already signed as maker and should not be held as material to him. The addition of the name of an alternative payee is material, since it changes his obligation. Paragraph (c) makes special mention of a change in the writing signed in order to cover occasional cases of addition of sticker clauses, scissoring or performing instruments where the separation is not authorized.

2. Paragraph (b) of subsection (1) is to be read together with Section 3–115 on incomplete instruments. Where an instrument contains blanks or is otherwise incomplete, it may be completed in accordance with the authority given and is then valid and effective as completed. If the completion is unauthorized and has the effect of changing the contract of any previous signer, this provision follows the generally accepted rule in treating it as a material alteration which may operate as a discharge.

3. Subsection (2) modifies the very rigorous rule of the original Section 124. The changes made are as follows:

a. A material alteration does not discharge any party unless it is made by the holder. Spoilation by any meddling stranger does not affect the rights of the holder. It is of course intended that the acts of the holder's authorized agent or employee, or of his confederates, are to be attributed to him.

b. A material alteration does not discharge any party unless it is made for a fraudulent purpose. There is no discharge where a blank is filled in the honest belief that it is authorized; or where a change is made with a benevolent motive such as a desire to give the obligor the benefit of a lower interest rate. Changes favorable to the obligor are unlikely to be made with any fraudulent intent; but if such an intent is found the alteration may operate as a discharge.

c. The discharge is a personal defense of the party whose contract is changed by the alteration, and anyone whose contract is not affected cannot assert it. The contract of any party is necessarily affected, however, by the discharge of any party against whom he has a right of recourse on the instrument. Assent to the alteration given before or after it is made will prevent the party from asserting the discharge. "Or is precluded from asserting the defense" is added in paragraph (a) to recognize the possibility of an estoppel or other ground barring the defense which does not rest on assent.

d. If the alteration is not material or if it is not made for a fraudulent purpose there is no discharge, and the instrument may be enforced according to its original tenor. Where blanks are filled or an incomplete instrument is otherwise completed there is no original tenor, but the instrument may be enforced according to the authority in fact given.

4. Subsection (3) combines the final sentences of the original Sections 14 and 124, and provides that a subsequent holder in due course takes free of the discharge in all cases. The provision is merely one form of the general rule governing the effect of discharge against a holder in due course (Section 3–602). The holder in due course may enforce the instrument according to its original tenor. In this connection reference should be made to the section giving the holder in due course the right, where the maker's or drawer's negligence has substantially contributed to the alteration, to enforce the instrument in its altered form (Section 3–406). Reference should also be made to Section 4–401 covering a bank's right to charge its customer's account in the case of altered instruments.

Where blanks are filled or an incomplete instrument is otherwise completed, this subsection follows the original Section 14 in placing the loss upon the party who left the instrument incomplete and permitting the holder to enforce it in its completed form. As indicated in the comment to Section 3–115 on incomplete instruments, this result is intended even though the instrument was stolen from the maker or drawer and completed after the theft; and the effect of this subsection, together with the section on incomplete instruments is to reverse the rule of the original Section 15.

There is no inconsistency between subsection (3) and paragraph (b) of subsection (2). The holder in due course may elect to enforce the instrument either as provided in that paragraph or as provided in subsection (3).

It should be noted that a purchaser who takes the instrument with notice of any material alterations, including the unauthorized completion of an incomplete instrument, takes notice of a claim or defense and cannot be a holder in due course (Section 3–304).

Cross References:

Sections 3–305, 3–306 and 3–307.
Point 2: Section 3–115.
Point 4: Sections 3–115, 3–304(2), 3–602 and 4–401.

Definitional Cross References:

"Contract". Section 1–201.
"Holder". Section 1–201.
"Holder in due course". Section 3–302.
"Instrument". Section 3–102.
"Party". Section 1–201.
"Person". Section 1–201.
"Signed". Section 1–201.
"Writing". Section 1–201.

Section 3–408. Consideration.

Want or failure of consideration is a defense as against any person not having the rights of a holder in due course (Section 3–305), except that no consideration is necessary for an instrument or obligation thereon given in payment of or as security for an antecedent obligation of any kind. Nothing in this section shall be taken to displace any statute outside this Act under which a promise is enforceable notwithstanding lack or failure of consideration. Partial failure of consideration is a defense pro tanto whether or not the failure is in an ascertained or liquidated amount.

New York Annotations

Accords generally with N.I.L., §§ 50, 51, and 54. Both the terms "value" and "consideration" are used in N.I.L., § 51, whereas the Code utilizes the term "consideration" as distinguished from "value". New York case law supports the Code provision that a pre-existing debt is sufficient consideration for the execution or transfer of a negotiable instrument. Kelso & Co. v. Ellis, 224 N.Y. 528, 121 N.E. 364 (1918).

Historical Note: The last two sentences were added at the suggestion of the Law Revision Commission to correlate with Section 3–306 and to clarify the status of failure of consideration as a defense. (1956 Recommendations, p. 110; Excerpts, p. 409.)

Official Uniform Comment

Prior Uniform Statutory Provision: Sections 24, 25 and 28, Uniform Negotiable Instruments Law.

Changes: Combined and reworded.

Purposes of Changes:

1. "Consideration" is distinguished from "value" throughout this Article. "Consideration" refers to what the obligor has received for his obligation, and is important only on the question of whether his obligation can be enforced against him.

2. The "except" clause is intended to remove the difficulties which have arisen where a note or a draft, or an indorsement of either, is given as payment or security for a debt already owed by the party giving it, or by a third person. The provision is intended to change the result of decisions holding that where no extension of time or other concession is given by the creditor the new obligation fails for lack of legal consideration. It is intended also to mean that an instrument given for more or less than the amount of a liquidated obligation does not fail by reason of the common law rule that an obligation for a lesser liquidated amount cannot be consideration for the surrender of a greater.

3. With respect to the necessity or sufficiency of consideration other obligations on an instrument are subject to the ordinary rules of contract law relating to contracts not under seal. Promissory estoppel or any other equivalent or substitute for consideration is to be recognized as in other contract cases. The provision of the original Section 28 as to absence or failure of consideration is now covered by the section dealing with the rights of one not a holder in due course; and the "presumption" of consideration in the original Section 24 is replaced by the provision relating to the burden of establishing defenses.

Cross References:

Point 1: Section 3–303.
Point 3: Sections 3–306(c) and 3–307(2).

Definitional Cross References:

"Holder in due course". Section 3–302.
"Instrument". Section 3–102.
"Person". Section 1–201.
"Rights". Section 1–201.

Section 3–409. Draft Not an Assignment.

(1) A check or other draft does not of itself operate as an assignment of any funds in the hands of the drawee available for its payment, and the drawee is not liable on the instrument until he accepts it.

(2) Nothing in this section shall affect any liability in contract, tort or otherwise arising from any letter of credit or other obligation or representation which is not an acceptance.

New York Annotations

(1) *Accord:* N.I.L., §§ 211 and 325.

(2) This subsection makes clear that this section does not in any way affect liability which may arise apart from the instrument itself. As to the nature of such liability, see Henderson v. Lincoln Rochester Trust Co., 303 N.Y. 27, 31, 100 N.E.2d 117, 119–120 (1951).

UCC

Official Uniform Comment

Prior Uniform Statutory Provision: Sections 127 and 189, Uniform Negotiable Instruments Law.

Changes: Combined and reworded; new provisions.

Purposes of Changes and New Matter:

The two original sections are combined, brought forward to appear in connection with acceptance, and reworded to remove uncertainties.

1. As under the original sections, a check or other draft does not of itself operate as an assignment in law or equity. The assignment may, however, appear from other facts, and particularly from other agreements, express or implied; and when the intent to assign is clear the check may be the means by which the assignment is effected.

2. The language of the original Section 189, that the drawee is not liable "to the holder", is changed as inaccurate and not intended. The drawee is not liable on the instrument until he accepts; but he remains subject to any other liability to the holder. In this connection reference should be made to Section 4–302 on the payor bank's liability for late return. Such a bank does not either make a prompt settlement or return on an item received by it will become liable to a holder of the item.

3. Subsection (2) is new. It is intended to make it clear that this section does not in any way affect any liability which may arise apart from the instrument itself. The drawee who fails to accept may be liable to the drawer or to the holder for breach of the terms of a letter of credit or any other agreement by which he is obligated to accept. He may be liable in tort or upon any other basis because of his representation that he has accepted, or that he intends to accept. The section leaves unaffected any liability of any kind apart from the instrument.

Cross References:

Sections 3–410, 3–411, 3–412 and 3–415.
Point 2: Section 4–302.

Definitional Cross References:

"Acceptance". Section 3–410.
"Check". Section 3–104.
"Contract". Section 1–201.
"Draft". Section 3–104.
"Instrument". Section 3–102.
"Letter of credit". Section 5–104.

Section 3–410. Definition and Operation of Acceptance.

(1) Acceptance is the drawee's signed engagement to honor the draft as presented. It must be written on the draft, and may consist of his signature alone. It becomes operative when completed by delivery or notification.

(2) A draft may be accepted although it has not been signed by the drawer or is otherwise incomplete or is overdue or has been dishonored.

(3) Where the draft is payable at a fixed period after sight and the acceptor fails to date his acceptance the holder may complete it by supplying a date in good faith.

New York Annotations

(1) First sentence *accords* with N.I.L., § 220 (writing required). Second sentence *accords* with N.I.L., §§ 220 and 221 and Spear v. Pratt, 2 Hill 582 (1842); but the requirement that the acceptance must be on the draft is *contra* to N.I.L., §§ 221 and 222. Third sentence *accords* with N.I.L., § 2.

(2) *Accord:* N.I.L., § 226.

(3) Similar to N.I.L., § 32, except that the Code provides that the holder may supply "a date in good faith," whereas the present law permits only the "true date" to be inserted. The last sentence of N.I.L., § 226, which the Comment states was intended to be changed, is merely omitted.

Official Uniform Comment

Prior Uniform Statutory Provision: Sections 132, 133, 134, 135, 136, 137, 138, 161–170, and 191, Uniform Negotiable Instruments Law.

Changes: Combined, reworded; original Sections 134, 135, 137 and 161–170 eliminated.

Purposes of Changes:

1. The original Sections 161–170 providing for the acceptance for honor are omitted from this Article. This ancient practice developed at a time when communications were slow, and particularly in overseas transactions there might be a delay of several months before the drawer could be notified of dishonor by nonacceptance and take steps to protect his credit. The need for intervention by a third party has passed with the development of cable transfer, the letter of credit, and numerous other devices by which a substitute arrangement is promptly made. The practice has been obsolete for many years, and the sections are therefore eliminated.

2. Under Section 3–417 a person obtaining acceptance gives a warranty against alteration of the instrument before acceptance.

3. Subsection (1) adopts the rule of Section 17 of the English Bills of Exchange Act that the acceptance must be written on the draft. It eliminates the original Sections 134 and 135, providing for "virtual" acceptance by a written promise to accept drafts to be drawn, and "collateral" acceptance by a separate writing. Both have been anomalous exceptions to the policy that no person is liable on an instrument unless his signature appears on it. Both are derived from a line of early American cases decided at a time when difficulties of communication, particularly overseas, might leave the holder in doubt for a long period whether the draft had been accepted. Such conditions have long since ceased to exist, and the "virtual" or "collateral" acceptance is now almost entirely obsolete. Good commercial and banking practice does not sanction acceptance by any separate writing because of the dangers and uncertainties arising when it becomes separated from the draft. The instrument is now forwarded to the drawee for his acceptance upon it, or reliance is placed upon the obligation of the separate writing itself, as in the case of a letter of credit.

Nothing in this section is intended to eliminate any liability of the drawee in contract, tort or otherwise arising from separate writing or any other obligation or representation, as provided in Section 3–409.

Subsection (1) likewise eliminates the original Section 137, providing for the acceptance by delay or refusal to return the instrument but the drawee may be liable for a conversion of the instrument under Section 3–419.

4. Subsection (1) states the generally recognized rule that the mere signature of the drawee on the instrument is sufficient acceptance. Customarily the signature is written vertically across the face of the instrument; but since the drawee has no reason

to sign for any other purpose his signature in any other place, even on the back of the instrument, is sufficient. It need not be accompanied by such words as "Accepted," "Certified," or "Goods." It must not, however, bear any words indicating an intent to refuse to honor the bill; and nothing in this provision is intended to change such decisions as Norton v. Knapp, 64 Iowa 112, 19 N.W. 867 (1884), holding that the drawee's signature accompanied by the words "Kiss my foot" is not an acceptance.

5. The final sentence of subsection (1) expressly states the generally recognized rule, implied in the definition of acceptance in the original Section 191, that an acceptance written on the draft takes effect when the drawee notifies the holder or gives notice according to his instructions. Acceptance is thus an exception to the usual rule that no obligation on an instrument is effective until delivery.

6. Subsection (3) changes the last sentence of the original Section 138. The purpose of the provision is to provide a definite date of payment where none appears on the instrument. An undated acceptance of a draft payable "thirty days after sight" is incomplete; and unless the acceptor himself writes in a different date the holder is authorized to complete the acceptance according to the terms of the draft by supplying a date of presentment. Any date which the holder chooses to write in is effective providing his choice of date is made in good faith. Any different agreement not written on the draft is not effective, and parol evidence is not admissable to show it.

Cross References:

Sections 3–411, 3–412 and 3–418.
Point 2: Section Point 3: Sections 3–401(1), 3–409(2) and 3–419.
Point 6: Section 3–412.

Definitional Cross References:

"Delivery". Section 1–201.
"Dishonor". Section 3–507.
"Draft". Section 3–104.
"Good faith". Section 1–201.
"Holder". Section 1–201.
"Honor". Section 1–201.
"Notification". Section 1–201.
"Presentment". Section 3–504.
"Signature". Section 3–401.
"Signed". Section 1–201.
"Written". Section 1–201.

Section 3–411. Certification of a Check.

(1) Certification of a check is acceptance. Where a holder procures certification the drawer and all prior indorsers are discharged.

(2) Unless otherwise agreed a bank has no obligation to certify a check.

(3) A bank may certify a check before returning it for lack of proper indorsement. If it does so the drawer is discharged.

New York Annotations

(1) *Accord:* N.I.L., §§ 323 and 324.
(2) *Accord:* Wachtel v. Rosen, 249 N.Y. 386, 164 N.E. 326 (1923).

(3) *Accord:* Lipten v. Columbia Trust Co., 194 App.Div. 384, 389, 185 N.Y.S. 198, 204 (1920). See also Meuer v. Phenix National Bank, 94 App.Div. 331, 88 N.Y.S. 83, Aff'd mem. 183 N.Y. 511, 76 N.E. 1100 (1905). Consistent with Section 3–410(2).

Official Uniform Comment

Prior Uniform Statutory Provision: Sections 187 and 188, Uniform Negotiable Instruments Law.

Changes: Combined and reworded; new provisions.

Purposes of Changes and New Matter:

1. The second sentence of subsection (1) continues the rule of original Section 188 that, while certification procured by a holder discharges the drawer and other prior parties, certification procured by the drawer leaves him liable. Under this provision any certification procured by a holder discharges the drawer and prior indorsers. Any indorsement made after a certification so procured remains effective; and where it is intended that any indorser shall remain liable notwithstanding certification, he may indorse with the words "after certification" to make his liability clear.

2. Subsection (2) is new. It states the generally recognized rule that in the absence of agreement a bank is under no obligation to certify a check, because it is a demand instrument calling for payment rather than acceptance. The bank may be liable for breach of any agreement with the drawer, the holder, or any other person by which it undertakes to certify. Its liability is not on the instrument, since the drawee is not so liable until acceptance (Section 3–409(1)). Any liability is for breach of the separate agreement.

3. Subsection (3) is new. It recognizes the banking practice of certifying a check which is returned for proper indorsement in order to protect the drawer against a longer contingent liability. It is consistent with the provision of Section 3–410(2) permitting certification although the check has not been signed or is otherwise incomplete.

Cross References:

Section 3–412, 3–413, 3–417 and 3–418.
Point 2: Section 3–409(1).
Point 3: Section 3–410(2).

Definitional Cross References:

"Acceptance". Section 3–410.
"Bank". Section 1–201.
"Check". Section 3–104.
"Holder". Section 1–201.

Section 3–412. Acceptance Varying Draft.

(1) Where the drawee's proffered acceptance in any manner varies the draft as presented the holder may refuse the acceptance and treat the draft as dishonored in which case the drawee is entitled to have his acceptance cancelled.

(2) The terms of the draft are not varied by an acceptance to pay at any particular bank or place in the United States, unless the acceptance states that the draft is to be paid only at such bank or place.

(3) Where the holder assents to an acceptance varying the terms of the draft each drawer and indorser who does not affirmatively assent is discharged.

New York Annotations

(1) *Accord:* N.I.L., § 230. The distinctions between various kinds of qualified acceptances in N.I.L., § 229, are eliminated, and the rule is made to apply to any "acceptance that in any manner varies the draft as presented." A provision is added that where the holder refuses the conditioned acceptance, the drawee is entitled to have his acceptance cancelled.

(2) *Accords* generally with N.I.L., § 228, except for the limitation "in the United States," which is new.

(3) *Accords* with N.I.L., § 230, insofar as drawers and indorsers are discharged where the holder assents to an acceptance varying the terms of the instrument. This subsection changes N.I.L., § 230, by requiring affirmative assent to acceptance.

Historical Note: This section was revised in part to meet policy and drafting criticisms made by the Law Revision Commission. (1956 Recommendations, pp. 111–112; Excerpts, p. 410.)

Official Uniform Comment

Prior Uniform Statutory Provision: Sections 139, 140, 141 and 142, Uniform Negotiable Instruments Law.

Changes:

Combined and reworded; law changed as to qualified acceptances.

Purposes of Changes:

1. The section applies to conditional acceptances, acceptances for part of the amount, acceptances to pay at a different time from that required by the draft, or to the acceptance of less than all of the drawees, all of which are covered by the original Section 141. It applies to any other engagement changing the essential terms of the draft.

2. Where the drawee offers such a varied engagement the holder has an election. He may reject the offer, insist on acceptance of the draft as presented, and treat the refusal to give it as a dishonor. In that event the drawee is not bound by his engagement, and is entitled to have it cancelled. After any necessary notice of dishonor and protest the holder may have his recourse against the drawer and indorsers.

If the holder elects to accept the offer, this section does not invalidate the drawer's varied engagement. It remains his effective obligation, which the holder may enforce against him. By his assent, however, the holder discharges any drawer or indorser who does not also assent. The rule of the original Section 142 is changed to require that the assent of the drawer or indorser be affirmatively expressed. Mere failure to object within a reasonable time is not assent which will prevent discharge.

3. The rule of original Section 140 that an acceptance to pay at a particular place is an unqualified acceptance is modified by the provision of subsection (2) that the terms of the draft are not varied by an acceptance to pay at any particular bank or place in the United States unless the acceptance states that the draft is to be paid only at such bank or place. Section 3–504(4) provides that a draft accepted payable at a bank in the United States must be presented at the bank designated [As amended 1962].

Cross References:

Sections 3–410 and 3–413.

Point 3: Section 3–504(4).

Definitional Cross References:

"Acceptance". Section 3–410.
"Bank". Section 1–201.
"Dishonor". Section 3–507.
"Draft". Section 3–104.
"Holder". Section 1–201.
"Term". Section 1–201.
"Written". Section 1–201.

Section 3–413. Contract of Maker, Drawer and Acceptor.

(1) The maker or acceptor engages that he will pay the instrument according to its tenor at the time of his engagement or as completed pursuant to Section 3–115 on incomplete instruments.

(2) The drawer engages that upon dishonor of the draft and any necessary notice of dishonor or protest he will pay the amount of the draft to the holder or to any indorser who takes it up. The drawer may disclaim this liability by drawing without recourse.

(3) By making, drawing or accepting the party admits as against all subsequent parties including the drawee the existence of the payee and his then capacity to indorse.

New York Annotations

(1) *Accord:* N.I.L., §§ 110 and 112. This section, read together with Section 3–410, changes the New York rule by making the acceptor of an altered instrument liable for the altered amount. See National Reserve Bank of City of New York v. Corn Exchange Bank, 171 App.Div. 195, 157 N.Y.S. 316 (1916). Effect widened by new rules of Sections 3–115 and 3–407.

(2) *Accord:* N.I.L., § 111.

(3) *Accord:* N.I.L., §§ 110, 111, and 112(2).

Historical Note: Pursuant to a Law Revision Commission suggestion, clarifying amendments to subsection (1) were made to conform to Section 3–115. (1956 Recommendations, p. 112; Excerpts, p. 410.)

Official Uniform Comment

Prior Uniform Statutory Provision: Sections 60, 61 and 62, Uniform Negotiable Instruments Law.

Changes: Combined and reworded.

Purposes of Changes:

The original sections are combined for convenience and condensed to avoid duplication of language. This section should be read in connection with the sections on incomplete instruments (3–115), negligence contributing to alteration or unauthorized signature (3–406), alteration (3–407), acceptances varying a draft (3–412) and finality of payment or acceptance (3–418). Thus a maker who signs an incomplete note engages under this section to pay it according to its tenor at the time he signs it, but by virtue of Sections 3–115 and 3–407 the note may thereafter be completed and enforced against him. In the same way, if the maker's negligence substantially contributes to alteration of the instrument, he will become liable on the note as altered under Section 3–406. When a holder assents to an acceptance varying a draft (Section 3–412) he can of course hold the acceptor only according to the form of the acceptance to which the holder agreed. Section 3–418 applies the rule of Price v. Neal both to the acceptance and the payment; thus an acceptor may not, after acceptance, assert that the drawer's signature is unauthorized.

Subsection (1) applies to all drafts (including checks) the rule that the acceptance relates to the instrument as it was at the time of its acceptance and not (in case of alteration before acceptance) to its original tenor. The cases on this point under the original act (all of which involved checks) have been in conflict. It should be noted that under Section 3–417 a person who obtains acceptance warrants to the acceptor that the instrument has not been materially altered.

Except as indicated in the foregoing comment the section makes no change in substance from the provision of the original act.

Cross References:

Sections 3–115, 3–406, 3–407, 3–412, 3–417 and 3–418.

Definitional Cross References:

"Contract". Section 1–201.
"Dishonor". Section 3–507.
"Draft". Section 3–104.
"Holder". Section 1–201.
"Instrument". Section 3–102.
"Notice of dishonor". Section 3–508.
"Party". Section 1–201.
"Protest". Section 3–509.

Section 3–414. Contract of Indorser; Order of Liability.

(1) Unless the indorsement otherwise specifies (as by such words as "without recourse") every indorser engages that upon dishonor and any necessary notice of dishonor and protest he will pay the instrument according to its tenor at the time of his indorsement to the holder or to any subsequent indorser who takes it up, even though the indorser who takes it up was not obligated to do so.

(2) Unless they otherwise agree indorsers are liable to one another in the order in which they indorse, which is presumed to be the order in which their signatures appear on the instrument.

New York Annotations

(1) *Accords* generally with N.I.L. §§ 116 (last paragraph), 68, and 115.

(2) *Accord:* N.I.L., § 118. As to the presumption that the order of indorsements is to be determined from the order in which the signatures appear on the instrument, see Moynihan v. McKeon, 16 Misc. 343, 38 N.Y.S. 61 (1896).

Official Uniform Comment

Prior Uniform Statutory Provision: Sections 38, 44, 66, 67 and 68, Uniform Negotiable Instruments Law.

Changes: Combined and reworded.

Purposes of Changes:

1. Subsection (1) states the contract of indorsement–that if the instrument is dishonored and any protest or notice of dishonor which may be necessary under Section 3–501 is given, the indorser will pay the instrument. The indorser's engagement runs to any holder (whether or not for value) and to any indorser subsequent to him who has taken the instrument up. An indorser may disclaim his liability on the contract of indorsement, but only if the indorsement itself so specifies. Since the disclaimer varies the written contract of indorsement, the disclaimer itself must be written on the instrument and cannot be proved by parol. The customary manner of disclaiming the indorser's liability under this section is to indorse "without recourse". Apart from such a disclaimer all indorsers incur this liability, without regard to whether or not the indorser transferred the instrument for value or received consideration for his indorsement.

Original Section 44, permitting a representative to indorse in such terms as to exclude personal liability, is omitted as unnecessary and included in the broader right to disclaim any liability. No change in the law is intended by this omission.

2. In addition to his liability on the contract of indorsement, an indorser, if a transferor, gives the warranties stated in Sections 3–417.

3. As in the case of acceptor's liability (Section 3–413), this section conditions the indorser's liability on the tenor of the instrument at the time of his indorsement. Thus if a person indorses an altered instrument he assumes liability as indorser on the instrument as altered.

4. Subsection (2) is intended to clarify existing law under original Section 68.

The section states two presumptions: One is that the indorsers are liable to one another in the order in which they have in fact indorsed. The other is that they have in fact indorsed in the order in which their names appear. Parol evidence is admissable to show that they have indorsed in another order, or that they have otherwise agreed as to their liability to one another.

The last sentence of the original Section 68 is now covered by Section 3–118(e)(Ambiguous Terms and Rules of Construction).

Cross References:

Point 1: Section 3–501.
Point 2: Section 3–417.
Point 3: Section 3–413.
Point 4: Section 3–118(e).

Definitional Cross References:

"Contract". Section 1–201.
"Dishonor". Section 3–507.
"Holder". Section 1–201.
"Instrument". Section 3–102.
"Notice of dishonor". Section 3–508.
"Presumed". Section 1–201.
"Protest". Section 3–509.
"Signature". Section 3–401.

Section 3–415. Contract of Accommodation Party.

(1) An accommodation party is one who signs the instrument in any capacity for the purpose of lending his name to another party to it.

(2) When the instrument has been taken for value before it is due the accommodation party is liable in the capacity in which he has signed even though the taker knows of the accommodation.

(3) As against a holder in due course and without notice of the accommodation oral proof of the accommodation is not admissible to give the accommodation party the benefit of discharges dependent on his character as such. In other cases the accommodation character may be shown by oral proof.

(4) An indorsement which shows that it is not in the chain of title is notice of its accommodation character.

(5) An accommodation party is not liable to the party accommodated, and if he pays the instrument has a right of recourse on the instrument against such party.

(6) An accommodation party warrants to any subsequent holder who is not the party accommodated and who takes the instrument in good faith that

(a) all signatures are genuine or authorized; and

(b) the instrument has not been materially altered; and

(c) all prior parties had capacity to contract; and

(d) he has no knowledge of any insolvency proceeding instituted with respect to the maker or acceptor or the drawer of an unaccepted instrument.

N.Y. Commission Comments

The Code as enacted in New York in 1962, added to Section 3–415, as it appears in the 1958 and 1962 Official Texts, a new subsection (6) for the purpose, as stated in the Commission's 1962 Report, of restoring "the warranty obligations of an accommodation endorser formerly imposed by Uniform Negotiable Instruments Law §§ 65, 66 and N.Y.N.I.L. §§ 115, 116."

"There seems to be no good reason why the holder of forged long term paper must await maturity and dishonor of the paper before enforcing the accommodation party's liability on it. The accommodation party may by then have disappeared or become insolvent."

New York Annotations

(1) *Accord:* N.I.L., § 55, except that the phrase "without receiving value therefor" is eliminated.

(2) *Accords* generally with N.I.L., § 55 (second sentence), except that the Code would make an indorser signing for accommodation, after delivery to the holder, liable, *Contra:* Produce Bank v. Bache, 30 Hun 351 (1883).

(3) The provision is new but accords generally with N.I.L., § 55. Parol evidence is admissible to show the liability and relation of the parties whose names appear upon the bill or note in all actions between themselves. Haddock, Blanchard & Co. v. Haddock, 192 N.Y. 499, 85 N.E. 682 (1908). However, parol evidence of an agreement to exhaust the payee's remedies against the accommodated maker is inadmissible in an action by the payee, who qualifies as a holder for value, against the accommodation indorser. Long Island Trust Co. v. Merz, 20 Misc.2d 342, 187 N.Y.S.2d 419 (1959).

(4) Appears to be contrary to N.I.L., §§ 113 and 114. But see, Haddock, Blanchard & Co. v. Haddock, *supra.*

(5) First clause accords with Callery v. Lyons, 292 N.Y. 15, 53 N.E.2d 376 (1944). Second clause appears to change the strict interpretation of N.I.L., § 202, found in Quimby v. Varnum, 190 Mass. 211, 76 N.E. 671 (1906). No post-N.I.L. cases have been found, but see Moynihan v. Mckeon, 16 Misc. 343, 38 N.Y.S. 61 (1896).

Historical Note: Subsection (1) was revised, after consideration of Law Revision Commission and American Bankers Association Committee comment, to improve the accuracy of the section's terminology, and in so doing reverts in part to the language of U.N.I.L., § 29 (N.I.L., § 55).

Official Uniform Comment

Prior Uniform Statutory Provision: Sections 28, 29 and 64, Uniform Negotiable Instruments Law.

Changes: Combined and Reworded; new provisions.

Purposes of Changes and New Matter: To make it clear that:

1. Subsection (1) recognizes that an accommodation party is always a surety (which includes a guarantor), and it is his only distinguishing feature. He differs from other sureties only in that his liability is on the instrument and he is a surety for another party to it. His obligation is therefore determined by the capacity in which he signs. An accommodation maker or acceptor is bound on the instrument without any resort to his principal, while an accommodation indorser may be liable only after presentment, notice of dishonor and protest. The subsection recognizes the defenses of a surety in accordance with the provisions subjecting one not a holder in due course to all simple contract defenses, as well as his rights against his principal after payment. Under subsection (3) except as against a holder in due course without notice of the accommodation, parol evidence is admissable to prove that the party has signed for accommodation. In any case, however, under subsection (4) an indorsement which is not in the chain of title (the irregular or anomalous indorsement) is notice to all subsequent takers of the instrument of the accommodation character of the indorsement.

2. Subsection (1) eliminates the language of the old Section 29 requiring that the accommodation party sign the instrument "without receiving value therefor." The essential characteristic is that the accommodation party is a surety, and not that he has signed gratuitously. He may be a paid surety, or receive other compensation from the party accommodated. He may even receive it from the payee, as where A and B buy goods and it is understood that A is to pay for all of them and that B is to sign a note only as a surety for A.

3. The obligation of the accommodation party is supported by any consideration for which the instrument is taken before it is due. Subsection (2) is intended to change occasional decisions holding that there is no sufficient consideration where an accommodation party signs a note after it is in the hands of a holder who has given value. The party is liable to the holder in such a case even though there is no extension of time or other concession. This is consistent with the provision as to antecedent obligations as consideration (Section 3–408). The limitation to "before it is due" is one of suretyship law, by which the obligation of surety is terminated at the time limit unless in the meantime the obligation of the principal has become effective.

4. As a surety the accommodation party is not liable to the party accommodated; but he is otherwise liable on the instrument in the capacity in which he has signed. This general statement of the rule makes unnecessary the detailed provisions of the original Section 64, which is therefore eliminated, without any change in substance.

5. Subsection (5) is intended to change the result of such decisions as Quimby v. Varnum, 190 Mass. 211, 76 N.E. 671 (1906), which held that an accommodation

indorser who paid the instrument could not maintain an action on it against the accommodated party since he had no "former rights" to which he was remitted. Under ordinary principles of suretyship the accommodation party who pays is subrogated to the rights of the holder paid, and should have his recourse on the instrument.

Cross References:

Sections 3–305, 3–408, 3–603, 3–604 and 3–606.
Point 1: Section 3–306(b).
Point 3: Section 3–408.

Definitional Cross References:

"Holder in due course". Section 3–302.
"Instrument". Section 3–102.
"Notice". Section 1–201.
"Party". Section 1–201.
"Presentment". Section 3–504.
"Signed". Section 1–201.
"Writing". Section 1–201.

Section 3–416. Contract of Guarantor.

(1) "Payment guaranteed' or equivalent words added to a signature mean that the signer engages that if the instrument is not paid when due he will pay it according to its tenor without resort by the holder to any other party.

(2) "Collection guaranteed" or equivalent words added to a signature mean that the signer engages that if the instrument is not paid when due he will pay it according to its tenor, but only after the holder has reduced his claim against the maker or acceptor to judgment and execution has been returned unsatisfied, or after the maker or acceptor has become insolvent or it is otherwise apparent that it is useless to proceed against him.

(3) Words of guaranty which do not otherwise specify guarantee payment.

(4) No words of guaranty added to the signature of a sole maker or acceptor affect his liability on the instrument. Such words added to the signature of one of two or more makers or acceptors create a presumption that the signature is for the accommodation of the others.

(5) When words of guaranty are used presentment, notice of dishonor and protest are not necessary to charge the user.

(6) Any guaranty written on the instrument is enforcible [sic] notwithstanding any statute of frauds.

New York Annotations

This section is new. It provides for words of guaranty added to a signature. No modern cases in New York were found on the effect of such a signature other than Peoples Trust Co. of Malone v. O'Neil, 273 N.Y. 312, 317-318, 7 N.E.2d 244, 246-247 (1937) (dissenting opinion). See generally, Brown v. Curtiss, 2 N.Y. 225, 228 (1849), and other New York cases collected in 21 A.L.R. 1375, 1388-1389.

Official Uniform Comment

Prior Statutory Provision: None.

Purposes: The section is new. It states the commercial understanding as to the meaning and effect of words of guaranty added to a signature.

An indorser who guarantees payment waives not only presentment, notice of dishonor and protest, but also all demand upon the maker or drawee. Words of guaranty do not affect the character of the indorsement as an indorsement (Section 3–202 (4)); but the liability of the indorser becomes indistinguishable from that of a co-maker. A guaranty of collection likewise waives formal presentment, notice of dishonor and protest, but requires that the holder first proceed against the maker or acceptor by suit and execution, or show that such proceeding would be useless.

Subsection (6) is concerned chiefly with the type of statute of frauds which provides that no promise to answer for debt, default or miscarriage of another is enforceable unless it is evidenced by a writing which states the consideration for the promise. It is unusual to state any consideration when a guaranty is added to a signature on a negotiable instrument, which in itself sufficiently shows the nature of the transaction; and such statutes have commonly been held not to apply to such guaranties.

Cross References:

Sections 3–202(4) and 3–414.

Definitional Cross References:

"Holder". Section 1–201.
"Insolvent". Section 1–201.
"Instrument". Section 3–102.
"Notice of dishonor". Section 3–508.
"Party". Section 1–201.
"Presumption". Section 1–201.
"Protest". Section 3–509.
"Signature". Section 3–401.
"Written". Section 1–201.

Section 3–417. Warranties on Presentment and Transfer.

(1) Any person who obtains payment or acceptance and any prior transferor warrants to a person who in good faith pays or accepts that

(a) he has a good title to the instrument or is authorized to obtain payment or acceptance on behalf of one who has a good title; and

(b) he has no knowledge that the signature of the maker or drawer is unauthorized, except that this warranty is not given by a holder in due course acting in good faith

(i) to a maker with respect to the maker's own signature; or

(ii) to a drawer with respect to the drawer's own signature, whether or not the drawer is also the drawee; or

(iii) to an acceptor of a draft if the holder in due course took the draft after the acceptance or obtained the acceptance without knowledge that the drawer's signature was unauthorized; and

(c) the instrument has not been materially altered, except that this warranty is not given by a holder in due course acting in good faith

UCC

(i) to the maker of a note; or

(ii) to the drawer of a draft whether or not the drawer is also the drawee; or

(iii) to the acceptor of a draft with respect to an alteration made prior to the acceptance if the holder in due course took the draft after the acceptance, even though the acceptance provided "payable as originally drawn" or equivalent terms; or

(iv) to the acceptor of a draft with respect to an alteration made after the acceptance.

(2) Any person who transfers an instrument and receives consideration warrants to his transferee and if the transfer is by indorsement to any subsequent holder who takes the instrument in good faith that

(a) he has a good title to the instrument or is authorized to obtain payment or acceptance on behalf of one who has a good title and the transfer is otherwise rightful; and

(b) all signatures are genuine or authorized; and

(c) the instrument has not been materially altered; and

(d) no defense of any party is good against him; and

(e) he has no knowledge of any insolvency proceeding instituted with respect to the maker or acceptor or the drawer of an unaccepted instrument.

(3) By transferring "without recourse" the transferor limits the obligation stated in subsection (2) (d) to a warranty that he has no knowledge of such a defense.

(4) A selling agent or broker who does not disclose the fact that he is acting only as such gives the warranties provided in this section, but if he makes such disclosure warrants only his good faith and authority.

New York Annotations

(1) This is a new provision stating an undertaking to a party who accepts or pays by one who obtains payment or acceptance or by any prior transferor.

(a) *Accords* generally with N.I.L., § 115, although the Code extends warranty to drawee, and with the result in Canal Bank v. Bank of Albany, 1 Hill 287 (1841). For discussion of varying theories of recovery, see Franklin Square National Bank v. Great Atlantic Building Material Supply Corp., 186 Misc. 524, 526, 60 N.Y.S.2d 352, 353, aff'd without opinion, 270 App. Div. 930, 62 N.Y.S.2d 617, aff'd, 296 N.Y. 644, 69 N.E.2d 684 (1946).

(b) This is new statutory law. The Comment suggests that the warranty and the exceptions to it stem from the common-law rule found in Price v. Neal, 3 Burr. 1354 (1762). This rule was early adopted by the New York courts, National Park Bank v. Ninth National Bank, 46 N.Y. 77 (1871), and has apparently not been affected by the enactment of the N.I.L. See Banca Commerciale Trust Co. v. Clarkson, 274 N.Y. 69, 73, 8 N.E.2d 281, 282 (1937), permitting a payor to recover from a bad-faith recipient of the proceeds of three checks on which the drawer's signature was forged and treating this as an exception to the rule of Price v. Neal.

(c) *Contra:* National Reserve Bank of City of New York v. Corn Exchange Bank, 171 App.Div. 195, 157 N.Y.S. 316 (1916) (check certified after being raised; payor permitted recovery after payment).

(2) *Accords* generally with N.I.L., §§ 115 and 116, except that the class of persons to whom warranties run is broadened. The language of subdivisions (2) (b) and (2) (c) is substituted for "genuine and what it purports to be" in N.I.L., § 115(1); and N.I.L., § 115(4), is changed by subdivision (2) (e) to a knowledge only of any insolvency proceeding.

(3) *Accord:* N.I.L., §§ 68 and 115, except that under N.I.L., § 115(3), the qualified indorser warrants against the defense of incapacity, and not against his knowledge of this defense.

(4) *Accord:* N.I.L., § 119, except that it is limited to a selling agent.

Historical Note: This section was entirely revised to achieve parallelism with Section 4–207. The Law Revision Commission approved this revision. (1956 Recommendations, pp. 115–116; Excerpts, p. 411.)

Official Uniform Comment

Prior Uniform Statutory Provision: Sections 65 and 69, Uniform Negotiable Instruments Law.

Changes: Combined and reworded; new provisions added.

Purposes of Changes and New Matter:

1. The obligations imposed by this section are stated in terms of warranty. Warranty terms, which are not limited to sale transactions, are used with the intention of bringing in all the usual rules of law applicable to warranties, and in particular the necessity of reliance in good faith and the availability of all remedies for breach of warranty, such as recission of the transaction or an action for damages. Like other warranties, those stated in this section may be disclaimed by agreement between the immediate parties. In the case of an indorser, disclaimer of his liability as a transferor, to be effective, must appear in the form of the indorsement, and no parol proof of "agreement otherwise" is admissible. For corresponding warranties in the case of items in the bank collection process, Section 4–207 should be consulted.

2. Subsection (1) is new. It is intended to state the undertaking to a party who accepts or pays of one who obtains payment or acceptance or of any prior transferor. It is closely connected with the following section on the finality of acceptance or payment (Section 3–418), and should be read together with it.

3. Subsection (1) (a) retains the generally accepted rule that the party who accepts or pays does not "admit" the genuineness of indorsements, and may recover from the person presenting the instrument when they turn out to be forged. The justification for the distinction between forgery of the signature of the drawer and forgery of an indorsement is that the drawee is in a position to verify the drawer's signature by comparison with one in his hands, but has ordinarily no opportunity to verify an indorsement.

4. Subsection (1) (b) recognizes and deals with competing equities of parties accepting or paying instruments bearing unauthorized maker's or drawer's signatures and those obtaining acceptances or receiving payment. The warranties prescribed and exceptions thereto follow closely principles established at common law, particularly, those under Price v. Neal, 3 Burr. 1354 (1762).

The basic warranty that the person obtaining payment or acceptance and any prior transferor warrants that he has no knowledge that the signature of the maker or drawer is unauthorized stems from the general principle that one who presents an instrument knowing that the signature of the maker or drawer is forged or unauthorized commits an obvious fraud upon the party to whom presentment is made. However, few cases present this simple fact situation. If the signature of a maker or drawer has been forged, the parties include the dishonest forger himself and usually one or more innocent holders taking from him. Frequently, the state of knowledge of a holder is difficult to determine and sometimes a holder takes such a forged instrument in perfect good faith but subsequently learns of the forgery. Since in different fact situations holders have equities of varying strength, it is necessary to have some exceptions to the basic warranty.

The exceptions apply only in favor of a holder in due course and, within the provisions of Section 3–201, to all subsequent transferees from a holder in due course. Since a condition of the status of a holder in due course under Section 3–302(1)(a) is that the holder takes the instrument without notice of any defense against it, this condition presupposes that at the time of taking such a holder had no knowledge of the unauthorized signature. Consequently, the warranty of subsection (1)(b) is pertinent in the case of a holder in due course only in the relatively few cases where he acquires knowledge of the forgery after the taking but before the presentment. In this situation the holder in due course must continue to act in good faith to be exempted from the basic warranty.

The first exemption from the warranty by such a holder, made by subparagraph (i), is that the warranty does not run to a maker of a note with respect to the maker's own signature. This codifies the rule of Price v. Neal, and related cases. Since a maker of a note is presumed to know his own signature, if he fails to detect a forgery of his own signature and pays the note, under the Price v. Neal principle he should not be permitted to recover such payment from a holder in due course acting in good faith. Similarly, under subparagraph (ii) a drawer of a draft is presumed to know his own signature and if he fails to detect a forgery of his signature and pays a draft he may not recover that payment from a holder in due course acting in good faith. This rule applies if the drawer pays the instrument as drawer and also if he pays the instrument as drawee in a case where he is both drawer and drawee.

Under the principle of Price v. Neal a drawee of a draft is presumed to know the signature of his customer, the drawer. However, under subsection (1)(b) and subparagraph (iii) of this subsection this presumption is not strong enough to deprive such a drawee (either in accepting or paying an instrument) of the warranty of no knowledge of the unauthorized drawer's signature, unless the holder in due course took the instrument and became such a holder after the drawee's acceptance; or obtained the acceptance without knowledge that the drawer's signature was unauthorized. In the former case, the holder taking after and thereby presumably in reliance on the acceptance should be protected as against the drawee who accepted without detecting the unauthorized signature. In the latter case the holder, having no knowledge of the unauthorized signature at the time of the drawee's acceptance, would not be charged with this warranty and would be entitled to enforce such acceptance under Section 3–418, even if thereafter he acquired knowledge of the unauthorized signature prior to enforcement of the acceptance. Such right of the holder to enforce the acceptance would be valueless if immediately upon enforcing it and obtaining payment the holder became obligated to return the payment by reason of breach of the warranty of no knowledge at the time of payment.

5. Subsection (1)(c) retains the common law rule, followed by several decisions under the original Act, which has permitted a party paying a materially altered instrument in good faith to recover, and a party who accepts such an instrument to avoid such acceptance. As in the case of subsection (1)(b) this warranty is not imposed against a holder in due course acting in good faith in favor of a maker of a note or a drawer of a draft on the ground that such maker or drawer should know the form and amount of the note or draft which he has signed. The exception made by subparagraph (iii) in the case of a holder in due course of a draft accepted after the

alteration follows the decisions in National City Bank of Chicago v. National Bank of Republic of Chicago, 300 Ill. 103, 132 N.E. 832, 22 A.L.R. 1153 (1921), and Wells Fargo Bank & Union Trust Company v. Bank of Italy, 214 Cal. 156, 4 P.2d 781 (1931), and is based on the principle that an acceptance is an undertaking relied upon in good faith by an innocent party. The attempt to avoid this result by certifying checks "payable as originally drawn" leaves the subsequent purchaser in uncertainty as to the amount for which the instrument in certified, and so defeats the entire purpose of certification, which is to obtain the definite obligation of the bank to honor a definite instrument. Subparagraph (iii) accordingly provides that such language is not sufficient to impose on the holder in due course the warranty of no material alteration where the holder took the draft after the acceptance and presumably in reliance on it.

Subparagraph (iv) of subsection (1)(c) exempts a holder in due course from the warranty of no material alteration to the acceptor of a draft with respect to an alteration made after the acceptance. A drawee accepting a draft has an opportunity of ascertaining the form and particularly the amount of the draft accepted. If, thereafter, the draft is materially altered and is thereupon presented for payment to the acceptor, the acceptor has the necessary information in its records to verify the form and particularly the amount of the draft. If in spite of this available information it pays the draft, there is as much reason to leave the responsibility for such payment upon the acceptor (as against a holder in due course acting in good faith) as there is in the case of a maker or drawer paying a materially altered note or draft.

6. Under Section 3–201 parties taking from or holding under a holder in due course, within the limits of that section, will have the same rights under Section 3–417(1) as a holder in due course. Of course such parties claiming under a holder in due course must act in good faith and be free from fraud, illegality and notice as provided in Section 3–201.

7. The liabilities imposed by subsection (2) in favor of the immediate transferee apply to all persons who transfer an instrument for consideration whether or not the transfer is accompanied by indorsement. Any consideration sufficient to support a simple contract will support those warranties.

8. Subsection (2) changes the original Section 65 to extend the warranties of any *indorser* beyond the immediate transferee in all cases. Where there is an indorsement the warranty runs with the instrument and the remote holder may sue the indorser-warrantor directly and thus avoid a multiplicity of suits which might be interrupted by the insolvency of an intermediate transferor. The language of subsections (2)(b) and (2)(c) is substituted for "genuine and what it purports to be" in the original Section 65(1). The language of subsection (2)(a) is substituted for that of Section 65(2) in order to cover the case of the agent who transfers for another.

9. Subsection (2)(d) resolves a conflict in the decisions as to whether the transferor warrants that there are no defenses to the instrument good against him. The position taken is that the buyer does not undertake to buy an instrument incapable of enforcement, and that in the absence of contrary understanding the warranty is implied. Even where the buyer takes as a holder in due course who will cut off the defense, he still does not undertake to buy a lawsuit with the necessity of proving his status. Subsection (3) however provides that an indorsement "without recourse" limits the (2)(d) warranty to one that the indorser has no knowledge of such defenses. With this exception the liabilities of a "without recourse" indorser under this section are the same as those of any other transferor. Under Section 3–414 "without recourse" in an indorsement is effective to disclaim the general contract of the indorser stated in that section.

10. Subsection (2)(e) is substituted for Section 65(4). The transferor does not warrant against difficulties of collection, apart from defenses, or against impairment of the credit of the obligor or even his insolvency in the commercial sense. The buyer

is expected to determine such questions for himself before he takes the obligation. If insolvency proceedings as defined in this Act (Section 1–201) have been instituted against the party who is expected to pay and the transferor knows it, the concealment of that fact amounts to a fraud upon the buyer, and the warranty against knowledge of such proceedings is provided accordingly.

11. Subsection (4) is substituted for Section 69 of the original Act. It applies only to a selling agent, as distinguished from an agent for collection. It follows the rule generally accepted that an agent who makes the disclosure warrants his good faith and authority and may not by contract assume a lesser warranty.

Cross References:

Sections 3–404, 3–405, 3–406, 3–414 and 4–207.
Point 1: Section 4–207.
Point 2: Section 3–418.
Point 4: Sections 3–201, 3–302 and 3–418.
Point 9: Section 3–414.
Point 10: Section 1–201.

Definitional Cross References:

"Acceptance". Section 3–410.
"Alteration". Section 3–407.
"Bank". Section 1–210.
"Draft". Section 3–104.
"Genuine". Section 1–201.
"Good faith". Section 1–201.
"Holder in due course". Section 3–302.
"Instrument". Section 3–102.
"Note". Section 3–104.
"Party". Section 1–201.
"Person". Section 1–201.
"Signature". Section 3–401.
"Term". Section 1–201.

Section 3–418. Finality of Payment or Acceptance.

Except for recovery of bank payments as provided in the Article on Bank Deposits and Collections (Article 4) and except for liability for breach of warranty on presentment under the preceding section, payment or acceptance of any instrument is final in favor of a holder in due course or a person who has in good faith changed his position in reliance on the payment.

New York Annotations

Accord: N.I.L., § 112 (as to an acceptor), except that New York apparently does not extend finality to a certification obtained by the drawer. Metropolitan Life Ins. Co. v. Bank of U.S., 259 N.Y. 365, 182 N.E. 18 (1932). Cf. Rosenbaum v. First Nat'l City Bank, 11 N.Y.2d 845, 182 N.E.2d 280, 227 N.Y.S.2d 670 (1962). As is indicated in the annotation to Section 3–417, the rule of Price v. Neal has been followed in New York and has been applied to cases of payment as well as acceptance. The Code makes payment final in favor of any holder in due course or any person who has in good faith changed his position in reliance on the payment, subject to the exceptions stated.

Historical Note: The phrase at the end of the section providing that payment is final in favor of a person who has in good faith changed his position in reliance on the payment was added at the suggestion of the Law Revision Commission. (1956 Recommendations, p. 116; Excerpts, p. 411.)

Official Uniform Comment

Prior Uniform Statutory Provision: Section 62, Uniform Negotiable Instruments Law.

Changes: Completely restated.

Purposes of Changes:

The rewording is intended to remove a number of uncertainties arising under the original section.

1. The section follows the rule of Price v. Neal, 3 Burr. 1354 (1762), under which a drawee who accepts or pays an instrument on which the signature of the drawer is forged is bound on his acceptance and cannot recover back his payment. Although the original Act is silent as to payment, the common law rule has been applied to it by all but a very few jurisdictions. The traditional justification for the result is that the drawee is in a superior position to detect a forgery because he has the maker's signature and is expected to know and compare it; a less fictional rationalization is that it is highly desirable to end the transaction on an instrument when it is paid rather than reopen and upset a series of commercial transactions at a later date when the forgery is discovered.

The rule as stated in the section is not limited to drawees, but applies equally to the maker of a note or to any other party who pays an instrument.

2. The section follows the decisions under the original Act applying the rule of Price v. Neal to the payment of overdrafts, or any other payment made in error as to the state of the drawer's account. The same argument for finality applies, with the additional reason that the drawee is responsible for knowing the state of the account before he accepts or pays.

3. The section follows decisions under the original Act, in making payment or acceptance final only in favor of a holder in due course, or a transferee who has the rights of a holder in due course under the shelter principle. If no value has been given for the instrument the holder loses nothing by the recovery of the payment or the avoidance of the acceptance, and is not entitled to profit at the expense of the drawee; and if he has given only an executory promise or credit he is not compelled to perform it after the forgery or other reason for recovery is discovered. If he has taken the instrument in bad faith or with notice he has no equities as against the drawee.

4. The section rejects decisions under the original Act permitting recovery on the basis of mere negligence of the holder in taking the instrument. If such negligence amounts to a lack of good faith as defined in this Act (Section 1–201) or to notice under the rules (Section 3–304) relating to notice to a purchaser of an instrument, the holder is not a holder in due course and is not protected; but otherwise the holder's negligence does not affect the finality of the payment or acceptance.

5. This section is to be read together with the preceding section, which states the warranties given by the person obtaining acceptance or payment. It is also limited by the bank collection provision (Section 4–301) permitting a payor bank to recover a payment improperly paid if it returns the item or sends notice of dishonor within the limited time provided in that section. But notice that the latter right is sharply limited in time, and terminates in any case when the bank has made final payment, as defined in Section 4–213.

Cross References:

Sections 3–302, 3–303 and 3–417.
Point 2: Section 3–201(1).
Point 4: Sections 1–201, 3–302 and 3–304.
Point 5: Sections 3–417, 4–213 and 4–301.

Definitional Cross References:

"Acceptance". Section 3–410.
"Account". Section 4–104.
"Bank". Section 1–201.
"Holder in due course". Section 3–302.
"Instrument". Section 3–102.
"Presentment". Section 3–504.

Section 3–419. Conversion of Instrument; Innocent Representative.

(1) An instrument is converted when

(a) a drawee to whom it is delivered for acceptance refuses to return it on demand; or

(b) any person to whom it is delivered for payment refuses on demand either to pay or to return it; or

(c) it is paid on a forged indorsement.

(2) In an action against a drawee under subsection (1) the measure of the drawee's liability is the face amount of the instrument. In any other action under subsection (1) the measure of liability is presumed to be the face amount of the instrument.

(3) Subject to the provisions of this Act concerning restrictive indorsements a representative, including a depositary or collecting bank, who has in good faith and in accordance with the reasonable commercial standards applicable to the business of such representative dealt with an instrument or its proceeds on behalf of one who was not the true owner is not liable in conversion or otherwise to the true owner beyond the amount of any proceeds remaining in his hands.

(4) An intermediary bank or payor bank which is not a depositary bank is not liable in conversion solely by reason of the fact that proceeds of an item indorsed restrictively (Sections 3–205 and 3–206) are not paid or applied consistently with the restrictive indorsement of an indorser other than its immediate transferor.

New York Annotations

(1) Subsections (1)(a) and (1)(b) reject the view that refusal to return or pay the instrument should constitute an acceptance. Compare N.I.L., § 225. The holder's recovery would now be limited to recovery in conversion, and demand becomes a prerequisite to such recovery. Subsection (1)(c) adopts the result in such cases as Henderson v. Lincoln Rochester Trust Co., 303 N.Y. 27, 100 N.E.2d 117 (1951), under which payment on a forged indorsement constitutes conversion of the instrument.

(2) Subsection (2) is new. Cf. Hillsley v. State Bank of Albany, 17 A.D.2d 686, 230 N.Y.S.2d 531 (1962).

(3) Subsection (3) protects to good-faith dispository and collecting bank from liability in conversion, subject to the indicated exceptions. The subsection is consistent with the rule under the N.I.L. with respect to good faith brokers dealing in negotiable securities. See Gruntal v. National Surety Co., 254 N.Y. 468, 173 N.E. 682 (1930).

(4) Amplifies the rule in Section 3–206(2) to ensure that the "neither given notice nor otherwise affected" phrase shall be understood to exclude liability in conversion.

Historical Note: Subsection (3) was changed and subsection (4) added to this section to effectuate the policy described under Section 3–205. The reference to reasonable commercial standards remains, as the standard for exemption from liability for conversion differs from the considerations applicable to Section 3–302. Further revision added "paid or" in subsection (4) to harmonize with Section 3–603. (1956 Recommendations, p. 117).

Official Uniform Comment

Prior Uniform Statutory Provision: Section 137, Uniform Negotiable Instruments Law.

Changes: Rule changed; new provisions.

Purposes of Changes and New Matter: To remove difficulties arising under the original section, and to cover additional situations:

1. The provision of the original Section 137 that refusal to return a bill presented for acceptance is deemed to be acceptance has led to difficulties. If the bill is accepted it is not dishonored, and the holder is left without recourse against the drawer and indorsers when he has most need for immediate recourse. The drawee does not in fact accept and does everything he can to display an intention not to accept; and the "acceptance" is useless to the holder for any purpose other than an action against the drawee, since he has nothing that he can negotiate. The original rule has therefore been changed (see Section 3–410).

2. A negotiable instrument is the property of the holder. It is a mercantile specialty which embodies rights against other parties, and a thing of value. This section adopts the generally recognized rule that a refusal to return it on demand is a conversion. The provision is not limited to drafts presented for acceptance, but extends to any instrument presented for payment, including a note presented to the maker. The action is not on the instrument, but in tort for its conversion.

The detention of an instrument voluntarily delivered is not wrongful unless and until there is demand for its return. Demand for a return at a particular time may, however, be made at the time of delivery; or it may be implied under the circumstances or understood as a matter of custom. If the holder is to call for the instrument and fails to do so, he is to be regarded as extending the time. "Refuses" is meant to cover any intentional failure to return the instrument, including its intentional destruction. It does not cover a negligent loss or destruction, or any other unintentional failure to return. In such a case the party may be liable in tort for any damage sustained as a result of his negligence, but he is not liable as a converter under this section.

3. Subsection (1)(c) is new. It adopts the prevailing view of decisions holding that payment on a forged indorsement is not an acceptance, but that even though made in good faith it is an exercise of dominion and control over the instrument inconsistent with the rights of the owner, and results in liability for conversion.

4. Subsection (2) is new. It adopts the rule generally applied to the conversion of negotiable instruments, that the obligation of any party on the instrument is presumed, in the sense that the term is defined in this Act (Section 1–201), to be worth its face value. Evidence is admissible to show that for any reason such as insolvency or the existence of a defense the obligation is in fact worth less, or even

that it is without value. In the case of the drawee, however, the presumption is replaced by a rule of absolute liability.

5. Subsection (3), which is new, is intended to adopt the rule of decisions which has held that a representative, such as a broker or depositary bank, who deals with a negotiable instrument for his principal in good faith is not liable to the true owner for conversion of the instrument or otherwise, except that he may be compelled to turn over to the true owner the instrument itself or any proceeds of the instrument remaining in his hands. The provisions of subsection (3) are, however, subject to the provisions of this Act concerning restrictive indorsements (Sections 3–205, 3–206 and related sections).

6. The provisions of this section are not intended to eliminate any liability on warranties of presentment and transfer (Section 3–417). Thus a collecting bank which had been subject to liability under this section, even though the collecting bank might not be liable directly to the owner of the instrument.

Cross References:

Sections 3–409, 3–410, 3–411 and 3–603.
Point 4: Section 1–201.
Point 5: Sections 1–201, 3–205 and 3–206.
Point 6: Section 3–417.

Definitional Cross References:

"Acceptance". Section 3–410.
"Action". Section 1–201.
"Bank". Section 1–201.
"Collecting bank". Sections 3–102 and 4–105.
"Depositary bank". Sections 3–102 and 4–105.
"Good faith". Section 3–102.
"Instrument". Section 3–102.
"Intermediary bank". Sections 3–102 and 4–105.
"On demand". Section 3–108.
"Person". Section 1–201.
"Presumed". Section 1–201.
"Representative". Section 1–201.

PART 5

PRESENTMENT, NOTICE OF DISHONOR AND PROTEST

Section 3–501. When Presentment, Notice of Dishonor, and Protest Necessary or Permissible.

(1) Unless excused (Section 3–511) presentment is necessary to charge secondary parties as follows:

(a) presentment for acceptance is necessary to charge the drawer and indorsers of a draft where the draft so provides, or is payable elsewhere than at the residence or place of business of the drawee, or its date of payment depends upon such presentment. The holder may at his option present for acceptance any other draft payable at a stated date;

(b) presentment for payment is necessary to charge any indorser;

(c) in the case of any drawer, the acceptor of a draft payable at a bank or the maker of a note payable at a bank, presentment for payment is necessary, but failure to make presentment discharges such drawer, acceptor or maker only as stated in Section 3–502(1) (b).

(2) Unless excused (Section 3–511)

(a) notice of any dishonor is necessary to charge any indorser;

(b) in the case of any drawer, the acceptor of a draft payable at a bank or the maker of a note payable at a bank, notice of any dishonor is necessary, but failure to give such notice discharges such drawer, acceptor or maker only as stated in Section 3–502(1) (b).

(3) Unless excused (Section 3–511) protest of any dishonor is necessary to charge the drawer and indorsers of any draft which on its face appears to be drawn or payable outside of the states and territories of the United States and the District of Columbia. The holder may at his option make protest of any dishonor of any other instrument and in the case of a foreign draft may on insolvency of the acceptor before maturity make protest for better security.

(4) Notwithstanding any provision of this section, neither presentment nor notice of dishonor nor protest is necessary to charge an indorser who has indorsed an instrument after maturity.

New York Annotations

(1)(a) *Accords* generally with N.I.L., §§ 240, and 247, except that the last sentence may change what appears to be the New York rule treating a refusal to accept a demand draft, other than a check, as a dishonor. Wachtel v. Rosen, 249 N.Y. 386, 388, 390, 164 N.E. 326, 327 (1928); N.I.L., § 111.

(b) *Accord:* N.I.L., § 130 (last sentence).

(c) This subparagraph, in conjunction with Section 3–502(1) (b), extends the rule of N.I.L., § 322, with certain modifications (see annotations to Section 3–502(1)(b) to the effect that drawers of checks are discharged only to the extent of the loss caused by the delay in presentment, to include acceptors of drafts and makers of notes payable at a bank. It thus changes the rule of some cases relying on N.I.L., § 130, that makers and acceptors of paper payable at banks are not discharged to any extent by a failure to make presentment. See, for example, Dubler v. Toscana Straw Goods Corporation, 142 Misc. 369, 254 N.Y.S. 464 (1932) (trade acceptance); compare Baldwin's Bank v. Smith, 215 N.Y. 76, 80, 109 N.E. 138, 139 (1915). Apart from these changes the present section is in accord with N.I.L., § 130.

(2)(a) *Accord:* N.I.L., § 160 (indorser).

(b) The persons entitled to notice of dishonor and the effect of failure to give such notice are the same as under Section 3–501(1)(c) above. The annotation under that section applies to this section as well.

(3) *Accord:* N.I.L., §§ 213 (as amended L. 1960, c. 362, § 1, eff. April 7, 1960, Redefinition of Inland Bills of Exchange Act) and 260. The last sentence is generally in accord with N.I.L., §§ 189 and 266.

(4) *Contra:* N.I.L., § 26 (last sentence). The former provision made overdue paper payable on demand as against the post-maturity indorser. The Code reverses this rule. No recent authorities were found, but see Moore v. Alexander, 63 App.Div. 100, 71 N.Y.S. 420 (1901) (pre-N.I.L. fact situation).

Historical Note: The word "made", found between the words "draft" and "payable" in the 1952 draft of subsections (1)(c) and 2(b), was deleted at the suggestion of the Law Revision Commission to cover the case of a draft accepted payable at a bank as well as drawn there payable. The addition of a clause at the end of the last sentence in subsection (3) is intended to provide for permissible "protest for better security", a practice common in certain foreign countries. (1956 Recommendations, p. 119; Excerpts, p. 411.)

Official Uniform Comment

Prior Uniform Statutory Provision: Sections 70, 89, 118, 129, 143, 144, 150, 151, 152, 157, 158 and 186, Uniform Negotiable Instruments Law.

Changes: Combined and simplified.

Purposes of Changes:

1. Part 5 simplifies the requirements of the original Act as to presentment for acceptance or payment, notice of dishonor and protest. This section assembles in one place all provisions as to when any such proceeding is necessary. It eliminates some of the requirements and simplifies others. The effect of unexcused delay in any such proceeding as a discharge is covered by the next section, and the sections following prescribe the details of the proceedings.

2. The words "Necessary to charge" are retained from the original Act. They mean that the necessary proceeding is a condition precedent to any right of action against the drawer or indorser. He is not liable and cannot be sued without the proceedings however long delayed. Under some circumstances delay is excused. If it is not excused it may operate as a discharge under the next section. Under some circumstances the proceeding may be entirely excused and the drawer or indorser is then liable as if the proceeding had been duly taken. Section 3–511 states the circumstances under which delay may be excused or the proceeding entirely excused.

3. Subsection (1)(a) retains the substance of the original Sections 143, 144 and 150. The last sentence of the subsection states the rule of the decisions both at common law and under the original Act, that the holder may at his option present any time draft for acceptance, and is not required to wait until the due date to know whether the drawee will accept it; but that if he does make presentment and acceptance is refused he must give notice of dishonor. There is no similar right to present for acceptance a draft payable on demand, since a demand draft entitles the holder to immediate payment but not to acceptance.

4. Subsections (1) (b) and (1) (c) on presentment for payment follow Section 70 of the original Act with one important change. Under the original Act and under this section ((1) (b)) presentment for payment is necessary (unless excused) to charge any drawer. Under the original Act drawers of drafts other than checks were wholly discharged by a failure to make due presentment but drawers of checks (Section 70 in conjunction with Section 186) were discharged only "to the extent of the loss caused by the delay"–that is to say, when insolvency of the drawee bank occurred after the time when presentment was due. The check rule of the original Act (somewhat modified–see Section 3–502(1)(b) and Comment thereto) is by subsection (1) (c) extended to all drawers, and also to the acceptors and makers of domiciled–"payable at a bank"–drafts and notes. Thus drawers of drafts other than checks are not, as they were under Section 70, wholly discharged by failure to make due presentment but, like drawers of checks, are discharged only as they may have suffered loss as provided in Section 3–502(1) (b). As to domiciled paper original Section 70 provided that ability and willingness to pay at the place named at maturity were "equivalent to a tender of payment"–that is to say would stop the running of interest, but had no other effect.

Accordingly cases have held that makers and acceptors of domiciled paper were not discharged to any extent by the holder's failure to make presentment even when the obligor had funds available in the paying bank on the date for presentment and the bank subsequently failed. Subsection (1)(c) applies the check rule to such makers and acceptors; the "tender" language of Section 70 is eliminated; and the result in the cases referred to in the preceding sentence is reversed. Under this section as under the original act presentment for payment is not necessary to charge primary parties (makers and acceptors of undomiciled paper).

5. Under subsection (2) the rules as to necessity of notice of dishonor run parallel with the rules as to necessity of presentment stated in subsection (1).

6. Under the original Sections 129 and 152 protest is required in the case of every "foreign draft", defined as a draft which on its face is not both drawn and payable "within this state." The result has been that upon dishonor in New York a check which appears on its face to be drawn in Jersey City must be protested in order to sue the drawer or any indorser. This has led to great inconvenience and expense of protest fees. The only function of protest is that of proof of dishonor, and it adds nothing to notice of dishonor as such.

Subsection (3) eliminates the requirement of protest except upon dishonor of a draft which on its face appears to be either drawn or payable outside of the states, territories, dependencies and possessions of the United States, the District of Columbia and the Commonwealth of Puerto Rico. The requirement is left as to such international drafts because it is generally required by foreign law, which this Article cannot affect. The formalities of protest are covered by Section 3–509 on protest, and substitutes for protest as proof of dishonor are provided for in Section 3–510 on evidence of dishonor and of notice. [This paragraph was amended in 1966].

This provision retains from the original Section 118 the rule permitting the holder at his option to make protest of any dishonor of any other instrument. Even where not required protest may have definite convenience where process does not run to another state and the taking of depositions is a slow and expensive matter. Even where the instrument is drawn and payable entirely within a state there may be convenience in saving the trip of a witness from Buffalo to New York to testify to dishonor, where the substitute evidence of dishonor and notice of dishonor cannot be relied on. Either required or optional protest is presumptive evidence of dishonor. (Section 3–510.)

7. The permissible "protest for better security" of original Section 158 is retained in the case of a foreign draft, as the practice is common in certain foreign countries.

8. Under the final sentence of Section 7 of the original Act an instrument indorsed when overdue became payable on demand as to the indorser. That language has been deleted from this Article–see Section 3–108 and Comment. It meant, among other things and in view of the provisions of the original Act as to demand paper, that such an indorser was discharged unless the instrument was presented for payment within a reasonable time after his indorsement. Presentment of overdue paper for the purpose of charging an indorser is unusual and not an expected commercial practice; the rule has been little more than a trap for those not familiar with the Act. Subsection (4), reversing the original Act, provides that as to indorsers after maturity neither presentment nor notice of dishonor nor protest is necessary; like primary parties therefore they will remain liable on the instrument for the period of the applicable statute of limitations.

Cross References:

Point 1: Sections 3–502 through 3–508.
Point 2: Sections 3–413, 3–414 and 3–511.
Point 3: Sections 3–413, 3–414 and 3–511.
Point 4: Section 3–502.
Point 6: Sections 3–413, 3–414, 3–509, 3–510 and 3–511.

Point 8: Section 3–108.

Definitional Cross References:

"Acceptance". Section 3–410.
"Bank". Section 1–201.
"Certificate of deposit". Section 3–104.
"Dishonor". Section 3–507.
"Draft". Section 3–104.
"Holder". Section 1–201.
"Instrument". Section 3–102.
"Note". Section 3–104.
"Notice of dishonor". Section 3–508.
"Party". Section 1–201.
"Presentment". Section 3–504.
"Protest". Section 3–509.
"Secondary party". Section 3–102.
"Signature". Section 3–401.

Section 3–502. Unexcused Delay; Discharge.

(1) Where without excuse any necessary presentment or notice of dishonor is delayed beyond the time when it is due

(a) any indorser is discharged; and

(b) any drawer or the acceptor of a draft payable at a bank or the maker of a note payable at a bank who because the drawee or payor bank becomes insolvent during the delay is deprived of funds maintained with the drawee or payor bank to cover the instrument may discharge his liability by written assignment to the holder of his rights against the drawee or payor bank in respect of such funds, but such drawer, acceptor or maker is not otherwise discharged.

(2) Where without excuse a necessary protest is delayed beyond the time when it is due any drawer or indorser is discharged.

New York Annotations

(1)(a) *Accord:* N.I.L., §§ 130–160, and 241.

(b) Extends the rule of N.I.L., § 322, to any drawer and to acceptors of drafts and makers of notes payable at a bank, and further limits the discharge of such latter persons to cases where the drawer or payor bank has become insolvent and only where the drawer, acceptor, or maker gives a written assignment of this right against the drawee or payor bank to the holder.

(2) *Accord:* N.I.L., § 260.

Historical Note: Subsection (1) (b) was revised for clarification and for consistency with Section 3–501. (1956 Recommendations, p. 119; Excerpts, p. 412.)

Official Uniform Comment

Prior Uniform Statutory Provision: Sections 7, 70, 89, 144, 150, 152 and 186, Uniform Negotiable Instruments Law.

Changes: Combined and simplified.

Purposes of Changes:

This section is the complement of the preceding section. It covers in one section widely scattered provisions of the original Act:

1. The circumstances under which presentment or notice of dishonor or protest or delay therein are excused are stated in Section 3–511. When not excused delay operates as a discharge as provided in this section.

2. Subsection (1)(b) applies to any drawer, as well as to the makers and acceptors of drafts and notes payable at a bank, the rule of the original Section 186 providing for discharge only where the drawer of a check has sustained loss through the delay. This section expressly limits the rule to loss sustained through insolvency of the drawee or payor which was the only type of loss to which the Section 186 rule has ever been applied in the cases arising under it.

The purpose of the rule is to avoid hardship upon the holder through complete discharge, and unjust enrichment of the drawer or other party who normally has received goods or other consideration for the issue of the instrument. He is "deprived of funds" in any case where bank failure or other insolvency of the drawee or payor has prevented him from receiving the benefit of funds which would have paid the instrument if it had been duly presented.

The original language discharging the drawer "to the extent of the loss caused by the delay" has not worked our satisfactorily in the decided cases, since the amount of the loss caused by the failure of a bank is almost never ascertainable at the time of suit and may not be ascertained until some years later. The decisions have turned upon burden of proof, and the drawer has seldom succeeded in proving his discharge. Subsection (1) (b) therefore substitutes a right to discharge liability by written assignment to the holder of rights against the drawee or payor as to the funds which cover the particular instrument. The assignment is intended to give the holder an effective right to claim against the drawee or payor.

3. Subsection (2) retains the rule of the original Section 152, that any unexcused delay of a required protest is a complete discharge of all drawers and indorsers.

Cross References:

Point 1: Section 3–511(1).
Point 2: Section 3–501.
Point 3: Section 3–509.

Definitional Cross References:

"Bank". Section 1–201.
"Draft". Section 3–104.
"Holder". Section 1–201.
"Insolvent". Section 1–201.
"Instrument". Section 3–102.
"Note". Section 3–104.
"Notice of dishonor". Section 3–508.
"Payor bank". Section 4–105.
"Presentment". Section 3–504.
"Protest". Section 3–509.
"Rights". Section 1–201.
"Signature". Section 3–401.
"Written". Section 1–201.

Section 3–503. Time of Presentment.

(1) Unless a different time is expressed in the instrument the time for any presentment is determined as follows:

(a) where an instrument is payable at or a fixed period after a stated date any presentment for acceptance must be made on or before the date it is payable;

(b) where an instrument is payable after sight it must either be presented for acceptance or negotiated within a reasonable time after date or issue whichever is later;

(c) where an instrument shows the date on which it is payable presentment for payment is due on that date;

(d) where an instrument is accelerated presentment for payment is due within a reasonable time after the acceleration;

(e) with respect to the liability of any secondary party presentment for acceptance or payment of any other instrument is due within a reasonable time after such party becomes liable thereon.

(2) A reasonable time for presentment is determined by the nature of the instrument, any usage of banking or trade and the facts of the particular case. In the case of an uncertified check which is drawn and payable within the United States and which is not a draft drawn by a bank the following are presumed to be reasonable periods within which to present for payment or to initiate bank collection:

(a) with respect to the liability of the drawer, thirty days after date or issue whichever is later; and

(b) with respect to the liability of an endorser, seven days after his indorsement.

(3) Where any presentment is due on a day which is not a full business day for either the person making presentment or the party to pay or accept, presentment is due on the next following day which is a full business day for both parties.

(4) Presentment to be sufficient must be made at a reasonable hour, and if at a bank during its banking day.

New York Annotations

(1)(a) and (b) *Accord:* N.I.L., §§ 240 and 241, except that as to situations specified in N.I.L., § 240(2) (express stipulation) and in N.I.L., § 240(3) (payable elsewhere than at drawee's home or office), the Code would require presentment on or before maturity rather than "within a reasonable time."

(c) *Accord:* N.I.L., § 131.

(d) This is new law.

(e) Changes the existing law found in N.I.L., § 131, which measures timely presentment from either date of issuance or date of last negotiation, by making the liability of secondary parties hinge upon the time when they become bound upon the instrument.

(2) *Accord:* N.I.L., § 4.

(a) and (b) N.I.L., § 4, makes no distinction between drawers and indorsers in defining reasonable time. Subsection (2)(a) greatly extends the period within which a check must be presented in order to charge the drawer and to that extent is contra to such cases as Hawks v. Board of Education, 241 App.Div. 880, 272 N.Y.S. 24 (1934), and Dehoust v. Lewis, 128 App.Div. 131, 112 N.Y.S. 559 (1908).

(3) Modifies existing law found in N.I.L., §§ 145 and 243, by eliminating the "half–day Saturday" provision and adding a test which involves the determination of whether a particular day is a "full business day for both parties." See also General Construction Law, §§ 24, 24–a, 25, and 25–a, and N.I.L., § 5.

(4) *Accord:* N.I.L., §§ 132(2), 135, and 242, except that the Code eliminates the last part of N.I.L., § 135, providing for the case where a person to make payment at a bank has no funds there to meet it.

Historical Note: Additions to subsections (1) (a) and (3) were made, pursuant to Law Revision Commission comment, for clarification. (1956 Recommendations, p. 120; Excerpts, p. 412.)

Official Uniform Comment

Prior Uniform Statutory Provision: Sections 71, 72, 75, 85, 86, 144, 145, 146, 186 and 193, Uniform Negotiable Instruments Law.

Changes: Combined and simplified; new provisions.

Purposes of Changes and New Matter:

1. This section states in one place all of the rules applicable to the time of presentment. Excused delay is covered by Section 3–511 on waiver and excuse, and the effect of unexcused delay by Section 3–502 on discharge.

The original Section 86, as to the determination of the time of payment by calculation from the day the time is to run, is omitted as superfluous. It states a rule universally applied to all time calculations in the law of contracts, and has no special application to negotiable instrument. No change in the law is intended.

2. Subsection (1) contains new provisions stating the commercial understanding as to the presentment of instruments payable after sight, and of accelerated paper.

3. Subsection (2) retains the substance of the original Section 193 as to the determination of a reasonable time. It provides specific time limits which are presumed, as that term is defined in this Act (Section 1–201), to be reasonable for uncertified checks drawn and payable within the continental limits of the United States. The court made time limit of one day after the receipt of the instrument found in decisions under the original Act has proved to be too short a time for some holders, such as the department store or other large business clearing many checks through its books shortly after the first of the month, as well as the farmer or other individual at a distance from a bank.

The time limit provided differs as to drawer and indorser. The drawer, who has himself issued the check and normally expects to have it paid and charged to his account is reasonably required to stand behind it for a longer period, especially in view of the protection now provided by Federal Deposit Insurance. The thirty days specified coincides with the time after which a purchaser has notice that a check has become stale (Section 3–304(3)(c)). The indorser, who has normally merely received the check and passed it on, and does not expect to have to pay it, is entitled to know more promptly whether it is to be dishonored, in order that he may have recourse against the person with whom he has dealt.

4. Subsection (3) replaces the original Sections 85 and 146. It is intended to make allowance for the increasing practice of closing banks or businesses on Saturday or other days of the week. It is not intended to mean that any drawee or obligor can avoid dishonor of instruments by extended closing.

5. Subsection (4) eliminates the provision of the original Section 75 permitting presentment "at any hour before the bank is closed" if the drawer has no funds in the bank. The change is made to avoid inconvenience to the bank.

"Banking day" is defined in Section 4–104.

Cross References:

Point 1: Sections 3–501, 3–502, 3–505, 3–506 and 3–511.
Point 3: Sections 1–201 and 3–304(3) (c).
Point 5: Section 4–104.

Definitional Cross References:

"Acceptance". Section 3–410.
"Bank". Section 1–201.
"Banking day". Section 4–104.
"Check". Section 3–104.
"Draft". Section 3–104.
"Instrument". Section 3–102.
"Issue". Section 3–102.
"Party". Section 1–201.
"Person". Section 1–201.
"Presentment". Section 3–504.
"Presumed". Section 1–201.
"Reasonable time". Section 1–201.
"Secondary party". Section 3–102.
"Usage of trade". Section 1–205.

Section 3–504. How Presentment Made.

(1) Presentment is a demand for acceptance or payment made upon the maker, acceptor, drawee or other payor by or on behalf of the holder.

(2) Presentment may be made

(a) by mail, in which event the time of presentment is determined by the time of receipt of the mail; or

(b) through a clearing house; or

(c) at the place of acceptance or payment specified in the instrument or if there be none at the place of business or residence of the party to accept or pay. If neither the party to accept or pay nor anyone authorized to act for him is present or accessible at such place presentment is excused.

(3) It may be made

(a) to any one of two or more makers, acceptors, drawees or other payors; or

(b) to any person who has authority to make or refuse the acceptance or payment.

(4) A draft accepted or a note made payable at a bank in the United Stated must be presented at such bank.

(5) In the cases described in Section 4–210 presentment may be made in the manner and with the result stated in that section.

Amended by Laws 1963, Ch. 1003, eff. Sept. 27, 1964.

New York Annotations

(1) *Accords* generally with N.I.L., §§ 132 and 242, but combines the definitions of presentment for payment and presentment for acceptance which were contained in separate sections of the N.I.L.

(2)(a) N.I.L., §§ 132 and 242, make no provision for presentment by mail unless such a provision is included by implication in the words "or some person authorized to receive payment on his behalf." Limited authority for presentment through the mails by a collecting bank is found in N.I.L., § 350–e(a). Language negative to the general proposition may be found in Gilpin v. Savage, 201 N.Y. 167, 171, 94 N.E. 656, 657 (1911).

(b) *Accord:* Columbia-Knickerbocker Trust Co. v. Miller, 215 N.Y. 191, 197, 109 N.E. 179, 180 (1915).

(c) Generally in accord with but more liberal than N.I.L., §§ 132 and 133. N.I.L., § 133(2) (presentment at address of payor indicated on instrument) and § 133(4) (presentment wherever payor found), are omitted.

(3)(a) *Contra:* N.I.L., §§ 138 and 242(1) (if the persons are not partners). *Accord:* N.I.L., § 137, as to partners where no place of presentment is specified.

(b) *Accord:* N.I.L., § 242. The rule is enlarged to include presentment for payment.

(4) *Accord:* N.I.L., §§ 133(1) and 135. Also see N.I.L., §§ 133(1) and 135. Also see N.I.L., §§ 130 and 147.

(5) See annotation to Section 4–210.

Historical Note: The following suggestions of the Law Revision Commission are incorporated in the present draft of the section:

(1) The term "or other payor" was inserted in subsections (1) and (3)(a);

(2) The last part of subsection (2)(a) was added;

(3) Subsection (2)(c) was modified by having it refer to the place of acceptance as well as the place of payment; and

(4) The last sentence was added to subsection (2)(c) to cover the situation where neither the proper nor authorized person is found at the place of presentment. (1956 Recommendations, pp. 120–121; Excerpts, pp. 412–413.)

Official Uniform Comment

Prior Uniform Statutory Provision: Sections 72, 73, 77, 78 and 145, Uniform Negotiable Instruments Law.

Changes: Combined and simplified.

Purposes of Changes:

1. This section is intended to simplify the rules as to how presentment is made and to make it clear that any demand upon the party to pay is a presentment no matter where or how. Former technical requirements of exhibition of the instrument and the like are not required unless insisted upon by the party to pay (Section 3–505).

2. Paragraph (a) of subsection (2) authorizes presentment by mail directly to the obligor. The presentment is sufficient and the instrument is dishonored by non-acceptance or nonpayment even though the party making presentment may be liable for improper collection methods. "Through a clearinghouse" means that presentment is not made when the demand reaches the clearing-house, but when it reaches the obligor. Section 4–210 should also be consulted for the methods of presenting which may properly be employed by a collecting bank. Subsection (5) of this section makes it clear that presentment made under Section 4–210 is proper presentment.

3. Paragraph (a) of subsection (3) eliminates the requirement of the original Sections 78 and 145(1) that presentment be made to each of two or more makers, acceptors or drawees unless they are partners or one has authority to act for the others. The holder is entitled to expect that any one of the named parties will pay or accept, and should not be required to go to the trouble and expense of making separate presentment to a number of them.

4. Section 3–412 provides that an acceptance made payable at a bank in the United States does not vary the draft. Subsection (4) of this Section makes it clear that a draft so accepted must be presented at the bank so designated. The same rule is applied to notes made payable at a bank. The rule of the subsection is in conformity with the provisions of Section 3–501 on presentment and Section 3–502 on the effect of failure to make presentment with reference to domiciled paper [This paragraph was amended in 1962].

Cross References:

Point 1: Sections 3–501, 3–502, 3–505 and 3–511.
Point 2: Section 4–210.
Point 5: Sections 3–412, 3–501 and 3–502.

Definitional Cross References:

"Acceptance". Section 3–410.
"Bank". Section 1–201.
"Clearing house". Section 4–104.
"Draft". Section 3–104.
"Holder". Section 1–201.
"Instrument". Section 3–102.
"Note". Section 3–104.
"Party". Section 1–201.
"Person". Section 1–201.

Section 3–505. Rights of Party to Whom Presentment Is Made.

(1) The party to whom presentment is made may without dishonor require

(a) exhibition of the instrument; and

(b) reasonable identification of the person making presentment and evidence of his authority to make it if made for another; and

(c) that the instrument be produced for acceptance or payment at a place specified in it, or if there be none at any place reasonable in the circumstances; and

(d) a signed receipt on the instrument for any partial or full payment and its surrender upon full payment.

(2) Failure to comply with any such requirement invalidates the presentment but the person presenting has a reasonable time in which to comply and the time for acceptance or payment runs from the time of compliance.

New York Annotations

(1)(a) N.I.L., § 134, is extended to cover presentment for acceptance as well as payment (compare N.I.L., §§ 242 and 243). The N.I.L. requires that the instrument be exhibited in all cases, whereas the Code merely requires exhibition when the party to whom presentment is made so desires.

(b) New statutory provision. No New York cases on point were found.

(c) Generally *accords* with N.I.L., § 133.

(d) Surrender of the instrument upon full payment is in accord with N.I.L., § 134. However, the right to demand a signed receipt is new and no New York cases on point were found.

(2) This provision is new and no New York cases on point were found.

Official Uniform Comment

Prior Uniform Statutory Provision: Section 74, Uniform Negotiable Instruments Law.

Changes: Expanded and modified.

Purposes of Changes: To supplement the provisions as to how presentment is made, by permitting the party to whom it is made to insist on additional requirements:

1. In the first instance a mere demand for acceptance or payment is sufficient presentment, and if the payment is unqualifiedly refused nothing more is required. The Party to whom presentment is made may, however, require exhibition of the instrument, its production at the proper place, identification of the party making presentment, and a signed receipt on the instrument, or its surrender on full payment. Failure to comply with any such requirement invalidates the presentment and means that the instrument is not dishonored. The time for presentment is, however, extended to give the person presenting a reasonable opportunity to comply with the requirements.

2. "Reasonable identification" means identification reasonable under all the circumstances. If the party on whom demand is made knows the person making presentment, no requirement of identification is reasonable, while if the circumstances are suspicious a great deal may be required. The requirement applies whether the instrument presented is payable to order or to bearer.

Cross References:

Point 1: Sections 3–504 and 3–506.

Definitional Cross References:

"Acceptance". Section 3–410.
"Dishonor". Section 3–507.
"Instrument". Section 3–102.
"Party". Section 1–201.
"Person". Section 1–201.
"Presentment". Section 3–504.
"Reasonable time". Section 1–204.
"Signed". Section 1–201.

Section 3–506. Time Allowed for Acceptance or Payment.

(1) Acceptance may be deferred without dishonor until the close of the next business day following presentment. The holder may also in a good faith effort to obtain acceptance and without either dishonor of the instrument or discharge of secondary parties allow postponement of acceptance for an additional business day.

(2) Except as a longer time is allowed in the case of documentary drafts drawn under a letter of credit, and unless an earlier time is agreed to by the party to pay, payment of an instrument may be deferred without dishonor pending reasonable examination to determine whether it is properly payable, but payment must be made in any event before the close of business on the day of presentment.

New York Annotations

(1) This subsection substitutes "the close of the next business day following presentment" for the 24-hour period in N.I.L., § 224. See also N.I.L., § 225. The provision for an "additional business day" thereafter is new.

(2) Compare N.I.L., § 143. No statute now fixes the time allowed for payment of negotiable instruments generally. N.I.L., § 224, applies to presentment for acceptance only. For present law governing time allowed in bank collections, see N.I.L., § 350–b(1).

Historical Note: Subsection (1) was amended by the elimination of the phrase "or for such longer time as the holder may allow" at the end of the first sentence, and by the addition of the second sentence in response to a suggestion by the Law Revision Commission. (1956 Recommendations, p. 122; Excerpts, p. 413.)

Official Uniform Comment

Prior Uniform Statutory Provision: Section 136, Uniform Negotiable Instruments Law.

Changes: Expanded.

Purposes of Changes: The original section covered only the time allowed to the drawee on presentment for acceptance. This section also covers the time allowed on presentment for payment.

Section 5–112 (Time Allowed for Honor) states the time, longer than here provided, during which a bank to which drafts are presented under a letter of credit may defer payment or acceptance without dishonor of the drafts. As to drafts drawn under a letter of credit Section 5–112 of course controls.

Section 4–301 on deferred posting should be consulted for the right of a payor bank to recover tentative settlements made by it on the day an item is received. That right does not survive final payment (Section 4–213).

Cross References: Sections 4–301 and 5–112.

Definitional Cross References:

"Acceptance". Section 3–410.
"Dishonor". Section 3–507.
"Documentary draft". Sections 3–102 and 4–104.
"Instrument". Section 3–102.
"Letter of credit". Section 5–103.
"Party". Section 1–201.
"Presentment". Section 3–504.

Section 3–507. Dishonor; Holder's Right of Recourse; Term Allowing Re-Presentment.

(1) An instrument is dishonored when

(a) a necessary or optional presentment is duly made and due acceptance or payment is refused or cannot be obtained within the prescribed time or in case of bank collections the instrument is seasonably returned by the midnight deadline (Section 4–301); or

(b) presentment is excused and the instrument is not duly accepted or paid.

(2) Subject to any necessary notice of dishonor and protest, the holder has upon dishonor an immediate right of recourse against the drawers and indorsers.

(3) Return of an instrument for lack of proper indorsement is not dishonor.

(4) A term in a draft or an indorsement thereof allowing a stated time for re-presentment in the event of any dishonor of the draft by nonacceptance if a time draft or by nonpayment if a sight draft gives the holder as against any secondary party bound by the term an option to waive the dishonor without affecting the liability of the secondary party and he may present again up to the end of the stated time.

New York Annotations

(1)(a) and (b) *Accord:* N.I.L., §§ 143 and 246. See also N.I.L., § 247.

(2) *Accord:* N.I.L., §§ 144 and 248.

(3) This is new and no New York cases directly in point were found. See Lipten v. Columbia Trust Co., 194 App.Div. 384, 185 N.Y.S. 198 (1920) (impliedly approving practice of certifying and returning a check where indorsement of payee was missing).

(4) This is new and no New York cases were found.

Official Uniform Comment

Prior Uniform Statutory Provision. Sections 83 and 149, Uniform Negotiable Instruments Law.

Changes: Reworded.

Purposes of Changes:

1. The language of the section is changed in accordance with the provisions of the preceding section as to the time allowed for acceptance or payment.

2. Subsection (3) is new. It states general banking and commercial understanding. The time within which a payor bank must return items, and the methods of returning, are stated in Section 4–301. Under Section 3–411 (3) a bank may certify an item so returned.

Cross References:

Point 1: Sections 3–503, 3–504, 3–505, 3–508 and 4–301.
Point 2: Sections 3–411(3), 4–301.

Definitional Cross References:

"Acceptance". Section 3–410.
"Bank". Section 1–201.
"Draft". Section 3–104.
"Holder". Section 1–201.

"Instrument". Section 3–102.
"Midnight deadline". Section 4–104.
"Notice of dishonor". Section 3–508.
"Presentment". Section 3–504.
"Protest". Section 3–509.
"Right". Section 1–201.
"Seasonably". Section 1–204.
"Secondary party". Section 3–102.
"Term". Section 1–201.

Section 3–508. Notice of Dishonor.

(1) Notice of dishonor may be given to any person who may be liable on the instrument by or on behalf of the holder or any party who has himself received notice, or any other party who can be compelled to pay the instrument. In addition an agent or bank in whose hands the instrument is dishonored may give notice to his principal or customer or to another agent or bank from which the instrument was received.

(2) Any necessary notice must be given by a bank before its midnight deadline and by any other person before midnight of the third business day after dishonor or receipt of notice of dishonor.

(3) Notice may be given in any reasonable manner. It may be oral or written and in any terms which identify the instrument and state that it has been dishonored. A misdescription which does not mislead the party notified does not vitiate the notice. Sending the instrument bearing a stamp, ticket or writing stating that acceptance or payment has been refused or sending a notice of debit with respect to the instrument is sufficient.

(4) Written notice is given when sent although it is not received.

(5) Notice to one partner is notice to each although the firm has been dissolved.

(6) When any party is in insolvency proceedings instituted after the issue of the instrument notice may be given either to the party or to the representative of his estate.

(7) When any party is dead or incompetent notice may be sent to his last known address or given to his personal representative.

(8) Notice operates for the benefit of all parties who have rights on the instrument against the party notified.

New York Annotations

(1) *Accord:* N.I.L., §§ 161, 162, 165, and 168, except that the Code would slightly broaden the provisions now found in §§ 161 and 165.

(2) This subsection extends the time in which to give notice of dishonor to midnight of the third business day after dishonor or receipt of notice thereof in the case of all except banks. Compare N.I.L., §§ 173–175. For banks (other than collecting banks

treated in Section 4–212) the time is midnight of the next banking day; compare N.I.L., § 174(1) ("the close of business hours on the day following").

(3) Generally in accord with N.I.L., §§ 166 and 167.

(4) *Accord:* N.I.L., § 176. See Sections 1–201(25) ("notice"), 1–201(26) ("notifies"), and 1–201(38) ("send"). See also N.I.L., § 179 (eliminated in the Code) to be compared with the foregoing definition of "send."

(5) *Accord:* N.I.L., § 170.

(6) Generally in *accord* with N.I.L., § 172.

(7) This subsection makes the notice to a personal representative of a party who is know to be dead permissive rather than mandatory as in N.I.L., § 169. The rule is broadened to include an incompetent party and to permit notice to be sent to his last known address.

(8) *Accord:* N.I.L., §§ 163 and 164.

Historical Note: Certain minor changes were made in response to suggestions made by the Law Revision Commission. (1956 Recommendations, p. 124; Excerpts, p. 413.)

Official Uniform Comment

Prior Uniform Statutory Provision: Sections 90 through 108, Uniform Negotiable Instruments Law.

Changes: Combined and simplified.

Purposes of Changes: To simplify notice of dishonor and eliminate many of the detailed requirements of the original Act:

1. Notice is normally given by the holder or by an indorser who has himself received notice. Subsection (1) is intended to encourage and facilitate notice of dishonor by permitting any party who may be compelled to pay the instrument to notify any party who may be liable on it. Thus an indorser may notify another indorser who is not liable to the one who gives notice, even when the latter has not received notice from any other party to the instrument.

2. Except as to collecting banks, as to whom Section 4–212 controls, the time within which necessary notice must be given is extended to three days after dishonor or receipt of notice from another party. In the case of individuals the one-day time limit of the original Act has proved too short in many cases. It is extended to give the party a margin of time within which to ascertain what is required of him and get out an ordinary business letter. This time leeway eliminates the elaborate provisions as to the time of mailing in the original Sections 103 and 104.

3. Subsection (3) retains the substance of the original Sections 95 and 96. The provision approves the bank practice of returning the instrument bearing a stamp, ticket or other writing, or a notice of debit of the account, as sufficient notice. Subsection (4) retains the substance of the original Section 105.

4. Subsection (7) permits notice to be sent to the last known address of a party who is dead or incompetent rather than to his personal representative. The provision is intended to save time, as the name of the personal representative often cannot easily be ascertained, and mail addressed to the original party will reach the representative.

Cross References:

Sections 3–501, 3–507 and 3–511.
Point 2: Section 4–212.

Definitional Cross References:

"Acceptance". Section 3–410.
"Bank". Section 1–201.
"Customer". Section 4–104.

"Dishonor". Section 3–507.
"Holder". Section 1–201.
"Insolvency proceedings". Section 1–201.
"Instrument". Section 3–102.
"Issue". Section 3–102.
"Midnight deadline". Section 4–104.
"Notifies". Section 1–201.
"Party". Section 1–201.
"Person". Section 1–201.
"Representative". Section 1–201.
"Rights". Section 1–201.
"Send". Section 1–201.
"Written" and "writing". Section 1–201.

Section 3–509. Protest; Noting for Protest.

(1) A protest is a certificate of dishonor made under the hand and seal of a United States consul or vice consul or a notary public or other person authorized to certify dishonor by the law of the place where dishonor occurs. It may be made upon information satisfactory to such person.

(2) The protest must identify the instrument and certify either that due presentment has been made or the reason why it is excused and that the instrument has been dishonored by non-acceptance or nonpayment.

(3) The protest may also certify that notice of dishonor has been given to all parties or to specified parties.

(4) Subject to subsection (5) any necessary protest is due by the time that notice of dishonor is due.

(5) If, before protest is due, an instrument has been noted for protest by the officer to make protest, the protest may be made at any time thereafter as of the date of the noting.

New York Annotations

(1) Protest may no longer be made by "any respectable resident of the place where the bill was dishonored", as under N.I.L., § 262 (2). In addition to a notary (*accord:* N.I.L., § 262(1)), it may be made by a United States consul or vice-consul or "other person authorized to certify dishonor by the law of the place where dishonor occurs." *Contra:* [Former] Civil Practice Act, § 369 [which became N.I.L. § 271]. N.I.L., § 264, as to where protest is to be made, is eliminated. The second sentence of subsection (1) would seem to change existing law which requires the notary to certify facts within his own knowledge. Littman v. Goldstein, 255 App. Div. 540, 8 N.Y.S.2d 490 (1938).

(2) *Accords* with, but is more liberal than, N.I.L., § 261, in that identification of the instrument is permitted by other means than annexation of the instrument or inclusion of a copy in the protest.

(3) This is new and no New York cases on point were found.

(4) Extends the time provided in N.I.L., § 263 ("day of its dishonor") by making protest due when notice of dishonor is due.

(5) *Accords* generally with the last sentence of N.I.L., § 263.

UCC

Official Uniform Comment

Prior Uniform Statutory Provision: Sections 153, 154, 155, 156, 158 and 160, Uniform Negotiable Instruments Law.

Changes: Combined and simplified.

Purposes of Changes:

1. Protest is not necessary except on drafts drawn or payable outside of the United States. Section 3–501(3) which also permits the holder at his option to make protest on dishonor of any other instrument. This section is intended to simplify either necessary or optional protest when it is made.

2. "Protest" has been used to mean the act of making protest, and sometimes loosely to refer to the entire process of presentment, notice of dishonor and protest. In this Article it is given its original, technical meaning, that of the official certificate of dishonor.

3. Subsection (1) adds to the notary public the United States consul or vice consul, and any other person authorized to certify dishonor by the law of the place where dishonor occurs. It eliminates the requirement of the original Section 156 that protest must be made at the place of dishonor. It eliminates also the provision of the original Section 154 permitting protest by "any respectable resident of the place where the bill is dishonored, in the presence of two or more credible witnesses." This has at least left uncertainty as to the identity and credibility of the persons certifying, and has almost never been used. Any necessary delay in finding the proper officer to make protest is excused under Section 3–511.

4. "Information satisfactory to such person" does away with the requirement occasionally stated, that the person making protest must certify as of his own knowledge. The requirement has been more honored in the breach than in the observance, and in practice protest has been made upon hearsay which the officer regards as reliable, upon the admission of the person who has dishonored, or at most upon re-presentment, which is only indirect proof of the original dishonor. There is seldom any possible motive for false protest, and the basis on which it is made is never questioned. Subsection (1) leaves to the certifying officer the responsibility for determining whether he has satisfactory information. The provision is not intended to affect any personal liability of the officer for making a false certificate.

5. The protest need not be in any particular form, so long as it certifies the matters stated in Subsection (2). It need not be annexed to the instrument, and may be forwarded separately; but annexation may identify the instrument. If the instrument is lost, destroyed, or wrongfully withheld, protest is still sufficient if it identifies the instrument; but the owner must prove his rights as in any action under this Article on a lost, destroyed or stolen instrument (Section 3–804).

6. Subsection (3) recognizes the practice of including in the protest a certification that notice of dishonor has been given to all parties or to specified parties. The next section makes such a certification presumptive evidence that the notice has been given.

7. Protest is normally forwarded with notice of dishonor. Subsection (4) extends the time for making a necessary protest to coincide with the time for giving notice of dishonor. Any delay due to circumstances beyond the holder's control is excused under Section 3–511 on waiver or excuse. Any protest which is not necessary but merely optional with the holder may be made at any time before it is used as evidence.

8. Subsection (5) retains from the original Section 155 the provision permitting the officer to note the protest and extend it formally later.

Cross References:

Point 1: Sections 3–501(3) and 3–511.

Point 3: Section 3–511 (1).
Point 5: Section 3–804.
Point 6: Section 3–510(a).
Point 7: Sections 3–508(2) and 3–511(1).

Definitional Cross References:

"Dishonor". Section 3–507.
"Instrument". Section 3–102.
"Notice of dishonor". Section 3–508.
"Party". Section 1–201.
"Person". Section 1–201.
"Presentment". Section 3–504.

Section 3–510. Evidence of Dishonor and Notice of Dishonor.

The following are admissible as evidence and create a presumption of dishonor and of any notice of dishonor therein shown:

(a) a document regular in form as provided in the preceding section which purports to be a protest;

(b) the purported stamp or writing of the drawee, payor bank or presenting bank on the instrument or accompanying it stating that acceptance or payment has been refused for reasons consistent with dishonor;

(c) any book or record of the drawee, payor bank, or any collecting bank kept in the usual course of business which shows dishonor, even though there is no evidence of who made the entry.

New York Annotations

(a) Generally in accord with [former] Civil Practice Act, §§ 368 and 369 [which became N.I.L. §§ 270, 271], except that under the present rule, in the case of a protest of a foreign bill, the law of the place of payment governs. The Code contains nothing comparable to the provision in [former] Civil Practice Act, § 368 [N.I.L. § 270], giving the party against whom the evidence is offered a means to destroy the force of the notarial certificate where he claims failure to receive notice.

(b) This is new and no New York cases were found.

(c) Generally in accord with, but broader than, Civil Practice Act, § 374–a [now CPLR 4518], in that the Code treats the evidence as presumptive rather than merely some evidence of the facts stated.

Official Uniform Comment

Prior Uniform Statutory Provision: None.

Purposes: This section is new. It states the effect of protest as evidence, and provides two substitutes for protest as proof of dishonor:

1. Paragraph (a) states the generally accepted rule that a protest is not only admissible as evidence, but creates a presumption, as that term is defined in this Act (Section 1–201), of the dishonor which it certifies. The rule is extended to include the giving of any notice of dishonor certified by the protest. The provision also relieves the holder of the necessity of proving that a document regular in form which purports to be a protest is authentic, or that the person making it was qualified. Nothing in

the provision is intended to prevent the obliger from overthrowing the presumption by evidence that there was in fact no dishonor, that notice was not given, or that the protest is not authentic or not made by a proper officer.

2. Paragraph (b) recognizes as the full equivalent of protest the stamp, ticket or other writing of the drawee, payor or presenting bank. The drawee's statement that payment is refused on account of insufficient funds always has been commercially acceptable as full proof of dishonor. It should be satisfactory evidence in any court. It is therefore made admissible, and creates a presumption of dishonor. The provision applies only where the stamp or writing states reasons for refusal which are consistent with dishonor. Thus the following reasons for refusal are not evidence of dishonor, but of justifiable refusal to pay or accept:

Indorsement missing
Signature missing
Signature illegible
Forgery
Payee altered
Date altered
Post dated
Not on us

On the other hand the following reasons are satisfactory evidence of dishonor, consistent with due presentment, and are within this provision:

Not sufficient funds
Account garnisheed
No account
Payment stopped

3. Paragraph (c) recognizes as the full equivalent of protest any books or records of the drawee, payor bank or any collecting bank kept in its usual course of business, even though there is no evidence of who made the entries. The provision, as well as that of paragraph (b), rests upon the inherent improbability that bank records, or those of the drawee, will show any dishonor which has not in fact occurred, or that the holder will attempt to proceed on the basis of dishonor if he could in fact have obtained payment.

Cross References:

Sections 3–501 and 3–508.
Point 1: Section 1–201.

Definitional Cross References:

"Acceptance". Section 3–410.
"Collecting bank". Section 4–105.
"Dishonor". Section 3–507.
"Instrument". Section 3–102.
"Notice of dishonor". Section 3–508.
"Payor bank". Section 4–105.
"Presumption". Section 1–201.
"Protest". Section 3–509.
"Writing". Section 1–201.

Section 3–511. Waived or Excused Presentment, Protest or Notice of Dishonor of Delay Therein.

(1) Delay in presentment, protest or notice of dishonor is excused when the party is without notice that it is due or when the delay is caused by circumstances

beyond his control and he exercises reasonable diligence after the cause of the delay ceases to operate.

(2) Presentment or notice or protest as the case may be is entirely excused when

(a) the party to be charged has waived it expressly or by implication either before or after it is due; or

(b) such party has himself dishonored the instrument or has countermanded payment or otherwise has no reason to expect or right to require that the instrument be accepted or paid; or

(c) by reasonable diligence the presentment or protest cannot be made or the notice given.

(3) Presentment is also entirely excused when

(a) the maker, acceptor or drawee of any instrument except a documentary draft is dead or in insolvency proceedings instituted after the issue of the instrument; or

(b) acceptance or payment is refused but not for want of proper presentment.

(4) Where a draft has been dishonored by nonacceptance a later presentment for payment and any notice of dishonor and protest for nonpayment are excused unless in the meantime the instrument has been accepted.

(5) A waiver of protest is also a waiver of presentment and of notice of dishonor even though protest is not required.

(6) Where a waiver of presentment or notice or protest is embodied in the instrument itself it is binding upon all parties; but where it is written above the signature of an indorser it binds him only.

New York Annotations

(1) Generally in *accord* with N.I.L., §§ 141 (presentment for payment), 184 (notice of dishonor), 244 (presentment where time is insufficient), and 267 (protest), except that the language "not imputable to his default, misconduct or negligence" has been deleted.

(2)(a) Generally in *accord* with N.I.L., §§ 142(3) (presentment for payment), 180 (notice of dishonor), 182 (protest), and 267 (protest).

(b) *Accord:* N.I.L., § 185(4), but the rule is here expanded to excuse presentment and protest as well as notice of dishonor. Compare N.I.L., §§ 139, 140, 186 (no similar language), and 267. Gonzalez v. Industrial Bank (of Cuba), 12 N.Y.2d 33, 186 N.E.2d 410, 234 N.Y.S.2d 210 (1962); Ellenbogen v. The State Bank, 119 Misc. 711, 197 N.Y.S. 278 (1922).

(c) Generally in *accord* with N.I.L., §§ 142(1), 183, and 267.

(3)(a) Excusing presentment for acceptance in case of drawee's death *accords* with N.I.L., § 245. The Code is *contra* to N.I.L., § 136 (presentment for payment when principal debtor dead). The provision as to insolvency proceedings is new and would change decisional law. Goldstein v. Brastone Corporation, 254 App.Div. 288, 4 N.Y.S. 2d 909, aff'd 279 N.Y. 775, 18 N.E.2d 862 (1939); Matter of Taylor, 174 Misc. 457, 21 N.Y.S.2d 245 (1940).

(b) *Accord:* N.I.L., § 245(3) (presentment for acceptance) The Code extends the rule to presentment for payment.

(4) *Accord:* N.I.L., §§ 187 and 248.

(5) *Accord:* N.I.L., § 182.

(6) *Accord:* N.I.L., § 181, except that language is added to make clear that the provision applies to waivers of protest and presentment as well as waiver of notice.

Historical Note: Pursuant to a comment by the Law Revision Commission, subsection (1) was revised by replacing the word "knowledge" (after "without") by "notice" to provide for an excuse to the party only when he has neither nor reason to know (Section 1–202(25)) that the prescribed diligence is due. The provision in subsection (6), consisting of N.I.L., § 181, literatim, was inserted to provide consistency with the N.I.L. in the matter in question. This addition and the elimination of the previous provision in subsection (6) were results of Law Revision Commission suggestions. (1956 Recommendations, pp. 125–126; Excerpts, pp. 414–415.)

Official Uniform Comment

Prior Uniform Statutory Provision: Sections 79, 80, 81, 82, 109, 111, 112, 113, 114, 115, 116, 130, 147, 148, 150, 151, 159, Uniform Negotiable Instruments Law.

Changes: Combined and simplified.

Purposes of Changes: This section combines widely scattered sections of the original act, and is intended to simplify the rules as to when presentment, notice or protest is excused:

1. The single term "excused" is substituted for "excused," dispensed with," "not necessary," "not required," as used variously in the original act. No change in meaning is intended.

2. Subsection (1) combines provisions found in the original Sections 81, 113, 147 and 159. Delay in making presentment either for payment or for acceptance, in giving notice of dishonor or in making protest is excused when the party has acted with reasonable diligence and the delay is not his fault. This is true where an instrument has been accelerated without his knowledge, or demand has been made by prior holder immediately before his purchase. It is true under any other circumstances where the delay is beyond his control. The words "not imputable to his default, misconduct or negligence" found in the original Sections 81, 113 and 159 are omitted as superfluous, but no change in substance is intended.

3. Any waived presentment, notice or protest is excused, as under the original Sections 82, 109, 110 and 111. The waiver may be express or implied, oral or written and before or after the proceeding waived is due. It may be, and often is, a term of the instrument when it is issued. Subsection (5) retains as standard commercial usage the meaning attached by the original Section 111 to "protest waived."

4. Paragraph (b) of subsection (2) combines the substance of provisions found in the original Sections 79, 80, 114, 115 and 130. A party who has no right to require or reason to expect that the instrument will be honored is not entitled to presentment, notice or protest. This is of course true where he has himself dishonored the instrument or has countermanded payment. It is equally true, for example, where he is an accommodated party and has himself broken the accommodation agreement.

5. Paragraph (c) of subsection (2) combines provisions found in the original Sections 82(1), 112 and 159. The excuse is established only by proof that reasonable diligence has been exercised without success, or that reasonable diligence would be in any case have been unsuccessful.

6. Paragraph (a) of subsection (3) is new. It excuses presentment in situations where immediate payment or acceptance is impossible or so unlikely that the holder cannot reasonably be expected to make presentment. He is permitted instead to have his immediate recourse upon the drawer or indorser, and let the latter file any necessary

claim in probate or insolvency proceedings. The exception for the documentary draft is to preserve any profit on the resale of goods for the creditors of the drawee if his representative can find the funds to pay.

7. Paragraph (b) of subsection (3) extends the original Section 148(3) to include any case where payment or acceptance is definitely refused and the refusal is not on the ground that there has been no proper presentment. The purpose of presentment is to determine whether or not the maker, accepter or drawee will pay or accept; and when that question is clearly determined the holder is not required to go through a useless ceremony. The provision applies to a definite refusal stating no reasons.

8. Subsection (4) retains the rule of the original Sections 116 and 151.

9. Subsection (6) retains the rule of original Section 110.

Cross References:

Sections 3–501, 3–502, 3–503, 3–507 and 3–509.

Definitional Cross References:

"Acceptance". Section 3–410.
"Dishonor". Section 3–507.
"Documentary draft". Section 4–104.
"Draft". Section 3–104.
"Insolvency proceedings". Section 1–201.
"Instrument". Section 3–102.
"Issue". Section 3–102.
"Notice of dishonor". Section 3–508.
"Party". Section 1–201.
"Presentment". Section 3–504.
"Protest". Section 3–509.
"Right". Section 1–201

PART 6

DISCHARGE

Section 3–601. Discharge of Parties.

(1) The extent of the discharge of any party from liability on an instrument is governed by the sections on

(a) payment or satisfaction (Section 3–603); or

(b) tender of payment (Section 3–604); or

(c) cancellation or renunciation (Section 3–605); or

(d) impairment or right of recourse or of collateral (Section 3–606), or

(e) reacquisition of the instrument by a prior party (Section 3–208); or

(f) fraudulent and material alteration (Section 3–407); or

(g) certification of a check (Section 3–411); or

(h) acceptance varying a draft (Section 3–412); or

(i) unexcused delay in presentment or notice of dishonor or protest (Section 3–502).

(2) Any party is also discharged from his liability on an instrument to another party by any other act or agreement with such party which would discharge his simple contract for the payment of money.

(3) The liability of all parties is discharged when any party who has himself no right of action or recourse the instrument

(a) reacquires the instrument in his own right; or

(b) is discharged under any provision of this Article, except as otherwise provided with respect to discharge for impairment of recourse or of collateral (Section 3–606).

New York Annotations

Generally in *accord* with N.I.L. §§ 200, 201, and 202. Where N.I.L., § 200, provides for the "discharge of the instrument," the Code provides only for the discharge of some or all of the parties thereto. The Code adds the phrase "or agreement with such party" to subsection (2) which otherwise conforms to N.I.L., § 200(4).

The term "any party who himself has no right of action or recourse on the instrument" is substituted in subsection (3) for the term "principal debtor" found in N.I.L., § 200(5). The Code would provide for the discharge of an accommodation maker or acceptor where the party accommodated is released. Compare Trietel v. Gibson, 131 Misc 377, 266 N.Y.S. 603 (1928) (dictum). See also Murray v. Judah, 6 Cow. 484 (1826).

Official Uniform Comment

Prior Uniform Statutory Provision: Sections 119, 120 and 121, Uniform Negotiable Instruments Law.

Changes: Portions of original sections combined and reworded; new provisions.

Purposes of Changes:

1. Subsection (1) contains an index referring to all of the sections of this Article which provide for the discharge of any party. The list is exclusive so far as the provisions of the Article are concerned, but it is not intended to prevent or affect any discharge arising apart from this statute, as for example a discharge in bankruptcy or a statutory provision for discharge if the instrument is negotiated in a gaming transaction.

2. A negotiable instrument is in itself merely a piece of paper bearing a writing, and strictly speaking is incapable of being discharged. The parties are rather discharged from liability on their contracts on the instrument. The language of the original Section 119 as to discharge of the instrument itself has left uncertainties as to the effect of the discharge upon the rights of a subsequent holder in due course. It is therefore eliminated, and this section now distinguishes instead between the discharge of a single party and the discharge of all parties.

So far as the discharge of any one party is concerned a negotiable instrument differs from any other contract only in the special rules arising out of its character to which paragraphs (a) to (i) of subsection (1) are an index, and in the effect of the discharge against a subsequent holder in due course (Section 3–602). Subsection (2) therefore retains from the original Section 119(4) the provision for discharge by "any other act which will discharge a simple contract for the payment of money," and specifically recognizes the possibility of a discharge by agreement.

The discharge of any party is a defense available to that party provided in sections on rights of those who are and are not holders in due course (Sections 3–305 and 3–306). He has the burden of establishing the defense (Section 3–307).

3. Subsection (3) substitutes for the "discharge of the instrument" the discharge of all parties from liability on their contracts on the instrument. It covers a part of the substance of the original Section 119(1), (2) and (5), the original Section 120(1) and the original Section 121(1) and (2). It states a general principle in lieu of the original detailed provisions. The principle is that all parties to an instrument are discharged when no party is left with rights against any other party on the paper.

When any party reacquires the instrument in his own right his own liability is discharged; and any intervening party to whom he was liable is also discharged as provided in Section 3–208 on reacquisition. When he is left with no right of action against an intervening party and no right of recourse against any prior party, all parties are obviously discharged. The instrument itself is not necessarily extinct, since it may be reissued or renegotiated with a new and further liability; and if it subsequently reaches the hands of a holder in due course without notice of the discharge he may still enforce it as provided in Section 3–602 on effect of discharge against a holder in due course.

Under Section 3–606 on impairment of recourse or collateral, the discharge of any party discharges those who have a right of recourse against him, except in the case of a release with reservation of rights or a failure to give notice of dishonor. A discharge of one who has himself no right of action or recourse on the instrument may thus discharge all parties. Again the instrument itself is not necessarily extinct, and if it is negotiated to a subsequent holder in due course without notice of the discharge he may enforce it as provided in Section 3–602 on effect of discharge against a holder in due course.

4. The language "any party who has himself no right of action or recourse on the instrument" is substituted for "principal debtor," which is not defined by the original Act and has been misleading. This Article also omits the original Section 192, defining the "person primarily liable." Under Section 3–415 on accommodation parties an accommodation maker or acceptor, although he is primarily liable on the instrument in the sense that he is obligated to pay it without recourse on another, has himself a right of recourse against the accommodated payee; and his reacquisition or discharge leaves the accommodated party liable to him. The accommodated payee, although he is not primarily liable to others, has no right of action or recourse against the accommodation maker, and his reacquisition or discharge may discharge all parties.

Cross References:

Sections 3–406, 3–411, 3–412, 3–509, 3–603, 3–604 and 3–605.
Point 2: Sections 3–305, 3–306, 3–307 and 3–602.
Point 3: Sections 3–208, 3–602 and 3–606.
Point 4: Section 3–415.

Definitional Cross References:

"Action". Section 1–201.
"Agreement". Section 1–201.
"Alteration". Section 3–407.
"Certification". Section 3–411.
"Check". Section 3–104.
"Contract". Section 1–201.
"Draft". Section 3–104.
"Instrument". Section 3–102.
"Money". Section 1–201.

"Notice of dishonor". Section 3–508.
"Party". Section 1–201.
"Presentment". Section 3–504.
"Rights". Section 1–201.

Section 3–602. Effect of Discharge Against Holder in Due Course.

No discharge of any party provided by this Article is effective against a subsequent holder in due course unless he has notice thereof when he takes the instrument.

New York Annotations

This is new and no New York cases directly in point have been found.

Official Uniform Comment

Prior Uniform Statutory Provision: None.

Purposes:

The section is intended to remove an uncertainty as to which the original Act is silent. It rests on the principle that any discharge of a party provided under any section of this Article is a personal defense of the party, which is cut off when a subsequent holder in due course takes the instrument without notice of the defense. Thus where an instrument is paid without surrender such a subsequent purchase cuts off the defense. This section applies only to discharges arising under the provisions of this Article, and it has no application to any discharge arising apart from it, such as a discharge in bankruptcy.

Under Section 3–304(1) (b) on notice to purchaser it is possible for a holder to take the instrument in due course even though he has notice that one or more parties have been discharged, so long as any party remains undischarged. Thus he may take with notice that an indorser of a note has been released, and still be a holder in due course as to the liability of the maker. In that event, the holder in due course is subject to the defense of the discharge of which he had notice when he took the instrument.

Cross References:

Sections 3–302, 3–304 and 3–601.

Definitional Cross References:

"Holder in due course". Section 3–302.
"Instrument". Section 3–102.
"Notice". Section 1–201.
"Party". Section 1–201.

Section 3–603. Payment or Satisfaction.

(1) The liability of any party is discharged to the extent of his payment or satisfaction to the holder even though it is made with knowledge of a claim of another person to the instrument unless prior to such payment or satisfaction the person making the claim either supplies indemnity deemed adequate by the party seeking the discharge or enjoins payment or satisfaction by order of a court

of competent jurisdiction in an action in which the adverse claimant and the holder are parties. This subsection does not, however, result in the discharge of the liability

(a) of a party who in bad faith pays or satisfies a holder who acquired the instrument by theft or who (unless having the rights of a holder in due course) holds through one who so acquired it; or

(b) of a party (other than an intermediary bank or a payor bank which is not a depository bank) who pays or satisfies the holder of an instrument which has been restrictively indorsed in a manner not consistent with the terms of such restrictive indorsement.

(2) Payment or satisfaction may be made with the consent of the holder by any person including a stranger to the instrument. Surrender of the instrument to such a person gives him the rights of a transferee (Section 3–201).

New York Annotations

(1) Modifies and presents a new scheme to replace N.I.L., §§ 90, 148, and 200, which provide that "payment in due course" discharges the payor lacking notice of a defect in the holder's title. This subsection would permit discharge of a party paying even with knowledge of an outstanding claim, unless the person claiming to be the "true owner" takes the action specified. Compare Banking Law, §§ 134(5) (6) (7), 171(5) (6) (7), and 239(5) (6) ("adverse claim" statutes as to banks or trust companies, private bankers, and savings banks).

(2) Modifies N.I.L., § 202, by omitting the provision that remits the payor to his former rights. N.I.L., §§ 90, 148, and 200 are also related to the rule presented by this subsection. N.I.L., §§ 300–306, dealing with the obsolete practice of payment for honor, are omitted.

Historical Note: The exceptions to subsection (1) as to cases involving stolen instruments and restrictively indorsed instruments were added at the suggestion of the Law Revision Commission to achieve conformity with Sections 3–306(d) and 3–206. (1956 Recommendations, pp. 127–128; Excerpts, pp. 414–416.)

Official Uniform Comment

Prior Uniform Statutory Provision: Sections 51, 88, 119, 121 and 171–177, Uniform Negotiable Instruments Law.

Changes: Parts of original sections combined and reworded, law changed.

Purposes of Changes: This Sections changes the law as follows:

1. It eliminates the: "payment in due course" found in the original Sections 51, 88 and 119. "Payment in due course" discharged all parties where it was made by one who has no right of recourse on the instrument; but this is true of any other discharge of such a party, and is now covered in Section 3–601(3) on discharge of parties. Such payment was effective as a discharge against a subsequent purchaser; but since it is made at or after maturity of the instrument a purchaser with notice of that fact cannot be a holder in due course, and one who takes without notice of the payment and maturity should be protected against failure to take up the instrument. The matter is now covered by Section 3–602.

2. The original Sections 171–177 provide for payment of a draft "for honor" after protest. The practice originated at a time when communications were slow and

difficult, and in overseas transactions there might be a delay of several months before the drawer could act upon any dishonor. It provided a method by which a third party might intervene to protect the credit of the drawer and at the same time his own rights. Cable, telegraph and telephone have made the practice obsolete for nearly a century, and it is today almost entirely unknown. It has been replaced by the cable transfer, the letter of credit and numerous other devices by which a substitute arrangement is promptly made. "Payment for honor" is therefore eliminated; and subsection (2) now provides that any person may pay with the consent of the holder.

3. Payment to the holder discharges the party who makes it from his own liability on the instrument, and a part payment discharges him pro tanto. The same is true of any other satisfaction. Subsection (1) changes the law by eliminating the requirement of the original Section 88 that the payment be made in good faith and without notice that the title of the holder is defective. It adopts as a general principle the position that a payor is not required to obey an order to stop payment received from an indorser. However, this general principle is qualified by the provisions of subsection (1)(a) and (b) respecting persons who acquire an instrument by theft, or through a restrictive indorsement (Section 3–205). These provisions are thus consistent with Section 3–306 covering the rights of one not a holder in due course.

When the party to pay is notified of an adverse claim to the instrument he has normally no means of knowing whether the assertion is true. The "unless" clause of subsection (1) follows statutes which may have been passed in many states on adverse claims to bank deposits. The paying party may pay despite notification of the adverse claim unless the adverse claimant supplies indemnity deemed adequate by the paying party or procures the issuance of process restraining payment in an action in which the adverse claimant and the holder of the instrument are both parties. If the paying party chooses to refuse payment and stand suit, even though not indemnified or enjoined, he is free to do so, although, under Section 3–306(d) on the rights of one not a holder in due course, except where theft or taking through a restrictive indorsement is alleged the payor must rely on the third party claimant to litigate the issue and may not himself defend on such a ground. His contract is to pay the holder of the instrument, and he performs it by making such payment. Except in cases of theft or restrictive indorsement there is no good reason to put him to inconvenience because of a dispute between two other parties unless he is indemnified or served with appropriate process.

4. With the elimination of "payment for honor", subsection (2) provides that with the consent of the holder payment may be made by anyone, including a stranger. The subsection omits the provision of the original Section 121 by which the payor is "remitted to his former rights". It rejects such decisions as Quimby v. Varnum, 190 Mass. 211, 76 N.E. 671 (1906), holding that an irregular indorser who makes payment cannot recover on the same instrument. The same result is reached under Section 3–415(5) on accommodation parties. Upon payment and surrender of the paper the payor succeeds to the rights of the holder, subject to the limitation found in Section 3–201 on transfer that one who has himself been a party to any fraud or illegality affecting the instrument or who as a prior holder had notice of a defense or claim against it cannot improve his position by taking from a later holder in due course.

5. Payment discharges the liability of the person making it. It discharges the liability of other parties only as

a. The discharge of the payor discharges others who have a right of recourse against him under Section 3–606; or

b. Reacquisition of the instrument discharges intervening parties under Section 3–208 on reacquisition; or

c. The discharge of one who has himself no right of recourse on the instrument discharges all parties under Section 3–601 on discharge of parties.

Cross References:

Sections 3–604 and 3–606.
Point 1: Section 3–601(3).
Point 3: Sections 3–205 and 3–306(d).
Point 4: Sections 3–201 and 3–415(5).
Point 5: Sections 3–606, 3–208, 3–601.

Definitional Cross References:

"Action". Section 1–201.
"Holder". Section 1–201.
"Instrument". Section 3–102.
"Order". Section 3–102.
"Party". Section 1–201.
"Person". Section 1–201.
"Rights". Section 1–201.

Section 3–604. Tender of Payment.

(1) Any party making tender of full payment to a holder when or after it is due is discharged to the extent of all subsequent liability for interest, costs and attorney's fees.

(2) The holder's refusal of such tender wholly discharges any party who has a right of recourse against the party making the tender.

(3) Where the maker or acceptor of an instrument payable otherwise than on demand is able and ready to pay at every place of payment specified in the instrument when it is due, it is equivalent to tender.

New York Annotations

(1) This is a new statutory provision, but it appears to be in *accord* with generally accepted rules relating to tender. See National Bank of Rochester v. Erion-Haines Realty Co., 213 App. Div. 54, 209 N.Y.S. 522 (1925).

(2) *Modifies* N.I.L., § 201(4). Where the holder refuses tender, the N.I.L. discharges all subsequent parties secondarily liable, whereas the Code discharges all parties, prior or subsequent, having recourse against the tendering party.

(3) *Accord:* N.I.L., § 130, but the rule is now expanded to include instruments payable at more than one place.

Official Uniform Comment

Prior Uniform Statutory Provisions: Sections 70 and 120, Uniform Negotiable Instruments Law.

Changes: Parts of original sections combined and reworded; new provisions.

Purposes of Changes and New Matter:

1. Subsection (1) is new. It states the generally accepted rule as to the effect of tender.

2. Subsection (2) rewords the original subsection 120(4). The party discharged is one who has a right of recourse against the party making tender, whether the latter be a prior party or a subsequent one who has been accommodated.

3. Subsection (3) rewords the final clause of the first sentence of the original Section 70. Where the instrument is payable at any one of two or more specified places, the maker or acceptor must be able and ready to pay at each of them. The language in original Section 70 was taken to mean that makers and acceptors of notes and drafts payable at a bank were not discharged by failure of a holder to make due presentment of such paper at the designated bank. This Article reverses that rule. See Sections 3–501 on necessity of presentment, 3–504 on how presentment is made, and 3–502 on effect of delay in presentment.

Cross References:

Section 3–601.
Point 3: Sections 3–501, 3–502 and 3–504.

Definitional Cross References:

"Holder". Section 1–201.
"Instrument". Section 3–102.
"On demand". Section 3–108.
"Party". Section 1–201.
"Right". Section 1–201.

Section 3–605. Cancellation and Renunciation.

(1) The holder of an instrument may even without consideration discharge any party

(a) in any manner apparent on the face of the instrument or the indorsement, as by intentionally cancelling the instrument or the party's signature by destruction or mutilation, or by striking out the party's signature; or

(b) by renouncing his rights by a writing signed and delivered or by surrender of the instrument to the party to be discharged.

(2) Neither cancellation nor renunciation without surrender of the instrument affects the title thereto.

New York Annotations

(1)(a) Generally in *accord* with N.I.L., §§ 78, 200(3), and 201(2).

(b) Generally in *accord* with N.I.L., § 203. The Code would require a signed writing as compared with the N.I.L.'s mere writing.

(2) This is new and no cases have been found directly in point. See, however, general discussions in Trietel v. Gibson, 131 Misc. 377, 379, 226 N.Y.S. 603, 605 (1928).

Historical Notes: Subsection (1)(a) was broadened by the addition of its present introductory phrase, and subsection (1)(b) was amended by requiring the delivery of the signed writing, at the suggestion of the Law Revision Commission. (1956 Recommendations, p. 128; Excerpts, p. 416.)

Official Uniform Comment

Prior Uniform Statutory Provision: Sections 48, 119(3), 120(2), 122 and 123, Uniform Negotiable Instruments Law.

Changes: Combined and reworded.

Purposes of Changes:

1. The original Act does not state how cancellation is to be effected, except as to striking indorsements under the original Section 48. It must be done in such a manner as to be apparent on the face of the instrument, and the methods stated, which are supported by the decisions, are exclusive.

2. Subsection (1)(b) restates the original Section 122. The provision as to "discharge of the instrument" is now covered by discharge. Section 3–601(3); that as to subsequent holders in due course by Section 3–602 on effect of discharge against a holder in due course.

3. Subsection (2) is new. It is intended to make it clear that the striking of an indorsement, or any other cancellation or renunciation, does not affect the title.

Cross References:

Point 2: Sections 3–601 and 3–602.

Definitional Cross References:

"Holder". Section 1–201.
"Instrument". Section 3–102.
"Party". Section 1–201.
"Rights". Section 1–201.
"Signature". Section 3–401.
"Signed". Section 1–201.
"Writing". Section 1–201.

Section 3–606. Impairment of Recourse or of Collateral.

(1) The holder discharges any party to the instrument to the extent that without such party's consent the holder

(a) without express reservation of rights releases or agrees not to sue any person against whom the party has to the knowledge of the holder a right of recourse or agrees to suspend the right to enforce against such person the instrument or collateral or otherwise discharges such person, except that failure or delay in effecting any required presentment, protest or notice of dishonor with respect to any such person does not discharge any party as to whom presentment, protest or notice of dishonor is effective or unnecessary; or

(b) unjustifiably impairs any collateral for the instrument given by or on behalf of the party or any person against whom he has a right of recourse.

(2) By express reservation of rights against a party with a right of recourse the holder preserves

(a) all his rights against such party as of the time when the instrument was originally due; and

(b) the right of the party to pay the instrument as of that time; and

(c) all rights of such party to recourse against others.

New York Annotations

(1)(a) Generally in *accord* with, but extends the rule of, N.I.L., § 201(3) (5) and (6). The Code would extend the discharge to any party to the instrument, including a primary party who signed as surety, whereas the N.I.L. provision is limited to persons "secondarily liable on the instrument." See National Citizens Bank v. Toplitz, 81 App. Div. 593, 81 N.Y.S. 422, aff'd on other grounds and expressly reserving this point, 178 N.Y. 464, 71 N.E.1 (1904). Neither N.I.L., § 201 (5), nor § 201(6), mentions consent or assent by a secondary party to the holder's release of the principal debtor or the extension of the principal debtor's time to pay as preventing the principal debtor's discharge. Compare U.N.I.L., § 120(6). The Code's phrase "without such party's consent" may change the present law in this respect.

(b) This is new but *accords* with general suretyship principles. See Exchange Bank v. Ludlum, 246 App. Div. 892, 285 N.Y.S. 862 (1936) (release of collateral); Cohen v. Rossmoore, 225 App. Div. 300, 233 N.Y.S. 196 (1929) (release of collateral).

(2) *Accords* generally with N.I.L., § 201(5) and (6), and Debtor and Creditor Law, § 234, but as distinct from N.I.L., § 201, applicable in terms not only to secondary parties but to "any party to the instrument."

Historical Note: The following suggestions of the Law Revision Commission were incorporated in the 1957 draft of this section: (1) extension of the suretyship defense of release of principal to the case of a principal bound otherwise than on the negotiable instrument in question; (2) provision that "without express reservation of rights" applies to one who "otherwise discharges"; (3) extension of the "except" clause in subsection (1)(a) to apply to presentment and protest as well as notice of dishonor; and (4) elimination of the provision in subsection (1)(c) of the previous draft as to notification of parties against whom rights are reserved. (1956 Recommendations, p. 129; Excerpts, p. 416.)

Official Uniform Comment

Prior Uniform Statutory Provision: Section 120, Uniform Negotiable Instruments Law.

Changes: Reworded; new provisions.

Purposes of Changes and New Matter: To make it clear that:

1. The words "any party to the instrument" remove an uncertainty arising under the original section. The suretyship defenses here provided are not limited to parties who are "secondary liable," but are available to any party who is in the position of surety, having a right of recourse either on the instrument or dehors it, including an accommodation maker or acceptor known to the holder to be so.

2. Consent may be given in advance, and is commonly incorporated in the instrument; or it may be given afterward. It requires no consideration, and operates as a waiver of the consenting party's right to claim his own discharge.

3. The words "to the knowledge of the holder" exclude the latent surety, as for example the accommodation maker where there is nothing on the instrument to show that he has signed for accommodation and the holder is ignorant of that fact. In such a case the holder is entitled to proceed according to what is shown by the face of the paper or what he otherwise knows, and does not discharge the surety when he acts in ignorance of the relation.

4. This section retains the right of the holder to release one party, or to postpone his time payment, while expressly reserving rights against others. Subsection (2), which is new, states the generally accepted rule as to the effect of such an express reservation of rights. [Comment 4 was amended in 1966.]

5. Paragraph (b) of subsection (1) is new. The suretyship defense stated has been generally recognized as available to indorsers or accommodation parties. As to when a holder's actions in dealing with collateral may be "unjustifiable", the section on rights and duties with respect to collateral in the possession of a secured party (Section 9–207) should be consulted.

Cross References:

Point 5: Section 9–207.

Definitional Cross References:

"Agreement". Section 1–201.
"Holder". Section 1–201.
"Instrument". Section 3–102.
"Notice of dishonor". Section 3–508.
"Party". Section 1–201.
"Person". Section 1–201.
"Rights". Section 1–201.

PART 7

ADVICE OF INTERNATIONAL SIGHT DRAFT

Section 3–701. Letter of Advice of International Sight Draft.

(1) A "letter of advice" is a drawer's communication to the drawee that a described draft has been drawn.

(2) Unless otherwise agreed when a bank receives from another bank a letter of advice of an international sight draft the drawee bank may immediately debit the drawer's account and stop the running of interest pro tanto. Such a debit and any resulting credit to any account covering outstanding drafts leaves in the drawer full power to stop payment or otherwise dispose of the amount and creates no trust or interest in favor of the holder.

(3) Unless otherwise agreed and except where a draft is drawn under a credit issued by the drawee, the drawee of an international sight draft owes the drawer no duty to pay an unadvised draft but if it does so and the draft is genuine, may appropriately debit the drawer's account.

Amended by Laws 1963, ch. 1003, eff. Sept. 27, 1964.

New York Annotations

This is new and no New York cases were found on this point. This section appears to state usual banking practice. See Equitable Trust Co. of New York v. First National Bank of Trinidad, Colo., 275 U.S. 359, 48 S. Ct. 167 (1927), reversing In re Gubelman, 13 F.2d 732 (2d Cir. 1926).

Historical Note: The previous Part 7, Collection of Documentary Drafts, was transferred to Article 4 at the suggestion of the Law Revision Commission. Former Section 3–806 was transferred to become the new Section 3–701 to avoid the inconvenience of renumbering the rest of Article 3. (1956 Recommendations, p. 130; Excerpts p. 417.)

Official Uniform Comment

Prior Uniform Statutory Provision: None.

Purposes: To recognize and clarify, in law, certain established practices of international banking.

1. Checks drawn by one international bank on the account it carries (in a currency foreign to itself) in another bank are still handled under practices which reflect older conditions, but which have a real, continuing reason in the typical, European rule that a bank paying a check in good faith and in ordinary course can charge its depositor's account notwithstanding forgery of a necessary indorsement. To decrease the risk that forgery will prove successful, the practice is to send a letter of advice that a draft has been drawn and will be forthcoming. Subsection 3 recognizes that a drawer who sends no such letter forfeits any rights for improper dishonor, while still permitting the drawee to protect his delinquent drawer's credit.

2. Subsection (2) clears up for American courts, the meaning of another international practice: that of charging the drawer's account on receipt of the letter of advice. This practice involves no conception of trust or the like and the rule of Section 3–409(1)(Draft not an assignment) still applies. The debit has to do with the payment of interest only. The section recognizes the fact.

Cross References:

Point 2: Section 3–409(1).

Definitional Cross References:

"Account". Section 4–104.
"Bank". Section 1–201.
"Credit". Section 5–103.
"Draft". Section 3–104.
"Genuine". Section 1–201.
"Holder". Section 1–201.

PART 8

MISCELLANEOUS

Section 3–801. Drafts in a Set.

(1) Where a draft is drawn in a set of parts, each of which is numbered and expressed to be an order only if no other part has been honored, the whole of the parts constitutes one draft but a taker of any part may become a holder in due course of the draft.

(2) Any person who negotiates, indorses or accepts a single part of a draft in a set thereby becomes liable to any holder in due course of that part as if it were the whole set, but as between different holders in due course to whom different parts have been negotiated the holder whose title first accrues has all rights to the draft and its proceeds.

(3) As against the drawee the first presented part of a draft drawn in a set is the part entitled to payment, or if a time draft to acceptance and payment. Acceptance of any subsequently presented part renders the drawee liable thereon under subsection (2). With respect both to a holder and to the drawer payment of a subsequently presented part of a draft payable at sight has the same effect as payment of a check notwithstanding an effective stop order (Section 4–407).

(4) Except as otherwise provided in this section, where any part of a draft in a set is discharged by payment or otherwise the whole draft is discharged.

New York Annotations

(1) First portion *accords* with N.I.L., § 310. The requirement that each of the parts must "be expressed to be on order only if no other part has been honored" is new but *accords* with commercial practice. See the exhibits in Kerr S.S. Co. v. Chartered Bank of India, Australia and China, 292 N.Y. 253, 54 N.E.2d 813 (1944)("pay this First of Exchange (Second being unpaid) to the order of."). The last phrase of the subsection is in *accord* with New York decisional law. Caras v. Thalmann, 138 App.Div. 297, 302, 123 N.Y.S. 97, 100 (1910); Durkin v. Cranston, 7 Johns.R. 442 (1811).

(2) *Accords* generally with N.I.L., §§ 311, 312, and 313.

(3) *Accords* generally with N.I.L., § 311 (last sentence), but the Code omits the "due course" requirement for payment of acceptance. See also N.I.L., § 313 (last sentence). The last sentence of the Code provision is new. For the effect of payment of a check notwithstanding an effective stop-order, see Section 4–407.

(4) *Accord:* N.I.L., § 315. See Casper v. Kuhne, 159 App. Div. 389, 144 N.Y.S. 502 (1913).

Historical Note: A cross reference to Section 4–407 was inserted in subsection (3) for clarification at the suggestion of the Law Revision Commission. (1956 Recommendations, p. 131; Excerpts, p. 418.)

Official Uniform Comment

Prior Uniform Statutory Provision: Sections 178–183, Uniform Negotiable Instruments Law.

Changes: Combined and reworded.

Purposes of Changes:

The revised language makes no important change in the substance, and is intended only as a clarification and supplementation of the original sections:

1. Draft in a set customarily contain such language as "Pay–this first of exchange(second unpaid)", with equivalent language in the second part. Today a part also commonly bears conspicuous indication of its number. At least the first factor is necessary to notify holder of his rights, and is therefore necessary in order to make this section apply. Subsection (1) so provides, thus stating in the statute a matter left previously to a commercial practice long uniform but expensive to establish in court.

2. The final sentence of subsection (3) is new. Payment of the part of the draft subsequently presented is improper and the drawee may not charge it to the account of the drawer, but someone has probably been unjustly enriched on the total transaction, at the expense of the drawee. So the drawee is like a bank which has paid a check over an effective stop payment order, and is subrogated as provided in that situation. Section 4–407.

3. A statement in a draft in a set of parts to the effect that the order is effective only if no other part has been honored does not render the draft nonnegotiable as conditional. See Section 3–112(1)(g).

Cross References:

Point 2: Section 4–407.
Point 3: Section 3–112.

Definitional Cross References:

"Acceptance". Section 3–410.

"Check". Section 3–104.
"Draft". Section 3–104.
"Holder". Section 1–201.
"Holder in due course". Section 3–302.
"Honor". Section 1–201.
"Person". Section 1–201.
"Rights". Section 1–201.

Section 3–802. Effect of Instrument on Obligation for Which It Is Given.

(1) Unless otherwise agreed where an instrument is taken for an underlying obligation

(a) the obligation is pro tanto discharged if a bank is drawer, maker or acceptor of the instrument and there is no recourse on the instrument against the underlying obligor; and

(b) in any other case the obligation is suspended pro tanto until the instrument is due or if it is payable on demand until its presentment. If the instrument is dishonored action may be maintained on either the instrument or the obligation; discharge of the underlying obligor on the instrument also discharges him on the obligation.

(2) The taking in good faith of a check which is not post-dated does not of itself so extend the time on the original obligation as to discharge a surety.

New York Annotations

(1)(a) This would change the present law that where a debtor executes and delivers an instrument for the same amount as either a contemporaneous or precedent debt, the presumption is that the instrument is not given in payment. Jagger Iron Co. v. Walker, 76 N.Y. 521 (1879) (contemporaneous debt); Cohen v. Rossmoore, 225 App. Div. 300, 233 N.Y.S. 196 (1929) (precedent debt). The same result follows where the debtor gives his creditor the instrument of a third party for a precedent debt. Dibble v. Richardson, 171 N.Y. 131, 138, 63 N.E. 829, 831 (1902). However, where the instrument of a third party is given concurrently with the creation of the debt, payment is presumed. Kirkham v. Bank of America, 26 App. Div. 110, 49 N.Y.S. 767, aff'd 165 N.Y. 132, 58 N.E. 753 (1900). The Code would now, under this subsection, limit the presumption of absolute payment to cases where the third party is a bank as drawer, maker, or acceptor of the instrument and there is no recourse on the instrument against the underlying obligor, but the presumption would be applicable regardless of whether the debt was contemporaneous or precedent.

(b) In *accord* with first sentence: Jagger Iron Co. v. Walker, *supra:* Hoar v. Union Mutual Life Ins. Co., 118 App. Div. 416, 420, 103 N.Y.S, 1059, 1061 (1907), but as noted above a change would result where the instrument of a third party is given simultaneously with the creation of the debt. Kirkham v. Bank of America, *supra.* In *accord* that on dishonor action may be maintained on either the instrument or the obligation, see Jagger Iron Co. v. Walker, *supra.* Generally in *accord* with last clause, see Sedwitz v. Arnold, 164 Misc. 892, 299 N.Y.S. 848 (1937).

(2) *Accord:* Fifth National Bank v. Woolsey, 31 App. Div. 61, 52 N.Y.S. 827 (1898) (demand note); Albany City F. Ins. Co. v. Devendorf, 43 Barb, 444 (1864) (inference that taking post-dated check payable at future time will discharge a surety).

Historical Note: At the suggestion of the Law Revision Commission, subsection (2) was amended as follows: (1) reference to Section 3–503(2) was eliminated, (2) the limitation to uncertified checks was removed, and (3) an exception with respect to postdated checks was inserted. Also subsection (3) of the previous draft, providing that a check reciting full satisfaction of an obligation discharges the obligation, was eliminated. (1956 Recommendations, pp. 131–132; Excerpts, p. 418.)

Official Uniform Comment

Prior Uniform Statutory Provision: None.

Purposes:

1. The section is new. It is intended to settle conflicts as to the effect of an instrument as payment of the obligation for which it is given.

2. Where a holder procures certification of a check the drawer is discharged under Section 3–411 on check certification. Thereafter the original obligation is regarded as paid, and the holder must look to the certifying bank. The circumstances may indicate a similar intent in other transactions, and the question may be one of fact for the jury. Subsection (1)(a) states a rule discharging the obligation pro tanto when the instrument taken carries the obligation of a bank as drawer, maker or acceptor and there is no recourse on the instrument against the underlying obligor.

3. It is commonly said that a check or other negotiable instrument is "conditional payment." By this it is normally meant that taking the instrument is a surrender of the right to sue on the obligation until the instrument is due, but if the instrument is not paid on due presentment the right to sue on the obligation is "revived." Subsection (1)(b) states this result in terms of suspension of the obligation, which is intended to include suspension of the running of the statute of limitations. On dishonor of the instrument the holder is given his option to sue either on the instrument or on the underlying obligation. If, however, the original obligor has been discharged on the instrument (see Section 3–601) he is also discharged on the original obligation.

4. Subsection (2) is intended to remove any implication that a check given in payment of an obligation discharges a surety. The check is taken as a means of immediate payment; the thirty day period for presentment specified in Section 3–503 does not affect the surety's liability.

Cross References:

Point 2: Sections 1–201, 3–411 and 3–601.
Point 4: Section 3–503.

Definitional Cross References:

"Action". Section 1–201.
"Bank". Section 1–201.
"Check". Section 3–104.
"Dishonor". Section 3–507.
"Good faith". Section 1–201.
"Instrument". Section 3–102.
"On demand". Section 3–108.
"Presentment". Section 3–504.

Section 3–803. Notice to Third Party.

Where a defendant is sued for breach of an obligation for which a third person is answerable over under this Article he may give the third person written notice of the litigation, and the person notified may then give similar notice to any other person who is answerable over to him under this Article. If the notice states that the person notified may come in and defend and that if the person notified does not do so he will in any action against him by the person giving the notice be bound by any determination of fact common to the two litigations, then unless after seasonable receipt of the notice the person notified does come in and defend he is so bound.

New York Annotations

This is new statutory material. Compare Section 2–607(5). "Vouching-in" is a recognized common-law device, but is available only against persons who will be directly responsible to the person first sued, if judgment goes against the person first sued. Hartford Accident & Indemnity Co. v. First Nat. Bank & Trust Co., 281 N.Y. 162, 22 N.E.2d 324 (1939). See also, Civil Practice Act, §§ 193-a [CPLR § 1007] (third-party practice) and 193-b [CPLR §§ 1012-1014] (intervention).

Historical Note: In response to criticism of the Law Revision Commission this section was entirely rewritten to conform to the rule of Hartford Accident & Indemnity Co. v. First Nat. Bank & Trust Co., supra. As revised, the section is limited to cases where the person notified is "answerable over" to the person giving the notice. (1956 Recommendations, pp 132-133; Excerpts, pp. 418-419.)

Official Uniform Comment

Prior Uniform Statutory Provision: None.

Purposes:

The section is new. It is intended to supplement, not to displace existing procedures for interpleader or joinder of parties.

The section conforms to the analogous provision in Section 2–607. It extends to such liabilities as those arising from forged indorsements even though not "on the instrument," and is intended to make it clear that the notification is not effective until received. In Hartford Accident & Indemnity Co. v. First Nat. Bank & Trust Co., 281 N.Y. 162, 22 N.E.2d 324, 123 A.L.R. 1149 (1939), the common-law doctrine of "vouching in" was held inapplicable where the party notified had no direct liability to the party giving notice. In that case the drawer of a check, sued by the payee whose indorsement had been forged, gave notice to a collecting bank. In a second action the drawee was held liable to the drawer; but in an action by the drawee for judgment over against the collecting bank the determinations of fact in the first action were held not conclusive. This section does not disturb this result; the section is limited to cases where the person notified is "answerable over" to the person giving notice.

Cross References:

Section 2–607.

Definitional Cross References:

"Action". Section 1–201.
"Defendant". Section 1–201.
"Instrument". Section 3–102.
"Notifies". Section 1–201.
"Person". Section 1–201.

"Right". Section 1–201.
"Seasonably". Section 1–204.
"Written". Section 1–201.

Section 3–804. Lost, Destroyed or Stolen Instruments.

The owner of an instrument which is lost, whether by destruction, theft or otherwise, may maintain an action in his own name and recover from any party liable thereon upon due proof of his ownership, the facts which prevent his production of the instrument and its terms. The court shall require security, in an amount fixed by the court not less than twice the amount allegedly unpaid on the instrument, indemnifying the defendant, his heirs, personal representatives, successors and assigns against loss, including costs and expenses, by reason of further claims on the instrument, but this provision does not apply where an action is prosecuted or defended by the state or by a public officer in its behalf.

Amended by Laws 1963, Ch. 1003, eff. Sept. 27, 1964.

N.Y. Commission Comments

The code, as enacted in New York in 1962 and as amended in 1963 by L. 1963, c. 1003, amended Section 3–804, as it appears in the 1958 and 1962 Official Texts, to read (brackets indicate omissions an italics additions):

"The owner of an instrument which is lost, whether by destruction, theft or otherwise, may maintain an action in his own name and recover from any party liable thereon upon due proof of his ownership, the facts which prevent his production of the instrument and its terms. The court [may] *shall* require security, *in an amount fixed by the court not less than twice the amount allegedly unpaid on the instrument,* indemnifying the defendant, *His heirs, personal representatives, successors and assigns* against loss, *including costs and expenses,* by reason of further claims on the instrument, *but this provision does not apply where an action is prosecuted or defended by the state or by a public officer in its behalf.* "

For the reasons stated in the Commission's 1962 and 1963 Reports to make the furnishing of security mandatory rather than discretionary and conform to old Civil Practice Act § 333, reenacted as Article 14-A of the New York Negotiable Instruments Law and repealed by L. 1963, c. 1003.

New York Annotations

Generally in *accord* with, but broader than, former N.I.L. § 272, which provided for proof of lost negotiable paper. New York decisional law provides a similar rule in respect of destroyed instruments, except that no security is required. Des Arts v. Leggett, 16 N.Y. 582 (1858); Scott v. Meeker, 20 Hun 161 (1880).

Official Uniform Comment

Prior Uniform Statutory Provision: None.

Purposes:

This section is new. It is intended to provide a method of recovery on instruments which are lost, destroyed or stolen. The plaintiff who claims to be the owner of such an instrument is not a holder as that term is defined in this Act, since he is not in possession of the paper, and he does not have the holder's prima facie right to recover under the section on the burden of establishing signatures. He must prove his case. He must establish the terms of the instrument and his ownership, and must account for its absence.

If the claimant testifies falsely, or if the instrument subsequently turns up in the hands of a holder in due course, the obligor may be subjected to double liability. The court is therefore authorized to require security indemnifying the obligor against loss by reason of such possibilities. There may be cases in which so much time has elapsed, or there is so little possible doubt as to the destruction of the instrument and its ownership that there is no good reason to require the security. The requirement is therefore not an absolute one, and the matter is left to the discretion of the court.

Cross References:

Sections 1–201 and 3–307.

Definitional Cross References:

"Action". Section 1–201.
"Defendant". Section 1–201.
"Instrument". Section 3–102.
"Party". Section 1–201.
"Term". Section 1–201.

Section 3–805. Instruments Not Payable to Order or to Bearer.

This Article applies to any instrument whose terms do not preclude transfer and which is otherwise negotiable within this Article but which is not payable to order or to bearer, except that there can be no holder in due course of such an instrument.

New York Annotations

This section is new and would bring non-negotiable instruments, insofar as their form permits, within the coverage of Article 3. However, since there cannot be a holder in due course of such an instrument the sections of the article peculiar to such holders do not apply. The present law would be changed where the common-law rule differs from the rules of the Code made applicable to such instruments. There is very little New York decisional law applicable to non-negotiable instruments. The decisional law rule as to an indorser's liability differs from the Code in that the indorser is considered by case law as in the position of a primary party, McMullen v. Rafferty, 89 N.Y. 456 (1882), and is generally not entitled to presentment or notice of dishonor, Seymour & Bouck v. Van Slyck, 8 Wend. 403, 422 (1832). There is no presumption of consideration as to non-negotiable instruments, St. Lawrence County Nat. Bank v. Watkins, 153 App. Div. 551, 138 N.Y.S. 116 (1912); Deyo v. Thompson, 53 App. Div. 9, 65 N.Y.S. 459 (1900), nor does possession create a presumption of title. Barrick v. Austin, 21 Barb. 241 (1855) (dictum). See generally, Willier, "Nonnegotiable Instruments," 11 Syracuse L. Rev. 13–26 (1960).

Official Uniform Comment

Prior Uniform Statutory Provision: None.

Purposes:

This section covers the "non-negotiable instrument." As it has been used by most courts, this term has been a technical one of art. It does not refer to a writing, such as a note containing an express condition, which is not negotiable and is entirely outside of the scope of this Article and to be treated as a simple contract. It refers to a particular type of instrument which meets all requirements as to form of a negotiable instrument except that it is not payable to order or to bearer. The typical example is the check reading merely "Pay John Doe."

Such a check is not a negotiable instrument under this Article. At the same time it is still a check, a mercantile specialty which differs in many respects from a simple contract. Commercial and banking practice treats it as a check, and a long line of decisions before and after the original Act have made it clear that it is subject to the law merchant as distinguished from ordinary contract law. Although the Negotiable Instruments Law has been held by its terms not to apply to such "non-negotiable instruments" it has been recognized as a codification and restatement of the law merchant, and has in fact been applied to them by analogy.

Thus the holder of the check reading "Pay A" establishes his case by production of the instrument and proof of signatures; and the burden of proving want of consideration or any other defense is upon the obligor. Such a check passes by indorsement and delivery without words of assignment, and the indorser undertakes greater liabilities than those of assignor. This section resolves the conflict in the decisions as to the extent of that undertaking by providing in effect that the indorser of such an instrument is not distinguished from any indorser of a negotiable instrument. The indorser is entitled to presentment, notice of dishonor and protest, and the procedure and liabilities in bank collection are the same. The rules as to alteration, the filling of blanks, accommodation parties, the liability of signing agents, discharge, and the like are those applied to negotiable instruments.

In short, the "non-negotiable instrument" is treated as negotiable instrument, so far as its form permits. Since it lacks words of negotiability there can be no holder in due course of such an instrument, and any provision of any section of this Article peculiar to a holder in due course cannot apply to it. With this exception, such instruments are covered by all sections of this Article.

Cross References:

Section 3–104.

Definitional Cross References:

"Bearer". Section 1–201.
"Holder in due course". Section 3–302.
"Instrument". Section 3–102.
"Term". Section 1–201.

ARTICLE 4

BANK DEPOSITS AND COLLECTIONS

PART 1

GENERAL PROVISIONS AND DEFINITIONS

PART 2

COLLECTION OF ITEMS: DEPOSITARY AND COLLECTING BANKS

PART 3

COLLECTION OF ITEMS: PAYOR BANKS

PART 4

RELATIONSHIP BETWEEN PAYOR BANK AND ITS CUSTOMER

PART 5

COLLECTION OF DOCUMENTARY DRAFTS

PART 1

GENERAL PROVISIONS AND DEFINITIONS

Section 4–101. Short Title.

This Article shall be known and may be cited as Uniform Commercial Code—Bank Deposits and Collections

New York Annotations

This is new, Article 4, dealing with bank deposits and collections, will replace Article 19–A of the N.I.L. (Bank Collection Code of the American Bankers Association, except for N.I.L., § 350–b, which is a modification of the ABA Deferred Posting Statute), and certain other provisions of the N.I.L. as they have been applied to this subject matter.

The Article is divided into two segments, one dealing with the bank collection process and the other with the relationship between banks and their customers. Although the Article has been subjected to extensive redrafting and revision, it is essentially a conservative statute, containing few major innovations. The attempt has been to codify with precision the well defined patterns of operation which are now existent in fact but only partially treated by present legislation. An attempt has been made to change or add to existing rules where greater certainty or a more workable result would be obtained. At the same time, it has been expressly recognized that much of this area is and will continue to be regulated by Federal Reserve rules and operating letters and by clearing house rules and banking usage (Section 4–103).

An illustrative of the more significant provisions relating to the collection process, the following may be noted: The extension of the presumption of agency without regard to the form of the indorsement (Section 4–201); the simplification of the bank to bank "indorsement" necessary for a "transfer" to a mere number (Section 4–206); the liberalization of the rule as to the proper media of remittance (Section 4–211(1)(b)); the provision for a clearcut test for when payment becomes final (Sec.4–213(1)) and for determining priority in stop payment and other situations (Section 4–303); the extension of authority to the bank to supply missing indorsements (Section 4–205(1)); the authority given to a collecting bank to grant a one-day extension to a payor bank for the purpose of securing payment of an item which would otherwise be dishonored (Section 4–108(1)).

Some notable provisions concerning the responsibility of a bank to its customer include: The limitation placed upon a bank to disclaim its responsibilities (Section 4–103(1)); the change in the risk of loss as to incomplete undelivered instruments (Section 4–402(2)(b)); see also Sections 3–115 and 3–407); the provision for definite rules and the shifting of the burden as to proving the fact of loss in stop payment cases (Section 4–403); the provision for a ten-day period after death during which a bank, even with knowledge, may pay or certify checks (Section 4–405 (2)); the extension of the time allowed a depositor to discover forged indorsements and the imposition of a duty of care and promptness in examining a statement and returned vouchers (Section 4–406); the provision for a right of subrogation in the bank on improper payment (over a stop order or otherwise) (Section 4–407).

A textual treatment of Article 4 may be found in Clark, Bailey and Young, Bank Deposits and Collections (under the UCC) (1959). For a discussion of the background and of the drafting of the Article, see Malcolm, "Article 4–A Battle with Complexity", 1952 Wis. L. Rev. 265.

Historical Note: Of the thirty-six sections found in the 1957 Draft of Article 4, including Sections 4—501 through 4—504 previously found in Part 7 of Article 3, fifteen were carried forward from the 1952 draft and were approved by the Law Revision Commission as they were set forth. Criticisms and suggestions were made with references to the remaining twenty-one sections, resulting in fifteen sections being revised to adopt the Law Revision Commission's suggestions or meet their criticisms and two other sections being revised to meet the Commission's criticisms at least in part. In the case of only four sections were the suggestions or criticisms not met.

Official Uniform Comment

The tremendous number of checks handled by banks and the countrywide nature of the bank collection process require uniformity in the law of bank collections. Individual Federal Reserve banks process as many as 1,000,000 items a day; large metropolitan banks average 300,000 a day; banks with less than $5,000,000 on deposit handle from 1,000 to 2,000 daily. There is needed a uniform statement of the principal rules of the bank collection process with ample provision for flexibility to meet the needs of the large volume handled and the changing needs and conditions that are bound to come with the years.

The American Bankers Association Bank Collection Code, enacted in eighteen states, has stated many of the bank collection rules that have developed, and more recently Deferred Posting statutes have developed and varied further rules. With items flowing in great volume not only in and around metropolitan and smaller centers but also continuously across state lines and back and forth across the entire country, a proper situation exists for uniform rules that will state in modern concepts at least some of the rights of the parties and in addition aid this flow and not interfere with its progress.

This Article adopts many of the rules of the American Bankers Association Code that are still in current operation, the principles and rules of the Deferred Posting and other statutes, codifies some rules established by court decisions and in addition states certain patterns and procedures that exist even though not heretofore covered by statute.

Section 4–102. Applicability.

(1) To the extent that items within this Article are also within the scope of Article 3 and 8, they are subject to the provisions of those Articles. In the event of conflict the provisions of this Article govern those of Article 3 but the provisions of Article 8 govern those of this Article.

(2) The liability of a bank for action or non-action with respect to any item handled by it for purposes of presentment, payment or collection is governed by the law of the place where the bank is located. In the case of action or non-action by or at a branch or separate office of a bank, its liability is governed by the law of the place where the branch or separate office is located.

New York Annotations

(1) This subsection merely declares the supremacy of Article 4 as against Article 3, and the supremacy of Article 8 as against Article 4.

(2) Although this subsection appears to state the generally accepted common-law conflict of law rule as followed in Old Company's Lehigh v. Meeker, 71 F.2d 280

(2d Cir. 1934) (applying the New York law of payment where a check deposited in Pennsylvania was payable in New York), it is probably contrary to Weissmann v. Banque de Bruxelles, 254 N.Y. 488, 173 N.E. 835 (1930), and Saint Nicholas Bank v. The State National Bank, 128 N.Y. 26, 27 N.E. 849 (1891).

Historical Note: In response to suggestions made by the Law Revision Commission, Subsection (1) was amended to provide for instances of conflict between Article 4 and Articles 8 and 3, and subsection (2) was amended to extend its application to all phases of the bank collection process. (1956 Recommendations, p. 134; Excerpts, pp. 419–420.)

Official Uniform Comment

Prior Uniform Statutory Provision: None.

Purposes:

1. The rules governing negotiable instruments, their transfer, and the contracts of the parties thereto apply to the items collected through banking channels wherever no specific provision is found in this Article. In the case of conflict, this Article governs. See Section 3–103(2).

Bonds and like instruments constituting investment securities under Article 8 may also be handled by banks for collection purposes. Various sections of Article 8 prescribe rules of transfer some of which (see Sections 8–304 and 8–306) may conflict with provisions of this Article (Sections 4–205 and 4–207). In the case of conflict Article 8 governs.

Section 4–208 deals specifically with overlapping problems and possible conflicts between this Article and Article 9. However, similar reconciling provisions are not necessary in the case of Article 5 and 7. Sections 4–301 and 4–302 are consistent with Section 5–112. In the case of Article 7 documents of title frequently accompany items but they are not themselves items. See Section 4–104(g).

2. Subsection (2) is designed to state a workable rule for the solution of otherwise vexatious problems of the conflicts of laws:

a. The routine and mechanical nature of bank collections makes it imperative that one law govern the activities of a bank. The requirement found in some cases that to hold an indorser notice must be given in accordance with the law of the place of indorsement, since that method of notice became an implied term of the indorser's contract, is more theoretical than practical.

b. Adoption of what is in essence a tort theory of the conflict of laws is consistent with the general theory of this Article that the basic duty of a collecting bank is one of good faith and the exercise of ordinary care. Justification lies in the fact that, in using an ambulatory instrument, the drawer, payee, and indorsers must know that action will be taken with respect to it in other jurisdictions. This is especially pertinent with respect to the law of the place of payment.

c. The phrase "action or non-action with respect to any item handled by it for purposes of presentment, payment or collection" is intended to make the conflicts rule of subsection (2) apply from the inception of the collection process of an item through all phrases of deposit, forwarding, presentment, payment and remittance or credit of proceeds. Specifically the subsection applies to the initial act of a depositary bank in receiving an item and to the incidents of such receipt. The conflict rule of Weissman v. Banque de Bruxelles, 254 N.Y. 488, 173 N.E. 835 (1930), is rejected. The subsection applies to questions of possible vicarious liability of a bank for action or non-action of sub-agents (see Section 4–202(3)) and tests these questions by the law of the state of the location of the bank which uses the sub-agent. The conflicts rule of St. Nicholas Bank of New York v. State Nat. Bank, 128 N.Y. 26, 27 N.E.849,

13 L.R.A. 241 (1891), is rejected. The subsection applies to action or non-action of a payor bank in connection with handling an item (see Sections 4–213(1), 4–301, 4–302, 4–303) as well as action or non-action of a collecting bank (Sections 4–201 through 4–214); to action or non-action of a bank which suspends payment or is affected by another bank suspending payment (Section 4–214); to action or non-action of a bank with respect to an item under the rules of Part 4 of Article 4.

d. Where subsection (2) makes this Article applicable, Section 4–103(1) leaves open the possibility of an agreement with respect to applicable law. Such freedom of agreement follows the general policy of Section 1–105.

Cross References:

Sections 1–105; 3–103(2) and Article 3; all sections of Article 4; 5–112; Article 7; 8–304 and 8–306; Article 9.

Definitional Cross References:

"Bank". Sections 1–201.
"Branch". Section 1–201.
"Item". Section 4–104.

Section 4–103. Variation by Agreement; Measure of Damages; Certain Action Constituting Ordinary Care.

(1) The effect of the provisions of this Article may be varied by agreement except that no agreement can disclaim a bank's responsibility for its own lack of good faith or failure to exercise ordinary care or can limit the measure of damages for such lack or failure; but the parties may by agreement determine the standards by which such responsibility is to be measured if such standards are not manifestly unreasonable.

(2) Federal Reserve regulations and operating letters, clearing house rules, and the like, have the effect of agreements under subsection (1), whether or not specifically assented by all parties interested in items handled.

(3) Action or non-action approved by this Article or pursuant to Federal Reserve regulations or operating letters constitutes the exercise of ordinary care and, in the absence of special instructions, action or non-action consistent with clearing house rules and the like or with a general banking usage not disapproved by this Article, prima facie constitutes the exercise of ordinary care.

(4) The specification or approval of certain procedures by this Article does not constitute disapproval of other procedures which may be reasonable under the circumstances.

(5) The measure of damages for failure to exercise ordinary care in handling an item is the amount of the item reduced by an amount which could not have been realized by the use of ordinary care, and where there is bad faith it includes other damages, if any, suffered by the party as a proximate consequence.

New York Annotations

(1) Generally in *accord* with present law in permitting variation by agreement, N.I.L. §§ 350–a, 350–b(4), but *contra* to the case law rule permitting banks to limit

their liability for lack of ordinary care where the limitation is explicit. Allen v. Merchants Bank, 22 Wend. 215 (1839); Briggs v. Central Nat'l Bank, 89 N.Y. 182 (1822); Isler v. National Park Bank, 239 N.Y. 462, 470, 147 N.E. 66, 69 (1925). Sustaining exculpation clauses in stop payment orders, see Gaita v. Windsor Bank, 251 N.Y. 152, 154–155, 167 N.E. 203, 204 (1929), and Seldowitz v. Manufacturer's Trust Company, 202 N.Y.S.2d 129 (1960).

(2) and (3) Generally in *accord:* Carson v. Federal Reserve Bank, 254 N.Y. 218, 172 N.E. 475 (1930) (Federal Reserve regulations and operating letters); O'Brien v. Grant, 146 N.Y. 163, 40 N.E. 871 (1895) (clearing house rules, but it has been held that banks which are not parties to clearing house agreements are not bound by their rules. Columbia Knickerbocker Trust Co. v. Miller, 215 N.Y. 191, 109 N.E. 179 (1915); First Nat. Bank v. National Park Bank, 181 App. Div. 103, 168 N.Y.S. 422 (1917). Practices observed by clearing house members have been held binding upon non-members where such practices are so well-established as to warrant an inference that the non-member contracted with them in mind. O'Brien v. Grant, *supra.* In such cases the burden of proof has been on the party seeking to give such a custom of usage binding effect as against a non-member. Albert v. State Bank, 78 Misc. 56, 138 N.Y.S. 237 (1912).

(4) This is new.

(5) The first part of the subsection appears to be generally in *accord* with decisional law. S. & M Allen v. Suydam & Boyd, 20 Wend. 321 (1838); First National Bank v. Fourth Nat'l Bank, 77 N.Y. 320 (1879); Mogul, Inc. v. Lavine, Inc., 247 N.Y. 20, 159 N.E. 708 (1928). The last part of the subsection is supported by a dictum in an early New York decision. Ayrault v. Pacific Bank, 6 Rob. 337, aff'd 47 N.Y. 570 (1872).

Historical Note: In accordance with a suggestion by the Law Revision Commission, subsection (1) was amended to include a provision that the parties may, by agreement, determine the standards by which obligations of ordinary care are to be measured if such standards are not manifestly unreasonable. (1956 Recommendations, p. 135; excerpts, pp. 420–421.)

Official Uniform Comment

Prior Uniform Statutory Provision: None; but see Sections 5 and 6 of the American Bankers Association Bank Collection Code.

Purposes:

1. Section 1–102 states the general principles and rules for variation of the effect of this Act by agreement and the limitations to this power. Section 4–103 states the specific rules for variation of Article 4 by agreement and also certain standards of ordinary care. In view of the technical complexity of the field of bank collections, the enormous number of items handled by banks, the certainty that there will be variations from the normal in each day's work in each bank, the certainty of changing conditions and the possibility of developing improved methods of collection to speed the process, it would be unwise to freeze present methods of operation by mandatory statutory rules. This section, therefore, permits within wide limits variation of provisions of the Article by agreement.

2. Subsection (1) confers blanket power to vary all provisions of the Article by agreements of the ordinary kind. The agreements may not disclaim a bank's responsibility for its own lack of good faith or failure to exercise ordinary care and may not limit the measure of damages for such lack of failure, but this subsection like Section 1–102(3) approves the practice of parties determining by agreement the standards by which such responsibility is to be measured. In the absence of a showing

that the standards manifestly are unreasonable, the agreement controls. Owners of items and other interested parties are not affected by agreements under this subsection unless they are parties to the agreement or are bound by adoption, ratification, estoppel or the like.

As here used "agreement" has the meaning given to it by Section 1–201(3). The agreement may be direct, as between the owner and the depositary bank; or indirect, as where the owner authorizes a particular type of procedure and any bank in the collection chain acts pursuant to such authorization. It may be with respect to a single item; or to all items handled for a particular customer, e.g., a general agreement between the depositary bank and the customer at the time a deposit account is opened. Legends on deposit tickets, collection letters and acknowledgement of items, coupled with action by the affected party constituting acceptance, adoption, ratification, estopped or the like, are agreements if they meet the tests of the definition of "agreement". See Section 1–201(3). First Nat. Bank of Denver v. Federal Reserve Bank, 6 F.2d 339 (8th Cir. 1925) (deposit slip); Jefferson County Bldg. Ass'n v. Southern Bank & Trust Co., 225 Ala. 25, 142 So.66 (1932) (signature card and deposit slip); Semington V. Stock Yards Nat. Bank, 162 Minn. 424, 203 N.W. 412 (1925) (passbook); Farmers State Bank v. Union Nat. Bank, 42 N.D. 449, 454, 173 N.W. 789, 790 (1919) (acknowledgement of receipt of item).

3. Subsection (1) (subject to its limitation with respect to good faith and ordinary care) goes far to meet the requirements of flexibility. However, it does not by itself confer fully effective flexibility. When it is recognized that banks handle probably 25,000,000 items every business day and that the parties interested in each item include the owner of the item, the drawer (if it is a check), all non–bank indorsers, the payor bank and from one to five or more collecting banks, it is obvious that it is impossible, practically, to obtain direct agreements from all of these parties on all items. En masse, the interested parties constitute virtually every adult person and business organization in the United States. On the other hand they may become bound to agreements on the principle that collecting banks acting as agents have authority to make binding agreements with respect to items handled. This conclusion was assumed but was not flatly decided in Federal Reserve Bank of Richmond v. Malloy, 264 U.S. 160, at 167, 44 S. Ct. 296, at 298, 68 L. Ed. 617, 31 A.L.R. 1261 (1924).

To meet this problem subsection (2) provides that official or quasi-official rules of collection, that is Federal Reserve regulations and operating letters, clearing house rules, and the like, have the effect of agreements under subsection (1), whether or not specifically assented to by all parties interested in items handled. Consequently, such official or quasi-official rules may, standing by themselves but subject to the good faith and ordinary care limitations, vary the effect of the provisions of Article 4.

Federal Reserve regulations. Various sections of the Federal Reserve Act (12 U.S.C.A. § 221 et seq.) authorize the Board of Governors of the Federal Reserve System to direct the Federal Reserve banks to exercise bank collection functions. For example, Section 16 (12 U.S.C.A. § 248(o)) authorizes the Board to require each Federal Reserve bank to exercise the functions of a clearing house for its members and Section 13 (12 U.S.C.A. § 342) authorizes each Federal Reserve to receive deposits from non-member banks solely for the purposes of exchange or of collection. Under this statutory authorization the Board has issued Regulation J (Check Clearing and Collection), which has been infrequently amended over the many years during which it has been in force. (Regulation G, issued under comparable statutory authority, covers the handling of "non-cash items"). Where regulations issued by the Board in pursuance of its statutory mandate may be said to have some force of law and constitute an effective means of maintaining flexibility, it is appropriate to provide that such regulations may vary this Article even though not specifically assented to by all parties interested in items handled.

Federal Reserve operating letters. The regulations of the Federal Reserve Board authorize the Federal Reserve banks to promulgate rules covering operating details. Regulation J, for example, provides that each bank may promulgate rules "not inconsistent with the terms of the law or of this regulation governing the sorting, listing, packaging and transmission of items and other details of its check clearing and collection operation. Such rules. . .shall be set forth. . .in. . .letters of instructions to. . .member and non-member clearing banks." The term "operating letters" means these "letters of instructions", sometimes called "operating circulars", issued by the Federal Reserve bank under the appropriate regulation of the Board. This Article recognizes such "operating letters" issued pursuant to the regulations and concerned with operating details as appropriate means, within their proper sphere, to vary the effect of the Article.

Clearing House Rules. Local clearing houses have long issued rules governing the details of clearing; hours of clearing, media of remittance, time for return of mis-sent items and the like. The case law has recognized such rules, within their proper sphere, as binding on affected parties and as appropriate sources for the courts to look to in filling out details of bank collection law. Subsection (2) in recognizing clearing house rules as a means of preserving flexibility continues the sensible approach indicated in the cases. Including in the term "clearing houses" are county and regional clearing houses as well as those within a single city or town. There is, of course, no intention of authorizing a local clearing house or a group of clearing houses to rewrite the basic law generally. The term "clearing house rules" should be understood in the light of functions the clearing houses have exercised in the past.

And the like. This phrase is to be construed in the light of the foregoing. "Federal Reserve regulations and operating letters" cover rules and regulations issued by public or quasi-public agencies under statutory authority. "Clearing house rules" cover rules issued by a group of banks which have associated themselves to perform through a clearing house some of their collection, payment and clearing functions. Other such agencies or associations may be established in the future whose rules and regulations could be appropriately looked on as constituting means of avoiding absolute statutory rigidity. The phrase "and the like" leaves open such possibilities of future development. An agreement between a number of banks, or even all banks in an area simply because they are banks, would not of itself, by virtue of the phrase "and the like," meet the purposes and objectives of subsection (2).

4. Under this Article banks come under the general obligations of the use of good faith and the exercise of ordinary care. "Good faith" is defined in this Act (Section 1–201(19) as "honesty in fact in the conduct or transaction concerned." The term "ordinary care" is not defined and is here used with its normal tort meaning and not in any special sense relating to bank collections. No attempt is made in the Article to define in toto what constitutes ordinary care or lack of it. Section 4–202 states respects in which collecting banks must use ordinary care. Subsection (3) of 4–103 provides that action or non–action approved by the Article or pursuant to Federal Reserve regulations or operating letters constitutes the exercise of ordinary care. Where Federal Reserve regulations and operating letters are issued pursuant to statutory mandate as indicated above, they constitute an affirmative standard of ordinary care equally with the provisions of Article 4 itself.

Subsection (3) further provides that, absent special instructions, action or non-action consistent with clearing house rules and the like or with a general banking usage not disapproved by the Article, prima facie constitutes the exercise of ordinary care. Clearing house rules and the phrase "and the like" have the significance set forth above in these Comments. The term "general banking usage" is not defined but should be taken to mean a general usage common to banks in the area concerned. See Section 1–205(2). Where the adjective "general" is used, the intention is to require a usage broader than a mere practice between two or three banks but it is not intended to

UCC

require anything as broad as country-wide usage. A usage followed generally throughout a state, a substantial portion of a state, a metropolitan area or the like would certainly be sufficient. Consistently with the principle of Section 1–205(3), action or non–action consistent with clearing house rules or the like or with such banking usages prima facie constitutes the exercise of ordinary care. However, the phrase "in the absence of special instructions" affords owners of items an opportunity to prescribe other standards and where there may be no direct supervision or control of clearing houses or banking usages by official supervisory authorities, the confirmation of ordinary care by compliance with these standards is prima facie only, thus conferring on the courts the ultimate power to determine ordinary care in any case where it should appear desirable to do so. The prima facie rule does, however, impose on the party contesting the standards to establish that they are unreasonable, arbitrary or unfair.

5. Subsection (4), in line with the flexible approach required for the bank collection process is designed to make clear that a novel procedure adopted by a bank is not to be considered unreasonable merely because that procedure is not specifically contemplated by this Article or by agreement, or because it has not yet been generally accepted as a bank usage. Changing conditions constantly call for new procedures and someone has to use the new procedure first. If such a procedure when called in question is found to be reasonable under the circumstances provided, of course, that it is not inconsistent with any provision of the Article or other law or agreement, the bank which has followed the new procedure should not be found to have failed in the exercise of ordinary care.

6. Subsection (5) sets forth a rule for determining the measure of damages which, under subsection (1) cannot be limited by agreement. In the absence of bad faith the maximum recovery is the amount of the item concerned. When it is established that some part or all of the item could not have been collected even by the use of ordinary care the recovery is reduced by the amount which would have been in any event uncollectible. This limitation on recovery follows the case law. Finally, when bad faith is established the rule opens to allow the recovery of other damages, whose "proximateness" is to be tested by the ordinary rules applied in comparable cases. Of course, it continues to be as necessary under subsection (5) as it has been under common law principles that, before the damage rule of the subsection becomes operative, liability of the bank and some loss to the customer or owner must be established.

Cross References:

Sections 1–102(3), 1–203, 1–205 and 4–202.

Definitional Cross References:

"Bank". Section 1–201.
"Good faith". Section 1–201.
"Item". Section 4–104.
"Usage". Section 1–205.

Section 4–104. Definitions and Index of Definitions.

(1) In this Article unless the context otherwise requires

(a) "Account" means any account with a bank and includes a checking, time, interest or savings account;

(b) "Afternoon" means the period of day between noon and midnight;

(c) "Banking day" means that part of any day on which a bank is open to the public for carrying on substantially all of its banking functions;

(d) "Clearing house" means any association of banks or other payors regularly clearing items;

(e) "Customer" means any person having an account with a bank or for whom a bank has agreed to collect items and includes a bank carrying an account with another bank;

(f) "Documentary draft" means any negotiable or non–negotiable draft with accompanying documents, securities or other papers to be delivered against honor of the draft;

(g) "Item" means any instrument for the payment of money even though it is not negotiable but does not include money;

(h) "Midnight deadline" with respect to a bank is midnight on its next banking day following the banking day on which it receives the relevant item or notice or from which the time for taking action commences to run, whichever is later;

(i) "Obligated bank" means the acceptor of a certified check, the issuer of a cashier's check, or the drawer of a teller's check;

(j) "Properly payable" includes the availability of funds for payment at the time of decision to pay or dishonor;

(k) "Remitter" means the buyer from the obligated bank of a cashier's check or a teller's check, and the drawer of a certified check;

(l) "Settle" means to pay in cash, by clearing house settlement, in a charge or credit or by remittance, or otherwise as instructed. A settlement may be either provisional or final;

(m) "Suspends payments" with respect to a bank means that it has been closed by order of the supervisory authorities, that a public officer has been appointed to take it over or that it ceases or refuses to make payments in the ordinary course of business.

(2) Other definitions applying to this Article and the sections in which they appear are:

"Collecting bank" Section 4–105.

"Depositary bank" Section 4–105.

"Intermediary bank" Section 4–105.

"Payor bank" Section 4–105.

"Presenting bank" Section 4–105.

"Remitting bank" Section 4–105.

(3) The following definitions in other Articles apply to this Article:

"Acceptance" Section 3–410.

"Certificate of deposit" Section 3–104.

"Certification" Section 3–411.

"Check" Section 3–104.

"Draft" Section 3–104.

"Holder in due course" Section 3–302.

"Notice of dishonor" Section 3–508.

"Presentment" Section 3–504.

"Protest" Section 3–509.

"Secondary party" Section 3–102.

(4) In addition Article 1 contains general definitions and principles of construction and interpretation applicable throughout this Article.

1990 Amendments: L. 1990, Ch. 568, eff. July 1, 1991, adding the definitions of "Obligated bank" and "Remitter."

New York Annotations

No attempt has been made to examine thoroughly the general body of New York statutory and common law to find statutes and cases defining and construing the terms defined in this and the succeeding section, as such statutes and cases would be of little significance. For comparative purposes, only, the following references are given:

(a) In re Fricke, 122 Misc. 427, 202 N.Y.S. 906 (1924); Rensselaer Glass Factory v. Reid, 5 Cowen 587 (1825).

(b) Compare General Construction Law, § 51, defining "night time."

(c) Hutchinson v. Manhattan Co., 150 N.Y. 250, 44 N.E. 775 (1896).

(d) Columbia-Knickerbocker Trust Company v. Miller, 215 N.Y. 191, 109 N.E. 179 (1915).

(g) N.I.L., § 350–b; Matter of Bank of United States, 243 App. Div. 287, 277 N.Y.S. 96 (1935).

(h) N.I.L., § 350–b(1).

(j) Gandolfo v. Appleton, 40 N.Y. 533 (1869); National Bank v. Norton, 1 Hill 572 (1841).

(k) Banking Law, § 606(f).

Historical Note: At the suggestion of the Law Revision Commission, the words "negotiable or non-negotiable" were added to paragraph (f) of subsection (1) to make clear that it is not the intention of Article 4 to restrict the term "documentary draft" to negotiable drafts. (1956 Recommendations, p. 137; Excerpts p. 421.)

Official Uniform Comment

Prior Uniform Statutory Provision: None.

Purposes:

1. Subsection (1)(c): "Banking Day". Under this definition that part of a business day when a bank is open only for limited functions, e.g., on Saturday evenings to receive deposits and cash checks, but with loan, bookkeeping and other departments closed, is not part of a banking day.

2. Subsection (1)(d): "Clearing House". Occasionally express companies, governmental agencies and other non-bank deal directly with a clearing house; hence the definition does not limit the term to an association of banks.

3. Subsection (1)(e): "Customer". It is to be noted that this term includes a bank carrying an account with another bank as well as the more typical non-bank customer or depositor.

4. Subsection (1)(g): The word "item" is chosen because it is "banking language" and includes non-negotiable as well as negotiable paper calling for money and also similar paper governed by the Article on Investment Securities (Article 8) as well as that governed by the Article on Commercial Paper (Article 3).

5. Subsection (1)(h): "Midnight Deadline." The use of this phrase is an example of the more mechanical approach used in this Article. Midnight is selected as a termination point or time limit to obtain greater uniformity and definiteness than would be possible from other possible termination points, such as the close of the banking day or business day.

6. Subsection (1)(j): The term "settle" is a new term in bank collection language that has substantial importance throughout. Article 4. In the American Bankers Association Bank Collection Code, in deferred posting statutes, in Federal Reserve regulations and operating letters, in clearing house rules, in agreements between banks and customers and in legends on deposit tickets and collection letters, there is repeated reference to "conditional" or "provisional" credits or payments. Tied in with this concept of credits or payments being in some way tentative, has been a related but somewhat different problem as to when an item is "paid" or "finally paid" either to determine the relative priority of the item as against attachment, stop payment orders and the like or in insolvency situations. There has been extensive litigation in the various states on these problems. To a substantial extent the confusion, the litigation and even the resulting court decisions fail to take into account that in the collection process some debits or credits are provisional or tentative and others are final and that very many debits or credits are provisional or tentative for awhile but later become final. Similarly, some cases fail to recognize that within a single bank, particularly a payor bank, each item goes through a series of processes and that in a payor bank most of these processes are preliminary to the basic act of payment or "final payment".

The term "settle" is used as a convenient term to characterize a broad variety of conditional, provisional, tentative and also final payments of items. Such a comprehensive term is needed because it is frequently difficult or unnecessary to determine whether a particular action is tentative or final or when a particular credit shifts from the tentative class to the final class. Therefore, its use throughout the Article indicates that in that particular context it is unnecessary or unwise to determine whether the debit or the credit or the payment is tentative or final. However, when qualified by the adjective "provisional" its tentative nature is intended, and when qualified by the adjective "final" its permanent nature is intended.

Examples of the various types of settlement contemplated by the term include payments in cash; the efficient but somewhat complicated process of payment through the adjustment and offsetting of balances through clearing houses; debits or credit entries in accounts between banks; the forwarding of various types of remittance instruments, sometimes to cover a particular item but more frequently to cover an entire group of items received on a particular day.

7. Subsection (1)(k): "Suspends payments". This term is designed to afford an objective test to determine when a bank is no longer operating as a part of the banking system.

Definitional Cross References:

"Bank". Section 1-201.
"Documents". Section 1-201.
"Money". Section 1-201.
"Negotiable". Section 3-104.

UCC

"Notice". Section 1-201.
"Person". Section 1-201.
"Securities". Section 8-102.

Section 4–105. "Depositary Bank"; "Intermediary Bank"; "Collecting Bank"; "Payor Bank"; "Presenting Bank"; "Remitting Bank".

In this Article unless the context otherwise requires:

(a) "Depositary bank" means the first bank to which an item is transferred for collection even though it is also the payor bank;

(b) "Payor bank" means a bank by which an item is payable as drawn or accepted;

(c) "Intermediary bank" means any bank to which an item is transferred in course of collection except the depositary or payor bank;

(d) "Collecting bank" means any bank handling the item for collection except the payor bank;

(e) "Presenting bank" means any bank presenting an item except a payor bank;

(f) "Remitting bank" means any payor or intermediary bank remitting for an item.

New York Annotations

See first part of annotation to Section 4–104. Comparable terminology has been used, though not defined, in the N.I.L.

(a) N.I.L. § 350–a.
(b) N.I.L., §§ 350–d and 350–j.
(c) N.I.L., § 350–e ("subsequent agent bank").
(d) N.I.L., §§ 350–c and 350–h.
(e) N.I.L., § 350–j (included in term "agent collecting bank").
(f) Compare N.I.L., § 350–1(3) ("agent collecting bank other than the drawer or payor").

Official Uniform Comment

Prior Uniform Statutory Provision: None.

Purposes:

1. The definitions in general exclude a bank to which an item is issued, as such bank does not take by transfer except in the particular case covered where the item is issued to a payee for collection, as where a corporation is transferring balances from one account to another. Thus, the definition of "depositary bank" does not include the bank to which a check is made payable where a check is given in payment of a mortgage. Such a bank has the status of a payee under Article 3 on Commercial Paper and not that of a collecting bank.

2. The term payor bank includes a drawee bank and also a bank at which an item is payable if the item constitutes an order on the bank to pay, for it is then "payable

by" the bank. If the "at" item is not an order in the particular state (See Section 3-121), then the bank is not a payor, but will be a presenting or collecting bank.

3. Items are sometimes drawn or accepted "payable through" a particular bank. Under this Section 3-120 the "payable through" bank (if it in fact handles the item) will be a collecting (and often a presenting) bank; it is not a "payor bank."

4. The term intermediary bank includes the last bank in the collection process where the payor is not a bank. Usually the last bank is also a presenting bank.

Cross References:

Article 3, especially Sections 3–120 and 3–121.

Definitional Cross References:

"Bank". Section 1–201.
"Customer". Section 4–104.
"Item". Section 4–104.

Section 4–106. Separate Office of a Bank.

A branch or separate office of a bank is a separate bank for the purpose of computing the time within which and determining the place at or to which action may be taken or notices or orders shall be given under this Article and under Article 3. The receipt of any notice or order by or the knowledge of one branch or separate office of a bank is not actual or constructive notice to or knowledge of any other branch or office of the same bank and does not impair the right of another branch or office to be a holder in due course of an item.

N.Y. Commission Comments

The code as enacted in New York in 1962 conforms to the 1962 Official Text of Section 4–106, except for the omission of the optional phrase "maintaining its own deposit ledgers" following "bank" at the beginning of the section, and the addition of the second sentence, for the reason stated in the Commission's 1962 Report: "The additions to Section 4–106 make explicit in respect of notices to branches what appears to be implicit under Section 4–106 of the 1958 Official Text when read together with Sections 1–201 (25) and (27), 3–304(6) and 4–102."

New York Annotations

New York law treats branch banks as separate entities for the collection process as well as other purposes (N.I.L., § 350; Chrzanowska v. Corn Exch. Bank, 173 App.Div. 285, 159 N.Y.S. 385, aff'd, 225 N.Y. 728, 122 N.E. 877 (1919); Cronan v. Schilling, 100 N.Y.S.2d 474 (1950)), though a bank and its branches are one for purposes of characterizing a draft drawn by a bank addressed to one of its branches as a draft drawn by a drawer on itself, giving rise to an immediate and primary liability on the part of the drawer bank. Cable and Wireless, Ltd. v. Yokohama Specie Bank, 191 Misc. 567, 573–579, 79, N.Y.S.2d 597, 604–609, aff'd, 304 N.Y. 574, 107 N.E.2d 75 (1952). Since no such requirement exists as that prescribed in the bracketed portion of the section [that the branch shall maintain its own deposit ledgers], New York law would be continued if the bracketed portion were omitted.

Historical Note: The bracketed phrase, "maintaining its own deposit ledgers", is to make it optional with the several states whether to require a branch to maintain its own deposit ledgers in order to be considered to be a separate bank for certain purposes under Article 4. In some states "maintaining its own deposit ledgers" is a satisfactory test. In other branch practices are such that this test would not be suitable. (1956 Recommendations, p. 138; Excerpts, p. 421.)

Official Uniform Comment

Prior Uniform Statutory Provision: None; but see Section 1, American Bankers Association Bank Collection Code.

Purposes:

1. A rule with respect to the status of a branch or separate office of a bank as a part of any statute on bank collections is highly desirable if not absolutely necessary. However, practices in the operations of branches and separate offices vary substantially in the different states and it has not been possible to find any single rule that is logically correct, fair in all situations and workable under all different types of practices.

2. In many states and for many purposes a branch or separate office of the bank needs to be treated as a separate bank. Many branches function as separate banks in the handling and payment of items and require time for doing so similar to that of a separate bank. This is particularly true where branch banking is permitted throughout a state or in different towns and cities. Similarly, where there is this separate functioning a particular branch or separate office is the only proper place for various types of action to be taken or orders or notices to be given. Examples include the drawing of a check on a particular branch by a customer whose account is carried at that branch; the presentment of that same check at that branch; the issuance of an order to the branch to stop payment on the check.

3. Section 1 of the American Bankers Association Bank Collection Code provides simply: "A branch or office of any such bank shall be deemed a bank." Although this rule appears to be brief and simple, as applied to particular sections of the ABA Code it produces illogical and, in some cases, unreasonable results. For example, under Section 11 of the ABA Code it seems anomalous for one branch of a bank to have charged an item to the account of the drawer and another branch to have the power to elect to treat the item as dishonored. Similar logical problems would flow from applying the same rule to Article 4. Warranties by one branch to another branch under Section 4–207 (each considered a separate bank) do not make sense.

4. Assuming that it is not desirable to make each branch a separate bank for all purposes, this Section provides that a branch or separate offices is a separate bank for certain purposes. In so doing the single legal entity of the bank as a whole is preserved, thereby carrying with it the liability of the institution as a whole on such obligations as it may be under. On the other hand, where the Article provides a number of time limits for different types of action by banks, of a branch functions as a separate bank, it should have the time limits available to a separate bank. Similarly if in its relations to customers a branch functions as a separate bank, notices and orders with respect to accounts of customers of the branch should be given at the branch. For example, whether a branch has notice sufficient to affect its status as a holder in due course of an item taken by it should depend upon what notice that branch has received with respect to the item. Similarly the receipt of a stop payment order at one branch should not be notice to another branch so as to impair the right of the second branch to be a holder in due course of the item, although in circumstances in which ordinary care requires the communication of a notice or order to the proper branch of a bank, such notice or order would be effective at such proper branch from the time it was or should have been received. See Section 1–201(27).

5. Whether a branch functions as a separate bank may vary depending upon the type of activity taking place and upon practices in the different states. If the activity is that of a payor bank paying items, a branch will usually function as a separate bank if it maintains its own deposit ledgers. Similarly whether a branch functions as a separate bank in the collection of items usually depends also on whether it maintains its own deposit ledgers. Conversely, if a particular bank having branches does all of its bookkeeping at its head office, the branches of that bank do not usually function as separate banks either in the payment or collection of items.

On the other hand, in its relations to customers a branch may function as a separate bank regardless of whether it maintains its own deposit ledgers. Checks may be drawn on a particular branch and notices and stop orders delivered to that branch even though all the bookkeeping is done at the head office or another branch.

Where the words "maintaining its own deposit ledgers" are bracketed, the option is given to each state enacting the Code to include these words as a test of separateness. In those states where the maintenance by a branch of its own deposit ledgers will serve as a satisfactory standard the bracketed words should be retained. In those states where these words will cause more problems than benefits, they may be deleted. Insofar as this latter rule allows extra time to banks maintaining branches where such extra time is not needed, it is not ideal. However, it has not been found possible to find a rule that will meet this problem and will work in all cases. Further, it is highly unlikely that large banks maintaining branches will needlessly take advantage of extra time under this rule.

Cross References:

Sections 3–504, 4–102(2).

Definitional Cross References:

"Bank". Section 1–201.
"Branch". Section 1–201.

Section 4–107. Time of Receipt of Items.

(1) For the purpose of allowing time to process items, prove balances and make the necessary entries on its books to determine its position for the day, a bank may fix an afternoon hour of 2 P.M. or later as a cut-off hour for the handling of money and items and the making of entries of its books.

(2) Any item or deposit of money received on any day after a cut-off hour so fixed or after the close of the banking day may be treated as being received at the opening of the next banking day.

New York Annotations

This section is similar to but broader than N.I.L., § 350–b(3) (iii) (deferred posting statute), in that it is applicable to all deposits, not being limited to the payment situation. The rule states a practice followed by many banks in large cities.

Official Uniform Comment

Prior Uniform Statutory Provision: None.

UCC

Purposes:

1. After an item has been received by a bank it goes through a series of processes varying with the type of item that it is. It moves from the teller's window, branch office, or mail desk at which it is received through settlement and proving departments until it is forwarded or presented to a clearing house or another bank, if it is a transit item, or until it reaches the bookkeeping department, if the bank receiving it is the payor bank. In addition, in order that the books of the bank always remain in balance while items are moving through it, the amount of each item is included in lists or proofs of debits or credits several times as it progresses through the bank. The running of proofs, the making of debit and credit entries in subsidiary and general ledgers and the striking of a general balance for each day requires a considerable amount of time. If these processes are to be completed on any particular day during normal working hours without the employment of night forces, a number of banks have found it necessary to establish a "cut-off hour" to allow time to obtain final figures to be incorporated into the bank's position for the day. Subsection (1) approves a cut-off hour of this type provided it is not earlier than 2 P.M. Subsection (2) provides that if such a cut-off hour is fixed, items received after the cut-off hour may be treated as being received at the opening of the next banking day. Where the number of items received either through the mail or over the counter tends to taper off radically as the afternoon hours progress, a 2 P.M. cut-off hour does not involve a large portion of the items received but at the same time permits a bank using such a cut-off hour to leave its doors open later in the afternoon without forcing into the evening the completion of its settling and proving process.

2. The alternative provision in Subsection (2) that items or deposits received after the close of the banking day may be treated as received at the opening of the next banking day is important in cases where a bank closes at twelve or one o'clock, e.g., on a Saturday, but continues to receive some items by mail or over the counter if, for example, it opens Saturday evening for the limited purpose or receiving deposits and cashing checks.

Definitional Cross References:

"Afternoon". Section 4–104.
"Bank". Section 1–201.
"Banking day". Section 4–104.
"Item". Section 4–104.
"Money". Section 1–201.

Section 4–108. Delays.

(1) Unless otherwise instructed, a collecting bank in a good faith effort to secure payment may, in the case of specific items and with or without the approval of any person involved, waive, modify or extend time limits imposed or permitted by this Act for a period not in excess of an additional banking day without discharge of secondary parties and without liability to its transferor or any prior party.

(2) Delay by a collecting bank or payor bank beyond time limits prescribed or permitted by this Act or by instructions is excused if caused by interruption of communication facilities, suspension of payments by another bank, war, emergency conditions or other circumstances beyond the control of the bank provided it exercises such diligence as the circumstances require.

New York Annotations

(1) This subsection extends the rule of N.I.L., § 350–d(2), applicable to "items drawn on a drawer other than a bank", to all "specific items".

(2) Although the language of this subsection is new, it appears to be generally consistent with present law. See N.I.L., §§ 350–d and 350–g.

Official Uniform Comment

Prior Uniform Statutory Provision: None.

Purposes:

1. Sections 4–202(2), 4–212, 4–301 and 4–302 prescribe various time limits for the handling of items. These are the limits of time within which a bank, in fulfillment of its obligation to exercise ordinary care, must handle items entrusted to it for collection or payment. Under Section 4–103 they may be varied by agreement or by Federal Reserve regulations or operating letters, clearing house rules, or the like.

2. Subsection (1) of this section permits a limited extension of these time limits in special cases. It permits collecting banks to grant, within a rather narrow field, an additional banking day and to do so with or without the approval of any interested party. Such one-day extension can only be granted in a good faith effort to secure payment and only with respect to specific items. It cannot be exercised if the customer instructs otherwise. Thus limited the escape provision should afford a limited degree of flexibility in special cases but should not interfere with the overall requirement and objective of speedy collections.

3. Notice that an extension granted under Subsection (1) is "without discharge of secondary parties". It therefore extends also the times for presentment or payment, as the case may be, specified in Article 3. See Sections 3–503 and 3–506. Where this Article and Article 3 conflict, this Article controls. See Sections 3–103(2) and 4–102(1).

4. Subsection (2) is another escape clause from time limits. This clause operates not only with respect to time limits imposed by the article itself but also time limits imposed by special instructions, by agreement or by Federal Reserve regulations or operating letters, clearing house rules or the like. The latter time limits are "permitted" by the Code. This clause operates, however, only in the types of situation specified. Examples of these situations include blizzards, floods, or hurricanes, and other "Act of God" events or conditions, and wrecks or disasters, interfering with mails; suspension of payments by another bank; abnormal operating conditions such as substantial increased volume or substantial shortage of personnel during war or emergency situations. When delay is sought to be excused under this subsection the bank must "exercise such diligence as the circumstances require" and it has the burden of proof. See Section 4–202(2).

Cross References:

Sections 3–103(2), 3–503, 3–506, 4–102(1), 4–103, 4–104, 4–202(2), 4–212, 4–213, 4–301, 4–302.

Definitional Cross References:

"Bank". Section 1–201.
"Banking day". Section 4–104.
"Collecting bank". Section 4–105.
"Good faith". Section 1–201.

"Item". Section 4–104.
"Party". Section 1–201.

Section 4–109. Process of Posting.

The "process of posting" means the usual procedure followed by a payor bank in determining to pay an item and in recording the payment including one or more of the following or other steps as determined by the bank:

(a) verification of any signature;

(b) ascertaining that sufficient funds are available;

(c) affixing a "paid" or other stamp.

(d) entering a charge or entry to a customer's account;

(e) correcting or reversing an entry or erroneous action with respect to the item.

Amended by Laws 1963, Ch. 1003, eff. Sept. 27, 1964.

Official Uniform Comment

Prior Uniform Statutory Provision: None.

Purposes:

Completion of the "process of posting" is one of the measuring points for determining when an item is finally paid (subsection (1) (c) of Section 4–213) and when knowledge, notice, stop order, legal process and set-off come too late to affect a payor bank's right or duty to pay an item (subsection (1) (d) of Section 4–303). This Section defines what is meant by the "process of posting". It is the "usual procedure followed by a payor bank in determining to pay an item and in recording the payment . . .". It involves the two basic elements of some decision to pay and some recording of the payment with a listing of some of the typical steps that might be involved. Procedures followed by banks in determining to pay an item and in recording the payment vary. Examples of some of these procedures will illustrate what is meant by completion of the "process of posting".

Example 1. A payor bank receives an item through the clearing on Monday morning. It is sorted under the name of the customer on Monday and under deferred posting routines (Section 4–301) reaches the bookkeeper for that customer on Tuesday morning. The bookkeeper examines the signature, verifies there are sufficient funds and decides at 11 a.m. on Tuesday to pay the item. A debit entry for or including the amount of the item is entered in the customer's account at 12 noon on Tuesday. The process of posting is completed at 12 noon on Tuesday.

Example 2. A payor bank with branches receives an item through the clearing on Monday morning. One branch does all the bookkeeping for itself and nine other branches. The item is sent to that branch and a provisional debit is entered to the customer's account for the amount of the item on Monday. After this entry is made the item is sent to the branch where the customer transacts business and at this branch a clerk verifies the signature on Tuesday, e.g. at 12 noon. If the clerk determines the signature is valid and makes a decision to pay, the process of posting is completed at 12 noon on Tuesday because there has been both a charge to the customer's account and a determination to pay. If, however, the clerk determines the signature is not valid or that the item should not be paid for some other reason, the item is then returned to the presenting bank through the clearing house and an offsetting credit entry is made in the customer's account by the bookkeeping branch. In this case there has been no determination to pay the item, no completion of the process of posting and no payment of the item.

Example 3. A payor bank receives in the mail on Monday an item drawn upon it. The item is sorted and otherwise processed on Monday and during Monday night is provisionally recorded on tape by an electronic computer as charged to the customer's account. On Tuesday a clerk examines the signature on the item and makes other checks to determine finally whether the item should be paid. If the clerk determines the signature is valid and makes a decision to pay and all processing of this item is complete, e.g., at 12 noon on Tuesday, the "process of posting" is completed at that time. If, however, the clerk determines the signature is not valid or that the item should not be paid for some other reason, the item is returned to the presenting bank and in the regular Tuesday night run of the computer the debit to the customer's account for the item is reversed or an offsetting credit entry is made. In this case, as in Example 2, there has been no determination to pay the item, no completion of the process of posting and no payment of the item.

Cross References:

Sections 4–213(1)(c), 4–303(1)(d).

Definitional Cross References:

"Account". Section 4–104(1)(a).
"Customer". Section 4–104(1)(e).
"Item". Section 4–104(1)(g).
"Payor bank". Section 4–105(b).

PART 2

COLLECTION OF ITEMS: DEPOSITARY AND COLLECTING BANKS

Section 4–201. Presumption and Duration of Agency Status of Collecting Banks and Provisional Status of Credits; Applicability of Article; Item Indorsed "Pay Any Bank".

(1) Unless a contrary intent clearly appears and prior to the time that a settlement given by a collecting bank for an item is or becomes final (subsection (3) of Section 4–211 and Sections 4–212 and 4–213) the bank is an agent or sub-agent of the owner of the item and any settlement given for the item is provisional. This provision applies regardless of the form of indorsement or lack of indorsement and even though credit given for the item is subject to immediate withdrawal as of right or is in fact withdrawn; but the continuance of ownership of an item by its owner and any rights of the owner to proceeds of the item are subject to rights of a collecting bank such as those resulting from outstanding advances on the item and valid rights of setoff. When an item is handled by banks for purposes of presentment, payment and collection, the relevant provisions of this Article apply even though action of parties clearly establishes that a particular bank has purchased the item and is the owner of it.

(2) After an item has been indorsed with the words "pay any bank" or the like, only a bank may acquire the rights of a holder

(a) until the item has been returned to the customer initiating collection; or

(b) until the item has been specially indorsed by a bank to a person who is not a bank.

New York Annotations

(1) The first provision of this subsection is similar to N.I.L., § 350–a, but thereafter the two statutes differ in that the present statute, unlike this subsection, places some emphasis on the type of indorsement on the instrument in determining whether a bank is an agent or owner. The subsection also provides that the presumptively provisional character of any settlement continues until the settlement is "final" and states that the continued ownership of an item by the owner and his right to proceeds are subject to the bank's rights resulting from outstanding advances and any right of set-off. Compare the last sentence of N.I.L., § 350–a.

(2) Similar in effect to N.I.L., § 350–c, except that this subsection permits a bank holding an item indorsed "pay any bank or banker" to transfer the item out of banking channels by special indorsement. In such a case the transferee could qualify as a holder in due course, but a bank making such a transfer would be liable to the customer if the transfer was prompted either by a lack of good faith or a lack of ordinary care. See Section 4–103. See also Sections 3–205 and 3–206, which continue to treat such an indorsement as "restrictive" but make some major changes in the law of restrictive indorsements.

Historical Note: Subsection (1) was completely revised to make clear the general status of collecting banks, the general nature of credits entered for items, and the extent to which the Article is applicable to all cases. Subsection (2) revived a type of provision appearing in some earlier drafts of the Article designed to protect ownership rights to an item once it enters bank collection channels. (1956 Recommendations, p. 140.)

Official Uniform Comment

Prior Uniform Statutory Provision: None; but see Sections 2 and 4 of the American Bankers Association Bank Collection Code.

Purposes:

1. This section states certain basic rules and presumptions of the bank collection process. One basic rule, appearing in the last sentence of subsection (1), is that, to the extent applicable, the provisions of the Article govern without regard to whether a bank handling an item owns the item or is an agent for collection. Historically, much time has been spent and effort expended in determining or attempting to determine whether a bank was a purchaser of an item or merely an agent for collection. See discussion of this subject and cases cited in 11 A.L.R. 1043, 16 A.L.R. 1084, 42 A.L.R. 492, 68 A.L.R. 725, 99 A.L.R. 486. See also Section 4 of the American Bankers Association Bank Collection Code. The general approach of Article 4, similar to that of other articles, is to provide, within reasonable limits, rules or answers to major problems known to exist in the bank collection process without regard to questions of status and ownership but to keep general principles such as status and ownership available to cover residual areas not covered by specific rules. In line with this approach, the last sentence of subsection (1) says in effect that Article 4 applies

to practically every item moving through banks for the purpose of presentment, payment or collection.

2. Within this general rule of broad coverage, the first two sentences of subsection (1) state a rule of status in terms of a strong presumption. "Unless a contrary intent clearly appears" the status of a collecting bank is that of an agent or sub-agent for the owner of the item. Although as indicated in Comment 1 it is much less important under Article 4 to determine status than has been the case heretofore, such status may have importance in some residual areas not covered by specific rules. Further, where status has been considered so important in the past, to omit all reference to it might cause confusion. The presumption of agency "applies regardless of the form of indorsement or lack of indorsement and even though credit given for the item is subject to immediate withdrawal as of right or is in fact withdrawn". Thus questions heretofore litigated as to whether ordinary indorsements "for deposit", "for collection" or in blank have the effect of creating an agency status or a purchase, no longer have significance in varying the prima facie rule of agency. Similarly, the nature of the credit given for an item or whether it is subject to immediate withdrawal as of right or is in fact withdrawn, do not rebut the general presumption. See A.L.R. references supra in Comment 1. A contrary intent can rebut the presumption but this must be clear. An example of a clear contrary intent would be if collateral papers established or the item bore a legend stating that the item was sold absolutely to the depositary bank.

3. The prima facie agency status of collecting banks is consistent with prevailing law and practice today. Section 2 of the American Bankers Association Bank Collection Code so provides. Legends on deposit tickets, collection letters and acknowledgments of items and Federal Reserve operating letters consistently so provide. The status is consistent with rights of charge-back (Section 4–212 and Section 11 of the ABA Code) and risk of loss in the event of insolvency (Section 4–214 and Section 13 of the ABA Code).

4. Affirmative statement of a prima facie agency status for collecting banks requires certain limitations and qualifications. Under current practices substantially all bank collections sooner or later merge into bank credits, at least if collection is effected. Usually, this takes place within a few days of the initiation of collection. An intermediary bank receives final collection and evidences the result of its collection by a "credit" on its books to the depositary bank. The depositary bank evidences the results of its collection by a "credit" in the account of its customer. As used in these instances the term "credit" clearly indicates a debtor-creditor relationship. At some stage in the bank collection process the agency status of a collecting bank changes to that of debtor, a debtor of its customer. Usually at about the same time it also becomes a creditor for the amount of the item, a creditor of some intermediary, payor or other bank. Thus the collection is completed, all agency aspects are terminated and the identity of the item has become completely merged in bank accounts, that of the customer with the depositary bank and that of one bank with another.

Although Section 4–213(1) provides that an item is finally paid when the payor bank takes certain action with respect to the item such final payment of the item may or may not result in the simultaneous final settlement for the item in the case of all prior parties. If a series of provisional debits and credits for the item have been entered in accounts between banks, the final payment of the item by the payor bank may result in the automatic firming up of all these provisional debits and credits for the item have been entered in accounts between banks, the final payment of the item by the payor bank may result in the automatic firming up of all these provisional debits and credits under Section 4–213(2), and the consequent receipt of final settlement for the item by each collecting bank and the customer of the depositary bank simultaneously with such action of the payor bank. However, if the payor bank

UCC

or some intermediary bank accounts for the item with a remittance draft, the next prior bank usually does not receive final settlement for the item until such remittance draft finally clears. See Section 4–211(3)(a). The first sentence of subsection (1) provides that the agency status of a collecting bank (whether intermediary or depositary) continues until the settlement *given by it for the item* is or becomes final, referring to Sections 4–211(3), 4–212, and 4–213. In the case of the series of provisional credits covered by Section 4–213(2), this could be simultaneously with the final payment of the item by the payor bank. In cases where remittance drafts are used or in straight non-cash collections, this would not be until the times specified in Sections 4–211(3) and 4–213(3).

A number of practical results flow from this rule continuing the agency status of a collecting bank until its settlement for the item is or becomes final, some of which are specifically set forth in this Article. One is that risk of loss continues in the owner of the item rather than the agent bank. See Section 4–212. Offsetting rights favorable to the owner are that pending such final settlement, the owner has the preference rights of Section 4–214 and the direct rights of Section 4–302 against the payor bank. It also follows from this rule that the dollar limitations of Federal Deposit Insurance are measured by the claim of the owner of the item rather than that of the collecting bank.

5. In those cases where some period of time elapses between the final payment of the item by the payor bank and the time that the settlement of the collecting bank is or becomes final, e.g., where the payor bank or an intermediary bank accounts for the item with a remittance draft or in straight non-cash collections, the continuance of the agency status of the collecting bank necessarily carries with it the continuance of the owner's status as principal. The second sentence of subsection (1) provides that whatever rights the owner has to proceeds of the item are subject to the rights of collecting banks for outstanding advances on the item and other valid rights, if any. The rule provides a sound rule to govern cases of attempted attachment of proceeds of a non-cash item in the hands of the payor bank as property of the absent owner. If a collecting bank has made an advance on an item which is still outstanding, its right to obtain reimbursement for this advance should be superior to the rights of the owner to the proceeds or to the rights of a creditor of the owner. The phrase "other valid rights, if any" is broad enough to cover legitimate rights of set-off accounts between banks without attempting to provide that all set-offs may be valid. An intentional crediting of proceeds of an item to the account of a prior bank known to be insolvent, for the purpose of acquiring a right of set-off, would not produce a valid set-off. See 8 Zollman, Banks and Banking (1936) Sec. 5443.

6. This section and Article 4 as a whole represent an intentional abandonment of the approach to bank collection problems appearing in Section 4 of the American Bankers Association Bank Collection Code. Where the tremendous volume of items handled makes impossible the examination by all banks of all indorsements on all items and where in fact this examination is not made, except perhaps by depositary banks, it is unrealistic to base the rights and duties of all banks in the collection chain on variations in the form of indorsements. It is anomalous to provide throughout the ABA Code that the prima facie status of collecting banks is that of agent or sub-agent but in Section 4 to provide that subsequent holders (sub-agents) shall have the right to rely on the presumption that the bank of deposit (the primary agent) is the owner of the item. It is unrealistic, particularly in this background, to base rights and duties on status of agent or owner. This Section 4–201 makes the pertinent provisions of Article 4 applicable to substantially all items handled by banks for presentment, payment or collection, recognizes the prima facie status of most banks as agents, and then seeks to state appropriate limits and some attributes to the general rules and presumptions so expressed.

7. Subsection (2) protects the ownership rights with respect to an item indorsed "pay any bank or banker" or in similar terms of a customer initiating collection or

of any bank acquiring a security interest under Section 4–208, in the event the item is subsequently acquired under improper circumstances by a person who is not a bank and transferred by that person to another person, whether or not a bank. Upon return to the customer initiating collection of an item so indorsed, the indorsement may be cancelled (Section 3–208). A bank holding an item so indorsed may transfer the item out of banking channels by special indorsement; however, under Section 4–103(5), such bank would be liable to the owner of the item for any loss resulting therefrom if the transfer had been made in bad faith or with lack of ordinary care. If briefer and more simple forms of bank indorsements are developed under Section 4–206 (e.g., the use of bank transit numbers in lieu of present lengthy forms of bank indorsements), a depositary bank having the transit number "X100" could make subsection (2) operative by indorsements such as "Pay any bank–X100".

Cross References:

Sections 3–206, 3–208, 4–103, 4–206, 4–208, 4–212, 4–213, 4–214 and 4–302.

Definitional Cross References:

"Bank". Section 1–201.
"Collecting Bank". Section 4–105.
"Customer". Section 4–104.
"Depository bank". Section 4–105.
"Holder". Section 1–201.
"Indorsements". Sections 3–202, 3–204, 3–205 and 3–206.
"Item". Section 4–104.
"Person". Section 1–201.
"Settle". Section 4–104.

Section 4–202. Responsibility for Collection; When Action Seasonable.

(1) A collecting bank must use ordinary care in

(a) presenting an item or sending it for presentment; and

(b) sending notice of dishonor or non-payment or returning an item other than a documentary draft to the bank's transferor or directly to the depositary bank under sub-section (2) of Section 4–212 after learning that the item has not been paid or accepted, as the case may be; and

(c) settling for an item when the bank receives final settlement; and

(d) making or providing for any necessary protest; and

(e) notifying its transferor of any loss or delay in transit within a reasonable time after discovery thereof.

(2) A collecting bank taking proper action before its midnight deadline following receipt of an item, notice or payment acts seasonably; taking proper action within a reasonably longer time may be seasonable but the bank has the burden of so establishing.

(3) Subject to subsection (1)(a), a bank is not liable for the insolvency, neglect, misconduct, mistake or default of another bank or person or for loss or destruction of an item in transit or in the possession of others.

New York Annotations

(1) Generally in *accord* with but more explicit than N.I.L., § 350–d. See also Florida Citrus Exchange v. Union Trust Co. of Rochester, 244 App.Div. 68, 278 N.Y.S. 313 (1935).

(2) This subsection adopts and applies to a "collecting Bank", as a prima facie test of when action is timely, the "midnight deadline" of N.I.L., § 350–b (deferred posting statute) applicable to a payor bank. The rule here adopted as applicable to all actions of a collecting bank is broader in scope than N.I.L., § 350–e, which is limited to forwarding and presentment.

(3) Generally in *accord* with N.I.L., § 350–d. See also Soma v. Handrulis, 252 App. Div. 332. 299 N.Y.S. 850, rev'd on other grounds, 277 N.Y. 223, 14 N.E.2d 46 (1938).

Historical Note: In conformity with suggestions made by the Law Revision Commission, the term "settlement" was substituted for the word "payment" at the end of subsection (1)(c), and the final phrase "or person or for loss, etc." was added to subsection (3) to conform to a similar provision in the ABA Bank Collection Code. (1956 Recommendations, p. 141; Excerpts, pp. 421–422.)

Official Uniform Comment

Prior Uniform Statutory Provision: None; but see Sections 5 and 6, American Bankers Association Bank Collection Code.

Purposes:

1. Subsection (1) states the basic responsibilities of a collecting bank. Of course, under Section 1–203 a collecting bank is subject to the standard requirement of good faith. By subsection (1) it must also use ordinary care in the exercise of its basic collection tasks. By Section 4–103(1) neither requirement may be disclaimed.

2. If the bank makes presentment itself, subsection 1(a) requires ordinary care with respect both to the time and manner of presentment. (Sections 3–503, 3–504, 4–210.) If it forwards the item to be presented the subsection requires ordinary care with respect to routing (Section 4–204), and also in the selection of intermediary banks or other agents.

3. Subsection (1) describes types of basic care. Subsection (2) deals with the time for taking action. It first prescribes the general standard for seasonable action, namely, for items received on Monday, proper action (such as forwarding or presenting) on Monday or Tuesday is seasonable. Although under current "production line" operations banks customarily move items along on regular schedules substantially briefer than two days, the subsections states an outside time within which a bank may know it has acted seasonably. To provide flexibility from this standard norm, the subsection further states that action within a reasonably longer time may be seasonable but the bank has the burden of proof. In the case of time items, action after the midnight deadline, but sufficiently in advance of maturity for proper presentation, is a clear example of a "reasonably longer time" that is seasonable. The standard of requiring action not later than Tuesday in the case of Monday items is also subject to possibilities of variation under the general provisions of Section 4–103, or under the special provisions regarding time of receipt of items (Section 4–107), and regarding delays (Section 4–108). This subsection (2) deals only with collecting banks. The time limits applicable to payor banks appear in Section 4–301 and 4–302.

4. At common law the so-called New York collection rule subjected the initial collecting bank to liability for the actions of subsequent banks in the collection chain; the so-called Massachusetts rule was that each bank, subject to the duty of selecting

proper intermediaries, was liable only for its own negligence. Subsection (3) adopts the Massachusetts rule. But since this is stated to be subject to subsection (1)(a) a collecting bank remains responsible for using ordinary care in selecting properly qualified intermediary banks and agents and in giving proper instruction to them.

Cross References:

Sections 1–203, 4–103, 4–107, 4–108, 4–301, and 4–302.

Definitional Cross References:

"Collecting bank". Section 4–105.
"Depositary bank". Section 4–105.
"Documentary draft". Section 4–104.
"Item". Section 4–104.
"Midnight deadline". Section 4–104.
"Presentment". Article 3, Part 5.
"Protest". Section 3–509.

Section 4–203. Effect of Instructions.

Subject to the provisions of Article 3 concerning conversion of instruments (Section 3–419) and the provisions of both Article 3 and this Article concerning restrictive indorsements only a collecting bank's transferor can give instructions which affect the bank or constitute notice to it and a collecting bank is not liable to prior parties for any action taken pursuant to such instructions or in accordance with any agreement with its transferor.

New York Annotations

This section is new but is to be compared with N.I.L., § 350–a (authority to follow instructions of immediate forwarding bank), and Florida Citrus Exchange v. Union Trust Co. of Rochester, 244 App. Div. 68, 278 N.Y.S. 313 (1935). This section should be read in connection with Section 4–205(2) which provides that intermediary or payor banks other than a depository bank are not given notice by prior restrictive indorsements, contrary to Soma v. Handrulis, 277 N.Y. 223, 14 N.E. 2d 46 (1938). See also Sections 3–205, 3–206, 3–419, and 3–603.

Historical Note: At the suggestion of the Law Revision Commission the "subject to" clause was added at the beginning of the section to reconcile with the new provisions as to "restrictive indorsements" referred to in the annotation. In addition, the word "collecting" was added to modify "bank" so as to afford consistency with Section 4–302. (1956 Recommendations, p. 141; Excerpts, p. 422.)

Official Uniform Comment

Prior Uniform Statutory Provision: None; but see Section 2 of the American Bankers Association Bank Collection Code.

Purposes:

This Section adopts a "chain of command" theory which renders it unnecessary for an intermediary or collecting bank to determine whether its transferor is "authorized" to give the instructions. Equally the bank is not put on notice of any "revocation of authority" or "lack of authority" by notice received from any other person. The desirability of speed in the collection process and the fact that, by reason of advances made, the transferor may have the paramount interest in the item requires the rule.

The Section is made subject to the provisions of Article 3 concerning conversion of instruments (Section 3–419) and other provisions of Article 3 and this Article concerning restrictive indorsements (Sections 3–205, 3–206, 3–419, 3–603, 4–205). Of course instructions from or an agreement with its transferor does not relieve a collecting bank of its general obligation to exercise good faith and ordinary care. See Section 4–103(1). If in any particular case a bank has exercised good faith and ordinary care and is relieved of responsibility by reason of instructions of or an agreement with its transferor, the owner of the item may still have a remedy for loss against the transferor (another bank) if such transferor has given wrongful instructions.

The rules of the Section are applied only to collecting banks. Payor banks always have the problem of making proper payment of an item; whether such payment is proper should be based upon all of the rules of Articles 3 and 4 and all of the facts of any particular case, and should not be dependent exclusively upon instructions from or an agreement with a person presenting the item.

Cross References:

Sections 3–205, 3–206, 3–419, 3–603, 4–103(1) and 4–205.

Definitional Cross References:

"Collecting bank". Section 4–105.
"Restrictive indorsement". Section 3–205.

Section 4–204. Methods of Sending and Presenting; Sending Direct to Payor Bank.

(1) A collecting bank must send items by reasonably prompt method taking into consideration any relevant instructions, the nature of the item, the number of such items on hand, and the cost of collection involved and the method generally used by it or others to present such items.

(2) A collecting bank may send

(a) any item direct to the payor bank;

(b) any item to any non-bank payor if authorized by its transferor; and

(c) any item other than documentary drafts to any non–bank payor, if authorized by Federal Reserve regulation or operating letter, clearing house rule or the like.

(3) Presentment may be made by a presenting bank at a place where the payor bank has requested that presentment be made.

New York Annotations

(1) Generally in *accord* with N.I.L., § 350–e, except that the Code provision sets forth specific factors to be considered.

(2) Generally in *accord* with N.I.L., § 350–e, except that the rule permitting direct sending to non-bank payors, now supported by Regulations G and J as to Federal Reserve banks, is extended to other non-bank payors where the transferor's authorization is obtained.

No New York cases on this point have been found.

Historical Note: While the present ABA Code in New York and other states makes no provision for forwarding certain items directly to non-bank payors (a clearing house practice of long standing in many cities), subsection (2) was added to provide affirmatively for clearing house practices of this kind where the practice is of such long standing and has worked as well as it has. (1956 Recommendations, p. 142; Excerpts, p. 422.)

Official Uniform Comment

Prior Uniform Statutory Provision: None; but see Section 6, American Bankers Association Bank Collection Code.

Purposes:

1. Subsection (1) prescribes the general standards applicable to proper sending or forwarding of items. Because of the many types of methods available and the desirability of preserving flexibility any attempt to prescribe limited or precise methods is avoided.

2. Subsection (2)(a) codifies the practice of direct mail, express, messenger or like presentment to payor banks. The practice is now country-wide and is justified by the need for speed, the general responsibility of banks, Federal Deposit Insurance protection and other reasons.

3. Full approval of the practice of direct sending is limited to cases where a bank is a payor. Where non-bank drawees or payors may be of unknown responsibility, substantial risks may be attached to placing in their hands the instruments calling for payments from them. This is obviously so in the case of documentary drafts. However, in some cities practices have long existed under clearing house procedures to forward certain types of items to certain non-bank payors. Examples include insurance loss drafts drawn by field agents on home offices. For the purpose of leaving the door open to legitimate practices of this kind, subsection (2)(c) affirmatively approves direct sending of any item other than documentary drafts to any non-bank payor, if authorized by Federal Reserve regulation or operation letter, clearing house rule or the like. On the other hand subsection (2)(b) approves sending any item direct to a non-bank payor if authorized by a collecting bank's transferor. This permits special instructions or agreements out of the norm and is consistent with the "chain of command" theory of Section 4–203. However, if a transferor other than the owner of the item, e.g., a prior collecting bank, authorizes a direct sending to a nonbank payor, such transferor assumes responsibility for the propriety or impropriety of such authorization.

4. Section 3–504 states how presentment is made and subsection (2) of that Section affirmatively approves three specific methods by which presentment may be made. The methods so specified are permissive and do not foreclose other possible methods. However, in view of the substantial increase in recent years of presentment at centralized bookkeeping centers and electronic processing centers maintained or used by payor banks, many of which are at locations other than the banks themselves, subsection (3) specifically approves presentment by a presenting bank at any place requested by the payor bank. [This paragraph was added in 1962.]

Cross References:

Sections 3–504, 4–501 and 4–502.

Definitional Cross References:

"Collecting bank". Section 4–105.

"Documentary draft". Section 4–104.
"Item". Section 4–104.
"Payor bank". Section 4–105.
"Presenting bank". Section 4–105.

Section 4–205. Supplying Missing Indorsements; No Notice From Prior Indorsements.

(1) A depositary bank which has taken an item for collection may supply any indorsement of the customer which is necessary to title unless the item contains the words "payee's indorsement required" or the like. In the absence of such a requirement a statement placed on the item by the depositary bank to the effect that the item was deposited by a customer or credited to his account is effective as the customer's indorsement.

(2) An intermediary bank, or payor bank which is not a depositary bank, is neither given notice nor otherwise affected by a restrictive indorsement of any person except the bank's immediate transferor.

New York Annotations

(1) This subsection, permitting the depository bank to supply the customer's missing indorsement, is new, but it reflects common banking practice. Compare N.I.L., §§ 60 and 79.

(2) This subsection would permit a collecting or payor bank to disregard conditions, trusts, and agencies created by the indorsement of any indorser except the immediate transferor. Compare N.I.L., §§ 66 and 67. This would change the rule of Soma v. Handrulis, 277 N.Y. 223, 14 N.E.2d 46 (1938), charging an intermediary bank with notice of the original depositor's interest by virtue of a restrictive ("for deposit") indorsement.

Historical Note: The revision of subsection (2), coupled with new language in Sections 3–205, 3–206, 3–419, and 4–203, left depositary banks responsible for acting consistently with restrictive indorsements, but, in the interest of speed and efficiency in the bank collection process, exempted from this responsibility intermediary banks and payor banks which are not depositary banks. (1956 Recommendations, p. 143.)

Official Uniform Comment

Prior Uniform Statutory Provision: None.

Purposes:

1. Subsection (1) is designed to speed up collections by eliminating any necessity to return to a non-bank depositor any items he may have failed to indorse.

2. For the purpose of permitting items to move rapidly through banking channels, intermediary banks and payor banks which are not also depositary banks are permitted to ignore restrictive indorsements of any person except the bank's immediate transferor. However, depositary banks may not so ignore restrictive indorsements. If an owner of an item indorses it "for deposit" or "for collection" he usually does so in the belief such indorsement will guard against further negotiation of the item to a holder in due course by a finder or a thief. This belief is reasonably justified if at least one bank in any chain of banks collecting the item has a responsibility to act consistently with the indorsement.

Cross References:

Sections 3–205, 3–206, 3–419, 3–603 and 4–203.

Definitional Cross References:

"Collecting bank". Section 4–105.
"Customer". Section 4–104.
"Depositary bank". Section 4–105.
"Intermediary bank". Section 4–105.
"Item". Section 4–104.
"Payor bank". Section 4–105.
"Restrictive indorsement". Section 3–205.

Section 4–206. Transfer Between Banks.

Any agreed method which identifies the transferor bank is sufficient for the item's further transfer to another bank.

New York Annotations

This section is new and is designed to simplify and expedite inter–bank transfer. Presumably any type of machine encoding or marking would suffice. Since the "transfer" between banks contemplated is not the same as an N.I.L. "negotiation", this provision is probably not inconsistent with N.I.L., § 60, requiring the indorsement of an order instrument for "negotiation".

Official Uniform Comment

Prior Uniform Statutory Provision: None.

Purposes:

This section is designed to permit the simplest possible form of transfer from one bank to another, once an item gets in the bank collection chain, provided only identity of the transferor bank is preserved. This is important for tracing purposes and if recourse is necessary. However, since the responsibilities of the various banks appear in the Article it becomes unnecessary to have liability or responsibility depend on more formal indorsements. Simplicity in the form of transfer is conducive to speed. Where the transfer is between banks this section takes the place of the more formal requirements of Section 3–202.

Cross References:

Section 3–201, 3–202.

Definitional Cross References:

"Bank". Section 1–201.
"Item". Section 4–104.

Section 4–207. Warranties of Customer and Collecting Bank on Transfer or Presentment of Items; Time for Claims.

(1) Each customer or collecting bank who obtains payment or acceptance of an item and each prior customer and collecting bank warrants to the payor bank or other payor who in good faith pays or accepts the item that

(a) he has a good title to the item or is authorized to obtain payment or acceptance on behalf of one who has a good title; and

(b) he has no knowledge that the signature of the maker or drawer is unauthorized, except that this warranty is not given by any customer or collecting bank that is a holder in due course and acts in good faith

(i) to a maker with respect to the maker's own signature; or

(ii) to a drawer with respect to the drawer's own signature, whether or not the drawer is also the drawee; or

(iii) to an acceptor of an item if the holder in due course took the item after the acceptance or obtained the acceptance without knowledge that the drawer's signature was unauthorized; and

(c) the item has not been materially altered, except that this warranty is not given by any customer or collecting bank that is a holder in due course and acts in good faith

(i) to the maker of a note; or

(ii) to the drawer of a draft whether or not the drawer is also the drawee; or

(iii) to the acceptor of an item with respect to an alteration made prior to the acceptance if the holder in due course took the item after the acceptance, even though the acceptance provided "payable as originally drawn" or equivalent terms; or

(iv) to the acceptor of an item with respect to an alteration made after the acceptance.

(2) Each customer and collecting bank who transfers an item and receives a settlement or other consideration for it warrants to his transferee and to any subsequent collecting bank who takes the item in good faith that

(a) he has a good title to the item or is authorized to obtain payment or acceptance on behalf of one who has a good title and the transfer is otherwise rightful; and

(b) all signatures are genuine or authorized; and

(c) the item has not been materially altered; and

(d) no defense of any party is good against him; and

(e) he has no knowledge of any insolvency proceeding instituted with respect to the maker or acceptor or the drawer of an unaccepted item.

In addition each customer and collecting bank so transferring an item and receiving a settlement or other consideration engages that upon dishonor and any necessary notice of dishonor and protest he will take up the item.

(3) The warranties and the engagement to honor set forth in the two preceding subsections arise notwithstanding the absence of indorsement or words of guaranty or warranty in the transfer or presentment and a collecting bank remains liable for their breach despite remittance to its transferor. Damages for breach

of such warranties or engagement to honor shall not exceed the consideration received by the customer or collecting bank responsible plus finance charges and expenses related to the item, if any.

(4) Unless a claim for breach of warranty under this section is made within a reasonable time after the person claiming learns of the breach, the person liable is discharged to the extent of any loss caused by the delay in making claim.

New York Annotations

(1) and (2). These subsections are virtually identical with subsections (1) and (2) of Section 3–417, except that they are limited to "customers and collecting banks" and they cover "items", a broader category than the instruments governed by Article 3. By contrast, Section 3–417(1) is applicable to "any person who obtains payment or acceptance and any prior transferor", and Section 3–417(2) is applicable only to "persons who transfer an instrument". See the annotations to subsections (1) and (2) of Section 3–417. The extension of the statutory warranty to operate in favor of the payor is new.

(3) The provision for a warranty remedy even in the absence of an indorsement is new. See, however, N.I.L., § 115 (Warranty; where negotiation by delivery). This subsection would limit recovery to the extent of "the consideration received by the customer or collecting bank responsible plus finance charges and expenses relating to the item, if any". Compare Corn Exchange Bank v. Nassau Bank, 91 N.Y. 74 (1883); Whitney v. National Bank, 45 N.Y. 303 (1871).

(4) This is new law.

Historical Note: Sections 3–417 and 4–207 were completely redrafted to remove inconsistencies between the two sections. The deletion of the warranty to payors of no knowledge of a stop payment order evidences no intent to change the common law insofar as there are common law decisions on the question. (1956 Recommendations, p. 146; Excerpts, p. 423.)

Official Uniform Comment

Prior Uniform Statutory Provision: None; but see American Bankers Association Bank Collection Code, Section 4.

Purposes:

1. Subject to certain exceptions peculiar to the bank collection process and except that they apply only to customers and collecting banks, the warranties and engagements to honor in this section are identical in substance with those provided in the Article on Commercial Paper (Article 3). See Sections 3–414, 3–417. For a more complete explanation of the purposes of these warranties and engagements see the Comments to Sections 3–414 and 3–417.

2. In addition to imposing upon customers and collecting banks the warranties and engagements imposed by the original Sections 65 and 66 of the Uniform Negotiable Instruments Law and those of Sections 3–414 and 3–417 of Article 3, with some variations, this Section 4–207 is intended to give the effect presently obtained in bank collections by the words "prior indorsements guaranteed" in collection transfers and presentments between banks. The warranties and engagements arise automatically as a part of the bank collection process. Receipt of a settlement or other consideration by a customer or collecting bank is a requirement but any settlement is sufficient regardless of whether the settlement is concurrent with the transfer as in the case

of a cash item, or delayed, as in the case of a non-cash straight collection item. Further, the warranties and engagements run with the item with the result that a collecting bank may sue a remote prior collecting bank or a remote customer and thus avoid multiplicity of suits. This section is also intended to make it clear that the so-called equitable defense of "payment over" does not apply to a collecting bank and that no statute of frauds provision will defeat recovery. Subsections (2) and (3) indicate that these results are intended notwithstanding the absence of indorsement or words of guarantee or warranty in a transfer or presentment. Consequently, if for purposes of simplification or the speeding up of the bank collection process, banks desire to cut down the length or size of indorsements (Section 4–206), they may do so and the standard warranties and engagements to honor still apply.

3. With respect to the exceptions to the warranties in favor of a holder in due course specified in sub-paragraphs (b) and (c) of subsection (1), collecting banks usually have holder in due course status (Sections 4–208, 4–209). However, if in any case there is a holder in due course but a subsequent collecting bank does not have holder in due course status (e.g., in a straight non-cash collection where no settlement of any kind is made until the bank itself receives final settlement) the bank still has the benefit of the exceptions (if it acts in good faith) under the shelter provisions of Section 3–201. It is to be noted that these shelter provisions, by virtue of successive transfers, benefit not only the immediate transferee from a holder in due course but also subsequent transferees.

4. In this section as in Section 3–417, the (a), (b) and (c) warranties to transferees and collecting banks under subsection (2) are in general similar to the (a), (b) and (c) warranties to payors under subsection (1); but the warranties to payors are less inclusive because of exceptions reflecting the rule of Price v. Neal, 3 Burr, 1354 (1762), and related principles. See Comment to Section 3–417. Thus collecting banks are given not only all the warranties given to payors by subsection (1), without those exceptions, but also the (d) and (e) warranties of subsection (2).

5. The last sentence of subsection (3) provides that damages for breach of warranties or the engagement to honor shall not exceed the consideration received by the customer or collecting bank responsible "plus finance charges and expenses related to the item, if any". The "expenses" referred to in this phrase may be ordinary collecting expenses and in appropriate cases could also include such expenses as attorneys fees. "Finance charges" are also referred to because in some cases interest or a finance charge is charged by the collecting bank for the time that the bank's advance on the item is outstanding prior to receipt of proceeds of collection. An example of this type of case would be where a bank undertakes a foreign collection in South America or Europe and makes an advance on the item at the time of receipt but may not receive proceeds of the foreign collection for three months or more.

Cross References:

Sections 3–201, 3–414, 3–417, 3–418, 4–206, 4–208, 4–209 and 4–406.

Definitional Cross References:

"Collecting bank". Section 4–105.
"Customer". Section 4–104.
"Draft". Section 3–104.
"Genuine". Section 1–201.
"Good faith". Section 1–201.
"Holder". Section 1–201.
"Holder in due course". Section 3–302.
"Insolvency proceedings". Section 1–201.
"Item". Section 4–104.

"Party". Section 1–201.
"Payor bank". Section 4–105.
"Person". Section 1–201.
"Presentment". Section 3–504.
"Protest". Section 3–509.
"Unauthorized signature". Section 1–201.

Section 4–208. Security Interest of Collecting Bank in Items, Accompanying Documents and Proceeds.

(1) A bank has a security interest in an item and any accompanying documents or the proceeds of either

(a) in case of an item deposited in an account to the extent to which credit given for the item has been withdrawn or applied;

(b) in case of an item for which it has given credit available for withdrawal as of right, to the extent of the credit given whether or not the credit is drawn upon and whether or not there is a right of charge–back; or

(c) if it makes an advance on or against the item.

(2) When credit which has been given for several items received at one time or pursuant to a single agreement is withdrawn or applied in part the security interest remains upon all the items, any accompanying documents or the proceeds of either. For the purpose of this section, credits first given are first withdrawn.

(3) Receipt by a collecting bank of a final settlement for an item is a realization on its security interest in the item, accompanying documents and proceeds. To the extent and so long as the bank does not receive final settlement for the item or give up possession of the item or accompanying documents for purposes other than collection, the security interest continues and is subject to the provisions of Article 9 except that

(a) no security agreement is necessary to make the security interest enforceable (subsection (1)(b) of Section 9–203); and

(b) no filing is required to perfect the security interest; and

(c) the security interest has priority over conflicting perfected security interests in the item, accompanying documents or proceeds.

New York Annotations

(1) *Accords* generally with result of N.I.L., § 350–a, except that the Code gives a security interest rather than title.

(2) New York decisional law has followed the "first-in, first-out" rule. Merchants National Bank v. Santa Maria Sugar Co., 162 App.Div. 248, 147 N.Y.S. 498, aff'd mem. 220 N.Y. 732, 116 N.E. 1061 (1917).

(3) This is new law and correlates the security interest of a collecting bank with the provisions of Article 9.

Historical Note: This section was completely revised to reflect more accurately the self-liquidating nature of a collecting bank's security interest, and to correlate such security interest with the provisions of Article 9. (1956 Recommendations, p. 148.)

Official Uniform Comment

Prior Uniform Statutory Provision: None; but see American Bankers Association Bank Collection Code, Section 2.

Purposes:

1. Subsection (1) states a rational rule for the interest of a bank in an item. The customer of the depositary bank is normally the owner of the item and the several collecting banks are his agents (Section 4–201). A collecting agent may properly make advances on the security of paper held by him for collection, and when he does acquires at common law a possessory lien for his advances. Subsection (1) applies an analogous principle to a bank in the collection chain which extends credit on items in the course of collection. The bank has a security interest to the extent stated in this section. To the extent of its security interest it is a holder for value (Section 3–303, 4–209) and a holder in due course if it satisfies the other requirements for that status (Section 3–302). Subsection (1) does not derogate from the banker's general common-law lien or right of set-off against indebtedness owing in deposit accounts. See Section 1–103. Rather subsection (1) specifically implements and extends the principle as a part of the bank collection process.

2. Subsection (2) spreads the security interest of the bank over all items in a single deposit or received under a single agreement and a single giving of credit. It also adopts the "first-in, first-out" rule.

3. Collection statistics establish that in excess of ninety-nine per cent of items handled for collection are in fact collected. The first sentence of subsection (3) reflects the fact that in such normal case the bank's security interest is self-liquidating. The remainder of the subsection correlates the security interest with the provisions of Article 9, particularly for use in the cases of non-collection where the security interest may be important.

Cross References:

Sections 3–302, 3–303, 4–201, 4–209, 9–203(1)(b) and 9–302.

Definitional Cross References:

"Account". Section 4–104.
"Agreement". Section 1–201.
"Bank". Section 1–201.
"Item". Section 4–104.
"Security interest". Section 1–201.
"Settlement". Section 4–104.

Section 4–209. When Bank Gives Value for Purposes of Holder in Due Course.

For purposes of determining its status as a holder in due course, the bank has given value to the extent that it has a security interest in an item provided that the bank otherwise complies with the requirements of Section 3–302 on what constitutes a holder in due course.

New York Annotations

Generally in accord with N.I.L., § 53. Under the N.I.L. a bank is treated as a holder for value only to the extent it permits actual withdrawals. Bath National Bank v. Sonnenstrahl, 249 N.Y. 391, 164 N.E. 327 (1928). See definition of "value" in Section 1–201(44)(a).

Official Uniform Comment

Prior Uniform Statutory Provision: Negotiable Instruments Law, Section 27.

Purposes:

The section completes the thought of the previous section and makes clear that a security interest in an item is "value" for the purpose of determining the holder's status as a holder in due course. The provision is in accord with the prior law (N.I.L. Section 27) and with Article 3 (Section 3–303). The section does not prescribe a security interest under Section 4–208 as a test of "value" generally because the meaning of "value" under other Articles is adequately defined in Section 1–201.

Cross References:

Sections 1–201, 3–302, 3–303 and 4–208.

Definitional Cross References:

"Bank". Section 1–201.
"Holder in due course". Section 3–302.
"Item". Section 4–104.
"Security interest". Section 1–201.

Section 4–210. Presentment by Notice of Item Not Payable by, Through or at a Bank; Liability of Secondary Parties.

(1) Unless otherwise instructed, a collecting bank may present an item not payable by, through or at a bank by sending to the party to accept or pay a written notice that the bank holds the item for acceptance or payment. The notice must be sent in time to be received on or before the day when presentment is due and the bank must meet any requirement of the party to accept or pay under Section 3–505 by the close of the bank's next banking day after it knows of the requirement.

(2) Where presentment is made by notice and neither honor nor request for compliance with a requirement under Section 3–505 is received by the close of business on the day after maturity or in the case of demand items by the close of business on the third banking day after notice was sent, the presenting bank may treat the item as dishonored and charge any secondary party by sending him notice of the facts.

New York Annotations

This section, validating notice presentment of items drawn on non-bank payors, represents a change from the present requirements governing presentment. See N.I.L.,

Article 8, particularly § 134 (Instrument must be exhibited). See also Parker v. Stroud, 98 N.Y. 379 (1885).

Official Uniform Comment

Prior Uniform Statutory Provision: None.

Purposes:

1. This section codifies a practice extensively followed in presentation of trade acceptances and documentary and other drafts drawn on non-bank payors. It imposes a duty on the payor to respond to the notice of the item if the item is not to be considered dishonored. Notice of such a dishonor charges parties secondarily liable. Presentment under this Section is good presentment under Article 3. See Section 3–504(5).

2. A drawee not receiving notice is not, of course, liable to the drawer for wrongful dishonor.

3. A bank so presenting an instrument must be sufficiently close to the drawee to be able to exhibit the instrument on the day it is requested to do so or the next business day at the latest.

Cross References:

Sections 3–501 through 3–508, 5–501 and 4–502.

Definitional Cross References:

"Acceptance". Section 3–410.
"Banking day". Section 4–104.
"Collecting bank". Section 4–105.
"Item". Section 4–104.
"Party". Section 1–201.
"Presentment". Section 3–504.
"Secondary party". Section 3–102.
"Send". Section 1–201.

Section 4–211. Media of Remittance; Provisional and Final Settlement in Remittance Cases.

(1) A collecting bank may take in settlement of an item

(a) a check of the remitting bank or of another bank on any bank except the remitting bank; or

(b) a cashier's check or similar primary obligation of a remitting bank which is a member of or clears through a member of the same clearing house or group as the collecting bank, or

(c) appropriate authority to charge an account of the remitting bank or of another bank with the collecting bank; or

(d) if the item is drawn: upon or payable by a person other than a bank, a cashier's check, certified check or other bank check or obligation.

(2) If before its midnight deadline the collecting bank properly dishonors a remittance check or authorization to charge on itself or presents or forwards

for collection a remittance instrument of or on another bank which is of a kind approved by subsection (1) or has not been authorized by it, the collecting bank is not liable to prior parties in the event of the dishonor of such check, instrument or authorization.

(3) A settlement for an item by means of a remittance instrument or authorization to charge is or becomes a final settlement as to both the person making and the person receiving the settlement

(a) if the remittance instrument or authorization to charge is of a kind approved by subsection (1) or has not been authorized by the person receiving the settlement and in either case the person receiving the settlement acts seasonably before its midnight deadline in presenting, forwarding for collection or paying the instrument or authorization,—at the time the remittance instrument or authorization is finally paid by the payor by which it is payable;

(b) if the person receiving the settlement has authorized remittance by a non-bank check or obligation or by a cashier's check or similar primary obligation of or a check upon the payor or other remitting bank which is not of a kind approved by subsection (1)(b),—at the time of the receipt of such remittance check or obligation; or

(c) if in a case not covered by sub-paragraphs (a) or (b) the person receiving the settlement fails to seasonably present, forward for collection, pay or return a remittance instrument or authorization to it to charge before its midnight deadline,—at such midnight deadline.

New York Annotations

(1)(a) Generally in *accord* with N.I.L., §§ 350–h and 350–i.

(b) This new law except as may be implied from the language of N.I.L., §§ 350–h and 350–i, approving "such method of settlement as may be customary."

(c) This is new law except as may be implied by custom (see comment to (b) next above) and by the proviso at the end of N.I.L., § 350–h.

(d) This is new law except as may be implied by custom (see comment to (b) above). See also N.I.L., § 350–h(b).

(2) This subsection complements subsection (1) by relieving a collecting bank from liability for taking a form of remittance approved in subsection (1), and would also permit a collecting bank to attempt to collect an improper remittance without liability for failure to collect. Compare N.I.L., §§ 350–h and 350–i.

(3) This subsection clarifies the question of when the remittance instrument becomes a final settlement. See N.I.L., §§ 350–b and 350–j; Jones v. Board of Education, 242 App.Div. 17, 272 N.Y.S. 5 (1934); United States Pipe & Foundry Co. v. City of Hornell, 146 Misc. 812, 263 N.Y.S. 89 (1933); In re Jayne & Mason, 140 Misc. 822, 251 N.Y.S. 768 (1931). The time of final settlement is involved in Sections 4–201, 4–212, 4–213, and 4–214.

Historical Note. The addition of subsection (3), in response to a criticism made by the Law Revision Commission, was designed to state more precisely when final settlement occurs in remittance cases. (1956 Recommendations, p. 150; Excerpts, pp. 424–425.)

Official Uniform Comment

Prior Uniform Statutory Provision: None; but see Sections 9 and 10, American Bankers Association Bank Collection Code.

Purposes:

1. Subsection (1) states various types of remittance instruments and authorities to charge which may be received by a collecting bank in a settlement for an item, without the collecting bank being responsible if such form of remittance is not itself paid. The action of the collecting bank in receiving these provisional forms of remittance is approved and the risk that they are not paid is placed on the owner of the item, and not on the collecting bank. Justification for these results lies in the fact that with the tremendous volume of items collected it is simply not mechanically feasible to remit or pay in money or other forms of technical "legal tender". Since it is not feasible for banks to perform their collection functions except with the use of these provisional remittances, they should not be penalized for acting in the only way they can act.

2. The first approved form of provisional remittance having these results is a check of the remitting bank or of another bank on any bank except the remitting bank (subsection (1)(a)). A check on the remitting bank itself is not approved because this would merely be substituting for the original item another time on the same payor.

3. A cashier's check or similar primary obligation of the remitting bank which is a member of or clears through a member of the same clearing house or group as the collecting bank is approved by subsection (1)(b) because this is just as speedy and effective a means of settlement through a clearing house as any other type of instrument or a check on another bank. On the other hand such cashier's checks or primary obligations are not approved for use, at the owner's risk, outside a single clearing house or clearing area because when so used they do not constitute a means of final settlement but merely substitute one item on the remitting bank for another one on the same bank. To the remitting bank they may have benefit in maintaining "float" or having the use of money even though drawn against, but this is not looked upon as sound practice.

4. Subsection (1)(d) recognizes and approves the general and consistent practice of collecting banks to accept cashier's checks, certified checks or other bank checks or obligations as a proper means of remittance from non-bank payors, with the owner of the original item carrying the risk of non-payment of these bank instruments rather than the collecting bank, to the extent there is any risk. Here again this rule and practice is justified by the fact that payment in money for all practical purposes is no longer feasible and consequently is not used except in rare instances. Subsection (1)(d) recognizes the standard medium that is used.

5. This section does not purport to deal with all kinds of settlements for items. It does not purport to deal with settlements for "cash items" (described in Comments to Section 4–212), settlements merely by debits and credits in accounts between banks (Section 4–213) or settlements through clearing houses. The section is limited to those situations where a collecting or payor bank or a non-bank payor receives an item and accounts for it by "remitting" or "sending back" something for the item, usually some form of a remittance instrument, order or authorization. Some specific rules are needed for remittance cases because of time required to process the remittance instrument.

Failure to mention in subsection (1) entries in accounts between banks and clearing house settlements carries no implication of impropriety of these types of provisional or final settlement. Approval of these means of settlement is evidenced by the definition of "settle" in Section 4–104(j), provision for charge-back and refund in Section 4–212, and provisions regarding settlements becoming final (Section 4–213).

Further, the specific listing in subsection (1) of certain usual types of remittances does not imply that all other types of remittance are improper (Section 4–103(4)).

6. Subsection (2) provides that if a remittance is one of the kinds approved by subsection (1) and the collecting bank receiving the item acts seasonably in handling it before the bank's midnight deadline, the bank is not liable to prior parties in the event of dishonor. The subsection also provides for an additional situation. If without any authorization whatsoever the payor or remitting bank or person remits with an improper remittance instrument, the collecting bank should not be penalized where it is without fault. Nevertheless, the owner of the item may not be served if the collecting bank rejects the improper instrument. In many cases the best course would be to collect the instrument as rapidly as possible. Subsection (2) provides that if this is done the collecting bank is not responsible in the event of dishonor.

7. Subsection (3) complements subsections (1) and (2) by providing when a settlement by means of a remittance instrument or authorization to charge becomes final. Subparagraph (a) provides that in situations specified in subsection (2) the settlement becomes final at the time the remittance instrument or authorization is finally paid by the payor by which it is payable. The standards determining this final payment are those prescribed in Section 4–213. Conversely, under subparagraph (b) if the person receiving the settlement has authorized remittance by certain specified media not approved by subsection (1) the settlement becomes final at the time of receipt of such check or obligation. In this event the person receiving the settlement assumes the risk that the remittance instrument is not itself paid. A prior course of dealing of receiving unapproved forms of remittances from the payor or remitting person in question would be the equivalent of an authorization and effective as such. Subparagraph (c) provides for most, if not all, remaining remittance situations. Here settlement becomes final at the midnight deadline of the person receiving the remittance.

Subsection (3) provides that the times of final settlement prescribed apply both to the person making and the person receiving the settlement. Further, by use of the term "person", these rules also apply to non-bank payors of items and non-bank customers for whom items are being collected, as well as to collecting and payor banks.

8. When settlement is by credit in an account with another bank Section 4–213 controls.

Cross References:

Section 4–213.

Definitional Cross References:

"Account". Section 4–104.
"Bank". Section 1–201.
"Clearing house". Section 4–104.
"Collecting bank". Section 4–105.
"Item". Section 4–104.
"Midnight deadline". Section 4–104.
"Money". Section 1–201.
"Payor bank." Section 4–105.
"Person". Section 1–201.
"Remitting bank". Section 5–105.
"Settle". Section 4–104.

Section 4–212. Right of Charge-Back or Refund.

(1) If a collecting bank has made provisional settlement with its customer for an item and itself fails by reason of dishonor, suspension of payments by

a bank or otherwise to receive a settlement for the item which is or becomes final, the bank may revoke the settlement given by it, charge back the amount of any credit given for the item to its customer's account or obtain refund from its customer, whether or not it is able to return the items if by its midnight deadline or within a longer reasonable time after it learns the facts it returns the item or sends notification of the facts. These rights to revoke, charge-back and obtain refund terminate if and when a settlement for the item received by the bank is or becomes final (subsection (3) of Section 4–211 and subsections (2) and (3) of Section 4–213).

(2) Within the time and manner prescribed by this section and Section 4–301, an intermediary or payor bank, as the case may be, may return an unpaid item directly to the depositary bank and may send for collection a draft on the depositary bank and obtain reimbursement. In such case, if the depositary bank has received provisional settlement for the item, it must reimburse the bank drawing the draft and any provisional credits for the item between banks shall become and remain final.

(3) A depositary bank which is also the payor may charge back the amount of an item to its customer's account or obtain refund in accordance with the section governing return of an item received by a payor bank for credit on its books (Section 4–301).

(4) The right to charge-back is not affected by

(a) prior use of the credit given for the item; or

(b) failure by any bank to exercise ordinary care with respect to the item but any bank so failing remains liable.

(5) A failure to charge-back or claim refund does not affect other rights of the bank against the customer or any other party.

(6) If credit is given in dollars as the equivalent of the value of an item payable in a foreign currency the dollar amount of any charge-back or refund shall be calculated on the basis of the buying sight rate for the foreign currency prevailing on the day when the person entitled to the charge-back or refund learns that it will not receive payment in ordinary course.

New York Annotations

(1) Generally in *accord* with but more liberal than N.I.L., §§ 350–a and 350–b.

(2) This optional provision is new law.

(3) This is a cross-reference provision to be read in conjunction with Section 4–301.

(4) and (5) These subsections contain new law as to which no New York authority was found.

(6) The New York courts have generally ruled that the breach date shall control what rate of exchange shall be applied in determining the dollar equivalent of a foreign currency and the foreign currency equivalent of U. S. dollars. Hoppe v. Russo Asiatic Bank, 235 N.Y. 37, 138 N.E. 497 (1923); DeSayve v. De La Valdene, 124 N.Y.S.2d 143, 154–155, aff'd 283 App.Div. 218, 130 N.Y.S.2d 865 (1954).

Historical Note: Changes in subsection (1), correlative with changes in Sections 4–211, 4–213, and 4–214, were designed to obtain greater precision and accuracy in provisions for final settlement and related rights of charge back, refund, and the like. Subsection (6) states the rate of exchange rule customarily followed today, in the absence of an agreement between the customer and the bank. Subsection (6) is applicable not only in cases where a credit entered is provisional, but also where it may be final but a right to a charge-back or refund still exists. (1956 Recommendations, p. 152; Excerpts, pp. 425–426.)

Official Uniform Comment

Prior Uniform Statutory Provision: None; but see Sections 2 and 11, American Bankers Association Bank Collection Code.

Purposes:

1. Under current bank practice, in a major portion of cases banks make provisional settlement for items when they are first received and then await subsequent determination of whether the item will be finally paid. This is the principal characteristic of what are referred to in banking parlance as "cash items". Statistically, this practice of settling provisionally first and then awaiting final payment is justified because more than ninety-nine per cent of such cash items are finally paid, with the result that in this great preponderance of cases it becomes unnecessary for the banks making the provisional settlements to make any further entries. In due course the provisional settlements become final simply with the lapse of time. However, in those cases where the item being collected is not finally paid or where for various reasons the bank making the provisional settlement does not itself receive final payment, under the American Bankers Association Bank Collection Code, under Federal Reserve Regulations and operating letters and under various types of agreements between banks and between customers and banks, provision is made for the reversal of the provisional settlements, charge-back of provisional credits and the right to obtain refund. Subsection (1) codifies and simplifies the statement of these rights.

2. Various causes of a bank not receiving final payment, with the resulting right of charge back or refund, are stated or suggested in subsection (1) These include dishonor of the original item; dishonor of a remittance instrument given for it; reversal of a provisional credit for the item; suspension of payments by another bank. The causes stated are illustrative; the right of charge-back or refund is stated to exist whether the failure to receive final payment in ordinary course arises through one of them "or otherwise."

3. The right of charge-back or refund exists if a collecting bank has made a provisional settlement for an item with its customer but terminates if and when a settlement received by the bank for the item is or becomes final. If the bank fails to receive such a final settlement the right of charge-back or refund must be exercised promptly after the bank learns the facts. The right exists (if so promptly exercised) whether or not the bank is able to return the item.

4. Subsection (2) is an affirmative provision for so-called "direct returns." This is a new practice that is currently in the process of developing in a few sections of the country. Its purpose is to speed up the return of unpaid items by avoiding handling by one or more intermediate banks. The subsection is bracketed because the practice is not yet well established and some bankers and bank lawyers would prefer to let the practice develop by agreement. The contention is made that substantive rights between banks may be affected, e.g. available set-offs, but proponents contend advantages of direct returns outweigh possible detriments. However, if the subsection were omitted, the election to use direct returns would be on the depositary bank and

it would probably be necessary for that bank to specifically authorize direct returns with each outgoing letter. This is a cumbersome way of meeting the problem. If the subsection is retained the payor bank, unless it has been specifically directed otherwise, will have the right to make the decision whether it will return an unpaid item directly. Since the subsection is permissive and its inclusion tends toward greater flexibility, its retention is recommended. The rule of subsection (4) relating to charge-back (as distinguished from claim for refund) applies irrespective of the cause of the nonpayment, and of the person ultimately liable for nonpayment. Thus charge-back is permitted even where nonpayment results from the depositary bank's own negligence. Any other rule would result in litigation based upon a claim for wrongful dishonor of other checks of the customer, with potential damages far in excess of the amount of the item. Any other rule would require a bank to determine difficult questions of fact. The customer's protection is found in the general obligation of good faith (Sections 1–203 and 4–103). If bad faith is established the customer's recovery "includes other damages, if any, suffered by the party as a proximate consequence" (Section 4–103(5) see also Section 4–402).

6. It is clear that the charge back does not relieve the bank from any liability for failure to exercise ordinary care in handling the item. The measure of damages for such failure is stated in Section 4–103(5).

7. Subsection (6) states a rule fixing the time for determining the rate of exchange if there is a charge-back or refund of a credit given in dollars for an item payable in a foreign currency. Compare Section 3–107(2). Fixing such a rule is desirable to avoid disputes. If in any case the parties wish to fix a different time for determining the rate of exchange, they may do so by agreement.

Cross References:

Sections 1–203, 3–107, 4–103, 4–211(3), 4–213(2) and (3), 4–402.

Definitional Cross References:

"Account". Section 4–104.
"Collecting bank". Section 4–105.
"Customer". Section 4–104.
"Depositary bank". Section 4–105.
"Intermediary bank". Section 4–105.
"Item". Section 4–104.
"Midnight deadline". Section 4–104.
"Payor bank". Section 1–201.
"Send". Section 1–201.
"Settlement". Section 4–104.
"Suspension of payment". Section 4–104.

Section 4–213. Final Payment of Item by Payor Bank; When Provisional Debits and Credits Become Final; When Certain Credits Become Available for Withdrawal.

(1) An item is finally paid by a payor bank when the bank has done any of the following, whichever happens first:

(a) paid the item in cash; or

(b) settled for the item without reserving a right to revoke the settlement and without having such right under statute, clearing house rule or agreement; or

(c) completed the process of posting the item to the indicated account of the drawer, maker or other person to be charged therewith; or

(d) made a provisional settlement for the item and failed to revoke the settlement in the time and manner permitted by statute, clearing house rule or agreement.

Upon a final payment under subparagraphs (b), (c) or (d) the payor bank shall be accountable for the amount of the item.

(2) If provisional settlement for an item between the presenting and payor banks is made through a clearing house or by debits or credits in an account between them, then to the extent that provisional debits or credits for the item are entered in accounts between the presenting and payor banks or between the presenting and successive prior collecting banks seriatim, they become final upon final payment of the item by the payor bank.

(3) If a collecting bank receives a settlement for an item which is or becomes final (subsection (3) of Section 4–211, subsection (2) of Section 4–213) the bank is accountable to its customer for the amount of the item and any provisional credit given for the item in an account with its customer becomes final.

(4) Subject to any right of the bank to apply the credit to an obligation of the customer, credit given by a bank for an item in an account with its customer becomes available for withdrawal as of right

(a) in any case where the bank has received a provisional settlement for the item,—when such settlement becomes final and the bank has had a reasonable time to learn that the settlement is final;

(b) in any case where the bank is both a depositary bank and a payor bank and the item is finally paid,—at the opening of the bank's second banking day following receipt of the item.

(5) A deposit of money in a bank is final when made but, subject to any right of the bank to apply the deposit to an obligation of the customer, the deposit becomes available for withdrawal as of right at the opening of the bank's next banking day following receipt of the deposit.

UCC

New York Annotations

(1) Generally *accords* with N.I.L., § 350–b, but is more explicit. The express reference to payment by cash is not found in the present statute but accords with the common-law rule. See Oddie v. National City Bank, 45 N.Y. 735 (1871) (dictum). Compare, Manufacturers Trust Company v. Diamond, 17 Misc.2d 909, 186 N.Y.S.2d 917 (1959).

(2) Generally in *accord* with Columbia-Knickerbocker Trust Co. v. Miller, 215 N.Y. 191, 109 N.E. 179 (1915), and Leonardi v. The Chase National Bank, 263 App.Div. 552, 33 N.Y.S.2d 706, motion for leave to appeal denied, 289 N.Y. 852, 43 N.E.2d 357 (1942).

(3), (4), and (5) These subsections are new law but are generally in accord with present law and banking practice. See N.I.L., §§ 350–b, 350–i, and 350–j. See also Leonardi v. Chase National Bank, *supra.*

Historical Note: Subsection (1)(d) was added to cover one additional situation not covered in previous drafts. Subsections (3), (4), and (5), in substitution for former subsection (3), were added, in correlation with changes in Sections 4–211, 4–212, and 4–214, to state with greater precision rules of final settlement and related rules as to when credit for an item in an account becomes available for withdrawal as of right. (1956 Recommendations, pp. 154–155; Excerpts, pp. 426–428.)

Official Uniform Comment

Prior Uniform Statutory Provision: None; but see Section 11, American Bankers Association Bank Collection Code.

Purposes:

1. By the definition and use of the term "settle" (Section 4–104(j)) this Article recognizes that various debits or credits, remittances, settlements or payments given for an item may be either provisional or final, that settlements sometimes are provisional and sometimes are final and sometimes are provisional for awhile but later become final. Subsection (1) of Section 4–213 defines when settlement for an item or other action with respect to it constitutes final payment.

Final payment of an item is important for a number of reasons. It is one of several factors determining the relative priorities between items and notices, stop-orders, legal process and set-offs (Section 4–303). It is the "end of the line" in the collection process and the "turn around" point commencing the return flow of proceeds. It is the point at which many provisional settlements become final. See Section 4–213(2). Final payment of an item by the payor bank fixes preferential rights under Section 4–214(1) and (2).

2. If an item being collected moves through several states, e.g., is deposited for collection in California, moves through two or three California banks to the Federal Reserve Bank of San Francisco, to the Federal Reserve Bank of Boston, to a payor bank in Maine, the collection process involves the eastward journey of the item from California to Maine and the westward journey of the proceeds from Maine to California. Subsection (1) adopts the basic policy that final payment occurs at some point in the processing of the item by the payor bank. This policy recognizes that final payment does not take place, in such hypothetical case, on the journey of the item eastward. It also adopts the view that neither does final payment occur on the journey westward because what in fact is journeying westward are *proceeds* of the item. Because the true tests of final payment are the same in all cases and to avoid the confusion resulting from variable standards, the rule basing final payment exclusively on action of the payor bank is not affected by whether payment is made by a remittance draft or whether such draft is itself paid. Consequently, subsection (1) rejects those cases which base time of payment of the item in remittance cases on whether the remittance draft was *accepted* by the presenting bank; Page v. Holmes-Darst Coal Co., 269 Mich. 159, 256 N.W. 840 (1934); Tobiason v. First State Bank of Ashby, 173 Minn. 533, 217 N.W. 934 (1928); Bohlig v. First Nat. Bank in Wadena, 233 Minn. 523, 48 N.W.2d 445 (1951); Dewey v. Margolis & Brooks, 195 N.C. 307, 142 S.E. 22 (1928); Texas Electric Service Co. v. Clark, 47 S.W.2d 483 (Tex. Civ. App. 1932); cf. Ellis Way Drug Co. v. McLean, 176 Miss. 830, 170 So. 288 (1936); 2 Paton's Digest 1332; or whether the remittance draft was itself *paid;* Cleve v. Craven Chemical Co., 18 F.2d 711 (4th Cir. 1927); Holdingford Milling Co. v. Hillman Farmers' Cooperative Creamery, 181 Minn. 212, 231 N.W. 928 (1930); or upon an election of a collecting bank under Section 11 of the American Bankers Association Bank Collection Code; United States Pipe & Foundry Co. v. City of Hornell, 146 Misc. 812, 263 N.Y.S. 89 (1933); Jones v. Board of Education, 242 App.Div. 17,

272 N.Y.S. 5 (1934); Matter of State Bank of Binghamton, 156 Misc. 353, 281 N.Y.S. 706 (1935); cf. Malcolm, Inc. v. Burlington City Loan & Trust Co., 115 N.J. Eq. 227, 170 A. 32 (1934). Of course, the time of payment of the remittance draft will be governed by subsection (1) but payment or nonpayment of the remittance draft will not change the time of payment of the original item.

3. In fixing the point of time within the payor bank when an item is finally paid, subsection (1) recognizes and is framed on the basis that in a payor bank an item goes through a series of processes before its handling is completed. The item is received first from the clearing house or over the counter or through the mail. When received over the counter, the bank may receipt for it in some way by making a notation in the customer's passbook or by receipting a duplicate deposit slip. After the initial receipt the item moves to the sorting and proving departments. When sorted and proved it may be photographed. Still later it moves to the bookkeeping department where it is examined for form and signature and compared against the ledger account of the customer to whom it is to be charged. If it is in good form and there are funds to cover it, it is posted to the drawer's account, either immediately or at a later time. If paid, it is so marked and fled with other items of the same customer. This process may take either a few hours or substantially all of the day of receipt and of the next banking day.

Within this period of processing by the payor bank subsection (1) first recognizes two types of overt external acts constituting final payment. Traditionally and under various decisions payment in cash of an item by a payor bank has been considered final payment. Chambers v. Miller, 13 C.B.N.S. 125 (Eng. 1862); Fedelity & Casualty Co. of New York v. Planens check, 200 Wis. 304, 309, 227 N.W. 387, 389, 71 A.L.R. 331 (1929); see Bellvue Bank of Allen Kimberly & Co. v. Security Nat. Bank of Sioux City, 168 Iowa 707, 712, 150 N.W. 1076, 1077 (1915); 1 Paton's Digest 1066. Subsection (1)(a) first recognizes and provides that payment of an item in cash by a payor bank is final payment.

4. Section 4–104(j) defines "settle" as meaning "to pay in cash, by clearing house settlement, in a charge or credit or by remittance, or otherwise as instructed. A settlement may be either provisional or final;" Subsection (1)(b) of Section 4–213 provides that an item is finally paid by a payor bank when the bank has "settled for the item without reserving a right to revoke the settlement and without having such right under statute, clearing house rule or agreement." Subsection (1)(b) provides in effect that if the payor bank finally settles for an item this constitutes final payment of the item. The subsection operates if nothing has occurred and no situation exists making the settlement provisional. If at the time of settlement the payor bank reserves a right to revoke the settlement, the settlement is provisional. In the alternative, if under statute, clearing house rule or agreement, a right of revocation of the settlement exists the settlement is provisional. Conversely, if there is an absence of a reservation of the right to revoke and also an absence of a right to revoke under statute, clearing house rule or agreement, the settlement is final and such final settlement constitutes final payment of the item.

A primary example of a statutory right on the part of the payor bank to revoke a settlement is the right to revoke conferred by Section 4–301. The underlying theory and reason for deferred posting statutes (Section 4–301) is to require a settlement on the date of receipt of an item but to keep that settlement provisional with the right to revoke prior to the midnight deadline. In any case where Section 4–301 is applicable, any settlement by the payor bank is provisional solely by virtue of the statute, subsection (1)(b) of Section 4–213 does not operate and such provisional settlement does not constitute final payment of the item.

A second important example of a right to revoke a settlement is that arising under clearing house rules. It is very common for clearing house rules to provide that items exchanged and settled for in a clearing, (e.g., before 10:00 a.m. on Monday) may be returned and the settlements revoked up to but not later than 2:00 p.m. on the same day (Monday) or under deferred posting at some hour on the next business day (e.g., 2:00 p.m. Tuesday). Under this type of rule the Monday morning settlement is provisional and being provisional does not constitute a final payment of the item.

An example of a reservation of a right to revoke a settlement is where the payor bank is also the depositary bank and has signed a receipt or duplicate deposit ticket or has made an entry in a passbook acknowledging receipt, for credit to the account of A, of a check drawn on it by B. If the receipt, deposit ticket, passbook or other agreement with A is to the effect that any credit so entered is provisional and may be revoked pending the time required by the payor bank to process the item to determine if it is in good form and there are funds to cover it, such reservation or agreement keeps the receipt or credit provisional and avoids it being either final settlement or final payment.

In other ways the payor bank may keep settlements provisional: by general or special agreement with the presenting party or bank; by simple reservation at the time the settlement is made; or otherwise. Thus a payor bank (except in the case of statutory provisions) has control whether a settlement made by it is provisional or final, by participating in general agreements or clearing house rules or by special agreement or reservation. If it fails to keep a settlement provisional and if no applicable statute keeps the settlement provisional, its settlement is final and, unless the item had previously been paid by one of the other methods prescribed in subsection (1), such final settlement constitutes final payment. In this manner payor banks may without difficulty avoid the effect of such cases as: Cohen v. First Nat. Bank of Nogales, 22 Ariz. 394, 400, 198 P. 122, 124, 15 A.L.R. 701 (1921); Briviesca v. Coronado, 19 Cal.2d 244, 120 P.2d 649 (1941); White Brokerage Co. v. Cooperman, 207 Minn. 239, 290 N.W. 790 (1940); Scotts Bluff County v. First Nat. Bank of Gering, 115 Neb. 273, 212 N.W. 617 (1927); Provident Savings Bank & Trust Co. v. Hildebrand, 49 Ohio App. 207, 196 N.E. 790, 791 (1934); Schaer v. First Nat. Bank of Brenham, 132 Tex. 499, 124 S.W.2d 108 (1939) (bill of exchange); Union State Bank of Lancaster v. Peoples State Bank of Lancaster, 192 Wis. 28, 33, 211 N.W. 931, 933 (1927); 1 Paton's Digest 1067.

5. If a payor bank has not previously paid an item in cash or finally settled for it, certain internal acts or procedures will produce final payment of the item. Exclusive of the external acts of payment in cash or final settlement, the key point at which the decision of the bank to pay or dishonor is made is when the bookkeeper for the drawer's account determines or verifies that the check is in good form and that there are sufficient funds in the drawer's account to cover it. Previous steps in the processing of an item are preliminary to this vital step and in no way indicate a decision to pay. However, a more tangible measuring point is desirable than a mere examination of the account of the person to be charged. The mechanical step that usually indicates that the examination has been completed and the decision to pay has been made is the posting of the item to the account to be charged. Therefore, subsection (1)(c) adopts as the third measuring point the completion of the process of posting. The phrase "completed the process of posting" is used rather than simple "posting" because under current machine operations posting is a process and something more than simply making entries on the customer's ledger. Subsection (1) follows fairly closely the New York statute, 37 McKinney's Consolidated Laws of New York, Negotiable Instruments, Art. 19–A, Sec. 350–b as amended by L. 1950, C. 153, Sec. 1. However, subsections (1)(a) and (b) furnish more precise rules for determining "final settlement" by the payor bank than does the New York statute in using the term "irrevocable credit", the definition of which is not helpful.

6. Subsection (1)(d) covers the situation where the payor bank makes a provisional settlement for an item, which settlement becomes final at a later time by reason of the failure of the payor bank to revoke it in the time and manner permitted by statute,

clearing house rule or agreement. An example of this type of situation is the clearing house settlement referred to in Comment 4. In the illustration there given if the time limit for the return of items received in the Monday morning clearing is 2:00 p.m. on Tuesday and the provisional settlement has not been revoked at that time in a manner permitted by the clearing house rules, the provisional settlement made on Monday morning becomes final at 2:00 p.m. on Tuesday. Subsection (1)(d) provides specifically that in this situation the item is finally paid at 2:00 p.m. Tuesday. If on the other hand a payor bank receives an item in the mail on Monday and makes some provisional settlement for the item on Monday, it has until midnight on Tuesday to return the item or give notice and revoke any settlement under Section 4–301. In this situation subsection (1)(d) of Section 4–213 provides that if the provisional settlement made on Monday is not revoked before midnight on Tuesday as permitted by Section 4–301, the item is finally paid at midnight on Tuesday even if the process of posting the item to the account of the drawer has not been completed at that time.

7. Subsection (1) provides that an item is finally paid by the payor bank when any one of the four events set forth in subparagraphs (a), (b), (c) and (d) have occurred, whichever happens first, and then provides that upon a final payment under subparagraphs (b), (c) or (d) the payor bank shall be accountable for the amount of the item. It is not made accountable if it has paid the item in cash because such payment is itself a sufficient accounting. The term "accountable" is used as imposing a duty to account, which duty is met if and when a settlement for the item satisfactorily clears. The fact that determination of the time of final payment is based exclusively upon action of the payor bank is not detrimental to the interests of owners of items or collecting banks because of the general obligations of payors to honor or dishonor and the time limits for action imposed by Sections 4–301 and 4–302.

8. Subsection (2) states the country-wide usage that when the item is finally paid by the payor bank under subsection (1) this final payment automatically without further action "firms up" other provisional settlements made for it. However, the subsection makes clear that this "firming up" occurs only where the settlement between the presenting and payor banks was made either through a clearing house or by debits and credits in accounts between them. It does not take place where the payor bank remits for the item with some form of remittance instrument. Further, the "firming up" continues only to the extent that provisional debits and credits are entered seriatim in accounts between banks which are successive to the presenting bank. The automatic "firming up" is broken at any time that any collecting bank remits for the item with a remittance draft, because final payment to the remittee then usually depends upon final payment of the remittance draft.

9. Subsection (3) states the general rule that if a collecting bank receives settlement for an item which is or becomes final, the bank is accountable to its customer for the amount of the item. One means of accounting is to remit to its customer the amount it has received on the item. If previously it gave to its customer a provisional credit for the item in an account its receipt of final settlement for the item "firms up" this provisional credit and makes it final. When this credit given by it so becomes final, in the usual case its agency status terminates and it becomes a debtor to its customer for the amount of the item. See Section 4–201(1). If the accounting is by a remittance instrument or authorization to charge further time will usually be required to complete its accounting (Section 4–211).

10. Subsection (4) states when certain credits given by a bank to its customer become available for withdrawal as of right. Subsection (4)(a) deals with the situation where a bank has given a credit (usually provisional) for an item to its customer and in turn has received a provisional settlement for the item from an intermediary or payor bank to which it has forwarded the item. In this situation before the provisional credit entered by the collecting bank in the account of its customer becomes available for withdrawal as of right, it is not only necessary that the provisional settlement

received by the bank for the item becomes final but also that the collecting bank has a reasonable time to learn that this is so. Hence, subsection (4)(a) imposes both of these conditions. If the provisional settlement received is a provisional debit or credit in an account with the intermediary or payor bank or a remittance instrument on some bank other than the collecting bank itself, the collecting bank will usually learn that this debit or credit is final or that the remittance instrument has been paid merely by not learning the opposite within a reasonable time. How much time is "reasonable" for these purposes will of course depend on the distance the item has to travel and the number of banks through which it must pass (having in mind not only travel time by regular lines of transmission but also the successive midnight deadlines of the several banks) and other pertinent facts. Also, if the provisional settlement received is some form of a remittance instrument or authorization to charge, the "reasonable" time depends on the identity and location of the payor of the remittance instrument, the means for clearing such instrument and other pertinent facts.

11. Subsection (4)(b) deals with the situation of a bank which is both a depositary bank and a payor bank. The subsection recognizes that where A and B are both customers of a depositary-payor bank and A deposits B's check on the depositary-payor in A's account on Monday, time must be allowed to permit the check under the deferred posting rules of Section 4–301 to reach the bookkeeper for B's account at some time on Tuesday, and if there are insufficient funds in B's account to reverse or charge back the provisional credit in A's account. Consequently this provisional credit in A's account does not become available for withdrawal as of right until the opening of business on Wednesday. If it is determined on Tuesday that there are insufficient funds in B's account to pay the check the credit to A's account can be reversed on Tuesday. On the other hand if the item is in fact paid on Tuesday, the rule of subsection (4)(b) is desirable to avoid uncertainty and possible disputes between the bank and its customer as to exactly what hour within the day the credit is available.

12. Subsection (5) recognizes that even when A makes a deposit of cash in his account on Monday it takes some period of time to record that cash deposit and communicate it to A's bookkeeper (the bookkeeper handling A's account) so that A's bookkeeper has a record of it when she considers whether there are available funds to pay A's check. Where as indicated in Comment 5 A's bookkeeper is the particular employee in the bank to determine, in most cases and subject to supervisory control, whether the item may be paid, the effectiveness of a deposit of cash as a basis for paying a check must of necessity rest upon when the record of that deposit reaches such bookkeeper rather than when it passes through the teller's window. Consequently, although the bank is charged with responsibility for cash deposited from the moment it is received on Monday the cash is not effective as a basis for paying checks until the opening of business on Tuesday.

Cross References:

Sections 3–418, 4–107, 4–201, 4–211, 4–212, 4–214, 4–301, 4–302, and 4–303.

Definitional Cross References:

"Account". Section 4–104.
"Agreement". Section 1–201.
"Banking day". Section 4–104.
"Clearing house". Section 4–104.
"Collecting bank". Section 4–105.
"Customer". Section 4–104.
"Depositary bank". Section 4–105.

"Item". Section 4–104.
"Money". Section 1–201.
"Notice". Section 1–201.
"Payor bank". Section 4–105.
"Presenting bank". Section 4–105.
"Settlement". Section 4–104.

Section 4–214. Insolvency and Preference.

(1) Any item in or coming into the possession of a payor or collecting bank which suspends payment and which item is not finally paid shall be returned by the receiver, trustee or agent in charge of the closed bank to the presenting bank or the closed bank's customer.

(2) If a payor bank finally pays an item and suspends payments without making a settlement for the item with its customer or the presenting bank which settlement is or becomes final, the owner of the item has a preferred claim against the payor bank.

(3) If a payor bank gives or a collecting bank gives or receives a provisional settlement for an item and thereafter suspends payments, the suspension does not prevent or interfere with the settlement becoming final if such finality occurs automatically upon the lapse of certain time or the happening of certain events (subsection (3) of Section 4–211, subsections (1)(d), (2) and (3) of Section 4–213).

(4) If a collecting bank receives from subsequent parties settlement for an item which settlement is or becomes final and suspends payments without making a settlement for the item with its customer which is or becomes final, the owner of the item has a preferred claim against such collecting bank.

New York Annotations

(1) Generally in *accord* with N.I.L., § 350–*1* (1), except that different terminology is used. The present statute uses the language: (1) "when a bank shall fail or be closed for business by law", (2) "the drawee or payor or any other agent collecting bank", and (3) "after an item shall be mailed or otherwise entrusted to it for collection or payment but before the actual collection or payment thereof", whereas the Code in the comparable portions of its subsection employs the following language—(1) "a bank which suspends payment", (2) "a payor or collecting bank", and (3) "any item in or coming into the possession which item is not finally paid."

(2) Generally in *accord* with N.I.L., § 350–*1* (2), except that different terminology is used and the Code abandons the trust theory found in the Bank Collection Code.

(3) This subsection is new and provides that suspension of payments does not prevent a settlement from becoming final, if such finality would otherwise occur automatically.

(4) Generally in *accord* with N.I.L., § 350–*1* (3), except that different terminology is used. The preference provisions are probably inapplicable to national banks because of the overriding preference provisions in the federal law. See Jennings v. U. S. Fidelity & Guaranty Co., 294 U.S. 216, 55 S. Ct. 394 (1935). Section 1–108, however, would preserve the applicability of Section 4–214 to state banks.

UCC

Historical Note: The changes state with greater precision rules applicable to insolvent banks. (1956 Recommendations, p. 155; Excerpts, p. 428.)

Official Uniform Comment

Prior Uniform Statutory Provision: None; but see Section 13, American Bankers Association Bank Collection Code.

Purposes:

1. The underlying purpose of the provisions of this section is not to confer upon banks, holders of items or anyone else preferential positions in the event of bank failures over general depositors or any other creditors of the failed banks. The purpose is to fix as definitely as possible the cut-off point of time for the completion or cessation of the collection process in the case of items that happen to be in such process at the time a particular bank suspends payments. It must be remembered that in bank collections as a whole and in the handling of items by an individual bank, items go through a whole series of processes. It must also be remembered that at any particular point of time a particular bank (at least one of any size) is functioning as a depositary bank for some items, as an intermediary bank for others, as a presenting bank for still others and as a payor bank for still others, and that when it suspends payments it will have close to its normal load of items working through its various processes. For the convenience of receivers, owners of items, banks, and in fact substantially everyone concerned, it is recognized that at the particular moment of time that a bank suspends payment, a certain portion of the items being handled by it have progressed far enough in the bank collection process that it is preferable to permit them to continue the remaining distance, rather than to send them back and reverse the many entries that have been made or the steps that have been taken with respect to them. Therefore, having this background and these purposes in mind, the section states what items must be turned backward at the moment suspension intervenes and what items have progressed far enough that the collection process with respect to them continues, with the resulting necessary statement of rights of various parties flowing from this prescription of the cut-off time.

2. The rules stated are similar to those stated in the American Bankers Association Bank Collection Code, but with the abandonment of any theory of trust. Although for practical purposes Federal Deposit Insurance affects materially the result of bank failures on holders of items and banks, no attempt is made to vary the rules of the section by reason of such insurance.

3. It is recognized that in view of Jennings v. United States Fidelity & Guaranty Co., 294 U.S. 216, 55 S.Ct. 394, 79 L.Ed. 869, 99 A.L.R. 1248 (1935), amendment of the National Bank Act would be necessary to have this section apply to national banks. But there is no reason why it should not apply to others. See Section 1–108.

Cross References:

Sections 1–108, 4–211(3) and 4–213.

Definitional Cross References:

"Collecting bank". Section 4–105.
"Customer". Section 4–104.
"Item". Section 4–104.
"Payor bank". Section 4–105.
"Presenting bank". Section 4–105.
"Settlement". Section 4–104.
"Suspends payment". Section 4–104.

PART 3

COLLECTION OF ITEMS: PAYOR BANKS

Section 4–301. Deferred Posting; Recovery of Payment by Return of Items; Time of Dishonor.

(1) Where an authorized settlement for a demand item (other than a documentary draft) received by a payor bank otherwise than for immediate payment over the counter has been made before midnight of the banking day of receipt the payor bank may revoke the settlement and recover any payment if before it has made final payment (subsection (1) of Section 4–213) and before its midnight deadline it

(a) returns the item; or

(b) sends written notice of dishonor or nonpayment if the item is held for protest or is otherwise unavailable for return.

(2) If a demand item is received by a payor bank for credit on its books it may return such item or send notice of dishonor and may revoke any credit given or recover the amount thereof withdrawn by its customer, if it acts within the time limit and in the manner specified in the preceding subsection.

(3) Unless previous notice of dishonor has been sent an item is dishonored at the time when for purposes of dishonor it is returned or notice sent in accordance with this section.

(4) An item is returned:

(a) as to an item received through a clearing house, when it is delivered to the presenting or last collecting bank or to the clearing house or is sent or delivered in accordance with its rules; or

(b) in all other cases, when it is sent or delivered to the bank's customer or transferor or pursuant to his instructions.

New York Annotations

(1) *Accords* generally with N.I.L., § 350–b (deferred posting statute), except that the Code excludes documentary drafts.

(2) *Accord:* N.I.L., § 350–b (1) and (2).

(3) *Accord:* N.I.L., § 350–b (2).

(4) This provision, establishing the time when an item is "returned", is new law, but would seem to codify existing practice and custom.

Historical Note: The words "a demand" were inserted before "item" in the opening phrase of subsection (2). The general deferred posting rules of Section 4–301(1) were limited to demand items and, therefore, the deferred posting rules of Section 4–301(2), applicable to depositary-payor banks, had to be similarly limited. (1956 Recommendations, p. 156.)

Official Uniform Comment

Prior Uniform Statutory Provision: None; but see American Bankers Association Model Deferred Posting Statute.

Purposes:

1. Deferred posting and delayed returns is that practice whereby a payor bank sorts and proves items received by it on the day they are received, e.g. Monday, but does not post the items to the customer's account or return "not good" items until the next day, e.g. Tuesday. The practice typifies "production line" methods currently used in bank collection and is based upon the necessity of an even flow of items through payor banks on a day by day basis in a manner which can be handled evenly by employee personnel without abnormal peak load periods, night work, and other practices objectionable to personnel. Since World War II statutes authorizing deferred posting and delayed returns have been passed in almost all of the forty-eight states. This section codifies the content of these statutes and approves the practice.

2. The time limits for action imposed by Subsection (1) are adopted by Subsection (2) for cases where the payor bank is also the depositary bank, but in this case the requirement of a settlement on the day of receipt is omitted.

3. Subsection (3) fixes a base point from which to measure the time within which notice of dishonor must be given. See Section 3–508.

4. Subsection (4) leaves banks free to agree upon the manner of returning items but establishes a precise time when an item is "returned". For definition of "sent" as used in subsections (a) and (b) see Section 1–201(38).

5. Obviously the section assumes that the item has not been "finally paid" under Section 4–213(1). If it has been, this section has no operation.

Cross References:

Sections 3–508, 4–213, 4–302.

Definitional Cross References:

"Banking day". Section 4–104.
"Clearing house". Section 4–104.
"Collecting bank". Section 4–105.
"Customer". Section 4–104.
"Documentary draft". Section 4–104.
"Item". Section 4–104.
"Midnight deadline". Section 4–104.
"Notice of dishonor". Section 3–508.
"Payor bank". Section 4–105.
"Presenting bank". Section 4–105.
"Sent". Section 1–201(38).
"Settlement". Section 4–104.

Section 4–302. Payor Bank's Responsibility for Late Return of Item.

In the absence of a valid defense such as breach of a presentment warranty (subsection (1) of Section 4–207), settlement effected or the like, if an item is presented on and received by a payor bank the bank is accountable for the amount of

(a) a demand item other than a documentary draft whether properly payable or not if the bank, in any case where it is not also the depositary bank, retains the item beyond midnight of the banking day of receipt without settling for it or, regardless of whether it is also the depositary bank, does not pay or return the item or send notice of dishonor until after its midnight deadline; or

(b) any other properly payable item unless within the time allowed for acceptance or payment of that item the bank either accepts or pays the item or returns it and accompanying documents.

New York Annotations

This section, providing the sanction to make Section 4–301 effective, is new law. N.I.L., § 350–b, is declarative of the bank's duty but is silent as to sanctions for non-compliance. See, however, N.I.L., § 225, which gives the drawee twenty-four hours to decide whether to accept a bill of exchange and provides that the drawee is deemed to have accepted the bill if he fails to return it within that period. In State Bank v. Weiss, 46 Misc. 93, 91 N.Y.S. 276 (1904), the court interpreted N.I.L., § 225, to mean that failure of a drawee bank to return checks presented for payment within twenty-four hours of their delivery, or to give proper notice of dishonor within such period, amounted to an acceptance. *Contra:* Matteson v. Moulton, 79 N.Y. 627 (1880) (contrary holding under an earlier statute similar to N.I.L., § 225).

Historical Note: The changes in this section were for clarification. (1956 Recommendations, p. 157; Excerpts, pp. 428–429.)

Official Uniform Comment

Prior Uniform Statutory Provision: None; but see American Bankers Association Model Deferred Posting Statute.

Purposes:

Under Section 4–301, time limits are prescribed within which a payor bank must take action if it receives an item payable by it. Section 4–302 states the rights of the customer if the payor bank fails to take the action required within the time limits prescribed.

Cross References:

Section 4–301.

Definitional Cross References:

"Acceptance". Section 3–410.
"Banking day". Section 4–104.
"Customer". Section 4–104.
"Depositary bank". 4–105
"Documentary draft". Section 4–104.
"Item". Section 4–104.
"Midnight deadline". Section 4–104.
"Notice of dishonor". Section 3–508.
"Payor bank". Section 4–105.
"Properly payable". Section 4–104.
"Settle". Section 4–104.

Section 4–303. When Items Subject to Notice, Stop-Order, Legal Process or Setoff; Order in Which Items May be Charged or Certified.

(1) Any knowledge, notice or stop-order received by, legal process served upon or setoff exercised by a payor bank, whether or not effective under other rules of law to terminate, suspend or modify the bank's right or duty to pay an item or to charge its customer's account for the item, comes too late to so terminate, suspend or modify such right or duty if the knowledge, notice, stop-order or legal process is received or served and a reasonable time for the bank to act thereon expires or the setoff is exercised after the bank has done any of the following:

(a) accepted or certified the item;

(b) paid the item in cash;

(c) settled for the item without reserving a right to revoke the settlement and without having such right under statute, clearing house rule or agreement;

(d) completed the process of posting the item to the indicated account of the drawer, maker or other person to be charged therewith or otherwise has evidenced by examination of such indicated account and by action its decision to pay the item; or

(e) become accountable for the amount of the item under subsection (1)(d) of Section 4–213 and Section 4–302 dealing with the payor bank's responsibility for late return of items.

(2) Subject to the provisions of subsection (1) items may be accepted, paid, certified or charged to the indicated account of its customer in any order convenient to the bank.

New York Annotations

(1)(a) Generally in *accord* with N.I.L., §§ 324 and 325–a. See also Carnegie Trust Co. v. New York First National Bank, 213 N.Y. 301, 107 N.E. 693 (1915), and Fiss Corp. v. National Safety Bank & Trust Co., 191 Misc. 397, 77 N.Y.S.2d 293 (1948).

(b) and (c) *Accord:* N.I.L., § 350–b.

(d) *Accord:* N.I.L., § 350–b, and First Nat. Bank v. National Park Bank, 181 App.Div. 103, 168 N.Y.S. 422 (1917) (supporting "omnibus" language in second part of this subparagraph).

(e) While no direct authority has been found, this subparagraph would appear to accord with a rule inferring liability from N.I.L., § 350–b.

(2) This is new law and no authority directly on point has been found.

Historical Note: In accordance with a suggestion of the Law Revision Commission, subsection (1) was revised, and the words "comes too late" were inserted to describe more aptly the rule and result intended. Subsection (1)(e) was changed to conform to new language in Section 4–213(1)(d). (1956 Recommendations, p. 158; Excerpts, p. 429.)

Official Uniform Comment

Prior Uniform Statutory Provision: None.

Purposes:

1. The comments to Section 4–213 describe the process through which an item passes in the payor bank. Prior to this process or at any time while it is going on, the payor bank may receive knowledge or a legal notice affecting the item, such as knowledge or notice that the drawer has filed a petition in bankruptcy or made an assignment for the benefit of creditors; may receive an order of the drawer stopping payment on the item; may have served on it an attachment of the account of the drawer; or the bank itself may exercise a right of setoff against the drawer's account. Each of these events affects the account of the drawer and may eliminate or freeze all or part of whatever balance is available to pay the item. Subsection (1) states the rule for determining the relative priorities between these various legal events and the item.

2. The rule is that if any one of several things has been done to the item or if it has reached any one of several stages in its processing at the time the knowledge, notice, stop-order or legal process is received or served and a reasonable time for the bank to act thereon expires or the setoff is exercised, the knowledge, notice, stop-order, legal process or setoff comes too late, the item has priority and a charge to the customer's account may be made and is effective. Certain of the tests determining the priority status of the item are the same as for final payment under Section 4–213(1), but additional tests apply in the context of the present section. The first event mentioned, namely, acceptance, means formal acceptance as that term is used and defined in Section 3–410. Certification is the type of certification defined in Section 3–411. Payment of the item in cash under Section 4–213(1)(a), final settlement for the item under Section 4–213(1)(b) and completion of the process of posting under Section 4–213(1)(c) all constitute final payment of the item and confer priority. After a cash payment, final settlement or the completion of the process of posting, and knowledge, notice, stop–order, legal process or setoff comes too late and cannot interfere with either payment of the item or a charge to the customer's account based upon such payment.

3. The sixth event conferring priority is stated by the language "or otherwise has evidenced by examination of such indicated account and by action its decision to pay the item." The general "omnibus" language is necessary to pick up other possible types of action impossible to specify particularly but where the bank has examined the account to see if there are sufficient funds and has taken some action indicating an intention to pay. An example is what has sometimes been called "sight posting" where the bookkeeper examines the account and makes a decision to pay but postpones a posting. The clause should be interpreted in the light of Nineteenth Ward Bank v. First Nat. Bank of South Weymouth, 184 Mass. 49, 67 N.E. 670 (1903). It is not intended to refer to various preliminary acts in no way close to a true decision of the bank to pay the item, such as receipt of the item over the counter for deposit, entry of a provisional credit in a passbook, or the making of a provisional settlement for the item through the clearing house, by entries in accounts, remittance or otherwise. All actions of this type are provisional and none of them evidences the bank's decision to pay the item. In this Section as in Section 4–213 reasoning such as appears in Cohen v. First Nat. Bank of Nogales, 22 Ariz. 394, 400, 198 P.122, 124, 15 A.L.R. 701 (1921); Briviesca v. Coronado, 19 Cal.2d 244, 120 P.2d 649 (1941); White Brokerage Co. v. Cooperman, 207 Minn. 239, 290 N.W. 790 (1940); Scotts Bluff County v. First Nat. Bank of Gering, 115 Neb. 273, 212 N.W. 617, 618 (1927); Provident Savings Bank & Trust Co. v. Hildebrand, 49 Ohio App. 207, 196 N.E. 790, 791 (1934); Schaer v. First Nat. Bank of Brenham, 132 Tex. 499, 124 S. W.2d

108 (1939) (bill of exchange); Union State Bank of Lancaster v. People's State Bank of Lancaster, 192 Wis. 28, 33, 211 N.W. 931, 933 (1927); 1 Paton's Digest 1067, is rejected.

4. The seventh and last event conferring priority for an item and a charge to the customer's account based upon the item is stated by the language "become accountable for the amount of the item under subsection (1)(d) of Section 4–213 and Section 4–302 dealing with the payor bank's responsibility for late return of items". Under Section 4–213(1)(d) if a payor bank makes a provisional settlement for an item and fails to revoke the settlement in the time and manner permitted by statute, clearing house rule or agreement, such combination of events constitutes final payment of the item. Under Section 4–302 a payor bank may also become accountable for the amount of an item in certain other situations even though there has been no provisional settlement for the item or such action as constitutes final payment under Section 4–213(1). Expiration of the deadlines under Sections 4–213(1)(d) or 4–302 with resulting accountability by the payor bank for the amount of the item, establish priority of the item over notices, stop-orders, legal process or setoff.

5. In the case of knowledge, notice, stop-orders and legal process the effective time for determining whether they were received too late to affect the payment of an item and a charge to the customer's account by reason of such payment, is receipt plus a reasonable amount of time for the bank to act on any of these communications. Usually a relatively short time is required to communicate to the bookkeeping department advice of one of these events but certainly some time is necessary. Compare Sections 1–201(27) and 4–403. In the case of setoff the effective time is when the setoff is actually made.

6. As between one item and another no priority rule is stated, other than the convenience rule of the bank. This rule is justified because of the impossibility of stating a rule that would be fair in all cases, having in mind the almost infinite number of combinations of large and small checks in relation to the available balance on hand in the drawer's account; the possible methods of receipt; and other difficulties. Further, where the drawer has drawn all checks, he should have funds available to meet all of them and has no basis for urging one should be paid before another; and the holders have no direct right against the payor bank in any event, unless of course, the bank has accepted, certified or finally paid a particular item, or has become liable for it under Section 4–302. Under subsection (2) the bank obviously has the right to pay items for which it is itself liable ahead of those for which it is not.

Cross References:

Sections 3–410, 3–411, 4–213(1), 4–301, and 4–302.

Definitional Cross References:

"Accepted". Section 3–410.
"Account". Section 4–104.
"Section Agreement". Section 1–201.
"Certified". Section 3–411.
"Clearing house". Section 4–104.
"Customer". Section 4–104.
"Item". Section 4–104.
"Notice". Section 1–201.
"Payor Bank". Section 4–105.
"Settle". Section 4–104.

PART 4

RELATIONSHIP BETWEEN PAYOR BANK AND ITS CUSTOMER

Section 4–401. When Bank May Charge Customer's Account.

(1) As against its customer, a bank may charge against his account any item which is otherwise properly payable from that account even though the charge creates an overdraft.

(2) A bank which in good faith makes payment to a holder may charge the indicated account of its customer according to

(a) the original tenor of his altered item; or

(b) the tenor of his completed item, even though the bank knows the item has been completed unless the bank has notice that the completion was improper.

New York Annotations

(1) *Accords* with common–law rule permitting a bank to recover the amount of an overdraft from the drawer. Payne v. Freer, 91 N.Y. 43, 48 (1883); Becker v. Fuller, 99 Misc. 672, 164 N.Y.S. 495 (1917).

(2)(a) In *accord,* permitting a bank to charge its customer's account according to the original tenor of his order, see Clark v. National Shoe & Leather Bank, 32 App. Div. 316, 52 N.Y.S. 1064, aff'd, 164 N.Y. 498, 58 N.E. 659 (1900).

(b) This subparagraph, together with Sections 3–115 and 3–407, would change New York law as to a right to enforce payment on an incomplete instrument which has not been delivered. See N.I.L. § 34.

Under the N.I.L. a person cannot qualify as a holder in due course if the instrument is completed in his presence, or if he knows that his transferor took it with blanks unfilled. Hunter v. Allen, 127 App.Div. 572, 111 N.Y.S. 820 (1908); Union Trust Co. of New Jersey v. McCrum, 145 App. Div. 409, 129 N.Y.S. 1078, aff'd, 207 N.Y. 721, 101 N.E. 1124 (1913).

Historical Note: The qualification of the rule of subsection (2)(b) adopts a suggestion made by the Law Revision Commission. (1956 Recommendations, p. 159; Excerpts, p. 430.)

Official Uniform Comment

Prior Uniform Statutory Provision: None.

Purposes:

1. It is fundamental that upon proper payment of a draft the drawee may charge the account of the drawer. This is true even though the draft is an overdraft since the draft itself authorizes the payment for the drawer's account and carries an implied promise to reimburse the drawee.

2. Subsection (2) parallels the provision which protects a holder in due course against discharge by reason of alteration and permits him to enforce the instrument to its original tenor. Section 3–407(3). It adopts the rule of cases extending the same protection to a drawee who pays in good faith. The subsection also follows the policy of Sections 3–115 and 3–407(3) by protecting the drawee who pays a completed instrument in good faith according to the instrument as completed.

Cross References:

Sections 3–115 and 3–407.

Definitional Cross References:

"Account". Section 4–104.
"Bank". Section 1–201.
"Customer". Section 4–104.
"Good faith". Section 1–201.
"Holder". Section 1–201.
"Item". Section 4–104.
"Property payable". Section 4–104.

Section 4–402. Bank's Liability to Customer for Wrongful Dishonor.

A payor bank is liable to its customer for damages proximately caused by the wrongful dishonor of an item. When the dishonor occurs through mistake liability is limited to actual damages proved. If so proximately caused and proved damages may include damages for an arrest or prosecution of the customer or other consequential damages. Whether any consequential damages are proximately caused by the wrongful dishonor is a question of fact to be determined in each case.

New York Annotations

This section accords with the present New York rule limiting recovery for innocent mistakes to actual damages proved. Citizens' National Bank v. Importers & Traders Bank, 119 N.Y. 195, 23 N.E. 540 (1890); Levine v. State Bank, 80 Misc. 524, 141 N.Y.S. 596 (1913), but would change the rule allowing nominal damages for a technical breach. Clark Co. v. Mt. Morris Bank, 85 App. Div. 362, 83 N.Y.S. 447, aff'd, 181 N.Y. 533, 73 N.E. 1133 (1905).

Also changed would be the special rule for fiduciaries permitting recovery of substantial damages for innocent mistakes without proof of actual injury. Nealis v. Industrial Bank of Commerce, 200 Misc. 406, 107 N.Y.S.2d 264 (1951).

The "trader rule", insofar as adopted in New York, is rejected. Wildenberger v. Ridgewood National Bank, 230 N.Y. 425, 130 N.E. 600 (1921).

No New York decisions have been found involving damages for arrest and prosecution caused by wrongful dishonor. See, however, Robbins v. Bankers Trust Co., 4 Misc. 2d 347, 157 N.Y.S.2d 56 (1956).

Historical Note: This section was completely revised to make clear that: (1) All damages, particularly those incident to arrest and prosecution, must be proximately caused by the wrongful dishonor; (2) the section abrogates decisional law that the dishonor is not the cause of arrest and prosecution. (1956 Recommendations, p. 159; Excerpts, p. 430.)

Official Uniform Comment

Prior Uniform Statutory Provision: None.

Purposes:

1. This section is new to the Uniform Laws, although similar statutory provisions are in existence in twenty-three jurisdictions.

2. The liability of the drawee for dishonor has sometimes been stated as one for breach of contract, sometimes for negligence or other breach of a tort duty, and sometimes as for defamation. This section does not attempt to specify a theory. "Wrongful dishonor" excludes any permitted or justified dishonor, as where the drawer has no credit extended by the drawee, or where the draft lacks a necessary indorsement or is not properly presented.

3. This section rejects decisions which have held that where the dishonored item has been drawn by a merchant, trader or fiduciary he is defamed in his business, trade or profession by a reflection on his credit and hence that substantial damages may be awarded on the basis of defamation "per se" without proof that damage has occurred. The merchant, trader and fiduciary are placed on the same footing as any other drawer and in all cases of dishonor by mistake damages recoverable are limited to those actually proved.

4. Wrongful dishonor is different from "failure to exercise ordinary care in handling an item", and the measure of damages is that stated in this section, not that stated in Section 4–103(5).

5. The fourth sentence of the section rejects decisions holding that as a matter of law the dishonor of a check is not the "proximate cause" of the arrest and prosecution of the customer, and leaves to determination in each case as a question of fact whether the dishonor is or may be the "proximate cause".

Definitional Cross References:

"Bank". Section 1–201.
"Customer". Section 4–104.
"Item". Section 4–104.

Section 4–403. Customer's Right to Stop Payment; Burden of Proof of Loss.

(1) A customer may by order to his bank stop payment of any item payable for his account but the order must be received at such time and in such manner as to afford the bank a reasonable opportunity to act on it prior to any action by the bank with respect to the item described in Section 4–303.

(2) A remitter or payee of a cashier's check or certified check may by order to the obligated bank stop payment of such a check, and a remitter or payee of a teller's check may order the obligated bank to order the payor bank to stop payment of such a check, at any time after ninety days from the date of issuance of either a cashier's check or teller's check, and date of certification of a certified check. The stop payment is effective if either the remitter or payee delivers to the obligated bank at a time and in a manner affording a reasonable opportunity to act before any of the actions described in Section 4-303(1) are taken: (i) a written order to stop payment, which shall describe the item with reasonable certainty, and (ii) an affidavit of the remitter or payee containing an averment that the check was destroyed, its whereabouts cannot be determined, or it is in the wrongful possession of an unknown person or a person that cannot be found or is not amenable to service of process.

(3) An oral order is binding upon the bank only for fourteen calendar days unless confirmed in writing within that period. A written order is effective for only six months unless renewed in writing.

UCC

(4) The burden of establishing the fact and amount of loss resulting from the payment of an item contrary to a binding stop payment order is on the customer, remitter or payee.

Amended by L. 1990, Ch. 568, eff. July 1, 1991, adding a new subdivision 2 and renumbering old subdivisions 2 and 3.

New York Annotations

(1) The first part of this subsection *accords* with the common-law rule that a drawer has the right to stop payment of a check at any time before it is certified (at the request of the holder) or paid. American Defense Society v. Sherman National Bank, 225 N.Y. 506, 122 N.E. 695 (1919). Although the common-law rule permitted a drawer to stop payment after the drawer had obtained certification, this rule has been abrogated by statute. N.I.L., § 325–a.

In *accord* with the requirement that the stop order be received "at such time as to afford the bank a reasonable opportunity to act on (such order) prior to any action by the bank with respect to the item", is the case of A. Sidney Davison Coal Co. v. National Park Bank, 201 App.Div. 309, 194 N.Y.S. 220 (1922). See also, Davis, Inc. v. Chemung Canal Trust Co., 9 A.D.2d 562, 189 N.Y.S.2d 320 (1959).

The general rule as to form and sufficiency of the order is that the notice must be clear and unambiguous and describe the check with reasonable accuracy. A. Sidney Davison Coal Co. v. National Park Bank, 201 App.Div. 309, 194 N.Y.S. 220 (1922); Levine v. Bank of United States, 132 Misc. 130, 229 N.Y.S. 108 (1928).

(2) Oral orders are effective in New York. K & K Silk Trimming Co., Inc. v. Garfield Nat. Bank, 127 Misc. 27, 215 N.Y.S. 269 (1926). The provisions imposing time limits on oral and written stop orders are new.

(3) This subsection would appear to be *contra* to the holding of American Defense Society v. Sherman National Bank of New York, 225 N.Y. 506, 122 N.E. 695 (1919), reaffirmed in Chase National Bank v. Battat, 297 N.Y. 185, 78 N.E.2d 465 (1948), that the customer's action is on his account for the amount of the check with no obligation to prove his actual loss as part of his prima facie case. The court in the American Defense Society case, *supra,* does state, however, that the customer may "not make a profit out of the bank's mistake and could only recover that which it lost". See Ted Granville Co. v. Chemical Bank & Trust Co., 8 Misc.2d 806, 160 N.Y.S.2d 959 (1957).

The doctrine of "ratification" is stated in the American Defense Society case, *supra,* by way of dictum. This rule would relieve the bank of liability for paying over a stop order where the customer "had credited itself upon its books with payment or had in any way recognized his receipt of the money"

Historical Note: Subsection (2) was changed to prescribe a flat fourteen-day period in which the customer must confirm in writing an oral stop payment order. This preserves the right of the customer to give an oral stop payment order but gives some protection to the bank against the uncertainties of oral orders by terminating the binding effect of an oral order unless it is confirmed in writing within fourteen days. (1956 Recommendations, p. 160.)

Official Uniform Comment

Prior Uniform Statutory Provision: None.

Purposes:

1. This section is new. It is intended to replace separate statutes in twenty-nine states which regulate stop-payment orders.

2. The position taken by this section is that stopping payment is a service which depositors expect and are entitled to receive from banks notwithstanding its difficulty, inconvenience and expense. The inevitable occasional losses through failure to stop should be borne by the banks as a cost of the business of banking.

3. Subsection (1) follows the decisions holding that a payee or indorsee has no right to stop payment. This is consistent with the provision governing payment or satisfaction. See Section 3–603. The sole exception to this rule is found in Section 4–405 on payment after notice of death, by which any person claiming an interest in the account can stop payment.

4. Payment is commonly stopped only on checks; but the right to stop payment is not limited to checks, and extends to any item payable by a bank. Where the maker of a note payable at a bank is in a position analogous to that of a drawer (Section 3–121) he may stop payment of the note. By analogy the rule extends to drawees other than banks.

5. There is no right to stop payment after certification of a check or other acceptance of a draft, and this is true no matter who procures the certification. See Sections 3–411 and 4–303. The acceptance is the drawee's own engagement to pay, and he is not required to impair his credit by refusing payment for the convenience of the drawer.

6. Normally a direction to stop payment is first given by telephone. Notwithstanding statutes which require a written order, banks customarily accept such directions, and have been held to waive the writing. Subsection (2) is intended to protect both parties by making the oral direction effective for only a short time during which the drawer must confirm it in writing, and by eliminating thereafter any claim of waiver by acceptance of the oral direction.

7. The existing statutes all specify a time limit after which any direction to stop payment becomes ineffective unless it is renewed in writing; and the majority of them have specified six months. The purpose of the provision is, of course, to facilitate stopping payment by clearing the records of the drawee of accumulated unrevoked stop orders, as where the drawer has found a lost instrument or has settled his controversy with the payee, but has failed to notify the drawee. The last sentence of subsection (2), together with the second clause in Section 4–404, rejects the reasoning of such cases as Goldberg v. Manufacturers Trust Company, 199 Misc. 167, 102 N.Y.S.2d 144 (1951).

8. A payment in violation of an effective direction to stop payment is an improper payment, even though it is made by mistake or inadvertence. Any agreement to the contrary is invalid under Section 4–103(1) if in paying the item over the stop payment order the bank has failed to exercise ordinary care. The drawee is, however, entitled to subrogation to prevent unjust enrichment (Section 4–407); retains common–law defenses, e.g., that by conduct in recognizing the payment the customer has ratified the bank's action in paying over a stop payment order (Section 1–103); and retains common-law rights, e.g., to recover money paid under a mistake (Section 1–103) in cases where the payment is not made final by Section 3–418. It has sometimes been said that payment cannot be stopped against a holder in due course (Sections 3–305, 3–413) and the drawee, if he pays, becomes subrogated to the rights of the holder in due course against the drawer. Section 4–407. Any defenses available against a holder in due course remain available to the drawer, but other defenses are cut off to the same extent as if the holder himself were bringing the action.

Cross References:

Point 3: Sections 3–603(1), 4–405.
Point 4: Section 3–121.
Point 5: Sections 3–411 and 4–303.
Point 8: Sections 3–305, 3–413, 3–418, 4–103 and 4–407.

Definitional Cross References:

"Account". Section 4–104.
"Bank". Section 1–201.
"Burden of establishing". Section 1–201.
"Customer". Section 4–104.
"Item". Section 4–104.
"Send". Section 1–201.

Section 4–404. Bank Not Obligated to Pay Check More Than Six Months Old.

A bank is under no obligation to a customer having a checking account to pay a check, other than a certified check, which is presented more than six months after its date, but it may charge its customer's account for a payment made thereafter in good faith.

New York Annotations

This is new law. There is decisional law authority to the effect that the presentment of a check dated more than two years previously puts the bank on inquiry to determine whether its customer still wants the check paid, Goldberg v. Manufacturers Trust Co., 199 Misc. 167, 102 N.Y.S.2d 144 (1951), and that a check presented 14 months after the date it bore must be presumed to be dishonored. Cowing v. Altman, 71 N.Y. 435 (1877). Compare Feller v. Manufacturers Trust Co., 4 A.D.2d 675, 163 N.Y.S.2d 512, aff'd mem. 4 N.Y.2d 951, 151 N.E.2d 619 (1958), where it was held that presentment of a check bearing a date five months earlier does not put the bank on inquiry.

Official Uniform Comment

Prior Uniform Statutory Provision: None.

Purposes:

This section incorporates a type of statute adopted in twenty-six jurisdictions. The time limit is set at six months because banking and commercial practice regards a check outstanding for longer than that period as stale, and a bank will normally not pay such a check without consulting the depositor. It is therefore not required to do so, but is given the option to pay because it may be in a position to know, as in the case of dividend checks, that the drawer wants payment made.

Certified checks are excluded from the section because they are the primary obligation of the certifying bank (Sections 3–411 and 3–413), which obligation runs direct to the holder of the check. The customer's account was charged when the check was certified.

Cross References:

Sections 3–411 and 3–413.

Definitional Cross References:

"Account". Section 4–104.
"Bank". Section 1–201.
"Check". Section 3–104.

"Customer". Section 4–104.
"Good faith". Section 1–201.
"Present". Section 3–504.

Section 4–405. Death or Incompetence of Customer.

(1) A payor or collecting bank's authority to accept, pay or collect an item or to account for proceeds of its collection if otherwise effective is not rendered ineffective by incompetence of a customer of either bank existing at the time the item is issued or its collection is undertaken if the bank does not know of an adjudication of incompetence. Neither death nor incompetence of a customer revokes such authority to accept, pay, collect or account until the bank knows of the fact of death or of an adjudication of incompetence and has reasonable opportunity to act on it.

(2) Even with knowledge a bank may for ten days after the date of death pay or certify checks drawn on or prior to that date unless ordered to stop payment by a person claiming an interest in the account.

New York Annotations

(1) This subsection is generally in accord with New York decisional law as to the authority of a bank to pay a depositor's checks until it has "knowledge" of the depositor's death. Glennan v. Rochester Trust & Safe Deposit Co., 209 N.Y. 12, 102 N.E. 537 (1913). Compare Matter of Graud's Estate, 43 N.Y.S.2d 803 (1943) (suggestion that notice, without actual knowledge, may be sufficient to charge the bank), but may change the New York rule as to the effect of a customer's death upon authority of a bank to collect. In re Hayward's Estate, 115 N.Y.S.2d 136 (1952). See, however, N.I.L., § 350–a.

The law in New York is unsettled as to whether a bank having knowledge of the actual insanity of its customer, not judicially declared incompetent, must honor his checks. Riley v. Albany Savings Bank, 36 Hun 513, aff'd, 103 N.Y. 669 (1886). Mace v. Rockland County Trust Co., 249 App.Div. 754, 291 N.Y.S. 835 (1935). Compare Wallis v. President of the Manhattan Company, 2 Hall 495 (1829).

There is authority that the adjudication of insanity itself is regarded as notice for the purpose of terminating the agency of a bank to deal with collateral, whether or not the bank, in fact, knows of the adjudication. McNerney v. Aetna Life Ins. Co., 284 App.Div. 21, 130 N.Y.S.2d 152, aff'd 308 N.Y. 916, 127 N.E.2d 79 (1955). The Code, in requiring actual knowledge of the adjudication, would change present law. The court in the McNerney case held that the bank's agency, as pledgee, was coupled with an interest and not revoked.

(2) This is new law and would change the present rule. Glennan v. Rochester Trust & Safe Deposit Co., *supra.*

Historical Note: Subsection (1) was changed to meet suggestions of the Law Revision Commission for more precise coverage of the subject matter involved. (1956 Recommendations, pp. 160–161; Excerpts, p. 431.)

Official Uniform Comment

Prior Uniform Statutory Provision: None.

Purposes:

1. This section is new, although similar statutory provisions are in existence in seven states.

2. Subsection (1) follows existing decisions which hold that a drawee (payor) bank is not liable for the payment of a check before it has notice of the death or incompetence of the drawer. The justice and necessity of the rule are obvious. A check is an order to pay which the bank must obey under penalty of possible liability for dishonor. Further, with the tremendous volume of items handled any rule which required banks to verify the continued life and competency of drawers would be completely unworkable.

One or both of these same reasons apply to other phases of the bank collection and payment process and the rule is made wide enough to apply to these other phases. It applies to all kinds of "items"; to "customers" who own items as well as "customers" who draw or make them; to the function of collecting items as well as the function of accepting or paying them; to the carrying out of instructions to account for proceeds even though these may involve transfers to third parties; to depositary and intermediary banks as well as payor banks; and to incompetency existing at the time of the issuance of an item or the commencement of the collection or payment process as well as to incompetency occurring thereafter. Further, the requirement of actual knowledge makes inapplicable the rule of some cases that an adjudication of incompetency is constructive notice to all the world because obviously it is as impossible for banks to keep posted on such adjudications (in the absence of actual knowledge) as it is to keep posted as to death of immediate or remote customers.

3. Subsection (2) provides a limited period after death during which a bank may continue to pay checks (as distinguished from other items) even though it has notice. The purpose of the provision, as of the existing statutes, is to permit holders of checks drawn shortly before death to cash them without the necessity of filing a claim in probate. The justification is that such checks normally are given in immediate payment of obligation, that there is almost never any reason why they should not be paid, and that filing in probate is a useless formality, burdensome to the holder, the executor, the court and the bank.

This section does not prevent an executor or administrator from recovering the payment from the holder of the check. It is not intended to affect the validity of any gift causa mortis or other transfer in contemplation of death, but merely to relieve the bank of liability for the payment.

4. Any surviving relative, creditor or other person who claims an interest in the account may give a direction to the bank not to pay checks, or not to pay a particular check. Such notice has the same effect as direction to stop payment. The bank has no responsibility to determine the validity of the claim or even whether it is "colorable". But obviously anyone who has an interest in the estate, including the person named as executor in a will, even if the will not yet been admitted to probate, is entitled to claim an interest in the account.

Definitional Cross References:

"Accept". Section 3–410.
"Bank". Section 1–201.
"Certify". Section 3–411.
"Check". Section 3–104.
"Customer". Section 4–104.
"Depositary bank". Section 4–105.
"Item". Section 4–104.
"Payor bank". Section 4–105.

UCC

Section 4–406. Customer's Duty to Discover and Report Unauthorized Signature or Alteration.

(1) When a bank sends to its customer a statement of account accompanied by items paid in good faith in support of the debit entries or holds the statement and items pursuant to a request or instructions of its customer or otherwise in a reasonable manner makes the statement and items available to the customer, the customer must exercise reasonable care and promptness to examine the statement and items to discover his unauthorized signature or any alteration on an item and must notify the bank promptly after discovery thereof.

(2) If the bank establishes that the customer failed with respect to an item to comply with the duties imposed on the customer by subsection (1) the customer is precluded from asserting against the bank

(a) his unauthorized signature or any alteration on the item if the bank also established that it suffered a loss by reason of such failure; and

(b) an unauthorized signature or alteration by the same wrongdoer on any other item paid in good faith by the bank after the first item and statement was available to the customer for a reasonable period not exceeding fourteen calendar days and before the bank receives notification from the customer of any such unauthorized signature or alteration.

(3) The preclusion under subsection (2) does not apply if the customer establishes lack of ordinary care on the part of the bank in paying the item(s).

(4) Without regard to care or lack of care of either the customer or the bank a customer who does not within one year from the time the statement and items are made available to the customer (subsection (1))discover and report his unauthorized signature or any alteration on the face or back of the item or does not within three years from that time discover and report any unauthorized indorsement is precluded from asserting against the bank such unauthorized signature or indorsement or such alteration.

(5) If under this section a payor bank has a valid defense against a claim of a customer upon or resulting from payment of an item and waives or fails upon request to assert the defense the bank may not assert against any collecting bank or other prior party presenting or transferring the item a claim based upon the unauthorized signature or alteration giving rise to the customer's claim.

New York Annotations

(1) New York decisional law accords in imposing a duty of reasonable care upon depositors to examine vouchers and to report unauthorized signatures and alterations. Critten v. Chemical National Bank, 171 N.Y. 219, 63 N.E. 969 (1902). The provision for holding the customer's statement and items pursuant to his instructions, or making the statement available to him, is new, and no relevant authority has been found.

(2)(a) Insofar as this subsection would preclude the depositor from recovering upon the check bearing the unauthorized signature or alteration, adopting a theory of estoppel, the present New York rule would be changed. Critten v. Chemical National

Bank, *supra.* See, however, Stella Flour & Feed Corp. v. National City Bank, 285 App.Div. 182, 185–186, 136 N.Y.S.2d 139, 143–144, aff'd, 308 N.Y. 1023, 127 N.E.2d 864 (1955).

(b) Generally in *accord:* Critten v. Chemical National Bank, supra.

(3) Generally in *accord:* Critten v. Chemical National Bank, supra; Gutfreund v. East River National Bank, 251 N.Y. 58, 167 N.E. 171 (1929).

(4) The one-year statute of limitations as to the drawer's signature and alterations is in accord with N.I.L., § 326. However, this subsection would extend the two-year statute of limitations as to forged or unauthorized indorsements, contained in N.I.L., § 43. to three years. The subsection differs from the present statutes, however, in that: (1) it applies to any "item", not merely checks; (2) it covers any alteration, not merely raising; and (3), in accordance with subsection (1), it applies where the bank merely holds the customer's statement and items pursuant to his request or otherwise makes them available to him.

(5) This subsection would change the rule of National Surety Corp. v. Federal Reserve Bank of New York, 188 Misc. 207, 70 N.Y.S.2d 636, aff'd, 188 Misc.2d 213, 70 N.Y.S.2d 642 (1946). See also, Travelers Indemnity Co. v. Szymanski, 207 Misc. 130, 136 N.Y.S.2d 790 (1954).

Historical Note: This section was completely revised, pursuant to criticisms of the law Revision Commission and others, to provide for the effect of the failure of the bank to exercise ordinary care between the customer and the bank. The revision also dealt somewhat more precisely with the time when the duty of the customer to examine his bank statement arises. (1956 Recommendations, pp. 162–163; Excerpts, pp. 431–432.)

Official Uniform Comment

Prior Uniform Statutory Provision: None.

Purposes:

1. This section is new to Uniform Laws. It is to replace statutes in forty jurisdictions dealing with the general subject of a depositor's duty to discover and report forgeries and alterations. In these statutes there is substantial variation in rules prescribed as to the following matters: application of the statute to unauthorized signatures, raised checks or altered checks; inclusion of special provisions with respect to fictitious payees; periods of time prescribed for termination of right of customer to assert claims against bank; time when limitation period begins to run; restriction of rights of customer stated in terms of liability for loss, preclusion of rights or limitations on time in which suits may be brought.

2. Subsection (1) states the general duty of a customer to exercise reasonable care and promptness to examine his bank statements and items to discover his unauthorized signature or any alteration. This duty becomes operative when the bank does any one of three things with respect to the statement of account and supporting items paid in good faith. The first action is the sending of the statement and items to the customer. The sending may be either by mailing or any other action within the definition of "send" (Section 1–201). The second action is the holding of such statement and items available for the customer pursuant to a request for instructions of the customer. The third action is stated as "or otherwise in a reasonable manner makes the statement and items available to the customer." Such wider residual language is desirable to cover unusual situations. An example might be where a bank knows a customer has left a former address but does not know any new address to which to send the statement or item or to obtain instructions from the customer. The third residual type of action, however, must be "reasonable" and any court has the

power to determine that a particular action or practice of a bank, other than sending statements and items or holding them pursuant to instructions, is not reasonable.

3. Subsection (2) states the effect of a failure of a customer to comply with subsection (1). The first effect stated in subparagraph (a) is that he is precluded from asserting against the bank his unauthorized signature and alteration if the bank establishes that it suffered a loss by reason of the customer's failure. The bank has the burden of establishing that it suffered some loss.

Under subparagraph (b) if, after the first item and statement becomes available plus a reasonable period not exceeding fourteen calendar days, the bank pays in good faith any other item on which there is an unauthorized signature or alteration by the same wrongdoer, which payment is prior to receipt by bank of notification of such unauthorized signature or alteration on the first item, the customer is precluded from asserting the additional unauthorized signature or alteration. This rule follows substantial case law that payment of an additional item or items bearing an unauthorized signature or alteration by the same wrongdoer is a loss suffered by the bank traceable to the customer's failure to exercise reasonable care in examining his statement and notifying the bank of objections to it. One of the most serious consequences of failure of the customer to comply with the requirements of subsection (1) is the opportunity presented to the wrongdoer to repeat his misdeeds. Conversely, one of the best ways to keep down losses in this type of situation is for the customer to promptly examine his statement and notify the bank of an unauthorized signature or alteration so that the bank will be alerted to stop payment of further items. Hence, the rule of subparagraph (b) is prescribed and to avoid dispute a specific time limit for action by the customer is designated, namely fourteen calendar days.

4. The two effects on the customer of his failure to comply with subsection (1) (subparagraphs (a) and (b) of subsection (2)) are stated in terms of preclusion from asserting a claim against the bank. However, these two effects occur only if the customer has failed to exercise reasonable care and promptness in examining his statement and items and notifying the bank as to this question of fact the burden is upon the bank to establish such failure. Further, even if the bank succeeds in establishing that the customer has failed to exercise ordinary care, if in turn the customer succeeds in establishing that the bank failed to exercise ordinary care in paying the item(s) the preclusion rule does not apply. This distribution of the burden of establishing between the customer and the bank provides reasonable equality of treatment and requires each person asserting negligence to establish such negligence rather than requiring either person to establish that his entire course of conduct constituted ordinary care.

5. Whether the preclusions rule of subsection (2) operates or does not operate depends upon determinations as to the ordinary care of the customer and possibly of the bank. However, subsection (4) places an absolute time limit on the right of a customer to make claim for payment of altered or forged paper without regard to care or lack of care of either the customer or the bank. In the case of alteration or the unauthorized signature of the customer himself the absolute time limit is one year. In the case of unauthorized indorsements it is three years. This recognizes that there is little excuse for a customer not detecting an alteration of his own check or a forgery of his own signature. However, he does not know the signatures of indorsers and may be delayed in learning that indorsements are forged. The three year absolute limit on the discovery of forged indorsements should be ample, because in the great preponderance of cases the customer will learn of the forged indorsements within this time and if in any exceptional case he does not, the balance in favor of a mechanical termination of the liability of the bank outweighs what few residuary risks the customer may still have. In thirteen of the existing statutes there are limitations on the liability of a bank for payment of items bearing forged indorsements which limitation periods range from thirty days to two years. In the remaining twenty-seven no provision is made for forged indorsements.

6. Nothing in this section is intended to affect any decision holding that a customer who has notice of something wrong with an indorsement must exercise reasonable care to investigate and to notify the bank. It should be noted that under the rules relating to impostors and signatures in the name of the payee (Section 3–405) certain forged indorsements on which the bank has paid the item in good faith may be treated as effective notwithstanding such discovery and notice. If the alteration or forgery results from the drawer's negligence the drawee who pays in good faith is also protected. Section 3–406.

7. The forty existing statutes on the subject as well as Section 4–406 evidence a public policy in favor of imposing on customers the duty of prompt examination of their bank statements and the notification of banks of forgeries and alterations and in favor of reasonable time limitations on the responsibility of banks for payment of forged or altered items. In two New York cases, however, it has been held that a payor bank may waive defenses of the kind prescribed by the section and ignore the public policy indicated by these defenses and recover the full amount of a forged or altered item from a collecting bank. Fallick v. Amalgamated Bank of New York, 232 App.Div. 127, 249 N.Y. S. 238 (1st Dep't 1931); National Surety Corp. v. Federal Reserve Bank of New York, 188 Misc. 207, 70 N.Y.S.2d 636 (1946), affirmed without opinion 188 Misc. 213, 70 N.Y.S.2d 642 (1946). Subsection (5) is intended to reject the holding of these and like cases. Although the principle of subsection (5) might well be applied to other types of claims of customers against banks and defenses to these claims, the rule of the subsection is limited to defenses of a payor bank under this section. No present need is known to give the rule wider effect.

Cross References:

Sections 3–404, 3–405, 3–406, 3–407, 3–417 and 4–207.

Definitional Cross References:

"Alteration". Section 3–407.
"Bank." Section 1–201.
"Collecting bank". Section 4–105.
"Customer". Section 4–104.
"Good faith". Section 1–201.
"Indorsement". Section 3–204.
"Payor bank". Section 4–105.
"Send". Section 1–201.
"Unauthorized signature". Section 1–201.

Section 4–407. Payor Bank's Right to Subrogation on Improper Payment.

If a payor bank has paid an item over the stop payment order of the drawer or maker or otherwise under circumstances giving a basis for objection by the drawer or maker, to prevent unjust enrichment and only to the extent necessary to prevent loss to the bank by reason of its payment of the item, the payor bank shall be subrogated to the rights

(a) of any holder in due course on the item against the drawer or maker; and

(b) of the payee or any other holder of the item against the drawer or maker either on the item or under the transaction out of which the item arose; and

(c) of the drawer or maker against the payee or any other holder of the item with respect to the transaction out of which the item arose.

New York Annotations

(a) and (b) These subparagraphs would change the New York rule denying the bank the right to be subrogated to the rights of a holder in due course, holder, or payee either in defending a suit brought by the bank's customer or in proceeding against the customer by way of counter-claim or otherwise Chase National Bank v. Battat, 297 N.Y. 185, 78 N.E.2d 465 (1948); Egerton v. Fulton National Bank, 43 How.Pr. 216 (1872); K & K Silk Trimming Co. v. Garfield Nat. Bank, 127 Misc. 27, 215 N.Y.S. 269 (1926). There are some cases, however, indicating that a right of subrogation may exist in favor of a bank claiming against its customer. See Schneider v. Irving Bank, 30 How.Pr. 190 (1865); K & K Silk Trimming Co. v. Garfield Nat. Bank, 127 Misc. 27, 31, 215 N.Y.S. 269, 273–274 (1926) (concurring opinion of Bijur, J.); Dousmanis v. Colonial Bank, 134 Misc. 472, 235 N.Y.S. 489 (1929).

(c) It is clear that a bank may recover a payment negligently made over a stop order from a payee who knew payment had been stopped at the time he was paid. Smith & McCrorken v. Chatham Phenix National Bank & Trust Co., 239 App.Div. 318, 267 N.Y.S. 153 (1933). See also, Chase National Bank v. Battat, 105 N.Y.S.2d 13 (1951). There is also authority supporting the right of a bank to recover from an apparently innocent payee where the bank overlooked the fact that the customer's account had been closed. Manufacturers Trust Company v. Diamond, 17 Misc.2d 909, 186 N.Y.S.2d 917 (1959). The court in the Diamond case, by way of dictum, indicated that recovery would be denied the bank if the payment had caused the payee prejudice or to change his position in reliance, citing National Bank of Commerce of New York v. National Mechanics' Banking Ass'n of New York, 55 N.Y. 211, 213 (1873). In both of these instances, however, the right of recovery was quasi-contractual rather than by way of subrogation. Compare Section 4–207.

Official Uniform Comment

Prior Uniform Statutory Provision: None.

Purposes.

1. Section 4–403 states that a stop payment order is binding on a bank. If a bank pays an item over such a stop order it is prima facie liable, but under subsection (3) of 4–403 the burden of establishing the fact and amount of loss from such payment is on the customer. A defense frequently interposed by a bank in an action against it for wrongful payment over a stop-order is that the drawer or maker suffered no loss because he would have been liable to a holder in due course in any event. On this argument some cases have held that payment cannot be stopped against a holder in due course. Payment can be stopped, but if it is, the drawer or maker is liable and the sound rule is that the bank is subrogated to the rights of the holder in due course. The preamble and subsection (a) of this Section state this rule.

2. Subsection (b) also subrogates the bank to the rights of the payee or other holder against the drawer or make either on the item or under the transaction out of which it arose. It may well be that the payee is not a holder in due course but still has good rights against the drawer. These may be on the check but also may not be as, for example, where the drawer buys goods from the payee and the goods are partially defective so that the payee is not entitled to the full price, but the goods are still worth a portion of the contract price. If the drawer retains the goods he is obligated to pay a part of the agreed price. If the bank has paid the check it should be subrogated to this claim of the payee against the drawer.

3. Subsection (c) subrogates the bank to the rights of the drawer or maker against the payee or other holder with respect to the transaction out of which the item arose.

If, for example the payee was a fraudulent salesman inducing the drawer to issue his check for defective securities, and the bank pays the check over a stop order but reimburses the drawer for such payment, the bank should have a basis for getting the money back from the fraudulent salesman.

4. The limitations of the preable prevent the bank itself from getting any double recovery or benefits out of its subrogation rights conferred by the section.

5. The spelling out of the affirmative rights of the bank in this section does not destroy other existing rights (Section 1–103). Among others these may include the defense of a payor bank that by conduct in recognizing the payment a customer has ratified the bank's action in paying in disregard of a stop payment order or rights to recover money paid under a mistake.

Cross References:

Section 4–403.

Definitional Cross References:

"Holder". Section 1–201.
"Holder in due course". Section 3–302.
"Item". Section 4–104.
"Payor bank". Section 4–105.

Section 4–408. Rights and Liabilities of Remitter or Payee With Respect to Cashier's Check, Teller's Check and Certified Check.

(1) This section applies if a cashier's check, teller's check or certified check is not presented for payment on or before ninety days from the date of issuance of a cashier's check or teller's check, or the date of certification of a certified check.

(2) The remitter or payee that causes payment of a cashier's check, teller's check or certified check to be stopped pursuant to Section 4–403(2) engages that upon dishonor of the check and any necessary notice of dishonor he will pay, subject to defenses, the amount of the check to any subsequent holder or indorser who takes it up.

(3) When a stop payment order pursuant to Section 4–403(2) becomes effective the obligated bank shall refund the amount of the item to the remitter or payee that issued the stop payment order, and shall have no further liability on the item.

Added by L. 1990, Ch. 568, eff. July 1, 1991.

PART 5

COLLECTION OF DOCUMENTARY DRAFTS

Section 4–501. Handling of Documentary Drafts; Duty to Send for Presentment and to Notify Customer of Dishonor.

A bank which takes a documentary draft for collection must present or send the draft and accompanying documents for presentment and upon learning that the draft has not been paid or accepted in due course must seasonably notify its customer of such fact even though it may have discounted or bought the draft or extended credit available for withdrawal as of right.

New York Annotations

This is new statutory law and there is no New York case law directly in point. There is decisional law authority requiring a bank taking any draft, not just documentary drafts, for collection to "present or send the draft for presentment". Fitelson v. State Bank, 207 App.Div. 702, 201 N.Y.S., 737 (1923); Fahy v. Irving Trust Co., 247 App.Div. 767, 286 N.Y.S. 578, aff'd mem. 272 N.Y. 475, 3 N.E.2d 876 (1936). Case law also accords in requiring timely notice. Fahy v. Irving Trust Co., supra; Van Brunt & Co. v. Guaranty Trust Co., 119 Misc. 422, 196 N.Y.S. 779, rev'd on other grounds, 207 App.Div. 847, 201 N.Y.S. 911 (1923).

Historical Note: Prior to 1951 Sections 4–501 through 4–504 were a part of Article 4. In 1951 when a decision was made temporarily not to go forward with Article 4, these four sections were shifted to Article 3. When it was decided in September 1951 to reinstate Article 4, the four sections were not transferred back to Article 4. However, as they clearly belong in Article 4, they were thereafter retransferred to Article 4. The minor changes in text in Sections 4–501 and 4–503 meet suggestions made by the Law Revision Commission. (1956 Recommendations, p. 164.)

Official Uniform Comment

Prior Uniform Statutory Provision: None.

Purposes:

To state the duty of a bank handling a documentary draft for a customer. "Documentary draft" is defined in Section 4–104. Notice that the duty stated exists even when the bank has bought the draft. This is because to the customer the draft normally represents an underlying commercial transaction, and if that is not going through as planned he should know it promptly.

Cross References:

In Article 4: Sections 4–201, 4–202, 4–203, 4–204 and 4–210.
In Article 5: Sections 5–110, 5–111, 5–112 and 5–113.

Definitional Cross References:

"Documentary draft". Sections 4–104, 5–103.

Section 4–502. Presentment of "On Arrival" Drafts.

When a draft or the relevant instructions require presentment "on arrival", "when goods arrive" or the like, the collecting bank need not present until in its judgment a reasonable time for arrival of the goods has expired. Refusal to pay or accept because the goods have not arrived is not dishonor; the bank must notify its transferor of such refusal but need not present the draft again until it is instructed to do so or learns of the arrival of the goods.

UCC

New York Annotations

This is new law. Although no New York authority has been found, it is believed that the statement that the collecting bank need not present a draft until in its judgment a reasonable time for arrival of the goods has expired would not change New York law. See 1 Paton's Dig. 703 (1940).

Historical Note: See Historical Note to Section 4–501.

Official Uniform Comment

Prior Uniform Statutory Provision: None.

Purposes:

The section is designed to establish a definite rule for "on arrival" drafts. The term includes not only drafts drawn payable "on arrival" but also drafts forwarded with instructions to present "on arrival". The term refers to the arrival of the relevant goods. Unless a bank has actual knowledge of the arrival of the goods, as for example, when it is the "notify" party on the bill of lading, the section only requires the exercise of such judgment in estimating time as a bank may be expected to have. Commonly the buyer-drawee will want the goods and will therefore call for the documents and take up the draft when they do arrive.

Cross References:

In Article 4: Sections 4–202 and 4–203.
In Article 5: Section 5–112.

Definitional Cross References:

"Collecting bank". Section 4–105.

Section 4–503. Responsibility of Presenting Bank for Documents and Goods; Report of Reasons for Dishonor; Referee in Case of Need.

Unless otherwise instructed and except as provided in Article 5 a bank presenting a documentary draft

(a) must deliver the documents to the drawee on acceptance of the draft if it is payable more than three days after presentment; otherwise, only on payment; and

(b) upon dishonor, either in the case of presentment for acceptance or presentment for payment, may seek and follow instructions from any referee in case of need designated in the draft or if the presenting bank does not choose to utilize his services it must use diligence and good faith to ascertain the reason for dishonor, must notify its transferor of the dishonor and of the results of its effort to ascertain the reasons therefor and must request instructions.

But the presenting bank is under no obligation with respect to goods represented by the documents except to follow any reasonable instructions seasonably received; it has a right to reimbursement for any expense incurred in following instructions and to prepayment of or indemnity for such expenses.

New York Annotations

The reference to Article 5 in the preamble covers drafts drawn under a letter of credit.

(a) Compare Personal Property Law, § 227, and Code Section 2–514.

(b) Generally in *accord* with N.I.L., § 215. The Code language makes it clear that the referee in case of need may give instructions. N.I.L., § 215, is silent as to his powers.

No New York authority was found as to the bank's obligations in respect of the goods or in respect of the duty to request instructions, although there is authority charging the bank with responsibility to give advice of nonpayment or non-acceptance of a draft, even in the absence of express instructions. Van Brunt & Co. v. Guaranty Trust Co., 119 Misc. 422, 196 N.Y.S. 779, rev'd on other grounds, 207 App.Div. 847, 201 N.Y.S. 911 (1923).

Historical Note: At the suggestion of the Law Revision Commission, subsection (a) was revised to conform with Section 2–514. See, also, Historical Note to Section 4–501. (1956 Recommendations, p. 165; Excerpts, p. 417.)

Official Uniform Comment

Prior Uniform Statutory Provision: Section 13(3), Uniform Negotiable Instruments Law.

Changes: Completely rewritten and enlarged.

Purposes:

1. To state the rules governing, in the absence of instructions, the duty of the presenting bank in case either of honor or of dishonor of a documentary draft. The section should be read in connection with Section 2–514 on when documents are deliverable on acceptance, when on payment.

2. If the draft is drawn under a letter of credit, Article 5 controls. See Sections 5–109 through 5–114.

Cross References:

Point 1. Section 2–514; see also Section 4–504.

Point 2. Article 5, especially Sections 5–109 through 5–114.

Definitional Cross References:

"Documentary draft". Sections 4–104, 5–103.

"Presenting bank". Section 4–105.

Section 4–504. Privilege of Presenting Bank to Deal with Goods; Security Interest for Expenses.

(1) A presenting bank which, following the dishonor of a documentary draft, has seasonably requested instructions but does not receive them within a reasonable time may store, sell, or otherwise deal with the goods in any reasonable manner.

(2) For its reasonable expenses incurred by action under subsection (1) the presenting bank has a lien upon the goods or their proceeds, which may be foreclosed in the same manner as an unpaid seller's lien.

New York Annotations

(1) This subsection would appear to set forth generally accepted rules of agency. No New York authority directly in point was found.

(2) There is no comparable existing statutory lien, and no New York decisional law directly in point was found. The reference to enforcement of seller's lien is apparently a reference to the seller's power of resale. See Section 2–706 and annotations thereto.

Historical Note: See Historical Note to Section 4–501.

Official Uniform Comment

Prior Uniform Statutory Provision: None.

Purposes:

To give the presenting bank, after dishonor, a privilege to deal with the goods in any commercially reasonable manner pending instructions from its transferor and, if still unable to communicate with its principal after a reasonable time, a right to realize its expenditures as if foreclosing on an unpaid seller's lien (Section 2–706). The provision includes situations in which storage of goods or other action becomes commercially necessary pending receipt of any requested instructions, even if the requested instructions are later received.

The "reasonable manner" referred to means one reasonable in the light of business factors and the judgment of a business man.

Cross References:

Sections 4–503 and 2–706.

Definitional Cross References:

"Presenting bank". Section 4–105.

"Documentary draft". Sections 4–104, 5–103.

ARTICLE 4A

FUNDS TRANSFERS

PART 1

SUBJECT MATTER AND DEFINITIONS

PART 2

ISSUE AND ACCEPTANCE OF PAYMENT ORDER

PART 3

EXECUTION OF SENDER'S PAYMENT ORDER BY RECEIVING BANK

PART 4

PAYMENT

PART 5

MISCELLANEOUS PROVISIONS

PART 1

SUBJECT MATTER AND DEFINITIONS

Section 4A–101. Short Title.

This Article may be cited as Uniform Commercial Code – Funds Transfers.

Added by Laws 1990, Ch. 208, eff. Jan. 1, 1991.

Section 4A–102. Subject Matter.

Except as otherwise provided in Section 4A–108, this Article applies to funds transfers defined in Section 4A–104.

Added by Laws 1990, Ch. 208, eff. Jan. 1, 1991.

Official Uniform Comment

Prior Uniform Statutory Provision: None.

Purposes:

Article 4A governs a specialized method of payment referred to in the Article as a funds transfer but also commonly referred to in the commercial community as a wholesale wire transfer. A funds transfer is made by means of one or more payment orders. The scope of Article 4A is determined by the definitions or "payment order" and "funds transfer" found in Section 4A-103 and Section 4A-104.

The funds transfer governed by Article 4A is in large part a product of recent and developing technological changes. Before this Article was drafted there was no comprehensive body of law—statutory or judicial—that defined the juridical nature of a funds transfer or the rights and obligations flowing from payment orders. Judicial authority with respect to funds transfers is sparse, undeveloped and not uniform. Judges have had to resolve disputes by referring to general principles of common law or equity, or they have sought guidance in statutes such as Article 4 which are applicable to other payment methods. But attempts to define rights and obligations in funds transfers by general principles or by analogy to rights and obligations in negotiable instrument law or the law of check collection have not been satisfactory.

In the drafting of Article 4A, a deliberate decision was made to write on a clean slate and to treat a funds transfer as a unique method of payment to be governed by unique rules that address the particular issues raised by this method of payment. A deliberate decision was also made to use precise and detailed rules to assign responsibility, define behaviorial norms, allocate risks and establish limits on liability, rather than to rely on broadly stated, flexible principles. In the drafting of these rules, a critical consideration was that the various parties to funds transfers need to be able to predict risk with certainty, to insure against risk, to adjust operational and security procedures, and to price funds transfer services appropriately. This consideration is particularly important given the very large amounts of money that are involved in funds transfers.

Funds transfer involve competing interests—those of the banks that provide funds transfer services and the commercial and financial organizations that use the services, as well as the public interest. These competing interests were represented in the drafting process and they were thoroughly considered. The rules that emerged represent a careful and delicate balancing of those interests and are intended to be the exclusive means of determining the rights, duties and liabilities of the affected parties in any situation covered by particular provisions of the Article. Consequently, resort to principles of law or equity outside of Article 4A is not appropriate to create rights, duties and liabilities inconsistent with those stated in this Article.

Section 4A–103. Payment Order–Definitions.

(1) In this article:

(a) "Payment order" means an instruction of a sender to a receiving bank, transmitted orally, electronically, or in writing, to pay, or to cause another bank to pay, a fixed or determinable amount of money to a beneficiary if:

(i) the instruction does not state a condition to payment to the beneficiary other than time of payment,

(ii) the receiving bank is to be reimbursed by debiting an account of, or otherwise receiving payment from, the sender, and

(iii) the instruction is transmitted by the sender directly to the receiving bank or to an agent, funds transfer system, or communication system for transmittal to the receiving bank.

(b) "Beneficiary" means the person to be paid by the beneficiary's bank.

(c) "Beneficiary's bank" means the bank identified in a payment order in which an account of the beneficiary is to be credited pursuant to the order or which otherwise is to make payment to the beneficiary if the order does not provide for payment to an account.

(d) "Receiving bank" means the bank to which the sender's instruction is addressed.

(e) "Sender" means the person giving the instruction to the receiving bank.

(2) If an instruction complying with paragraph (a) of subsection (1) is to make more than one payment to a beneficiary, the instruction is a separate payment order with respect to each payment.

(3) A payment order is issued when it is sent to the receiving bank.

Added by Laws 1990, Ch. 208, eff. Jan. 1, 1991.

Official Uniform Comment

Prior Uniform Statutory Provision: None.

Purposes:

This section is discussed in the Comment following Section 4A–104.

Section 4A–104. Funds Transfer–Definitions.

In this Article:

(1) "Funds transfer" means the series of transactions, beginning with the originator's payment order, made for the purpose of making payment to the beneficiary of the order. The term includes any payment order issued by the originator's bank or an intermediary bank intended to carry out the originator's payment order. A funds transfer is completed by acceptance by the beneficiary's bank of a payment order for the benefit of the beneficiary of the originator's payment order.

(2) "Intermediary bank" means a receiving bank other than the originator's bank or the beneficiary's bank.

(3) "Originator" means the sender of the first payment order in a funds transfer.

(4) "Originator's bank" means (a) the receiving bank to which the payment order of the originator is issued if the originator is not a bank, or (b) the originator if the originator is a bank.

Added by Laws 1990, Ch. 208, eff. Jan. 1, 1991.

Official Uniform Comment

Prior Uniform Statutory Provision: None.

Purposes:

1. Article 4A governs a method of payment in which the person making payment (the "originator") directly transmits an instruction to a bank either to make payment to the person receiving payment (the "beneficiary") or to instruct some other bank to make payment to the beneficiary. The payment from the originator to the beneficiary occurs when the bank that is to pay the beneficiary becomes obligated to pay the beneficiary. There are two basic definitions: "Payment order" stated in Section 4A-103 and "Funds transfer" stated in section 4A-104. These definitions, other related definitions, and the scope of Article 4A can best be understood in the context of specific fact situations. Consider the following cases:

Case #1. X, which has an account in Bank A, instructs that bank to pay $1,000,000 to Y's account in Bank A. Bank A carries out X's instruction by making a credit of $1,000,000 to Y's account and notifying Y that the credit is available for immediate withdrawal. The instruction by X to Bank A is a "payment order" which was issued when it was sent to Bank A. Section 4A-103(a)(1) and (c). X is the "sender" of the payment order and Bank A is the "receiving bank." Section 4A-103(a)(5) and (a)(4). Y is the "beneficiary" of the payment order and Bank A is the "beneficiary's bank." Section 4A-103(a)(2) and (a)(3). When Bank A notified Y of receipt of the payment order, Bank A "accepted" the payment order. Section 4A-209(b)(1). When Bank a accepted the order it incurred an obligation to Y to pay the amount of the order. Section 4A-404(a). When Bank A accepted X's order, X incurred an obligation to pay Bank A the amount of the order. Section 4A-402(b). Payment from X to Bank A would normally be made by a debit to X's account in Bank A. Section 4A-403(a)(3). At the time Bank A incurred the obligation to pay Y, payment of $1,000,000 by X to Y was also made. Section 4A-406(a). Bank A paid Y when it gave notice to Y of a withdrawable credit of $1,000,000 to Y's account. Section 4A 405(a). The overall transaction, which comprises the acts of X and Bank A, in which the payment by X to Y is accomplished is referred to as the "funds transfer." Section 4A-104(a). In this case only one payment order was involved in the funds transfer. A one-payment-order funds transfer is usually referred to as a "book transfer" because the payment is accomplished by the receiving bank's debiting the account of the sender and crediting the account of the beneficiary in the same bank. X, in addition to being the sender of the payment order to Bank A, is the "originator" of the funds transfer. section 4A-104(c). Bank A is the "originator's bank" in the funds transfer as well as the beneficiary's back. Section 4A-104(d).

Case #2. Assume the same facts as in Case #1 except that X instructs Bank A to pay $1,000,000 to Y's account in Bank B. With respect to this payment order, X is the sender, Y is the beneficiary, and Bank A is the receiving bank. Bank A carries out X's order by instructing Bank B to pay 41,000,000 to Y's account. This instruction is a payment order in which Bank A is the sender, Bank B is the receiving bank, and Y is the beneficiary. When Bank A issued its payment order to Bank B, Bank A "executed" X's order. Section 4A-301(a). In the funds transfer, X is the originator, Bank A is the originator's bank, and Bank B is the beneficiary's bank. When Bank A executed X's order, X incurred an obligation to pay Bank A the amount of the order. Section 4A-402(c). When Bank B accepts the payment order issued to it by Bank A, Bank B incurs an obligation to Y to pay the amount of the order (Section 4A-404(a)) and Bank A incurs an obligation to pay Bank B. Section 4A402(b).

Acceptance by Bank B also results in payment of $1,000,000 by X to Y. Section 4A-406(a). In this case two payment orders are involved in the funds transfer.

Case #3. Assume the same facts as in Case #2 except that Bank A does not execute X's payment order by issuing a payment order to Bank B. One bank will not normally act to carry out a funds transfer for another bank unless there is a preexisting arrangement between the banks for transmittal of payment orders and settlement of accounts. For example, if Bank B is a foreign bank with which Bank A has no relationship, Bank A can utilize a bank that is a correspondent of both Bank A and Bank B. Assume Bank A issues a payment order to Bank C to pay $1,000,000 to Y's account in Bank B. With respect to this order, Bank A is the sender, Bank C is the receiving bank, and Y is the beneficiary. Bank C will execute the payment order of Bank A by issuing a payment order to Bank B to pay $1,000,000 to Y's account in bank B. With respect to Bank C's payment order, Bank C is the sender, Bank B is the receiving bank, and Y is the beneficiary. Payment of $1,000,000 by X to Y occurs when Bank B accepts the payment order issued to it by Bank C. In this case the funds transfer involves three payment orders. In thc funds transfer, X is the originator, Bank A is the originator's bank, Bank B is the beneficiary's bank, and Bank C is an "intermediary bank." Section 4A-104(b). In some cases there may be more than one intermediary bank, and in those cases each intermediary bank is treated like Bank C in Case #3.

As the three cases demonstrate, a payment under Article 4A involves an overall transaction, the funds transfer, in which the originator, X, is making payment to the beneficiary, Y, but the funds transfer may encompass a series of payment orders that are issued in order to effect the payment initiated by the originator's payment order.

In some cases the originator and the beneficiary may be the same person. This will occur, for example, when a corporation orders a bank to transfer funds from an account of the corporation in that bank to another account of the corporation in that bank or in some other bank. In some funds transfers the first bank to issue a payment order is a bank that is executing a payment order of a customer that is not a bank. In this case the customer is the originator. In other cases, the first bank to issue a payment order is not acting for a customer, but is making a payment for its own account. In that event the first bank to issue a payment order is the originator as well as the originator's bank.

2. "Payment order" is defined in Section 4A-103(a)(1) as an instruction to a bank to pay, or to cause another bank to pay, a fixed or determinable amount of money. The bank to which the instruction is addressed is known as the "receiving bank." Section 4A-103(a)(4). "Bank" is defined in Section 4A-105(a)(2). The effect of this definition is to limit Article 4A to payments made through the banking system. A Transfer of funds made by an entity outside the banking system is excluded. A transfer or funds through an entity other than a bank is usually a consumer transaction involving relatively small amounts of money and a single contract carried out by transfers of cash or a cash equivalent such as a check. Typically, the transferor delivers cash or a check to the company making the transfer, which agrees to pay a like amount to a person designated by the transferor. Transactions covered by Article 4A typically involve very large amounts of money in which several transactions involving several banks may be necessary to carry out the payment. Payments are normally made by debits or credits to bank accounts. Originators and beneficiaries are almost always business organizations and the transfers are usually made to pay obligations. Moreover, these transactions are frequently done on the basis of very short-term credit granted by the receiving bank to the sender of the payment order. Wholesale wire transfers involve policy questions that are distinct from those involved in consumer-based transactions by non banks.

3. Further limitations on the scope of Article 4A are found in the three requirements found in subparagraphs (i), (ii), and (iii) of Section 4A-103(a)(1). Subparagraph (i)

states that the instruction to pay is a payment order only if it "does not state a condition to payment to the beneficiary other than time of payment." An instruction to pay a beneficiary sometimes is subject to a requirement that the beneficiary perform some act such as delivery of documents. For example, a New York bank may have issued a letter of credit in favor of X, a California seller of goods to be shipped to the New York bank's customer in New York. The terms of the letter of credit provide for payment to X if documents are presented to prove shipment of the goods. Instead of providing for presentment of the documents to the New York bank, the letter of credit states that they may be presented to a California bank that acts as an agent for payment. The New York bank sends an instruction to the California bank to pay X upon presentation of the required documents. The instruction is not covered by Article 4A because payment to the beneficiary is conditional upon receipt of shipping documents. The function of banks in a funds transfer under Article 4A is comparable to the role of banks in the collection and payment of checks in that it is essentially mechanical in nature. The low price and high speed that characterize funds transfers reflect this fact. Conditions to payment by the California bank other than time of payment impose responsibilities on that bank that go beyond those in Article 4A funds transfers. Although the payment by the New York bank to X under the letter of credit is not covered by Article 4A, if X is paid by the California bank, payment of the obligation of the New York bank to reimburse the California bank could be made by an Article 4A funds transfer. In such a case there is a distinction between the payment by the New York bank to X under the letter of credit and the payment by the New York bank to he California bank. For example, if the New York bank pays its reimbursement obligation to the California bank by a Fedwire naming the California bank as beneficiary (see Comment 1 to § 4A-107), payment is made to the California bank rather than to X. That payment is governed by Article 4A and it could be made either before or after payment by the California bank to X. The payment by the New York bank to X under the letter of credit is not governed by Article 4A and it occurs when the California bank, as agent of the New York bank, pays X. No payment order was involved in that transaction. In this example, if the New York bank had erroneously sent an instruction to the California bank unconditionally instructing payment to X, the instruction would have been an Article 4A payment order. If the payment order was accepted (§ 4A-209(b)) by the California bank, a payment by the New York bank to X would have resulted (§ 4A-406(a)). But Article 4a would not prevent recovery of funds from X on the basis that X was not entitled to retain the funds under the law of mistake and restitution, letter of credit law or other applicable law.

4. Transfers of funds made through the banking system are commonly referred to as either "credit" transfers or "debit" transfers. In a credit transfer the instruction to pay is given by the person making payment. In a debit transfer the instruction to pay is given by the person receiving payment. The purpose of subparagraph (ii) of subsection (a)(1) of § 4A-103 is to include credit transfers in Article 4A and to exclude debit transfers. All of the instructions to pay in the three cases described in Comment 1 fall within subparagraph (ii). Take Case #2 as an example. With respect to X's instruction given to Bank A, Bank A will be reimbursed by debiting X's account or otherwise receiving payment from X. With respect to Bank A's instruction to Bank B, Bank B will be reimbursed by receiving payment from Bank A. In a debit transfer, a creditor, pursuant to authority front he debtor, is enabled to draw on the debtor's bank account by issuing an instruction to pay to the debtor's bank. If the debtor's bank pays, it will be reimbursed by the debtor rather than by the person giving the instruction. For example, the holder of an insurance policy may pay premiums by authorizing the insurance company to order the policyholder's bank to pay the insurance company. The order to pay may be in the form of a draft covered by Article 3, or it might be an instruction to pay that is not an instrument under the Article.

the bank receives reimbursement by debiting the policyholder's account. or, a subsidiary corporation may make payments to its parent by authorizing the parent to order the subsidiary's bank to pay the parent from the subsidiary's account. These transactions are not covered by Article 4A because subparagraph (2) is not satisfied. Article 4A is limited to transactions in which the account to be debited by the receiving bank is that of the person in whose name the instruction is given.

If the beneficiary of funds a transfer is the originator of the transfer, the transfer is governed by Article 4A if it is a credit transfer in form. If it is in the form of a debit transfer it is not governed by Article 4A. For example, Corporation has accounts in Bank A and Bank B. Corporation instructs Bank A to pay to Corporation's account in Bank B. The funds transfer is governed by Article 4A. Sometimes, Corporation will authorize Bank B to draw on Corporation's account in Ban A for the purpose of transferring funds into Corporation's account in Bank B. If Corporation also makes an agreement with Bank A under which Bank A is authorized to follow instructions of Bank B, as agent of Corporation, to transfer funds from Customer's account in Bank a, the instruction of Bank B is a payment order of Customer and is governed by Article 4A. This kind of transaction is known in the wire-transfer business as a "draw-down transfer." If Corporation does not make such an agreement with Bank A and Bank B instructs Bank A to make the transfer, the order is in form a debit transfer and is not governed by Article 4A. These debit transfers are normally ACH transactions in which Bank A relies on Bank B's warranties pursuant to ACH rules, including the warranty that the transfer is authorized.

5. The principal effect of subparagraph (iii) of subsection (a) of § 4A-103 is to exclude from Article 4A payments made by check or credit care. In those cases the instruction of the debtor to the bank on which the check is drawn or to which the credit care slip is to be presented is contained in the check or credit card slip signed by the debtor. The instruction is not transmitted by the debtor directly to the debtor's bank. Rather, the instruction is delivered or otherwise transmitted by the debtor to the creditor who then presents it to the bank either directly or through bank collection channels. These payments are governed by Articles 3 and 4 and federal law. There are, however, limited instances in which the paper on which a check is printed can be used as the means of transmitting a payment order that is covered by Article 4A. Assume that Originator instructs Originator's Bank to pay $10,000 to the account of Beneficiary in Beneficiary's Bank. Since the amount of Originator's payment order is small, if Originator's Bank and Beneficiary's Bank do not have an account relationship, Originator's Bank may execute Originator's order by issuing a teller's check payable to Beneficiary's Bank for $10,000 along with instructions to credit Beneficiary's account in that amount. The instruction to Beneficiary's Bank to credit Beneficiary's account is a payment order. The check is the means by which Originator's Bank pays its obligation as sender of the payment order. The instruction of Originator's Bank to Beneficiary's Bank might be given in a letter accompanying the check or it may be written on the check itself. In either case the instruction to Beneficiary's Bank is a payment order but the check itself (which is an order to pay addressed to the drawee rather than the Beneficiary's Bank) is an instrument under Article 3 and is not a payment order. The check can be both the means by which Originator's Bank pays its obligation under § 4A-402(b) to Beneficiary's Bank and the means by which the instruction to Beneficiary's Bank is transmitted.

6. Most payments covered by Article 4A are commonly referred to as wire transfers and usually involve some kind of electronic transmission, but the applicability of the Article 4A does not depend upon the means used to transmit the instruction of the sender. Transmission may be by letter or other written communication, oral communication or electronic communication. An oral communication is normally given by telephone. Frequently the message is recorded by the receiving bank to provide evidence of the transaction, but apart from problems of proof there is no

need to record the oral instruction. Transmission of an instruction may be a direct communication between the sender and the receiving bank or through an intermediary such as an agent of the sender, a communication system such as international cable, or a funds transfer system such as CHIPS, SWIFT or an automated clearing house.

Section 4A–105. Other Definitions.

(1) In this Article:

(a) "Authorized account" means a deposit account of a customer in a bank designated by the customer as a source of payment of payment orders issued by the customer to the bank. If a customer does not so designate an account, any account of the customer is an authorized account if payment of a payment order from that account is not inconsistent with a restriction on the use of that account.

(b) "Bank" means a person engaged in the business of banking and includes a savings bank, savings and loan association, credit union, and trust company. A branch or separate office of a bank is a separate bank for purposes of this article.

(c) "Customer" means a person, including a bank, having an account with a bank or from whom a bank has agreed to receive payment orders.

(d) "Funds-Transfer business day" of a receiving bank means the part of a day during which the receiving bank is open for the receipt, processing, and transmittal of payment orders and cancellations and amendments of payment orders.

(e) "Funds-Transfer system" means a wire transfer network, automated clearing house, or other communication system of a clearing house or other association of banks through which a payment order by a bank may be transmitted to the bank to which the order is addressed.

(f) "Good faith" means honesty in fact and the observance of reasonable commercial standards of fair dealing.

(g) "Prove" with respect to a fact means to meet the burden of establishing the fact (subsection (8) of section 1-201).

(2) Other definitions applying to this Article and the sections in which they appear are:

"Acceptance". Section 4A–209

"Beneficiary". Section 4A–103

"Beneficiary's bank". Section 4A 103

"Executed". Section 4A–301

"Execution date". Section 4A–301

"Funds transfer". Section 4A–104

"Funds-transfer system rule". Section 4A–501

"Intermediary bank". Section 4A–104

"Originator". Section 4A–104

"Originator's bank". Section 4A–104

"Payment by beneficiary's bank to beneficiary". Section 4A–405

"Payment by originator to beneficiary". Section 4A–406

"Payment by sender to receiving bank". Section 4A–403

"Payment date". Section 4A–401

"Payment order". Section 4A–103

"Receiving bank". Section 4A–103

"Security procedure". Section 4A–201

"Sender". Section 4A–103

(3) The following definitions in Article 4 apply to this Article:

"Clearing house". Section 4–104

"Item". Section 4–104

"Suspends payments". Section 4–104

(4) In addition Article 1 contains general definitions and principles of construction and interpretation applicable throughout this Article.

Added by Laws 1990, Ch. 208, eff. Jan. 1, 1991.

Official Uniform Comment

Prior Uniform Statutory Provision: None.

Purposes:

1. The definition of "bank" in subsection (a)(2) includes some instructions that are not commercial banks. The definition reflects the fact that many financial institutions now perform functions previously restricted to commercial banks, including acting on behalf of customers in funds transfers. Since many funds transfers involve payment orders to or from foreign countries the definition also covers foreign banks. The definition also includes Federal Reserve Banks. Funds transfers carried out by Federal Reserve Banks are described in Comments 1 and 2 to § 4A-107.

2. Funds transfer business is frequently transacted by banks outside of general banking hours. Thus, the definition of banking day in § 4A-104(1)(c) cannot be used to describe when a bank is open for funds transfer business. Subsection (a)(4) defines a new term, "funds transfer business day," which is applicable to Article 4A. The definition states, "is open for the receipt, processing, and transmittal of payment orders and cancellations and amendments of payment orders." In some cases it is possible to electronically transmit payment orders and other communications to a receiving bank at any time. If the receiving bank is not open for the processing of an order when it is received, the communication is stored in the receiving bank's computer for retrieval when the receiving bank is open for processing. The use of the conjunctive makes clear that the defined term is limited to the period during which all functions of the receiving bank can be performed, i.e., receipt, processing, and transmittal of payment orders, cancellations and amendments.

3. Subsection (a)(5) defines "funds transfer system." The term includes a system such as CHIPS which provides for transmission of a payment order as well as settlement of the obligation of the sender to pay the order. It also includes automated clearing houses, operated by a clearing house or other association of banks, which process and transmit payment orders of banks to other banks. In addition the term includes organizations that provide only transmission services such as SWIFT. The definition also includes the wire transfer network and automated clearing houses of Federal Reserve Banks. Systems of the Federal Reserve Banks, however, are treated differently from systems of other associations of banks. Funds transfer systems other than systems of the Federal Reserve Banks are treated in Article 4A as a means of communication of payment orders between participating banks. § 4A-206. The Comment to that section and the Comment to § 4A-107 explain how Federal Reserve Banks function under Article 4A. Funds transfer systems are also able to promulgate rules binding on participating banks that, under § 4A-501, may supplement or in some cases may even override provisions of Article 4A.

4. Subsection (d) incorporates definitions stated in Article 1 as well as principles of construction and interpretation stated in that Article. Included is § 1-103. the last paragraph of the Comment to § 4A-102 is addressed to the issue of the extent to which general principles of law and equity should apply to situations covered by provisions of Article 4A.

Section 4A–106. Time Payment Order is Received.

(1) The time of receipt of a payment order or communication cancelling or amending a payment order is determined by the rules applicable to receipt of a notice stated in subsection (27) of Section 1-201. A receiving bank may fix a cut-off time or times on a funds-transfer business day for the receipt and processing of payment orders and communications cancelling or amending payment orders. Different cut-off times may apply to payment orders, cancellations, or amendments, or to different categories of payment orders, cancellations, or amendments. A cut-off time may apply to senders generally or different cut-off times may apply to different senders or categories of payment orders. If a payment order or communication cancelling or amending a payment order is received after the close of a funds-transfer business day or after the appropriate cut-off time on a funds-transfer business day, the receiving bank may treat the payment order or communication as received at the opening of the next funds-transfer business day.

(2) If this Article refers to an execution date or payment date or states a day on which a receiving bank is required to take action, and the date or day does not fall on a funds-transfer business day, the next day that is a funds-transfer business day is treated as the date or day stated, unless the contrary is stated in this Article.

Added by Laws 1990, Ch. 208, eff. Jan. 1, 1991.

Official Uniform Comment

Prior Uniform Statutory Provision: None.

Purposes:

The time that a payment order is received by a receiving bank usually defines the payment date or the execution date of a payment order. § 4A-401 and § 4A-301.

the time of receipt of a payment order, or communication cancelling or amending a payment order is defined in subsection (a) by reference to the rules stated in § 1-201(27). Thus, time of receipt is determined by the same rules that determine when a notice is received. Time of receipt, however, may be altered by a cut-off time.

Section 4A–107. Federal Reserve Regulations and Operating Circulars.

Regulations of the Board of Governors of the Federal Reserve System and operating circulars of the Federal Reserve Banks supersede any inconsistent provision of this Article to the extent of the inconsistency.

Added by Laws 1990, Ch. 208, eff. Jan. 1, 1991.

Official Uniform Comment

Prior Uniform Statutory Provision: None.

Purposes:

1. Funds transfers under Article 4A may be made, in whole or in part, by payment orders through a Federal Reserve Bank in what is usually referred to as a transfer by Fedwire. If Bank A, which has an account in Federal Reserve Bank X, wants to pay $1,000,000 to Bank B, which has an account in Federal Reserve Bank Y, Bank A can issue an instruction to Reserve Bank X requesting a debit of $1,000,000 to Bank A's Reserve account and an equal credit to Bank B's Reserve account. Reserve Bank X will debit Bank A's account and will credit the account of Reserve Bank Y. Reserve Bank X will issue an instruction to reserve Bank Y requesting a debit of $1,000,000 to the account of Reserve Bank X and an equal credit to Bank B's account in Reserve Bank Y. Reserve Bank Y will make the requested debit and credit and will give Bank B an advice of credit. The definition of "bank: in § 4A-105(a)(2) includes both Reserve Bank X and Reserve Bank Y. Bank A's instruction to Reserve Bank X to pay money to Bank B is a payment order under § 4A-103(a)(1). Bank A is the sender and Reserve Bank X is the receiving bank. Bank B is the beneficiary of Bank A's order and of the funds transfer. Bank A is the originator of the funds transfer and is also the originator's bank. § 4A-104(c) and (d). Reserve Bank X, an intermediary bank under§ 4A-104(b), executes Bank A's order by sending a payment order to Reserve Bank Y instructing that bank to credit the Federal Reserve account of Bank B. Reserve Bank Y is the beneficiary's bank.

Suppose the transfer of funds from Bank A to Bank B is part of a larger transaction in which Originator, a customer of Bank A, wants to pay Beneficiary, a customer of Bank B. Originator issues a payment order to Bank A to pay $1,000,000 to the account of Beneficiary in Bank B. Bank A may execute Originator's order by means of Fedwire which simultaneously transfers $1,000,000 from Bank A to Bank B and carries a message instructing Bank B to pay $1,000,000 to the account of Y. The Fedwire transfer is carried out as described in the previous paragraph, except that the beneficiary of the funds transfer is Beneficiary rather than Bank B. Reserve Bank X and Reserve Bank Y are intermediary banks. When Reserve Bank Y advises Bank B of the credit to its Federal Reserve account it will also instruct Bank B to pay to the account of Beneficiary. The instruction is a payment order to Bank B which is the beneficiary's bank. When Reserve Bank Y advises Bank B of the credit to its Federal Reserve account Bank B receives payment of the payment order issued to it by Reserve Bank Y. § 4A-403(a)(1). The payment order is automatically accepted by Bank B at the time it receives the payment order of Reserve Bank Y. § 4A-209(b)(2). At the time of acceptance by Bank B payment by originator to Beneficiary also occurs. Thus, in a Fedwire transfer, payment to the beneficiary's bank, acceptance by the beneficiary's bank and payment by the originator to the beneficiary all occur simultaneously by operation of law at the time the payment order to the beneficiary's bank is received.

If Originator orders payment to the account of Beneficiary in Bank C rather than Bank B, the analysis is somewhat modified. Bank A may not have any relationship with Bank C and may not be able to make payment directly to Bank C. In that case, Bank A could send a Fedwire instructing Bank B to instruct Bank C to pay Beneficiary. The analysis is the same as the previous case except that Bank B is an intermediary bank and Bank C is the beneficiary's bank.

2. A funds transfer can also be made through a Federal Reserve Bank in an automated clearing house transaction. In a typical case, Originator instructs Originator's Bank to pay to the account of Beneficiary in Beneficiary's Bank. Originator's instruction to pay a particular beneficiary is transmitted to Originator's Bank along with many other instructions for payment to other beneficiaries by many different beneficiary's banks. All of these instructions are contained in a magnetic tape or other electronic device. Transmission of instructions to the various beneficiary's banks requires that Originator's instructions be processed and repackaged with instructions of other originators so that all instructions to a particular beneficiary's bank are transmitted together to that bank. The repackaging is done in processing centers usually referred to as automated clearing houses. Automated clearing houses are operated either by Federal Reserve Banks or by other associations of banks. If Originator's Bank chooses to execute Originator's instructions by transmitting them to a Federal Reserve Bank for processing by the Federal Reserve Bank, the transmission to the Federal Reserve Bank results in the issuance of payment orders by Originator's Bank to the Federal Reserve Bank, which is an intermediary bank. Processing by the Federal Reserve Bank will result in the issuance of payment orders by the Federal Reserve Bank to Beneficiary's Bank as well as payment orders to other beneficiary's banks making payments to carry out Originator's instructions.

3. Although the terms of Article 4A apply to funds transfers involving Federal Reserve Banks, federal preemption would make ineffective any Article 4A provision that conflicts with federal law. The payments activities of the Federal Reserve Banks are governed by regulations of the Federal Reserve Board and by operating circulars issued by the Reserve Banks themselves. In some instances, the operating circulars are issued pursuant to a Federal Reserve Board regulation. In other cases, the Reserve Bank issues the operating circular under its own authority under the Federal Reserve Act, subject to review by the Federal Reserve Board. § 4A-107 states that Federal Reserve Board regulations and operating circulars of the Federal Reserve Banks supersede any inconsistent provision of Article 4A to the extent of the inconsistency. Federal Reserve Board regulations, being valid exercises of regulatory authority pursuant to a federal statute, take precedence over state law if there is an inconsistency. Childs v. Federal Reserve Bank of Dallas, 719 F.2d 812 (5the cir. 1983), re. den. 724 F.2d 127 (5the Cir. 1984). § 4A-107 treats operating circulars as having the same effect whether issued under the Reserve Bank's own authority or under a Federal Reserve Board regulation.

Section 4A-108. Exclusion of Consumer Transactions Governed by Federal Law.

This Article does not apply to a funds transfer any part of which is governed by the Electronic Fund Transfer Act of 1978 (Title XX, Public Law 95-630, 92 Stat. 3728, 15 U.S.C. § 1693 et seq.) as amended from time to time.

UCC

Added by Laws 1990, Ch. 208, eff. Jan. 1, 1991.

Official Uniform Comment

Prior Uniform Statutory Provision: None.

Purposes:

The Electronic Fund Transfer Act of 1978 is a federal statute that covers a wide variety of electronic funds transfers involving consumers. The types of transfers covered by the federal statute are essentially different from the wholesale wire transfers that are the primary focus of Article 4A. § 4A-108 excludes a funds transfer from Article 4A if any part of the transfer is covered by the federal law. Existing procedures designed to comply with federal law will not be affected by Article 4A. The effect of § 4A-108 is to make Article 4A and EFTA mutually exclusive. For example, if a funds transfer is to a consumer account in the beneficiary's bank and the funds transfer is made in part by use of Fedwire and in part by means of an automated clearing house, EFTA applies to the ACH part of the transfer but not to the Fedwire part. Under § 4A-108, Article 4A does not apply to any part of the transfer. However, in the absence of any law to govern the part of the funds transfer that is not subject to EFTA, a court might apply appropriate principles from Article 4A by analogy.

PART 2

ISSUE AND ACCEPTANCE OF PAYMENT ORDER

Section 4A–201. Security Procedure.

"Security procedure" means a procedure established by agreement of a customer and a receiving bank for the purpose of (1) verifying that a payment order or communication amending or cancelling a payment order is that of the customer, or (2) detecting error in the transmission or the content of the payment order or communication. A security procedure may require the use of algorithms or other codes, identifying words or numbers, encryption, callback procedures, or similar security devices. Comparison of a signature on a payment order or communication with an authorized specimen signature of the customer is not by itself a security procedure.

Added by Laws 1990, Ch. 208, eff. Jan. 1, 1991.

Official Uniform Comment

Prior Uniform Statutory Provision: None.

Purposes:

A large percentage of payment orders and communications amending or cancelling payment orders are transmitted electronically and it is standard practice to use security procedures that are designed to assure the authenticity of the message. Security procedures can also be used to detect error in the content of messages or to detect payment orders that are transmitted by mistake as in the case of multiple transmission of the same payment order. Security procedures might also apply to communications that are transmitted by telephone or in writing. § 4A-201 defines these security procedures. The definition of security procedure limits the term to a procedure "established by agreement of a customer and a receiving bank." The term does not apply to procedures that the receiving bank may follow unilaterally in processing payment orders. The question of whether loss that may result from the transmission of a spurious or erroneous payment order will be borne by the receiving bank or the sender or purported sender is affected by whether a security procedure was or was not in effect and whether there was or was not compliance with the procedure. Security procedures are referred to in §§ 4A-202 and 4A-203, which deal with authorized and verified payment orders, and § 4A-205, which deals with erroneous payment orders.

Section 4A–202. Authorized and Verified Payment Orders.

(1) A payment order received by the receiving bank is the authorized order of the person identified as sender if that person authorized the order or is otherwise bound by it under the law of agency.

(2) If a bank and its customer have agreed that the authenticity of payment orders issued to the bank in the name of the customer as sender will be verified pursuant to a security procedure, a payment order received by the receiving bank is effective as the order of the customer, whether or not authorized, if (a) the security procedure is a commercially reasonable method of providing security against unauthorized payment orders, and (b) the bank proves that it accepted the payment order in good faith and in compliance with the security procedure and any written agreement or instruction of the customer restricting acceptance of payment orders issued in the name of the customer. The bank is not required to follow an instruction that violates a written agreement with the customer or notice of which is not received at a time and in a manner affording the bank a reasonable opportunity to act on it before the payment order is accepted.

(3) Commercial reasonableness of a security procedure is a question of law to be determined by considering the wishes of the customer expressed to the bank, the circumstances of the customer known to the bank, including the size, type, and frequency of payment orders normally issued by the customer to the bank, alternative security procedures offered to the customer, and security procedures in general use by customers and receiving banks similarly situated. A security procedure is deemed to be commercially reasonable if (a) the security procedure was chosen by the customer after the bank offered, and the customer refused, a security procedure that was commercially reasonable for that customer, and (b) the customer expressly agreed in writing to be bound by any payment order, whether or not authorized, issued in its name and accepted by the bank in compliance with the security procedure chosen by the customer.

(4) The term "sender" in this Article includes the customer in whose name a payment order is issued if the order is the authorized order of the customer under subsection (1), or it is effective as the order of the customer under subsection (2).

(5) This section applies to amendments and cancellations of payment orders to the same extent it applies to payment orders.

(6) Except as provided in this section and in paragraph (a) of subsection (l) of Section 4A–203, rights and obligations arising under this section or Section 4A–203 may not be varied by agreement.

Added by Laws 1990, Ch. 208, eff. Jan. 1, 1991.

Official Uniform Comment

Prior Uniform Statutory Provision: None.

Purposes:

This section is discussed in the Comment following Section 4A–203.

Section 4A–203. Unenforceability of Certain Verified Payment Orders.

(1) If an accepted payment order is not, under subsection (1) of Section 4A–202, an authorized order of a customer identified as sender, but is effective as an order of the customer pursuant to subsection (2) of Section 4A–202, the following rules apply:

(a) By express written agreement, the receiving bank may limit the extent to which it is entitled to enforce or retain payment of the payment order.

(b) The receiving bank is not entitled to enforce or retain payment of the payment order if the customer proves that the order was not caused, directly or indirectly, by a person (i) entrusted at any time with duties to act for the customer with respect to payment orders or the security procedure, or (ii) who obtained access to transmitting facilities of the customer or who obtained, from a source controlled by the customer and without authority of the receiving bank, information facilitating breach of the security procedure, regardless of how the information was obtained or whether the customer was at fault. Information includes any access device, computer software, or the like.

(2) This section applies to amendments of payment orders to the same extent it applies to payment orders.

Added by Laws 1990, Ch. 208, eff. Jan. 1, 1991.

Official Uniform Comment

Prior Uniform Statutory Provision: None.

Purposes:

1. Some person will always be identified as the sender of a payment order. Acceptance of the order by the receiving bank is based on a belief by the bank that the order was authorized by the person identified as the sender. If the receiving bank is the beneficiary's bank acceptance means that the receiving bank is obliged to pay the beneficiary. If the receiving bank is not the beneficiary's bank, acceptance means that the receiving bank has executed the sender's order and is obliged to pay the bank that accepted the order issued in execution of the sender's order. In either case the receiving bank may suffer a loss unless it is entitled to enforce payment of the payment order that is accepted. If the person identified as the sender of the order refuses to

pay on the ground that the order was not authorized by that person, what are the rights of the receiving bank? In the absence of a statute or agreement that specifically addresses the issue, the question usually will be resolved by the law of agency. In some cases, the law of agency works well. For example, suppose the receiving bank executes a payment order given by means of a letter apparently written by a corporation that is a customer of the bank and apparently signed by an officer of the corporation. If the receiving bank acts solely on the basis of the letter, the corporation is not bound as the sender of the payment order unless the signature was that of the officer and the officer was authorized to act for the corporation in the issuance of payment orders, or some other agency doctrine such as apparent authority or estoppel causes the corporation to be bound. Estoppel can be illustrated by the following example. Suppose P is aware that A, who is unauthorized to act for P, has fraudulently misrepresented to T that A is authorized to act for P. T believes A and is about to rely on the misrepresentation. If P does not notify T of the true facts although P could easily do so, P may be estopped from denying A's lack of authority. A similar esult could follow if the failure to notify T is the result of negligence rather than a deliberate decision. Restatement, Second, Agency § 8B. Other equitable principles such as subrogation or restitution might also allow a receiving bank to recover with respect to an unauthorized payment order that it accepted. In Gatoil (U.S.A.), Inc. v. Forest Hill State Bank, 1 U.C.C. Rep. Serv.2d 171 (D. Md. 1986), a joint venturer not authorized to order payments from the account of the joint venture, ordered a funds transfer from the account. The transfer paid a bona fide debt of the joint venture. Although the transfer was unauthorized the court refused to require recredit of the account because the joint venture suffered no loss. The result can be rationalized on the basis of subrogation of the receiving bank to the right of the beneficiary of the funds transfer to receive the payment from the joint venture.

But in most cases these legal principles give the receiving bank very little protection in the case of an authorized payment order. Cases like those just discussed are not typical of the way that most payment orders are transmitted and accepted, and such cases are likely to become even less common. Given the large amount of the typical payment order, a prudent receiving bank will be unwilling to accept a payment order unless it has assurance that the order is what it purports to be. This assurance is normally provided by security procedures described in § 4A-201.

In a very large percentage of cases covered by Article 4A, transmission of the payment order is made electronically. The receiving bank may be required to act on the basis of a message that appears on a computer screen. Common law concepts of authority of agent to bind principal are not helpful. There is no way of determining the identity or the authority of the person who caused the message to be sent. The receiving bank is not relying on the authority of any particular person to act for the purported sender. The case is not comparable to payment of a check by the drawee bank on the basis of a signature that is forged. Rather, the receiving bank relies on a security procedure pursuant to which the authenticity of the message can be "tested" by various devices which are designed to provide certainty that the message is that of the sender identified in the payment order. In the wire transfer business the concept of "authorized" is different from that found in agency law. In that business a payment order is treated as the order of the person in whose name it is issued if it is properly tested pursuant to a security procedure and the order passes the test.

§ 4A-202 reflects the reality of the wire transfer business. A person in whose name a payment order is issued is considered to be the sender of the order if the order is "authorized" as stated in subsection (a) or if the order is "verified" pursuant to a security procedure in compliance with subsection (b). If subsection (b) does not apply, the question of whether the customer is responsible for the order is determined by the law of agency. The issue is one of actual or apparent authority of the person who caused the order to be issued in the name of the customer. In some cases the law of agency might allow the customer to be bound by an unauthorized order if conduct of the customer can be used to find an estoppel against the customer to deny that the order was unauthorized. If the customer is bound by the order under any of these agency doctrines, subsection (a) treats the order as authorized and thus the customer is deemed to be the sender of the order. In most cases, however, subsection (b) will apply. In that event there is no need to make an agency law analysis to determine authority. Under § 4A-202, the issue of liability of the purported sender of the payment order will be determined by agency law only if the receiving bank did not comply with subsection (b).

2. The scope of § 4A-202 can be illustrated by the following cases. *Case #1*. A payment order purporting to be that of Customer is received by Receiving Bank but the order was fraudulently transmitted by a person who had no authority to act for Customer. *Case #2*. An authentic payment order was sent by Customer, but before the order was received by Receiving Bank the order was fraudulently altered by an unauthorized person to change the beneficiary. *Case #3*. An authentic payment order was received by Receiving Bank, but before the order was executed by Receiving Bank a person who has no authority to act for Customer fraudulently sent a communication purporting to amend the order by changing the beneficiary. In each case Receiving Bank acted on the fraudulent communication by accepting the payment order. These cases are all essentially similar and they are treated identically by § 4A-202. In each case Receiving Bank acted on a communication that it thought was authorized by Customer when in fact the communication was fraudulent. No distinction is made between Case #1 in which Customer took no part at all in the transaction and Case #2 and Case #3 in which an authentic order was fraudulently altered or amended by an unauthorized person. If subsection (b) does not apply, each case is governed by subsection (a). If there are no additional facts on which an estoppel might be found, Customer is not responsible in Case #1 for the fraudulently issued payment order, in Case #2 for the fraudulent alteration or in Case #3 for the fraudulent amendment. Thus, in each case Customer is not liable to pay the order and Receiving Bank takes the loss. The only remedy of Receiving Bank is to seek recovery from the person who received payment as beneficiary of the fraudulent order. If there was verification in compliance with subsection (b), Customer will take the loss unless § 4A-203 applies.

3. Subsection (b) of § 4A-202 is based on the assumption that losses due to fraudulent payment orders can best be avoided by the use of commercially reasonable security procedures, and that the use of such procedures should be encouraged. The subsection is designed to protect both the customer and the receiving bank. A receiving bank needs to be able to rely on objective criteria to determine whether it can safely act on a payment order. Employees of the bank can be trained to "test" a payment order according to the various steps specified in the security procedure. The bank is responsible for the acts of these employees. Subsection (b)(ii) requires the bank to prove that it accepted the payment order in good faith and "in compliance with the security procedure." If the fraud was not detected because the bank's employee did not perform the acts required by the security procedure, the bank has not complied. Subsection (b)(ii) also requires the bank to prove that it complied with any agreement or instruction that restricts acceptance of payment orders issued in the name of the customer. A customer may want to protect itself by imposing limitations on acceptance of payment orders by the bank. For example, the customer may prohibit the bank from accepting a payment order that is not payable from an authorized account, that exceeds the credit balance in specified accounts of the customer, or that exceeds some other amount. Another limitation may relate to the beneficiary. The customer may provide the bank with a list of authorized beneficiaries and prohibit acceptance of any payment order to a beneficiary not appearing on the list. Such limitations may

be incorporated into the security procedure itself or they may be covered by a separate agreement or instruction. In either case, the bank must comply with the limitations if the conditions stated in subsection (b) are met. Normally limitations on acceptance would be incorporated into an agreement between the customer and the receiving bank, ut in some cases the instruction might be unilaterally given by the customer. If standing instructions or an agreement state limitations on the ability of the receiving bank to act, provision must be made for later modification of the limitations. Normally this would be done by an agreement that specifies particular procedures to be followed. Thus, subsection (b) states that the receiving bank is not required to follow an instruction that violates a written agreement. The receiving bank is not bound by an instruction unless it has adequate notice of it. Subsections (25), (26) and (27) of § 1-201 apply.

Subsection (b)(i) assures that the interests of the customer will be protected by providing an incentive to a bank to make available to the customer a security procedure that is commercially reasonable. If a commercially reasonable security procedure is not made available to the customer, subsection (b) does not apply. The result is that subsection (a) applies and the bank acts at its peril in accepting a payment order that may be unauthorized. Prudent banking practice may require that security procedures be utilized in virtually all cases except for those in which personal contact between the customer and the bank eliminates the possibility of an unauthorized order. The burden of making available commercially reasonable security procedures is imposed on receiving banks because they generally determine what security procedures can be sued and are in the best position to evaluate the efficacy of procedures offered to customers to combat fraud. The burden on the customer is to supervise its employees to assure compliance with the security procedure and to safeguard confidential security information and access to transmitting facilities so that the security procedure cannot be breached.

4. The principal issue that is likely to arise in litigation involving subsection (b) is whether the security procedure in effect when a fraudulent payment order was accepted was commercially reasonable. The concept of what is commercially reasonable in a given case is flexible. Verification entails labor and equipment costs that can vary greatly depending upon the degree of security that is sought. A customer that transmits very large numbers of payment orders in very large amounts may desire and may reasonably expect to be provided with state-of-the-art procedures that provide maximum security. But the expense involved may make use of a state-of-the-art procedure infeasible for a customer that normally transmits payments orders infrequently or in relatively low amounts. Another variable is the type of receiving bank. It is reasonable to require large money center banks to make available state-of-the-art security procedures. On the other hand, the same requirement may not be reasonable for a small country bank. A receiving bank might have several security procedures that are designed to meet the varying needs of different customers. The type of payment order is another variable. For example, in a wholesale wire transfer, each payment order is normally transmitted electronically and individually. A testing procedure will be individually applied to each payment order. In funds transfers to be made by means of an automated clearing house many payment orders are incorporated into an electronic device such as a magnetic tape that is physically delivered. Testing of the individual payment orders is not feasible. Thus, a different kind of security procedure must be adopted to take into account the different mode of transmission.

The issue of whether a particular security procedure is commercially reasonable is a question of law. Whether the receiving bank complied with the procedure is a question of fact. It is appropriate to make the finding concerning commercial reasonability a matter of law because security procedures are likely to be standardized in the banking industry and a question of law standard leads to more predictability concerning the level of security that a bank must offer to its customers. The purpose of subsection (b) is to encourage banks to institute reasonable safeguards against fraud but not to make them insurers against fraud. A security procedure it not commercially unreasonable simply because another procedure might have been better or because the judge deciding the question would have opted for a more stringent procedure. The standard is not whether the security procedure is the best available. Rather it is whether the procedure is reasonable for the particular customer and the particular bank, which is a lower standard. On the other hand, a security procedure that fails to meet prevailing standards of good banking practice applicable to the particular bank should not be held to be commercially reasonable. Subsection (c) states factors to be considered by the judge in making the determination of commercial reasonableness. Sometimes an informed customer refuses a security procedure that is commercially reasonable and suitable for that customer and insists on using a higher-risk procedure because it is more convenient or cheaper. In that case, under the last sentence of subsection (c), the customer has voluntarily assumed the risk of failure of the procedure and cannot shift the loss to the bank. But this result follows only if the customer expressly agrees in writing to assume that risk. It is implicit in the last sentence of subsection (c) that a bank that accedes to the wishes of its customer in this regard is not acting in bad faith by so doing so long as the customer is made aware of the risk. In all cases, however, a receiving bank cannot get the benefit of subsection (b) unless it has made available to the customer a security procedure that is commercially reasonable and suitable for use by that customer. In most cases, the mutual interest of bank and customer to protect against fraud should lead to agreement to a security procedure which is commercially reasonable.

5. The effect of § 4A-202(b) is to place the risk of loss on the customer if an unauthorized payment order is accepted by the receiving bank after verification by the bank in compliance with a commercially reasonable security procedure. An exception to this result is provided by § 4A-203(a)(2). The customer may avoid the loss resulting from such a payment order if the customer can prove that the fraud was not committed by a person described in that subsection. Breach of a commercially reasonable security procedure requires that the person committing the fraud have knowledge of how the procedure works and knowledge of codes, identifying devices, and the like. That person may also need access to transmitting facilities through an access device or other software in order to breach the security procedure. This confidential information must be obtained either from a source controlled by the customer or from a source controlled by the receiving bank. If the customer can prove that the person committing the fraud did not obtain the confidential information from an agent or former agent of the customer or from a source controlled by the customer, the loss is shifted to the bank. "Prove" is defined in § 4A-105(a)(7). Because of bank regulation requirements, in this kind of case there will always be a criminal investigation as well as an internal investigation of the bank to determine the probable explanation for the breach of security. Because a funds transfer fraud usually will involve a very large amount of money, both the criminal investigation and the internal investigation are likely to be thorough. In some cases there may be an investigation by bank examiners as well. Frequently, these investigations will develop evidence of who is at fault and the cause of the loss. The customer will have access to evidence developed in these investigations and that evidence can be used by the customer in meeting its burden of proof.

6. The effect of § 4A-202(b) may also be changed by an agreement meeting the requirements of § 4A-203(a)(1). Some customers may be unwilling to take all or part of the risk of loss with respect to unauthorized payment orders even if all of the requirements of § 4A-202(b) are met. By virtue of § 4A-203(a)(1), a receiving bank may assume all of the risk of loss with respect to unauthorized payment orders or the customer and bank may agree that losses from unauthorized payment orders are to be divided as provided in the agreement.

7. In a large majority of cases the sender of a payment order is a bank. In many cases in which there is a bank sender, both the sender and the receiving bank will be members of a funds transfer system over which the payment order is transmitted. Since § 4A-202(f) does not prohibit a funds transfer system rule from varying rights and obligations under § 4A-202, a rule of the funds transfer system can determine how loss due to an unauthorized payment order from a participating bank to another participating bank is to be allocated. A funds transfer system rule, however, cannot change the rights of a customer that is not a participating bank. § 4A-501(b). § 4A-202(f) also prevents variation by agreement except to the extent stated.

Section 4A–204. Refund of Payment and Duty of Customer to Report with Respect to Unauthorized Payment Order.

(1) If a receiving bank accepts a payment order issued in the name of its customer as sender which is (a) not authorized and not effective as the order of the customer under Section 4A–202, or (b) not enforceable, in whole or in part, against the customer under Section 4A–203, the bank shall refund any payment of the payment order received from the customer to the extent the bank is not entitled to enforce payment and shall pay interest on the refundable amount calculated from the date the bank received payment to the date of the refund. However, the customer is not entitled to interest from the bank on the amount to be refunded if the customer fails to exercise ordinary care to determine that the order was not authorized by the customer and to notify the bank of the relevant facts within a reasonable time not exceeding ninety days after the date the customer received notification from the bank that the order was accepted or that the customer's account was debited with respect to the order. The bank is not entitled to any recovery from the customer on account of a failure by the customer to give notification as stated in this section.

(2) Reasonable time under subsection (1) may be fixed by agreement as stated in subsection (1) of Section 1-204, but the obligation of a receiving bank to refund payment as stated in subsection (1) may not otherwise be varied by agreement.

Added by Laws 1990, Ch. 208, eff. Jan. 1, 1991.

Official Uniform Comment

Prior Uniform Statutory Provision: None.

Purposes:

1. With respect to unauthorized payment orders, in a very large percentage of cases a commercially reasonable security procedure will be in effect. § 4A-204 applies only to cases in which (i) no commercially reasonable security procedure is in effect, (ii) the bank did not comply with a commercially reasonable security procedure that was in effect, (iii) the sender can prove, pursuant to § 4A-203(a)(2), that the culprit did not obtain confidential security information controlled by the customer, or (iv) the bank, pursuant to § 4A-203(a)(1) agreed to take all or part of the loss resulting from an unauthorized payment order. In each of these cases the bank takes the risk of loss with respect to an unauthorized payment order because the bank is not entitled to payment from the customer with respect to the order. The bank normally debits the

customer's account or otherwise receives payment from the customer shortly after acceptance of the payment order. Subsection (a) of § 4A-204 states that the bank must recredit the account or refund payment to the extent the bank is not entitled to enforce payment.

2. § 4A-204 is designed to encourage a customer to promptly notify the receiving bank that it has accepted an unauthorized payment order. Since cases of unauthorized payment orders will almost always involve fraud, the bank's remedy is normally to recover from the beneficiary of the unauthorized order if the beneficiary was party to the fraud. This remedy may not be worth very much and it may not make any difference whether or not the bank promptly learns about the fraud. But in some cases prompt notification may make it easier for the bank to recover some part of its loss from the culprit. The customer will routinely be notified of the debit to its account with respect to an unauthorized order or will otherwise be notified of acceptance of the order. The customer has a duty to exercise ordinary care to determine that the order was unauthorized after it has received notification from the bank, and to advise the bank of the relevant facts within a reasonable time not exceeding 90 days after receipt of notification. Reasonable time is not defined and it may depend on the facts of the particular case. If a payment order for $1,000,000 is wholly unauthorized, the customer should normally discover t in far less than 90 days. If a $1,000,000 payment order was authorized but the name of the beneficiary was fraudulently changed, a much longer period may be necessary to discover the fraud. But in any event, if the customer delays more than 90 days the customer's duty has not been met. The only consequence of a failure of the customer to perform this duty is a loss of interest on the refund payable by the bank. A customer that acts promptly is entitled to interest from the time the customer's account was debited or the customer otherwise made payment. The rate of interest is stated in § 4A-506. If the customer fails to perform the duty, no interest is recoverable for any part of the period before the bank learns that it accepted an unauthorized order. But the bank is not entitled to any recovery from the customer based on negligence for failure to inform the bank. Loss of interest is in the nature of a penalty on the customer designed to provide an incentive for the customer to police its account. There is no intention to impose a duty on the customer that might result in shifting loss from the unauthorized order to the customer.

Section 4A–205. Erroneous Payment Orders.

(1) If an accepted payment order was transmitted pursuant to a security procedure for the detection of error and the payment order (i) erroneously instructed payment to a beneficiary not intended by the sender, (ii) erroneously instructed payment in an amount greater than the amount intended by the sender, or (iii) was an erroneously transmitted duplicate of a payment order previously sent by the sender, the following rules apply:

(a) If the sender proves that the sender or a person acting on behalf of the sender pursuant to Section 4A–206 complied with the security procedure and that the error would have been detected if the receiving bank had also complied, the sender is not obliged to pay the order to the extent stated in paragraphs (b) and (c).

(b) If the funds transfer is completed on the basis of an erroneous payment order described in clause (i) or (iii) of subsection (1), the sender is not obliged to pay the order and the receiving bank is entitled to recover from the beneficiary any amount paid to the beneficiary to the extent allowed by the law governing mistake and restitution.

(c) If the funds transfer is completed on the basis of a payment order described in clause (ii) of subsection (1), the sender is not obliged to pay the order to the extent the amount received by the beneficiary is greater than the amount intended by the sender. In that case, the receiving bank is entitled to recover from the beneficiary the excess amount received to the extent allowed by the law governing mistake and restitution.

(2) If (i) the sender of an erroneous payment order described in subsection (1) is not obliged to pay all or part of the order, and (ii) the sender receives notification from the receiving bank that the order was accepted by the bank or that the sender's account was debited with respect to the order, the sender has a duty to exercise ordinary care, on the basis of information available to the sender, to discover the error with respect to the order and to advise the bank of the relevant facts within a reasonable time, not exceeding ninety days, after the bank's notification was received by the sender. If the bank proves that the sender failed to perform that duty, the sender is liable to the bank for the loss the bank proves it incurred as a result of the failure, but the liability of the sender may not exceed the amount of the sender's order.

(3) This section applies to amendments to payment orders to the same extent it applies to payment orders.

Added by Laws 1990, Ch. 208, eff. Jan. 1, 1991.

Official Uniform Comment

Prior Uniform Statutory Provision: None.

Purposes:

1. This section concerns error in the content or in the transmission of payment orders. It deals with three kinds of error. *Case #1.* The order identifies a beneficiary not intended by the sender. For example, Sender intends to wire funds to a beneficiary identified only by an account number. The wrong account number is stated in the order. *Case #2.* The error is in the amount of the order. For example, Sender intends to wire $1,000 to Beneficiary. Through error, the payment order instructs payment of $1,000,000. *Case #3.* A payment order is sent to the receiving bank and then, by mistake, the same payment order is sent to the receiving bank again. In Case #3, the receiving bank may have no way of knowing whether the second order is a duplicate of the first or is another order. Similarly, in Case #1 and Case #2, the receiving bank may have no way of knowing that the error exists. In each case, if this section does not apply and the funds transfer is completed, Sender is obliged to pay the order. § 4A-402. Sender's remedy, based on payment by mistake, is to recover from the beneficiary that received payment.

Sometimes, however, transmission of payment orders of the sender to the receiving bank is made pursuant to a security procedure designed to detect one or more of the errors described above. Since "security procedure" is defined by § 4A-201 as "a procedure established by agreement of a customer and a receiving bank for the purpose of * * * detecting error * * *," § 4A-205 does not apply if the receiving bank and the customer did not agree to the establishment of a procedure for detecting error. A security procedure may be designed to detect an account number that is not one to which Sender normally makes payment. In that case, the security procedure may require a special verification that payment to the stated account number was intended. In the case of dollar amounts, the security procedure may require different codes for different dollar amounts. If a $1,000,000 payment order contains a code that is inappropriate for that amount, the error in amount should be detected. In the case of duplicate orders, the security procedure may require that each payment order be identified by a number or code that applies to no other order. If the number or code of each payment order received is registered in a computer base, the receiving bank can quickly identify a duplicate order. The three cases covered by this section are essentially similar. In each, if the error is not detected, some beneficiary will receive funds that the beneficiary was not intended to receive. If this section applies, the risk of loss with respect to the error of the sender is shifted to the bank which has the burden of recovering the funds from the beneficiary. The risk of loss is shifted to the bank only if the sender proves that the error would have been detected if there had been compliance with the procedure and that the sender (or an agent under § 4A-206) complied. In the case of a duplicate order or a wrong beneficiary, the sender doesn't have to pay the order. In the case of an overpayment, the sender does nt have to pay the order to the extent of the overpayment. If subsection (a)(1) applies, the position of the receiving bank is comparable to that of a receiving bank that erroneously executes a payment order as stated in § 4A-303. However, failure of the sender to timely report the error is covered by § 4A-205(b) rather than by § 4A-304 which applies only to erroneous execution under § 4A-303. A receiving bank to which the risk of loss is shifted by subsection (a)(1) or (2) is entitled to recover the amount erroneously paid to the beneficiary to the extent allowed by the law of mistake and restitution. Rights of the receiving bank against the beneficiary are similar to those of a receiving bank that erroneously executes a payment order as stated in § 4A-303. Those rights are discussed in Comment 2 to § 4A-303.

2. A security procedure established for the purpose of detecting error is not effective unless both sender and receiving bank comply with the procedure. Thus, the bank undertakes a duty of complying with the procedure for the benefit of the sender. This duty is recognized in subsection (a)(1). The loss with respect to the sender's error is shifted to the bank if the bank fails to comply with the procedure and the sender (or an agent under § 4A-206) does comply. Although the customer may have been negligent in transmitting the erroneous payment order, the loss is put on the bank on a last-clear-chance theory. A similar analysis applies to subsection (b). If the loss with respect to an error is shifted to the receiving bank and the sender is notified by the bank that the erroneous payment order was accepted, the sender has a duty to exercise ordinary care to discover the error and notify the bank of the relevant facts within a reasonable time not exceeding 90 days. If the bank can prove that the sender failed in this duty it is entitled to compensation for the loss incurred as a result of the failure. Whether the bank is entitled to recover from the sender depends upon whether the failure to give timely notice would have made any difference. If the bank could not have recovered from the beneficiary that received payment under the erroneous payment order even if timely notice had been given, the sender's failure to notify did not cause any loss of the bank.

3. § 4A-205 is subject to variation by agreement under § 4A-501. Thus, if a receiving bank and its customer have agreed to a security procedure for detection of error, the liability of the receiving bank for failing to detect an error of the customer as provided in § 4A-205 may be varied as provided in an agreement of the bank and the customer.

Section 4A–206. Transmission of Payment Order Through Funds-Transfer or Other Communication System.

(1) If a payment order addressed to a receiving bank is transmitted to a funds-transfer system or other third-party communication system for transmittal to the

bank, the system is deemed to be an agent of the sender for the purpose of transmitting the payment order to the bank. If there is a discrepancy between the terms of the payment order transmitted to the system and the terms of the payment order transmitted by the system to the bank, the terms of the payment order of the sender are those transmitted by the system. This section does not apply to a funds-transfer system of the Federal Reserve Banks.

(2) This section applies to cancellations and amendments of payment orders to the same extent it applies to payment orders.

Added by Laws 1990, Ch. 208, eff. Jan. 1, 1991.

Official Uniform Comment

Prior Uniform Statutory Provision: None.

Purposes.

1. A payment order may be issued to a receiving bank directly by delivery of a writing or electronic device or by an oral or electronic communication. If an agent of the sender is employed to transmit orders on behalf of the sender, the sender is bound by the order transmitted by the agent on the basis of agency law. § 4A-206 is application of that principle to cases in which a funds transfer or communication system acts as an intermediary in transmitting the sender's order to the receiving bank. the intermediary is deemed to be an agent of the sender for the purpose of transmitting payment orders and related messages for the sender. § 4A-206 deals with error by the intermediary.

2. Transmission by an automated clearing house of an association of banks other than the Federal Reserve Banks is an example of a transaction covered by § 4A-206. Suppose Originator orders Originator's Bank to cause a large number of payments to be made to many accounts in banks in various parts of the country. These payment orders are electronically transmitted to Originator's Bank and stored in an electronic device that is held by Originator's Bank. Or, transmission of the various payment orders is made by delivery to Originator's Bank of an electronic device containing the instruction of the bank. In either case the terms of the various payment orders by Originator are determined by the information contained in the electronic device. In order to execute the various orders, the information in the electronic device must be processed. For example, if some of the orders are for payments to accounts in Bank X and some to accounts in Bank Y, Originator's Bank will execute these orders of Originator by issuing a series of payment orders to Bank X covering all payments to accounts in that bank, and by issuing a series of payment orders to Bank Y covering all payments to accounts in that bank. The orders to Bank X may be transmitted together by means of an electronic device, and those to Bank Y may be included in another electronic device. Typically, this processing is done by an automated clearing house acting for a group of banks including Originator's Bank. The automated clearing house is a funds transfer system. § 4A-105(a)(5). Originator's Bank delivers Originator's electronic device or transmits the information contained in the device to the funds transfer system for processing into payments orders of Originator's Bank to the appropriate beneficiary's banks. The processing may result in an erroneous payment order. Originator's Bank, by use of Originator's electronic device, may have given information to the funds transfer system instructing payment of $1,000,00 to an account in Bank X, but because of human error or an equipment malfunction the processing may have converted that instruction into an instruction to Bank X to make a payment of $1,000,000. Under § 4A-206, Originator's Bank issued a payment order

for $1,000,000 to Bank X when the erroneous information was sent to Bank X. Originator's Bank is responsible for the error of the automated clearing house. The liability of the funds transfer system that made the error is not governed by Article 4A. It is left to the law of contract, a funds transfer system rule, or other applicable law.

In the hypothetical case just discussed, if the automated clearing house is operated by a Federal Reserve Bank, the analysis is different. § 4A-206 does not apply. Originator's Bank will execute Originator's payment orders by delivery or transmission of the electronic information to the federal Reserve Bank for processing. The result is that Originator's Bank has issued payment orders to the Federal Reserve Bank which, in this case, is acting as an intermediary bank. When the Federal Reserve Bank has processed the information given to it by Originator's Bank it will issue payment orders to the various beneficiary's banks. If the processing results in an erroneous payment order, the Federal Reserve Bank has erroneously executed the payment order of Originator's Bank and the case is governed by § 4A-303.

Section 4A–207. Misdescription of Beneficiary.

(1) Subject to subsection (2), if, in a payment order received by the beneficiary's bank, the name, bank account number, or other identification of the beneficiary refers to a nonexistent or unidentifiable person or account, no person has rights as a beneficiary of the order and acceptance of the order cannot occur.

(2) If a payment order received by the beneficiary's bank identifies the beneficiary both by name and by an identifying or bank account number and the name and number identify different persons, the following rules apply:

(a) Except as otherwise provided in subsection (3), if the beneficiary's bank does not know that the name and number refer to different persons, it may rely on the number as the proper identification of the beneficiary of the order. The beneficiary's bank need not determine whether the name and number refer to the same person.

(b) If the beneficiary's bank pays the person identified by name or knows that the name and number identify different persons, no person has rights as beneficiary except the person paid by the beneficiary's bank if that person was entitled to receive payment from the originator of the funds transfer. If no person has rights as beneficiary, acceptance of the order cannot occur.

(3) If (i) a payment order described in subsection (2) is accepted, (ii) the originator's payment order described the beneficiary inconsistently by name and number, and (iii) the beneficiary's bank pays the person identified by number as permitted by paragraph (a) of subsection (2), the following rules apply:

(a) If the originator is a bank, the originator is obliged to pay its order.

(b) If the originator is not a bank and proves that the person identified by number was not entitled to receive payment from the originator, the originator is not obliged to pay its order unless the originator's bank proves that the originator, before acceptance of the originator's order, had notice that payment of a payment order issued by the originator might be made by the beneficiary's bank on the basis of an identifying or bank account number even if it identifies a person different from the named beneficiary. Proof of notice may be made by any admissible evidence. The originator's bank satisfies the burden of proof if it proves that the originator, before the payment order was accepted, signed a writing stating the information to which the notice relates.

(4) In a case governed by paragraph (a) of subsection (2), if the beneficiary's bank rightfully pays the person identified by number and that person was not entitled to receive payment from the originator, the amount paid may be recovered from that person to the extent allowed by the law governing mistake and restitution as follows:

(a) If the originator is obliged to pay its payment order as stated in subsection (3), the originator has the right to recover.

(b) If the originator is not a bank and is not obliged to pay its payment order, the originator's bank has the right to recover.

Added by Laws 1990, Ch. 208, eff. Jan. 1, 1991.

Official Uniform Comment

Prior Uniform Statutory Provision: None.

Purposes:

1. Subsection (a) deals with the problem of payment orders issued to the beneficiary's bank for payment to nonexistent or unidentifiable persons or accounts. Since it is not possible in that case for the funds transfer to be completed, subsection (a) states that the order cannot be accepted. Under § 4A-402(c), a sender of a payment order is not obliged to pay its order unless the beneficiary's bank accepts a payment order instructing payment to the beneficiary of that sender's order. Thus, if the beneficiary of a funds transfer is non-existent or unidentifiable, each sender in the funds transfer that has paid its payment order is entitled to get its money back.

2. Subsection (b), which takes precedence over subsection (a), deals with the problem of payment orders in which the description of the beneficiary does not allow identification of the beneficiary because the beneficiary is described by name and by an identifying number or an account number and the name and number refer to different persons. A very large percentage of payment orders issued to the beneficiary's bank by another bank are processed by automated means using machines capable of reading orders on standard formats that identify the beneficiary by an identifying number or the number of a bank account. The processing of the order by the beneficiary's bank and the crediting of the beneficiary's account are done by use of the identifying or bank account number without human reading of the payment order itself. The process is comparable to that used in automated payment of checks. The standard format, however, may also allow the inclusion of the name of the beneficiary and other information which can be useful to the beneficiary's bank and the beneficiary but which plays no part in the process of payment. If the beneficiary's bank has both the account number and name of the beneficiary supplied by the originator of the funds transfer, it is possible for the beneficiary's bank to determine whether the name and number refer to the same person, but if a duty to make that determination is imposed on the beneficiary's bank the benefits of automated payment are lost. Manual handling of payment orders is both expensive and subject to human error. If payment orders can be handled on an automated basis there are substantial

economies of operation and the possibility of clerical error is reduced. Subsection (b) allows banks to utilize automated processing by allowing banks to act on the basis of the number without regard to the name if the bank does not know that the name and number refer to different persons. "Know" is defined in § 1-201(25) to mean actual knowledge, and § 1-201(27) states ruls for determining when an organization has knowledge of information received by the organization. The time of payment is the pertinent time at which knowledge or lack of knowledge must be determined.

Although the clear trend is for beneficiary's banks to process payment orders by automated means, § 4A-207 is not limited to cases in which processing is done by automated means. A bank that processes by semi-automated means or even manually may rely on number as stated in § 4A-207.

In cases covered by subsection (b) the erroneous identification would in virtually all cases be the identifying or bank account number. In the typical case the error is made by the originator of the funds transfer. The originator should know the name of the person who is to receive payment and can further identify that person by an address that would normally be known to the originator. It is not unlikely, however, that the originator may not be sure whether the identifying or account number refers to the person the originator intends to pay. Subsection (b)(1) deals with the typical case in which the beneficiary's bank pays on the basis of the account number and is not aware at the time of payment that the named beneficiary is not the holder of the account which was paid. In some cases the false number will be the result of error by the originator. In other cases fraud is involved. For example, Doe is the holder of shares in Mutual Fund. Thief, impersonating Doe, requests redemption of the shares and directs Mutual Fund to wire the redemption proceeds to Doe's account #12345 in Beneficiary's Bank. Mutual Fund originates a funds transfer by issuing a payment order to Originator's Bank to make the payment to Doe's account #12345 in Beneficiary's Bank. Originator's Bank executes the order by issuing a conforming payment order to Beneficiary's Bank which makes payment to account #12345. That account is the account of Roe rather than Doe. Roe might be a person acting in concert with Thief or Roe might be an innocent third party. Assume that Roe is a gem merchant that agreed to sell gems to Thief who agreed to wire the purchase price to Roe's account in Beneficiary's Bank. Roe believed that the credit to Roe's account was a transfer of funds from Thief and released the gems to Thief in good faith in reliance on the payment. The case law is unclear on the responsibility of a beneficiary's bank in carrying out a payment order in which the identification of the beneficiary by name and number is conflicting. See Securities Fund Services, Inc. v. American National Bank, 542 F. Supp. 323 (N.D. Ill. 1982) and Bradford Trust Co. v. Texas American Bank, 790 F.2d 407 (5the Cir. 1986). § 4A-207 resolves the issue.

If Beneficiary's Bank did not know about the conflict between the name and number, subsection (b)(1) applies. Beneficiary's Bank has no duty to determine whether there is a conflict and it may rely on the number as the proper identification of the beneficiary of the order. When it accepts the order, it is entitled to payment from Originator's Bank. § 4A-402(b). On the other hand, if Beneficiary's Bank knew about the conflict between the name and number and nevertheless paid Roe, subsection (b)(2) applies. Under that provision, acceptance of the payment order of Originator's Bank did not occur because there is no beneficiary of that order. Since acceptance did not occur Originator's Bank is not obliged to pay Beneficiary's Bank. § 4A-402(b). Similarly, Mutual Fund is excused from its obligation to pay Originator's Bank. § 4A-402(c). Thus, Beneficiary's Bank takes the loss. Its only cause of action is against Thief. Roe is not obliged to return the payment to the beneficiary's bank because Roe received the payment in good faith and for value. Article 4A makes irrelevant the issue of whether Mutual Fund was or was not negligent in issuing its payment order.

3. Normally, subsection (b)(1) will apply to the hypothetical case discussed in Comment 2. Beneficiary's Bank will pay on the basis of the number without knowledge of the conflict. In that case subsection (c) places the loss on either Mutual Fund or Originator's Bank. It is not unfair to assign the loss to Mutual Fund because it is the person who dealt with the impostor and it supplied the wrong account number. It could have avoided the loss if it had not used an account number that it was not sure was that of Doe. Mutual Fund, however, may not have been aware of the risk involved in giving both name and number. Subsection (c) is designed to protect the originator, Mutual Fund, in this case. Under that subsection, the originator is responsible for the inconsistent description of the beneficiary if it had notice that the order might be paid by the beneficiary's bank on the basis of the number. If the originator is a bank, the originator always has that responsibility. The rational is that any bank should know how payment orders are processed and paid. If the originator is not a bank, the originator's bank must prove that its customer, the originator, had notice. Notice can be proved by any admissible evidence, but the bank can always prove notice by providing the customer with a written statement of the required information and obtaining the customer's signature to the statement. That statement will then apply to any payment order accepted by the bank thereafter. The information need not be supplied more than once.

In the hypothetical case of Originator's Bank made the disclosure stated in the last sentence of subsection (c)(2), Mutual Fund must pay Originator's Bank. Under subsection (d)(1), Mutual Fund has an action to recover from Roe if recovery from Roe is permitted by the law governing mistake and restitution. Under the assumed facts Roe should be entitled to keep the money as a person who took it in good faith and for value since it was taken as payment for the gems. In that case, Mutual Fund's only remedy is against Thief. If Roe was not acting in good faith, Roe has to return the money to Mutual Fund. If Originator's Bank does not prove that Mutual Fund had notice as stated in subsection (c)(2), Mutual Fund is not required to pay Originator's Bank. Thus, the risk of loss falls on Originator's Bank whose remedy is against Roe or Thief as stated above. Subsection (d)(2).

Section 4A–208. Misdescription of Intermediary Bank or Beneficiary's Bank.

(1) This subsection applies to a payment order identifying an intermediary bank or the beneficiary's bank only by an identifying number.

(a) The receiving bank may rely on the number as the proper identification of the intermediary or beneficiary's bank and need not determine whether the number identifies a bank.

(b) The sender is obliged to compensate the receiving bank for any loss and expenses incurred by the receiving bank as a result of its reliance on the number in executing or attempting to execute the order.

(2) This subsection applies to a payment order identifying an intermediary bank or the beneficiary's bank both by name and an identifying number if the name and number identify different persons.

(a) If the sender is a bank, the receiving bank may rely on the number as the proper identification of the intermediary or beneficiary's bank if the receiving bank, when it executes the sender's order, does not know that the name and number identify different persons. The receiving bank need not determine

UCC

whether the name and number refer to the same person or whether the number refers to a bank. The sender is obliged to compensate the receiving bank for any loss and expenses incurred by the receiving bank as a result of its reliance on the number in executing or attempting to execute the order.

(b) If the sender is not a bank and the receiving bank proves that the sender, before the payment order was accepted, had notice that the receiving bank might rely on the number as the proper identification of the intermediary or beneficiary's bank even if it identifies a person different from the bank identified by name, the rights and obligations of the sender and the receiving bank are governed by paragraph (a) of subsection (2), as though the sender were a bank. Proof of notice may be made by any admissible evidence. The receiving bank satisfies the burden of proof if it proves that the sender, before the payment order was accepted, signed a writing stating the information to which the notice relates.

(c) Regardless of whether the sender is a bank, the receiving bank may rely on the name as the proper identification of the intermediary or beneficiary's bank if the receiving bank, at the time it executes the sender's order, does not know that the name and number identify different persons. The receiving bank need not determine whether the name and number refer to the same person.

(d) If the receiving bank knows that the name and number identify different persons, reliance on either the name or the number in executing the sender's payment order is a breach of the obligation stated in paragraph (a) of subsection (1) of Section 4A–302.

Added by Laws 1990, Ch. 208, eff. Jan. 1, 1991.

Official Uniform Comment

Prior Uniform Statutory Provision: None.

Purposes:

1. This section addresses an issue similar to that addressed by § 4A-207. Because of automation in the processing of payment orders, a payment order may identify the beneficiary's bank or an intermediary bank by an identifying number. The bank identified by number might or might not also be identified by name. The following two cases illustrate § 4A-208(a) and (b):

Case #1. Originator's payment order to Originator's Bank identifies the beneficiary's bank as Bank A and instructs payment to Account #12345 in that bank. Originator's Bank executes Originator's order by issuing a payment order to Intermediary Bank. In the payment order to Originator's Bank the beneficiary's bank is identified as Bank A but is also identified by number, #67890. The identifying number refers to Bank B rather than Bank A. If processing by Intermediary Bank of the payment order of Originator's Bank is done by automated means, Intermediary Bank, in executing the order, will rely on the identifying number and will issue a payment order to Bank B rather than Bank A. If there is an Account #12345 in Bank B, the payment order of Intermediary Bank would normally be accepted and payment would be made to a person not intended by Originator. In this case, § 4A-208(b)(1) puts the risk of loss on Originator's Bank. Intermediary Bank may rely on the number

$67890 as the proper identification of the beneficiary's bank. Intermediary Bank has properly executed the payment order of Originator's Bank. By using the wrong number to describe the beneficiary's bank, originator's Bank has improperly executed Originator's payment order because the payment order of Originator's Bank provides for payment to the wrong beneficiary, the holder of Account #12345 in Bank B rather than the holder of Account #12345 in Bank A. § 4A-302(a)(1) and § 4A-303(c). Originator's Bank is not entitled to payment from Originator but is required to pay Intermediary Bank. § 4A-303(c) and § 4A-402(c). Intermediary Bank is also entitled to compensation for any loss and expenses resulting from the error by Originator's Bank.

If there is no Account #12345 in Bank B, the result is that there is no beneficiary of the payment order issued by Originator's Bank and the funds transfer will not be completed. Originator's Bank is not entitled to payment from Originator and Intermediary bank is not entitled to payment from Originator's Bank. § 4A-402(c). Since Originator's Bank improperly executed Originator's payment order it may be liable for damages under § 4A-305. As stated above, Intermediary Bank is entitled to compensation for loss and expenses resulting from the error by Originator's Bank.

Case #2. Suppose the same payment order by Originator to originator's Bank as in Case #1. In executing the payment order Originator's Bank issues a payment order to Intermediary Bank in which the beneficiary's bank is identified only by #67890. That number does not refer to Bank A. Rather, it identifies a person that is not a bank. If processing by Intermediary Bank of the payment order of Originator's Bank is done by automated means, Intermediary Bank will rely on the number #67890 to identify the beneficiary's bank. Intermediary Bank has no duty to determine whether the number identifies a bank. The funds transfer cannot be completed in this case because no bank is identified as the beneficiary's bank. Subsection (a) puts the risk of loss on Originator's Bank. Originator's Bank is not entitled to payment from Originator. § 4A-402(c). Originator's Bank has improperly executed Originator's payment order and may be liable for damages under § 4A-305. Originator's Bank is obliged to compensate Intermediary Bank for loss and expenses resulting from the error by Originator's Bank.

Subsection (a) also applies if #67890 identifies a bank, but the bank is not Bank A. Intermediary Bank may rely on the number as the proper identification of the beneficiary's bank. If the bank to which Intermediary Bank sends its payment order accepts the order, Intermediary Bank is entitled to payment from Originator's Bank, but Originator's Bank is not entitled to payment from Originator. The analysis is similar to that in Case #1.

2. Subsection (b)(2) of § 4A-208 addresses cases in which an erroneous identification of a beneficiary's bank or intermediary bank by name and number is made in a payment order of a sender that is not a bank. Suppose Originator issues a payment order to Originator's Bank that instructs that bank to use an intermediary bank identified as Bank A and by an identifying number, #67890. The identifying number refers to Bank B. Originator intended to identify Bank A as intermediary bank. If Originator's Bank relied on the number and issued a payment order to Bank B the rights of Originator's Bank depend upon whether the proof of notice stated in subsection (b)(2) is made by Originator's Bank. If proof is made, originator's Bank's rights are governed by subsection (b)(1) of § 4A-208. Originator's Bank is not liable for breach of § 4A-302(a)(1) and is entitled to compensation from Originator for any loss and expenses resulting from Originator's error. If notice is not proved, Originator's bank may not rely on the number in executing Originator's payment order. Since Originator's Bank does not get the benefit of subsection (b)(1) in that case, Originator's Bank improperly executed Originator's payment order and is in breach of the obligation stated in § 4A-302(a)(1). If notice is not given, Originator's Bank can rely on the name if it is not aware of the conflict in name and number. Subsection (b)(3).

3. Although the principal purpose of § 4A-208 is to accommodate automated processing of payment orders, § 4A-208 applies regardless of whether processing is done by automation, semi-automated means or manually.

Section 4A–209. Acceptance of Payment Order.

(1) Subject to subsection (4), a receiving bank other than the beneficiary's bank accepts a payment order when it executes the order.

(2) Subject to subsections (3) and (4), a beneficiary's bank accepts a payment order at the earliest of the following times:

(a) When the bank (i) pays the beneficiary as stated in subsection (1) or (2) of Section 4A–405, or (ii) notifies the beneficiary of receipt of the order or that the account of the beneficiary has been credited with respect to the order unless the notice indicates that the bank is rejecting the order or that funds with respect to the order may not be withdrawn or used until receipt of payment from the sender of the order;

(b) When the bank receives payment of the entire amount of the sender's order pursuant to paragraph (a) or (b) of subsection (1) of Section 4A–403; or

(c) The opening of the next funds-transfer business day of the bank following the payment date of the order if, at that time, the amount of the sender's order is fully covered by a withdrawable credit balance in an authorized account of the sender or the bank has otherwise received full payment from the sender, unless the order was rejected before that time or is rejected within (i) one hour after that time, or (ii) one hour after the opening of the next business day of the sender following the payment date if that time is later. If notice of rejection is received by the sender after the payment date and the authorized account of the sender does not bear interest, the bank is obliged to pay interest to the sender on the amount of the order for the number of days elapsing after the payment date to the day the sender receives notice or learns that the order was not accepted, counting that day as an elapsed day. If the withdrawable credit balance during that period falls below the amount of the order, the amount of interest payable is reduced accordingly.

(3) Acceptance of a payment order cannot occur before the order is received by the receiving bank. Acceptance does not occur under paragraph (b) or (c) of subsection (2) if the beneficiary of the payment order does not have an account with the receiving bank, the account has been closed, or the receiving bank is not permitted by law to receive credits for the beneficiary's account.

(4) A payment order issued to the originator's bank cannot be accepted until the payment date if the bank is the beneficiary's bank, or the execution date if the bank is not the beneficiary's bank. If the originator's bank executes the originator's payment order before the execution date or pays the beneficiary of the originator's payment order before the payment date and the payment order is subsequently cancelled pursuant to subsection (2) of Section 4A–211, the bank may recover from the beneficiary any payment received to the extent allowed by the law governing mistake and restitution.

Added by Laws 1990, Ch. 208, eff. Jan. 1, 1991.

Official Uniform Comment

Prior Uniform Statutory Provision: None.

Purposes:

1. This section treats the sender's payment order as a request by the sender to the receiving bank to execute or pay the order and that request can be accepted or rejected by the receiving bank. § 4A-209 defines when acceptance occurs. § 4A-210 covers rejection. Acceptance of the payment order imposes an obligation on the receiving bank to the sender if the receiving bank is not the beneficiary's bank, or to the beneficiary if the receiving bank is the beneficiary's bank. These obligations are stated in § 4A-302 and § 4A-404.

2. Acceptance by a receiving bank other than the beneficiary's bank is defined in § 4A-209(a). That subsection states the only way that a bank other than the beneficiary's bank can accept a payment order. A payment order to a bank other than the beneficiary's bank is, in effect, a request that the receiving bank execute the sender's order by issuing a payment order to the beneficiary's bank or to an intermediary bank. Normally, acceptance occurs at the time of execution, but there is an exception stated in subsection (d) and discussed in Comment 9. Execution occurs when the receiving bank "issues a payment order intended to carry out" the sender's order. § 4A-301(a). In some cases the payment order issued by the receiving bank may not conform to the sender's order. For example, the receiving bank might make a mistake in the amount of its order, or the order might be issued to the wrong beneficiary's bank or for the benefit of the wrong beneficiary. In all of these cases there is acceptance of the sender's order by the bank when the receiving bank issues its order intended to carry out the sender's order, even though the bank's payment order does not in fact carry out the instruction of the sender. Improper execution of the sender's order may lead to liability to the sender for damages or it may mean that the sender is not obliged to pay its payment order. These matters are covered in § 4A-303, § 4A-305, and § 4A-402.

3. A receiving bank has no duty to accept a payment order unless the bank makes an agreement, either before or after issuance of the payment order, to accept it, or acceptance is required by a funds transfer system rule. If the bank makes such an agreement it incurs a contractual obligation based on the agreement and may be held liable for breach of contract if a failure to execute violates the agreement. In many cases a bank will enter into an agreement with its customer to govern the rights and obligations of the parties with respect to payment orders issued to the bank by the customer or, in cases in which the sender is also a bank, there may be a funds transfer system rule that governs the obligations of a receiving bank with respect to payment orders transmitted over the system. Such agreements or rules can specify the circumstances under which a receiving bank is obliged to execute a payment order and can define the extent of liability of the receiving bank for breach of the agreement or rule. § 4A-305(d) states the liability for breach of an agreement to execute a payment order.

4. In the case of a payment order issued to the beneficiary's bank, acceptance is defined in § 4A-209(b). The function of a beneficiary's bank that receives a payment order is different from that of a receiving bank that receives a payment order for execution. In the typical case, the beneficiary's bank simply receives payment from the sender of the order, credits the account of the beneficiary and notifies the beneficiary of credit. Acceptance by the beneficiary's bank does not create any obligation to the sender. Acceptance by the beneficiary's bank means that the bank

is liable to the beneficiary for the amount of the order. § 4A-404(a). There are three ways in which the beneficiary's bank can accept a payment order which are described in the following comments.

5. Under § 4A-209(b)(1), the beneficiary's bank can accept a payment order by paying the beneficiary. In the normal case of crediting an account of the beneficiary, payment occurs when the beneficiary is given notice of the right to withdraw the credit, the credit is applied to a debt of the beneficiary, or "funds with respect to the order" are otherwise made available to the beneficiary. § 4A-405(a). The quoted phrase covers cases in which funds are made available to the beneficiary as a result of receipt of a payment order for the benefit of the beneficiary but the release of funds is not expressed as payment of the order. For example, the beneficiary's bank might express a release of funds equal to the amount of the order as a "loan" that will be automatically repaid when the beneficiary's bank receives payment by the sender of the order. If the release of funds is designated as a loan pursuant to a routine practice of the bank, the release is conditional payment of the order rather than a loan, particularly if normal incidents of a loan such as the signing of a loan agreement or note and the payment of interest are not present. Such a release of funds is payment to the beneficiary under § 4A-405(a). Under § 4A-405(c) the bank cannot recover the money from the beneficiary if the bank does not receive payment from the sender of the payment order that it accepted. Exceptions to this rule are stated in § 4A-405(d) and (e). The beneficiary's bank may also accept by notifying the beneficiary that the order has been received. "Notifies" is defined in § 1-201(26). In some cases a beneficiary's bank will receive a payment order during the day but settlement of the sender's obligation to pay the order will not occur until the end of the day. If the beneficiary's bank wants to defer incurring liability to the beneficiary until the beneficiary's bank receives payment, it can do so. The beneficiary's bank incurs no liability to the beneficiary with respect to a payment order that it receives until it accepts the order. If the bank does not accept pursuant to subsection (b)(1), acceptance does not occur until the end of the day when the beneficiary's bank receives settlement. If the sender settles, the payment order will be accepted under subsection (b)(2) and the funds will be released to the beneficiary the next morning. If the sender doesn't settle, no acceptance occurs. In either case the beneficiary's bank suffers no loss.

6. In most cases the beneficiary's bank will receive a payment order from another bank. If the sender is a bank and the beneficiary's bank receives payment from the sender by final settlement through the Federal Reserve System or a funds transfer system (§ 4A-403(a)(1)) or, less commonly, through credit to an account of the beneficiary's bank with the sender or another bank (§ 4A-403(a)(2)), acceptance by the beneficiary's bank occurs at the time payment is made. § 4A-209(b)(2). A minor exception to this rule is stated in § 4A-209(c). § 4A-209(b)(2) results in automatic acceptance of payment orders issued to a beneficiary's bank by means of Fedwire because the Federal Reserve account of the beneficiary's bank is credited and final payment is made to that bank when the payment order is received.

Subsection (b)(2) would also apply to cases in which the beneficiary's bank mistakenly pays a person who is not the beneficiary of the payment order issued to the beneficiary's bank. For example, suppose the payment order provides for immediate payment to Account #12345. The beneficiary's bank erroneously credits Account #12346 and notifies the holder of that account of the credit. No acceptance occurs in this case under subsection (b)(1) because the beneficiary of the order has not been paid or notified. The holder of Account #12345 is the beneficiary of the order issued to the beneficiary's bank. But acceptance will normally occur if the beneficiary's bank takes no other action, because the bank will normally receive settlement with respect to the payment order. At that time the bank has accepted because the sender paid its payment order. The bank is liable to pay the holder of Account #12345. The bank has paid the holder of Account #12346 by mistake, and has a right to recover the payment if the credit is withdrawn, to the extent provided in the law governing mistake and restitution.

7. Subsection (b)(3) covers cases of inaction by the beneficiary's bank. It applies whether or not the sender is a bank and covers a case in which the sender and the beneficiary both have accounts with the receiving bank and payment will be made by debiting the account of the sender and crediting the account of the beneficiary. Subsection (b)(3) is similar to subsection (b)(2) in that it bases acceptance by the beneficiary's bank on payment by the sender. Payment by the sender is effected by a debit to the sender's account if the account balance is sufficient to cover the amount of the order. On the payment date (§ 4A-401) of the order the beneficiary's bank will normally credit the beneficiary's account and notify the beneficiary of receipt of the order if it is satisfied that the sender's account balance covers the order or is willing to give credit to the sender. In some cases, however, the bank may not be willing to give credit to the sender and it may not be possible for the bank to determine until the end of the day on the payment date where there are sufficient good funds in the sender's account. There may be various transactions during the day involving funds going into and out of the account. Some of these transactions may occur late in the day or after the close of the banking day. To accommodate this situation, subsection (b)(3) provides that the status of the account is determined at the opening of the next funds transfer business day of the beneficiary's bank after the payment date of the order. If the sender's account balance is sufficient to cover the order, the beneficiary's bank has a source of payment and the result in almost all cases is that the bank accepts the order at that time if it did not previously accept under subsection (b)(1). In rare cases, a bank may want to avoid acceptance under subsection (b)(3) by rejecting the order as discussed in Comment 8.

8. § 4A-209 is based on a general principle that a receiving bank is not obliged to accept a payment order unless it has agreed or is bound by a funds transfer system rule to do so. Thus, provision is made to allow the receiving bank to prevent acceptance of the order. This principle is consistently followed if the receiving bank is not the beneficiary's bank. If the receiving bank is not the beneficiary's bank, acceptance is in the control of the receiving bank because it occurs only if the order is executed. But in the case of the beneficiary's bank acceptance can occur by passive receipt of payment under subsection (b)(2) or (3). In the case of a payment made by Fedwire acceptance cannot be prevented. In other cases the beneficiary's bank can prevent acceptance by giving notice of rejection to the sender before payment occurs under § 4A-403(a)(1) or (2). A minor exception to the ability of the beneficiary's bank to reject is stated in § 4A-502(c)(3).

Under subsection (b)(3) acceptance occurs at the opening of the next funds transfer business day of the beneficiary's bank following the payment date unless the bank rejected the order before that time or it rejects within one hour after that time. In some cases the sender and the beneficiary's bank may not be in the same time zone or the beginning of the business day of the sender and the funds transfer business day of the beneficiary's bank may not coincide. For example, the sender may be located in California and the beneficiary's bank in New York. Since in most cases notice of rejection would be communicated electronically or by telephone, it might not be feasible for the bank to give notice before one hour after the opening of the funds transfer business day in New York because at that hour, the sender's business day may not have started in California. For that reason, there are alternative deadlines stated in subsection (b)(3). In the case stated, the bank acts in time if it gives notice within one hour after the opening of the business day of the sender. But if the notice of rejection is received by the sender after the payment date, the bank is obliged to pay interest to the sender if the sender's account does not bear interest. In that case the bank had the use of funds of the sender that the sender could reasonably assume would be used to pay the beneficiary. The rate of interest is stated in § 4A-506. If

UCC

the sender receives notice on the day after the payment date the sender is entitled to one day's interest. If receipt of notice is delayed for more than one day, the sender is entitled to interest for each additional day of delay.

9. Subsection (d) applies only to a payment order by the originator of a funds transfer to the originator's bank and it refers to the following situation. On April 1, Originator instructs Bank A to make a payment on April 15 to the account of Beneficiary in Bank B. By mistake, on April 1, Bank A executes Originator's payment order by issuing a payment order to Bank B instructing immediate payment to Beneficiary. Bank B credited Beneficiary's account and immediately released the funds to Beneficiary. Under subsection (d) no acceptance by Bank A occurred on April 1 when Originator's payment order was executed because acceptance cannot occur before the execution date which in this case would be April 15 or shortly before that date. § 4A-301(b). Under § 4A-402(c), Originator is not obliged to pay Bank A until the order is accepted and that can't occur until the execution date. But Bank A is required to pay Bank B when Bank B accepted Bank A's order on April 1. Unless Originator and Beneficiary are the same person, in almost all cases Originator is paying a debt owed Beneficiary and early payment does not injure Originator because Originator does not have to pay Bank A until the execution date. § 4A-402(c). Bank A takes the interest loss. But suppose that on April 3, Originator concludes that no debt was owed to Beneficiary or that the debt was less than the amount of the payment order. Under § 4A-211(b) Originator can cancel its payment order if Bank a has not accepted. If early execution of Originator's payment order is acceptance, Originator can suffer a loss because cancellation after acceptance is not possible without the consent of Bank A and Bank B. § 4A-211(c). If Originator has to pay Bank A, Originator would be required to seek recovery of the money from Beneficiary. Subsection (d) prevents this result and puts the risk of loss on Bank A by providing that the early execution does not result in acceptance until the execution date. Since on April 3 Originator's order was not yet accepted, Originator can cancel it under § 4A-211(b). The result is that Bank A is not entitled to payment from Originator but is obliged to pay Bank B. Bank A has paid Beneficiary by mistake. If Originator's payment order is cancelled, Bank A becomes the originator of an erroneous funds transfer to Beneficiary. Bank A has the burden of recovering payment from Beneficiary on the basis of a payment by mistake. If Beneficiary received the money in good faith in payment of a debt owed to Beneficiary by Originator, the law of mistake and restitution may allow Beneficiary to keep all or part of the money received. If Originator owed money to Beneficiary, Bank A has paid originator's debt and, under the law of restitution, which applies pursuant to § 1-103, Bank A is subrogated to Beneficiary's rights against Originator on the debt.

If Bank A is the Beneficiary's bank and Bank A credited Beneficiary's account and released the funds to Beneficiary on April 1, the analysis is similar. If Originator's order is cancelled, Bank A has paid Beneficiary by mistake. The right of Bank A to recover the payment from Beneficiary is similar to Bank A's rights in the preceding paragraph.

Section 4A-210. Rejection of Payment Order.

(1) A payment order is rejected by the receiving bank by a notice of rejection transmitted to the sender orally, electronically, or in writing. A notice of rejection need not use any particular words and is sufficient if it indicates that the receiving bank is rejecting the order or will not execute or pay the order. Rejection is effective when the notice is given if transmission is by a means that is reasonable in the circumstances. If notice of rejection is given by a means that is not reasonable, rejection is effective when the notice is received. If an agreement

of the sender and receiving bank establishes the means to be used to reject a payment order, (i) any means complying with the agreement is reasonable and (ii) any means not complying is not reasonable unless no significant delay in receipt of the notice resulted from the use of the noncomplying means.

(2) This subsection applies if a receiving bank other than the beneficiary's bank fails to execute a payment order despite the existence on the execution date of a withdrawable credit balance in an authorized account of the sender sufficient to cover the order. If the sender does not receive notice of rejection of the order on the execution date and the authorized account of the sender does not bear interest, the bank is obliged to pay interest to the sender on the amount of the order for the number of days elapsing after the execution date to the earlier of the day the order is cancelled pursuant to subsection (4) of Section 4A–211 or the day the sender receives notice or learns that the order was not executed, counting the final day of the period as an elapsed day. If the withdrawable credit balance during that period falls below the amount of the order, the amount of interest is reduced accordingly.

(3) If a receiving bank suspends payments, all unaccepted payment orders issued to it are deemed rejected at the time the bank suspends payments.

(4) Acceptance of a payment order precludes a later rejection of the order. Rejection of a payment order precludes a later acceptance of the order.

Added by Laws 1990, Ch. 208, eff. Jan. 1, 1991.

Official Uniform Comment

Prior Uniform Statutory Provision: None.

Purposes.

1. With respect to payment orders issued to a receiving bank other than the beneficiary's bank, notice or rejection is not necessary to prevent acceptance of the order. Acceptance can occur only if the receiving bank executes the order. § 4A-209(a). but notice of rejection will routinely be given by such a bank in cases in which the bank cannot or is not willing to execute the order for some reason. There are many reasons why a bank doesn't execute an order. The payment order may not clearly instruct the receiving bank because of some ambiguity in the order or an internal consistency. In some cases, the receiving bank may not be able to carry out the instruction because of equipment failure, credit limitations on the receiving bank, or some other factor which makes proper execution of the order infeasible. In those cases notice of rejection is a means of informing the sender of the facts so that a corrected payment order can be transmitted or the sender can seek alternate means of completing the funds transfer. The other major reason for not executing an order is that the sender's account is insufficient to cover the order and the receiving bank is not willing to give credit to the sender. If the sender's account is sufficient to cover the order and the receiving bank chooses not to execute the order, notice of rejection is necessary to prevent liability to pay interest to the sender if the case falls within § 4A-210(b) which is discussed in Comment 3.

2. A payment order to the beneficiary's bank can be accepted by inaction of the bank. § 4A-209(b)(2) and (3). To prevent acceptance under those provisions it is necessary for the receiving bank to send notice of rejection before acceptance occurs.

Subsection (a) of § 4A-210 states the rule that rejection is accomplished by giving notice or rejection. This incorporates the definitions in § 1-201(26). Rejection is effective when notice is given if it is given by a means that is reasonable in the circumstances. Otherwise it is effective when the notice is received. The question when rejection is effective is important only in the relatively few cases under subsection (b)(2) and (3) in which a notice of rejection is necessary to prevent acceptance. The question of whether a particular means is reasonable depends on the facts in a particular case. In a very large percentage of cases the sender and the receiving bank will be in direct electronic contact with each other and in those cases a notice of rejection can be transmitted instantaneously. Since time is of the essence in a large proportion of funds transfers, some quick means of transmission would usually be required, but this is not always the case. The parties may specify by agreement the means by which communication between the parties is to be made.

3. Subsection (b) deals with cases in which a sender does not learn until after the execution date that the sender's order has not been executed. It applies only to cases in which the receiving bank was assured of payment because the sender's account was sufficient to cover the order. Normally, the receiving bank will accept the sender's order if it is assured of payment, but there may be some cases in which the bank chooses to reject. Unless the receiving bank had obligated itself by agreement to accept, the failure to accept is not wrongful. There is no duty of the receiving bank to accept the payment order unless it is obliged to accept by express agreement. § 4A–212. But even if the bank has not acted wrongfully, the receiving bank had the use of the sender's money that the sender could reasonably assume was to be the source of payment of the funds transfer. Until the sender learns that the order was not accepted the sender is denied the use of that money. Subsection (b) obliges the receiving bank to pay interest to the sender as restitution unless the sender receives notice of rejection on the execution date. The time of receipt of notice is determined pursuant to § 1-201(27). The rate of interest is stated in § 4A-506. If the sender receives notice on the day after the execution date, the sender is entitled to one day's interest. If receipt of notice is delayed for more than one day, the sender is entitled to interest for each additional day of delay.

4. Subsection (d) treats acceptance and rejection as mutually exclusive. If a payment order has been accepted, rejection of that order comes impossible. If a payment order has been rejected it cannot be accepted later by the receiving bank. Once notice of rejection has been given, the sender may have acted on the notice by making the payment through other channels. If the receiving bank wants to act on a payment order that it has rejected it has to obtain the consent of the sender. In that case the consent of the sender would amount to the giving of a second payment order that substitutes for the rejected first order. If the receiving bank suspends payments (§ 4–104(1)(k)), subsection (c) provides that unaccepted payment orders are deemed rejected at the time suspension of payments occurs. This prevents acceptance by passage of time under § 4A-209(b)(3).

Section 4A–211. Cancellation and Amendment of Payment Order.

(1) A communication of the sender of a payment order cancelling or amending the order may be transmitted to the receiving bank orally, electronically, or in writing. If a security procedure is in effect between the sender and the receiving bank, the communication is not effective to cancel or amend the order unless the communication is verified pursuant to the security procedure or the bank agrees to the cancellation or amendment.

(2) Subject to subsection (1), a communication by the sender cancelling or amending a payment order is effective to cancel or amend the order if notice

of the communication is received at a time and in a manner affording the receiving bank a reasonable opportunity to act on the communication before the bank accepts the payment order.

(3) After a payment order has been accepted, cancellation or amendment of the order is not effective unless the receiving bank agrees or a funds-transfer system rule allows cancellation or amendment without agreement of the bank.

(a) With respect to a payment order accepted by a receiving bank other than the beneficiary's bank, cancellation or amendment is not effective unless a conforming cancellation or amendment of the payment order issued by the receiving bank is also made.

(b) With respect to a payment order accepted by the beneficiary's bank, cancellation or amendment is not effective unless the order was issued in execution of an unauthorized payment order, or because of a mistake by a sender in the funds transfer which resulted in the issuance of a payment order (i) that is a duplicate of a payment order previously issued by the sender, (ii) that orders payment to a beneficiary not entitled to receive payment from the originator, or (iii) that orders payment in an amount greater than the amount the beneficiary was entitled to receive from the originator. If the payment order is cancelled or amended, the beneficiary's bank is entitled to recover from the beneficiary any amount paid to the beneficiary to the extent allowed by the law governing mistake and restitution.

(4) An unaccepted payment order is cancelled by operation of law at the close of the fifth funds-transfer business day of the receiving bank after the execution date or payment date of the order.

(5) A cancelled payment order cannot be accepted. If an accepted payment order is cancelled, the acceptance is nullified and no person has any right or obligation based on the acceptance. Amendment of a payment order is deemed to be cancellation of the original order at the time of amendment and issue of a new payment order in the amended form at the same time.

(6) Unless otherwise provided in an agreement of the parties or in a funds-transfer system rule, if the receiving bank, after accepting a payment order, agrees to cancellation or amendment of the order by the sender or is bound by a funds-transfer system rule allowing cancellation or amendment without the bank's agreement, the sender, whether or not cancellation or amendment is effective, is liable to the bank for any loss and expenses, including reasonable attorney's fees, incurred by the bank as a result of the cancellation or amendment or attempted cancellation or amendment.

(7) A payment order is not revoked by the death or legal incapacity of the sender unless the receiving bank knows of the death or of an adjudication of incapacity by a court of competent jurisdiction and has reasonable opportunity to act before acceptance of the order.

(8) A funds-transfer system rule is not effective to the extent it conflicts with paragraph (b) of subsection (3).

Added by Laws 1990, Ch. 208, eff. Jan. 1, 1991.

Official Uniform Comment

Prior Uniform Statutory Provision: None.

Purposes:

1. This section deals with cancellation and amendment of payment orders. It states the conditions under which cancellation or amendment is both effective and rightful. There is no concept of wrongful cancellation or amendment of a payment order. If the conditions stated in this section are not met the attempted cancellation or amendment is not effective. If the stated conditions are met the cancellation or amendment is effective and rightful. The sender of a payment order may want to withdraw or change the order because the sender has had a change of mind about the transaction or because the payment order was erroneously issued or for any other reason. One common situation is that of multiple transmission of the same order. The sender that mistakenly transmits the same order twice wants to correct the mistake by cancelling the duplicate order. Or, a sender may have intended to order a payment of $1,000,000 but mistakenly issued an order to pay $10,000,000. In this case the sender might try to correct the mistake by cancelling the order and issuing another order in the proper amount. Or, the mistake could be corrected by amending the order to change it to the proper amount. Whether the error is corrected by amendment or cancellation and reissue the net result is the same. This result is stated in the last sentence of subsection (e).

2. Subsection (a) allows a cancellation or amendment of a payment order to be communicated to the receiving bank "orally, electronically, or in writing." The quoted phrase is consistent with the language of § 4A-103(a) applicable to payment orders. Cancellations and amendments are normally subject to verification pursuant to security procedures to the same extent as payment orders. Subsection (a) recognizes this fact by providing that in cases in which there is a security procedure in effect between the sender and the receiving bank the bank is not bound by a communication cancelling or amending an order unless verification has been made. This is necessary to protect the bank because under subsection (b) a cancellation or amendment can be effective by unilateral action of the sender. Without verification the bank cannot be sure whether the communication was or was not effective to cancel or amend a previously verified payment order.

3. If the receiving bank has not yet accepted the order, there is no reason why the sender should not be able to cancel or amend the order unilaterally so long as the requirements of subsection (a) and (b) are met. If the receiving bank has accepted the order, it is possible to cancel or amend but only if the requirements of subsection (c) are met.

First consider the case of a receiving bank other than the beneficiary's bank. If the bank has not yet accepted the order, the sender can unilaterally cancel or amend. the communication amending or cancelling the payment order must be received in time to allow the bank to act on it before the bank issues its payment order in execution of the sender's order. The time that the sender's communication is received is governed by § 4A-106. If a payment order does not specify a delayed payment date or execution date, the order will normally be executed shortly after receipt. Thus, as a practical matter, the sender will have very little time in which to instruct cancellation or amendment before acceptance. In addition, a receiving bank will normally have cut-off times for receipt of such communications, and the receiving bank is not obliged to act on communications received after the cut-off hour. Cancellation by the sender after execution of the order by the receiving bank requires the agreement of the bank unless a funds transfer rule otherwise provides. Subsection (c). Although execution of the sender's pose liability on the receiving bank does not itself impose liability on the receiving bank (under § 4A-402 no liability is incured by the receiving bank to pay its order until it is accepted), it would commonly be the case that acceptance follows shortly after issuance. thus, as a practical matter, a receiving bank that has executed a payment order will incur a liability to the next bank in the chain before it would be able to act on the cancellation request of its customer. It is unreasonable to impose on the receiving bank a risk of loss with respect to a cancellation request without the consent of the receiving bank.

The statute does not state how or when the agreement of the receiving bank must be obtained for cancellation after execution. the receiving bank's consent could be obtained at the time cancellation occurs or it could be based on a preexisting agreement. Or, a funds transfer system rule could provide that cancellation can be made unilaterally by the sender. By virtue of that rule any receiving bank covered by the rule is bound. § 4A-501. If the receiving bank has already executed the sender's order, the bank would not consent to cancellation unless the bank to which the receiving bank has issued its payment order consents to cancellation of that order. It makes no sense to allow cancellation of a payment order unless all subsequent payment orders in the funds transfer that were issued because of the cancelled payment order are also cancelled. Under subsection (c)(1), if a receiving bank consents to cancellation of the payment order after it is executed, the cancellation is not effective unless the receiving bank also cancels the payment order issued by the bank.

4. With respect to a payment order issued to the beneficiary's bank, acceptance is particularly important because it creates liability to pay the beneficiary, it defines when the originator pays its obligation to the beneficiary, and it defines when any obligation for which the payment is made is discharged. Since acceptance affects the rights of the originator and the beneficiary it is not appropriate to allow the beneficiary's bank to agree to cancellation or amendment except in unusual cases. Except as provided in subsection (c)(2), cancellation or amendment after acceptance by the beneficiary's bank is not possible unless all parties affected by the order agree. Under subsection (c)(2), cancellation or amendment is possible only in the four cases stated. The following examples illustrate subsection (c)(2):

Case #1. Originator's Bank executed a payment order issued in the name of its customer as sender. The order was not authorized by the customer and was fraudulently issued. Beneficiary's Bank accepted the payment order issued by Originator's Bank. Under subsection (c)(2) Originator's Bank can cancel the order if Beneficiary's Bank consents. It doesn't make any difference whether the payment order that Originator's Bank accepted was or was not enforceable against the customer under § 4A-202(b). Verification under that provision is important in determining whether Originator's Bank or the customer has the risk of loss, but it has no relevance under § 4A-211(c)(2). Whether or not verified, the payment order was not authorized by the customer. Cancellation of the payment order to Beneficiary's Bank causes the acceptance of Beneficiary's Bank to be nullified. Subsection (e). Beneficiary's Bank is entitled to recover payment from the beneficiary to the extent allowed by the law of mistake and restitution. In this kind of case the beneficiary is usually a party to the fraud who has no right to receive or retain payment of the order.

Case #2. Originator owed Beneficiary $1,000,000 and order Bank A to pay that amount to the account of Beneficiary in Bank B. Bank a issued a complying order to Bank B, but by mistake issued a duplicate order as well. Bank B accepted both orders. Under subsection (c)(2)(i) cancellation of the duplicate order could be made by Bank A with the consent of Bank B. Beneficiary has no right to receive or retain payment of the duplicate payment order if only $1,000,000 was owed by Originator to Beneficiary. If Originator owed $2,000,000 to Beneficiary, the law of restitution might allow Beneficiary to retain the $1,000,000 paid by Bank B on the duplicate

UCC

order. In that case Bank B is entitled to reimbursement from Bank A under subsection (f).

Case #3. Originator owed $1,000,000 to X. Intending to pay X, Originator ordered Bank A to pay $1,000,000 to Y's account in Bank B. Bank A issued a complying payment order to Bank B which Bank B accepted by releasing the $1,000,000 to Y. Under subsection (c)(2)(ii) Bank A can cancel its payment order to Bank B with the consent of Bank B if Y was not entitled to receive payment from Originator. Originator can also cancel its order to Bank A with Bank A's consent. Subsection (c)(1). Bank B may recover the $1,000,000 from Y unless the law of mistake and restitution allows Y to retain some or all of the amount paid. If no debt was owed to Y, Bank B should have a right of recover.

Case #4. Originator owed Beneficiary $10,000. By mistake Originator Ordered Bank A to pay $1,000,000 to the account of Beneficiary in Bank B. Bank A issued a complying order to Bank B which accepted by notifying Beneficiary of its right to withdraw $1,000,000. cancellation is permitted in this case under subsection (c)(2)(iii). If bank B paid Beneficiary it is entitled to recover the payment except to the extent the law of mistake and restitution allows Beneficiary to retain payment. In this case Beneficiary might be entitled to retain $10,000, the amount of the debt owed to Beneficiary. If Beneficiary may retain $10,000, Bank B would be entitled to $10,000 from Bank A pursuant to subsection (f). In this case Originator also cancelled its order. Thus Bank A would be entitled to $10,000 from Originator pursuant to subsection (f).

5. Unless constrained by a funds transfer system rule, a receiving bank may agree to cancellation or amendment of the payment order under subsection (c) but is not required to do so regardless of the circumstances. If the receiving bank has incurred liability as a result of its acceptance of the sender's order, there are substantial risks in agreeing to cancellation or amendment. This is particularly true for a beneficiary's bank. Cancellation or amendment after acceptance by the beneficiary's bank can be made only in the four cases stated and the beneficiary's bank may not have any way of knowing whether the requirements of subsection (c) have been met or whether it will be able to recover payment from the beneficiary that received payment. Even with indemnity the beneficiary's bank may be reluctant to alienate its customer, the beneficiary, by denying the customer the funds. Subsection (c) leaves the decision to the beneficiary's bank unless the consent of the beneficiary's bank is not required under a funds transfer system rule or other interbank agreement. If a receiving bank agrees to cancellation or amendment under subsection (c)(1) or (2), it is automatically entitled to indemnification from the sender under subsection (f). The indemnification provisions recognizes that a sender has no right to cancel a payment order after it is accepted by the receiving bank. If the receiving bank agrees to cancellation, it is doing so as an accommodation to the sender and it should not incur a risk of loss in doing so.

6. Acceptance by the receiving bank of a payment order issued by the sender is comparable to acceptance of an offer under the law of contracts. Under that law the death or legal incapacity of an offeror terminates the offer even though the offeree has no notice of the death or incapacity. Restatement Second, Contracts § 48. Comment a. to that section state that the "rule seems to be a relic of the obsolete view that a contract requires a "meeting of minds,' and it is out of harmony with the modern doctrine that a manifestation of assent is effective without regard to actual mental assent." Subsection (g), which reverses the Restatement rule in the case of a payment order, is similar to § 4-405(1) which applies to checks. Subsection (g) does not address the effect of the bankruptcy of the sender of a payment order before the order is accepted, but the principle of subsection (g) has been recognized in Bank of Marin v. England, 385 U.S. 99 (1966). Although Bankruptcy Code § 542(c) may not have been drafted with wire transfers in mind, its language can be read to allow

the receiving bank to charge the sender's account for the amount of the payment order if the receiving bank executed it in ignorance of the bankruptcy.

7. Subsection (d) deals with stale payment orders. Payment orders normally are executed on the execution date or the day after. An order issued to the beneficiary's bank is normally accepted on the payment date or the day after. If a payment order is not accepted on its execution or payment date or shortly thereafter, it is probable that there was some problem with the terms of the order or the sender did not have sufficient funds or credit to cover the amount of the order. Delayed acceptance of such an order is normally not contemplated, but the order may not have been cancelled by the sender. Subsection (d) provides for cancellation by operation of law to prevent an unexpected delayed acceptance.

8. A funds transfer system rule can govern rights and obligations between banks that are parties to payment orders transmitted over the system even if the rule conflicts with Article 4A. In some cases, however, a rule governing a transaction between two banks can affect a third party in an unacceptable way. Subsection (h) deals with such a case. A funds transfer system rule cannot allow cancellation of a payment order accepted by the beneficiary's bank if the rule conflicts with subsection (c)(2). Because rights of the beneficiary and the originator are directly affected by acceptance, subsection (c)(2) severely limits cancellation. These limitations cannot be altered by funds transfer system rule.

UCC

Section 4A–212. Liability and Duty of Receiving Bank Regarding Unaccepted Payment Order.

If a receiving bank fails to accept a payment order that it is obliged by express agreement to accept, the bank is liable for breach of the agreement to the extent provided in the agreement or in this article, but does not otherwise have any duty to accept a payment order or, before acceptance, to take any action, or refrain from taking action, with respect to the order except as provided in this article or by express agreement. Liability based on acceptance arises only when acceptance occurs as stated in Section 4A–209, and liability is limited to that provided in this Article. A receiving bank is not the agent of the sender or beneficiary of the payment order it accepts, or of any other party to the funds transfer, and the bank owes no duty to any party to the funds transfer except as provided in this article or by express agreement.

Added by Laws 1990, Ch. 208, eff. Jan. 1, 1991.

Official Uniform Comment

Prior Uniform Statutory Provision: None.

Purposes:

With limited exceptions stated in this Article, the duties and obligations of receiving banks that carry out a funds transfer arise only as a result of acceptance of payment orders or of agreements made by receiving banks. Exceptions are stated in § 4A-209(b)(3) and § 4A-210(b). A receiving bank is not like a collecting bank under Article 4. No receiving bank, whether it be an originating bank, an intermediary bank or a beneficiary's bank, is an agent for any other party in the funds transfer.

PART 3

EXECUTION OF SENDER'S PAYMENT ORDER BY RECEIVING BANK

Section 4A–301. Execution and Execution Date.

(1) A payment order is "executed" by the receiving bank when it issues a payment order intended to carry out the payment order received by the bank. A payment order received by the beneficiary's bank can be accepted but cannot be executed.

(2) "Execution date" of a payment order means the day on which the receiving bank may properly issue a payment order in execution of the sender's order. The execution date may be determined by instruction of the sender but cannot be earlier than the day the order is received and, unless otherwise determined, is the day the order is received. If the sender's instruction states a payment date, the execution date is the payment date or an earlier date on which execution is reasonably necessary to allow payment to the beneficiary on the payment date.

Added by Laws 1990, Ch. 208, eff. Jan. 1, 1991.

Official Uniform Comment

Prior Uniform Statutory Provision: None.

Purposes:

1. The terms "executed," "execution" and "execution date" are used only with respect to a payment order to a receiving bank other than the beneficiary's bank. The beneficiary's bank can accept the payment order that it receives, but it does not execute the order. Execution refers to the act of the receiving bank in issuing a payment order "intended to carry out" the payment order that the bank received. A receiving bank has executed an order even if the order issued by the bank does not carry out the order received by the bank. For example, the bank may have erroneously issued an order to the wrong beneficiary, or in the wrong amount or to the wrong beneficiary's bank. In each of these cases execution has occurred but the execution is erroneous. Erroneous execution is covered in § 4A-303.

2. "Execution date" refers to the time a payment order should be executed rather than the day it is actually executed. Normally the sender will not specify an execution date, but most payment orders are meant to be executed immediately. Thus, the execution date is normally the day the order is received by the receiving bank. It is common for the sender to specify a "payment date" which is defined in § 4A-401 as "the day on which the amount of the order is payable to the beneficiary by the beneficiary's bank." Except for automated clearing house transfers, if a funds transfer is entirely within the United States and the payment is to be carried out electronically, the execution date is the payment date unless the order is received after the payment date. if the payment is to be carried out through an automated clearing house, execution may occur before the payment date. In an ACH transfer the beneficiary is usually paid one or two days after issue of the originator's payment order. The execution date is determined by the stated payment date and is a date before the payment date on which execution is reasonably necessary to allow payment on the payment date. A funds transfer system rule could also determine the execution date

of orders received by the receiving bank if both the sender and the receiving bank are participants in the funds transfer system. The execution date can be determined by the payment order itself or by separate instructions of the sender or an agreement of the sender and the receiving bank. The second sentence of subsection (b) must be read in the light of § 4A-106 which states that if a payment order is received after the cut-off time of the receiving bank it may be treated by the bank as received at the opening of the next funds transfer business day.

3. Execution on the execution date is timely, but the order can be executed before or after the execution date. § 4A-209(d) and § 4A-402(c) state the consequences of early execution and § 4A-305(a) states the consequences of late execution.

Section 4A–302. Obligations of Receiving Bank in Execution of Payment Order.

(1) Except as provided in subsections (2) through (4); if the receiving bank accepts a payment order pursuant to subsection (1) of Section 4A–209, the bank has the following obligations in executing the order:

(a) The receiving bank is obliged to issue, on the execution date, a payment order complying with the sender's order and to follow the sender's instructions concerning (i) any intermediary bank or funds-transfer system to be used in carrying out the funds transfer, or (ii) the means by which payment orders are to be transmitted in the funds transfer. If the originator's bank issues a payment order to an intermediary bank, the originator's bank is obliged to instruct the intermediary bank according to the instruction of the originator. An intermediary bank in the funds transfer is similarly bound by an instruction given to it by the sender of the payment order it accepts.

(b) If the sender's instruction states that the funds transfer is to be carried out telephonically or by wire transfer or otherwise indicates that the funds transfer is to be carried out by the most expeditious means, the receiving bank is obliged to transmit its payment order by the most expeditious available means, and to instruct any intermediary bank accordingly. If a sender's instruction states a payment date, the receiving bank is obliged to transmit its payment order at a time and by means reasonably necessary to allow payment to the beneficiary on the payment date or as soon thereafter as is feasible.

(2) Unless otherwise instructed, a receiving bank executing a payment order may (i) use any funds-transfer system if use of that system is reasonable in the circumstances, and (ii) issue a payment order to the beneficiary's bank or to an intermediary bank through which a payment order conforming to the sender's order can expeditiously be issued to the beneficiary's bank if the receiving bank exercises ordinary care in the selection of the intermediary bank. A receiving bank is not required to follow an instruction of the sender designating a funds-transfer system to be used in carrying out the funds transfer if the receiving bank, in good faith, determines that it is not feasible to follow the instruction or that following the instruction would unduly delay completion of the funds transfer.

(3) Unless paragraph (b) of subsection (1) applies or the receiving bank is otherwise instructed, the bank may execute a payment order by transmitting its

payment order by first class mail or by any means reasonable in the circumstances. If the receiving bank is instructed to execute the sender's order by transmitting its payment order by a particular means, the receiving bank may issue its payment order by the means stated or by any means as expeditious as the means stated.

(4) Unless instructed by the sender (i) the receiving bank may not obtain payment of its charges for services and expenses in connection with the execution of the sender's order by issuing a payment order in an amount equal to the amount of the sender's order less the amount of the charges, and (ii) may not instruct a subsequent receiving bank to obtain payment of its charges in the same manner.

Added by Laws 1990, Ch. 208, eff. Jan. 1, 1991.

Official Uniform Comment

Prior Uniform Statutory Provision: None.

Purposes:

1. In the absence of agreement, the receiving bank is not obliged to execute an order of the sender. § 4A-212. § 4A-302 states the manner in which the receiving bank may execute the sender's order if execution occurs. Subsection (a)(1) states the residual rule. The payment order issued by the receiving bank must comply with the sender's order and, unless some other rule is stated in the section, the receiving bank is obliged to follow any instruction of the sender concerning which funds transfer system is to be sued, which intermediary banks are to be sued, and what means of transmission is to be used. The instruction of the sender may be incorporated in the payment order itself or may be given separately. For example, there may be a master agreement between the sender and receiving bank containing instructions governing payment orders to be issued from time to time by the sender to the receiving bank. In most funds transfers, speed is a paramount consideration. A sender that wants assurance that the funds transfer will be expeditiously completed can specify the means to be used. The receiving bank can follow the instructions literally or it can use an equivalent means. For example, if the sender instructs the receiving bank to transmit by telex, the receiving bank could use telephone instead. Subsection (c). In most cases the sender will not specify a particular means but will use a general term such as "by wire" or "wire transfer" or "as soon as possible." These words signify that the sender wants a same-day transfer. In these cases the receiving bank is required to use a telephonic or electronic communication to transmit its order and is also required to instruct any intermediary bank which it issues its order to transmit by similar means. Subsection (a)(2). In other cases, such as an automated clearing house transfer, a same-day transfer is not contemplated. Normally the sender's instruction or the context in which the payment order is received makes clear the type of fund transfer that is appropriate. If the sender states a payment date with respect to the payment order, the receiving bank is obliged to execute the order at a time and in a manner to meet the payment date if that is feasible. Subsection (a)(2). This provision would apply to many ACH transfers made to pay recurring debts of the sender. In other cases, involving relatively small amounts, time may not be an important factor and cost may be a more important element. Fast means, such as telephone or electronic transmission, are more expensive than slow means such as mailing. Subsection (c) states that in the absence of instructions the receiving bank is given discretion to

decide. It may issue its payment order by first class mail or by any means reasonable in the circumstances. § 4A-305 states the liability of a receiving bank for breach of the obligations stated in § 4A-302.

2. Subsection (b) concerns the choice of intermediary banks to be sued in completing the funds transfer, and the funds transfer system to be used. If the receiving bank is not instructed about the matter, it can issue an order directly to the beneficiary's bank or can issue an order to an intermediary bank. The receiving bank also has discretion concerning use of a funds transfer system. In some cases it may be reasonable to use either an automated clearing house system or a wire transfer system such as Fedwire or CHIPS. Normally, the receiving bank will follow the instruction of the sender in these matters, but in some cases it may be prudent for the bank not to follow instructions. The sender may have designated a funds transfer system to be used in carrying out the funds transfer, but it may not be feasible to use the designated system because of some impediment such as a computer breakdown which prevents prompt execution of the order. the receiving bank is permitted to use an alternate means of transmittal in a good faith effort to execute the order expeditiously. The same leeway is not given to the receiving bank if the sender designates an intermediary bank through which the funds transfer is to be routed. The sender's designation of that intermediary bank may mean that the beneficiary's bank is expecting to obtain a credit from that intermediary bank and may have relied on that anticipated credit. If the receiving bank uses another intermediary bank the expectations of the beneficiary's bank may not be realized. The receiving bank could choose to route the transfer to another intermediary bank and then to the designated intermediary bank if there was some reason such as a lack of a correspondent-bank relationship or a bilateral credit limitation, but the designated intermediary bank cannot be circumvented. To do so violates the sender's instructions.

3. The normal rule, under subsection (a)(1), is that the receiving bank, in executing a payment order, is required to issue a payment order that complies as to amount with that of the sender's order. In most cases the receiving bank issues an order equal to the amount of the sender's order and makes a separate charge for services and expenses in executing the sender's order. In some cases, particularly if it is an intermediary bank that is executing an order, charges are collected by deducting them from the amount of the payment order issued by the executing bank. If that is done, the amount of the payment order accepted by the beneficiary's bank will be slightly less than the amount of the originator's payment order. For example, Originator, in order to pay an obligation of $1,000,000 owed to Beneficiary, issues a payment order to Originator's Bank to pay $1,000,000 to the account of Beneficiary in Beneficiary's Bank. Originator's Bank issues a payment order to Intermediary Bank for $1,000,000 and debits Originator's account for $1,000,010. The extra $10 is the fee of Originator's Bank. Intermediary Bank executes the payment order or Originator's Bank by issuing a payment order to Beneficiary's Bank for $999,990, but under § 4A-402(c) is entitled to receive $1,000,000 from Originator's Bank. The $10 difference is the fee of Intermediary Bank. Beneficiary's Bank credits Beneficiary's account for $999,990. When Beneficiary's Bank accepts the payment order of Intermediary Bank the result is a payment of $999,990 from Originator to Beneficiary. § 4A-406(a). If that payment discharges the $1,000,000 debt, the effect is that Beneficiary has paid the charges of Intermediary Bank and Originator has paid the charges of Originator's Bank. Subsection (d) of § 4A-302 allows Intermediary Bank to collect its charges by deducting them from the amount of the payment order, but only if instructed to do so by Originator's Bank. Originator's Bank is not authorized to give that instruction to Intermdiary Bank unless Originator authorized the instruction. Thus, Originator can control how the charges of Originator's Bank and Intermediary Bank are to be paid. Subsection (d) does not apply to charges of Beneficiary's Bank to Beneficiary.

In the case discussed in the preceding paragraph the $10 charge is trivial in relation to the amount of the payment and it may not be important to Beneficiary how the

UCC

charge is paid. But it may be very important if the $1,000,000 obligation represented the price of exercising a right such as an option favorable to Originator and unfavorable to Beneficiary. Beneficiary might well argue that it was entitled to receive $1,000,000. If the option was exercised shortly before its expiration date, the result could be loss of the option benefit because the required payment of $1,000,000 was not made before the option expired. § 4A-406(c) allows Originator to preserve the option benefit. The amount received by Beneficiary is deemed to be $1,000,000 unless Beneficiary demands the $10 and Originator does not pay it.

Section 4A–303. Erroneous Execution of Payment Order.

(1) A receiving bank that (i) executes the payment order of the sender by issuing a payment order in an amount greater than the amount of the sender's order, or (ii) issues a payment order in execution of the sender's order and then issues a duplicate order, is entitled to payment of the amount of the sender's order under subsection (3) of Section 4A–402 if that subsection is otherwise satisfied. The bank is entitled to recover from the beneficiary of the erroneous order the excess payment received to the extent allowed by the law governing mistake and restitution.

(2) A receiving bank that executes the payment order of the sender by issuing a payment order in an amount less than the amount of the sender's order is entitled to payment of the amount of the sender's order under subsection (3) of Section 4A–402 if (i) that subsection is otherwise satisfied and (ii) the bank corrects its mistake by issuing an additional payment order for the benefit of the beneficiary of the sender's order. If the error is not corrected, the issuer of the erroneous order is entitled to receive or retain payment from the sender of the order it accepted only to the extent of the amount of the erroneous order. This subsection does not apply if the receiving bank executes the sender's payment order by issuing a payment order in an amount less than the amount of the sender's order for the purpose of obtaining payment of its charges for services and expenses pursuant to instruction of the sender.

(3) If a receiving bank executes the payment order of the sender by issuing a payment order to a beneficiary different from the beneficiary of the sender's order and the funds transfer is completed on the basis of that error, the sender of the payment order that was erroneously executed and all previous senders in the funds transfer are not obliged to pay the payment orders they issued. The issuer of the erroneous order is entitled to recover from the beneficiary of the order the payment received to the extent allowed by the law governing mistake and restitution.

Added by Laws 1990, Ch. 208, eff. Jan. 1, 1991.

Official Uniform Comment

Prior Uniform Statutory Provision: None.

Purposes:

1. § 4A-303 states the effect of erroneous execution of a payment order by the receiving bank. Under § 4A-402(c) the sender of a payment order is obliged to pay

the amount of the order to the receiving bank if the bank executes the order, but the obligation to pay is excused if the beneficiary's bank does not accept a payment order instructing payment to the beneficiary of the sender's order causes the wrong beneficiary to be apid, the sender is not required to pay. If erroneous execution causes the wrong amount to be paid the sender is not obliged to pay the receiving bank an amount in excess of the amount of the sender's order. § 4A-303 takes precedence over § 4A-402(c) and states the liability of the sender and the rights of the receiving bank in various cases of erroneous execution.

2. Subsections (a) and (b) deal with cases in which the receiving bank executes by issuing a payment order in the wrong amount. If Originator ordered Originator's Bank to pay $1,000,000 to the account of Beneficiary in Beneficiary's Bank, but Originator's Bank erroneously instructed Beneficiary's Bank to pay $2,000,000 to Beneficiary's account, subsection (a) applies. If Beneficiary's bank accepts the order of Originator's Bank, Beneficiary's Bank is entitled to receive $2,000,000 from Originator's Bank, but Originator's Bank is entitled to receive only $1,000,000 from Originator. Originator's Bank is entitled to recover the overpayment from Beneficiary to the extent allowed by law governing mistake and restitution. Originator's Bank would normally have a right to recover the overpayment from Beneficiary, but in usual cases the law of restitution might allow Beneficiary to keep all or part of the overpayment. For example, if Originator owed $2,000,000 to Beneficiary and Beneficiary received the extra $1,000,000 in good faith in discharge of the debt, Beneficiary may be allowed to keep it. In this case Originator's Bank has paid an obligation of Originator and under the law of restitution, which applies through § 1-103, Originator's Bank would be subrogated to Beneficiary's rights against Originator on the obligation paid by Originator's Bank.

If Originator's Bank erroneously executed Originator's order by instructing Beneficiary's Bank to pay less than $1,000,000, subsection (b) applies. If Originator's Bank corrects its error by issuing another payment order to Beneficiary's Bank that results in payment of $1,000,000 to Beneficiary, Originator's Bank is entitled to payment of $1,000,000 from Originator. If the mistake is not corrected, Originator's Bank is entitled to payment from Originator only in the amount of the order issued by Originator's Bank.

3. Subsection (a) also applies to duplicate payment orders. Assume Originator's Bank properly executes Originator's $1,000,000 payment order and then by mistake issues a second $1,000,000 payment order in execution of Originator's order. If Beneficiary's Bank accepts both orders issued by Originator's bank, Beneficiary's Bank is entitled to receive $2,000,000 from Originator's Bank but Originator's Bank is entitled to receive only $1,000,000 from Originator. The remedy of Originator's Bank is the same as that of a receiving bank that executes by issuing an order in an amount greater than the sender's order. It may recover the overpayment from Beneficiary to the extent allowed by the law governing mistake and restitution and in a proper case as stated in Comment 2 may have subrogation rights if it is not entitled to recover from Beneficiary.

4. Suppose Originator instructs Originator's bank to pay $1,000,000 to Account #12345 in Beneficiary's Bank. Originator's Bank erroneously instructs Beneficiary's Bank to pay $1,000,000 to Account #12346 and Beneficiary's Bank accepted. Subsection (c) covers this case. Originator is not obliged to pay its payment order, but Originator's Bank is required to pay $1,000,000 to Beneficiary's Bank. The remedy of Originator's Bank is to recover $1,000,000 front he holder of Account #12346 that received payment by mistake. Recovery based on the law of mistake and restitution is described in Comment 2.

Section 4A–304. Duty of Sender to Report Erroneously Executed Payment Order.

If the sender of a payment order that is erroneously executed as stated in Section 4A–303 receives notification from the receiving bank that the order was executed or that the sender's account was debited with respect to the order, the sender has a duty to exercise ordinary care to determine, on the basis of information available to the sender, that the order was erroneously executed and to notify the bank of the relevant facts within a reasonable time not exceeding ninety days after the notification from the bank was received by the sender. If the sender fails to perform that duty, the bank is not obliged to pay interest on any amount refundable to the sender under subsection (4) of Section 4A402 for the period before the bank learns of the execution error. The bank is not entitled to any recovery from the sender on account of a failure by the sender to perform the duty stated in this section.

Added by Laws 1990, Ch. 208, eff. Jan. 1, 1991.

Official Uniform Comment

Prior Uniform Statutory Provision: None.

Purposes:

This section is identical in effect to § 4A-204 which applies to unauthorized orders issued in the name of a customer of the receiving bank. The rational is stated in Comment 2 to § 4A-204.

Section 4A–305. Liability for Late or Improper Execution or Failure to Execute Payment Order.

(1) If a funds transfer is completed but execution of a payment order by the receiving bank in breach of Section 4A–302 results in delay in payment to the beneficiary, the bank is obliged to pay interest to either the originator or the beneficiary of the funds transfer for the period of delay caused by the improper execution. Except as provided in subsection (3), additional damages are not recoverable.

(2) If execution of a payment order by a receiving bank in breach of Section 4A–302 results in (i) noncompletion of the funds transfer, (ii) failure to use an intermediary bank designated by the originator, or (iii) issuance of a payment order that does not comply with the terms of the payment order of the originator, the bank is liable to the originator for its expenses in the funds transfer and for incidental expenses and interest losses, to the extent not covered by subsection (1), resulting from the improper execution. Except as provided in subsection (3), additional damages are not recoverable.

(3) In addition to the amounts payable under subsections (1) and (2), damages, including consequential damages, are recoverable to the extent provided in an express written agreement of the receiving bank.

(4) If a receiving bank fails to execute a payment order it was obliged by express agreement to execute, the receiving bank is liable to the sender for its expenses in the transaction and for incidental expenses and interest losses resulting from the failure to execute. Additional damages, including consequential damages, are recoverable to the extent provided in an express written agreement of the receiving bank, but are not otherwise recoverable.

(5) Reasonable attorney's fees are recoverable if demand for compensation under subsection (1) or (2) is made and refused before an action is brought on the claim. If a claim is made for breach of an agreement under subsection (4) and the agreement does not provide for damages, reasonable attorney's fees are recoverable if demand for compensation under subsection (4) is made and refused before an action is brought on the claim.

(6) Except as stated in this section, the liability of a receiving bank under subsections (1) and (2) may not be varied by agreement.

Added by Laws 1990, Ch. 208, eff. Jan. 1, 1991.

Official Uniform Comment

Prior Uniform Statutory Provision: None.

Purposes:

1. Subsection (a) covers cases of delay in completion of a funds transfer resulting from an execution by a receiving bank in breach of § 4A-302(a). The receiving bank is obliged to pay interest on the amount of the order for the period of the delay. The rate of interest is stated in § 4A-506. With respect to wire transfers (other than ACH transactions) within the United States, the expectations is that the funds transfer will be completed the same day. In those cases, the originator can reasonably expect that the originator's account will be debited on the same day as the beneficiary's account is credited. If the funds transfer is delayed, compensation can be paid either to the originator or to the beneficiary. The normal practice is to compensate the beneficiary's bank to allow that bank to compensate the beneficiary by back-valuing the payment by the number of days of delay. Thus, the beneficiary is in the same position that it would have been in if the funds transfer had been completed on the same day. Assume on Day 1, Originator's Bank issues its payment order to Intermediary Bank which is received on that day. Intermediary Bank does not execute that order until Day 2 when it issues an order to Beneficiary's Bank which is accepted on that day. Intermediary Bank does not execute that order until Day 2 when it issues an order to Beneficiary's Bank which is accepted on that day. Intermediary Bank complies with subsection (a) by paying one day's interest to Beneficiary's Bank for the account of Beneficiary.

2. Subsection (b) applies to cases of breach of § 4A-302 involving more than mere delay. In those cases the bank is liable for damages for improper execution but they are limited to compensation for interest losses and incidental expenses of the sender resulting from the breach, the expenses of the sender in the funds transfer and attorney's fees. This subsection reflects the judgment that imposition of consequential damages on a bank for commission of an error is not justified.

The leading common law case on the subject of consequential damages is Evra Corp. v. Swiss Bank Corp., 673 F.2d 951 (7the Cir. 1982), in which Swiss Bank, an intermediary bank, failed to execute a payment order. Because the beneficiary did not receive timely payment the originator did not receive timely payment the originator loss a valuable ship charter. The lower court awarded the originator $2.1 million for loss profits even though the amount of the payment order was only $27,000. The Seventh Circuit reversed, in part on the basis of the common law rule of Hadley v. Baxendale that consequential damages may not be awarded unless the defendant is put on notice of the special circumstances giving rise to them. Swiss Bank may have known that the originator was paying the shipowner for the hire of a vessel but did not know that a favorable charter would be loss if the payment was delayed. "Electronic payments are not so unusual as to automatically place a bank on notice of extraordinary consequences if such a transfer goes awry. Swiss Bank did not have enough information to infer that if it loss a $27,000 payment order it would face liability in excess of $2 million." 673 F.2d at 956.

If *Evra* means that consequential damages can be imposed if the culpable bank has notice particular circumstances giving rise to the damages, it does not provide an acceptable solution to the problem of bank liability for consequential damages. In the typical case transmission of the payment order is made electronically. Personnel of the receiving bank that process payment orders are not the appropriate people to evaluate the risk of liability for consequential damages in relation to the price charged for the wire transfer service. Even if notice is received by higher level management personnel who could make an appropriate decision whether the risk is justified by the price, liability based on notice would require evaluation of payment orders on an individual basis. This kind of evaluation is inconsistent with the high-speed, low-price, mechanical nature of the processing system that characterizes wire transfers. Moreover, in *Evra* the culpable bank was an intermediary bank with which the originator did not deal. Notice to the originator's bank would not bind the intermediary bank, and it seems impractical for the originator's bank to convey notice of this kind to intermediary banks in the funds transfer. The success of the wholesale wire transfer industry has largely been based on its ability to effect payment at low cost and great speed. Both of these essential aspects of the modern wire transfer system would be adversely affected by a rule that imposed on banks liability for consequential damages. A banking industry amicus brief in *Evra* stated: "Whether banks can continue to make EFT services available on a widespread basis, by charging reasonable rates, depends on whether they can do so without incurring unlimited consequential risks. Certainly, no bank would handle for $3.25 a transaction entailing potential liability in the millions of dollars."

As the court in *Evra* also noted, the originator of the funds transfer is in the best position to evaluate the risk that a funds transfer will not be made on time and to manage that risk by issuing a payment order in time to allow monitoring of the transaction. The originator, by asking the beneficiary, can quickly determine if the funds transfer has been completed. If the originator has sent the payment order at a time that allows a reasonable margin for correcting error, no loss is likely to result if the transaction is monitored. The other published cases on this issue reach the *Evra* result. Central Coordinates, Inc. v. Morgan Guaranty Trust Co., 40 U.C.C. Rep. Serv. 1340 (N.Y. Supp. Ct. 1985), and Gatoil (U.S.A.), Inc. v. Forest Hill State Bank, 1 U.C.C. Rep. Serv.2d 171 (D. Md. 1986).

Subsection (c) allows the measure of damages in subsection (b) to be increased by an express written agreement of the receiving bank, An originator's bank might be willing to assume additional responsibilities and incur additional liability in exchange for a higher fee.

3. Subsection (d) governs cases in which a receiving bank has obligated itself by express agreement to accept payment orders of a sender. In the absence of such an agreement there is no obligation by a receiving bank to accept a payment order. § 4A-212. The measure of damages for breach of an agreement to accept a payment order is the same as that stated in subsection (b). As in the case of subsection (b), additional

damages, including consequential damages, may be recovered to the extent stated in an express written agreement of the receiving bank.

4. Reasonable attorney's fees are recoverable only in cases in which damages are limited to statutory damages stated in subsection (a), (b) and (d). If additional damages are recoverable because provided for by an express written agreement, attorney's fees are not recoverable. The rationale is that there is no need for statutory attorney's fees in the latter case, because the parties have agreed to a measure of damages which may or may not provide for attorney's fees.

5. The effect of subsection (f) is to prevent reduction of a receiving bank's liability under § 4A-305.

PART 4

PAYMENT

Section 4A–401. Payment Date.

"Payment date" of a payment order means the day on which the amount of the order is payable to the beneficiary by the beneficiary's bank. The payment date may be determined by instruction of the sender but cannot be earlier than the day the order is received by the beneficiary's bank and, unless otherwise determined, is the day the order is received by the beneficiary's bank.

Added by Laws 1990, Ch. 208, eff. Jan. 1, 1991.

Official Uniform Comment

Prior Uniform Statutory Provision: None.

Purposes:

"Payment date" refers to the day the beneficiary's bank is to pay the beneficiary. the payment date may be expressed in various ways so long as it indicates the day the beneficiary is to receive payment. For example, in ACH transfers the payment date is the equivalent of "settlement date" or "effective date." Payment date applies to the payment order issued to the beneficiary's bank, but a payment order issued to a receiving bank other than the beneficiary's bank may also state a date for payment to the beneficiary. In the later case, the statement of a payment date is to instruct the receiving bank concerning time of execution of the sender's order. § 4A-301(b).

Section 4A–402. Obligation of Sender to Pay Receiving Bank.

(1) This Section is subject to Sections 4A–205 and 4A–207.

(2) With respect to a payment order issued to the beneficiary's bank, acceptance of the order by the bank obliges the sender to pay the bank the amount of the order, but payment is not due until the payment date of the order.

(3) This subsection is subject to subsection (5) and to Section 4A–303. With respect to a payment order issued to a receiving bank other than the beneficiary's bank, acceptance of the order by the receiving bank obliges the sender to pay the bank the amount of the sender's order. Payment by the sender is not due until the execution date of the sender's order. The obligation of that sender to

pay its payment order is excused if the funds transfer is not completed by acceptance by the beneficiary's bank of a payment order instructing payment to the beneficiary of that sender's payment order.

(4) If the sender of a payment order pays the order and was not obliged to pay all or part of the amount paid, the bank receiving payment is obliged to refund payment to the extent the sender was not obliged to pay. Except as provided in Sections 4A–204 and 4A–304, interest is payable on the refundable amount from the date of payment.

(5) If a funds transfer is not completed as stated in subsection (3) and an intermediary bank is obliged to refund payment as stated in subsection (4) but is unable to do so because not permitted by applicable law or because the bank suspends payments, a sender in the funds transfer that executed a payment order in compliance with an instruction, as stated in paragraph (a) of subsection (1) of Section 4A–302, to route the funds transfer through that intermediary bank is entitled to receive or retain payment from the sender of the payment order that it accepted. The first sender in the funds transfer that issued an instruction requiring routing through that intermediary bank is subrogated to the right of the bank that paid the intermediary bank to refund as stated in subsection (4).

(6) The right of the sender of a payment order to be excused from the obligation to pay the order as stated in subsection (3) or to receive refund under subsection (4) may not be varied by agreement.

Added by Laws 1990, Ch. 208, eff. Jan. 1, 1991.

Official Uniform Comment

Prior Uniform Statutory Provision: None.

Purposes:

1. Subsection (b) states that the sender of a payment order to the beneficiary's bank must pay the order when the beneficiary's bank accepts the order. At that point the beneficiary's bank is obliged to pay the beneficiary. § 4A-404(a). The last clause of subsection (b) covers a case of premature acceptance by the beneficiary's bank. In some funds transfers, notably automated clearing house transfers, a beneficiary's bank may receive a payment order with a payment date after the day the order is received. the beneficiary's bank might accept the order before the payment date by notifying the beneficiary of receipt of the order. Although the acceptance obliges the beneficiary's bank to pay the beneficiary, payment is not due until the payment date. The last clause of subsection (b) is consistent with that result. the beneficiary's bank is also not entitled to payment from the sender until the payment date.

2. Assume that Originator instructs Bank A to order immediate payment to the account of Beneficiary in Bank B. Execution of Originator's payment order by Bank A is acceptance under § 4A-209(a). Under the second sentence of § 4A-402(c) the acceptance creates an obligation of Originator to Pay Bank A the amount of the order. The last clause of that sentence deals with attempted funds transfers that are not completed. In that event the obligation of the sender to pay its payment order is excused. Originator makes payment to Beneficiary when Bank B, the beneficiary's bank, accepts a payment order for the benefit of Beneficiary. § 4A-406(a). If that

acceptance by Bank B does not occur, the funds transfer has miscarried because Originator has not paid Beneficiary. Originator doesn't have to pay its payment order, and if it has already paid it is entitled to refund of the payment with interest. The rate of interest is stated in § 4A-506. This "money-back guarantee" is an important protection of Originator. Originator is assured that it will not lose its money if something goes wrong in the transfer. For example, risk of loss resulting from payment to the wrong beneficiary is borne by some bank, not by Originator. The most likely reason for noncompletion is a failure to execute or an erroneous execution of a payment order by Bank A or an intermediary bank. Bank A may have issued its payment order to the wrong bank or it may have identified the wrong beneficiary in its order. The money-back guarantee is particularly important to Originator if noncompletion of the funds transfer is due to the fault of an intermediary bank rather than Bank A. In that case Bank A must refund payment to Originator, and Bank A has the burden of obtaining refund from the intermediary bank that it paid.

Subsection (c) can result in loss if an intermediary bank suspends payments. Suppose originator instructs Bank A to apy to Beneficiary's account in Bank B and to use Bank C as an intermediary bank. Bank A executes Originator's order by issuing a payment order to Bank C. Bank A pays Bank C. Bank C fails to execute the order of Bank A and suspends payments. Under subsections (c) and (d), Originator is not obliged to pay Bank A and is entitled to refund from Bank A of any payment that it may have made. Bank A is entitled to a refund from Bank C, but Ban C is insolvent. Subsection (e) deals with this case. Bank A was required to issue its payment order to Bank C because Bank C was designated as an intermediary bank by Originator. § 4A-302(a)(1). In this case Originator takes the risk of insolvency of Bank C. Under subsection (e), Bank A is entitled to payment from Originator and originator is subrogated to the right of Bank A under subsection (d) to refund of payment form Bank C.

3. A payment order is not like a negotiable instrument on which the drawer or maker has liability. Acceptance of the order by the receiving bank creates an obligation of the sender to pay the receiving bank the amount of the order. That is the extent of the sender's liability to the receiving bank and no other person has any rights against the sender with respect to the sender's order.

Section 4A–403. Payment by Sender to Receiving Bank.

(1) Payment of the sender's obligation under Section 4A–402 to pay the receiving bank occurs as follows:

(a) If the sender is a bank, payment occurs when the receiving bank receives final settlement of the obligation through a federal reserve bank or through a funds-transfer system.

(b) If the sender is a bank and the sender (i) credited an account of the receiving bank with the sender, or (ii) caused an account of the receiving bank in another bank to be credited, payment occurs when the credit is withdrawn or, if not withdrawn, at midnight of the day on which the credit is withdrawable and the receiving bank learns of that fact.

(c) If the receiving bank debits an account of the sender with the receiving bank, payment occurs when the debit is made to the extent the debit is covered by a withdrawable credit balance in the account.

(2) If the sender and receiving bank are members of a funds-transfer system that nets obligations multilaterally among participants, the receiving bank

receives final settlement when settlement is complete in accordance with the rules of the system. The obligation of the sender to pay the amount of a payment order transmitted through the funds-transfer system may be satisfied, to the extent permitted by the rules of the system, by setting off and applying against the sender's obligation the right of the sender to receive payment from the receiving bank of the amount of any other payment order transmitted to the sender by the receiving bank through the funds-transfer system. The aggregate balance of obligations owed by each sender to each receiving bank in the funds-transfer system may be satisfied, to the extent permitted by the rules of the system, by setting off and applying against that balance the aggregate balance of obligations owed to the sender by other members of the system. The aggregate balance is determined after the right of setoff stated in the second sentence of this subsection has been exercised.

(3) If two banks transmit payment orders to each other under an agreement that settlement of the obligations of each bank to the other under Section 4A–402 will be made at the end of the day or other period, the total amount owed with respect to all orders transmitted by one bank shall be set off against the total amount owed with respect to all orders transmitted by the other bank. To the extent of the setoff, each bank has made payment to the other.

(4) In a case not covered by subsection (1), the time when payment of the sender's obligation under subsection (2) or subsection (3) of Section 4A–402 occurs is governed by applicable principles of law that determine when an obligation is satisfied.

Added by Laws 1990, Ch. 208, eff. Jan. 1, 1991.

Official Uniform Comment

Prior Uniform Statutory Provision: None.

Purposes:

1. This section defines when a sender pays the obligation stated in § 4A-402. If a group of two or more banks engage in funds transfers with each other, the participating banks will sometimes be senders and sometimes receiving banks. With respect to payment orders other than Fedwires, the amounts of the various payment orders may be credited and debited to accounts of one bank with another or to a clearing house account of each bank and amounts owed and amounts due are netted. Settlement is made through a Federal Reserve Bank by charges to the Federal Reserve accounts of the net debtor banks and credits to the Federal Reserve accounts of the net creditor banks. In the case of Fedwires the sender's obligation is settled by a debit to the Federal Reserve account of the sender and a credit to the Federal Reserve account of the receiving bank at the time the receiving bank receives the payment order. Both of these cases are covered by subsection (a)(1). When the Federal Reserve settlement becomes final the obligation of the sender under § 4A-402 is paid.

2. In some cases a bank does not settle an obligation owed to another bank through a Federal Reserve Bank. This is the case if one of the banks is a foreign bank without access to the Federal Reserve payment system. In this kind of case, payment is usually made by credits or debits to accounts of the two banks with each other or to accounts

of the two banks in a third bank. Suppose Bank B has an account in Bank A. Bank A advises Bank B that its account in Bank A has been credited $1,000,000 and that the credit is immediately withdrawable. Bank A also instructs Bank B to pay $1,000,000 to the account of Beneficiary in Bank B. This case is covered by subsection (a)(2). Bank B may want to immediately withdraw this credit. For example, it might do so by instructing Bank A to debit the account and pay some third party. Payment by Bank A to Bank B of Bank A's payment order occurs when the withdrawal is made. Suppose Bank B does not withdraw the credit. Since Bank B is the beneficiary's bank, one of the effects of receipt of payment by Bank B is that acceptance of Bank A's payment order automatically occurs at the time of payment. § 4A-209(b)(2). Acceptance means that Bank B is obliged to pay $1,000,000 to Beneficiary. § 4A-404(a). Subsection (a)(2) of § 4A-403 states that payment does not occur until midnight if the credit is not withdrawn. This allows Bank B an opportunity to reject the order if it does not have time to withdraw the credit to its account and it is not willing to incur the liability to Beneficiary before it has use of the funds represented by the credit.

3. Subsection (a)(3) applies to a case in which the sender (bank or nonbank) has a funded account in the receiving bank. If Sender has an account in Bank and issues a payment order to Bank, Bank can obtain payment form Sender by debiting the account of Sender, which pays its § 4A-402 obligation to Bank when the debit is made.

4. Subsection (b) deals with multilateral settlements made through a funds transfer system and is based on the CHIPS settlement system. In a funds transfer system such as CHIPS, which allows the various banks that transmit payment orders over the system to settle obligations at the end of each day, settlement is not based on individual payment orders. Each bank using the system engages in funds transfers with many other banks using the system. Settlement for any participant is based on the net credit or debit position of that participant with all other banks using the system. Subsection (b) is designed to make clear that the obligations of any sender are paid when the net position of that sender is settled in accordance with the rules of the funds transfer system. This provision is intended to invalidate any argument, based on common-law principles, that multilateral netting is not valid because mutuality netting is not valid because mutuality of obligation is not present. Subsection (b) dispenses with any mutuality of obligation requirements. Subsection (c) applies to case in which two banks send payment orders to each other during the day and settle with each other at the end of the day or at the end of some other period. It is similar to subsection (b) in that it recognizes that a sender's obligation to pay a payment order is satisfied by a setoff. The obligations of each bank as sender to the other as receiving bank are obligations of the bank itself and not as representative of customers. These two sections are important in the case of insolvency of a bank. They make clear that liability under § 4A-402 is based on the net position of the insolvent bank after setoff.

5. Subsection (d) relates to the uncommon case in which the sender doesn't have an account relationship with the receiving bank and doesn't settle through a Federal Reserve Bank. An example would be a customer that pays over the counter for a payment order that customer issues to the receiving bank. Payment would normally be by cash, check or bank obligation. When payment occurs is determined by law outside Article 4A.

Section 4A–404. Obligation of Beneficiary's Bank to Pay and Give Notice to Beneficiary.

(1) Subject to subsection (5) of Section 4A–211 and subsections (4) and (5) of Section 4A–405, if a beneficiary's bank accepts a payment order, the bank

UCC

is obliged to pay the amount of the order to the beneficiary of the order. Payment is due on the payment date of the order, but if acceptance occurs on the payment date after the close of the funds-transfer business day of the bank, payment is due on the next funds-transfer business day. If the bank refuses to pay after demand by the beneficiary and receipt of notice of particular circumstances that will give rise to consequential damages as a result of nonpayment, the beneficiary may recover damages resulting from the refusal to pay to the extent the bank had notice of the damages, unless the bank proves that it did not pay because of a reasonable doubt concerning the right of the beneficiary to payment.

(2) If a payment order accepted by the beneficiary's bank instructs payment to an account of the beneficiary, the bank is obliged to notify the beneficiary of receipt of the order before midnight of the next funds-transfer business day following the payment date. If the payment order does not instruct payment to an account of the beneficiary, the bank is required to notify the beneficiary only if notice is required by the order. Notice may be given by first class mail or any other means reasonable in the circumstances. If the bank fails to give the required notice, the bank is obliged to pay interest to the beneficiary on the amount of the payment order from the day notice should have been given until the day the beneficiary learned of receipt of the payment order by the bank. No other damages are recoverable. Reasonable attorney's fees are also recoverable if demand for interest is made and refused before an action is brought on the claim.

(3) The right of a beneficiary to receive payment and damages as stated in subsection (1) may not be varied by agreement or a funds-transfer system rule. The right of a beneficiary to be notified as stated in subsection (2) may be varied by agreement of the beneficiary or by a funds-transfer system rule if the beneficiary is notified of the rule before initiation of the funds transfer.

Added by Laws 1990, Ch. 208, eff. Jan. 1, 1991.

Official Uniform Comment

Prior Uniform Statutory Provision: None.

Purposes:

1. The first sentence of subsection (a) states the time when the obligation of the beneficiary's bank arises. The second and third sentences state when the beneficiary's bank must make funds available to the beneficiary. They also state the measure of damages for failure, after demand, to comply. Since the Expedited Funds Availability Act, 12 U.S.C. 4001 et seq., also governs funds availability in a funds transfer, the second and third sentences of subsection (a) may be subject to preemption by that Act.

2. Subsection (a) provides that the beneficiary's of an accepted payment order may recover consequential damages if the beneficiary's bank refuses to pay the order after demand by the beneficiary if the bank at that time had notice of the particular circumstances giving rise to the damages. Such damages are recoverable only to the extent the bank had "notice of the damages." The quoted phrase requires that the bank have notice of the general type or nature of the damages that will be suffered

as a result of the refusal to pay and their general magnitude. There is no requirement that the bank have notice of the exact or even the approximate amount of the damages, but if the amount of damages is extraordinary the bank is entitled to notice of that fact. For example, in Evra Corp. v. Swiss Bank Corp., 673 F.2d 951 (7th Cir. 1982), failure to complete a funds transfer of only $27,000 required to retain rights to a very favorable ship charter resulted in a claim for more than $2,000,000 of consequential damages. Since it is not reasonably foreseeable that a failure to make a relatively small payment will result in damages of this magnitude, notice is not sufficient if the beneficiary's bank has notice only that the $27,000 is necessary to retain rights on a ship charter. The bank is entitled to notice that an exceptional amount of damages will result as well. For example, there would be adequate notice if the bank had been made aware that damages of $1,000,000 or more might result.

3. Under the last clause of subsection (a) the beneficiary's bank is not liable for damages if its refusal to pay was "because of a reasonable doubt concerning the right of the beneficiary to payment." Normally there will not be any question about the right of the beneficiary to receive payment. Normally, the bank should be able to determine whether it has been accepted, the first sentence of subsection (a) states that the bank is obliged to pay. There may be uncommon cases, however, in which there is doubt whether acceptance occurred. For example, if acceptance is based on receipt of payment by the beneficiary's bank under § 4A-403(a)(1) or (2), there may be cases in which the bank is not certain that payment has been received. There may also be cases in which there is doubt about whether the person demanding payment is the person identified in the payment order as beneficiary of the order.

The last clause of subsection (a) does not apply to cases in which a funds transfer is being used to pay an obligation and a dispute arises between the originator and the beneficiary concerning whether the obligation is in fact owed. For example, the originator may try to prevent payment to the beneficiary by the beneficiary's bank by alleging that the beneficiary is not entitled to payment because of fraud against the originator or a breach of contract relating to the obligation. The fraud or breach of contract claim of the originator may be grounds for recovery by the originator from the beneficiary after the beneficiary is paid, but it does not affect the obligation of the beneficiary's bank to pay the beneficiary. Unless the payment order has been cancelled pursuant to § 4A-211(c), there is no excuse for refusing to pay the beneficiary and, in a proper case, the refusal may result in consequential damages. Except in the case of a book transfer, in which the beneficiary's bank is also the originator's bank, the originator of a funds transfer cannot cancel a payment order to the beneficiary's bank, with or without the consent of that bank, because the originator is not the sender of that order. Thus, the beneficiary's bank may safely ignore any instruction by the originator to withhold payment to the beneficiary.

4. Subsection (b) states the duty of the beneficiary's bank to notify the beneficiary of receipt of the order. If acceptance occurs under § 4A-209(b)(1) the beneficiary is normally notified. Thus, subsection (b) applies primarily to cases in which acceptance occurs under § 4A-209(b)(2) or (3). Notice under subsection (b) is not required if the person entitled to the notice agrees or a funds transfer system rule provides that notice is not required and the beneficiary is given notice of the rule. In ACH transactions the normal practice is not to give notice to the beneficiary unless notice is requested by the beneficiary. This practice can be continued by adoption of a funds transfer system rule. Subsection (a) is not subject to variation by agreement or by a funds transfer system rule.

Section 4A–405. Payment by Beneficiary's Bank to Beneficiary.

(1) If the beneficiary's bank credits an account of the beneficiary of a payment order, payment of the bank's obligation under subsection (1) of Section 4A–404

occurs when and to the extent (i) the beneficiary is notified of the right to withdraw the credit, (ii) the bank lawfully applies the credit to a debt of the beneficiary, or (iii) funds with respect to the order are otherwise made available to the beneficiary by the bank.

(2) If the beneficiary's bank does not credit an account of the beneficiary of a payment order, the time when payment of the bank's obligation under subsection (1) of Section 4A–404 occurs is governed by principles of law that determine when an obligation is satisfied.

(3) Except as stated in subsections (4) and (5), if the beneficiary's bank pays the beneficiary of a payment order under a condition to payment or agreement of the beneficiary giving the bank the right to recover payment from the beneficiary if the bank does not receive payment of the order, the condition to payment or agreement is not enforceable.

(4) A funds-transfer system rule may provide that payments made to beneficiaries of funds transfers made through the system are provisional until receipt of payment by the beneficiary's bank of the payment order it accepted. A beneficiary's bank that makes a payment that is provisional under the rule is entitled to refund from the beneficiary if (i) the rule requires that both the beneficiary and the originator be given notice of the provisional nature of the payment before the funds transfer is initiated, (ii) the beneficiary, the beneficiary's bank and the originator's bank agreed to be bound by the rule, and (iii) the beneficiary's bank did not receive payment of the payment order that it accepted. If the beneficiary is obliged to refund payment to the beneficiary's bank, acceptance of the payment order by the beneficiary's bank is nullified and no payment by the originator of the funds transfer to the beneficiary occurs under Section 4A–406.

(5) This subsection applies to a funds transfer that includes a payment order transmitted over a funds-transfer system that (i) nets obligations multilaterally among participants, and (ii) has in effect a loss-sharing agreement among participants for the purpose of providing funds necessary to complete settlement of the obligations of one or more participants that do not meet their settlement obligations. If the beneficiary's bank in the funds transfer accepts a payment order and the system fails to complete settlement pursuant to its rules with respect to any payment order in the funds transfer, (i) the acceptance by the beneficiary's bank is nullified and no person has any right or obligation based on the acceptance, (ii) the beneficiary's bank is entitled to recover payment from the beneficiary, (iii) no payment by the originator to the beneficiary occurs under Section 4A–406, and (iv) subject to subsection (5) of Section 4A–402, each sender in the funds transfer is excused from its obligation to pay its payment order under subsection (3) of Section 4A–402 because the funds transfer has not been completed.

Added by Laws 1990, Ch. 208, eff. Jan. 1, 1991.

Official Uniform Comment

Prior Uniform Statutory Provision: None.

Purposes:

1. This section defines when the beneficiary's bank pays the beneficiary and when the obligation of the beneficiary's bank under § 4A-404 to pay the beneficiary is satisfied. In almost all cases the bank will credit an account of the beneficiary when it receives a payment order. In the typical case the beneficiary is paid when the beneficiary is given notice of the right to withdraw the credit. Subsection (a)(i). In some cases payment might be made to the beneficiary not by releasing funds to the beneficiary, but by applying the credit to a debt of the beneficiary. Subsection (a)(ii). In this case the beneficiary gets the benefit of the payment order because a debt of the beneficiary has been satisfied. The two principal cases in which payment will occur in this manner are setoff by the beneficiary's bank and payment of the proceeds of the payment order to a garnishing creditor of the beneficiary. These cases are discussed in Comment 2 to § 4A-502.

2. If a beneficiary's bank releases funds to the beneficiary before it receives payment from the sender of the payment order, it assumes the risk that the sender may not pay the sender's order because of suspension of payments or other reason. Subsection (c). As stated in Comment 5 to § 4A-209, the beneficiary's bank can protect itself against this risk by delaying acceptance. But if the bank accepts the order it is obliged to pay the beneficiary. If the beneficiary's bank has given the beneficiary notice of the right to withdraw a credit made to the beneficiary's account, the beneficiary has received payment from the bank. Once payment has been made to the beneficiary with respect to an obligation incurred by the bank under § 4A-404(a), the payment cannot be recovered by the beneficiary's bank unless subsection (d) or (e) applies. Thus, a right to withdraw a credit cannot be revoked if the right to withdraw constituted payment of the bank's obligation. This principle applies even if funds were released as a "loan" (see Comment 5 to § 4A-209), or were released subject to a condition that they would be repaid in the event the bank does not receive payment from the sender of the payment order, or the beneficiary agreed to return the payment if the bank did not receive payment from the sender.

3. Subsection (c) is subject to an exception stated in subsection (d) which is intended to apply to automated clearing house transfers. ACH transfers are made in batches. A beneficiary's bank will normally accept, at the same time and as part of a single batch, payment orders with respect to many different originator's banks. Comment 2 to § 4A-206. the custom in ACH transactions is to release funds to the beneficiary early on the payment date even though settlement to the beneficiary's bank does not occur until later in the day. the understanding is that payments to beneficiaries are provisional until the beneficiary's bank receives settlement. This practice is similar to what happens when a depositary bank releases funds with respect to a check forwarded for collection. If the check is dishonored the bank is entitled to recover the funds from the customer. ACH transfers are widely perceived as check substitutes. § 4A-405(d) allows the funds transfer system to adopt a rule making payments to beneficiaries provisional. If such a rule is adopted, a beneficiary's bank that releases funds to the beneficiary will be able to recover the payment if it doesn't receive payment of the payment order that it accepted. There are two requirements with respect to the funds transfer system rule. The beneficiary, the beneficiary's bank and the originator's bank must all agree to be bound by the rule and the rule must require that both the beneficiary and the originator be given notice of the provisional nature of the payment before the funds transfer is initiated. There is no requirement that the notice be given with respect to a particular funds transfer. Once notice of the provisional nature of the payment has been given, the notice is effective for all

subsequent payments to or form the person to whom the notice was given. Subsection (d) provides only that the funds transfer system rule must require notice to the beneficiary and the originator. The beneficiary's bank will know what the rule requires, but it has no way of knowing whether the originator's bank complied with the rule. Subsection (d) does not require proof that the originator received notice. If the originator's bank failed to give the required notice and the originator suffered as a result, the appropriate remedy is an action by the originator against the originator's bank based on that failure. But the beneficiary's bank will not be able to get the benefit of subsection (d) unless the beneficiary had notice of the provisional nature of the payment because subsection (d) requires an agreement by the beneficiary to be bound by the rule. Implicit in an agreement to be bound by a rule that notice be given of what the rule provides. The notice can be part of the agreement or separately given. For example, notice can be given by providing a copy of the system's operating rules.

With respect to ACH transfers made through a Federal Reserve Bank acting as an intermediary bank, the Federal Reserve Bank is obliged under § 4A-402(b) to pay a beneficiary's bank that accepts the payment order. Unlike Fedwire transfers, under current ACH practice a Federal Reserve Bank that processes a payment order does not obligate itself to pay if the originator's bank failed to pay the Federal Reserve Bank. It is assumed that the Federal Reserve will use its right of preemption which is recognized in § 4A-107 to disclaim the § 4A-402(b) obligation in ACH transactions if it decides to retain the provisional payment rule.

4. Subsection (e) is another exception to subsection (c). It refers to funds transfer systems having loss-sharing rules described in the subsection. CHIPS has proposed a rule that fits the description. Under the CHIPS loss-sharing rule the CHIPS banks will have agreed to contribute funds to allow the system to settle for payment orders sent over the system during the day in the event that one or more banks are unable to meet their settlement obligations. Subsection (e) applies only if CHIPS fails to settle despite the loss-sharing rule. Since funds under the loss-sharing rule will be instantly available to CHIPS and will be in an amount sufficient to cover any failure that can be reasonably anticipated, it is extremely unlikely that CHIPS would ever fail to settle. Thus, subsection (e) addresses an event that should never occur. If that event were to occur, all payment orders made over the system would be cancelled under the CHIPS rule. Thus, no bank would receive settlement, whether or not a failed bank was involved in a particular funds transfer. Subsection (e) provides that each funds transfer in which there is a payment order with respect to which there is a settlement failure is unwound. Acceptance by the beneficiary's bank in each funds transfer is nullified. The consequences of nullification are that the beneficiary has no right to receive or retain payment by the beneficiary's bank, no payment is made by the originator to the beneficiary and each sender in the funds transfer is, subject to § 4A-402(e), not obliged to pay its payment order and is entitled to refund under § 4A-402(d) if it has already paid.

Section 4A–406. Payment by Originator to Beneficiary; Discharge of Underlying Obligation.

(1) Subject to subsection (5) of Section 4A–211 and subsections (4) and (5) of Section 4A–405, the originator of a funds transfer pays the beneficiary of the originator's payment order (i) at the time a payment order for the benefit of the beneficiary is accepted by the beneficiary's bank in the funds transfer and (ii) in an amount equal to the amount of the order accepted by the beneficiary's bank, but not more than the amount of the originator's order.

(2) If payment under subsection (1) is made to satisfy an obligation, the obligation is discharged to the same extent discharge would result from payment

to the beneficiary of the same amount in money, unless (i) the payment under subsection (1) was made by a means prohibited by the contract of the beneficiary with respect to the obligation, (ii) the beneficiary, within a reasonable time after receiving notice of receipt of the order by the beneficiary's bank, notified the originator of the beneficiary's refusal of the payment, (iii) funds with respect to the order were not withdrawn by the beneficiary or applied to a debt of the beneficiary, and (iv) the beneficiary would suffer a loss that could reasonably have been avoided if payment had been made by a means complying with the contract. If payment by the originator does not result in discharge under this section, the originator is subrogated to the rights of the beneficiary to receive payment from the beneficiary's bank under subsection (1) of Section 4A–404.

(3) For the purpose of determining whether discharge of an obligation occurs under subsection (2), if the beneficiary's bank accepts a payment order in an amount equal to the amount of the originator's payment order less charges of one or more receiving banks in the funds transfer, payment to the beneficiary is deemed to be in the amount of the originator's order unless upon demand by the beneficiary the originator does not pay the beneficiary the amount of the deducted charges.

(4) Rights of the originator or of the beneficiary of a funds transfer under this section may be varied only by agreement of the originator and the beneficiary.

Added by Laws 1990, Ch. 208, eff. Jan. 1, 1991.

Official Uniform Comment

Prior Uniform Statutory Provision: None.

Purposes:

1. Subsection (a) states the fundamental rule of Article 4A that payment by the originator to the beneficiary is accomplished by providing to the beneficiary the obligation of the beneficiary's bank to pay. Since this obligation arises when the beneficiary's bank accepts a payment order, the originator pays the beneficiary at the time of acceptance and in the amount of the payment order accepted.

2. In a large percentage of funds transfers, the transfer is made to pay an obligation of the originator. Subsection (a) states that the beneficiary is paid by the originator when the beneficiary's bank accepts a payment order for the benefit of the beneficiary. When that happens the effect under subsection (b) is to substitute the obligation of the beneficiary's bank for the obligation of the originator. The effect is similar to that under Article 3 if a cashier's check payable to the beneficiary had been taken by the beneficiary. Normally, payment by funds transfer is sought by the beneficiary because it puts money into the hands of the beneficiary more quickly. As a practical matter the beneficiary and the originator will nearly always agree to the funds transfer in advance. Under subsection (b) acceptance by the beneficiary's bank will result in discharge of the obligation for which payment was made unless the beneficiary had made a contract with respect to the obligation which does not permit payment by the means used. Thus, if there is no contract of the beneficiary with respect to the means of payment of the obligation, acceptance by the beneficiary's bank of a payment order to the account of the beneficiary can result in discharge.

3. Suppose Beneficiary's contract stated that payment of an obligation owed by Originator was to be made by a cashier's check of Bank A. Instead Originator paid by a funds transfer to Beneficiary's account in Bank B. Bank B accepted a payment order for the benefit of Beneficiary by immediately notifying Beneficiary that the funds were available for withdrawal. Before Beneficiary had a reasonable opportunity to withdraw the funds Bank B suspended payments. Under the unless clause of subsection (b) Beneficiary is not required to accept the payment as discharging the obligation owed by Originator to Beneficiary if Beneficiary's contract means that Beneficiary was not required to accept payment by wire transfer. Beneficiary could refuse the funds transfer as payment of the obligation and could resort to rights under the underlying contract to enforce the obligation. The rationale is that Originator cannot impose the risk of Bank B's insolvency on Beneficiary if Beneficiary had specified another means of payment that did not entail that risk. If Beneficiary is required to accept Originator's payment, Beneficiary would suffer a loss that would not have occurred if payment had been made by a cashier's check on Bank A, and Bank A has not suspended payments. In this case Originator will have to pay twice. It is obliged to pay the amount of a its payment order to the bank that accepted it and has to pay the obligation it owes to Beneficiary which has not been discharged. Under the last sentence of subsection (b) originator is subrogated to Beneficiary's right to receive payment from Bank B under § 4A-404(a).

4. Suppose Beneficiary's contract called for payment by a Fedwire transfer to Bank B, but the payment order accepted by Bank B was not a Fedwire transfer. Before the funds were withdrawn by Beneficiary, Bank B suspended payments. The sender of the payment order to Bank B paid the amount of the order to Bank B. In this case the payment by Originator did not comply with Beneficiary's contract, but the noncompliance did not result in a loss to Beneficiary as required by subsection (b)(iv). A Fedwire transfer avoids the risk of insolvency of the sender of the payment order to Bank B, but it does not affect the risk that Bank B will suspend payments before withdrawal of the funds by Beneficiary. Thus, the unless clause of subsection (b) is not applicable and the obligation owed to Beneficiary is discharged.

5. Charges of receiving banks in a funds transfer normally are nominal in relationship to the amount being paid by the originator to the beneficiary. Wire transfers are normally agreed to in advance and the parties may agree concerning how these charges are to be divided between the parties. Subsection (c) states a rule that applies in the absence of agreement. In some funds transfers charges of banks that execute payment orders are collected by deducting the charges from the amount of the payment order issued by the bank, i.e. the bank issues a payment order that is slightly less than the amount of the payment order that is being executed. The process is described in Comment 3 to § 4A-302. The result in such a case is that the payment order accepted by the beneficiary's bank will be slightly less than the amount of the originator's order. Subsection (c) recognizes the principle that a beneficiary is entitled to full payment of a debt paid by wire transfer as a condition to discharge. On the other hand, Subsection (c) prevents a beneficiary from denying the originator the benefit of the payment by asserting that discharge did not occur because deduction of bank charges resulted in less than full payment. The typical case is one in which the payment is made to exercise a valuable right such as an option which is unfavorable to the beneficiary. Subsection (c) allows discharge notwithstanding the deduction unless the originator fails to reimburse the beneficiary for the deducted charges after demand by the beneficiary.

PART 5

MISCELLANEOUS PROVISIONS

Section 4A–501. Variation by Agreement and Effect of Funds-Transfer System Rule.

(1) Except as otherwise provided in this article, the rights and obligations of a party to a funds transfer may be varied by agreement of the affected party.

(2) "Funds-Transfer system rule" means a rule of an association of banks (i) governing transmission of payment orders by means of a funds-transfer system of the association or rights and obligations with respect to those orders, or (ii) to the extent the rule governs rights and obligations between banks that are parties to a funds transfer in which a federal reserve bank, acting as an intermediary bank, sends a payment order to the beneficiary's bank. Except as otherwise provided in this article, a funds transfer system rule governing rights and obligations between participating banks using the system may be effective even if the rule conflicts with this article and indirectly affects another party to the funds transfer who does not consent to the rule. A funds-transfer system rule may also govern rights and obligations of parties other than participating banks using the system to the extent stated in subsection (3) of Section 4A–404, subsection (4) of Section 4A–405, and subsection (3) of Section 4A–507.

Added by Laws 1990, Ch. 208, eff. Jan. 1, 1991.

Official Uniform Comment

Prior Uniform Statutory Provision: None.

Purposes:

1. This section is designed to give some flexibility to Article 4A. Funds transfer system rules govern rights and obligations between banks that use the system. They may cover a wide variety of matters such as form and content of payment orders, security procedures, indemnity rights, compensation rules for delays in completion of a funds transfer, time and method of settlement, credit restrictions with respect to senders of payment orders and risk allocation with respect to suspension of payments by a participating bank. Funds transfer system rules can be very effective in supplementing the provisions of Article 4A and in filing gaps that may be present in Article 4A. To the extent they do not conflict with Article 4A there is no problem with respect to their effectiveness. In that case they merely supplement Article 4A. § 4A-501 goes further. It states that unless the contrary is stated, funds transfer system rules can override provisions of Article 4A. Thus, rights and obligations of a sender bank and a receiving bank with respect to each other can be different from that stated in Article 4A to the extent a funds transfer system rule applies. Since funds transfer system rules are defined as those governing the relationship between participating banks, a rule can have a direct effect only on participating banks. But a rule that affects the conduct of a participating bank may indirectly affect the rights of nonparticipants such as the originator or beneficiary of a funds transfer, and such a rule can be effective even though it may affect nonparticipants without their consent. For example, a rule might prevent execution of a payment order or might allow

UCC

cancellation of a payment order with the result that a funds transfer is not completed or is delayed. But a rule purporting to define rights and obligations of nonparticipants in the system would not be effective to alter Article 4A rights because the rule is not within the definition of funds transfer system rule. Rights and obligations arising under Article 4A may also be varied by agreement of the affected parties, except to the extent Article 4A otherwise provides. Rights and obligations arising under Article 4A can also be changed by Federal Reserve regulations and operating circulars of Federal Reserve Banks. § 4A-107.

2. Subsection (b)(ii) refers to ACH transfers. Whether an ACH transfer is made through an automated clearing house of a Federal Reserve Bank or through an automated clearing house of another association of banks, the rights and obligations of the originator's bank and the beneficiary's bank are governed by uniform rules adopted by various associations of banks in various parts of the nation. With respect to transfers in which a Federal Reserve Bank acts as intermediary bank these rules may be incorporated, in whole or in part, in operating circulars of the Federal Reserve Bank. Even if not so incorporated these rules can still be binding on the association banks. If a transfer is made through a Federal Reserve Bank, the rules are effective under subsection (b)(ii). If the transfer is not made through a Federal Reserve Bank, the association rules are effective under subsection (b)(i).

Section 4A–502. Credit or Process Served on Receiving Bank; Set Off by Beneficiary's Bank.

(1) As used in this section, "creditor process" means levy, attachment, garnishment, notice of lien, sequestration, or similar process issued by or on behalf of a creditor or other claimant with respect to an account.

(2) This subsection applies to creditor process with respect to an authorized account of the sender of a payment order if the creditor process is served on the receiving bank. For the purpose of determining rights with respect to the creditor process, if the receiving bank accepts the payment order the balance in the authorized account is deemed to be reduced by the amount of the payment order to the extent the bank did not otherwise receive payment of the order, unless the creditor process is served at a time and in a manner affording the bank a reasonable opportunity to act on it before the bank accepts the payment order.

(3) If a beneficiary's bank has received a payment order for payment to the beneficiary's account in the bank, the following rules apply:

(a) The bank may credit the beneficiary's account. The amount credited may be set off against an obligation owed by the beneficiary to the bank or may be applied to satisfy creditor process served on the bank with respect to the account.

(b) The bank may credit the beneficiary's account and allow withdrawal of the amount credited unless creditor process with respect to the account is served at a time and in a manner affording the bank a reasonable opportunity to act to prevent withdrawal.

(c) If creditor process with respect to the beneficiary's account has been served and the bank has had a reasonable opportunity to act on it, the bank may not reject the payment order except for a reason unrelated to the service of process.

(4) Creditor process with respect to a payment by the originator to the beneficiary pursuant to a funds transfer may be served only on the beneficiary's bank with respect to the debt owed by that bank to the beneficiary. Any other bank served with the creditor process is not obliged to act with respect to the process.

Added by Laws 1990, Ch. 208, eff. Jan. 1, 1991.

Official Uniform Comment

Prior Uniform Statutory Provision: None.

Purposes:

1. When a receiving bank accepts a payment order, the bank normally receives payment from the sender by debiting an authorized account of the sender. In accepting the sender's order the bank may be relying on a credit balance in the account. If creditor process is served on the bank with respect to the account before the bank accepts the order but the bank employee responsible for the acceptance was not aware of the creditor process at the time the acceptance occurred, it is unjust to the bank to allow the creditor process to take the credit balance on which the bank may have relied. Subsection (b) allows the bank to obtain payment from the sender's account in this case. Under that provision, the balance in the sender's account to which the creditor process applies is deemed to be reduced by the amount of the payment order unless there was sufficient time for notice of the service of creditor process to be received by personnel of the bank responsible for the acceptance.

2. Subsection (c) deals with payment orders issued to the beneficiary's bank. The bank may credit the beneficiary's account when the order is received, but under § 4A-404(a) the bank incurs no obligation to pay the beneficiary until the order is accepted pursuant to § 4A-209(b). Thus, before acceptance, the credit to the beneficiary's account is provisional. But under § 4A-209(b) acceptance occurs if the beneficiary's bank pays the beneficiary pursuant to § 4A-405(a). Under that provision, payment occurs if the credit to the beneficiary's account is applied to a debt of the beneficiary. Subsection (c)(1) allows the bank to credit the beneficiary's account with respect to a payment order and to accept the order by setting off the credit against an obligation owed to the bank or applying the credit to creditor process with respect to the account.

Suppose a beneficiary's bank receives a payment order for the benefit of a customer. Before that bank accepts the order, the bank learns that creditor process has been served on the bank with respect to the customer's account. Normally there is no reason for a beneficiary's bank to reject a payment order, but if the beneficiary's account is garnished, the bank may be faced with a difficult choice. If it rejects the order, the garnishing creditor's potential recovery of funds of the beneficiary is frustrated. It may be faced with a claim by the creditor that the rejection was a wrong to the creditor. If the bank accepts the order, the effect is to allow the creditor to seize funds of its customer, the beneficiary. Subsection (c)(3) gives the bank no choice in this case. It provides that it may not favor its customer over the creditor by rejecting the order. The beneficiary's bank may rightfully reject only if there is an independent basis for rejection.

3. Subsection (c)(2) is similar to subsection (b). Normally the beneficiary's bank will release funds to the beneficiary shortly after acceptance or it will accept by releasing funds. Since the bank is bound by a garnishment order served before funds are released to the beneficiary, the bank might suffer a loss if funds were released without knowledge that a garnishment order had been served. Subsection (c)(2)

protects the bank if it did not have adequate notice of the garnishment when the funds were released.

4. A creditor may want to reach funds involved in a funds transfer. The creditor may try to do so by serving process on the originator's bank, an intermediary bank or the beneficiary's bank. The purpose of subsection (d) is to guide the creditor and the court as to the proper method of reaching the funds involved in a funds transfer. A creditor of the originator in the originator's bank before the funds transfer is initiated, but that levy is subject to the limitations stated in subsection (b). The creditor of the originator cannot reach any other funds because no property of the originator is being transferred. A creditor of the beneficiary cannot levy on property of the originator and until the funds transfer is completed by acceptance by the beneficiary's bank payment order for the benefit of the beneficiary, the beneficiary has no property interest in the funds transfer which the beneficiary's creditor can reach. A creditor of the beneficiary that wants to reach the funds to be received by the beneficiary must serve creditor process on the beneficiary's bank to reach the obligation of the beneficiary's bank to pay the beneficiary which arises upon acceptance by the beneficiary's bank under § 4A-404(a).

5. "Creditor process" is defined in subsection (a) to cover a variety of devices by which a claimant to a bank account can seize the account. Procedure and nomenclature varies widely from state to state. The term used in § 4A-502 is a generic term.

Section 4A–503. Injunction or Restraining Order With Respect to Funds Transfer.

For proper cause and in compliance with applicable law, a court may restrain (i) a person from issuing a payment order to initiate a funds transfer, (ii) an originator's bank from executing the payment order of the originator, or (iii) the beneficiary's bank from releasing funds to the beneficiary or the beneficiary from withdrawing the funds. A court may not otherwise restrain a person from issuing a payment order, paying or receiving payment of a payment order, or otherwise acting with respect to a funds transfer.

Added by Laws 1990, Ch. 208, eff. Jan. 1, 1991.

Official Uniform Comment

Prior Uniform Statutory Provision: None.

Purposes:

This section is related to § 4A-502(d) and to Comment 4 of § 4A-502. It is designed to prevent interruption of a funds transfer after it has been set in motion. the initiation of a funds transfer can be prevented by enjoining the originator or the originator's bank from issuing a payment order. After the funds transfer is completed by acceptance of a payment order by the beneficiary's bank, that bank can be enjoined from releasing funds to the beneficiary or the beneficiary can be enjoined from withdrawing the funds. No other injunction is permitted. In particular, intermediary banks are protected, and injunctions against the originator and the originator's bank are limited to issuance of a payment order. Except for the beneficiary's bank, nobody can be enjoined from paying a payment order, and no receiving bank can be enjoined from receiving payment from the sender of the order that it accepted.

Section 4A–504. Order in Which Items and Payment Orders May Be Charged to Account; Order of Withdrawals From Account.

(1) If a receiving bank has received more than one payment order of the sender or one or more payment orders and other items that are payable from the sender's account, the bank may charge the sender's account with respect to the various orders and items in any sequence.

(2) In determining whether a credit to an account has been withdrawn by the holder of the account or applied to a debt of the holder of the account, credits first made to the account are first withdrawn or applied.

Added by Laws 1990, Ch. 208, eff. Jan. 1, 1991.

Official Uniform Comment

Prior Uniform Statutory Provision: None.

Purposes:

1. Subsection (a) concerns priority among various obligations that are to be paid from the same amount. A customer may have written checks on its account with the receiving bank and may have issued one or more payment orders payable from the same account. If the account balance is not sufficient to cover all of the checks and payment orders, some checks may be dishonored and some payment orders may not be accepted. Although there is no concept of wrongful dishonor of a payment order in Article 4A in the absence of an agreement to honor by the receiving bank, some rights and obligations may depend on the amount in the customer's account. § 4A-209(b)(3) and § 4A-210(b). Whether dishonor of a check is wrongful also may depend upon the balance in the customer's account. Under subsection (a), the bank is not required to consider the competing items and payment orders in any particular order. Rather it may charge the customer's account for the various items and orders in any order. Suppose there is $12,000 in the customer's account. If a check for $5,000 is presented for payment and the bank receives a $10,000 payment order from the customer, the bank could dishonor the check and accept the payment order. Dishonor of the check is not wrongful because the account balance was less than the amount of the check after the bank charged the account $10,000 on account of the payment order. Or, the bank could pay the check and not execute the payment order because the amount of the order is not covered by the balance in the account.

2. Subsection (b) follows § 4A-208(b) in using the first-in-first-out rule for determining the order in which credits to an account are withdrawn.

Section 4A–505. Preclusion of Objection to Debit of Customer's Account.

If a receiving bank has received payment from its customer with respect to a payment order issued in the name of the customer as sender and accepted by the bank, and the customer received notification reasonably identifying the order, the customer is precluded from asserting that the bank is not entitled to retain the payment unless the customer notifies the bank of the customer's objection to the payment within one year after the notification was received by the customer.

UCC

Added by Laws 1990, Ch. 208, eff. Jan. 1, 1991.

Official Uniform Comment

Prior Uniform Statutory Provision: None.

Purposes:

This section is in the nature of a statute of repose for objecting to debits made to the customer's account. A receiving bank that executes payment orders of a customer may have received payment from the customer by debiting the customer's account with respect to a payment order that the customer was not required to pay. For example, the payment order may not have been authorized or verified pursuant to § 4A-202 or the funds transfer may not have been completed. In either case the receiving bank is obliged to refund the payment to the customer and this obligation to refund payment cannot be varied by agreement. § 4A-204 and § 4A-402. Refund may also be required if the receiving bank is not entitled to payment from the customer because the bank erroneously executed a payment order. § 4A-303. A similar analysis applies to that case. § 4A-402(d) and (f) require refund and the obligation to refund may not be varied by agreement. Under § 4A-505, however, the obligation to refund may not be asserted by the customer if the customer has not objected to the debiting of the account within one year after the customer received notification of the debit.

Section 4A–506. Rate of Interest.

(1) If, under this article, a receiving bank is obliged to pay interest with respect to a payment order issued to the bank, the amount payable may be determined (i) by agreement of the sender and receiving bank, or (ii) by a funds-transfer system rule if the payment order is transmitted through a funds-transfer system.

(2) If the amount of interest is not determined by an agreement or rule as stated in subsection (1), the amount is calculated by multiplying the applicable federal funds rate by the amount on which interest is payable, and then multiplying the product by the number of days for which interest is payable. The applicable federal funds rate is the average of the federal funds rates published by the federal reserve bank of New York for each of the days for which interest is payable divided by 360. The federal funds rate for any day on which a published rate is not available is the same as the published rate for the next preceding day for which there is a published rate. If a receiving bank that accepted a payment order is required to refund payment to the sender of the order because the funds transfer was not completed, but the failure to complete was not due to any fault by the bank, the interest payable is reduced by a percentage equal to the reserve requirement on deposits of the receiving bank.

Added by Laws 1990, Ch. 208, eff. Jan. 1, 1991.

Official Uniform Comment

Prior Uniform Statutory Provision: None.

Purposes:

1. A receiving bank is required to pay interest on the amount of a payment order received by the bank in a number of situations. Sometimes the interest is payable

to the sender and in other cases it is payable to either the originator or the beneficiary of the funds transfer. The relevant provisions are § 4A-204(a), § 4A-209(b)(3), § 4A-201(b), § 4A-305(a), § 4A-402(d), and § 4A-404(b). the rate of interest may be governed by a funds transfer system rule or by agreement as stated in subsection (a). If subsection (a) doesn't apply, the rate is determined under subsection (b). Subsection (b) is illustrated by the following example. A bank is obliged to pay interest on $1,000,000 for three days, July 3, July 4, and July 5. The published Fed Funds rate is.082 for July 3 and.081 for July 5. There is no published rate for July 4 because that day is not a banking day. The rate for July 3 applies to July 4. The applicable Fed Funds rate is.08167 (the average of.082,.082, and.081) divided by 360 which equals.0002268. The amount of interest payable is $1,000,000 X.0002268 X 3 = $680.40.

2. In some cases, interest is payable in spite of the fact that there is no fault by the receiving bank. the last sentence of subsection(b) applies to those cases. For example, a funds transfer might not be completed because the beneficiary's bank rejected the payment order issued to it by the originator's bank or intermediary bank. § 4A-402(c) provides that the originator is not obliged to pay its payment order and § 4A-402(d) provides that the originator's bank must refund any payment received plus interest. The requirement to pay interest in this case is not based on fault by the originator's bank. Rather, it is based on restitution. Since the originator's bank had the use of the originator's money, it is required to pay the originator for the value of that use. The value of that use is not determined by multiplying the interest rate by the refundable amount because the originator's bank is required to deposit with the Federal Reserve a percentage of the bank's deposits as a reserve requirement. Since that deposit does not bear interest, the bank had use of the refundable amount reduced by a percentage equal to the reserve requirement. If the reserve requirement is 12%, the amount of interest payable by the bank under the formula stated in subsection (b) is reduced by 12%.

Section 4A–507. Choice of Law.

(1) The following rules apply unless the affected parties otherwise agree or subsection (3) applies:

(a) The rights and obligations between the sender of a payment order and the receiving bank are governed by the law of the jurisdiction in which the receiving bank is located.

(b) The rights and obligations between the beneficiary's bank and the beneficiary are governed by the law of the jurisdiction in which the beneficiary's bank is located.

(c) The issue of when payment is made pursuant to a funds transfer by the originator to the beneficiary is governed by the law of the jurisdiction in which the beneficiary's bank is located.

(2) If the parties described in each paragraph of subsection (1) have made an agreement selecting the law of a particular jurisdiction to govern rights and obligations between each other, the law of that jurisdiction governs those rights and obligations, whether or not the payment order or the funds transfer bears a reasonable relation to that jurisdiction.

(3) A funds-transfer system rule may select the law of a particular jurisdiction to govern (i) rights and obligations between participating banks with respect to

payment orders transmitted or processed through the system, or (ii) the rights and obligations of some or all parties to a funds transfer any part of which is carried out by means of the system. A choice of law made pursuant to clause (i) is binding on participating banks. A choice of law made pursuant to clause (ii) is binding on the originator, other sender, or a receiving bank having notice that the funds-transfer system might be used in the funds transfer and of the choice of law by the system when the originator, other sender, or receiving bank issued or accepted a payment order. The beneficiary of a funds transfer is bound by the choice of law if, when the funds transfer is initiated, the beneficiary has notice that the funds-transfer system might be used in the funds transfer and of the choice of law by the system. The law of a jurisdiction selected pursuant to this subsection may govern, whether or not that law bears a reasonable relation to the matter in issue.

(4) In the event of inconsistency between an agreement under subsection (2) and a choice-of-law rule under subsection (3), the agreement under subsection (2) prevails.

(5) If a funds transfer is made by use of more than one funds-transfer system and there is inconsistency between choice-of-law rules of the systems, the matter in issue is governed by the law of the selected jurisdiction that has the most significant relationship to the matter in issue.

Added by Laws 1990, Ch. 208, eff. Jan. 1, 1991.

Official Uniform Comment

Prior Uniform Statutory Provision: None.

Purposes:

1. Funds transfers are typically interstate or international in character. If part of a funds transfer is governed by Article 4A and another part is governed by other law, the rights and obligations of parties to the funds transfer may be unclear because there is no clear consensus in various jurisdictions concerning the juridical nature of the transaction. Unless all of a funds transfer is governed by a single law it may be very difficult to predict the result if something goes wrong in the transfer. § 4A-507 deals with this problem. Subsection (b) allows parties to a funds transfer to make a choice-of-law agreement. Subsection (c) allows a funds transfer system to select the law of a particular jurisdiction to govern funds transfers carried out by means of the system. Subsection (a) states residual rules if no choice of law has occurred under subsection (b) or subsection (c).

2. Subsection (a) deals with three sets of relationships. Rights and obligations between the sender of a payment order and the receiving bank are governed by the law of the jurisdiction in which the receiving bank is located. If the receiving bank is the beneficiary's bank the rights and obligations of the beneficiary are also governed by the law of the jurisdiction in which the receiving bank is located. Suppose Originator, located in Canada, sends a payment order to Originator's Bank located in a state in which Article 4A has been enacted. The order is for payment to an account of Beneficiary in a bank in England. Under subsection (a)(1), the rights and obligations of Originator and Originator's bank toward each other are governed by Article 4A if an action is brought in a court in the Article 4A state. If an action is brought in

a Canadian court, the conflict of laws issue will be determined by Canadian law which might or might not apply the law of the state in which Originator's bank is located. If that law is applied, the execution of originator's order will be governed by Article 4A, but with respect to the payment order of Originator's Bank to the English bank, Article 4A may or may not be applied with respect to the rights and obligations between the two banks. The result may depend upon whether action is brought in a court in the state in which Originator's Bank is located or in an English court. Article 4A is binding only on a court tin a state that enacts it. It can have extraterritorial effect only to the extent courts of another jurisdiction are willing to apply it. Subsection (c) also bears on the issues discussed in this Comment.

Under § 4A-406 payment by the originator to the beneficiary of the funds transfer occurs when the beneficiary's bank accepts a payment order for the benefit of the beneficiary. A jurisdiction in which Article 4A is not in effect may follow a different rule or it may not have a clear rule. Under § 4A-507(a)(3) the issue is governed by the law of the jurisdiction in which the beneficiary's bank is located. Since the payment to the beneficiary is made through the beneficiary's bank it is reasonable that the issue of when payment occurs be governed by the law of the jurisdiction in which the bank is located. Since it is difficult in many cases to determine where a beneficiary is located, the location of the beneficiary's bank provides a more certain rule.

3. Subsection (b) deals with choice-of-law agreements and it gives maximum freedom of choice. Since the law of funds transfers is not highly developed in the case law there may be a strong incentive to choose the law of a jurisdiction in which Article 4A is in effect because it provides a greater degree of certainly with respect to the rights of various parties. With respect to commercial transactions, it is often said that "[u]uniformity and predictability based upon commercial convenience are the prime considerations in making the choice of governing law...." R. Leflar, American Conflicts Law, § 185 (1977). Subsection (b) is derived in part from recently enacted choice-of-law rules in the States of New York and California. N.Y. Gen. Obligations Law 5-1401 (McKinney's 1989 Supp.) and California Civil Code § 1646.5. This broad endorsement of freedom of contract is an enhancement of the approach taken by Restatement (Second) of Conflict of Laws § 187(b) (1971). The Restatement recognizes the basic right of freedom of contract, but the freedom granted the parties may be more limited than the freedom granted here. Under the formulation of the Restatement, if there is no substantial relationship to the jurisdiction whose law is selected and there is no "other" reasonable basis for the parties' choice, then the selection of the parties need not be honored by a court. Further, if the choice is violative of a fundamental policy of a state which has a materially greater interest than the chosen state, the selection could be disregarded by a court. Those limitations are not found in subsection (b).

4. Subsection (c) may be the most important provision in regard to creating uniformity of law in funds transfers. Most rights stated in Article 4A regard parties who are in privity of contract such as originator and beneficiary, sender and receiving bank, and beneficiary's bank and beneficiary. Since they are in privity they can make a choice of law by agreement. But that is not always the case. For example, an intermediary bank that improperly executes a payment order is not in privity with either the originator or the beneficiary. The ability of a funds transfer system to make a choice of law by rule is a convenient way of dispensing with individual agreements and to cover cases in which agreements are not feasible. It is probable that funds transfer systems will adopt a governing law to increase the certainty of commercial transactions that are effected over such systems. A system rule might adopt the law of an Article 4A state to govern transfers on the system in order to provide a consistent, unitary, law governing all transfers made on the system. To the extent such system rules develop, individual choice-of-law agreements become unnecessary.

Subsection (c) has broad application. A system choice of law applies not only to rights and obligations between banks that use the system, but may also apply to other parties to the funds transfer so long as some part of the transfer was carried out over the system. The originator and any other sender or receiving bank in the funds transfer is bound if at the time it issues or accepts a payment order it had notice that the funds transfer involved use of the system and that the system chose the law of a particular jurisdiction. Under § 4A-107, the Federal Reserve by regulation could make a similar choice of law to govern funds transfers carried out by use of Federal Reserve Banks. Subsection (d) is a limitation on subsection (c). If parties have made a choice-of-law agreement that conflicts with a choice of law made under subsection (c), the agreement prevails.

5. Subsection (e) addresses the case in which a funds transfer involves more than one funds transfer system and the systems adopt conflicting choice-of-law rules. The rule that has the most significant relationship to the matter at issue prevails. For example, each system should be able to make a choice of law governing payment orders transmitted over that system without regard to a choice of law made by another system.

ARTICLE 5

LETTERS OF CREDIT

Section 5–101. Short Title.

This article may be cited as "Uniform Commercial Code—Letters of Credit".

Added by Laws 2000, Ch. 471, eff. Nov. 1, 2000.

Official Comment

The Official Comment to the original Section 5-101 was a remarkably brief inaugural address. Noting that letters of credit had not been the subject of statutory enactment and that the law concerning them had been developed in the cases, the Comment stated that Article 5 was intended "within its limited scope" to set an independent theoretical frame for the further development of letters of credit. That statement addressed accurately conditions as they existed when the statement was made, nearly half a century ago. Since Article 5 was originally drafted, the use of letters of credit has expanded and developed, and the case law concerning these developments is, in some respects, discordant.

Revision of Article 5 therefore has required reappraisal both of the statutory goals and of the extent to which particular statutory provisions further or adversely affect achievement of those goals.

The statutory goal of Article 5 was originally stated to be: (1) to set a substantive theoretical frame that describes the function and legal nature of letters of credit; and (2) to preserve procedural flexibility in order to accommodate further development of the efficient use of letters of credit. A letter of credit is an idiosyncratic form of undertaking that supports performance of an obligation incurred in a separate financial, mercantile, or other transaction or arrangement. The objectives of the original and revised Article 5 are best achieved (1) by defining the peculiar characteristics of a letter of credit that distinguish it and the legal consequences of its use from other forms of assurance such as secondary guarantees, performance bonds, and insurance policies, and from ordinary contracts, fiduciary engagements, and escrow arrangements; and (2) by preserving flexibility through variation by agreement in order to respond to and accommodate developments in custom and usage that are not inconsistent with the essential definitions and substantive mandates of the statute. No statute can, however, prescribe the manner in which such substantive rights and duties are to be enforced or imposed without risking stultification of wholesome developments in the letter of credit mechanism. Letter of credit law should remain responsive to commercial reality and in particular to the customs and expectations of the international banking and mercantile community. Courts should read the terms of this article in a manner consistent with these customs and expectations.

The subject matter in Article 5, letters of credit, may also be governed by an international convention that is now being drafted by UNCITRAL, the draft Convention on Independent Guarantees and Standby Letters of Credit. The Uniform Customs and Practice is an international body of trade practice that is commonly adopted by international and domestic letters of credit and as such is the "law of the transaction" by agreement of the parties. Article 5 is consistent with and was influenced by the rules in the existing version of the UCP. In addition to the UCP and the international convention, other bodies of law apply to letters of credit. For example, the federal bankruptcy law applies to letters of credit with respect to applicants and beneficiaries that are in bankruptcy; regulations of the Federal Reserve Board and the Comptroller of the Currency lay out requirements for banks that issue letters of credit and describe how letters of credit are to be treated for calculating asset risk and for the purpose of loan limitations. In addition there is an array of anti-boycott and other similar laws that may affect the issuance and performance of letters of credit. All of these laws are beyond the scope of Article 5, but in certain circumstances they will override Article 5.

Section 5–102. Definitions.

(a) In this article:

(1) "Adviser" means a person who, at the request of the issuer, a confirmer, or another adviser, notifies or requests another adviser to notify the beneficiary that a letter of credit has been issued, confirmed, or amended.

(2) "Applicant" means a person at whose request or for whose account a letter of credit is issued. The term includes a person who requests an issuer to issue a letter of credit on behalf of another if the person making the request undertakes an obligation to reimburse the issuer.

(3) "Beneficiary" means a person who under the terms of a letter of credit is entitled to have its complying presentation honored. The term includes a person to whom drawing rights have been transferred under a transferable letter of credit.

(4) "Confirmer" means a nominated person who undertakes, at the request or with the consent of the issuer, to honor a presentation under a letter of credit issued by another.

(5) "Dishonor" of a letter of credit means failure to timely honor or to take an interim action, such as acceptance of a draft, that may be required by the letter of credit.

(6) "Document" means a draft or other demand, document of title, investment security, certificate, invoice, or other record, statement, or representation of fact, law, right, or opinion:

(i) which is presented in a written or other medium permitted by the letter of credit or, unless prohibited by the letter of credit, by the standard practice referred to in subsection (e) of Section 5–108; and

(ii) which is capable of being examined for compliance with the terms and conditions of the letter of credit. A document may not be oral.

(7) "Good faith" means honesty in fact in the conduct or transaction concerned.

(8) "Honor" of a letter of credit means performance of the issuer's undertaking in the letter of credit to pay or deliver an item of value. Unless the letter of credit otherwise provides, "honor" occurs:

(i) upon payment,

(ii) if the letter of credit provides for acceptance, upon acceptance of a draft and, at maturity, its payment, or

(iii) if the letter of credit provides for incurring a deferred obligation, upon incurring the obligation and, at maturity, its performance.

(9) "Issuer" means a bank or other person that issues a letter of credit, but does not include an individual who makes an engagement for personal, family, or household purposes.

(10) "Letter of credit" means a definite undertaking that satisfies the requirements of Section 5–104 by an issuer to a beneficiary at the request or for the account of an applicant or, in the case of a financial institution, to itself or for its own account, to honor a documentary presentation by payment or delivery of an item of value.

(11) "Nominated person" means a person whom the issuer:

(i) designates or authorizes to pay, accept, negotiate, or otherwise give value under a letter of credit, and

(ii) undertakes by agreement or custom and practice to reimburse.

(12) "Presentation" means delivery of a document to an issuer or nominated person for honor or giving of value under a letter of credit.

(13) "Presenter" means a person making a presentation as or on behalf of a beneficiary or nominated person.

(14) "Record" means information that is inscribed on a tangible medium, or that is stored in an electronic or other medium and is retrievable in perceivable form.

(15) "Successor of a beneficiary" means a person who succeeds to substantially all of the rights of a beneficiary by operation of law, including a corporation with or into which the beneficiary has been merged or consolidated, an administrator, executor, personal representative, trustee in bankruptcy, debtor in possession, liquidator, and receiver.

(b) Definitions in other articles applying to this article and the sections in which they appear are:

"Accept" or "Acceptance"	Section 3–410
"Value"	Sections 3–303, 4–209.

(c) Article 1 contains certain additional general definitions and principles of construction and interpretation applicable throughout this article.

Added by Laws 2000, Ch. 471, eff. Nov. 1, 2000.

Official Comment

1. Since no one can be a confirmer unless that person is a nominated person as defined in Section 5-102(a)(11), those who agree to "confirm" without the designation or authorization of the issuer are not confirmers under Article 5. Nonetheless, the undertakings to the beneficiary of such persons may be enforceable by the beneficiary as letters of credit issued by the "confirmer" for its own account or as guarantees or contracts outside of Article 5.

2. The definition of "document" contemplates and facilitates the growing recognition of electronic and other nonpaper media as "documents," however, for the time being, data in those media constitute documents only in certain circumstances. For example, a facsimile received by an issuer would be a document only if the letter of credit explicitly permitted it, if the standard practice authorized it and the letter did not prohibit it, or the agreement of the issuer and beneficiary permitted it. The fact that data transmitted in a nonpaper (unwritten) medium can be recorded on paper by a recipient's computer printer, facsimile machine, or the like does not under current practice render the data so transmitted a "document." A facsimile or S.W.I.F.T. message received directly by the issuer is in an electronic medium when it crosses the boundary of the issuer's place of business. One wishing to make a presentation by facsimile (an electronic medium) will have to procure the explicit agreement of the issuer (assuming that the standard practice does not authorize it). Where electronic transmissions are authorized neither by the letter of credit nor by the practice, the beneficiary may transmit the data electronically to its agent who may be able to put it in written form and make a conforming presentation.

3. "Good faith" continues in revised Article 5 to be defined as "honesty in fact." "Observance of reasonable standards of fair dealing" has not been added to the definition. The narrower definition of "honesty in fact" reinforces the "independence principle" in the treatment of "fraud," "strict compliance," "preclusion," and other tests affecting the performance of obligations that are unique to letters of credit. This narrower definition — which does not include "fair dealing" — is appropriate to the decision to honor or dishonor a presentation of documents specified in a letter of credit. The narrower definition is also appropriate for other parts of revised Article

5 where greater certainty of obligations is necessary and is consistent with the goals of speed and low cost. It is important that U.S. letters of credit have continuing vitality and competitiveness in international transactions.

For example, it would be inconsistent with the "independence" principle if any of the following occurred: (i) the beneficiary's failure to adhere to the standard of "fair dealing" in the underlying transaction or otherwise in presenting documents were to provide applicants and issuers with an "unfairness" defense to dishonor even when the documents complied with the terms of the letter of credit; (ii) the issuer's obligation to honor in "strict compliance in accordance with standard practice" were changed to "reasonable compliance" by use of the "fair dealing" standard, or (iii) the preclusion against the issuer (Section 5-108(d)) were modified under the "fair dealing" standard to enable the issuer later to raise additional deficiencies in the presentation. The rights and obligations arising from presentation, honor, dishonor and reimbursement, are independent and strict, and thus "honesty in fact" is an appropriate standard.

The contract between the applicant and beneficiary is not governed by Article 5, but by applicable contract law, such as Article 2 or the general law of contracts. "Good faith" in that contract is defined by other law, such as Section 2-103(1)(b) or Restatement of Contracts 2d, § 205, which incorporate the principle of 'fair dealing'in most cases, or a State's common law or other statutory provisions that may apply to that contract.

The contract between the applicant and the issuer (sometimes called the "reimbursement" agreement) is governed in part by this article (e.g., Sections 5-108(i), 5-111(b), and 5-103(c)) and partly by other law (e.g., the general law of contracts). The definition of good faith in Section 5-102(a)(7) applies only to the extent that the reimbursement contract is governed by provisions in this article; for other purposes good faith is defined by other law.

4. Payment and acceptance are familiar modes of honor. A third mode of honor, incurring an unconditional obligation, has legal effects similar to an acceptance of a time draft but does not technically constitute an acceptance. The practice of making letters of credit available by "deferred payment undertaking" as now provided in UCP 500 has grown up in other countries and spread to the United States. The definition of "honor" will accommodate that practice.

5. The exclusion of consumers from the definition of "issuer" is to keep creditors from using a letter of credit in consumer transactions in which the consumer might be made the issuer and the creditor would be the beneficiary. If that transaction were recognized under Article 5, the effect would be to leave the consumer without defenses against the creditor. That outcome would violate the policy behind the Federal Trade Commission Rule in 16 CFR Part 433. In a consumer transaction, an individual cannot be an issuer where that person would otherwise be either the principal debtor or a guarantor.

6. The label on a document is not conclusive; certain documents labelled "guarantees" in accordance with European (and occasionally, American) practice are letters of credit. On the other hand, even documents that are labelled "letter of credit" may not constitute letters of credit under the definition in Section 5-102(a). When a document labelled a letter of credit requires the issuer to pay not upon the presentation of documents, but upon the determination of an extrinsic fact such as applicant's failure to perform a construction contract, and where that condition appears on its face to be fundamental and would, if ignored, leave no obligation to the issuer under the document labelled letter of credit, the issuer's undertaking is not a letter of credit. It is probably some form of suretyship or other contractual arrangement and may be enforceable as such. See Sections 5-102(a)(10) and 5-103(d). Therefore, undertakings whose fundamental term requires an issuer to look beyond documents and beyond conventional reference to the clock, calendar, and practices concerning

the form of various documents are not governed by Article 5. Although Section 5-108(g) recognizes that certain nondocumentary conditions can be included in a letter of credit without denying the undertaking the status of letter of credit, that section does not apply to cases where the nondocumentary condition is fundamental to the issuer's obligation. The rules in Sections 5-102(a)(10), 5-103(d), and 5-108(g) approve the conclusion in *Wichita Eagle & Beacon Publishing Co. v. Pacific Nat. Bank*, 493 F.2d 1285 (9th Cir. 1974).

The adjective "definite" is taken from the UCP. It approves cases that deny letter of credit status to documents that are unduly vague or incomplete. *See, e.g.*, *Transparent Prods. Corp. v. Paysaver Credit Union*, 864 F.2d 60 (7th Cir. 1988). Note, however, that no particular phrase or label is necessary to establish a letter of credit. It is sufficient if the undertaking of the issuer shows that it is intended to be a letter of credit. In most cases the parties' intention will be indicated by a label on the undertaking itself indicating that it is a "letter of credit," but no such language is necessary.

A financial institution may be both the issuer and the applicant or the issuer and the beneficiary. Such letters are sometimes issued by a bank in support of the bank's own lease obligations or on behalf of one of its divisions as an applicant or to one of its divisions as beneficiary, such as an overseas branch. Because wide use of letters of credit in which the issuer and the applicant or the issuer and the beneficiary are the same would endanger the unique status of letters of credit, only financial institutions are authorized to issue them.

In almost all cases the ultimate performance of the issuer under a letter of credit is the payment of money. In rare cases the issuer's obligation is to deliver stock certificates or the like. The definition of letter of credit in Section 5-102(a)(10) contemplates those cases.

7. Under the UCP any bank is a nominated bank where the letter of credit is "freely negotiable." A letter of credit might also nominate by the following: "We hereby engage with the drawer, indorsers, and bona fide holders of drafts drawn under and in compliance with the terms of this credit that the same will be duly honored on due presentation" or "available with any bank by negotiation." A restricted negotiation credit might be "available with x bank by negotiation" or the like.

Several legal consequences may attach to the status of nominated person. First, when the issuer nominates a person, it is authorizing that person to pay or give value and is authorizing the beneficiary to make presentation to that person. Unless the letter of credit provides otherwise, the beneficiary need not present the documents to the issuer before the letter of credit expires; it need only present those documents to the nominated person. Secondly, a nominated person that gives value in good faith has a right to payment from the issuer despite fraud. Section 5-109(a)(1).

8. A "record" must be in or capable of being converted to a perceivable form. For example, an electronic message recorded in a computer memory that could be printed from that memory could constitute a record. Similarly, a tape recording of an oral conversation could be a record.

9. Absent a specific agreement to the contrary, documents of a beneficiary delivered to an issuer or nominated person are considered to be presented under the letter of credit to which they refer, and any payment or value given for them is considered to be made under that letter of credit. As the court held in *Alaska Textile Co. v. Chase Manhattan Bank, N.A.*, 982 F.2d 813, 820 (2d Cir. 1992), it takes a "significant showing" to make the presentation of a beneficiary's documents for "collection only" or otherwise outside letter of credit law and practice.

10. Although a successor of a beneficiary is one who succeeds "by operation of law," some of the successions contemplated by Section 5-102(a)(15) will have resulted from voluntary action of the beneficiary such as merger of a corporation. Any merger makes the successor corporation the "successor of a beneficiary" even though the

transfer occurs partly by operation of law and partly by the voluntary action of the parties. The definition excludes certain transfers, where no part of the transfer is "by operation of law" — such as the sale of assets by one company to another.

11. "Draft" in Article 5 does not have the same meaning it has in Article 3. For example, a document may be a draft under Article 5 even though it would not be a negotiable instrument, and therefore would not qualify as a draft under Section 3-104(e).

Section 5–103. Scope.

(a) This article applies to letters of credit and to certain rights and obligations arising out of transactions involving letters of credit.

(b) The statement of a rule in this article does not by itself require, imply, or negate application of the same or a different rule to a situation not provided for, or to a person not specified, in this article.

(c) with the exception of this subsection, subsections (a) and (d) of this section, paragraphs (9) and (10) of subsection (a) of Section 5–102, subsection (d) of Section 5–106, and subsection (d) of Section 5–114, and except to the extent prohibited in subsection (3) of Section 1–102 and subsection (d) of Section 5–117, the effect of this article may be varied by agreement or by a provision stated or incorporated by reference in an undertaking. A term in an agreement or undertaking generally excusing liability or generally limiting remedies for failure to perform obligations is not sufficient to vary obligations prescribed by this article.

(d) Rights and obligations of an issuer to a beneficiary or a nominated person under a letter of credit are independent of the existence, performance, or nonperformance of a contract or arrangement out of which the letter of credit arises or which underlies it, including contracts or arrangements between the issuer and the applicant and between the applicant and the beneficiary.

Added by Laws 2000, Ch. 471, eff. Nov. 1, 2000.

Official Comment

1. Sections 5-102(a)(10) and 5-103 are the principal limits on the scope of Article 5. Many undertakings in commerce and contract are similar, but not identical to the letter of credit. Principal among those are "secondary," "accessory," or "suretyship" guarantees. Although the word "guarantee" is sometimes used to describe an independent obligation like that of the issuer of a letter of credit (most often in the case of European bank undertakings but occasionally in the case of undertakings of American banks), in the United States the word "guarantee" is more typically used to describe a suretyship transaction in which the "guarantor" is only secondarily liable and has the right to assert the underlying debtor's defenses. This article does not apply to secondary or accessory guarantees and it is important to recognize the distinction between letters of credit and those guarantees. It is often a defense to a secondary or accessory guarantor's liability that the underlying debt has been discharged or that the debtor has other defenses to the underlying liability. In letter of credit law, on the other hand, the independence principle recognized throughout Article 5 states that the issuer's liability is independent of the underlying obligation. That the beneficiary

may have breached the underlying contract and thus have given a good defense on that contract to the applicant against the beneficiary is no defense for the issuer's refusal to honor. Only staunch recognition of this principle by the issuers and the courts will give letters of credit the continuing vitality that arises from the certainty and speed of payment under letters of credit. To that end, it is important that the law not carry into letter of credit transactions rules that properly apply only to secondary guarantees or to other forms of engagement.

2. Like all of the provisions of the Uniform Commercial Code, Article 5 is supplemented by Section 1-103 and, through it, by many rules of statutory and common law. Because this article is quite short and has no rules on many issues that will affect liability with respect to a letter of credit transaction, law beyond Article 5 will often determine rights and liabilities in letter of credit transactions. Even within letter of credit law, the article is far from comprehensive; it deals only with "certain" rights of the parties. Particularly with respect to the standards of performance that are set out in Section 5-108, it is appropriate for the parties and the courts to turn to customs and practice such as the Uniform Customs and Practice for Documentary Credits, currently published by the International Chamber of Commerce as I.C.C. Pub. No. 500 (hereafter UCP). Many letters of credit specifically adopt the UCP as applicable to the particular transaction. Where the UCP are adopted but conflict with Article 5 and except where variation is prohibited, the UCP terms are permissible contractual modifications under Sections 1-102(3) and 5-103(c). See Section 5-116(c). Normally Article 5 should not be considered to conflict with practice except when a rule explicitly stated in the UCP or other practice is different from a rule explicitly stated in Article 5.

Except by choosing the law of a jurisdiction that has not adopted the Uniform Commercial Code, it is not possible entirely to escape the Uniform Commercial Code. Since incorporation of the UCP avoids only "conflicting" Article 5 rules, parties who do not wish to be governed by the nonconflicting provisions of Article 5 must normally either adopt the law of a jurisdiction other than a State of the United States or state explicitly the rule that is to govern. When rules of custom and practice are incorporated by reference, they are considered to be explicit terms of the agreement or undertaking.

Neither the obligation of an issuer under Section 5-108 nor that of an adviser under Section 5-107 is an obligation of the kind that is invariable under Section 1-102(3). Section 5-103(c) and Comment 1 to Section 5-108 make it clear that the applicant and the issuer may agree to almost any provision establishing the obligations of the issuer to the applicant. The last sentence of subsection (c) limits the power of the issuer to achieve that result by a nonnegotiated disclaimer or limitation of remedy.

What the issuer could achieve by an explicit agreement with its applicant or by a term that explicitly defines its duty, it cannot accomplish by a general disclaimer. The restriction on disclaimers in the last sentence of subsection (c) is based more on procedural than on substantive unfairness. Where, for example, the reimbursement agreement provides explicitly that the issuer need not examine any documents, the applicant understands the risk it has undertaken. A term in a reimbursement agreement which states generally that an issuer will not be liable unless it has acted in "bad faith" or committed "gross negligence" is ineffective under Section 5-103(c). On the other hand, less general terms such as terms that permit issuer reliance on an oral or electronic message believed in good faith to have been received from the applicant or terms that entitle an issuer to reimbursement when it honors a "substantially" though not "strictly" complying presentation, are effective. In each case the question is whether the disclaimer or limitation is sufficiently clear and explicit in reallocating a liability or risk that is allocated differently under a variable Article 5 provision.

Of course, no term in a letter of credit, whether incorporated by reference to practice rules or stated specifically, can free an issuer from a conflicting contractual obligation to its applicant. If, for example, an issuer promised its applicant that it would pay only against an inspection certificate of a particular company but failed to require such a certificate in its letter of credit or made the requirement only a nondocumentary condition that had to be disregarded, the issuer might be obliged to pay the beneficiary even though its payment might violate its contract with its applicant.

3. Parties should generally avoid modifying the definitions in Section 5-102. The effect of such an agreement is almost inevitably unclear. To say that something is a "guarantee" in the typical domestic transaction is to say that the parties intend that particular legal rules apply to it. By acknowledging that something is a guarantee, but asserting that it is to be treated as a "letter of credit," the parties leave a court uncertain about where the rules on guarantees stop and those concerning letters of credit begin.

4. Section 5-102(2) and (3) of Article 5 are omitted as unneeded; the omission does not change the law.

Section 5–104. Formal Requirements.

A letter of credit, confirmation, advice, transfer, amendment, or cancellation may be issued in any form that is a record and is authenticated:

(a) by a signature, or

(b) in accordance with the agreement of the parties or the standard practice referred to in subsection (e) of Section 5–108.

Added by Laws 2000, Ch. 471, eff. Nov. 1, 2000.

Official Comment

1. Neither Section 5-104 nor the definition of letter of credit in Section 5-102(a)(10) requires inclusion of all the terms that are normally contained in a letter of credit in order for an undertaking to be recognized as a letter of credit under Article 5. For example, a letter of credit will typically specify the amount available, the expiration date, the place where presentation should be made, and the documents that must be presented to entitle a person to honor. Undertakings that have the formalities required by Section 5-104 and meet the conditions specified in Section 5-102(a)(10) will be recognized as letters of credit even though they omit one or more of the items usually contained in a letter of credit.

2. The authentication specified in this section is authentication only of the identity of the issuer, confirmer, or adviser.

An authentication agreement may be by system rule, by standard practice, or by direct agreement between the parties. The reference to practice is intended to incorporate future developments in the UCP and other practice rules as well as those that may arise spontaneously in commercial practice.

3. Many banking transactions, including the issuance of many letters of credit, are now conducted mostly by electronic means. For example, S.W.I.F.T. is currently used to transmit letters of credit from issuing to advising banks. The letter of credit text so transmitted may be printed at the advising bank, stamped "original" and provided to the beneficiary in that form. The printed document may then be used as a way of controlling and recording payments and of recording and authorizing assignments of proceeds or transfers of rights under the letter of credit. Nothing in this section should be construed to conflict with that practice.

To be a record sufficient to serve as a letter of credit or other undertaking under this section, data must have a durability consistent with that function. Because consideration is not required for a binding letter of credit or similar undertaking (Section 5-105) yet those undertakings are to be strictly construed (Section 5-108), parties to a letter of credit transaction are especially dependent on the continued availability of the terms and conditions of the letter of credit or other undertaking. By declining to specify any particular medium in which the letter of credit must be established or communicated, Section 5-104 leaves room for future developments.

Section 5–105. Consideration.

Consideration is not required to issue, amend, transfer, or cancel a letter of credit, advice, or confirmation.

Added by Laws 2000, Ch. 471, eff. Nov. 1, 2000.

Official Comment

It is not to be expected that any issuer will issue its letter of credit without some form of remuneration. But it is not expected that the beneficiary will know what the issuer's remuneration was or whether in fact there was any identifiable remuneration in a given case. And it might be difficult for the beneficiary to prove the issuer's remuneration. This section dispenses with this proof and is consistent with the position of *Lord Mansfield in Pillans v. Van Mierop,* 97 Eng. Rep. 1035 (K.B. 1765) in making consideration irrelevant.

Section 5–106. Issuance, Amendment, Cancellation, and Duration.

(a) A Letter of credit is issued and becomes enforceable according to its terms against the issuer when the issuer sends or otherwise transmits it to the person requested to advise or to the beneficiary. A letter of credit is revocable only if it so provides.

(b) After a letter of credit is issued, rights and obligations of a beneficiary, applicant, confirmer, and issuer are not affected by an amendment or cancellation to which that person has not consented except to the extent the letter of credit provides that it is revocable or that the issuer may amend or cancel the letter of credit without that consent.

(c) If there is no stated expiration date or other provision that determines its duration, a letter of credit expires one year after its stated date of issuance or, if none is stated, after the date on which it is issued.

(d) A letter of credit that states that it is perpetual expires five years after its stated date of issuance, or if none is stated, after the date on which it is issued.

Added by Laws 2000, Ch. 471, eff. Nov. 1, 2000.

Official Comment

1. This section adopts the position taken by several courts, namely that letters of credit that are silent as to revocability are irrevocable. *See, e.g., Weyerhaeuser Co. v. First Nat. Bank,* 27 UCC Rep. Serv. 777 (S.D. Iowa 1979); *West Va. Hous. Dev. Fund v. Sroka,* 415 F. Supp. 1107 (W.D. Pa. 1976). This is the position of the current UCP (500). Given the usual commercial understanding and purpose of letters of credit, revocable letters of credit offer unhappy possibilities for misleading the parties who deal with them.

2. A person can consent to an amendment by implication. For example, a beneficiary that tenders documents for honor that conform to an amended letter of credit but not to the original letter of credit has probably consented to the amendment. By the same token an applicant that has procured the issuance of a transferable letter of credit has consented to its transfer and to performance under the letter of credit by a person to whom the beneficiary's rights are duly transferred. If some, but not all of the persons involved in a letter of credit transaction consent to performance that does not strictly conform to the original letter of credit, those persons assume the risk that other nonconsenting persons may insist on strict compliance with the original letter of credit. Under subsection (b) those not consenting are not bound. For example, an issuer might agree to amend its letter of credit or honor documents presented after the expiration date in the belief that the applicant has consented or will consent to the amendment or will waive presentation after the original expiration date. If that belief is mistaken, the issuer is bound to the beneficiary by the terms of the letter of credit as amended or waived, even though it may be unable to recover from the applicant.

In general, the rights of a recognized transferee beneficiary cannot be altered without the transferee's consent, but the same is not true of the rights of assignees of proceeds from the beneficiary. When the beneficiary makes a complete transfer of its interest that is effective under the terms for transfer established by the issuer, adviser, or other party controlling transfers, the beneficiary no longer has an interest in the letter of credit, and the transferee steps into the shoes of the beneficiary as the one with rights under the letter of credit. Section 5-102(a)(3). When there is a partial transfer, both the original beneficiary and the transferee beneficiary have an interest in performance of the letter of credit and each expects that its rights will not be altered by amendment unless it consents.

The assignee of proceeds under a letter of credit from the beneficiary enjoys no such expectation. Notwithstanding an assignee's notice to the issuer of the assignment of proceeds, the assignee is not a person protected by subsection (b). An assignee of proceeds should understand that its rights can be changed or completely extinguished by amendment or cancellation of the letter of credit. An assignee's claim is precarious, for it depends entirely upon the continued existence of the letter of credit and upon the beneficiary's preparation and presentation of documents that would entitle the beneficiary to honor under Section 5-108.

3. The issuer's right to cancel a revocable letter of credit does not free it from a duty to reimburse a nominated person who has honored, accepted, or undertaken a deferred obligation prior to receiving notice of the amendment or cancellation. Compare UCP Article 8.

4. Although all letters of credit should specify the date on which the issuer's engagement expires, the failure to specify an expiration date does not invalidate the letter of credit, or diminish or relieve the obligation of any party with respect to the letter of credit. A letter of credit that may be revoked or terminated at the discretion of the issuer by notice to the beneficiary is not "perpetual

Section 5–107. Confirmer, Nominated Person, and Advisor.

(a) A confirmer is directly obligated on a letter of credit and has the rights and obligations of an issuer to the extent of its confirmation. The confirmer also has rights against and obligations to the issuer as if the issuer were an applicant and the confirmer had issued the letter of credit at the request and for the account of the issuer.

(b) A nominated person who is not a confirmer is not obligated to honor or otherwise give value for a presentation.

(c) A person requested to advise may decline to act as an adviser. An adviser that is not a confirmer is not obligated to honor or give value for a presentation. An adviser undertakes to the issuer and to the beneficiary accurately to advise the terms of the letter of credit, confirmation, amendment, or advice received by that person and undertakes to the beneficiary to check the apparent authenticity of the request to advise. Even if the advice is inaccurate, the letter of credit, confirmation, or amendment is enforceable as issued.

(d) A person who notifies a transferee beneficiary of the terms of a letter of credit, confirmation, amendment, or advice has the rights and obligations of an adviser under subsection (c) of this section. The terms in the notice to the transferee beneficiary may differ from the terms in any notice to the transferor beneficiary to the extent permitted by the letter of credit, confirmation, amendment, or advice received by the person who so notifies.

Added by Laws 2000, Ch. 471, eff. Nov. 1, 2000.

Official Comment

1. A confirmer has the rights and obligations identified in Section 5-108. Accordingly, unless the context otherwise requires, the terms "confirmer" and "confirmation" should be read into this article wherever the terms "issuer" and "letter of credit" appear.

A confirmer that has paid in accordance with the terms and conditions of the letter of credit is entitled to reimbursement by the issuer even if the beneficiary committed fraud (see Section 5-109(a)(1)(ii)) and, in that sense, has greater rights against the issuer than the beneficiary has. To be entitled to reimbursement from the issuer under the typical confirmed letter of credit, the confirmer must submit conforming documents, but the confirmer's presentation to the issuer need not be made before the expiration date of the letter of credit.

A letter of credit confirmation has been analogized to a guarantee of issuer performance, to a parallel letter of credit issued by the confirmer for the account of the issuer or the letter of credit applicant or both, and to a back-to-back letter of credit in which the confirmer is a kind of beneficiary of the original issuer's letter of credit. Like letter of credit undertakings, confirmations are both unique and flexible, so that no one of these analogies is perfect, but unless otherwise indicated in the letter of credit or confirmation, a confirmer should be viewed by the letter of credit issuer and the beneficiary as an issuer of a parallel letter of credit for the account of the original letter of credit issuer. Absent a direct agreement between the applicant and a confirmer, normally the obligations of a confirmer are to the issuer not the applicant, but the applicant might have a right to injunction against a confirmer under Section 5-109 or warranty claim under Section 5-110, and either might have claims against the other under Section 5-117.

2. No one has a duty to advise until that person agrees to be an adviser or undertakes to act in accordance with the instructions of the issuer. Except where there is a prior agreement to serve or where the silence of the adviser would be an acceptance of an offer to contract, a person's failure to respond to a request to advise a letter of credit does not in and of itself create any liability, nor does it establish a relationship of issuer and adviser between the two. Since there is no duty to advise a letter of credit in the absence of a prior agreement, there can be no duty to advise it timely or at any particular time. When the adviser manifests its agreement to advise by actually doing so (as is normally the case), the adviser cannot have violated any duty

to advise in a timely way. This analysis is consistent with the result of *Sound of Market Street v. Continental Bank International,* 819 F.2d 384 (3d Cir. 1987) which held that there is no such duty. This section takes no position on the reasoning of that case, but does not overrule the result. By advising or agreeing to advise a letter of credit, the adviser assumes a duty to the issuer and to the beneficiary accurately to report what it has received from the issuer, but, beyond determining the apparent authenticity of the letter, an adviser has no duty to investigate the accuracy of the message it has received from the issuer. "Checking" the apparent authenticity of the request to advise means only that the prospective adviser must attempt to authenticate the message (e.g., by "testing" the telex that comes from the purported issuer), and if it is unable to authenticate the message must report that fact to the issuer and, if it chooses to advise the message, to the beneficiary. By proper agreement, an adviser may disclaim its obligation under this section.

3. An issuer may issue a letter of credit which the adviser may advise with different terms. The issuer may then believe that it has undertaken a certain engagement, yet the text in the hands of the beneficiary will contain different terms, and the beneficiary would not be entitled to honor if the documents it submitted did not comply with the terms of the letter of credit as originally issued. On the other hand, if the adviser also confirmed the letter of credit, then as a confirmer it will be independently liable on the letter of credit as advised and confirmed. If in that situation the beneficiary's ultimate presentation entitled it to honor under the terms of the confirmation but not under those in the original letter of credit, the confirmer would have to honor but might not be entitled to reimbursement from the issuer.

4. When the issuer nominates another person to "pay," "negotiate," or otherwise to take up the documents and give value, there can be confusion about the legal status of the nominated person. In rare cases the person might actually be an agent of the issuer and its act might be the act of the issuer itself. In most cases the nominated person is not an agent of the issuer and has no authority to act on the issuer's behalf. Its "nomination" allows the beneficiary to present to it and earns it certain rights to payment under Section 5-109 that others do not enjoy. For example, when an issuer issues a "freely negotiable credit," it contemplates that banks or others might take up documents under that credit and advance value against them, and it is agreeing to pay those persons but only if the presentation to the issuer made by the nominated person complies with the credit. Usually there will be no agreement to pay, negotiate, or to serve in any other capacity by the nominated person, therefore the nominated person will have the right to decline to take the documents. It may return them or agree merely to act as a forwarding agent for the documents but without giving value against them or taking any responsibility for their conformity to the letter of credit.

Section 5–108. Issuer's Rights and Obligations.

(a) Except as otherwise provided in Section 5–109, an issuer shall honor a presentation that, as determined by the standard practice referred to in subsection (e) of this section, appears on its face strictly to comply with the terms and conditions of the letter of credit. Except as otherwise provided in Section 5–113 and unless otherwise agreed with the applicant, an issuer shall dishonor a presentation that does not appear so to comply.

(b) An issuer has a reasonable time after presentation, but not beyond the end of the seventh business day of the issue after the day of its receipt of documents:

(1) to honor,

(2) if the letter of credit provides for honor to be completed more than seven business days after presentation, to accept a draft or incur a deferred obligation, or

(3) to give notice to the presenter of discrepancies in the presentation.

(c) Except as otherwise provided in subsection of this section, an issuer is precluded from asserting as a basis for dishonor any discrepancy if timely notice is not given, or any discrepancy not stated in the notice if timely notice is given.

(d) Failure to give the notice specified in subsection (b) of this section or to mention fraud, forgery, or expiration in the notice does not preclude the issuer from asserting as a basis for dishonor fraud or forgery as described in subsection (a) of Section 5–109 or expiration of the letter of credit before presentation.

(e) An issuer shall observe standard practice of financial institutions that regularly issue letters of credit.

(f) An issuer is not responsible for:

(1) the performance or nonperformance of the underlying contract, arrangement, or transaction,

(2) an act or omission of others, or

(3) observance or knowledge of the usage of a particular trade other than the standard practice referred to in subsection (e) of this section.

(g) If an undertaking constituting a letter of credit under paragraph (10) of subsection (a) of Section 5–102 contains nondocumentary conditions, an issuer shall disregard the nondocumentary conditions and treat them as if they were not stated.

(h) An issuer that has dishonored a presentation shall return the documents or hold them at the disposal of, and send advice to that effect to, the presenter.

(i) An issuer that has honored a presentation as permitted or required by this article:

(1) is entitled to be reimbursed by the applicant in immediately available funds not later than the date of its payment of funds;

(2) takes the documents free of claims of the beneficiary or presenter;

(3) is precluded from asserting a right of recourse on a draft under Sections 3–414 and 3–415;

(4) except as otherwise provided in Sections 5–110 and 5–117, is precluded from restitution of money paid or other value given by mistake to the extent the mistake concerns discrepancies in the documents or tender which are apparent on the face of the presentation; and

(5) is discharged to the extent of its performance under the letter of credit unless the issuer honored a presentation in which a required signature of a beneficiary was forged.

Added by Laws 2000, Ch. 471, eff. Nov. 1, 2000.

Official Comment

1. This section combines some of the duties previously included in Sections 5-114 and 5-109. Because a confirmer has the rights and duties of an issuer, this section applies equally to a confirmer and an issuer. See Section 5-107(a).

The standard of strict compliance governs the issuer's obligation to the beneficiary and to the applicant. By requiring that a "presentation" appear strictly to comply, the section requires not only that the documents themselves appear on their face strictly to comply, but also that the other terms of the letter of credit such as those dealing with the time and place of presentation are strictly complied with. Typically, a letter of credit will provide that presentation is timely if made to the issuer, confirmer, or any other nominated person prior to expiration of the letter of credit. Accordingly, a nominated person that has honored a demand or otherwise given value before expiration will have a right to reimbursement from the issuer even though presentation to the issuer is made after the expiration of the letter of credit. Conversely, where the beneficiary negotiates documents to one who is not a nominated person, the beneficiary or that person acting on behalf of the beneficiary must make presentation to a nominated person, confirmer, or issuer prior to the expiration date.

This section does not impose a bifurcated standard under which an issuer's right to reimbursement might be broader than a beneficiary's right to honor. However, the explicit deference to standard practice in Section 5-108(a) and (e) and elsewhere expands issuers' rights of reimbursement where that practice so provides. Also, issuers can and often do contract with their applicants for expanded rights of reimbursement. Where that is done, the beneficiary will have to meet a more stringent standard of compliance as to the issuer than the issuer will have to meet as to the applicant. Similarly, a nominated person may have reimbursement and other rights against the issuer based on this article, the UCP, bank-to-bank reimbursement rules, or other agreement or undertaking of the issuer. These rights may allow the nominated person to recover from the issuer even when the nominated person would have no right to obtain honor under the letter of credit.

The section adopts strict compliance, rather than the standard that commentators have called "substantial compliance," the standard arguably applied in *Banco Espanol de Credito v. State Street Bank and Trust Co.,* 385 F.2d 230 (1st Cir. 1967) and *Flagship Cruises Ltd. v. New England Merchants Nat. Bank,* 569 F.2d 699 (1st Cir. 1978). Strict compliance does not mean slavish conformity to the terms of the letter of credit. For example, standard practice (what issuers do) may recognize certain presentations as complying that an unschooled layman would regard as discrepant. By adopting standard practice as a way of measuring strict compliance, this article indorses the conclusion of the court in *New Braunfels Nat. Bank v. Odiorne,* 780 S.W.2d 313 (Tex. Ct. App. 1989) (beneficiary could collect when draft requested payment on "Letter of Credit No. 86-122-5" and letter of credit specified "Letter of Credit No. 86-122-S" holding strict compliance does not demand oppressive perfectionism). The section also indorses the result in *Tosco Corp. v. Federal Deposit Ins. Corp.,* 723 F.2d 1242 (6th Cir. 1983). The letter of credit in that case called for "drafts Drawn under Bank of Clarksville Letter of Credit Number 105." The draft presented stated "drawn under Bank of Clarksville, Clarksville, Tennessee letter of Credit No. 105." The court correctly found that despite the change of upper case "L" to a lower case "l" and the use of the word "No." instead of "Number," and despite the addition of the words "Clarksville, Tennessee," the presentation conformed. Similarly a document addressed by a foreign person to General Motors as "Jeneral Motors" would strictly conform in the absence of other defects.

Identifying and determining compliance with standard practice are matters of interpretation for the court, not for the jury. As with similar rules in Sections 4A-202(c) and 2-302, it is hoped that there will be more consistency in the outcomes and speedier resolution of disputes if the responsibility for determining the nature and scope of standard practice is granted to the court, not to a jury. Granting the court authority to make these decisions will also encourage the salutary practice of courts' granting summary judgment in circumstances where there are no significant factual disputes. The statute encourages outcomes such as *American Coleman Co. v. Intrawest Bank,* 887 F.2d 1382 (10th Cir. 1989), where summary judgment was granted.

In some circumstances standards may be established between the issuer and the applicant by agreement or by custom that would free the issuer from liability that it might otherwise have. For example, an applicant might agree that the issuer would have no duty whatsoever to examine documents on certain presentations (e.g., those below a certain dollar amount). Where the transaction depended upon the issuer's payment in a very short time period (e.g., on the same day or within a few hours of presentation), the issuer and the applicant might agree to reduce the issuer's responsibility for failure to discover discrepancies. By the same token, an agreement between the applicant and the issuer might permit the issuer to examine documents exclusively by electronic or electro-optical means. Neither those agreements nor others like them explicitly made by issuers and applicants violate the terms of Section 5-108(a) or (b) or Section 5-103(c).

2. Section 5-108(a) balances the need of the issuer for time to examine the documents against the possibility that the examiner (at the urging of the applicant or for fear that it will not be reimbursed) will take excessive time to search for defects. What is a "reasonable time" is not extended to accommodate an issuer's procuring a waiver from the applicant. See Article 14c of the UCP.

Under both the UCC and the UCP the issuer has a reasonable time to honor or give notice. The outside limit of that time is measured in business days under the UCC and in banking days under the UCP, a difference that will rarely be significant. Neither business nor banking days are defined in Article 5, but a court may find useful analogies in Regulation CC, 12 CFR 229.2, in state law outside of the Uniform Commercial Code, and in Article 4.

Examiners must note that the seven-day period is not a safe harbor. The time within which the issuer must give notice is the lesser of a reasonable time or seven business days. Where there are few documents (as, for example, with the mine run standby letter of credit), the reasonable time would be less than seven days. If more than a reasonable time is consumed in examination, no timely notice is possible. What is a "reasonable time" is to be determined by examining the behavior of those in the business of examining documents, mostly banks. Absent prior agreement of the issuer, one could not expect a bank issuer to examine documents while the beneficiary waited in the lobby if the normal practice was to give the documents to a person who had the opportunity to examine those together with many others in an orderly process. That the applicant has not yet paid the issuer or that the applicant's account with the issuer is insufficient to cover the amount of the draft is not a basis for extension of the time period.

This section does not preclude the issuer from contacting the applicant during its examination; however, the decision to honor rests with the issuer, and it has no duty to seek a waiver from the applicant or to notify the applicant of receipt of the documents. If the issuer dishonors a conforming presentation, the beneficiary will be entitled to the remedies under Section 5-111, irrespective of the applicant's views.

Even though the person to whom presentation is made cannot conduct a reasonable examination of documents within the time after presentation and before the expiration date, presentation establishes the parties' rights. The beneficiary's right to honor or the issuer's right to dishonor arises upon presentation at the place provided in the letter of credit even though it might take the person to whom presentation has been made several days to determine whether honor or dishonor is the proper course. The issuer's time for honor or giving notice of dishonor may be extended or shortened by a term in the letter of credit. The time for the issuer's performance may be otherwise modified or waived in accordance with Section 5-106.

The issuer's time to inspect runs from the time of its "receipt of documents." Documents are considered to be received only when they are received at the place specified for presentation by the issuer or other party to whom presentation is made.

Failure of the issuer to act within the time permitted by subsection (b) constitutes dishonor. Because of the preclusion in subsection (c) and the liability that the issuer may incur under Section 5-111 for wrongful dishonor, the effect of such a silent dishonor may ultimately be the same as though the issuer had honored, i.e., it may owe damages in the amount drawn but unpaid under the letter of credit.

3. The requirement that the issuer send notice of the discrepancies or be precluded from asserting discrepancies is new to Article 5. It is taken from the similar provision in the UCP and is intended to promote certainty and finality.

The section thus substitutes a strict preclusion principle for the doctrines of waiver and estoppel that might otherwise apply under Section 1-103. It rejects the reasoning in *Flagship Cruises Ltd. v. New England Merchants' Nat'l Bank,* 569 F.2d 699 (1st Cir. 1978) and *Wing On Bank Ltd. v. American Nat'l Bank & Trust Co.,* 457 F.2d 328 (5th Cir. 1972) where the issuer was held to be estopped only if the beneficiary relied on the issuer's failure to give notice.

Assume, for example, that the beneficiary presented documents to the issuer shortly before the letter of credit expired, in circumstances in which the beneficiary could not have cured any discrepancy before expiration. Under the reasoning of Flagship and Wing On, the beneficiary's inability to cure, even if it had received notice, would absolve the issuer of its failure to give notice. The virtue of the preclusion obligation adopted in this section is that it forecloses litigation about reliance and detriment.

Even though issuers typically give notice of the discrepancy of tardy presentation when presentation is made after the expiration of a credit, they are not required to give that notice and the section permits them to raise late presentation as a defect despite their failure to give that notice.

4. To act within a reasonable time, the issuer must normally give notice without delay after the examining party makes its decision. If the examiner decides to dishonor on the first day, it would be obliged to notify the beneficiary shortly thereafter, perhaps on the same business day. This rule accepts the reasoning in cases such as *Datapoint Corp. v. M & I Bank,* 665 F. Supp. 722 (W.D. Wis. 1987) and *Esso Petroleum Canada, Div. of Imperial Oil, Ltd. v. Security Pac. Bank,* 710 F. Supp. 275 (D. Ore. 1989).

The section deprives the examining party of the right simply to sit on a presentation that is made within seven days of expiration. The section requires the examiner to examine the documents and make a decision and, having made a decision to dishonor, to communicate promptly with the presenter. Nevertheless, a beneficiary who presents documents shortly before the expiration of a letter of credit runs the risk that it will never have the opportunity to cure any discrepancies.

5. Confirmers, other nominated persons, and collecting banks acting for beneficiaries can be presenters and, when so, are entitled to the notice provided in subsection (b). Even nominated persons who have honored or given value against an earlier presentation of the beneficiary and are themselves seeking reimbursement or honor need notice of discrepancies in the hope that they may be able to procure complying documents. The issuer has the obligations imposed by this section whether the issuer's performance is characterized as "reimbursement" of a nominated person or as "honor."

6. In many cases a letter of credit authorizes presentation by the beneficiary to someone other than the issuer. Sometimes that person is identified as a "payor" or

"paying bank," or as an "acceptor" or "accepting bank," in other cases as a "negotiating bank," and in other cases there will be no specific designation. The section does not impose any duties on a person other than the issuer or confirmer, however a nominated person or other person may have liability under this article or at common law if it fails to perform an express or implied agreement with the beneficiary.

7. The issuer's obligation to honor runs not only to the beneficiary but also to the applicant. It is possible that an applicant who has made a favorable contract with the beneficiary will be injured by the issuer's wrongful dishonor. Except to the extent that the contract between the issuer and the applicant limits that liability, the issuer will have liability to the applicant for wrongful dishonor under Section 5-111 as a matter of contract law. A good faith extension of the time in Section 5-108(b) by agreement between the issuer and beneficiary binds the applicant even if the applicant is not consulted or does not consent to the extension.

The issuer's obligation to dishonor when there is no apparent compliance with the letter of credit runs only to the applicant. No other party to the transaction can complain if the applicant waives compliance with terms or conditions of the letter of credit or agrees to a less stringent standard for compliance than that supplied by this article. Except as otherwise agreed with the applicant, an issuer may dishonor a noncomplying presentation despite an applicant's waiver.

Waiver of discrepancies by an issuer or an applicant in one or more presentations does not waive similar discrepancies in a future presentation. Neither the issuer nor the beneficiary can reasonably rely upon honor over past waivers as a basis for concluding that a future defective presentation will justify honor. The reasoning of *Courtaulds of North Am. Inc. v. North Carolina Nat'l Bank,* 528 F.2d 802 (4th Cir. 1975) is accepted and that expressed in *Schweibish v. Pontchartrain State Bank*, 389 So. 2d 731 (La. App. 1980) and *Titanium Metals Corp. v. Space Metals, Inc.*, 529 P.2d 431 (Utah 1974) is rejected.

8. The standard practice referred to in subsection (e) includes (i) international practice set forth in or referenced by the Uniform Customs and Practice, (ii) other practice rules published by associations of financial institutions, and (iii) local and regional practice. It is possible that standard practice will vary from one place to another. Where there are conflicting practices, the parties should indicate which practice governs their rights. A practice may be overridden by agreement or course of dealing. See Section 1-205(4).

9. The responsibility of the issuer under a letter of credit is to examine documents and to make a prompt decision to honor or dishonor based upon that examination. Nondocumentary conditions have no place in this regime and are better accommodated under contract or suretyship law and practice. In requiring that nondocumentary conditions in letters of credit be ignored as surplusage, Article 5 remains aligned with the UCP (see UCP 500 Article 13c), approves cases like *Pringle-Associated Mortgage Corp. v. Southern Nat'l Bank*, 571 F.2d 871, 874 (5th Cir. 1978), and rejects the reasoning in cases such as *Sherwood & Roberts, Inc. v. First Sec. Bank*, 682 P.2d 149 (Mont. 1984).

Subsection (g) recognizes that letters of credit sometimes contain nondocumentary terms or conditions. Conditions such as a term prohibiting "shipment on vessels more than 15 years old," are to be disregarded and treated as surplusage. Similarly, a requirement that there be an award by a "duly appointed arbitrator" would not require the issuer to determine whether the arbitrator had been "duly appointed." Likewise a term in a standby letter of credit that provided for differing forms of certification depending upon the particular type of default does not oblige the issuer independently to determine which kind of default has occurred. These conditions must be disregarded by the issuer. Where the nondocumentary conditions are central and fundamental to the issuer's obligation (as for example a condition that would require the issuer to determine in fact whether the beneficiary had performed the underlying contract or whether the applicant had defaulted) their inclusion may remove the undertaking from the scope of Article 5 entirely. See Section 5-102(a)(10) and Comment 6 to Section 5-102.

Subsection (g) would not permit the beneficiary or the issuer to disregard terms in the letter of credit such as place, time, and mode of presentation. The rule in subsection (g) is intended to prevent an issuer from deciding or even investigating extrinsic facts, but not from consulting the clock, the calendar, the relevant law and practice, or its own general knowledge of documentation or transactions of the type underlying a particular letter of credit.

Even though nondocumentary conditions must be disregarded in determining compliance of a presentation (and thus in determining the issuer's duty to the beneficiary), an issuer that has promised its applicant that it will honor only on the occurrence of those nondocumentary conditions may have liability to its applicant for disregarding the conditions.

10. Subsection (f) condones an issuer's ignorance of "any usage of a particular trade"; that trade is the trade of the applicant, beneficiary, or others who may be involved in the underlying transaction. The issuer is expected to know usage that is commonly encountered in the course of document examination. For example, an issuer should know the common usage with respect to documents in the maritime shipping trade but would not be expected to understand synonyms used in a particular trade for product descriptions appearing in a letter of credit or an invoice.

11. Where the issuer's performance is the delivery of an item of value other than money, the applicant's reimbursement obligation would be to make the "item of value" available to the issuer.

12. An issuer is entitled to reimbursement from the applicant after honor of a forged or fraudulent drawing if honor was permitted under Section 5-109(a).

13. The last clause of Section 5-108(i)(5) deals with a special case in which the fraud is not committed by the beneficiary, but is committed by a stranger to the transaction who forges the beneficiary's signature. If the issuer pays against documents on which a required signature of the beneficiary is forged, it remains liable to the true beneficiary.

Section 5–109. Fraud and Forgery.

(a) If a presentation is made that appears on its face strictly to comply with the terms and conditions of the letter of credit, but a required document is forged or materially fraudulent, or honor of the presentation would facilitate a material fraud by the beneficiary on the issuer or applicant:

(1) the issuer shall honor the presentation, if honor is demanded by:

(i) a nominated person who has given value in good faith and without notice of forgery or material fraud,

(ii) a confirmer who has honored its confirmation in good faith,

(iii) a holder in due course of a draft drawn under the letter of credit which was taken after acceptance by the issuer or nominated person, or

(iv) an assignee of the issuer's or nominated person's deferred obligation that was taken for value and without notice of forgery or material fraud after the obligation was incurred by the issuer or nominated person; and

(2) the issuer, acting in good faith, may honor or dishonor the presentation in any other case.

(b) If an applicant claims that a required document is forged or materially fraudulent or that honor of the presentation would facilitate a material fraud by the beneficiary on the issuer or applicant, a court of competent jurisdiction may temporarily or permanently enjoin the issuer from honoring a presentation or grant similar relief against the issuer or other persons only if the court finds that:

(1) the relief is not prohibited under the law applicable to an accepted draft or deferred obligation incurred by the issuer;

(2) a beneficiary, issuer, or nominated person who may be adversely affected is adequately protected against loss that it may suffer because the relief is granted;

(3) all of the conditions to entitle a person to the relief under the law of this state have been met; and

(4) on the basis of the information submitted to the court, the applicant is more likely than not to succeed under its claim of forgery or material fraud and the person demanding honor does not qualify for protection under paragraph (1) of subsection (a) of this section.

Added by Laws 2000, Ch. 471, eff. Nov. 1, 2000.

Official Comment

1. This recodification makes clear that fraud must be found either in the documents or must have been committed by the beneficiary on the issuer or applicant. *See Cromwell v. Commerce & Energy Bank*, 464 So. 2d 721 (La. 1985).

Secondly, it makes clear that fraud must be "material." Necessarily courts must decide the breadth and width of "materiality." The use of the word requires that the fraudulent aspect of a document be material to a purchaser of that document or that the fraudulent act be significant to the participants in the underlying transaction. Assume, for example, that the beneficiary has a contract to deliver 1,000 barrels of salad oil. Knowing that it has delivered only 998, the beneficiary nevertheless submits an invoice showing 1,000 barrels. If two barrels in a 1,000 barrel shipment would be an insubstantial and immaterial breach of the underlying contract, the beneficiary's act, though possibly fraudulent, is not materially so and would not justify an injunction. Conversely, the knowing submission of those invoices upon delivery of only five barrels would be materially fraudulent. The courts must examine the underlying transaction when there is an allegation of material fraud, for only by examining that transaction can one determine whether a document is fraudulent or the beneficiary has committed fraud and, if so, whether the fraud was material.

Material fraud by the beneficiary occurs only when the beneficiary has no colorable right to expect honor and where there is no basis in fact to support such a right to honor. The section indorses articulations such as those stated in *Intraworld Indus. v. Girard Trust Bank*, 336 A.2d 316 (Pa. 1975), *Roman Ceramics Corp. v. People's Nat'l Bank*, 714 F.2d 1207 (3d Cir. 1983), and similar decisions and embraces certain decisions under Section 5-114 that relied upon the phrase "fraud in the transaction." Some of these decisions have been summarized as follows in *Ground Air Transfer v. Westate's Airlines*, 899 F.2d 1269, 1272-73 (1st Cir. 1990):

We have said throughout that courts may not "normally" issue an injunction because of an important exception to the general 'no injunction'rule. The exception, as we also explained in *Itek*, 730 F.2d at 24-25, concerns "fraud" so serious as to make it obviously pointless and unjust to permit the beneficiary to obtain the money. Where the circumstances "plainly" show that the underlying contract forbids the beneficiary to call a letter of credit, *Itek*, 730 F.2d at 24; where they show that the contract deprives the beneficiary of even a "colorable" right to do so, *id.*, at 25; where the contract and circumstances reveal that the beneficiary's demand for payment has "absolutely no basis in fact," *id.*; see *Dynamics Corp. of Am.*, 356 F. Supp. at 999; where the beneficiary's conduct has "so vitiated the entire transaction that the legitimate purposes of the independence of the issuer's obligation would no longer be served," *Itek*, 730 F.2d at 25 (quoting *Roman Ceramics Corp. v. Peoples Nat'l Bank*, 714 F.2d 1207, 1212 n.12, 1215 (3d Cir. 1983) (quoting *Intraworld Indus.*, 336 A.2d at 324-25)); then a court may enjoin payment.

2. Subsection (a)(2) makes clear that the issuer may honor in the face of the applicant's claim of fraud. The subsection also makes clear what was not stated in former Section 5-114, that the issuer may dishonor and defend that dishonor by showing fraud or forgery of the kind stated in subsection (a). Because issuers may be liable for wrongful dishonor if they are unable to prove forgery or material fraud, presumably most issuers will choose to honor despite applicant's claims of fraud or forgery unless the applicant procures an injunction. Merely because the issuer has a right to dishonor and to defend that dishonor by showing forgery or material fraud does not mean it has a duty to the applicant to dishonor. The applicant's normal recourse is to procure an injunction, if the applicant is unable to procure an injunction, it will have a claim against the issuer only in the rare case in which it can show that the issuer did not honor in good faith.

3. Whether a beneficiary can commit fraud by presenting a draft under a clean letter of credit (one calling only for a draft and no other documents) has been much debated. Under the current formulation it would be possible but difficult for there to be fraud in such a presentation. If the applicant were able to show that the beneficiary were committing material fraud on the applicant in the underlying transaction, then payment would facilitate a material fraud by the beneficiary on the applicant and honor could be enjoined. The courts should be skeptical of claims of fraud by one who has signed a "suicide" or clean credit and thus granted a beneficiary the right to draw by mere presentation of a draft.

4. The standard for injunctive relief is high, and the burden remains on the applicant to show, by evidence and not by mere allegation, that such relief is warranted. Some courts have enjoined payments on letters of credit on insufficient showing by the applicant. For example, in *Griffin Cos. v. First Nat'l Bank*, 374 N.W.2d 768 (Minn. App. 1985), the court enjoined payment under a standby letter of credit, basing its decision on plaintiff's allegation, rather than competent evidence, of fraud.

There are at least two ways to prohibit injunctions against honor under this section after acceptance of a draft by the issuer. First is to define honor (see Section 5-102(a)(8)) in the particular letter of credit to occur upon acceptance and without regard to later payment of the acceptance. Second is explicitly to agree that the applicant has no right to an injunction after acceptance/— whether or not the acceptance constitutes honor.

5. Although the statute deals principally with injunctions against honor, it also cautions against granting "similar relief" and the same principles apply when the applicant or issuer attempts to achieve the same legal outcome by injunction against presentation (see *Ground Air Transfer Inc. v. Westates Airlines, Inc.*, 899 F.2d 1269 (1st Cir. 1990)), interpleader, declaratory judgment, or attachment. These attempts should face the same obstacles that face efforts to enjoin the issuer from paying. Expanded use of any of these devices could threaten the independence principle just as much as injunctions against honor. For that reason courts should have the same hostility to them and place the same restrictions on their use as would be applied

to injunctions against honor. Courts should not allow the "sacred cow of equity to trample the tender vines of letter of credit law."

6. Section 5-109(a)(1) also protects specified third parties against the risk of fraud. By issuing a letter of credit that nominates a person to negotiate or pay, the issuer (ultimately the applicant) induces that nominated person to give value and thereby assumes the risk that a draft drawn under the letter of credit will be transferred to one with a status like that of a holder in due course who deserves to be protected against a fraud defense.

7. The "loss" to be protected against — by bond or otherwise under subsection (b)(2) — includes incidental damages. Among those are legal fees that might be incurred by the beneficiary or issuer in defending against an injunction action.

Section 5–110. Warranties.

(a) If its presentation is honored, the beneficiary warrants:

(1) to the issuer, any other person to whom presentation is made, and the applicant that there is no fraud or forgery of the kind described in subsection (a) of Section 5–109; and

(2) to the applicant that the drawing does not violate any agreement between the applicant and beneficiary or any other agreement intended by them to be augmented by the letter of credit.

(b) The warranties in subsection (a) of this section are in addition to warranties arising under articles 3, 4, 7 and 8 because of the presentation or transfer of documents covered by any of those articles.

Added by Laws 2000, Ch. 471, eff. Nov. 1, 2000.

Official Comment

1. Since the warranties in subsection (a) are not given unless a letter of credit has been honored, no breach of warranty under this subsection can be a defense to dishonor by the issuer. Any defense must be based on Section 5-108 or 5-109 and not on this section. Also, breach of the warranties by the beneficiary in subsection (a) cannot excuse the applicant's duty to reimburse.

2. The warranty in Section 5-110(a)(2) assumes that payment under the letter of credit is final. It does not run to the issuer, only to the applicant. In most cases the applicant will have a direct cause of action for breach of the underlying contract. This warranty has primary application in standby letters of credit or other circumstances where the applicant is not a party to an underlying contract with the beneficiary. It is not a warranty that the statements made on the presentation of the documents presented are truthful nor is it a warranty that the documents strictly comply under Section 5-108(a). It is a warranty that the beneficiary has performed all the acts expressly and implicitly necessary under any underlying agreement to entitle the beneficiary to honor. If, for example, an underlying sales contract authorized the beneficiary to draw only upon "due performance" and the beneficiary drew even though it had breached the underlying contract by delivering defective goods, honor of its draw would break the warranty. By the same token, if the underlying contract authorized the beneficiary to draw only upon actual default or upon its or a third party's determination of default by the applicant and if the beneficiary drew in violation of its authorization, then upon honor of its draw the warranty would be breached. In many cases, therefore, the documents presented to

the issuer will contain inaccurate statements (concerning the goods delivered or concerning default or other matters), but the breach of warranty arises not because the statements are untrue but because the beneficiary's drawing violated its express or implied obligations in the underlying transaction.

3. The damages for breach of warranty are not specified in Section 5-111. Courts may find damage analogies in Section 2-714 in Article 2 and in warranty decisions under Articles 3 and 4.

Unlike wrongful dishonor cases — where the damages usually equal the amount of the draw — the damages for breach of warranty will often be much less than the amount of the draw, sometimes zero. Assume a seller entitled to draw only on proper performance of its sales contract. Assume it breaches the sales contract in a way that gives the buyer a right to damages but no right to reject. The applicant's damages for breach of the warranty in subsection (a)(2) are limited to the damages it could recover for breach of the contract of sale. Alternatively assume an underlying agreement that authorizes a beneficiary to draw only the "amount in default." Assume a default of $200,000 and a draw of $500,000. The damages for breach of warranty would be no more than $300,000.

Section 5–111. Remedies.

(a) If an issuer wrongfully dishonors or repudiates its obligation to pay money under a letter of credit before presentation, the beneficiary, successor, or nominated person presenting on its own behalf may recover from the issuer the amount that is the subject of the dishonor or repudiation. If the issuer's obligation under the letter of credit is not for the payment of money, the claimant may obtain specific performance or, at the claimant's election, recover an amount equal to the value of performance from the issuer. In either case, the claimant may also recover incidental but not consequential damages. The claimant is not obligated to take action to avoid damages that might be due from the issuer under this subsection. If, although not obligated to do so, the claimant avoids damages, the claimant's recovery from the issuer must be reduced by the amount of damages avoided. The issuer has the burden of proving the amount of damages avoided. In the case of repudiation the claimant need not present any document.

(b) If an issuer wrongfully dishonors a draft or demand presented under a letter of credit or honors a draft or demand in breach of its obligation to the applicant, the applicant may recover damages resulting from the breach, including incidental but not consequential damages, less any amount saved as a result of the breach.

(c) If an adviser or nominated person other than a confirmer breaches an obligation under this article or an issuer breaches an obligation not covered in subsection (a) or (b) of this section, a person to whom the obligation is owed may recover damages resulting from the breach, including incidental but not consequential damages, less any amount saved as a result of the breach. To the extent of the confirmation, a confirmer has the liability of an issuer specified in this subsection and subsections (a) and (b) of this section.

(d) An issuer, nominated person, or adviser who is found liable under subsection (a), (b) or (c) of this section shall pay interest on the amount owed thereunder from the date of wrongful dishonor or other appropriate date.

(e) Damages that would otherwise be payable by a party for breach of an obligation under this article may be liquidated by agreement or undertaking, but only in an amount or by a formula that is reasonable in light of the harm anticipated.

Added by Laws 2000, Ch. 471, eff. Nov. 1, 2000.

Official Comment

1. The right to specific performance is new. The express limitation on the duty of the beneficiary to mitigate damages adopts the position of certain courts and commentators. Because the letter of credit depends upon speed and certainty of payment, it is important that the issuer not be given an incentive to dishonor. The issuer might have an incentive to dishonor if it could rely on the burden of mitigation falling on the beneficiary, (to sell goods and sue only for the difference between the price of the goods sold and the amount due under the letter of credit). Under the scheme contemplated by Section 5-111(a), the beneficiary would present the documents to the issuer. If the issuer wrongfully dishonored, the beneficiary would have no further duty to the issuer with respect to the goods covered by documents that the issuer dishonored and returned. The issuer thus takes the risk that the beneficiary will let the goods rot or be destroyed. Of course the beneficiary may have a duty of mitigation to the applicant arising from the underlying agreement, but the issuer would not have the right to assert that duty by way of defense or setoff. See Section 5-117(d). If the beneficiary sells the goods covered by dishonored documents or if the beneficiary sells a draft after acceptance but before dishonor by the issuer, the net amount so gained should be subtracted from the amount of the beneficiary's damages — at least where the damage claim against the issuer equals or exceeds the damage suffered by the beneficiary. If, on the other hand, the beneficiary suffers damages in an underlying transaction in an amount that exceeds the amount of the wrongfully dishonored demand (e.g., where the letter of credit does not cover 100 percent of the underlying obligation), the damages avoided should not necessarily be deducted from the beneficiary's claim against the issuer. In such a case, the damages would be the lesser of (i) the amount recoverable in the absence of mitigation (that is, the amount that is subject to the dis honor or repudiation plus any incidental damages) and (ii) the damages remaining after deduction for the amount of damages actually avoided.

A beneficiary need not present documents as a condition of suit for anticipatory repudiation, but if a beneficiary could never have obtained documents necessary for a presentation conforming to the letter of credit, the beneficiary cannot recover for anticipatory repudiation of the letter of credit. *Doelger v. Battery Park Bank*, 201 A.D. 515, 194 N.Y.S. 582 (1922) and *Decor by Nikkei Int'l, Inc. v. Federal Rep. of Nigeria*, 497 F. Supp. 893 (S.D.N.Y. 1980), *aff'd*, 647 F.2d 300 (2d Cir. 1981), *cert. denied*, 454 U.S. 1148 (1982). The last sentence of subsection (c) does not expand the liability of a confirmer to persons to whom the confirmer would not otherwise be liable under Section 5-107.

Almost all letters of credit, including those that call for an acceptance, are "obligations to pay money" as that term is used in Section 5-111(a).

2. What damages "result" from improper honor is for the courts to decide. Even though an issuer pays a beneficiary in violation of Section 5-108(a) or of its contract with the applicant, it may have no liability to an applicant. If the underlying contract has been fully performed, the applicant may not have been damaged by the issuer's breach. Such a case would occur when A contracts for goods at $100 per ton, but, upon delivery, the market value of conforming goods has decreased to $25 per ton.

If the issuer pays over discrepancies, there should be no recovery by A for the price differential if the issuer's breach did not alter the applicant's obligation under the underlying contract, i.e., to pay $100 per ton for goods now worth $25 per ton. On the other hand, if the applicant intends to resell the goods and must itself satisfy the strict compliance requirements under a second letter of credit in connection with its sale, the applicant may be damaged by the issuer's payment despite discrepancies because the applicant itself may then be unable to procure honor on the letter of credit where it is the beneficiary, and may be unable to mitigate its damages by enforcing its rights against others in the underlying transaction. Note that an issuer found liable to its applicant may have recourse under Section 5-117 by subrogation to the applicant's claim against the beneficiary or other persons.

One who inaccurately advises a letter of credit breaches its obligation to the beneficiary, but may cause no damage. If the beneficiary knows the terms of the letter of credit and understands the advice to be inaccurate, the beneficiary will have suffered no damage as a result of the adviser's breach.

3. Since the confirmer has the rights and duties of an issuer, in general it has an issuer's liability, see subsection (c). The confirmer is usually a confirming bank. A confirming bank often also plays the role of an adviser. If it breaks its obligation to the beneficiary, the confirming bank may have liability as an issuer or, depending upon the obligation that was broken, as an adviser. For example, a wrongful dishonor would give it liability as an issuer under Section 5-111(a). On the other hand a confirming bank that broke its obligation to advise the credit but did not commit wrongful dishonor would be treated under Section 5-111(c).

4. Consequential damages for breach of obligations under this article are excluded in the belief that these damages can best be avoided by the beneficiary or the applicant and out of the fear that imposing consequential damages on issuers would raise the cost of the letter of credit to a level that might render it uneconomic. *A fortiori* punitive and exemplary damages are excluded, however, this section does not bar recovery of consequential or even punitive damages for breach of statutory or common law duties arising outside of this article.

5. The section does not specify a rate of interest. It leaves the setting of the rate to the court. It would be appropriate for a court to use the rate that would normally apply in that court in other situations where interest is imposed by law.

6. The court must award attorney's fees to the prevailing party, whether that party is an applicant, a beneficiary, an issuer, a nominated person, or adviser. Since the issuer may be entitled to recover its legal fees and costs from the applicant under the reimbursement agreement, allowing the issuer to recover those fees from a losing beneficiary may also protect the applicant against undeserved losses. The party entitled to attorneys' fees has been described as the "prevailing party." Sometimes it will be unclear which party "prevailed," for example, where there are multiple issues and one party wins on some and the other party wins on others. Determining which is the prevailing party is in the discretion of the court. Subsection (e) authorizes attorney's fees in all actions where a remedy is sought "under this article." It applies even when the remedy might be an injunction under Section 5-109 or when the claimed remedy is otherwise outside of Section 5-111. Neither an issuer nor a confirmer should be treated as a "losing" party when an injunction is granted to the applicant over the objection of the issuer or confirmer; accordingly neither should be liable for fees and expenses in that case.

"Expenses of litigation" is intended to be broader than "costs." For example, expense of litigation would include travel expenses of witnesses, fees for expert witnesses, and expenses associated with taking depositions.

7. For the purposes of Section 5-111(f) "harm anticipated" must be anticipated at the time when the agreement that includes the liquidated damage clause is executed or at the time when the undertaking that includes the clause is issued. See Section 2A-504.

Section 5–112. Transfer of letter of credit.

(a) Except as otherwise provided in Section 5–113, unless a letter of credit provides that it is transferable, the right of a beneficiary to draw or otherwise demand performance under a letter of credit may not be transferred.

(b) Even if a letter of credit provides that it is transferable, the issuer may refuse to recognize or carry out a transfer if:

(1) the transfer would violate applicable law; or

(2) the transferor or transferee has failed to comply with any requirement stated in the letter of credit or any other requirement relating to transfer imposed by the issuer which is within the standard practice referred to in subsection (e) of Section 5–108 or is otherwise reasonable under the circumstances.

Added by Laws 2000, Ch. 471, eff. Nov. 1, 2000.

Official Comment

1. In order to protect the applicant's reliance on the designated beneficiary, letter of credit law traditionally has forbidden the beneficiary to convey to third parties its right to draw or demand payment under the letter of credit. Subsection (a) codifies that rule. The term "transfer" refers to the beneficiary's conveyance of that right. Absent incorporation of the UCP (which make elaborate provision for partial transfer of a commercial letter of credit) or similar trade practice and absent other express indication in the letter of credit that the term is used to mean something else, a term in the letter of credit indicating that the beneficiary has the right to transfer should be taken to mean that the beneficiary may convey to a third party its right to draw or demand payment. Even in that case, the issuer or other person controlling the transfer may make the beneficiary's right to transfer subject to conditions, such as timely notification, payment of a fee, delivery of the letter of credit to the issuer or other person controlling the transfer, or execution of appropriate forms to document the transfer. A nominated person who is not a confirmer has no obligation to recognize a transfer.

The power to establish "requirements" does not include the right absolutely to refuse to recognize transfers under a transferable letter of credit. An issuer who wishes to retain the right to deny all transfers should not issue transferable letters of credit or should incorporate the UCP. By stating its requirements in the letter of credit an issuer may impose any requirement without regard to its conformity to practice or reasonableness. Transfer requirements of issuers and nominated persons must be made known to potential transferors and transferees to enable those parties to comply with the requirements. A common method of making such requirements known is to use a form that indicates the information that must be provided and the instructions that must be given to enable the issuer or nominated person to comply with a request to transfer.

2. The issuance of a transferable letter of credit with the concurrence of the applicant is ipso facto an agreement by the issuer and applicant to permit a beneficiary to transfer its drawing right and permit a nominated person to recognize and carry out that transfer without further notice to them. In international commerce, transferable letters of credit are often issued under circumstances in which a nominated person or adviser is expected to facilitate the transfer from the original beneficiary to a transferee and to deal with that transferee. In those circumstances it is the responsibility of the nominated person or adviser to establish procedures satisfactory to protect itself

against double presentation or dispute about the right to draw under the letter of credit. Commonly such a person will control the transfer by requiring that the original letter of credit be given to it or by causing a paper copy marked as an original to be issued where the original letter of credit was electronic. By keeping possession of the original letter of credit the nominated person or adviser can minimize or entirely exclude the possibility that the original beneficiary could properly procure payment from another bank. If the letter of credit requires presentation of the original letter of credit itself, no other payment could be procured. In addition to imposing whatever requirements it considers appropriate to protect itself against double payment the person that is facilitating the transfer has a right to charge an appropriate fee for its activity.

"Transfer" of a letter of credit should be distinguished from "assignment of proceeds." The former is analogous to a novation or a substitution of beneficiaries. It contemplates not merely payment to but also performance by the transferee. For example, under the typical terms of transfer for a commercial letter of credit, a transferee could comply with a letter of credit transferred to it by signing and presenting its own draft and invoice. An assignee of proceeds, on the other hand, is wholly dependent on the presentation of a draft and invoice signed by the beneficiary.

By agreeing to the issuance of a transferable letter of credit, which is not qualified or limited, the applicant may lose control over the identity of the person whose performance will earn payment under the letter of credit.

Section 5–113. Transfer by Operation of Law.

(a) A successor of a beneficiary may consent to amendments, sign and present documents, and receive payment or other items of value in the name of the beneficiary without disclosing its status as a successor.

(b) A successor of a beneficiary may consent to amendments, sign and present documents, and receive payment or other items of value in its own name as the disclosed successor of the beneficiary. Except as otherwise provided in subsection (e) of this section, an issuer shall recognize a disclosed successor of a beneficiary as beneficiary in full substitution for its predecessor upon compliance with the requirements for recognition by the issuer of a transfer of drawing rights by operation of law under the standard practice referred to in subsection (e) of Section 5–108 or, in the absence of such a practice, compliance with other reasonable procedures sufficient to protect the issuer.

(c) An issuer is not obliged to determine whether a purported successor is a successor of a beneficiary or whether the signature of a purported successor is genuine or authorized.

(d) Honor of a purported successor's apparently complying presentation under subsection (a) or (b) of this section has the consequences specified in subsection (i) of Section 5–108 even if the purported successor is not the successor of a beneficiary. Documents signed in the name of the beneficiary or of a disclosed successor by a person who is neither the beneficiary nor the successor of the beneficiary are forged documents for the purposes of Section 5–109.

(e) An issuer whose rights of reimbursement are not covered by subsection (d) of this section or substantially similar law and any confirmer or nominated person may decline to recognize a presentation under subsection (b) of this section.

(f) A beneficiary whose name is changed after the issuance of a letter of credit has the same rights and obligations as a successor of a beneficiary under this section.

Added by Laws 2000, Ch. 471, eff. Nov. 1, 2000.

Official Comment

This section affirms the result in *Pastor v. National Rep. Bank of Chicago*, 76 Ill. 2d 139, 390 N.E.2d 894 (Ill. 1979) and *Federal Deposit Ins. Co. v. Bank of Boulder*, 911 F.2d 1466 (10th Cir. 1990).

An issuer's requirements for recognition of a successor's status might include presentation of a certificate of merger, a court order appointing a bankruptcy trustee or receiver, a certificate of appointment as bankruptcy trustee, or the like. The issuer is entitled to rely upon such documents which on their face demonstrate that presentation is made by a successor of a beneficiary. It is not obliged to make an independent investigation to determine the fact of succession.

Section 5-114. Assignment of Proceeds.

(a) In this section, "proceeds of a letter of credit" means the cash, check, accepted draft, or other item of value paid or delivered upon honor or giving of value by the issuer or any nominated person under the letter of credit. The term does not include a beneficiary's drawing rights or documents presented by the beneficiary.

(b) A beneficiary may assign its right to part or all of the proceeds of a letter of credit. The beneficiary may do so before presentation as a present assignment of its right to receive proceeds contingent upon its compliance with the terms and conditions of the letter of credit.

(c) An issuer or nominated person need not recognize an assignment of proceeds of a letter of credit until it consents to the assignment.

(d) An issuer or nominated person has no obligation to give or withhold its consent to an assignment of proceeds of a letter of credit, but consent may not be unreasonably withheld if the assignee possesses and exhibits the letter of credit and presentation of the letter of credit is a condition to honor.

(e) Rights of a transferee beneficiary or nominated person are independent of the beneficiary's assignment of the proceeds of a letter of credit and are superior to the assignee's right to the proceeds.

(f) Neither the rights recognized by this section between an assignee and an issuer, transferee beneficiary, or nominated person nor the issuer's or nominated person's payment of proceeds to an assignee or a third person affect the rights between the assignee and any person other than the issuer, transferee beneficiary, or nominated person. The mode of creating and perfecting a security interest in or granting an assignment of a beneficiary's rights to proceeds is governed by article 9 or other law. Against persons other than the issuer, transferee beneficiary, or nominated person, the rights and obligations arising upon the creation of a security interest or other assignment of a beneficiary's right to proceeds and its perfection are governed by article 9 or other law.

Added by Laws 2000, Ch. 471, eff. Nov. 1, 2000.

Official Comment

1. Subsection (b) expressly validates the beneficiary's present assignment of letter of credit proceeds if made after the credit is established but before the proceeds are realized. This section adopts the prevailing usage — "assignment of proceeds" — to an assignee. That terminology carries with it no implication, however, that an assignee acquires no interest until the proceeds are paid by the issuer. For example, an "assignment of the right to proceeds" of a letter of credit for purposes of security that meets the requirements of Section 9-203(1) would constitute the present creation of a security interest in that right. This security interest can be perfected by possession (Section 9-305) if the letter of credit is in written form. Although subsection (a) explains the meaning of " 'proceeds' of a letter of credit," it should be emphasized that those proceeds also may be Article 9 proceeds of other collateral. For example, if a seller of inventory receives a letter of credit to support the account that arises upon the sale, payments made under the letter of credit are Article 9 proceeds of the inventory, account, and any document of title covering the inventory. Thus, the secured party who had a perfected security interest in that inventory, account, or document has a perfected security interest in the proceeds collected under the letter of credit, so long as they are identifiable cash proceeds (Section 9-306(2), (3)). This perfection is continuous, regardless of whether the secured party perfected a security interest in the right to letter of credit proceeds.

2. An assignee's rights to enforce an assignment of proceeds against an issuer and the priority of the assignee's rights against a nominated person or transferee beneficiary are governed by Article 5. Those rights and that priority are stated in subsections (c), (d), and (e). Note also that Section 4-210 gives first priority to a collecting bank that has given value for a documentary draft.

3. By requiring that an issuer or nominated person consent to the assignment of proceeds of a letter of credit, subsections (c) and (d) follow more closely recognized national and international letter of credit practices than did prior law. In most circumstances, it has always been advisable for the assignee to obtain the consent of the issuer in order better to safeguard its right to the proceeds. When notice of an assignment has been received, issuers normally have required signatures on a consent form. This practice is reflected in the revision. By unconditionally consenting to such an assignment, the issuer or nominated person becomes bound, subject to the rights of the superior parties specified in subsection (e), to pay to the assignee the assigned letter of credit proceeds that the issuer or nominated person would otherwise pay to the beneficiary or another assignee.

Where the letter of credit must be presented as a condition to honor and the assignee holds and exhibits the letter of credit to the issuer or nominated person, the risk to the issuer or nominated person of having to pay twice is minimized. In such a situation, subsection (d) provides that the issuer or nominated person may not unreasonably withhold its consent to the assignment.

Section 5–115. Statute of limitations.

An action to enforce a right or obligation arising under this article must be commenced within one year after the expiration date of the relevant letter of credit or one year after the cause of action accrues, whichever occurs later. A cause of action accrues when the breach occurs, regardless of the aggrieved party's lack of knowledge of the breach.

Added by Laws 2000, Ch. 471, eff. Nov. 1, 2000.

Official Comment

1. This section is based upon Sections 4-111 and 2-725(2).

2. This section applies to all claims for which there are remedies under Section 5-111 and to other claims made under this article, such as claims for breach of warranty under Section 5-110. Because it covers all claims under Section 5-111, the statute of limitations applies not only to wrongful dishonor claims against the issuer but also to claims between the issuer and the applicant arising from the reimbursement agreement. These might be for reimbursement (issuer v. applicant) or for breach of the reimbursement contract by wrongful honor (applicant v. issuer).

3. The statute of limitations, like the rest of the statute, applies only to a letter of credit issued on or after the effective date and only to transactions, events, obligations, or duties arising out of or associated with such a letter. If a letter of credit was issued before the effective date and an obligation on that letter of credit was breached after the effective date, the complaining party could bring its suit within the time that would have been permitted prior to the adoption of Section 5-115 and would not be limited by the terms of Section 5-115.

Section 5–116. Choice of law and forum.

(a) The liability of an issuer, nominated person, or adviser for action or omission is governed by the law of the jurisdiction chosen by an agreement in the form of a record signed or otherwise authenticated by the affected parties in the manner provided in Section 5–104 or by a provision in the person's letter of credit, confirmation, or other undertaking. The jurisdiction whose law is chosen need not bear any relation to the transaction.

(b) Unless subsection (a) of this section applies, the liability of an issuer, nominated person, or adviser for action or omission is governed by the law of the jurisdiction in which the person is located. The person is considered to be located at the address indicated in the person's undertaking. If more than one address is indicated, the person is considered to be located at the address from which the person's undertaking was issued. For the purpose of jurisdiction, choice of law, and recognition of interbranch letters of credit, but not enforcement of a judgement, all branches of a bank are considered separate juridical entities and a bank is considered to be located at the place where its relevant branch is considered to be located under this subsection.

(c) Except as otherwise provided in this subsection, the liability of an issuer, nominated person, or adviser is governed by any rules of custom or practice, such as the uniform customs and practice for documentary credits, to which the letter of credit, confirmation, or other undertaking is expressly made subject. If (1) this article would govern the liability of an issuer, nominated person, or adviser under subsection (a) or (b) of this section, (2) the relevant undertaking incorporates rules of custom or practice, and (3) there is conflict between this article and those rules as applied to that undertaking, those rules govern except to the extent of any conflict with the nonvariable provisions specified in subsection (c) of Section 5–103.

(d) If there is conflict between this article and article 3, 4, 4A or 9, this article governs.

(e) The forum for settling disputes arising out of an undertaking within this article may be chosen in the manner and with the binding effect that governing law may be chosen in accordance with subsection (a) of this section.

Added by Laws 2000, Ch. 471, eff. Nov. 1, 2000.

Official Comment

1. Although it would be possible for the parties to agree otherwise, the law normally chosen by agreement under subsection (a) and that provided in the absence of agreement under subsection (b) is the substantive law of a particular jurisdiction not including the choice of law principles of that jurisdiction. Thus, two parties, an issuer and an applicant, both located in Oklahoma might choose the law of New York. Unless they agree otherwise, the section anticipates that they wish the substantive law of New York to apply to their transaction and they do not intend that a New York choice of law principle might direct a court to Oklahoma law. By the same token, the liability of an issuer located in New York is governed by New York substantive law — in the absence of agreement — even in circumstances in which choice of law principles found in the common law of New York might direct one to the law of another State. Subsection (b) states the relevant choice of law principles and it should not be subordinated to some other choice of law rule. Within the States of the United States renvoi will not be a problem once every jurisdiction has enacted Section 5-116 because every jurisdiction will then have the same choice of law rule and in a particular case all choice of law rules will point to the same substantive law.

Subsection (b) does not state a choice of law rule for the "liability of an applicant." However, subsection (b) does state a choice of law rule for the liability of an issuer, nominated person, or adviser, and since some of the issues in suits by applicants against those persons involve the "liability of an issuer, nominated person, or adviser," subsection (b) states the choice of law rule for those issues. Because an issuer may have liability to a confirmer both as an issuer (Section 5-108(a), Comment 5 to Section 5-108) and as an applicant (Section 5-107(a), Comment 1 to Section 5-107, Section 5-108(i)), subsection (b) may state the choice of law rule for some but not all of the issuer's liability in a suit by a confirmer.

2. Because the confirmer or other nominated person may choose different law from that chosen by the issuer or may be located in a different jurisdiction and fail to choose law, it is possible that a confirmer or nominated person may be obligated to pay (under their law) but will not be entitled to payment from the issuer (under its law). Similarly, the rights of an unreimbursed issuer, confirmer, or nominated person against a beneficiary under Section 5-109, 5-110, or 5-117, will not necessarily be governed by the same law that applies to the issuer's or confirmer's obligation upon presentation. Because the UCP and other practice are incorporated in most international letters of credit, disputes arising from different legal obligations to honor have not been frequent. Since Section 5-108 incorporates standard practice, these problems should be further minimized — at least to the extent that the same practice is and continues to be widely followed.

3. This section does not permit what is now authorized by the nonuniform Section 5-102(4) in New York. Under the current law in New York a letter of credit that incorporates the UCP is not governed in any respect by Article 5. Under revised Section 5-116 letters of credit that incorporate the UCP or similar practice will still be subject to Article 5 in certain respects. First, incorporation of the UCP or other practice does not override the nonvariable terms of Article 5. Second, where there is no conflict between Article 5 and the relevant provision of the UCP or other practice, both apply. Third, practice provisions incorporated in a letter of credit will not be effective if they fail to comply with Section 5-103(c). Assume, for example, that a practice provision purported to free a party from any liability unless it were "grossly negligent" or that the practice generally limited the remedies that one party might have against another. Depending upon the circumstances, that disclaimer or limitation of liability might be ineffective because of Section 5-103(c).

Even though Article 5 is generally consistent with UCP 500, it is not necessarily consistent with other rules or with versions of the UCP that may be adopted after Article 5's revision, or with other practices that may develop. Rules of practice incorporated in the letter of credit or other undertaking are those in effect when the letter of credit or other undertaking is issued. Except in the unusual cases discussed in the immediately preceding paragraph, practice adopted in a letter of credit will override the rules of Article 5 and the parties to letter of credit transactions must be familiar with practice (such as future versions of the UCP) that is explicitly adopted in letters of credit.

4. In several ways Article 5 conflicts with and overrides similar matters governed by Articles 3 and 4. For example, "draft" is more broadly defined in letter of credit practice than under Section 3-104. The time allowed for honor and the required notification of reasons for dishonor are different in letter of credit practice than in the handling of documentary and other drafts under Articles 3 and 4.

5. Subsection (e) must be read in conjunction with existing law governing subject matter jurisdiction. If the local law restricts a court to certain subject matter jurisdiction not including letter of credit disputes, subsection (e) does not authorize parties to choose that forum. For example, the parties' agreement under Section 5-116(e) would not confer jurisdiction on a probate court to decide a letter of credit case.

If the parties choose a forum under subsection (e) and if — because of other law — that forum will not take jurisdiction, the parties' agreement or undertaking should then be construed (for the purpose of forum selection) as though it did not contain a clause choosing a particular forum. That result is necessary to avoid sentencing the parties to eternal purgatory where neither the chosen State nor the State which would have jurisdiction but for the clause will take jurisdiction — the former in disregard of the clause and the latter in honor of the clause.

Section 5–117. Subrogation of issuer, applicant, and nominated person.

(a) An issuer that honors a beneficiary's presentation is subrogated to the rights of the beneficiary to the same extent as if the issuer were a secondary obligor of the underlying obligation owed to the beneficiary and of the applicant to the same extent as if the issuer were the secondary obligor of the underlying obligation owed to the applicant.

(b) An applicant that reimburses an issuer is subrogated to the rights of the issuer against any beneficiary, presenter, or nominated person to the same extent as if the applicant were the secondary obligor of the obligations owed to the issuer and has the rights of subrogation of the issuer to the rights of the beneficiary stated in subsection (a) of this section.

(c) A nominated person who pays or gives value against a draft or demand presented under a letter of credit is subrogated to the rights of:

(1) the issuer against the applicant to the same extent as if the nominated person were a secondary obligor of the obligation owed to the issuer by the applicant;

(2) the beneficiary to the same extent as if the nominated person were a secondary obligor of the underlying obligation owed to the beneficiary; and

(3) the applicant to the same extent as if the nominated person were a secondary obligor of the underlying obligation owed to the applicant.

(d) Notwithstanding any agreement or term to the contrary, the rights of subrogation stated in subsections (a) and (b) of this section do not arise until the issuer honors the letter of credit or otherwise pays and the rights in subsection (c) of this section do not arise until the nominated person pays or otherwise gives value. Until then, the issuer, nominated person, and the applicant do not derive under this section present or prospective rights forming the basis of a claim, defense, or excuse.

Added by Laws 2000, Ch. 471, eff. Nov. 1, 2000.

Official Comment

1. By itself this section does not grant any right of subrogation. It grants only the right that would exist if the person seeking subrogation "were a secondary obligor." (The term "secondary obligor" refers to a surety, guarantor, or other person against whom or whose property an obligee has recourse with respect to the obligation of a third party. See Restatement of the Law Third, Suretyship § 1 (1995).) If the secondary obligor would not have a right to subrogation in the circumstances in which one is claimed under this section, none is granted by this section. In effect, the section does no more than to remove an impediment that some courts have found to subrogation because they conclude that the issuer's or other claimant's rights are "independent" of the underlying obligation. If, for example, a secondary obligor would not have a subrogation right because its payment did not fully satisfy the underlying obligation, none would be available under this section. The section indorses the position of Judge Becker in *Tudor Dev. Group, Inc. v. United States Fidelity and Guar.*, 968 F.2d 357 (3rd Cir. 1991).

2. To preserve the independence of the letter of credit obligation and to insure that subrogation not be used as an offensive weapon by an issuer or others, the admonition in subsection (d) must be carefully observed. Only one who has completed its performance in a letter of credit transaction can have a right to subrogation. For example, an issuer may not dishonor and then defend its dishonor or assert a setoff on the ground that it is subrogated to another person's rights. Nor may the issuer complain after honor that its subrogation rights have been impaired by any good faith dealings between the beneficiary and the applicant or any other person. Assume, for example, that the beneficiary under a standby letter of credit is a mortgagee. If the mortgagee were obliged to issue a release of the mortgage upon payment of the underlying debt (by the issuer under the letter of credit), that release might impair

the issuer's rights of subrogation, but the beneficiary would have no liability to the issuer for having granted that release.

Section 5–118. Applicability.

This article applies to a letter of credit that is issued on or after the effective date of this article. This article does not apply to a transaction, event, obligation, or duty arising out of or associated with a letter of credit that was issued before the effective date of this article.

Added by Laws 2000, Ch. 471, eff. Nov. 1, 2000.

Section 5–119. Savings Clause.

A transaction arising out of or associated with a letter of credit that was issued before the effective date of this article and the rights, obligations, and interests flowing from that transaction are governed by any statute or other law amended or repealed by the chapter of the laws which added this article as if repeal or amendment had not occurred and may be terminated, completed, consummated, or enforced under that statute or other law

Added by Laws 2000, Ch. 471, eff. Nov. 1, 2000.

ARTICLE 6
BULK TRANSFERS

Section 6–101. Short Title.

This Article shall be known and may be cited as Uniform Commercial Code Bulk Transfers.

N.Y. Commission Comments

Article 6–Bulk Transfers is, in some respects, narrower and, in other respects, broader than pre-Code law governing bulk transfers, i.e., Personal Property Law § 44. *Transfer of goods and/or fixtures in bulk,* and Lien Law § 240-a. *Chattel mortgages on stocks of merchandise,* both repealed by L.1962, c. 553, which enacted the Code.

Article 6 is narrower than pre-Code law in that a bulk transfer subject to Article 6 does not include:

1. under Code § 6–102(2), a transfer of "equipment" [See Code § 9–109(2)] unless it is made in connection with a bulk transfer of inventory [See Code § 9–109(4)] and then only if the transfer is a transfer of a substantial part of the equipment of an enterprise while, under Personal Property Law § 44, a bulk transfer included a transfer of fixtures either alone or together with merchandise.

2. under Code § 6–103(7), a "transfer to a new business enterprise organized to take over and continue the business, if public notice of the transaction is given and the new enterprise assumes the debts of the transferor and he receives nothing from the transaction except an interest in the new enterprise junior to the claims of creditors," while Personal Property Law § 44 contained no such exclusion; or

3. under Code § 6–103(1), a transfer "made to give security for the performance of an obligation," while a chattel mortgage on a stock of merchandise was subject to Lien Law § 270-a.

Moreover, the requirements under Code § 6–104(1)(b) for "a schedule of the property transferred sufficient to identify it," are much more easily met than that of Personal Property Law § 44 and Lien Law § 230-a for a "full and detailed inventory, showing the quantity and, so far as is possible with the exercise of reasonable diligence, the cost price to the seller * * * of each article to be included in the sale."

On the other hand, Article 6 is broader than pre-Code law governing bulk transfers in that:

1. under Code § 6–104(3), the list of creditors of the transferor which he is required to furnish to the transferee, must contain "the names of all persons who are known to the transferor to assert claims against him even though such claims are disputed," while, under Personal Property Law § 44, a creditor included only one whose debt was liquidated.

2. under Code § 6–107(1) and (2) the contents of the notice to creditors is somewhat more detailed than under Personal Property Law § 44 and Lien Law § 230-a, which required a notification to creditors of the proposed sale or mortgage "and of the price, terms and conditions thereof."

Attention is called to the fact that L. 1962, c. 552, the companion bill to the Code, added to the Penal Law a new § 940-b. "*Bulk transfers of personal property; duties of parties; penalties for violation,*" having no counterpart in prior law and imposing criminal sanctions for the violation by transferors, auctioneers and transferees (except purchasers at auction) of the duties imposed upon them by Article 6–Bulk Transfers. [*Editor's Note: Penal Law § 940-b has been repealed.*]

New York Annotations

For an exhaustive discussion of the bulk sale laws, see Miller, "Bulk Sale Laws," 1954 Wash. U.L.Q. 1, 132, 283. For discussion of the Code provisions, see Miller, "The Effect of Bulk Sales Article on Existing Commercial Practices," 16 Law & Contemp. Prob. 267 (1951); Billig, "Article 6–Order Out of Chaos; A Bulk Transfers Article Emerges," 1952 Wis. L.Rev. 312; Weintraub and Levin, "Bulk Sales Law and Adequate Protection of Creditors," 65 Harv. L.Rev. 418 (1952). The language of the Comment to this section was quoted in Sternberg v. Rubenstein, 305 N.Y. 235, 239, 112 N.E.2d 210 (1953).

Article 6 would replace the New York bulk sales statute, Personal Property Law, § 44, and would also require the repeal of Lien Law, § 230-a, since this Article excludes transfers made as security. For the most part the Article is substantially declaratory of existing law. Its innovations include an expansion of coverage by the inclusion of provisions for auction sales in Section 6–108, the provision for a short, six-months' statute of limitations in Section 6–111, and the expansion of the class of protected creditors in Section 6–109. An optional provision in Section 6–106 would also be a major innovation in New York since it imposes a duty upon the transferee to assure that the proceeds of the sale are applied to the transferee's debts.

In addition, the Article limits its coverage to sellers whose principal business is the sale of merchandise from stock, including those who manufacture what they sell, and a transfer of equipment can be within the Article only if made in connection with a bulk transfer of inventory. Thus barber shops and laundries are excluded. There are also some new specific exclusions in subsections (5), (6), and (7) of Section 6–103.

The balance of the Article clarifies and simplifies the procedural steps in the preparation of the schedule, in the content of the notice to creditors, and otherwise, necessary to be followed if civil liability is to be avoided.

Historical Note: The Law Revision Commission said of Article 6: "The Commission's criticisms of Article 6 are limited to some questions of phraseology. It believes that the Article is properly included in a uniform commercial code and would improve the law." 1956 Report, p. 38. After that Report four of this Article's eleven sections were rewritten in their present form to meet most of the Commission's suggestions.

Official Uniform Comment

Prior Uniform Statutory Provision: None.

Purposes:

1. This Article attempts to simplify and make uniform the bulk sales laws of the states that adopt this Act.

2. Many states have bulk sales laws, of varying type and coverage. Their central purpose is to deal with two common forms of commercial fraud, namely:

(a) The merchant, owing debts, who sells out his stock in trade to a friend for less than it is worth, pays his creditors less than he owes them, and hopes to come back into the business through the back door some time in the future.

(b) The merchant, owing debts, who sells out his stock in trade to anyone for any price, pockets the proceeds, and disappears leaving his creditors unpaid.

3. The first is one form of fraudulent conveyance. The substantive law concerning it has been codified by the Commissioners in the Uniform Fraudulent Conveyance Act. No change in that Act is proposed. The contribution of the bulk sales laws to the problem is in the requirement that creditors receive advance notice of bulk sales. Having such notice, they can investigate the price and other circumstances of the sale before it occurs, and determine then instead of later whether they should try to stop it. This is a valuable policing measure, and is continued. To be effective, it requires a longer notice than five days. This Article therefore follows in this respect those laws which require a longer notice (Section 6–105, 6–108).

4. The second form of fraud suggested above represents the major bulk sales risk, and its prevention is the central purpose of the existing bulk sales laws and of this Article. Advance notice to the seller's creditors of the impending sale is an important protection against it, since with notice the creditors can take steps to impound the proceeds if they think it necessary. In many states, typified for instance by New York, such notice is substantially the only protection which bulk sales statutes give. Other states, typified for instance by Pennsylvania, give additional protection by imposing on the buyer an obligation to ensure that the money that he pays to his indebted seller is in fact applied to pay the seller's debts. This Article requires notice to creditors (Section 6–105) and if bracketed Section 6–106 is enacted it imposes the other obligation also.

5. These are the affirmative reasons for a law such as this Article. The objections are chiefly delay and red tape on legitimate transactions, and the possibility of a trap for the unwary buyer. It is hard to avoid the latter danger. But to minimize both it and the former the transactions subject to the Article are identified as clearly as possible and are limited to those which carry the dangers to be guarded against (Sections 6–102 and 6–103), and the sanctions are such as to permit honest and solvent buyers and sellers to put through transactions promptly without undue risk. Section 6–104 through 6–108.

Cross References:

Point 3: Sections 6–105 and 6–108.
Point 4: Sections 6–105 and 6–106.
Point 5: Sections 6–102, 6–103, 6–104 through 6–108.

Section 6–102. "Bulk Transfer"; Transfers of Equipment; Enterprises Subject to This Article; Bulk Transfers Subject to This Article.

(1) A "bulk transfer" is any transfer in bulk and not in the ordinary course of the transferor's business of a major part of the materials, supplies, merchandise or other inventory (Section 9–109) of an enterprise subject to this Article. "Bulk transfer" shall also include a transfer out of the ordinary course of business of a major part of the goods, wares and merchandise of a restaurant, or other food dispensing establishment.

(2) A transfer of a substantial part of the equipment (Section 9–109) of such an enterprise or of the equipment of a restaurant or other food dispensing establishment is a bulk transfer if it is made in connection with a bulk transfer of inventory, but not otherwise.

(3) The enterprises subject to this Article are all those whose principal business is the sale or rental of merchandise from stock, including those who manufacture what they sell and restaurants or other food dispensing establishments.

(4) Except as limited by the following section all bulk transfers of goods located within this state are subject to this Article.

Amended by Laws 1970, Ch. 574, eff. 120th day after May 8, 1970, Laws 1974, Ch. 613.

New York Annotations

(1) Subject to the exclusions in Section 6–103 the transaction within the Article is any transfer of a major part of the defined assets and not any "part or the whole of a stock of merchandise or of fixtures, or merchandise and fixtures." "Obviously the term major part means more than one-half of the transferor's total stock." 1952 Wis.L.Rev. 312, 318; 1954 Wash.U.L.Q. 283, 313. Neither the Code nor the New York statute makes an attempt to define "in bulk and not in the ordinary course of the transferor's business." See Sternberg v. Rubenstein, 305 N.Y. 235, 112 N.E.2d 210 (1953).

(2) The inclusion of sales of equipment only where there is a transfer of a substantial part of such equipment together with a bulk transfer of inventory, changes New York law. Personal Property Law, § 44, includes sales of "fixtures" alone or with merchandise, and the term "fixtures" has been said to be "all such things as are customarily and necessarily employed in the trade or traffic of the merchandise." Davignon v. Raquette River Paper Co., 269 App.Div. 889, 56 N.Y.S.2d 249, appeal dismissed, 295 N.Y. 569, 64 N.E.2d 279 (1945). See Section 9–109 for a definition of "equipment" as well as of "inventory."

(3) This changes New York law. Under Personal Property Law, § 44, the inclusion of bulk sales of "fixtures" alone extends the coverage to businesses which have no merchandise. Stumpp & Walter Co v. Napanoch Country Club, Inc., 198 Misc. 600, 102 N.Y.S.2d 489 (1950). The inclusion of manufacturers is consistent with New York law, Mosson v. Kriser, 212 App.Div. 282, 208 N.Y.S. 566 (1925), even though there is dictum that raw materials are not "merchandise", Mott v. Reeves, 125 Misc. 511, 515, 211 N.Y.S. 375, 379, aff'd, 217 App.Div. 718, 215 N.Y.S. 889, aff'd 246 N.Y. 567, 159 N.E. 654 (1927).

(4) This provision seems to be in accord with New York law. See Rosenbaum v. Consolidated Products Co., Inc., 81 N.Y.S.2d 571, aff'd 276 App. Div. 1069, 96 N.Y.S.2d 490 (1950), where a bulk sale of property located in Massachusetts was made between two New York corporations by a bill of sale delivered in New York; the court held that the transfer was subject to the law of the situs of the property and that compliance with New York law was not necessary.

Official Uniform Comment

Prior Uniform Statutory Provision: None.

Purposes:

1. Much of the litigation under the existing laws has dealt with the kinds of businesses and the kinds of transfers covered. This section defines these matters.

2. The businesses covered are defined in subsection (3). Notice that they do not include farming nor contracting nor professional services, nor such things as cleaning shops, barber shops, pool halls, hotels, restaurants, and the like whose principal business is the sale not of merchandise but of services. While some bulk sales risk exists in the excluded businesses, they have in common the fact that unsecured credit is not commonly extended on the faith of a stock of merchandise.

3. The transfers included are of "materials, supplies, merchandise or other inventory" that is, of goods. Transfers of investment securities are not covered by the Article, nor are transfers or money, accounts receivable, chattel paper, contract rights, negotiable instruments, nor things in action generally. Such transfers are dealt with in other Articles, and are not believed to carry any major bulk sales risk.

4. The kinds of transfers covered are identified in paragraph (1). They are believed to be those that carry the major bulk sales risks. They are further limited by the section following.

Cross References:

Point 3: Articles 3, 4, 8 and 9.

Point 4: Section 6 103.

Section 6–103. Transfers Excepted From This Article.

The following transfers are not subject to this Article:

(1) Those made to give security for the performance of an obligation;

(2) General assignments for the benefit of all the creditors of the transferor, and subsequent transfers by the assignee thereunder;

(3) Transfers in settlement or realization of a lien or other security interests;

(4) Sales by executors, administrators, receivers, trustees in bankruptcy, or any public officer under judicial process;

(5) Sales made in the course of judicial or administrative proceedings for the dissolution or reorganization of a corporation and of which notice is sent to the creditors of the corporation pursuant to order of the court or administrative agency;

(6) Transfers to a person maintaining a known place of business in this State who becomes bound to pay the debts of the transferor in full and gives public notice of that fact, and who is solvent after becoming so bound;

(7) A transfer to a new business enterprise organized to take over and continue the business, if public notice of the transaction is given and the new enterprise assumes the debts of the transferor and he receives nothing from the transaction except an interest in the new enterprise junior to the claims of creditors;

(8) Transfers of property which is exempt from execution.

Public notice under subsection (6) or subsection (7) may be given by publishing once a week for two consecutive weeks in a newspaper of general circulation where the transferor had its principal place of business in this state an advertisement including the names and addresses of the transferor and transferee and the effective date of the transfer.

Amended by Laws 1963, Ch. 1003, eff. Sept. 27, 1964.

New York Annotations

(1) The exclusion of transfers for security purposes is contrary to New York law and requires the repeal of Lien Law, § 230–a, the Bulk Mortgage Statute. See Section 9–111. However, it should be noted that this exclusion is not without precedent in the New York law. See Lien Law, § 230–c(7), exempting chattel mortgages by a dealer, and In re Rosom Utilities, 105 F.2d 132 (2d Cir. 1939), exempting purchase money chattel mortgages. For a complete discussion of the exemption in the Code, see statement of Professor Bunn before the Law Revision Commission, 1954 Leg. Doc. No. 65(E), p. 24.

(2) The exclusion of general assignments for the benefit of creditors is in accord with New York law. Personal Property Law, § 44(2).

(3) This may change existing law since it has been held that a transfer in settlement of an execution lien, not made as a judicial sale, was subject to the Bulk Sales Act. Leonard v. Fink, 119 Misc. 370, 196 N.Y.S. 316 (1922).

(4) In *accord* with the New York statute, except that no exclusion is made in the Code of sales by "committees of incompetents." Personal Property Law, § 44(2).

(5) To the extent that the subparagraph excludes sales under judicial process, it is in *accord* with the prior law. Personal Property Law, § 44(2). But to the extent that it excludes such sales controlled by administrative bodies, it is new.

(6) This is new. Compare, Lowendahl v. L. VanBokkelen Inc., 139 Misc. 857, 248 N.Y.S. 553, aff'd 234 App.Div. 749, 254 N.Y.S. 917, aff'd, 260 N.Y. 557, 184 N.E. 90 (1932); and see Gabbe v. Kleban Drug Corp., 6 Misc.2d 457, 161 N.Y.S.2d 245 (1957).

(7) This is new, but the subparagraph is in *accord* with the exclusion of the sale of a partner's interest in the partnership stock to a fellow partner. Citizens Trust Co. of Binghamton v. Merselis, 148 Misc. 676, 266 N.Y.S. 353, aff'd per curiam, 244 App. Div. 845, 279 N.Y.S. 324, aff'd mem., 271 N.Y. 539, 2 N.E.2d 684 (1935).

(8) This is new. While there are no New York cases on the point, the principle is consonant with existing law. See 59 Commercial Law Journal 92 (1954).

Historical Note: Subparagraph (5) was amended: (1) To limit the exception of judicial and administrative proceedings, (2) to make the requirement that the notice be sent, rather than received, (3) to eliminate the question of fact whether the notice ordered by the court or administrative agency is "substantially equivalent to that provided in this Article," and (4) to put the words "or reorganization" where they belong. This follows a Law Revision Commission suggestion. (1956 Recommendations, p. 187; Excerpts, pp. 437–8.)

Official Uniform Comment

Prior Uniform Statutory Provision: None.

Purposes:

1. The section defines the transfers which although within the general definition of the previous section ought not to be subjected to the requirements of this Article.

2. Some of the existing Bulk Sales laws cover "bulk mortgages" as well as outright sales. In this Code security interests of all kinds in personal property are regulated by Article 9, Secured Transactions. Subsection (1) of this section therefore excludes all transfers for security from the operation of this Article. See also Sec. 9–111.

3. The exclusions described in subsections (2), (3), (4), (5) and (8) are believed to explain themselves.

4. Subsection (6) will exclude a great many transactions from the requirements of this Article. It is believed the exclusion is justified, and that it removes many of the objections to a law of this character. The transactions excluded are outright sales, since that is the only kind of a transaction in which the transferee is likely to bind himself to pay the transferor's debts. The purpose of this Article on outright sales is to give the seller's creditors a reasonable chance to collect their debts. (See Sections 6–104 through 6–108). If the buyer is willing to assume personal liability for those debts, and is himself solvent after such assumption, there is no reason to subject the transaction to the delay and red tape which this Article imposes.

5. Subsection (7) deals with certain changes in the ownership of a business, as by incorporation, change of membership of a firm, or transfer from a sole proprietor to a firm. The exclusion is believed to be justified within the limits stated in the subsection. Notice that in all the transactions to which the subsection applies (a) both the original debtor and the new enterprise are personally bound to pay the debts, (b) the property subject to the debts before the transfer is still subject to them, and (c) the original debtor has taken nothing out of the transaction except an interest (shares in a corporation, an interest in a firm, or a subordinated obligation) which is junior to the debts.

Cross References:

Point 1: Section 6–102.
Point 2: Section 9–111 and Article 9 generally.
Point 4: Sections 6–104 through 6–108.

Definitional Cross References:

"Creditor." Sections 1–201 and 6–109.
"Person." Section 1–201.

Section 6–104. Schedule of Property; List of Creditors.

(1) Except as provided with respect to auction sales (Section 6–108), a bulk transfer subject to this Article is ineffective against any creditor of the transferor unless:

(a) The transferee requires the transferor to furnish a list of his existing creditors prepared as stated in this section; and

(b) The parties prepare a schedule of the property transferred sufficient to identify it; and

(c) The transferee preserves the list and schedule for six months next following the transfer and permits inspection of either or both and copying therefrom at all reasonable hours by any creditor of the transferor, or files the list and schedule in the department of state.

(2) The list of creditors must be signed and sworn to or affirmed by the transferor or his agent. It must contain the names and business addresses of all creditors of the transferor, with the amounts when known, and also the names of all persons who are known to the transferor to assert claims against him even though such claims are disputed. If the transferor is the obligor of an outstanding issue of bonds, debentures or the like as to which there is an indenture trustee, the list of creditors need include only the name and address of the indenture trustee and the aggregate outstanding principal amount of the issue.

(3) Responsibility for the completeness and accuracy of the list of creditors rests on the transferor, and the transfer is not rendered ineffective by errors or omissions therein unless the transferee is shown to have had knowledge.

Amended by Laws 1963, Ch. 1003, eff. Sept. 27, 1964.

N.Y. Commission Comments

The Department of State has been specified in subsection (1)(c) of Section 6–104 as the public office where lists of creditors and schedules of property transferred may be filed.

New York Annotations

(1) This is declaratory of the New York statute. The term "ineffective", although more precise, can be equated with "void" as used in Personal Property Law, § 44. "Void" is not given a literal meaning, i.e., of no effect except as between the parties. Schwartz v. A. J. Armstrong Co., Inc., 179 F. 2d 766 (2d Cir. 1950); City of New York v. Johnson, 137 F.2d 163 (2d Cir. 1943). The sanctions for noncompliance are discussed at the end of the annotations to this Article.

(a) This is in substantial *accord* with the New York statute. Personal Property Law, § 44.

(b) This is, for the most part, new. Personal Property Law, § 44, requires the transferor, rather than the parties, to "make and deliver to the purchaser, transferee or assignee a full and detailed inventory, showing the quantity and, so far as possible with the exercise of reasonable diligence, the cost price to the seller, transferor, or assignor of each article to be included in the sale." The Code requirement of a schedule sufficient to identify the property is less demanding.

(c) This is new in part. The list and schedule must be filed or be available for examination by the creditors during the short period of limitations provided in Section 6–110 "to aid in carrying out the policies of the Uniform Fraudulent Conveyance Act and of the Bankruptcy Act." No filing requirements are contained in the Bulk Sales Act although Personal Property Law, § 44, calls for retention of the inventory for ninety days.

(2) This is new to the extent that it adds to "creditors" persons "who are known to the transferor to assert claims against him even though such claims are disputed"; and also insofar as it requires listing of the amount due "when known." Under the New York statute one is not a creditor if the amount of the debt is not liquidated.

Wolfe v. Bellfair Hat Co., Inc., 47 N.Y.S.2d 908 (1944); Borenstein v. Buffalo Hat Co., Inc., 33 N.Y.S. 60 (1942). See annotation to Section 6–109.

(3) New to the statute, but declaratory of the New York law. Klein v. Schwartz, 128 N.Y.S.2d 177 (1953); Carl Ahlers, Inc. v. Dingott, 173 Misc. 873, 18 N.Y.S.2d 434 (1940); Mascus v. Knitzer, 168 Misc. 9, 4 N.Y.S.2d 308 (1938). See also, Willner Butter & Egg Corp. v. Roth, 192 Misc. 970, 83 N.Y.S.2d 16 (1948), wherein an omitted creditor was held not entitled to relief where the buyer, without actual knowledge of any creditors of the seller, obtained the seller's affidavit listing his creditors, and provided for payment of those creditors.

Official Uniform Comment

Prior Uniform Statutory Provision: None.

Purposes:

1. The section describes the information that must be compiled and kept available to creditors on all bulk transfers subject to this Article except those made by sale at auction. Additional requirements for particular kinds of transfers are stated in the succeeding Sections (6–105 through 6–107). The section on auction sales (Section 6–108) imposes similar requirements, but on different people and with a different sanction.

2. Except for the accuracy of the list of creditors, the sanction for non-compliance with the present section is that the transfer is ineffective against creditors of the transferor. The creditors referred to are those holding claims based on transactions or events occurring before the transfer (Section 6–109). Any such creditor or creditors may therefore disregard the transfer and levy on the goods as still belonging to the transferor, or a receiver representing them can take them by whatever procedure the local law provides. But it follows also that if the debts of the transferor are paid as they mature disregard of the requirements of the section creates no liability. And a defect can always be cured by paying off the unpaid creditors.

3. The sanction for the accuracy of the list of creditors is the criminal law of the state relative to false swearing, made applicable by subsection (2).

Cross References:

Point 1: Sections 6–105 through 6–108.
Point 2: Section 6–109.

Definitional Cross References:

"Bulk transfer." Section 6–102.
"Creditor." Section 1–201 and 6–109.
"Party." Section 1–201.
"Person." Section 1–201.
"Signed." Section 1–201.

Section 6–105. Notice to Creditors.

In addition to the requirements of the preceding section, any bulk transfer subject to this Article except one made by auction sale (Section 6–108) is ineffective against any creditor of the transferor unless at least ten days before he takes possession of the goods or pays for them, whichever happens first, the transferee gives notice of the transfer in the manner and to the persons hereafter provided (Section 6–107).

New York Annotations

This section is substantially in *accord* with Personal Property Law, § 44. Both provide for a ten-day notice to creditors. The Code removes an ambiguity by adding the language "whichever happens first" in requiring notice ten days before a transfer of possession or payment.

Historical Note: By the adoption of the possession or payment test and by the definition of "notice" in Section 1–201(26), the objections of the Law Revision Commission to this section have been met. (1956 Recommendations, p. 188; Excerpts, p. 438.)

Official Uniform Comment

Prior Uniform Statutory Provision: None.

Purposes:

1. This section is the heart of the Article. It requires notice to creditors of all bulk transfers subject to the Article, except those made by auction sale. The contents of the notice, the persons to whom it must be given, and the manner of giving it are stated in Section 6–107. The section on auction sales (Section 6–108) also calls for notice, but by a different person and with a different sanction.

2. The notice in all cases must be given ten days in advance. See Points 3 and 4 to Section 6–101.

3. The sanction for noncompliance with the section is that the transfer is ineffective against creditors. Comment 2 to Section 6–104 applies.

Cross References:

Point 1: Sections 6–107 and 6–108.
Point 2: Points 3 and 4 to Section 6–101.
Point 3: Comment 2 to Section 6–104.

Definitional Cross References:

"Bulk transfer." Section 6–102.
"Creditor." Sections 1–201 and 6–109.

Section 6–106. Application of the Proceeds.

N.Y. Commission Comments

Optional Section 6–106, relating to application of the proceeds, has been omitted in the New York Code. To keep the numbering of Sections consistent with the 1958 and 1962 Official Texts, the remaining sections of the Article have not been renumbered.

Section 6–107. The Notice.

(1) The notice to creditors (Section 6–105) shall state:

(a) that a bulk transfer is about to be made; and

(b) the names and business addresses of the transferor and transferee, and all other business names and addresses used by the transferor within three years last past so far as known to the transferee; and

(c) whether or not all the debts of the transferor are to be paid in full as they fall due as a result of the transaction, and if so, the address to which creditors should send their bills.

(2) If the debts of the transferor are not to be paid in full as they fall due or if the transferee is in doubt on that point then the notice shall state further:

(a) the location and general description of the property to be transferred and the estimated total of the transferor's debts;

(b) the address where the schedule of property and list of creditors (Section 6–104) may be inspected;

(c) whether the transfer is to pay existing debts and if so the amount of such debts and to whom owing; and

(d) whether the transfer is for new consideration and if so the amount of such consideration and the time and place of payment.

(3) The notice in any case shall be delivered personally or sent by registered or certified mail to all the persons shown on the list of creditors furnished by the transferor (Section 6–104) and to all other persons who are known to the transferee to hold or assert claims against the transferor, but, if the transferor is the obligor of an outstanding issue of bonds, debendtures or the like as to which is an indenture trustee, no notice need be delivered or sent to holders of the bonds, debentures or the like.

Amended by Laws 1963, Ch. 1003, eff. Sept. 27, 1964.

N.Y. Commission Comments

Optional paragraph (e) of subsection (2) of Section 6–107: "(e) if for new consideration the time and place where creditors of the transferor are to file their claims." has been omitted in the New York Code.

In addition, L. 1963, c. 1003, added "but if the transferor * * * debentures or the like" at the end of subsection (3) of Section 6–107, as it appears in the 1958 and 1962 Official Texts and as enacted in New York in 1962, to conform to the amendment of subsection (2) of Section 6–104 of the 1958 Official Text by the Permanent Editorial Board 1962 Report, incorporated in the New York Code by L. 1963 c. 1003.

New York Annotations

This section, in part, is new. It provides in subsection (1) and (2) for two alternative forms of notice, depending upon whether the transferor's debts are to be paid in full or the transferee is in doubt on that point. No such distinction exists in the prior statute.

Subsection (3), dealing with the method by which the notice is to be communicated to creditors, is substantially declaratory of the prior statute. The requirement that such notice shall be sent to any person known to the transferee to hold claims against the transferor is in accord with the prior statute. See Goros v. T. & F. Snack Bar, Inc., 145 N.Y.S.2d 582 (1955).

Official Uniform Comment

Prior Uniform Statutory Provision: None.

Purposes:

1. This section specifies the contents of the notice to be given on all transfers covered by Section 6–105 (that is, all transfers subject to the Article except those made by auction sale) and the manner in which it is to be given.

2. Under the section, if the debts of the transferor are to be paid in full as they fall due, a short form of notice is provided. This facilitates honest and solvent transactions.

3. If the transfer is by auction sale Section 6–108 applies.

4. Subsection (2)(e) is a corollary of Section 6–106 and should be omitted if that section is. See note to Section 6–106.

Cross References:

Point 1: Section 6–105.
Point 3: Section 6–108.
Point 4: Note to Section 6–106.

Definitional Cross References:

"Bulk transfer." Section 6–105.
"Creditor." Sections 1–201 and 6–109.
"Person." Section 1–201.

Section 6–108. Auction Sales; "Auctioneer."

(1) A bulk transfer is subject to this Article even though it is by sale at auction, but only in the manner and with the results stated in this section.

(2) The transferor shall furnish a list of his creditors and assist in the preparation of a schedule of the property to be sold, both prepared as before stated (Section 6–104).

(3) The person or persons other than the transferor who direct, control or are responsible for the auction are collectively called the "auctioneer." The auctioneer shall:

(a) receive and retain the list of creditors and prepare and retain the schedule of property for the period stated in this Article (Section 6–104); and

(b) give notice of the auction personally or by registered or certified mail at least ten days before it occurs to all persons shown on the list of creditors and to all other persons who are known to him to hold or assert claim against the transferor, but, if the transferor is the obligor of an outstanding issue of bonds, debentures or the like as to which there is an indenture trustee, no notice need be delivered or sent to holders of the bonds, debentures or the like.

(4) Failure of the auctioneer to perform any of these duties does not affect the validity of the sale or the title of the purchasers, but if the auctioneer knows that the auction constitutes a bulk transfer such failure renders the auctioneer liable to the creditors of the transferor as a class for the sums owing to them from the transferor up to but not exceeding the net proceeds of the auction. If the auctioneer consists of several persons their liability is joint and several.

Amended by Laws 1963, Ch. 1003, eff. Sept. 27, 1964.

N.Y. Commission Comments

Optional paragraph (c) of section (3) of Section 6–108: "(c) assure that the net proceeds of the auction are applied as provided in this Article (Section 6–106)." has been omitted in the New York Code.

In addition, L. 1963, c. 1003, added "but if the transferor * * * debentures or the like" at the end of paragraph (b) of subsection (3) of Section 6–108, as it appears in the 1958 and 1962 Official Texts and as enacted in New York in 1962, to conform to the amendment of subsection (2) of Section 6–104 of the 1958 Official Text by the Permanent Editorial Board 1962 Report, incorporated in the New York Code by L. 1963, c. 1003.

New York Annotations

This section makes Article 6 applicable to sales at auction, and is new. Auction sales have been held to be not within the Bulk Sales Law. Wolfe v. Bellfair Hat Co., Inc., 47 N.Y.S.2d 908 (1944); Lowe v. Fairberg, 245 App. Div. 731, 280 N.Y.S. 615, aff'd, 270 N.Y. 590, 1 N.E.2d 344 (1936). The definition of "auctioneer" in subsection (3) is broad enough to include the transferor's lawyer if he directs, controls, or is responsible for the auction.

Subsection (4) is the only provision in the Article which imposes a sanction for non-compliance specifically and in defined terms. The validity of the auction sale may not be affected by non-compliance. The auctioneer, and those who by definition are associated with him in joint and several liability, may be accountable to the "creditors . . . as a class", but such liability is limited to the net proceeds of the auction.

Historical Note: The changes in subsection (4) relieve the auctioneer of the stated liability when he does know that the auction constitutes a bulk sale. It appears that in some cases, as for instance when the goods are simply received on consignment for sale, he may not know. (1956 Recommendations, p. 191; Excerpts, p. 439.)

Official Uniform Comment

Prior Uniform Statutory Provision: None.

Purposes:

1. The section is intended to make appropriate application of the requirements of this Article to auction sales. It is clear that the provisions of the four previous sections in their literal form cannot be applied directly to an auction, since neither the price nor the identity of the purchaser or purchasers can be known until the sale occurs. But it is equally clear that if auctions were excluded entirely from the transfers covered by this Article the way would be open to a debtor to carry out a bulk transfer of his property without notice to his creditors and without any duty upon anyone to see to the application of the proceeds. The section attempts to meet this situation by imposing the obligations stated in the section upon the persons there described.

2. Since the obligation to give advance notice, etc., cannot rest upon bidders at an auction it is clear that the sale must be effective so far as they are concerned whether or not the section is complied with. Subsection (4) therefore states a sanction which does not affect the purchasers. Notice that the sanction applies only "if the auctioneer knows that the auction constitutes a bulk transfer." No doubt in some cases, as for instance when goods are simply received on consignment for sale, he may not know.

3. Subsection (3)(c) is a corollary of Section 6–106 and should be omitted if that section is. See note to that section.

Cross References:

Point 1: Sections 6–104 through 6–107.
Point 2: Sections 6–104 through 6–107.
Point 3: Section 6–106 and Note thereto.

Definitional Cross References:

"Bulk transfer." Section 6–102.
"Creditor." Sections 1–201 and 6–109.
"Person." Section 1–201.
"Purchaser." Section 1–201.

Section 6–109. What Creditors Protected.

(1) The creditors of the transferor mentioned in this Article are those holding claims based on transactions or events occurring before the bulk transfer, but creditors who become such after notice to creditors is given (Sections 6–105 and 6–107) are not entitled to notice.

N.Y. Commission Comments

Optional subsection (2): "(2) Against the aggregate obligation imposed by the provisions of this Article concerning the application of the proceeds (Section 6–106 and subsection (3)(c) of 6–108) the transferee or auctioneer is entitled to credit for sums paid to particular creditors of the transferor, not exceeding the sums believed in good faith at the time of the payment to be properly payable to such creditors." has been omitted in the New York Code.

New York Annotations

The New York statute contains no provision like the second clause of Section 6–109(1), dispensing with notice to persons whose claims arise after the notice is given. To the extent that this section defines the creditors who are protected as those existing at the time of the bulk transfer, it is declaratory of the New York law. Modern Truck Renting Service Corp. v. Admiration Coat, Apron and Towel Supply Co., Inc., 107 N.Y.S.2d 253, aff'd, 279 App.Div. 754, 109 N.Y.S.2d 180 (1951); American Mercantile Co., Inc. v. Wohlmuth, 280 App.Div. 571, 116 N.Y.S.2d 71 (1952); Costello v. Emmick, 122 Misc. 114, 203 N.Y.S. 123 (1923). But to the extent–as suggested in 16 Law & Contemp.Prob. 267, 280 (1951)–that the word "claims" is broad enough to include "claims whether are in tort or contract, are liquidated or unliquidated, are secured or unsecured, are contingent or fixed, are presently due or not," this section changes the law. See, 3 Williston, Sales, Sec. 643a (1948). Comment 1 states that creditors with unliquidated claims are within the protected group. This is consistent with the requirements in Section 6–104 that all listed creditors must include all persons "known to the transferor to assert claims against him even though such claims are disputed"; and in Section 6–107 that all listed persons must receive notice of the transfer. Under the New York law the protected creditor must be one who has a fixed debt, capable of being definitely ascertained, i.e., an existing obligation liquidated in amount. Wolfe v. Bellfair Hat Co., Inc., 47 N.Y.S.2d 908 (1944) (breach of contract of employment); S. Silberstein & Sons, Inc., v. Cohen,

222 App.Div. 249, 225 N.Y.S. 549 (1927). Holders of contingent unliquidated claims are not within the statute. Adams-Flanigan Co. v. Baselice, 180 App.Div. 342, 167 N.Y.S. 948, aff'd mem., 228 N.Y. 542, 126 N.E. 898 (1920)(holder's claim against tenant under lease where there was no breach prior to bulk sale). A liquidated unmatured claim (holder of unmatured note gainst the maker)will bring the creditor within the protected class under prior law. Terris v. Julian Food Corp., 247 App.Div. 799, 286 N.Y.S. 146, aff'd, 272 N.Y. 650, 5 N.E.2d 376 (1936); Himmelstein v. Bach, 261 App.Div. 57, 24 N.Y.S.2d 696 (1941). Compare § 1 of the Uniform Fraudulent Conveyances Act, Debtor and Creditor Law, § 270.

Official Uniform Comment

Prior Uniform Statutory Provision: None.

Purposes:

1. Subsection (1) identifies the creditors who may have rights under the various provisions of this Article. The claims referred to of course include liquidated claims.
2. Subsection (2) gives the transferee or auctioneer appropriate credit for honest payments to particular creditors. If Section 6–106 is omitted this subsection should be also. See note to that section.

Cross References:

Point 1: Sections 6–104 through 6–108.
Point 2: Section 6–106 and Note thereto.

Definitional Cross References:

"Auctioneer." Section 6–108.
"Bulk transfer." Section 6–102.
"Creditors." Section 1–201.
"Good faith." Section 1–201.

Section 6–110. Subsequent Transfers.

When the title of a transferee to property is subject to a defect by reason of his non-compliance with the requirements of this Article, then:

(1) a purchaser of any of such property from such transferee who pays no value or who takes with notice of such non-compliance takes subject to such defect, but

(2) a purchaser for value in good faith and without such notice takes free of such defect.

New York Annotations

This provision is new and the question has not been litigated under the Bulk Sales Act. However, in protecting a subsequent good faith purchaser for value without notice of any non-compliance, the Code adopts the generally accepted principle in respect of fraudulent conveyances that a transferee, holding property as a result of a fraudulent conveyance, can pass unimpaired title to a bona fide purchaser for value without notice. Anderson v. Roberts, 18 Johns. 515 (1820); Heroy v. Kerr, 2 Abb.Dec. 359,

41 N.Y. (2 Keyes) 582 (1866). See also, § 9 of the Uniform Fraudulent Conveyance Act, Debtor and Creditor Law § 278.

Historical Note: Revision of the details of definition of the kind of purchaser protected, and the addition of a definition of value in Section 1-201(44) met the Law Revision Commission's suggestions. (1956 Recommendations, p. 191; Excerpts, p. 440.)

Official Uniform Comment

Prior Uniform Statutory Provision: None.

Purposes:

1. The section deals with subsequent transfers by the transferee.
2. The second transfer may of course be a "bulk transfer" subject to this Article. Whether it is or not will depend on its own character under sections 6-102 and 6-103.

Cross References:

Point 2: Sections 6-102 and 6-103.

Definitional Cross References:

"Good faith." Section 1-201.
"Notice." Section 1-201.
"Purchaser." Section 1-201.
"Value." Section 1-201.

Section 6-111. Limitation of Actions and Levies.

No action under this Article shall be brought nor levy made more than six months after the date on which the transferee took possession of the goods unless the transfer has been concealed. If the transfer has been concealed, actions may be brought or levies made within six months after its discovery.

New York Annotations

This section is new. It has been held in New York that there is no short statute of limitations fixed for maintaining an action to have the proceeds held for the benefit of creditors on the ground that the notice required by the Bulk Sales Act had not been given, Ogdensburg Wholesale Mercantile Co., Inc. v. Curry 148 Misc. 806, 266 N.Y.S. 222, aff'd 241 App.Div. 786, 270 N.Y.S. 1018 (1934). In addition, the three-year period of limitation in Civil Practice Act, § 49(3), where the action is based upon a statute which provides a penalty or forfeiture, has been held to be inapplicable. Blatt v. Eakin, 166 F.Supp. 4 (E.D.N.Y. 1958). There is also a three-year statutory period for an action against an executor, administrator, or receiver in Civil Practice Act, § 49(5); but it is doubtful if this applies to a suit upon which the transferee becomes the receiver. Personal Property Law, § 44(3). Thus, it appears that the appropriate limitation is the ten-year period provided under Civil Practice Act, § 53, which has been held to be applicable to actions to set aside fraudulent conveyances. Buttles v. Smith, 281 N.Y. 226, 22 N.E.2d 350 (1939); Hearn 45 St. Corp. v. Jano, 283 N.Y. 139, 27 N.E.2d 814 (1940). The period of limitation under this ten-year section begins to run from the time the cause of action accrues, not from the time of its discovery as under the Code. Compare Civil Practice Act, § 48(5).

Historical Note: The explicit exclusion of levy of execution on the goods after the short period of limitation stems from a suggestion of the Law Revision Commission. (Excerpts. p. 440; Recommendations, p. 192.)

Official Uniform Comment

Prior Uniform Statutory Provision: None.

Purposes:

1. This Article imposes unusual obligations on buyers of property. A short statute of limitations is therefore appropriate.

2. The main sanction for non-compliance with the Article is that the transfer "is ineffective against any creditor of the transferor." Sections 6–104, 6–105. This means, e.g., that a judgement creditor of the transferor may levy execution on the property. See Comment 2 to Section 6–104.

In such a case, which may be expected to be frequent, no "action under this Article" will be necessary. The action will have been brought and prosecuted to judgement on whatever the claim was. The only thing done "under this Article" will be the levy and resulting sale.

The short statute of limitations is therefore made applicable to the levies as well as actions. "Levy", which is not a defined term in the Code, should be read broadly as including not only levies of execution proper but also attachment, garnishment, trustee process, receivership, or whatever proceeding, under the state's practice, is used to apply a debtor's property to payment of his debts.

Definitional Cross References:

"Action." Section 1–201.

Section 6–112. Liability of Transferee for Sales and Compensating Use Taxes.

For provisions of the tax law with respect to transfers in bulk, including but not limited to provisions relating to notice requirements and liability of a transferee for sales and compensating use taxes due and owing by a transferor or other persons, see subdivision (c) of section eleven hundred forty-one of such law.

Added by Laws 1979, Ch. 231, eff. June 14, 1979.

ARTICLE 7

WAREHOUSE RECEIPTS, BILLS OF LADING AND OTHER DOCUMENTS OF TITLE

PART 1

GENERAL

PART 2

WAREHOUSE RECEIPTS: SPECIAL PROVISIONS

PART 3

BILLS OF LADING: SPECIAL PROVISIONS

PART 4

WAREHOUSE RECEIPTS AND BILLS OF LADING: GENERAL OBLIGATIONS

PART 5

WAREHOUSE RECEIPTS AND BILLS OF LADING: NEGOTIATION AND TRANSFER

PART 6

WAREHOUSE RECEIPTS AND BILLS OF LADING: MISCELLANEOUS PROVISIONS

PART 1

GENERAL

Section 7–101. Short Title.

This Article shall be known and may be cited as Uniform Commercial Code–Documents of Title.

New York Annotations

Scope: This Article consolidates and revises provisions of three Uniform Acts which appear in the New York Statutes as follows:

(1) Uniform Warehouse Receipts Act (General Business Law, §§ 90 et seq.);

(2) Uniform Bills of Lading Act (Personal Property Law, §§ 187 et seq.); and

(3) Uniform Sales Act (Personal Property Law, §§ 82–158).

All three of these statutes would be repealed by the Code except for criminal provisions which are not contained in the Code. Few basic changes are made. The general scope of Article 7 is quite like that of the first two acts listed. Article 7 is also designed to replace §§ 27 through 40 of the Uniform Sales Act. Those sections are presently in the New York statute (Personal Property Law, §§ 108–121), but a statutory declaration was made that the Sales Act provisions do not repeal or limit the Warehouse Receipts or Bills of Lading statutes (Personal Property Law, § 158).

"Document of Title": The Code definition of "document of title" is substantially the same as that in the Sales Act. It includes warehouse receipts, bills of lading, delivery orders, and other documents treated in the current course of business as evidencing the right to control the goods they cover. Sections 1–201(15); 7–102(1)(e); Personal Property Law, § 156. The Code includes general provisions for all documents of title, a number of special provisions for warehouse receipts and bills of lading, and some specific provisions not found in present law governing delivery orders (Sections 7–102(1)(d), (g), 7–502(1)(d), 7–503(2)), through bills of lading (Section 7–302), destination bills of lading (Section 7–305), and bills of lading issued by freight forwarders (Sections 1–201(6), 7–503(3)).

Applicability: The Federal Government has pre-empted the field of bills of lading in interstate and international shipments, and the enactment of the Code in New York would not alter this fact. (See 49 U.S.C.A. §§ 81 et seq.)

Sources: For a complete treatment of Article 7, see Braucher, Documents of Title (Under the UCC) (1958).

Historical Note: The Law Revision Commission reported, "Article 7 contains a significant change in the concept of 'due negotiation' and some important exceptions to the doctrine of caveat emptor.—Apart from these innovations, Article 7 makes relatively few basic changes in present law." 1956 Report, p. 48. Either during or after the Law Revision study of the Code, twenty-nine of the Article's forty sections were revised or rewritten for clarification. Approximately two-thirds of the Commission's suggestions were followed in whole, or in major part.

Official Uniform Comment

This Article is a consolidation and revision of the Uniform Warehouse Receipts Act and Uniform Bills of Lading Act, and embraces also the provisions of the Uniform Sales Act relating to the negotiation of documents of title. The only substantial omissions of material covered in the previous uniform acts are the criminal provisions found in the Warehouse Receipts and Bills of Lading acts. These criminal provisions are inappropriate to a Commercial Code, and for the most part duplicate portions of the ordinary criminal law relating to frauds.

The Article does not attempt to define the tort liability of bailees, except to hold certain classes of bailees to a minimum standard of reasonable care. For important classes of bailees, liabilities in case of loss, damage or destruction, as well as other legal questions associated with particular documents of title, are governed by federal statutes, international treaties, and in some case regulatory state laws, which supersede the provisions of this Article in case of inconsistency. See Section 7-103.

Section 7-102. Definitions and Index of Definitions.

(1) In this Article, unless the context otherwise requires:

(a) "Bailee" means the person who by a warehouse receipt, bill of lading or other document of title acknowledges possession of goods and contracts to deliver them.

(b) "Consignee" means the person named in a bill to whom or to whose order the bill promises delivery.

(c) "Consignor" means the person named in a bill as the person from whom the goods have been received for shipment.

(d) "Delivery order" means a written order to deliver goods directed to a warehouseman, carrier or other person who in the ordinary course of business issues warehouse receipts or bills of lading.

(e) "Document" means document of title as defined in the general definitions in Article 1 (Section 1-201).

(f) "Goods" means all things which are treated as movable for the purposes of a contract of storage or transportation.

(g) "Issuer" means a bailee who issues a document except that in relation to an unaccepted delivery order it means the person who orders the possessor of goods to deliver. Issuer includes any person for whom an agent or employee purports to act in issuing a document if the agent or employee has real or apparent authority to issue documents, notwithstanding that the issuer received no goods or that the goods were misdescribed or that in any other respect the agent or employee violated his instructions.

(h) "Warehouseman" is a person engaged in the business of storing goods for hire.

(2) Other definitions applying to this Article or to specified Parts thereof, and the sections in which they appear are:

"Duly negotiate." Section 7-501.

"Person entitled under the document." Section 7-403(4).

(3) Definitions in other Articles applying to this Article and the sections in which they appear are:

"Contract for sale." Section 2-106.

"Overseas." Section 2–323.

"Receipt" of goods. Section 2–103.

(4) In addition Article 1 contains general definitions and principles of construction and interpretation applicable throughout this Article.

New York Annotations

(a) "Bailee." This definition goes beyond the concepts of present law by making the issuer of a document of title a bailee without reference to possessory transfer.

(b) "Consignee." Substantially the same definition appears in Personal Property Law. § 239.

(c) "Consignor." *Accord:* Personal Property Law, § 239.

(d) "Delivery order." This term is new to the statutes, although the Uniform Sales Act, § 76 (Personal Property Law, § 156) defines "document of title to goods" as including an "order for delivery of the goods."

(e) "Document." See annotation to Section 7–101.

(f) "Goods." The definition here is narrower than that in Section 2–105 of the Code since the subject matter of a sale may properly include items which are neither stored nor transported, e. g., unborn young of animals; standing timber.

(g) "Issuer." New, but see Personal Property Law, § 209, and General Business Law, §§ 90 and 137.

(h) "Warehouseman." This definition is broader than the present provision of General Business Law, § 142, which limits the term to those lawfully engaged in the business. The Code theory is that a person engaged in the warehousing business should be subject to terms of the statute regardless of the legality of his activity. See Comment 2.

Historical Note: A new definition of "goods" was added as subsection (1)(f), and the related cross-reference to Section 2–501 deleted from subsection (3) at the suggestion of the Law Revision Commission. Subsection (1)(g), formerly (1)(f), was changed to meet the fear, expressed on behalf of the Pennsylvania State Chamber of Commerce, that a person such as a connecting carrier might be held to be a "bailee" and therefore an "issuer" even though it issued no document. As to deletion of the definition of "value" in former subsection (1)(g), see Section 1–201(44). (1956 Recommendations, p. 194; Excerpts, p. 440.)

Official Uniform Comment

Prior Uniform Statutory Provision: Section 76, Uniform Sales Act; Section 58, Uniform Warehouse Receipts Act; Sections 1 and 53, Uniform Bills of Lading Act.

Changes: Applicable definitions from the uniform acts have been consolidated and revised; definition of delivery order is new.

Purposes of Changes and New Matter:

1. "Bailee" was not defined in the old uniform acts. It is used in this Article as a blanket term to designate carriers, warehousemen and others who normally issue documents of title on the basis of goods which they have received. The definition does not, however, require actual possession of the goods. If a bailee acknowledges possession when he does not have it he is bound by sections of this Article which declare the "bailee's" obligations. (See definition of "Issuer" in this section and Sections 7–203 and 7–301 on liability in case of non-receipt.)

2. The definition of warehouse receipt contained in the general definitions section of this Act (Section 1–201) eliminates the requirement of the Uniform Warehouse

Receipts Act that the issuing warehouseman be "lawfully engaged" in business. The warehouseman's compliance with applicable state regulations such as the filing of a bond has no bearing on the substantive issues dealt with in this Article. Certainly the issuer's violations of law should not diminish his responsibility on documents he has put in commercial circulation. The Uniform Warehouse Receipts Act requirement that the warehouseman be engaged "for profit" has also been eliminated in view of the existence of state operated and co-operative warehouses. But it is still essential that the business be storing goods "for hire" (Section 1–201 and this section). A person does not become a warehouseman by storing his own goods.

3. Delivery orders, which were included without qualification in the Uniform Sales Act definition of the document of title, must be treated differently in this consolidation or provisions from the three uniform acts. When a delivery order has been accepted by the bailee it is for practical purposes indistinguishable from a warehouse receipt. Prior to such acceptance there is no basis for imposing obligations on the bailee other than the ordinary obligation of contract which the bailee may have assumed to the depositor of the goods.

Cross References:

Point 1: Sections 7–203 and 7–301.
Point 2: Section 1–201 and 7–203.
See general comment to document of title in Section 1–201.

Definitional Cross References:

"Bill of lading." Section 1–201.
"Contract." Section 1–201.
"Contract for sale." Section 2–106.
"Delivery." Section 1–201.
"Document of title." Section 1–201.
"Person." Section 1–201.
"Purchase." Section 1–201.
"Receipt of goods." Section 2–103.
"Right." Section 1–201.
"Warehouse receipt." Section 1–201.
"Written." Section 1–201.

Section 7–103. Relation of Article to Treaty, Statute, Tariff, Classification or Regulation.

To the extent that any treaty or statute of the United States, regulatory statute of this State or tariff, classification or regulation filed or issued pursuant thereto is applicable, the provisions of this Article are subject thereto.

New York Annotations

Existing legislation dealing generally with warehouse receipts, bills of lading, or other documents has not been interpreted as overruling regulatory requirements concerning specific types of transactions, and this provision makes explicit this rule of construction. The Code provisions are subject to federal statutes such as the Federal Bills of Lading Act (see annotation to Section 7–101, *supra*), the Carriage of Goods by Sea Act (46 U.S.C.A. §§ 1300–1315, regulating ocean bills of lading), and the United States Warehouse Act (7 U.S.C.A. §§ 241–273, regulating federally licensed warehouses). The Code would not affect such New York statutes as Alcoholic

Beverage Control Law, §§ 90, 96, 96-a, and 102, or Agriculture and Markets Law, §§ 16(15), 20, and 258–a. Nor would the Code affect Public Service Law, §§ 63–1 through 63–bb, regulating motor carriers transporting property for compensation. See Stepnoski v. Feinberg, 7 A.D.2d 777, 179 N.Y.S.2d 908 (1958).

Similarly the Code would not affect the provisions of § 365 of the Penal Law requiring a carrier to take up a bill of lading, either order or straight, upon delivery of the goods where the document is not marked "not negotiable." Colgate v. Pennsylvania Co., 102 N.Y. 120, 6 N.E.2d 114 (1886); Mairs v. B. & O. R. Co., 175 N.Y. 409, 67 N.E. 901 (1903).

Official Uniform Comment

Prior Uniform Statutory Provision: None.

Purposes:

1. To make clear what would of course be true without the Section, that applicable Federal statutes (such as those fixing or authorizing a commission to fix rates and prescribe services, authorizing different charges for goods of different values, and limiting liability for loss to the declared value on which the charge was based) are not affected by the Article and are controlling on the matters which they cover. Notice that the reference is not only to such statutes, but to tariffs, classifications and regulations filed or issued pursuant to them.

Cross References:

Sections 7–201, 7–202, 7–204, 7–206, 7–309, 7–401, and 7–403.

Definitional Cross References:

"Bill of lading." Section 1–201.

Section 7–104. Negotiable and Non-Negotiable Warehouse Receipt, Bill of Lading or Other Document of Title.

(1) A warehouse receipt, bill of lading or other document of title is negotiable

(a) if by its terms the goods are to be delivered to bearer or to the order of a named person; or

(b) where recognized in overseas trade, if it runs to a named person or assigns.

(2) Any other document is non-negotiable. A bill of lading in which it is stated that the goods are consigned to a named person is not made negotiable by a provision that the goods are to be delivered only against a written order signed by the same or another named person.

New York Annotations

Generally in *accord,* Personal Property Law, §§ 108 and 188, General Business Law, § 92. The Warehouse Receipts and Sales Acts provide for "bearer" documents of title (General Business Law, § 92, and Personal Property Law, § 108). The Bills of Lading Act does not (Personal Property Law, § 188). The Code eliminates the discrepancy, and provides for bearer bills of lading and bearer warehouse receipts.

Although the Code sets out the phrase "Non-Negotiable Bill of Lading" as an example in the definition of "conspicuous" in Section 1–201(10), the requirement of present law that issuers plainly mark non-negotiable documents as such is omitted. (Personal Property Law, § 194, and General Business Law, § 94.) Also omitted without apparent change in the law, is the provision stating that such a marking does not impair the negotiability of a document which runs to order or bearer. (Personal Property Law, §§ 111, 191, and General Business Law, § 92.) See Gubelman v. Panama Railway Co., 192 App.Div. 165, 182 N.Y.S. 403, aff'd 232 N.Y. 566, 134 N.E. 574 (1921).

Unlike existing law, the Code provides for negotiable documents running to "X or assigns" where these are recognized in overseas trade.

Historical Note: Supp. No. 1 changed subsection (1)(a) to conform to the style in setting formal requirements in such sections as Section 3–110, and to avoid the possibility that a document might be held negotiable which provides for delivery to order or bearer only upon written instructions of a named person. The change in subsection (2) meets the desire expressed on behalf of the Pennsylvania State Chamber of Commerce for further clarification on the same point. (1956 Recommendations, p. 195.)

Official Uniform Comment

Prior Uniform Statutory Provision: Sections 27 and 76, Uniform Sales Act; Sections 2, 3, 4, and 5, Uniform Warehouse Receipts Act; Sections 2, 3, 4, 5 and 53, Uniform Bills of Lading Act

Changes: Consolidated and rewritten.

Purposes of Changes:

This Article deals with a class of commercial paper representing commodities in storage of transportation. This "commodity paper" is to be distinguished from what might be called "money paper" dealt with in the Article of this Act on Commercial Paper (Article 3) and "investment paper" dealt with in the Article of this Act on Investment Securities (Article 8). The class of "commodity paper" is designated "document of title" following the terminology of the Uniform Sales Act Section 76. Section 1–201. The distinctions between negotiable and nonnegotiable documents in this section makes the most important subclassification employed in the Article, in that the holder of negotiable documents may acquire more rights than his transferor had (See Section 7–502).

A document of title is negotiable only if it satisfies this section. "Deliverable upon proper indorsement and surrender of this receipt" will not render a document negotiable. Bailees often include such provisions as a means of insuring return of nonnegotiable receipts for record purposes. Such language may be regarded as insistence by the bailee upon a particular kind of receipt in connection with delivery of goods. Subsections (1)(a) and (b) make it clear that a document is not negotiable which provides for delivery to order or bearer only if written to that effect are given by a named person.

Cross References:

Section 7–502.

Definitional Cross References:

"Bearer." Section 1–201.
"Bill of lading." Section 1–201.
"Delivery." Section 1–201.
"Document of title." Section 1–201.
"Overseas." Section 2–323.

"Person." Section 1–201.
"Warehouse receipt." Section 1–201.

Section 7–105. Construction Against Negative Implication.

The omission from either Part 2 or Part 3 of this Article of a provision corresponding to a provision made in the other Part does not imply that a corresponding rule of law is not applicable.

New York Annotations

This is new. See Section 1–103.

Historical Note: Supp. No. 1 inserted this section to avoid any impairment, for example, of any common-law right of indemnity a warehouseman may have corresponding to Section 7–301(3), or of any contractual security interest a carrier might have corresponding to Section 7–209(2). (1956 Recommendations, p. 196.)

Official Uniform Comment

Prior Uniform Statutory Provision: None.

Purposes:

To avoid any impairment, for example, of any common-law right of indemnity a warehouseman may have corresponding to Section 7–301(5), or of any contractual security interest a carrier might have corresponding to Section 7–209(2).

Cross References: Parts 2 and 3 of Article 7.

PART 2

WAREHOUSE RECEIPTS: SPECIAL PROVISIONS

Section 7–201. Who May Issue a Warehouse Receipt; Storage Under Government Bond.

(1) A warehouse receipt may be issued by any warehouseman.

(2) Where goods including distilled spirits and agricultural commodities are stored under a statute requiring a bond against withdrawal or a license for the issuance of receipts in the nature of warehouse receipts, a receipt issued for the goods has like effect as a warehouse receipt even though issued by a person who is the owner of the goods and is not a warehouseman.

New York Annotations

(1) *Accord:* General Business Law, § 90.

(2) This is new. See Section 7–401(d).

Historical Note: Subsection (2) was added to cover receipts issued by the owner for whiskey or other goods stored in bonded warehouses under such statutes as 26 U.S.C. chapter 26. Limitations on the transfer of the receipts, and criminal sanctions for violations of such limitations are not impaired. Section 7–103. Compare Section 7–401(d) on the liability of the issuer in such cases. (1956 Recommendations, p. 196.)

Official Uniform Comment

Prior Uniform Statutory Provision: Section 1, Uniform Warehouse Receipts Acts.

Changes: Provision added to cover storage under government bond or under licensing statute.

Purposes:

It is not intended by reenactment of subsection (1) to repeal any provisions of special licensing or other statutes regulating who may become a warehouseman. See Section 10–103. Subsection (2) covers receipts issued by the owner for whiskey or other goods stored in bonded warehouses under such statutes as 26 U.S.C. Chapter 26. Limitations on the transfer of the receipts and criminal sanctions for violation of such limitations are not impaired. Section 7–103. Compare Section 7–401(d) on the liability of the issuer in such cases.

Cross References:

Sections 7–103, 7–401, 10–103.

Definitional Cross References:

"Warehouse receipt." Section 1–201.
"Warehouseman." Section 7–102.

Section 7–202. Form of Warehouse Receipt; Essential Terms; Optional Terms.

(1) A warehouse receipt need not be in any particular form.

(2) Unless a warehouse receipt embodies within its written or printed terms each of the following, the warehouseman is liable for damages caused by the omission to a person injured thereby:

(a) the location of the warehouse where the goods are stored;

(b) the date of issue of the receipt;

(c) the consecutive number of the receipt;

(d) a statement whether the goods received will be delivered to the bearer, to a specified person, or to a specified person or his order;

(e) the rate of storage and handling charges, except that where goods are stored under a field warehousing arrangement a statement of that fact is sufficient on a non-negotiable receipt;

(f) a description of the goods or of the packages containing them;

(g) the signature of the warehouseman, which may be made by his authorized agent;

(h) if the receipt is issued for goods of which the warehouseman is owner, either solely or jointly or in common with others, the fact of such ownership; and

(i) a statement of the amount of advances made and of liabilities incurred for which the warehouseman claims a lien or security interest (Section 7–209). If the precise amount of such advances made or of such liabilities incurred is, at the time of the issue of the receipt, unknown to the warehouseman or to his agent who issues it, a statement of the fact that advances have been made or liabilities incurred and the purpose thereof is sufficient.

(3) A warehouseman may insert in his receipt any other terms which are not contrary to the provisions of this Act and do not impair his obligation of delivery (Section 7–403) or his duty of care (Section 7–204). Any contrary provisions shall be ineffective.

New York Annotations

This section is generally in accord with General Business Law, § 91. However, the Code here imposes liability on a warehouseman for damages caused by the omission of required terms from any warehouse receipt, while present law imposes such liability only when such a term is absent from a negotiable receipt. (General Business Law, § 91). Further, the reference to handling charges and the exception of field warehousing in subsection (2)(e) are new. The same is true of the reference to "security interest" in subsection (2)(i).

Historical Note: Supp. No. 1 changed the preamble of subsection (2) by substituting "damages" for "any loss", to avoid the possibility of change in well-established rules of damages. See also Sections 7–204(1), 7–210(4), 7–308(3), and 7–402. A further change followed a recommendation of the Law Revision Commission that an exception be added to subsection (2)(e) for the complex rate arrangements of field warehouse companies. (1956 Recommendations, p. 197; Excerpts, p. 442.)

Official Uniform Comment

Prior Uniform Statutory Provision: Section 2, Uniform Warehouse Receipts Act.

Changes: Exemption for field warehouse receipts added in subsection (2).

Purposes:

To make clear that the formal requirements of the Uniform Warehouse Receipts Act are continued but not to displace particular legislation requiring other or different specifications of form. See Sections 7–103 and 10–103. This section does not require that a receipt be issued but states formal requirements for those which are issued.

Cross References:

Sections 7–103 and 10–103.

Definitional Cross References:

"Bearer." Section 1–201.
"Delivery." Section 1–201.
"Goods." Section 7–102.
"Person." Section 1–201.
"Security interest." Section 1–201.
"Term." Section 1–201.
"Warehouse receipt." Section 7–102.
"Warehouseman." Section 7–102.

"Written." Section 1–201.

Section 7–203. Liability for Non-Receipt or Misdescription.

A party to or purchaser for value in good faith of a document of title other than a bill of lading relying in either case upon the description therein of the goods may recover from the issuer damages caused by the non-receipt or misdescription of the goods, except to the extend that the document conspicuously indicates that the issuer does not know whether any part or all of the goods in fact were received or conform to the description, as where the description is in terms of marks or labels or kind, quantity or condition, or the receipt or description is qualified by "contents, condition and quality unknown", "said to contain" or the like, if such indication be true, or the party or purchaser otherwise has notice.

New York Annotations

This section generally *accords* with General Business Law, § 106. The Code section adds a requirements that the notation of the issuer's lack of knowledge on the receipt must be "conspicuous." See Section 1–201(10). Further, the Code makes the issuer liable to a "party to or purchaser for value in good faith of a document", while under existing law the issuer is liable to any "holder", i.e. one who has "possession of such receipt and a right of property therein." (General Business Law, § 142.)

Historical Note: Supp. No. 1 inserted provision for "contents, condition and quality unknown", a form of words very widely used in standard forms of warehouse receipts. (1956 Recommendations, p. 198.)

Official Uniform Comment

Prior Uniform Statutory Provision: Section 20, Uniform Warehouse Receipts Act.

Changes: New Section confined to problem of non-receipt and misdescription.

Purposes of Changes and New Matter:

This section is a simplified restatement of existing law as to the method by which a bailee may avoid responsibility for the accuracy of descriptions which are made by or in reliance upon information furnished by the depositor. The issuer is liable on documents issued by an agent, contrary to his instructions of his principal, without receiving goods. No disclaimer of the latter liability is permitted.

Cross References:

Sections 7–301 and 7–203.

Definitional Cross References:

"Conspicuous." Section 1–201.
"Document." Section 7–102.
"Document of title." Section 1–201.
"Goods." Section 7–102.
"Issuer." Section 7–102.
"Notice." Section 1–201.

"Party." Section 1–201.
"Purchaser." Section 1–201.
"Receipt of goods." Section 2–103.
"Value." Section 1–201.

Section 7–204. Duty of Care; Contractual Limitation of Warehouseman's Liability.

(1) A warehouseman is liable for damages for loss of or injury to the goods caused by his failure to exercise such care in regard to them as a reasonably careful man would exercise under like circumstances but unless otherwise agreed he is not liable for damages which could not have been avoided by the exercise of such care.

(2) Damages may be limited by a term in the warehouse receipt or storage agreement limiting the amount of liability in case of loss or damage, and setting forth a specific liability per article or item, or value per unit of weight, beyond which the warehouseman shall not be liable; provided, however, that such liability may on written request of the bailor at the time of signing such storage agreement or within a reasonable time after receipt of the warehouse receipt be increased on part or all of the goods thereunder, in which event increased rates may be charged based on such increased valuation, but that no such increase shall be permitted contrary to a lawful limitation of liability contained in the warehouseman's tariff, if any. No such limitation is effective with respect to the warehouseman's liability for conversion to his own use.

(3) Reasonable provisions as to the time and manner of presenting claims and instituting actions based on the bailment may be included in the warehouse receipt or tariff.

N.Y. Commission Comments

Subsection (4) of the Official Text [(4) This section does not impair or repeal * * *.] has been omitted from the New York Code as inapplicable.

New York Annotations

Subsection (1) is generally in *accord* with General Business Law, § 107, although the standard of care in the Code is "a reasonably careful manin like circumstances" as compared with the standard of "a reasonably careful owner" in the present law.

Subsection (2) is new to the statutes and deals with the question of enforcing contract provisions limiting damages in case of loss or damage to the goods. See General Business Law, § 91. Such clauses have been sustained in New York where it is clear that a contract has been made. Rapp v. Washington Storage and Warehouse and Van Co., 75 Misc. 16, 134 N.Y.S. 855 (1911); David v. United Security Associated Warehouses, Inc., 86 N.Y.S.2d 236 (1949). Compare, Klar v. H. & M. Parcel Room, 270 App. Div. 538, 61 N.Y.S.2d 285, aff'd 296 N.Y. 1044, 73 N.E.2d 912 (1953) (no contract in fact).

Subsection (3) provides for inclusion in the receipt or tariff of reasonable terms specifying the time and place for presenting claims. The provision is new but is consistent with General Business Law, § 91, and New York case law dealing with bills of lading and limits on the time for bringing suit, e.g., Jones v. Cunard Steamship Co., Ltd., 238 App. Div. 172, 263 N.Y.S. 769 (1933).

Historical Note: As to the change to terminology of damages law in subsection (1), see Section 7–202. Subsection (3) was changed to its present form as a result of proposals on behalf of the Pennsylvania State Chamber of Commerce to avoid any implied invitation to the development of a common-law rule imposing insurer's liability on a warehouseman. Compare Section 7–309. (1956 Recommendations, p. 199.)

Official Uniform Comment

Prior Uniform Statutory Provisions: Sections 3 and 21, Uniform Warehouse Receipts Act.

Changes: Consolidated and rewritten; material on limitation of remedy is new.

Purposes of Changes:

The old uniform acts provided that receipts could not contain terms impairing the obligation of reasonable care. Whether this is violated by a stipulation that in case of loss the bailee's liability is limited to stated amounts has been much controverted. The section is intended to eliminate that controversy by setting forth the conditions under which liability is so limited. However, as subsection (4) makes clear, the states as well as the federal government may supplement this section with more rigid standards of responsibility for some or all bailees.

Cross References:

Sections 7–103 and 10–103.

Definitional Cross References:

"Action." Section 1–201.
"Agreed." Section 1–201.
"Goods." Section 7–102.
"Reasonable time." Section 1–204.
"Sign." Section 1–201.
"Term." Section 1–201.
"Value." Section 1–201.
"Warehouse receipt." Section 1–201.
"Warehouseman." Section 7–102.
"Written." Section 1–201.

Section 7–205. Title Under Warehouse Receipt Defeated in Certain Cases.

A buyer in the ordinary course of business of fungible goods sold and delivered by a warehouseman who is also in the business of buying and selling such goods takes free of any claim under a warehouse receipt even though it has been duly negotiated.

New York Annotations

There is presently no statutory provision like this section which is aimed primarily at the receipt issued by a dealer in grain. In theory the section would change the

New York law, although there are no cases exactly on point. Cf. Kimberly v. Patchin, 19 N.Y. 330 (1859). The current doctrine is that the holder of a receipt may now trace and recover the goods from a bona fide purchaser from the dealer-warehouseman. This section is a particular application to fungible goods of the general policy, expressed in Section 2–403(2), that entrusting possession of goods to a merchant who deals in such goods gives the merchant power to transfer all rights to a buyer in the ordinary course of business. See Section 1–201(9) for the definition of the protected class, and note that this section calls for delivery.

Historical Note: Subsection (2) and Section 9–305(2) were deleted to remove the requirement of filing to perfect a security interests under a field warehousing arrangement. That requirement had been disapproved by the Law Revision Commission and was thought disadvantageous to banking by a committee of the American Bankers Association. (1956 Recommendations, p. 200; Excerpts, p. 442.)

Official Uniform Comment

Prior Uniform Statutory Provision: None.

Purposes:

The typical case covered by this section is that of the warehouseman-dealer in grain, and the substantive question at issue is whether in case the warehouseman becomes insolvent the receipt holders shall be able to trace and recover the grain shipped to farmers and other purchasers from the elevator. This was possible under the old acts, although the courts were eager to find estoppels to prevent it. The practical difficulty of tracing fungible grain means that the preservation of this theoretical right adds little to the commercial acceptability of negotiable grain receipts, which really circulate on the credit of the warehouseman. Moreover, on default of the warehouseman, the receipt holders at least share in what grain remains, whereas retaking the grain from a good faith cash purchaser reduces him completely to the status of general creditor in a situation where there was very little he could do to guard against the loss. Compare 15 U.S.C. Section 714p, enacted in 1955.

Cross References:

Sections 2–403 and 9–307.

Definitional Cross References:

"Buyer in ordinary course of business." Section 1–201.
"Delivery." Section 1–201.
"Duly negotiate." Section 7–501.
"Fungible" goods. Section 1–201.
"Goods." Section 7–102.
"Value." Section 1–201.
"Warehouse receipt." Section 1–201.
"Warehouseman." Section 7–102.

Section 7–206. Termination of Storage at Warehouseman's Option.

(1) A warehouseman may on notifying the person on whose account the goods are held and any other person known to claim an interest in the goods require payment of any charges and removal of the goods from the warehouse at the termination of the period of storage fixed by the document, or, if no period is fixed, within a stated period not less than thirty days after the notification. If

the goods are not removed before the date specified in the notification, the warehouseman may sell them in accordance with the provisions of the section on enforcement of a warehouseman's lien (Section 7–210).

(2) If a warehouseman in good faith believes that the goods are about to deteriorate or decline in value to less than the amount of his lien within the time prescribed in subsection (1) for notification, advertisement and sale, the warehouseman may specify in the notification any reasonable shorter time for removal of the goods and in case the goods are not removed, may sell them at public sale held not less than one week after a single advertisement or posting.

(3) If as a result of a quality or condition of the goods of which the warehouseman had no notice at the time of deposit the goods are a hazard to other property or to the warehouse or to persons, the warehouseman may sell the goods at public or private sale without advertisement on reasonable notification to all persons known to claim an interest in the goods. If the warehouseman after a reasonable effort is unable to sell the goods he may dispose of them in any lawful manner and shall incur no liability by reason of such disposition.

(4) The warehouseman must deliver the goods to any person entitled to them under this Article upon due demand made at any time prior to sale or other disposition under this section.

(5) The warehouseman may satisfy his lien from the proceeds of any sale or disposition under this section but must hold the balance for delivery on the demand of any person to whom he would have been bound to deliver the goods.

New York Annotations

(1) Since there is no existing statute imposing upon the warehouseman a duty to continue storage, he has the right of a bailee (in the absence of an agreement as to a minimum storage period) to terminate storage at any time upon reasonable notice to the bailor. Emerald and Phoenix Brewing Co. v. Leonard, 22 Misc. 120, 48 N.Y.S. 706 (1897). The Code provides him with a procedure for enforcing this right by sale without risking substantial liability. Note that the section permits termination of indefinite storage arrangements even where the storage charges are paid.

(2) This subsection is comparable to General Business Law, § 119. However, the Code makes the following changes: (1) A decline in the market value of the goods gives rise to the same rights as the deterioration of the intrinsic nature or quality of the goods. The latter instance seems to be the only case where the special procedure is now authorized. (2) The Code requires a public sale within one week after advertisement or posting (which follows reasonable notice to remove). Present law permits public or private sale, without advertisement, promptly after failure to remove. (3) The Code limits to hazardous goods the privilege of disposing of the goods in any lawful manner after an unsuccessful attempt to sell. (See subsection (3).) Present law extends that right to goods merely deteriorating in value.

(3) This provision is generally in *accord* with General Business Law, § 119. Unlike present law, the subsection limits its application to cases where the warehouseman had no notice of the hazardous nature of the goods, and does not limit the kinds of hazards covered to goods which by their "odor, leakage, inflammability or explosive nature" are liable to cause harm.

(4) Section 119 of the General Business Law also gives a right of redemption, but the Code provision is somewhat broader since the subsection permits "any person entitled" to redeem the goods, while present law gives that right literally only to those entitled to notice. Further, the Code permits redemption at any time prior to "sale or other disposition", while present law purports to cut off the right at the end of the time specified in the warehouseman's notice to remove. Compare, General Business Law, § 118.

(5) *Accord:* General Business Law, §§ 118 and 119.

Official Uniform Comment

Prior Uniform Statutory Provision: Section 34, Uniform Warehouse Receipts Act.

Changes: Rewritten and expanded to define the warehouseman's right to terminate storage not only where the goods are perishable or hazardous as in Uniform Warehouse Receipts Act, Section 34, but also for any other reason including decline in value of the goods imperilling the warehouseman's security for charges.

Purposes of Changes:

1. Most warehousing is for an indefinite term, the bailor being entitled to delivery on reasonable demand. It is necessary to define the warehouseman's power to terminate bailment, since it would be commercially intolerable to allow warehousemen to order removal of the goods on short notice. The thirty day period provided where the document does not carry its own period of termination corresponds to commercial practice of computing rates on a monthly basis. The right to terminate under subsection (1) includes a right to require payment of "any charges", but does not depend on the existence of unpaid charges.

2. In permitting expeditious disposition of perishable and hazardous goods Uniform Warehouse Receipts Act, Section 34, made no distinction between cases where the warehouseman knowingly undertook to store such goods and cases where the goods were discovered to be of that character subsequent to storage. The former situation presents no such emergency as justifies the summary power of removal and sale. Subsection (2) and (3) distinguish between the two situations.

3. Protection of his lien is the only interest which the warehouseman has to justify summary sale of goods which are not hazardous. This same interest must be recognized when the stored goods, although not perishable, decline in market value to a point which threatens the warehouseman's security.

4. The right to order removal of stored goods is subject to provisions of the public warehousing laws of some states forbidding warehousemen from discriminating among customers. Nor does the section relieve the warehouseman of any obligation under the state laws to secure the approval of a public official before disposing of deteriorating goods. Such regulatory statutes and the regulations under them remain in force and operative. Section 7–103, 10–103.

Cross References:

Sections 7–103, 7–403, 10–103.

Definitional Cross References:

"Delivery." Section 1–201.
"Document." Section 7–102.
"Good faith." Section 1–201.
"Goods." Section 7–102.
"Notice." Section 1–201.
"Notification." Section 1–201.

"Person." Section 1–201.
"Reasonable time." Section 1–204.
"Value." Section 1–201.
"Warehouseman." Section 7–102.

Section 7–207. Goods Must Be Kept Separate; Fungible Goods.

(1) Unless the warehouse receipt otherwise provides, a warehouseman must keep separate the goods covered by each receipt so as to permit at all times identification and delivery of those goods except that different lots of fungible goods may be commingled.

(2) Fungible goods so commingled are owned in common by the persons entitled thereto and the warehouseman is severally liable to each owner for that owner's share. Where because of overissue a mass of fungible goods is insufficient to meet all the receipts which the warehouseman has issued against it, the persons entitled include all holders to whom overissued receipts have been duly negotiated.

New York Annotations

(1) This subsection is generally in *accord* with General Business Law, §§ 108 and 109. However, the Code specifically permits commingling of fungible goods, whereas existing law permits such commingling only where "authorized by agreement or by custom." Further, when read with the definition of fungible goods (Section 1–201(17)), the Code permits commingling not only of goods fungible by nature or usage, but also of goods made fungible by a particular contract or document.

(2) Sections 108 and 109 of the General Business Law permit "depositors" of the mingled goods to share in the mass of fungible goods and the claims against the warehouseman. The Code makes it clear that all persons to whom overissued warehouse receipts have been duly negotiated–including a bona fide purchaser of a negotiable receipt which did not in fact represent a deposit–have those rights.

Official Uniform Comment

Prior Uniform Statutory Provision: Sections 22, 23 and 24, Uniform Warehouse Receipts Act.

Changes: Consolidated and revised; holders of overissued receipts permitted to share in mass of fungible goods.

Purposes of Changes:

No change of substance is made other than the explicit statement that holders to whom overissued receipts have been duly negotiated shall share in a mass of fungilbe goods. Where individual ownership interests are merged into claims on a common fund, as is necessarily the case with fungible goods, there is no policy reason for discriminating between successive purchasers of similar claims.

Definitional Cross References:

"Delivery." Section 1–201.
"Duly negotiate." Section 7–501.
"Fungible" goods. Section 1–201.

"Goods." Section 7–102.
"Holder." Section 1–201.
"Person." Section 1–201.
"Warehouse receipt." Section 1–201.
"Warehouseman." Section 7–102.

Section 7–208. Altered Warehouse Receipts.

Where a blank in a negotiable warehouse receipt has been filled in without authority, a purchaser for value and without notice of the want of authority may treat the insertion as authorized. Any other unauthorized alteration leaves any receipt enforceable against the issuer according to its original tenor.

New York Annotations

This section is comparable to General Business Law, § 99. Two changes would be made. Existing law would apparently classify the unauthorized filling in of blanks as an unauthorized alteration which does not bind the warehouseman even where he is responsible for the issuance of a receipt with a blank. In cases involving blanks the Code holds the warehouseman responsible for the receipts, as altered, to a bona fide purchaser for value of a negotiable receipt. This follows existing law as to negotiable instruments (Negotiable Instruments Law, § 33, and Code Sections 3–407(3) and 8–206). Compare Section 7–306 as to bills of lading. Secondly, as to both negotiable and non-negotiable receipts, the Code gives any holder, including a person who made a fraudulent alteration, or a purchaser with notice thereof, the right to enforce the receipt against the issuer according to its original tenor. Existing law is somewhat ambiguous on this question.

Official Uniform Comment

Prior Uniform Statutory Provision: Section 13, Uniform Warehouse Receipts Act.

Changes: Generally revised and simplified, explicit treatment of the situation where a blank in an executed document is filed without authority.

Purposes of Changes:

1. The execution of warehouse receipts in blank is a dangerous practice. As between the issuer and an innocent purchaser the risks should clearly fall on the former.

2. An unauthorized alteration whether made with or without fraudulent intent does not relieve the issuer of his liability on the warehouse receipt as originally executed. The unauthorized alteration itself is of course ineffective against the warehouseman.

Definitional Cross References:

"Issuer." Section 7–102.
"Notice." Section 1–201.
"Purchaser." Section 1–201.
"Value." Section 1–201.
"Warehouse receipt." Section 1–201.

Section 7–209. Lien of Warehouseman.

(1) A warehouseman has a lien against the bailor on the goods covered by a warehouse receipt or on the proceeds thereof in his possession for charges

UCC

for storage or transportation (including demurrage and terminal charges), insurance, labor, or charges present or future in relation to the goods, and for expenses necessary for preservation of the goods or reasonably incurred in their sale pursuant to law. If the person on whose account the goods are held is liable for like charges or expenses in relation to other goods whenever deposited and it is stated in the receipt that a lien is claimed for charges and expenses in relation to other goods, the warehouseman also has a lien against him for such charges and expenses whether or not the other goods have been delivered by the warehouseman. But against a person to whom a negotiable warehouse receipt is duly negotiated a warehouseman's lien is limited to charged in an amount or at a rate specified on the receipt or if no charges are so specified then to a reasonable charge for storage of the goods covered by the receipt subsequent to the date of the receipt.

(2) The warehouseman may also reserve a security interest against the bailor for a maximum amount specified on the receipt for charges other than those specified in subsection (1), such as for money advanced and interest. Such a security interest is governed by the Article on Secured Transactions (Article 9).

(3) A warehouseman's lien for charges and expenses under subsection (1) or a security interest under subsection (2) is also effective against any person who so entrusted the bailor with possession of the goods that a pledge of them by him to a good faith purchaser for value would have been valid but is not effective against a person as to whom the document confers no right in the goods covered by it under section 7–503.

(4) A warehouseman loses his lien on any goods which he voluntarily delivers or which he unjustifiably refuses to deliver.

New York Annotations

This section rewrites, with the changes indicated below, the rules of law relating to warehouseman's liens now found in General Business Law, §§ 112–117. Under the Code one must distinguish a specific lien, a general lien, and a security interest in cases involving negotiable and non-negotiable receipts.

Charges covered. The first sentence of subsection (1) provides for a specific lien, which attaches automatically, is limited to the usual charges arising out of a storage arrangement, and covers such charges only in relation to the particular goods stored under the receipt. Where the goods are stored under a non-negotiable receipt, the warehouseman may make the specific lien into a general lien, i.e. one covering charges on other goods, by a notation on the receipt that the lien is claimed for such charges and expenses in relation to other goods even these previously surrendered. Present law seems to create such a general lien in cases involving non-negotiable documents without the requirement of the notation. General Business Law, § 113. Compare Chemical Nat'l Bank v. New York Dock Co., 203 App.Div. 108, 196 N.Y.S. 414, aff'd 236 N.Y. 560, 142 N.E. 283 (1923). The same rules apply to negotiable receipts, except that, as against a person to whom the receipt has been "duly negotiated" (Section 7–501), the lien is limited to the amount or rate specified on the receipt. Here the notation must be more particular and if no such notation is made the lien is limited to "a reasonable charge for storage of the goods covered by the receipt subsequent to the date of the receipt." Present law seems to protect negotiable receipts rather than holders. General Business Law, § 115, requires a notation, but literally calls for no specific enumeration of amounts or rates where the added claims are within the class of charges enumerated in § 112 of the same law. But see, Metropolitan Commercial Corp. v. Larkin Co., 257 App.Div. 612, 15 N.Y.S.2d 18, leave to appeal denied, 283 N.Y. 779 (1940).

Advances. First it must be noted that Section 7–202 of the Code and General Business Law, § 91, both require a statement of the amount or the fact of advances for which the warehouseman claims a lien or a security interest. Both of these requirements relate not to enforcement of such interests but to the liability of the warehouseman for damages incurred by their omission. The Code here contains the requirement, new at least for non-negotiable documents, that the maximum amount of charges for which a security interest is claimed must be specified on the receipt. See, General Business Law, §§ 112 and 115. The theory here is that the advance, unlike charges, is not directly related to the storage contract and should be governed by Article 9. Comment 2. Compare Section 9–113.

Depositor's interest in goods. As under present law a warehouseman's lien claim or security interest is under subsection (3) effective against the owner of the goods in the case of unauthorized bailment only where the depositor would have had power to pledge the goods. See General Business Law, § 113. Contract Sections 7–307 and 7–503.

Loss of lien. Subsection (4) is in accord with General Business Law, § 114.

Historical Note: Supp. No. 1 changed subsection (4) to meet objections that the bailee might lose his lien by involuntary surrender under court order. Compare Section 7–307. Further changes adopt the substance of the recommendations made on behalf of the Pennsylvania State Chamber of Commerce that the lien given by subsection (1), so far as it affects goods covered by a non-negotiable receipt, be made a "general" rather than a "specific" lien. This change is a partial return to the policy of the Uniform Warehouse Receipts Act; it made inappropriate the special priority formerly granted by subsection (3) and Section 9–310. Accordingly, the priority provisions of § 28(b) of the Uniform Warehouse Receipts Act were substituted. Various changes in wording for clarification and articulation of the relationship of this section to Article 9 follow the suggestion of the Law Revision Commission. (1956 Recommendations, p. 202; Excerpts, pp. 443–4.)

Official Uniform Comment

Prior Uniform Statutory Provision: Sections 27 through 32, Uniform Warehouse Receipts Act.

Changes: Rewritten.

Purposes of Changes:

1. Subsection (1) defines the warehouseman's statutory lien. A specific lien attaches automatically, without express notation on the receipt, to goods stored under a non-negotiable receipt. That lien is limited to the usual charges arising out of a storage transaction; by notation on the receipt it can be made a general lien extending to like charges in relation to other goods. The same rules apply where the receipt is negotiable, except that as against a holder by due negotiation the lien is limited to the amount or rate specified on the receipt, or, if none is specified, to a reasonable charge for storage of the specific goods after the date of receipt.

2. Subsection (2) provides for a security interest based upon agreement. Such a security interest arises out of relations between parties other than bailment for storage or transportation, as where the bailee assumes the role of financier or performs a

manufacturing operation, extending credit in reliance upon goods covered by the receipt. Such a security interest is not a statutory lien. Compare Sections 9–102(2) and 9–310. It is governed in all respects by Article 9, except that subsection (2) requires that the receipt specify a maximum amount and limits the security interests to the amount specified.

3. Subsections (1) and (2) validate the lien and security interest "against the bailor." As against third parties, subsection (3)(a) continues the rule under the prior uniform statutory provision that to validate the lien the owner must have entrusted the goods to the depositor, and that the circumstances must be such that a pledge by the depositor to a good faith purchaser for value would have been valid. Thus the owner's interest will not be subjected to a lien or security interest arising out of a deposit of his goods by a thief. The warehouseman may be protected because of the actual, implied or apparent authority of the depositor, because of a Factor's Act, or because of other circumstances which would protect a bona fide pledgee, unless those circumstances are denied in effect under Section 7–503. Where the third party is the holder of a security interest, the rights of the warehouseman depend on the priority given to the hypothetical bona fide pledgee by Article 9, particularly Section 9–312. Thus the special priority granted to statutory liens by Sections 9–310 does not apply to liens under subsection (1) of this section, since subsection (3) "expressly provides otherwise" within the meaning of Section 9–310. As to household goods, however, subsection (3)(b) makes the warehouseman's lien "for charges and expenses in relation to the goods" effective against all persons if the depositor was the legal possessor. The purpose of exception is to permit the warehouseman to accept household goods for storage in sole reliance upon the value of the goods themselves, especially in situations of family emergency. [This paragraph was amended in 1966].

4. It is unnecessary to state here, as in Uniform Warehouse Receipts Act 31, that a bailee with a valid lien need not deliver until the lien is satisfied. Section 7–403 provides that a person demanding delivery under a document must be prepared to satisfy the bailee's lien.

5. Where goods have been stored under a non-negotiable warehouse receipt and are sold by the person to whom the receipt has been issued, frequently the goods are not withdrawn by the new owner. The obligations of the seller of the goods in this situation are set forth in Section 2–503(4) on tender of delivery and include procurement of an acknowledgement by the bailee of the buyer's right to possession acknowledgement can be withheld until storage charges have been paid or provided for. The statutory lien for charges on the goods sold, granted by the first sentence of subsection (1), continues valid unless the bailee gives it up. But once a new receipt is issued to the buyer, the buyer becomes "the person on whose account the goods are held" under the second sentence of subsection (1); unless he undertakes liability for charges in relation to other goods stored by the seller, there is no general lien against the buyer for such charges. Of course, the bailee may preserve the general lien in such a case either by arrangement by which the buyer "is liable for" such charges, or by serving a security interest under subsection (2).

Cross References:

Point 2: Sections 9–102(2) and 9–310.
Point 3: Sections 7–503, 9–310 and 9–312.
Point 4: Section 7–403.
Point 5: Section 2–503.

Definitional Cross References:

"Deliver." Section 1–201.
"Document." Section 7–102.

"Goods." Section 7–102.
"Money." Section 1–201.
"Person." Section 1–201.
"Purchaser." Section 1–201.
"Right." Section 1–201.
"Security interest." Section 1–201.
"Value." Section 1–201.
"Warehouse receipt." Section 1–201.
"Warehouseman." Section 7–102.

Section 7–210. Enforcement of Warehouseman's Lien.

(1) Except as provided in subsection (2), a warehouseman's lien may be enforced by public or private sale of the goods in bloc or in parcels, at any time or place and on any terms which are commercially reasonable, after notifying all persons known to claim an interest in the goods. Such notification must include a statement of the amount due, the nature of the proposed sale and the time and place of any public sale, and, unless the goods are perishable or threaten to decline speedily in value, it shall state that any person claiming an interest in the goods is entitled to bring a proceeding under section 7–211 within ten days of the service of the notice if he disputes the validity of the lien or the amount claimed. The fact that a better price could have been obtained by a sale at a different time or in a different method from that selected by the warehouseman is not of itself sufficient to establish that the sale was not made in a commercially reasonable manner. If the warehouseman either sells the goods in the usual manner in any recognized market therefor, or if he sells at the price current in such market at the time of his sale, or if he has otherwise sold in conformity with commercially reasonable practices among dealers in the type of goods sold, he has sold in a commercially reasonable manner. A sale of more goods than apparently necessary to be offered to insure satisfaction of the obligation is not commercially reasonable except in cases covered by the preceding sentence.

(2) A warehouseman's lien on goods other than goods stored by a merchant in the course of his business may be enforced only as follows:

(a) all persons known to claim an interest in the goods must be notified.

(b) the notification must be delivered in person or sent by registered or certified letter to the last known address of any person to be notified.

(c) the notification must include an itemized statement of the claim, a description of the goods subject to the lien, a demand for payment within a specified time not less than ten days after receipt of the notification, a conspicuous statement that unless the claim is paid within that time the goods will be advertised for sale and sold by auction at a specified time and place, and a statement that any person claiming an interest in the goods is entitled to bring a proceeding under section 7–211 within ten days of the service of the notice if he disputes the validity of the lien or the amount claimed.

(d) the sale must conform to the terms of the notification.

(e) the sale must be held at the nearest suitable place to that where the goods are held or stored.

(f) after the expiration of the time given in the notification, an advertisement of the sale must be published once a week for two weeks consecutively in a newspaper of general circulation where the sale is to be held. The advertisement must include a description of the goods, the name of the person on whose account they are being held, and the time and place of the sale. The sale must take place at least fifteen day after the first publication. If there is no newspaper of general circulation where the sale is to be held, the advertisement must be posted at least ten days before the sale in not less than six conspicuous places in the neighborhood of the proposed sale.

(3) Before any sale pursuant to this section any person claiming a right in the goods may pay the amount necessary to satisfy the lien and the reasonable expenses incurred under this section. In that event the goods must not be sold, but must be retained by the warehouseman subject to the terms of the receipt and this Article.

(4) The warehouseman may buy at any public sale pursuant to this section.

(5) A purchaser in good faith of goods sold to enforce a warehouseman's lien takes the goods free of any rights of persons against whom the lien was valid, despite noncompliance by the warehouseman with the requirements of this section.

(6) The warehouseman may satisfy his lien from the proceeds of any sale pursuant to this section but must hold the balance, if any, for delivery on demand to any person to whom he would have been bound to deliver the goods.

(7) The rights provided by this section shall be in addition to all other rights allowed by law to a creditor against his debtor.

(8) Where a lien is on goods stored by a merchant in the course of his business the lien may be enforced in accordance with either subsection (1) or (2).

(9) The warehouseman is liable for damages caused by failure to comply with the requirements for sale under this section and in case of willful violation is liable for conversion.

Amended by Laws 1963, Ch. 1003, eff. Sept. 27, 1964, Laws 1982, Ch. 528, eff. Sept. 1, 1982.

New York Annotations

(1) and (8) Subsection (1) is new to the statues. In a case where the lien arises out of storage of goods by a merchant in the course of his business, the Code permits the warehouseman to choose between a modified version of existing procedure (subsection (2)) and a new simplified procedure based on "commercial reasonableness" (subsection (8)). This new procedure requires notice to all persons claiming an interest in the goods, but reduces the technical requirements as to such notice, and the sale, e.g. the sale may be "public or private" and may be "in bloc or in parcels." For the purposes of Article 2, at least, "merchant" is defined in Section 2–104.

(2) The Code here provides a method of lien enforcement much like that of General Business Law, § 118, and requires a public sale on notice, and after publication. It is optional in commercial storage cases (see subsection (1) *supra*) and mandatory in all others. See Lake v. Dye, 232 N.Y. 209, 133 N.E. 448 (1921), on ineffective waiver.

(3) General Business Law, § 118, is generally in accord except for the fact that the Code requires the warehouseman to retain the goods upon payment, while the present statute permits delivery to the person paying if such person is entitled under the document.

(4) The Code in permitting the warehouseman to bid at any proper public sale clarifies a point upon which there is doubt under present law. Jones v. Nat'l Chatauqua County Bank of Jamestown, 272 App.Div. 521, 74 N.Y.S.2d 498 (1947) (agreement might authorize pledgee to buy at public sale).

(5) This is new to the statute and conforms to Section 9–504(4). Present law apparently gives a bona fide purchaser for value at a non-conforming sale no rights to the goods.

(6) *Accord:* General Business Law, § 118.

(7) *Accord:* General Business Law, § 117.

(9) Existing law makes a sale not complying with the statute a conversion, leaving the bailee liable for the full value of the goods. Lake v. Dye, *supra.* The Code in such a case is in *accord* with existing law only to the extent that the violation is willful; in non-willful cases the Code limits the warehouseman's liability to actual damages.

Historical Note: Supp. No. 1 changed "bid" to "buy" in subsection (4) to conform to Section 9–504(2). The first sentence of former subsection (4) was renumbered as subsection (9) because it was unrelated to the second sentence. As to the change in the wording of subsection (9), see Section 7–202(2). (1956 Recommendations, p. 205.)

Official Uniform Comment

Prior Uniform Statutory Provision: Section 33, Uniform Warehouse Receipts Act.

Changes: Rewritten; simplified foreclosure proceeding provided for all liens other than warehousemen's lien in non-commercial storage.

Purpose of Changes:

1. Subsection (1) makes "commercial reasonableness" the standard of foreclosure proceedings in all cases except non-commercial storage with a warehouseman. The latter category embraces principally storage of household goods by private owners; and for such cases the detailed provisions as to notification, publication and public sale, found in Section 33 of the Uniform Warehouse Receipts Act are retained in subsection (2). The swifter, more flexible procedure of subsection (1) is appropriate to commercial storage. Compare seller's power of resale on breach by buyer under the provisions of the Article on Sales (Section 2–706).

2. The provisions of subsections (4) and (5) permitting the bailee to bid at public sales and confirming the title of purchase at foreclosure sales are designed to secure more bidding and better prices.

Cross References:

Section 7–403.

Definitional Cross References:

"Bill of lading." Section 1–201.

"Conspicuous." Section 1–201.

UCC

"Creditor." Section 1–201.
"Delivery." Section 1–201.
"Document." Section 7–102.
"Good faith." Section 1–201.
"Goods." Section 7–102.
"Notification." Section 1–201.
"Notifies." Section 1–201.
"Person." Section 1–201.
"Purchaser." Section 1–201.
"Rights." Section 1–201.
"Term." Section 1–201.
"Warehouseman." Section 7–102.

Section 7–211. Proceeding to Determine Validity of Lien.

Within ten days after service of the notice of sale, a person claiming an interest in the goods may commence a special proceeding to determine the validity of the lien. The special proceeding may be brought in any court which would have jurisdiction to render a judgment for a sum equal to the amount of the lien. If the person shall show that the warehouseman is not entitled to claim a lien in the goods, or that all or part of the amount claimed by the warehouseman has not been properly charged to the account of such person, or, as the case may be, that all or part of such amount exceeds the fair and reasonable value of the services performed by the warehouseman, the court shall direct the entry of judgment cancelling the lien or reducing the amount claimed thereunder accordingly. If the warehouseman shall establish the validity of the lien, in whole or in part, the judgment shall fix the amount thereof, and shall provide that the sale may proceed upon the expiration of five days after service of a copy of the judgment together with notice of entry thereof upon the person, unless the goods are redeemed prior thereto pursuant to subsection (3) of section 7–210. If the lien is cancelled, the judgment shall provide that, upon service of a copy of the judgment together with notice of entry thereof upon the warehouseman, the person shall be entitled to possession of the property.

Added by Laws 1982, Ch. 528, eff. Sept. 1, 1982.

PART 3

BILLS OF LADING: SPECIAL PROVISIONS

Section 7–301. Liability for Non-Receipt or Misdescription; "Said to Contain"; "Shipper's Load and Count"; Improper Handling.

(1) A consignee of a non-negotiable bill who has given value in good faith or a holder to whom a negotiable bill has been duly negotiated relying in either case upon the description therein of the goods, or upon the date therein shown, may recover from the issuer damages caused by the misdating of the bill or the non-receipt or misdescription of the goods, except to the extent that the

document indicates that the issuer does not know whether any part or all of the goods in fact were received or conform to the description, as where the description is in terms of marks or labels or kind, quantity, or condition or the receipt or description is qualified by "contents or condition of contents of packages unknown", "said to contain", "shipper's weight, load and count" or the like, if such indication be true.

(2) When goods are loaded by an issuer who is a common carrier, the issuer must count the packages of goods if package freight and ascertain the kind and quantity if bulk freight. In such cases "shipper's weight, load and count" or other words indicating that the description was made by the shipper are ineffective except as to freight concealed by packages.

(3) When bulk freight is loaded by a shipper who makes available to the issuer adequate facilities for weighing such freight, an issuer who is a common carrier must ascertain the kind and quantity within a reasonable time after receiving the written request of the shipper to do so. In such cases "shipper's weight" or other words of like purport are ineffective.

(4) The issuer may be inserting in the bill the words "shipper's weight, load and count" or other words of like purport indicate that the goods were loaded by the shipper; and if such statement be true the issuer shall not be liable for damages caused by the improper loading. But their omission does not imply liability for such damages.

(5) The shipper shall be deemed to have guaranteed to the issuer the accuracy at the time of shipment of the description, marks, labels, number, kind, quantity, condition and weight, as furnished by him; and the shipper shall indemnify the issuer against damage caused by inaccuracies in such particulars. The right of the issuer to such indemnity shall in no way limit his responsibility and liability under the contract of carriage to any person other than the shipper.

New York Annotations

Generally, it must be noted that, unlike Section 7–201 as to warehouse receipts, the Code here makes no provision for the formal details of a bill of lading. Present law contains such requisites in Personal Property Law, § 188. Compare, General Business Law, § 398, Public Service Law, § 38, and Canal Law, § 76.

(1) Generally this subsection is in *accord* with Personal Property Law, § 209. The Code's specific reference to misdating is not in the Uniform Act but is contained in the New York law. The class of persons to whom an issuer is liable is more restricted under the Code than under existing law. In the case of a negotiable bill the holder not only must have given value in good faith, but also must have had the bill "duly negotiated" to him. See Section 7–501(4).

(2) and (3) These provisions are generally in *accord* with the 1941 New York modification of the Uniform Bills of Lading Act, § 23 (Personal Property Law, § 209). See Fenderson v. Lehigh Valley R. Co., 163 App.Div. 107, 148 N.Y.S. 494 (1914).

(4) *Accord:* Personal Property Law, § 209. The Code leaves open the question whether the issuer escapes losses caused by improper loading by a shipper where there is no notation indicating loading by the shipper.

(5) This subsection is new. The Code provides an absolute liability on the shipper to indemnify the carrier against damages caused by inaccuracies in particulars furnished by the shipper regarding the goods. Such indemnity is not explicitly provided for in existing law and could be obtained only with difficulty.

Historical Note: Supp. No. 1 added provisions as to misdating to conform to the policy of the amendment to the Federal Bills of Lading Act by 44 Stat. 1450 (1927), as amended 49 U.S.C.A. § 102, after the holding in Browne v. Union Pac. R. R., 113 Kan. 726, 216 P. 299, aff'd on other grounds, 267 U.S. 255, 45 S.Ct. 315, 69 L. Ed. 601 (1925). The other change in subsection (1), also made in Supp. No. 1, makes express provision for a standard phrase used in uniform railroad bills of lading. Further revision also followed recommendations of the Law Revision Commission in inserting new subsections (2) and (3) to conform to the policy of the Federal Bills of Lading Act, 49 U.S.C.A. §§ 100, 101, and the laws of several states. See, e.g., N.Y. Pers. Prop. Law, § 209; Report of N.Y. Law Revision Commission, N.Y. Leg. Doc. (1941) No. 65 (F). The change in former subsection (2), now renumbered (4), was proposed on behalf of the Pennsylvania State Chamber of Commerce to avoid any implication that decisions such as Modern Tool Corp. v. Penna. R. R., 100 F. Supp. 595 (D.N.J. 1951), are disapproved. (1956 Recommendations, p. 206; Excerpts, p. 444.)

Official Uniform Comment

Prior Uniform Statutory Provision: Section 23, Uniform Bills of Lading Act.
Changes: Rewritten in part.

Purposes of Changes:

1. The provision as to misdating in subsection (1) conforms to the policy of the amendment to the Federal Bills of Lading Act by 44 Stat. 1450 (1927), as amended 49 U.S.C. Section 102, after the holding in Browne v. Union Pac. R. Co., 113 Kan. 726, 216 P. 299 (1923), affirmed on other grounds 267 U.S.255, 45 S.Ct. 315, 69 L. Ed. 601 (1925). Subsections (2) and (3) conform to the policy of the Federal Bills of Lading Act, 49 U.S.C. Sections 100, 101, and the laws of several states. See, e.g. N.Y. Pers. Prop. Law Section 209; Report of N.Y. Law Revision Commission, N.Y. Leg. Doc. (1941) No. 65(F).

2. The language of the old Uniform Act suggested that a carrier is ordinarily liable for damage caused by improper loading, but may relieve himself of liability by disclosing on the bill that shipper actually loaded. A more accurate statement of the law is that the carrier is not liable for losses caused by act or default of the shipper, which would include improper loading. There is some question whether under present law a carrier is liable even to a good faith purchaser of a negotiable bill for such losses, if the shipper's faulty loading in fact caused the loss. It is this doubtful liability which subsection (4) permits the carrier to bar by disclosure of shipper's loading. There is no implication that decisions such as Modern Tool Corp. v. Pennsylvania R. Co., 100 F.Supp. 595 (D.N.J. 1951), are disapproved.

3. This section is a simplified restatement of existing law as to the method by which a bailee may avoid responsibility for the accuracy of descriptions which are made by or in reliance upon information furnished by the depositor or shipper. The issuer is liable on documents issued by an agent, contrary to instructions of his principal, without receiving goods. No disclaimer of this liability is permitted since it is not a matter either of the care of the goods or their description.

4. The shipper's erroneous report to the carrier concerning the goods may cause damage to the carrier. Subsection (5) therefore provides appropriate indemnity.

Cross References:

Sections 7–203 and 7–309.

Definitional Cross References:

"Bill of lading." Section 1–201.
"Consignee." Section 7–102.
"Document." Section 7–102.
"Duly negotiate." Section 7–501.
"Good faith." Section 1–201.
"Goods." Section 7–102.
"Holder." Section 1–201.
"Issuer." Section 7–102.
"Notice." Section 1–201.
"Party." Section 1–201.
"Purchaser." Section 1–201.
"Receipt of goods." Section 2–103.
"Value." Section 1–201.

Section 7–302. Through Bills of Lading and Similar Documents.

(1) The issuer of a through bill of lading or other document embodying an undertaking to be performed in part by persons acting as its agents or by connecting carriers is liable to anyone entitled to recover on the document for any breach by such other persons or by a connecting carrier of its obligation under the document but to the extent that the bill covers an undertaking to be performed overseas or in territory not contiguous to the continental United States or an undertaking including matters other than transportation this liability may be varied by agreement of the parties.

(2) Where goods covered by a through bill of lading or other document embodying an undertaking to be performed in part by persons other than the issuer are received by any such person, he is subject with respect to his own performance while the goods are in his possession to the obligation of the issuer. His obligation is discharged by delivery of the goods to another such person pursuant to the document, and does not include liability for breach by any other such persons or by the issuer.

(3) The issuer of such through bill of lading or other document shall be entitled to recover from the connecting carrier of such other person in possession of the goods when the breach of the obligation under the document occurred, the amount it may be required to pay to anyone entitled to recover on the document therefor, as may be evidenced by any receipt, judgment, or transcript thereof, and the amount of any expense reasonably incurred by it in defending any action brought by anyone entitled to recover on the document therefor.

New York Annotations

(1) No comparable state statutory rule now exists. Where the common law imposed liability on the issuer for the faults of the connecting carrier only where "contracted

for", the Code places such liability squarely on the issuing carrier, giving him in subsection (3) a right of recourse against the appropriate connecting carrier. Compare Burtis v. Buffalo State Line R. Co., 24 N.Y. 269 (1862), and Root v. The Great Western R. R. Co., 45 N.Y. 524 (1871), with Van Santvoord v. St. John & Tousey, 6 Hill 157 (1849). See Public Service Law, § 41, for the rule on routing by shipper.

(2) Placing upon the connecting carrier, while the goods are in his possession, the same individual obligation as is borne by the issuing carrier, is consistent with present New York law. Pacific Coast Borax Co. v. Shippers Navigation Co., Inc., et al., 108 Misc. 198, 178 N.Y.S. 182 (1919); Remington v. Barrett, 196 App.Div. 838, 188N.Y.S. 174, aff'd 235 N.Y. 519, 139 N.E. 717 (1921).

(3) New York law is consistent with the issuer's right to recover from the connecting carrier for the amount the issuer is required to pay to anyone entitled to recover under the document as a result of the connecting carrier's breach of obligation. Germini v. Southern Pacific Co. et al., 209 App.Div. 442, 204 N.Y.S. 603 (1924); Railroad Law, § 70. Evidencing the amount of recovery by receipt and the recovery of expenses, appear to be new.

Historical Note: Supp. No. 1, inserted in subsection (2) the words "while the goods are in its possession" to make it clear that a connecting carrier is not responsible for defaults of prior or subsequent carriers. Further revision of that subsection, following a recommendation of the Law Revision Commission, made it clear that the connecting carrier is subject to common-law obligations as well as those stated in the document, and that the connecting carrier is not subject to vicarious liability, for example, where the issuer incurs liability for misdescription under Section 7–301. (1956 Recommendations, p. 207; Excerpts, p. 445.)

Official Uniform Comment

Prior Uniform Statutory Provision: None.

Purposes:

1. The purpose of this section is to subject the initial carrier under a through bill to suit for breach of the contract of carriage by any connecting carrier and to make it clear that any such connecting carrier holds the goods on terms which are defined by the document of title even though such connecting carrier did not issue the document. Since the connecting carrier does hold on the terms of the document, it must honor a proper demand for delivery or a diversion order just as the original bailee would have to. Similarly it has the benefits of the excuses for nondelivery and limitations of liability provided for the original bailee. Unlike the original bailee-issuer, the connecting carrier's responsibility is limited to the period while the goods are in its possession. The section is patterned generally after the Interstate Commerce Act, but does not impose any obligation to issue through bills.

2. The reference to documents other than through bills looks to the possibility that multi-purpose documents may come into use, e.g., combination warehouse receipts and bills of lading.

3. Where the obligations or standards applicable to different parties bound by a document of title are different, the initial carrier's responsibility for portions of the journey not on its own lines will be determined by the standards appropriate to the connecting carrier. Thus a land carrier issuing a through bill of lading involving water carriage at a later stage will have the benefit of the water carrier's immunity from liability for negligence of its servants in navigating the vessel, where the law provides such an immunity for water carriers and the loss occurred while the goods were in the water carrier's possession.

4. Under Subsection (1) the issuer of a through bill of lading may become liable for the fault of another person. Subsection (3) gives it appropriate rights of recourse.

Definitional Cross References:

"Agreement." Section 1–201.
"Bailee." Section 7–102.
"Bill of lading." Section 1–201.
"Delivery." Section 1–201.
"Document." Section 7–102.
"Goods." Section 7–102.
"Issuer." Section 7–102.
"Overseas." Section 2–323.
"Party." Section 1–201.
"Person." Section 1–201.

Section 7–303. Diversion; Reconsignment; Change of Instructions.

(1) Unless the bill of lading otherwise provides, the carrier may deliver the goods to a person or destination other than that stated in the bill or may otherwise dispose of the goods on instructions from

(a) the holder of a negotiable bill; or

(b) the consignor on a non-negotiable bill notwithstanding contrary instructions from the consignee; or

(c) the consignee on a non-negotiable bill in the absence of contrary instructions from the consignor, if the goods have arrived at the billed destination or if the consignee is in possession of the bill; or

(d) the consignee on a non-negotiable bill if he is entitled as against the consignor to dispose of them.

(2) Unless such instructions are noted on a negotiable bill of lading, a person to whom the bill is duly negotiated can hold the bailee according to the original terms.

New York Annotations

Existing statutory law does not deal expressly with the subject matter of this section. The privilege of the carrier to permit a change of instructions now depends strictly upon whether the ultimate result is a "justified delivery," i.e. delivery to the holder of an order bill, the consignee of a straight bill, or a person lawfully entitled to possession of the goods. Personal Property Law, §§ 198 and 199.

Negotiable bills; Since the Code permits a change of instructions to be made only by the holder and requires notation of such changes on the bill, there is no change in existing law. Knight v. Delaware & Hudson Co., 178 App. Div. 518, 165 N.Y.S. 583 (1917).

Non-negotiable bills. With respect to non-negotiable bills the Code makes a modification in existing law and gives the carrier more freedom to comply with the instructions of the consignor and less freedom to obey the orders of the consignee. Under present law, delivery to the consignee on a straight bill is "justified" and the carrier is immune from liability even though the consignee was not really entitled to the goods. Thus the carrier could divert at the request of the consignee regardless of where the goods were located, or who had the document, or whether the consignor had issued contrary instructions. The last aspect was modified where the consignor's instructions were a proper stoppage in transit under §§ 138–140 of the Personal Property Law. See annotation to Section 2–705. Under the Code, however, the carrier cannot, without taking the risk that the consignee may not be entitled to the goods, divert at the request of the consignee before arrival of the goods at destination, unless the consignee has possession of the bill. In any event, the carrier cannot make a diversion free of that risk where the consignor has given conflicting instructions. Under present New York law, the carrier cannot comply with changed instructions from the consignor (except for proper stoppage in transit) without taking the risk that the consignor had no right to make that change. Under the Code the carrier is privileged to comply with changed instructions from the consignor.

Historical Note: Supp. No. 1 made it clear that the instructions referred to in subsection (2) are diversion instructions and the like rather than ventilation, refrigeration, or heating instructions, and limited the subsection to cases of due negotiation. Further revision followed recommendations of the Law Revision Commission in clarifying subsections (1)(b) and (1)(d) so as to avoid conflict with the right of stoppage under Section 2–705 in cases where the consignee "owns" the goods, and to make it clear that the carrier may follow the consignor's instructions notwithstanding contrary orders from the consignee. (1956 Recommendations, p. 208; Excerpts, p. 445.)

Official Uniform Comment

Prior Uniform Statutory Provision: None.

Purposes:

1. The old Acts contained no reference to diversion, a very common commercial practice which defeats delivery to the consignee originally named in a bill of lading. The carrier was protected under the heading of "justified delivery" if the substituted consignee who received delivery was "a person lawfully entitled to possession of the goods." Cf. subsection (1)(d). This in turn depended on whether the person ordering the diversion was the owner of the goods or empowered to dispose of them, which again might depend upon whether under sales law title had passed from the consignor-seller to the consignee-buyer. The carrier is plainly not in a position to decide such questions when directed by the person with whom it has contracted for transportation to change the destination of the goods in transit. Carriers may as a business matter be willing to accept instructions from consignees in which case, as under the old uniform acts, the carrier will be liable for misdelivery if the consignee was not the owner or otherwise empowered to dispose of the goods. The section imposes no duty on carriers to undertake diversion; it is of course subject to the provisions of filed tariffs. Section 7–103.

2. It should be noted that the section provides only an immunity for carriers against liability for "misdelivery." It does not, for example, defeat the title to the goods which the consignee-buyer may have acquired from the consignor-seller upon delivery of the goods to the carrier under a non-negotiable bill of lading. Thus if the carrier, upon instructions from the consignor, returns the goods to him, the consignee may recover the goods from the consignor or his insolvent estate. However, under certain circumstances, the consignee's title may be defeated by diversion of the goods in transit to a different consignee.

Cross References:

Point 2: Sections 7–403 and 7–504(3).

Definitional Cross References:

"Bailee." Section 7–102.

"Bill of lading." Section 1–201.
"Consignee." Section 7–102.
"Consignor." Section 7–102.
"Delivery." Section 1–201.
"Goods." Section 7–102.
"Holder." Section 1–201.
"Notice." Section 1–201.
"Person." Section 1–201.
"Purchaser." Section 1–201.
"Term." Section 1–201.

Section 7–304. Bills of Lading in a Set.

(1) Except where customary in overseas transportation, a bill of lading must not be issued in a set of parts. The issuer is liable for damages caused by violation of this subsection.

(2) Where a bill of lading is lawfully drawn in a set of parts, each of which is numbered and expressed to be valid only if the goods have not been delivered against any other part, the whole of the parts constitute one bill.

(3) Where a bill of lading is lawfully issued in a set of parts and different parts are negotiated to different persons, the title of the holder to whom the first due negotiation is made prevails as to both the document and the goods even though any later holder may have received the goods from the carrier in good faith and discharged the carrier's obligation by surrender of his part.

(4) Any person who negotiates or transfers a single part of a bill of lading drawn in a set is liable to holders of that part as if it were the whole set.

(5) The bailee is obliged to deliver in accordance with Part 4 of this Article against the first presented part of a bill of lading lawfully drawn in a set. Such delivery discharges the bailee's obligation on the whole bill.

New York Annotations

(1) In Personal Property Law, § 192, negotiable bills in parts or sets are prohibited where transportation is to ". . . any place in the United Stated on the continent of North America, except Alaska . . ." This section of the Code prohibits both negotiable and non-negotiable bills in a set of parts except "where customary in overseas transportation", and "overseas" is defined in Sections 7–102(3) and 2–323 as a sea or air shipment subject by usage to "practices characteristic of deep water commerce." The unlawful issuance of such bills makes the carrier liable for damages under the Code, while existing law makes him liable to a purchaser of a part for value and in good faith.

(2), (3), (4), and (5) The statutory definition of the legal effect of lawfully issued bills in a set of parts is new.

Official Uniform Comment

Prior Uniform Statutory Provision: Section 6, Uniform Bills of Lading Act.

Changes: This section adds to existing legislation, which merely prohibits bills in a set in ordinary domestic trade, a statement of the legal effect of a lawfully issued set.

Purposes of Changes:

The statement of the legal effect of a lawfully issued set is in *accord* with existing commercial law relating to maritime and other overseas bills. This law has been codified in the Hague and Warsaw Conventions and in the Carriage of Goods by Sea Act, the provisions of which would ordinarily govern in situations where bills in a set are recognized by this Article.

Cross Reference:

Section 10–103.

Definitional Cross References:

"Bailee." Section 7–102.
"Bill of lading." Section 7–102.
"Delivery." Section 1–201.
"Document." Section 7–102.
"Duly negotiate." Section 7–501.
"Good faith." Section 1–201.
"Goods." Section 7–102.
"Holder." Section 1–201.
"Issuer." Section 7–102.
"Overseas." Section 2–323.
"Person." Section 1–201.
"Receipt of goods." Section 2–103.

Section 7–305. Destination Bills.

(1) Instead of issuing a bill of lading to the consignor at the place of shipment a carrier may at the request of the consignor procure the bill to be issued at destination or at any other place designated in the request.

(2) Upon request of anyone entitled as against the carrier to control the goods while in transit and on surrender of any outstanding bill of lading or other receipt covering such goods, the issuer may procure a substitute bill to be issued at any place designated in the request.

New York Annotations

There is no comparable statutory provision in New York and no cases were found concerning the carrier's right to issue destination bills. Public Service Law, § 38, is silent on the question, and the Code merely authorizes the parties to use such a device to facilitate the use of order bills in connection with fast shipments which may now be delayed pending receipt of documents.

Official Uniform Comment

Prior Uniform Statutory Provision: None.

Purposes:

This proposal is designed to facilitate the use of order bills in connection with fast shipments. Use of order bills on high speed shipments is impeded by the fact that the goods may arrive at destination before the documents, so that no one is ready to take delivery from the carrier. This is especially inconvenient for carriers by truck and air, who do not have terminal facilities where shipment can be held to await consignee's appearance. Order bills would be useful to take advantage of bank collection. This may be preferable to C.O.D. shipment in which the carrier, e.g. a truck driver, is the collecting and remitting agent. Financing of shipments under this plan would be handled as follows: seller at San Francisco delivers the goods to an airline with instructions to issue a bill in New York to a named bank. Seller receives a receipt embodying this undertaking to issue a destination bill. Airline wires its New York freight agent to issue the bill as instructed by the seller. Seller wires the New York bank a draft on buyer. New York bank indorses the bill to buyer when he honors the draft. Normally seller would act through his own bank in San Francisco, which would extend him credit in reliance on the airline's contract to deliver a bill to the order of its New York correspondent. This section is entirely permissive; it imposes no duty to issue such bills. Whether a connecting carrier will act as issuing agent is left to agreement between carriers.

Definitional Cross References:

"Bill of lading." Section 1–201.
"Consignor." Section 7–102.
"Goods." Section 7–102.
"Issuer." Section 7–102.
"Receipt of goods." Section 2–103.

Section 7–306. Altered Bills of Lading.

An unauthorized alteration or filling in of a bank in a bill of lading leaves the bill enforceable according to its original tenor.

New York Annotations

This section is generally in *accord* with Personal Property law § 202. Under the Code the authority for alterations need not be "in writing or noted on the bill," as required by the present law. See Section 7–208 for the somewhat different rules as to altered warehouse receipts.

Official Uniform Comment

Prior Uniform Statutory Provision: Section 16, Uniform Bills of Lading Act.

Changes: Generally revised and simplified; explicit treatment of the situation where a blank in an executed document is filled without authority.

Purposes of Changes:

An unauthorized alteration whether made with or without fraudulent intent does not relieve the issuer of his liability on the document as originally executed. Uniform Warehouse Receipts Act 13 excused the issuer from any liability to a fraudulent alterer, other than the liability to deliver the goods according to the terms of the original document. It is difficult to conceive what liability the draftsman intended to excuse. Uniform Bills of Lading Act 16 contains no such excuse provision, and is followed in this respect in the present section. Uniform Bills of Lading Act 16 characterizes an unauthorized alteration as "void" but apparently nothing more was intended than that the alteration did not change the obligation of the issuer. This is sufficiently covered by the terms of this section. Moreover cases are conceivable in which an alteration would not be "void"; for example, an alteration made by common consent of a transferor and transferee of a document might evidence an enforceable contract between them. The same rule is made applicable to the filling in of blanks, a matter on which the prior Acts were silent.

Definitional Cross References:

"Bill of lading." Section 1–201.
"Issuer." Section 7–102.

Section 7–307. Lien of Carrier.

(1) A carrier has a lien on the goods covered by a bill of lading for charges subsequent to the date of its receipt of the goods for storage or transportation (including demurrage and terminal charges) and for expenses necessary for preservation of the goods incident to their transportation or reasonably incurred in their sale pursuant to law. But against a purchaser for value of a negotiable bill of lading a carrier's lien is limited to charges stated in the bill or the applicable tariffs, or if no charges are stated then to a reasonable charge.

(2) A lien for charges and expenses under subsection (1) on goods which the carrier was required by law to receive for transportation is effective against the consignor or any person entitled to the goods unless the carrier had notice that the consignor lacked authority to subject the goods to such charges and expenses. Any other lien under subsection (1) is effective against the consignor and any person who permitted the bailor to have control or possession of the goods unless the carrier had notice that the bailor lacked such authority.

(3) A carrier loses his lien on any goods which he voluntarily delivers or which he unjustifiably refuses to deliver.

New York Annotations

(1) The first sentence of this subsection gives a carrier, issuing a bill of lading, a specific possessory statutory lien for the enumerated charges and expenses. The Code clearly extends the carrier's lien to demurrage charges, while New York law has denied a lien position for such charges under the common-law carrier's lien. Compare Personal Property Law, § 212, and Troy Waste Mfg. Co. v. N. Y. C. and H. R. R. Co., 158 App.Div. 352, 143 N.Y.S. 420, appeal dismissed, 216 N.Y. 632, 110 N.E. 1050 (1914). Unlike the present law the subsection expressly provides lien rights in transaction involving non-negotiable bills. Personal Property Law, § 212. Presently the only statutory lien explicitly recognized is for a truckman and a drayman under Lien Law, § 187. The last sentence of the subsection introduces a new distinction between negotiable bills held by purchasers for value an other negotiable bills. In the former case the Code limits the carrier lien to charges stated in the bill or applicable tariff or, if no charges are stated, to a reasonable charge. Personal Property Law, § 212.

(2) Present law does not protect the carrier's lien on goods consigned by a thief. Van Buskirk v. Purinton, 2 Hall 601 (N.Y. Super. Ct. 1829). The Code would protect the lien against any person, including one holding a recorded security interest, who entrusted the goods to the bailor. See Section 9–310. Further, in the ordinary case of a common carrier required by law to receive the goods, the Code would protect

his lien even though the consignor was a thief. In either case there is no protection for the lien if the carrier has notice of the lack of authority. See Section 1–201(25).

(3) This subsection is a new statutory control of carrier's liens, but is in *accord* with existing New York case law, e.g. Neustadt v. Lehigh Valley Railroad Co., 159 App.Div. 667, 144 N.Y.S. 911 (1913).

Note: This section is similar in some respects to Section 7–209 relating to warehouseman's liens. The instant section, however, does not authorize a general lien to cover charges on other goods, nor does it specifically permit a carrier's lien to secure money lent. Under Section 7–105 no negative implication is to be drawn from the fact that such security is provided for in Section 7–209.

Historical Note: Subsection (1) was revised to make it clear that the lien attaches only to the goods covered by the bill, and this meets a suggestion of the Law Revision Commission. Subsection (2) was revised to limit the bailee's lien on stolen goods to goods which the carrier had a duty to receive; in the absence of such a duty, as recommended by the Law Revision Commission, the lien was made invalid if the owner did not put the depositor in control of the goods. (1956 Recommendations, p. 210; Excerpts, pp. 445–6.)

UCC

Official Uniform Comment

Prior Uniform Statutory Provision: Sections 27 through 32, Uniform Warehouse Receipts Act.

Changes: Rewritten; lien extended to carrier. Lien of common carrier validated unless carrier had notice that consignor lacked authority to subject the goods to charges and expenses. Where the carrier is not required by law to receive the goods for transportation, lien validated against anyone who permitted the bailor to have possession even if he had no real or apparent authority.

Purposes of Changes:

The section is intended to give carriers a specific statutory lien for charges and expenses similar to that given to warehousemen by the first sentence of Section 7–209. But since carriers do not commonly claim a lien for charges in relation to other goods or lend money on the security of goods in their hands, provisions for a general lien or a security interest similar to those in Section 7–209(1) and (2) are omitted. See Comment to Section 7–105. Since the lien given by this section is specific, and the storage or transportation often preserves or increases the value of the goods, subsection (2) validates the lien against anyone who permitted the bailor to have possession of the goods. Where the carrier is required to receive the goods for transportation, the owner's interest may be subjected to charges and expenses arising out of deposit of his goods by a thief. Cf. Section 9–310. The crucial mental element is the carrier's knowledge or reason to know of the bailor's lack of authority.

Cross References:

Sections 7–209, 9–102(2) and 9–310.

Definitional Cross References:

"Bill of lading." Section 1–201.
"Consignor." Section 7–102.
"Delivery." Section 1–201.
"Goods." Section 7–102.
"Person." Section 1–201.
"Purchaser." Section 1–201.
"Value." Section 1–201.

Section 7–308. Enforcement of Carrier's Lien.

(1) A carrier's lien may be enforced by public or private sale of the goods, in bloc or in parcels, at any time or place and on any terms which are commercially reasonable, after notifying all persons known to claim an interest in the goods. Such notification must include a statement of the amount due, the nature of the proposed sale and the time and place of any public sale. The fact that a better price could have been obtained by a sale at a different time or in a different method from that selected by the carrier is not of itself sufficient to establish that the sale was not made in a commercially reasonable manner. If the carrier either sells the goods in the usual manner in any recognized market therefor or if he sells at the price current in such market at the time of his sale or if he has otherwise sold in conformity with commercially reasonable practices among dealers in the type of goods sold he has sold in a commercially reasonable manner. A sale of more goods than apparently necessary to be offered to ensure satisfaction of the obligation is not commercially reasonable except in cases covered by the preceding sentence.

(2) Before any sale pursuant to this section any person claiming a right in the goods may pay the amount necessary to satisfy the lien and the reasonable expenses incurred under this section. In that event the goods must not be sold, but must be retained by the carrier subject to the terms of the bill and this Article.

(3) The carrier may buy at any public sale pursuant to this section.

(4) A purchaser in good faith of goods sold to enforce a carrier's lien takes the goods free of any rights of persons against whom the lien was valid, despite noncompliance by the carrier with the requirements of this section.

(5) The carrier may satisfy his lien from the proceeds of any sale pursuant to this section but must hold the balance, if any, for delivery on demand to any person to whom he would have been bound to deliver the goods.

(6) The rights provided by this section shall be in addition to all other rights allowed by law to a creditor against his debtor.

(7) A carrier's lien may be enforced in accordance with either subsection (1) or the procedure set forth in subsection (2) of Section 7–210.

(8) The carrier is liable for damages caused by failure to comply with the requirements for sale under this section and in case of willful violation is liable for conversion.

New York Annotations

(1) Although the Uniform Bills of Lading Act contains no provision governing the enforcement of the common law carrier's lien, there are several relevant statutory provisions:

(a) Lien Law, §§ 200–210, govern realization at least for liens created by that chapter. See the definition of "lienor" in Lien Law, § 2, as well as § 205. The lien of truckman under Lien Law, § 187, may be so enforced.

(b) General Business Law, §§ 285–287, with respect to express companies, and Railroad Law, § 68, with respect to railroads and other transportation companies, provide that where such firms have unclaimed freight for one year the goods may be sold at public auction. In both statutes there are provisions for disposing of perishables promptly.

(c) General Business Law, §§ 280–284, provide for public sale of unclaimed freight held by proprietors of stage, canal, and steamboat lines. Further, Personal Property Law, § 213, provides that a carrier shall not be liable for failure to deliver after the goods have been "lawfully sold" to satisfy a carrier's lien. However, nowhere is the term "lawfully sold" defined by statute

If the Code does not repeal the statutes collected under (b) and (c), *supra,* these provisions may continue to provide a method alternative to that provided by this section. The Code provision is designed to eliminate ambiguity and uncertainty in situations not covered by those sections. Under this subsection the test of "commercial reasonableness" would determine the whether, where, when, and how of the sale. See Section 7–210 for the same test in enforcement of warehouseman's liens.

(2) through (8) These are new as to bills of lading. They are virtually identical to subsections (3) through (9) of Section 7–210 governing warehouseman's liens. Note that subsection (7) permits enforcement under the more controlled terms of Section 7–210(2).

Historical Note: "Bid" was changed to "buy" in subsection (3) and the first sentence of that subsection moved to new subsection (8). See Section 7–210(4). Supp. No. 1 also added new subsection (7) to give carriers the same alternative procedure available to warehousemen. (1956 Recommendations, p. 211.)

Official Uniform Comment

Prior Uniform Statutory Provision: Section 33, Uniform Warehouse Receipts Act.

Changes: Rewritten; provisions extended to carriers' liens; simplified foreclosure proceeding provided.

Purposes of Changes:

This section is intended to give the carrier an enforcement procedure of his lien coextensive with that given the warehousemen in cases other than those covering noncommercial storage by him. See Comment to Section 7–210.

Cross Reference:

Section 7–210.

Definitional Cross References:

"Bill of lading." Section 1–201.
"Creditor." Section 1–201.
"Delivery." Section 1–201.
"Good faith." Section 1–201.
"Goods." Section 7–102.
"Notification." Section 1–201.
"Notifies." Section 1–201.
"Person." Section 1–201.
"Purchaser." Section 1–201.
"Rights." Section 1–201.
"Term." Section 1–201.

UCC

Section 7–309. Duty of Care; Contractual Limitation of Carrier's Liability.

(1) A carrier who issues a bill of lading whether negotiable or non-negotiable must exercise the degree of care in relation to the goods which a reasonably careful man would exercise under like circumstances. This subsection does not repeal or change any law or rule of law which imposes liability upon a common carrier for damages not caused by its negligence.

(2) Damages may be limited by a provision that the carrier's liability shall not exceed a value stated in the document if the carrier's rates are dependent upon value and the consignor by the carrier's tariff is afforded an opportunity to declare a higher value or a value as lawfully provided in the tariff, or where no tariff is filed he is otherwise advised of such opportunity; but no such limitation is effective with respect to the carrier's liability for conversion to its own use.

(3) Reasonable provisions as to the time and manner of presenting claims and instituting actions based on the shipment may be included in a bill of lading or tariff.

New York Annotations

Whereas § 3 of the Uniform Bills of Lading Act (Personal Property Law, § 189) leaves in doubt the propriety of attempts to limit financial responsibility, or to specify the time and method of making claims, the Code declares that such provisions are proper within prescribed limits. Section 1–102(3) generally permits variation by agreement but prohibits disclaimers of the standards of care imposed by the Code. The Code rule is consistent with New York case law, National Blouse Corp. v. Felson, 274 App.Div. 164, 79 N.Y.S.2d 765, aff'd, 299 N.Y. 612, 86 N.E.2d 177 (1949); Murphy v. Export Steamship Corp., 151 Misc. 655, 271 N.Y.S. 880 (1934).

The standard of care imposed by subsection (1) is that of a "reasonably careful man under like circumstances", while Personal Property Law, § 189, speaks of the standard of a "reasonably careful manin regard to similar goods of his own." Note that subsection (1) also explicitly continues any stricter rule of law imposing liability on a carrier, e. g. Public Service Law, § 38.

Historical Note: The changes were proposed on behalf of the Pennsylvania State Chamber of Commerce. The change from "vary with" to "are dependent upon" in new subsection (2) conforms to the language of 49 U.S.C. § 20(11). The other changes (e.g. the addition of the last sentence to subsection (1)) avoid any implied invitation to the development of a common-law rule imposing insurer's liability on carriers other than common carriers. Compare Section 7 204. (1956 Recommendations, p. 212.)

Official Uniform Comment

Prior Uniform Statutory Provision: Section 3, Uniform Bills of Lading Act.
Changes: Consolidated and rewritten.

Purposes of Changes:

The old uniform act provided that bills of lading could not contain terms impairing the obligation of reasonable care. Whether this is violated by a stipulation that in case of loss the bailee's liability is limited to stated amounts has been much controverted. For interstate rail transportation the matter is settled by the Carmack Amendment to the Interstate Commerce Act (See 49 U.S.C.A. § 20(11)). The present section is a generalized version of the Interstate Commerce Act provisions. The obligation of due care is radically qualified, in the case of maritime bills and international airbills, by federal legislation and treaty. All this special legislation would remain in effect even if Congress enacts this Code, including the present Article. See Section 7-103.

Subsection (1) does not impair any rule of law imposing the liability of an insurer on a common carrier in intrastate commerce. Subsection (2), however, applies to such liability as well as to liability based on negligence. The entire section is subject under Section 7-103 to applicable provisions in filed tariffs, such as the common disclaimer of responsibility for undeclared articles of extraordinary value, hidden from view. Tariffs which lawfully provide a maximum unit value beyond which goods are not taken fall within the same principle, and are expressly covered by the words "value as lawfully provided in the tariff."

Cross Reference:

Section 7–103.

Definitional Cross References:

"Action." Section 1–201.
"Bill of lading." Section 1–201.
"Consignor." Section 7–102.
"Document." Section 7–102.
"Goods." Section 7–102.
"Value." Section 1–201.

PART 4

WAREHOUSE RECEIPTS AND BILLS OF LADING: GENERAL OBLIGATIONS

Section 7–401. Irregularities in Issue of Receipt or Bill or Conduct of Issuer.

The obligations imposed by this Article on an issuer apply to a document of title regardless of the fact that

(a) the document may not comply with the requirements of this Article or of any other law or regulation regarding its issue, form or content; or

(b) the issuer may have violated laws regulating the conduct of his business; or

(c) the goods covered by the document were owned by the bailee at the time the document was issued; or

(d) the person issuing the document does not come within the definition of warehouseman if it purports to be a warehouse receipt.

New York Annotations

(a) As to the effect of failure to comply with the requirements of this Article, see annotation to Section 7–202. The Code rule on the obligation imposed by Article 7 is new but is consistent with Joseph v. Viane, Inc., 118 Misc. 344, 194 N.Y.S. 235, aff'd, 206 App.Div. 698, 199 N.Y.S. 930 (1923) (non-complying warehouse receipt treated as negotiable document). No cases were found on the effect of noncompliance with other laws as to form or content.

(b) This subparagraph is consistent with Siebert v. Erie R. Co., 189 App. Div. 586, 179, N.Y.S. 136, aff'd, 232 N.Y. 517, 134 N.E. 553 (1921) (carrier liable for goods received from shipper who was given illegal preference).

(c) Compare, as to warehouse receipts, General Business Law, §§ 91 and 137, requiring the statement of the warehouseman's ownership on the receipt and making non-compliance a crime. The Code makes no criminal provision on any matter.

(d) This subparagraph guards against a narrow application of the duties imposed by Article 7 where the person issuing the document purports to issue a warehouse receipt. See annotation to Section 7–102(h).

Historical Note: Subparagraph (d) was changed in response to a question of the Law Revision Commission to make it clear that the issuer's liability is not defeated merely because he is not engaged in the business of storing goods for hire. (1956 Recommendations, p. 213; Excerpts, p. 446.)

Official Uniform Comment

Prior Uniform Statutory Provision: Section 20, Uniform Warehouse Receipts Act; Section 23, Uniform Bills of Lading Act.

Changes: Most of the material is new; the uniform act sections cited deal only with non-receipt and misdescription.

Purposes of Changes and New Matter:

The bailee's liability on his document despite non-receipt or misdescription of the goods is affiliated in Section 7-203 and 7-301. The purpose of this section is to make it clear that regardless of irregularities a document which falls within the definition of document of title imposes on the issuer the obligations stated in this Article. For example, a bailee will not be permitted to avoid his obligation to deliver the goods (Section 7-403) or his obligation of due care with respect to them. (Sections 7-204 and 7-309) by taking the position that no valid "document" was issued because he failed to file a statutory bond or did not pay stamp taxes or did not disclose the place of storage in the document. Sanctions against violations of statutory or administrative duties with respect to documents should be limited to revocation of license or other measures prescribe by the regulation imposing the duty. As to the continuing vitality of regulations, in addition to those found in this Article, of documents of title, see Sections 7-103 and 10-103.

Cross References:

Sections 7–103, 7–203, 7–204, 7–301, 7–309 and 10–103.

Definitional Cross References:

"Bailee." Section 7–102.
"Document." Section 7–102.
"Document of title." Section 1–201.
"Goods." Section 7–102.

"Issuer." Section 7–102.
"Person." Section 1–201.
"Warehouse receipt." Section 1–201.
"Warehouseman." Section 7–102.

Section 7–402. Duplicate Receipt or Bill; Overissue.

Neither a duplicate nor any other document of title purporting to cover goods already represented by an outstanding document of the same issuer confers any right in the goods, except as provided in the case of bills in a set, overissue of documents for fungible goods and substitutes for lost, stolen or destroyed documents. But the issuer is liable for damages caused by his overissue or failure to identify a duplicate document as such by conspicuous notation on its face.

New York Annotations

The section expands the present rules of Personal Property Law, § 193, and General Business Law, § 93, which apply only to negotiable documents, to make the issuer of non-marked non-negotiable documents liable for damages caused by overissuance or his failure to note a duplicate conspicuously. "Conspicuous" is defined in Section 1–201(10). The provision that unmarked duplicates confer no rights in goods is new, but probably states existing law. See 2 Williston, Sales, Sec. 441 (1948). The exception for fungible goods applies only to warehouse receipts (Section 7–207(2)). Note that this section does not cover disputes between holders of documents not "of the same issuer." See Section 7–503.

Historical Note: See Historical Note to Section 7–202(2) for the explanation of the change from "resulting from" to "caused by" in the second sentence. (1956 Recommendations, p. 213.)

Official Uniform Comment

Prior Uniform Statutory Provision: Section 6, Uniform Warehouse Receipts Act; Section 7, Uniform Bills of Lading Act.

Changes: Consolidated and rewritten.

Purposes of Changes:

1. This section treats a duplicate which is not properly identified as such like any other overissue of documents: a purchaser of such a document acquires no title but only a cause of action for damages against the person who made his deception possible, except in the cases noted in the section. But parts of a bill lawfully issued in a set of parts are not "overissue" (Section 7-304). Of course, if the issuer has clearly indicated that a document is a duplicate so that no one can be deceived by it, and in fact the duplicate is a correct copy of the original, the warehouseman is not liable for preparing and delivering such a duplicate copy.

2. The section applies to non-negotiable documents to the extent of providing an action for damages for one who acquires an unmarked duplicate from a transferor who knew the facts and would therefore himself have had no cause of action against the issuer of the duplicate. Ordinarily the transferee of a nonnegotiable document acquires only the rights of his transferor.

3. Overissue is defined so as to exclude the common situation where two valid documents of different issuers are outstanding for the same goods at the same time. Thus freight forwarders commonly issue bills of lading to their customers for small

shipments to be combined into carload shipments for which the railroad will issue a bill of lading to the forwarder. So also a warehouse receipt may be outstanding against goods, and the holder of the receipt may issue delivery orders against the same goods. In these cases dealings with the subsequently issued documents may be effective to transfer title; e.g. negotiation of a delivery order will effectively transfer title in the ordinary case where no dishonesty has occurred and the goods are available to satisfy the orders. Section 7-503 provides for cases of conflict between documents of different issuers.

Cross References:

Point 1: Sections 7–207, 7–304, and 7–601.
Point 3: Section 7–503.

Definitional Cross References:

"Bill of lading." Section 1–201.
"Conspicuous." Section 1–201.
"Document." Section 7–102.
"Document of title." Section 1–201.
"Fungible" goods. Section 1–201.
"Goods." Section 7–102.
"Issuer." Section 7–102.
"Right." Section 1–201.

Section 7–403. Obligation of Warehouseman or Carrier to Deliver; Excuse.

(1) The bailee must deliver the goods to a person entitled under the document who complies with subsections (2) and (3), unless and to the extent that the bailee establishes any of the following:

(a) delivery of the goods to a person whose receipt was rightful as against the claimant;

(b) damage to or delay, loss or destruction of the goods for which the bailee is not liable, but the burden of establishing negligence in such cases is on the person entitled under the document;

(c) previous sale or other disposition of the goods in lawful enforcement of a lien or on warehouseman's lawful termination of storage;

(d) the exercise by a seller of his right to stop delivery pursuant to the provisions of the Article on Sales (Section 2–705);

(e) a diversion, reconsignment or other disposition pursuant to the provisions of this Article (Section 7–303) or tariff regulating such right;

(f) release, satisfaction or any other fact affording a personal defense against the claimant;

(g) any other lawful excuse.

(2) A person claiming goods covered by a document of title must satisfy the bailee's lien where the bailee so requests or where the bailee is prohibited by law from delivering the goods until the charges are paid.

(3) Unless the person claiming is one against whom the document confers no right under Section 7–503(1), he must surrender for cancellation or notation of partial deliveries any outstanding negotiable document covering the goods, and the bailee must cancel the document or conspicuously note the partial delivery thereon or be liable to any person to whom the document is duly negotiated.

(4) "Person entitled under the document" means holder in the case of a negotiable document, or the person to whom delivery is to be made by terms of or pursuant to written instructions under a non-negotiable document.

Amended by Laws 1963, Ch. 1003, eff. Sept. 27, 1964.

N.Y. Commission Comments

The New York Code as amended by L. 1963, c. 1003, includes the optional language [as to the burden of establishing negligence] at the end of paragraph (b) of subsection (1) of this section.

New York Annotations

(1)(a) *Accord:* Personal Property Law, §§ 197 and 198; General business Law, §§ 95 and 96.

(b) *Accord:* Personal Property Law, § 197; General Business Law, §§ 95 and 107. The New York Code as amended by L.1963 c. 1003, includes the optional language in paragraph (b) of Subsection (1), designed to adopt the rule on burden of proof laid down for carriers in federal cases. The optional rule is consistent with New York law as to warehousemen and carriers other than common carriers. Personal Property Law, § 197, and General Business Law, § 95, clearly state that the bailee must establish the existence of a lawful excuse, such as loss by theft or destruction by fire. If the warehouseman shows a loss of the goods from fire or theft, he satisfies the duty of explanation, and the owner must show that such loss was occasioned by the negligence of the warehouseman. Draper v. Delaware & Hudson Canal Co., 118 N.Y. 118 (1889) (under bill of lading providing that after arrival of goods, although they remain in the cars, carrier's liability should be that of a warehouseman and not a carrier; liability for loss by fire depended on affirmative proof of negligence); Caldwell v. N. J. Steamboat Co., 47 N.Y. 282 (1872) (liability for personal injuries suffered during steamboat trip; steamboat company's liability was not as insurer, and burden was on plaintiff to establish negligence).

Where the liability of a common carrier is not validly limited by statute or contract, it is liable as insurer (Merritt v. Earle, 29 N.Y. 115 (1864)), and has the burden of establishing the facts by which it is entitled to any exception from an insurer's liability. That is, it must show that it was free from any neglect concurring in or contributing to a loss claimed to result from an act of God. Michaels v. New York Central R.R. Co., 30 N.Y. 564 (1864).

(c) *Accord:* Personal Property Law, § 213, and General Business Law, § 121.

(d) This seems to be in *accord* with the implications of §§ 95 and 133 of the General Business Law; and §§ 197 and 228 of the Personal Property Law. See Personal Property Law, §§ 138-140, particularly § 140(2).

(e) See annotation to Section 7–303.

(f) and (g) These subparagraphs seem to be in *accord* with Personal Property Law, § 140, which retains traditional defenses for the bailee.

(2) Generally this subsection is in *accord* with Personal Property Law, § 197, and General Business Law, § 95. The Code requires the bailee to request satisfaction of the lien except where the bailee is prohibited by law from delivering before payment. The present statute seems to make an offer to satisfy the lien a condition precedent to the duty to deliver regardless of any request.

(3) This provision generally restates existing New York law. Personal Property Law, §§ 200 and 201; and General Business Law, § 98. The Code makes it clear that an outstanding negotiable document need not be surrendered if the claimant is the true owner and the document has been procured by a thief. The requirement of surrender of a negotiable document for notation of partial deliveries makes explicit the requirement clearly implied in the current statutes. "Conspicuous" is defined in Section 1–201(10).

(4) Generally in *accord* with Personal Property Law, § 198, and General Business Law, § 96. The Code makes it clear that the bailee must deliver to the holder of a delivery order executed by a consignee in a non-negotiable document. See Bank of America v. Whitney-Central Nat'l Bank, 291 Fed. 929 (5th Cir. 1923) (N.Y. law). As to the effect of instructions given to a carrier under a non-negotiable bill of lading, see annotations to Section 7–303.

Historical Note: Supp. No. 1 added the bracketed provision in subsection (1)(b), stating the rule laid down for carriers in many federal cases. State decisions are in conflict as to both carriers and warehousemen. Particular states may prefer to adopt the federal rule.

Supp. No. 1 also added new subsection (1)(g) to protect the bailee from liability in cases of compulsion of legal process, disposition of hazardous goods, and other situations which might be held not to afford a "personal defense" under subsection (1)(f).

Supp. No. 1 revised subsections (2) and (3) to dispense with a request by the bailee when the carrier is forbidden by law to deliver without payment of charges, and to protect the bailee from liability for misdelivery when goods held under a negotiable document are lawfully sold to enforce the bailee's lien. (1956 Recommendations, p. 214.)

Official Uniform Comment

Prior Uniform Statutory Provision: Sections 8 through 12, 16 and 19, Uniform Warehouse Receipts Act; Sections 11 through 15, 19 and 22, Uniform Bills of Lading Act.

Changes: Consolidated and rewritten.

Purposes of Changes:

1. The general and primary purpose of this revision is to simplify the statement of the bailee's obligation on the document. The interrelations of the separate sections of the old uniform acts dealing with "obligation to deliver," "justification in delivering," and "liability for misdelivery" are obscure. The present section is constructed on the basis of stating what previous deliveries or other circumstances operate to excuse the bailee's normal obligation on the document. Accordingly, "justified" deliveries under the old uniform acts now find their place as "excuse" under subsection (1). Unjustified deliveries, i.e., "misdeliveries" under the old acts, are simply omitted from the list of excuses, thus permitting the normal obligation on the document to be asserted.

2. The principal case covered by subsection (1)(a) is delivery to a person whose title is paramount to the rights represented by the document. For example, if a thief deposits stolen goods in a warehouse and takes a negotiable receipt, the warehouseman

is not liable on the receipt if he has surrendered the goods to the true owner, even though the receipt is held by a good faith purchaser. See Section 7-503(1). However, if the owner entrusted the goods to a person with power of disposition, and that person deposited the goods and took a negotiable document, the owner's receipt would not be rightful as against a holder to whom the negotiable document was duly negotiated, and delivery to the owner would not give the bailee a defense against such a holder. See Sections 7-502 (1)(b), 7-503(1)(a).

3. Subsection (1)(b) amounts to a cross reference to all the tort law that determines the varying responsibilities and standards of care applicable to commercial bailees. A restatement of this tort law would be beyond the scope of this Act. Much of the applicable law as to responsibility of bailees for the preservation of the goods and limitation of liability in case of loss has been codified for particular classes of bailees in interstate and foreign commerce by federal legislation and treaty and for intrastate carriers and other bailees by the regulatory state laws preserved by Section 7-103. In the absence of governing legislation the common law will prevail subject to the minimum standard of reasonable care prescribed by Sections 7-204 and 7-309 of this Article. The optional language in subsection (1)(b) states the rule laid down for interstate carriers in many federal cases. State decisions are in conflict as to both carriers and warehousemen. Particular states may prefer to adopt the federal rule.

4. Subsection (2) eliminates the implication of the old uniform acts that a request for delivery must be accompanied by a formal tender of the amount of the charges due. Rather, the bailee must request payment of the amount of his lien when asked to deliver, and only in case this request is refused is he justified in declining to deliver because of nonpayment of charges. Where delivery without payment is forbidden by law, the request is treated as implicit. Such a prohibition reflects a policy of uniformity to prevent discrimination by failure to request payment in particular cases.

5. Subsection (3) states the obvious duty of a bailee to take up a negotiable document or note partial deliveries conspicuously thereon, and the result of failure in that duty. It is subject to only one exception, that stated in subsection 1(a) of this section and in Section 7-503(1). It is limited to cases of delivery to a claimant; it has no application, for example, where goods held under a negotiable document are lawfully sold to enforce the bailee's lien.

Cross References:

Point 2: Section 7–502 and 7–503.
Point 3: Section 7–103, 7–204, 7–309 and 10–103.
Point 5: Section 7–503(1).

Definitional Cross References:

"Bailee." Section 7–102.
"Conspicuous." Section 1–201.
"Delivery." Section 1–201.
"Document." Section 7–102.
"Document of title." Section 1–201.
"Duly negotiate." Section 7–501.
"Goods." Section 7–102.
"Person." Section 1–201.
"Receipt of goods." Section 2–103.
"Right." Section 1–201.
"Terms." Section 1–201.
"Warehouseman." Section 7–102.
"Written." Section 1–201.

Section 7–404. No Liability for Good Faith Delivery Pursuant to Receipt or Bill.

A bailee who in good faith including observance of reasonable commercial standards has received goods and delivered or otherwise disposed of them according to the terms of the document of title or pursuant to this Article is not liable therefor. This rule applies even though the person from whom he received the goods had no authority to procure the document or to dispose of the goods and even though the person to whom he delivered the goods had no authority to receive them.

New York Annotations

This section makes explicit the implication of the present statutes (Personal Property Law, § 199, and General Business Law, § 97). The Code confers immunity on the bailee even where the depositor was a thief. Present statutes do not clearly so provide, but the result is consistent with Restatement, Torts, § 235. Further, the section protects the bailee in delivering to a holder of a document even though the holder is not entitled to the goods. Such protection is limited to the bailee who follows the terms of the document or this Article "in good faith including the observance of reasonable commercial standards." Contrast, Section 1–201(19). Present law would deny any protection to a bailee if the true owner requested the bailee not to deliver. Personal Property Law, §§ 198 and 199. General Business Law, §§ 96 and 97.

Historical Note: The section was revised for clarification to meet criticism by the Law Revision Commission directed at this section 7–501(4). The changes make it clear that the section applies to a delivery to a fraudulent holder of a valid document as well as to a holder of an invalid document. The Commission had read Section 7–501(4) as permitting delivery to the holder of a negotiable document after an adverse claim had been made by another person; this section, as revised, makes it clear that the non-liability of the bailee in such a case depends on good faith. (1956 Recommendations, p. 215; Excerpts, p. 447.)

Official Uniform Comment

Prior Uniform Statutory Provision: Section 10, Uniform Warehouse Receipts Act; Section 13, Uniform Bills of Lading Act.

Changes: Consolidated and rewritten.

Purposes of Changes:

The generalized test of good faith and observance of reasonable commercial standards is substituted for the attempts to particularize what constitutes good faith in the cited sections of the old uniform acts. The section states explicitly what is perhaps an implication from the old acts that the common law rule of "innocent conversion" by unauthorized "intermeddling" with another's property is inapplicable to the operations of commercial carriers and warehousemen, who in good faith and with reasonable observance of commercial standards perform obligations which they have assumed and which generally they are under a legal compulsion to assume. The section applies to delivery to a fraudulent holder of a valid document as well as to delivery to the holder of an invalid document.

Definitional Cross References:

"Bailee." Section 7–102.

"Delivery." Section 1–201.
"Document of title." Section 1–201.
"Good faith." Section 1–201.
"Goods." Section 7–102.
"Person." Section 1–201.
"Receipt of goods." Section 2–103.
"Term." Section 1–201.

PART 5

WAREHOUSE RECEIPTS AND BILLS OF LADING: NEGOTIATION AND TRANSFER

Section 7–501. Form of Negotiation and Requirements of "Due Negotiation."

(1) A negotiable document of title running to the order of a named person is negotiated by his indorsement and delivery. After his indorsement in blank or to bearer any person can negotiate it by delivery alone.

(2)(a) A negotiable document of title is also negotiated by delivery alone when by its original terms it runs to bearer;

(b) When a document running to the order of a named person is delivered to him the effect is the same as if the document had been negotiated.

(3) Negotiation of a negotiable document of title after it has been indorsed to a specified person requires indorsement by the special indorsee as well as delivery.

(4) A negotiable document of title is "duly negotiated" when it is negotiated in the manner stated in this section to a holder who purchases it in good faith without notice of any defense against or claim to it on the part of any person and for value, unless it is established that the negotiation is not in the regular course of business or financing or involves receiving the document in settlement or payment of a money obligation.

(5) Indorsement of a non-negotiable document neither makes it negotiable nor adds to the transferee's rights.

(6) The naming in a negotiable bill of a person to be notified of the arrival of the goods does not limit the negotiability of the bill nor constitute notice to a purchaser thereof of any interest of such person in the goods.

Amended by Laws, Ch. 1003, eff. Sept. 27, 1964.

New York Annotations

(1) *Accord:* Personal Property Law, §§ 109 and 110 (Uniform Sales Act); Personal Property Law, § § 214, 215, and 217 (Uniform Bills of Lading Act); General Business Law, §§ 122 and 124 (Uniform Warehouse Receipts Act).

(2)(a) *Accord* as to warehouse receipts: General Business Law, § 122. As noted in the annotation to Section 7–104 the Code, unlike present law, recognizes bearer bills of lading in intrastate transactions.

(b) This provision extends to documents of title the rule that a payee of a negotiable instrument can, if he meets all other requirements, be a holder in due course entitled to rights created by negotiation. See annotation to Section 3–302(2). This result, not expressly adopted in the present statutes, is to enable the person named in the document, whether he is a depositor, buyer, or financing bank to claim the rights created by negotiation. For examples of such rights, see Sections 7–207(2), 7–304(3) and (4), and 7–502.

(3) The Code adopts the doctrine that the last indorsement controls. *Accord:* Personal Property Law, §§ 109, 215, and General Business Law, § 122. The definition of "holder" in Section 1–201(20) is limited by and must read in light of this section.

(4) The present statutes use the purchase "duly negotiated" without defining the term. Personal Property Law, §§ 114 and 218; General Business Law, § 125. Existing statutes, however, do provide that named defects, e.g. fraud, accident or duress, do not impair the effectiveness of the negotiation if the transferee pays value without notice of the defect (Personal Property Law, §§ 119 and 224; General Business Law, § 131). The Code here adds the tests that, to qualify, a transfer must be in "good faith" and in the "regular course of business or financing", and that the transaction does not involve receiving the document in settlement or payment of money obligation. Under Section 1–201(44) a pre-existing debt is "value", and the fifth paragraph of Comment 1 indicates that definition is to be applied here. Present law is in accord: Personal Property Law, §§ 156 and 239; and General Business Law, § 142. The Code makes a further distinction, however, in eliminating from the class of "duly negotiated" transfers those transactions in which a document is taken in payment of, rather than as security for, a money debt.

(5) *Accord:* Personal Property Law, §§ 112 and 216; and General Business Law, § 123.

(6) *Accord:* Personal Property Law, § 195.

Historical Note: Supp. No. 1 deleted the reference to "reasonable commercial standards" in subsection (4) to conform to a change made in Section 3–302(1)(b) on commercial paper. The change in that same subsection from "current course of business" to "regular course of business" was suggested by the Law Revision Commission to avoid any implication of a time factor or of a requirement of "new value." At the same time new language was added to make it clear that payment of a debt by a delivery of a document of title is not treated as in regular course. The last clause of subsection (4) was deleted to meet a criticism by the Law Revision Commission; at the same time Section 7–404 was revised to make clear its application to the situation formerly covered by the deleted clause. The reference to "notice" in subsection (4) was added for clarification on the recommendation of the Pennsylvania State Chamber of Commerce. (1956 Recommendations, p. 216; Excerpts, p. 447.)

Official Uniform Comment

Prior Uniform Statutory Provision: Sections 28, 29, 31, 32 and 38, Uniform Sales Act; Sections 37, 38, 39, 40 and 47, Uniform Warehouse Receipts Act; Sections 9, 28, 29, 30, 31 and 38, Uniform Bills of Lading Act.

Changes: Consolidated and rewritten.

Purposes of Changes:

1. In general this section is intended to clarify the language of the old acts and to restate the effect of the better decisions thereunder. An important new concept is added, however, in the requirement of "regular course of business of financing"

to effect the "due negotiation" which will transfer greater rights than those held by the person negotiating. The foundation of the mercantile doctrine of good faith purchase for value has always been, as shown by the case situations, the furtherance and protection of the regular course of trade. The reason for allowing a person, in bad faith or in error, to convey away rights which are not his own has from the beginning been to make possible the speedy handling of the great run of commercial transactions which are patently usual and normal.

There are two aspects to the usual and normal course of mercantile dealings, namely, the person making the transfer and the nature of the transaction itself. The first question which arises is: Is the transferor a person with whom it is reasonable to deal as having full powers? In regard to documents of title the only holder whose possession appears, commercially, to be in order is almost invariably a person in the trade. No commercial purpose is served by allowing a tramp or a professor to "duly negotiate" and order bill of lading for hides or cotton not his own, and since such a transfer is obviously not in the regular course of business, it is excluded from the scope of the protection of subsection (4).

The second question posed by the "regular course" qualification is: Is the transaction one which is normally proper to pass full rights without inquiry, even though the transferor himself may not have such rights to pass, and even though he may be acting in breach of duty? In raising this question the "regular course" criterion has the further advantage of limiting, the effective wrongful disposition to transactions whose protection will really further trade. Obviously, the snapping up of goods for quick resale at a price suspiciously below the market deserves no protection as a matter of policy: it is also clearly outside the range of regular course.

Any notice from the face of the document sufficient to put a merchant on inquiry as to the "regular course" quality of the transaction will frustrate a "due negotiation." Thus irregularity of the document on its face or unexplained staleness of a bill of lading may appropriately be recognized as negating a negotiation in "regular" course.

A pre-existing claim constitutes value, and "due negotiation" does not require "new value." A usual and ordinary transaction in which documents are received as security for credit previously extended may be in "regular" course, even though there is a demand for additional collateral because the creditor "deems himself insecure." But the matter has moved out of the regular course of financing if the debtor is thought to be insolvent, the credit previously extended is in effect cancelled, and the creditor snatches a plank in the shipwreck under the guise of a demand for additional collateral. Where a money debt is "paid" in commodity paper, any question of "regular" course disappears, as the case is explicitly excepted from "due negotiation."

2. Negotiation under this section may be made by any holder no matter how he acquired possession of the document. The present section follows in this respect the Uniform Bills of Lading Act and amendments of the original Uniform Sales Act and Uniform Warehouse Receipts Act proposed by the Commissioners on Uniform State Laws in 1922.

3. Subsection (2)(b) makes explicit a matter upon which the intent of the old acts was clear but the language somewhat obscure: a negotiation results from a delivery to a banker or buyer to whose order the document has been taken by the person making the bailment. There is no presumption of irregularity in such a negotiation; it may very well be in "regular course."

4. This Article does not contain any provision creating a presumption of due negotiation to, and full rights in, a holder of a document of title akin to that created by Section 16, 24 and 59 of the Negotiable Instruments Law. But the reason of the provisions of this Act (Section 1-202) on the prima facie authenticity and accuracy of third party documents, joins with the reason of the present section to work such a presumption in favor of any person who has power to make a due negotiation. It would not make sense for this Act to authorize a purchaser to indulge the presumption of regularity if the courts were not also called upon to do so.

Cross References:

Point 1: Sections 7–502 and 7–503.
Point 2: Section 7–502.

Definitional Cross References:

"Bearer." Section 1–201.
"Delivery." Section 1–201.
"Document." Section 7–102.
"Document of title." Section 1–201.
"Good faith." Section 1–201.
"Holder." Section 1–201.
"Notice." Section 1–201.
"Person." Section 1–201.
"Purchase." Section 1–201.
"Rights." Section 1–201.
"Term." Section 1–201.
"Value." Section 1–201.

Section 7–502. Rights Acquired by Due Negotiation.

(1) Subject to the following section and to the provisions of Section 7–205 on fungible goods, a holder to whom a negotiable document of title has been duly negotiated acquires thereby:

(a) title to the document;

(b) title to the goods;

(c) all rights accruing under the law of agency or estoppel, including rights to goods delivered to the bailee after the document was issued; and

(d) the direct obligation of the issuer to hold or deliver the goods according to the terms of the document free of any defense or claim by him except those arising under the terms of the document or under this Article. In the case of a delivery order the bailee's obligation occurs only upon acceptance and the obligation acquired by the holder is that the issuer and any indorser will procure the acceptance of the bailee.

(2) Subject to the following section, title and rights so acquired are not defeated by any stoppage of the goods represented by the document or by surrender of such goods by the bailee, and are not impaired even though the negotiation or any prior negotiation constituted a breach of duty or even though any person has been deprived of possession of the document by misrepresentation, fraud, accident, mistake, duress, loss, theft or conversion, or even though a previous sale or other transfer of the goods or document has been made to a third person.

New York Annotations

This section must be read together with Sections 7–503 and 7–205.

(1)(a) and (b) Under the present New York rules a person to whom a negotiable document has been duly negotiated acquires "such title to the goods" as his transferor, or the consignor and consignee, or the depositor or the person named in the receipt "had or had ability to convey to a purchaser in good faith for value." Personal Property Law, §§ 114 and 218; an General Business Law, § 125. The Code restates these rules and makes it clear that such a transferee also gets a protected position as to the document. To the extent that the section enlarges the transferee's rights to the goods it is consistent with the language of "absolute title" in Commercial Savings Bank of Grand Rapids v. Mann, 206 App. Div. 297, 200 N.Y.S. 587, aff'd, 238 N.Y. 559, 144 N.E. 890 (1924).

(c) The subparagraph is in accord with the leading case on "feeding" a negotiable bill of lading by a subsequent receipt of the goods. Baldwin v. Childs, 249 N.Y. 212, 163 N.E. 737 (1928).

(d) Delivery orders are recognized in the definition of "document of title" in Uniform Sales Act, § 76 (Personal Property Law, § 156). The rights of a transferee of a non-negotiable delivery order depend upon notification of the bailee rather than acceptance. See Sections 7–504(2) and 2–503(4). Cundill V. Lewis, 245 N.Y. 383, 157 N.E. 502 (1927). In the language of the present statute the holder is apparently given the direct obligation of the bailee, assuming that the bailee and the issuer are the same person. Personal Property Law, § 114. The Code clarifies this situation by treating negotiable delivery orders separately and making the bailee's obligation depend upon his acceptance.

(2) Comment 4 states that this subsection "adds nothing to the effect of the rules stated in subsection (1), but it has been included since such explicit references were relied upon under the prior acts to preserve the rights of a purchaser by due negotiation unimpaired." The subsection restates Personal Property Law, §§ 119, 224, and 228; and General Business Law, §§ 131 and 133. Together with subsection 1(d) this subsection rejects the notion that delivery of the goods to a prior holder of a negotiable document "spends" so that a subsequent purchaser acquires no right to the goods. Compare National Commercial Bank v. Lackawanna Transportation Co., 59 App. Div. 270, 69 N.Y.S. 396, aff'd, 172 N.Y. 596, 64 N.E. 1123 (1902).

Historical Note: Supp. No. 1 changed subsection (1)(c) to refer expressly to the case of "feeding" referred to in Comment 2. Subsection (1)(d) was also changed and the postamble deleted to make it clear that the provision as to delivery orders applies only to delivery orders in negotiable form, to avoid impairment of the holder's rights against persons other than the bailee, and to subject the holder to such defenses as non-negligent destruction even though not apparent on the face of the document. The last sentence of subsection (d) also seems to be directed to a Law Revision Commission comment.

Further revision deleted the reference to "field warehouse receipts" in the preamble to subsection (1) to conform to the deletion of Section 7–205(2). At the same time the words "apparent on its face" were deleted from subsection (1)(d), at the suggestion of the Law Revision Commission, as covered by the words "arising under the terms." The cross-reference in subsection (2) was made necessary by changes in Section 7–503 to meet criticism by the Law Revision Commission with respect to delivery orders. (1956 Recommendations, p. 218; Excerpts, p. 448.)

Official Uniform Comment

Prior Uniform Statutory Provision: Sections 20(4), 25, 33, 38 and 62, Uniform Sales Act; Sections 41, 47, 48 and 49, Uniform Warehouse Receipts Act; Sections 32, 38, 39, 40 and 42, Uniform Bills of Lading Act.

Changes: Rewritten.

Purposes of Changes:

1. The several necessary qualifications of the broad principle that the holder of a document acquired in a due negotiation is the owner of the document and the goods have been brought together in the next section.

2. Subsection (1)(c) covers the case of "feeding" of a duly negotiated document by subsequent delivery to the bailee of such goods as the document falsely purported to cover; the bailee in such case is estopped as against the holder of the document.

3. The explicit statement in subsection (1)(d) of the bailee's direct obligation to the holder precludes the defense, sometimes successfully asserted under the old acts, that the document in question was "spent" after the carrier had delivered the goods to a previous holder. But the holder is subject to such defenses as non-negligent destruction even though not apparent on the face of the document, and the bailee's obligation is of course subject to lawful provisions in filed classifications and tariffs. See Section 7-103, 7-403. The sentence on delivery orders applies only to delivery orders in negotiable form which have been duly negotiated. On delivery orders, see also Section 7-503(2) and Comment.

4. Subsection (2) condenses and continues the law of a number of sections of the prior acts which gave full effect to the issuance or due negotiation of a negotiable document. The subsection adds nothing to the effect of the rules stated in subsection (1), but it has been included since such explicit references were relied upon under the prior acts to preserve the rights of a purchaser by due negotiation unimpaired. The listing is not exhaustive. Only those matters have been repeated in this subsection which were explicitly reserved in the prior acts except in the case of stoppage in transit. Here, the language has been broadened to include "any stoppage" lest an inference be drawn that a stoppage of the goods before or after transit might cut off otherwise impair the purchaser's rights.

Cross References:

Sections 7–103, 7–205, 7–403 and 7–503.

Definitional Cross References:

"Bailee." Section 7–102.
"Delivery." Section 1–201.
"Delivery order." Section 7–102.
"Document." Section 7–102.
"Document of title." Section 1–201.
"Duly negotiate." Section 7–501.
"Fungible." Section 1–201.
"Goods." Section 7–102.
"Holder." Section 1–201.
"Issuer." Section 7–102.
"Person." Section 1–201.
"Rights." Section 1–201.
"Term." Section 1–201.
"Warehouse receipt." Section 1–201.

Section 7–503. Document of Title to Goods Defeated in Certain Cases.

(1) A document of title confers no right in goods against a person who before issuance of the document had a legal interest or a perfected security interest in them and who neither

(a) delivered or entrusted them or any document of title covering them to the bailor or his nominee with actual or apparent authority to ship, store or sell or with power to obtain delivery under this Article (Section 7–403) or with power of disposition under this Act (Section 2–403 and 9–307) or other statute or rule of law; nor

(b) acquiesced in the procurement by the bailor of his nominee of any document of title.

(2) Title to goods based upon an unaccepted delivery order is subject to the rights of anyone to whom a negotiable warehouse receipt or bill of lading covering the goods has been duly negotiated. Such a title may be defeated under the next section to the same extent as the rights of the issuer or a transferee from the issuer.

(3) Title to goods based upon a bill of lading issued to a freight forwarder is subject to the rights of anyone to whom a bill issued by the freight forwarder is duly negotiated; but delivery by the carrier in accordance with Part 4 of this Article pursuant to its own bill of lading discharges the carrier's obligation to deliver.

New York Annotations

(1) As noted in the annotation to Section 7–502(1)(a) and (b), present New York law gives the transferee, to whom the document was duly negotiated, such rights against the true owner as the consignor or the depositor or the person entitled under the document, or the transferee, could convey. Where the depositor of the goods has a defective title, the Code expands the ability of the person in possession to give title to a "buyer in ordinary course of business." See Sections 2–403 and 9–307. Further, the reference to a power in the depositor under "other statute or rule of law" would make applicable the Factor's Act, Personal Property Law, § 43. In addition this subsection protects the purchaser by due negotiation where the true owner "acquiesced" in the procurement of any document of title. The change in emphasis will probably expand the protection of the document holder's title, although one can find a similar approach in present law, e.g. B. W. Dyer & Co. v. Monitz, Wollack & Colodney, 16 Misc.2d 1033, 184 N.Y.S.2d 445 (1959). Of course, in the absence of such authority, power of disposition, or acquiescence, a thief cannot deposit the goods and acquire power to give good title through the document. See Moors v. Kidder, 106 N.Y. 32, 12 N.E. 818 (1887).

(2) There is no present statutory provision like this subsection, and no New York cases on the points could be found.

(3) This subsection is also new. Note that the carrier is here protected by "delivery pursuant to its own bill of lading." See Section 1–201(19) where "good faith" is defined as honesty in fact, and Section 7–404 which requires "good faith, including the observance of reasonable commercial standards."

Historical Note: Supp. No. 1 changed the last sentence of the section to avoid any requirement that a non-negotiable bill of lading be surrendered.

Subsections (1) and (2) were changed for clarification in response to criticism by the Law Revision Commission. The changes in subsection (1) made it clear that a perfected security interest is not defeated merely because it is not a legal interest, that "entrusting" of goods and that "power of disposition" includes power given by the Code or other statute. The words "or pursuant to a contract for sale" were deleted to avoid defeat of a perfected security interest retained by a seller in goods not sold to a merchant.

Further changes met criticism by the Law Revision Commission directed at changes made by Supp. No. 1 in the provisions of Section 7–502 affecting delivery orders. Under subsection (1) of this section a delivery order issued by a person having no right in or power over the goods is ineffective unless the owner acts as provided in subsection (1)(a) or (b). Thus the rights of a transferee of a non-negotiable warehouse receipt can be defeated by a delivery order subsequently issued by the transferor only if the transferee "delivers or entrusts" to the "person procuring" the delivery order or "acquiesces" in his procurement. Similarly, a second delivery order issued by the same issuer for the same goods will ordinarily be subject to the first, both under this section and under Section 7–402. Once a delivery order is validly issued, it may nevertheless be defeated under subsection (2) in much the same way that the rights of a transferee may be defeated under Section 7–504. But an accepted delivery order has the same effect as a document issued by the bailee. (1956 Recommendations, p. 219; Excerpts, p. 449.)

Official Uniform Comment

Prior Uniform Statutory Provision: Section 33, Uniform Sales Act; Section 41, Uniform Warehouse Receipts Act; Section 32, Uniform Bills of Lading Act.

Changes: Subsection (1) narrows, as compared to the cited sections, the occasions for defeating the document holder's title.

Purposes of Changes:

1. In general it may be said that the title of a purchaser by due negotiation prevails over almost any interest in the goods which existed prior to the procurement of the document of title if the possession of the goods by the person obtaining the document derived from any action by the prior claimant which introduced the goods into the stream of commerce or carried them along that stream. A thief of the goods cannot indeed by shipping or storing them to his own order acquire power to transfer them to a good faith purchaser. Nor can a tenant or mortgagor defeat any rights of a landlord or mortgagee which have been perfected under the local law merely by wrongfully shipping or storing a portion of the crop or other goods. However, "acquiescence" by the landlord or tenant does not require active consent under subsections (1)(b) and knowledge of the likelihood of storage or shipment with no objection or effort to control it is sufficient to defeat this rights as against one who takes by "due" negotiation of a negotiable document.

On the other hand, where goods are delivered to a factor for sale, even though the factor has made no advances and is limited in his duty to sell for cash, the goods are "entrusted" to him "with actual . . . authority . . . to sell" under subsection (1)(a), and if he procures a negotiable document of title he can transfer the owner's interest to a purchaser by due negotiation. Further, where the factor is in the business of selling, goods entrusted to him simply for safekeeping or storage may be entrusted under circumstances which give him "apparent authority to ship, store or sell" under subsection (1)(a), or power of disposition under Section 2-403, 7-205 or 9-307, or under a statute such as the earlier Factors Acts, or under a rule of law giving effect to apparent ownership. See Section 1-103.

Persons having an interest in goods also frequently deliver or entrust them to agents or servants other than factors for the purpose of shipping or warehousing or under circumstances reasonably contemplating such action. Rounding out the case law development under the prior Acts, this Act is clear that such persons assume full risk that the agent to whom the goods are so delivered may ship or store in breach of duty, take a document to his own order and then proceed to misappropriate it. This Act makes no distinction between possession or merely custody in such situations and finds no exception in the case of larceny by a bailee or the like. The safeguard in such situations lies in the requirement that a due negotiation can occur only "in the regular course of business or financing" and that the purchase be in good faith and without notice. See Section 7-501. Documents of title have no market among the commercially inexperienced and the commercially experienced do not take them without inquiry from persons known to be truck drivers or petty clerks even though such persons purport to be operating in their own names.

Again, where the seller allows a buyer to receive goods under a contract for sale, though as a "conditional delivery" or under "cash sale" terms and on explicit agreement for immediate payment, the buyer thereby acquires power to defeat the seller's interest by transfer of the goods to certain good faith purchasers. See Section 2-403. Both in policy and under the language of subsection (1)(a) that same power must be extended to accomplish the same result if the buyer procures a negotiable document of title to the goods and duly negotiates it.

2. Under subsection (1) a delivery order issued by a person having no right in or power over the goods is ineffective unless the owner acts as provided in subsection (1)(a) or (b). Thus the rights of a transferee of a non-negotiable warehouse receipt can be defeated by a delivery order subsequently issued by the transferor only if the transferee "delivers or entrusts" to the "person procuring" the delivery order or "acquiesces" in his procurement. Similarly, a second delivery order issued by the same issuer for the same goods will ordinarily be subject to the first, both under this section and under Section 7-402. After a delivery order is validly issued but before it is accepted, it may nevertheless be defeated under subsection (2) in much the same way that the rights of a transferee may be defeated under Section 7-504. For example, a buyer in ordinary course from the issuer may defeat the rights of the holder of a prior delivery order if the bailee receives notification of the buyer's rights before notification of the holder's rights. Section 7-504(2)(b). But an accepted delivery order has the same effect as a document issued by the bailee.

3. Under subsection (3) a bill of lading issued to a freight forwarder is subordinated to the freight forwarder's certificate, since the bill on its face gives notice of the fact that a freight forwarder is in the picture and has in all probability issued a certificate. But the carrier is protected in following the terms of its own bill of lading.

Cross References:

Point 1: Sections 2–403, 7–205, 7–501, 9–307, and 9–309.
Point 2: Sections 7–402 and 7–504.
Point 3: Sections 7–402, 7–403 and 7–404.

Definitional Cross References:

"Contract for sale." Section 2–106.
"Delivery." Section 1–201.
"Delivery order." Section 7–102.
"Document." Section 7–102.
"Document of title." Section 1–201.
"Duly negotiate." Section 7–501.
"Goods." Section 7–102.
"Person." Section 1–201.
"Right." Section 1–201.
"Warehouse receipt." Section 1–201.

Section 7–504. Rights Acquired in the Absence of Due Negotiation; Effect of Diversion; Seller's Stoppage of Delivery.

(1) A transferee of a document, whether negotiable or non-negotiable, to whom the document has been delivered but not duly negotiated, acquires the title and rights which his transferor had or had actual authority to convey.

(2) In the case of a non-negotiable document, until but not after the bailee receives notification of the transfer, the rights of the transferee may be defeated

(a) by those creditors of the transferor who could treat the sale as void under Section 2–402; or

(b) by a buyer from the transferor in ordinary course of business if the bailee has delivered the goods to the buyer or received notification of his rights; or

(c) as against the bailee by good faith dealings of the bailee with the transferor.

(3) A diversion or other change of shipping instructions by the consignor in a non-negotiable bill of lading which causes the bailee not to deliver to the consignee defeats the consignee's title to the goods if they have been delivered to a buyer in ordinary course of business and in any event defeats the consignee's rights against the bailee.

(4) Delivery pursuant to a non-negotiable document may be stopped by a seller under Section 2–705, and subject to the required of due notification there provided. A bailee honoring the seller's instructions is entitled to be indemnified by the seller against any resulting loss or expense.

New York Annotations

(1) Generally in *accord:* Personal Property Law, §§ 115 and 219; and General Business Law, § 126. Gass v. Astoria Veneer Mills, 134 App.Div. 184, 118 N.Y.S. 982 (1909). Note that the rule of this subsection applies to non-negotiable documents and to negotiable documents which have not been duly negotiated.

(2) Under Personal Property Law, §§ 115 and 219, and General Business Law, § 126, until the bailee is notified, the title of a transferee of a non-negotiable document may be defeated by attaching creditors of the transferor. California Packing Corp. v. Kelly Storage etc. Co., 188 App.Div. 475, 177 N.Y.S. 37 (1919) (documentary transfer for security). The Code makes provision for such defeat only where the creditor may treat the sale as void under Section 2–402. See Section 9–305 for a similar requirement of notification of the bailee for perfecting security interests. Section 1–201(25), (26), and (27) define "notification."

The existing statutes also make the rights of the transferee defeaslble by a bona fide purchaser from the transferor if such a purchaser gives the first notice to the bailee. The Code establishes such a protection only for purchasers who qualify as "buyers in the ordinary course of business." Thus the Code rule, unlike prior law, does not apply to successive sales by a non-merchant, nor to a subsequent purchaser for security or in satisfaction of a money debt. Note further that the purchaser must take delivery under this subsection if notice has not been received. Compare Sections 1–201(9) and 2–403. This subsection together with Section 2–503(4) continues the present rule that the transferee's right can be defeated by the protected kind of subsequent purchaser only if the purchaser gives the first notice to the bailee.

The Code makes it clear that the transferee's right can be defeated before notification, by the bailee himself purchasing in good faith or by the bailee delivering to the person to whom the goods are deliverable under the non-negotiable document. See Gubelman v. Panama R. Co., 192 App.Div. 165, 182 N.Y.S. 403, aff'd 232 N.Y. 566, 134 N.E. 574 (1921). Compare General Business Law, § 102, and Personal Property Law, § 205.

(3) This subsection departs from present New York law. In the usual sales transaction calling for shipment of goods, title passes to the vendee upon delivery of the goods to a carrier for shipment. Personal Property Law, § 100, Rule 4(2). Diversion to another purchaser by the consignor-seller cannot defeat the rights of the consignee-buyer named in the non-negotiable bill of lading unless the buyer has lost these rights against the seller (e.g. by stoppage in transit) or is precluded from denying the seller's authority. Personal Property Law, §§ 104 and 138. See Bailey v. Hudson River R.R. Co., 49 N.Y. 70 (1872); Hunter v. Payne, 113 Misc. 385, 184 N.Y.S. 433, aff'd 197 App.Div. 919, 188 N.Y.S. 926 (1920). The Code changes this result. See annotation to Section 7–303.

(4) *Accord:* Personal Property Law, §§ 139 and 140. The Code adds the carrier's express right to indemnity where the seller's request to stop is honored. See annotation to Section 2–705.

Historical Note: Subsection (2) was revised at the suggestion of the Law Revision Commission and for clarification. The changes made it clear that paragraph (b) is limited to buyers in ordinary course and to cases where the bailee has delivered or received notification; the deletion of the reference to Section 2–403 made it clear that possession of the goods by the transferor is not required. The change in paragraph (c) avoids any possibility that the transferee's rights against a fraudulent transferor might be cut off. At the time subsection (3) was revised to make applicable the definition of "buyer in ordinary course of business." (1956 Recommendations, p. 220; Excerpts, p. 450.)

Official Uniform Comment

Prior Uniform Statutory Provision: Section 34, Uniform Sales Act; Sections 41(b) and 42, Uniform Warehouse Receipts Act; Sections 32(b) and 33, Uniform Bills of Lading Act.

Changes: Generally rewritten; Subsection (3) is new.

Purposes of Changes and New Matter:

1. Under the general principles controlling negotiable documents, it is clear that in the absence of due negotiation a transferor cannot convey greater rights than he himself has, even when the negotiation is formally perfect. This section recognizes the transferor's power to transfer rights which he himself has or has "actual authority to convey." Thus, where a negotiable document of title is being transferred the operation of the principle of estoppel is not recognized, as contrasted with situations involving the transfer of the goods themselves. (Compare Section 2-403 on good faith purchase of goods.)

A necessary part of the price for the protection of regular dealings with negotiable documents of title is an insistence that no dealing which is in any way irregular shall be recognized as a good faith purchase of the document or of any rights pertaining to it. So, where the transfer of a negotiable document fails as a negotiation because a requisite indorsement is forged or otherwise missing, the purchaser in good faith and for value may be in the anomalous position of having less rights, in part, than if he had purchased the goods themselves. True, his rights are not subject to defeat by attachment of the goods or surrender of them to his transferor [Contrast subsection

(2)]; but on the other hand, he cannot acquire enforceable rights to control or receive the goods over the bailee's objection merely by giving notice to the bailee. Similarly, a consignee who makes payment to his consignor against a straight bill of lading can thereby acquire the position of a good faith purchaser of goods under provisions of the Article of this Act on Sales (Section 2-403), whereas the same payment made in good faith against an unindorsed order bill would not have such effect. The appropriate remedy of a purchaser in such a situation is to regularize his status by compelling indorsement of the document (see Section 7-506).

2. As in the case of transfer–as opposed to "due negotiation"–negotiable documents, subsection (1) empowers the transferor of a non-negotiable document to transfer only such rights as he himself has or has "actual authority" to convey. In contrast to situations involving the goods themselves the operation of estoppel or agency principles is not here recognized to enable the transferor to convey greater rights than he actually has. Subsection (2) makes it clear, however, that the transferee of a nonnegotiable document may acquire rights greater in some respects than those of his transferor by giving notice of the transfer to the bailee.

3. Subsection (3) is in part a reiteration of the carrier's immunity from liability if it honors instructions of the consignor to divert, but there is added a provision protecting the title of the substituted consignee if the latter is a buyer in ordinary course of business. A typical situation would be where a manufacturer, having shipped a lot of standardized goods to A on nonnegotiable bill of lading, diverts the goods to customer B who pays for them. Under orthodox passage-of-title-by-appropriation doctrine A might reclaim the goods from B. However, no consideration of commercial policy supports this involvement of an innocent third party in the default of the manufacturer on his contract to A; and the common commercial practice of diverting goods in transit suggests a trade understanding in accordance with this subsection.

4. Subsection (4) gives the carrier an express right to indemnity where he honors a seller's request to stop delivery.

5. Section 1–201(27) gives the bailee protection, if due diligence is exercised, similar to that found in the third paragraph of Section 33, Uniform Bills of Lading Act, where the bailee's organization has not had time to act on a notification.

Cross References:

Point 1: Sections 2–403 and 7–506.
Point 2: Section 2–403.
Point 3: Sections 7–303 and 7–403(1)(e).
Point 4: Sections 2–705 and 7–403(1)(d).

Definitional Cross References:

"Bailee." Section 7–102.
"Bill of lading." Section 1–201.
"Buyer in ordinary course of business." Section 1–201.
"Consignee." Section 7–102.
"Consignor." Section 7–102.
"Creditor." Section 1–201.
"Delivery." Section 1–201.
"Document." Section 7–102.
"Duly negotiate." Section 7–501.
"Good faith." Section 1–201.
"Goods." Section 7–102.
"Honor." Section 1–201.
"Notification." Section 1–201.
"Purchaser." Section 1–201.

"Rights." Section 1–201.

Section 7–505. Indorser Not a Guarantor for Other Parties.

The indorsement of a document of title issued by a bailee does not make the indorser liable for any default by the bailee or by previous indorsers.

New York Annotations

Accord: Personal Property, §§ 118 and 222; General Business Law, § 129.

Official Uniform Comment

Prior Uniform Statutory Provision: Section 37, Uniform Sales Act; Section 45, Uniform Warehouse Receipts Act; Section 36, Uniform Bills of Lading Act.

Changes: No substantial change.

Purposes of Changes:

The indorsement of a document of title is generally understood to be directed towards perfecting the transferee's rights rather than towards assuming additional obligations. The language of the present section, however, does not preclude the one case in which an indorsement given for value guarantees future action, namely, that in which the bailee has not yet become liable upon the document at the time of the indorsement. Under such circumstances the indorser, of course, engages that appropriate honor of the document by the bailee will occur. See Section 7-502(1)(d) as to negotiable delivery orders. However, even in such a case, once the bailee attorns to the transferee, the indorser's obligation has been fulfilled and the policy of this section excludes any continuing obligation on the part of the indorser for the bailee's ultimate actual performance.

Cross Reference:

Section 7–502.

Definitional Cross References:

"Bailee." Section 7–102.
"Document of title." Section 1–201.
"Party." Section 1–201.

Section 7–506. Delivery Without Indorsement; Right to Compel Indorsement.

The transferee of a negotiable document of title has a specifically enforceable right to have his transferor supply any necessary indorsement but the transfer becomes a negotiation only as of the time the indorsement is supplied.

New York Annotations

Generally, this section is in *accord* with Personal Property Law, §§ 116 and 220, and General Business Law, § 127. The Code eliminates the requirement of present law that the person seeking relief must be a transferee for value.

UCC

Official Uniform Comment

Prior Uniform Statutory Provision: Section 35, Uniform Sales Act; Section 43, Uniform Warehouse Receipts Act; Section 34, Uniform Bills of Lading Act.

Changes: Consolidated and rewritten; former requirement that transfer be "for value" eliminated.

Purposes of Changes:

1. From a commercial point of view the intention to transfer a negotiable document of title which requires an indorsement for its transfer, is incompatible with an intention to withhold such indorsement and so defeat the effective use of the document. This position is sustained by the absence of any reported case applying the prior provisions in almost forty years of decisions. Further, the preceding section and the Comment thereto make it clear that an indorsement generally imposes no responsibility on the indorser.

2. Although this section provides that delivery of a document of title without the necessary indorsement is effective as a transfer, the transferee, of course, has not regularized his position until such indorsement is supplied. Until this is done he cannot claim rights under due negotiation within the requirements of this Article (subsection (4) of Section 7-501) on "due negotiation." Similarly, despite the transfer to him of his transferor's title, he cannot demand the goods from the bailee until the negotiation has been completed and the document is in proper form for surrender. See Section 7-403(2).

Cross References:

Point 1: Section 7–505.
Point 2: Sections 7–510(4) and 7–403(2).

Definitional Cross References:

"Document of title." Section 1–201.
"Rights." Section 1–201.

Section 7–507. Warranties on Negotiation or Transfer of Receipt or Bill.

Where a person negotiates or transfers a document of title for value otherwise than as a mere intermediary under the next following section, then unless otherwise agreed he warrants to his immediate purchaser only in addition to any warranty made in selling the goods

(a) that the document is genuine; and

(b) that he has no knowledge of any fact which would impair its validity or worth; and

(c) that his negotiation or transfer is rightful and fully effective with respect to the title to the document and the goods it represents.

New York Annotations

Personal Property Law, §§ 117 and 221, and General Business Law, § 128, are generally in accord with this section. The Code leaves warranties connected with the goods to the sales provisions of Article 2, Section 2–312 through 2–318. See Kingdom of Sweden v. New York Trust Co., 197 Misc. 431, 96 N.Y.S.2d 779 (1949). Compare Stanford Seed Co. v. Balfour Gurhrie & Co., Ltd., 27 Misc.2d 147, 208 N.Y.S.2d 996 (1960), and "genuine" in Section 1–201(18).

Historical Note: The preamble was received at the suggestion of the Law Revision Commission to state explicitly that the warranties do not run to remote holders or transferees. (1956 Recommendations, p. 221; Excerpts, p. 450.)

Official Uniform Comment

Prior Uniform Statutory Provision: Section 36, Uniform Sales Act; Section 44, Uniform Warehouse Receipts Act; Section 35, Uniform Bills of Lading Act.

Changes: Consolidated and rewritten without change in policy.

Purposes of Changes:

1. This section omits provisions of the prior acts on warranties as to the goods as unnecessary and incomplete. It is unnecessary because such warranties derive from the contract of sale and not from the transfer of the documents. The fact that transfer of control occurs by way of a document of title does not limit or displace the ordinary obligations of a seller. The former provision, moreover, was incomplete because it did not expressly include all of the warranties which might rest upon a seller under such circumstances. This Act handles the problem by means of the precautionary reference to "any warranty made in selling the goods." If the transfer of documents attends or follows the making of a contract for the sale of goods, the general obligations on warranties as to the goods (Sections 2-312 through 2-318) are brought to bear as well as the special warranties under this section.

2. The limited warranties of a delivering or collecting intermediary are stated in Section 7–508.

Cross References:

Point 1: Sections 2–312 through 2–318.

Point 2: Section 7–508.

Definitional Cross References:

"Document." Section 7–102.
"Document of title." Section 1–201.
"Genuine." Section 1–201.
"Goods." Section 7–102.
"Person." Section 1–201.
"Purchaser." Section 1–201.
"Value." Section 1–201.

Section 7–508. Warranties of Collecting Bank as to Documents.

A collecting bank or other intermediary known to be entrusted with documents on behalf of another or with collection of a draft or other claim against delivery of documents warrants by such delivery of the documents only its own good faith and authority. This rule applies even though the intermediary has purchased or made advances against the claim or draft to be collected.

New York Annotations

Although no reference is made to existing acts in the sponsors' Comments, the section is in general *accord* with Personal Property Law, § 223, and General Business Law, § 130. (Uniform Bills of Lading Act, § 37, and Uniform Warehouse Receipts Act, § 46). The Code spells out affirmative warranties of good faith and authority while the present statutes negative warranties of genuineness, quality, or quantity. The present statutes apply to a "mortgagee, pledge, or holder for security," while the Code rule applies explicitly also to a holder for collection. For relevant case material, see annotation to Section 5–111.

Official Uniform Comment

Prior Uniform Statutory Provision: None.

Purposes:

1. To state the limited warranties given with respect to the documents accompanying a documentary draft.

2. In warranting its authority a bank only warrants its authority from its transferor. See Section 4–203. It does not warrant the genuineness or effectiveness of the document. Compare Section 7-507.

3. Other duties and rights of banks handling documentary drafts for collection are stated in Article 4, Part 5.

Cross References:

Sections 4–203 and 7–507, 4–501 through 4–504.

Definitional Cross References:

"Collecting bank." Section 4–105.
"Delivery." Section 1–201.
"Document." Section 7–102.
"Draft." Section 5–103.
"Good faith." Section 1–201.

Section 7–509. Receipt or Bill; When Adequate Compliance With Commercial Contract.

The question whether a document is adequate to fulfill the obligations of a contract for sale or the conditions of a credit is governed by the Articles on Sales (Article 2) and on Letters of Credit (Article 5).

New York Annotations

No comparable explicit provision for referring such questions to other bodies of law now exists.

Official Uniform Comment

Prior Uniform Statutory Provision: None.

Purposes:

To cross-refer to the Articles of this Act which deal with the substantive issued of the type of document of title required under the contract entered into by the parties.

Cross References:

Articles 2 and 5.

Definitional Cross References:

"Contract for sale." Section 2–106.
"Document." Section 7–102.

PART 6

WAREHOUSE RECEIPTS AND BILLS OF LADING: MISCELLANEOUS PROVISIONS

Section 7–601. Lost and Missing Documents.

(1) If a document has been lost, stolen or destroyed, a court may order delivery of the goods or issuance of a substitute document and the bailee may without liability to any person comply with such order. If the document was negotiable the claimant must post security approved by the court to indemnify any person who may suffer loss as a result of non-surrender of the document. If the document was not negotiable, such security may be required at the discretion of the court. The court may also in its discretion order payment of the bailee's reasonable costs and counsel fees.

(2) A bailee who without court order delivers goods to a person claiming under a missing negotiable document is liable to any person injured thereby, and if the delivery is not in good faith becomes liable for conversion. Delivery in good faith is not conversion if made in accordance with a filed classification or tariff or, where no classification or tariff is filed, if the claimant posts security with the bailee in an amount at least double the value of the goods at the time of posting to indemnify any person injured by the delivery who files a notice of claim within one year after the delivery.

New York Annotations

(1) Personal Property Law, § 203, and General Business Law, § 100, make provision for judicial orders of delivery as to "lost or destroyed" negotiable documents. The Code extends these provisions to non-negotiable and to stolen documents. In addition, the Code, unlike the present statutes, permits the bailee to comply with a court order "without liability to any person"; the holder's recourse is thus limited to the bond.

(2) When a negotiable document is missing, the present statutes do not authorize a delivery without court order. Delivery without a court order, under the Code, as under the present statutes, may subject the bailee to liability to persons injured by the failure to cancel the document. Personal Property Law, § 200; General Business Law, § 98; and Code Section 7–403(3). The bailee will therefore usually insist on

the posting of some security such as a bond. Furthermore, this subsection limits the bailee's liability for conversion in such cases. (Personal Property Law, § 199, and General Business Law, § 97). Liability for conversion is imposed, as under present law, for delivery in bad faith. However, the Code eliminates liability for conversion if the bailee delivers in good faith, in accordance with a filed classification or tariff, or in the absence of such a filing upon the posting of the described security. See Penal Law, § 365, for the criminal sanction.

Historical Note: Supp. No. 1 changed subsection (2). The changes, (1) made the same provisions for carriers and for warehousemen, both where tariffs are filed and where they are not, (2) made it clear that the posting of security under this section bears only on liability for conversion, (3) provided that the beneficiary of the posted security is any person injured, and (4) placed a time limit on the posted security. (1956 Recommendations, p. 223.)

Official Uniform Comment

Prior Uniform Statutory Provision: Section 14, Uniform Warehouse Receipts Act; Section 17, Uniform Bills of Lading Act.

Changes: General Revision. Principal innovations include: affirmation of bailee's privilege to deliver to claimant without resort to judicial proceedings if the bailee acts in good faith and is willing to take the full risk of loss in case the lost document turns up in the hands of an innocent purchaser; explicit authorization to the court to order bailee to issue a substitute document rather than make physical delivery of the goods; inclusion of "stolen" as well as lost documents; extension of section to non-negotiable documents.

Purposes of Changes:

The purposes of the changes insofar as they are not self-evident are as follow:

1. As to bailee's privilege to deliver without court order, doubt had arisen as to the propriety of such action under Section 54 of the Uniform Warehouse Receipts Act, which made it a crime to deliver goods covered by negotiable receipts without taking up the receipts "except in the cases provided for in Section 14" (the lost receipts section). This has been interpreted by one court as exempting from criminal liability only if the judicial procedure of Section 14 was followed. Dahl v. Winter-Truesdell-Diercks Co., 61 N.D. 84, 237 N.W. 202 (1931). Although the criminal provisions are not being re-enacted in this Act (and the Uniform Bills of Lading Act never did include such a criminal provision), it seems advisable to clarify the legality of the well established commercial practice of bailees to make delivery where they are satisfied that the claimant is the person entitled under a lost document. Since the bailee remains liable on the document in such cases, he will usually insist that the claimant provide an indemnity bond.

2. The old acts provide only for compulsory delivery of goods; this Section provides also for compulsory issuance of a substitute document. If continuance of the bailment is desirable there is no reason to require the goods to be withdrawn and redeposited in order to secure a negotiable document. The present acts would probably be so interpreted. Section 20 of the Federal Warehouse Act and some state laws expressly require issuance of a new receipt of proof of loss and posting of bond.

3. Claimants on non-negotiable instruments are permitted to avail themselves of this procedure because straight bills of lading sometimes contain provisions that the goods shall not be delivered except upon production of the bill. If the carrier should choose to insist upon production of the bill, the consignee should have some means of compelling delivery on satisfactory proof of entitlement.

Ordinarily no security would be necessary to indemnify a bailee in delivering to the person named in a non-negotiable document. But disputes as to ability may arise, in which case if there is a reasonable doubt on the point the bailee should be protected against the possibility that the missing document would, in the hands of an innocent purchaser for value, be held negotiable.

4. It seems unnecessary to state, as do the present acts, that the court shall act "on satisfactory proof of such loss or destruction." The right of action created by the section is conditioned on a document being lost, stolen or destroyed. Plaintiff must of course bring himself within the section. There is nothing in the language of the old acts to suggest that they intended to impose anything but the normal burden of proof on the plaintiff in such proceedings.

5. Subsection (2) makes it clear that after delivery without court order the bailee remains liable for actual damages. Liability for conversion is provided where the delivery is dishonest, but excluded where a filed classification or tariff is followed in good faith, or where the described bond is posted in good faith and no classification or tariff is filed. Liability for conversion in other cases is left to judicial decision.

Definitional Cross References:

"Bailee." Section 7–102.
"Bill of lading." Section 1–201.
"Delivery." Section 1–201.
"Document." Section 7–102.
"Good faith." Section 1–201.
"Goods." Section 7–102.
"Person." Section 1–201.
"Warehouse receipt." Section 1–201.
"Warehouseman." Section 7–102.

Section 7–602. Attachment of Goods Covered by a Negotiable Document.

Except where the document was originally issued upon delivery of the goods by a person who had no power to dispose of them, no lien attaches by virtue of any judicial process to goods in the possession of a bailee for which a negotiable document of title is outstanding unless the document be first surrendered to the bailee or its negotiation enjoined, and the bailee shall not be compelled to deliver the goods pursuant to process until the document is surrendered to him or impounded by the court. One who purchases the document for value without notice of the process or injunction takes free of the lien imposed by judicial process.

New York Annotations

Generally in *accord* with Personal Property Law, §§ 120 and 210, and General Business Law, § 110. The Code, like present law, protects bailees from attachment of goods in the absence of control of the negotiable document. Meyers Lumber Co. v. Wayne Machinery Co., Inc., 123 Misc.517, 206 N.Y.S. 1 (1924); Goldstein v. Societa Veneziana, 193 App. Div. 168, 183 N.Y.S. 460 (1920). Further, the Code, like present law, does not apply that protection where the person asserting rights has a claim independent of and adverse to the document. Salant v. Pennsylvania R. Co., 188 App.Div. 851, 177 N.Y.S. 475, aff'd 231 N.Y. 607, 132 N.E. 907 (1921). The protection extended to purchasers of the document accords with Civil Practice Act, § 917 [now CPLR § 6214].

Historical Note: The word order was revised at the suggestion of the Law Revision Commission to make the "except" clause applicable to the compulsion of the bailee as well as to the denial of lien. (1956 Recommendations, p. 223; Excerpts, p. 451.)

Official Uniform Comment

Prior Uniform Statutory Provisions: Section 25, Uniform Warehouse Receipts Act; Section 24, Uniform Bills of Lading Act.

Changes: Consolidated and rewritten.

Purposes of Changes:

1. The purpose of the section is to protect the bailee from conflicting claims of the document holder and the judgment creditors of the person who deposited the goods. The rights of the former prevail unless, in effect, the judgment creditors immobilize the negotiable document. However, if the document was issued upon deposit of the goods by a person who had no power to dispose of the goods so that the document is ineffective to pass title, judgment liens are valid to the extent of the debtor's interest in the goods.

2. The last sentence covers the possibility that the holder of a document who has been enjoined from negotiating it will violate the injunction by negotiating to an innocent purchaser for value. In such case the lien will be defeated.

Cross Reference:

Point 1: Section 7–503.

Definitional Cross References:

"Bailee." Section 7–102.
"Delivery." Section 1–201.
"Document." Section 7–102.
"Goods." Section 7–102.
"Notice." Section 1–201.
"Person." Section 1–201.
"Purchase." Section 1–201.
"Value." Section 1–201.

Section 7–603. Conflicting Claims; Interpleader.

If more than one person claims title or possession of the goods, the bailee is excused from delivery until he has had a reasonable time to ascertain the validity of the adverse claims or to bring an action to compel all claimants to interplead and may compel such interpleader, either in defending an action for non-delivery of the goods, or by original action, whichever is appropriate.

New York Annotations

Accord: Personal Property Law, §§ 206 and 207; General Business Law, §§ 103 and 104. United Shoe Repairing Machine Co v. Dochtermann, etc. Co., 186 App.Div. 359, 174 N.Y.S. 284 (1919); Manhattan Storage, etc. Co. v. Benguiat Art Museum, 155 App.Div. 196, 139 N.Y.S. 1073 (1913); Rosenberg v. Viane, Inc., 109 Misc. 215, 179 N.Y.S. 447 (1919); Zuber v. Mehrle, 112 N.Y.S. 1093 (1908).

Historical Note: Supp. No. 1 added affirmative authorization for interpleader similar to that found in the prior acts. (1956 Recommendations, p. 223.)

Official Uniform Comment

Prior Uniform Statutory Provision: Sections 16 and 17, Uniform Warehouse Receipts Act; Sections 20 and 21, Uniform Bills of Lading Act.

Changes: Consolidation without substantial change.

Purposes of Changes:

The section enables a bailee faced with conflicting claims to the goods to compel the claimants to litigate their claims with each other rather than with him.

Definitional Cross References:

"Action." Section 1–201.
"Bailee." Section 7–102.
"Delivery." Section 1–201.
"Goods." Section 7–102.
"Person." Section 1–201.
"Reasonable time." Section 1–204.

ARTICLE 8

INVESTMENT SECURITIES

[*Article 8 repealed and a new Article 8 added by Laws 1997, Ch. 566, § 5, eff. Oct. 10, 1997.*]

PART 1

SHORT TITLE AND GENERAL MATTERS

PART 2

ISSUE AND ISSUER

PART 3

TRANSFER OF CERTIFICATED AND UNCERTIFICATED SECURITIES

PART 4

REGISTRATION

PART 5

SECURITY ENTITLEMENTS

PART 6

TRANSITION PROVISIONS FOR REVISED ARTICLE 8 AND FOR THE CONFORMING AMENDMENTS TO ARTICLES 1, 5, 9 AND 13

PART 1

SHORT TITLE AND GENERAL MATTERS

Section 8–101. Short Title.

This article may be cited as Uniform Commercial Code–Investment Securities.

Added by Laws 1997, Ch. 566, § 5, eff. Oct. 10, 1997.

Legislative Intent

Legislative intent and declaration. The legislature finds and declares that a revised article eight of the uniform commercial code is needed to provide clarity and certainty regarding the rules that govern how interests in securities are evidenced and how they are transferred in the current securities market. The existing law fails to clearly define such rules when an interest is held through an intermediary, rather than by holding a certificate or by registration with the issuer of securities. The revisions to article 8 of the uniform commercial code proposed by the national conference of commissioners on uniform state laws in 1994 will clarify the law regarding these issues. The legislature intends by adopting those revisions to promote uniformity with the laws of other states so that the securities market will function in such a way that it will be more stable, and so that investors, both individual and corporate, will be more secure and their rights and interests better protected.

Article 8 of the uniform commercial code as revised is not intended to constitute a comprehensive body of law governing the relationship between brokers and their customers nor to be a body of regulatory law to police against improper conduct by brokers or other intermediaries. Many, if not most, aspects of the relationship between brokers and customers are governed by the common law of contract and agency, supplemented or supplanted by federal and state regulatory law. Article 8 of the uniform commercial code does not take the place of this body of common and regulatory law. It simply deals with the mechanisms by which interests in securities are transferred and the rights and duties of those who are involved in the transfer process. It does not, for the most part, deal with the process of entering into contracts for the transfer of securities or regulate the rights and duties of those involved in the contracting process. Sections of article 8 of the uniform commercial code presume the active regulation of the securities industry. The legislature enacts article 8 of the uniform commercial code with the expectation of continued active oversight by agencies of the federal and state governments and the continued availability of the securities investor protection corporation (SIPC) established pursuant to 15 United States Code § 78-ccc, et seq., and the SIPC fund, established pursuant to 15 United States Code § 78-ddd, to protect investors from loss. If the federal or state government alters or reduces its role as protector of shareholders and other participants in the securities market, then the state may need to enact laws in addition to article 8 of the uniform commercial code to address these issues. Except as otherwise expressly provided in this act, the provisions of this act are not intended to change or to control the definitions of the terms "security" and "commodity" contained in any other laws, including but not limited to, the general business law.

Notwithstanding the work done by the uniform commissioners, the legislature finds that there is a lack of clarity in some of the provisions that may raise questions about how particular provisions are to be interpreted. Of particular concern is the situation envisioned by subsections (d) and (e) of section 8-503 of the uniform commercial code involving a purchase (including the taking of a security interest) of a financial asset, e.g., stock, from a securities intermediary, e.g., broker, that sells or pledges that asset in violation of its obligations to an entitlement holder, e.g., customer, who has paid in full and owns the stock. When the purchaser or lender gives value for and obtains control of the financial asset and has not acted in "collusion" with the securities intermediary, then the entitlement holder is limited to remedies against the wrongful intermediary and is without recourse against the purchaser. The term "collusion" is, however, nowhere defined within the text of article 8 of the uniform commercial code, though used elsewhere. See, subsection 2 of section 8-115 of the uniform commercial code.

The legislature intends collusion to include acting in concert, acting by conspiratorial arrangement, or acting by agreement for the purpose of violating the entitlement holder's rights or with actual knowledge that the securities intermediary is violating those rights. Under this standard, "collusion" includes transactions with a securities intermediary in which the purchaser has actual knowledge that the securities intermediary has violated or is violating an entitlement holder's property interest. The legislature intends that the purchaser's knowledge will be judged on a subjective, not an objective basis. When considering whether a purchaser has the requisite actual knowledge of the wrongdoing, the legislature intends that the purchaser be charged with possession of information that is brought to the purchaser's attention or that is contained in communications made or sent to the purchaser but that the purchaser has declined to receive or to communicate to persons within its own organization who are conducting the transaction. Nevertheless, nothing in this standard imposes a duty of inquiry. Thus, for example, a purchaser's knowledge of the precarious financial situation of the financial intermediary coupled with rumors, allegations, or reports of suspected wrongdoing does not amount to collusion. As used in this act, the collusion standard strikes a balance between two competing goals – the need for liquidity and finality in the market for financial assets and the need for assurance that the rules that protect liquidity and finality are not subject to abuse by a purchaser who is willing to participate with or assist an intermediary for the purpose of violating the rights of an intermediary's customers, or a purchaser who acts with actual knowledge of an intermediary's wrongdoing.

Sections 8-504 through 8-508 of the uniform commercial code impose on securities intermediaries certain duties to obtain and maintain financial assets in favor of entitlement holders. These duties implement one of the central tenets of the indirect holding system, that the intermediary undertakes to hold financial assets corresponding to the securities entitlements of its entitlement holders. Because the entitlement holder receives a package of rights that can be asserted directly only against the intermediary, it is essential for the securities intermediary to take appropriate steps to ensure that the entitlement holders receive the full benefit of the economic and other rights that comprise ownership of a security.

A securities intermediary complies with its duties to obtain and maintain financial assets in favor of entitlement holders if it acts as agreed upon between the parties or, in the absence of agreement, if it exercises due care in accordance with reasonable commercial standards. The agreement/due care provisions are intended to provide sufficient flexibility to accommodate these general duties in the wide variety of circumstances that may be encountered in the modern securities holding system. In particular, there may be instances in which a securities intermediary may need to define the exact scope of its duties with respect to the securities. One example would be the holding of foreign securities through a foreign intermediary, in which the risk of loss or destruction of securities is unusually large.

In any case, a securities intermediary's duties with respect to securities entitlements are subject to the general obligation of good faith under section 1-203 of the uniform commercial code, which is defined for purposes of article 8 of the uniform commercial code as requiring honesty in fact and the observance of reasonable commercial standards of fair dealing. Consequently, any agreement with respect to the duties to obtain and maintain securities entitlements is subject to an obligation to observe reasonable commercial standards of fair dealing. An agreement is not, however, subject to the statutory standard of due care, which is applicable only in the absence of agreement as to the standard of due care. Consequently, it may be possible under these provisions for a securities intermediary to contract out of its obligation to exercise due care in accordance with reasonable commercial standards in special circumstances.

The legislature recognizes that investors who hold securities through the indirect holding system expect that a securities intermediary will comply with its duty to obtain and maintain securities entitlements on behalf of its investor. This is the expectation against which the good faith performance of these duties must be tested. It is the intention of the legislature that, in the absence of special circumstances that make it financially unreasonable for an intermediary to provide the customer with the same level of care for particular securities as it does for securities generally, a standard of performance that materially alters a securities intermediary's obligations from those called for under the "due care" standard would be difficult to justify, and the ability to enter into an agreement concerning the securities intermediary's duties with respect to or maintaining securities should not reduce the intermediary's duty to exercise due care with respect to obtaining and maintaining securities entitlements. However, when special circumstances exist that make it financially unreasonable for an intermediary to provide the customer with the level of care for particular securities that it provides for securities generally and the customer still desires the intermediary to act for him or her regarding these securities, it may be appropriate by contract to alter the level of care. An example of unusual circumstances would be securities held outside the United States under conditions that would materially interfere with the usual exercise of due care.

Finally, shares in cooperative apartments present issues unique to New York State, which require special treatment in article 8 of the uniform commercial code. The legislature has consulted the report issued by the Committee on Uniform State Laws and the Banking Law Committee of the Association of the Bar of the City of New York issued on February 21, 1996, and has incorporated its recommendations regarding a special provision in the New York uniform commercial code governing shares in a cooperative apartment. These issues are addressed in subsection (b) of section 8-113, section 9-115, and subsection 7 of section 9-304 of the uniform commercial code.

Section 8–102. Definitions.

(a) In this article:

(1) "Adverse claim" means a claim that a claimant has a property interest in a financial asset and that it is a violation of the rights of the claimant for another person to hold, transfer, or deal with the financial asset.

(2) "Bearer form", as applied to a certificated security, means a form in which the security is payable to the bearer of the security certificate according to its terms but not by reason of an indorsement.

(3) "Broker" means a person defined as a broker or dealer under the federal securities laws, but without excluding a bank acting in that capacity.

(4) "Certificated security" means a security that is represented by a certificate.

(5) "Clearing corporation" means:

(i) a person that is registered as a "clearing agency" pursuant to 15 United States Code, 78-c(a)(23), as from time to time amended;

(ii) a federal reserve bank; or

(iii) any other person that provides clearance or settlement services with respect to financial assets that would require it to register as a clearing agency under the federal securities laws but for an exclusion or exemption from the registration requirement, if its activities as a clearing corporation, including promulgation of rules, are subject to regulation by a federal or state governmental authority.

(6) "Communicate" means to:

(i) send a signed writing; or

(ii) transmit information by any mechanism agreed upon by the persons transmitting and receiving the information.

(7) "Entitlement holder" means a person identified in the records of a securities intermediary as the person having a security entitlement against the securities intermediary. If a person acquires a security entitlement by virtue of Section 8–501(b)(2) or (3), that person is the entitlement holder.

(8) "Entitlement order" means a notification communicated to a securities intermediary directing transfer or redemption of a financial asset to which the entitlement holder has a security entitlement.

(9) "Financial asset", except as otherwise provided in Section 8–103, means:

(i) a security;

(ii) an obligation of a person or a share, participation, or other interest in a person or in property or an enterprise of a person, which is, or is of a type, dealt in or traded on financial markets, or which is recognized in any area in which it is issued or dealt in as a medium for investment; or

(iii) any property that is held by a securities intermediary for another person in a securities account if the securities intermediary has expressly agreed with the other person that the property is to be treated as a financial asset under this article. As context requires, the term means either the interest itself or the means by which a person's claim to it is evidenced, including a certificated or uncertificated security, a security certificate, or a security entitlement.

(10) "Good faith", for purposes of the obligation of good faith in the performance or enforcement of contracts or duties within this Article, means honesty in fact and the observance of reasonable commercial standards of fair dealing.

(11) "Indorsement" means a signature that alone or accompanied by other words is made on a security certificate in registered form or on a separate document for the purpose of assigning, transferring, or redeeming the security or granting a power to assign, transfer, or redeem it.

(12) "Instruction" means a notification communicated to the issuer of an uncertificated security which directs that the transfer of the security be registered or that the security be redeemed.

(13) "Registered form", as applied to a certificated security, means a form in which:

(i) the security certificate specifies a person entitled to the security; and

(ii) a transfer of the security may be registered upon books maintained for that purpose by or on behalf of the issuer, or the security certificate so states.

(14) "Securities intermediary" means:

(i) a clearing corporation; or

(ii) a person, including a bank or broker, that in the ordinary course of its business maintains securities accounts for others and is acting in that capacity.

(15) "Security", except as otherwise provided in Section 8–103, means an obligation of an issuer or a share, participation, or other interest in an issuer or in property or an enterprise of an issuer:

(i) which is represented by a security certificate in bearer or registered form, or the transfer of which may be registered upon books maintained for that purpose by or on behalf of the issuer;

(ii) which is one of a class or series or by its terms is divisible into a class or series of shares, participations, interests, or obligations; and

(iii) which:

(A) is, or is of a type, dealt in or traded on securities exchanges or securities markets; or

(B) is a medium for investment and by its terms expressly provides that it is a security governed by this Article.

(16) "Security certificate" means a certificate representing a security.

(17) "Security entitlement" means the rights and property interest of an entitlement holder with respect to a financial asset specified in Part 5.

(18) "Uncertificated security" means a security that is not represented by a certificate.

(b) Other definitions applying to this Article and the sections in which they appear are:

"Appropriate Person".	Section 8–107.
"Control".	Section 8–106.
"Delivery".	Section 8–301.
"Investment Company Security".	Section 8–103.
"Issuer".	Section 8–201.
"Overissue".	Section 8–210.
"Protected Purchaser".	Section 8–303.
"Securities Account".	Section 8–501.

(c) In addition, Article 1 contains general definitions and principles of construction and interpretation applicable throughout this Article.

(d) The characterization of a person, business, or transaction for purposes of this Article does not determine the characterization of the person, business, or transaction for purposes of any other law, regulation, or rule.

Added by Laws 1997, Ch. 566, § 5, eff. Oct. 10, 1997. See legislative history following § 8–101 for explanation of legislative intent.

Official Comment

1. "Adverse claim." The definition of the term "adverse claim" has two components. First, the term refers only to property interests. Second, the term means not merely that a person has a property interest in a financial asset but that it is a violation of the claimant's property interest for the other person to hold or transfer the security or other financial asset.

The term adverse claim is not, of course, limited to ownership rights, but extends to other property interests established by other law. A security interest, for example, would be an adverse claim with respect to a transferee from the debtor since any effort by the secured party to enforce the security interest against the property would be an interference with the transferee's interest.

The definition of adverse claim in the prior version of Article 8 might have been read to suggest that any wrongful action concerning a security, even a simple breach of contract, gave rise to an adverse claim. Insofar as such cases as *Fallon v. Wall Street Clearing Corp.*, 586 N.Y.S.2d 953, 182 A.D.2d 245, (1992) and *Pentech Intl. v. Wall St. Clearing Co.*, 983 F.2d 441 (2d Cir. 1993), were based on that view, they are rejected by the new definition which explicitly limits the term adverse claim to property interests. Suppose, for example, that A contracts to sell or deliver securities to B, but fails to do so and instead sells or pledges the securities to C. B, the promisee, has an action against A for breach of contract, but absent unusual circumstances the action for breach would not give rise to a property interest in the securities. Accordingly, B does not have an adverse claim. An adverse claim might, however, be based upon principles of equitable remedies that give rise to property claims. It would, for example, cover a right established by other law to rescind a transaction in which securities were transferred. Suppose, for example, that A holds securities and is induced by B's fraud to transfer them to B. Under the law of contract or restitution, A may have a right to rescind the transfer, which gives A a property claim to the securities. If so, A has an adverse claim to the securities in B's hands. By contrast, if B had committed no fraud, but had merely committed a breach of contract in connection with the transfer from A to B, A may have only a right to damages for breach, not a right to rescind. In that case, A would not have an adverse claim to the securities in B's hands.

2. "Bearer form." The definition of "bearer form" has remained substantially unchanged since the early drafts of the original version of Article 8. The requirement that the certificate be payable to bearer by its terms rather than by an indorsement has the effect of preventing instruments governed by other law, such as chattel paper or Article 3 negotiable instruments, from being inadvertently swept into the Article 8 definition of security merely by virtue of blank indorsements. Although the other elements of the definition of security in Section 8-102(a)(14) probably suffice for that purpose in any event, the language used in the prior version of Article 8 has been retained.

3. "Broker." Broker is defined by reference to the definitions of broker and dealer in the federal securities laws. The only difference is that banks, which are excluded from the federal securities law definition, are included in the Article 8 definition when they perform functions that would bring them within the federal securities law definition if it did not have the clause excluding banks. The definition covers both those who act as agents ("brokers" in securities parlance) and those who act as principals ("dealers" in securities parlance). Since the definition refers to persons "defined" as brokers or dealers under the federal securities law, rather than to persons required to "register" as brokers or dealers under the federal securities law, it covers not only registered brokers and dealers but also those exempt from the registration requirement, such as purely intrastate brokers. The only substantive rules that turn on the defined term broker are one provision of the section on warranties, Section 8-108(i), and the special perfection rule in Article 9 for security interests granted by brokers, Section 9-115(4)(c).

4. "Certificated security." The term "certificated security" means a security that is represented by a security certificate.

5. "Clearing corporation." The definition of clearing corporation limits its application to entities that are subject to a rigorous regulatory framework. Accordingly, the definition includes only federal reserve banks, persons who are registered as "clearing agencies" under the federal securities laws (which impose a comprehensive system of regulation of the activities and rules of clearing agencies), and other entities subject to a comparable system of regulatory oversight.

6. "Communicate." The term "communicate" assures that the Article 8 rules will be sufficiently flexible to adapt to changes in information technology. Sending a signed writing always suffices as a communication, but the parties can agree that a different means of transmitting information is to be used. Agreement is defined in Section 1-201(3) as "the bargain of the parties in fact as found in their language or by implication from other circumstances including course of dealing or usage of trade or course of performance." Thus, use of an information transmission method might be found to be authorized by agreement, even though the parties have not explicitly so specified in a formal agreement. The term communicate is used in Sections 8-102(a)(7) (definition of entitlement order), 8-102(a)(11) (definition of instruction), and 8-403 (demand that issuer not register transfer).

7. "Entitlement holder." This term designates those who hold financial assets through intermediaries in the indirect holding system. Because many of the rules of Part 5 impose duties on securities intermediaries in favor of entitlement holders, the definition of entitlement holder is, in most cases, limited to the person specifically designated as such on the records of the intermediary. The last sentence of the definition covers the relatively unusual cases where a person may acquire a security entitlement under Section 8-501 even though the person may not be specifically designated as an entitlement holder on the records of the securities intermediary.

A person may have an interest in a security entitlement, and may even have the right to give entitlement orders to the securities intermediary with respect to it, even though the person is not the entitlement holder. For example, a person who holds securities through a securities account in its own name may have given discretionary trading authority to another person, such as an investment adviser. Similarly, the control provisions in Section 8-106 and the related provisions in Article 9 are designed to facilitate transactions in which a person who holds securities through a securities account uses them as collateral in an arrangement where the securities intermediary has agreed that if the secured party so directs the intermediary will dispose of the positions. In such arrangements, the debtor remains the entitlement holder but has agreed that the secured party can initiate entitlement orders.

8. "Entitlement order." This term is defined as a notification communicated to a securities intermediary directing transfer or redemption of the financial asset to which an entitlement holder has a security entitlement. The term is used in the rules for the indirect holding system in a fashion analogous to the use of the terms "indorsement" and "instruction" in the rules for the direct holding system. If a person directly holds a certificated security in registered form and wishes to transfer it, the means of transfer is an indorsement. If a person directly holds an uncertificated security and wishes to transfer it, the means of transfer is an instruction. If a person holds a security entitlement, the means of disposition is an entitlement order. As noted in Comment 6, an entitlement order need not be initiated by the entitlement holder in order to be effective, so long as the entitlement holder has authorized the other party to initiate entitlement orders. See Section 8-107(b).

9. "Financial asset." The definition of "financial asset," in conjunction with the definition of "securities account" in Section 8-501, sets the scope of the indirect holding system rules of Part 5 of Revised Article 8. The Part 5 rules apply not only to securities held through intermediaries, but also to other financial assets held through intermediaries. The term financial asset is defined to include not only securities but also a broader category of obligations, shares, participations, and interests.

Having separate definitions of security and financial asset makes it possible to separate the question of the proper scope of the traditional Article 8 rules from the question of the proper scope of the new indirect holding system rules. Some forms of financial assets should be covered by the indirect holding system rules of Part 5, but not by the rules of Parts 2, 3, and 4. The term financial asset is used to cover such property. Because the term security entitlement is defined in terms of financial assets rather than securities, the rules concerning security entitlements set out in Part 5 of Article 8 and in Revised Article 9 apply to the broader class of financial assets.

The fact that something does or could fall within the definition of financial asset does not, without more, trigger Article 8 coverage. The indirect holding system rules of Revised Article 8 apply only if the financial asset is in fact held in a securities account, so that the interest of the person who holds the financial asset through the securities account is a security entitlement. Thus, questions of the scope of the indirect holding system rules cannot be framed as "Is such-and-such a 'financial asset' under Article 8?" Rather, one must analyze whether the relationship between an institution and a person on whose behalf the institution holds an asset falls within the scope of the term securities account as defined in Section 8-501. That question turns in large measure on whether it makes sense to apply the Part 5 rules to the relationship.

The term financial asset is used to refer both to the underlying asset and the particular means by which ownership of that asset is evidenced. Thus, with respect to a certificated security, the term financial asset may, as context requires, refer either to the interest or obligation of the issuer or to the security certificate representing that interest or obligation. Similarly, if a person holds a security or other financial asset through a securities account, the term financial asset may, as context requires, refer either to the underlying asset or to the person's security entitlement.

10. "Good faith." Good faith is defined in Article 8 for purposes of the application to Article 8 of Section 1-203, which provides that "Every contract or duty within this Act imposes an obligation of good faith in its performance or enforcement." The sole function of the good faith definition in Revised Article 8 is to give content to the Section 1-203 obligation as it applies to contracts and duties that are governed by Article 8. The standard is one of "reasonable commercial standards of fair dealing." The reference to commercial standards makes clear that assessments of conduct are to be made in light of the commercial setting. The substantive rules of Article 8 have been drafted to take account of the commercial circumstances of the securities holding and processing system. For example, Section 8-115 provides that a securities intermediary acting on an effective entitlement order, or a broker or other agent acting as a conduit in a securities transaction, is not liable to an adverse claimant, unless the claimant obtained legal process or the intermediary acted in collusion with the wrongdoer. This, and other similar provisions, see Sections 8-404 and 8-503(e), do not depend on notice of adverse claims, because it would impair rather than advance the interest of investors in having a sound and efficient securities clearance and settlement system to require intermediaries to investigate the propriety of the transactions they are processing. The good faith obligation does not supplant the standards of conduct established in provisions of this kind.

In Revised Article 8, the definition of good faith is not germane to the question whether a purchaser takes free from adverse claims. The rules on such questions as whether a purchaser who takes in suspicious circumstances is disqualified from protected purchaser status are treated not as an aspect of good faith but directly in the rules of Section 8-105 on notice of adverse claims.

11. "Indorsement" is defined as a signature made on a security certificate or separate document for purposes of transferring or redeeming the security. The definition is adapted from the language of Section 8-308(1) of the prior version and from the definition of indorsement in the Negotiable Instruments Article, see Section 3-204(a). The definition of indorsement does not include the requirement that the signature be made by an appropriate person or be authorized. Those questions are treated in the separate substantive provision on whether the indorsement is effective, rather than in the definition of indorsement. See Section 8-107.

12. "Instruction" is defined as a notification communicated to the issuer of an uncertificated security directing that transfer be registered or that the security be redeemed. Instructions are the analog for uncertificated securities of indorsements of certificated securities.

13. "Registered form." The definition of "registered form" is substantially the same as in the prior version of Article 8. Like the definition of bearer form, it serves primarily to distinguish Article 8 securities from instruments governed by other law, such as Article 3.

14. "Securities intermediary." A "securities intermediary" is a person that in the ordinary course of its business maintains securities accounts for others and is acting in that capacity. The most common examples of securities intermediaries would be clearing corporations holding securities for their participants, banks acting as securities custodians, and brokers holding securities on behalf of their customers. Clearing corporations are listed separately as a category of securities intermediary in subparagraph (i) even though in most circumstances they would fall within the general definition in subparagraph (ii). The reason is to simplify the analysis of arrangements such as the NSCC-DTC system in which NSCC performs the comparison, clearance, and netting function, while DTC acts as the depository. Because NSCC is a registered clearing agency under the federal securities laws, it is a clearing corporation and hence a securities intermediary under Article 8, regardless of whether it is at any particular time or in any particular aspect of its operations holding securities on behalf of its participants.

The terms securities intermediary and broker have different meanings. Broker means a person engaged in the business of buying and selling securities, as agent for others or as principal. Securities intermediary means a person maintaining securities accounts for others. A stockbroker, in the colloquial sense, may or may not be acting as a securities intermediary.

The definition of securities intermediary includes the requirement that the person in question is "acting in the capacity" of maintaining securities accounts for others. This is to take account of the fact that a particular entity, such as a bank, may act in many different capacities in securities transactions. A bank may act as a transfer agent for issuers, as a securities custodian for institutional investors and private investors, as a dealer in government securities, as a lender taking securities as collateral, and as a provider of general payment and collection services that might be used in connection with securities transactions. A bank that maintains securities accounts for its customers would be a securities intermediary with respect to those accounts; but if it takes a pledge of securities from a borrower to secure a loan, it is not thereby acting as a securities intermediary with respect to the pledged securities, since it holds them for its own account rather than for a customer. In other circumstances, those two functions might be combined. For example, if the bank is a government securities dealer it may maintain securities accounts for customers and also provide the customers with margin credit to purchase or carry the securities, in much the same way that brokers provide margin loans to their customers.

15. "Security." The definition of "security" has three components. First, there is the subparagraph (i) test that the interest or obligation be fully transferable, in the sense that the issuer either maintains transfer books or the obligation or interest is represented by a certificate in bearer or registered form. Second, there is the subparagraph (ii) test that the interest or obligation be divisible, that is, one of a class or series, as distinguished from individual obligations of the sort governed by ordinary contract law or by Article 3. Third, there is the subparagraph (iii) functional test, which generally turns on whether the interest or obligation is, or is of a type, dealt in or traded on securities markets or securities exchanges. There is, however, an "opt-in" provision in subparagraph (iii) which permits the issuer of any interest or obligation that is "a medium of investment" to specify that it is a security governed by Article 8.

The divisibility test of subparagraph (ii) applies to the security — that is, the underlying intangible interest — not the means by which that interest is evidenced. Thus, securities issued in book-entry only form meet the divisibility test because the underlying intangible interest is divisible via the mechanism of the indirect holding system. This is so even though the clearing corporation is the only eligible direct holder of the security.

The third component, the functional test in subparagraph (iii), provides flexibility while ensuring that the Article 8 rules do not apply to interests or obligations in circumstances so unconnected with the securities markets that parties are unlikely to have thought of the possibility that Article 8 might apply. Subparagraph (iii)(A) covers interests or obligations that either are dealt in or traded on securities exchanges or securities markets, or are of a type dealt in or traded on securities exchanges or securities markets. The "is dealt in or traded on" phrase eliminates problems in the characterization of new forms of securities which are to be traded in the markets, even though no similar type has previously been dealt in or traded in the markets. Subparagraph (iii)(B) covers the broader category of media for investment, but it applies only if the terms of the interest or obligation specify that it is an Article 8 security. This opt-in provision allows for deliberate expansion of the scope of Article 8.

Section 8-103 contains additional rules on the treatment of particular interests as securities or financial assets.

16. "Security certificate." The term "security" refers to the underlying asset, e.g., 1000 shares of common stock of Acme, Inc. The term "security certificate" refers to the paper certificates that have traditionally been used to embody the underlying intangible interest.

17. "Security entitlement" means the rights and property interest of a person who holds securities or other financial assets through a securities intermediary. A security entitlement is both a package of personal rights against the securities intermediary and an interest in the property held by the securities intermediary. A security entitlement is not, however, a specific property interest in any financial asset held by the securities intermediary or by the clearing corporation through which the securities intermediary holds the financial asset. See Sections 8-104(c) and 8-503. The formal definition of security entitlement set out in subsection (a)(16) of this section is a cross-reference to the rules of Part 5. In a sense, then, the entirety of Part 5 is the definition of security entitlement. The Part 5 rules specify the rights and property interest that comprise a security entitlement.

18. "Uncertificated security." The term "uncertificated security" means a security that is not represented by a security certificate. For uncertificated securities, there is no need to draw any distinction between the underlying asset and the means by which a direct holder's interest in that asset is evidenced. Compare "certificated security" and "security certificate."

Definitional Cross References

"Agreement"–Section 1-201(3)
"Bank"–Section 1-201(4)
"Person"–Section 1-201(30)
"Send"–Section 1-201(38)
"Signed"–Section 1-201(39)
"Writing"–Section 1-201(46)

Section 8–103. Rules for Determining Whether Certain Obligations and Interests Are Securities or Financial Assets.

(a) A share or similar equity interest issued by a corporation, business trust, joint stock company, or similar entity is a security.

(b) an "investment company security" is a security. "investment company security" means a share or similar equity interest issued by an entity that is registered as an investment company under the federal investment company laws, an interest in a unit investment trust that is so registered, or a face-amount certificate issued by a face-amount certificate company that is so registered. Investment company security does not include an insurance policy or endowment policy or annuity contract issued by an insurance company.

(c) An interest in a partnership or limited liability company is not a security unless it is dealt in or traded on securities exchanges or in securities markets, its terms expressly provide that it is a security governed by this Article, or it is an investment company security. However, an interest in a partnership or limited liability company is a financial asset if it is held in a securities account.

(d) A writing that is a security certificate is governed by this Article and not by Article 3, even though it also meets the requirements of that Article. However, a negotiable instrument governed by Article 3 is a financial asset if it is held in a securities account.

(e) An option or similar obligation issued by a clearing corporation to its participants is not a security, but is a financial asset.

(f) A commodity contract, as defined in Section 9–115, is not a security or a financial asset.

Added by Laws 1997, Ch. 566, § 5, eff. Oct. 10, 1997. See legislative history following § 8–101 for explanation of legislative intent.

Official Comment

1. This section contains rules that supplement the definitions of "financial asset" and "security" in Section 8-102. The Section 8-102 definitions are worded in general terms, because they must be sufficiently comprehensive and flexible to cover the wide variety of investment products that now exist or may develop. The rules in this section are intended to foreclose interpretive issues concerning the application of the general definitions to several specific investment products. No implication is made about the application of the Section 8-102 definitions to investment products not covered by this section.

2. Subsection (a) establishes an unconditional rule that ordinary corporate stock is a security. That is so whether or not the particular issue is dealt in or traded on securities exchanges or in securities markets. Thus, shares of closely held corporations are Article 8 securities.

3. Subsection (b) establishes that the Article 8 term "security" includes the various forms of the investment vehicles offered to the public by investment companies registered as such under the federal Investment Company Act of 1940, as amended. This clarification is prompted principally by the fact that the typical transaction in shares of open-end investment companies is an issuance or redemption, rather than a transfer of shares from one person to another as is the case with ordinary corporate stock. For similar reasons, the definitions of indorsement, instruction, and entitlement order in Section 8-102 refer to "redemptions" as well as "transfers," to ensure that the Article 8 rules on such matters as signature guaranties, Section 8-306, assurances, Sections 8-402 and 8-507, and effectiveness, Section 8-107, apply to directions to redeem mutual fund shares. The exclusion of insurance products is needed because some insurance company separate accounts are registered under the Investment Company Act of 1940, but these are not traded under the usual Article 8 mechanics.

4. Subsection (c) is designed to foreclose interpretive questions that might otherwise be raised by the application of the "of a type" language of Section 8-102(a)(15)(iii) to partnership interests. Subsection (c) establishes the general rule that partnership interests or shares of limited liability companies are not Article 8 securities unless they are in fact dealt in or traded on securities exchanges or in securities markets. The issuer, however, may explicitly "opt-in" by specifying that the interests or shares are securities governed by Article 8. Partnership interests or shares of limited liability companies are included in the broader term "financial asset." Thus, if they are held through a securities account, the indirect holding system rules of Part 5 apply, and the interest of a person who holds them through such an account is a security entitlement.

5. Subsection (d) deals with the line between Article 3 negotiable instruments and Article 8 investment securities. It continues the rule of the prior version of Article 8 that a writing that meets the Article 8 definition is covered by Article 8 rather than Article 3, even though it also meets the definition of negotiable instrument. However,

subsection (d) provides that an Article 3 negotiable instrument is a "financial asset" so that the indirect holding system rules apply if the instrument is held through a securities intermediary. This facilitates making items such as money market instruments eligible for deposit in clearing corporations.

6. Subsection (e) is included to clarify the treatment of investment products such as traded stock options, which are treated as financial assets but not securities. Thus, the indirect holding system rules of Part 5 apply, but the direct holding system rules of Parts 2, 3, and 4 do not.

7. Subsection (f) excludes commodity contracts from all of Article 8. However, the Article 9 rules on security interests in investment property do apply to security interests in commodity positions. See Section 9-115 and Comment 8 thereto. "Commodity contract" is defined in Section 9-115.

Definitional Cross References

"Clearing corporation"–Section 8-102(a)(5)
"Commodity contract"–Section 9-115
"Financial asset"–Section 8-102(a)(9)
"Security"–Section 8-102(a)(15)
"Security certificate"–Section 8-102(a)(16)

Section 8–104. Acquisition of Security or Financial Asset or Interest Therein.

(a) A person acquires a security or an interest therein, under this Article, if:

(1) the person is a purchaser to whom a security is delivered pursuant to Section 8–301; or

(2) the person acquires a security entitlement to the security pursuant to Section 8–501.

(b) A person acquires a financial asset, other than a security, or an interest therein, under this Article, if the person acquires a security entitlement to the financial asset.

(c) A person who acquires a security entitlement to a security or other financial asset has the rights specified in Part 5, but is a purchaser of any security, security entitlement, or other financial asset held by the securities intermediary only to the extent provided in Section 8–503.

(d) Unless the context shows that a different meaning is intended, a person who is required by other law, regulation, rule, or agreement to transfer, deliver, present, surrender, exchange, or otherwise put in the possession of another person a security or financial asset satisfies that requirement by causing the other person to acquire an interest in the security or financial asset pursuant to subsection (a) or (b).

Added by Laws 1997, Ch. 566, § 5, eff. Oct. 10, 1997. See legislative history following § 8–101 for explanation of legislative intent.

Official Comment

1. This section lists the ways in which interests in securities and other financial assets are acquired under Article 8. In that sense, it describes the scope of Article

8. Subsection (a) describes the two ways that a person may acquire a security or interest therein under this Article: (1) by delivery (Section 8-301), and (2) by acquiring a security entitlement. Each of these methods is described in detail in the relevant substantive provisions of this Article. Part 3, beginning with the definition of "delivery" in Section 8-301, describes how interests in securities are acquired in the direct holding system. Part 5, beginning with the rules of Section 8-501 on how security entitlements are acquired, describes how interests in securities are acquired in the indirect holding system.

Subsection (b) specifies how a person may acquire an interest under Article 8 in a financial asset other than a security. This Article deals with financial assets other than securities only insofar as they are held in the indirect holding system. For example, a bankers' acceptance falls within the definition of "financial asset," so if it is held through a securities account the entitlement holder's right to it is a security entitlement governed by Part 5. The bankers' acceptance itself, however, is a negotiable instrument governed by Article 3, not by Article 8. Thus, the provisions of Parts 2, 3, and 4 of this Article that deal with the rights of direct holders of securities are not applicable. Article 3, not Article 8, specifies how one acquires a direct interest in a bankers' acceptance. If a bankers' acceptance is delivered to a clearing corporation to be held for the account of the clearing corporation's participants, the clearing corporation becomes the holder of the bankers' acceptance under the Article 3 rules specifying how negotiable instruments are transferred. The rights of the clearing corporation's participants, however, are governed by Part 5 of this Article.

2. The distinction in usage in Article 8 between the term "security" (and its correlatives "security certificate" and "uncertificated security') on the one hand, and "security entitlement" on the other, corresponds to the distinction between the direct and indirect holding systems. For example, with respect to certificated securities that can be held either directly or through intermediaries, obtaining possession of a security certificate and acquiring a security entitlement are both means of holding the underlying security. For many other purposes, there is no need to draw a distinction between the means of holding. For purposes of commercial law analysis, however, the form of holding may make a difference. Where an item of property can be held in different ways, the rules on how one deals with it, including how one transfers it or how one grants a security interest in it, differ depending on the form of holding.

Although a security entitlement is means of holding the underlying security or other financial asset, a person who has a security entitlement does not have any direct claim to a specific asset in the possession of the securities intermediary. Subsection (c) provides explicitly that a person who acquires a security entitlement is a "purchaser" of any security, security entitlement, or other financial asset held by the securities intermediary only in the sense that under Section 8-503 a security entitlement is treated as a *sui generis* form of property interest.

3. Subsection (d) is designed to ensure that parties will retain their expected legal rights and duties under Revised Article 8. One of the major changes made by the revision is that the rules for the indirect holding system are stated in terms of the "security entitlements" held by investors, rather than speaking of them as holding direct interests in securities. Subsection (d) is designed as a translation rule to eliminate problems of co-ordination of terminology, and facilitate the continued use of systems for the efficient handling of securities and financial assets through securities intermediaries and clearing corporations. The efficiencies of a securities intermediary or clearing corporation are, in part, dependent on the ability to transfer securities credited to securities accounts in the intermediary or clearing corporation to the account of an issuer, its agent, or other person by book entry in a manner that permits exchanges, redemptions, conversions, and other transactions (which may be governed by pre-existing or new agreements, constitutional documents, or other instruments) to occur and to avoid the need to withdraw from immobilization in an

intermediary or clearing corporation physical securities in order to deliver them for such purposes. Existing corporate charters, indentures and like documents may require the "presentation," "surrender," "delivery," or "transfer" of securities or security certificates for purposes of exchange, redemption, conversion or other reason. Likewise, documents may use a wide variety of terminology to describe, in the context for example of a tender or exchange offer, the means of putting the offeror or the issuer or its agent in possession of the security. Subsection (d) takes the place of provisions of prior law which could be used to reach the legal conclusion that book-entry transfers are equivalent to physical delivery to the person to whose account the book entry is credited.

Definitional Cross References

"Delivery"–Section 8-301
"Financial asset"–Section 8-102(a)(9)
"Person"–Section 1-201(30)
"Purchaser"–Section 1-201(33) & 8-116
"Security"–Section 8-102(a)(15)
"Security entitlement"–Section 8-102(a)(17)

Section 8–105. Notice of Adverse Claim.

(a) A person has notice of an adverse claim if:

(1) the person knows of the adverse claim;

(2) the person is aware of facts sufficient to indicate that there is a significant probability that the adverse claim exists and deliberately avoids information that would establish the existence of the adverse claim; or

(3) the person has a duty, imposed by statute or regulation, to investigate whether an adverse claim exists, and the investigation so required would establish the existence of the adverse claim.

(b) Having knowledge that a financial asset or interest therein is or has been transferred by a representative imposes no duty of inquiry into the rightfulness of a transaction and is not notice of an adverse claim. However, a person who knows that a representative has transferred a financial asset or interest therein in a transaction that is, or whose proceeds are being used, for the individual benefit of the representative or otherwise in breach of duty has notice of an adverse claim.

(c) An act or event that creates a right to immediate performance of the principal obligation represented by a security certificate or sets a date on or after which the certificate is to be presented or surrendered for redemption or exchange does not itself constitute notice of an adverse claim except in the case of a transfer more than:

(1) one year after a date set for presentment or surrender for redemption or exchange; or

(2) six months after a date set for payment of money against presentation or surrender of the certificate, if money was available for payment on that date.

(d) A purchaser of a certificated security has notice of an adverse claim if the security certificate:

(1) whether in bearer or registered form, has been indorsed "for collection" or "for surrender" or for some other purpose not involving transfer; or

(2) is in bearer form and has on it an unambiguous statement that it is the property of a person other than the transferor, but the mere writing of a name on the certificate is not such a statement.

(e) Filing of a financing statement under Article 9 is not notice of an adverse claim to a financial asset.

Added by Laws 1997, Ch. 566, § 5, eff. Oct. 10, 1997. See legislative history following § 8–101 for explanation of legislative intent.

Official Comment

1. The rules specifying whether adverse claims can be asserted against persons who acquire securities or security entitlements, Sections 8-303, 8-502, and 8-510, provide that one is protected against an adverse claim only if one takes without notice of the claim. This section defines notice of an adverse claim.

The general Article 1 definition of "notice" in Section 1-201(25) – which provides that a person has notice of a fact if "from all the facts and circumstances known to him at the time in question he has reason to know that it exists" – does not apply to the interpretation of "notice of adverse claims." The Section 1-201(25) definition of "notice" does, however, apply to usages of that term and its cognates in Article 8 in contexts other than notice of adverse claims.

2. This section must be interpreted in light of the definition of "adverse claim" in Section 8-102(a)(1). "Adverse claim" does not include all circumstances in which a third party has a property interest in securities, but only those situations where a security is transferred in violation of the claimant's property interest. Therefore, awareness that someone other than the transferor has a property interest is not notice of an adverse claim. The transferee must be aware that the transfer violates the other party's property interest. If A holds securities in which B has some form of property interest, and A transfers the securities to C, C may know that B has an interest, but infer that A is acting in accordance with A's obligations to B. The mere fact that C knew that B had a property interest does not mean that C had notice of an adverse claim. Whether C had notice of an adverse claim depends on whether C had sufficient awareness that A was acting in violation of B's property rights. The rule in subsection (b) is a particularization of this general principle.

3. Paragraph (a)(1) provides that a person has notice of an adverse claim if the person has knowledge of the adverse claim. Knowledge is defined in Section 1-201(25) as actual knowledge.

4. Paragraph (a)(2) provides that a person has notice of an adverse claim if the person is aware of a significant probability that an adverse claim exists and deliberately avoids information that might establish the existence of the adverse claim. This is intended to codify the "willful blindness" test that has been applied in such cases. See *May v. Chapman*, 16 M. & W. 355, 153 Eng. Rep. 1225 (1847); *Goodman v. Simonds*, 61 U.S. 343 (1857).

The first prong of the willful blindness test of paragraph (a)(2) turns on whether the person is aware facts sufficient to indicate that there is a significant probability that an adverse claim exists. The "awareness" aspect necessarily turns on the actor's state of mind. Whether facts known to a person make the person aware of a "significant probability" that an adverse claim exists turns on facts about the world and the conclusions that would be drawn from those facts, taking account of the experience and position of the person in question. A particular set of facts might indicate a significant probability of an adverse claim to a professional with considerable experience in the usual methods and procedures by which securities transactions are conducted, even though the same facts would not indicate a significant probability of an adverse claim to a non-professional.

The second prong of the willful blindness test of paragraph (a)(2) turns on whether the person "deliberately avoids information" that would establish the existence of the adverse claim. The test is the character of the person's response to the information the person has. The question is whether the person deliberately failed to seek further information because of concern that suspicions would be confirmed.

Application of the "deliberate avoidance" test to a transaction by an organization focuses on the knowledge and the actions of the individual or individuals conducting the transaction on behalf of the organization. Thus, an organization that purchases a security is not willfully blind to an adverse claim unless the officers or agents who conducted that purchase transaction are willfully blind to the adverse claim. Under the two prongs of the willful blindness test, the individual or individuals conducting a transaction must know of facts indicating a substantial probability that the adverse claim exists and deliberately fail to seek further information that might confirm or refute the indication. For this purpose, information known to individuals within an organization who are not conducting or aware of a transaction, but not forwarded to the individuals conducting the transaction, is not pertinent in determining whether the individuals conducting the transaction had knowledge of a substantial probability of the existence of the adverse claim. Cf. Section 1-201(27). An organization may also "deliberately avoid information" if it acts to preclude or inhibit transmission of pertinent information to those individuals responsible for the conduct of purchase transactions.

5. Paragraph (a)(3) provides that a person has notice of an adverse claim if the person would have learned of the adverse claim by conducting an investigation that is required by other statute or regulation. This rule applies only if there is some other statute or regulation that explicitly requires persons dealing with securities to conduct some investigation. The federal securities laws require that brokers and banks, in certain specified circumstances, check with a stolen securities registry to determine whether securities offered for sale or pledge have been reported as stolen. If securities that were listed as stolen in the registry are taken by an institution that failed to comply with requirement to check the registry, the institution would be held to have notice of the fact that they were stolen under paragraph (a)(3). Accordingly, the institution could not qualify as a protected purchaser under Section 8-303. The same result has been reached under the prior version of Article 8. See *First Nat'l Bank of Cicero v. Lewco Securities*, 860 F.2d 1407 (7th Cir. 1988).

6. Subsection (b) provides explicitly for some situations involving purchase from one described or identifiable as a representative. Knowledge of the existence of the representative relation is not enough in itself to constitute "notice of an adverse claim" that would disqualify the purchaser from protected purchaser status. A purchaser may take a security on the inference that the representative is acting properly. Knowledge that a security is being transferred to an individual account of the representative or that the proceeds of the transaction will be paid into that account is not sufficient to constitute "notice of an adverse claim," but knowledge that the proceeds will be applied to the personal indebtedness of the representative is. See *State Bank of Binghamton v. Bache*, 162 Misc. 128, 293 N.Y.S. 667 (1937).

7. Subsection (c) specifies whether a purchaser of a "stale" security is charged with notice of adverse claims, and therefore disqualified from protected purchaser status under Section 8-303. The fact of "staleness" is viewed as notice of certain defects

UCC

after the lapse of stated periods, but the maturity of the security does not operate automatically to affect holders' rights. The periods of time here stated are shorter than those appearing in the provisions of this Article on staleness as notice of defects or defenses of an issuer (Section 8-203) since a purchaser who takes a security after funds or other securities are available for its redemption has more reason to suspect claims of ownership than issuer's defenses. An owner will normally turn in a security rather than transfer it at such a time. Of itself, a default never constitutes notice of a possible adverse claim. To provide otherwise would not tend to drive defaulted securities home and would serve only to disrupt current financial markets where many defaulted securities are actively traded. Unpaid or overdue coupons attached to a bond do not bring it within the operation of this subsection, though they may be relevant under the general test of notice of adverse claims in subsection (a).

8. Subsection (d) provides the owner of a certificated security with a means of protection while a security certificate is being sent in for redemption or exchange. The owner may endorse it "for collection" or "for surrender," and this constitutes notice of the owner's claims, under subsection (d).

Definitional Cross References

"Adverse claim"–Section 8-102(a)(1)
"Bearer form"–Section 8-102(a)(2)
"Certificated security"–Section 8-102(a)(4)
"Financial asset"–Section 8-102(a)(9)
"Knowledge"–Section 1-201(25)
"Person"–Section 1-201(30)
"Purchaser"–Section 1-201(33) & 8-116
"Registered form"–Section 8-102(a)(13)
"Representative"–Section 1-201(35)
"Security certificate"–Section 8-102(a)(16)

Section 8-106. Control.

(a) A purchaser has "control" of a certificated security in bearer form if the certificated security is delivered to the purchaser.

(b) A purchaser has "control" of a certificated security in registered form if the certificated security is delivered to the purchaser, and:

(1) the certificate is indorsed to the purchaser or in blank by an effective indorsement; or

(2) the certificate is registered in the name of the purchaser, upon original issue or registration of transfer by the issuer.

(c) A purchaser has "control" of an uncertificated security if:

(1) the uncertificated security is delivered to the purchaser; or

(2) the issuer has agreed that it will comply with instructions originated by the purchaser without further consent by the registered owner.

(d) A purchaser has "control" of a security entitlement if:

(1) the purchaser becomes the entitlement holder; or

(2) the securities intermediary has agreed that it will comply with entitlement orders originated by the purchaser without further consent by the entitlement holder.

(e) If an interest in a security entitlement is granted by the entitlement holder to the entitlement holder's own securities intermediary, the securities intermediary has control.

(f) A purchaser who has satisfied the requirements of subsection (c)(2) or (d)(2) has control even if the registered owner in the case of subsection (c)(2) or the entitlement holder in the case of subsection (d)(2) retains the right to make substitutions for the uncertificated security or security entitlement, to originate instructions or entitlement orders to the issuer or securities intermediary, or otherwise to deal with the uncertificated security or security entitlement.

(g) An issuer or a securities intermediary may not enter into an agreement of the kind described in subsection (c)(2) or (d)(2) without the consent of the registered owner or entitlement holder, but an issuer or a securities intermediary is not required to enter into such an agreement even though the registered owner or entitlement holder so directs. An issuer or securities intermediary that has entered into such an agreement is not required to confirm the existence of the agreement to another party unless requested to do so by the registered owner or entitlement holder.

Added by Laws 1997, Ch. 566, § 5, eff. Oct. 10, 1997. See legislative history following § 8–101 for explanation of legislative intent.

Official Comment

1. The concept of "control" plays a key role in various provisions dealing with the rights of purchasers, including secured parties. See Sections 8-303 (protected purchasers); 8-503(e) (purchasers from securities intermediaries); 8-510 (purchasers of security entitlements from entitlement holders); 9-115(4) (perfection of security interests); 9-115(5) (priorities among conflicting security interests).

Obtaining "control" means that the purchaser has taken whatever steps are necessary, given the manner in which the securities are held, to place itself in a position where it can have the securities sold, without further action by the owner.

2. Subsection (a) provides that a purchaser obtains "control" with respect to a certificated security in bearer form by taking "delivery," as defined in Section 8-301. Subsection (b) provides that a purchaser obtains "control" with respect to a certificated security in registered form by taking "delivery," as defined in Section 8-301, provided that the security certificate has been indorsed to the purchaser or in blank. Section 8-301 provides that delivery of a certificated security occurs when the purchaser obtains possession of the security certificate, or when an agent for the purchaser (other than a securities intermediary) either acquires possession or acknowledges that the agent holds for the purchaser.

3. Subsection (c) specifies the means by which a purchaser can obtain control over uncertificated securities which the transferor holds directly. Two mechanisms are possible.

Under subsection (c)(1), securities can be "delivered" to a purchaser. Section 8-301(b) provides that "delivery" of an uncertificated security occurs when the purchaser becomes the registered holder. So far as the issuer is concerned, the purchaser would then be entitled to exercise all rights of ownership. See Section 8-207. As between the parties to a purchase transaction, however, the rights of the purchaser are determined by their contract. Cf. Section 9-202. Arrangements covered by this paragraph are analogous to arrangements in which bearer certificates are delivered to a secured party – so far as the issuer or any other parties are concerned, the secured party appears to be the outright owner, although it is in fact holding as collateral property that belongs to the debtor.

Under subsection (c)(2), a purchaser has control if the issuer has agreed to act on the instructions of the purchaser, even though the owner remains listed as the registered owner. The issuer, of course, would be acting wrongfully against the registered owner if it entered into such an agreement without the consent of the registered owner. Subsection (g) makes this point explicit. The subsection (c)(2) provision makes it possible for issuers to offer a service akin to the registered pledge device of the 1978 version of Article 8, without mandating that all issuers offer that service.

4. Subsection (d) specifies the means by which a purchaser can obtain control over a security entitlement. Two mechanisms are possible, analogous to those provided in subsection (c) for uncertificated securities. Under subsection (d)(1), a purchaser has control if it is the entitlement holder. This subsection would apply whether the purchaser holds through the same intermediary that the debtor used, or has the securities position transferred to its own intermediary.

Subsection (d)(2) provides that a purchaser has control if the securities intermediary has agreed to act on entitlement orders originated by the purchaser, even though the transferor remains listed as the entitlement holder. This section specifies only the minimum requirements that such an arrangement must meet to confer "control‘; the details of the arrangement can be specified by agreement. The arrangement might cover all of the positions in a particular account or subaccount, or only specified positions. There is no requirement that the control party's right to give entitlement orders be exclusive. The arrangement might provide that only the control party can give entitlement orders, or that either the entitlement holder or the control party can give entitlement orders. See subsection (f).

The following examples illustrate the rules of subsection (d):

Example 1. Debtor grants Alpha Bank a security interest in 1000 shares of XYZ Co. stock that Debtor holds through an account with Able & Co. Alpha Bank also has an account with Able. Debtor instructs Able to transfer the shares to Alpha Bank, and Able does so. Alpha Bank has control of the 1000 shares under subsection (d)(1), because Alpha Bank is the entitlement holder.

Example 2. Debtor grants Alpha Bank a security interest in 1000 shares of XYZ Co. stock that Debtor holds through an account with Able & Co. Alpha Bank does not have an account with Able. Alpha Bank uses Beta Bank as its securities custodian. Debtor instructs Able to transfer the shares to Beta Bank, for the account of Alpha Bank, and Able does so. Alpha Bank has control of the 1000 shares under subsection (d)(1), because Alpha Bank is the entitlement holder.

Example 3. Debtor grants Alpha Bank a security interest in 1000 shares of XYZ Co. stock that Debtor holds through an account with Able & Co. Debtor, Able, and Alpha Bank enter into an agreement under which Debtor will continue to receive dividends and distributions, and will continue to have the right to direct dispositions, but Alpha Bank also has the right to direct dispositions. Alpha Bank has control of the 1000 shares under subsection (d)(2).

Example 4. Able & Co., a securities dealer, grants Alpha Bank a security interest in 1000 shares of XYZ Co. stock that Able holds through an account with Clearing Corporation. Able causes Clearing Corporation to transfer the shares into Alpha Bank's account at Clearing Corporation. Alpha Bank has control of the 1000 shares under subsection (d)(1).

Example 5. Able & Co., a securities dealer, grants Alpha Bank a security interest in 1000 shares of XYZ Co. stock that Able holds through an account with Clearing Corporation. Alpha Bank does not have a account with Clearing Corporation. It holds its securities through Beta Bank, which does have an account with Clearing Corporation.

Able causes Clearing Corporation to transfer the shares into Beta Bank's account at Clearing Corporation. Beta Bank credits the position to Alpha Bank's account with Beta Bank. Alpha Bank has control of the 1000 shares under subsection (d)(1).

Example 6. Able & Co. a securities dealer, grants Alpha Bank a security interest in 1000 shares of XYZ Co. stock that Able holds through an account with Clearing Corporation. Able causes Clearing Corporation to transfer the shares into a pledge account, pursuant to an agreement under which Able will continue to receive dividends, distributions, and the like, but Alpha Bank has the right to direct dispositions. Alpha Bank has control of the 1000 shares under subsection (d)(2).

Example 7. Able & Co. a securities dealer, grants Alpha Bank a security interest in 1000 shares of XYZ Co. stock that Able holds through an account with Clearing Corporation. Able, Alpha, and Clearing Corporation enter into an agreement under which Clearing Corporation will act on instructions from Alpha with respect to the XYZ Co. stock carried in Able's account, but Able will continue to receive dividends, distributions, and the like, and will also have the right to direct dispositions. Alpha Bank has control of the 1000 shares under subsection (d)(2).

Example 8. Able & Co. a securities dealer, holds a wide range of securities through its account at Clearing Corporation. Able enters into an arrangement with Alpha Bank pursuant to which Alpha provides financing to Able secured by securities identified as the collateral on lists provided by Able to Alpha on a daily or other periodic basis. Able, Alpha, and Clearing Corporation enter into an agreement under which Clearing Corporation agrees that if at any time Alpha directs Clearing Corporation to do so, Clearing Corporation will transfer any securities from Able's account at Alpha's instructions. Because Clearing Corporation has agreed to act on Alpha's instructions with respect to any securities carried in Able's account, at the moment that Alpha's security interest attaches to securities listed by Able, Alpha obtains control of those securities under subsection (d)(2). There is no requirement that Clearing Corporation be informed of which securities Able has pledged to Alpha.

5. For a purchaser to have "control" under subsection (c)(2) or (d)(2), it is essential that the issuer or securities intermediary, as the case may be, actually be a party to the agreement. If a debtor gives a secured party a power of attorney authorizing the secured party to act in the name of the debtor, but the issuer or securities intermediary does not specifically agree to this arrangement, the secured party does not have "control" within the meaning of subsection (c)(2) or (d)(2) because the issuer or securities intermediary is not a party to the agreement. The secured party does not have control under subsection (c)(1) or (d)(1) because, although the power of attorney might give the secured party authority to act on the debtor's behalf as an agent, the secured party has not actually become the registered owner or entitlement holder.

6. Subsection (e) provides that if an interest in a security entitlement is granted by an entitlement holder to the securities intermediary through which the security entitlement is maintained, the securities intermediary has control. A common transaction covered by this provision is a margin loan from a broker to its customer.

7. The term "control" is used in a particular defined sense. The requirements for obtaining control are set out in this section. The concept is not to be interpreted by reference to similar concepts in other bodies of law. In particular, the requirements for "possession" derived from the common law of pledge are not to be used as a basis for interpreting subsection (c)(2) or (d)(2). Those provisions are designed to supplant the concepts of "constructive possession" and the like. A principal purpose of the "control" concept is to eliminate the uncertainty and confusion that results from attempting to apply common law possession concepts to modern securities holding practices.

The key to the control concept is that the purchaser has the present ability to have the securities sold or transferred without further action by the transferor. There is no requirement that the powers held by the purchaser be exclusive. For example, in a secured lending arrangement, if the secured party wishes, it can allow the debtor to retain the right to make substitutions, or to direct the disposition of the uncertificated security or security entitlement. Subsection (f) is included to make clear the general point stated in subsection (c) that the test of control is whether the purchaser has obtained the requisite power, not whether the debtor has retained other powers. There is no implication that retention by the debtor of powers other than those mentioned in subsection (f) is inconsistent with the purchaser having control.

Definitional Cross References

"Bearer form"–Section 8-102(a)(2)
"Certificated security"–Section 8-102(a)(4)
"Delivery"–Section 8-301
"Effective"–Section 8-107
"Entitlement holder"–Section 8-102(a)(7)
"Entitlement order"–Section 8-102(a)(8)
"Indorsement"–Section 8-102(a)(11)
"Instruction"–Section 8-102(a)(12)
"Purchaser"–Section 1-201(33) & 8-116
"Registered form"–Section 8-102(a)(13)
"Securities intermediary"–Section 8-102(a)(14)
"Security entitlement"–Section 8-102(a)(17)
"Uncertificated security"–Section 8-102(a)(18)

Section 8–107. Whether Indorsement, Instruction, or Entitlement Order is Effective.

(a) "Appropriate person" means:

(1) with respect to an indorsement, the person specified by a security certificate or by an effective special indorsement to be entitled to the security;

(2) with respect to an instruction, the registered owner of an uncertificated security;

(3) with respect to an entitlement order, the entitlement holder;

(4) if the person designated in paragraph (1), (2), or (3) is deceased, the designated person's successor taking under other law or the designated person's personal representative acting for the estate of the decedent; or

(5) if the person designated in paragraph (1), (2), or (3) lacks capacity, the designated person's guardian, conservator, or other similar representative who has power under other law to transfer the security or financial asset.

(b) An indorsement, instruction, or entitlement order is effective if:

(1) it is made by the appropriate person;

(2) it is made by a person who has power under the law of agency to transfer the security or financial asset on behalf of the appropriate person, including, in the case of an instruction or entitlement order, a person who has control under Section 8–106(c)(2) or (d)(2); or

(3) the appropriate person has ratified it or is otherwise precluded from asserting its ineffectiveness.

(c) An indorsement, instruction, or entitlement order made by a representative is effective even if:

(1) the representative has failed to comply with a controlling instrument or with the law of the state having jurisdiction of the representative relationship, including any law requiring the representative to obtain court approval of the transaction; or

(2) the representative's action in making the indorsement, instruction, or entitlement order or using the proceeds of the transaction is otherwise a breach of duty.

(d) If a security is registered in the name of or specially indorsed to a person described as a representative, or if a securities account is maintained in the name of a person described as a representative, an indorsement, instruction, or entitlement order made by the person is effective even though the person is no longer serving in the described capacity.

(e) Effectiveness of an indorsement, instruction, or entitlement order is determined as of the date the indorsement, instruction, or entitlement order is made, and an indorsement, instruction, or entitlement order does not become ineffective by reason of any later change of circumstances.

Added by Laws 1997, Ch. 566, § 5, eff. Oct. 10, 1997. See legislative history following § 8–101 for explanation of legislative intent.

Official Comment

1. This section defines two concepts, "appropriate person" and "effective." Effectiveness is a broader concept than appropriate person. For example, if a security or securities account is registered in the name of Mary Roe, Mary Roe is the "appropriate person," but an indorsement, instruction, or entitlement order made by John Doe is "effective" if, under agency or other law, Mary Roe is precluded from denying Doe's authority. Treating these two concepts separately facilitates statement of the rules of Article 8 that state the legal effect of an indorsement, instruction, or entitlement order. For example, a securities intermediary is protected against liability if it acts on an effective entitlement order, but has a duty to comply with an entitlement order only if it is originated by an appropriate person. See Sections 8-115 and 8-507.

One important application of the "effectiveness" concept is in the direct holding system rules on the rights of purchasers. A purchaser of a certificated security in registered form can qualify as a protected purchaser who takes free from adverse claims under Section 8-303 only if the purchaser obtains "control." Section 8-106 provides that a purchaser of a certificated security in registered form obtains control if there has been an "effective" indorsement.

2. Subsection (a) provides that the term "appropriate person" covers two categories: (1) the person who is actually designated as the person entitled to the security or security entitlement, and (2) the successor or legal representative of that person if that person has died or otherwise lacks capacity. Other law determines who has power to transfer a security on behalf of a person who lacks capacity. For example, if securities are registered in the name of more than one person and one of the designated persons dies, whether the survivor is the appropriate person depends on the form of tenancy. If the two were registered joint tenants with right of survivorship, the survivor would have that power under other law and thus would be the "appropriate person."

If securities are registered in the name of an individual and the individual dies, the law of decedents' estates determines who has power to transfer the decedent's securities. That would ordinarily be the executor or administrator, but if a "small estate statute" permits a widow to transfer a decedent's securities without administration proceedings, she would be the appropriate person. If the registration of a security or a securities account contains a designation of a death beneficiary under the Uniform Transfer on Death Security Registration Act or comparable legislation, the designated beneficiary would, under that law, have power to transfer upon the person's death and so would be the appropriate person. Article 8 does not contain a list of such representatives, because any list is likely to become outdated by developments in other law.

3. Subsection (b) sets out the general rule that an indorsement, instruction, or entitlement order is effective if it is made by the appropriate person or by a person who has power to transfer under agency law or if the appropriate person is precluded from denying its effectiveness. The control rules in Section 8-106 provide for arrangements where a person who holds securities through a securities intermediary, or holds uncertificated securities directly, enters into a control agreement giving the secured party the right to initiate entitlement orders of instructions. Paragraph 2 of subsection (b) states explicitly that an entitlement order or instruction initiated by a person who has obtained such a control agreement is "effective."

Subsections (c), (d), and (e) supplement the general rule of subsection (b) on effectiveness. The term "representative," used in subsections (c) and (d), is defined in Section 1-201(35).

4. Subsection (c) provides that an indorsement, instruction, or entitlement order made by a representative is effective even though the representative's action is a violation of duties. The following example illustrates this subsection:

Example 1. Certificated securities are registered in the name of John Doe. Doe dies and Mary Roe is appointed executor. Roe indorses the security certificate and transfers it to a purchaser in a transaction that is a violation of her duties as executor.

Roe's indorsement is effective, because Roe is the appropriate person under subsection (a)(4). This is so even though Roe's transfer violated her obligations as executor. The policies of free transferability of securities that underlie Article 8 dictate that neither a purchaser to whom Roe transfers the securities nor the issuer who registers transfer should be required to investigate the terms of the will to determine whether Roe is acting properly. Although Roe's indorsement is effective under this section, her breach of duty may be such that her beneficiary has an adverse claim to the securities that Roe transferred. The question whether that adverse claim can be asserted against purchasers is governed not by this section but by Section 8-303. Under Section 8-404, the issuer has no duties to an adverse claimant unless the claimant obtains legal process enjoining the issuer from registering transfer.

5. Subsection (d) deals with cases where a security or a securities account is registered in the name of a person specifically designated as a representative. The following example illustrates this subsection:

Example 2. Certificated securities are registered in the name of "John Jones, trustee of the Smith Family Trust." John Jones is removed as trustee and Martha Moe is appointed successor trustee. The securities, however, are not reregistered, but remain registered in the name of "John Jones, trustee of the Smith Family Trust." Jones indorses the security certificate and transfers it to a purchaser.

Subsection (d) provides that an indorsement by John Jones as trustee is effective even though Jones is no longer serving in that capacity. Since the securities were registered in the name of "John Jones, trustee of the Smith Family Trust," a purchaser, or the issuer when called upon to register transfer, should be entitled to assume without further inquiry that Jones has the power to act as trustee for the Smith Family Trust.

Note that subsection (d) does not apply to a case where the security or securities account is registered in the name of principal rather than the representative as such. The following example illustrates this point:

Example 3. Certificated securities are registered in the name of John Doe. John Doe dies and Mary Roe is appointed executor. The securities are not reregistered in the name of Mary Roe as executor. Later, Mary Roe is removed as executor and Martha Moe is appointed as her successor. After being removed, Mary Roe indorses the security certificate that is registered in the name of John Doe and transfers it to a purchaser.

Mary Roe's indorsement is not made effective by subsection (d), because the securities were not registered in the name of Mary Roe as representative. A purchaser or the issuer registering transfer should be required to determine whether Roe has power to act for John Doe. Purchasers and issuers can protect themselves in such cases by requiring signature guaranties. See Section 8-306.

6. Subsection (e) provides that the effectiveness of an indorsement, instruction, or entitlement order is determined as of the date it is made. The following example illustrates this subsection:

Example 4. Certificated securities are registered in the name of John Doe. John Doe dies and Mary Roe is appointed executor. Mary Roe indorses the security certificate that is registered in the name of John Doe and transfers it to a purchaser. After the indorsement and transfer, but before the security certificate is presented to the issuer for registration of transfer, Mary Roe is removed as executor and Martha Moe is appointed as her successor.

Mary Roe's indorsement is effective, because at the time Roe indorsed she was the appropriate person under subsection (a)(4). Her later removal as executor does not render the indorsement ineffective. Accordingly, the issuer would not be liable for registering the transfer. See Section 8-404.

Definitional Cross References

"Entitlement order"–Section 8-102(a)(8)
"Financial asset"–Section 8-102(a)(9)
"Indorsement"–Section 8-102(a)(11)
"Instruction"–Section 8-102(a)(12)
"Representative"–Section 1-201(35)
"Securities account"–Section 8-501
"Security"–Section 8-102(a)(15)
"Security certificate"–Section 8-102(a)(16)
"Security entitlement"–Section 8-102(a)(17)
"Uncertificated security"–Section 8-102(a)(18)

Section 8–108. Warranties in Direct Holding.

(a) A person who transfers a certificated security to a purchaser for value warrants to the purchaser, and an indorser, if the transfer is by indorsement, warrants to any subsequent purchaser, that:

(1) the certificate is genuine and has not been materially altered;

(2) the transferor or indorser does not know of any fact that might impair the validity of the security;

(3) there is no adverse claim to the security;

(4) the transfer does not violate any restriction on transfer;

(5) if the transfer is by indorsement, the indorsement is made by an appropriate person, or if the indorsement is by an agent, the agent has actual authority to act on behalf of the appropriate person; and

(6) the transfer is otherwise effective and rightful.

(b) A person who originates an instruction for registration of transfer of an uncertificated security to a purchaser for value warrants to the purchaser that:

(1) the instruction is made by an appropriate person, or if the instruction is by an agent, the agent has actual authority to act on behalf of the appropriate person;

(2) the security is valid;

(3) there is no adverse claim to the security; and

(4) at the time the instruction is presented to the issuer:

(i) the purchaser will be entitled to the registration of transfer;

(ii) the transfer will be registered by the issuer free from all liens, security interests, restrictions, and claims other than those specified in the instruction;

(iii) the transfer will not violate any restriction on transfer; and

(iv) the requested transfer will otherwise be effective and rightful.

(c) A person who transfers an uncertificated security to a purchaser for value and does not originate an instruction in connection with the transfer warrants that:

(1) the uncertificated security is valid;

(2) there is no adverse claim to the security;

(3) the transfer does not violate any restriction on transfer; and

(4) the transfer is otherwise effective and rightful.

(d) A person who indorses a security certificate warrants to the issuer that:

(1) there is no adverse claim to the security; and

(2) the indorsement is effective.

(e) A person who originates an instruction for registration of transfer of an uncertificated security warrants to the issuer that:

(1) the instruction is effective; and

(2) at the time the instruction is presented to the issuer the purchaser will be entitled to the registration of transfer.

(f) A person who presents a certificated security for registration of transfer or for payment or exchange warrants to the issuer that the person is entitled to the registration, payment, or exchange, but a purchaser for value and without notice of adverse claims to whom transfer is registered warrants only that the person has no knowledge of any unauthorized signature in a necessary indorsement.

(g) If a person acts as agent of another in delivering a certificated security to a purchaser, the identity of the principal was known to the person to whom the certificate was delivered, and the certificate delivered by the agent was received by the agent from the principal or received by the agent from another person at the direction of the principal, the person delivering the security certificate warrants only that the delivering person has authority to act for the principal and does not know of any adverse claim to the certificated security.

(h) A secured party who redelivers a security certificate received, or after payment and on order of the debtor delivers the security certificate to another person, makes only the warranties of an agent under subsection (g).

(i) Except as otherwise provided in subsection (g), a broker acting for a customer makes to the issuer and a purchaser the warranties provided in subsections (a) through (f). A broker that delivers a security certificate to its customer, or causes its customer to be registered as the owner of an uncertificated security, makes to the customer the warranties provided in subsection (a) or (b), and has the rights and privileges of a purchaser under this section. The warranties of and in favor of the broker acting as an agent are in addition to applicable warranties given by and in favor of the customer.

Added by Laws 1997, Ch. 566, § 5, eff. Oct. 10, 1997. See legislative history following § 8–101 for explanation of legislative intent.

Official Comment

1. Subsections (a), (b), and (c) deal with warranties by security transferors to purchasers. Subsections (d) and (e) deal with warranties by security transferors to issuers. Subsection (f) deals with presentment warranties.

2. Subsection (a) specifies the warranties made by a person who transfers a certificated security to a purchaser for value. Paragraphs (3), (4), and (5) make explicit several key points that are implicit in the general warranty of paragraph (6) that the transfer is effective and rightful. Subsection (b) sets forth the warranties made to a purchaser for value by one who originates an instruction. These warranties are quite similar to those made by one transferring a certificated security, subsection (a), the principal difference being the absolute warranty of validity. If upon receipt of the instruction the issuer should dispute the validity of the security, the burden of proving validity is upon the transferor. Subsection (c) provides for the limited circumstances in which an uncertificated security could be transferred without an instruction, see Section 8-301(b)(2). Subsections (d) and (e) give the issuer the benefit of the warranties of an indorser or originator on those matters not within the issuer's knowledge.

3. Subsection (f) limits the warranties made by a purchaser for value without notice whose presentation of a security certificate is defective in some way but to whom the issuer does register transfer. The effect is to deny the issuer a remedy against such a person unless at the time of presentment the person had knowledge of an unauthorized signature in a necessary indorsement. The issuer can protect itself by refusing to make the transfer or, if it registers the transfer before it discovers the defect, by pursuing its remedy against a signature guarantor.

4. Subsection (g) eliminates all substantive warranties in the relatively unusual case of a delivery of certificated security by an agent of a disclosed principal where the agent delivers the exact certificate that it received from or for the principal. Subsection

(h) limits the warranties given by a secured party who redelivers a certificate. Subsection (i) specifies the warranties of brokers in the more common scenarios.

5. Under Section 1-102(3) the warranty provisions apply "unless otherwise agreed" and the parties may enter into express agreements to allocate the risks of possible defects. Usual estoppel principles apply with respect to transfers of both certificated and uncertificated securities whenever the purchaser has knowledge of the defect, and these warranties will not be breached in such a case.

Definitional Cross References

"Adverse claim"–Section 8-102(a)(1)
"Appropriate person"–Section 8-107
"Broker"–Section 8-102(a)(3)
"Certificated security"–Section 8-102(a)(4)
"Indorsement"–Section 8-102(a)(11)
"Instruction"–Section 8-102(a)(12)
"Issuer"–Section 8-201
"Person"–Section 1-201(30)
"Purchaser"–Section 1-201(33) & 8-116
"Secured party"–Section 9-105(1)(m)
"Security"–Section 8-102(a)(15)
"Security certificate"–Section 8-102(a)(16)
"Uncertificated security"–Section 8-102(a)(18)
"Value"–Section 1-201(44) & 8-116

Section 8–109. Warranties in Indirect Holding.

(a) A person who originates an entitlement order to a securities intermediary warrants to the securities intermediary that:

(1) the entitlement order is made by an appropriate person, or if the entitlement order is by an agent, the agent has actual authority to act on behalf of the appropriate person; and

(2) there is no adverse claim to the security entitlement.

(b) A person who delivers a security certificate to a securities intermediary for credit to a securities account or originates an instruction with respect to an uncertificated security directing that the uncertificated security be credited to a securities account makes to the securities intermediary the warranties specified in Section 8-108(a) or (b).

(c) If a securities intermediary delivers a security certificate to its entitlement holder or causes its entitlement holder to be registered as the owner of an uncertificated security, the securities intermediary makes to the entitlement holder the warranties specified in Section 8–108(a) or (b).

Added by Laws 1997, Ch. 566, § 5, eff. Oct. 10, 1997. See legislative history following § 8–101 for explanation of legislative intent.

Official Comment

1. Subsection (a) provides that a person who originates an entitlement order warrants to the securities intermediary that the order is authorized, and warrants the

absence of adverse claims. Subsection (b) specifies the warranties that are given when a person who holds securities directly has the holding converted into indirect form. A person who delivers a certificate to a securities intermediary or originates an instruction for an uncertificated security gives to the securities intermediary the transfer warranties under Section 8-108. If the securities intermediary in turns delivers the certificate to a higher level securities intermediary, it gives the same warranties.

2. Subsection (c) states the warranties that a securities intermediary gives when a customer who has been holding securities in an account with the securities intermediary requests that certificates be delivered or that uncertificated securities be registered in the customer's name. The warranties are the same as those that brokers make with respect to securities that the brokers sell to or buy on behalf of the customers. See Section 8-108(i).

3. As with the Section 8-108 warranties, the warranties specified in this section may be modified by agreement under Section 1-102(3).

Definitional Cross References

"Adverse claim"–Section 8-102(a)(1)
"Appropriate person"–Section 8-107
"Entitlement holder"–Section 8-102(a)(7)
"Entitlement order"–Section 8-102(a)(8)
"Instruction"–Section 8-102(a)(12)
"Person"–Section 1-201(30)
"Securities account"–Section 8-501
"Securities intermediary"–Section 8-102(a)(14)
"Security certificate"–Section 8-102(a)(16)
"Uncertificated security"–Section 8-102(a)(18)

Section 8–110. Applicability; Choice of Law.

(a) The local law of the issuer's jurisdiction, as specified in subsection (d), governs:

(1) the validity of a security;

(2) the rights and duties of the issuer with respect to registration of transfer;

(3) the effectiveness of registration of transfer by the issuer;

(4) whether the issuer owes any duties to an adverse claimant to a security; and

(5) whether an adverse claim can be asserted against a person to whom transfer of a certificated or uncertificated security is registered or a person who obtains control of an uncertificated security.

(b) The local law of the securities intermediary's jurisdiction, as specified in subsection (e), governs:

(1) acquisition of a security entitlement from the securities intermediary;

(2) the rights and duties of the securities intermediary and entitlement holder arising out of a security entitlement;

(3) whether the securities intermediary owes any duties to an adverse claimant to a security entitlement; and

(4) whether an adverse claim can be asserted against a person who acquires a security entitlement from the securities intermediary or a person who purchases a security entitlement or interest therein from an entitlement holder.

(c) The local law of the jurisdiction in which a security certificate is located at the time of delivery governs whether an adverse claim can be asserted against a person to whom the security certificate is delivered.

(d) "Issuer's jurisdiction" means the jurisdiction under which the issuer of the security is organized or, if permitted by the law of that jurisdiction, the law of another jurisdiction specified by the issuer. An issuer organized under the law of this state may specify the law of another jurisdiction as the law governing the matters specified in subsection (a)(2) through (5).

(e) The following rules determine a "securities intermediary's jurisdiction" for purposes of this section:

(1) if an agreement between the securities intermediary and its entitlement holder specifies that it is governed by the law of a particular jurisdiction, that jurisdiction is the securities intermediary's jurisdiction.

(2) If an agreement between the securities intermediary and its entitlement holder does not specify the governing law as provided in paragraph (1), but expressly specifies that the securities account is maintained at an office in a particular jurisdiction, that jurisdiction is the securities intermediary's jurisdiction.

(3) If an agreement between the securities intermediary and its entitlement holder does not specify a jurisdiction as provided in paragraph (1) or (2), the securities intermediary's jurisdiction is the jurisdiction in which is located the office identified in an account statement as the office serving the entitlement holder's account.

(4) If an agreement between the securities intermediary and its entitlement holder does not specify a jurisdiction as provided in paragraph (1) or (2) and an account statement does not identify an office serving the entitlement holder's account as provided in paragraph (3), the securities intermediary's jurisdiction is the jurisdiction in which is located the chief executive office of the securities intermediary.

(f) A securities intermediary's jurisdiction is not determined by the physical location of certificates representing financial assets, or by the jurisdiction in which is organized the issuer of the financial asset with respect to which an entitlement holder has a security entitlement, or by the location of facilities for data processing or other record keeping concerning the account.

Added by Laws 1997, Ch. 566, § 5, eff. Oct. 10, 1997. See legislative history following § 8–101 for explanation of legislative intent.

Official Comment

1. This section deals with applicability and choice of law issues concerning Article 8. The distinction between the direct and indirect holding systems plays a significant

role in determining the governing law. An investor in the direct holding system is registered on the books of the issuer and/or has possession of a security certificate. Accordingly, the jurisdiction of incorporation of the issuer or location of the certificate determine the applicable law. By contrast, an investor in the indirect holding system has a security entitlement, which is a bundle of rights against the securities intermediary with respect to a security, rather than a direct interest in the underlying security. Accordingly, in the rules for the indirect holding system, the jurisdiction of incorporation of the issuer of the underlying security or the location of any certificates that might be held by the intermediary or a higher tier intermediary, do not determine the applicable law.

The phrase "local law" refers to the law of a jurisdiction other than its conflict of laws rules. See Restatement (Second) of Conflict of Laws § 4.

2. Subsection (a) provides that the law of an issuer's jurisdiction governs certain issues where the substantive rules of Article 8 determine the issuer's rights and duties. Paragraph (1) of subsection (a) provides that the law of the issuer's jurisdiction governs the validity of the security. This ensures that a single body of law will govern the questions addressed in Part 2 of Article 8, concerning the circumstances in which an issuer can and cannot assert invalidity as a defense against purchasers. Similarly, paragraphs (2), (3), and (4) of subsection (a) ensure that the issuer will be able to look to a single body of law on the questions addressed in Part 4 of Article 8, concerning the issuer's duties and liabilities with respect to registration of transfer.

Paragraph (5) of subsection (a) applies the law of an issuer's jurisdiction to the question whether an adverse claim can be asserted against a purchaser to whom transfer has been registered, or who has obtained control over an uncertificated security. Although this issue deals with the rights of persons other than the issuer, the law of the issuer's jurisdiction applies because the purchasers to whom the provision applies are those whose protection against adverse claims depends on the fact that their interests have been recorded on the books of the issuer.

The principal policy reflected in the choice of law rules in subsection (a) is that an issuer and others should be able to look to a single body of law on the matters specified in subsection (a), rather than having to look to the law of all of the different jurisdictions in which security holders may reside. The choice of law policies reflected in this subsection do not require that the body of law governing all of the matters specified in subsection (a) be that of the jurisdiction in which the issuer is incorporated. Thus, subsection (d) provides that the term "issuer's jurisdiction" means the jurisdiction in which the issuer is organized, or, if permitted by that law, the law of another jurisdiction selected by the issuer. Subsection (d) also provides that issuers organized under the law of a State which adopts this Article may make such a selection, except as to the validity issue specified in paragraph (1). The question whether an issuer can assert the defense of invalidity may implicate significant policies of the issuer's jurisdiction of incorporation. See, e.g., Section 8-202 and Comments thereto.

Although subsection (a) provides that the issuer's rights and duties concerning registration of transfer are governed by the law of the issuer's jurisdiction, other matters related to registration of transfer, such as appointment of a guardian for a registered owner or the existence of agency relationships, might be governed by another jurisdiction's law. Neither this section nor Section 1-105 deals with what law governs the appointment of the administrator or executor; that question is determined under generally applicable choice of law rules.

3. Subsection (b) provides that the law of the securities intermediary's jurisdiction governs the issues concerning the indirect holding system that are dealt with in Article 8. Paragraphs (1) and (2) cover the matters dealt with in the Article 8 rules defining the concept of security entitlement and specifying the duties of securities intermediaries. Paragraph (3) provides that the law of the security intermediary's jurisdiction

determines whether the intermediary owes any duties to an adverse claimant. Paragraph (4) provides that the law of the security intermediary's jurisdiction determines whether adverse claims can be asserted against entitlement holders and others.

Subsection (e) determines what is a "securities intermediary's jurisdiction." The policy of subsection (b) is to ensure that a securities intermediary and all of its entitlement holders can look to a single, readily-identifiable body of law to determine their rights and duties. Accordingly, subsection (e) sets out a sequential series of tests to facilitate identification of that body of law. Paragraph (1) of subsection (e) permits specification of the governing law by agreement. Because the policy of this section is to enable parties to determine, in advance and with certainty, what law will apply to transactions governed by this Article, the validation of selection of governing law by agreement is not conditioned upon a determination that the jurisdiction whose law is chosen bear a "reasonable relation" to the transaction. See Section 4A-507; compare Section 1-105(1). That is also true with respect to the similar provisions in subsection (d) of this section and in Section 9-103(6).

Subsection (f) makes explicit a point that is implicit in the Article 8 description of a security entitlement as a bundle of rights against the intermediary with respect to a security or other financial asset, rather than as a direct interest in the underlying security or other financial asset. The governing law for relationships in the indirect holding system is not determined by such matters as the jurisdiction of incorporation of the issuer of the securities held through the intermediary, or the location of any physical certificates held by the intermediary or a higher tier intermediary.

4. Subsection (c) provides a choice of law rule for adverse claim issues that may arise in connection with delivery of security certificates in the direct holding system. It applies the law of the place of delivery. If a certificated security issued by an Idaho corporation is sold, and the sale is settled by physical delivery of the certificate from Seller to Buyer in New York, under subsection (c), New York law determines whether Buyer takes free from adverse claims. The domicile of Seller, Buyer, and any adverse claimant is irrelevant.

5. The following examples illustrate how a court in a jurisdiction which has enacted this section would determine the governing law:

Example 1. John Doe, a resident of Kansas, maintains a securities account with Able & Co. Able is incorporated in Delaware. Its chief executive offices are located in Illinois. The office where Doe transacts business with Able is located in Missouri. The agreement between Doe and Able specifies that it is governed by Illinois law. Through the account, Doe holds securities of a Colorado corporation, which Able holds through Clearing Corporation. The rules of Clearing Corporation provide that the rights and duties of Clearing Corporation and its participants are governed by New York law. Subsection (a) specifies that a controversy concerning the rights and duties as between the issuer and Clearing Corporation is governed by Colorado law. Subsections (b) and (e) specify that a controversy concerning the rights and duties as between the Clearing Corporation and Able is governed by New York law, and that a controversy concerning the rights and duties as between Able and Doe is governed by Illinois law.

Example 2. Same facts as to Doe and Able as in Example 1. Through the account, Doe holds securities of a Senegalese corporation, which Able holds through Clearing Corporation. Clearing Corporation's operations are located in Belgium, and its rules and agreements with its participants provide that they are governed by Belgian law. Clearing Corporation holds the securities through a custodial account at the Paris branch office of Global Bank, which is organized under English law. The agreement between Clearing Corporation and Global Bank provides that it is governed by French law. Subsection (a) specifies that a controversy concerning the rights and duties as between the issuer and Global Bank is governed by Senegalese law. Subsections (b) and (e) specify that a controversy concerning the rights and duties as between Global Bank and Clearing Corporation is governed by French law, that a controversy concerning the rights and duties as between Clearing Corporation and Able is governed by Belgian law, and that a controversy concerning the rights and duties as between Able and Doe is governed by Illinois law.

6. To the extent that this section does not specify the governing law, general choice of law rules apply. For example, suppose that in either of the examples in the preceding Comment, Doe enters into an agreement with Roe, also a resident of Kansas, in which Doe agrees to transfer all of his interests in the securities held through Able to Roe. Article 8 does not deal with whether such an agreement is enforceable or whether it gives Roe some interest in Doe's security entitlement. This section specifies what jurisdiction's law governs the issues that are dealt with in Article 8. Article 8, however, does specify that securities intermediaries have only limited duties with respect to adverse claims. See Section 8-115. Subsection (b)(3) of this section provides that Illinois law governs whether Able owes any duties to an adverse claimant. Thus, if Illinois has adopted Revised Article 8, Section 8-115 as enacted in Illinois determines whether Roe has any rights against Able.

7. The choice of law provisions concerning security interests in securities and security entitlements are set out in Section 9-103(6).

Definitional Cross References

"Adverse claim"–Section 8-102(a)(1)
"Agreement"–Section 1-201(3)
"Certificated security"–Section 8-102(a)(4)
"Entitlement holder"–Section 8-102(a)(7)
"Financial asset"–Section 8-102(a)(9)
"Issuer"–Section 8-201
"Person"–Section 1-201(30)
"Purchase"–Section 1-201(32)
"Securities intermediary"–Section 8-102(a)(14)
"Security"–Section 8-102(a)(15)
"Security certificate"–Section 8-102(a)(16)
"Security entitlement"–Section 8-102(a)(17)
"Uncertificated security"–Section 8-102(a)(18)

Section 8–111. Clearing Corporation Rules.

A rule adopted by a clearing corporation governing rights and obligations among the clearing corporation and its participants in the clearing corporation is effective even if the rule conflicts with this article and affects another party who does not consent to the rule.

Added by Laws 1997, Ch. 566, § 5, eff. Oct. 10, 1997. See legislative history following § 8–101 for explanation of legislative intent.

Official Comment

1. The experience of the past few decades shows that securities holding and settlement practices may develop rapidly, and in unforeseeable directions. Accordingly, it is desirable that the rules of Article 8 be adaptable both to ensure that commercial law can conform to changing practices and to ensure that commercial law does not operate as an obstacle to developments in securities practice. Even if practices were unchanging, it would not possible in a general statute to specify in

detail the rules needed to provide certainty in the operations of the clearance and settlement system.

The provisions of this Article and Article 1 on the effect of agreements provide considerable flexibility in the specification of the details of the rights and obligations of participants in the securities holding system by agreement. See Sections 8-504 through 8-509, and Section 1-102(3) and (4). Given the magnitude of the exposures involved in securities transactions, however, it may not be possible for the parties in developing practices to rely solely on private agreements, particularly with respect to matters that might affect others, such as creditors. For example, in order to be fully effective, rules of clearing corporations on the finality or reversibility of securities settlements must not only bind the participants in the clearing corporation but also be effective against their creditors. Section 8-111 provides that clearing corporation rules are effective even if they indirectly affect third parties, such as creditors of a participant. This provision does not, however, permit rules to be adopted that would govern the rights and obligations of third parties other than as a consequence of rules that specify the rights and obligations of the clearing corporation and its participants.

2. The definition of clearing corporation in Section 8-102 covers only federal reserve banks, entities registered as clearing agencies under the federal securities laws, and others subject to comparable regulation. The rules of registered clearing agencies are subject to regulatory oversight under the federal securities laws.

Definitional Cross References

"Clearing corporation"–Section 8-102(a)(5)

Section 8–112. Creditor's Legal Process.

(a) The interest of a debtor in a certificated security may be reached by a creditor only by actual seizure of the security certificate by the officer making the attachment or levy, except as otherwise provided in subsection (d). However, a certificated security for which the certificate has been surrendered to the issuer may be reached by a creditor by legal process upon the issuer.

(b) The interest of a debtor in an uncertificated security may be reached by a creditor only by legal process upon the issuer at its chief executive office in the united states, except as otherwise provided in subsection (d).

(c) The interest of a debtor in a security entitlement may be reached by a creditor only by legal process upon the securities intermediary with whom the debtor's securities account is maintained, except as otherwise provided in subsection (d).

(d) The interest of a debtor in a certificated security for which the certificate is in the possession of a secured party, or in an uncertificated security registered in the name of a secured party, or a security entitlement maintained in the name of a secured party, may be reached by a creditor by legal process upon the secured party.

(e) A creditor whose debtor is the owner of a certificated security, uncertificated security, or security entitlement is entitled to aid from a court of competent jurisdiction, by injunction or otherwise, in reaching the certificated security, uncertificated security, or security entitlement or in satisfying the claim by means allowed at law or in equity in regard to property that cannot readily be reached by other legal process.

Added by Laws 1997, Ch. 566, § 5, eff. Oct. 10, 1997. See legislative history following § 8–101 for explanation of legislative intent.

Official Comment

1. In dealing with certificated securities the instrument itself is the vital thing, and therefore a valid levy cannot be made unless all possibility of the certificate's wrongfully finding its way into a transferee's hands has been removed. This can be accomplished only when the certificate is in the possession of a public officer, the issuer, or an independent third party. A debtor who has been enjoined can still transfer the security in contempt of court. See *Overlock v. Jerome-Portland Copper Mining Co.*, 29 Ariz. 560, 243 P. 400 (1926). Therefore, although injunctive relief is provided in subsection (e) so that creditors may use this method to gain control of the certificated security, the security certificate itself must be reached to constitute a proper levy whenever the debtor has possession.

2. Subsection (b) provides that when the security is uncertificated and registered in the debtor's name, the debtor's interest can be reached only by legal process upon the issuer. The most logical place to serve the issuer would be the place where the transfer records are maintained, but that location might be difficult to identify, especially when the separate elements of a computer network might be situated in different places. The chief executive office is selected as the appropriate place by analogy to Section 9-103(3)(d). See Comment 5(c) to that section. This section indicates only how attachment is to be made, not when it is legally justified. For that reason there is no conflict between this section and *Shaffer v. Heitner*, 433 U.S. 186 (1977).

3. Subsection (c) provides that a security entitlement can be reached only by legal process upon the debtor's security intermediary. Process is effective only if directed to the debtor's own security intermediary. If Debtor holds securities through Broker, and Broker in turn holds through Clearing Corporation, Debtor's property interest is a security entitlement against Broker. Accordingly, Debtor's creditor cannot reach Debtor's interest by legal process directed to the Clearing Corporation. See also Section 8-115.

4. Subsection (d) provides that when a certificated security, an uncertificated security, or a security entitlement is controlled by a secured party, the debtor's interest can be reached by legal process upon the secured party. This section does not attempt to provide for rights as between the creditor and the secured party, as, for example, whether or when the secured party must liquidate the security.

Definitional Cross References

"Certificated security"–Section 8-102(a)(4)
"Issuer"–Section 8-201
"Secured party"–Section 9-105(1)(m)
"Securities intermediary"–Section 8-102(a)(14)
"Security certificate"–Section 8-102(a)(16)
"Security entitlement"–Section 8-102(a)(17)
"Uncertificated security"–Section 8-102(a)(18)

Section 8–113. Statute of Frauds Generally Inapplicable.

(a) Except as provided in subsection (b), a contract or modification of a contract for the sale or purchase of a security is enforceable whether or not there is a writing signed or record authenticated by a party against whom enforcement is sought, even if the contract or modification is not capable of performance within one year of its making.

(b) A contract for the sale of a security constituting an ownership interest or a proprietary lease or either of the foregoing from a corporation or partnership formed for the purpose of cooperative ownership of real property is not enforceable by way of action or defense unless:

(1) there is some writing signed by the party against whom enforcement is sought which describes the security and states its price; or

(2) the party against whom enforcement is sought admits in its pleading, testimony, or otherwise in court that a contract was made for the sale of the security and the admission describes the security and states its price.

Added by Laws 1997, Ch. 566, § 5, eff. Oct. 10, 1997. See legislative history following § 8–101 for explanation of legislative intent.

Official Comment

This section provides that the statute of frauds does not apply to contracts for the sale of securities, reversing prior law which had a special statute of frauds in Section 8-319 (1978). With the increasing use of electronic means of communication, the statute of frauds is unsuited to the realities of the securities business. For securities transactions, whatever benefits a statute of frauds may play in filtering out fraudulent claims are outweighed by the obstacles it places in the development of modern commercial practices in the securities business.

Definitional Cross References

"Action"–Section 1-201(1)
"Contract"–Section 1-201(11)
"Writing"–Section 1-201(46)

Section 8–114. Evidentiary Rules Concerning Certificated Securities.

The following rules apply in an action on a certificated security against the issuer:

(1) Unless specifically denied in the pleadings, each signature on a security certificate or in a necessary indorsement is admitted.

(2) If the effectiveness of a signature is put in issue, the burden of establishing effectiveness is on the party claiming under the signature, but the signature is presumed to be genuine or authorized.

(3) If signatures on a security certificate are admitted or established, production of the certificate entitles a holder to recover on it unless the defendant establishes a defense or a defect going to the validity of the security.

(4) If it is shown that a defense or defect exists, the plaintiff has the burden of establishing that the plaintiff or some person under whom the plaintiff claims is a person against whom the defense or defect cannot be asserted.

Added by Laws 1997, Ch. 566, § 5, eff. Oct. 10, 1997. See legislative history following § 8–101 for explanation of legislative intent.

Official Comment

This section adapts the rules of negotiable instruments law concerning procedure in actions on instruments, see Section 3-308, to actions on certificated securities governed by this Article. An "action on a security" includes any action or proceeding brought against the issuer to enforce a right or interest that is part of the security, such as an action to collect principal or interest or a dividend, or to establish a right to vote or to receive a new security under an exchange offer or plan of reorganization. This section applies only to certificated securities; actions on uncertificated securities are governed by general evidentiary principles.

Definitional Cross References

"Action"–Section 1-201(1)
"Burden of establishing"–Section 1-201(8)
"Certificated security"–Section 8-102(a)(4)
"Indorsement"–Section 8-102(a)(11)
"Issuer"–Section 8-201
"Presumed"–Section 1-201(31)
"Security"–Section 8-102(a)(15)
"Security certificate"–Section 8-102(a)(16)

Section 8–115. Securities Intermediary and Others Not Liable to Adverse Claimant.

A securities intermediary that has transferred a financial asset pursuant to an effective entitlement order, or a broker or other agent or bailee that has dealt with a financial asset at the direction of its customer or principal, is not liable to a person having an adverse claim to the financial asset, unless the securities intermediary, or broker or other agent or bailee:

(1) took the action after it had been served with an injunction, restraining order, or other legal process enjoining it from doing so, issued by a court of competent jurisdiction, and had a reasonable opportunity to act on the injunction, restraining order, or other legal process; or

(2) acted in collusion with the wrongdoer in violating the rights of the adverse claimant; or

(3) in the case of a security certificate that has been stolen, acted with notice of the adverse claim.

Added by Laws 1997, Ch. 566, § 5, eff. Oct. 10, 1997. See legislative history following § 8–101 for explanation of legislative intent.

Official Comment

1. Other provisions of Article 8 protect certain purchasers against adverse claims, both for the direct holding system and the indirect holding system. See Sections 8-303 and 8-502. This section deals with the related question of the possible liability of a person who acted as the "conduit" for a securities transaction. It covers both securities intermediaries – the "conduits" in the indirect holding system – and brokers or other agents or bailees – the "conduits" in the direct holding system. The following examples illustrate its operation:

Example 1. John Doe is a customer of the brokerage firm of Able & Co. Doe delivers to Able a certificate for 100 shares of XYZ Co. common stock, registered in Doe's name and properly indorsed, and asks the firm to sell it for him. Able does so. Later, John Doe's spouse Mary Doe brings an action against Able asserting that Able's action was wrongful against her because the XYZ Co. stock was marital property in which she had an interest, and John Doe was acting wrongfully against her in transferring the securities.

Example 2. Mary Roe is a customer of the brokerage firm of Baker & Co. and holds her securities through a securities account with Baker. Roe instructs Baker to sell 100 shares of XYZ Co. common stock that she carried in her account. Baker does so. Later, Mary Roe's spouse John Roe brings an action against Baker asserting that Baker's action was wrongful against him because the XYZ Co. stock was marital property in which he had an interest, and Mary Roe was acting wrongfully against him in transferring the securities.

Under common law conversion principles, Mary Doe might be able to assert that Able & Co. is liable to her in Example 1 for exercising dominion over property inconsistent with her rights in it. On that or some similar theory John Roe might assert that Baker is liable to him in Example 2. Section 8-115 protects both Able and Baker from liability.

2. The policy of this section is similar to that of many other rules of law that protect agents and bailees from liability as innocent converters. If a thief steals property and ships it by mail, express service, or carrier, to another person, the recipient of the property does not obtain good title, even though the recipient may have given value to the thief and had no notice or knowledge that the property was stolen. Accordingly, the true owner can recover the property from the recipient or obtain damages in a conversion or similar action. An action against the postal service, express company, or carrier presents entirely different policy considerations. Accordingly, general tort law protects agents or bailees who act on the instructions of their principals or bailors. See Restatement (Second) of Torts § 235. See also UCC Section 7-404.

3. Except as provided in paragraph 3, this section applies even though the securities intermediary, or the broker or other agent or bailee, had notice or knowledge that another person asserts a claim to the securities. Consider the following examples:

Example 3. Same facts as in Example 1, except that before John Doe brought the XYZ Co. security certificate to Able for sale, Mary Doe telephoned or wrote to the firm asserting that she had an interest in all of John Doe's securities and demanding that they not trade for him.

Example 4. Same facts as in Example 2, except that before Mary Roe gave an entitlement order to Baker to sell the XYZ Co. securities from her account, John Roe telephoned or wrote to the firm asserting that he had an interest in all of Mary Roe's securities and demanding that they not trade for her.

Section 8-115 protects Able and Baker from liability. The protections of Section 8-115 do not depend on the presence or absence of notice of adverse claims. It is essential to the securities settlement system that brokers and securities intermediaries be able to act promptly on the directions of their customers. Even though a firm has notice that someone asserts a claim to a customer's securities or security entitlements, the firm should not be placed in the position of having to make a legal judgment about the validity of the claim at the risk of liability either to its customer or to the third party for guessing wrong. Under this section, the broker or securities intermediary is privileged to act on the instructions of its customer or entitlement holder, unless it has been served with a restraining order or other legal process enjoining it from doing so. This is already the law in many jurisdictions. For example a section of the New York Banking Law provides that banks need not recognize any adverse claim to funds or securities on deposit with them unless they have been served with legal process. N.Y. Banking Law § 134. Other sections of the UCC embody a similar policy. See Sections 3-602, 5-114(2)(b).

Paragraph (1) of this section refers only to a court order enjoining the securities intermediary or the broker or other agent or bailee from acting at the instructions of the customer. It does not apply to cases where the adverse claimant tells the intermediary or broker that the customer has been enjoined, or shows the intermediary or broker a copy of a court order binding the customer.

Paragraph (3) takes a different approach in one limited class of cases, those where a customer sells stolen certificated securities through a securities firm. Here the policies that lead to protection of securities firms against assertions of other sorts of claims must be weighed against the desirability of having securities firms guard against the disposition of stolen securities. Accordingly, paragraph (3) denies protection to a broker, custodian, or other agent or bailee who receives a stolen security certificate from its customer, if the broker, custodian, or other agent or bailee had notice of adverse claims. The circumstances that give notice of adverse claims are specified in Section 8-105. The result is that brokers, custodians, and other agents and bailees face the same liability for selling stolen certificated securities that purchasers face for buying them.

4. As applied to securities intermediaries, this section embodies one of the fundamental principles of the Article 8 indirect holding system rules – that a securities intermediary owes duties only to its own entitlement holders. The following examples illustrate the operation of this section in the multi-tiered indirect holding system:

Example 5. Able & Co., a broker-dealer, holds 50,000 shares of XYZ Co. stock in its account at Clearing Corporation. Able acquired the XYZ shares from another firm, Baker & Co., in a transaction that Baker contends was tainted by fraud, giving Baker a right to rescind the transaction and recover the XYZ shares from Able. Baker sends notice to Clearing Corporation stating that Baker has a claim to the 50,000 shares of XYZ Co. in Able's account. Able then initiates an entitlement order directing Clearing Corporation to transfer the 50,000 shares of XYZ Co. to another firm in settlement of a trade. Under Section 8-115, Clearing Corporation is privileged to comply with Able's entitlement order, without fear of liability to Baker. This is so even though Clearing Corporation has notice of Baker's claim, unless Baker obtains a court order enjoining Clearing Corporation from acting on Able's entitlement order.

Example 6. Able & Co., a broker-dealer, holds 50,000 shares of XYZ Co. stock in its account at Clearing Corporation. Able initiates an entitlement order directing Clearing Corporation to transfer the 50,000 shares of XYZ Co. to another firm in settlement of a trade. That trade was made by Able for its own account, and the proceeds were devoted to its own use. Able becomes insolvent, and it is discovered that Able has a shortfall in the shares of XYZ Co. stock that it should have been carrying for its customers. Able's customers bring an action against Clearing Corporation asserting that Clearing Corporation acted wrongfully in transferring the XYZ shares on Able's order because those were shares that should have been held by Able for its customers. Under Section 8-115, Clearing Corporation is not liable to Able's customers, because Clearing Corporation acted on an effective entitlement order of its own entitlement holder, Able. Clearing Corporation's protection against liability does not depend on the presence or absence of notice or knowledge of the claim by Clearing Corporation.

5. If the conduct of a securities intermediary or a broker or other agent or bailee rises to a level of complicity in the wrongdoing of its customer or principal, the policies that favor protection against liability do not apply. Accordingly, paragraph (2) provides that the protections of this section do not apply if the securities intermediary or broker or other agent or bailee acted in collusion with the customer or principal in violating of the rights of another person. The collusion test is intended to adopt a standard akin to the tort rules that determine whether a person is liable as an aider or abettor for the tortious conduct of a third party. See Restatement (Second) of Torts § 876.

Knowledge that the action of the customer is wrongful is a necessary but not sufficient condition of the collusion test. The aspect of the role of securities intermediaries and brokers that Article 8 deals with is the clerical or ministerial role of implementing and recording the securities transactions that their customers conduct. Faithful performance of this role consists of following the instructions of the customer. It is not the role of the record-keeper to police whether the transactions recorded are appropriate, so mere awareness that the customer may be acting wrongfully does not itself constitute collusion. That, of course, does not insulate an intermediary or broker from responsibility in egregious cases where its action goes beyond the ordinary standards of the business of implementing and recording transactions, and reaches a level of affirmative misconduct in assisting the customer in the commission of a wrong.

Definitional Cross References

"Broker"–Section 8-102(a)(3)
"Effective"–Section 8-107
"Entitlement order"–Section 8-102(a)(8)
"Financial asset"–Section 8-102(a)(9)
"Securities intermediary"–Section 8-102(a)(14)
"Security certificate"–Section 8-102(a)(16)

Section 8–116. Securities Intermediary as Purchaser for Value.

A securities intermediary that receives a financial asset and establishes a security entitlement to the financial asset in favor of an entitlement holder is a purchaser for value of the financial asset. A securities intermediary that acquires a security entitlement to a financial asset from another securities intermediary acquires the security entitlement for value if the securities intermediary acquiring the security entitlement establishes a security entitlement to the financial asset in favor of an entitlement holder.

Added by Laws 1997, Ch. 566, § 5, eff. Oct. 10, 1997. See legislative history following § 8–101 for explanation of legislative intent.

Official Comment

1. This section is intended to make explicit two points that, while implicit in other provisions, are of sufficient importance to the operation of the indirect holding system that they warrant explicit statement. First, it makes clear that a securities intermediary that receives a financial asset and establishes a security entitlement in respect thereof in favor of an entitlement holder is a "purchaser" of the financial asset that the securities intermediary received. Second, it makes clear that by establishing a security entitlement in favor of an entitlement holder a securities intermediary gives value

for any corresponding financial asset that the securities intermediary receives or acquires from another party, whether the intermediary holds directly or indirectly.

In many cases a securities intermediary that receives a financial asset will also be transferring value to the person from whom the financial asset was received. That, however, is not always the case. Payment may occur through a different system than settlement of the securities side of the transaction, or the securities might be transferred without a corresponding payment, as when a person moves an account from one securities intermediary to another. Even though the securities intermediary does not give value to the transferor, it does give value by incurring obligations to its own entitlement holder. Although the general definition of value in Section 1-201(44)(d) should be interpreted to cover the point, this section is included to make this point explicit.

2. The following examples illustrate the effect of this section:

Example 1. Buyer buys 1000 shares of XYZ Co. common stock through Buyer's broker Able & Co. to be held in Buyer's securities account. In settlement of the trade, the selling broker delivers to Able a security certificate in street name, indorsed in blank, for 1000 shares XYZ Co. stock, which Able holds in its vault. Able credits Buyer's account for securities in that amount. Section 8-116 specifies that Able is a purchaser of the XYZ Co. stock certificate, and gave value for it. Thus, Able can obtain the benefit of Section 8-303, which protects purchasers for value, if it satisfies the other requirements of that section.

Example 2. Buyer buys 1000 shares XYZ Co. common stock through Buyer's broker Able & Co. to be held in Buyer's securities account. The trade is settled by crediting 1000 shares XYZ Co. stock to Able's account at Clearing Corporation. Able credits Buyer's account for securities in that amount. When Clearing Corporation credits Able's account, Able acquires a security entitlement under Section 8-501. Section 8-116 specifies that Able acquired this security entitlement for value. Thus, Able can obtain the benefit of Section 8-502, which protects persons who acquire security entitlements for value, if it satisfies the other requirements of that section.

Example 3. Thief steals a certificated bearer bond from Owner. Thief sends the certificate to his broker Able & Co. to be held in his securities account, and Able credits Thief's account for the bond. Section 8-116 specifies that Able is a purchaser of the bond and gave value for it. Thus, Able can obtain the benefit of Section 8-303, which protects purchasers for value, if it satisfies the other requirements of that section.

Definitional Cross References

"Financial asset"–Section 8-102(a)(9)
"Securities intermediary"–Section 8-102(a)(14)
"Security entitlement"–Section 8-102(a)(17)
"Entitlement holder"–Section 8-102(a)(7)

PART 2

ISSUE AND ISSUER

Section 8–201. Issuer.

(a) With respect to an obligation on or a defense to a security, an "issuer" includes a person that:

(1) places or authorizes the placing of its name on a security certificate, other than as authenticating trustee, registrar, transfer agent, or the like, to evidence

a share, participation, or other interest in its property or in an enterprise, or to evidence its duty to perform an obligation represented by the certificate;

(2) creates a share, participation, or other interest in its property or in an enterprise, or undertakes an obligation, that is an uncertificated security;

(3) directly or indirectly creates a fractional interest in its rights or property, if the fractional interest is represented by a security certificate; or

(4) becomes responsible for, or in place of, another person described as an issuer in this section.

(b) With respect to an obligation on or defense to a security, a guarantor is an issuer to the extent of its guaranty, whether or not its obligation is noted on a security certificate.

(c) With respect to a registration of a transfer, issuer means a person on whose behalf transfer books are maintained.

Added by Laws 1997, Ch. 566, § 5, eff. Oct. 10, 1997. See legislative history following § 8–101 for explanation of legislative intent.

Official Comment

1. The definition of "issuer" in this section functions primarily to describe the persons whose defenses may be cut off under the rules in Part 2. In large measure it simply tracks the language of the definition of security in Section 8-102(a)(15).

2. Subsection (b) distinguishes the obligations of a guarantor as issuer from those of the principal obligor. However, it does not exempt the guarantor from the impact of subsection (d) of Section 8-202. Whether or not the obligation of the guarantor is noted on the security is immaterial. Typically, guarantors are parent corporations, or stand in some similar relationship to the principal obligor. If that relationship existed at the time the security was originally issued the guaranty would probably have been noted on the security. However, if the relationship arose afterward, e.g., through a purchase of stock or properties, or through merger or consolidation, probably the notation would not have been made. Nonetheless, the holder of the security is entitled to the benefit of the obligation of the guarantor.

3. Subsection (c) narrows the definition of "issuer" for purposes of Part 4 of this Article (registration of transfer). It is supplemented by Section 8-407.

Definitional Cross References

"Person"–Section 1-201(30)
"Security"–Section 8-102(a)(15)
"Security certificate"–Section 8-102(a)(16)
"Uncertificated security"–Section 8-102(a)(18)

Section 8–202. Issuer's Responsibility and Defenses; Notice of Defect or Defense.

(a) Even against a purchaser for value and without notice, the terms of a certificated security include terms stated on the certificate and terms made part of the security by reference on the certificate to another instrument, indenture, or document or to a constitution, statute, ordinance, rule, regulation, order, or the like, to the extent the terms referred to do not conflict with terms stated on the certificate. A reference under this subsection does not of itself charge a purchaser for value with notice of a defect going to the validity of the security, even if the certificate expressly states that a person accepting it admits notice. The terms of an uncertificated security include those stated in any instrument, indenture, or document or in a constitution, statute, ordinance, rule, regulation, order, or the like, pursuant to which the security is issued.

(b) The following rules apply if an issuer asserts that a security is not valid:

(1) a security other than one issued by a government or governmental subdivision, agency, or instrumentality, even though issued with a defect going to its validity, is valid in the hands of a purchaser for value and without notice of the particular defect unless the defect involves a violation of a constitutional provision. In that case, the security is valid in the hands of a purchaser for value and without notice of the defect, other than one who takes by original issue.

(2) Paragraph (1) applies to an issuer that is a government or governmental subdivision, agency, or instrumentality only if there has been substantial compliance with the legal requirements governing the issue or the issuer has received a substantial consideration for the issue as a whole or for the particular security and a stated purpose of the issue is one for which the issuer has power to borrow money or issue the security.

(c) Except as otherwise provided in Section 8–205, lack of genuine ness of a certificated security is a complete defense, even against a purchaser for value and without notice.

(d) All other defenses of the issuer of a security, including nondelivery and conditional delivery of a security, are ineffective against a purchaser for value who has taken the security without notice of the particular defense.

(e) This section does not affect the right of a party to cancel a contract for a security "when, as and if issued" or "when distributed" in the event of a material change in the character of the security that is the subject of the contract or in the plan or arrangement pursuant to which the security is to be issued or distributed.

(f) If a security is held by a securities intermediary against whom an entitlement holder has a security entitlement with respect to the security, the issuer may not assert any defense that the issuer could not assert if the entitlement holder held the security directly.

Added by Laws 1997, Ch. 566, § 5, eff. Oct. 10, 1997. See legislative history following § 8–101 for explanation of legislative intent.

Official Comment

1. In this Article the rights of the purchaser for value without notice are divided into two aspects, those against the issuer, and those against other claimants to the security. Part 2 of this Article, and especially this section, deal with rights against the issuer.

Subsection (a) states, in accordance with the prevailing case law, the right of the issuer (who prepares the text of the security) to include terms incorporated by adequate reference to an extrinsic source, so long as the terms so incorporated do not conflict with the stated terms. Thus, the standard practice of referring in a bond or debenture to the trust indenture under which it is issued without spelling out its necessarily complex and lengthy provisions is approved. Every stock certificate refers in some manner to the charter or articles of incorporation of the issuer. At least where there is more than one class of stock authorized applicable corporation codes specifically require a statement or summary as to preferences, voting powers and the like. References to constitutions, statutes, ordinances, rules, regulations or orders are not so common, except in the obligations of governments or governmental agencies or units; but where appropriate they fit into the rule here stated.

Courts have generally held that an issuer is estopped from denying representations made in the text of a security. *Delaware-New Jersey Ferry Co. v. Leeds*, 21 Del.Ch. 279, 186 A. 913 (1936). Nor is a defect in form or the invalidity of a security normally available to the issuer as a defense. *Bonini v. Family Theatre Corporation*, 327 Pa. 273, 194 A. 498 (1937); *First National Bank of Fairbanks v. Alaska Airmotive*, 119 F.2d 267 (C.C.A.Alaska 1941).

2. The rule in subsection (a) requiring that the terms of a security be noted or referred to on the certificate is based on practices and expectations in the direct holding system for certificated securities. This rule does not express a general rule or policy that the terms of a security are effective only if they are communicated to beneficial owners in some particular fashion. Rather, subsection (a) is based on the principle that a purchaser who does obtain a certificate is entitled to assume that the terms of the security have been noted or referred to on the certificate. That policy does not come into play in a securities holding system in which purchasers do not take delivery of certificates.

The provisions of subsection (a) concerning notation of terms on security certificates are necessary only because paper certificates play such an important role for certificated securities that a purchaser should be protected against assertion of any defenses or rights that are not noted on the certificate. No similar problem exists with respect to uncertificated securities. The last sentence of subsection (a) is, strictly speaking, unnecessary, since it only recognizes the fact that the terms of an uncertificated security are determined by whatever other law or agreement governs the security. It is included only to preclude any inference that uncertificated securities are subject to any requirement analogous to the requirement of notation of terms on security certificates.

The rule of subsection (a) applies to the indirect holding system only in the sense that if a certificated security has been delivered to the clearing corporation or other securities intermediary, the terms of the security should be noted or referred to on the certificate. If the security is uncertificated, that principle does not apply even at the issuer-clearing corporation level. The beneficial owners who hold securities through the clearing corporation are bound by the terms of the security, even though they do not actually see the certificate. Since entitlement holders in an indirect holding system have not taken delivery of certificates, the policy of subsection (a) does not apply.

3. The penultimate sentence of subsection (a) and all of subsection (b) embody the concept that it is the duty of the issuer, not of the purchaser, to make sure that the security complies with the law governing its issue. The penultimate sentence of subsection (a) makes clear that the issuer cannot, by incorporating a reference to a statute or other document, charge the purchaser with notice of the security's invalidity. Subsection (b) gives to a purchaser for value without notice of the defect the right to enforce the security against the issuer despite the presence of a defect that otherwise would render the security invalid. There are three circumstances in which a purchaser

does not gain such rights: first, if the defect involves a violation of constitutional provisions, these rights accrue only to a subsequent purchaser, that is, one who takes other than by original issue. This Article leaves to the law of each particular State the rights of a purchaser on original issue of a security with a constitutional defect. No negative implication is intended by the explicit grant of rights to a subsequent purchaser.

Second, governmental issuers are distinguished in subsection (b) from other issuers as a matter of public policy, and additional safeguards are imposed before governmental issues are validated. Governmental issuers are estopped from asserting defenses only if there has been substantial compliance with the legal requirements governing the issue or if substantial consideration has been received and a stated purpose of the issue is one for which the issuer has power to borrow money or issue the security. The purpose of the substantial compliance requirement is to make certain that a mere technicality as, e.g., in the manner of publishing election notices, shall not be a ground for depriving an innocent purchaser of rights in the security. The policy is here adopted of such cases as *Tommie v. City of Gadsden*, 229 Ala. 521, 158 So. 763 (1935), in which minor discrepancies in the form of the election ballot used were overlooked and the bonds were declared valid since there had been substantial compliance with the statute.

UCC

A long and well established line of federal cases recognizes the principle of estoppel in favor of purchasers for value without notices where municipalities issue bonds containing recitals of compliance with governing constitutional and statutory provisions, made by the municipal authorities entrusted with determining such compliance. *Chaffee County v. Potter*, 142 U.S. 355 (1892); *Oregon v. Jennings*, 119 U.S. 74 (1886); *Gunnison County Commissioners v. Rollins*, 173 U.S. 255 (1898). This rule has been qualified, however, by requiring that the municipality have power to issue the security. *Anthony v. County of Jasper*, 101 U.S. 693 (1879); *Town of South Ottawa v. Perkins*, 94 U.S. 260 (1876). This section follows the case law trend, simplifying the rule by setting up two conditions for an estoppel against a governmental issuer: (1) substantial consideration given, and (2) power in the issuer to borrow money or issue the security for the stated purpose. As a practical matter the problem of policing governmental issuers has been alleviated by the present practice of requiring legal opinions as to the validity of the issue. The bulk of the case law on this point is nearly 100 years old and it may be assumed that the question now seldom arises.

Section 8-210, regarding overissue, provides the third exception to the rule that an innocent purchase for value takes a valid security despite the presence of a defect that would otherwise give rise to invalidity. See that section and its Comment for further explanation.

4. Subsection (e) is included to make clear that this section does not affect the presently recognized right of either party to a "when, as and if" or "when distributed" contract to cancel the contract on substantial change.

5. Subsection (f) has been added because the introduction of the security entitlement concept requires some adaptation of the Part 2 rules, particularly those that distinguish between purchasers who take by original issue and subsequent purchasers. The basic concept of Part 2 is to apply to investment securities the principle of negotiable instruments law that an obligor is precluded from asserting most defenses against purchasers for value without notice. Section 8-202 describes in some detail which defenses issuers can raise against purchasers for value and subsequent purchasers for value. Because these rules were drafted with the direct holding system in mind, some interpretive problems might be presented in applying them to the indirect holding. For example, if a municipality issues a bond in book-entry only form, the only direct "purchaser" of that bond would be the clearing corporation. The policy of precluding the issuer from asserting defenses is, however, equally applicable. Subsection (f) is

designed to ensure that the defense preclusion rules developed for the direct holding system will also apply to the indirect holding system.

Definitional Cross References

"Certificated security"–Section 8-102(a)(4)
"Notice"–Section 1-201(25)
"Purchaser"–Section 1-201(33) & 8-116
"Security"–Section 8-102(a)(15)
"Uncertificated security"–Section 8-102(a)(18)
"Value"–Section 1-201(44) & 8-116

Section 8–203. Staleness as Notice of Defect or Defense.

After an act or event, other than a call that has been revoked, creating a right to immediate performance of the principal obligation represented by a certificated security or setting a date on or after which the security is to be presented or surrendered for redemption or exchange, a purchaser is charged with notice of any defect in its issue or defense of the issuer, if the act or event:

(1) requires the payment of money, the delivery of a certificated security, the registration of transfer of an uncertificated security, or any of them on presentation or surrender of the security certificate, the money or security is available on the date set for payment or exchange, and the purchaser takes the security more than one year after that date; or

(2) is not covered by subsection (1) and the purchaser takes the security more than two years after the date set for surrender or presentation or the date on which performance became due.

Added by Laws 1997, Ch. 566, § 5, eff. Oct. 10, 1997. See legislative history following § 8–101 for explanation of legislative intent.

Official Comment

1. The problem of matured or called securities is here dealt with in terms of the effect of such events in giving notice of the issuer's defenses and not in terms of "negotiability'. The substance of this section applies only to certificated securities because certificates may be transferred to a purchaser by delivery after the security has matured, been called, or become redeemable or exchangeable. It is contemplated that uncertificated securities which have matured or been called will merely be canceled on the books of the issuer and the proceeds sent to the registered owner. Uncertificated securities which have become redeemable or exchangeable, at the option of the owner, may be transferred to a purchaser, but the transfer is effectuated only by registration of transfer, thus necessitating communication with the issuer. If defects or defenses in such securities exist, the issuer will necessarily have the opportunity to bring them to the attention of the purchaser.

2. The fact that a security certificate is in circulation long after it has been called for redemption or exchange must give rise to the question in a purchaser's mind as to why it has not been surrendered. After the lapse of a reasonable period of time a purchaser can no longer claim "no reason to know" of any defects or irregularities in its issue. Where funds are available for the redemption the security certificate is

normally turned in more promptly and a shorter time is set as the "reasonable period" than is set where funds are not available.

Defaulted certificated securities may be traded on financial markets in the same manner as unmatured and undefaulted instruments and a purchaser might not be placed upon notice of irregularity by the mere fact of default. An issuer, however, should at some point be placed in a position to determine definitely its liability on an invalid or improper issue, and for this purpose a security under this section becomes "stale" two years after the default. A different rule applies when the question is notice not of issuer's defenses but of claims of ownership. Section 8-105 and Comment.

3. Nothing in this section is designed to extend the life of preferred stocks called for redemption as "shares of stock" beyond the redemption date. After such a call, the security represents only a right to the funds set aside for redemption.

Definitional Cross References

"Certificated security"–Section 8-102(a)(4)
"Notice"–Section 1-201(25)
"Purchaser"–Section 1-201(33) & 8-116
"Security"–Section 8-102(a)(15)
"Security certificate"–Section 8-102(a)(16)
"Uncertificated security"–Section 8-102(a)(18)

Section 8–204. Effect of Issuer's Restriction on Transfer.

A restriction on transfer of a security imposed by the issuer, even if otherwise lawful, is ineffective against a person without knowledge of the restriction unless:

(1) the security is certificated and the restriction is noted conspicuously on the security certificate; or

(2) the security is uncertificated and the registered owner has been notified of the restriction.

Added by Laws 1997, Ch. 566, § 5, eff. Oct. 10, 1997. See legislative history following § 8–101 for explanation of legislative intent.

Official Comment

1. Restrictions on transfer of securities are imposed by issuers in a variety of circumstances and for a variety of purposes, such as to retain control of a close corporation or to ensure compliance with federal securities laws. Other law determines whether such restrictions are permissible. This section deals only with the consequences of failure to note the restriction on a security certificate.

This section imposes no bar to enforcement of a restriction on transfer against a person who has actual knowledge of it.

2. A restriction on transfer of a certificated security is ineffective against a person without knowledge of the restriction unless the restriction is noted conspicuously on the certificate. The word "noted" is used to make clear that the restriction need not be set forth in full text. Refusal by an issuer to register a transfer on the basis of an unnoted restriction would be a violation of the issuer's duty to register under Section 8-401.

3. The policy of this section is the same as in Section 8-202. A purchaser who takes delivery of a certificated security is entitled to rely on the terms stated on the

certificate. That policy obviously does not apply to uncertificated securities. For uncertificated securities, this section requires only that the registered owner has been notified of the restriction. Suppose, for example, that A is the registered owner of an uncertificated security, and that the issuer has notified A of a restriction on transfer. A agrees to sell the security to B, in violation of the restriction. A completes a written instruction directing the issuer to register transfer to B, and B pays A for the security at the time A delivers the instruction to B. A does not inform B of the restriction, and B does not otherwise have notice or knowledge of it at the time B pays and receives the instruction. B presents the instruction to the issuer, but the issuer refuses to register the transfer on the grounds that it would violate the restriction. The issuer has complied with this section, because it did notify the registered owner A of the restriction. The issuer's refusal to register transfer is not wrongful. B has an action against A for breach of transfer warranty, see Section 8-108(b)(4)(iii). B's mistake was treating an uncertificated security transaction in the fashion appropriate only for a certificated security. The mechanism for transfer of uncertificated securities is registration of transfer on the books of the issuer; handing over an instruction only initiates the process. The purchaser should make arrangements to ensure that the price is not paid until it knows that the issuer has or will register transfer.

4. In the indirect holding system, investors neither take physical delivery of security certificates nor have uncertificated securities registered in their names. So long as the requirements of this section have been satisfied at the level of the relationship between the issuer and the securities intermediary that is a direct holder, this section does not preclude the issuer from enforcing a restriction on transfer. See Section 8-202(a) and Comment 2 thereto.

5. This section deals only with restrictions imposed by the issuer. Restrictions imposed by statute are not affected. See *Quiner v. Marblehead Social Co.*, 10 Mass. 476 (1813); *Madison Bank v. Price*, 79 Kan. 289, 100 P. 280 (1909); *Healey v. Steele Center Creamery Ass'n*, 115 Minn. 451, 133 N.W. 69 (1911). Nor does it deal with private agreements between stockholders containing restrictive covenants as to the sale of the security.

Definitional Cross References

"Certificated security"–Section 8-102(a)(4)
"Conspicuous"–Section 1-201(10)
"Issuer"–Section 8-201
"Knowledge"–Section 1-201(25)
"Notify"–Section 1-201(25)
"Purchaser"–Section 1-201(33) & 8-116
"Security"–Section 8-102(a)(15)
"Security certificate"–Section 8-102(a)(16)
"Uncertificated security"–Section 8-102(a)(18)

Section 8–205. Effect of Unauthorized Signature on Security Certificate.

An unauthorized signature placed on a security certificate before or in the course of issue is ineffective, but the signature is effective in favor of a purchaser for value of the certificated security if the purchaser is without notice of the lack of authority and the signing has been done by:

(1) an authenticating trustee, registrar, transfer agent, or other person entrusted by the issuer with the signing of the security certificate or of similar security certificates, or the immediate preparation for signing of any of them; or

(2) an employee of the issuer, or of any of the persons listed in subsection (1), entrusted with responsible handling of the security certificate.

Added by Laws 1997, Ch. 566, § 5, eff. Oct. 10, 1997. See legislative history following § 8–101 for explanation of legislative intent.

Official Comment

1. The problem of forged or unauthorized signatures may arise where an employee of the issuer, transfer agent, or registrar has access to securities which the employee is required to prepare for issue by affixing the corporate seal or by adding a signature necessary for issue. This section is based upon the issuer's duty to avoid the negligent entrusting of securities to such persons. Issuers have long been held responsible for signatures placed upon securities by parties whom they have held out to the public as authorized to prepare such securities. See *Fifth Avenue Bank of New York v. The Forty-Second & Grand Street Ferry Railroad Co.*, 137 N.Y. 231, 33 N.E. 378, 19 L.R.A. 331, 33 Am.St.Rep. 712 (1893); *Jarvis v. Manhattan Beach Co.*, 148 N.Y. 652, 43 N.E. 68, 31 L.R.A. 776, 51 Am.St.Rep. 727 (1896). The "apparent authority" concept of some of the case-law, however, is here extended and this section expressly rejects the technical distinction, made by courts reluctant to recognize forged signatures, between cases where forgers sign signatures they are authorized to sign under proper circumstances and those in which they sign signatures they are never authorized to sign. *Citizens' & Southern National Bank v. Trust Co. of Georgia*, 50 Ga.App. 681, 179 S.E. 278 (1935). Normally the purchaser is not in a position to determine which signature a forger, entrusted with the preparation of securities, has "apparent authority" to sign. The issuer, on the other hand, can protect itself against such fraud by the careful selection and bonding of agents and employees, or by action over against transfer agents and registrars who in turn may bond their personnel.

2. The issuer cannot be held liable for the honesty of employees not entrusted, directly or indirectly, with the signing, preparation, or responsible handling of similar securities and whose possible commission of forgery it has no reason to anticipate. The result in such cases as *Hudson Trust Co. v. American Linseed Co.*, 232 N.Y. 350, 134 N.E. 178 (1922), and *Dollar Savings Fund & Trust Co. v. Pittsburgh Plate Glass Co.*, 213 Pa. 307, 62 A. 916, 5 Ann.Cas. 248 (1906) is here adopted.

3. This section is not concerned with forged or unauthorized indorsements, but only with unauthorized signatures of issuers, transfer agents, etc., placed upon security certificates during the course of their issue. The protection here stated is available to all purchasers for value without notice and not merely to subsequent purchasers.

Definitional Cross References

"Certificated security"–Section 8-102(a)(4)
"Issuer"–Section 8-201
"Notice"–Section 1-201(25)
"Purchaser"–Section 1-201(33) & 8-116
"Security certificate"–Section 8-102(a)(14)
"Unauthorized signature"–Section 1-201(43)

Section 8–206. Completion or Alteration of Security Certificate.

(a) If a security certificate contains the signatures necessary to its issue or transfer but is incomplete in any other respect:

(1) any person may complete it by filling in the blanks as authorized; and

(2) even if the blanks are incorrectly filled in, the security certificate as completed is enforceable by a purchaser who took it for value and without notice of the incorrectness.

(b) A complete security certificate that has been improperly altered, even if fraudulently, remains enforceable, but only according to its original terms.

Added by Laws 1997, Ch. 566, § 5, eff. Oct. 10, 1997. See legislative history following § 8–101 for explanation of legislative intent.

Official Comment

1. The problem of forged or unauthorized signatures necessary for the issue or transfer of a security is not involved here, and a person in possession of a blank certificate is not, by this section, given authority to fill in blanks with such signatures. Completion of blanks left in a transfer instruction is dealt with elsewhere (Section 8-305(a)).

2. Blanks left upon issue of a security certificate are the only ones dealt with here, and a purchaser for value without notice is protected. A purchaser is not in a good position to determine whether blanks were completed by the issuer or by some person not authorized to complete them. On the other hand the issuer can protect itself by not placing its signature on the writing until the blanks are completed or, if it does sign before all blanks are completed, by carefully selecting the agents and employees to whom it entrusts the writing after authentication. With respect to a security certificate that is completed by the issuer but later is altered, the issuer has done everything it can to protect the purchaser and thus is not charged with the terms as altered. However, it is charged according to the original terms, since it is not thereby prejudiced. If the completion or alteration is obviously irregular, the purchaser may not qualify as a purchaser who took without notice under this section.

3. Only the purchaser who physically takes the certificate is directly protected. However, a transferee may receive protection indirectly through Section 8-302(a).

4. The protection granted a purchaser for value without notice under this section is modified to the extent that an overissue may result where an incorrect amount is inserted into a blank (Section 8-210).

Definitional Cross References

"Notice"–Section 1-201(25)
"Purchaser"–Section 1-201(33) & 8-116
"Security certificate"–Section 8-102(a)(16)
"Unauthorized signature"–Section 1-201(43)
"Value"–Section 1-201(44) & 8-116

Section 8–207. Rights and Duties of Issuer with Respect to Registered Owners.

(a) Before due presentment for registration of transfer of a certificated security in registered form or of an instruction requesting registration of transfer of an uncertificated security, the issuer or indenture trustee may treat the registered owner as the person exclusively entitled to vote, receive notifications, and otherwise exercise all the rights and powers of an owner.

(b) This article does not affect the liability of the registered owner of a security for a call, assessment, or the like.

Added by Laws 1997, Ch. 566, § 5, eff. Oct. 10, 1997. See legislative history following § 8-101 for explanation of legislative intent.

Official Comment

1. Subsection (a) states the issuer's right to treat the registered owner of a security as the person entitled to exercise all the rights of an owner. This right of the issuer is limited by the provisions of Part 4 of this article. Once there has been due presentation for registration of transfer, the issuer has a duty to register ownership in the name of the transferee. Section 8-401. Thus its right to treat the old registered owner as exclusively entitled to the rights of ownership must cease.

The issuer may under this section make distributions of money or securities to the registered owners of securities without requiring further proof of ownership, provided that such distributions are distributable to the owners of all securities of the same issue and the terms of the security do not require surrender of a security certificate as a condition of payment or exchange. Any such distribution shall constitute a defense against a claim for the same distribution by a person, even if that person is in possession of the security certificate and is a protected purchaser of the security. See PEB Commentary No. 4, dated March 10, 1990.

2. Subsections (a) is permissive and does not require that the issuer deal exclusively with the registered owner. It is free to require proof of ownership before paying out dividends or the like if it chooses to. *Barbato v. Breeze Corporation*, 128 N.J.L. 309, 26 A.2d 53 (1942).

3. This section does not operate to determine who is finally entitled to exercise voting and other rights or to receive payments and distributions. The parties are still free to incorporate their own arrangements as to these matters in seller-purchaser agreements which may be definitive as between them.

4. No change in existing state laws as to the liability of registered owners for calls and assessments is here intended; nor is anything in this section designed to estop record holders from denying ownership when assessments are levied if they are otherwise entitled to do so under state law. See *State ex rel. Squire v. Murfey, Blosson & Co.*, 131 Ohio St. 289, 2 N.E.2d 866 (1936); *Willing v. Delaplaine*, 23 F.Supp. 579 (1937).

5. No interference is intended with the common practice of closing the transfer books or taking a record date for dividend, voting, and other purposes, as provided for in by-laws, charters, and statutes.

Definitional Cross References

"Certificated security"–Section 8-102(a)(4)
"Instruction"–Section 8-102(a)(12)
"Issuer"–Section 8-201
"Registered form" –Section 8-102(a)(13)
"Security"–Section 8-102(a)(15)
"Uncertificated security"–Section 8-102(a)(18)

Section 8–208. Effect of Signature of Authenticating Trustee, Registrar, or Transfer Agent.

(a) A person signing a security certificate as authenticating trustee, registrar, transfer agent, or the like, warrants to a purchaser for value of the certificated security, if the purchaser is without notice of a particular defect, that:

(1) the certificate is genuine;

(2) the person's own participation in the issue of the security is within the person's capacity and within the scope of the authority received by the person from the issuer; and

(3) the person has reasonable grounds to believe that the certificated security is in the form and within the amount the issuer is authorized to issue.

(b) Unless otherwise agreed, a person signing under subsection (a) does not assume responsibility for the validity of the security in other respects.

Added by Laws 1997, Ch. 566, § 5, eff. Oct. 10, 1997. See legislative history following § 8–101 for explanation of legislative intent.

Official Comment

1. The warranties here stated express the current understanding and prevailing case law as to the effect of the signatures of authenticating trustees, transfer agents, and registrars. See *Jarvis v. Manhattan Beach Co.*, 148 N.Y. 652, 43 N.E. 68, 31 L.R.A. 776, 51 Am.St.Rep. 727 (1896). Although it has generally been regarded as the particular obligation of the transfer agent to determine whether securities are in proper form as provided by the by-laws and Articles of Incorporation, neither a registrar nor an authenticating trustee should properly place a signature upon a certificate without determining whether it is at least regular on its face. The obligations of these parties in this respect have therefore been made explicit in terms of due care. See *Feldmeier v. Mortgage Securities, Inc.*, 34 Cal.App.2d 201, 93 P.2d 593 (1939).

2. Those cases which hold that an authenticating trustee is not liable for any defect in the mortgage or property which secures the bond or for any fraudulent misrepresentations made by the issuer are not here affected since these matters do not involve the genuineness or proper form of the security. *Ainsa v. Mercantile Trust Co.*, 174 Cal. 504, 163 P. 898 (1917); *Tschetinian v. City Trust Co.*, 186 N.Y. 432, 79 N.E. 401 (1906); *Davidge v. Guardian Trust Co. of New York*, 203 N.Y. 331, 96 N.E. 751 (1911).

3. The charter or an applicable statute may affect the capacity of a bank or other corporation undertaking to act as an authenticating trustee, registrar, or transfer agent. See, for example, the Federal Reserve Act (U.S.C.A., Title 12, Banks and Banking, Section 248) under which the Board of Governors of the Federal Reserve Bank is authorized to grant special permits to National Banks permitting them to act as trustees. Such corporations are therefore held to certify as to their legal capacity to act as well as to their authority.

4. Authenticating trustees, registrars, and transfer agents have normally been held liable for an issue in excess of the authorized amount. *Jarvis v. Manhattan Beach Co.*, supra; *Mullen v. Eastern Trust & Banking Co.*, 108 Me. 498, 81 A. 948 (1911). In imposing upon these parties a duty of due care with respect to the amount they are authorized to help issue, this section does not necessarily validate the security, but merely holds persons responsible for the excess issue liable in damages for any loss suffered by the purchaser.

5. Aside from questions of genuineness and excess issue, these parties are not held to certify as to the validity of the security unless they specifically undertake to do so. The case law which has recognized a unique responsibility on the transfer agent's part to testify as to the validity of any security which it countersigns is rejected.

6. This provision does not prevent a transfer agent or issuer from agreeing with a registrar of stock to protect the registrar in respect of the genuineness and proper

form of a security certificate signed by the issuer or the transfer agent or both. Nor does it interfere with proper indemnity arrangements between the issuer and trustees, transfer agents, registrars, and the like.

7. An unauthorized signature is a signature for purposes of this section if and only if it is made effective by Section 8-205.

Definitional Cross References

"Certificated security"–Section 8-102(a)(4)
"Genuine"–Section 1-201(18)
"Issuer"–Section 8-201
"Notice"–Section 1-201(25)
"Purchaser"–Section 1-201(33) & 8-116
"Security"–Section 8-102(a)(15)
"Security certificate"–Section 8-102(a)(16)
"Uncertificated security"–Section 8-102(a)(18)
"Value"–Section 1-201(44) & 8-116

Section 8–209. Issuer's Lien.

A lien in favor of an issuer upon a certificated security is valid against a purchaser only if the right of the issuer to the lien is noted conspicuously on the security certificate.

Added by Laws 1997, Ch. 566, § 5, eff. Oct. 10, 1997. See legislative history following § 8–101 for explanation of legislative intent.

Official Comment

This section is similar to Sections 8-202 and 8-204 which require that the terms of a certificated security and any restriction on transfer imposed by the issuer be noted on the security certificate. This section differs from those two sections in that the purchaser's knowledge of the issuer's claim is irrelevant. "Noted" makes clear that the text of the lien provisions need not be set forth in full. However, this would not override a provision of an applicable corporation code requiring statement in haec verba. This section does not apply to uncertificated securities. It applies to the indirect holding system in the same fashion as Sections 8-202 and 8-204, see Comment 2 to Section 8-202.

Definitional Cross References

"Certificated security"–Section 8-102(a)(4)
"Issuer"–Section 8-201
"Purchaser"–Section 1-201(33) & 8-116
"Security"–Section 8-102(a)(15)
"Security certificate"–Section 8-102(a)(16)

Section 8–210. Overissue.

(a) In this section, "overissue" means the issue of securities in excess of the amount the issuer has corporate power to issue, but an overissue does not occur if appropriate action has cured the overissue.

(b) Except as otherwise provided in subsections (c) and (d), the provisions of this Article which validate a security or compel its issue or reissue do not apply to the extent that validation, issue, or reissue would result in overissue.

(c) If an identical security not constituting an overissue is reasonably available for purchase, a person entitled to issue or validation may compel the issuer to purchase the security and deliver it if certificated or register its transfer if uncertificated, against surrender of any security certificate the person holds.

(d) If a security is not reasonably available for purchase, a person entitled to issue or validation may recover from the issuer the price the person or the last purchaser for value paid for it with interest from the date of the person's demand.

Added by Laws 1997, Ch. 566, § 5, eff. Oct. 10, 1997. See legislative history following § 8–101 for explanation of legislative intent.

Official Comment

1. Deeply embedded in corporation law is the conception that "corporate power" to issue securities stems from the statute, either general or special, under which the corporation is organized. Corporation codes universally require that the charter or articles of incorporation state, at least as to capital shares, maximum limits in terms of number of shares or total dollar capital. Historically, special incorporation statutes are similarly drawn and sometimes similarly limit the face amount of authorized debt securities. The theory is that issue of securities in excess of the authorized amounts is prohibited. See, for example, *McWilliams v. Geddes & Moss Undertaking Co.*, 169 So. 894 (1936, La.); *Crawford v. Twin City Oil Co.*, 216 Ala. 216, 113 So. 61 (1927); *New York and New Haven R.R. Co. v. Schuyler*, 34 N.Y. 30 (1865). This conception persists despite modern corporation codes under which, by action of directors and stockholders, additional shares can be authorized by charter amendment and thereafter issued. This section does not give a person entitled to validation, issue, or reissue of a security, the right to compel amendment of the charter to authorize additional shares. Therefore, in a case where issue of an additional security would require charter amendment, the plaintiff is limited to the two alternate remedies set forth in subsections (c) and (d). The last clause of subsection (a), which is added in Revised Article 8, does, however, recognize that under modern conditions, overissue may be a relatively minor technical problem that can be cured by appropriate action under governing corporate law

2. Where an identical security is reasonably available for purchase, whether because traded on an organized market, or because one or more security owners may be willing to sell at a not unreasonable price, the issuer, although unable to issue additional shares, will be able to purchase them and may be compelled to follow that procedure. *West v. Tintic Standard Mining Co.*, 71 Utah 158, 263 P. 490 (1928).

3. The right to recover damages from an issuer who has permitted an overissue to occur is well settled. *New York and New Haven R.R. Co. v. Schuyler*, 34 N.Y. 30 (1865). The measure of such damages, however, has been open to question, some courts basing them upon the value of stock at the time registration is refused; some upon the value at the time of trial; and some upon the highest value between the time of refusal and the time of trial. *Allen v. South Boston Railroad*, 150 Mass. 200, 22 N.E. 917, 5 L.R.A. 716, 15 Am.St.Rep. 185 (1889); *Commercial Bank v. Kortright*, 22 Wend. (N.Y.) 348 (1839). The purchase price of the security to the last purchaser who gave value for it is here adopted as being the fairest means of reducing the

possibility of speculation by the purchaser. Interest may be recovered as the best available measure of compensation for delay.

Definitional Cross References

"Issuer"–Section 8-201
"Security"–Section 8-102(a)(15)
"Security certificate"–Section 8-102(a)(16)
"Uncertificated security"–Section 8-102(a)(18)

PART 3

TRANSFER OF CERTIFICATED AND UNCERTIFICATED SECURITIES

Section 8–301. Delivery.

(a) Delivery of a certificated security to a purchaser occurs when:

(1) the purchaser acquires possession of the security certificate;

(2) another person, other than a securities intermediary, either acquires possession of the security certificate on behalf of the purchaser or, having previously acquired possession of the certificate, acknowledges that it holds for the purchaser; or

(3) a securities intermediary acting on behalf of the purchaser acquires possession of the security certificate, only if the certificate is in registered form and has been specially indorsed to the purchaser by an effective indorsement.

(b) Delivery of an uncertificated security to a purchaser occurs when:

(1) the issuer registers the purchaser as the registered owner, upon original issue or registration of transfer; or

(2) another person, other than a securities intermediary, either becomes the registered owner of the uncertificated security on behalf of the purchaser or, having previously become the registered owner, acknowledges that it holds for the purchaser.

Added by Laws 1997, Ch. 566, § 5, eff. Oct. 10, 1997. See legislative history following § 8–101 for explanation of legislative intent.

Official Comment

1. This section specifies the requirements for "delivery" of securities. Delivery is used in Article 8 to describe the formal steps necessary for a purchaser to acquire a direct interest in a security under this Article. The concept of delivery refers to the implementation of a transaction, not the legal categorization of the transaction which is consummated by delivery. Issuance and transfer are different kinds of transaction, though both may be implemented by delivery. Sale and pledge are different kinds of transfers, but both may be implemented by delivery.

2. Subsection (a) defines delivery with respect to certificated securities. Paragraph (1) deals with simple cases where purchasers themselves acquire physical possession

of certificates. Paragraphs (2) and (3) of subsection (a) specify the circumstances in which delivery to a purchaser can occur although the certificate is in the possession of a person other than the purchaser. Paragraph (2) contains the general rule that a purchaser can take delivery through another person, so long as the other person is actually acting on behalf of the purchaser or acknowledges that it is holding on behalf of the purchaser. Paragraph (2) does not apply to acquisition of possession by a securities intermediary, because a person who holds securities through a securities account acquires a security entitlement, rather than having a direct interest. See Section 8-501. Subsection (a)(3) specifies the limited circumstances in which delivery of security certificates to a securities intermediary is treated as a delivery to the customer.

3. Subsection (b) defines delivery with respect to uncertificated securities. Use of the term "delivery" with respect to uncertificated securities, does, at least on first hearing, seem a bit solecistic. The word "delivery" is, however, routinely used in the securities business in a broader sense than manual tradition. For example, settlement by entries on the books of a clearing corporation is commonly called "delivery," as in the expression "delivery versus payment." The diction of this section has the advantage of using the same term for uncertificated securities as for certificated securities, for which delivery is conventional usage. Paragraph (1) of subsection (b) provides that delivery occurs when the purchaser becomes the registered owner of an uncertificated security, either upon original issue or registration of transfer. Paragraph (2) provides for delivery of an uncertificated security through a third person, in a fashion analogous to subsection (a)(2).

Definitional Cross References

"Certificated security"–Section 8-102(a)(4)
"Effective"–Section 8-107
"Issuer"–Section 8-201
"Purchaser"–Section 1-201(33) & 8-116
"Registered form" –Section 8-102(a)(13)
"Securities intermediary"–Section 8-102(a)(14)
"Security certificate"–Section 8-102(a)(16)
"Special indorsement"–Section 8-304(a)
"Uncertificated security"–Section 8-102(a)(18)

Section 8–302. Rights of Purchaser.

(a) Except as otherwise provided in subsections (b) and (c), upon delivery of a certificated or uncertificated security to a purchaser, the purchaser acquires all rights in the security that the transferor had or had power to transfer.

(b) A purchaser of a limited interest acquires rights only to the extent of the interest purchased.

(c) A purchaser of a certificated security who as a previous holder had notice of an adverse claim does not improve its position by taking from a protected purchaser.

Added by Laws 1997, Ch. 566, § 5, eff. Oct. 10, 1997. See legislative history following § 8–101 for explanation of legislative intent.

Official Comment

1. Subsection (a) provides that if a certificated or uncertificated security is delivered (Section 8-301) to a purchaser in a transfer, the purchaser acquires all rights that the

transferor had or had power to transfer. This statement of the familiar "shelter" principle is qualified by the exceptions that a purchaser of a limited interest acquires only that interest, subsection (b), and that a person who does not qualify as a protected purchaser cannot improve its position by taking from a subsequent protected purchaser, subsection (c).

2. Although this section provides that a purchaser acquires a property interest in a certificated or uncertificated security upon "delivery," it does not state that a person can acquire an interest in a security only by delivery. Article 8 is not a comprehensive codification of all of the law governing the creation or transfer of interests in securities. For example, the grant of a security interest is a transfer of a property interest, but the formal steps necessary to effectuate such a transfer are governed by Article 9 not by Article 8. Under the Article 9 rules, a security interest in a certificated or uncertificated security can be created by execution of a security agreement under Section 9-203 and can be perfected by filing. A transfer of an Article 9 security interest can be implemented by an Article 8 delivery, but need not be.

Similarly, Article 8 does not determine whether a property interest in certificated or uncertificated security is acquired under other law, such as the law of gifts, trusts, or equitable remedies. Nor does Article 8 deal with transfers by operation of law. For example, transfers from decedent to administrator, from ward to guardian, and from bankrupt to trustee in bankruptcy are governed by other law as to both the time they occur and the substance of the transfer. The Article 8 rules do, however, determine whether the issuer is obligated to recognize the rights that a third party, such as a transferee, may acquire under other law. See Sections 8-207, 8-401, and 8-404.

Definitional Cross References

"Certificated security"–Section 8-102(a)(4)
"Notice of adverse claim"–Section 8-105
"Protected purchaser"–Section 8-303
"Purchaser"–Section 1-201(33) & 8-116
"Uncertificated security"–Section 8-102(a)(18)
"Delivery"–Section 8-301

Section 8–303. Protected Purchaser.

(a) "Protected purchaser" means a purchaser of a certificated or uncertificated security, or of an interest therein, who:

(1) gives value;

(2) does not have notice of any adverse claim to the security; and

(3) obtains control of the certificated or uncertificated security.

(b) In addition to acquiring the rights of a purchaser, a protected purchaser also acquires its interest in the security free of any adverse claim.

Added by Laws 1997, Ch. 566, § 5, eff. Oct. 10, 1997. See legislative history following § 8–101 for explanation of legislative intent.

Official Comment

1. Subsection (a) lists the requirements that a purchaser must meet to qualify as a "protected purchaser." Subsection (b) provides that a protected purchaser takes its

interest free from adverse claims. "Purchaser" is defined broadly in Section 1-201. A secured party as well as an outright buyer can qualify as a protected purchaser. Also, "purchase" includes taking by issue, so a person to whom a security is originally issued can qualify as a protected purchaser.

2. To qualify as a protected purchaser, a purchaser must give value, take without notice of any adverse claim, and obtain control. Value is used in the broad sense defined in Section 1-201(44). See also Section 8-116 (securities intermediary as purchaser for value). Adverse claim is defined in Section 8-102(a)(1). Section 8-105 specifies whether a purchaser has notice of an adverse claim. Control is defined in Section 8-106. To qualify as a protected purchaser there must be a time at which all of the requirements are satisfied. Thus if a purchaser obtains notice of an adverse claim before giving value or satisfying the requirements for control, the purchaser cannot be a protected purchaser. See also Section 8-304(d).

The requirement that a protected purchaser obtain control expresses the point that to qualify for the adverse claim cut-off rule a purchaser must take through a transaction that is implemented by the appropriate mechanism. By contrast, the rules in Part 2 provide that any purchaser for value of a security without notice of a defense may take free of the issuer's defense based on that defense. See Section 8-202.

3. The requirements for control differ depending on the form of the security. For securities represented by bearer certificates, a purchaser obtains control by delivery. See Sections 8-106(a) and 8-301(a). For securities represented by certificates in registered form, the requirements for control are: (1) delivery as defined in Section 8-301(b), plus (2) either an effective indorsement or registration of transfer by the issuer. See Section 8-106(b). Thus, a person who takes through a forged indorsement does not qualify as a protected purchaser by virtue of the delivery alone. If, however, the purchaser presents the certificate to the issuer for registration of transfer, and the issuer registers transfer over the forged indorsement, the purchaser can qualify as a protected purchaser of the new certificate. If the issuer registers transfer on a forged indorsement, the true owner will be able to recover from the issuer for wrongful registration, see Section 8-404, unless the owner's delay in notifying the issuer of a loss or theft of the certificate results in preclusion under Section 8-406.

For uncertificated securities, a purchaser can obtain control either by delivery, see Sections 8-106(c)(1) and 8-301(b), or by obtaining an agreement pursuant to which the issuer agrees to act on instructions from the purchaser without further consent from the registered owner, see Section 8-106(c)(2). The control agreement device of Section 8-106(c)(2) takes the place of the "registered pledge" concept of the 1978 version of Article 8. A secured lender who obtains a control agreement under Section 8-106(c)(2) can qualify as a protected purchaser of an uncertificated security.

4. This section states directly the rules determining whether one takes free from adverse claims without using the phrase "good faith." Whether a person who takes under suspicious circumstances is disqualified is determined by the rules of Section 8-105 on notice of adverse claims. The term "protected purchaser, which replaces the term "bona fide purchaser" used in the prior version of Article 8, is derived from the term "protected holder" used in the Convention on International Bills and Notes prepared by the United Nations Commission on International Trade Law ("UNCITRAL").

Definitional Cross References

"Adverse claim"–Section 8-102(a)(1)
"Certificated security"–Section 8-102(a)(4)
"Control"–Section 8-106
"Notice of adverse claim"–Section 8-105
"Purchaser"–Section 1-201(33) & 8-116

"Uncertificated security"–Section 8-102(a)(18)
"Value"–Section 1-201(44) & 8-116

Section 8–304. Indorsement.

(a) An indorsement may be in blank or special. An indorsement in blank includes an indorsement to bearer. A special indorsement specifies to whom a security is to be transferred or who has power to transfer it. A holder may convert a blank indorsement to a special indorsement.

(b) An indorsement purporting to be only of part of a security certificate representing units intended by the issuer to be separately transferable is effective to the extent of the indorsement.

(c) An indorsement, whether special or in blank, does not constitute a transfer until delivery of the certificate on which it appears or, if the indorsement is on a separate document, until delivery of both the document and the certificate.

(d) If a security certificate in registered form has been delivered to a purchaser without a necessary indorsement, the purchaser may become a protected purchaser only when the indorsement is supplied. However, against a transferor, a transfer is complete upon delivery and the purchaser has a specifically enforceable right to have any necessary indorsement supplied.

(e) An indorsement of a security certificate in bearer form may give notice of an adverse claim to the certificate, but it does not otherwise affect a right to registration that the holder possesses.

(f) Unless otherwise agreed, a person making an indorsement assumes only the obligations provided in Section 8–108 and not an obligation that the security will be honored by the issuer.

Added by Laws 1997, Ch. 566, § 5, eff. Oct. 10, 1997. See legislative history following § 8–101 for explanation of legislative intent.

Official Comment

1. By virtue of the definition of indorsement in Section 8-102 and the rules of this section, the simplified method of indorsing certificated securities previously set forth in the Uniform Stock Transfer Act is continued. Although more than one special indorsement on a given security certificate is possible, the desire for dividends or interest, as the case may be, should operate to bring the certificate home for registration of transfer within a reasonable period of time. The usual form of assignment which appears in the back of a stock certificate or in a separate "power" may be filled up either in the form of an assignment, a power of attorney to transfer, or both. If it is not filled up at all but merely signed, the indorsement is in blank. If filled up either as an assignment or as a power of attorney to transfer, the indorsement is special.

2. Subsection (b) recognizes the validity of a "partial" indorsement, e.g., as to fifty shares of the one hundred represented by a single certificate. The rights of a transferee under a partial indorsement to the status of a protected purchaser are left to the case law.

3. Subsection (c) deals with the effect of an indorsement without delivery. There must be a voluntary parting with control in order to effect a valid transfer of a

certificated security as between the parties. *Levey v. Nason*, 279 Mass. 268, 181 N.E. 193 (1932), and *National Surety Co. v. Indemnity Insurance Co. of North America*, 237 App.Div. 485, 261 N.Y.S. 605 (1933). The provision in Section 10 of the Uniform Stock Transfer Act that an attempted transfer without delivery amounts to a promise to transfer is omitted. Even under that Act the effect of such a promise was left to the applicable law of contracts, and this Article by making no reference to such situations intends to achieve a similar result. With respect to delivery there is no counterpart to subsection (d) on right to compel indorsement, such as is envisaged in *Johnson v. Johnson*, 300 Mass. 24, 13 N.E.2d 788 (1938), where the transferee under a written assignment was given the right to compel a transfer of the certificate.

4. Subsection (d) deals with the effect of delivery without indorsement. As between the parties the transfer is made complete upon delivery, but the transferee cannot become a protected purchaser until indorsement is made. The indorsement does not operate retroactively, and notice may intervene between delivery and indorsement so as to prevent the transferee from becoming a protected purchaser. Although a purchaser taking without a necessary indorsement may be subject to claims of ownership, any issuer's defense of which the purchaser had no notice at the time of delivery will be cut off, since the provisions of this Article protect all purchasers for value without notice (Section 8-202).

The transferee's right to compel an indorsement where a security certificate has been delivered with intent to transfer is recognized in the case law. See *Coats v. Guaranty Bank & Trust Co.*, 170 La. 871, 129 So. 513 (1930). A proper indorsement is one of the requisites of transfer which a purchaser of a certificated security has a right to obtain (Section 8-307). A purchaser may not only compel an indorsement under that section but may also recover for any reasonable expense incurred by the transferor's failure to respond to the demand for an indorsement.

5. Subsection (e) deals with the significance of an indorsement on a security certificate in bearer form. The concept of indorsement applies only to registered securities. A purported indorsement of bearer paper is normally of no effect. An indorsement "for collection," "for surrender" or the like, charges a purchaser with notice of adverse claims (Section 8-105(d)) but does not operate beyond this to interfere with any right the holder may otherwise possess to have the security registered.

6. Subsection (f) makes clear that the indorser of a security certificate does not warrant that the issuer will honor the underlying obligation. In view of the nature of investment securities and the circumstances under which they are normally transferred, a transferor cannot be held to warrant as to the issuer's actions. As a transferor the indorser, of course, remains liable for breach of the warranties set forth in this Article (Section 8-108).

Definitional Cross References

Bearer form"–Section 8-102(a)(2)
Certificated security"–Section 8-102(a)(4)
Indorsement"–Section 8-102(a)(11)
Purchaser"–Section 1-201(33) & 8-116
Registered form" –Section 8-102(a)(13)
Security certificate"–Section 8-102(a)(16)

Section 8–305. Instruction.

(a) If an instruction has been originated by an appropriate person but is incomplete in any other respect, any person may complete it as authorized and the issuer may rely on it as completed, even though it has been completed incorrectly.

(b) Unless otherwise agreed, a person initiating an instruction assumes only the obligations imposed by Section 8–108 and not an obligation that the security will be honored by the issuer.

Added by Laws 1997, Ch. 566, § 5, eff. Oct. 10, 1997. See legislative history following § 8–101 for explanation of legislative intent.

Official Comment

1. The term instruction is defined in Section 8-102(a)(12) as a notification communicated to the issuer of an uncertificated security directing that transfer be registered. Section 8-107 specifies who may initiate an effective instruction.

Functionally, presentation of an instruction is quite similar to the presentation of an indorsed certificate for reregistration. Note that instruction is defined in terms of "communicate," see Section 8-102(a)(6). Thus, the instruction may be in the form of a writing signed by the registered owner or in any other form agreed upon by the issuer and the registered owner. Allowing nonwritten forms of instructions will permit the development and employment of means of transmitting instructions electronically.

When a person who originates an instruction leaves a blank and the blank later is completed, subsection (a) gives the issuer the same rights it would have had against the originating person had that person completed the blank. This is true regardless of whether the person completing the instruction had authority to complete it. Compare Section 8-206 and its Comment, dealing with blanks left upon issue.

2. Subsection (b) makes clear that the originator of an instruction, like the indorser of a security certificate, does not warrant that the issuer will honor the underlying obligation, but does make warranties as a transferor under Section 8-108.

Definitional Cross References

"Appropriate person"–Section 8-107
"Instruction"–Section 8-102(a)(12)
"Issuer"–Section 8-201

Section 8–306. Effect of Guaranteeing Signature, Indorsement, or Instruction.

(a) A person who guarantees a signature of an indorser of a security certificate warrants that at the time of signing:

(1) the signature was genuine;

(2) the signer was an appropriate person to indorse, or if the signature is by an agent, the agent had actual authority to act on behalf of the appropriate person; and

(3) the signer had legal capacity to sign.

(b) A person who guarantees a signature of the originator of an instruction warrants that at the time of signing:

(1) the signature was genuine;

(2) the signer was an appropriate person to originate the instruction, or if the signature is by an agent, the agent had actual authority to act on behalf of the appropriate person, if the person specified in the instruction as the registered owner was, in fact, the registered owner, as to which fact the signature guarantor does not make a warranty; and

(3) the signer had legal capacity to sign.

(c) A person who specially guarantees the signature of an originator of an instruction makes the warranties of a signature guarantor under subsection (b) and also warrants that at the time the instruction is presented to the issuer:

(1) the person specified in the instruction as the registered owner of the uncertificated security will be the registered owner; and

(2) the transfer of the uncertificated security requested in the instruction will be registered by the issuer free from all liens, security interests, restrictions, and claims other than those specified in the instruction.

(d) A guarantor under subsections (a) and (b) or a special guarantor under subsection (c) does not otherwise warrant the rightfulness of the transfer.

(e) A person who guarantees an indorsement of a security certificate makes the warranties of a signature guarantor under subsection (a) and also warrants the rightfulness of the transfer in all respects.

(f) A person who guarantees an instruction requesting the transfer of an uncertificated security makes the warranties of a special signature guarantor under subsection (c) and also warrants the rightfulness of the transfer in all respects.

(g) An issuer may not require a special guaranty of signature, a guaranty of indorsement, or a guaranty of instruction as a condition to registration of transfer.

(h) The warranties under this section are made to a person taking or dealing with the security in reliance on the guaranty, and the guarantor is liable to the person for loss resulting from their breach. An indorser or originator of an instruction whose signature, indorsement, or instruction has been guaranteed is liable to a guarantor for any loss suffered by the guarantor as a result of breach of the warranties of the guarantor.

Added by Laws 1997, Ch. 566, § 5, eff. Oct. 10, 1997. See legislative history following § 8–101 for explanation of legislative intent.

Official Comment

1. Subsection (a) provides that a guarantor of the signature of the indorser of a security certificate warrants that the signature is genuine, that the signer is an appropriate person or has actual authority to indorse on behalf of the appropriate person, and that the signer has legal capacity. Subsection (b) provides similar, though not identical, warranties for the guarantor of a signature of the originator of an instruction for transfer of an uncertificated security.

Appropriate person is defined in Section 8-107(a) to include a successor or person who has power under other law to act for a person who is deceased or lacks capacity.

Thus if a certificate registered in the name of Mary Roe is indorsed by Jane Doe as executor of Mary Roe, a guarantor of the signature of Jane Doe warrants that she has power to act as executor.

Although the definition of appropriate person in Section 8-107(a) does not itself include an agent, an indorsement by an agent is effective under Section 8-107(b) if the agent has authority to act for the appropriate person. Accordingly, this section provides an explicit warranty of authority for agents.

2. The rationale of the principle that a signature guarantor warrants the authority of the signer, rather than simply the genuineness of the signature, was explained in the leading case of *Jennie Clarkson Home for Children v. Missouri, K. & T. R. Co.*, 182 N.Y. 47, 74 N.E. 571, 70 A.L.R. 787 (1905), which dealt with a guaranty of the signature of a person indorsing on behalf of a corporation. "If stock is held by an individual who is executing a power of attorney for its transfer, the member of the exchange who signs as a witness thereto guaranties not only the genuineness of the signature affixed to the power of attorney, but that the person signing is the individual in whose name the stock stands. With reference to stock standing in the name of a corporation, which can only sign a power of attorney through its authorized officers or agents, a different situation is presented. If the witnessing of the signature of the corporation is only that of the signature of a person who signs for the corporation, then the guaranty is of no value, and there is nothing to protect purchasers or the companies who are called upon to issue new stock in the place of that transferred from the frauds of persons who have signed the names of corporations without authority. If such is the only effect of the guaranty, purchasers and transfer agents must first go to the corporation in whose name the stock stands and ascertain whether the individual who signed the power of attorney had authority to so do. This will require time, and in many cases will necessitate the postponement of the completion of the purchase by the payment of the money until the facts can be ascertained. The broker who is acting for the owner has an opportunity to become acquainted with his customer, and may readily before sale ascertain, in case of a corporation, the name of the officer who is authorized to execute the power of attorney. It was therefore, we think, the purpose of the rule to cast upon the broker who witnesses the signature the duty o f ascertaining whether the person signing the name of the corporation had authority to so do, and making the witness a guarantor that it is the signature of the corporation in whose name the stock stands."

3. Subsection (b) sets forth the warranties that can reasonably be expected from the guarantor of the signature of the originator of an instruction, who, though familiar with the signer, does not have any evidence that the purported owner is in fact the owner of the subject uncertificated security. This is in contrast to the position of the person guaranteeing a signature on a certificate who can see a certificate in the signer's possession in the name of or indorsed to the signer or in blank. Thus, the warranty in paragraph (2) of subsection (b) is expressly conditioned on the actual registration's conforming to that represented by the originator. If the signer purports to be the owner, the guarantor under paragraph (2), warrants only the identity of the signer. If, however, the signer is acting in a representative capacity, the guarantor warrants both the signer's identity and authority to act for the purported owner. The issuer needs no warranty as to the facts of registration because those facts can be ascertained from the issuer's own records.

4. Subsection (c) sets forth a "special guaranty of signature" under which the guarantor additionally warrants both registered ownership and freedom from undisclosed defects of record. The guarantor of the signature of an indorser of a security certificate effectively makes these warranties to a purchaser for value on the evidence of a clean certificate issued in the name of the indorser, indorsed to the indorser or indorsed in blank. By specially guaranteeing under subsection (c), the guarantor warrants that the instruction will, when presented to the issuer, result in the requested registration free from defects not specified.

5. Subsection (d) makes clear that the warranties of a signature guarantor are limited to those specified in this section and do not include a general warranty of rightfulness. On the other hand subsections (e) and (f) provide that a person guaranteeing an indorsement or an instruction does warrant that the transfer is rightful in all respects.

6. Subsection (g) makes clear what can be inferred from the combination of Sections 8-401 and 8-402, that the issuer may not require as a condition to transfer a guaranty of the indorsement or instruction nor may it require a special signature guaranty.

7. Subsection (h) specifies to whom the warranties in this section run, and also provides that a person who gives a guaranty under this section has an action against the indorser or originator for any loss suffered by the guarantor.

Definitional Cross References

"Appropriate person"–Section 8-107
"Genuine"–Section 1-201(18)
"Indorsement"–Section 8-102(a)(11)
"Instruction"–Section 8-102(a)(12)
"Issuer"–Section 8-201
"Security certificate"–Section 8-102(a)(16)
"Uncertificated security"–Section 8-102(a)(18)

Section 8–307. Purchaser's Right to Requisites for Registration of Transfer.

Unless otherwise agreed, the transferor of a security on due demand shall supply the purchaser with proof of authority to transfer or with any other requisite necessary to obtain registration of the transfer of the security, but if the transfer is not for value, a transferor need not comply unless the purchaser pays the necessary expenses. If the transferor fails within a reasonable time to comply with the demand, the purchaser may reject or rescind the transfer.

Added by Laws 1997, Ch. 566, § 5, eff. Oct. 10, 1997. See legislative history following § 8–101 for explanation of legislative intent.

Official Comment

1. Because registration of the transfer of a security is a matter of vital importance, a purchaser is here provided with the means of obtaining such formal requirements for registration as signature guaranties, proof of authority, transfer tax stamps and the like. The transferor is the one in a position to supply most conveniently whatever documentation may be requisite for registration of transfer, and the duty to do so upon demand within a reasonable time is here stated affirmatively. If an essential item is peculiarly within the province of the transferor so that the transferor is the only one who can obtain it, the purchaser may specifically enforce the right to obtain it. Compare Section 8-304(d). If a transfer is not for value the transferee need not pay expenses.

2. If the transferor's duty is not performed the transferee may reject or rescind the contract to transfer. The transferee is not bound to do so. An action for damages for breach of contract may be preferred.

Definitional Cross References

"Purchaser"–Section 1-201(33) & 8-116

"Security"–Section 8-102(a)(15)
"Value"–Section 1-201(44) & 8-116

PART 4

REGISTRATION

Section 8–401. Duty of Issuer to Register Transfer.

(a) If a certificated security in registered form is presented to an issuer with a request to register transfer or an instruction is presented to an issuer with a request to register transfer of an uncertificated security, the issuer shall register the transfer as requested if:

(1) under the terms of the security the person seeking registration of transfer is eligible to have the security registered in its name;

(2) the indorsement or instruction is made by the appropriate person or by an agent who has actual authority to act on behalf of the appropriate person;

(3) reasonable assurance is given that the indorsement or instruction is genuine and authorized (section 8–402);

(4) any applicable law relating to the collection of taxes has been complied with;

(5) the transfer does not violate any restriction on transfer imposed by the issuer in accordance with Section 8–204;

(6) a demand that the issuer not register transfer has not become effective under Section 8–403, or the issuer has complied with Section 8–403(b) but no legal process or indemnity bond is obtained as provided in Section 8–403(d); and

(7) the transfer is in fact rightful or is to a protected purchaser.

(b) If an issuer is under a duty to register a transfer of a security, the issuer is liable to a person presenting a certificated security or an instruction for registration or to the person's principal for loss resulting from unreasonable delay in registration or failure or refusal to register the transfer.

Added by Laws 1997, Ch. 566, § 5, eff. Oct. 10, 1997. See legislative history following § 8–101 for explanation of legislative intent.

Official Comment

1. This section states the duty of the issuer to register transfers. A duty exists only if certain preconditions exist. If any of the preconditions do not exist, there is no duty to register transfer. If an indorsement on a security certificate is a forgery, there is no duty. If an instruction to transfer an uncertificated security is not originated by an appropriate person, there is no duty. If there has not been compliance with applicable tax laws, there is no duty. If a security certificate is properly indorsed but nevertheless the transfer is in fact wrongful, there is no duty unless the transfer is to a protected purchaser (and the other preconditions exist).

This section does not constitute a mandate that the issuer must establish that all preconditions are met before the issuer registers a transfer. The issuer may waive the reasonable assurances specified in paragraph (a)(3). If it has confidence in the responsibility of the persons requesting transfer, it may ignore questions of compliance with tax laws. Although an issuer has no duty if the transfer is wrongful, the issuer has no duty to inquire into adverse claims, see Section 8-404.

2. By subsection (b) the person entitled to registration may not only compel it but may hold the issuer liable in damages for unreasonable delay.

3. Section 8-201(c) provides that with respect to registration of transfer, "issuer" means the person on whose behalf transfer books are maintained. Transfer agents, registrars or the like within the scope of their respective functions have rights and duties under this Part similar to those of the issuer. See Section 8-407.

Definitional Cross References

"Appropriate person"–Section 8-107
"Certificated security"–Section 8-102(a)(4)
"Genuine"–Section 1-201(18)
"Indorsement"–Section 8-102(a)(11)
"Instruction"–Section 8-102(a)(12)
"Issuer"–Section 8-201
"Protected purchaser"–Section 8-303
"Registered form" –Section 8-102(a)(13)
"Uncertificated security"–Section 8-102(a)(18)

Section 8–402. Assurance That Indorsement or Instruction Is Effective.

(a) An issuer may require the following assurance that each necessary indorsement or each instruction is genuine and authorized:

(1) in all cases, a guaranty of the signature of the person making an indorsement or originating an instruction including, in the case of an instruction, reasonable assurance of identity;

(2) if the indorsement is made or the instruction is originated by an agent, appropriate assurance of actual authority to sign;

(3) if the indorsement is made or the instruction is originated by a fiduciary pursuant to Section 8–107(a)(4) or (a)(5), appropriate evidence of appointment or incumbency;

(4) if there is more than one fiduciary, reasonable assurance that all who are required to sign have done so; and

(5) if the indorsement is made or the instruction is originated by a person not covered by another provision of this subsection, assurance appropriate to the case corresponding as nearly as may be to the provisions of this subsection.

(b) An issuer may elect to require reasonable assurance beyond that specified in this section.

(c) In this section:

(1) "Guaranty of the signature" means a guaranty signed by or on behalf of a person reasonably believed by the issuer to be responsible. An issuer may adopt standards with respect to responsibility if they are not manifestly unreasonable.

(2) "Appropriate evidence of appointment or incumbency" means:

(i) in the case of a fiduciary appointed or qualified by a court, a certificate issued by or under the direction or supervision of the court or an officer thereof and dated within 6 months before the date of presentation for transfer; or

(ii) in any other case, a copy of a document showing the appointment or a certificate issued by or on behalf of a person reasonably believed by an issuer to be responsible or, in the absence of that document or certificate, other evidence the issuer reasonably considers appropriate.

Added by Laws 1997, Ch. 566, § 5, eff. Oct. 10, 1997. See legislative history following § 8–101 for explanation of legislative intent.

Official Comment

1. An issuer is absolutely liable for wrongful registration of transfer if the indorsement or instruction is ineffective. See Section 8-404. Accordingly, an issuer is entitled to require such assurance as is reasonable under the circumstances that all necessary indorsements are effective, and thus to minimize its risk. This section establishes the requirements the issuer may make in terms of documentation which, except in the rarest of instances, should be easily furnished. Subsection (b) provides that an issuer may require additional assurances if that requirement is reasonable under the circumstances, but if the issuer demands more than reasonable assurance that the instruction or the necessary indorsements are genuine and authorized, the presenter may refuse the demand and sue for improper refusal to register. Section 8-401(b).

2. Under subsection (a)(1), the issuer may require in all cases a guaranty of signature. See Section 8-306. When an instruction is presented the issuer always may require reasonable assurance as to the identity of the originator. Subsection (c) allows the issuer to require that the person making these guaranties be one reasonably believed to be responsible, and the issuer may adopt standards of responsibility which are not manifestly unreasonable. Regulations under the federal securities laws, however, place limits on the requirements transfer agents may impose concerning the responsibility of eligible signature guarantors. See 17 CFR 240.17Ad-15.

3. This section, by paragraphs (2) through (5) of subsection (a), permits the issuer to seek confirmation that the indorsement or instruction is genuine and authorized. The permitted methods act as a double check on matters which are within the warranties of the signature guarantor. See Section 8-306. Thus, an agent may be required to submit a power of attorney, a corporation to submit a certified resolution evidencing the authority of its signing officer to sign, an executor or administrator to submit the usual "short-form certificate," etc. But failure of a fiduciary to obtain court approval of the transfer or to comply with other requirements does not make the fiduciary's signature ineffective. Section 8-107(c). Hence court orders and other controlling instruments are omitted from subsection (a).

Subsection (a)(3) authorizes the issuer to require "appropriate evidence" of appointment or incumbency, and subsection (c) indicates what evidence will be "appropriate'. In the case of a fiduciary appointed or qualified by a court that evidence will be a court certificate dated within sixty days before the date of presentation, subsection (c)(2)(i). Where the fiduciary is not appointed or qualified by a court, as in the case of a successor trustee, subsection (c)(2)(ii) applies. In that case, the issuer may require a copy of a trust instrument or other document showing the appointment, or it may require the certificate of a responsible person. In the absence of such a document or certificate, it may require other appropriate evidence. If the security is registered in the name of the fiduciary as such, the person's signature is effective even though the person is no longer serving in that capacity, see Section 8-107(d), hence no evidence of incumbency is needed.

4. Circumstances may indicate that a necessary signature was unauthorized or was not that of an appropriate person. Such circumstances would be ignored at risk of absolute liability. To minimize that risk the issuer may properly exercise the option given by subsection (b) to require assurance beyond that specified in subsection (a). On the other hand, the facts at hand may reflect only on the rightfulness of the transfer. Such facts do not create a duty of inquiry, because the issuer is not liable to an adverse claimant unless the claimant obtains legal process. See Section 8-404.

Definitional Cross References

"Appropriate person"–Section 8-107
"Genuine"–Section 1-201(18)
"Indorsement"–Section 8-102(a)(11)
"Instruction"–Section 8-102(a)(12)
"Issuer"–Section 8-201

Section 8–403. Demand That Issuer Not Register Transfer.

(a) A person who is an appropriate person to make an indorsement or originate an instruction may demand that the issuer not register transfer of a security by communicating to the issuer a notification that identifies the registered owner and the issue of which the security is a part and provides an address for communications directed to the person making the demand. The demand is effective only if it is received by the issuer at a time and in a manner affording the issuer reasonable opportunity to act on it.

(b) If a certificated security in registered form is presented to an issuer with a request to register transfer or an instruction is presented to an issuer with a request to register transfer of an uncertificated security after a demand that the issuer not register transfer has become effective, the issuer shall promptly communicate, to the person who initiated the demand at the address provided in the demand and to the person who presented the security for registration of transfer or initiated the instruction requesting registration of transfer, a notification stating that:

(1) the certificated security has been presented for registration of transfer or the instruction for registration of transfer of the uncertificated security has been received;

(2) a demand that the issuer not register transfer had previously been received; and

(3) the issuer will withhold registration of transfer for a period of time stated in the notification in order to provide the person who initiated the demand an opportunity to obtain legal process or an indemnity bond.

(c) The period described in subsection (b)(3) may not exceed 30 days after the date of communication of the notification. A shorter period may be specified by the issuer if it is not manifestly unreasonable.

(d) An issuer is not liable to a person who initiated a demand that the issuer not register transfer for any loss the person suffers as a result of registration of a transfer pursuant to an effective indorsement or instruction if the person who initiated the demand does not, within the time stated in the issuer's communication, either:

(1) obtain an appropriate restraining order, injunction, or other process from a court of competent jurisdiction enjoining the issuer from registering the transfer; or

(2) file with the issuer an indemnity bond, sufficient in the issuer's judgment to protect the issuer and any transfer agent, registrar, or other agent of the issuer involved from any loss it or they may suffer by refusing to register the transfer.

(e) This section does not relieve an issuer from liability for registering transfer pursuant to an indorsement or instruction that was not effective.

Added by Laws 1997, Ch. 566, § 5, eff. Oct. 10, 1997. See legislative history following § 8–101 for explanation of legislative intent.

Official Comment

1. The general rule under this Article is that if there has been an effective indorsement or instruction, a person who contends that registration of the transfer would be wrongful should not be able to interfere with the registration process merely by sending notice of the assertion to the issuer. Rather, the claimant must obtain legal process. See Section 8-404. Section 8-403 is an exception to this general rule. It permits the registered owner–but not third parties–to demand that the issuer not register a transfer.

2. This section is intended to alleviate the problems faced by registered owners of a certificated securities who lose or misplace their certificates. A registered owner who realizes that a certificate may have been lost or stolen should promptly report that fact to the issuer, lest the owner be precluded from asserting a claim for wrongful registration. See Section 8-406. The usual practice of issuers and transfer agents is that when a certificate is reported as lost, the owner is notified that a replacement can be obtained if the owner provides an indemnity bond. See Section 8-405. If the registered owner does not plan to transfer the securities, the owner might choose not to obtain a replacement, particularly if the owner suspects that the certificate has merely been misplaced.

Under this section, the owner's notification that the certificate has been lost would constitute a demand that the issuer not register transfer. No indemnity bond or legal process is necessary. If the original certificate is presented for registration of transfer, the issuer is required to notify the registered owner of that fact, and defer registration of transfer for a stated period. In order to prevent undue delay in the process of registration, the stated period may not exceed thirty days. This gives the registered owner an opportunity to either obtain legal process or post an indemnity bond and thereby prevent the issuer from registering transfer.

3. Subsection (e) makes clear that this section does not relieve an issuer from liability for registering a transfer pursuant to an ineffective indorsement. An issuer's liability for wrongful registration in such cases does not depend or the presence or absence of notice that the indorsement was ineffective. Registered owners who are confident that they neither indorsed the certificates, nor did anything that would preclude them from denying the effectiveness of another's indorsement, see Sections

8-107(b) and 8-406, might prefer to pursue their rights against the issuer for wrongful registration rather than take advantage of the opportunity to post a bond or seek a restraining order when notified by the issuer under this section that their lost certificates have been presented for registration in apparently good order.

Definitional Cross References

"Appropriate person"–Section 8-107
"Certificated security"–Section 8-102(a)(4)
"Communicate"–Section 8-102(a)(6)
"Effective"–Section 8-107
"Indorsement"–Section 8-102(a)(11)
"Instruction"–Section 8-102(a)(12)
"Issuer"–Section 8-201
"Registered form" –Section 8-102(a)(13)
"Uncertificated security"–Section 8-102(a)(18)

Section 8–404. Wrongful Registration.

(a) Except as otherwise provided in Section 8–406, an issuer is liable for wrongful registration of transfer if the issuer has registered a transfer of a security to a person not entitled to it, and the transfer was registered:

(1) pursuant to an ineffective indorsement or instruction;

(2) after a demand that the issuer not register transfer became effective under Section 8–403(a) and the issuer did not comply with Section 8–403(b);

(3) after the issuer had been served with an injunction, restraining order, or other legal process enjoining it from registering the transfer, issued by a court of competent jurisdiction, and the issuer had a reasonable opportunity to act on the injunction, restraining order, or other legal process; or

(4) by an issuer acting in collusion with the wrongdoer.

(b) An issuer that is liable for wrongful registration of transfer under subsection (a) on demand shall provide the person entitled to the security with a like certificated or uncertificated security, and any payments or distributions that the person did not receive as a result of the wrongful registration. If an overissue would result, the issuer's liability to provide the person with a like security is governed by Section 8–210.

(c) Except as otherwise provided in subsection (a) or in a law relating to the collection of taxes, an issuer is not liable to an owner or other person suffering loss as a result of the registration of a transfer of a security if registration was made pursuant to an effective indorsement or instruction.

Added by Laws 1997, Ch. 566, § 5, eff. Oct. 10, 1997. See legislative history following § 8–101 for explanation of legislative intent.

Official Comment

1. Subsection (a)(1) provides that an issuer is liable if it registers transfer pursuant to an indorsement or instruction that was not effective. For example, an issuer that

registers transfer on a forged indorsement is liable to the registered owner. The fact that the issuer had no reason to suspect that the indorsement was forged or that the issuer obtained the ordinary assurances under Section 8-402 does not relieve the issuer from liability. The reason that issuers obtain signature guaranties and other assurances is that they are liable for wrongful registration.

Subsection (b) specifies the remedy for wrongful registration. Pre-Code cases established the registered owner's right to receive a new security where the issuer had wrongfully registered a transfer, but some cases also allowed the registered owner to elect between an equitable action to compel issue of a new security and an action for damages. Cf. *Casper v. Kalt-Zimmers Mfg. Co.*, 159 Wis. 517, 149 N.W. 754 (1914). Article 8 does not allow such election. The true owner of a certificated security is required to take a new security except where an overissue would result and a similar security is not reasonably available for purchase. See Section 8-210. The true owner of an uncertificated security is entitled and required to take restoration of the records to their proper state, with a similar exception for overissue.

2. Read together, subsections (c) and (a) have the effect of providing that an issuer has no duties to an adverse claimant unless the claimant serves legal process on the issuer to enjoin registration. Issuers, or their transfer agents, perform a record keeping function for the direct holding system that is analogous to the functions performed by clearing corporations and securities intermediaries in the indirect holding system. This section applies to the record-keepers for the direct holding system the same standard that Section 8-115 applies to the record-keepers for the indirect holding system. Thus, issuers are not liable to adverse claimants merely on the basis of notice. As in the case of the analogous rules for the indirect holding system, the policy of this section is to protect the right of investors to have their securities transfers processed without the disruption or delay that might result if the record-keepers risked liability to third parties. It would be undesirable to apply different standards to the direct and indirect holding systems, since doing so might operate as a disincentive to the development of a book-entry direct holding system.

3. This section changes prior law under which an issuer could be held liable, even though it registered transfer on an effective indorsement or instruction, if the issuer had in some fashion been notified that the transfer might be wrongful against a third party, and the issuer did not appropriately discharge its duty to inquire into the adverse claim. See Section 8-403 (1978).

The rule of former Section 8-403 was anomalous inasmuch as Section 8-207 provides that the issuer is entitled to "treat the registered owner as the person exclusively entitled to vote, receive notifications, and otherwise exercise all the rights and powers of an owner." Under Section 8-207, the fact that a third person notifies the issuer of a claim does not preclude the issuer from treating the registered owner as the person entitled to the security. See *Kerrigan v. American Orthodontics Corp.*, 960 F.2d 43 (7th Cir. 1992). The change made in the present version of Section 8-404 ensures that the rights of registered owners and the duties of issuers with respect to registration of transfer will be protected against third-party interference in the same fashion as other rights of registered ownership.

Definitional Cross References

"Certificated security"–Section 8-102(a)(4)
"Effective"–Section 8-107
"Indorsement"–Section 8-102(a)(11)
"Instruction"–Section 8-102(a)(12)
"Issuer"–Section 8-201
"Security"–Section 8-102(a)(15)
"Uncertificated security"–Section 8-102(a)(18)

Section 8–405. Replacement of Lost, Destroyed, or Wrongfully Taken Security Certificate.

(a) If an owner of a certificated security, whether in registered or bearer form, claims that the certificate has been lost, destroyed, or wrongfully taken, the issuer shall issue a new certificate if the owner:

(1) so requests before the issuer has notice that the certificate has been acquired by a protected purchaser;

(2) files with the issuer a sufficient indemnity bond; and

(3) satisfies other reasonable requirements imposed by the issuer.

(b) If, after the issue of a new security certificate, a protected purchaser of the original certificate presents it for registration of transfer, the issuer shall register the transfer unless an overissue would result. In that case, the issuer's liability is governed by Section 8–210. In addition to any rights on the indemnity bond, an issuer may recover the new certificate from a person to whom it was issued or any person taking under that person, except a protected purchaser.

Added by Laws 1997, Ch. 566, § 5, eff. Oct. 10, 1997. See legislative history following § 8–101 for explanation of legislative intent.

Official Comment

1. This section enables the owner to obtain a replacement of a lost, destroyed or stolen certificate, provided that reasonable requirements are satisfied and a sufficient indemnity bond supplied.

2. Where an "original" security certificate has reached the hands of a protected purchaser, the registered owner– who was in the best position to prevent the loss, destruction or theft of the security certificate– is now deprived of the new security certificate issued as a replacement. This changes the pre-UCC law under which the original certificate was ineffective after the issue of a replacement except insofar as it might represent an action for damages in the hands of a purchaser for value without notice. *Keller v. Eureka Brick Mach. Mfg. Co.*, 43 Mo.App. 84, 11 L.R.A. 472 (1890). Where both the original and the new certificate have reached protected purchasers the issuer is required to honor both certificate unless an overissue would result and the security is not reasonably available for purchase. See Section 8-210. In the latter case alone, the protected purchaser of the original certificate is relegated to an action for damages. In either case, the issuer itself may recover on the indemnity bond.

Definitional Cross References

"Bearer form"–Section 8-102(a)(2)
"Certificated security"–Section 8-102(a)(4)
"Issuer"–Section 8-201
"Notice"–Section 1-201(25)
"Overissue"–Section 8-210
"Protected purchaser"–Section 8-303
"Registered form"–Section 8-102(a)(13)
"Security certificate"–Section 8-102(a)(16)

Section 8–406. Obligation to Notify Issuer of Lost, Destroyed, or Wrongfully Taken Security Certificate.

If a security certificate has been lost, apparently destroyed, or wrongfully taken, and the owner fails to notify the issuer of that fact within a reasonable time after the owner has notice of it and the issuer registers a transfer of the security before receiving notification, the owner may not assert against the issuer a claim for registering the transfer under Section 8–404 or a claim to a new security certificate under Section 8–405.

Added by Laws 1997, Ch. 566, § 5, eff. Oct. 10, 1997. See legislative history following § 8–101 for explanation of legislative intent.

Official Comment

An owner who fails to notify the issuer within a reasonable time after the owner knows or has reason to know of the loss or theft of a security certificate is estopped from asserting the ineffectiveness of a forged or unauthorized indorsement and the wrongfulness of the registration of the transfer. If the lost certificate was indorsed by the owner, then the registration of the transfer was not wrongful under Section 8-404, unless the owner made an effective demand that the issuer not register transfer under Section 8-403.

Definitional Cross References

"Issuer"–Section 8-201
"Notify"–Section 1-201(25)
"Security certificate"–Section 8-102(a)(16)

Section 8–407. Authenticating Trustee, Transfer Agent, and Registrar.

A person acting as authenticating trustee, transfer agent, registrar, or other agent for an issuer in the registration of a transfer of its securities, in the issue of new security certificates or uncertificated securities, or in the cancellation of surrendered security certificates has the same obligation to the holder or owner of a certificated or uncertificated security with regard to the particular functions performed as the issuer has in regard to those functions.

Added by Laws 1997, Ch. 566, § 5, eff. Oct. 10, 1997. See legislative history following § 8–101 for explanation of legislative intent.

Official Comment

1. Transfer agents, registrars, and the like are here expressly held liable both to the issuer and to the owner for wrongful refusal to register a transfer as well as for wrongful registration of a transfer in any case within the scope of their respective functions where the issuer would itself be liable. Those cases which have regarded these parties solely as agents of the issuer and have therefore refused to recognize their liability to the owner for mere non-feasance, i.e., refusal to register a transfer, are rejected. *Hulse v. Consolidated Quicksilver Mining Corp.*, 65 Idaho 768, 154 P.2d 149 (1944); *Nicholson v. Morgan*, 119 Misc. 309, 196 N.Y.Supp. 147 (1922); *Lewis v. Hargadine-McKittrick Dry Goods Co.*, 305 Mo. 396, 274 S.W. 1041 (1924).

2. The practice frequently followed by authenticating trustees of issuing certificates of indebtedness rather than authenticating duplicate certificates where securities have been lost or stolen became obsolete in view of the provisions of the Section 8-405, which makes express provision for the issue of substitute securities. It is not a breach of trust or lack of due diligence for trustees to authenticate new securities. Cf. *Switzerland General Ins. Co. v. N.Y.C. & H.R.R. Co.*, 152 App.Div. 70, 136 N.Y.S. 726 (1912).

Definitional Cross References

"Certificated security"–Section 8-102(a)(4)
"Issuer"–Section 8-201
"Security"–Section 8-102(a)(15)
"Security certificate"–Section 8-102(a)(16)
"Uncertificated security"–Section 8-102(a)(18)

PART 5

SECURITY ENTITLEMENTS

Section 8–501. Securities Account; Acquisition of Security Entitlement From Securities Intermediary.

(a) "Securities account" means an account to which a financial asset is or may be credited in accordance with an agreement under which the person maintaining the account undertakes to treat the person for whom the account is maintained as entitled to exercise the rights that comprise the financial asset.

(b) Except as otherwise provided in subsections (d) and (e), a person acquires a security entitlement if a securities intermediary:

(1) indicates by book entry that a financial asset has been cred ited to the person's securities account;

(2) receives a financial asset from the person or acquires a financial asset for the person and, in either case, accepts it for credit to the person's securities account; or

(3) becomes obligated under other law, regulation, or rule to credit a financial asset to the person's securities account.

(c) If a condition of subsection (b) has been met, a person has a security entitlement even though the securities intermediary does not itself hold the financial asset.

(d) If a securities intermediary holds a financial asset for another person, and the financial asset is registered in the name of, payable to the order of, or specially indorsed to the other person, and has not been indorsed to the securities intermediary or in blank, the other person is treated as holding the financial asset directly rather than as having a security entitlement with respect to the financial asset.

(e) Issuance of a security is not establishment of a security entitlement.

Added by Laws 1997, Ch. 566, § 5, eff. Oct. 10, 1997. See legislative history following § 8–101 for explanation of legislative intent.

Official Comment

1. Part 5 rules apply to security entitlements, and Section 8-501(b) provides that a person has a security entitlement when a financial asset has been credited to a "securities account." Thus, the term "securities account" specifies the type of arrangements between institutions and their customers that are covered by Part 5. A securities account is a consensual arrangement in which the intermediary undertakes to treat the customer as entitled to exercise the rights that comprise the financial asset. The consensual aspect is covered by the requirement that the account be established pursuant to agreement. The term agreement is used in the broad sense defined in Section 1-201(3). There is no requirement that a formal or written agreement be signed.

As the securities business is presently conducted, several significant relationships clearly fall within the definition of a securities account, including the relationship between a clearing corporation and its participants, a broker and customers who leave securities with the broker, and a bank acting as securities custodian and its custodial customers. Given the enormous variety of arrangements concerning securities that exist today, and the certainty that new arrangements will evolve in the future, it is not possible to specify all of the arrangements to which the term does and does not apply.

Whether an arrangement between a firm and another person concerning a security or other financial asset is a "securities account" under this Article depends on whether the firm has undertaken to treat the other person as entitled to exercise the rights that comprise the security or other financial asset. Section 1-102, however, states the fundamental principle of interpretation that the Code provisions should be construed and applied to promote their underlying purposes and policies. Thus, the question whether a given arrangement is a securities account should be decided not by dictionary analysis of the words of the definition taken out of context, but by considering whether it promotes the objectives of Article 8 to include the arrangement within the term securities account.

The effect of concluding that an arrangement is a securities account is that the rules of Part 5 apply. Accordingly, the definition of "securities account" must be interpreted in light of the substantive provisions in Part 5, which describe the core features of the type of relationship for which the commercial law rules of Revised Article 8 concerning security entitlements were designed. There are many arrangements between institutions and other persons concerning securities or other financial assets which do not fall within the definition of "securities account" because the institutions have not undertaken to treat the other persons as entitled to exercise the ordinary rights of an entitlement holder specified in the Part 5 rules. For example, the term securities account does not cover the relationship between a bank and its depositors or the relationship between a trustee and the beneficiary of an ordinary trust, because those are not relationships in which the holder of a financial asset has undertaken to treat the other as entitled to exercise the rights that comprise the financial asset in the fashion contemplated by the Part 5 rules.

In short, the primary factor in deciding whether an arrangement is a securities account is whether application of the Part 5 rules is consistent with the expectations of the parties to the relationship. Relationships not governed by Part 5 may be governed by other parts of Article 8 if the relationship gives rise to a new security, or may be governed by other law entirely.

2. Subsection (b) of this section specifies what circumstances give rise to security entitlements. Paragraph (1) of subsection (b) sets out the most important rule. It turns

on the intermediary's conduct, reflecting a basic operating assumption of the indirect holding system that once a securities intermediary has acknowledged that it is carrying a position in a financial asset for its customer or participant, the intermediary is obligated to treat the customer or participant as entitled to the financial asset. Paragraph (1) does not attempt to specify exactly what accounting, record-keeping, or information transmission steps suffice to indicate that the intermediary has credited the account. That is left to agreement, trade practice, or rule in order to provide the flexibility necessary to accommodate varying or changing accounting and information processing systems. The point of paragraph (1) is that once an intermediary has acknowledged that it is carrying a position for the customer or participant, the customer or participant has a security entitlement. The precise form in which the intermediary manifests that acknowledgment is left to private ordering.

Paragraph (2) of subsection (b) sets out a different operational test, turning not on the intermediary's accounting system but on the facts that accounting systems are supposed to represent. Under paragraph (b)(2) a person has a security entitlement if the intermediary has received and accepted a financial asset for credit to the account of its customer or participant. For example, if a customer of a broker or bank custodian delivers a security certificate in proper form to the broker or bank to be held in the customer's account, the customer acquires a security entitlement. Paragraph (b)(2) also covers circumstances in which the intermediary receives a financial asset from a third person for credit to the account of the customer or participant. Paragraph (b)(2) is not limited to circumstances in which the intermediary receives security certificates or other financial assets in physical form. Paragraph (b)(2) also covers circumstances in which the intermediary acquires a security entitlement with respect to a financial asset which is to be credited to the account of the intermediary's own customer. For example, if a customer transfers her account from Broker A to Broker B, she acquires security entitlements against Broker B once the clearing corporation has credited the positions to Broker B's account. It should be noted, however, that paragraph (b)(2) provides that a person acquires a security entitlement when the intermediary not only receives but also accepts the financial asset for credit to the account. This limitation is included to take account of the fact that there may be circumstances in which an intermediary has received a financial asset but is not willing to undertake the obligations that flow from establishing a security entitlement. For example, a security certificate which is sent to an intermediary may not be in proper form, or may represent a type of financial asset which the intermediary is not willing to carry for others. It should be noted that in all but extremely unusual cases, the circ umstances covered by paragraph (2) will also be covered by paragraph (1), because the intermediary will have credited the positions to the customer's account.

Paragraph (3) of subsection (b) sets out a residual test, to avoid any implication that the failure of an intermediary to make the appropriate entries to credit a position to a customer's securities account would prevent the customer from acquiring the rights of an entitlement holder under Part 5. As is the case with the paragraph (2) test, the paragraph (3) test would not be needed for the ordinary cases, since they are covered by paragraph (1).

3. In a sense, Section 8-501(b) is analogous to the rules set out in the provisions of Sections 8-313(1)(d) and 8-320 of the prior version of Article 8 that specified what acts by a securities intermediary or clearing corporation sufficed as a transfer of securities held in fungible bulk. Unlike the prior version of Article 8, however, this section is not based on the idea that an entitlement holder acquires rights only by virtue of a "transfer" from the securities intermediary to the entitlement holder. In the indirect holding system, the significant fact is that the securities intermediary has undertaken to treat the customer as entitled to the financial asset. It is up to the securities intermediary to take the necessary steps to ensure that it will be able to perform its undertaking. It is, for example, entirely possible that a securities

intermediary might make entries in a customer's account reflecting that customer's acquisition of a certain security at a time when the securities intermediary did not itself happen to hold any units of that security. The person from whom the securities intermediary bought the security might have failed to deliver and it might have taken some time to clear up the problem, or there may have been an operational gap in time between the crediting of a customer's account and the receipt of securities from another securities intermediary. The entitlement holder's rights against the securities intermediary do not depend on whether or when the securities intermediary acquired its interests. Subsection (c) is intended to make this point clear. Subsection (c) does not mean that the intermediary is free to create security entitlements without itself holding sufficient financial assets to satisfy its entitlement holders. The duty of a securities intermediary to maintain sufficient assets is governed by Section 8-504 and regulatory law. Subsection (c) is included only to make it clear the question whether a person has acquired a security entitlement does not depend on whether the intermediary has complied with that duty.

4. Part 5 of Article 8 sets out a carefully designed system of rules for the indirect holding system. Persons who hold securities through brokers or custodians have security entitlements that are governed by Part 5, rather than being treated as the direct holders of securities. Subsection (d) specifies the limited circumstance in which a customer who leaves a financial asset with a broker or other securities intermediary has a direct interest in the financial asset, rather than a security entitlement.

The customer can be a direct holder only if the security certificate, or other financial asset, is registered in the name of, payable to the order of, or specially indorsed to the customer, and has not been indorsed by the customer to the securities intermediary or in blank. The distinction between those circumstances where the customer can be treated as direct owner and those where the customer has a security entitlement is essentially the same as the distinction drawn under the federal bankruptcy code between customer name securities and customer property. The distinction does not turn on any form of physical identification or segregation. A customer who delivers certificates to a broker with blank indorsements or stock powers is not a direct holder but has a security entitlement, even though the broker holds those certificates in some form of separate safe-keeping arrangement for that particular customer. The customer remains the direct holder only if there is no indorsement or stock power so that further action by the customer is required to place the certificates in a form where they can be transferred by the broker.

The rule of subsection (d) corresponds to the rule set out in Section 8-301(a)(3) specifying when acquisition of possession of a certificate by a securities intermediary counts as "delivery" to the customer.

5. Subsection (e) is intended to make clear that Part 5 does not apply to an arrangement in which a security is issued representing an interest in underlying assets, as distinguished from arrangements in which the underlying assets are carried in a securities account. A common mechanism by which new financial instruments are devised is that a financial institution that holds some security, financial instrument, or pool thereof, creates interests in that asset or pool which are sold to others. In many such cases, the interests so created will fall within the definition of "security" in Section 8-102(a)(15). If so, then by virtue of subsection (e) of Section 8-501, the relationship between the institution that creates the interests and the persons who hold them is not a security entitlement to which the Part 5 rules apply. Accordingly, an arrangement such as an American depositary receipt facility which creates freely transferable interests in underlying securities will be issuance of a security under Article 8 rather than establishment of a security entitlement to the underlying securities.

The subsection (e) rule can be regarded as an aspect of the definitional rules specifying the meaning of securities account and security entitlement. Among the key components of the definition of security in Section 8-102(a)(15) are the "transferability" and "divisibility" tests. Securities, in the Article 8 sense, are fungible interests or obligations that are intended to be tradable. The concept of security entitlement under Part 5 is quite different. A security entitlement is the package of rights that a person has against the person's own intermediary with respect to the positions carried in the person's securities account. That package of rights is not, as such, something that is traded. When a customer sells a security that she had held through a securities account, her security entitlement is terminated; when she buys a security that she will hold through her securities account, she acquires a security entitlement. In most cases, settlement of a securities trade will involve termination of one person's security entitlement and acquisition of a security entitlement by another person. That transaction, however, is not a "transfer" of the same entitlement from one person to another. That is not to say that an entitlement holder cannot transfer an interest in her security entitlement as such; granting a security interest in a security entitlement is such a transfer. On the other hand, the nature of a security entitlement is that the intermediary is undertaking duties only to the person identified as the entitlement holder.

Definitional Cross References

"Financial asset"–Section 8-102(a)(9)
"Indorsement"–Section 8-102(a)(11)
"Securities intermediary"–Section 8-102(a)(14)
"Security"–Section 8-102(a)(15)
"Security entitlement"–Section 8-102(a)(17)

Section 8–502. Assertion of Adverse Claim Against Entitlement Holder.

An action based on an adverse claim to a financial asset, whether framed in conversion, replevin, constructive trust, equitable lien, or other theory, may not be asserted against a person who acquires a security entitlement under Section 8–501 for value and without notice of the adverse claim.

Added by Laws 1997, Ch. 566, § 5, eff. Oct. 10, 1997. See legislative history following § 8–101 for explanation of legislative intent.

Official Comment

1. The section provides investors in the indirect holding system with protection against adverse claims by specifying that no adverse claim can be asserted against a person who acquires a security entitlement under Section 8-501 for value and without notice of the adverse claim. It plays a role in the indirect holding system analogous to the rule of the direct holding system that protected purchasers take free from adverse claims (Section 8-303).

This section does not use the locution "takes free from adverse claims" because that could be confusing as applied to the indirect holding system. The nature of indirect holding system is that an entitlement holder has an interest in common with others who hold positions in the same financial asset through the same intermediary. Thus, a particular entitlement holder's interest in the financial assets held by its intermediary is necessarily "subject to" the interests of others. See Section 8-503. The rule stated in this section might have been expressed by saying that a person who acquires a security entitlement under Section 8-501 for value and without notice of adverse claims takes "that security entitlement" free from adverse claims. That formulation has not been used, however, for fear that it would be misinterpreted as suggesting that the person acquires a right to the underlying financial assets that could not be affected by the competing rights of others claiming through common or higher tier intermediaries. A security entitlement is a complex bundle of rights. This section does not deal with the question of what rights are in the bundle. Rather, this section provides that once a person has acquired the bundle, someone else cannot take it away on the basis of assertion that the transaction in which the security entitlement was created involved a violation of the claimant's rights.

2. Because securities trades are typically settled on a net basis by book-entry movements, it would ordinarily be impossible for anyone to trace the path of any particular security, no matter how the interest of parties who hold through intermediaries is described. Suppose, for example, that S has a 1000 share position in XYZ common stock through an account with a broker, Able & Co. S's identical twin impersonates S and directs Able to sell the securities. That same day, B places an order with Baker & Co., to buy 1000 shares of XYZ common stock. Later, S discovers the wrongful act and seeks to recover "her shares." Even if S can show that, at the stage of the trade, her sell order was matched with B's buy order, that would not suffice to show that "her shares" went to B. Settlement between Able and Baker occurs on a net basis for all trades in XYZ that day; indeed Able's net position may have been such that it received rather than delivered shares in XYZ through the settlement system.

In the unlikely event that this was the only trade in XYZ common stock executed in the market that day, one could follow the shares from S's account to B's account. The plaintiff in an action in conversion or similar legal action to enforce a property interest must show that the defendant has the an item of property that belongs to the plaintiff. In this example, B's security entitlement is not the same item of property that formerly was held by S, it is a new package of rights that B acquired against Baker under Section 8-501. Principles of equitable remedies might, however, provide S with a basis for contending that if the position B received was the traceable product of the wrongful taking of S's property by S's twin, a constructive trust should be imposed on B's property in favor of S. See G. Palmer, The Law of Restitution § 2.14. Section 8-502 ensures that no such claims can be asserted against a person, such as B in this example, who acquires a security entitlement under Section 8-501 for value and without notice, regardless of what theory of law or equity is used to describe the basis of the assertion of the adverse claim.

In the above example, S would ordinarily have no reason to pursue B unless Able is insolvent and S's claim will not be satisfied in the insolvency proceedings. Because S did not give an entitlement order for the disposition of her security entitlement, Able must recredit her account for the 1000 shares of XYZ common stock. See Section 8-507(b).

3. The following examples illustrate the operation of Section 8-502.

Example 1. Thief steals bearer bonds from Owner. Thief delivers the bonds to Broker for credit to Thief's securities account, thereby acquiring a security entitlement under Section 8-501(b). Under other law, Owner may have a claim to have a constructive trust imposed on the security entitlement as the traceable product of the bonds that Thief misappropriated. Because Thief was himself the wrongdoer, Thief obviously had notice of Owner's adverse claim. Accordingly, Section 8-502 does not preclude Owner from asserting an adverse claim against Thief.

Example 2. Thief steals bearer bonds from Owner. Thief owes a personal debt to Creditor. Creditor has a securities account with Broker. Thief agrees to transfer the bonds to Creditor as security for or in satisfaction of his debt to Creditor. Thief does so by sending the bonds to Broker for credit to Creditor's securities account. Creditor thereby acquires a security entitlement under Section 8-501(b). Under other law, Owner may have a claim to have a constructive trust imposed on the security entitlement as the traceable product of the bonds that Thief misappropriated. Creditor acquired the security entitlement for value, since Creditor acquired it as security for or in satisfaction of Thief's debt to Creditor. See Section 1-201(44). If Creditor did not have notice of Owner's claim, Section 8-502 precludes any action by Owner against Creditor, whether framed in constructive trust or other theory. Section 8-105 specifies what counts as notice of an adverse claim.

Example 3. Father, as trustee for Son, holds XYZ Co. shares in a securities account with Able & Co. In violation of his fiduciary duties, Father sells the XYZ Co. shares and uses the proceeds for personal purposes. Father dies, and his estate is insolvent. Assume–implausibly–that Son is able to trace the XYZ Co. shares and show that the "same shares" ended up in Buyer's securities account with Baker & Co. Section 8-502 precludes any action by Son against Buyer, whether framed in constructive trust or other theory, provided that Buyer acquired the security entitlement for value and without notice of adverse claims.

Example 4. Debtor holds XYZ Co. shares in a securities account with Able & Co. As collateral for a loan from Bank, Debtor grants Bank a security interest in the security entitlement to the XYZ Co. shares. Bank perfects by a method which leaves Debtor with the ability to dispose of the shares. See Section 9-115. In violation of the security agreement, Debtor sells the XYZ Co. shares and absconds with the proceeds. Assume–implausibly–that Bank is able to trace the XYZ Co. shares and show that the "same shares" ended up in Buyer's securities account with Baker & Co. Section 8-502 precludes any action by Bank against Buyer, whether framed in constructive trust or other theory, provided that Buyer acquired the security entitlement for value and without notice of adverse claims.

Example 5. Debtor owns controlling interests in various public companies, including Acme and Ajax. Acme owns 60% of the stock of another public company, Beta. Debtor causes the Beta stock to be pledged to Lending Bank as collateral for Ajax s debt. Acme holds the Beta stock through an account with a securities custodian, C Bank, which in turn holds through Clearing Corporation. Lending Bank is also a Clearing Corporation participant. The pledge of the Beta stock is implemented by Acme instructing C Bank to instruct Clearing Corporation to debit C Bank's account and credit Lending Bank's account. Acme and Ajax both become insolvent. The Beta stock is still valuable. Acme s liquidator asserts that the pledge of the Beta stock for Ajax s debt was wrongful as against Acme and seeks to recover the Beta stock from Lending Bank. Because the pledge was implemented by an outright transfer into Lending Bank's account at Clearing Corporation, Lending Bank acquired a security entitlement to the Beta stock under Section 8-501. Lending Bank acquired the security entitlement for value, since it acquired it as security for a debt. See Section 1-201(44). If Lending Bank did not have notice of Acme's claim, Section 8-502 will preclude any action by Acme against Lending Bank, whether framed in constructive trust or other theory.

4. Although this section protects entitlement holders against adverse claims, it does not protect them against the risk that their securities intermediary will not itself have sufficient financial assets to satisfy the claims of all its entitlement holders. Suppose that Customer A holds 1000 shares of XYZ Co. stock in an account with her broker, Able & Co. Able in turn holds 1000 shares of XYZ Co. through its account with Clearing Corporation, but has no other positions in XYZ Co. shares, either for other customers or for its own proprietary account. CUstomer B places an order with Able for the purchase of 1000 shares of XYZ Co. stock, and pays the purchase price. Able credits B's account with a 1000 share position in XYZ Co. stock, but Able does not itself buy any additional XYZ Co. shares. Able fails, having only 1000 shares to satisfy the claims of A and B. Unless other insolvency law establishes a different distributional rule, A and B would share the 1000 shares held by Able pro rata, without regard to the time that their respective entitlements were established. See Section 8-503(b). Section 8-502 protects entitlement holders, such as A and B, against adverse

claimants. In this case, however, the problem that A and B face is not that someone is trying to take away their entitlements, but that the entitlements are not worth what they thought. The only role that Section 8-502 plays in this case is to preclude any assertion that A has some form of claim against B by virtue of the fact that Able's establishment of an entitlement in favor of B diluted A's rights to the limited assets held by Able.

Definitional Cross References

"Adverse Claim"–Section 8-102(a)(1)
"Financial asset"–Section 8-102(a)(9)
"Notice of adverse claim"–Section 8-105
"Security entitlement"–Section 8-102(a)(17)
"Value"–Section 1-201(44) & 8-116

Section 8–503. Property Interest of Entitlement Holder in Financial Asset Held by Securities Intermediary.

(a) To the extent necessary for a securities intermediary to satisfy all security entitlements with respect to a particular financial asset, all interests in that financial asset held by the securities intermediary are held by the securities intermediary for the entitlement holders, are not property of the securities intermediary, and are not subject to claims of creditors of the securities intermediary, except as otherwise provided in Section 8–511.

(b) An entitlement holder's property interest with respect to a particular financial asset under subsection (a) is a pro rata property interest in all interests in that financial asset held by the securities intermediary, without regard to the time the entitlement holder acquired the security entitlement or the time the securities intermediary acquired the interest in that financial asset.

(c) An entitlement holder's property interest with respect to a particular financial asset under subsection (a) may be enforced against the securities intermediary only by exercise of the entitlement holder's rights under sections 8–505 through 8–508.

(d) An entitlement holder's property interest with respect to a particular financial asset under subsection (a) may be enforced against a purchaser of the financial asset or interest therein only if:

(1) insolvency proceedings have been initiated by or against the securities intermediary;

(2) the securities intermediary does not have sufficient inter ests in the financial asset to satisfy the security entitle ments of all of its entitlement holders to that financial asset;

(3) the securities intermediary violated its obligations under Section 8–504 by transferring the financial asset or inter est therein to the purchaser; and

(4) the purchaser is not protected under subsection (e). The trustee or other liquidator, acting on behalf of all entitlement holders having security entitlements with respect to a particular financial asset, may recover the financial asset, or

interest therein, from the purchaser. If the trustee or other liquidator elects not to pursue that right, an entitlement holder whose security entitlement remains unsatisfied has the right to recover its interest in the financial asset from the purchaser.

(e) An action based on the entitlement holder's property interest with respect to a particular financial asset under subsection (a), whether framed in conversion, replevin, constructive trust, equitable lien, or other theory, may not be asserted against any purchaser of a financial asset or interest therein who gives value, obtains control, and does not act in collusion with the securities intermediary in violating the securities intermediary's obligations under Section 8–504.

Added by Laws 1997, Ch. 566, § 5, eff. Oct. 10, 1997. See legislative history following § 8–101 for explanation of legislative intent.

Official Comment

1. This section specifies the sense in which a security is an interest in the property held by the securities intermediary. It expresses the ordinary understanding that securities that a firm holds for its customers are not general assets of the firm subject to the claims of creditors. Since securities intermediaries generally do not segregate in such fashion that one could identify particular securities as the ones held for customers, it would not be realistic for this section to state that "customer's securities" are not subject to creditors' claims. Rather subsection (a) provides that to the extent necessary to satisfy all customer claims, all units of that security held by the firm are held for the entitlement holders, are not property of the securities intermediary, and are not subject to creditors' claims, except as otherwise provided in Section 8-511.

An entitlement holder's property interest under this section is an interest with respect to a specific issue of securities or financial assets. For example, customers of a firm who have positions in XYZ common stock have security entitlements with respect to the XYZ common stock held by the intermediary, while other customers who have positions in ABC common stock have security entitlements with respect to the ABC common stock held by the intermediary.

Subsection (b) makes clear that the property interest described in subsection (a) is an interest held in common by all entitlement holders who have entitlements to a particular security or other financial asset. Temporal factors are irrelevant. One entitlement holder cannot claim that its rights to the assets held by the intermediary are superior to the rights of another entitlement holder by virtue of having acquired those rights before, or after, the other entitlement holder. Nor does it matter whether the intermediary had sufficient assets to satisfy all entitlement holders claims at one point, but no longer does. Rather, all entitlement holders have a pro rata interest in whatever positions in that financial asset the intermediary holds.

Although this section describes the property interest of entitlement holders in the assets held by the intermediary, it does not necessarily determine how property held by a failed intermediary will be distributed in insolvency proceedings. If the intermediary fails and its affairs are being administered in an insolvency proceeding, the applicable insolvency law governs how the various parties having claims against the firm are treated. For example, the distributional rules for stockbroker liquidation proceedings under the Bankruptcy Code and Securities Investor Protection Act ("SIPA") provide that all customer property is distributed pro rata among all customers in proportion to the dollar value of their total positions, rather than dividing the property on an issue by issue basis. For intermediaries that are not subject to the

Bankruptcy Code and SIPA, other insolvency law would determine what distributional rule is applied.

2. Although this section recognizes that the entitlement holders of a securities intermediary have a property interest in the financial assets held by the intermediary, the incidents of this property interest are established by the rules of Article 8, not by common law property concepts. The traditional Article 8 rules on certificated securities were based on the idea that a paper certificate could be regarded as a nearly complete reification of the underlying right. The rules on transfer and the consequences of wrongful transfer could then be written using the same basic concepts as the rules for physical chattels. A person's claim of ownership of a certificated security is a right to a specific identifiable physical object, and that right can be asserted against any person who ends up in possession of that physical certificate, unless cut off by the rules protecting purchasers for value without notice. Those concepts do not work for the indirect holding system. A security entitlement is not a claim to a specific identifiable thing; it is a package of rights and interests that a person has against the person's securities intermediary and the property held by the intermediary. The idea that discrete objects might be traced through the hands a different persons has no place in the Revised Article 8 rules for the indirect holding system. The fundamental principles of the indirect holding system rules are that an entitlement holder's own intermediary has the obligation to see to it that the entitlement holder receives all of the economic and corporate rights that comprise the financial asset, and that the entitlement holder can look only to that intermediary for performance of the obligations. The entitlement holder cannot assert rights directly against other persons, such as other intermediaries through whom the intermediary holds the positions, or third parties to whom the intermediary may have wrongfully transferred interests, except in extremely unusual circumstances where the third party was itself a partic ipant in the wrongdoing. Subsections (c) through (e) reflect these fundamental principles.

Subsection (c) provides that an entitlement holder's property interest can be enforced against the intermediary only by exercise of the entitlement holder's rights under Sections 8-505 through 8-508. These are the provisions that set out the duty of an intermediary to see to it that the entitlement holder receives all of the economic and corporate rights that comprise the security. If the intermediary is in insolvency proceedings and can no longer perform in accordance with the ordinary Part 5 rules, the applicable insolvency law will determine how the intermediary's assets are to be distributed.

Subsections (d) and (e) specify the limited circumstances in which an entitlement holder's property interest can be asserted against a third person to whom the intermediary transferred a financial asset that was subject to the entitlement holder's claim when held by the intermediary. Subsection (d) provides that the property interest of entitlement holders cannot be asserted against any transferee except in the circumstances therein specified. So long as the intermediary is solvent, the entitlement holders must look to the intermediary to satisfy their claims. If the intermediary does not hold financial assets corresponding to the entitlement holders' claims, the intermediary has the duty to acquire them. See Section 8-504. Thus, paragraphs (1), (2), and (3) of subsection (d) specify that the only occasion in which the entitlement holders can pursue transferees is when the intermediary is unable to perform its obligation, and the transfer to the transferee was a violation of those obligations. Even in that case, a transferee who gave value and obtained control is protected by virtue of the rule in subsection (e), unless the transferee acted in collusion with the intermediary.

Subsections (d) and (e) have the effect of protecting transferees from an intermediary against adverse claims arising out of assertions by the intermediary's entitlement holders that the intermediary acted wrongfully in transferring the financial assets. These rules, however, operate in a slightly different fashion than traditional adverse claim cut-off rules. Rather than specifying that a certain class of transferee takes free from all claims, subsections (d) and (e) specify the circumstances in which this particular form of claim can be asserted against a transferee. Revised Article 8 also contains general adverse claim cut-off rules for the indirect holding system. See Sections 8-502 and 8-510. The rule of subsections (d) and (e) takes precedence over the general cut-off rules of those sections, because Section 8-503 itself defines and sets limits on the assertion of the property interest of entitlement holders. Thus, the question whether entitlement holders' property interest can be asserted as an adverse claim against a transferee from the intermediary is governed by the collusion test of Section 8-503(e), rather than by the "without notice" test of Sections 8-502 and 8-510.

3. The limitations that subsections (c) through (e) place on the ability of customers of a failed intermediary to recover securities or other financial assets from transferees are consistent with the fundamental policies of investor protection that underlie this Article and other bodies of law governing the securities business. The commercial law rules for the securities holding and transfer system must be assessed from the forward-looking perspective of their impact on the vast number of transactions in which no wrongful conduct occurred or will occur, rather than from the *post hoc* perspective of what rule might be most advantageous to a particular class of persons in litigation that might arise out of the occasional case in which someone has acted wrongfully. Although one can devise hypothetical scenarios where particular customers might find it advantageous to be able to assert rights against someone other than the customers' own intermediary, commercial law rules that permitted customers to do so would impair rather than promote the interest of investors and the safe and efficient operation of the clearance and settlement system. Suppose, for example, that Intermediary A transfers securities to B, that Intermediary A acted wrongfully as against its customers in so doing, and that after the transaction Intermediary A did not have sufficient securities to satisfy its obligations to its entitlement holders. Viewed solely from the standpoint of the customers of Intermediary A, it would seem that permitting the property to be recovered from B, would be good for investors. That, however, is not the case. B may itself be an intermediary with its own customers, or may be some other institution through which individuals invest, such as a pension fund or investment company. There is no reason to think that rules permitting customers of an intermediary to trace and recover securities that their intermediary wrongfully transferred work to the advantage of investors in general. To the contrary, application of such rules would often merely shift losses from one set of investors to another. The uncertainties that would result from rules permitting such recoveries would work to the disadvantage of all participants in the securities markets.

The use of the collusion test in Section 8-503(e) furthers the interests of investors generally in the sound and efficient operation of the securities holding and settlement system. The effect of the choice of this standard is that customers of a failed intermediary must show that the transferee from whom they seek to recover was affirmatively engaged in wrongful conduct, rather than casting on the transferee any burden of showing that the transferee had no awareness of wrongful conduct by the failed intermediary. The rule of Section 8-503(e) is based on the long-standing policy that it is undesirable to impose upon purchasers of securities any duty to investigate whether their sellers may be acting wrongfully.

Rather than imposing duties to investigate, the general policy of the commercial law of the securities holding and transfer system has been to eliminate legal rules that might induce participants to conduct investigations of the authority of persons transferring securities on behalf of others for fear that they might be held liable for participating in a wrongful transfer. The rules in Part 4 of Article 8 concerning transfers by fiduciaries provide a good example. Under *Lowry v. Commercial &*

Farmers' Bank, 15 F. Cas. 1040 (C.C.D. Md. 1848) (No. 8551), an issuer could be held liable for wrongful transfer if it registered transfer of securities by a fiduciary under circumstances where it had any reason to believe that the fiduciary may have been acting improperly. In one sense that seems to be advantageous for beneficiaries who might be harmed by wrongful conduct by fiduciaries. The consequence of the *Lowry* rule, however, was that in order to protect against risk of such liability, issuers developed the practice of requiring extensive documentation for fiduciary stock transfers, making such transfers cumbersome and time consuming. Accordingly, the rules in Part 4 of Article 8, and in the prior fiduciary transfer statutes, were designed to discourage transfer agents from conducting investigations into the rightfulness of transfers by fiduciaries.

The rules of Revised Article 8 implement for the indirect holding system the same policies that the rules on protected purchasers and registration of transfer adopt for the direct holding system. A securities intermediary is, by definition, a person who is holding securities on behalf of other persons. There is nothing unusual or suspicious about a transaction in which a securities intermediary sells securities that it was holding for its customers. That is exactly what securities intermediaries are in business to do. The interests of customers of securities intermediaries would not be served by a rule that required counterparties to transfers from securities intermediaries to investigate whether the intermediary was acting wrongfully against its customers. Quite the contrary, such a rule would impair the ability of securities intermediaries to perform the function that customers want.

The rules of Section 8-503(c) through (e) apply to transferees generally, including pledgees. The reasons for treating pledgees in the same fashion as other transferees are discussed in the Comments to Section 8-511. The statement in subsection (a) that an intermediary holds financial assets for customers and not as its own property does not, of course, mean that the intermediary lacks power to transfer the financial assets to others. For example, although Article 9 provides that for a security interest to attach the debtor must have "rights" in the collateral, see Section 9-203, the fact that an intermediary is holding a financial asset in a form that permits ready transfer means that it has such rights, even if the intermediary is acting wrongfully against its entitlement holders in granting the security interest. The question whether the secured party takes subject to the entitlement holder's claim in such a case is governed by Section 8-511, which is an application to secured transactions of the general principles expressed in subsections (d) and (e) of this section.

Definitional Cross References

"Control"–Section 8-106
"Entitlement holder"–Section 8-102(a)(7)
"Financial asset"–Section 8-102(a)(9)
"Insolvency proceedings"–Section 1-201(22)
"Purchaser"–Section 1-201(33) & 8-116
"Securities intermediary"–Section 8-102(a)(14)
"Security entitlement"–Section 8-102(a)(17)
"Value"–Section 1-201(44) & 8-116

Section 8–504. Duty of Securities Intermediary to Maintain Financial Asset.

(a) A securities intermediary shall promptly obtain and thereafter maintain a financial asset in a quantity corresponding to the aggregate of all security entitlements it has established in favor of its entitlement holders with respect to that financial asset. The securities intermediary may maintain those financial assets directly or through one or more other securities intermediaries.

(b) Except to the extent otherwise agreed by its entitlement holder, a securities intermediary may not grant any security interests in a financial asset it is obligated to maintain pursuant to subsection (a).

(c) A securities intermediary satisfies the duty in subsection (a) if:

(1) the securities intermediary acts with respect to the duty as agreed upon by the entitlement holder and the securities intermediary; or

(2) in the absence of agreement, the securities intermediary exercises due care in accordance with reasonable commercial standards to obtain and maintain the financial asset.

(d) This section does not apply to a clearing corporation that is itself the obligor of an option or similar obligation to which its entitlement holders have security entitlements.

Added by Laws 1997, Ch. 566, § 5, eff. Oct. 10, 1997. See legislative history following § 8–101 for explanation of legislative intent.

Official Comment

1. This section expresses one of the core elements of the relationships for which the Part 5 rules were designed, to wit, that a securities intermediary undertakes to hold financial assets corresponding to the security entitlements of its entitlement holders. The locution "shall promptly obtain and shall thereafter maintain" is taken from the corresponding regulation under federal securities law, 17 C.F.R. § 240.15c3-3. This section recognizes the reality that as the securities business is conducted today, it is not possible to identify particular securities as belonging to customers as distinguished from other particular securities that are the firm's own property. Securities firms typically keep all securities in fungible form, and may maintain their inventory of a particular security in various locations and forms, including physical securities held in vaults or in transit to transfer agents, and book entry positions at one or more clearing corporations. Accordingly, this section states that a securities intermediary shall maintain a quantity of financial assets corresponding to the aggregate of all security entitlements it has established. The last sentence of subsection (a) provides explicitly that the securities intermediary may hold directly or indirectly. That point is implicit in the use of the term "financial asset," inasmuch as Section 8-102(a)(9) provides that the term "financial asset" may refer either to the underlying asset or the means by which it is held, including both security certificates and security entitlements.

2. Subsection (b) states explicitly a point that is implicit in the notion that a securities intermediary must maintain financial assets corresponding to the security entitlements of its entitlement holders, to wit, that it is wrongful for a securities intermediary to grant security interests in positions that it needs to satisfy customers' claims, except as authorized by the customers. This statement does not determine the rights of a secured party to whom an securities intermediary wrongfully grants a security interest; that issue is governed by Sections 8-503 and 8-511.

Margin accounts are common examples of arrangements in which an entitlement holder authorizes the securities intermediary to grant security interests in the positions held for the entitlement holder. Securities firms commonly obtain the funds needed to provide margin loans to their customers by "rehypothecating" the customers' securities. In order to facilitate rehypothecation, agreements between margin customers and their brokers commonly authorize the broker to commingle securities of all margin customers for rehypothecation to the lender who provides the financing. Brokers commonly rehypothecate customer securities having a value somewhat greater than the amount of the loan made to the customer, since the lenders who provide the necessary financing to the broker need some cushion of protection against the risk of decline in the value of the rehypothecated securities. The extent and manner in which a firm may rehypothecate customers' securities are determined by the agreement between the intermediary and the entitlement holder and by applicable regulatory law. Current regulations under the federal securities laws require that brokers obtain the explicit consent of customers before pledging customer securities or commingling different customers' securities for pledge. Federal regulations also limit the extent to which a broker may rehypothecate customer securities to 110% of the aggregate amount of the borrowings of all customers.

3. The statement in this section that an intermediary must obtain and maintain financial assets corresponding to the aggregate of all security entitlements it has established is intended only to capture the general point that one of the key elements that distinguishes securities accounts from other relationships, such as deposit accounts, is that the intermediary undertakes to maintain a direct correspondence between the positions it holds and the claims of its customers. This section is not intended as a detailed specification of precisely how the intermediary is to perform this duty, nor whether there may be special circumstances in which an intermediary's general duty is excused. Accordingly, the general statement of the duties of a securities intermediary in this and the following sections is supplemented by two other provisions. First, each of Sections 8-504 through 8-508 contains an "agreement/due care" provision. Second, Section 8-509 sets out general qualifications on the duties stated in these sections, including the important point that compliance with corresponding regulatory provisions constitutes compliance with the Article 8 duties.

4. The "agreement/due care" provision in subsection (c) of this section is necessary to provide sufficient flexibility to accommodate the general duty stated in subsection (a) to the wide variety of circumstances that may be encountered in the modern securities holding system. For the most common forms of publicly traded securities, the modern depository-based indirect holding system has made the likelihood of an actual loss of securities remote, though correctable errors in accounting or temporary interruptions of data processing facilities may occur. Indeed, one of the reasons for the evolution of book-entry systems is to eliminate the risk of loss or destruction of physical certificates. There are, however, some forms of securities and other financial assets which must still be held in physical certificated form, with the attendant risk of loss or destruction. Risk of loss or delay may be a more significant consideration in connection with foreign securities. An American securities intermediary may well be willing to hold a foreign security in a securities account for its customer, but the intermediary may have relatively little choice of or control over foreign intermediaries through which the security must in turn be held. Accordingly, it is common for American securities intermediaries to disclaim responsibility for custodial risk of holding through foreign intermediaries.

Subsection (c)(1) provides that a securities intermediary satisfies the duty stated in subsection (a) if the intermediary acts with respect to that duty in accordance with the agreement between the intermediary and the entitlement holder. Subsection (c)(2) provides that if there is no agreement on the matter, the intermediary satisfies the subsection (a) duty if the intermediary exercises due care in accordance with reasonable commercial standards to obtain and maintain the financial asset in question. This formulation does not state that the intermediary has a universally applicable statutory duty of due care. Section 1-102(3) provides that statutory duties of due care cannot be disclaimed by agreement, but the "agreement/due care" formula contemplates that there may be particular circumstances where the parties do not wish to create a specific duty of due care, for example, with respect to foreign securities. Under subsection (c)(1), compliance with the agreement constitutes satisfaction of the subsection (a) duty, whether or not the agreement provides that the intermediary will exercise due care.

In each of the sections where the "agreement/due care" formula is used, it provides that entering into an agreement and performing in accordance with that agreement is a method by which the securities intermediary may satisfy the statutory duty stated in that section. Accordingly, the general obligation of good faith performance of statutory and contract duties, see Sections 1-203 and 8-102(a)(10), would apply to such an agreement. It would not be consistent with the obligation of good faith performance for an agreement to purport to establish the usual sort of arrangement between an intermediary and entitlement holder, yet disclaim altogether one of the basic elements that define that relationship. For example, an agreement stating that an intermediary assumes no responsibilities whatsoever for the safekeeping any of the entitlement holder's securities positions would not be consistent with good faith performance of the intermediary's duty to obtain and maintain financial assets corresponding to the entitlement holder's security entitlements.

To the extent that no agreement under subsection (c)(1) has specified the details of the intermediary's performance of the subsection (a) duty, subsection (c)(2) provides that the intermediary satisfies that duty if it exercises due care in accordance with reasonable commercial standards. The duty of care includes both care in the intermediary's own operations and care in the selection of other intermediaries through whom the intermediary holds the assets in question. The statement of the obligation of due care is meant to incorporate the principles of the common law under which the specific actions or precautions necessary to meet the obligation of care are determined by such factors as the nature and value of the property, the customs and practices of the business, and the like.

5. This section necessarily states the duty of a securities intermediary to obtain and maintain financial assets only at the very general and abstract level. For the most part, these matters are specified in great detail by regulatory law. Broker-dealers registered under the federal securities laws are subject to detailed regulation concerning the safeguarding of customer securities. See 17 C.F.R. § 240.15c3-3. Section 8-509(a) provides explicitly that if a securities intermediary complies with such regulatory law, that constitutes compliance with Section 8-503. In certain circumstances, these rules permit a firm to be in a position where it temporarily lacks a sufficient quantity of financial assets to satisfy all customer claims. For example, if another firm has failed to make a delivery to the firm in settlement of a trade, the firm is permitted a certain period of time to clear up the problem before it is obligated to obtain the necessary securities from some other source.

6. Subsection (d) is intended to recognize that there are some circumstances, where the duty to maintain a sufficient quantity of financial assets does not apply because the intermediary is not holding anything on behalf of others. For example, the Options Clearing Corporation is treated as a "securities intermediary" under this Article, although it does not itself hold options on behalf of its participants. Rather, it becomes the issuer of the options, by virtue of guaranteeing the obligations of participants in the clearing corporation who have written or purchased the options cleared through it. See Section 8-103(e). Accordingly, the general duty of an intermediary under subsection (a) does not apply, nor would other provisions of Part 5 that depend upon the existence of a requirement that the securities intermediary hold financial assets, such as Sections 8-503 and 8-508.

Definitional Cross References

"Agreement"–Section 1-201(3)
"Clearing corporation"–Section 8-102(a)(5)
"Entitlement holder"–Section 8-102(a)(7)
"Financial asset"–Section 8-102(a)(9)
"Securities intermediary"–Section 8-102(a)(14)
"Security entitlement"–Section 8-102(a)(17)

Section 8–505. Duty of Securities Intermediary with Respect to Payments and Distributions.

(a) A securities intermediary shall take action to obtain a payment or distribution made by the issuer of a financial asset. A securities intermediary satisfies the duty if:

(1) the securities intermediary acts with respect to the duty as agreed upon by the entitlement holder and the securities intermediary; or

(2) in the absence of agreement, the securities intermediary exercises due care in accordance with reasonable commercial standards to attempt to obtain the payment or distribution.

(b) A securities intermediary is obligated to its entitlement holder for a payment or distribution made by the issuer of a financial asset if the payment or distribution is received by the securities intermediary.

Added by Laws 1997, Ch. 566, § 5, eff. Oct. 10, 1997. See legislative history following § 8–101 for explanation of legislative intent.

Official Comment

1. One of the core elements of the securities account relationships for which the Part 5 rules were designed is that the securities intermediary passes through to the entitlement holders the economic benefit of ownership of the financial asset, such as payments and distributions made by the issuer. Subsection (a) expresses the ordinary understanding that a securities intermediary will take appropriate action to see to it that any payments or distributions made by the issuer are received. One of the main reasons that investors make use of securities intermediaries is to obtain the services of a professional in performing the record-keeping and other functions necessary to ensure that payments and other distributions are received.

2. Subsection (a) incorporates the same "agreement/due care" formula as the other provisions of Part 5 dealing with the duties of a securities intermediary. See Comment 4 to Section 8-504. This formulation permits the parties to specify by agreement what action, if any, the intermediary is to take with respect to the duty to obtain payments and distributions. In the absence of specification by agreement, the intermediary satisfies the duty if the intermediary exercises due care in accordance with reasonable commercial standards. The provisions of Section 8-509 also apply to the Section 8-505 duty, so that compliance with applicable regulatory requirements constitutes compliance with the Section 8-505 duty.

3. Subsection (b) provides that a securities intermediary is obligated to its entitlement holder for those payments or distributions made by the issuer that are in fact received by the intermediary. It does not deal with the details of the time and manner of payment. Moreover, as with any other monetary obligation, the obligation

to pay may be subject to other rights of the obligor, by way of set-off counterclaim or the like. Section 8-509(c) makes this point explicit.

Definitional Cross References

"Agreement"–Section 1-201(3)
"Entitlement holder"–Section 8-102(a)(7)
"Financial asset"–Section 8-102(a)(9)
"Securities intermediary"–Section 8-102(a)(14)
"Security entitlement"–Section 8-102(a)(17)

Section 8–506. Duty of Securities Intermediary to Exercise Rights as Directed by Entitlement Holder.

A securities intermediary shall exercise rights with respect to a financial asset if directed to do so by an entitlement holder. A securities intermediary satisfies the duty if:

(1) the securities intermediary acts with respect to the duty as agreed upon by the entitlement holder and the securities intermediary; or

(2) in the absence of agreement, the securities intermediary either places the entitlement holder in a position to exercise the rights directly or exercises due care in accordance with reasonable commercial standards to follow the direction of the entitlement holder.

Added by Laws 1997, Ch. 566, § 5, eff. Oct. 10, 1997. See legislative history following § 8–101 for explanation of legislative intent.

Official Comment

1. Another of the core elements of the securities account relationships for which the Part 5 rules were designed is that although the intermediary may, by virtue of the structure of the indirect holding system, be the party who has the power to exercise the corporate and other rights that come from holding the security, the intermediary exercises these powers as representative of the entitlement holder rather than at its own discretion. This characteristic is one of the things that distinguishes a securities account from other arrangements where one person holds securities "on behalf of" another, such as the relationship between a mutual fund and its shareholders or a trustee and its beneficiary.

2. The fact that the intermediary exercises the rights of security holding as representative of the entitlement holder does not, of course, preclude the entitlement holder from conferring discretionary authority upon the intermediary. Arrangements are not uncommon in which investors do not wish to have their intermediaries forward proxy materials or other information. Thus, this section provides that the intermediary shall exercise corporate and other rights "if directed to do so" by the entitlement holder. Moreover, as with the other Part 5 duties, the "agreement/due care" formulation is used in stating how the intermediary is to perform this duty. This section also provides that the intermediary satisfies the duty if it places the entitlement holder in a position to exercise the rights directly. This is to take account of the fact that some of the rights attendant upon ownership of the security, such as rights to bring derivative and other litigation, are far removed from the matters that intermediaries are expected to perform.

3. This section, and the two that follow, deal with the aspects of securities holding that are related to investment decisions. For example, one of the rights of holding a particular security that would fall within the purview of this section would be the right to exercise a conversion right for a convertible security. It is quite common for investors to confer discretionary authority upon another person, such as an investment adviser, with respect to these rights and other investment decisions. Because this section, and the other sections of Part 5, all specify that a securities intermediary satisfies the Part duties if it acts in accordance with the entitlement holder's agreement, there is no inconsistency between the statement of duties of a securities intermediary and these common arrangements.

4. Section 8-509 also applies to the Section 8-506 duty, so that compliance with applicable regulatory requirements constitutes compliance with this duty. This is quite important in this context, since the federal securities laws establish a comprehensive system of regulation of the distribution of proxy materials and exercise of voting rights with respect to securities held through brokers and other intermediaries. By virtue of Section 8-509(a), compliance with such regulatory requirement constitutes compliance with the Section 8-506 duty.

Definitional Cross References

"Agreement"–Section 1-201(3)
"Entitlement holder"–Section 8-102(a)(7)
"Financial asset"–Section 8-102(a)(9)
"Securities intermediary"–Section 8-102(a)(14)
"Security entitlement"–Section 8-102(a)(17)

Section 8–507. Duty of Securities Intermediary to Comply with Entitlement Order.

(a) A securities intermediary shall comply with an entitlement order if the entitlement order is originated by the appropriate person, the securities intermediary has had reasonable opportunity to assure itself that the entitlement order is genuine and authorized, and the securities intermediary has had reasonable opportunity to comply with the entitlement order. A securities intermediary satisfies the duty if:

(1) the securities intermediary acts with respect to the duty as agreed upon by the entitlement holder and the securities intermediary; or

(2) in the absence of agreement, the securities intermediary exercises due care in accordance with reasonable commercial standards to comply with the entitlement order.

(b) if a securities intermediary transfers a financial asset pursuant to an ineffective entitlement order, the securities intermediary shall reestablish a security entitlement in favor of the person entitled to it, and pay or credit any payments or distributions that the person did not receive as a result of the wrongful transfer. If the securities intermediary does not reestablish a security entitlement, the securities intermediary is liable to the entitlement holder for damages.

Added by Laws 1997, Ch. 566, § 5, eff. Oct. 10, 1997. See legislative history following § 8–101 for explanation of legislative intent.

UCC

Official Comment

1. Subsection (a) of this section states another aspect of duties of securities intermediaries that make up security entitlements – the securities intermediary's duty to comply with entitlement orders. One of the main reasons for holding securities through securities intermediaries is to enable rapid transfer in settlement of trades. Thus the right to have one's orders for disposition of the security entitlement honored is an inherent part of the relationship. Subsection (b) states the correlative liability of a securities intermediary for transferring a financial asset from an entitlement holder's account pursuant to an entitlement order that was not effective.

2. The duty to comply with entitlement orders is subject to several qualifications. The intermediary has a duty only with respect to an entitlement order that is in fact originated by the appropriate person. Moreover, the intermediary has a duty only if it has had reasonable opportunity to assure itself that the order is genuine and authorized, and reasonable opportunity to comply with the order. The same "agreement/due care" formula is used in this section as in the other Part 5 sections on the duties of intermediaries, and the rules of Section 8-509 apply to the Section 8-507 duty.

3. Appropriate person is defined in Section 8-107. In the usual case, the appropriate person is the entitlement holder, see Section 8-107(a)(3). Entitlement holder is defined in Section 8-102(a)(7) is the person "identified in the records of a securities intermediary as the person having a security entitlement." Thus, the general rule is that an intermediary's duty with respect to entitlement orders runs only to the person with whom the intermediary has established a relationship. One of the basic principles of the indirect holding system is that securities intermediaries owe duties only to their own customers. See also Section 8-115. The only situation in which a securities intermediary has a duty to comply with entitlement orders originated by a person other than the person with whom the intermediary established a relationship is covered by Section 8-107(a)(4) and (a)(5), which provide that the term "appropriate person" includes the successor or personal representative of a decedent, or the custodian or guardian of a person who lacks capacity. If the entitlement holder is competent, another person does not fall within the defined term "appropriate person" merely by virtue of having power to act as an agent for the entitlement holder. Thus, an intermediary is not required to determine at its peril whether a person who purports to be authorized to act for an entitlement holder is in fact authorized to do so. If an entitlement holder wishes to be able to act through agents, the entitlement holder can establish appropriate arrangements in advance with the securities intermediary.

One important application of this principle is that if an entitlement holder grants a security interest in its security entitlements to a third-party lender, the intermediary owes no duties to the secured party, unless the intermediary has entered into a "control" agreement in which it agrees to act on entitlement orders originated by the secured party. See Section 8-106. Even though the security agreement or some other document may give the secured party authority to act as agent for the debtor, that would not make the secured party an "appropriate person" to whom the security intermediary owes duties. If the entitlement holder and securities intermediary have agreed to such a control arrangement, then the intermediary's action in following instructions from the secured party would satisfy the subsection (a) duty. Although an agent, such as the secured party in this example, is not an "appropriate person," an entitlement order is "effective" if originated by an authorized person. See Section 8-107(a) and (b). Moreover, Section 8-507(a) provides that the intermediary satisfies its duty if it acts in accordance with the entitlement holder's agreement.

4. Subsection (b) provides that an intermediary is liable for a wrongful transfer if the entitlement order was "ineffective." Section 8-107 specifies whether an entitlement order is effective. An "effective entitlement order" is different from an

"entitlement order originated by an appropriate person." An entitlement order is effective under Section 8-107(b) if it is made by the appropriate person, or by a person who has power to act for the appropriate person under the law of agency, or if the appropriate person has ratified the entitlement order or is precluded from denying its effectiveness. Thus, although a securities intermediary does not have a duty to act on an entitlement order originated by the entitlement holder's agent, the intermediary is not liable for wrongful transfer if it does so.

Subsection (b), together with Section 8-107, has the effect of leaving to other law most of the questions of the sort dealt with by Article 4A for wire transfers of funds, such as allocation between the securities intermediary and the entitlement order of the risk of fraudulent entitlement orders.

5. The term entitlement order does not cover all directions that a customer might give a broker concerning securities held through the broker. Article 8 is not a codification of all of the law of customers and stockbrokers. Article 8 deals with the settlement of securities trades, not the trades. The term entitlement order does not refer to instructions to a broker to make trades, that is, enter into contracts for the purchase or sale of securities. Rather, the entitlement order is the mechanism of transfer for securities held through intermediaries, just as indorsements and instructions are the mechanism for securities held directly. In the ordinary case the customer's direction to the broker to deliver the securities at settlement is implicit in the customer's instruction to the broker to sell. The distinction is, however, significant in that this section has no application to the relationship between the customer and broker with respect to the trade itself. For example, assertions by a customer that it was damaged by a broker's failure to execute a trading order sufficiently rapidly or in the proper manner are not governed by this Article.

Definitional Cross References

"Agreement"–Section 1-201(3)
"Appropriate person"–Section 8-107
"Effective"–Section 8-107
"Entitlement holder"–Section 8-102(a)(7)
"Entitlement order"–Section 8-102(a)(8)
"Financial asset"–Section 8-102(a)(9)
"Securities intermediary"–Section 8-102(a)(14)
"Security entitlement"–Section 8-102(a)(17)

Section 8–508. Duty of Securities Intermediary to Change Entitlement Holder's Position to Other Form of Security Holding.

A securities intermediary shall act at the direction of an entitlement holder to change a security entitlement into another available form of holding for which the entitlement holder is eligible, or to cause the financial asset to be transferred to a securities account of the entitlement holder with another securities intermediary. A securities intermediary satisfies the duty if:

(1) the securities intermediary acts as agreed upon by the entitlement holder and the securities intermediary; or

(2) in the absence of agreement, the securities intermediary exercises due care in accordance with reasonable commercial standards to follow the direction of the entitlement holder.

UCC

Added by Laws 1997, Ch. 566, § 5, eff. Oct. 10, 1997. See legislative history following § 8–101 for explanation of legislative intent.

Official Comment

1. This section states another aspect of the duties of securities intermediaries that make up security entitlements – the obligation of the securities intermediary to change an entitlement holder's position into any other form of holding for which the entitlement holder is eligible or to transfer the entitlement holder's position to an account at another intermediary. This section does not state unconditionally that the securities intermediary is obligated to turn over a certificate to the customer or to cause the customer to be registered on the books of the issuer, because the customer may not be eligible to hold the security directly. For example, municipal bonds are now commonly issued in "book-entry only" form, in which the only entity that the issuer will register on its own books is a depository.

If security certificates in registered form are issued for the security, and individuals are eligible to have the security registered in their own name, the entitlement holder can request that the intermediary deliver or cause to be delivered to the entitlement holder a certificate registered in the name of the entitlement holder or a certificate indorsed in blank or specially indorsed to the entitlement holder. If security certificates in bearer form are issued for the security, the entitlement holder can request that the intermediary deliver or cause to be delivered a certificate in bearer form. If the security can be held by individuals directly in uncertificated form, the entitlement holder can request that the security be registered in its name. The specification of this duty does not determine the pricing terms of the agreement in which the duty arises.

2. The same "agreement/due care" formula is used in this section as in the other Part 5 sections on the duties of intermediaries. So too, the rules of Section 8-509 apply to the Section 8-508 duty.

Definitional Cross References

"Agreement"–Section 1-201(3)
"Entitlement holder"–Section 8-102(a)(7)
"Financial asset"–Section 8-102(a)(9)
"Securities intermediary"–Section 8-102(a)(14)
"Security entitlement"–Section 8-102(a)(17)

Section 8–509. Specification of Duties of Securities Intermediary by Other Statute or Regulation; Manner of Performance of Duties of Securities Intermediary and Exercise of Rights of Entitlement Holder.

(a) If the substance of a duty imposed upon a securities intermediary by sections 8–504 through 8–508 is the subject of other statute, regulation, or rule, compliance with that statute, regulation, or rule satisfies the duty.

(b) To the extent that specific standards for the performance of the duties of a securities intermediary or the exercise of the rights of an entitlement holder are not specified by other statute, regulation, or rule or by agreement between the securities intermediary and entitlement holder, the securities intermediary shall perform its duties and the entitlement holder shall exercise its rights in a commercially reasonable manner.

(c) The obligation of a securities intermediary to perform the duties imposed by sections 8–504 through 8–508 is subject to:

(1) rights of the securities intermediary arising out of a secu rity interest under a security agreement with the entitlement holder or otherwise; and

(2) rights of the securities intermediary under other law, regulation, rule, or agreement to withhold performance of its duties as a result of unfulfilled obligations of the entitle ment holder to the securities intermediary.

(d) Sections 8–504 through 8–508 do not require a securities intermediary to take any action that is prohibited by other statute, regulation, or rule.

Added by Laws 1997, Ch. 566, § 5, eff. Oct. 10, 1997. See legislative history following § 8–101 for explanation of legislative intent.

Official Comment

This Article is not a comprehensive statement of the law governing the relationship between broker-dealers or other securities intermediaries and their customers. Most of the law governing that relationship is the common law of contract and agency, supplemented or supplanted by regulatory law. This Article deals only with the most basic commercial/property law principles governing the relationship. Although Sections 8-504 through 8-508 specify certain duties of securities intermediaries to entitlement holders, the point of these sections is to identify what it means to have a security entitlement, not to specify the details of performance of these duties.

For many intermediaries, regulatory law specifies in great detail the intermediary's obligations on such matters as safekeeping of customer property, distribution of proxy materials, and the like. To avoid any conflict between the general statement of duties in this Article and the specific statement of intermediaries' obligations in such regulatory schemes, subsection (a) provides that compliance with applicable regulation constitutes compliance with the duties specified in Sections 8-504 through 8-508.

Definitional Cross References

"Agreement"–Section 1-201(3)
"Entitlement holder"–Section 8-102(a)(7)
"Securities intermediary"–Section 8-102(a)(14)
"Security agreement"–Section 9-105(1)(l)
"Security interest"–Section 1-201(37)

Section 8–510. Rights of Purchaser of Security Entitlement from Entitlement Holder.

(a) An action based on an adverse claim to a financial asset or security entitlement, whether framed in conversion, replevin, constructive trust, equitable lien, or other theory, may not be asserted against a person who purchases a security entitlement, or an interest therein, from an entitlement holder if the purchaser gives value, does not have notice of the adverse claim, and obtains control.

(b) If an adverse claim could not have been asserted against an entitlement holder under Section 8–502, the adverse claim cannot be asserted against a person who purchases a security entitlement, or an interest therein, from the entitlement holder.

(c) In a case not covered by the priority rules in Article 9, a purchaser for value of a security entitlement, or an interest therein, who obtains control has priority over a purchaser of a security entitlement, or an interest therein, who does not obtain control. Purchasers who have control rank equally, except that a securities intermediary as purchaser has priority over a conflicting purchaser who has control unless otherwise agreed by the securities intermediary.

Added by Laws 1997, Ch. 566, § 5, eff. Oct. 10, 1997. See legislative history following § 8–101 for explanation of legislative intent.

Official Comment

1. This section specifies certain rules concerning the rights of persons who purchase interests in security entitlements from entitlement holders. The rules of this section are provided to take account of cases where the purchaser's rights are derivative from the rights of another person who is and continues to be the entitlement holder.

2. Subsection (a) provides that no adverse claim can be asserted against a purchaser of an interest in a security entitlement if the purchaser gives value, obtains control, and does not have notice of the adverse claim. The primary purpose of this rule is to give adverse claim protection to persons who take security interests in security entitlements and obtain control, but do not themselves become entitlement holders.

The following examples illustrate subsection (a):

Example 1. X steals a certificated bearer bond from Owner. X delivers the certificate to Able & Co. for credit to X's securities account. Later, X borrows from Bank and grants bank a security interest in the security entitlement. Bank obtains control under Section 8-106(d)(2) by virtue of an agreement in which Able agrees to comply with entitlement orders originated by Bank. X absconds.

Example 2. Same facts as in Example 1, except that Bank does not obtain a control agreement. Instead, Bank perfects by filing a financing statement.

In both of these examples, when X deposited the bonds X acquired a security entitlement under Section 8-501. Under other law, Owner may be able have a constructive trust imposed on the security entitlement as the traceable product of the bonds that X misappropriated. X granted a security interest in that entitlement to Bank. Bank was a purchaser of an interest in the security entitlement from X. In Example 1, although Bank was not a person who acquired a security entitlement from the intermediary, Bank did obtain control. If Bank did not have notice of Owner's claim, Section 8-510(a) precludes Owner from asserting an adverse claim against Bank. In Example 2, Bank had a perfected security interest, but did not obtain control. Accordingly, Section 8-510(a) does not preclude Owner from asserting its adverse claim against Bank.

3. Subsection (b) applies to the indirect holding system a limited version of the "shelter principle." The following example illustrates the relatively limited class of cases for which it may be is needed:

Example 3. Thief steals a certificated bearer bond from Owner. Thief delivers the certificate to Able & Co. for credit to Thief's securities account. Able forwards the certificate to a clearing corporation for credit to Able's account. Later Thief instructs Able to sell the positions in the bonds. Able sells to Baker & Co., acting as broker for Buyer. The trade is settled by book-entries in the accounts of Able and Baker at the clearing corporation, and in the accounts of Thief and Buyer at Able and Baker respectively. Owner may be able to reconstruct the trade records to show that settlement occurred in such fashion that the "same bonds" that were carried in Thief's account at Able are traceable into Buyer's account at Baker. Buyer later decides to donate the bonds to Alma Mater University and executes an assignment of its rights as entitlement holder to Alma Mater.

Buyer had a position in the bonds, which Buyer held in the form of a security entitlement against Baker. Buyer then made a gift of the position to Alma Mater. Although Alma Mater is a purchaser, Section 1-201(33), it did not give value. Thus, Alma Mater is a person who purchased a security entitlement, or an interest therein, from an entitlement holder (Buyer). Buyer was protected against Owner's adverse claim by the Section 8-502 rule. Thus, by virtue of the Section 8-510(b), Owner is also precluded from asserting an adverse claim against Alma Mater.

4. Subsection (c) specifies a priority rule for cases where an entitlement holder transfers conflicting interests in the same security entitlement to different purchasers. It follows the same principle as the Article 9 priority rule for investment property, that is, control trumps non-control. Indeed, the most significant category of conflicting "purchasers" may be secured parties. Priority questions for security interests, however, are governed by the rules in Article 9. Subsection (c) applies only to cases not covered by the Article 9 rules. It is intended primarily for disputes over conflicting claims arising out of repurchase agreement transactions that are not covered by the other rules set out in Article 8 and 9.

The following example illustrates subsection (c):

Example 4. Dealer holds securities through an account at Alpha Bank. Alpha Bank in turns holds through a clearing corporation account. Dealer transfers securities to RP1 in a "hold in custody" repo transaction. Dealer then transfers the same securities to RP2 in another repo transaction. The repo to RP2 is implemented by transferring the securities from Dealer's regular account at Alpha Bank to a special account maintained by Alpha Bank for Dealer and RP2. The agreement among Dealer, RP2, and Alpha Bank provides that Dealer can make substitutions for the securities but RP2 can direct Alpha Bank to sell any securities held in the special account. Dealer becomes insolvent. RP1 claims a prior interest in the securities transferred to RP2.

In this example Dealer remained the entitlement holder but agreed that RP2 could initiate entitlement orders to Dealer's security intermediary, Alpha Bank. If RP2 had become the entitlement holder, the adverse claim rule of Section 8-502 would apply. Even if RP2 does not become the entitlement holder, the arrangement among Dealer, Alpha Bank, and RP2 does suffice to give RP2 control. Thus, under Section 8-510(c), RP2 has priority over RP1, because RP2 is a purchaser who obtained control, and RP1 is a purchaser who did not obtain control. The same result could be reached under Section 8-510(a) which provides that RP1's earlier in time interest cannot be asserted as an adverse claim against RP2. The same result would follow under the Article 9 priority rules if the interests of RP1 and RP2 are characterized as "security interests," see Section 9-115(5)(a). The main point of the rules of Section 8-510(c) is to ensure that there will be clear rules to cover the conflicting claims of RP1 and RP2 without characterizing their interests as Article 9 security interests.

The priority rules in Article 9 for conflicting security interests also include a default rule of pro rata treatment for cases where multiple secured parties have obtained control but omitted to specify their respective rights by agreement. See Section 9-115(5)(b) and Comment 6 to Section 9-115. Because the purchaser priority rule in Section 8-510(c) is intended to track the Article 9 priority rules, it too has a pro rata rule for cases where multiple non-secured party purchasers have obtained control but omitted to specify their respective rights by agreement.

Definitional Cross References

"Adverse claim"–Section 8-102(a)(1)

"Control"–Section 8-106
"Entitlement holder"–Section 8-102(a)(7)
"Notice of adverse claim"Section 8-105
"Purchase"–Section 1-201(32)
"Purchaser"–Section 1-201(33) & 8-116
"Securities intermediary"–Section 8-102(a)(14)
"Security entitlement"–Section 8-102(a)(17)
"Value"–Section 1-201(44) & 8-116

Section 8–511. Priority among Security Interests and Entitlement Holders.

(a) Except as otherwise provided in subsections (b) and (c), if a securities intermediary does not have sufficient interests in a particular financial asset to satisfy both its obligations to entitlement holders who have security entitlements to that financial asset and its obligation to a creditor of the securities intermediary who has a security interest in that financial asset, the claims of entitlement holders, other than the creditor, have priority over the claim of the creditor.

(b) A claim of a creditor of a securities intermediary who has a security interest in a financial asset held by a securities intermediary has priority over claims of the securities intermediary's entitlement holders who have security entitlements with respect to that financial asset if the creditor has control over the financial asset.

(c) If a clearing corporation does not have sufficient financial assets to satisfy both its obligations to entitlement holders who have security entitlements with respect to a financial asset and its obligation to a creditor of the clearing corporation who has a security interest in that financial asset, the claim of the creditor has priority over the claims of entitlement holders.

Added by Laws 1997, Ch. 566, § 5, eff. Oct. 10, 1997. See legislative history following § 8–101 for explanation of legislative intent.

Official Comment

1. This section sets out priority rules for circumstances in which a securities intermediary fails leaving an insufficient quantity of securities or other financial assets to satisfy the claims of its entitlement holders and the claims of creditors to whom it has granted security interests in financial assets held by it. Subsection (a) provides that entitlement holders' claims have priority except as otherwise provided in subsection (b), and subsection (b) provides that the secured creditor's claim has priority if the secured creditor obtains control, as defined in Section 8-106. The following examples illustrate the operation of these rules.

Example 1. Able & Co., a broker, borrows from Alpha Bank and grants Alpha Bank a security interest pursuant to a written agreement which identifies certain securities that are to be collateral for the loan, either specifically or by category. Able holds these securities in a clearing corporation account. Able becomes insolvent and it is discovered that Able holds insufficient securities to satisfy the claims of customers who have paid for securities that they held in accounts with Able and the collateral claims of Alpha Bank. Alpha Bank's security interest in the security entitlements that Able holds through the clearing corporation account may be perfected under the automatic perfection rule of Section 9-115(4)(c), but Alpha Bank did not obtain control under Section 8-106. Thus, under Section 8-511(a) the entitlement holders' claims have priority over Alpha Bank's claim.

Example 2. Able & Co., a broker, borrows from Beta Bank and grants Beta Bank a security interest in securities that Able holds in a clearing corporation account. Pursuant to the security agreement, the securities are debited from Alpha's account and credited to Beta's account in the clearing corporation account. Able becomes insolvent and it is discovered that Able holds insufficient securities to satisfy the claims of customers who have paid for securities that they held in accounts with Able and the collateral claims of Alpha Bank. Although the transaction between Able and Beta took the form of an outright transfer on the clearing corporation's books, as between Able and Beta, Able remains the owner and Beta has a security interest. In that respect the situation is no different than if Able had delivered bearer bonds to Beta in pledge to secure a loan. Beta's security interest is perfected, and Beta obtained control. See Sections 8-106 and 9-115. Under Section 8-511(b), Beta Bank's security interest has priority over claims of Able's customers.

The result in Example 2 is an application to this particular setting of the general principle expressed in Section 8-503, and explained in the Comments thereto, that the entitlement holders of a securities intermediary cannot assert rights against third parties to whom the intermediary has wrongfully transferred interests, except in extremely unusual circumstances where the third party was itself a participant in the transferor's wrongdoing. Under subsection (b) the claim of a secured creditor of a securities intermediary has priority over the claims of entitlement holders if the secured creditor has obtained control. If, however, the secured creditor acted in collusion with the intermediary in violating the intermediary's obligation to its entitlement holders, then under Section 8-503(e), the entitlement holders, through their representative in insolvency proceedings, could recover the interest from the secured creditor, that is, set aside the security interest.

2. The risk that investors who hold through an intermediary will suffer a loss as a result of a wrongful pledge by the intermediary is no different than the risk that the intermediary might fail and not have the securities that it was supposed to be holding on behalf of its customers, either because the securities were never acquired by the intermediary or because the intermediary wrongfully sold securities that should have been kept to satisfy customers' claims. Investors are protected against that risk by the regulatory regimes under which securities intermediaries operate. Intermediaries are required to maintain custody, though clearing corporation accounts or in other approved locations, of their customers' securities and are prohibited from using customers' securities in their own business activities. Securities firms who are carrying both customer and proprietary positions are not permitted to grant blanket liens to lenders covering all securities which they hold, for their own account or for their customers. Rather, securities firms designate specifically which positions they are pledging. Under SEC Rules 8c-1 and 15c2-1, customers' securities can be pledged only to fund loans to customers, and only with the consent of the customers. Customers' securities cannot be pledged for loans for the firm's proprietary business; only proprietary positions can be pledged for proprietary loans. SEC Rule 15c3-3 implements these prohibitions in fashion tailored to modern securities firm accounting systems by requiring brokers to maintain a sufficient inventory of securities, free from any liens, to satisfy the claims of all of their customers for fully paid and excess margin securities. Revised Article 8 mirrors that requirement, specifying in Section 8-504 that a securities intermediary must maintain a sufficient quantity of investment property to satisfy all security entitlements, and may not grant security interests in the positions it is required to hold for customers, except as authorized by th e customers.

If a failed brokerage has violated the customer protection regulations and does not have sufficient securities to satisfy customers claims, its customers are protected against loss from a shortfall by the Securities Investor Protection Act ('SIPA'). Securities firms required to register as brokers or dealers are also required to become members of the Securities Investor Protection Corporation ('SIPC'), which provides their customers with protection somewhat similar to that provided by FDIC and other deposit insurance programs for bank depositors. When a member firm fails, SIPC is authorized to initiate a liquidation proceeding under the provisions of SIPA. If the assets of the securities firm are insufficient to satisfy all customer claims, SIPA makes contributions to the estate from a fund financed by assessments on its members to protect customers against losses up to $500,000 for cash and securities held at member firms.

Article 8 is premised on the view that the important policy of protecting investors against the risk of wrongful conduct by their intermediaries is sufficiently treated by other law.

3. Subsection (c) sets out a special rule for secured financing provided to enable clearing corporations to complete settlement. The reasons that secured financing arrangements are needed in such circumstances are explained in Comment 7 to Section 9-115. In order to permit clearing corporations to establish liquidity facilities where necessary to ensure completion of settlement, subsection (c) provides a priority for secured lenders to such clearing corporations. Subsection (c) does not turn on control because the clearing corporation may be the top tier securities intermediary for the securities pledged, so that there may be no practicable method for conferring control on the lender.

Definitional Cross References

"Clearing corporation"–Section 8-102(a)(5)
"Control"–Section 8-106
"Entitlement holder"–Section 8-102(a)(7)
"Financial asset"–Section 8-102(a)(9)
"Securities intermediary"–Section 8-102(a)(14)
"Security entitlement"–Section 8-102(a)(17)
"Security interest"–Section 1-201(37)
"Value"–Section 1-201(44) & 8-116

PART 6

TRANSITION PROVISIONS FOR REVISED ARTICLE 8 AND FOR THE CONFORMING AMENDMENTS TO ARTICLES 1, 5, 9 AND 13

Section 8–601. Savings Clause; Effect on Prior Perfected Security Interest.

(a) As used in this part, the term "this act" means that chapter of the laws of 1997 which repealed former Article 8 of this code, added this article to this code, and made conforming amendments to provisions of other articles of this code.

(b) This act does not affect an action or proceeding commenced before this act takes effect. An oral contract or a modification of contract entered into before the date this act takes effect does not become enforceable by reason of operation of Section 8–113.

(c) If a security interest in a security is perfected at the date this Act takes effect, and the action by which the security interest was perfected would suffice to perfect a security interest under this Act, no further action is required to continue perfection. If a security interest in a security is perfected at the date this Act takes effect but the action by which the security interest was perfected would not suffice to perfect a security interest under this Act, the security interest remains perfected for a period of 12 months after the effective date of this Act and continues perfected thereafter if appropriate action to perfect under this Act is taken within that period. If a security interest is perfected at the date this Act takes effect and the security interest can be perfected by filing under this Act, a financing statement signed by the secured party instead of by the debtor may be filed within that period to continue perfection or thereafter to perfect.

Added by Laws 1997, Ch. 566, § 5, eff. Oct. 10, 1997. See legislative history following § 8–101 for explanation of legislative intent.

Section 8–602. Cross-References to Former Article 8; Meaning or Interpretation.

(a) Any reference made in law to a bond or other security or instrument to be issued hereafter under the authority of such law as being a negotiable instrument or security under former Article 8 of this code shall be deemed to mean and refer to such bond or other security or instrument issued on or after the effective date of this act as being one to be governed by the provisions of this new Article 8.

(b) The provisions of subsection (a) shall not be deemed to impair in any manner the obligations of any bond or other security or instrument previously issued and in existence on the effective date of this Act and the same shall continue to be governed by its covenants. The provisions of this Act shall apply to such previously issued and existing bond or other security or instrument only to the extent that the provisions of this Act can be harmonized with the provisions of covenants existing on the effective date of this Act to which such bond or other security or instrument is subject on such date, without impairing its obligations.

Added by Laws 1997, Ch. 566, § 5, eff. Oct. 10, 1997. See legislative history following § 8–101 for explanation of legislative intent.

Official Comment

If the State has adopted the Uniform Act for the Simplification of Fiduciary Security Transfers, or similar legislation, it should be repealed.

ARTICLE 9
SECURED TRANSACTIONS; SALES OF ACCOUNTS, CONTRACT RIGHTS AND CHATTEL PAPER

PART 1

SHORT TITLE, APPLICABILITY AND DEFINITIONS

PART 2

VALIDITY OF SECURITY AGREEMENT AND RIGHTS OF PARTIES THERETO

PART 3

RIGHTS OF THIRD PARTIES; PERFECTED AND UNPERFECTED SECURITY INTERESTS; RULES OF PRIORITY

PART 4

FILING

PART 5

DEFAULT

PART 1

SHORT TITLE, APPLICABILITY AND DEFINITIONS

Section 9–101. Short Title.

This Article shall be known and may be cited as Uniform Commercial Code—Secured Transactions.

New York Annotations

The basic policy of Article 9 is to eliminate technical distinctions between forms of security devices such as chattel mortgages, conditional sales, trust receipts, and to substitute one uniform set of rules for all security transactions which would vary in certain respects depending upon the functional nature and the subject matter of the transaction. The elimination of these distinctions will remove traps based upon formal technicalities, resulting from the unrelated development of the law pertaining to various types of security transactions in personal property, and not upon any apparent fundamental public policy. Where functional differences are important the Code preserves those distinctions in a somewhat different terminology, e.g. purchase money security interests.

To implement this basic policy, Article 9 in general either carries forward into all fields of security transactions principles which have been formulated in some fields of New York law, or plugs gaps in certain fields in respect of problems for which there is now no satisfactory answer in New York law, or (in surprisingly few situations) adopts rules which are probably contrary to all New York precedents.

Thus, many of the provisions of Article 9 merely apply to all fields of security transactions in personal property those principles which have already been established by the most recently adopted New York statutes, namely, the Factor's Lien Act, the Uniform Trust Receipts Act, and the Dealer's Chattel Mortgage Act. Accordingly, provisions permitting the acquisition of a lien on after-acquired property (see annotations to Section 9–204) without cumbersome and expensive paper work, or creating a security interest to secure future advances, or relating to filing of a simple financing statement, or governing the effect of a filing or lack of filing and setting out rights as to proceeds of collateral, although they may change New York rules in respect of some security devices, are founded on the present policies either of the Factor's Lien Act or of the Uniform Trust Receipts Act, or both. On "general intangibles" the Code, to a considerable extent, codifies the law worked out on a case by case approach over the last century in the various jurisdictions.

Section 9–205 abrogates Benedict v. Ratner principles which were adopted as part of New York law, but which have been repeatedly diminished in vitality by statute.

The gaps in New York law which are plugged by the provisions of Article 9 are many and are pointed out in the annotations which follow.

For a textual treatment of this Article, see, Spivack, Secured Transactions (Under the Uniform Commercial Code) (1960). Helpful law review materials include: Gilmore and Axelrod, "Chattel Security," 57 Yale L.J. 517, 761 (1948) (non-Code law); Coogan, "Article 9 of the Uniform Commercial Code; Priorities Among Secured Creditors and the Floating Lien," 72 Harv.L.Rev. 838 (1959); Coogan and Bok, "The Impact of Article 9 of the Uniform Commercial Code on the Corporate Indenture," 69 Yale L.J. 203 (1959); Hanna, "The Secured Creditor in Bankruptcy," 14 Rutgers L.Rev. 471 (1960); and Kennedy, "The Trustee in Bankruptcy Under the Uniform Commercial Code; Some Problems Suggested by Articles 2 and 9," 14 Rutgers L. Rev. 518 (1960).

Historical Note: The Law Revision Commission reported that "Article 9 would accomplish a significant reform of the law of personal property security. The Commission believes that the approach taken by Article 9 as a whole is sound in theory and satisfactorily developed in most of its elements." 1956 Report, p. 60. Either during or after the Commission study 46 of the Article's 54 sections were revised by the sponsors. At that time more than 80% of the Law Revision Commission's suggestions were adopted wholly or in part.

Official Uniform Comment

This Article sets out a comprehensive scheme for the regulation of security interests impersonal property and fixtures. It supersedes prior legislation dealing with such security devices as chattel mortgages, conditional sales, trust receipts, factor's liens and assignments of accounts receivable (see Note to Section 9–102).

Consumer installment sales and consumer loans present special problems of a nature which makes special regulation of them inappropriate in a general commercial codification. Many states now regulate such loans and sales under small loan acts, retail installment selling acts and the like. The National Conference of Commissioners on Uniform State Laws has proposed a Uniform Consumer Credit Code dealing with this subject. While this Article applies generally to security interests in consumer goods, it is not designed to supersede such regulatory legislation (see Notes to Section 9–102 and 9–203). Nor is this Article designed as a substitute for small loan acts or retail installment selling acts in any state which does not presently have such legislation.

Pre-Code law recognized a wide variety of security devices, which came into use at various times to make possible different types of secured financing. Differences between one device and another persisted, in formal requisites, in the secured party's rights against the debtor and third parties, in the debtor's rights against the secured party, and in filing requirements, although many of those differences no longer served any useful function. Thus an unfiled chattel mortgage was by the law of many states "void" against creditors generally; a conditional sale, often available as a substitute for the chattel mortgage, was in some states valid against all creditors without filing, and in states where filing is required was, if unfiled, void only against lien creditors. The recognition of so many separate security devices had the result that half a dozen filing systems covering chattel security devices might be maintained within a state, some on a county basis, others on a state-wide basis, each of which had to be separately checked to determine a debtor's status.

Nevertheless, despite the great number of security devices there remained gaps in the structure. In many states, for example, a security interest could not be taken in inventory or a stock in trade although there was a real need for such financing. It was often baffling to try to maintain a technically valid security interest when financing a manufacturing process, where the collateral starts out a raw materials, becomes work in process and ends as finished goods. Furthermore, it was by no means clear, even to specialists, how under pre-Code law a security interest might be taken in many finds of intangible property—such as television or motion picture rights—which have come to be an important source of commercial collateral.

While the chattel mortgage was adaptable for use in almost any situation where goods are collateral, there were limitations, sometimes highly technical, on the use of other devices, such as the conditional sale and particularly the trust receipt. The cases are many in which a security transaction described by the parties as a conditional sale or a trust receipt was later determined by a court to be something else, usually a chattel mortgage. The consequence of such a determination was typically to void the security interest against creditors because the security agreement was not filed as a chattel mortgage (even though it may have been filed as a conditional sale or a trust receipt). The already mentioned difficulty of financing on the security of inventory has been got around to some extent by the device known as "field warehousing" as well as by the use of the trust receipt. After 1940 a number of states generally authorized inventory financing by enacting statutes, similar although not uniform, known as "factor's lien" acts. Also after 1940 the increasingly important business of lending against accounts receivable inspired new statutes in that field in more than thirty states.

The growing complexity of financing transactions forced legislatures to keep piling new statutory provisions on top of our inadequate and already sufficiently complicated nineteenth-century structure of security law. The results of this continuing development were increasing costs to both parties and increasing uncertainty as to their rights and the rights of third parties dealing with them.

The aim of this Article is to provide a simple and unified structure within which the immense variety of present-day secured financing transactions can go forward with less cost and with greater certainty.

Under this Article the traditional distinctions among security devices, based largely on form, are not retained; the Article applies to all transactions intended to create security interests impersonal property and fixtures, and the single term "security interest" substitutes for the variety of descriptive terms which had grown up at common law and under a hundred-year accretion of statutes. This does not mean that the old forms may not be used, and Section 9–102(2) makes it clear that they may be.

This Article does not determine whether "title" to collateral is in the secured party or in the debtor and adopts neither a "title theory" nor a "lien theory" of security interests. Rights, obligations and remedies under the Article do not depend on the location of title (Section 9–202). The location of title may become important for other purposes—as, for example, in determining the incidence of taxation— and in such a case the parties are left free to contract as they will. In this connection the use of a form which has traditionally been regarded as determinative of title (e.g., the conditional sale) would reasonably be regarded as evidencing the parties' intention with respect to title to the collateral.

Under the Article distinctions based on form (except as between pledge and non-possessory interests) are no longer controlling. For some purposes there are distinctions based on the type of property which constitutes the collateral–industrial and commercial equipment, business inventory, farm products, consumer goods, accounts receivable, documents of title and other intangibles– and, where appropriate, the Article states special rules applicable to financing transactions involving a particular type of property. Despite the statutory simplification a greater degree of flexibility in the financing transaction is allowed than is possible under existing law. The scheme of the Article is to make distinctions, where distinctions are necessary, along functional rather than formal lines.

This has made possible a radical simplification in the formal requisites for creation of a security interest.

A more rational filing system replaces the present system of different files for each security device which is subject to filing requirements. Thus not only is the information contained in the files made more accessible but the cost of procuring credit information, and, incidentally, of maintaining the files, is greatly reduced.

The Article's flexibility and simplified formalities should make it possible for new forms of secured financing, as they develop, to fit comfortably under its provisions, thus avoiding the necessity, so apparent in recent years, of year by year passing new statutes and tinkering with the old ones to allow legitimate business transactions to go forward. The rules set out in this Article are principally concerned with the limits of the secured party's protection against purchasers from and creditors of the debtor. Except for procedure on default, freedom of contract prevails between the immediate parties to the security transaction.

Section 9–102. Policy and Subject Matter of Article.

(1) Except as otherwise provided Section 9–104 on excluded transactions, this Article applies

(a) to any transaction (regardless of its form) which is intended to create a security interest in personal property or fixtures including goods, documents, instruments, general intangibles, chattel paper or accounts; and also

(b) to any sale of accounts or chattel paper.

(2) This Article applies to security interests created by contract including pledge, assignment, chattel mortgage, chattel trust, trust deed, factor's lien, equipment trust, conditional sale, trust receipt, other lien or title retention contract and lease or consignment intended as security. This Article does not apply to statutory liens except as provided in Section 9–310.

(3) The application of this Article to a security interest in a secured obligation is not affected by the fact that the obligation is itself secured by a transaction or interest to which this Article does not apply.

1977 Amendment

Section 9–102 was amended by L. 1977, Ch. 866, effective July 2, 1978. The Section title deleted "scope" and substituted "subject matter" in its place. The words "contract rights" were deleted from paragraphs (a) and (b). Subsection (1) was further amended to conform to the changes in Sections 9–103 and 9–104.

New York Annotations

(1) Note that the term "security interest" is defined in Section 1–201(37). It should also be noted that some agreements, such as certain types of leases or consignments, which formerly were drafted so as not to constitute chattel mortgages, conditional sales, or trust receipts might now under appropriate circumstances constitute "security agreements" within the meaning of Section 1–201(37) and accordingly become subject to the provisions of Article 9. Further, under Section 2–326(3)(c) some consignment sales, which do not create a "security interest", must nevertheless be filed under Article 9.

(2) This subsection makes it clear that the devices dealt with in Article 9 are contractual and that the Article does not apply to statutory liens except in Section 9–310.

(3) This subsection makes it clear that, although real estate mortgages are not governed by the Code, a pledge of a note secured by such a mortgage is within Article 9.

Historical Note: Subsection (1) was changed by adding an explicit reference to Section 9–103 to avoid possible conflict or inconsistency between Section 9–102 and Section 9–103; to include "fixtures" as to which, under revised Section 9–313, it is possible to acquire a security interest in certain kinds of fixtures which are "in place"; to include the new category of collateral denominated "general intangibles" defined in revised Section 9–106; and to conform clause (b) of the subsection to the revision in the definition of a "security interest" in Section 1–201(37) by deleting the undefined concept of a "financing" buyer of accounts, chattel paper, or contract rights so that the Article, except as otherwise excluded, applies to all sales of such kinds of collateral.

Subsection (2) was changed to negate the idea that a security interest under Article 9 is a statutory lien in line with the decision in the case of In re Tele-Tone Radio Corp., 133 F.Supp.739 (D.N.J.1955), and to delete the words "bailment lease", since true leases are frequently referred to as such and this phrase is unnecessary, its subject matter being included in the concept of a lease intended as security.

Subsection (3) was added to make clear the fact that Article 9 does apply to a note, bond, or other instrument which falls within one of the categories of collateral as defined in the Article, even though the instrument is otherwise secured by an interest to which the Article does not apply, such as a real estate mortgage. (1956 Recommendations, pp. 254–255.)

Official Uniform Comment

Prior Uniform Statutory Provision: None.

Purposes:

The main purpose of this Section is to bring all consensual security interests in personal property and fixtures under this Article, except for certain types of transactions excluded by Section 9–104. In addition certain sales of accounts and chattel paper are brought within this Article to avoid difficult problems of distinguishing between transactions intended for security and those not so intended. As to security interests in fixtures created under the law applicable to real estate, see Section 9–313(1).

1. Except for sales of accounts and chattel paper, the principal test whether a transaction comes under this Article is: is the transaction intended to have effect as security? For example, Section 9–104 excludes certain transactions where the security interest (such as an artisan's lien) arises under statute or common law by reason of status and not by consent of the parties. Transactions in the form of consignments or leases are subject to this Article if the understanding of the parties or the effect of the arrangement shows that a security interest was intended. (As to consignments the provisions of Sections 2–326, 9–114 and 9–408 should be consulted.)When it is found that a security interest as defined in Section 1–201(37) was intended, this Article applies regardless of the form of the transaction or the name by which the parties may have christened it. The list of traditional security devices in subsection (2) is illustrative only; other old devices, as well as any new ones which the ingenuity of lawyers may invent, are included, so long as the requisite intent is found. The controlling definition is that contained in subsection (1).

The Article does not in terms abolish existing security devices. The conditional sale or bailment-lease, for example, is not prohibited; but even though it is used, the rules of this Article govern.

2. If an obligation is to repay money lent and is not part of chattel paper, it is either an instrument or a general intangible. A sale of an instrument or general intangible is not within this Article, but a transfer intended to have effect as security for an obligation of the transferor is covered by subsection 1(a). In either case the nature of the transaction is not affected by the fact that collateral is transferred with the instrument or general intangible. Such a transfer is treated as a transfer by operation of law, whether or not it is articulated in the agreement.

An assignment of accounts or chattel paper as security for an obligation is covered by subsection (1)(a). Commercial financing on the basis of accounts and chattel paper is often so conducted that the distinction between a security transfer and a sale is blurred, and a sale of such property is therefore covered by subsection (1)(b) whether intended for security or not, unless excluded by Section 9–104. The buyer then is treated as a secured party, and his interest as a security interest. See Sections 9–105(1)(m), 1–201(37). Certain sales which have nothing to do with commercial financing transactions are excluded by Section 9–104(f); compare Spurlin v. Sloan, 368 S.W.2d 314 (Ky. 1963). See also Section 9–302(1)(e), exempting from filing casual or isolated assignments, and Section 9–302(2), preserving the perfected status of a security interest against the original debtor when a secured party assigns his interest.

3. In general, problems of choice of law in this Article as to the validity of security agreements are governed by Section 1–105. Problems of choice of law as to perfection of security interests and the effect of perfection or non-perfection thereof, including rules requiring reperfection, are governed by Section 9–103.

4. An illustration of subsection (3) is as follows: The owner of Blackacre borrows $10,000 from his neighbor, and secures his note by a mortgage on Blackacre. This Article is not applicable to the creation of the real estate mortgage. Nor is it applicable to a sale of the note by the mortgagee, even though the mortgage continues to secure the note. However, when the mortgagee pledges the note to secure his own obligation to X, this Article applies to the security interest thus created, which is a security interest in an instrument even though the instrument is secured by a real estate mortgage. This Article leaves the other law the question of the effect on rights under the mortgage of delivery or non-delivery of the mortgage or of recording or non-recording of an assignment of the mortgagee's interest. See Section 9–104(j). But under Section 3–304(5) recording of the assignment does not of itself prevent X from holding the note in due course.

5. While most sections of this Article apply to a security interest without regard to the nature of the collateral or its use, some sections state special rules with reference

to particular types of collateral. An index of sections where such special rules are stated follows:

ACCOUNTS

Section	
9–102(1)(b)	Sale of accounts subject to Article
9–103(1)	When Article applies; conflict of laws rules
9–104(f)	Certain sales of accounts excluded from Article
9–106	Definitions
9–205	Permissible for debtor to make collections
9–206(1)	Agreement not to assert defenses against assignee
9–301(1)(d)	Unperfected security interest subordinate to certain transferees
9–302(1)(e)	What assignments need not be filed
9–306(5)	Rule when goods whose sale gave rise to an account return to seller's possession
9–318(1)	Rights of assignee subject to defenses
9–318(2)	Modification of contract after assignment of contract right
9–318(3)	When account debtor may pay assignor
9–318(4)	Term prohibiting assignment ineffective
9–401	Place of filing
9–502	Collection rights of secured party
9–504(2)	Rights on default where underlying transaction was sale of accounts or contract rights

CHATTEL PAPER

9–102(1)(b)	Sale subject to Article
9–104(f)	Certain sales excluded from Article
9–105(1)(b)	Definition
9–205	Permissible for debtor to make collections
9–206(1)	Agreement not to assert defenses against assignee
9–207(1)	Duty of secured party in possession to preserve rights against prior parties
9–301(1)(c)	Unperfected security interest subordinate to certain transferees
9–304(1)	Perfection by filing
9–305	When possession by secured party perfects security interest
9–306(5)	Rule when goods whose sale results in chattel paper return to seller's possession
9–308	When purchasers of chattel paper have priority over security interest
9–318(1)	Rights of assignee subject to defenses
9–318(3)	When account debtor may pay assignor
9–502	Collection rights of secured party
9–504(2)	Rights on default where underlying transaction was sale

DOCUMENTS AND INSTRUMENTS

9–105(1)(e)	Definition of document (and see 1–201)
9–105(1)(g)	Definition of instrument
9–206(1)	Rule where buyer of goods signs both negotiable instrument and security agreement
9–207(1)	Duty of secured party in possession of instrument, to preserve rights against prior parties

UCC

9–301(1)(c)	Unperfected security interest subordinate to certain transferees
9–302(1)(b) and (f)	What interests need not be filed
9–304(1)	How security interest can be perfected
9–304(2, 3)	Perfection of security interest in goods in possession of issuer of negotiable document or of other bailee
9–304(4, 5)	Perfection of security interest in instruments or negotiable documents without filing or transfer of possession
9–305	When possession by secured party perfects security interest
9–308	When purchasers of instruments have priority over security interest
9–309	When purchasers of negotiable instruments or negotiable documents have priority over security interest
9–501(1)	Rights on default where collateral is documents
9–502	Collection rights of secured party

GENERAL INTANGIBLES

9–103(2)	When Article applies; conflict of laws rules
9–105	Obligor is "account debtor"
9–106	Definition
9–301(1)(d)	Unperfected security interest subordinate to certain transferees
9–318(1)	Rights of assignee subject to defenses
9–318(3)	When account debtor may pay assignor
9–502	Collection rights of secured party

GOODS

(See also Consumer Goods, Equipment, Farm Products, Inventory)

9–103	When Article applies with regard to goods of a type normally used in more than one jurisdiction; goods covered by certificate of title; conflict of laws rules
9–105(1)(h)	Definition
9–109	Classification of goods as consumer goods, equipment, farm products and inventory
9–203	Formal requisites of security agreement covering certain types of goods (crops or timber)
9–204	Validity of after-acquired property clause covering certain types of goods (crops, consumer goods)
9–205	Permissible for debtor to accept returned goods
9–206(2)	When security agreement can limit or modify warranties on sale
9–301(1)(c)	Unperfected security interest subordinate to certain transferees
9–304(2, 3)	Perfection of security interest in goods in possession of issuer of negotiable document or of other bailee
9–304(5)	Perfection of security interest without filing or transfer of possession where goods in possession of certain bailees
9–305	When possession by secured party perfects security interest
9–306(5)	Rule when goods whose sale gave rise to account or chattel paper return to seller's possession
9–307	When buyers of goods from debtor take free of security interest
9–313	Goods which are or become fixtures
9–314	Goods affixed to other goods
9–315	Goods commingled in a product
9–401(1)	Place of filing for fixtures

9–402	Form of financing statement covering fixtures
9–504(1)	Sale of goods by secured party after default subject to Article 2 (Sales)
	CONSUMER GOODS
9–109(1)	Definition
9–203(2)	Transaction, although subject to this Article, may also be subject to certain regulatory statutes
9–204(2)	Validity of after-acquired property clause
9–206(1)	Buyer's agreement not to assert defenses against an assignee subject to statute or decision which establishes rule for buyers of consumer goods
9–302(1)(d)	When filing not required
9–307(2)	When buyers from debtor take free of security interest
9–401(1)(a)	Place of filing
9–505(1)	Secured party's duty to dispose of repossessed consumer goods
9–507(1)	Secured party's liability for improper disposition of consumer goods after default
	EQUIPMENT
9–103(2)	When Article applies with regard to certain types of equipment normally used in more than one jurisdiction; conflict of laws rules
9–109(2)	Definition
9–302(1)(c)	When filing not required to perfect security interest in certain farm equipment
9–307(2)	When buyers of certain farm equipment from debtor take free of security interest
9–401(1)	Place of filing for equipment used in farming operation
9–503	Secured party's right after default to remove or to render equipment unusable
	FARM PRODUCTS
9–109(3)	Definition
9–203(1)(b)	Formal requisites of security agreement covering crops
9–307	When a buyer of farm products takes free of security interest
9–312(2)	Priority of secured party who gives new value to enable debtor to produce crops
9–401(1)	Place of filing
9–402(1) and (3)	Form of financing statement covering crops
	INVENTORY
9–103(3)	When Article applies with regard to certain types of inventory normally used in more than one jurisdiction; conflict of laws rules
9–109(4)	Definition
9–114	Consigned goods
9–306(5)	Rule where goods whose sale gave rise to account or chattel paper return to seller's possession
9–307(1)	When buyers from debtor take free of security interest
9–312(3), 9–304(5)	When purchase money security interest takes priority over conflicting security interest
9–408	Financing statements covering consigned or leased goods

Cross References:

Sections 9–103 and 9–104.

Point 1: Section 2–326
Point 2: Section 1–105.

Definitional Cross References:

"Account." Section 9–106.
"Chattel paper." Section 9–105.
"Contract." Section 1–201.
"Document." Section 9–105.
"General intangibles." Section 9–106.
"Goods." Section 9–105.
"Instrument." Section 9–105.
"Security interest." Section 1–201.

Section 9–103. Perfection of Security Interests in Multiple State Transactions.

Documents, instruments, letters of credit, and ordinary goods.

(1)(a) This subsection applies to documents, instruments, rights to proceeds of written letters of credit, and goods other than those covered by a certificate of title described in subsection (2), mobile goods described in subsection (3), and minerals described in subsection (5).

(b) Except as otherwise provided in this subsection, perfection and the effect of perfection non-perfection of a security interest in collateral are governed by the law of the jurisdiction where the collateral is when the last event occurs on which is based the assertion that the security interest is perfected or unperfected.

(c) If the parties to a transaction creating a purchase money security interest in goods in one jurisdiction understand at the time that the security interest attaches that the goods will be kept in another jurisdiction, then the law of the other jurisdiction governs the perfection and the effect of perfection or non-perfection of the security interest from the time it attaches until thirty days after the debtor receives possession of the goods and thereafter if the goods are taken to the other jurisdiction before the end of the thirty-day period.

(d) When collateral is brought into and kept in this state while subject to a security interest perfected under the law of the jurisdiction from which the collateral was removed, the security interest remains perfected, but if action is required by Part 3 of this Article to perfect the security interest,

(i) if the action is not taken before the expiration of the period of perfection in the other jurisdiction or the end of four months after the collateral is brought into this state, whichever period first expires, the security interest becomes unperfected at the end of that period and is thereafter deemed to have been unperfected as against a person who became a purchaser after removal;

(ii) if the action is taken before the expiration of the period specified in subparagraph (i), the security interest continues perfected thereafter;

(iii) for the purpose of priority over a buyer of consumer goods (subsection (2) of Section 9-307), the period of the effectiveness of a filing in the jurisdiction from which the collateral is removed is governed by the rules with respect to perfection in subparagraphs (i) and (ii).

(2) Certificate of title.

(a) This subsection applies to goods covered by a certificate of title issued under a statute of this state or of another jurisdiction under the law of which indication of a security interest on the certificate is required as a condition of perfection.

(b) Except as otherwise provided in this subsection, perfection and the effect of perfection or non-perfection of the security interest are governed by the law (including the conflict of laws rules) of the jurisdiction issuing the certificate until four months after the goods are removed from that jurisdiction and thereafter until the goods are registered in another jurisdiction, but in any event not beyond surrender of the certificate. After the expiration of that period, the goods are not covered by the certificate of title within the meaning of this section.

(c) Except with respect to the rights of a buyer described in the next paragraph, a security interest, perfected in another jurisdiction otherwise than by notation on a certificate of title, in goods brought into this state and thereafter covered by a certificate of title issued by this state is subject to the rules stated in paragraph (d) of subsection (1).

(d) If goods are brought into this state while a security interest therein is perfected in any manner under the law of the jurisdiction from which the goods are removed and a certificate of title is issued by this state and the certificate does not show that the goods are subject to the security interest or that they may be subject to security interests not shown on the certificate, the security interest is subordinate to the rights of a buyer of the goods who is not in the business offsetting goods of that kind to the extent that he gives value and receives delivery of the goods after issuance of the certificate and without knowledge of the security interest.

(3) Accounts, general intangibles and mobile goods.

(a) This subsection applies to accounts (other than an account described in subsection (5) on minerals) and general intangibles, other than uncertificated securities and to goods which are mobile and which are of a type normally used in more than one jurisdiction, such as motor vehicles, trailers, rolling stock, airplanes, shipping containers, road building and construction machinery and commercial harvesting machinery and the like, if the goods are equipment or are inventory leased or held for lease by the debtor to others, and are not covered by a certificate of title described in subsection (2).

(b) The law (including the conflict of laws rules) of the jurisdiction in which the debtor is located governs the perfection and the effect of perfection or non-perfection of the security interest.

(c) If, however, the debtor is located in a jurisdiction which is not a part of the United States, and which does not provide for perfection of the security

UCC

interest by filing or recording in that jurisdiction, the law of the jurisdiction in the United States in which the debtor has its major executive office in the United States governs the perfection and the effect of perfection or non-perfection of the security interest through filing. In the alternative, if the debtor is located in a jurisdiction which is not a part of the United States or Canada and the collateral is accounts or general intangibles for money due or to become due, the security interest may be perfected by notification to the account debtor. As used in this paragraph, "United States" includes its territories and possessions and the Commonwealth of Puerto Rico.

(d) A debtor shall be deemed located at his place of business if he has one, at his chief executive office if he has more than one place of business, otherwise at his residence. If, however, the debtor is a foreign air carrier under the Federal Aviation Act of 1958, as amended, it shall be deemed located at the designated office of the agent upon whom service of process may be made on behalf of the foreign air carrier.

(e) A security interest perfected under the law of the jurisdiction of the location of the debtor is perfected until the expiration of four months after a change of the debtor's location to another jurisdiction, or until perfection would have ceased by the law of the first jurisdiction, whichever period first expires. Unless perfected in the new jurisdiction before the end of that period, it becomes unperfected thereafter and is deemed to have been unperfected as against a person who became a purchaser after the change.

(4) Chattel paper.

The rules stated for goods in subsection (1) apply to a possessory security interest in chattel paper. The rules stated for accounts in subsection (3) apply to a non-possessory security interest in chattel paper, but the security interest may not be perfected by notification to the account debtor.

(5) Minerals.

Perfection and the effect of perfection or non-perfection of a security interest which is created by a debtor who has an interest in minerals or the like (including oil and gas) before extraction and which attaches thereto as extracted, or which attaches to an account resulting from the sale thereof at the well head or mine head are governed by the law (including the conflict of laws rules) of the jurisdiction wherein the well head or mine head is located.

(6) Investment property.

(a) This subsection applies to investment property.

(b) Except as otherwise provided in paragraph (f), during the time that a security certificate is located in a jurisdiction, perfection of a security interest, the effect of perfection or non-perfection, and the priority of a security interest in the certificated security represented thereby are governed by the local law of that jurisdiction.

(c) Except as otherwise provided in paragraph (f), perfection of a security interest, the effect of perfection or non-perfection, and the priority of a security interest in an uncertificated security are governed by the local law of the issuer's jurisdiction as specified in Section 8–110(d).

(d) Except as otherwise provided in paragraph (f), perfection of a security interest, the effect of perfection or non-perfection, and the priority of a security interest in a security entitlement or securities account are governed by the local law of the securities intermediary's jurisdiction as specified in Section 8–110(e).

(e) Except as otherwise provided in paragraph (f), perfection of a security interest, the effect of perfection or non-perfection, and the priority of a security interest in a commodity contract or commodity account are governed by the local law of the commodity intermediary's jurisdiction. The following rules determine a "commodity intermediary's jurisdiction" for purposes of this paragraph:

(i) If an agreement between the commodity intermediary and commodity customer specifies that it is governed by the law of a particular jurisdiction, that jurisdiction is the commodity intermediary's jurisdiction.

(ii) If an agreement between the commodity intermediary and commodity customer does not specify the governing law as provided in subparagraph (i), but expressly specifies that the commodity account is maintained at an office in a particular jurisdiction, that jurisdiction is the commodity intermediary's jurisdiction.

(iii) if an agreement between the commodity intermediary and commodity customer does not specify a jurisdiction as provided in subparagraphs (i) or (ii), the commodity intermediary's jurisdiction is the jurisdiction in which is located the office identified in an account statement as the office serving the commodity customer's account.

(iv) If an agreement between the commodity intermediary and commodity customer does not specify a jurisdiction as provided in subparagraphs (i) or (ii) and an account statement does not identify an office serving the commodity customer's account as provided in subparagraph (iii), the commodity intermediary's jurisdiction is the jurisdiction in which is located the chief executive office of the commodity intermediary.

(f) Perfection of a security interest by filing, automatic perfection of a security interest in investment property granted by a broker or securities intermediary, and automatic perfection of a security interest in a commodity contract or commodity account granted by a commodity intermediary are governed by the local law of the jurisdiction in which the debtor is located.

Added by Laws 1977, Ch. 866, eff. July 2, 1978; **amended** by Laws 1982, Ch. 928, eff. Dec. 21, 1982 and deemed to have been in full force and effect on and after Sept. 1, 1982; L. 1997, Ch. 566, eff. Oct. 10, 1997; L. 2000, Ch. 471, eff. Nov. 1, 2000.

New York Annotations

Choice of law. The rules applicable to Article 9 (see also Sections 9–102 and 9-104) are designed to assure as far as possible that the domestic law of a single jurisdiction will apply to a given security transaction regardless of the forum in which the case is litigated. (See Section 1–105.) This section as a whole has no present counterpart in statutory or caselaw.

(1) Some New York authorities suggest that as between the assignor and the assignee many issues relating to the assignment are governed by the law of the place of assignment, e. g. Barry v. Equitable Life Assurance Society, 59 N.Y. 587 (1875). There is authority that the law of the place of performance may govern performance, while interpretation and validity may be referred to the place where the contract was made. Swift and Co. v. Bankers Trust Co., 280 N.Y. 135, 19 N.E.2d 992 (1939); Union National Bank v. Chapman, 169 N.Y. 538, 62 N.E. 672 (1902). Sometimes intention is controlling, and the test may also be expressed in terms of "the most significant contracts." Wilson v. Lewiston Mill Co., 150 N.Y. 314, 44 N.E. 959 (1896); Rubin v. Irving Trust Co., 305 N.Y. 288, 113 N.E. 2d 424 (1953). "Office where the assignor of accounts keeps his records concerning them" is defined in Section 9–105(j) of the New York Code, a definition not contained in the 1958 and 1962 Official Texts.

(2) "General intangibles" is defined in Section 9–106, and the classification of goods as "inventory" or "equipment" is explained in Section 9–109(2) and (4). As to railroad rolling stock, aircraft, and motor vehicles of interstate carriers, see the annotations to Sections 9–104(e) and 9–302(3) for federal aspects of perfection. To the extent that the chief place of business of the debtor is not the same as the place where the equipment is located at the time of the creation of the security interest, this subsection changes New York law. See, e. g. Goetschius v. Brightman, 245 N.Y. 186, 156 N.E. 660 (1927); Youssoupoff v. Widener, 246 N.Y. 174, 158 N.E. 64 (1927). The effect of this subsection should ordinarily be to facilitate this kind of transaction. Note that "chief place of business" is not a defined term.

The last sentence of Subsection (2) conforms to an optional provision offered by the 1962 Official Text and is designed to facilitate loans secured by aircraft owned by foreign carriers making regular flights to the United States. See also the Geneva Convention 4(2) United States Treaties and Other International Agreements 1831 (1953); Treaties, Information and Agreements Series No. 2847.

(3) The first sentence states New York law, since local filing requirements have been held not to apply to valid security interests created elsewhere. Goetschius v. Brightman, *supra.* However, the balance of the subsection works a change in the present rules as to conditional sales. Prior to 1960 a conditional seller who received notice that the goods had been moved from outside the state to a place in this state was required to file in New York within ten days. Personal Property Law, § 74 (prior to 1960). In 1960 that provision was omitted and a requirement was substituted that the seller must refile upon ten days' notice that the buyer changed his residence from outside the state to a place within the state (L.1960, c 1004, Sec 4, eff. Oct. 1, 1960). Under the Code the test is again the fact that the goods are brought into the state. The secured party must perfect within four months after such date, and his knowledge of the removal becomes immaterial. Thus the subsection effects a compromise between the claims of local creditors and purchasers and those of out-of-state lenders. Compare the annotation to Section 9–401. The Code provision is discussed in Churchill Motors v. A. C. Lohman, 16 A.D.2d 560, 229 N.Y.S.2d 570 (3rd Dept. 1962).

(4) This rule is new and is designed to give effect to certificate of title laws requiring compliance therewith to perfect security interests.

(5) New York Code Section 9–103(5) is new. It conforms in part to optional Subsection (5) offered by the 1962 Official Text with respect to the perfection of security interests in accounts and contract rights "if the office where the assignor . . . keeps his records concerning them is not located in . . . the United States." The Official Text of Subsection (5) requires notification to the account debtor for the perfection of the assignment of such accounts and contract rights. New York Code Section 9–103(5) explicitly provides for such perfection upon attachment without filing and without notification to the account debtor.

(6) New York Code Section 9–103(6) is new and has no counterpart in the 1958 and 1962 Official Texts. It provides for the continued validity and perfection of a security interest in accounts, contract rights and general intangibles notwithstanding the removal, after the attachment of the security interest, to another jurisdiction of the debtor's chief place of business with respect to general intangibles or the office where the debtor keeps his records concerning them with respect to accounts or contract rights.

Historical Note: The word "jurisdiction" was substituted for "state" to cover the possibility of conflicts between the law of not only the various states of the United States but foreign provinces or countries.

Subsection (2) was changed for clarification to include within its application the new category of collateral designated as "general intangibles", and also to make it applicable not only to "equipment" but also to certain types of goods classified as inventory of the debtor by reason of their being leased. The last sentence gives to those states which adopt the Code a more positive and certain means of establishing the validity and perfection of a security interest in mobile property where the law in other states having reference to a transaction is not clear either as to conflicts rule or otherwise.

The changes in subsection (3) were merely clarifying and followed suggestions of the Law Revision Commission.

Subsection (4) is new and avoids the possible necessity of duplicating perfection in the case of vehicles subject to a certificate of title law requiring compliance therewith to perfect security interests. The certificate of title law requirements are adopted as the test for perfection. (1956 Recommendations, pp. 256–257; Excerpts, pp. 464–465.)

Official Uniform Comment

Prior Uniform Statutory Provisions: Paragraph 1(d): Section 14, Uniform Conditional Sales Act.

Purposes:

1. The general rules on choice of law between the original parties in section 1–105 apply to this Article. However, when conflicting claims to collateral arise, the question depends on *perfection* of security interests, and thus on the effect of perfection or non-perfection. These problems are dealt with in this section. The general rule (paragraph (1)(b) is that these questions are governed by the law of the jurisdiction where the collateral is when the last event occurs on which is based the assertion that the security interest is perfected or unperfected. This event will frequently be the filing. If the last event is not filing and perfection is through filing, the filing required is in the jurisdiction where the collateral is when the last event occurs; prior filing in another jurisdiction is not effective and is not saved by the four-month rule discussed below, which applies only when the security interest was *perfected* in the jurisdiction from which the collateral was removed. If the security interest was perfected in one jurisdiction and then removed to another jurisdiction, maintenance

of perfection in the latter jurisdiction or failure to do so is the "last event" to which the basic rule refers.

There are, however, exceptions to this basic rule:

2. If the parties to a transaction creating a purchase money security interest in goods understand when the security interest attaches that the collateral will be kept in another jurisdiction, the law of that jurisdiction governs perfection and the effect of perfection or non-perfection until 30 days after the debtor receives possession of the goods (paragraph (1)(c)). A filing in that jurisdiction perfects the security interest even before the goods are removed. The 30-day period is not a period of grace during which filing is unnecessary or has retroactive effect, but merely states the period during which the other jurisdiction is the place of filing. The effect of late filing is governed by other provisions, such as Sections 9–301 and 9–312.

3. If the goods reach that jurisdiction within the 30 days, the effectiveness of the filing in that jurisdiction continues without interruption. If the collateral is not kept in that jurisdiction before the end of the 30-day period, paragraph (1)(c) ceases to be applicable and thereafter the law of the jurisdiction where the collateral is controls perfection. A failure of the collateral to reach the intended destination jurisdiction before the expiration of the 30-day period because of a conflicting claim or otherwise may cause disappointment of expectations that the law of the destination jurisdiction will govern continuously, and caution may dictate filing both in that jurisdiction and in the jurisdiction where the security interest attaches. This section uses the concepts that goods are "kept" in a state or "brought" into a state, and related terms. These concepts imply a stopping place of a permanent nature in the state, not merely transit or storage intended to be transitory.

4.(a) Where the collateral is an automobile or other goods covered by a certificate of title issued by any state and the security interest is perfected by notation on the certificate of title, perfection is controlled by the certificate of title rather than by the law of the state wherein the security interest attached (subsection (2)).

(b) It has long been hoped that "exclusive certificate of title laws" would provide a sure means of controlling property interests in goods like automobiles, which because of their nature cannot readily be controlled by local or statewide filing alone. In theory the certificate of title should control the property interests in the vehicle wherever the vehicle may be. However, two circumstances operate to prevent the perfect operation of the certificate of title device:

First, some states have never adopted certificate of title laws. This results in a problem in the issuance of a certificate of title when the vehicle moves from a non-certificate to a certificate state, because the certificate-issuing officer is in no position to conduct a complete search to ascertain the condition of the title in a state of origin which requires no filing or in which filing could be in any one or more of several localities. Also, it seems that when a vehicle moves from a certificate to a non-certificate state, the officers issuing a new registration for the vehicle are not always meticulous to notify secured parties shown on the certificate to give them a chance to perfect their security interests in the non-certificate state when a new registration is issued. Moreover, some vehicles like mobile homes are not always registered and title certificates are not always issued even in a state which may have certificate laws applicable thereto, because the certificate laws may apply only if the mobile homes use the highways. Registration plates of a mobile home having a certificate could be removed and there would be nothing visible to show that a certificate has ever been issued for it.

Second, various fraudulent devices based on allegations of loss of the certificate of title enable a dishonest person to obtain both an original and a duplicate of title; to have a security interest shown on only one thereof; and then to effect a transfer into a new state on the basis of the clean certificate, no matter how diligent the officers in the second may be.

Given these practical problems, the choice of applicable rules of law after interstate removals of vehicles subject to certificate of title laws is most difficult. This Article provides the rules set forth below.

(c) The security interest perfected by notation on a certificate of title will be recognized without limit as to time; but, of course, perfection by this method ceases if the certificate of title is surrendered (paragraph (2)(b)). Since the secured party ordinarily holds the certificate, surrender thereof could not occur without his action in the matter in some respect. If the vehicle is reregistered in another jurisdiction while the secured party still holds the certificate, a danger of deception to third parties arises. The section provides that the certificate ceases to control after 4 months following removal if reregistration has occurred, but during the 4 months the secured party has the same protection for cases of interstate removal as is set forth in paragraph (1)(d) of the section and Comment 7, subject to additional limitation if the reregistration also involves anew "clean" certificate of title in the removal jurisdiction and a non-professional buyer buys while that new certificate is outstanding. See paragraph (2)(d) and Comment 4(e).

(d) If a vehicle not described in the preceding paragraph (i.e., not covered by a certificate of title) is removed to a certificate state and a certificate is issued therefor, the holder of a security interest has the same 4-month protection, subject to the provision discussed in the next paragraph of Comment.

(e) Where "this state" issues a certificate of title on collateral that has come from another state subject to a security interest perfected in any manner, problems will arise if this state, from whatever cause, fails to show on its certificate the security interest perfected in the other jurisdiction. This state will have every reason, nevertheless, to make its certificate of title reliable to the type of person who most needs to rely on it. Paragraph (2)(d) of the section therefore provides that the security interest perfected in the other jurisdiction is subordinate to the rights of a limited class of persons buying the goods while there is a clean certificate of title issued by this state, without knowledge of the security interest perfected in the other jurisdiction. The limited class are buyers who are non-professionals, i.e., not dealers and not secured parties, because these are ordinarily professionals. The protective rule mentioned does not apply if this state adopts a device used under some certificate of title laws, namely, stating on the certificate of title that the vehicle may be subject to security interests not shown on the certificate, where the collateral came from a non-certificate state.

In any event the security interest perfected out of state becomes unperfected unless reperfected in this state under the usual 4-month rule (paragraph (2)(d) of the section). States which place a cautionary statement on a certificate of title coming from a non-certificate state make provision to reissue the certificate without the caution after four months.

One difficulty is that no state's certificate of title law makes any provision by which a foreign security interest may be reperfected in that state, without the cooperation of the owner or other person holding the certificate in temporarily surrendering the certificate. But that cooperation is not likely to be forth coming from an owner who wrongfully procured the issuance of a new certificate not showing the out-of-state security interest, or from a local secured party finding himself in a priority contest with the out-of-state secured party. The only solution for the out-of-state secured party under present certificate of title laws seems to be reperfect by possession, i.e., by repossessing the goods.

5. The general rules of the section based on location of the collateral could not be applied to certain types of intangible collateral which have no location in any realistic sense, or to certain movable chattels which have no permanent location.

(a) For accounts and general intangibles there is no indispensable or symbolic document which represents the underlying claim, whose endorsement or delivery is the one effectual means of transfer. There is a considerable body of case law dealing with the situs of choses in action such as these. This case law is in the highest degree confused, contradictory and uncertain: it affords no base on which to build a statutory rule.

An account arises typically out of a sale; the contract of sale may be executed in State A, the goods shipped from a warehouse in State B to buyer (account debtor) in State C. The account may then be assigned to an assignee in State D. The seller-assignor may keep his principal records in State E. Under the non-notification system of accounts financing, the seller-assignor, despite the assignment, bills and collects from the account debtor; under notification financing the account debtor makes payment to the assignee, but the bills may be prepared and sent out by either assignor or assignee. The contacts of the transaction are with many jurisdictions: to which one is it appropriate to look for the governing law? Even more complicated situations may be anticipated when the collateral consists of novel or uncommon types of personal property, which fall within the definition of general intangibles.

If we bear in mind that out principal question is where certain financing statements shall be filed, two things become clear. *First:* since the purpose of filing is to allow subsequent creditors of the *debtor-assignor* to determine the true status of his affairs, the place chosen must be one which such creditors would normally associate with the assignor; thus the place of business of the assignee and the places of business or residences of the various account debtors must be rejected in ordinary situations. *Second:* the place chosen must be one which can be determined with the least possible risk of error. The place chosen by subsection (3) is the debtor's location, which is ordinarily the location of its chief executive office. This concept is discussed below.

(b) Another class of collateral for which a special rule is stated in subsection (3) is mobile goods of types which are normally moved for use from one jurisdiction to another. Such goods are generally classified as equipment; sometimes they may be classified as inventory, for example, goods leased by a professional lessor. Subsection (3) provides that a security interest in such equipment or inventory is subject to this Article when the debtor's location, i.e., ordinarily its chief executive office, is in this state.

While automobiles are obviously mobile goods, they will in most cases be covered by subsection (2) of this section and therefore excluded from subsection (3) by paragraph (a) thereof. If an automobile is not covered by a certificate of title and is classified as equipment or as inventory under lease, it will be subject to subsection (3). Automobiles and other mobile goods which are classified as consumer goods are not subject to subsection (3).

The rule of subsection (3) applies to goods of a type "normally used" in more than one jurisdiction; there is no requirement that particular goods be in fact used out of state. Thus, if an enterprise whose chief executive office is in State X keeps in State Y goods of the type covered by subsection (3), the rule of subsection (3) requires filing in State X even though the goods never leave State Y.

(c) "Chief executive office" does not mean the place of incorporation; it means the place from which in fact the debtor manages the main part of this business operations. This is the place where persons dealing with the debtor would normally look for credit information, and is the appropriate place for filing. The term "chief executive office" is not defined in this Section or elsewhere in this Act. Doubt may arise as to which is the "chief executive office" of a multi-state enterprise, but it would be rare that there could be more than two possibilities. A secured party in such a case may easily protect himself at no great additional burden by filing in each possible place. The subsection states a rule which will be simple to apply in most cases, and which makes it possible to dispense with much burdensome and useless filing.

(d) If the location of the debtor is moved after a security interest has been perfected in another jurisdiction, the secured party has four months within which to refile, unless the perfection in the original jurisdiction would have expired earlier (paragraph (3)(e)).

(e) Under subsection (3) each state other than that of the debtor's location in effect disclaims jurisdiction over certain accounts and general intangibles which, by common law rules, might be held to be within its jurisdiction; in the same way there is a disclaimer of jurisdiction over mobile chattels, even though they may be physically located within the state much of the time. If the jurisdiction whose law controls under this rule is a United States jurisdiction or has enacted legislation permitting perfection of the security interest by filing or recording in that jurisdiction, the law of that jurisdiction will be recognized in the disclaiming jurisdiction as perfecting the security interest. The jurisdiction of the debtor's location may not, however, have such legislation. For example, mobile equipment is used in New York; the debtor's chief place of business is in a Canadian jurisdiction which will not permit or recognize filing as to property not physically located therein. Paragraph (3)(c) solves this difficulty by permitting perfection through filing in the jurisdiction in the United States in which the debtor has its major executive office in the United States. Where the debtor is not located in the United States or Canada and the collateral is accounts or general intangibles for money due or to become due, the secured party may alternatively perfect by notification to account debtors.

(f) A sentence in paragraph (3)(d) provides a special rule for security interests in airplanes owned by a foreign air carrier. Without that sentence subsection (3) might refer such a case to the law of a foreign nation whose law is difficult or impossible to ascertain. The sentence clears up such doubts by treating as the location of the carrier the office designated for service of process in the United States under the Federal Aviation Act of 1958. To the extent that it is applicable, the Convention on the International Recognition of Rights in Aircraft (Geneva Convention) supersedes state legislation on this subject, as set forth in Section 9–302(3), but some nations are not parties to that Convention.

6. Subsection (4) deals with chattel paper, a semi-intangible security interest which may be perfected either by possession or by filing (Sections 9–304(1), 9–305). As to possessory security, subsection (4) provides that chattel paper shall be subject to the same rule as goods in subsection (1). As to non-possessory security, subsection (4) provides that it shall be subject to the same rule as the intangibles under subsection (3), except that notification to the account debtor is ruled out as an optional means of perfection under paragraph (3)(c). The reason for thesis that a different alternative, possession, is available for chattel paper.

7. In addition to the foregoing rules defining which jurisdiction governs perfection of a security interest in the first instance, "this state" (i.e., a destination state after removal) adds its own rules requiring reperfection following removal of collateral other than that described in subsections (2), (3), and (5). "This state" will for four months recognize perfection under the law of the jurisdiction from which the collateral came, unless the remaining period of effectiveness of the perfection in that jurisdiction was less than four months (paragraph (1)(d)). After the four month period or the remaining period of effectiveness, whichever is shorter, the secured party must comply with perfection requirements in this state. This rule differs from the former rule of Section 14 of the Uniform Conditional Sales Act. Under that section a conditional seller was required to file within 10 days after he "received notice" that the goods had been removed into this state. Apparently, under the Uniform Conditional Sales Act, if the seller never "received notice" his interest continued or became perfected in this state without filing. Paragraph (1)(d) proceeds on the theory that not only the secured party whose collateral has been removed but also creditors of and purchasers from the debtor "in this state" should be considered.

The four-month period is long enough for a secured party to discover in most cases that the collateral has been removed and refile in this state; thereafter, if he has not done so, his interest, although originally perfected in the jurisdiction from which the collateral was removed, is subject to defeat here by purchasers of the collateral. Compare the situation arising under Section 9–403(2) when a filing lapses.

UCC

It should be noted that a "purchaser" includes a secured party. Section 1–201(32) and (33). The rights of a purchaser with a security interest against an unperfected security interest are governed by Section 9–312.

In case of delay beyond the four-month period, there is no "relation back"; and this is also true where the security interest is perfected for the first time in this state.

If the removal occurs within a short period, like two weeks, before the lapse of the filing in the original state, the secured party has only that period, not the full four months, to reperfect in "this state". But ordinarily he would have filed a continuation statement in the original jurisdiction; and he may do so to avoid lapse and allow himself the full four months if he is searching for the collateral and needs more time.

Paragraph (1)(d) does not apply to the case of goods removed from one filing district to another within this state (see subsection (3) of Section 9–401), but only to property brought into this state from another jurisdiction.

8. Subsection (5) deals with problems relating to the financing of minerals (including oil and gas) as these products come from the ground. In some cases rights in oil and gas in the groundwave been split into a large variety of interests. As the oil or gas issues from the ground, it may be encumbered by the group of persons having interests therein. Or the product may be sold at minehead or wellhead and the resulting accounts assigned. The question arises as to the place of filing. The usual rule of this section in subsection (2) would make the place to search for encumbrances on the accounts the locations of the respective assignors; but the assignors might be a number of individuals located throughout the country. To avoid the difficult problems of search thus created, subsection (5) provides that the place for filing with respect to security interests in the minerals as they issue from the ground at minehead or wellhead or in the accounts arising out of the sale of the minerals at minehead or wellhead shall be in the state where the minehead or wellhead is located. Section 9–401 similarly provides that the place to file within the state is in the real property records in the county where the minehead or wellhead is located. These rules conform to pre-Code practice and to practice which seems to have continued in the early Code period before express provision was made for these situations.

The term "at wellhead" is intended to encompass arrangements based on sale of the product as soon as it issues from the ground and is measured, without technical distinctions as to whether title passes at the "Christmas tree" or the far side of a gathering tank or at some other point. The term "at minehead" is a comparable concept.

Cross References:

Sections 1–105, 9–302 and 9–401.

Definitional Cross References:

"Accounts." Section 9–106.
"Attaches." Section 9–203.
"Chattel Paper." Section 9–105.
"Collateral." Section 9–105.
"Consumer Goods." Section 9–109.
"Debtor." Section 9–105.
"Document." Section 9–105.
"Equipment." Section 9–109.
"General intangibles." Section 9–106.
"Goods." Section 9–105.
"Instrument." Section 9–109.
"Purchase money security interest." Section 9–107.

"Purchaser." Section 1–201(33).
"Security interest." Section 1–201(37).

Section 9–104. Transactions Excluded From Article.

This Article does not apply

(a) to a security interest subject to any statute of the United States to the extent that such statute governs the rights of parties to and third parties affected by transactions in particular types of property; or

(b) to a landlord's lien; or

(c) to a lien given by statute or other rule of law for services or materials except as provided in Section 9-310 on priority of such liens; or

(d) to a transfer of a claim for wages, salary or other compensation of an employee; or

(e) to any security interest created or granted by a government, governmental subdivision, agency, department, commission, board, authority, public benefit corporation or other governmental entity to the extent that the creation, validity, enforceability, perfection or priority of such security interest is expressly governed by any other law of this state; or

(f) to a sale of accounts or chattel paper as part of a sale of the business out of which they arose, or an assignment of accounts or chattel paper which is for the purpose of collection only, or a transfer of a right to payment under a contract to an assignee who is also to do the performance under the contract or a transfer of a single account to an assignee in whole or partial satisfaction of a preexisting indebtedness; or

(g) to a transfer of an interest or claim in or under any policy of insurance or contract for an annuity including a variable annuity, except as provided with respect to proceeds (Section 9-306) and priorities in proceeds (Section 9-312); or

(h) to a right represented by a judgment (other than a judgment taken on a right to payment which was collateral); or

(i) to any right of set-off; or

(j) except to the extent that provision is made for fixtures in Section 9-313 or for a security interest in shares or other ownership interests evidenced by stock certificates or other instruments, and a leasehold evidenced by a proprietary lease or either of the foregoing from a corporation or partnership formed for the purpose of cooperative ownership of real property, to the creation or transfer of an interest in or lien on real estate, including a lease or rents thereunder; or

(k) to a transfer in whole or in part of any claim arising out of tort; or

(l) to a transfer of an interest in any deposit account (subsection (1) of Section 9–105), except as provided with respect to proceeds (Section 9–306) and priorities in proceeds (Section 9–312); or

(m) to a transfer of an interest in a letter of credit other than the rights to proceeds of a written letter of credit.

Amended by Laws 1977, Ch. 866, eff. July 2, 1978; Laws 1988, Ch. 333, eff. Aug. 24, 1988, and applicable to any security interest obtained, continued or consolidated on rafter such effective date, and shall not affect security interests obtained prior to such effective date by means other than filing; L. 2000, Ch. 471, eff. Nov. 1, 2000.

New York Annotations

Generally, four classes of transactions are excluded from Article 9: (1) those which relate to areas with a well developed body of law and special policy (clauses c, e, g, k, and the last clause of k); (2) those which relate closely to real estate (clauses b and j); (3) where the particular assets are not used commercially for borrowing (clauses d, h, and k); and (4) those covered by a federal statute (clause a).

(a) In addition to the material in Comment 1, see the perfecting provisions of federal law as to motor vehicles of interstate carriers. Interstate Commerce Act, § 213, 72 Stat. 812, 49 U.S.C. § 313 (1958). Under this statute perfection by filing under the Code would have a national effect on subsequent parties.

(b) There is no recognition of a landlord's lien in New York statutes, although Lien Law, § 181, gives a statutory lien to the "keeper of a hotel, apartment hotel, inn, boardinghouse, rooming house, or lodging house except an immigrant lodging house." See Section 9-310.

(c) See the annotation to Section 9–310 for a representative collection of the statutory liens, omitted from Article 9, save for that priority rule. This clause should make it as clear as is possible under state law that the Code's security interest is not a statutory lien under § 67 of the Bankruptcy Act.

(d) Personal Property Law, §§ 46–49–b, Banking Law, §§ 355 and 356, and Labor Law, § 197, regulating wage assignments would be unaffected by the Code.

(e) Conditional sales of railway stock are now governed by Personal Property Law, § 68, but to a large extent this statute has been superseded by the federal statute referred to in Comment 5 and would be repealed by the Code.

(f) Since Section 9–102 brings under Code coverage even outright sales of these intangibles, it is necessary to exclude those transfers which are wholly unconnected with commercial financing. The common law will continue to govern these assignments.

(g)–(k) are self-explanatory. Subsection (g) in the New York Code specifically excludes contracts for an annuity including a variable annuity, an exclusion not explicitly provided for in the 1958 and 1962 Official Texts.

Historical Note: Changes were made for greater clarification and precision as to the types of transactions entirely excluded from the operation of Article 9, and the additional exclusion of rent and tort-claim assignments follows the suggestion of the Law Revision Commission. (1956 Recommendations, p. 258; Excerpts, p. 466.)

Official Uniform Comment

Prior Uniform Statutory Provisions: None.

Purposes:

1. Where a federal statute regulates the incidents of security interests in particular types of property, those security interests are of course governed by the federal statute and excluded from this Article. The Ship Mortgage Act, 1920, is an example of such a federal act. The present provisions of the Federal Aviation Act of 1958 (49 U.S.C.

§ 1403 et seq.) call for registration of title to and liens upon aircraft with the Civil Aeronautics Administrator and such registration is recognized as equivalent to filing under this Article (Section 9–302(3)); but to the extent that the Federal Aviation Act does not regulate the rights of parties to and third parties affected by such transactions, security interests in aircraft remain subject to this Article.

Although the Federal Copyright Act contains provisions permitting the mortgage of a copyright and for the recording of an assignment of a copyright (17 U.S.C. §§ 28, 30) such a statute would not seem to contain sufficient provisions regulating the rights of the parties and third parties to exclude security interests in copyrights from the provisions of this Article. Compare Republic Pictures Corp. v. Security-First National Bank of Los Angeles, 197 F.2d 767 (9th Cir. 1952). Compare also with respect to patents, 35 U.S.C. § 47. The filing provisions under these Acts, like the filing provisions of the Federal Aviation Act, are recognized as the equivalent to filing under this Article. Section 9–302(3) and (4).

Even such a statute as the Ship Mortgage Act is far from a comprehensive regulation of all aspects of ship mortgage financing. That Act contains provisions on formal requisites, on recordation and on foreclosure but not much more. If problems arise under a ship mortgage which are not covered by the Act, the federal admiralty court must decide whether to improvise an answer under "federal law" or to follow the law of some state with which the mortgage transaction has appropriate contacts. The exclusionary language in paragraph (a) is that this Article does not apply to such security interest "to the extent" that the federal statute governs the rights of the parties. Thus if the federal statute contained no relevant provision, this Article could be looked to for an answer.

2. Except for fixtures (Section 9–313), the Article applies only to security interests in personal property. The exclusion of landlord's liens by paragraph (b) and of leases and other interests in or liens on real estate by paragraph (j) merely reiterates the limitations on coverage already made explicit in Section 9–102(3). See Comment 4 to that section.

3. In all jurisdictions liens are given suppliers of many types of services and materials either by statute or by common law. It was thought to be both inappropriate and unnecessary for this Article to attempt a general codification of that lien structure which is in considerable part determined by local conditions and which is far removed from ordinary commercial financing. Moreover, federal law may displace state law in situations such as admiralty liens. Paragraph (c) therefore excludes statutory liens from the Article. Section 9–310 states a rule for determining priorities between such liens and the consensual security interests covered by this Article.

4. In many states assignments of wage claims and the like are regulated by statute. Such assignments present important social problems whose solution should be a matter of local regulation. Paragraph (d) therefore excludes them from this Article.

5. Certain governmental borrowings include collateral in the form of assignments of water, electricity or sewer charges, rents on dormitories or industrial buildings, tools, etc. Since these assignments are usually governed by special provisions of law, these governmental transfers are excluded from this Article.

6. In general sales as well as security transfers of accounts and chattel paper are within the Article (see Section 9–102). Paragraph (f) excludes from the Article certain transfers of such intangibles which, by their nature, have nothing to do with commercial financing transactions.

Similarly, this paragraph excludes from the Article such transactions as that involved in Lyon v. Ty-Wood Corporation, 212 Pa. Super. 69, 239 A.2d 819 (1968) and Spurlin v. Sloan, 368 S.W.2d 314 (Ky. 1963).

7. Rights under life insurance and other policies, and deposit accounts, are often put up as collateral. Such transactions are often quite special, do not fit easily under a general commercial statute and are adequately covered by existing law. Paragraphs

(g) and (l) make appropriate exclusions, but provision is made for coverage of deposit accounts and certain insurance money as proceeds.

8. The remaining exclusions go to other types of claims which do not customarily serve as commercial collateral: judgments under paragraph (h), set-offs under paragraph (i) and tort claim sunder paragraph (k).

Cross References:

Point 1: Section 9–302(3).
Point 2: Sections 9–102(3) and 9–313.
Point 3: Sections 9–102(2) and 9–310.
Point 6: Section 9–102.

Definitional Cross References:

"Account." Section 9–106.
"Chattel paper." Section 9–105.
"Contract." Section 1–201.
"Deposit account." Section 9–105.
"Party." Section 1–201.
"Rights." Section 1–201.
"Security interest." Section 1–201.

Section 9–105. Definitions and Index of Definitions.

(1) In this Article unless the context otherwise requires:

(a) "Account debtor" means the person who is obligated on an account, chattel paper or general intangible;

(b) "Chattel paper" means a writing or writings which evidence both a monetary obligation and a security interest in or a lease of specific goods, but a charter or other contract involving these or hire of a vessel is not chattel paper. When a transaction is evidenced both by such a security agreement or a lease and by an instrument or a series of instruments, the group of writings taken together constitutes chattel paper;

(c) "Collateral" means the property subject to a security interest, and includes accounts and chattel paper which have been sold;

(d) "Debtor" means the person who owes payment or other performance of the obligation secured, whether or not he owns or has rights in the collateral, and includes the seller of accounts or chattel paper. Where the debtor and the owner of the collateral are not the same person, the term "debtor" means the owner of the collateral in any provision of the Article dealing with the collateral, the obligor in any provision dealing with the obligation, and may include both where the context so requires;

(e) "Deposit account" means a demand, time, savings, passbook or like account maintained with a bank, savings and loan association, credit union or like organization, other than an account evidenced by a certificate of deposit;

(f) "Document" means document of title as defined in the general definitions of Article 1 (Section 1-201), and a receipt of the kind described in subsection (2) of Section 7-201;

(g) "Encumbrance" includes real estate mortgages and other liens on real estate and all other rights in real estate that are not ownership interests;

(h) "Goods" includes all things which are movable at the time the security interest attaches or which are fixtures (Section 9–313), but does not include money, documents, instruments, investment property, accounts, chattel paper, general intangibles, or minerals or the like (including oil and gas) before extraction. "Goods" also includes standing timber which is to be cut and removed under a conveyance or contract for sale, the unborn young of animals, and growing crops;

(i) "Instrument" means a negotiable instrument (defined in Section 3–104), or any other writing which evidences a right to the payment of money and is not itself a security agreement or lease and is of a type which is in ordinary course of business transferred by delivery with any necessary indorsement or assignment. The term does not include investment property;

(j) "Mortgage" means a consensual interest created by a real estate mortgage, a trust deed on real estate, or the like;

(k) An advance is made "pursuant to commitment" if the secured party has bound himself to make it, whether or not a subsequent event of default or other event not within his control has relieved or may relieve him from his obligation;

(l) "Security agreement" means an agreement which creates or provides for a security interest;

(m) "Secured party" means a lender, seller or other person in whose favor there is a security interest, including a person to whom accounts or chattel paper have been sold. When the holders of obligations issued under an indenture of trust, equipment trust agreement or the like are represented by a trustee or other person, the representative is the secured party;

(n) "Transmitting utility" means any person primarily engaged in the railroad, street railway or trolley bus business, the electric or electronics communications transmission business, the transmission of goods by pipeline, or the transmission or the production and transmission of electricity, steam, gas or water, or the provision of sewer service.

(2) Other definitions applying to this Article and the sections in which they appear are:

"Account".	Section 9–106.
"Attach".	Section 9–203.
"Commodity Contract".	Section 9–115.
"Commodity Customer".	Section 9–115.
"Commodity Intermediary".	Section 9–115.
"Construction mortgage".	Section 9–313(1).
"Consumer goods".	Section 9–109(1).
"Control".	Section 9–115.
"Equipment".	Section 9–109(2).
"Farm products".	Section 9–109(3).

"Fixture".	Section 9–313(1).
"Fixture filing".	Section 9–313(1).
"General intangibles".	Section 9–106.
"Inventory".	Section 9–109(4).
"Investment property".	Section 9–115.
"Lien creditor".	Section 9–301(3).
"Proceeds".	Section 9–306(1).
"Purchase money security interest".	Section 9–107.
"United States".	Section 9–103.

(3) The following definitions in other Articles apply to this Article:

"Broker".	Section 8–102.
"Certificated security".	Section 8–102.
"Check".	Section 3–104.
"Clearing corporation".	Section 8–102.
"Contract for sale".	Section 2–106.
"Control".	Section 8–106.
"Delivery".	Section 8–301.
"Entitlement holder".	Section 8–102.
"Financial asset".	Section 8–102.
"Holder in due course".	Section 3–302.
"Letter of credit".	Section 5–102.
"Note".	Section 3–104.
"Proceeds of a letter of credit".	Section 5–114(A).
"Sale".	Section 2–106.
"Securities intermediary".	Section 8–102.
"Security".	Section 8–102.
"Security certificate".	Section 8–102.
"Security entitlement".	Section 8–102.
"Uncertificated security".	Section 8–102.

Amended by Laws 1977, Ch. 866, eff. July 2, 1978; Laws 1982, Ch. 928, eff. Dec. 21, 1982 and deemed to have been in full force and effect on and after Sept. 1, 1982; L. 1997, Ch. 566, eff. Oct. 10, 1997; L. 2000, Ch. 471, eff. Nov. 1, 2000.

New York Annotations

(1)(a) "Account debtor." This definition would be new to the statutes, since New York has no existing statute governing accounts receivable financing in general. To the extent that the Factor's Lien Act deals with accounts it leaves the term undefined. Personal Property Law, § 45.

(b) "Chattel paper." There is no comparable statutory definition under existing law.

(c) and (d) "Collateral" and "Debtor." Although these words have a common business meaning, there is no statute which defines them for secured transactions.

(e) "Document." This definition is similar to that contained in the Uniform Trust Receipts Act, Personal Property Law, § 51(2).

(f) "Goods." This definition is in scope much like the definition in the Uniform Trust Receipts Act, Personal Property Law, § 51 (4), which, however, uses the general phrase "chattels personal." As in the case of the Uniform Trust Receipts Act, the term excludes money and things in action. Unlike the Uniform Trust Receipts Act the term includes fixtures, growing crops and the unborn young of animals. Section 9–313 should be consulted for the detailed treatment of fixtures.

Care must be taken to compare this definition of goods with that contained in Section 2–105, with the realization that Article 2 applies to the sales aspects of any transaction, and Article 9 applies to the security interest aspects (see Section 2–102).

(g) "Instrument." The Code definition is similar in scope to that contained in Personal Property Law, § 51(5).

(h) and (i) "Security agreement" and "secured party." There are no comparable definitions in New York law, since the existing method is to deal with the agreements and parties in accordance with the type of device used, i.e. "chattel mortgage", "chattel mortgagee", "conditional sales contract", "conditional vendor", etc. Note that "security interest" is defined in Section 1–201(37).

(j) Subsection (j) is new and is not contained in the 1958 and 1962 Official Texts. It clarifies the application of Section 9–103(1).

Historical Note: Clause (a) of subsection (1) was changed because of the new category of collateral called "general intangibles."

Clause (b) of subsection (1) was changed to define more sharply the distinction between "chattel paper" and "instrument"; to delete, in accordance with a suggestion of the Law Revision Commission, the uncertain test of delivery in ordinary course of business; and to broaden the application of the term to include not only the writing which gives rise to a security interest in specific goods but also a lease of specific goods by reason of the change in Section 9–109(4) which includes within the meaning of the word "inventory" goods leased or held for lease.

The changes in clauses (c), (d), (e) were clarifying. Clause (d) follows a suggestion of the Law Revision Commission in clarifying the term "debtor" where one person owns the collateral and another owes the debt. The change in clause (f) was necessitated by the new category of collateral called "general intangibles", and to include fixtures within the term "goods" so as to be consistent with Section 9–313. (1956 Recommendations, p. 260; Excerpts, p.466.)

Official Uniform Comment

Prior Uniform Statutory Provisions: Various.

Purposes:

1. *General.* It is necessary to have a set of terms to describe the parties to a secured transaction, the agreement itself, and the property involved therein; but the selection of the set of terms applicable to any one of the existing forms (e.g., mortgagor and mortgagee) might carry to some extent the implication that the existing law referable to that form was to be used for the construction and interpretation of this Article. Since it is desired to avoid any such implication, a set of terms has been chosen which have no common law or statutory roots tying them to a particular form.

In place of such terms as "chattel mortgage," "conditional sale," "assignment of accounts receivable," "trust receipt," etc., this Article substitutes the general term "security agreement" defined in paragraph (1)(l). In place of "mortgagor," "mortgagee," "conditional vendee,""conditional vendor," etc., this Article substitutes "debtor", defined in paragraph (1)(d), and "secured party", defined in paragraph (1)(m). The property subject to the security agreement is "collateral", defined in paragraph (1)(c). The interest in the collateral which is conveyed by the debtor to the secured party is a "security interest", defined in Section 1–201 (37).

2. *Parties.* The parties to the security agreement are the "debtor" and the"secured party."

"*Debtor*": In all but a few cases the person who owes the debt and the person whose property secures the debt will be the same. Occasionally, one person furnishes security for another's debt, and sometimes property is transferred subject to a secured debt of the transferor which the transferee does not assume; in such cases, under the second sentence of the definition, the term "debtor" may, depending upon the context, include either or both such persons. Section 9–112 sets out special rules which are applicable where collateral is owned by a person who does not owe a debt.

"*Secured Party*": The term includes any person in whose favor there is a security interest (defined in Section 1–201). The term is used equally to refer to a person who as a seller retains a lien on or title to goods sold, to a person whose interest arises initially from a loan transaction, and to an assignee of either. Note that a seller is a "secured party" in relation to his customer; the seller becomes a "debtor" if he assigns the chattel paper as collateral. This is also true of a lender who assigns the debt as collateral. With the exceptions stated in Section 9–104(f) the Article applies to any sale of accounts or chattel paper: the term "secured party" includes an assignee or such intangibles whether by sale or for security, to distinguish him from the payee of the account, for example, who becomes a "debtor" by pledging the account as security for a loan.

On the applicability of the terms "debtor" and "secured party" to consignments and leases see Section 9–408 and Comment thereto.

"*Account debtor*": Where the collateral is an account, chattel paper or general intangible the original obligor is called the "account debtor", defined in paragraph (1)(a).

3. *Property subject to the security agreement.* "*Collateral*", defined in paragraph (1)(c), is a general term for the tangible and intangible property subject to a security interest. For some purposes the Code makes distinctions between different types of collateral and therefore further classification of collateral is necessary. Collateral which consists of tangible property is "goods", defined in paragraph (1)(h); and "goods" are again subdivided in Section 9–109. For purposes of this Article all intangible collateral fits one of five categories, two of which, "accounts", and "general intangibles" are defined in the following Section 9–106; the other three, "documents", "instruments" and "chattel paper", are defined in paragraphs (1)(f), (1)(i) and (1)(b) of this section.

"Goods": the definition in paragraph (1)(h) is similar to that contained in Section 2–105 except that the Sales Article definition refers to "time of identification to the contract for sale", while this definition refers to "the time the security interest attaches."

For the treatment of fixtures, Section 9–313 should be consulted, it will be noted that the treatment of fixtures under Section 9–313 does not at all points conform to their treatment under Section 2–107 (goods to be severed from realty). Section 2–107 relates to sale of such goods; Section 9–313 to security interests in them. The discrepancies between the two sections arise from the differences in the types of interest covered. A comparable discrepancy exists as to minerals. In the case of timber, both sections treat it as goods if it is to be severed under a contract of sale, but not otherwise.

If in any state minerals before severance are deemed to be personal property, they fall outside the Article's definition of "goods" and would therefore fall in the catch-all definition, "general intangibles", in Section 9–106. The special provisions of Section 9–103(5) would not apply and those of Section 9–103(3) would apply. The resulting problems should be considered locally.

For the purpose of this Article, goods are classified as "consumer goods", "equipment", "farm products", and "inventory"; those terms are defined in Section 9–109. When the general term "goods" is used in this Article, it includes, as may be appropriate in the context, the subclasses of goods defined in Section 9–109.

"Instrument": the term as defined in paragraph (1)(i) includes not only negotiable instruments and investment securities but also any other intangibles evidenced by writings which are in ordinary course of business transferred by delivery. As in the

case of chattel paper "delivery" is only the minimum stated and may be accompanied by other steps.

If a writing is itself a security agreement or lease with respect to specific goods it is not an instrument although it otherwise meets the term of the definition. See Comment below on "chattel paper."

The fact that an instrument is secured by collateral, whether the collateral be other instruments, documents, goods, accounts or general intangibles, does not change the character of the principal obligation as an instrument or convert the combination of instrument and collateral into a separate Code classification of personal property. The single qualification to this principle is that an instrument which is secured by chattel paper is itself part of the chattel paper, while also retaining its identity as an instrument.

"Document": See the Comments under Section 1–201(15) and 7–201.

"Chattel paper": To secure his own financing a secured party may wish to borrow against or sell the security agreement itself along with his interest in the collateral which he has received from his debtor. Since the refinancing of paper secured by specific goods presents some problems of its own, the term "chattel paper" is used to describe this kind of collateral. The Comments under Section 9–308 further describe this concept.

Charters of vessels are excluded from the definition of chattel paper because they fit undertoe definition of accounts. See Comment to Section 9–106. The term "charter" as used herein and in Section 9–106 includes bareboat charters, time charters, successive voyage charters, contracts of affreightment, contracts of carriage, and all other arrangements for use of vessels.

4. The following transactions illustrate the use of the term "chattel paper" and some of the other terms defined in this section.

A dealer sells a tractor to a farmer on conditional sales contract or purchase money security interest. The conditional sales contract is a "security agreement", the farmer is the "debtor", the dealer is the "secured party" and the tractor is the type of "collateral" defined in Section 9–109 as "equipment." But now the dealer transfers the contract to his bank, either by outright sale or to secure a loan. Since the conditional sales contract is a security agreement relating to specific equipment, the conditional sales contract is now the type of collateral called "chattel paper." In this transaction between the dealer and his bank, the bank is the "secured party", the dealer is the "debtor", and the farmer is the "account debtor."

Under the definition of "security interest" in Section 1–201(37) a lease does not create a security interest unless intended as security. Whether or not the lease itself is a security agreement, it is chattel paper when transferred if it relates to specific goods. Thus, if the dealer enters a straight lease of the tractor to the farmer (not intended as security), and then arranges tomorrow money on the security of the lease, the lease is chattel paper.

Security agreement of the type formerly known as chattel mortgages and conditional sales contracts are frequently executed in connection with a negotiable note or a series of such notes. Under the definitions in paragraphs (1)(b) and (1)(i) the rules applicable to chattel paper, rather than those relating to instruments, are applicable to the group of writings (contract plus note)taken together.

5. *Miscellaneous definitions.*

"*Deposit account*" is a type of collateral excluded from this Article under Section 9–104(1), except when it constitutes proceeds of other collateral under Section 9–306.

The terms "encumbrance" and "mortgage" are defined for use in the section on fixtures, Section 9–113.

The term "transmitting utility" is defined to designate a special class of debtors for whom separate filing rules are provided in Part 4, thus obviating all local filing and particularly the several local filings that would be necessary under the usual rules of Section 9–401 for the fixture collateral of a far-flung public utility debtor. See Comments under Sections 9–401 and 9–403.

The term "pursuant to commitment" is defined for use in the rules relating to priority of future advances in Sections 9–301(4), 9–307(3), and 9–312(7).

6. Comments to the definitions indexed in subsections (2) and (3) follow the sections in which the definitions are contained.

Cross References:

Point 2: Sections 9–104(f) and 9–112.
Point 3: Sections 2–105, 2–107, 9–106, 9–109, 9–303, and 9–313.

Definitional Cross References:

"Account." Section 9–106.
"Agreement." Section 1–201.
"Document of title." Sections 1–201, 7–201.
"General intangibles." Section 9–106.
"Holder." Section 1–201.
"Money." Section 1–201.
"Negotiable instrument." Section 3–104.
"Person." Section 1–201.
"Representative." Section 1–201.
"Rights." Section 1–201.
"Security." Section 8–102.
"Security interest." Section 1–201.
"Writing." Section 1–201.

Section 9—106. Definitions: "Account"; "General Intangibles".

"Account" means any right to payment for goods sold or leased or for services rendered which is not evidenced by an instrument or chattel paper, whether or not it has been earned by performance. "General intangibles" means any personal property (including things in action) other than goods, accounts, chattel paper, documents, instruments, investment property, rights to proceeds of written letters of credit, and money. All rights to payment earned or unearned under a charter or other contract involving the use or hire of a vessel and all rights incident to the charter or contract are accounts.

Amended by Laws 1977, Ch. 866, eff. July 2, 1978; L. 1997, Ch. 566, eff. Oct. 1, 1997; L. 2000, Ch. 471, eff. Nov. 1, 2000.

New York Annotations

The Code's classification of intangibles should contribute to removing much of the ambiguity now present in the assignment law of New York. An "account" under the Code is the next thing to money in the till, and its use here is comparable to its undefined use in Personal Property Law, § 45 (factor's liens). A "contract right" is also concerned only with money payments and is one degree less definite; the contract exists but since the goods are not delivered or the services are not yet rendered, the money is not yet due and it is not an "account." The value of the contract right may be diminished by the prospects of nonfulfillment of the conditions, but it is nonetheless a species of property which may now be assigned. Cooper v. Douglass, 44 Barb. 409 (1864); Seamon v. Federated Films, Inc., 142 N.Y.S.2d 324

(1955). Cf. Rockmore v. Lehman, 129 F.2d 892 (2d Cir. 1942). "General intangibles" is a term by which the Code leaves room for expansion of recognition of commercially significant assets as assignable property. Compare General Business Law, § 365 (trade and service marks). New York has recognized some kinds of future intangibles as being presently assignable, as in the case of assignments of wages even in the absence of a contract of employment. Compare Field v. City of N.Y., 6 N.Y. 179 (1852), and Matter of Black, 138 App. Div. 562, 123 N.Y.S. 371 (1910). See Section 9-104(d). The cases are collected in the majority and dissenting opinions in City of New York v. Bedford Bar & Grill, Inc., 2 N.Y. 2d 429, 141 N.E.2d 575 (1957).

Historical Note: The third sentence, relating to rights to wages, salary, other compensation or rights represented by a judgment, was deleted since Section 9–104(d) and (h) now entirely exclude such rights from the operation of Article 9.

The new term "general intangibles" brings under Article 9 miscellaneous types of rights which are personal property and which are used or may become customarily used as commercial security. Examples are good will, literary rights, copyrights, trademarks, patents, rights to performance and others, to the extent that any of same are not governed by statutes of the United States. See Section 9–104(a). This Article solves the problems of filing and perfecting security interests in these types of intangibles under Section 9–103(2), 9–302, and 9–401(1)(a) or (c).

It should be noted that this new definition of "general intangibles" does not apply to types of property which are specifically excluded from the coverage of Article 9 under Section 9–104. (1956 Recommendations, p. 261.)

UCC

Official Uniform Comment

Prior Uniform Statutory Provision: None.

Purposes:

The terms defined in this section round out the classification of intangibles: see the definitions of "document", "chattel paper" and "instrument" in Section 9–105. Those three terms cover the various categories of commercial paper which are either negotiable or to a greater or less extent dealt with as if negotiable. The term "account" covers most choses in action which may be the subject of commercial financing transactions but which are not evidenced by an indispensable writing. The term "general intangibles" brings under this Article miscellaneous types of contractual rights and other personal property which are used or may become customarily used as commercial security. Examples are goodwill, literary rights and rights to performance. Other examples are copyrights, trademarks and patents, except to the extent that they may excluded by Section 9–104(a). This Article solves the problems of filing security interests in these types of intangibles (Sections 9–103(3) and 9–401). Note that this catch-all definition does not apply to money or to types of intangibles which are specifically excluded from the coverage of the Article (Section 9–104) and note also that under Section 9–302 filing under a federal statute may satisfy the filing requirements of this Article.

A right to the payment of money is frequently buttressed by ancillary covenants to insure the preservation of collateral, such as covenants in a purchase agreement, note or mortgage requiring insurance on the collateral or forbidding removal of the collateral; or covenants to preserve credit-worthiness of the promisor, such as covenants restricting dividends, etc. While these miscellaneous ancillary rights might conceivably be thought to fall within the definition of "general intangibles", it is not the intention of the Code to treat them separately and require the perfection of assignment thereof by filing in the manner required for perfection of an assignment of general intangibles. Whatever perfection is required for the perfection of an assignment of the right to the payment of money will also carry these ancillary rights.

Similarly, when the right to the payment of money is not yet earned by performance, there are frequently ancillary rights designed to assure that an assignee may complete the performance and crystallize the right to payment of money. Such rights are frequently present in a "maintenance" lease where the lessor has continuing duties to perform, or in a ship charter. These ancillary rights, if considered in the abstract, might be thought to be "general intangibles", since they do not themselves involve the payment of money; but it is not the intent of the Code to split up the rights to the payment of money and its ancillary supports, and thereby multiply the problem of perfection of assignments. Therefore, all rights of the lessor in a lease are to be perfected as "chattel paper", and all rights of the owner in a ship charter are to be perfected as "accounts."

"Account" is defined as a right to payment for goods sold or leased or services rendered; the ordinary commercial account receivable. In some special cases a right to receive money not yet earned by performance crystallizes not into an account but into a general intangible for it is aright to payment of money that is not "for goods sold or leased or for services rendered." Examples of such rights are the right to receive payment of a loan not evidenced by an instrument or chattel paper; a right to receive partial refund of purchase prices paid by reason of retroactive volume discounts; rights to receive payment under licenses of patents and copyrights, exhibition contracts, etc.

This Article rejects any lingering common law notion that only rights already earned can be assigned. In the triangular arrangement following assignment, there is reason to allow the original parties–assignor and account debtor–more flexibility in modifying the underlying contract before performance than after performance (see Section 9–318). It will, however, be found that in most situations the same rules apply to accounts both before and after performance.

Cross References:

Sections 9–103(2), 9–104, 9–302(3), 9–318 and 9–401.

Definitional Cross References:

"Chattel paper." Section 9–105.
"Contract." Section 1–201.
"Document." Section 9–105.
"Goods." Section 9–105.
"Instrument." Section 9–105.

Section 9–107. Definitions: "Purchase Money Security Interest".

A security interest is a purchase money security interest" to the extent that it is

(a) taken or retained by the seller of the collateral to secure all or part of its price; or

(b) taken by a person who by making advances or incurring an obligation gives value to enable the debtor to acquire rights in or the use of collateral if such value is in fact so used.

New York Annotations

In practice most purchase money security interests are represented by conditional sales and trust receipts. There is some indication in present law that a security interest in newly acquired assets may constitute a preferred category. For example, such security interests may be perfected under less stringent filing requirements providing for filing during periods of grace. Personal Property Law, § 65 (conditional sales), and Personal Property Law, §§ 58 and 58-e (trust receipts). All chattel mortgages now have a similar grace period under Lien Law, § 230.

Special treatment of purchase money transactions is also evident in the statutory rules for realization upon chattel mortgage purchase money security under Lien Law, §§ 239 et seq., and in the judicial exclusion of purchase money transactions from Lien Law, § 230-a (Bulk Mortgage Law). In re Rosom Utilities, Inc., 105 F.2d 132 (2d Cir. 1939).

Historical Note: Subparagraph was deleted for the reason that by permitting a ten-day grace period for the debtor taking possession of the newly acquired collateral, it extended the purchase money security interest concept too far. The deleted subparagraph unnecessarily created difficult problems in the determination of priorities between conflicting security interests since it made priorities in affected cases depend upon the accident of whose money, as between competing secured parties, was actually used. (1956 Recommendations, p.262.)

Official Uniform Comment

Prior Uniform Statutory Provision: None.

Purposes:

1. Under existing rules of law and under this Article purchase money obligations often have priority over other obligations. Thus a purchase money obligation has priority over an interest acquired under an after-acquired property clause (Section 9–312(3) and (4)); where filing is required a grace period of ten days is allowed against creditors and transferees in bulk (Section 9–301(2)); and in some instances filing may not be necessary (Section 9–302(1)(d)).

Under this section a seller has a purchase money security interest if he retains a security interest in the goods; a financing agency has a purchase money security interest when it advances money to the seller, taking back an assignment of chattel paper, and also when it makes advances to the buyer (e.g., on chattel mortgage) to enable him to buy, and he uses the money for that purpose.

2. When a purchase money interest is claimed by a secured party who is not a seller, he must of course have given present consideration. This section therefore provides that the purchase money party must be one who give value "by making advances or incurring an obligation": the quoted language excludes from the purchase money category an security interest taken as security for or in satisfaction of a preexisting claim or antecedent debt.

Cross References:

Point 1: Sections 9–301, 9–302 and 9–312.
Point 2: Section 9–108.

Definitional Cross References:

"Collateral." Section 9–105.
"Debtor." Section 9–105.
"Person." Section 1–201.
"Rights." Section 1–201.
"Security interest." Section 1–201.
"Value." Section 1–201.

Section 9–108. When After-Acquired Collateral Not Security for Antecedent Debt.

Where a secured party makes an advance, incurs an obligation, releases a perfected security interest, or otherwise gives new value which is to be secured in whole or in part by after-acquired property his security interest in the after-acquired collateral shall be deemed to be taken for new value and not as security for an antecedent debt if the debtor acquires his rights in such collateral either in the ordinary course of his business or under a contract of purchase made pursuant to the security agreement within a reasonable time after new value is given.

New York Annotations

This section, together with Section 9–201 and Section 9–204, validates after-acquired property clauses and generally places security acquired pursuant to an after-acquired property clause on the same footing for most practical purposes with security existing at the time of the security agreement. The changes made in New York law, in respect of after-acquired property clauses relating to personal property, are discussed in the annotation to Section 9–204.

Note that this section applies only to property acquired in the manner specified in the last phrase of the section and by no means relates to all after-acquired property. Further, this section does not restore the "relation back" doctrine of cases like Sexton v. Kessler, 225 U.S. 90, 32Sup.Ct. 657 (1912), where, under a less stringent Bankruptcy Act, perfection within the four-months' period "related back" to a period prior thereto, even though the secured party had neglected to make use of legal means of perfecting his security interest at the earlier date. Compare, § 601(6) of the present Bankruptcy Act.

It should be noted that if the contract were actually in existence at the time a security agreement was executed, then it should be possible to draft a security agreement which would minimize if not eliminate a preference question. Rights in existence or potential existence are assigned initially, and the receipt of the goods or the making of the contract at a later time is in effect a substitution of other collateral. See the excellent discussion on this point in Rockmore v. Lehman, 129 F.2d 892 (2d Cir. 1942), reversing the contrary result in Rockmore v. Lehman, 128 F.2d 564 (2d Cir. 1942). See also Wolf v. Aero Factors Corp., 221 F.2d 291 (2d Cir. 1955).

Historical Note: Former subsection (1) was deleted in its entirety, since the definition of "value" has been transferred to a new Section 1–201(44). Changes in former subsection (2), which is now the entire section, were for greater precision. Both changes follow suggestions of the Law Revision Commission. (1956 Recommendations, p. 263; Excerpts, p.467.)

Official Uniform Comment

Prior Uniform Statutory Provision: None.

Purposes:

1. Many financing transactions contemplate that the collateral will include both the debtor's existing assets and also assets thereafter acquired by him in the operation of his business. This Article generally validates such after-acquired property interests (see Section 9–204 and Comment) although they may be subordinated to later purchase money interests under Section 9–312(3) and (4).

Interests in after-acquired property have never been considered as involving transfers of property for antecedent debt merely because of the after-acquired feature, nor should they be so considered. The section makes explicit what has been true under the case law: and after-acquired property interest is not, by virtue of that fact alone, security for a pre-existing claim. This rule is of importance principally in insolvency proceedings under the federal Bankruptcy Act or state statutes which make certain transfers for antecedent debt voidable as preferences. The determination of when a transfer is for antecedent debt is largely left by the Bankruptcy Act to state law.

Two tests must be met under this section for an interest in after-acquired property to be one not taken for an antecedent debt. *First:* the secured party must, at the inception of the transaction, have given new value in some form. *Second:* the after-acquired property must come in either in the ordinary course of the debtor's business or as an acquisition which is made under a contract of purchase entered into within a reasonable time after the giving of new value and pursuant to the security agreement. The reason for the first test needs no comment. The second is in line with limitations which judicial construction has placed on the operation of after-acquired property clauses. Their coverage has been in many cases restricted to subsequent ordinary course acquisitions: this Article does not go so far (see Section 9–204 and Comment), but it does deny present value status to out of ordinary course acquisition not made pursuant to the original loan agreement. This solution gives the secured party full protection as to the collateral which he may be reasonably thought to have contracted for; it gives other creditors the possibility, under the law of preferences, of subjecting to their claims windfall or uncontemplated acquisitions shortly before bankruptcy.

2. The term "value" is defined in Section 1–201(44) and discussed in the accompanying Comment. In this section and in other sections of this Article the term "new value" is used but is left without statutory definition. The several illustrations of "new value" given in the text of this section (making an advance, incurring an obligation, releasing a perfected security interest) as well as the "purchase money security interest" definition in Section 9–107 indicate the nature of the concept. In other situations it is left to the courts to distinguish between "new" and "old" value, between present considerations and antecedent debt.

Cross References:

Point 1: Sections 9–204 and 9–312.
Point 2: Section 9–107.

Definitional Cross References:

"Collateral." Section 9–105.
"Contract." Section 1–201.
"Debtor." Section 9–105.
"Purchase." Section 1–201.
"Rights." Section 1–201.
"Secured party." Section 9–105.
"Security agreement." Section 9–105.
"Security interest." Section 1–201.
"Value." Section 1–201.

Section 9–109. Classification of Goods; "Consumer Goods"; "Equipment"; "Farm Products"; "Inventory".

Goods are

(1) "consumer goods" if they are used or bought for use primarily for personal, family or household purposes;

(2) “equipment” if they are used or bought for use primarily in business (including farming or a profession) or by a debtor who is a non-profit organization or a governmental subdivision or agency or if the goods are not included in the definitions of inventory, farm products or consumer goods;

(3) “farm products if they are crops or livestock or supplies used or produced in farming operations or if they are products of crops or livestock in their unmanufactured states (such as ginned cotton, wool-clip, maple syrup, milk and eggs), and if they are in the possession of a debtor engaged in raising, fattening, grazing or other farming operations. If goods are farm products they are neither equipment nor inventory;

(4) “inventory” if they are held by a person who holds them for sale or lease or to be furnished under contracts of service or if he has so furnished them, or if they are raw materials, work in process or materials used or consumed in a business. Inventory of a person is not to be classified as his equipment.

New York Annotations

The division into various classifications is new but statutory precedent for such division is not hard to find. Inventory may be compared to “merchandise” in Personal Property Law, § 45 (Factor’s Lien), and a security interest in such collateral is now most likely to be covered by a trust receipt under Personal Property Law, § 52, or a factor’s lien. Inventory is also similar to the definition of “goods” in the recently expanded provision for chattel mortgages by dealers. Lien Law, § 230-c. Note that equipment may not be covered by the latter laws, and through the tests imposed by subsection 3 of Personal Property Law, § 52, equipment is excluded from the collateral subject to a trust receipt. Farm products have an antecedent in Lien Law, § 230-b, providing special rules for chattel mortgages of crops and livestock. Consumer goods are in a sense similar to the class of collateral isolated in personal Property Law, § 301 (Motor Vehicle Retail Instalment Sales Act), Personal Property Law, § 401 (Retail Instalment Sales Act), and Lien Law, § 239 (chattel mortgages to secure unpaid purchase price for $5, 000 or less, where purchase not for a commercial or business use.)

Historical Note: The definition of “farm products” was broadened in subparagraph (3) to include such goods in the possession of any farmer and not merely the farmer who grew or used the products. In subparagraph (4) the definition of “inventory” was broadened to include goods held by a debtor for lease as well as for sale, and goods which have been furnished under a contract of service or lease. The latter change meets a suggestion of the Law revision Commission. Subparagraphs (3) and (4) now make it clear that “farm products” are not inventory, and that inventory of a person who is engaged in the business of selling or leasing goods is not his equipment. (1956 Recommendations, pp. 263-264; Excerpts, p.468.)

Official Uniform Comment

Prior Uniform Statutory Provision: None.

Purposes:

1. This section classifies goods as consumer goods, equipment, farm products and inventory. The classification is important in many situations: it is relevant, for

example, in determining the rights of persons who buy from a debtor goods subject to a security interest (Section 9–307), in certain questions of priority (Section 9–312), in determining the place of filing (Section 9–401) and in working out rights after default (Part 5). Comment 5 to Section 9–102 contains an index of the special rules applicable to different classes of collateral.

2. The classes of goods are mutually exclusive; the same property cannot at the same time and as to the same person be both equipment and inventory, for example. In borderline cases—a physician's car or a farmer's jeep which might be either consumer goods or equipment—the principal use to which the property is put should be considered as determinative. Goods can fall into different classes at different times; a radio is inventory in the hands of a dealer and consumer goods in the hands of a householder.

3. The principal test to determine whether goods are inventory is that they are held for immediate or ultimate sale. Implicit in the definition is the criterion that the prospective sale is in the ordinary course of business. Machinery used in manufacturing, for example, is equipment and not inventory even though it is the continuing policy of the enterprise to sell machinery when it becomes obsolete. Goods to be furnished under a contract of service are inventory even though the arrangement under which they are furnished is not technically a sale. When an enterprise is engaged in the business of leasing a stock of products to users (for example, the fleet of cars owned by a car rental agency), that stock is also included within the definition of "inventory." It should be noted that one class of goods which is not held for disposition to a purchaser or user is included in inventory: "Materials used or consumed in a business." Examples of this class of inventory are fuel to be used in operations, scrap metal produced in the course of manufacture, and containers to be used to package the goods. In general it may be said that goods used in a business are equipment when they are fixed assets or have, as identifiable units, a relatively long period of use; but are inventory, even though not held for sale, if they are used up or consumed in a short period of time in the production of some end product.

4. Goods are "farm products" only if they are in the possession of a debtor engaged in farming operations. Animals in a herd of livestock are covered whether they are acquired by purchase or result from natural increase. Products of crops or livestock remain farm products so long as they are in the possession of a debtor engaged in farming operations and have not been subjected to a manufacturing process. The terms "crops", "livestock" and "farming operations" are not defined; however, it is obvious from the text that "farming operations" includes raising livestock as well as crops; similarly, since eggs are products of livestock, livestock includes fowl. When crops or livestock or their products come into the possession of a person not engaged in farming operations they cease to be "farm products." If they come into the possession of a marketing agency for sale or distribution or of a manufacturer or processor as raw materials, they become inventory.

Products of crops or livestock, even though they remain in the possession of a person engaged in farming operations, lose their status as farm products if they are subjected to a manufacturing process. What is and what is not a manufacturing operation is not determined by this Article. At one end of the scale some processes are so closely connected with farming–such as pasteurizing milk or boiling sap to produce maple syrup or maple sugar–that they would not rank as manufacturing. On the other hand an extensive canning operation would be manufacturing. The line is one for the courts to draw. After farm products have been subjected to a manufacturing operation, they become inventory if held for sale.

Note that the buyer in ordinary course who under Section 9–307 takes free of a security interest in goods held for sale does not include one who buys farm products from a person engaged in farming operations.

5. The principal definition of equipment is a negative one: goods used in a business (including farming or a profession) which are not inventory and not farm products.

Trucks, rolling stock, tools, machinery are typical. It will be noted furthermore that any goods which are not covered by one of the other definitions in this section are to be treated as equipment.

Cross References:

Point 1: Sections 9–102, 9–307, 9–312, 9–401 and Part 5.
Point 3: Section 9–307.
Point 4: Section 9–307.

Definitional Cross References:

"Contract." Section 1–201.
"Debtor." Section 9–105.
"Goods." Section 9–105.
"Organization." Section 1–201.
"Person." Section 1–201.
"Sale." Sections 2–106 and 9–105.

Section 9–110. Sufficiency of Description.

For the purposes of this Article any description of personal property or, except as otherwise required by subsection (1) of Section 9–402 relating to the contents of a financing statement, real estate is sufficient whether or not it is specific if it reasonably identifies what is described.

Amended by Laws 1964, Ch. 476, eff. Sept. 27, 1964.

New York Annotations

In. cases involving chattel mortgages, a general description of the mortgaged property has been held to be reasonable identification without an enumeration and description of the specific articles mortgaged. E.g., Conkling v. Shelley, 28 N.Y. 360 (1863). The principles enunciated in such cases seem to be in accord with the purposes set forth in the Comment to Section 9-110.

The New York Factor's Lien Act, Personal Property Law, § 45, requires the general character of merchandise to be included in the recording of the factor's lien. As for trust receipts, Personal Property Law, § 58-e, calls for a description of the kind of goods covered or to be covered by the agreement. See also Personal Property Law, § 67, as to a conditional sales contract's description of realty where fixtures are involved.

In transactions governed by the Retail Instalment Sales Act the contract must contain an adequate description of the goods, including make and model, if any, where the goods are customarily sold by make and model. Personal Property Law, § 402(3).

Historical Note: This section was changed to make simplicity of description, for the purposes of this Article only, applicable to real as well as personal property. (1956 Recommendations, p. 264.)

Official Uniform Comment

Prior Uniform Statutory Provision: None.

Purposes:

The requirement of description of collateral (see Section 9–203 and Comment thereto) is evidentiary. The test of sufficiency of a description laid down by this section is that the description do the job assigned to it–that it make possible the identification of the thing described. Under this rule courts should refuse to follow the holdings, often found in the older chattel mortgage cases, that descriptions are insufficient unless they are of the most exact and detailed nature, the so-called "serial number" test. The same test of reasonable identification applies where a description of real estate is required in a financing statement. See Section 9–402.

Cross References:

Sections 9–203 and 9–402.

Section 9–111. Applicability of Bulk Transfer Laws.

The creation of a security interest is not a bulk transfer under Article 6 (see Section 6–103).

New York Annotations

This section is inconsistent with present New York law and requires the repeal of Lien Law, § 230–a (Bulk Mortgage Law). However, it should be noted that this exclusion is not without precedent in the New York law. See Lien Law, § 230-c(7), exempting chattel mortgages by dealers, and In re Rosom Utilities, 105 F.2d 132 (2d Cir. 1939), exempting purchase money chattel mortgages. For a complete discussion of the exemption in the Code, see statement of Professor Bunn before the Law Revision Commission, 1954 Leg.Doc.No.65(E), p.24. See also Section 6–103.

Official Uniform Comment

Prior Uniform Statutory Provision: None.

Purposes:

The bulk transfer laws, which have been almost everywhere enacted, were designed to prevent a once prevalent type of fraud which seems to have flourished particularly in the retail field: the owner of a debt-burdened enterprise would sell it to an unwary purchaser and then remove himself, with the purchase price and his other assets, beyond the reach of process. The creditors would find themselves with no recourse unless they could establish that the purchaser assumed existing debts. The bulk transfer laws, which require advance notice of sale to all known creditors, seem to have been successful in preventing such frauds.

There has been disagreement whether the bulk transfer laws should be applied to security as well as to sale transactions. In most states security transactions have not been covered; in a few states the opposite result has been reached either by judicial construction or by express statutory provision. Whatever the reasons may be, it seems to be true that the bulk transfer type of fraud has not often made its appearance in the security field: it may be that lenders of money are more inclined to investigate a potential borrower than are purchasers of retail stores to determine the true state of their vendor's affairs. Since compliance with the bulk transfer laws is onerous and expensive, legitimate financing transactions should not be required to comply when there is no reason to believe that other creditors will be prejudiced.

This section merely reiterates the provisions of Article 6 on Bulk Transfers which provides in Section 6–103(1) that transfers "made to give security for the performance of an obligation" are not subject to that Article.

Cross Reference:

Section 6–103(1).

Definitional Cross Reference:

"Security interest." Section 1–201.

Section 9–112. Where Collateral Is Not Owned by Debtor.

Unless otherwise agreed, when a secured party knows that collateral is owned by a person who is not the debtor, the owner of the collateral is entitled to receive from the secured party any surplus under Section 9–502(2) or under Section 9–504(1), and is not liable for the debt or for any deficiency after resale, and he has the same right as the debtor

(a) to receive statements under Section 9–208;

(b) to receive notice of and to object to a secured party's proposal to retain the collateral in satisfaction of the indebtedness under Section 9–505;

(c) to redeem the collateral under Section 9–506;

(d) to obtain injunctive or other relief under Section 9–507(1); and

(e) to recover losses caused to him under Section 9–208 (2).

New York Annotations

There is no comparable provision in existing New York law.

Historical Note: The revision of this section was to obtain greater clarity, to make it clear that an owner of collateral who is not the debtor is not liable under Sections 9–502(2) and 9–504(1), and to achieve consistency with Section 9–506 under which such an owner has a right of redemption. The Law Revision Commission had suggested such a clarification. (1956 Recommendations, p. 265; Excerpts, p. 468.)

Official Uniform Comment

Prior Uniform Statutory Provision: None.

Purposes:

Under the definition of Section 9–105, in any provisions of the Article dealing with the collateral the term "debtor" means the owner of the collateral even though he is not the person who owes payment or performance of the obligation secured. The section covers several situations in which the implications of this definition are specifically set out.

The duties which this section imposes on a secured party toward such an owner of collateral are conditioned on the secured party's knowledge of the true state of facts. Short of such knowledge he may continue to deal exclusively with the person who owes the obligation. Nor does the section suggest that the secured party is under any duty of inquiry. It does not purport to cut across the law of conversion or of ultra vires. Whether a person who does not own property has authority to encumber it for his own debts and whether a person is free to encumber his property as collateral for the debts of another, are matters to be decided under other rules of law and are not covered by this section.

The section does not purport to be an exhaustive treatment of the subject. It isolates certain problems which may be expected to arise and states rules as to them. Others will no doubt arise: their solution is left to the courts.

Cross References:

Sections 9–105, 9–208 and Part 5.

Definitional Cross References:

"Collateral." Section 9–105.
"Debtor." Section 9–105.
"Notice." Section 1–201.
"Person." Section 1–201.
"Receive notice." Section 1–201.
"Right." Section 1–201.
"Secured party." Section 9–105.

Section 9–113. Security Interests Arising Under Article on Sales.

[Editor's note: The following is effective until and including June 29, 1995.]

A security interest arising solely under the Article on Sales (Article 2) is subject to the provisions of this Article except that to the extent that and so long as the debtor does not have or does not lawfully obtain possession of the goods

(a) no security agreement is necessary to make the security interest enforceable; and

(b) no filing is required to perfect the security interest; and

(c) the rights of the secured party on default by the debtor are governed by the Article on Sales (Article 2).

[Editor's note: The following takes effect June 30, 1995.]

A security interest arising solely under the Article on Sales (Article 2) or the Article on Leases (Article 2A) is subject to the provisions of this Article except that to the extent that and so long as the debtor does not have or does not lawfully obtain possession of the goods

(a) no security agreement is necessary to make the security interest enforceable; and

(b) no filing is required to perfect the security interest; and

(c) the rights of the secured party on default by the debtor are governed (i) by the Article on Sales (Article 2) in the case of a security interest arising solely under such Article or (ii) by the Article on Leases (article 2A) in the case of a security interest arising solely under such Article.

New York Annotations

See the New York annotations to the various sections of the article on sales (Article 2) referred to in the Comments to this Section 9–113. Also see the annotations to Sections 2–326, 2–402, 2–403, and 2–502 and 2–716. In some of these cases what may appear to be a "security interest" is excluded from Section 1–201 (37). Note should also be taken of the fact that the "creditor" may be the buyer, and the "debtor" may be the seller. (E. g., Sections 2–502, 2–711.) Finally, when the debtor "lawfully" obtains possession, Article 9 rules apply.

Historical Note: This new section clarifies the application of Article 9 to security interests created by Article 2 on sales, and follows a suggestion of the Law Revision Commission as to the need for such a provision. Conforming changes were made in Sections 2–401, 2–402, and 2–506. While Article 9 applies to security interests arising under Article 2, If the debtor has not obtained or is not in possession of the goods, the former requisites of Article 9 as to a written security agreement and as to filing are obviated and on default by the debtor the secured party's rights are governed by Article 2 on sales and not by Part 5 of Article 9. Of course, if the debtor obtains or has possession of the goods, then all provisions of Article 9 are applicable. (1956 Recommendations, p. 265; 1956 Report, p. 31.)

Official Uniform Comment

Prior Uniform Statutory Provision: None.

Purposes:

1. Under the provisions of Article 2 on Sales, a seller of goods may reserve a security interest (see, e.g., Sections 2–401 and 2–505); and in certain circumstances, whether or not a security interest is reserved, the seller has rights of resale and stoppage under Sections 2–703, 2–705 and 2–706 which are similar to the rights of a secured party. Similarly, under such sections as Sections 2–506, 2–707 and 2–711, a financing agency, an agent, a buyer or another person may have a security interest or other right in goods similar to that of a seller. The use of the term "security interest" in the Sales Article is meant to bring the interests so designated within this Article. This section makes it clear, however, that such security interests are exempted from certain provisions of this Article. Compare Section 4–208(3), making similar special provisions for security interests arising in the bank collection process.

2. The security interests to which this section applies commonly arise by operation of law in the course of a sales transaction. Since the circumstances under which they arise are defined in the Sales Article, there is no need for the "security agreement" defined in Section 9–105(1)(l) and required by Section 9–203 (1) and paragraph (a) dispenses with such requirements. The requirement of filing may be inapplicable under Sections 9–302 (1)(a) and (b), 9–304 and 9–305, where the goods are in the possession of the secured party or of a bailee other than the debtor. To avoid difficulty in the residual cases, as for example where a bailee does not receive notification of the secured party's interest until after the security interest arises, paragraph (b)dispenses with any filing requirement. Finally, paragraph makes inapplicable the default provisions of Part 5 of this Article, since the Sales Article contains detailed provisions governing stoppage of delivery and resale after breach. See Section 2–705, 2–706, 2–707(2) and 2–711(3).

3. These limitations on the applicability of this Article to security interests arising under the Sales Article are appropriate only so long as the debtor does not have or lawfully obtain possession of the goods. Compare Section 56(b) of the Uniform Sales Act. A secured party who wishes to retain a security interest after the debtor lawfully

obtains possession must comply fully with all the provisions of this Article and ordinarily must file a financing statement to perfect his interest. This is the effect of the "except' clause in the preamble to this section. Note that in the case of a buyer who has a security interest in rejected goods under Section 2–711(3), the buyer is the "secured party" and the seller is the "debtor."

4. This section applies only to a "security interest." The definition of "security interest" in Section 1–201(37) expressly excludes the special property interest of a buyer of goods on identification under Section 2–401(1). The seller's interest after identification and before delivery may be more than a security interest by virtue of explicit agreement under Section 2–401(1) or 2–501(1), by virtue of the provisions of Section 2–401(2), (3) or (4), or by virtue of substitution pursuant to Section 2–501(2). In such cases, Article 9 is inapplicable by the terms of Section 9–102(1)(a).

5. Where there is a "security interest", this section applies only if the security interest arises "solely" under the Sales Article. Thus Section 1–201(37) permits a buyer to acquire by agreement a security interest in goods not in his possession or control; such a security interest does not impair his rights under the Sales Article, but any rights based on the security agreement are fully subject to this Article without regard to the limitations of this section. Similarly, a seller who reserves a security interest by agreement does not lose his rights under the Sales Article, but rights other than those conferred by the Sales Article depend on full compliance with this Article.

Cross References:

Point 1: Sections 2–401, 2–505, 2–506, 2–705, 2–706, 2–707, 2–711(3), 4–208(3).

Point 2: Sections 2–705, 2–706, 2–707(2), 2–711(3), 9–203(1), 9–302(1)(a) and (b), 9–304, 9–305 and Part 5.

Point 3: Section 2–711(3).

Point 4: Sections 2–401, 2–501 and 9–102(1)(a).

Definitional Cross References:

"Agreement." Section 1–201(3).
"Debtor." Section 9–105.
"Goods." Section 9–105.
"Rights." Section 1–201.
"Secured party." Section 9–105.
"Security agreement." Section 9–105.
"Security interest." Section 1–201.

Section 9–114. Consignment.

(1) A person who delivers goods under a consignment which is not a security interest and who would be required to file under this Article by paragraph of subdivision three of Section 2-326 has priority over a secured party who is or becomes a creditor of the consignee and who would have a perfected security interest in the goods if they were the property of the consignee, and also has priority with respect to identifiable cash proceeds received on or before delivery of the goods to a buyer, if

(a) the consignor complies with the filing provisions of the Article on Sales with respect to consignments (Paragraph of subdivision three of Section 2-326) before the consignee receives possession of the goods; and

(b) the consignor gives notification in writing to the holder of the security interest if the holder has filed a financing statement covering the same types of goods before the date of the filing made by the consignor; and

(c) the holder of the security interest receives the notification within five years before the consignee receives possession of the goods; and

(d) the notification states that the consignor expects to deliver goods on consignment to the consignee, describing the goods by item or type.

(2) In the case of a consignment which is not a security interest and in which the requirements of the preceding subsection have not been met, a person who delivers goods to another is subordinate to a person who would have a perfected security interest in the goods if they were the property of the debtor.

Added by Laws 1977, Ch. 866, eff. July 2, 1978.

Official Uniform Comment

Prior Uniform Statutory Provision: None.

Purposes:

1. This section requires that where goods are furnished to a merchant under the arrangement known as consignment rather than in a security transaction, the consignor must, in order to protect his position as against an inventory secured party of the consignee, give to that party the same notice and at the same time that he would give to that party if that party had filed first with respect to inventory and if the consignor were furnishing the goods under an inventory security agreement instead of under a consignment.

For the distinction between true consignment and security arrangements, see Section 1–201(37). For the assimilation of consignments under certain circumstances to goods on sale or return and the requirements of filing in the case of consignments, see Section 2–326.

The requirements of notice in this section conform closely to the concepts and the language of Section 9–312(3), which should be consulted together with the relevant Comments.

Except in the limited cases of identifiable cash proceeds received on or before delivery of the goods to a buyer, no attempt has been made to provide rules as to perfection of a claim to proceeds of consignments (compare Section 9–306) or the priority thereof (compare Section 9–312). It is believed that under many true consignments the consignor acquires a claim for an agreed amount against the consignee at the moment of sale, and does not look to the proceeds of sale. In contrast to the assumption of this Article that rights to proceeds of security interests under Section 9–306 represent the presumed intent of the parties (compare Section 9–203(3)), the Article goes on the assumption that if consignors intend to claim the proceeds of sale, they will do so by expressly contracting for them and will perfect their security interests therein.

Cross References:

Sections 2–326 and 9–312(3).

Definitional Cross References:

"Consignment." Section 1–201(37).

"Debtor." Section 9–105.
"Goods." Section 9–105.
"Notification." Section 1–201(26).
"Proceeds." Section 9–306.
"Security interest." Section 1–201(37).

Section 9–115. Investment Property.

(1) In this Article:

(a) "Commodity account" means an account maintained by a commodity intermediary in which a commodity contract is carried for a commodity customer.

(b) "Commodity contract" means a commodity futures contract, an option on a commodity futures contract, a commodity option, or other contract that, in each case, is:

(i) traded on or subject to the rules of a board of trade that has been designated as a contract market for such a contract pursuant to the federal commodities laws; or

(ii) traded on a foreign commodity board of trade, exchange, or market, and is carried on the books of a commodity intermediary for a commodity customer.

(c) "Commodity customer" means a person for whom a commodity intermediary carries a commodity contract on its books.

(d) "Commodity intermediary" means:

(i) a person who is registered as a futures commission merchant under the federal commodities laws; or

(ii) a person who in the ordinary course of its business provides clearance or settlement services for a board of trade that has been designated as a contract market pursuant to the federal commodities laws.

(e) "Control" with respect to a certificated security, uncertificated security, or security entitlement has the meaning specified in Section 8–106. A secured party has control over a commodity contract if by agreement among the commodity customer, the commodity intermediary, and the secured party, the commodity intermediary has agreed that it will apply any value distributed on account of the commodity contract as directed by the secured party without further consent by the commodity customer. If a commodity customer grants a security interest in a commodity contract to its own commodity intermediary, the commodity intermediary as secured party has control. A secured party has control over a securities account or commodity account if the secured party has control over all security entitlements or commodity contracts carried in the securities account or commodity account.

(f) "Investment property" means:

(i) a security, whether certificated or uncertificated;

(ii) a security entitlement;

UCC

(iii) a securities account;

(iv) a commodity contract; or

(v) a commodity account.

(2) Attachment or perfection of a security interest in a securities account is also attachment or perfection of a security interest in all security entitlements carried in the securities account. Attachment or perfection of a security interest in a commodity account is also attachment or perfection of a security interest in all commodity contracts carried in the commodity account.

(3) A description of collateral in a security agreement or financing statement is sufficient to create or perfect a security interest in a certificated security, uncertificated security, security entitlement, securities account, commodity contract, or commodity account whether it describes the collateral by those terms, or as investment property, or by description of the underlying security, financial asset, or commodity contract. A description of investment property collateral in a security agreement or financing statement is sufficient if it identifies the collateral by specific listing, by category, by quantity, by a computational or allocational formula or procedure, or by any other method, if the identity of the collateral is objectively determinable.

(4) Perfection of a security interest in investment property is governed by the following rules:

(a) A security interest in investment property may be perfected by control.

(b) Except as otherwise provided in paragraphs (c) and (d), a security interest in investment property may be perfected by filing.

(c) If the debtor is a broker or securities intermediary, a security interest in investment property is perfected when it attaches. The filing of a financing statement with respect to a security interest in investment property granted by a broker or securities intermediary has no effect for purposes of perfection or priority with respect to that security interest.

(d) If a debtor is a commodity intermediary, a security interest in a commodity contract or a commodity account is perfected when it attaches. The filing of a financing statement with respect to a security interest in a commodity contract or a commodity account granted by a commodity intermediary has no effect for purposes of perfection or priority with respect to that security interest.

(5) Priority between conflicting security interests in the same investment property is governed by the following rules:

(a) A security interest of a secured party who has control over investment property has priority over a security interest of a secured party who does not have control over the investment property.

(b) Except as otherwise provided in paragraphs (c) and (d), conflicting security interests of secured parties each of whom has control rank equally.

(c) Except as otherwise agreed by the securities intermediary, a security interest in a security entitlement or a securities account granted to the debtor's own securities intermediary has priority over any security interest granted by the debtor to another secured party.

(d) Except as otherwise agreed by the commodity intermediary, a security interest in a commodity contract or a commodity account granted to the debtor's own commodity intermediary has priority over any security interest granted by the debtor to another secured party.

(e) Conflicting security interests granted by a broker, a securities intermediary, or a commodity intermediary which are perfected without control rank equally.

(f) In all other cases, priority between conflicting security interests in investment property is governed by Section 9–312(5), (6), and (7). Section 9–312(4) does not apply to investment property.

(6) If a security certificate in registered form is delivered to a secured party pursuant to agreement, a written security agreement is not required for attachment or enforceability of the security interest, delivery suffices for perfection of the security interest, and the security interest has priority over a conflicting security interest perfected by means other than control, even if a necessary indorsement is lacking.

(7) The perfection and priority rules in this section do not apply to security interests in shares or other ownership interests evidenced by stock certificates or other instruments of a corporation or partnership formed for the purposes of cooperative ownership of real property governed by Section 9–304(7).

Added by Laws 1997, Ch. 566, eff. Oct. 10, 1997.

Section 9–116. Security Interest Arising in Purchase or Delivery of Financial Asset.

(1) If a person buys a financial asset through a securities intermediary in a transaction in which the buyer is obligated to pay the purchase price to the securities intermediary at the time of the purchase, and the securities intermediary credits the financial asset to the buyer's securities account before the buyer pays the securities intermediary, the securities intermediary has a security interest in the buyer's security entitlement securing the buyer's obligation to pay. A security agreement is not required for attachment or enforceability of the security interest, and the security interest is automatically perfected.

(2) If a certificated security, or other financial asset represented by a writing which in the ordinary course of business is transferred by delivery with any necessary indorsement or assignment is delivered pursuant to an agreement between persons in the business of dealing with such securities or financial assets and the agreement calls for delivery versus payment, the person delivering the certificate or other financial asset has a security interest in the certificated security or other financial asset securing the seller's right to receive payment. A security agreement is not required for attachment or enforceability of the security interest, and the security interest is automatically perfected.

Added by Laws 1997, Ch. 566, eff. Oct. 10, 1997.

PART 2

VALIDITY OF SECURITY AGREEMENT AND RIGHTS OF PARTIES THERETO

Section 9–201. General Validity of Security Agreement.

Except as otherwise provided by this Act a security agreement is effective according to its terms between the parties against purchasers of the collateral and against creditors. Nothing in the Article validates any charge or practice illegal under any statute or regulation thereunder governing usury, small loans, retail installment sales, or the like, or extends the application of any such statute or regulation to any transaction not otherwise subject thereto.

New York Annotations

The emphasis here and throughout the Code is on the effectiveness of a security instrument, whereas older statutory provisions are often phrased in negative terms. Compare Lien Law, § 230 (chattel mortgages) with Personal Property Law, § 64 (conditional sales).

Historical Note: The phrase "rule of law" had been criticized by the Law revision Commission as vague and the section was changed so as to substitute "statute or regulation thereunder" in the last sentence. (1956 Recommendations, p. 266; Excerpts, p.468.)

Official Uniform Comment

Prior Uniform Statutory Provisions: Section 4, Uniform Conditional Sales Act; Section 3, Uniform Trust Receipts Act.

Changes: Rewritten; no change in substance.

Purposes of Changes:

This section states the general validity of a security agreement. In general the security agreement is effective between the parties; it is likewise effective against third parties. Exceptions to this general rule arise where there is a specific provision in any Article of this Act, for example, where Article 1 invalidates a disclaimer of the obligations of good faith, etc. (Section 1–102(3)), or this Article subordinates the security interest because it has not been perfected (Section 9–301) or for other reasons (see Section 9–312 on priorities) or defeats the security interest where certain types of claimants are involved (for example Section 9–307 on buyers of goods). As pointed out in the Note to Section 9–102, there is no intention that the enactment of this Article should repeal retail installment selling acts or small loan acts. Nor of course are the usury laws of any state repealed. These are mentioned in the text of Section 9–201 as examples of applicable laws, outside this Code entirely, which might invalidate the terms of a security agreement.

Cross References:

Sections 1–102(3), 9–301, 9–307 and 9–312.

Definitional Cross References:

"Collateral." Section 9–105.
"Creditor." Section 1–201.
"Party." Section 1–201.
"Purchaser." Section 1–201.
"Security agreement." Section 9–105.

Section 9–202. Title to Collateral Immaterial.

Each provision of this Article with regard to rights, obligations and remedies applies whether title to collateral is in the secured party or in the debtor.

New York Annotations

New York has adopted the title theory of chattel mortgages. Parshall v. Eggert, 54 N.Y. 18 (1873). It is difficult to find many cases where this theory is determinative of results in light of the extensive statutory controls. See, Barrett Mfg. Co. v. Van Ronk, 212 N.Y. 90, 105 N.E. 811 (1914). The question may be important procedurally, Spencer v. Standard Chemicals and Metals Corp., 237 N.Y. 479, 143 N.E. 651 (1924), or for tax purposes, Prudential Insurance Co. of America v. McGoldrick, 256 App. Div. 205, 9 N.Y.S.2d 515, aff'd, 281 N.Y.595, 22 N.E.2d 166 (1939).

Official Uniform Comment

Prior Uniform Statutory Provision: None.

Purposes:

The rights and duties of the parties to a security transaction and of third parties are stated In this Article without reference to the location of "title" to the collateral. Thus the incidents of a security interest which secures the purchase price of goods are the same under this Article whether the secured party appears to have retained title or the debtor appears to have obtained title and then conveyed it or a lien to the secured party. This Article in no way determines which line of interpretation (title theory v. lien theory or retained title v. conveyed title) should be followed in cases where the applicability of some other rule of law depends upon who has title. Thus if a revenue law imposes a tax on the "legal" owner of goods or if a corporation law makes a vote of the stockholders prerequisite to a corporation "giving" a security interest but not if it acquires property "subject" to a security interest, this Article does not attempt to define whether the secured party is a "legal" owner or whether the transaction "gives" a security interest for the purpose of such laws. Other rules of law of the agreement of the parties determine the location of "title" for such purposes.

Petitions for reclamation brought by a secured party in his debtor's insolvency proceedings have often been granted or denied on a title theory: where the secured party has title, reclamation will be granted; where he has "merely a lien", reclamation may be denied. For the treatment of such petitions under this Article, see Point 1 of Comment to Section 9–507.

Cross References:

Sections 2–401 and 2–507.

Definitional Cross References:

"Collateral." Section 9–105.

"Debtor." Section 9–105.
"Remedy." Section 1–201.
"Rights." Section 1–201.
"Secured party." Section 9–105.

Section 9–203. Attachment and Enforceability of Security Interest; Proceeds; Formal Requisites.

(1) Subject to the provisions of Section 4–208 on the security interest of a collecting bank, Sections 9–115 and 9–116 on security interests in investment property, and Section 9–113 on a security interest arising under the Article on Sales, a security interest is not enforceable against the debtor or third parties with respect to the collateral and does not attach unless:

(a) The collateral is in the possession of the secured party pursuant to agreement, the collateral is investment property and the secured party has control pursuant to agreement, or the debtor has signed a security agreement which contains a description of the collateral and in addition, when the security interest covers crops growing or to be grown or timber to be cut, a description of the land concerned;

(b) value has been given; and

(c) the debtor has rights in the collateral.

(2) A security interest attaches when it becomes enforceable against the debtor with respect to the collateral. Attachment occurs as soon as all of the events specified in subsection (1) have taken place unless explicit agreement postpones the time of attaching.

(3) Unless otherwise agreed a security agreement gives the secured party the rights to proceeds provided by Section 9–306.

(4) A transaction, although subject to this Article, is also subject to article nine of the personal property law cited as the motor vehicle retail instalment sales act, article ten of the personal property law cited as the retail instalment sales act, article nine of the banking law relating to licensed lenders, article eleven-B of the banking law relating to sales finance companies, article twelve-B of the banking law relating to insurance premium finance agencies, and article five of the general business law relating to collateral loan brokers, and in the case of conflict between the provisions of this Article and any such statute, the provisions of such statute control. Failure to comply with any applicable statute has only the effect which is specified therein.

Amended by Laws 1977, Ch. 866, eff. July 2, 1978; Laws 1982, Ch. 928, eff. Dec. 21, 1982 and deemed to have been in full force and effect on and after Sept. 1, 1982; L. 1983, Ch. 321, eff. June 21, 1983; L. 1997, Ch. 566, eff. Oct. 10, 1997.

New York Annotations

(1)(a) In general this subsection states the present New York law as to pledges. Furthermore, possession taken under an unfilled chattel mortgage makes recording unnecessary (Lien Law, § 230).

(b) The requirement of a written security agreement containing a description of collateral, imposed by subsection (1)(b) where the collateral is not in possession of the third party, is generally in accord with present New York law. Thus a factor's lien (Personal Property Law, § 45) and a trust receipt transaction (Personal Property Law, § 52) must be in writing and contain a description of the collateral. To the extent that chattel mortgages must be recorded the agreement must obviously be in writing (Lien Law, § 230). A conditional sale contract must also be in writing to qualify for recording (Personal Property Law, § 65). Apparently an oral chattel mortgage or conditional sale was valid at common law as between the parties. See Jones, Chattel Mortgages and Conditional Sales, Section 2. Alexander v. Kellner, 131 App. Div. 809, 116 N.Y.S. 98 (1909). Under the Code no change will be made in the special formal requisites under Personal Property Law, § 64-a, Lien Law, § 239-I, the Motor Vehicle Retail Instalment Sales Act (Personal Property Law, Art. 9), the Retail Instalment Sales Act (Personal Property Law, Art. 10), Banking Law, §§ 340–357 (small loans), and the usury laws. See Section 9–210 and subsection(2).

Although there is no general requirement of a description of the real estate where the collateral is crops, gas, or minerals to be extracted, or timber to be cut, the Code requirement is similar to the provision for conditional sales of fixtures, Personal Property Law, § 67. The law governing agricultural mortgages (N.Y. Unconsol. Laws, § 2 (McKinney), Lien Law, § 230-b) specifically rejects the requirement of a seal or an acknowledgment.

As to assignments of accounts or contract rights see Risley v. Phenix Bank, 83 N.Y. 318 (1881); Superior Brassiere Co., Inc. v. Zimetbaum, 214 App. Div. 525, 212 N.Y.S. 473 (1925).Note that security interest is defined in Section 1–201(37).

Historical Note: Changes have been made for clarification and precision. In particular, in subsection (1) the security interest of a collecting bank under Article 4 and a security interest under Article 2 on sales are recognized as needing treatment apart from general security interests in regard to requirements for enforceability. In clause (b) the insertion of the words "or timber to be cut" was to conform to Section 9–204(2)(b), and in claiming the proceeds of collateral the new sentence makes it unnecessary to try and describe the proceeds because of the impossibility of being certain in advance as to the form of the proceeds.

The changes in subsection (2) specifically subject a non-complying transaction to the consequence of non-compliance stated in the applicable statute, but not to any general rule that an illegal contract is void. The Law Revision Commission suggestions as to this section have thus been met. (1956 Recommendations, p. 267; Excerpts, p. 469.)

Official Uniform Comment

Prior Uniform Statutory Provision: Section 2, Uniform Trust Receipts Act.

Purposes:

1. Subsection (1) states three basic prerequisites to the existence of a security interest: agreement, value, and collateral. In addition, the agreement must be in writing unless the collateral is in the possession of the secured party (including an agent on his behalf see Comment 2 to section 9–305). When all of these elements exist, the security agreement becomes enforceable between the parties and is said to "attach." Perfection of a security interest (see Section 9–303) will in many cases depend on the additional step of filing a financing statement (see Section 9–302) or possession of the collateral (Sections 9–304 (1) and 9–305). Section 9–301 states who will take priority over a security interest which has attached but which has not been perfected. Subsection (2) states a rule of construction under which the security interest, unless

UCC

postponed by explicit agreement, attaches automatically when the stated events have occurred.

2. As to the type of description of collateral in a written security agreement which will satisfy the requirements of this section, see Section 9–110 and Comment thereto.

In the case of crops growing or to be grown or timber to be cut the best identification is by describing the land, and subsection (1)(a) requires such a description.

3. One purpose of the formal requisites stated in subsection (1)(a) is evidentiary. The requirements of written record minimizes the possibility of future dispute as to the terms of a security agreement and as to what property stands as collateral for the obligation secured. Where the collateral is in the possession of the secured party, the evidentiary need for a written record is much less than where the collateral is in the debtor's possession; customarily, of course, as a matter of business practice the written record will be kept, but, in this Article as at common law, the writing is not a formal requisite. Subsection (1)(a), therefore, dispenses with the written agreement–and thus with signature and description–if the collateral is in the secured party's possession.

4. The definition of "security agreement" (Section 9–105) is "an agreement which creates or provides for a security interest." Under that definition the requirement of this section that the debtor sign a security agreement is not intended to reject, and does not reject, the deeply rooted doctrine that a bill of sale although absolute in form may be shown to have been in fact given as security. Under this Article as under prior law a debtor may show by parol evidence that a transfer purporting to be absolute was in fact for security and may then, on payment of the debt, assert his fundamental right to return of the collateral and execution of an acknowledgment of satisfaction.

5. The formal requisite of a writing stated in this section is not only a condition to the enforceability of a security interest against third parties, it is in the nature of a Statue of Frauds. Unless the secured party is in possession of the collateral, his security interest, absent a writing which satisfies paragraph (1)(a), is not enforceable even against the debtor, and cannot be made so on any theory of equitable mortgage or the like. If he has advanced money, he is of course a creditor and, like any creditor, is entitled after judgment to appropriate process to enforce his claim against his debtor's assets; he will not, however, have against his debtor the rights given a secured party be Part 5 of this Article on Default. The theory of equitable mortgage, insofar as it has operated to allow creditors to enforce informal security agreements against debtors, may well have developed as a necessary escape from the elaborate requirements of execution, acknowledgment and the like which the nineteenth century chattel mortgage acts vainly relied on as a deterrent to fraud. Since this Article reduces formal requisites to a minimum, the doctrine is no longer necessary or useful. More harm than good would result from allowing creditors to establish a secured status by parol evidence after they have neglected the simple formality of obtaining a signed writing.

6. Subsection (4) states that the provisions of regulatory statutes covering the field of consumer finance prevail over the provisions of this Article in case of conflict. The second sentence of the subsection is added to make clear that no doctrine of total voidness for illegality is intended: failure to comply with the applicable regulatory statute has whatever effect may be specified in that statute, but no more.

Cross References:

Sections 4–208 and 9–113.
Point 1: Section 9–110.
Point 5: Part 5.

Definitional Cross References:

"Collateral." Section 9–105.

"Debtor." Section 9–105.
"Party." Section 1–201.
"Proceeds." Section 9–306.
"Secured party." Section 9–105.
"Security agreement." Section 9–105.
"Security interest." Section 1–201.
"Signed." Section 1 201.

Section 9–204. After-Acquired property; Future Advances.

(1) Except as provided in subsection (2), a security agreement may provide that any or all obligations covered by the security agreement are to be secured by after-acquired collateral.

(2) No security interest attaches under an after-acquired property clause to consumer goods other than accessions (Section 9-314) when given as additional security unless the debtor acquires rights in them within ten days after the secured party gives value.

(3) Obligations covered by a security agreement may include future advances or other value whether or not the advances or value are given pursuant to commitment (subsection (1) of Section 9-105).

Amended by Laws 1977, Ch. 866, eff. July 2, 1978.

New York Annotations

General comment. In general, this section and Sections 9-108, 9-201, and 9-303, make possible in respect of all classes of security the creation (without further act at the time the property comes into existence or into the possession of the debtor) of a security interest in after-acquired property in a manner permitted by present New York law only as to certain collateral, e.g. crops, livestock, and perhaps inventory. Article 9 follows present New York law in some cases and makes substantial changes in others.

Chattel mortgages. With special exceptions, current New York law protects an attaching creditor against a chattel mortgagee who claims solely under an after-acquired property clause in a recorded mortgage, since the recording is not constructive notice to the creditor. Rochester Distilling Co. v. Rasey, 142 N.Y. 570, 37 N.E. 632 (1894). The result is apparently different where the contest is between a bona fide purchaser and such a mortgagee. Kribbs v. Alford, 120 N.Y. 519, 24 N.E. 811 (1890). Thus, a trustee in bankruptcy prevailed over the mortgagee in Zartman v. First Nat'l Bank, 189 N.Y. 267, 82 N.E. 127 (1907).

Crops and livestock. By special statute certain agricultural mortgages may now create an effective security interest by the operation of an after-acquired property provision even beyond the one year limit in subsection (4)(a) of this section. N.Y. Unconsol. Laws, § 1 (McKinney). This statute apparently makes obsolete the more limited provisions of Lien Law, § 230-b, which creates a one-year limitation.

Mortgages of real and personal property. Such mortgages recorded in the realty records when made by a Rural Electric Cooperative effectively cover after-acquired property. Rural Electric Cooperative Law, § 63. Further, under Lien Law, § 231, supplemental mortgages covering after-acquired property may be recorded with the original corporate mortgage of real and personal property to secure payment of bonds, notes or other evidences of indebtedness.

Utility or railroad mortgages. Where there are general mortgages by such firms, it is well settled that after-acquired property necessary to the operation of the firm may be effectively included within the mortgage without any additional action by the mortgagee. Ithaca Trust Co. v. Ithaca Traction Corp., 248 N.Y. 322, 162 N.E. 93 (1928); Platt v. N.Y. & Sea Beach Railway Co., 9 App. Div. 87, 41 N.Y.S. 42, aff'd, 153 N.Y. 670, 48 N.E. 1106 (1897).

Factor's liens. Although the matter is not free from doubt, Personal Property Law, § 45, seems to give effect to an after-acquired property clause except in the case of accounts which must be either specially assigned or as to which the account debtors must be notified. Compare, In re Comet Textile Co., 15 F.Supp. 963 (S.D.N.Y.), aff'd, 91 F.2d 1008 (2d Cir. 1937), and Irving Trust Co. v. Commercial Factors Corp., 68 F.2d 864 (2d Cir. 1934).

Trust receipts. Personal Property Law, § 54, makes a contract to give a trust receipt equivalent to a trust receipt; thus it would appear that after-acquired collateral could be subjected to the entruster's security interest.

Accounts receivable and contract rights. The existing New York law on the effect of an assignment of a future account or contract right is very confused. The Code permits such an assignment to be effective when the account comes into existence or when the contract is made. Note the definition of these two kinds of intangibles in Section 9–106. The requirement of the Factor's Lien Act is noted above. Under a relatively recent New York case, City of New York v. Bedford Bar & Grill, Inc. 2 N.Y.2d 429, 141 N.E.2d 575 (1957), the confusion in present law is demonstrated in a 4 to 2 decision where both the majority and minority relied on the same kind of cases. The majority concluded that a bank, claiming as assignee of the right to a liquor license refund, was subordinated to the claim of a judgment lienor. The case may be of limited value, since it appears that the assignment was completed before the application for license was made, and a concept of safeguarding the public obligor or debtor may be an unspoken premise. See, Note, 43 Cornell L.Q. 289 (1957).

Consumer goods. Subsection (4)(b), containing a ten-day limit on after-acquired property provisions where consumer goods are given as additional security, must be read in light of Personal Property Law, § 410, which as to retail instalment sales provides for conspicuous disclosure of such a provision. The Code security interest will be subjected to that requirement. Section 9–201. On the other hand, Personal Property Law, § 66-a, precluding additions to filed conditional sales, would be repealed by the Code.

Future advances. New York law permits the securing of future advances by chattel mortgage. Brown v. Kiefer, 71 N.Y. 610 (1877). See N.Y. Unconsol. Laws, § 3 (McKinney) (agricultural mortgages). Determining the relative rights between a future advance lender and a creditor, where no commitment has been made for the advance, will involve an analysis of "obligation" in Section 1–201(37), the definition of security interest, and the general provisions of Section 9–201.

Historical Note: The changes in subsections (1), (3), (4)(b), and (5) were for clarification.

The changes in subsection (4)(a) widen the language to encompass deeds of trust used in many states, as well as mortgages, and broaden the exception to permit attachment under an after-acquired property clause to crops after the one-year period when given in conjunction with a land improvement transaction.

Former subsection (6) dealing with a financing buyer was deleted in its entirety. Under the revisions of Sections 1–201(37) and 2–401, identification of goods to a contract for sale gives the buyer a "special property" which is not a "security interest." The buyer may also acquire a security interest but in order to do so must comply with the normal requirements of this Article. This change conforms to the Law Revision Commission's suggestion. (1956 Recommendations, p.269; Excerpts, pp. 469 and 470.)

Official Uniform Comment

Prior Uniform Statutory Provision: None.

Purposes:

1. Subsection (1) makes clear that a security interest arising by virtue of an after-acquired property clause has equal status with a security interest in collateral in which the debtor has right sat the time value is given under the security agreement. That is to say: the security interest in after–acquired property is not merely an "equitable" interest; no further action by the secured party—such as the taking of a supplemental agreement covering the new collateral—is required. This does not however mean that the interest is proof against subordination or defeat: Section 9–108 should be consulted on when a security interest in after-acquired collateral is not security for antecedent debt, and Section 9–312(3) and (4) on when such a security interest may be subordinated to a conflicting purchase money security interest in the same collateral.

2. This Article accepts the principle of a "continuing general lien." It rejects the doctrine–of which the judicial attitude toward after-acquired property interests was one expression–that there is reason to invalidate as a matter of law what has been variously called the floating charge, the free-handed mortgage and the lien on a shifting stock. This Article validates a security interest in the debtor's existing and future assets, even though (see Section 9–205) the debtor has liberty to use or dispose of collateral without being required to account for proceeds or substitute new collateral. (See further, however, Section 9–306 on Proceeds and Comment thereto.)

The widespread nineteenth century prejudice against the floating charge was based on a feeling, often inarticulate in the opinions, that a commercial borrower should not be allowed to encumber all his assets present and future, and that for the protection not only of the borrower but of his other creditors a cushion of free assets should be preserved. That inarticulate premise has much to recommend it. This Article decisively rejects it not on the ground that it was wrong in policy but on the ground that it was not effective. In pre-Code law there was a multiplication of security devices designed to avoid the policy: field warehousing, trust receipts, factor's lien acts and so on. The cushion of free assets was not preserved. In almost every state it was possible before the Code for the borrower to give a lien on everything he held or would have. There have no doubt been sufficient economic reasons for the change. This Article, in expressly validating the floating charge, merely recognizes an existing state of things. The substantive rules of law set forth in the balance of the Article are designed to achieve the protection of the debtor and the equitable resolution of the conflicting claims of creditors which the old rules no longer give.

Notice that the question of assignment of future accounts is treated like any other case of after-acquired property: no periodic list of accounts is required by this Act. Where less than all accounts are assigned such a list may of course be necessary to permit identification of the particular accounts assigned.

3. Subsection (1) has been already referred to in connection with after-acquired property. It also serves to validate the so-called "cross-security" clause under which collateral acquired at anytime may secure advances whenever made.

4. Subsection (2) limits the operation of the after-acquired property clause against consumers. No such interest can be claimed as additional security in consumer goods (defined in Section 9–109), except accessions (see Section 9–314), acquired more than ten days after the giving of value.

5. Under subsection (3) collateral may secure future as well as present advances when the security agreement so provides. At common law and under chattel mortgage statutes there seems to have been a vaguely articulated prejudice against future advance agreements comparable to the prejudice against after-acquired property interests. Although only a very few jurisdictions went to the length of invalidating

interests claimed by virtue of future advances, judicial limitations severely restricted the usefulness of such arrangements. A common limitation was that an interest claimed in collateral existing at the time the security transaction was entered into for advances made thereafter was good only to the extent that the original security agreement specified the amount of such later advances and even the times at which they should be made. In line with the policy of this Article toward after-acquired property interests this subsection validates the future advance interest, provided only that the obligation be covered by the security agreement.

The effect of after-acquired property and future advance clauses in the security agreement should not be confused with the use of financing statements in notice filing. The references toaster-acquired property clauses and future advances clauses in Section 9–204 are limited to security agreements. This section follows Section 9–203, the section requiring a written security agreement, and its purpose is to make clear that confirmatory agreements are not necessary where the basic agreement has the clauses mentioned. This section has no reference to the operation of financing statements. The filing of a financing statement is effective to perfect security interests as to which the other required elements for perfection exist, whether the security agreement involved is one existing at the date of filing with an after-acquired property clause or a future advance clause, or whether the applicable security agreement is executed later. Indeed, Section 9–402(1) expressly contemplates that a financing statement may be filed when there is no security agreement. There is no need to refer to after-acquired property or future advances in the financing statement.

As in the case of interests in after-acquired collateral, a security interest based on future advances may be subordinated to conflicting interests in the same collateral. See Sections 9–301(4); 9–307(3); 9–312(3), (4) and (7).

Cross References:

Point 1: Sections 9–108 and 9–312.
Point 2: Sections 9–205 and 9–306.
Point 4: Sections 9–109 and 9–314.
Point 5: Sections 9–301(4); 9–307(3); 9–312(3), (4), and (7).

Definitional Cross References:

"Account." Section 9–106.
"Agreement." Section 1–201.
"Collateral." Section 9–105.
"Consumer goods." Section 9–109.
"Contract." Section 1–201.
"Debtor." Section 9–105.
"Purchase." Section 1–201.
"Pursuant to commitment." Section 9–105.
"Rights." Section 1–201.
"Secured party." Section 9–105
"Security agreement." Section 9–105
"Security interest." Section 1–201.
"Value." Section 1–201.

Section 9–205. Use or Disposition of Collateral Without Accounting Permissible.

A security interest is not invalid or fraudulent against creditors by reason of liberty in the debtor to use, commingle or dispose of all or part of the collateral (including returned or repossessed goods) or to collect or compromise accounts or chattel paper, or to accept the return of goods or make repossessions, or to use, commingle or dispose of proceeds, or by reason of the failure of the secured party to require the debtor to account for proceeds or replace collateral. This section does not relax the requirements of possession where perfection of a security interest depends upon possession of the collateral by the secured party or by a bailee.

1977 Amendment

Section 9–205 was amended by L. 1977, ch. 866, effective July 2, 1978, to delete the words "contract rights," from the first sentence.

New York Annotations

This section expressly rejects the rule that the debtor's unrestricted dominion over the collateral renders the security agreement void. Benedict v. Ratner, 268 U.S. 353, 45 S.Ct. 566, 69 L. Ed. 991 (1925). In New York the development of this fraud-in-law doctrine has been a history of the erosion of the general rule through special legislative enactments. The Code provision in effect represents a case of the exceptions swallowing the general rule.

The courts adopted, as part of the common law, the notion that any agreement between a mortgagee and a mortgagor that the mortgagor is free to sell, use, or dispose of the collateral and proceeds as the mortgagor sees fit and for his own benefit, renders the mortgage void as to creditors, e.g. Zartman v. First Nat'l Bank, 189 N.Y. 267, 82 N.E. 127 (1907); Skilton v. Coddington, 185 N.Y. 80, 77 N.E. 790 (1906); Wood v. Lowry & Douglass, 17 Wend. 492 (1837).

Thereafter, Benedict v. Ratner, *supra,* applied that same notion to the intangibles assigned in an accounts receivable transaction.

The legislature in Lien Law, § 230–b, and N.Y. Unconsol. Laws, § 4 (McKinney), explicitly limited the rule by permitting the uncontrolled sale of mortgaged chattels in agricultural transactions if the proceeds of such mortgage are applied on the debt or are invested in the remaining property subject to the mortgage. Similarly in the Factor's Lien Act the legislature specifically excepted from the rule those cases where goods are returned to the assignor by the account debtor, or where the assignor makes an adjustment with the account debtor. Personal Property Law, § 45(3) (par. 4). Compare Bloch v. Mills Factors Corp., 131 F.2d 562 (2d Cir. 1943) (prior statute).

The Code makes it clear that this fraud-in-law rule does not apply to any transactions now governed by the Factor's Lien Act or the Trust Receipts Act. Compare In re Cut Rate Furniture Co., 163 F.Supp. 360 (N.D.N.Y. 1958), and McCloskey v. Schroder Banking Corp., 7 Misc.2d 501, 168 N.Y.S.2d 522 (1957). Furthermore, the Code eliminates the possibility of a negative inference that the invalidating rule might apply to such transactions because of the express abrogation of the rule in relation to some aspects of Factor's Liens and Trust Receipts. See Personal Property Law, §§ 45 and 58-a. Manchester Nat'l Bank v. Roche, 186 F.2d 827 (1st Cir. 1951). See Section 9–306(4) for the limited rights of the secured party as to proceeds left in the debtor's control.

The legislature further limited the effect of the fraud-in-law rule in the Motor Vehicle Retail Instalment Sales Act and the Retail Instalment Sales Act by explicitly validating as against the assignor's creditors the assignment of covered contracts even where the assignor retains control of repossessed goods or of the payments under such a contract. Personal Property Law, §§ 302(10) and 411.

Historical Note: The last sentence has been added in view of the deletion of Section 9–305(2) which formerly required filing for a field warehouse arrangement. As a result, it was necessary to make it clear that the requirements of possession are not watered down by this section. In other words, where the security interest is perfected by filing, the secured party may allow the debtor to use, commingle, or dispose of collateral without invalidating the security interest by application of the doctrine of Benedict v. Ratner, 268 U.S. 353, 45 S.Ct. 566, 69 L.Ed. 991 (1925). But in a pledge or warehouse operation, similar freedom would negate the requisite actual and exclusive possession of the secured party or bailee. (1956 Recommendations, pp. 269-270.)

Official Uniform Comment

Prior Uniform Statutory Provision: None.

Purposes:

1. This Article expressly validates the floating charge or lien on a shifting stock. (See Sections 9–201, 9–204, and Comment to Section 9–204.) This section provides that a security interest is not invalid or fraudulent by reason of liberty in the debtor to dispose of the collateral without being required to account for proceeds or substitute new collateral. It repeals the rule of Benedict v. Ratner, 268 U.S. 353, 45 S.Ct. 566, 69 L.Ed. 991 (1925), and other cases which held such arrangements void as a matter of law because the debtor was given unfettered dominion or control over the collateral. The principle effect of the Benedict rule has been, not to discourage or eliminate security transactions in inventory and accounts receivable–on the contrary such transactions have vastly increased in volume–but rather to force financing arrangements in this field toward a self-liquidating basis. Furthermore, several lower court cases drew implications from Justice Brandeis' opinion in Benedict v. Ratner which required lenders operating in this field to observe a number of needless and costly formalities: for example it was thought necessary for the debtor to make daily remittances to the lender of all collections received, even though the amount remitted is immediately returned to the debtor in order to keep the loan at an agreed level.

2. The Benedict rule was, in the accounts receivable field, repealed in many of the state accounts receivable statutes enacted after 1943, and, in the inventory field, by some of the factor's lien statutes. (Benedict v. Ratner purported to state the law of New York and not a rule of federal bankruptcy law. Since its acceptance is a matter of state law, it can of course be rejected by state statute.)

3. The requirement of "policing" is the substance of the Benedict rule. While this section repeals Benedict in matters of form, the filing requirements (Section 9–302) give other creditors the opportunity to ascertain from public sources whether property of their debtor or prospective debtor is subject to secured claims, and the provisions about proceeds (Section 9–306(4)) enable creditors to claim collections which were made by the debtor more than 10 days before insolvency proceedings and commingled or deposited in a bank account before institution of the insolvency proceedings. The repeal of the Benedict rule under this section must be read in the light of these provisions.

4. Other decisions reaching results like that in the Benedict case, but relating to other aspects of dominion (of which Lee v. State Bank & Trust Co., 54 F.2d 518 (2d Circ. 1931), is an example) are likewise rejected.

5. Nothing in Section 9–205 prevents such "policing" or dominion as the secured party and the debtor may agree upon; business and not legal reasons will determine the extent to which strict accountability, segregation of collections, daily reports and the like will be employed.

6. The last sentence is added to make clear that the section does not mean that the holder of an unfilled security interest, whose perfection depends on possession of the collateral by the secured party or by a bailee (such as a field warehouseman), can allow the debtor access to and control over the goods without thereby losing his perfected interest. The common law rules on the degree and extent of possession which are necessary to perfect a pledge interest or to constitute a valid field warehouse are not relaxed by this or any other section of this Article.

Cross References:

Point 1: Sections 9–201 and 9–204.
Point 3: Sections 9–302 and 9–306(4).
Point 6: Sections 9–304 and 9–305.

Definitional Cross References:

"Account." Section 9–106.
"Chattel paper." Section 9–105.
"Collateral." Section 9–105.
"Creditor." Section 1–201.
"Debtor." Section 9–105.
"Goods." Section 9–105.
"Proceeds." Section 9–306.
"Secured party." Section 9–105.
"Security interest." Section 1–201.

Section 9–206. Agreement Not to Assert Defenses Against Assignee; Modification of Sales Warranties Where Security Agreement Exists.

(1) Subject to any statute or decision which establishes a different rule for buyers or lessees of consumer goods, an agreement by a buyer or lessee that he will not assert against an assignee any claim or defense which he may have against the seller or lessor is enforceable by an assignee who takes his assignment for value, in good faith and without notice of a claim or defense, except as to defenses of a type which may be asserted against a holder in due course of a negotiable instrument under the Article on Commercial Paper (Article 3). A buyer who as part of one transaction signs both a negotiable instrument and a security agreement makes such an agreement.

(2) When a seller retains a purchase money security interest in goods the Article on Sales (Article 2) governs the sale and any disclaimer, limitation or modification of the seller's warranties.

Amended by Laws 1963, Ch. 1003, eff. Sept. 27, 1964.

New York Annotations

(1) In New York the Motor Vehicle Retail Installment Sales Act prohibits the execution of a note which cuts off the buyer's defenses in litigation with third parties. Personal Property Law, § 302(9). On the other hand, the Retail Instalment Sales Act merely prohibits a general waiver of defenses. Personal Property Law, § 403(3). However, these same sections validate a contract provision which protects an assignee

under the contract, in good faith, for value and without notice of the claim within ten days after mailing a notice of the transfer to the buyer. The form and content of this notice are specified in the statute which calls for a specific disclosure of the effect of the notice. Both of these statutes exclude from their coverage, sales for a commercial or business use. This represents a policy determination similar to that of Section 9–206 (1) which limits protection to buyers of consumer goods. Personal Property Law, §§ 301(4) and 401(1).

(2) This subsection is in accord with present New York law in providing that a sale offends is governed by the law of sales although the seller retains a security interest. Personal Property Law, §§ 62 and 63.

Historical Note: The changes made conform to the suggestions of the Law Revision Commission. Former subsection (1), giving special treatment as a matter of uniform policy to defenses asserted by reason of defects in consumer goods, has been deleted. As a consequence, under former subsection (2), now subsection (1), each state is free to establish any such rules by statute or decision in conformity with local policy. Former subsection (3), now subsection (2), has been revised for clarity. (1956 Recommendations, p. 271; Excerpts, p.470.)

Official Uniform Comment

Prior Uniform Statutory Provision: Section 2, Uniform Conditional Sales Act.

Changes: Rewritten and new material added.

Purposes of Changes and New Matter:

1. Clauses are frequently inserted in installment purchase contracts under which the conditional vendee agrees not to assert defenses against an assignee of the contract. These clause shave led to litigation and their present status under the case law is in confusion. In some jurisdictions they have been held void as attempts to create negotiable instruments outside the framework of Article 3 or on grounds of public policy; in others they have been allowed to operate to cut off at least defenses based on breach of warranty. Under subsection (1) such clauses in a security agreement are validated outside the consumer field, but only as to defenses which could be cut off if a negotiable instrument were used. This limitation is important since if the clauses were allowed to have full effect as typically drafted, they would operate to cut off real as well as personal defenses. The execution of a negotiable note in connection with a security agreement is given like effect as the execution of an agreement containing a waiver of defense clause. The same rules are made applicable to leases as to security agreements, whether or not the lease is intended as security.

2. This Article takes no position on the controversial question whether a buyer of consumer goods may effectively waive defenses by contractual clause or by execution of a negotiable note. In some states such waivers have been invalidated by statute. In other states the course of judicial decision has rendered them ineffective or unreliable—courts have found that the assignee is not protected against the buyer's defense by a clause in the contract or that the holder of a note, by reason of his too close connection with the underlying transaction, does not have the rights of aloha in due course. This Article neither adopts nor rejects the approach taken in such statutes and decisions, except that the validation of waivers in subsection (1) is expressly made "subject to any statute or decision" which may restrict the waiver's effectiveness in the case of a buyer of consumer goods.

3. Subsection (2) makes clear, as did Section 2 of the Uniform Conditional Sales Act, that purchase money security transactions are sales, and warranty rules for sales are applicable. It also prevents buyer from inadvertently abandoning his warranties by a "no warranties" term in the security agreement when warranties have already

been created under the sales arrangement. Where the sales arrangement and the purchase money security transaction are evidenced by only one writing, that writing may disclaim, limit or modify warranties to the extent permitted by Article 2.

Cross References:

Point 1: Section 3–305
Point 2: Section 9–203(2)
Point 3: Sections 2–102 and 2–316.

Definitional Cross References:

"Agreement." Section 1–201.
"Consumer goods." Section 9–109.
"Good faith." Section 1–201.
"Goods." Section 9–105.
"Holder." Section 1–201.
"Holder in due course." Sections 3–302 and 9–105.
"Negotiable instrument." Section 3–104.
"Notice." Section 1–201.
"Purchase money security interest." Section 9–107.
"Sale." Sections 2–106 and 9–105.
"Security agreement." Section 9–105.
"Security interest." Section 1–201.
"Value." Section 1–201.

Section 9–207. Rights and Duties When Collateral Is in Secured Party's Possession.

(1) A secured party must use reasonable care in the custody and preservation of collateral in his possession. In the case of an instrument or chattel paper reasonable care includes taking necessary steps to preserve rights against prior parties unless otherwise agreed.

(2) Unless otherwise agreed, when collateral is in the secured party's possession

(a) reasonable expenses (including the cost of any insurance and payment of taxes or other charges) incurred in the custody, preservation, use or operation of the collateral are chargeable to the debtor and are secured by the collateral;

(b) the risk of accidental loss or damage is on the debtor to the extent of any deficiency in any effective insurance coverage;

(c) the secured party may hold as additional security any increase or profits (except money) received from the collateral, but money so received, unless remitted to the debtor, shall be applied in reduction of the secured obligation;

(d) the secured party must keep the collateral identifiable but fungible collateral may be commingled;

(e) the secured party may repledge the collateral upon terms which do not impair the debtor's right to redeem it.

(3) A secured party is liable for any loss caused by his failure to meet any obligation imposed by the preceding subsections but does not lose his security interest.

(4) A secured party may use or operate the collateral for the purpose of preserving the collateral or its value or pursuant to the order of a court of appropriate jurisdiction or, except in the case of consumer goods, in the manner and to the extent provided in the security agreement.

New York Annotations

(1) *Accord:* As to the general duty of reasonable care: Willets v. Hatch, 132 N.Y.41, 30 N.E. 251 (1892); Ouderkirk v. Central Nat'l Bank, 119 N.Y. 263, 23 N.E. 875 (1890). See, Restatement, Security, §§ 17, 18. Entrusters in possession, after default, have the same general rights and duties as a pledgee. Personal Property Law, § 56(3).

(2)(a) Generally in *accord:* Personal Property Law, § 80–a (conditional sales); Personal Property Law, § 56(3)(b) (trust receipts); Lien Law, § 329-c (purchase money chattel mortgage for $3,000 or less).

(b) Generally in *accord:* Personal Property Law, § 103 (conditional vendee). Insurance policies should be examined in light of this section. Compare Section 2–510.

(c) *Accord:* Brightson v. Claflin, 225 N.Y. 469; 122 N.E. 458 (1919) (dividends on pledged stock).

(d) The rule stated in this clause is similar to present statutory provisions as to warehouseman. General Business Law, §§ 108 and 109.

(e) See Restatement, Security, § 22, which states that a pledgee without authorization has no privilege to use pledged chattel.

(3) This may change New York law which apparently forfeits the pledgee's security interest for failing in his duty toward collateral in his possession. Compare Wood v. Fisk, 215 N.Y. 233,109 N.E. 177 (1915), with Content v. Banner, 184 N.Y. 121, 76 N.E. 913 (1906).

(4) This is new. See Restatement, Security, § 22, and Historical Note, *infra.*

Historical Note: The addition of "effective" prior to "insurance" in subsection (2)(b) was for clarification and to conform with Section 2–510. (1956 Recommendations.) In 1958 the section was further revised to make it clear that operation of collateral is permissible under the circumstances stated in the new subsection (4), whether before or after default, and that expenses of such operation may be paid or provided for. The deleted cross-reference to Part 5 in subsection (2) was confusing in view of the re-reference in Section 9–501(2) and the restrictions upon variation by agreement in Section 9–501(3). The result was doubt in some quarters as to the validity after default of some provisions apparently permitted in the security agreement under the "unless otherwise agreed" language of subsection (2), including especially provisions permitting operation of the collateral. Such provisions are common in trust indentures securing corporate bonds, and are particularly important when the collateral is a going business. There never was any intention under the Code to interfere with the right to operate in the circumstances stated in the new subsection (4). See Sections 1–102(3) and 1–103. (1958 Supplement, p. 13; 1956 Recommendations, p. 272; Excerpts, p. 470.)

Official Uniform Comment

Prior Uniform Statutory Provision: None.

Purposes:

1. Subsection (1) states the duty to preserve collateral imposed on a pledge at common law. See Restatement of Security, §§ 17, 18. In many cases a secured party having collateral in his possession may satisfy this duty by notifying the debtor of

any act which must be taken and allowing the debtor to perform such act himself. If the secured party himself takes action, his reasonable expenses may be added to the secured obligation.

Under Section 1–102(3) the duty to exercise reasonable care may not be disclaimed by agreement, although under that section the parties remain free to determine by agreement, in any manner not manifestly unreasonable, what shall constitute reasonable care in a particular case.

2. Subsection (2) states rules, which follow common law precedents, and which apply, unless there is agreement otherwise, in typical situations during the period while the secured party is in possession of the collateral.

3. The right of a secured party holding instruments or documents to have them indorsed or transferred to him or his order is dealt with in the relevant sections of Articles 3 (Commercial Paper), 7 (Warehouse Receipts, Bills of Lading and Other Documents) and 8 (Investment Securities). (Sections 3–201, 7–506, 8–307.)

4. This section applies when the secured party has possession of the collateral before default, as a pledge, and also when he has taken possession of the collateral after default. See Section 9–501(1) and (2). Subsection (4) permits operation of the collateral in the circumstances stated, and subsection (2)(a) authorizes payment of or provisions for expenses of such operation. Agreements providing for such operation are common in trust indentures securing corporate bonds and are particularly important when the collateral is a going business. Such an agreement cannot of course disclaim the duty of care established by subsection (1), not can it waive or modify the rights of the debtor contrary to Section 9–501(3).

Cross References:

Point 1: Section 1–102(3).
Point 3: Sections 3–201, 7–506 and 8–307.
Point 4: Section 9–501(2) and Part 5.

Definitional Cross References:

"Chattel paper." Section 9–105.
"Collateral." Section 9–105.
"Debtor." Section 9–105.
"Instrument." Section 9–105.
"Money." Section 1–201.
"Party." Section 1–201.
"Secured party." Section 9–105.
"Security interest." Section 1–201.

Section 9–208. Request for Statement of Account or List of Collateral.

(1) A debtor may sign a statement indicating what he believes to be the aggregate amount of unpaid indebtedness as of a specified date and may send it to the secured party with a request that the statement be approved or corrected and returned to the debtor. When the security agreement or any other record kept by the secured party identifies the collateral a debtor may similarly request the secured party to approve or correct a list of the collateral.

(2) The secured party must comply with such a request within two weeks after receipt by sending a written correction or approval. If the secured party claims a security interest in all of a particular type of collateral owned by the debtor he may indicate that fact in his reply and need not approve or correct

UCC

an itemized list of such collateral. If the secured party without reasonable excuse fails to comply he is liable for any loss caused to the debtor thereby; and if the debtor has properly included in his request a good faith statement of the obligation or a list of the collateral or both the secured party may claim a security interest only as shown in the statement against persons misled by his failure to comply. If he no longer has an interest in the obligation or collateral at the time the request is received he must disclose the name and address of any successor in interest known to him and he is liable for any loss caused to the debtor as a result of failure to disclose. A successor in interest is not subject to this section until a request is received by him.

(3) A debtor is entitled to such a statement once every six months without charge. The secured party may require payment of a charge not exceeding $10 for each additional statement furnished.

New York Annotations

This section has some limited counterparts in present New York law. Under Lien Law, § 230-c(5), relating to chattel mortgages by dealers, an interested third party may demand, with the written consent of the dealer, that the mortgagee disclose the specified items which are subject to the lien of the mortgagee. A similar provision was added to the trust receipts law in 1961. Laws 1961, ch. 401, eff. Oct. 1, 1961. In addition, under the Motor Vehicle Instalment Sales Act, Personal Property Law, § 302(12), the buyer is entitled upon request to a written statement of the payments and the unpaid balance. Similarly under the Retail Instalment Sales Act, a holder must supply at the request of the buyer a statement of account without charge once a year. Additional statements may be obtained for a fee of not more than one dollar. Personal Property Law, § 407. The Code provides a time limit of six months and a maximum fee of ten dollars for additional statements.

Official Uniform Comment

Prior Uniform Statutory Provision: None.

Purposes:

1. To provide a procedure whereby a debtor may obtain from the secured party a statement of the amount due on the obligation and in some cases a statement of the collateral.

2. The financing statement required to be filed under this Article (see Section 9-402) may disclose only that a secured party may have a security interest in specified types of collateral owned by the debtor. Unless a copy of the security agreement itself is filed as the financing statement third parties are told neither the amount of the obligation secured nor which particular assets are covered. Since subsequent creditors and purchasers may legitimately need more detailed information, it is necessary to provide a procedure under which the secured party will be required to make disclosure. On the other hand, the secured party should not be under a duty to disclose details of business operations to any casual inquirer or competitor who asks for them. This section gives the right to demand disclosure only to the debtor, who will typically request a statement in connection with negotiations with subsequent creditors and purchasers, or for the purpose of establishing his credit standing and proving which of his assets are free of the security interest. The secured party is further protected

against onerous requests by the provisions that he need furnish a statement of collateral only when his own records identify the collateral and that if he claims all of a particular type of collateral owned by the debtor he is not required to approve an itemized list.

Cross Reference:

Point 2: Section 9–402.

Definitional Cross References:

"Collateral." Section 9–105.
"Debtor." Section 9–105.
"Good faith." Section 1–201.
"Know." Section 1–201.
"Person." Section 1–201.
"Receive." Section 1–201.
"Secured party." Section 9–105.
"Security agreement." Section 9–105.
"Security interest." Section 1–201.
"Send." Section 1–201.
"Written." Section 1–201.

UCC

PART 3

RIGHTS OF THIRD PARTIES; PERFECTED AND UNPERFECTED SECURITY INTERESTS; RULES OF PRIORITY

Section 9–301. Persons Who Take Priority Over Unperfected Security Interests; Right of "Lien Creditor".

(1) Except as otherwise provided in subsection (2), an unperfected security interest is subordinate to the rights of

(a) persons entitled to priority under Section 9-312;

(b) a person who becomes a lien creditor before the security interest is perfected;

(c) in the case of goods, instruments, documents, and chattel paper, a person who is not a secured party and who is a transferee in bulk or other buyer not in ordinary course of business, or is a buyer of farm products in ordinary course of business, to the extent that he gives value and receives delivery of the collateral without knowledge of the security interest and before it is perfected;

(d) in the case of accounts, and general intangibles, and investment property, a person who is not a secured party and who is a transferee to the extent that he gives value without know ledge of the security interest and before it is perfected.

(2) If the secured party files with respect to a purchase money security interest before or within twenty days after the debtor receives possession of the collateral, he takes priority over the rights of a transferee in bulk or of a lien creditor which arise between the time the security interest attaches and the time of filing.

(3) A "lien creditor" means a creditor who has acquired a lien on the property involved by attachment, levy or the like and includes as assignee for benefit of creditors from the time of assignment, and a trustee in bankruptcy from the date of the filing of the petition or a receiver inequity from the time of appointment.

(4) A person who becomes a lien creditor while a security interest is perfected takes subject to the security interest only to the extent that it secures advances made before he becomes a lien creditor or within 45 days thereafter or made without knowledge of the lien or pursuant to a commitment entered into without knowledge of the lien.

Amended: by Laws 1977, Ch. 866, eff. July 2, 1978; Laws 1985, Ch. 717, eff. Aug. 31, 1985, and applicable to collateral received by a debtor on or after that date; L. 1997, Ch. 566, eff. Oct. 10, 1997.

New York Annotations

(1)(a) Annotations to this Section 9–301 should be read with the annotations to succeeding sections of Part 3.

(b) This paragraph states a single rule for determining the effect of failure to perfect a security interest in personal property where delivery, filing, or some other action is necessary to make the security good against creditors. The rule adopted is similar to that presently in effect for conditional sales, Personal Property Law, § 65, under which the creditor without notice must assert his legal process against the goods before the contract is recorded. The present statute also provides for a ten-day period for filing, as does subsection (2) of this section, in purchase money transactions. In the case of chattel mortgages the Code rejects the New York case law founded upon Karst v. Gane, 136 N.Y. 316, 32 N.E. 1073 (1893), under which a chattel mortgage unfilled beyond a reasonable time is not valid against creditors who extended credit prior to the filing even though those creditors had no lien prior to filing. Lien Law, § 230, was amended to provide a ten-day grace period for filing, but it is uncertain whether the rule of Karst v. Gane still might not permit creditors to reach the collateral even after filing where filing is delayed more than ten days. The Code removes that doubt by requiring the creditor to obtain his lien prior to perfection. This is also similar to the present rule for trust receipts. Personal Property Law, § 58(2) and (3). Under both the present law and under Article 9, the creditor who fails to perfect is just another general creditor as against lien creditor without knowledge of the security arrange-ment. Note that "knowledge" is defined in Section 1–201(25). See also Quinn v. Quinn, 17 A.D.2d 1028, 235 N.Y.S.2d 609 (1962). See the annotation under paragraph (d) below for the status of an unperfected security interest in accounts, contract rights and general intangibles.

(c) Under the authority cited above, an unrecorded chattel mortgage or conditional sale is not effective against purchasers without notice. See also Rand's Discount Co. v. Universal C. I. T. Credit Corp., 9 N.Y.2d 454, 174 N.E.2d 509 (1961). As to trust receipts see Personal Property Law, §§ 58 (2), 58-a(2)(b), for a similar rule.

(d) The general rule under existing New York law is that no steps need be taken for the perfection of an interest in these intangibles. Consequently, no precise body of law has developed for a failure to perfect. See the annotation to Section 9–401 for a list of special requirements for filing transfers of accounts.

(2) Most purchase money security transactions have been in the form of a conditional sale or trust receipt. (See Section 9–107.) This provision is derived from

the Uniform Conditional sales Act, Personal Property Law, § 65, which in New York permits a ten-day period of grace which cuts off all intervening interests, and from the Uniform Trust Receipts Act, Personal Property Law, § 58-a, which in New York now provides a twenty-one day grace period that does not cut off purchasers who took delivery prior to the filing. (Laws of 1961, ch. 19, eff. July 1, 1961.) Under this subsection the grace period will operate against lien creditors and transferees in bulk. See the comparable period in Section 9–312(4) which operates against other secured parties in cases where there is a conflict with a purchase money security interest in collateral other than inventory. Cf. § 60(a) of the Bankruptcy Act.

(3) Substantially the same definition appears in the Uniform Trust Receipts Act, Personal Property Law, § 51(6). There is no conflict with Debtor and Creditor Law, § 15(b), as to the right of an assignee for the benefit of creditors to assail a preference. Compare § 70 of the Bankruptcy Act.

Historical Note: Subsection (1) was changed in 1956 to transfer all questions of priority to Section 9–312. Former clause (d) was split into clauses and (d) because delivery is an inappropriate concept for intangible collateral.

The last sentence of subsection (3) was omitted in 1956 because it involved varying local procedural rules as to the time a creditor obtains a lien by legal process. The suggestions of the Law Revision Commission were followed in making this revision. (1956 Recommendations, p.274; Excerpts, p. 470.)

In. 1958 subsection (2) was revised to make the ten-day period run from the time the debtor takes possession rather than the time the secured party gives value. Cf. Sections 9–312(3) and (4). (1958 Supplement, p. 15.)

Official Uniform Comment

Prior Uniform Statutory Provision: Sections 8(2) and 9(2)(b), Uniform Trust Receipts Act; Section 5, Uniform Conditional Sales Act.

Purposes:

1. This section lists the classes of persons who take priority over an unperfected security interest. As in Section 60 of the Federal Bankruptcy Act, the term "perfected" is used to describe a security interest in personal property which cannot be defeated in insolvency proceedings or in general by creditors. A security interest is "perfected" when the secured party has taken whatever steps are necessary to give him such an interest. These steps are explained in the five following sections (9–302 through 9–306).

2. Section 9–312 states general rules for the determination of priorities among conflicting security interests and in addition refers to other sections which state special rules of priority in a variety of situations. The interests given priority under Section 9–312 and the other sections therein cited take such priority in general even over a perfected security interest. A fortiori they take priority over an unperfected security interest, and paragraph (1)(a) of this section so states.

3. Paragraph (1)(b) provides that an unperfected security interest is subordinate to the rights of lien creditors. The section rejects the rule applied in many jurisdictions in pre-Code law that an unperfected security interest is subordinated to all creditors, but requires the lien obtained by legal proceedings to attach to the collateral before the security interest is perfected. The section subordinates the unperfected security interest but does not subordinate the secured debt to the lien.

4. Paragraphs (1)(c) and (1)(d) deal with purchasers (other than secured parties) of collateral who would take subject to a perfected security interest but who are by these subsections given priority over an unperfected security interest. In the cases of goods and of intangibles of the type whose transfer is effected by physical delivery

of the representative piece of paper (instruments, documents and chattel paper) the purchaser who takes priority must both give value and receive delivery of the collateral without knowledge of the existing security interest and before perfection (paragraph (1)(c)). Thus even if the purchaser gave value without knowledge and before perfection, he would take subject to the security interest if perfection occurred before physical delivery of the collateral to him. The paragraph (1)(c) rule is obviously not appropriate where the collateral consists of intangibles and there is no representative piece of paper whose physical delivery is the only or the customary method of transfer. Therefore with respect to such intangibles (accounts and general intangibles), paragraph (1)(d) gives priority to any transferee who has given value without knowledge and before perfection of the security interest.

The term "buyer in ordinary course of business" referred to in paragraph (1)(c) is defined in Section 1–201(9).

Other secured parties are excluded from paragraphs (1)(c) and (1)(d) because their priorities are covered in Section 9–312 (see point 2 of this Comment).

5. Except to the extent provided in subsection (2), this Article does not permit a secured party to file or take possession after another interest has received priority under subsection (1) and thereby protect himself against the intervening interest. A few chattel mortgage statutes did have grace periods, i.e., a filing within x days after the mortgage was given related back to the day the mortgage was given. The Uniform Conditional sales Act has a ten-day period which cut off all intervening interests. The Uniform Trust Receipts Act had a thirty-day period but did not cut off the interest of a purchaser who took delivery before the filing.

Subsection (2) gives a grace period for perfection by filing as to purchase money security interests only (that term is defined in Section 9–107). The grace period runs for ten days after the debtor receives possession of the collateral but operates to cut off only the interests of intervening lien creditors or bulk purchasers.

6. Subsection (3) defines "lien creditor", following in substance the provisions of the Uniform Trust Receipts Act.

7. Subsection (4) deals with the question whether advances under an existing security interest in collateral, made after rights of lien creditors have attached to that collateral, will take precedence over rights of lien creditors. See related problems in Sections 9–307(3) and 9–312(7). In this section, because of the impact of the rule chosen on the question whether the security interest for future advances is "protected" under Sections 6323(c)(2) and (d) of the Internal Revenue Code as amended by the Federal Tax Lien Act of 1966, the priority of the security interest for future advances over a judgment lien is made absolute for 45 days regardless of knowledge of the secured party concerning the judgment lien. If, however, the advance is made after the 45 days, the advance will not have priority unless it was made or committed without knowledge or the lien obtained by legal proceedings. The importance of the rule chosen for actual conflicts between secured parties making subsequent advances and judgment lien creditors may not be great; but the rule chosen for the first 45 days is important in effectuating the interest of the Federal Tax Lien Act of 1966.

Cross References:

Section 9–312.
Point 1: Sections 9–302 through 9–306.
Point 7: Sections 9–204, 9–307(3) and 9–312(7).

Definitional Cross References:

"Account." Section 9–106.
"Buyer in ordinary course of business." Section 1–201.
"Chattel paper." Section 9–105.

"Collateral." Section 9–105.
"Creditor." Section 1–201.
"Delivery." Section 1–201.
"Document." Section 9–105.
"General intangibles." Section 9–106.
"Goods." Section 9–105.
"Instrument." Section 9–105.
"Knowledge." Section 1–201.
"Person." Section 1–201.
"Purchase money security interest." Section 9–107.
"Pursuant to commitment." Section 9–105.
"Representative." Section 1–201.
"Rights." Section 1–201.
"Secured party." Section 9–105.
"Security interest." Section 1–201.
"Value." Section 1–201.

Section 9–302. When Filing Is Required to Perfect Security Interest; Security Interests to Which Filing Provisions of This Article Do Not Apply.

(1) A financing statement must be filed to perfect all security interests except the following:

(a) a security interest in collateral in possession of the secured party under Section 9–305;

(b) a security interest temporarily perfected in instruments, certificated securities, or documents without delivery under Section 9–304 or in proceeds for a 10 day period under Section 9–306;

(c) a security interest created by an assignment of a beneficial interest in a trust or a decedent's estate;

(d) a purchase money security interest in consumer goods; but filing is required to perfect such a security interest in a motor vehicle required to be licensed or registered in this state unless it is perfected in accordance with Article forty-six of the vehicle and traffic law; and fixture filing is required for priority over conflicting interests in fixtures to the extent provided in Section 9–313;

(e) an assignment of accounts which does not alone or in conjunction with other assignments to the same assignee transfer a significant part of the outstanding accounts of the assignor;

(f) a security interest of a collecting bank (Section 4–208) or arising under the Article on Sales (see Section 9–113) or covered in subsection (3) of this section;

(g) an assignment for the benefit of all the creditors of the transferor, and subsequent transfers by the assignee there under;

(h) a security interest in accounts or rights under a contract for the performance of labor or the furnishing of materials for the improvement of real property or for a public improvement perfected prior to September twenty-seventh, nineteen hundred sixty-four by a filing in accordance with Section fifteen or Section sixteen of the lien law;

(i) a security interest in personal property under a mortgage or a supplemental mortgage creating a lien upon real and personal property executed by a corporation and recorded prior to September twenty-seventh, nineteen hundred sixty-four as a mortgage of real property in accordance with Section two hundred thirty-one of the lien law; or

(j) A security interest in investment property which is perfected without filing under Section 9–115 or Section 9–116.

(1-A) However, and notwithstanding the provisions of subsection (1), filing in accordance with the provisions of Part 4, but only in the department of state, is required to perfect a security interest in

(a) accounts or rights under a contract for the performance of labor or the furnishing of materials for the improvement of real property or for a public improvement as to which a filing is required and is made on or after September twenty-seventh, nineteen hundred sixty-four in accordance with Section fifteen or Section sixteen of the lien law; and

(b) personal property including goods which are or are to become fixtures under a mortgage or a supplemental mortgage creating a lien upon real and personal property executed by a corporation and on or after September twenty-seventh, nineteen hundred sixty-four recorded as a mortgage of real property in accordance with Section one hundred ninety of the lien law.

(2) If a secured party assigns a perfected security interest, no filing under the Article is required in order to continue the perfected status of the security interest against creditors of and transferees from the original debtor.

(3) The filing of a financing statement otherwise required by this Article is not necessary or effective to perfect a security interest in property subject to

(a) a statute or treaty of the United States which provides for a national or international registration or a national or international certificate of title or which specifies a place of filing different from that specified in this Article for filing of the security interest; or

(b) the following statutes of this state: article forty-six of the vehicle and traffic law; but during any period in which collateral is inventory held for sale by a person who is in the business of selling goods of that kind, the filing provisions of this Article (Part 4) apply to a security interest in that collateral created by him as debtor; or

(c) a certificate of title statute of another jurisdiction under the law of which indication of a security interest on the certificate is required as a condition of perfection (subsection (2) of Section 9-103).

(4) Compliance with a statute or treaty described in subsection (3) is equivalent to the filing of a financing statement under this Article, and a security

interest in property subject to the statute or treaty can be perfected only by compliance therewith except as provided in Section 9–103on multiple state transactions. Duration and renewal of perfection of a security interest perfected by compliance with the statute or treaty are governed by the provisions of the statute or treaty; in other respects the security interest is subject to this Article.

Amended by Laws 1977, Ch. 866, eff. July 2, 1978; Laws 1982, Ch. 928, eff. Dec. 21, 1982 and deemed to have been in full force and effect on and after Sept. 1, 1982; L. 1997, Ch. 566, eff. Oct. 1, 1997.

New York Annotations

Two important differences should be noted between the requirements of this section and those of present New York law. First, requirements of filing are dependent upon the nature of the transaction and the collateral (e.g. "consumer goods", "inventory", "purchase money") rather than the type of legal device used (e.g. chattel mortgage, conditional sale). Further, the security agreement itself need not be recorded as is presently required in respect of chattel mortgages (other than dealer's chattel mortgages) and conditional sales; instead a simple "financing statement" (see Section 9–402) or a copy of the security agreement may be filed. See annotation to Section 9–401 as to the place of filing. Note also that a security agreement, even though not perfected, is effective to the extent provided in Section 9–301.

(1) The following transactions require filing to perfect a security interest under present New York law; chattel mortgages (lien Law, § 230, in the absence of an actual change of possession); dealer's chattel mortgage (Lien Law, § 230-c); conditional sales contracts (Personal Property Law, § 65); trust receipts (Personal Property Law, § 58), and inventory or accounts receivable liens under the Factor's Lien Act (Personal Property Law, § 45).

The following transactions do not require filing to perfect a security interest under present New York law even where the collateral is not in the possession of the secured party; more assignments of accounts receivable and other rights under contracts, and consignments, leases, bailments, and other transactions intended as security devices. On accounts: Fortunato v. Patten, 147 N.Y.277, 41 N.E.572 (1895). But see Lien Law, §§ 13, 15, 16 and 25, and Personal Property Law, § 45. On consignments: Compare Ginsburg v. Martin, 122 Misc.468, 203 N.Y.S. 110 (1924) with Liebowitz v. Voiello, 107 F.2d 914 (2d Cir. 1939) (not a true consignment). Subsection (1) would now require filing in connection with any such transaction unless the collateral involved is of a type which is specifically exempted from filing by this subsection. See Section 2–326 as to consignments not intended to be security devices.

(a) Present New York law is in *accord;* see annotation to Section 9–203(1)(a). Furthermore, certain mortgages of stocks or bonds to be delivered to the lender on the same day are exempt from recording (Lien Law, § 230).

(b) See annotation to Sections 9–304 and 9–306.

(c) and (d) These exceptions represent a change from present New York statutory provisions which require filing in all conditional sale and non-possessory chattel mortgage transactions. See annotations to Section 9–401.

(e) and (f) Probably no change from present law.

(g), (h), (j) and (k). These paragraphs, having no counterparts in the 1958 and 1962 Official Texts, relate to specialized transactions governed by other statutory provisions. Note that perfection of post-Code transactions within the scope of paragraphs (j) and (k) require filing in accordance with Part 4 of Article 9 in the Department of State.

(i) This paragraph has no counterpart in the 1958 and 1962 Official Texts. It conforms to Subsection (5) of New York Code Section 9–103.

(2) Although present law requires recording of an assignment of a chattel mortgage prior to satisfaction of the debt, the requirement does not affect the perfected status of the mortgage. In re Industrial Sapphire Mfg. Co., 182 F.2d 589 (3rd Cir. 1950) (N.Y. law); Lien Law, § 232-a. A similar provision exists for agricultural mortgages, N.Y. Unconsol. Laws, § 8. (McKinney.)

(3) and (4) Obviously the "central filing" which would excuse filing under Part 4 is central filing under another statute. The enactment of the Code in New York might result in the repeal of present central filing systems, and there would then be neither any such "other central filing" system nor any title certificate on which security interests would be recorded. On the other hand, the Code could be enacted in New York and special filing offices like that provided in Lien Law, § 232, for canal boats, tugs, scows, and similar crafts, could be retained. See also, Personal Property Law, § 66 (conditional sales). Note that the sponsor's text provides alternative sections dealing with the applicability of Article 9 where another form of central filing is available. Under Alternate A no Code filing would be required where a local statute provides for central filing or the indication of the security interest on a certificate of title, while under Alternate B the exception from Code filing would not apply to motor vehicles which are held as inventory.

Historical Note: This section was rewritten for clarity and meets the suggestions of the Law Revision Commission. The new alternative subsection (3)(b) is designed (in the case of a vehicle not classified as inventory) to eliminate the requirement of filing in those states where a statute requires a certificate of title for the vehicle and permits but does not require a notation of security interests on the certificate. In some states the Motor Vehicle Code provides for the notation of encumbrances on certificate of title by the issuance and marking of a duplicate Certificate of Title. (1956 Recommendations, p. 276; Excerpts, p. 471.)

Official Uniform Comment

Prior Uniform Statutory Provision: Section 5, Uniform Conditional Sales Act; Section 8, Uniform Trust Receipts Act.

Purposes:

1. Subsection (1) states the general rule that to perfect a security interest under this Article a financing statement must be filed. Paragraphs (1)(a) through (1)(g) exempt from the filing requirement the transactions described. Subsection (3) further sets out certain transactions to which the filing provisions of this Article do not apply, but it does not defer to another state statute on the filing of inventory security interests. The cases recognized are those where suitable alternative systems for giving public notice of a security interest are available. Subsection (4) states the consequence of such other form of notice.

Section 9–303 states the time when a security interest is perfected by filing or otherwise. Part 4 of the Article deals with the mechanics of filing: place of filing, form of financing statement and so on.

2. As at common law, there is no requirement of filing when the secured party has possession of the collateral in a pledge transaction (paragraph (1)(a)), Section 9–305 should be consulted on what collateral may be pledged and on the requirements of possession.

3. Under this Article, as under the Uniform Trust Receipts Act, filing is not effective to perfect a security interest in instruments. See Section 9–304(1).

4. Where goods subject to a security interest are left in the debtor's possession, the only permanent exception from the general filing requirement is that stated in

paragraph (1)(d): purchase money security interests in consumer goods. For temporary exceptions, see Sections 9–304(5)(a) and 9–306.

In many jurisdictions under prior law security interests in consumer goods under conditional sale or bailment leases were not subject to filing requirements. Paragraph (1)(d) follows the policy of those jurisdictions. The paragraph changes prior law in jurisdictions where all conditional sales and bailment leases were subject to a filing requirement, except that filing is required for purchase money security interests in consumer fixtures to attain priority under Section 9–313 against real estate interests.

Although the security interests described in paragraph (1)(d) are perfected without filing. Section 9–307(2) provides that unless a financing statement is filed certain buyers may take free of the security interest even though perfected. See that section and the Comment thereto.

On filing for security interests in motor vehicles under certificate of title laws see subsection (3) of this section.

5. A financing statement must be filed to perfect a security interest in accounts except for the transaction described in paragraphs (1)(e) and (g). It should be noted that this Article applies to sales of accounts and chattel paper as well as to transfers thereof for security (Section 9–102(1)(b)); the filing requirement of this section applies both to sales and to transfers thereof for security. In this respect this Article follows many of the pre-Code statutes regulating assignments of accounts receivable.

Over forty jurisdictions had enacted accounts receivable statutes. About half of these statutes required filing to protect or perfect assignments; of the remainder, one was so-called "book-marking" statute and the others validated assignments without filing. This Article adopts the filing requirement, on the theory that there is no valid reason why public notice is less appropriate for assignments of accounts than for any other type of nonpossessory interest. Section 9–305, furthermore, excludes accounts from the types of collateral which may be the subject of a possessory security interest: filing is thus the only means of perfection contemplated by this Article. See Section 9–306 on accounts as proceeds.

The purpose of the subsection (1)(e) exemption is to save from *ex post facto* invalidation casual or isolated assignments: some accounts receivable statutes were so broadly drafted that all assignments, whatever their character or purpose, fell within their filing provisions. Under such statutes many assignments which no one would think of filing might have been subject to invalidation. The paragraph (1)(e) exemption goes to that type of assignment. Any person who regularly takes assignments of any debtor's accounts should file. In this connection Section 9–104(f) which excludes certain transfers of accounts from the Article should be consulted.

Assignments of interests in trusts and estates are not required to be filed because they are often not thought of as collateral comparable to the types dealt with by this Article. Assignments for the benefit of creditors are not required to be filed because they are not financing transactions and the debtor will not ordinarily be engaging in further credit transactions.

6. With respect to the paragraph (1)(f) exemptions, see the sections cited therein and Comments thereto.

7. The following example will explain the operation of subsection (2): Buyer buys goods from seller who retains a security interest in them which he perfects. Seller assigns the perfected security interest to X. The security interest, in X's hands and without further steps on his part, continues perfected against *Buyer's* transferees and creditors. If, however, the assignments from Seller to X was itself intended for security (or was a sale of accounts or chattel paper), X must take whatever steps may be required for perfection in order to be protected against *Seller's* transferees and creditors.

8. Subsection (3) exempts from the filing provisions of this Article transactions as to which an adequate system of filing, state or federal, has been set up outside

UCC

this Article and subsection (4) makes clear that when such a system exists perfection of a relevant security interest can be had only through compliance with that system (i.e., filing under this Article is not a permissible alternative).

Examples of the type of federal statute referred to in paragraph (3)(a) are the provisions of 17 U.S.C. §§ 28, 30 (copyrights), 49 U.S.C. § 1403 (aircraft), 49 U.S.C. § 20 railroads). The Assignment of Claims Act of 1940, as amended, provides for notice to contracting and disbursing officers and to sureties on bonds but does not establish a national filing system and therefore is not within the scope of paragraph (3)(a). An assignee of a claim against the United States, who must of course comply with the Assignment of Claims Act, must also file this Article in order to perfect his security interest against creditors and transferees of his assignor.

Some states have enacted central filing statutes with respect to security transactions in kinds of property which are of special importance in the local economy. Subsection (3) adopts such statutes as the appropriate filing system for such property.

In addition to such central filing statutes many states have enacted certificate of title laws covering motor vehicles and the like. Subsection (3) exempts transactions covered by such laws from the filing requirements of this Article.

For a discussion of the operation of state motor vehicle certificate of title laws in interstate contexts, see Comment 4 to Section 9–103.

9. Perfection of a security interest under a state or federal statute of the type referred to in subsection (3) has all the consequences of perfection under the provisions of this Article, Subsection (4).

Cross References:

Point 1: Section 9–303 and Part 4.
Point 2: Section 9–305.
Point 3: Section 9–304(1).
Point 4: Section 9–307(2).
Point 5: Sections 9–102(1)(b), 9–104(f) and 9–305.
Point 6: Sections 4–208 and 9–113.

Definitional Cross References:

"Account." Section 9–106.
"Collateral." Section 9–105.
"Consumer goods." Section 9–109.
"Creditor." Section 1–201.
"Debtor." Section 9–105.
"Delivery." Section 1–201.
"Document." Section 9–105.
"Equipment." Section 9–109.
"Fixture." Section 9–313.
"Fixture filing." Section 9–313.
"Instrument." Section 9–105.
"Inventory." Section 9–109.
"Proceeds." Section 9–306.
"Purchase." Section 1–201.
"Purchase money security interest." Section 9–107.
"Sale." Section 2–106 and 9–105.
"Secured party." Section 9–105.
"Security interest." Section 1–201.

Section 9–303. When Security Interest Is Perfected; Continuity of Perfection.

(1) A security interest is perfected when it has attached and when all of the applicable steps required for perfection have been taken. Such steps are specified in Sections 9–103, 9–115, 9–302, 9–304, 9–305, and 9–306. If such steps are taken before the security interest attaches, it is perfected at the time when it attaches.

(2) If a security interest is originally perfected in any way permitted under this Article and is subsequently perfected in some other way under this Article, without an intermediate period when it was unperfected, the security interest shall be deemed to be perfected continuously for the purposes of this Article.

Amended by Laws 1963, Ch. 1003, eff. Sept. 27, 1964; L. 1997, Ch. 566, eff. Oct. 10, 1997.

New York Annotations

(1) Except as noted in the annotations to Section 9–204 in respect of after-acquired property, subsection (1) is generally in accord with the theory of present New York filing statutes. Lien Law, § 230 (chattel mortgages); Lien Law, § 230-c (dealer's chattel mortgages); Personal Property Law, § 66 (conditional sales); Personal Property Law, § 58-e (trust receipts); Personal Property Law, § 45 (factor's liens). Subsection (1) becomes significant in determining priorities under Section 9–312(5)(b), which adopts for certain cases a "first to perfect" rule.

(2) There is no direct counterpart in New York statutes but this subsection probably represents present law as to certain security interests originally perfected by possession but which are subsequently recorded, Lien Law, § 230 (chattel mortgage) and Personal Property Law, § 45 (factor's lien).

Historical Note: This section and the following section were completely rewritten and reorganized for clarity. It appears that the new section meets the suggestions of the Law Revision Commission.

Filing is now permitted as a means of perfecting a security interest in negotiable documents, thus continuing the policy established by the Uniform Trust Receipts Act. New Section 9–304(2) states the relationship between a security interest in the negotiable document and a security interest in the goods subject thereto. New Section 9–304(3) deals with the comparable relationship between goods and non-negotiable documents.

Former provisions in Section 9–304 for a temporary 21-day period for perfection of an interest in instruments or documents, or the goods controlled by the documents, have been clarified and rewritten in Section 9–304(5). (1956 Recommendations, p. 277; Excerpts, pp.472 and 473.)

Official Uniform Comment

Prior Uniform Statutory Provision: None.

Purposes:

1. The term "attach" is used in this Article to describe the point at which property becomes subject to a security interest. The requisites for attachment are stated in Section 9–203. When it attaches a security interest may be either perfected or

unperfected: "Perfected" means that the secured party has taken all the steps required by this Article as specified in the several sections listed in subsection (1). A perfected security interest may still be or become subordinate to other interests (see Section 9–312) but in general after perfection the secured party is protected against creditors and transferees of the debtor and in particular against any representative of creditors in insolvency proceedings instituted by or against the debtor. Subsection (1) states the truism that the time of perfection is when the security interest has attached and any necessary steps for perfection (such as taking possession or filing) have been taken. If the steps for perfection have been taken in advance (as when the secured party files a financing statement before giving value or before the debtor acquires rights in the collateral), then the interest is perfected automatically when it attaches.

2. The following example will illustrate the operation of subsection (2): A bank which has issued a letter of credit honors drafts drawn under the credit and receives possession of the negotiable bill of lading covering the goods shipped. Under Sections 9–304(2) and 9–305 the bank now has a perfected security interest in the document and the goods. The bank releases the bill of lading to the debtor for the purpose of procuring the goods from the carrier and selling them. Under Section 9–304(5) the bank continues to have a perfected security interest in the document and goods for 21 days. The bank files before the expiration of the 21 day period. Its security interest now continues perfected for as long as the filing is good. The goods are sold by the debtor. The bank continues to have a security interest in the proceeds of the sale to the extent stated in Section 9–306.

If the successive stages of the bank's security interest succeed each other without an intervening gap, the security interest is "continuously perfected" and the date of perfection is when the interest first became perfected (i.e., in the example given, when the bank received possession of the bill of lading against honor of the drafts). If, however, there is a gap between stages–for example, if the bank does not file until after the expiration of the 21 day period specified in Section 9–304(5), the collateral still being in the debtor's possession–then, the chain being broken, the perfection is no longer continuous. The date of perfection would now be the date of filing (after expiration of the 21 day period); the bank's interest might now become subject to attack under Section 60 of the Federal Bankruptcy Act and would be subject to any interests arising during the gap period which under Section 9–301 take priority over an unperfected security interest.

The rule of subsection (2) would also apply to the case of collateral brought into this state subject to a security interest which became perfected in another state or jurisdiction. See Section 9–103(1)(d).

Cross References:

Sections 9–302, 9–304, 9–305 and 9–306.
Point 1: Sections 9–204 and 9–312.
Point 2: Sections 9–103(1)(d) and 9–301.

Definitional Cross References:

"Attach." Section 9–203.
"Security interest." Section 1–201.

Section 9–304. Perfection of Security Interest in Instruments, Documents, Proceeds of a Written Letter of Credit, and Goods Covered by Documents; Perfection by Permissive Filing; Temporary Perfection Without Filing or Transfer of Possession.

(1) A security interest in chattel paper or negotiable documents may be perfected by filing. A security interest in the rights to proceeds of a written letter of credit can be perfected only by the secured party's taking possession of the letter of credit. A security interest in money or instruments (other than instruments which constitute part of chattel paper) can be perfected only by the secured party's taking possession, except as provided in subsections (4), (5) and (7) of this section and subsections (2) and (3) of Section 9–306 on proceeds.

(2) During the period that goods are in the possession of the issuer of a negotiable document therefor, a security interest in the goods is perfected by perfecting a security interest int. document, and any security interest in the goods otherwise perfected during such period is subject thereto.

(3) A security interest in goods in the possession of a bailee other than one who has issued a negotiable document therefor is perfected by issuance of a document in the name of the secured party or by the bailee's receipt of notification of the secured party's interest or by filing as to the goods.

(4) A security interest in instruments, certificated securities, or negotiable documents is perfected without filing or the taking of possession for a period of 21 days from the time it attaches to the extent that it arises for new value given under a written security agreement.

(5) A security interest remains perfected for a period of 21 days without filing where a secured party having a perfected security interest in an instrument, a certificated security, a negotiable document or goods in possession of a bailee other than one who has issued a negotiable document therefor

(a) makes available to the debtor the goods or documents representing the goods for the purpose of ultimate sale or exchange or for the purpose of loading, unloading, storing, shipping, transshipping, manufacturing, processing or otherwise dealing with them in a manner preliminary to their sale or exchange, but priority between conflicting security interests in the goods is subject to subsection (3) of Section 9-312; or

(b) delivers the instrument or certificated security to the debtor for the purpose of ultimate sale or exchange or of presentation, collection, renewal or registration of transfer.

(6) After the 21 day period in subsections (4) and (5) perfection depends upon compliance with applicable provisions of this Article.

(7) Notwithstanding the provisions of Section 9–305 of this code, or any provision of this section to the contrary, a security interest in shares or other ownership interests evidenced by stock certificates or other instruments, and a

leasehold evidenced by a proprietary lease or either of the foregoing from a corporation or partnership formed for the purpose of cooperative ownership of real property, or in such stock certificates alone can be perfected only by filing in accordance with paragraph (b) of subsection one of Section 9–401 of this code. Such filing must identify the real estate or house or building owned by such corporation or partnership with a description sufficient for its identification.

Amended by Laws 1977, Ch. 866, eff. July 2, 1978; Laws 1982, Ch. 928, eff. Dec. 21, 1982 and deemed to have been in full force and effect on and after Sept. 1, 1982; Laws 1988, Ch. 333 eff. Oct. 1, 1988, and applicable to any security interest obtained, continued or consolidated on or after such effective date by means other than filing; L. 1997, Ch. 566, eff. Oct. 1, 1997; L. 2000, Ch. 471, eff. Nov. 1, 2000.

New York Annotations

Since the Uniform Trust Receipts Act has been law in New York since 1934, Personal Property Law, §§ 50-58-m, there is little to add to the discussion of this statute in the Comments to this section. The New York legislature in 1961 amended the trust receipts provision to permit a twenty-one rather than a thirty-day period in accord with subsection (5). (Laws 1961, ch. 19, eff. July 1, 1961.) See Lien Law, § 230, for a somewhat analogous temporary perfection as to certain corporate transactions involving release of security to a successor trustee.

Historical Note: See Historical Note under Section 9–303. (1956 Recommendations, p. 279.)

Official Uniform Comment

Prior Uniform Statutory Provision: Sections 3 and 8(1), Uniform Trust Receipts Act.

Purposes:

1. For most types of property, filing and taking possession are alternative methods of perfection. For some types of intangibles (i.e., accounts and general intangibles) filing is the only available method (see Section 9–305 and point 1 of Comment thereto). With respect to instruments subsection (1) provides that, except for the cases of "temporary perfection" covered in subsections (4) and (5), taking possession is the only available method; this provision follows the Uniform Trust Receipts Act. The rule is based on the thought that where the collateral consists of instruments, it is universal practice for the secured party to take possession of them in pledge; any surrender of possession to the debtor is for a short time; therefore it would be unwise to provide the alternative of perfection for a long period by filing which, since it in no way corresponds with commercial practice, would serve no useful purpose. For similar reasons, filing is not permitted as to money. Perfection of security interests in certificated securities, which are covered by the definition of instruments, is governed by Section 8-321 and, therefore, excluded from this section.

Subsection (1) further provides that filing is available as a method of perfection for security interests in chattel paper and negotiable documents, which also come within Section 9–305 on perfection by possession. Chattel paper is sometimes delivered to the assignee, sometimes left int. hands of the assignor for collection; subsection (1) allows the assignee to perfect his interest by filing in the latter case. Negotiable documents may be, and usually are, delivered to the secured party; subsection (1) follows the Uniform Trust Receipts Act in allowing filing as an alternative method of perfection. Perfection of an interest in goods through a non-negotiable document is covered in subsection (3).

2. Subsection (2), following prior law and consistently with the provisions of Article 7, takes the position that, so long as a negotiable document covering goods is outstanding, title to the goods is, so to say, locked up in the document and the proper way of dealing with such goods is through the document. Perfection therefore is to be made with respect to the document and, when made, automatically carries over to the goods. Any interest perfected directly in the goods while the document is outstanding (for example, a chattel mortgage type of security interest on goods in a warehouse) is subordinated to an outstanding negotiable document.

3. Subsection (3) takes a different approach to the problem of goods covered by a non-negotiable document or otherwise in the possession of a bailee who has not issued a negotiable document. Here title to the goods is not looked on as being locked up in the document and the secured party may perfect his interest directly in the goods by filing as to them. The subsection states two other methods of perfection: issuance of the document in the secured party's name (as consignee of a straight bill of lading or the person to whom delivery would be made under a non-negotiable warehouse receipt) and receipt of notification of the secured party's interest by the bailee which, under Section 9–305, is looked on as equivalent to taking possession by the secured party.

4. Subsections (4) and (5) follow the Uniform Trust Receipts Act in giving perfected status to security interests in instruments and documents for a short period although there has been no filing and the collateral is in the debtor's possession. The period of 21 days is chosen to conform to the provisions of Section 60 of the Federal Bankruptcy Act. There are a variety of legitimate reasons–some of them are described in subsection (5)(a) and (5)(b)–why such collateral has to be temporarily released to a debtor and no useful purpose would be served by cluttering the files with records of such exceedingly short term transactions. Under subsection (4) the 21 day perfection runs from the date of attachment; there is no limitation on the purpose for which the debtor is in possession but the secured party must be given new value under a written security agreement. Under subsection (5) the 21 day perfection runs from the date a secured party who already has a perfected security interest turns over the collateral to the debtor (an example is a bank which has acquired a bill of lading by honoring drafts drawn under a letter of credit and subsequently turns over the bill of lading to its customer); there is no new value requirement but the turnover must be for one or more of the purposes stated in subsections (5)(a) and (5)(b). Note that while subsection (4) is restricted to instruments and *negotiable* documents, subsection (5) extends to goods covered by non-negotiable documents as well. Thus the letter of credit bank referred to in the example could make a subsection (5) turnover without regard to the form of the bill of lading, provided that, in the case of a non-negotiable document, it had previously perfected its interest under one of the methods stated in subsection (3). But note that the discussion of subsection (5) in this Comment deals only with perfection. Priority of a security interest in inventory after surrender of the document depends on compliance with the requirements of Section 9–312(3) on notice to prior inventory financer.

Finally, it should be noted that the 21 days applies only to the documents and to the goods obtained by surrender thereof. If the goods are sold, the security interest will continue in proceeds for only 10 days under Section 9–306, unless a further perfection occurs as to the security interest in proceeds.

Cross References:

Article 7 and Sections 9–303, 9–305 and 9–312(3).

UCC

Definitional Cross References:

"Chattel paper." Section 9–105.
"Debtor." Section 9–105.
"Document." Section 9–105.
"Goods." Section 9–105.
"Instrument." Section 9–105.
"Receives." notification. Section 1–201.
"Sale." Sections 2–106 and 9–105.
"Secured party." Section 9–105.
"Security agreement." Section 9–105.
"Security interest." Section 1–201.
"Value." Section 1–201.
"Written." Section 1–201.

Section 9—305. When Possession by Secured Party Perfects Security Interest Without Filing.

A security interest in goods, instruments, money, negotiable documents, or chattel paper may be perfected by the secured party's taking possession of the collateral. A security interest in the right to proceeds of a written letter of credit may be perfected by the secured party's taking possession of the letter of credit. If such collateral other than goods covered by a negotiable document is held by a bailee, the secured party is deemed to have possession from the time the bailee receives notification of the secured party's interest. A security interest is perfected by possession from the time possession is taken without relation back and continues only so long as possession is retained, unless otherwise specified in this Article. The security interest may be otherwise perfected as provided in this Article before or after the period of possession by the secured party.

Amended by Laws 1977, Ch. 866, eff. July 2, 1978; Laws 1982, Ch. 928, eff. Dec. 21, 1982 and deemed to have been in full force and effect on and after Sept. 1, 1982; L. 1997, Ch. 566, eff. Oct. 1, 1997; L. 2000, Ch. 471, eff. Nov. 1, 2000.

New York Annotations

This section states the usual New York rule as to the effect of possession taken by a secured party. See McCoy v. American Express Co., 253 N.Y. 477, 171 N.E. 749 (1930) (pledge), and Lien Law, § 230 (chattel mortgage). The time of perfection is the same as that provided by the Uniform Trust Receipts Act, Personal Property Law, § 53. Compare § 60(a) of the Bankruptcy Act.

Furthermore, this section validates, without filing, security interests in goods arising from field warehousing arrangements, provided sufficient control is passed to the agent. See Friedman, "Field Warehousing", 42 Col.L. Rev. 991 (1942), and Comment, 69 Yale L.J. 663 (1960). Note the last sentence of Section 9–205.

Historical Note: The present section is a clarification of former subsection (1), and meets the suggestions of the Law Revision Commission. Former subsection (2), which required filing for field warehousing arrangements, has been eliminated and the validity of field warehouse arrangements is left dependent, as at common law, on the validity of the possessory arrangements. Compare discussion under Section 9–205. (1956 Recommendations, p. 280; Excerpts, p. 473.)

Official Uniform Comment

Prior Uniform Statutory Provision: None.

Purposes:

1. As under the common law of pledge, no filing is required by this Article to perfect a security interest where the secured party has possession of the collateral. Compare Section 9–302(1)(a). This section permits a security interest to be perfected by transfer of possession only when the collateral is goods, instruments, documents or chattel paper: that is to say, accounts and general intangibles are excluded. See Section 5–116 for the special case of assignments of letters and advices of credit. A security interest in accounts and general intangibles–property not ordinarily represented by any writing whose delivery operates to transfer the claim–may under this Article be perfected only by filing, and this rule would not be affected by the fact that a security agreement or other writing described the assignment of accounts which are out of the ordinary course of financing: such exempted assignments are perfected when they attach under Section 9–303(1); they do not fall within this section.

2. Possession may be by the secured party himself or by an agent on his behalf: it is of course clear, however, that the debtor or a person controlled by him cannot qualify as such an agent for the secured party. See also the last sentence of Section 9–205. Where the collateral (except for goods covered by a negotiable document) is held by a bailee, the time of perfection of the security interest, under the second sentence of the section, is when the bailee receives notification of the secured party's interest: this rule rejects the common law doctrine that it is necessary for the bailee to attorn to the secured party or acknowledge that he now holds on his behalf.

3. The third sentence of the section rejects the "equitable pledge" theory of relation back, under which the taking possession was deemed to relate back to the date of the original security agreement. The relation back theory has had little vitality since the 1938 revision of the Federal Bankruptcy Act, which introduced in Section 60a provisions designed to make such interests voidable as preferences in bankruptcy proceedings. This section now brings state law into conformity with the overriding federal policy: where a pledge transaction is contemplated, perfection dates only from the time possession is taken, although a security interest may attach, unperfected, before that under the rules stated in Section 9–204. The only exception to this rule is the short twenty-one day period of perfection provided in Section 9–304(4) and (5) during which a debtor may have possession of specified collateral in which there is a perfected security interest.

Cross References:

Sections 5–116, 9–204, 9–302, 9–303 and 9–304.

Definitional Cross References:

"Chattel paper." Section 9–105.
"Collateral." Section 9–105.
"Documents." Section 9–105.
"Goods." Section 9–105.
"Instruments." Section 9–105.
"Receives notification." Section 1–201.
"Secured party." Section 9–105.
"Security interest." Section 1–201.

Section 9–306. "Proceeds"; Secured Party's Rights on Disposition of Collateral.

(1) "Proceeds" includes whatever is received upon the sale, exchange, collection, or other disposition of collateral or proceeds. Insurance payable by reason of loss or damage to the collateral is proceeds, except to the extent that it is payable to a person other than a party to the security agreement. Any payments or distributions made with respect to investment property collateral are proceeds. Money, checks, deposit accounts, and the like, are "cash proceeds". All other proceeds are "non-cash proceeds".

(2) Except where this Article otherwise provides, a security interest continues in collateral notwithstanding sale, exchange or other disposition thereof unless the disposition was authorized by the secured party in the security agreement or otherwise, and also continues in any identifiable proceeds including collections received by the debtor.

(3) The security interest in proceeds is a continuously perfected security interest if the interest in the original collateral was perfected but it ceases to be a perfected security interest and becomes unperfected 10 days after receipt of the proceeds by the debtor unless:

(a) A filed financing statement covers the original collateral and the proceeds are collateral in which a security interest may be perfected by filing in the office or offices where the financing statement has been filed and, if the proceeds are acquired with cash proceeds, the description of collateral in the financing statement indicates the types of property constituting the proceeds; or

(b) a filed financing statement covers the original collateral and the proceeds are identifiable cash proceeds; or

(c) the original collateral was investment property and the proceeds are identifiable cash proceeds; or

(d) the security interest in the proceeds is perfected before the expiration of the 10 day period.

Except as provided in this section, a security interest in proceeds can be perfected only by the methods or under the circumstances permitted in this Article for original collateral of the same type.

(4) In the event of insolvency proceedings instituted by or against a debtor, a secured party with a perfected security interest in proceeds has a perfected security interest only in the following proceeds: (a) in identifiable non-cash proceeds and in separate deposit accounts containing only proceeds;

(b) in identifiable cash proceeds in the form of money which is neither commingled with other money nor deposited in a deposit account prior to the insolvency proceedings;

(c) in identifiable cash proceeds in the form of checks and the like which are not deposited in a deposit account prior to the insolvency proceedings; and

(d) in all cash and deposit accounts of the debtor in which proceeds have been commingled with other funds, but the perfected security interest under this paragraph (d) is

(i) subject to any right of set-off; and

(ii) limited to an amount not greater than the amount of any cash proceeds received by the debtor within ten days before the institution of the insolvency proceedings less the sum of (I) the payments to the secured party on account of cash proceeds received by the debtor during such period and (II) the cash proceeds received by the debtor during such period to which the secured party is entitled under paragraphs (a) through of this subsection (4).

(5) If a sale of goods results in an account or chattel paper which is transferred by the seller to a secured party, and if the goods are returned to or are repossessed by the seller or the secured party, the following rules determine priorities:

(a) If the goods were collateral at the time of sale for an indebtedness of the seller which is still unpaid, the original security interest attaches again to the goods and continues as a perfected security interest if it was perfected at the time when the goods were sold. If the security interest was originally perfected by a filing which is still effective nothing further is required to continue the perfected status; in any other case, the secured party must take possession of the returned or repossessed goods or must file.

(b) An unpaid transferee of the chattel paper has a security interest in the goods against the transferor. Such security interest is prior to a security interest asserted under paragraph (a) to the extent that the transferee of the chattel paper was entitled to priority under Section 9–308.

(c) An unpaid transferee of the account has a security interest in the goods against the transferor. Such security interest is subordinate to a security interest asserted under paragraph (a).

(d) A security interest of an unpaid transferee asserted under paragraph (b) or must be perfected for protection against creditors of the transferor and purchasers of the returned or repossessed goods.

Amended by Laws 1977, Ch. 866, eff. July 2, 1978; L. 1997, Ch. 566, eff. Oct. 1, 1997.

New York Annotations

(1) For the concept of "proceeds", see Tradesman's Nat'l Bank v. Nat'l Surety Co., 169 N.Y. 563, 62 N.E. 670 (1902).

(2) and (3) These subsections adopt as to security agreements generally a scheme, in respect of proceeds realized by a debtor on a sale or other disposition of collateral, which is generally similar to that adopted in the Uniform Trust Receipts Act, Personal Property Law, § 58–b. The present New York rules as to proceeds in other types of security transactions, which have not been developed in such a comprehensive manner as in Article 9, as as follows:

Chattel mortgages. Present New York law is similar to subsection (2) in that the security interest of the mortgagee continues in the original collateral unless the sale by the mortgagor was expressly or impliedly permitted by the mortgagee. Mortgages recorded under Lien Law, § 230, are still governed by Utica Trust & Deposit Co. v. Decker, 244 N.Y. 340, 155 N.E. 665 (1927), which refused to estop the chattel mortgagee who entrusted possession to a dealer and recovered the collateral from a subsequent purchaser. Cf. Zendman v. Harry Winston, Inc., 305 N.Y. 180, 111 N.E.2d 871 (1953) (N.J. law). On the other hand, if a mortgage is filed under Lien Law, § 230–c, the buyer in ordinary course is protected. Lien Law, § 230–c(6). There is apparently no New York law on cash proceeds, and on non-cash proceeds it would appear that the after-acquired property provisions would govern. See annotation to Section 9–204. See also Section 9–307.

Conditional sales. Under Personal Property Law, § 69, a conditional seller's interest continues in the goods sold unless the seller has expressly or impliedly consented to a resale. This is consistent with subsection (2) but the rule will be altered by this section's reference to other Code sections. See annotation to Section 9–307(1) and (2). There appears to be no New York authority on cash proceeds arising from a conditional sale.

Inventory liens. Under the Factor's Lien Act (Personal Property Law, § 45) it is provided, as in subsection (2), that a security interest attaches to identifiable proceeds resulting from the sale of inventory. However, the Code provision in subsection (2) that the security interest attaches to accounts as proceeds without further action by the parties is somewhat more generous to secured parties than the present law which requires either an additional assignment of the subsequent accounts or notice to the account debtor. Personal Property Law, § 45. See also, Irving Trust Co. v. Commercial Factors Corp., 68 F.2d 864 (2d Cir. 1934). The effect of the reference in subsection (2) to other provisions of Article 9 is that the secured party's interest in the inventory would not continue when the inventory is sold to a buyer in ordinary course of business. See Section 9–307(1). Although there is no specific protection of such persons in the present statute, it is probable that the factor's lien would be subordinated to the buyer's claim.

(4) Substantially similar provisions are made in the Uniform Trust Receipts Act, Personal Property Law, § 58–b. There is no similar statutory scheme in other New York statutes.

(5) This subsection will provide rules of law for a situation for which there is no present New York authority.

Historical Note: The entire section has been rewritten for clarity and meets the suggestions of the Law Revision Commission. The subject matter of old subsection (4) has been dealt with in Section 9–308. Former subsection (2) dealing with cash proceeds upon insolvency has been rewritten to permit the retention of the security interest in identifiable cash proceeds, and to give a security interest in all unidentifiable cash and bank accounts received by the debtor but limited to the net amount of cash proceeds received and retained by the debtor within ten days prior to the insolvency proceedings. (1956 Recommendations, p. 284; Excerpts, p.474.)

Official Uniform Comment

Prior Uniform Statutory Provision: Section 10, Uniform Trust Receipts Act.

Purposes:

1. This section states a secured party's right to the proceeds received by a debtor on disposition of collateral and states when his interest in such proceeds is perfected.

It makes clear that insurance proceeds from casualty loss of collateral are proceeds within the meaning of this section.

As to the proceeds of consigned goods, see Section 9–114 and the Comment thereto.

2. (a) Whether a debtor's sale of collateral was authorized or unauthorized, prior law generally gave the secured party a claim to the proceeds. Sometimes it was said that the security interest attached to the "property" received in substitution; sometimes it was said the debtor held the proceeds as "trustee" or "agent" for the secured party. Whatever the formulation of the rule, the secured party, if he could identify the proceeds, could reclaim them or their equivalent from the debtor or his trustee in bankruptcy. This section provides new rules for insolvency proceedings. Paragraphs 4(a) through substitute specific rules of identification for general principles of tracing. Paragraph 4(d) limits the security interest in proceeds not within these rules to an amount of the debtor's cash and deposit accounts not greater than cash proceeds received within ten days of insolvency proceedings less the cash proceeds during this period already paid over and less the amounts for which the security interest is recognized under paragraphs 4(a) through (c).

(b) Subsections (2) and (3) make clear that the four-month period for calculating a voidable preference in bankruptcy begins with the date of the secured party's obtaining the security interest in the original collateral and not with the date of his obtaining control of the proceeds. The interest in the proceeds "continues" as a perfected interest if the original interest was perfected; but the interest ceases to be perfected after the expiration of ten days unless a filed financing statement covered the original collateral and the proceeds are collateral of a type as to which a security interest could be perfected by a filing in the same office or unless the secured party perfects his interest in the proceeds themselves—i.e., by filing a financing statement covering them or by taking possession. See Section 9–312(6) and Comment thereto for priority of rights in proceeds perfected by a filing as to original collateral.

(c) Where cash proceeds are covered into the debtor's checking account and paid out in the operation of the debtor's business, recipients of the funds of course take free of any claim which the secured party may have in them as proceeds. What has been said relates to payments and transfers in ordinary course. The law of fraudulent conveyances would not doubt in appropriate cases support recovery of proceeds by a secured party from a transferee out of ordinary course or otherwise in collusion with the debtor to defraud the secured party.

3. In most cases when a debtor makes an unauthorized disposition of collateral, the security interest, under prior law and under this Article, continues in the original collateral in the hands of the purchaser or other transferee. That is to say, since the transferee takes subject to the security interest, the secured party may repossess the collateral from him or in an appropriate case maintain an action for conversion. Subsection (2) codifies this rule. The secured party may claim both proceeds and collateral, but may of course have only one satisfaction.

In many cases a purchaser or other transferee of collateral will take free of a security interest: in such cases the secured party's only right will be to proceeds. The transferee will take free whenever the disposition was authorized; the authorization may be contained in the security agreement or otherwise given. The right to proceeds, either under the rules of this section or under specific mention thereof in a security agreement or financing statement does not in itself constitute an authorization of sale.

Section 9–301 states when transferees take free of unperfected security interests. Sections 9–307 on goods, 9–308 on chattel paper and instruments and 9–309 on negotiable instruments, negotiable documents and securities state when purchasers of such collateral take free of a security interest even though perfected and even though the disposition was not authorized.

4. Subsection (5) states rules to determine priorities when collateral which has been sold is returned to the debtor: for example goods returned to a department store by a dissatisfied customer. The most typical problems involve sale and return of inventory, but the subsection can also apply to equipment. Under the rule of Benedict v. Ratner, failure to segregate such returned goods sometimes led to invalidation of

the entire security arrangement. This Article rejects the Benedict v. Ratner line of cases (see Section 9–205 and Comment). Subsection (5)(a) of this section reinforces the rule of Section 9–205: as between secured party and debtor (and debtor's trustee in bankruptcy) the original security interest continues on the returned goods. Whether or not the security interest in the returned goods is perfected depends upon factors stated in the text.

Paragraphs (5)(b), and (d) deal with a different aspect of the returned goods situation. Assume that a dealer has sold an automobile and transferred the chattel paper or the account arising on the sale to Bank X (which had not previously financed the car as inventory). Thereafter the buyer of the automobile rightfully rescinds the sale, say for breach of warranty, and the car is returned to the dealer. Paragraph (5)(b) gives the bank as transferee of the chattel paper or the account a security interest in the car against the dealer. For protection against dealer's creditors or purchasers from him (other than buyers in the ordinary course of business, see Section 9–307), Bank X as the transferee, under paragraph (5)(d), must perfect its interest by taking possession of the car or by filing as to it. Perfection of his original interest in the chattel paper or the account does not automatically carry over to the returned car, as it does under paragraph (5)(a) where the secured party originally financed the dealer's inventory.

In the situation covered by (5)(b) and (5)(c) a secured party who financed the inventory and a secured party to whom the chattel paper or the account was transferred may both claim the returned goods–the inventory financer under paragraph (5)(a), the transferee under paragraphs(5)(b) and (5)(c). With respect to chattel paper, Section 9–308 regulates the priorities. With respect to an account, paragraph (5)(c) subordinates the security interest of the transferee of the account to that of the inventory financer. However, if the inventory security interest was unperfected, the transferee's interest could become entitled to priority under the rules stated in Section 9–312(5).

In cases of repossession by the dealer and also in cases where the chattel was returned to the dealer by the voluntary act of the account debtor, the dealer's position may be that of a mere custodian; he may be an agent for resale, but without any other obligation to the holder of the chattel paper; he may be obligated to repurchase the chattel, the chattel paper or the account from the secured party or to hold it as collateral for a loan secured by a transfer of the chattel paper of the account.

If the dealer thereafter sells the chattel to a buyer in ordinary course of business in any of the foregoing cases the buyer is fully protected under Section 2–403(2) as well as under Section 9–307(1), whichever is technically applicable.

Cross References:

Sections 9–307, 9–308 and 9–309.
Point 3: Sections 1–205 and 9–301.
Point 4: Sections 2–403(2), 9–205 and 9–312.

Definitional Cross References:

"Account." Section 9–106.
"Bank." Section 1–201.
"Chattel paper." Section 9–105.
"Check." Sections 3–104 and 9–105.
"Collateral." Section 9–105.
"Creditors." Section 1–201.
"Debtor." Section 9–105.
"Deposit account." Section 9–105.
"Goods." Section 9–105.

"Insolvency proceedings." Section 1–201.
"Money." Section 1–201.
"Purchaser." Section 1–201.
"Sale." Sections 2–106 and 9–105.
"Secured party." Section 9–105.
"Security agreement." Section 9–105.
"Security interest." Section 1–201.

Section 9–307. Protection of Buyers of Goods.

(1) A buyer in ordinary course of business (subsection (9) of Section 1–201) other than a person buying farm products from a person engaged in farming operations takes free of a security interest created by his seller even though the security interest is perfected and even though the buyer knows of its existence.

(2) In the case of consumer goods, a buyer takes free of a security interest even though perfected if he buys without knowledge of the security interest, for value and for his own personal, family or household purposes unless prior to the purchase the secured party has filed a financing statement covering such goods.

(3) A buyer other than a buyer in ordinary course of business (subsection (1) of this section) takes free of a security interest to the extent that it secures future advances made after the secured party acquires knowledge of the purchase, or more than 45 days after the purchase, whichever first occurs, unless made pursuant to a commitment entered into without knowledge of the purchase and before the expiration of the 45 day period.

Amended by Laws 1977, Ch. 866, eff. July 2, 1978.

New York Annotations

(1) The Code adopts a rule similar to the Uniform Trust Receipts Act (Personal Property Law, § 58–a (2)(a)(i)), the chattel mortgage law in respect of dealers (Lien Law, § 230–c) and the Uniform Conditional Sales Act (Personal Property Law, § 69).

The theory of subsection (1) is consistent in principle with what the New York rule is or has been in many transactions, namely: where the debtor has express, implied, or apparent authority to sell the collateral, a buyer in the ordinary course of business takes free of the security interest. Generally, the Code expands the buyer's protection. By definition (Section 1–201(9)) the seller must be one "engaged in the business of selling goods of that kind," and other secured creditors are not "buyers." Thus the subsection does not create rules of priority and will usually, but not always, affect inventory only.

Chattel mortgages. A "buyer in the ordinary course of business" will apparently acquire title superior to the perfected security interest of a mortgagee under the dealers chattel mortgage law, Lien Law, § 230–c. Mortgagees under chattel mortgages recorded under Lien Law, § 230, are not estopped from claiming the goods from a buyer merely because the goods were entrusted to a dealer. Utica Trust & Deposit Co. v. Decker, 244 N.Y. 340, 155 N.E. 665 (1927); Merchants Bank of New York v. McKenna, 212 N.Y.S.2d 541(1961). The Code will change this rule.

Conditional sales. Accord: Personal Property Law, § 69.Under the Code, transfers for security are explicitly not included under the term "buyer in ordinary course."

The Court of Appeals recently interpreted § 65 of the Personal Property Law in a similar fashion. See Rand's Discount Co. v. Universal C. I. T. Credit Corp., 9 N.Y.2d 454, 174 N.E.2d 509 (1961). See Section 9–312.

Consignments. Where a consignee is given authority to sell, a purchaser takes free of the consignor's claim even though the consignee exceeds the scope of his authority. Personal Property Law, § 43.

Inventory lien. There is no explicit provision in Personal Property Law, § 45, safeguarding the position of buyers in the ordinary course of business. However, it would appear from the materials collected above that in the usual case the factor would be precluded from asserting his lien against such a buyer.

(2) There are no special New York rules relating to buyers of consumer goods and farm equipment. It will be recalled that under Section 9–302 filing is not necessary to perfect a purchase money security interest with respect to most consumer goods (motor vehicles and fixtures excepted) and certain farm equipment. By taking the additional step of filing, the secured party can protect himself against the limited risk he otherwise runs under this subsection.

Historical Note: The former preamble has been omitted because the definition of "buyer in ordinary course of business" limits subsection (1) to inventory cases. Other changes are for clarification of buyer in ordinary course, and meet the suggestions of the Law Revision Commission. (1956 Recommendations, p. 284; Excerpts, p. 475.)

Official Uniform Comment

Prior Uniform Statutory Provision: Section 9, Uniform Conditional Sales Act; Section 9(2), Uniform Trust Receipts Act.

Purposes:

1. This section states when buyers of goods take free of a security interest even though perfected. A buyer who takes free of a perfected security interest of course takes free of an unperfected one. Section 9–301 should be consulted to determine what purchasers, in addition to the buyers covered in this section, take free of an unperfected security interest.

Article 2 (Sales) states general rules on purchase of goods from a seller with defective or voidable title (Section 2–403).

2. The definition of "buyer in ordinary course of business" in Section 1–201(9) restricts the application of subsection (1) to buyers (except pawnbrokers) "from a person in the business of selling goods of that kind": thus the subsection applies, in the terminology of this Article, primarily to inventory. Subsection (1) further excludes from its operation buyers of "farm products", defined in Section 9–109(3), from a person engaged in farming operations. The buyer in ordinary course of business is defined as one who buys "in good faith and without knowledge that the sale to him is in violation of the ownership rights or security interest of a third party." This section provides that such a buyer takes free of a security interest, even though perfected, and although he knows the security interest exists. Reading the two provisions together, it results that the buyer takes free if he merely knows that there is a security interest which covers the goods but takes subject if he knows, in addition, that the sale is in violation of some term in the security agreement not waived by the words or conduct of the secured party.

The limitations which this section imposes on the persons who may take free of a security interest apply of course only to unauthorized sales by the debtor. If the secured party has authorized sale in the security agreement or otherwise, the buyer takes free without regard to the limitations of this section. Section 9–306 states the right of a secured party to the proceeds of a sale, authorized or unauthorized.

3. Subsection (2) deals with buyers of "consumer goods" (defined in Section 9–109).Under Section 9–301(1)(d) no filing is required to perfect a purchase money interest in consumer goods subject to this subsection except motor vehicles required to be registered; filing is required to perfect security interests in such goods other than purchase money interests and, for motor vehicles, even in the case of purchase money interests. (The special case of fixtures has added complications that are apart from the point of this discussion.)

Under subsection (2) a buyer of consumer goods takes free of a security interest even though perfected a) if he buys without knowledge of the security interest, b) for value, c) for his own personal, family, or household purposes and d) before a financing statement is filed.

As to purchase money security interests which are perfected without filing under Section 9–302(1)(d): A secured party may file a financing statement (although filing is not required for perfection). If he does file, all buyers take subject to the security interest. If he does not file, a buyer who meets the qualifications stated in the preceding paragraph takes free of the security interest.

As to security interests which can be perfected only by filing under Section 9–302: This category includes all non-purchase money interests, and all interests, whether or not purchase money, in motor vehicles, as well as interests which may be and are filed, though filing was not required for perfection under Section 9–302. (Note that under Section 9–302 (3)the filing provisions of this Article do not apply when a state has enacted a certificate of title law. Thus where motor vehicles are concerned, in a state having such a certificate of title law, perfection will be under that law.) So long as the security interest remains unperfected, not only the buyers described in subsection (2) but the purchasers described in Section 9–301 will take free of the interest. After a financing statement has been filed or after compliance with the certificate of title law all subsequent buyers, under the rule of subsection (2), are subject to the security interest.

4. Although a buyer is of course subject to the Code's system of notice from filing or possession, subsection (3) makes clear that he will not be subject to future advances under a security interest after the secured party has knowledge that the buyer has purchased the collateral and in any event after 45 days after the purchase unless the advances were made pursuant to a commitment entered into before the expiration of the 45 days and without knowledge of the purchase. Of course, a buyer in ordinary course who takes free of the security interest under subsection (1) is not subject to any future advances. Compare Sections 9–301(4) and 9–312(7).

Cross References:

Point 1: Sections 2–403 and 9–301.
Point 2: Section 9–306.
Point 3: Sections 9–301 and 9–302.
Point 4: Sections 9–301(4) and 9–312(7).

Definitional Cross References:

"Buyer in ordinary course of business." Section 1–201.
"Consumer goods." Section 9–109.
"Goods." Section 9–105.
"Knows" and "Knowledge." Section 1–201.
"Person." Section 1–201.
"Purchase." Section 1–201.
"Pursuant to commitment." Section 9–105.
"Secured party." Section 9–105.
"Security interest." Section 1–201.

"Value." Section 1–201.

Section 9–308. Purchase of Chattel Paper and Instruments.

A purchaser of chattel paper or an instrument who gives new value and takes possession of it in the ordinary course of his business has priority over a security interest in the chattel paper or instrument

(a) which is perfected under Section 9-304 (permissive filing and temporary perfection) or under Section 9-306 (perfection as to proceeds) if he acts without knowledge that the specific paper or instrument is subject to a security interest; or

(b) which is claimed merely as proceeds of inventory subject to a security interest (Section 9-306) even though he knows that the specific paper or instrument is subject to the security interest.

Amended by Laws 1977, Ch. 866, eff. July 2, 1978.

New York Annotations

New, but compare Uniform Trust Receipts Law, Personal Property Law, § 58–a(1)(a). It is not clear whether the provisions of Lien Law, § 232–a,governing filing of assignments of a chattel mortgage, are designed to permit the assignee to file and protect himself against subsequent transferees of the actual papers.

Historical Note: This section was completely rewritten. The first sentence now makes it clear that an interest in chattel paper or non-negotiable instruments based on possession will have priority over security interests based on filing, or on temporary perfection under Section 9–304 without filing. The second sentence deals with the subject matter of former Section 9–306(4) and makes it clear that a security interest in chattel paper for new value outranks a security interest based merely on a claim to proceeds of inventory which had been subject to the new security interest. The changes meet the suggestions of the Law Revision Commission. (1956 Recommendations, p. 285; Excerpts, p. 475.)

Official Uniform Comment

Prior Uniform Statutory Provision: Sections 9(a) and 10 of Uniform Trust Receipts Act.

Purposes:

1. Chattel paper is defined (Section 9–105) as "a writing or writings which evidence both a monetary obligation and a security interest in or a lease of specific goods." Such paper has become an important class of collateral in financing arrangements, which may–as in the automobile and some other fields–follow an earlier financing arrangement covering inventory or which may begin with the chattel paper itself.

Arrangements where the chattel paper is delivered to the secured party who then makes collections, as well as arrangements where the debtor, whether or not he is left in possession of the paper, makes the collections, are both widely used, and are known respectively as notification (or "direct collection") and non-notification (or "indirect collection") arrangements. In the automobile filed, for example, when a car is sold to a consumer buyer under an installment purchase agreement and the resulting chattel paper is assigned, the assignee usually takes possession, the obligor is notified of the assignment and is directed to make payments to the assignee. In the furniture field, for an example on the other hand, the chattel paper may be left in the dealer's hands or delivered to the assignee; in either case the obligor may not be notified, and payments are made to the dealer-assignor who receives them under a duty to remit to his assignee. The widespread use of both methods of dealing with chattel paper is recognized by the provisions of this Article, which permit perfection of a chattel paper security interest either by filing or by taking possession.

2. Although perfection by filing is permitted as to chattel paper, certain purchasers of chattel paper allowed to remain in the debtor's possession take free of the security interest despite the filing.

Clause (b) of the section deals with the case where the security interest in the chattel paper is claimed merely as proceeds—i.e., on behalf of an inventory financer who has not by some new transaction with the debtor acquired a specific interest in the chattel paper. In that case a purchaser, even though he knows of the inventory financer's proceeds interest, takes priority provided he gives new value and takes possession of the paper in the ordinary course of his business.

The same basic rule applies in favor of a purchaser of other instruments who claims priority against a proceeds interest therein of which he has knowledge. Thus a purchaser of a negotiable instrument might prevail under clause (b) even though his knowledge of the conflicting proceeds claim precluded his having holder in due course status under Section 9–309.

3. Clause (a) deals with the case where the non-possessory security interest in the chattel paper is more than a mere claim to proceeds—i.e., exists in favor of a secured party who has given value against the paper, whether or not he financed the inventory whose sale gave rise to it. In this case the purchaser, to take priority, must not only give new value and take possession in the ordinary course of his business; he must also take without knowledge of the existing security interest. Thus a secured party, who has a specific interest in the chattel paper and not merely a claim to proceeds, and who wishes to leave the paper in the debtor's possession can, because of the knowledge requirement, protect himself against purchasers by stamping or noting on the paper the fact that it has been assigned to him.

4. It should be noted that under Section 9–304(1) a security interest in an instrument, negotiable or non-negotiable, cannot be perfected by filing (except where the instrument constitutes part of chattel paper). Thus the only types of perfected non-possessory security interest that can arise in an instrument are the temporary 21 day perfection provided for in Section 9–304(4) and (5) or the 10 day perfection in proceeds of Section 9–306. Where such a perfected interest exists in a non-negotiable instrument, purchasers will take free if they qualify under clause (a) of the section.

Cross References:

Point 1: Sections 9–304(1) and 9–305.
Point 2: Section 9–306.
Point 4: Sections 9–304 and 9–306.

Definitional Cross References:

"Chattel paper." Section 9–105.
"Instrument." Section 9–105.
"Inventory." Section 9–109.
"Knowledge." Section 1–201.
"Proceeds." Section 9–306.
"Purchaser." Section 1–201.
"Security interest." Section 1–201.
"Value." Section 1–201.

Section 9–309. Protection of Purchasers of Instruments, Documents and Securities.

Nothing in this Article limits the rights of a holder in due course of a negotiable instrument (Section 3–302) or a holder to whom a negotiable document of title has been duly negotiated (Section 7–501) or a protected purchaser of a security (Section 8–303) and such holders or purchasers take priority over an earlier security interest even though perfected. Filing under this Article does not constitute notice of the security interest to such holders or purchasers.

Amended by Laws 1982, Ch. 928, eff. Dec. 21, 1982 and deemed to have been in full force and effect on and after Sept. 1, 1982.

New York Annotations

Compare the Uniform Trust Receipts Act, Personal Property Law, § 58–a(1)(a).

Historical Note: The section was changed for clarification and consistency in cross-references, and to omit a reference to former Section 9–206(1). (1956 Recommendations, p. 286; Excerpts, p. 476.)

Official Uniform Comment

Prior Uniform Statutory Provision: Section 9(a), Uniform Trust Receipts Act.

Purposes:

1. Under this Article as at common law and under prior statutes the rights of purchasers of negotiable paper, including negotiable documents of title and investment securities, are determined by the rules of holding in due course and the like which are applicable to the type of paper concerned. (Articles 3, 7, and 8.) This section, as did Section 9(a) of the Uniform Trust Receipts Act, makes explicit the rule which was implicitly but universally recognized under the earlier statutes.

2. Under Section 9–304(1) filing is ineffective to perfect a security interest in instruments (including securities) except those instruments which are part of chattel paper, and of course is ineffective to constitute notice to subsequent purchasers. Although filing is permissible as a method of perfection for a security interest in documents, this section follows the policy of the Uniform Trust Receipts Act in providing that the filing does not constitute notice to purchasers

Cross References:

Articles 3, 7, and 8 and Sections 9–304(1) and 9–308.

Definitional Cross References:

"Bona fide purchaser." Section 8–302.
"Document of title." Section 1–201.
"Duly negotiated." Section 7–501.
"Holder." Section 1–201.
"Holder in due course." Sections 3–302 and 9–105.
"Negotiable instrument." Sections 3–104 and 9–105.
"Notice." Section 1–201.
"Purchaser." Section 1–201.
"Security." Sections 8–102 and 9–105.

"Security interest." Section 1–201.

Section 9–310. Priority of Certain Liens Arising by Operation of Law.

When a person in the ordinary course of his business furnishes services or materials with respect to goods subject to a security interest, a lien upon goods in the possession of such person given by statute or rule of law for such materials or services takes priority over a perfected security interest unless the lien is statutory and the statute expressly provides otherwise.

New York Annotations

The provisions of this section seem analogous to those of the Uniform Trust Receipts Act, Personal Property Law, § 58–c, which provide that specific liens arising out of contractual dealings of the trustee in respect of the goods prevail against the entruster.

As to the creation and existence of liens resulting from the furnishing of services or materials in respect of goods subject to a security interest, this section looks to existing law. It attempts only to establish the priority of such liens over perfected security interests in the goods unless the lien is statutory and the statute expressly provides otherwise.

Presently New York statutes give a variety of such liens to creditors in possession of goods. In most cases the lien arises if the services or materials were furnished at the request of the legal or equitable owner. In any event, the fact that title to the goods is in the secured party is seldom material to the possessory liens. For example under Lien Law, § 184, the garage man's lien on motor vehicles, aircraft, motor cycles, or motor boats for supplies, storage, or labor takes priority over a conditional seller or a mortgagee. Temporary surrender of possession apparently does not destroy the lien, but surrender of possession thirty days after accrual of the lien makes the lien void as to prior conditional sellers or mortgagees. Water town Nat'l Bank v. Van Cortlandt Garage, 273 App. Div. 826, 76 N.Y.S.2d 393 (1948). Default by a conditional buyer does not affect a lien arising for services provided at his request. Motor Discount Corp. v. Scappy & Peck Auto Body, 12 N.Y.2d 227, 188 N.E.2d 907 (1963).

A similar explicit priority over security interests is given by Lien Law, § 183 (veterinarian or agistor's lien); General Business Law, § 113(b) (warehouseman's lien). Under Lien Law, § 181 (innkeeper's lien), there is no requirement that the guest own the property subjected to the lien, and security interests have been subordinated to the statutory lien where the lienor has no knowledge of the prior security interest. Waters & Co. v. Gerard, 189 N.Y. 302, 82 N.E. 143 (1907).

To the extent that the creation of common law possessory liens required the consent of the legal title holder, this section leaves the prior law unchanged in respect of the creation and existence of such liens. See Lien Law, § 180, declaratory of the common law artisan's lien. Tucker v. Werner, 2 Misc. 193, 21 N.Y.S. 264 (1892) (implied consent).

Statutes creating non-possessory liens, such as Lien Law, § 182, are not within this section of the Code.

Official Uniform Comment

Prior Uniform Statutory Provision: Section 11, Uniform Trust Receipts Act.

Purposes:

1. To provide that liens securing claims arising from work intended to enhance or preserve the value of the collateral take priority over an earlier security interest even though perfected.

2. Apart from the Uniform Trust Receipts Act which had a section similar to this one, there was generally no specific statutory rule as to priority between security devices and liens for services or materials. Under chattel mortgage or conditional sales law many decisions made the priority of such liens turn on whether the secured party did or did not have "title." This section changes such rules and makes the lien for services or materials prior in all cases where they are furnished in the ordinary course of the lienor's business and the goods involved are in the lienor's possession. Some of the statutes creating such liens expressly make the lien subordinate to a prior security interest. This section does not repeal such statutory provisions. If the statute creating the lien is silent, even though it has been construed by decision to make the lien subordinate to the security interest, this section provides a rule of interpretation that the lien should take priority over the security interest.

Cross References:

Sections 9–102(2), 9–104 and 9–312(1).

Definitional Cross References:

"Goods." Section 9–105.
"Person." Section 1–201.
"Security interest." Section 1–201.

Section 9–311. Alienability of Debtor's Rights: Judicial Process.

The debtor's rights in collateral may be voluntarily or involuntarily transferred (by way of sale, creation of a security interest, attachment, levy, garnishment or other judicial process) notwithstanding a provision in the security agreement prohibiting any transfer or making the transfer constitute a default.

New York Annotations

The provisions of this section as to voluntary transfers seem to be generally in *accord* with New York law. Thus a chattel mortgagor may convey or mortgage his right to redeem, Tremaine v. Mortimer, 128 N.Y. 1, 27 N.E. 1060 (1891). If the mortgage makes such a transfer ineffective, the mortgagee may repossess. Liebman v. Brockway Motor Truck Corp., 140 Misc. 73, 249 N.Y.S. 39 (1930). Further, a conditional buyer of personal property may, upon notifying the conditional seller, transfer his interest in the goods sold. Personal Property Law, § 73. Even where the resale is unauthorized, the sub-buyer obtains all the interest that the original buyer than holds. Powers v. Burdick, 126 App.Div. 179, 110 N.Y.S. 883 (1908).

On voluntary transfers, see Civil Practice Act, § 688 [now CPLR § 5232], permitting levy to be made on the interest of a chattel mortgagor or conditional buyer even after default, if the debtor is still in possession.

Historical Note: At the suggestion of the Law Revision Commission the section now specifies the alien ability of the debtor's interest after the creation of a security interest. (1956 Recommendations, p. 286; Excerpts, p. 476.)

Official Uniform Comment

Prior Uniform Statutory Provision: None.

Purposes:

1. To make clear that in all security transactions under this Article, the debtor has an interest (whether legal title or an equity) which he can dispose of and which his creditors can reach.

2. Some jurisdictions have held that when a mortgagee or conditional seller has "title" to the collateral, creditors may not proceed against the mortgagor's or vendee's interest by levy, attachment or other judicial judicial process. This section changes those rules by providing that in all security interests the debtor's interest in the collateral remains subject to claims of creditors who take appropriate action. It is left to the law of each state to determine the form of "appropriate process."

3. Where the security interest is in inventory, difficult problems arise with reference to attachment and levy. Assume that a debt of $100,000 is secured by inventory worth twice that amount. If by attachment or levy certain units of the inventory are seized, the determination of the debtor's equity in the units seized is not a simple matter. The section leaves the solution of this problem to the courts. Procedures such as marshalling may be appropriate.

Cross References:

Sections 9–301(4), 9–307(3) and 9–312(7).

Definitional Cross References:

"Collateral." Section 9–105.
"Debtor." Section 9–105.
"Rights." Section 1–201.
"Sale." Sections 2–106 and 9–105.
"Security agreement." Section 9–105.
"Security interest." Section 1–201.

Section 9–312. Priorities Among Conflicting Security Interests in the Same Collateral.

(1) The rules of priority stated in other sections of this Part and in the following sections shall govern when applicable: Section 4–210 with respect to the security interests of collecting banks in items being collected, accompanying documents and proceeds; Section 9–103 on security interests related to other jurisdictions; Section 9–114 on consignments; Section 9–115 on security interests in investment property.

(2) A perfected security interest in crops for new value given to enable the debtor to produce the crops during the production season and given not more than three months before the crops become growing crops by planting or otherwise takes priority over an earlier perfected security interest to the extent that such earlier interest secures obligations due more than six months before the crops become growing crops by planting or otherwise, even though the person giving new value had knowledge of the earlier security interest.

(3) A perfected purchase money security interest in inventory has priority over a conflicting security interest in the same inventory and also has priority

in identifiable cash proceeds received on or before the delivery of the inventory to a buyer if

(a) the purchase money security interest is perfected at the time the debtor receives possession of the inventory; and

(b) the purchase money secured party gives notification in writing to the holder of the conflicting security interest if the holder had filed a financing statement covering the same types of inventory (i) before the date of the filing made by the purchase money secured party, or (ii) before the beginning of the 21 day period where the purchase money security interest is temporarily perfected without filing or possession (subsection (5) of Section 9-304); and

(c) the holder of the conflicting security interest receives the notification within five years before the debtor receives possession of the inventory; and

(d) the notification states that the person giving the notice has or expects to acquire a purchase money security interest in inventory of the debtor, describing such inventory by item or type.

(4) A purchase money security interest in collateral other than inventory has priority over a conflicting security interest in the same collateral or its proceeds if the purchase money security interest is perfected at the time the debtor receives possession of the collateral or within twenty days thereafter.

(5) In all cases not governed by other rules stated in this section (including cases of purchase money security interests which do not qualify for the special priorities set forth in subsections (3) and (4) of this section), priority between conflicting security interests in the same collateral shall be determined according to the following rules:

(a) Conflicting security interests rank according to priority in time of filing or perfection. Priority dates from the time a filing is first made covering the collateral or the time the security interest is first perfected, whichever is earlier, provided that there is no period thereafter when there is neither filing nor perfection.

(b) So long as conflicting security interests are unperfected, the first to attach has priority.

(6) For the purposes of subsection (5) a date of filing or perfection as to collateral is also a date of filing or perfection as to proceeds.

(7) If future advances are made while a security interest is perfected by filing, the taking of possession, or under Section 9–115 or Section 9–116 on investment property, the security interest has the same priority for the purposes of subsection (5) or Section 9–115(5) with respect to the future advances as it does with respect to the first advance. If a commitment is made before or while the security interest is so perfected, the security interest has the same priority with respect to advances made pursuant thereto. In other cases a perfected security interest has priority from the date the advance is made.

Amended by Laws 1977, Ch. 866, eff. July 2, 1978; Laws 1982, Ch. 928, eff. Dec. 21, 1982 and deemed to have been in full force and effect on and after Sept. 1, 1982; Laws 1985, Ch. 717, eff. Aug. 31, 1985, and applicable to collateral received by a debtor on or after that date; L. 1997, Ch. 566, eff. Oct. 1, 1997.

New York Annotations

(1) All questions of priority not treated directly in this section 9–312 are collected by cross-reference in this subsection.

(2) This subsection, of very limited application, probably changes present New York law. See Lien Law, § 230–b, and N.Y. Unconsol. Laws, § 1 (McKinney).

(3) and (4) New as to mechanics, but since purchase money security interests are likely to be represented by conditional sales or trust receipts, as to both of which "relation back" is permitted, the result under the Code will not be too different from that under present law. See Personal Property Law, §§ 65 and 58. Note that there is no period of grace for perfecting a purchase money security interest in inventory collateral under the priority provision of Section 9 312(3), but that such a period is given under Section 9–301(2) in relation to lien creditors and bulk transferees. Compare, Chase Nat'l Bank v. Sweezy, 281 N.Y.S. 487, aff'd 236 App.Div. 835, 259 N.Y.S. 1010, aff'd, 261 N.Y. 710, 185 N.E. 803 (1933).

A conditional seller's interest is apparently prior to that of a mortgagee under an after-acquired property clause, whether or not the contract is filed. Washington Trust Co. v. Morse Iron Works, 106 App.Div. 195, 200, 94 N.Y.S. 495, 498–499, modified, 187 N.Y. 307,79 N.E. 1022 (1906); New York & Suburban Federal Savings & Loan Ass'n v. Crescent Const. Corp., 196 Misc. 532, 92 N.Y.S.2d 533 (1949); Diana Paper Co. v. Wheeler-Green Electric Co., 228 App.Div. 577, 240 N.Y.S. 108 (1930). However, if the prior mortgagee makes further advances before the contract is filed, he attains the status of a subsequent mortgagee and prevails. New York & Suburban Federal Savings & Loan Ass'n v. Crescent Const.Corp., *supra,* Central Chandelier Co. v. Irving Trust Co., 259 N.Y. 343, 182 N.E. 10 (1932). See Personal Property Law, § 67.

(5)(a) and (b) the rule of priority in order of filing or of perfection is for the most part in *accord* with New York law. Order of filing would appear to be the test under Personal Property Law § 65, for conditional sales contracts but, as to chattel mortgages, an unfilled first mortgage will not gain priority over a second mortgage made in good faith and for a fair consideration where the first mortgage is thereafter recorded before the second. Witherbee v. Taft, 51 App.Div. 87, 64 N.Y.S. 347 (1900); Huber v. Ehlers, 76 App.Div. 602, 79 N.Y.S. 150 (1902). Priority under the Factor's Lien Act seems to be from the time of perfection, Personal property Law, § 45. Compare the Uniform Trust Receipts Act, Personal Property Law, §§ 57, 58–e(4), and 58–f. Where the dispute involves an unfilled conditional sale contract for resale and a subsequent chattel mortgage, the issue is decided in favor of the mortgagee. Rand's Discount Co. v. Universal C. I. T. Credit Corp., 9 N.Y.2d 454, 174 N.E.2d 599 (1961).

(c) Present New York law seems to give priority to a second chattel mortgage in good faith for a fair consideration where the first mortgage was not filed, even though the second mortgage is not filed. Witherbee v. Taft, 51 App. Div. 87, 64 N.Y.S. 347 (1900).

(6) No comparable provision in present law.

Historical Note: The section was entirely rewritten for clarification and to remove previous inconsistencies. All questions of priority are collected by cross-references in subsection (1) or directly into this section. Suggestions of the Law Revision Commission were followed in subsections (3) and (4). (1956 Recommendations, p. 290; Excerpts, p. 476.)

In 1958 further changes were made in subsections (3)(b) and in the preamble to subsection (5) to preserve the integrity of the first-to-file rule of priority stated in subsection (5)(a) and the first-to-perfect rule of subsection (5)(b). In Point 4 of the Comment it was erroneously stated that the first-to-file rule had no application if either security interest was a purchase money interest. That interpretation would in some cases be contrary to the policy of Section 9–301 in respect of late filing. Suppose, for example, that A delivery collateral to X (debtor) on February 1, retaining a purchase money security interest, but does not file until February 15. B takes a non-purchase-money security interest in the same collateral and promptly files on April 1.Subsections (3) and (4) do not give priority to A because of his late perfection, and thus the case is "not governed by" those subsections. The changes make clear what was originally intended, that A has priority under the first-to-file rule of subsection (5)(a). The 1958 change in subsection (4) permits a ten-day grace period for priority purposes, and conforms to the business practice of filing after delivery in cases of purchase money security interests in collateral other than inventory. Compare Section 9–301(2). In the 1953 edition of the Code, enacted in Pennsylvania, Section 9–312(4) provided for such a grace period as against claims under an after-acquired property clause. The change makes the grace period applicable also as against subsequent security agreements under a prior filing. (1958 Supplement, p. 17.)

Official Uniform Comment

Prior Uniform Statutory Provision: None.

Purposes:

1. In a variety of situations two or more people may claim an interest in the same property. The several sections specified in subsection (1) contain rules for determining priorities between security interests and such other claims in the situations covered in those sections. For cases not covered in those sections this section states general rules of priority between conflicting security interests.

2. Subsection (2) gives priority to a new value security interest in crops based on a current crop production loan over an earlier security interest in the crop which secured obligations (such as rent, interest or mortgage principal amortization) due more than six months before the crops become growing crops. This priority is not affected by the fact that the person making the crop loan knew of the earlier security interest.

3. Subsections (3) and (4) give priority to a purchase money security interest (defined in Section 9–107) under certain conditions over non-purchase money interests, which in this context will usually be interests asserted under after-acquired property clauses. See Section 9–204 on the extent to which after-acquired property interests are validated and Section 9–108 on when a security interest in after-acquired property is deemed taken for new value.

Prior law, under one or another theory, usually contrived to protect purchase money interests over after-acquired property interests (to the extent to which the after acquired property interest was recognized at all). For example, in the field of industrial equipment financing it was possible, by manipulation of title theory, for the purchase money financer of new equipment (under conditional sale or equipment trust) to protect himself against the claims of prior mortgagees or bondholders under an after-acquired clause in the mortgage or trust indenture: the result was arrived at on the theory that since "title" to the equipment was never in the vendee or lessee there was nothing for the lien of the mortgage to attach to. While this Article broadly validates the after-acquired property interest, it also recognized as sound the preference which prior law gave to the purchase money interest. That policy is carried out in subsections (3) and (4).

Subsection (4) states a general rule applicable to all types of collateral except inventory: the purchase money interest takes priority if it is perfected when the debtor receives possession of the collateral or within ten days thereafter. As to the ten day grace period, compare Section 9–301(2). The perfection requirement means that the purchase money secured party either has filed a financing statement before that time or has a temporarily perfected interest in goods covered by documents under Section 9–304(4) and (5) (which is continued in a perfected status by filing before the expiration of the 21 day period specified in that section). There is no requirement that the purchase money secured party be without notice or knowledge of the other interest; he takes priority although he knows of it or it has been filed.

Under subsection (3) the same rule of priority, but without the ten day grace period for filing, applies to a purchase money security interest in inventory, with the additional requirement that the purchase money secured party give notification, as stated in subsection (3), to any other secured party who filed earlier for the same item or type of inventory. The reason for the additional requirement of notification is that typically the arrangement between an inventory secured party and his debtor will require the secured party to make periodic advances against incoming inventory or periodic releases of old inventory as new inventory is received. A fraudulent debtor may apply to the secured party for advances even though he has already given a security interest in the inventory to another secured party. The notification requirement protects the inventory financer in such a situation: if he has received notification, he will presumably not make an advance; if he has not received notification (or if the other interest does not qualify as a purchase money interest), any advance he may make will have priority. Since an arrangement for periodic advances against incoming property is unusual outside the inventory field, no notification requirement is included in subsection (4).

Where the purchase money inventory financing began by possession of a negotiable document of title by the secured party, he must in order to retain priority give the notice required by subsection (3) at or before the usual time, i.e., when the debtor gets possession of the inventory, even though his security interest remains perfected for 21 days under Section 9–304(5).

When under these rules the purchase money secured party has priority over another secured party, the question arises whether this priority extends to the proceeds of the original collateral. Under subsection (4) which deals with non-inventory collateral and where there was no ordinary expectation that the goods would be sold, the section gives an affirmative answer. In the case of inventory collateral under subsection (3), where it was expected that the goods would be sold and where financing frequently is based on the resulting accounts, chattel paper, or other proceeds, the subsection gives an answer limited to the preservation of the purchase money priority only in so far as the proceeds are cash received on or before the delivery of the inventory to a buyer, that is, without the creation of an intervening account to which conflicting rights might attach. The conflicting rights to proceeds consisting of account are governed by subsection (5). See Comment 8.

The foregoing rules applicable to purchase money security interests in inventory apply also to the rights in consigned merchandise. See Section 9–114.

4. Subsection (5) states a rule for determining priority between conflicting security interests in cases not covered in the sections referred to in subsection (1) or in subsections (2), (3) and (4) of this section. Note that subsection (5) applies to cases of purchase money security interests which do not qualify for the special priorities set forth in subsections (3) and (4).

There is a single priority rule based on precedence in the time as of which the competing parties either filed their security interests or perfected their security interests. The form of the claim to priority, i.e., filing or perfection, may shift from time to time, and the rank will be based on the first filing or perfection so long as

UCC

there is no intervening period without filing or perfection. Filing may occur as to particular collateral before the collateral comes into existence. Under the standards of Section 9–203 perfection cannot occur as to particular collateral until the collateral itself (and not prior collateral) comes into existence and the debtor has rights therein; but under subsection (6) of this section the secured party's priority may date from his time of perfection as to the prior collateral, if perfection or filing has been continuously maintained. Subsection (6) provides that a date of filing or perfection as to original collateral is also a date of filing or perfection as to proceeds. This rule should also be read with Section 9–306, which makes it unnecessary to claim proceeds expressly in a financing statement and provides in effect that a filing as to original collateral is also a filing as to proceeds (with exceptions therein stated).Thus, if a financing statement is filed covering inventory, then (subject to the exception involving multistate problems) this filing is also a filing as to the resulting accounts and constitutes the date of filing as to the accounts.

The party who may have had a prior security interest in inventory or may have had the only such security interest does not automatically for that reason have priority as to the accounts. His claim to accounts may or may not have priority over competing filed claims to accounts. The priority is based on precedence as to the accounts under the rules stated in the preceding paragraph.

5. The operation of this section is illustrated by the examples set forth under this and the succeeding Points.

Example 1. A files against X (debtor) on February 1. B files against X on March 1. B makes a non-purchase money advance against certain collateral on April 1. A makes an advance against the same collateral on May 1. A has priority even though B's advance was made earlier and was perfected when made. It makes no difference whether or not A knew of B's interest when he made his advance.

The problem stated in the example is peculiar to a notice filing system under which filing may be made before the security interest attaches (see Section 9–402). The Uniform Trust Receipts Act, which first introduced such a filing system, contained no hint of a solution and case law under it was unpredictable. This Article follows several of the accounts receivable statutes in determining priority by order of filing. The justification for the rule lies in the necessity of protecting the filing system–that is, of allowing the secured party who has first filed to make subsequent advances without each time having, as a condition of protection, to check for filings later than his. Note, however, that his protection is not absolute: if, in the example, B's advance creates a purchase money security interest, he has priority under subsection (4), or, in the case of inventory, under subsection (3) provided he has properly notified A. (See further Example 3 below.)

Example 2. A and B make non-purchase money advances against the same collateral. The collateral is in the debtor's possession and neither interest is perfected when the second advance is made. Whichever secured party first perfects his interest (by taking possession of the collateral or by filing) takes priority and it makes no difference whether or not he knows of the other interest at the same time he perfects his own.

This result may be regarded as an adoption, in this type of situation, of the idea, deeply rooted at common law, of a race of diligence among creditors. Subsection (5)(b) adds the thought that so long as neither of the interests is perfected, the one which first attached (i.e., under the advance first made) has priority. The last mentioned rule may be thought to be of merely theoretical interest, since it is hard to imagine a situation where the case would come into litigation without either A or B having perfected his interest. If neither interest had been perfected at the time of the filing of a petition in bankruptcy, of course neither would be good against the trustee in bankruptcy.

Example 3. A has a temporarily perfected (21 day) security interest, unfilled, in a negotiable document in the debtor's possession under Section 9–304(4) or (5). On the fifth day files and thus perfects a security interest in the same document. On the tenth day A files. A has priority, whether or not he knows of B's interest when he files, because he perfected first and has maintained continuous perfection or filing.

6. The application of the priority rules to after-acquired property must be considered separately for each item of collateral. Priority does not depend only on time of perfection, but may also be based on priority in filing before perfection.

Example 4: On February 1 A makes advances to X under a security agreement which covers "all the machinery in X's plant" and contains an after-acquired property clause. A promptly files his financing statement. On March 1 X acquires a new machine, B makes an advance against it and files his financing statement. On April 1 A, under the original security agreement, makes an advance against the machine acquired March 1. If B's advance creates a purchase money security interest, he has priority under subsection (4) (provided he filed before X received possession of the machine or within ten days thereafter). If B's advance, although he gave new value, did not create a purchase money interest, A has priority as to both of his advances by virtue of his priority in filing, although the parties perfected simultaneously on March 1 as to the new machine.

The application of the priority rules to proceeds presents special features discussed in Comment 8.

7. The application of the priority rules to future advances is complicated. In general, since any secured party must operate in reference to the Code's system of notice, he takes subject to future advances under a priority security interest while it is perfected through filing or possession, whether the advances are committed or non-committed, and to any advances subsequently made "pursuant to commitment" (Section 9–105) during that period. In the rare case when a future advance is made without commitment while the security interest is perfected temporarily without either filing or possession, the future advance has priority from the date it is made. These rules are more liberal toward the priority of future advances than the corresponding rules applicable to an intervening buyer (Section 9–307(3)) because of the different characteristics of the intervening party. Compare the corresponding rule applicable to an intervening judgment creditor. (Section 9–301(4)).

Example 5. On February 1 A makes an advance against machinery in the debtor's possession and files his financing statement. On March 1 B makes an advance against the same machinery and files his financing statement. On April 1 A makes a further advance, under the original security agreement, against the same machinery (which is covered by the original financing statement and thus perfected when made). A has priority over B both as to the February 1 and as to the April 1 advance and it makes no difference whether or not A knows of B's intervening advance when he makes his second advance.

A wins, as to the April 1 advance, because he first filed even though B's interest attached, and indeed was perfected, before the April 1 advance. The same rule would apply if either A or B had perfected through possession. Section 9–204(3) and the Comment thereto should be consulted for the validation of future advances.

The same result would be reached even though A's April 1 advance was not under the original security agreement, but was under a new security agreement under A's same financing statement or during the continuation of A's possession.

8. The application of the priority rules of subsections (5) and (6) to proceeds is shown by the following examples:

Example 6. A files a financing statement covering a described type of inventory then owned or thereafter acquired. B subsequently takes a purchase money security interest in certain inventory described in A's financing statement and achieves priority over A under subsection (3) as to this inventory. This inventory is then sold, producing proceeds.

If the proceeds of the inventory are instruments or chattel paper, the rights of A and B on the one hand and any adverse claimant to these proceeds on the other are

UCC

governed by Sections 9–308 and 9–309. If the proceeds are cash, subsection (3) indicates that B's priority as to the inventory carries over to the cash. Proceeds which are accounts constitute different collateral and the priorities as to the original collateral do not control the priority as to the accounts. Under Sections 9–306 and 9–312(6), A's first filing as to the inventory constitutes a first filing as to the accounts, provided that the same filing office would be appropriate for filing as to accounts under the rules of Section 9–306(3). Therefore, A has priority as to the accounts.

Many parties financing inventory are quite content to protect their first security interest in the inventory itself, realizing that when inventory is sold, someone else will be financing the accounts and the priority for inventory will not run forward to the accounts. Indeed, the cash supplied by the accounts financer will be used to pay the inventory financing. In some situations, the party financing the inventory on a purchase money basis makes contractual arrangements that the proceeds of accounts financing by another be devoted to paying off the first inventory security interest.

Example 7. In the foregoing case, if B had filed directly as to accounts, the date of that filing as to accounts would be compared with the date of A's first filing as to the inventory, and the first-to-file rule would prevail.

Subsection (6) provides that a filing as to original collateral determines the date of a filing as to the proceeds thereof. This rule implies, of course, that the filing as to the original collateral is effective as to proceeds under the rule of Section 9–306(3).

Example 8. If C had filed as to accounts in Example 6 above before either A or B had filed as to inventory, C's first filing as to accounts would have priority over the filings of A and B, which would also constitute filings as to accounts under the rule just mentioned. A's and B's position as to the inventory gives them no automatic claim to the proceeds of the inventory consisting of accounts against someone who has filed earlier as to accounts. If, on the other hand, either A's or B's filings as to the inventory constituted good filings as to accounts and these filings preceded C's direct filings as to accounts, A or B would outrank C as to the accounts.

If the filings as to inventory were not effective under subsection (6) for filing as to accounts because a filing for accounts would have to be in a different filing office under Section 9–103(3), these inventory filings would nevertheless be effective for 10 days as to accounts. If the perfection of the security interest in accounts was continued within the 10 days by appropriate filings, then A and B's interests in the accounts would date from the date of filing as to inventory.

Cross References:

Sections 9–204(1) and 9–303.

Point 1: Sections 4–208, 9–114, 9–301, 9–304, 9–306, 9–307, 9–308,9–309, 9–310, 9–313, 9–314, 9–315 and 9–316.

Point 3: Sections 9–108, 9–204, 9–304(4) and (5).

Points 4 to 7: Sections 9–204, 9–301(4), 9–304(4) and (5), 9–306, 9–307(3) and 9–402(1).

Point 8: Sections 9–103(6) and 9–306(3).

Definitional Cross References:

"Chattel paper." Section 9–105.

"Collateral." Section 9–105.

"Collecting bank." Section 4–105.

"Debtor." Section 9–105.

"Documents." Section 9–105.

"Give notice." Section 1–201.

"Goods." Section 9–105.

"Instruments." Section 9–105.

"Inventory." Section 9–109.
"Knowledge." Section 1–201.
"Person." Section 1–201.
"Proceeds." Section 9–306.
"Purchase money security interest." Section 9–107.
"Pursuant to commitment." Section 9–105.
"Receives notification." Section 1–201.
"Secured party." Section 9–105.
"Security." Sections 8–102 and 9–105.
"Security interest." Section 1–201.
"Value." Section 1–201.

Section 9–313. Priority of Security Interests in Fixtures.

(1) In this section and in the provisions of Part 4 of this Article referring to fixture filing, unless the context otherwise requires

(a) goods are "fixtures" when they become so related to particular real estate that an interest in them arises under real estate law

(b) a "fixture filing" is the filing, in the office where a mortgage on the real estate would be recorded or registered, of a financing statement covering goods which are or are to become fixtures and conforming to the requirements of subsection (5) of Section 9–402

(c) a mortgage is a "construction mortgage" to the extent that it secures an obligation incurred for the construction of an improvement on land including the acquisition cost of the land, if the recorded writing so indicates.

(2) A security interest under this Article may be created in goods which are fixtures or may continue in goods which become fixtures, but no security interest exists under this Article in ordinary building materials incorporated into an improvement on land.

(3) This Article does not prevent creation of an encumbrance upon fixtures pursuant to real estate law.

(4) A perfected security interest in fixtures has priority over the conflicting interest of an encumbrancer or owner of the real estate where

(a) the security interest is a purchase money security interest, the interest of the encumbrancer or owner arises before the goods become fixtures, the security interest is perfected by a fixture filing before the goods become fixtures or within ten days thereafter, and the debtor has an interest of record in the real estate or is in possession of the real estate; or

(b) the security interest is perfected by a fixture filing before the interest of the encumbrancer or owner is of record, the security interest has priority over any conflicting interest of a predecessor in title of the encumbrancer or owner, and the debtor has an interest of record in the real estate or is in possession of the real estate; or

(c) the fixtures are readily removable factory or office machines or readily removable replacements of domestic appliances which are consumer goods, and before the goods become fixtures the security interest is perfected by any method permitted by this Article; or

(d) the conflicting interest is a lien on the real estate obtained by legal or equitable proceedings after the security interest was perfected by any method permitted by this Article.

(5) A security interest in fixtures, whether or not perfected, has priority over the conflicting interest of an encumbrancer or owner of the real estate where

(a) the encumbrancer or owner has consented in writing to the security interest or has disclaimed an interest in the goods as fixtures; or

(b) the debtor has a right to remove the goods as against the encumbrancer or owner. If the debtor's right terminates, the priority of the security interest continues for a reasonable time.

(6) Notwithstanding paragraph (a) of subsection (4) but otherwise subject to subsections (4) and (5), a security interest in fixtures is subordinate to a construction mortgage recorded before the goods become fixtures if the goods become fixtures before the completion of the construction. To the extent that it is given to refinance a construction mortgage, a mortgage has this priority to the same extent as the construction mortgage.

(7) In cases not within the preceding subsections, a security interest in fixtures is subordinate to the conflicting interest of an encumbrancer or owner of the related real estate who is not the debtor.

(8) When the secured party has priority over all owners and encumbrancers of the real estate, he may, on default, subject to the provisions of Part 5, remove his collateral from the real estate but he must reimburse any encumbrancer or owner of the real estate who is not the debtor and who has not otherwise agreed for the cost of repair of any physical injury, but not for any diminution in value of the real estate caused by the absence of the goods removed or by any necessity of replacing them. A person entitled to reimbursement may refuse permission to remove until the secured party gives adequate security for the performance of this obligation.

Amended by Laws 1977, Ch. 866, eff. July 2, 1978.

New York Annotations

Present New York law. Security interests in fixture-type items are presently handled through the use of either a chattel mortgage or a conditional sale. Neither the Factor's Lien Act, nor the Uniform Trust Receipts Act, nor the pledge is adapted to this kind of collateral.

Classification of the collateral. Subsection (1) probably makes no change in existing New York law. Like Personal Property Law, § 67 (Uniform Conditional Sales Act), the Code leaves to existing law the question of when chattels become fixtures. The Code makes it clear that the section does not apply to structural materials. This has been said to be the present rule. See Ford v. Cobb, 20 N.Y. 344 (1859); Voorhees v. McGinnis, 48 N.Y. 278 (1872). At the opposite end of the spectrum there are some chattels which, it is said, cannot become fixtures under existing law even after attachment to the realty, e.g., gas ranges. See Madfes v. Beverly Development Corp., 251 N.Y. 12, 166 N.E. 787 (1929). It is apparently the intermediate class which this section will affect in New York. Met. Concert Co. v. Sperry, 58 Hun 470, 9St.Rep. 342, aff'd, 120 N.Y. 620, 23 N.E. 1152 (1890) (theater seats). Where there is doubt as to the classification of the collateral as personalty or realty, filing should be made dually.

Under present New York law the rules relating to conditionally sold goods which become part of the realty are codified under Personal Property Law, § 67, while there are similar common law rules for chattel mortgage collateral that becomes part of the realty.

When chattels serving a collateral under a chattel mortgage become a part of the realty in such a way that they cannot be detached without being destroyed or materially injured, or without the destruction of, or material injury to the things real with which they are connected, the chattel mortgage holder loses his claim. Ford v. Cobb, 20 N.Y. 344, 348 (1859). But where the removal of the chattels will not take away or destroy that which is essential to the support of the main building or other part of the real estate to which they were attached, the chattel mortgagee's interest will prevail over the prior real estate mortgagee, without filing, if the parties intended that the chattel should remain personal property. Tifft v. Horton, 53 N.Y. 377 (1873).

Under Personal Property Law, § 67 (conditional sales), if the goods are not severable without material injury to the freehold, the reservation of property is void against any person who has not assented to it. If they are severable, and if there is a failure to file properly, the conditional seller's interest will be void as against subsequent purchasers and the owner of realty who is not the buyer of the goods. Of course, failure to file a chattel mortgage invalidates the security interest as to creditors and subsequent purchasers and mortgagees. Lien Law, § 230.

Contrary to Section 9–313(4)(b), judgment creditors do not benefit by the failure to file under Personal Property Law, § 67; Prudence-Bonds Corp. v. 1000 Island House Co.,141 Misc. 39, 252 N.Y.S. 60 (1930). Under Lien Law, § 230, they would prevail.

A prior mortgagee who makes an advance after the goods become fixtures is deemed a subsequent purchaser within Personal Property Law, § 67, so as to prevail against an unfilled conditional sales contract. Central Chandelier Co. v. Irving Trust Co., 259 N.Y. 343, 182 N.E. 10 (1932).

In New York the "material injury" test is clearly a physical test. See Modern Security Co. v. Thwaites, 138 Misc. 469, 246 N.Y.S. 405, determination aff'd 234 App.Div. 671, 252 N.Y.S. 930 (1931). As Comment 5 adequately points out, subsection (5) changes current law in abandoning the "material injury" rule by permitting a secured party with priority to sever and remove his collateral, subject, however, to a duty to reimburse other real estate claimants.

Historical Note: The revisions were primarily for clarification. The first sentence of subsection (1) makes it clear that no security interest in the goods as chattels may be retained in goods which become an integral part of real estate. The new subsection (3) permits creation of a chattel interest in goods even after they have become fixtures, with the consent of all parties then interested in the real estate. (1956 Recommendations, p. 291.)

Official Uniform Comment

Prior Uniform Statutory Provision: Section 7, Uniform Conditional Sales Act.

Purposes:

1. Section 9–313 deals with the problem that certain goods which are the subject of chattel financing become so affixed or otherwise so related to real estate that they

become part of the real estate, and that chattel interests would be subordinate to real estate interests except as protected by the priorities regulated by the section. These goods are called "fixtures." Some fixtures also retain their chattel nature in that a chattel financing with respect to them may exist and may continue to be recognized, if notice thereof is given to real estate interests in accordance with this section. But this concept does not apply if the goods are integrally incorporated into the real estate.

The term "fixture filing" has been introduced and defined. It emphasizes that when a filing is intended to give the priority advantages herein discussed against real estate interests, the filing must (except as stated below) be for record in the real estate records and indexed therein, so that it will be found in a real estate search.

Since the determination in advance of judicial decision of the question whether goods have become fixtures is a difficult one, no inference may be drawn from a fixture filing that the secured party concedes that the goods are or will become fixtures. The fixture filing may be merely precautionary.

2. "Fixture" is defined to include any goods which become so related to particular real estate that an interest in them arises under real estate law and therefore, goods integrally incorporated into the real estate are clearly fixtures. But under subsection (2) no security interest exists under Article 9 in ordinary building materials incorporated into an improvement on land.

Goods may be technically "ordinary guilding materials," e.g., window glass, but if they are incorporated into a structure which as a whole has not become an integral part of the real estate, the rules applicable to the ordinary building materials follow the rules applicable to the structure itself. The outstanding examples presenting this kind of problem are the modern "mobile homes" and the modern prefabricated steel buildings usable as warehouses, garages, factories, etc. In the case of the mobile homes, most of them are erected on leased land and the right of the debtor under a mobile home purchase contract to remove the goods as lessee will make clear that his secured party ordinarily has a similar right. See paragraph (5)(b).

In cases where mobile homes or prefabricated steel buildings are erected by a person having an ownership interest in the land, the question into which category the buildings fall is one determined by local law. In general, the governing local law will not be that applicable in determining whether goods have become real property between landlord and tenant, or between mortgagor and mortgagee, or between grantor and grantee, but rather that applicable in a three-party situation, determining whether chattel financing can survive as against parties who acquire rights through the affixation of the goods to the real estate.

The assertion that no security interest exists in ordinary building materials is only for the operation of the priority provisions of this section. It is without prejudice to any rights which the secured party may have against the debtor himself if he incorporated the goods into real estate or against any party guilty of wrongful incorporation thereof in violation of the secured party's rights.

3. Under these concepts the section recognizes three categories of goods: (1) those which retain their chattel character entirely and are not part of the real estate; (2) ordinary building materials which have become an integral part of the real estate and cannot retain their chattel character for purposes of finance; and (3) an intermediate class which has become real estate for certain purposes, but as to which chattel financing may be preserved. This third and intermediate class is the primary subject of this section. The demarcation between these classifications is not delineated by this section.

4. In considering fixture priority problems, there will always first be a preliminary question whether real estate interests per se have an interest in the goods as part of real estate. If not, it is immaterial, so far as concerns real estate parties as such, whether a chattel security interest is perfected or unperfected. In no event does a real estate party acquire an interest in a "pure" chattel just because a security interest therein

is unperfected. If on the other hand real estate law gives real estate parties an interest in the goods, a conflict arises and this section states the priorities.

(a) The principal exception to the general rule of priority stated in Comment 4(b) based on time of filing or recording is a priority given in paragraph (4)(a) to purchase money security interests in fixtures as against prior recorded real estate interests, provided that the purchase money security interest is filed as a fixture filing in the real estate records before the goods become fixtures or within 10 days thereafter. This priority corresponds to one given in Section 9–312(4), and the 10 days of grace represents a reduction of the purchase money priority as against prior interests in the real estate under the present Section 9–313, where the purchase money priority exists even though the security interest is never filed.

It should be emphasized that this purchase money priority with the 10-day grace period for filing is limited to rights against prior real estate interests. There is no such priority with the 10-day grace period as against subsequent real estate interests. The fixture security interest can defeat subsequent real estate interests only if it is filed first and prevails under the usual conveyancing rule recognized in paragraph (4)(b).

(b) The general principle of priority announced in this section is set forth in paragraph (4)(b). It is basically that a fixture filing gives to the fixture security interest priority as against other real estate interests according to the usual priority rule of conveyancing, that is, the first to file or record prevails. An apparent limitation to this principle set forth in paragraph (4)(b),namely that the secured party must have had priority over any interest of a predecessor in title of the conflicting encumbrancer or owner, is not really a limitation, but is an expression of the usual rule that a person must be entitled to transfer what he has. Thus, if the fixture security interest is subordinate to a mortgage, it is subordinate to an interest of an assignee of the mortgage even though the assignment is a later recorded instrument. Similarly if the fixture security interest is subordinate to the rights of an owner, it is subordinate to a subsequent grantee of the owner and likewise subordinate to a subsequent mortgagee of the owner.

(c) A qualification to the rule based on priority of filing or recording is paragraph (4)(d), where priority based on precedence in filing or recording is preserved, but there is no requirement that as against a judgment lien or of the real estate, the prior filing of the fixture security interest must be in the real estate records. The fixture security interest if perfected first should prevail even though not filed or recorded in real estate records, because generally a judgment creditor is not a reliance creditor who would have searched records. Thus, even a prior filing in the chattel records protects the priority of a fixture security interest against a subsequent judgment lien.

It is hoped that this rule will have the effect of preserving a fixture security interest so filed against invalidation by a trustee in bankruptcy. That would, of course, be the result under Section 60a of the Bankruptcy Act if the time of perfection of the fixture security interest were measured by the judgment creditor test applicable to personal property. It would not be the result if the time of perfection were measured by the purchaser test applicable to real estate. Since the fixture security interest arises against the goods in their capacity as chattels, the bankruptcy courts should apply the judgment creditor test. The effectiveness of the drafting to achieve its purpose cannot be known certainly until the courts adjudicate the question or until it is settled by amendment to Section 60a of the Bankruptcy Act.

The phrase "lien by legal or equitable proceedings" is suggested by Section 70c of the Bankruptcy Act, and is intended to encompass all liens on real estate obtained by any of the creditor action therein described.

(d) A special exception to the usual rule of priority based on precedence in time is the one of paragraph (4)(c) in favor of holders of security interests in factory and office machines, and in certain replacement domestic appliances, as discussed below.

This is not as broad an exception as it might seem. To repeat, a fixture conflict is not reached if the goods are held as a matter of local law not to have become part of the real estate, which will frequently be the holding for goods of these types. If the opposite is held, the rule of paragraph (4)(c) operates only if the fixture security interest is perfected before the goods become fixtures. Having been perfected, it would of course have priority over subsequent real estate interests under the rule of paragraph (4)(b). Since it would in almost all cases be a purchase money security interest, it would also have priority over other real estate interests under the purchase-money priority of paragraph (4)(a), discussed in paragraph (a) above. The rule is stated separately because the permitted perfection is by any method permitted by the Article, and not exclusively by fixture filing in the real estate records. This rule is made necessary by the confusions of the law as to whether certain machinery and appliances become fixtures.

As an additional point, in the case of machinery, the separate statement of this rule makes clear that it is not overridden by the construction mortgage priority of subsection (6) discussed in Comment 4(e) below, as would have been true if reliance had been solely on the purchase money priority. Factory and office machines are not always financed as part of a construction mortgage, and the mortgagee should be alert to conflicting chattel financing of these machines.

As to appliances, the rule stated is limited to readily removable replacements, not original installations, of appliances which are consumer goods in the hands of the debtor (Section 9–109). To facilitate financing of original appliances in new dwellings as part of the real estate financing of the dwellings, no special priority is given to chattel financing of original appliances. The section leaves to other law of the state the question whether original installations are fixtures to which the protection accorded by this section to construction mortgages would be applicable. Likewise, it is recognized that (when not supplied by tenants) appliances in commercial apartment buildings are intended as permanent improvements, and no special rule is stated for appliances in that case. The special priority rule here stated in favor of chattel financing is limited to situations where the installation of appliances may not be intended to be permanent, i.e., replacement appliances used by the debtor or his family (consumer goods). The principal effect of the rule is to make clear that a secured party financing occasional replacements of domestic appliances in noncommercial owner-occupied contexts need not concern himself with real estate descriptions or records; indeed, for a purchase-money replacement of consumer goods, perfection without any filing will be possible. (The priority of the construction mortgage has no application to replacement appliances.)

(e) The purchase money priority presents a difficult problem in relation to construction mortgages. The latter will ordinarily have been recorded even before the commencement of delivery of materials to the job, and therefore would be prior in rank to the fixture security interests were it not for the problem of the purchase money priority. Subsection (6) expressly gives priority to the construction mortgage recorded before the filing of the fixture security interest, but this priority of a construction mortgage applies only during the construction period leading to the completion of the improvement. As to additions to the building made long after completion of the improvement, the construction priority will not apply simply because the additions are financed by the real estate mortgagee under an open end clause of his construction mortgage. In such case, the applicable principles will be those of paragraphs (4)(a) and (4)(b). Are financing of a construction mortgage has the same priority as the mortgage itself.

The phrase "an obligation incurred for the construction of an improvement" covers both optional advances and advances pursuant to commitment, and both types of advances have the same priority under the section.

5. The section makes it impossible for a fixture supplier to retain a security interest against a contractor, to the possible surprise and deception of real estate interests,

unless the debtor has an interest of record in the real estate. See paragraphs (4)(a) and (b).

On the other hand, these paragraphs do recognize that fixture filing may be necessary when the debtor is in possession of the real estate (e.g., a lessee) even without an interest of record. This possibility of a filing against a debtor who is not in the real estate chain of title makes it necessary to require the furnishing of the name of a record owner in such cases. See Sections 9–402(3), item 3; 9–402(5); 9–403(7).

6. The status of fixtures installed by tenants (as well as such persons as licensees and holders of easements) is defined by paragraph (5)(b) to the effect that if the debtor (tenant or other interest mentioned) has the right to remove the fixture as against a real estate interest, the secured party has priority over that real estate interest.

7. Real estate lenders and title companies will have little difficulty in locating relevant fixture security interests applicable to particular parcels of real estate because of the provisions as to real estate description in fixture filings, the indexing thereof, and other related provisions in Part 4 of Article 9.

8. Real estate lending is typically long-term, and is usually done by institutional investors who can afford to take a long view of the matter rather than concentrating on the results of any particular case. It is apparent that the rule which permits and encourages purchase money fixture financing, which in contrast is typically short-term, will result in the modernization and improvement of real estate rather than in its deterioration and will on balance benefit long-term real estate lenders. Because of the short-term character of the chattel financing, it will rarely produce any conflict in fact with the real estate lender. The contrary rule would chill the availability of short-term credit for modernization of real estate by installation of new fixtures and in the long run could not help real estate lenders.

9. Subsection (8) is an important departure from Section 7 of the Uniform Conditional Sales Act and from much other conditional sales legislation. Under the Uniform Conditional Sales Act a conditional vendor could not sever and remove the affixed chattel if a "material injury to the freehold" would result. The courts of various jurisdictions were in sharp disagreement on the meaning of "material injury"; some held that only physical injury was meant; others adopted the so-called "institutional theory" and denied removal whenever the "going value" of the structure would be materially diminished by the removal. Under these rules the conditional vendor either could not remove at all, or, if he could, could damage the structure on removal without becoming accountable to the real estate claimant. The situation was complicated by the fact that it became increasingly difficult to predict what types of goods the courts in a given jurisdiction would hold to subject to removal.

Subsection (8) abandons the "material injury to the freehold" rule. Instead a secured party entitled to priority may in all cases sever and remove his collateral, subject, however, to a duty to reimburse any real estate claimant (other than the debtor himself) for any physical injury caused by the removal. The right to reimbursement is implemented by the last sentence of subsection (8) which gives the real estate claimant a statutory right to security or indemnity failing which he may refuse permission to remove. The subsection (8) rule thus accomplishes two things: it puts an end to the uncertainty which has grown up under the "material injury" rule, while at the same time it protects the real estate claimant under the reimbursement provisions.

Cross References:

Sections 2–107, 9–102(1), 9–104(j) and 9–312(1), and Parts 4 and 5.

Definitional Cross References:

"Collateral." Section 9–105.

UCC

"Contract." Section 1–201.
"Creditor." Section 1–201.
"Debtor." Section 9–105.
"Encumbrance." Section 9–105.
"Goods." Section 9–105.
"Knowledge." Section 1–201.
"Mortgage." Section 9–105.
"Person." Section 1–201.
"Purchase." Section 1–201.
"Purchaser." Section 1–201.
"Secured party." Section 9–105.
"Security interest." Section 1–201.
"Value." Section 1–201.
"Writing." Section 1–201.

Section 9–314. Accessions.

(1) A security interest in goods which attaches before they are installed in or affixed to other goods takes priority as to the goods installed or affixed (called in this section "accessions") over the claims of all persons to the whole except as stated in subsection (3) and subject to Section 9–315(1).

(2) A security interest which attaches to goods after they become part of whole is valid against all persons subsequently acquiring interests in the whole except as stated in subsection (3) but is invalid against any person with an interest in the whole at the time the security interest attaches to the goods who has not in writing consented to the security interest or disclaimed an interest in the goods as part of the whole.

(3) The security interests described in subsections (1) and (2) do not take priority over

(a) a subsequent purchaser for value of any interest in the whole; or

(b) a creditor with a lien on the whole subsequently obtained by judicial proceedings; or

(c) a creditor with a prior perfected security interest in the whole to the extent that he makes subsequent advances

if the subsequent purchase is made, the lien by judicial proceedings obtained or the subsequent advance under the prior perfected security interest is made or contracted for without knowledge of the security interest and before it is perfected. A purchaser of the whole at a foreclosure sale other than the holder of a perfected security interest purchasing at his own foreclosure sale is a subsequent purchaser within this section.

(4) When under subsections (1) or (2) and (3) a secured party has an interest in accessions which has priority over the claims of all persons who have interests in the whole, he may on default subject to the provisions of Part 5 remove his collateral from the whole but he must reimburse any encumbrancer or owner of the whole who is not the debtor and who has not otherwise agreed for the cost of repair of any physical injury but not for any diminution in value of the

whole caused by the absence of the goods removed or by any necessity for replacing them. A person entitled to reimbursement may refuse permission to remove until the secured party gives adequate security for the performance of this obligation.

New York Annotations

(1), (2), and (3) Under present New York law it appears that the conditional seller of accessories under a filed contract may recapture the goods from a conditional seller of the whole. John W. Snyder, Inc. v. Aker, 134 Misc. 721, 236 N.Y.S. 28 (1929); Meisel Tire Co. v. Mar-Bel Trading Co., 155 Misc. 664, 280 N.Y.S. 335 (1935). There is some indication that where the accessory contract is not filed, the conditional seller of the whole may prevail as a subsequent purchaser at a sale after repossession. The Code conforms in general to these results and in subsection (4) imposes a duty upon the supplier of the accessory to reimburse for the cost of repair of any physical injury upon severance from the whole.

Historical Note: The changes followed suggestions of the Law Revision Commission and were principally for clarification and to conform the structure and language of this section as closely as possible to Section 9–313. (1956 Recommendations, p. 293; Excerpts, p. 479.)

Official Uniform Comment

Prior Uniform Statutory Provision: None.

Purposes:

1. To state when a secured party claiming an interest in goods installed in or affixed to other goods is entitled to priority over a party with a security interest in the whole.
2. This section changes prior law in that the secured party claiming an interest in a part (e.g., a new motor in an old car) is entitled to priority and has a right to remove even though under other rules of law the part now belongs to the whole.
3. This section does not apply to goods which, for example, are so commingled in a manufacturing process that their original identity is lost. That type of situation is covered in Section 9–315. Section 9–315 should also be consulted for the effect of a financing statement which claims both component parts and the resulting product.

Cross References:

Sections 9–203(1), 9–303 and 9–312(1) and Part 5.
Point 3: Section 9–315.

Definitional Cross References:

"Collateral." Section 9–105.
"Creditor." Section 1–201.
"Debtor." Section 9–105.
"Goods." Section 9–105.
"Knowledge." Section 1–201.
"Person." Section 1–201.
"Purchaser." Section 1–201.
"Secured party." Section 9–105.
"Security interest." Section 1–201.
"Value." Section 1–201.

UCC

"Writing." Section 1–201.

Section 9–315. Priority When Goods Are Commingled or Processed.

(1) If a security interest in goods was perfected and subsequently the goods or a part thereof have become part of a product or mass, the security interest continues in the product or mass if

(a) the goods are so manufactured, processed, assembled or commingled that their identity is lost in the product or mass; or

(b) a financing statement covering the original goods also covers the product into which the goods have been manufactured, processed or assembled.

In a case to which paragraph (b) applies, no separate security interest in that part of the original goods which has been manufactured, processed or assembled into the product may be claimed under Section 9–314.

(2) When under subsection (1) more than one security interest attaches to the product or mass, they rank equally according to the ratio that the cost of the goods to which each interest originally attached bears to the cost of the total product or mass.

New York Annotations

(1) This subsection seems to be in *accord* with the principle of prior New York law, e.g. Dunning v. Stearns, 9 Barb. 630 (1850). Under Personal Property Law, § 58–b, an entruster under a trust receipt may be entitled to a security interest in processed goods as proceeds from raw materials subject to the trust receipts.

(2) *Accord* in principle with Dunning v. Stearns, *supra.*

Historical Note: Subsection (1) has been rewritten to recognize that the principle of the section should be applicable to situations of small components and parts built into a unit like a radio, even though their identity may not be lost. In such a case Section 9–315, rather than Section 9–314 on accessions, will be applicable, if the financing statement claims an interest in the product. (1956 Recommendations, p. 294.)

Official Uniform Comment

Prior Uniform Statutory Provision: None.

Purposes:

1. To state when a secured party whose collateral contributes to a product has priority over others who have conflicting claims in the same product.

2. This section changes the law in some jurisdictions where a security interest in goods (e.g., raw materials) was lost when the goods lost their identity by being commingled or processed. Under this section the security interest continues in the resulting mass or product in the cases stated in subsection (1).

3. This section applies not only to cases where flour, sugar and eggs are commingled into cake mix or cake, but also to cases where components are assembled into a machine. In the latter case a secured party is put to an election at the time of filing, by the last sentence of subsection (1), whether to claim under this section or to claim a security interest in one component under Section 9–314.

4. Subsection (2) is new and is needed because under subsection (1) it is possible to have more than one secured party claiming an interest in a product. The rule stated treats all such interests as being of equal priority entitled to share ratably in the product.

Cross References:

Sections 9–203(1), 9–303, 9–312(1) and 9–314.

Definitional Cross References:

"Goods." Section 9–105.
"Security interest." Section 1–201.

Section 9–316. Priority Subject to Subordination.

Nothing in this Article prevents subordination by agreement by any person entitled to priority.

New York Annotations

This section merely recognizes the general principle that a person entitled to priority may subordinate his interest by agreement. See as to certain agricultural mortgages. N.Y. Unconsol. Laws, § 1 (McKinney).

Official Uniform Comment

Prior Uniform Statutory Provision: None.

Purposes:

The several preceding sections deal elaborately with questions of priority. This section is inserted to make it entirely clear that a person entitled to priority may effectively agree to subordinate his claim. Only the person entitled to priority may make such an agreement: his rights cannot be adversely affected by an agreement to which he is not a party.

Cross References:

Sections 1–102 and 9–312(1).

Definitional Cross References:

"Agreement." Section 1–201.
"Person." Section 1–201.

Section 9–317. Secured Party Not Obligated on Contract of Debtor.

The mere existence of a security interest or authority given to the debtor to dispose of or use collateral does not impose contract or tort liability upon the secured party for the debtor's acts or omissions.

New York Annotations

Generally in *accord* with Personal Property Law, § 58–d (Uniform Trust Receipts Act). There is in the present law a possible difficulty in connection with conditional sale contracts assigned to a bank or finance company as security for a loan to the dealer. Personal property Law, § 62, makes the "seller" liable to the buyer for breach of contract or warranty, and Personal Property Law, § 61, defines "seller" as including the legal successor in interest of the original seller. Thus in theory the financer may be liable for any breach of contract. The Code clearly rejects this result. See also Section 9–206.

Historical Note: Although a specific clarification of this section, suggested by the Law Revision Commission, was not adopted, the section was redrafted. (1956 Recommendations, p. 294; Excerpts, p. 479.)

Official Uniform Comment

Prior Uniform Statutory Provision: Section 12, Uniform Trust Receipts Act.

Purposes:

There were a few common law decisions, mostly in cases involving trust receipts, which suggested, if they did not hold, that a secured party who gave his debtor liberty of sale might be liable (for example, for breach of warranty) on the debtor's contracts of sale. The theory was grounded on the law of agency; the debtor being regarded as selling agent for the secured party as principal. This section rejects that theory. Section 12 of the Uniform Trust Receipts Act provided that the entruster was not subject to liability, merely because of his status as entruster, on sale of the goods subject to trust receipt. This section adopts the policy of the prior act and states it in general terms.

Cross Reference:

Section 2–210(4).

Definitional Cross References:

"Collateral." Section 9–105.
"Contract." Section 1–201.
"Debtor." Section 9–105.
"Secured party." Section 9–105.
"Security interest." Section 1–201.

Section 9–318. Defenses Against Assignee; Modification of Contract After Notification of Assignment; Term Prohibiting Assignment Ineffective; Identification and Proof of Assignment.

(1) Unless an account debtor has made an enforceable agreement not to assert defenses or claims arising out of a sale as provided in Section 9 206 the rights of an assignee are subject to

(a) all the terms of the contract between the account debtor and assignor and any defense or claim arising therefrom; and

(b) any other defense or claim of the account debtor against the assignor which accrues before the account debtor receives notification of the assignment.

(2) So far as the right to payment or a part thereof under an assigned contract has not been fully earned by performance, and notwithstanding notification of

the assignment, any modification of or substitution for the contract made in good faith, in accordance with reasonable commercial standards and without material adverse effect upon the assignee's rights under or the assignor's ability to perform the contract, is effective against an assignee unless the account debtor has otherwise agreed but the assignee acquires corresponding rights under the modified or substituted contract. The assignment may provide that such modification or substitution is a breach by the assignor.

(3) The account debtor is authorized to pay the assignor until the account debtor receives notification that the amount due or to become due has been assigned and that payment is to be made to the assignee. A notification which does not reasonably identify the rights assigned is ineffective. If requested by the account debtor, the assignee must seasonably furnish reasonable proof that the assignment has been made and unless he does so the account debtor may pay the assignor.

(4) A term in any contract between an account debtor and an assignor is ineffective if it prohibits assignment of an account or prohibits creation of a security interest in a general intangible for money due or to become due or requires the account debtor's consent to such assignment or security interest.

Amended by Laws 1977, Ch. 866, eff. July 2,1978.

New York Annotations

(1)(a) This subsection substantially restates New York law to the effect that the assignee takes subject to the terms of the contract and stands in the place of the assignor. Seibert v. Dunn, 216 N.Y. 237, 110 N.E. 447 (1915). Compare Collens v. Philipsborn's Inc., 209 App.Div. 483,205 N.Y.S. 21, aff'd, 239 N.Y. 611, 147 N.E. 217 (1925) (dictum that assignment cuts off executory contract rights of the debtor).

(b) Substantially in *accord:* Personal Property Law, § 41(3) ("uses existing" rather than "accrues"); Civil Practice Act, § 267 (1) [now CPLR § 3019] (time of assignment rather than notice is crucial); Golden v. D.R. Paskie& Co., Inc., 205 App.Div. 610, 200 N.Y.S. 123 (1923). See Restatement, Contracts, § 167(1) (1932) and New York Annotations.

(2) The freedom of modification and substitution allowed here is for the protection of the obligor and would apparently modify exiting law or at least existing policy. See Collens v. Philipsborn's Inc., *supra;* Madison Industrial Corp. v. Elisberg, 152 Misc. 167, 271 N.Y.S. 891 (1934). Compare Personal Property Law, § 41(3).

(3) It is clear that a debtor after notice of the assignment must pay the assignee and will not be protected if he pays the assignor. Weniger v. Fourteenth St. Store, 191 N.Y. 423, 84 N.E. 394 (1908). Note the requirements, again for the protection of the account debtor, that the notice must reasonably identify the rights assigned and that the account debtor may demand proof of the assignment. In Gibraltar Realty Corp. v. Mount Vernon Trust Co., 276 N.Y. 353, 12 N.E. 2d 438 (1938), a similar approach was followed as to notice of an assignment of a bank account.

(4) Present New York law states that it gives effect to a provision prohibiting an assignment of an account or contract right. Allhusen v. Caristo Construction Corp., 303 N.Y. 446, 103 N.E.2d 891 (1951). The Code rejects that rule and thus favors accounts receivable financing. Note that the Code protects the account debtor, or obligor, from certain risks under subsections (2) and (3). Further, the present law is only altered as to accounts and contract rights. Note that "contract right" is defined

in Section 9–106 in a limited way as a "right to *payment*under a contract not yet earned by performance" [Emphasis supplied.]

Historical Note: Clarifying changes were made in subsections (1)(b), (3), and (4) which followed in part suggestions of the Law Revision Commission. (1956 Recommendations, p.295; Excerpts, p. 480.)

Official Uniform Comment

Prior Uniform Statutory Provision: Section 9(3), Uniform Trust Receipts Act.

Purposes:

1. Subsection (1) makes no substantial change in prior law. An assignee has traditionally been subject to defenses or setoffs existing before an account debtor is notified of the assignment. When the account debtor's defenses on an assigned claim arise from the contract between him and the assignor, it makes no difference whether the breach giving rise to the defense occurs before or after the account debtor is notified of the assignment (paragraph) (1)(a)). The account debtor may also have claims against the assignor which arise independently of that contract: an assignee is subject to all such claims which accrue before, and free of all those which accrue after, the account debtor is notified (paragraph (1)(b)). The account debtor may waive his right to assert claims or defenses against an assignee to the extent provided in Section 9–206.

2. Prior law was in confusion as to whether modification of an executory contract by account debtor and assignor without the assignee's consent was possible after notification of an assignment. Subsection (2) makes good faith modifications by assignor and account debtor without the assignee's consent effective against the assignee even after notification. This rule may do some violence to accepted doctrines of contract law. Nevertheless it is a sound and indeed necessary rule in view of the realities of large scale procurement. When for example it becomes necessary for a government agency to cut back or modify existing contracts, comparable agreements must be made promptly in hundreds and even thousands of subcontracts lying in many tiers below the prime contract. Typically the right to payments under these subcontracts will have been assigned. The government, as sovereign, might have the to amend or terminate existing contracts apart from statute. This subsection gives the prime contractor (the account debtor) the right to make the required arrangements directly with his subcontractors without undertaking the task of procuring assents from the many banks to whom rights under the contracts may have been assigned. Assignees are protected by the provision which gives them automatically corresponding rights under the modified or substituted contract. Notice that subsection (2) applies only so far as the right to payment has not been earned by performance, and therefore its application ends entirely when the work is done or the goods furnished.

3. Subsection (3) clarifies the right of an account debtor to make payment to his seller-assignor in an "indirect collection" situation (see Comment to Section 9–308). So long as the assignee permits the assignor to collect claims or leaves him in possession of chattel paper which does not indicate that payment is to be made at some place other than the assignor's place of business, the account debtor may pay the assignor even though he may know of the assignment. In such a situation an assignee who wants to take over collections must notify the account debtor to make further payments to him.

4. Subsection (4) breaks sharply with the older contract doctrines by denying effectiveness to contractual terms prohibiting assignment of sums due and to become due under contracts of sale, construction contracts and the like. Under the rule as stated, an assignment would be effective even if made to an assignee who took with

full knowledge that the account debtor had sought to prohibit or restrict assignment of the claims.

It is only for the past hundred years that our law has recognized the possibility of assigning choses in action. The history of this development, at law and equity, is in broad outline well known. Lingering traces of the absolute common law prohibition have survived almost to our own day.

There can be no doubt that a term prohibiting assignment of proceeds was effective against an assignee with notice through the nineteenth century and well into the twentieth. Section 151 of the Restatement of Contracts (1932) so states the law without qualification, but the changing character of the law is shown in the proposed Section 154 of the Restatement, Second, Contracts.

The original rule of law has been progressively undermined by a process of erosion which began much earlier than the cited section of the Restatement of Contracts would suggest. The cases are legion in which courts have construed the heart out of prohibitory or restrictive terms and held the assignment good. The cases are not lacking where courts have flatly held assignments valid without bothering to construe away the prohibition. See 4 Corbin on Contracts (1951) §§ 872, 873. Such cases as Allhusen v. Caristo Const. Corp., 303 N.Y. 446, 103 N.E.2d 891 (1952), are rejected by this subsection.

This gradual and largely unacknowledged shift in legal doctrine has taken place in response to economic need: as accounts and other rights under contracts have become the collateral which secures an ever increasing number of financing transactions, it has been necessary to reshape the law so that these intangibles, like negotiable instruments and negotiable documents of title, can be freely assigned.

Subsection (4) thus states a rule of law which is widely recognized in the cases and which corresponds to current business practices. It can be regarded as a revolutionary departure only by those who still cherish the hope that we may yet return to the views entertained some two hundred years ago by the Court of King's Bench.

5. The Federal Assignment of Claims Act of 1940–to which of course this section is subject–requires that assignments of claims against the United States be filed as provided in that Act. Many large business enterprises, situated like the United States in that claims against them are held by hundreds or thousands of subcontractors or suppliers, often require in their contract of purchase order forms that assignments against them be filed in a prescribed way. Subsection (3) requires reasonable identification of the account assigned and recognizes the right of an account debtor to require reasonable proof of the making of the assignment and to that extent validates such requirements in contracts or purchase order forms. If the notification does not contain such reasonable identification or if such reasonable proof is not furnished on request, the account debtor may disregard the assignment and make payment to the assignor. What is "reasonable" is not left to the arbitrary decision of the account debtor; if there is doubt as to the adequacy either of a notification or of proof submitted after request, the account debtor may not be safe in disregarding it unless he has notified the assignee with commercial promptness as to the respects in which identification or proof is considered defective.

6. If the thing to be assigned is the beneficiary's right under a letter of credit, Section 5–116 should be consulted.

Cross References:

Point 1: Section 9–206.
Point 3: Sections 9–205 and 9–308.
Point 4: Section 2–210(2) and (3).
Point 6: Section 5–116.

UCC

Definitional Cross References:

"Account." Section 9–106.
"Account debtor." Section 9–105.
"Agreement." Section 1–201.
"Contract." Section 1–201.
"Good faith." Section 1–201.
"Party." Section 1–201.
"Receives." notification. Section 1–201.
"Rights." Section 1–201.
"Sale." Sections 2–106 and 9–105.
"Seasonably." Section 1–204.
"Term." Section 1–201.

PART 4

FILING

Section 9–401. Place of Filing; Erroneous Filing; Removal of Collateral.

(1) The proper place to file in order to perfect a security interest is as follows:

(a) when the collateral is equipment used in farming operations, or farm products, or accounts, or general intangibles arising from or relating to the sale of farm products by a farmer, or consumer goods, then in the office of the filing officer in the county of the debtor's residence if the debtor is a resident of this state, and, in addition to any other filing when the collateral is crops, in the office of the filing officer in the county where the land on which the crops are growing or to be grown is located;

(b) when the collateral is timber to be cut or is minerals or the like (including oil and gas) or accounts subject to subsection (5) of Section 9–103, or when the financing statement is filed as a fixture filing (Section 9–313) and the collateral is goods which are or are to become fixtures, or when the collateral is an ownership interest evidenced by certificates of stock or other instruments, and a leasehold evidenced by a proprietary lease, or either of the foregoing, from a corporation or partnership formed for the purpose of cooperative ownership of real estate, then in the office where a mortgage on the real estate concerned would be filed, recorded or registered, viz., in the office of the recording officer in the county where the real estate or house or building owned by such corporation or partnership is located;

(c) in all other cases, in the department of state and in addition, if the debtor has a place of business in this state and in only one county of this state, also in the office of the filing officer of such county;

(d) for the purposes of paragraph (a) of this subsection, a foreign corporation which is authorized to do business in this state is deemed a resident of this state and the residence of a debtor which is

(i) a domestic corporation, is the county in which the office of the corporation is to be located as specified in its certificate of incorporation or most recently, filed certificate of amendment thereto;

(ii) a foreign corporation, is the county in which the office of the corporation within the state is to be located as specified in its application for authority to do business in this state or most recently filed amendment thereto;

(iii) a partnership and has filed in the office of the clerk of a county of the state a certificate under section four hundred forty of the former penal law as in force and effect immediately prior to September first, nineteen hundred sixty-seven, or under section one hundred thirty of the general business law, is that county.

(2) A filing which is made in good faith in an improper place or not in all of the places required by this section is nevertheless effective with regard to any collateral as to which the filing complied with the requirements of this Article and is also effective with regard to collateral covered by the financing statement against any person who has knowledge of the contents of such financing statement.

(3) A filing which is made in the proper place in this state continues effective even thought the debtor's residence or place of business or the location of the collateral or its use, whichever controlled the original filing, is thereafter changed.

(4) The rules stated in Section 9–103 determine whether filing is necessary in this state.

(5) Notwithstanding the preceding subsections, and subject to subsection (3) of Section 9-302, the proper place to file in order to perfect a security interest in collateral, including fixtures, of a transmitting utility is the department of state. This filing constitutes a fixture filing (Section 9-313) as to the collateral described therein which is or is to become fixtures.

(6) Except as otherwise provided in paragraph (d) of subsection (1), for the purposes of this section the residence of an organization is its place of business if it has one or its chief executive office if it has more than one place of business.

(7) In this Part, the term "filing officer" or "recording officer" means the county clerk of the county, except in the counties of Bronx, Kings, New York and Queens where it means the city register in the county; and the term "filing officer" includes the secretary of state where a filing is made in the department of state.

Amended by Laws 1977, Ch. 866, eff. July 2, 1978; Laws 1988, Ch. 333, eff. Aug. 24, 1988, and applicable to any security interest obtained, continued or consolidated on or after such effective date, and shall not affect security interests obtained prior to such effective date by means other than filing.

New York Annotations

Present New York Law, except in the case of canal boats and certain other craft, conditional sales of railroad rolling stock, and dealer's chattel mortgages, makes no explicit distinction as to the type of collateral and the nature of the collateral in determining the place of filing. On the other hand, Section 9–401 uses the type and nature of the collateral to determine whether filing should be central, local, or both. As will be seen from the following analysis, the existing New York filing system is complex, contains many pitfalls for unwary creditors, both secured and unsecured, and varies with the type of device used as well as the geographic allocation of the collateral or the debtor.

(1)(c) In providing for central filing of certain agreements, this subsection follows § 13 of the Uniform Trust Receipts Act (Personal Property Law, § 58–e(1));the New York provision for chattel mortgages by dealers (Lien Law, § 230–c); and the provisions for conditional sales of railroad equipment or rolling stock (Personal Property Law, § 68).

There is also precedent for central filing in Lien Law, § 232, and Personal Property Law, § 66, by which chattel mortgages and conditional sales covering canal boats, and certain other craft are filed in the office of the Superintendent of Public Works. There seems to be no reason why, if desired, this place of filing could not be continued under the Code.

New York does not presently have any general requirements of filing in relation to assignments of accounts, contract rights, or general intangibles. However, filing is necessary for accounts financing of real estate improvements contracts under Lien Law, §§ 15 and 16. See also Lien Law, § 73. Furthermore, accounts receivable financing under the Factor's Lien Act includes a requirement of filing. Although functionally similar to the trust receipt and dealer's chattel mortgage, both of which are not centrally filed, the Factor's Lien Act requires local filing (Personal Property Law, § 45) in the city or town where the merchandise is to be kept and also where the debtor's principal office or place of business is or shall be located.

The theory of central filing is that since filing seems to have its chief value in giving information to credit agencies, central filing is preferable except where the nature of the transaction or the kind of collateral is related to a particular locality. The Code offers a bracketed optional provision under which there must be a supplemental county filing, if all the debtor's places of business are in a single county.

Subsection (1)(a) here provides for county filing in situations where the demand for credit information arises locally. Under present New York law there is a mixture of city and town filing with county filing.

Chattel mortgages. Under Lien Law, § 232, where the mortgagor is a resident of the state, chattel mortgages must be recorded, in the absence of a transfer of possession, on the records of the city or town where the mortgage is executed. If the mortgagor is a non-resident of the state at that time, recording must be made in the city or town where the property then is located. Filing is made in the office of the town or city clerk with two major exceptions. First, filing is made on a county-wide basis where the controlling geographical unit is Nassau county or New York City (Bronx, Kings, New York, Richmond, and Queens Counties). In Kings, Queens, New York, and Bronx Counties the proper place is the office of the city register in each county; while in Richmond and Nassau Counties the proper place is the office of the county clerk. On other special requirement exists where the goods are situate in New York City at the time of the execution of the mortgage. In such cases the filing must take place both at the mortgagor's residence in this state, if any, and in the county in New York City where the goods are located.

Second, where the proper place of filing is a city or town in which there is a county clerk's office, then filing must be in the county office. No distinction is presently drawn for the filing of agricultural mortgages. Other exceptions to these filing requirements are noted in the first paragraph of this annotation.

Conditional sales. With the exception of special provisions for railroad equipment and rolling stock (Personal Property Law, § 68), canal boats and certain other craft

(Personal Property Law, § 66), and fixture-type items (Personal Property Law, § 67), the present rules for the place of filing conditional sales contracts are substantially the same as described in the treatment of chattel mortgages. (Personal Property Law, § 66.) One must also file a conditional sales contract of goods furnished under a public contract with public offices of the state or political subdivisions in order to preserve its effectiveness against the state or political subdivision thereof. (Personal Property Law, § 65–a.)

As noted above, filing under the Code is determined by the classification of collateral, which in some cases depends on the character of the user. Under Section 9–302 filing is not required to perfect a purchase money security interest in certain farm equipment nor to perfect a purchase money security interest in consumer goods other than motor vehicles and fixtures. But under Section 9–307(2) such security interest in consumer goods could be defeated by one who buys without knowledge, etc. To protect against this risk, filing, even with respect to such purchase money security interests, is required and Section 9–401 states where that filing should be made. Security interests created in consumer goods or farm equipment already owned by the borrower are not excepted. At present most of such purchase money security interests are represented by conditional sales, which generally must be recorded to prevail against third parties. Filing with respect to accounts, contract rights, or general intangibles (Section 9–106) arising from or relating to the sale of farm products by a farmer is new.

The subsection does not deal with the situation where there are multiple debtors. See Lien Law, § 232, and Personal Property Law, § 66.

The requirement of dual filing in the case of crop collateral, where the land is in one county but the debtor resides elsewhere, is new, but is analogous to what is required by the Factor's Lien Act, Personal Property Law, § 45.

(1)(b) Where the collateral is goods which are to be affixed to realty, the Code follows the Uniform Conditional Sales Act, Personal Property Law, § 67. See also Lien Law, § 231, and Rural Electric Co-operative Law, § 63.

(2) This subsection is probably intended to emphasize the rule stated in Section 9–301(1)that actual knowledge in the absence of perfection of a security interests may be decisive in determining rights against third parties. Compare the different effect of such knowledge insertions 9–312 and 9–307. The Code provision that incomplete compliance with filing requirements may still be partially effective, seems to be a change in New York law. See Petition of Turchin, 260 App.Div. 447, 23 N.Y.S.2d 144 (1940), where it was held that partial compliance with Lien Law, § 232, did not make the filing effective in any respect. It should be noted that subsection (2) deals with filing in an improper place. Such filing is effective under the Code to the extent it is territorially proper. See further on present New York law, Harnischfeger Sales Corp. v. Spellman, 160 Misc. 350, 289 N.Y.S. 352, aff'd 256 App. Div. 879, 9 N.Y.S.2d 241 (1939); Creamery Package Mfg. Co. v. Horton, 178 App.Div. 467, 165 N.Y.S. 257 (1917); S.S.Silver Co. v. Cafe Charing, 264 App.Div. 790, 34 N.Y.S.2d (1942); Mack v. Phelan, 92 N.Y. 20 (1883). In New York one with actual notice cannot successfully defeat an adverse interest on the ground of improper filing.

(3) Two alternatives are presented for this subsection. The first alternative, adopted in New York, states that once filing has been effected in the Code state, it "remains effective even thought the debtor's residence or place of business or the location of the collateral is thereafter changed." The other provides that the original filing remains effective for 120 days after the change, but thereafter is ineffective unless a copy is filed in the new county.

The first alternative is in accord with present New York law with regard to removal under a chattel mortgage. Apparently, the constructive notice, imparted by the initial proper recording of a chattel mortgage, reaches whatever town, county, or state to

UCC

which the property may be removed and no further record is necessary after the removal. Nichols v. Mase, 94 N.Y. 160 (1883); Farnham v. Eichin, 230 App.Div. 639, 246 N.Y.S. 133 (1930).

The second alternative, not adopted in New York, is similar to the present requirements as to a conditional sales and factor's liens. Personal Property Law, § 74, requires that a conditional seller file a copy of the conditional sales contract in the district to which the good shave been removed within ten days, if he has actual notice of such removal and of the new filing district. Personal Property Law, § 45, in specifying the place required for filing, expressly provides for refilling on removal by requiring filing "in every town or city where the merchandise is or at any time shall be located, kept or stored, and also in the town or city where the principal office or place of business of the lienor is or at any time shall be located."

(4) See annotation to Section 9–103.

Historical Note: Subsection (1) has been changed for simplification and clarification.

The changes in subsection (2) were for clarification and, in states such as Pennsylvania adopting dual filing (i.e. both central and local filing with respect to equipment, accounts, etc.), the section now makes it clear that filing to be effective in respect of a particular item of collateral must have been made in both places. It was never intended that filing in only one of two required places in respect of a particular item of collateral should be effective except as against one with actual knowledge.

Subsection (3) has been changed to make it clear that a change in use of collateral which would have the effect of changing its classification does not impair the effectiveness of a prior filing. The change meets certain criticisms which have been made.

The alternative subsection (3) has been changed for clarification and also to provide for anew perfection after the expiration of the four-month period for refilling. (1956 Recommendations, p. 298.)

Official Uniform Comment

Prior Uniform Statutory Provision: Section 4, Uniform Trust Receipts Act; Sections 6 and 7, Uniform Conditional Sales Act.

Purposes:

1. Under chattel mortgage acts, the Uniform Conditional Sales Act and other conditional sales legislation the geographical unit for filing or recording was local: the county or township in which the mortgagor or vendee resided or in which the goods sold or mortgaged were kept. the Uniform Trust Receipts Act used the state as the geographic filing unit: under that Act statements of trust receipt financing were filed with an official in the state capital and were not filed locally. The state-wide filing system of the Trust Receipts Act has been followed in many accounts receivable and factor's lien acts.

Both systems have their advocates and both their own advantages and drawbacks. The principal advantage of state-wide filing is ease of access to the credit information which the files exist to provide. Consider for example the national distributor who wishes to have current information about the credit standing of the thousands of persons he sells to on credit. The more completely the files are centralized on a state-wide basis, the easier and cheaper it becomes to procure credit information; the more the files are scattered in local filing units, the more burdensome and costly. On the other hand, it can be said that most credit inquiries about local businesses, farmers and consumers come from local sources; convenience is served by having the files locally available and there is not great advantage in centralized filing.

This section does not attempt to resolve the controversy between advocates of a completely centralized state-wide filing system and those of a large degree of local autonomy. Instead the section is drafted in a series of alternatives; local considerations of policy will determine the choice to be made.

2. Fortunately there is general agreement that the proper filing place for security interests in fixtures is in the office where a mortgage on the real estate concerned would be filed or recorded, and paragraph (1)(a) in the First Alternative and paragraph (1)(b) in the Second and Third Alternatives so provide. This provision follows the Uniform Conditional Sales Act. Note that there is no requirement for an additional filing with the chattel records.

3. In states where it is felt wise to preserve local filing for transactions of essentially local interest, either the Second or Third Alternative of subsection (1) should be adopted. Paragraph (1)(a) in both alternatives provides county (township, etc.) filing for consumer goods transactions and for agricultural transactions (farm equipment, farm products, farm accounts and crops). Note that the subsection departs from Section 6 of the Uniform Conditional Sales Act and adopts instead the policy of many chattel mortgage acts in selecting the county of the debtor's residence, rather than the county where the goods are located, as the normal filing place. Where, however, the debtor is an out-of-state resident, the filing must of necessity be in the county where the goods are, and the subsection so provides. Though not expressly stated, it is evident that filing for an assignment of accounts arising from the sale of farm products by a farmer who is not a resident must be in the county where the debtor keeps his farm products. In the case of crops growing or to be grown, where the land is in one county and the debtor's residence in another, filing must be made in both counties. Neither this filing for crops in the county where the land is nor the requirements that the security agreement (Section 9–203(1)(a)) and the financing statement (Section 9–402(1) and (3)) contain a description of the real estate to the conclusion that a financing statement for a security interest in crops must be filed in the real estate records. This Article follows pre-Code law which recognized such a financing as a chattel mortgage. The policy of the subsection is to require filing in the place or places where a creditor would normally look for information concerning interests created by the debtor.

For some incorporated farmers, reference to residence is an anomaly. Therefore subsection (6) provides that the residence of an organization is its place of business, or its chief executive office if it has more than one place of business. Compare Section 9–103(3), which reaches essentially the same concept as a definition of the "location" of a debtor.

4. It is thought that sound policy requires a state-wide filing system for all transactions except the essentially local ones covered in paragraph (1)(a) of the Second and Third Alternatives and land-related transactions covered in paragraph (1)(b) of the Second and Third Alternatives. Paragraph (1)(c) so provides in both alternatives, as does paragraph (1)(b) in the First Alternative. In a state which has adopted either the Second or Third Alternative, central filing would be required when the collateral was goods except consumer goods, farm equipment or farm products (including crops), or was documents or chattel paper or was accounts or general intangibles, unless related to a farm. Note that the filing provisions of this Article do not apply to instruments (see Section 9–304).

If the Third Alternative subsection (1) is adopted, then local filing, in addition to the central filing, is required in all the cases stated in the preceding paragraph, with respect to any debtor whose places of business within the state are all within a single county (township, etc.) or a debtor who is not engaged in business. The last event test stated in Section 9–103(1)(b) and Comment thereto applies to determine whether local filing is required under the present section, as well as to determine in which state filing is required.

UCC

In states where the arguments for a completely centralized set of files (except for fixtures) prevail, the First Alternative subsection (1) should be adopted. That alternative provides for exclusive central filing of all security interests except those in fixtures.

5. When a secured party has in good faith attempted to comply with filing requirements but has not done so correctly, subsection (2) makes his filing effective in so far as it was proper, and also makes it good for all collateral covered by the financing statement against any person who actually knows the contents of the improperly filed statement. The subsection rejects the occasional decisions that an improperly filed record is ineffective to give notice to a person who knows of it. But if the Third Alternative subsection (1) is adopted, the requirements of paragraph (1)(c) are not complied with unless there is a filing in both offices specified; filing in only one of two required places is not effective except as actual knowledge of the contents of the defective financing statement.

6. Subsection (3) deals with change of residence or place of business or the location or use of goods after a proper filing has been made. The subsection is important only when local filing is required, and covers only changes between local filing units in the state. For changes of location between states see Section 9–103(1)(d).

Subsection (3) is presented in alternative forms. Under the first no new filing is required in the county to which collateral has been removed. Under alternative subsection (3) the original filing lapses four months after the change in location; this is basically the same rule that is applied by Section 9–103(1)(d) to the case of collateral brought into the state subject to a security interest which attached elsewhere.

7. The usual filing rules do not apply well for a transmitting utility (defined in Section 9–105). Many pre-Code statutes provided special filing rules for railroads and in some cases for other public utilities to avoid the requirements for filing with legal descriptions in every county in which such debtors had property. The Code recreates and broadens these provisions by subsection (5) of this section, which provides that for transmitting utilities the filing need only be in the state office of the Secretary of State. The nature of the debtor will inform persons searching the record as to where to make a search.

Cross References:

Sections 9–302, 9–304 and 9–307(2).
Point 2: Section 9–313.
Point 6: Section 9–103(3)
Point 7: Sections 9–402(5) and 9–403(6).

Definitional Cross References:

"Account." Section 9–106.
"Collateral." Section 9–105.
"Consumer goods." Section 9–109.
"Debtor." Section 9–105.
"Equipment." Section 9–109.
"Farm products." Section 9–109.
"Financing statement." Section 9–402.
"Fixture filing." Section 9–313.
"Good faith." Section 1–201.
"Goods." Section 9–105.
"Knowledge." Section 1–201.
"Person." Section 1–201.
"Secured party." Section 9–105.
"Security interest." Section 1–201.

"Signed." Section 1–201.
"Transmitting utility." Section 9–105.

Section 9–402. Formal Requisites of Financing Statement; Amendments; Mortgage as Financing Statement.

(1) A financing statement is sufficient if it gives the names of the debtor and the secured party, is signed by the debtor, gives an address of the secured party from which information concerning the security interest may be obtained, gives a mailing address of the debtor and contains a statement indicating the types, or describing the items, of collateral. A financing statement may be filed before a security agreement is made or a security interest otherwise attaches. When the financing statement covers crops growing or to be grown, or timber to be cut, or minerals or the like (including oil and gas), or accounts subject to subsection (5) of Section 9–103, or when the financing statement is filed as a fixture filing (Section 9–313) and the collateral is goods which are or are to become fixtures, the statement must also contain a brief description sufficient for the identification of the real estate concerned, show the name of a record owner, and also comply with subsection (5). For the purposes of this section, the location of the real estate by reference to a book and page number in a deed or mortgage index maintained in the County Clerk's office in the county where the property is situate or by street and number and town or city, or, if the real estate is in the city of New York, by county is a sufficient description, except that if the real estate is in the city of New York or counties of Nassau or Onondaga, where the block system of recording or registering and indexing conveyances is in use, the statement must also specify the block in which the real estate is situated. A copy of the security agreement is sufficient as a financing statement if it contains the above information and is signed by the debtor. A carbon, photographic or other reproduction of a security agreement or a financing statement is sufficient as a financing statement if the security agreement so provides or if the original has been filed in this state. A financing statement to be filed in the department of state need contain neither a description of the real estate concerned nor the name of a record owner.

(2) A financing statement which otherwise complies with subsection (1) is sufficient when it is signed by the secured party instead of the debtor if it is filed to perfect a security interest in

(a) collateral already subject to a security interest in another jurisdiction when it is brought into this state, or when the debtor's location is changed to this state. Such a financing statement must state that the collateral was brought into this state or that the debtor's location was changed to this state under such circumstances; or

(b) proceeds under Section 9–306 if the security interest in the original collateral was perfected. Such a financing statement must describe the original collateral; or

(c) collateral as to which the filing has lapsed; or

UCC

(d) collateral acquired after a change of name, identity or corporate structure of the debtor (subsection (7)); or

(e) collateral under a security agreement signed by the debtor and authorizing the secured party to file a financing statement. Such a financing statement must state that it is filed in accordance with a security agreement signed by the debtor and authorizing the filing of the statement and may be filed by either the original secured party or by the assignee; the statement therein indicating the types, or describing the items, of collateral must be limited to the types, or description of items, of collateral under the security agreement.

(3) A form substantially as follows is sufficient to comply with subsection (1):

Name of debtor (or assignor) . . . .

Address . . . .

Name of secured party (or assignee) . . . .

Address . . . .

1. This financing statement covers the following types (or items) of property: (Describe) . . . .

2. One of the following statements, if applicable:

The above described crops are growing or are to be grown on:

The above described goods are or are to become fixtures on:

The above described timber is standing on:

The above described minerals or the like (including oil and gas) or accounts will be financed at the well head or mine head of the well or mine located on:

and, in addition:

(Describe Real Estate) . . . . and the financing statement is to be indexed in the real estate records. The name of a record owner is . . . .

3. (If products of collateral are claimed.) Products of the collateral are also covered. (use whichever is applicable)

Signature of Debtor (or Assignor)

Signature of Secured Party (or Assignee)

(4) A financing statement may be amended by filing a writing signed by both the debtor and the secured party. An amendment does not extend the period of effectiveness of a financing statement. If any amendment adds collateral, it is effective as to the added collateral only from the filing date of the amendment. In this Article, unless the context otherwise requires, the term "financing statement" means the original financing statement and any amendments.

(5) A financing statement covering crops growing or to be grown, or timber to be cut, or minerals or the like (including oil and gas), or accounts subject to subsection (5) of Section 9–103, or a financing statement filed as a fixture filing (Section 9–313) where the debtor is not a transmitting utility, must show that it covers this type of collateral, must recite that it is to be indexed in the real estate records, and the financing statement must contain a description of the real estate sufficient for its identification and must show the name of a record owner.

(6) A mortgage is effective as a financing statement filed as a fixture filing from the date of its recording if (a) the goods are described in the mortgage by item or type, (b) the goods are or are to become fixtures related to the real estate described in the mortgage, the mortgage complies with the requirements for a financing statement in this section other than a recital that it is to be indexed in the real estate records, and (d) the mortgage is duly recorded. No fee with reference to the financing statement is required other than the regular recording and satisfaction fees with respect to the mortgage.

(7) A financing statement sufficiently shows the name of the debtor if it gives the individual, partnership or corporate name of the debtor, whether or not it adds other trade names or the names of partners. Where the debtor so changes his name or in the case of an organization its name, identity or corporate structure that a filed financing statement becomes seriously misleading, the filing is not effective to perfect a security interest in collateral acquired by the debtor more than four months after the change, unless a new appropriate financing statement is filed before the expiration of that time. A filed financing statement remains effective with respect to collateral transferred by the debtor even though the secured party knows of or consents to the transfer.

(8) A financing statement substantially complying with the requirements of this section is effective even though it contains minor errors which are not seriously misleading.

Amended by Laws 1977, Ch. 866, eff. July 2, 1978.

New York Annotations

(1), (3), and (4) The form of the financing statement provided in the Code now exists in substance in most modern security statutes, including Personal Property Law, § 58–e (trust receipts); Personal Property Law, § 45 (factor's lien); and Lien Law, § 230–c (mortgage statement in lieu of filing mortgages by dealers).

Other provisions of present law call for the filing of the contract itself or a copy thereof. Personal Property Law, §§ 65, 65–a, 67 (conditional sales); Lien Law, §§ 230, 230–b (chattel mortgages).

The result of Section 9–402 in this situation would be to simplify and reduce the size of the instrument which must be filed. Under some circumstances, a single filing under the Code might take the place of many separate filings, particularly where after-acquired property is involved. The requirement of a description of the realty in the case of fixtures is in *accord* with Personal Property Law, § 67 (conditional sales).

The Code provision does place more emphasis on the importance of signatures, although there are the following provisions: Personal Property Law, § 58–e (signature of entruster and trustee); Personal Property Law, § 64–a (signature of conditional buyer of goods for non-commercial use); Personal Property Law, § 45 (Name of lienor); Personal Property Law, § 302(1) (motor vehicle retail installment contracts); Lien Law § 239–i (signature of mortgagor of goods sold for non-commercial use); Lien Law, § 230–b (signed by mortgagor and witness); Lien Law, § 230–c (signed by mortgagee and dealer).

This signature requirement for the financing statement is not apparently intended as a Statute of Frauds, since Section 9–203, which provides for the formal requirement of the security agreement itself, is intended to be "in the nature of a Statute of Frauds" and requires only the signature of the debtor. See Comment 5 to Section 9–203. However, the express requirement in Section 9–402 of the signatures of both the debtor and the secured party apparently would result in an unperfected security interest if one failed to sign. The counselling point is that where the agreement itself is filed, care must be taken to assure that both parties sigh the agreement.

(2) There is nothing comparable to this subsection in the present law.

(5) Under Personal Property Law, § 45, a liberal construction is required so that a typographical error in the lienor's name, subsequently corrected, which did not mislead, was held not to invalidate a factor's lien. Bloch Bros. Paper Co. v. Efficient Direct Mail Service, 198 Misc.669, 102 N.Y.S.2d 1003 (1950).

Historical Note: Subsection (1) has been changed for clarification and also to eliminate the necessity of an itemized description of collateral affixed or to be affixed to real estate, which it is believed, imposes an unnecessary burden in cases of extensive installations as, for example, in a large housing development. A new subsection (4) has been added to provide additional flexibility through the use of amending statements. A new subsection (5) has been added, in *accord* with a Law Revision Commission suggestion, to make it clear that an immaterial error should not have the devastating effect reached in GMAC v. Haley, 329 Mass.559, 109 N.E.2d 143 (1952). (1956 Recommendations, p. 300; Excerpts p. 481.)

Official Uniform Comment

Prior Uniform Statutory Provision: Sections 13(3), 13(4), Uniform Trust Receipts Act.

Purposes:

1. Subsection (1) sets out the simple formal requisites of a financing statement under this Article. These requirements are: (1) signature of the debtor; (2) addresses of both parties; (3) a description of the collateral by type or item.

Where the collateral is crops growing or to be grown or when the financing statement is filed as a fixture filing (section 9–313) or when the collateral is timber to be cut or minerals or the like (including oil and gas) financed at wellhead or minehead or accounts resulting from the sale thereof, the financing statement must also contain a description of the lands concerned. On description generally, see Section 9–110 and Comment 5 to the present section. An important distinction must be drawn, however, between the function of the description of land in reference to crops and its function in the other cases mentioned. For crops it is merely part of the description of the crops concerned, and the security interest in crops is a Code security interest, like the pre-Code "crop mortgage" which was a chattel mortgage. In contrast, in the other cases mentioned the function of the description of land is to have the financing statement filed in the county where the land is situated and in the realty records, as distinguished from the chattel records. chattel records. Subsection (3) suggests a form which complies with the statutory requirements and makes clear that for the types of collateral mentioned other than crops, the financing statement containing a description of the land concerned is to go in the realty records. Note also subsection (5) on the adequacy of the description of land where the filing is to be in the real estate records. See also Section 9–403(7) on the indexing of these filings in the real estate records.

A copy of the security agreement may be filed in place of a separate financing statement, if it contains the required information and signature.

2. This section adopts the system of "notice filing" which proved successful under the Uniform Trust Receipts Act. What is required to be filed is not, as under chattel mortgage and conditional sales acts, the security agreement itself, but only a simple notice which may be filed before the security interest attaches or thereafter. The notice itself indicates merely that the secured party who has filed may have a security interest in the collateral described. Further inquiry from the parties concerned will be necessary to disclose the complete state of affairs. Section 9–208 provides a statutory procedure under which the secured party, at the debtor's request, may be required to make disclosure. Notice filing has proved to be of great use in financing transactions involving inventory, accounts and chattel paper, since it obviates the necessity of refiling on each of a series of transactions in a continuing arrangement where the collateral changes from day to day. Where other types of collateral are involved, the alternative procedure of filing a signed copy of the security agreement may prove to be simplest solution. Sometimes more than one copy of a financing statement or of a security agreement used as a financing agreement is needed for filing. In such a case the section permits use of a carbon copy or photographic copy of the paper, including signatures.

However, even in the case of filings that do not necessarily involve a series of transactions the financing statement is effective to encompass transactions under a security agreement not in existence and not contemplated at the time the notice was filed, if the description of collateral in the financing statement is broad enough to encompass them. Similarly, the financing statement is valid to cover after-acquired property and future advances under security agreements whether or not mentioned in the financing statement.

3. This section departs from the requirements of many pre-Code chattel mortgage statutes that the instrument filed be acknowledged of witnessed or accompanied by affidavits of good faith. Those requirements did not seem to have been successful as a deterrent to fraud; their principal effect was to penalize good faith mortgagees who had inadvertently failed to comply with the statutory niceties. They are here abandoned in the interest of a simplified and workable filing system.

4. Subsection (2) allows the secured party to file a financing statement signed only by himself where the filing is required by any of the events listed, each of which occurs after the commencement of the financing, and therefore under circumstances where the cooperation of the debtor is not certain. Section 9–401(3), alternative provision, contains similar permission on removal between counties in this state. The secured party should not be penalized for failure to make a timely filing by reason of difficulty in procuring the signature of a possibly reluctant or hostile debtor. Financing statements filed under this subsection must explain the circumstances under which they are filed with the signature of the secured party rather than that of the debtor.

In contrast to the signatures on original financing statements, an amendment to a financing statement must be signed by both parties, to preclude either from adversely affecting the interests of the other.

The reference in subsection (4) to the amendment which "adds collateral" refers to additional types of collateral. A security interest of additional units of a type of collateral already described can be created under an after-acquired property clause or a new security agreement. See Comment 5 to Section 9–204. On priorities in such cases see Section 9–312 and Comments thereto.

5. A description of real estate must be sufficient to identify it. See Section 9–110. This formulation rejects the view that the real estate description must be by metes and bounds, or otherwise conforming to traditional real estate practice in conveyancing, but of course the incorporation of such a description by reference to the recording data of deed, mortgage or other instrument containing the description should suffice under the most stringent standards. The proper test is that a description of real estate must be sufficient so that the fixture financing statement will fit into the real estate search system and the financing statement be found by a real estate searcher. Optional language has been added by which the test of adequacy of the description is whether it would be adequate in a mortgage of the real estate. As suggested in the Note, more detail may required if there is a tract indexing system or a land registration system.

Where the debtor does not have an interest of record in the real estate, a fixture financing statement must show the name of a record owner, and Section 9–403(7) requires the financing statement to be indexed in the name of the owner. Thus the fixture financing statement will fit into the real estate search system.

6. A real estate mortgage may provide that it constitutes a security agreement with respect to fixtures (or other goods) in conformity with this Article. Combined mortgages on real estate and chattels are common and useful for certain purposes. This section goes further and makes provision that the recording of the real estate mortgage (if it complies with the requirements of a financing statement) shall constitute the filing of a financing statement as to the fixtures (but not, of course, as to the other goods). Section 9–403(6) makes the usual five-year maximum life for financing statements inapplicable to real estate mortgages which operate as financing statements under Section 9–402(6), and they are effective for the duration of the real estate recording.

Of course, if a combined mortgage covers chattels which are not fixtures, a regular chattel filing is necessary, and subsection (6) is inapplicable to such chattels. Likewise, filing as a "fixture filing" provided in Section 9–401 does not apply to true chattels.

7. Section (7) undertakes to deal with some of the problems as to who is the debtor. In the case of individuals, it contemplates filing only in the individual name, not in a trade name. In the case of partnerships it contemplates filing in the partnership name, not in the names of any of the partners, and not in any other trade names. Trade names are deemed to be too uncertain and too likely not to be known to the secured party or person searching the record to form the basis for a filing system. However, provision is made in Section 9–403(5) for indexing in a trade name if the secured party so desires.

Subsection (7) also deals with the case of a change of name of a debtor and provides some guidelines where mergers or other changes of corporate structure of the debtor occur with the result that a filed financing statement might become seriously misleading. Not all cases can be imagined and covered by statutes in advance; however, the principle sought to be achieved by the subsection is that after a change which would be seriously misleading the old financing statement is not effective as to new collateral acquired more than four months after the change, unless a new appropriate financing statement is filed before the expiration of four months. The old financing statement, if legally still valid under the circumstances, would continue to protect collateral acquired before the change and, if still operative under the particular circumstances, would also protect collateral acquired within four months. Obviously, the subsection does not undertake to state whether the old security agreement continues to operate between the secured party and the party surviving the corporate change of the debtor.

8. Subsection (7) also deals with a different problem, namely whether a new filing is necessary where the collateral has been transferred from one debtor to another. This question has been much debated both in pre-Code law and under the Code. This Article now answers the question in the negative. Thus, any person searching the

condition of the ownership of a debtor must make inquiry as to the debtor's source of title, and must search in the name of a former owner if circumstances seem to require it.

9. Subsection (8) is in line with the policy of this Article to simplify formal requisites and filing requirements and is designed to discourage the fanatical and impossibly refined reading of such statutory requirements in which courts have occasionally indulged themselves. As an example of the sort of reasoning which this subsection rejects, see General Motor Acceptance Corporation v. Haley, 329 Mass. 559, 109 N.E.2d 143 (1952).

Cross References:

Point 1: Section 9–110.
Point 2: Section 9–208.
Point 4: Sections 9–103, 9–306 and 9–401(3).
Point 5: Section 9–110.
Point 6: Section 9–403(6).
Point 7: Section 9–403(8).
Point 8: Section 9–311.

Definitional Cross References:

"Collateral." Section 9–105.
"Debtor." Section 9–105.
"Fixture." Section 9–313.
"Fixture filing." Section 9–313.
"Goods." Section 9–105.
"Party." Section 1–201.
"Proceeds." Section 9–306.
"Secured party." Section 9–105.
"Security agreement." Section 9–105.
"Security interest." Section 1–201.
"Signed." Section 1–201.
"Transmitting utility." Section 9–105.

Section 9–403. What Constitutes Filing; Duration of Filing; Effect of Lapsed Filing; Duties of Filing Officer

(1) Presentation for filing of a financing statement and tender of the filing or processing fee or acceptance of the statement by the filing officer constitutes filing under this Article.

(2) Except as provided in subsection (6) a filed financing statement is effective for a period of five years from the date of filing. The effectiveness of a filed financing statement lapses on the expiration of the five year period unless a continuation statement is filed prior to the lapse. If a security interest perfected by filing exists at the time insolvency proceedings are commenced by or against the debtor, the security interest remains perfected until termination of the insolvency proceedings and thereafter for a period of sixty days or until expiration of the five year period, whichever occurs later. Upon lapse the security interest becomes unperfected, unless it is perfected without filing. If the security interest becomes unperfected upon lapse, it is deemed to have been unperfected as against a person who became a purchaser or lien creditor before lapse.

(3) A continuation statement may be filed by the secured party within six months prior to the expiration of the five year period specified in subsection (2). Any such continuation statement must be signed by the secured party, identify the original statement by file number and state that the original statement is still effective. A continuation statement signed by a person other than the secured party of record must be accompanied by a separate written statement of assignment signed by the secured party of record and complying with subsection (2) of Section 9–405, including payment of the required fee. Upon timely filing of the continuation statement, the effectiveness of the original statement is continued for five years after the last date to which the filing was effective where upon it lapses in the same manner as provided in subsection (2) unless another continuation statement is filed prior to such lapse. Succeeding continuation statements may be filed in the same manner to continue the effectiveness of the original statement. Unless a statute on disposition of public records provides otherwise, the filing officer may remove a lapsed statement from the files and destroy it immediately or inactivate the computerized index record of the financing statement immediately if he or she has retained a microfilm, other photographic record or computerized image of the record, or in other cases after one year after the lapse. The filing officer shall so arrange matters by physical annexation of financing statements to continuation statements or other related filings, or by other means, automated or otherwise, that if he or she physically destroys or inactivates the computerized index record of the financing statements of a period more than five years past, those which have been continued by a continuation statement or which are still effective under subsection (6) shall be retained.

(4)(a) A filing officer shall: (i) mark each statement with a consecutive file number and with the date of filing and shall hold the statement or a photographic or microfilm copy thereof for public disclosure or (ii) create a computerized record of the financing statement, assign a consecutive file number to each statement and enter the date of filing by using automated methods and shall hold such computerized record of the statement for public disclosure.

(b) If the filing system is manual, consecutive filing numbers for statements filed in each calendar year shall begin with the numeral "one" preceded by the last two digits of the calendar year in which filing occurs. If the filing system is computerized, consecutive filing numbers shall be assigned and the date on which such filings occur shall be assigned to the computerized records. In addition the filing officer shall index the statements according to the name of the debtor and shall note in the index the file number.

(c) In addition, with respect to a financing statement to which subsection (7) applies, the filing officer, other than the secretary of state, shall also index the statement according to subsection (7).

(5) The secretary of state shall prescribe, pursuant to the provisions of section ninety-six-o of the executive law, the uniform fee for filing, indexing and furnishing filing data for an original or a continuation statement on a form

conforming to standards prescribed by the secretary of state, and the fee if the statement otherwise conforms to the requirements of Section 9–402, plus, in either case, an additional fee:

(a) if the statement covers collateral which is crops or goods which are or are to become fixtures and is not filed in the office of the secretary of state and, in addition,

(b) if the real estate is in the city of New York or the county of Nassau, any block fees allowed by the administrative code of the city of New York or the Nassau county administrative code, and

(c) for each additional person, firm or organization, beyond the first, named as a debtor in the statement.

(6) A county clerk may adopt a new indexing system utilizing electro-mechanical, electronic or any other method he deems suitable for maintaining the indexes.

(7) If the debtor is a transmitting utility (subsection (5) of Section 9–401) and a filed financing statement so states, it is effective for a period of five years from the date of filing unless continued. Any financing statement which states that the debtor is a transmitting utility and which is filed prior to January first, nineteen hundred ninety, shall lapse on January second, nineteen hundred ninety-five, unless a continuation statement is filed on or before January first, nineteen hundred ninety-five, and such statement if continued shall remain effective in accordance with the provisions of subsection (3). A real estate mortgage which is effective as a fixture filing under subsection (6) of Section 9–402 remains effective as a fixture filing until the mortgage is released or satisfied of record or its effectiveness otherwise terminates as to the real estate.

(8) When a financing statement covers crops growing or to be grown, or timber to be cut, or minerals or like (including oil and gas), or accounts subject to subsection (5) of Section 9–103, or is filed as a fixture filing, the filing officer shall index it according to the name of any owner of the real estate shown on the financing statement, and if the real estate is in the city of New York or in Nassau, Onondaga or any other county where the block system of recording or registering and indexing conveyances is in use, according to the block in which the real estate is situated; the filing officer may index such statements according to the names of the record owners of the real estate in a single consolidated index installed and maintained by him pursuant to section five hundred twenty-nine of the county law.

(9) When a financing statement covers shares of other ownership interests evidenced by stock certificates or other instruments, and a leasehold evidenced by a proprietary lease, or either of the foregoing, from a corporation or partnership formed for the purpose of cooperative ownership of real property and the filed financing statement so states, it is effective until a termination statement is filed.

UCC

(10) No financing statement, security agreement, or other related statement shall be accepted for filing unless it is typed or printed in black ink and in the determination of the filing officer it can be legibly read, scanned, interpreted or reproduced by the technology employed by the department of state.

Amended by Laws 1977, Ch. 866, eff. July 2, 1978; Laws 1982, Ch. 692, eff. Aug. 21, 1982; Laws 1986, Ch. 453, eff. July 21, 1986; Laws 1988, Ch. 333, eff. Aug. 24, 1988, and applicable to any security interest obtained, continued or consolidated on or after such effective date, and shall not affect security interests obtained prior to such effective date by means other than filing; Laws 1990, Ch. 561, eff. July 18, 1990; Laws 1991, Ch. 648, eff. July 26, 1991, Laws 1996, Ch. 309, eff. July 13, 1996.

New York Annotations

(1) The rule of this subsection that "presentation for filing of a financing statement and tender of the filing fee or acceptance of the statement by the filing officer constitutes filing" is directly in *accord* with present New York law. Matter of Labb, 42 F. Supp. 542 (W.D.N.Y. 1941); Personal Property Law § 58–e(4); Lien Law, § 230–c.

(2) and (3) These subsections are similar in principle to present requirements that in order to preserve validity under a conditional sale, chattel mortgage, or trust receipt transactions there must be refiling within a specified time.

Under Personal Property Law, § 71, and Lien Law, § 235, a property filed conditional sale contract is valid for three years and then for successive three-year periods upon are filing. See also Lien Law § 230–c(4) (one year).

Personal Property Law, § 58–e(4) and (5), makes the trust receipt statement good for one year and permits renewal for subsequent one-year periods. Notwithstanding the foregoing general provisions, certain transactions under existing law have special rules on refiling. Lien Law, § 236 (mortgage recording on canal boats and certain other craft effective until debt is paid), and Rural Electric Co-operative Law, § 63 (no refiling needed on such transactions); Personal Property Law, §§ 68, 71 (conditional sales of railroad rolling stock–fifteen years). The factor's lien under Personal Property Law, § 45, "shall be deemed to be and remain in full force and effect under this act without further or other filing."

As to combined real estate and chattel corporate mortgages, the present law would be changed, since financing statements would have to be filed under the Code. Realty recording is now sufficient under Lien Law, § 231, in cases of corporate mortgages to secure bonds, notes, or other evidences of indebtedness, and under Rule Electric Cooperative Law, § 63.

The rule that upon a lapsed filing the security interest becomes unperfected with regard to rights which accrue thereafter, clarifies an obscure area under existing law. In New York today, if there is a failure to refile a chattel mortgage, it "shall be invalid as against creditors of the mortgagor, and against subsequent purchasers or mortgagees in good faith" Lien Law, § 235. It has been held that a creditor whose lien attached during the validity of a prior chattel mortgage can attack the mortgage on the ground that it was not subsequently refiled. Thompson v. Van Vechten, 27 N.Y. 568 (1863). But in Lockhart v. Garden City Bank &Trust Co., 116 F.2d 658 (2d Cir. 1940), a bankruptcy case, the opposite result was reached. Compare Benedict v. Zutes, 88 Misc. 214, 150 N.Y.S. 147 (1914), questioned in Weissglass Gold Seal Dairy Corp. v. First National Bank of Fleischmanns, 263 App.Div. 744, 31 N.Y.S.2d 58 (1941).

The same question is not perfectly clear under Personal Property Law, §§ 65 and 71, as to conditional sales. However, since an amended filing if subordinate to an attaching or levying creditor without notice, Matter of Herlihy, 38 N.Y.S.2d 663

(1942), it is probable that a creditor put on constructive notice by the original filing could not attack the failure to refile. American Laundry Machinery Co. v. Larson, 217 Wis. 208, 257 N.W. 608 (1934). The same reasoning and results would probably apply to trust receipts refiling under Personal Property Law, §§ 58, 58–e(4) and (5).

(4) The duties of the filing officers prescribed in subsection (4) are substantially the same as those prescribed in Personal Property Law, §§ 58–e(3), 70, 45, and Lien Law, § 233. Note, however, the special provisions under existing law relating to New York City filing and endorsements.

Historical Note: Subsection (2) was changed to impose a maximum period of five years for the effectiveness of a filed financing statement not specifying a maturity date and a maximum period of sixty days beyond a specified maturity date of five years or less in place of the former indefinite provisions. The changes were designed to make searches for filed statements less burdensome.

Subsection (3) was changed to make it clear that a continuation statement must be filed within the six months preceding the lapse of effectiveness provided in subsection (2), and that, when there has been a timely filing of a continuation statement, effectiveness is extended for an additional period of five years from the date when the prior effectiveness would otherwise have lapsed, rather than from the date of filing of the continuation statement. Provision was also made for the filing of additional continuation statements.

Subsection (4) was changed to eliminate the requirement that the filing officer index in the name of the secured party. The Secretary of State of Pennsylvania suggested the change.

UCC

Official Uniform Comment

Prior Uniform Statutory Provision: Sections 13(3), 13(4), Uniform Trust Receipts Act; Section 10, Uniform Conditional Sales Act.

Purposes:

1. Prior law was not always clear whether a mortgage filed for record gave constructive notice from the time of presentation to the filing officer or only from time of indexing. Subsection (1) adopts the former position.

2. Prior statutes have usually limited the effectiveness of a filing to a specified period of time after which refiling is necessary. Subsection (2) follows the same policy, establishing five years as the filing period, with an exception for the cases mentioned in subsection (6). Subsection (3) provides for the filing of one or more continuation statements (which need be signed only by the secured party) if it is desired to continue the effectiveness of the original filing.

The theory of this Article is that the public files of financing statements are self-clearing, because the filing officer may automatically discard each financing statement after a period of five years plus the year after lapse required by subsection (3), unless a continuation statement is filed, or the financing statement is still effective under subsection (6). This theory materially lessens the tension that would otherwise exist to have the files cleared by termination statements under Section 9–404. Similarly, a person searching the files need not go back past this five years plus one year, and if indices are arranged by years, he has a limited and defined search problem. The section asks the filing officer to attach financing statements whose life has been continued by continuation statements to the latter statements, so that anything contained in the files of old year scan be discarded.

Subsection (6) provides certain special filing rules, namely, filings against transmitting utilities (Section 9–105), for which financing statements are filed in the office of the [Secretary of State]; and real estate mortgages which serve as fixture financing statements and which are filed in the real estate records. In both of these cases the financing statement is valid for the life of the obligations secured. No confusion as to the required scope of search should result, because of the special nature of the filing involved.

3. Under subsection (2) the security interest becomes unperfected when filing lapses. Thereafter, the interest of the secured party is subject to defeat by purchasers and lienors even though before lapse the conflicting interest may have been junior. Compare the situation arising under Section 9–103(1)(d) when a perfected security interest under the law of another jurisdiction is not perfected in this state within four months after the property is brought into this state.

Thus if A and B both make purchase money advances against the same collateral, and both perfect security interests by filing, A who files first is entitled to priority under Section 9–312(5). But if no continuation statement is filed, A's filing may lapse first. So long as B's interest remains perfected thereafter, he is entitled to priority over A's unperfected interest. This rule avoids the circular priority which arose under some prior statutes, under which A was subordinate to the debtor's trustee in bankruptcy, A retained priority over B, and B's interest was valid against the trustee in bankruptcy. In re Andrews, 172 F.2d 996 (7th Cir. 1949).

4. Subsection (7) makes clear that the filings in real estate records (Sections 9–401 and 9–402(3) and (5)) shall be indexed in the real estate records, where they will be found by a real estate searcher. Where the debtor is not an owner of record, the financing statement must show the name of an owner of record, and the statement is to be indexed in his name. See Sections 9–313(4)(b) and (c); 9–402(3); 9–402(5).

Cross References:

Point 3: Sections 9–103(3), 9–301 and 9–312(5).
Point 4: Sections 9–313(4)(b) and (c), 9–401(1), 9–402(3) and (5), and 9–405(2).

Definitional Cross References:

"Debtor." Section 9–105.
"Financing statement." Section 9–402.
"Fixture." Section 9–313.
"Fixture filing." Section 9–313.
"Secured party." Section 9–105.
"Security interest." Section 1–201.
"Transmitting utility." Section 9–105.

Section 9–404. Termination Statement.

(1) If a financing statement covering consumer goods is filed on or after September first of the year in which the act to amend the uniform commercial code to insert this section becomes effective, then within one month or within ten days following written demand by the debtor after there is no outstanding secured obligation and no commitment to make advances, incur obligations or otherwise give value, the secured party must file with each filing officer with whom the financing statement was filed, a termination statement to the effect that he no longer claims a security interest under the financing statement, which shall be identified by file number. In other cases whenever there is no outstanding secured obligation and no commitment to make advances, incur obligations or otherwise give value the secured party must on written demand by the debtor send the debtor, for each filing officer with whom the financing statement was

filed, a termination statement to the effect that he no longer claims a security interest under the financing statement, which shall be identified by file number. A termination statement signed by a person other than the security party of record must be accompanied by a separate written statement of assignment signed by the secured party of record and complying with subsection (2) of Section 9–405, including payment of the required fee. If the affected secured party fails to file such a termination statement as required by this subsection, or to send such termination statement as required by this subsection, or to send such a termination statement within ten days after proper demand therefor, he shall be liable to the debtor for one hundred dollars, and in addition for any loss caused to the debtor by such failure.

(2) On presentation to the filing officer of such a termination statement he or she must note it in the index or, in the case of a computerized index, he or she must enter the termination information in the index. If a filing officer, other than the secretary of state, has received the termination statement in duplicate, he or she shall return one copy of the termination statement or shall deliver or send a computerized image of the first page of the filing of the termination statement to the secured party or to such other person as the secured party filing such statement may direct stamped to show the date of receipt thereof. The secretary of state shall deliver or send a computerized image of the first page of the filing of the termination statement to the secured party or to such other person as the secured party filing such statement may direct which shall show the date of filing thereof. If the filing officer has a microfilm, other photographic record or computerized image of the financing statement, and of any related continuation statement, statement of assignment and statement of release, he or she may, if the filing system is manual, remove the originals from the files at any time after receipt of the termination statement, or if the filing system is computerized, he or she may inactivate the computerized index records from the computer files at any time after receipt of the termination statement. If the filing officer has no such microfilm or other record, he or she may, if the filing system is manual, remove the originals from the files at any time after one year after receipt of the termination statement, or, if the filing system is computerized, he or she may inactivate and/or delete the computerized records from the computer files at any time after one year after receipt of the termination statement.

(3) The secretary of state shall prescribe, pursuant to the provisions of section ninety-six-o of the executive law, if the termination statement is in the standard form prescribed by the secretary of state, the uniform fee for filing and indexing the termination statement and returning any duplicate thereof to the secured party and, other fees, plus in each case the fee for each name more than one against which the termination statement is required to be indexed.

Amended by Laws 1977, Ch. 866, eff. July 2, 1978; Laws 1982, Ch. 692, eff. Aug. 21, 1982; Laws 1986, Ch. 453, eff. July 21, 1986; Laws 1990, Ch. 561, eff. January 1, 1991; Laws 1996, Ch. 309, eff. July 13, 1996.

New York Annotations

Since under Article 9 there may be filing before the execution of any security agreements, the debtor must have a method available to clear the record. This section provides that technique and while it is quite similar to Personal Property Law, § 72, there is presently no explicit provision for a demand by the buyer for such a termination statement under conditional sales law. In addition, under existing law, it is the seller who must file. Fees for such filing are handles in Personal Property Law, § 70. Penalties are not so severe, a $5 plus damages provision is now made in Personal Property Law, § 72.

This Code provision is similar in some respects to Lien Law, § 238, and Personal property Law, § 45. Under these sections the debtor may demand a certificate setting forth such payment or satisfaction and the debtor must file this certificate in order to get a discharge of record. Unlike Personal Property Law, § 72, Lien Law, § 238, provides no penalty for noncompliance. Analogies are not to be made between two sections, Broadway Concessions, Inc. v. Mullin, 88 N.Y.S.2d 7 (1949). Fees are provided for in Lien Law § 234 and 234–a.

The provisions of the Code are also analogous to Lien Law, § 230–c(5), which permits any interested person to demand from the dealer's mortgagee a statement of the specific goods covered by the mortgagee's filing, and the recent amendment of Personal Property Law, § 58–e, providing a similar right to trust receipt transactions (Laws 1961, ch. 401, eff. Oct. 1, 1961).

Historical Note: Subsection (1) was changed for clarification and also to provide a chain of title in the case of an assignment, the latter change having been suggested by the Pennsylvania Department of State. Subsection (2) was changed to permit the filing officer to retain the termination statement as evidence of his authority to act in reliance upon it. Subsection (3) was changed in the light of Pennsylvania experience to restrict filing officers to the fee provided here. (1956 Recommendations, p. 303.)

In 1958 Subsection (2) was further amended. The changes eliminated the reference to statutes on disposition of public records, and directed return of related statements together with the financing statement. (1958 Supplement, p. 18.)

Official Uniform Comment

Prior Uniform Statutory Provision: Section 12, Uniform Conditional Sales Act.

Purposes:

1. To provide a procedure for noting discharge of the secured obligation on the records and for noting that a financing arrangement has been terminated.

Since most financing statements expire in five years unless a continuation statement is filed (Section 9–403), no compulsion is placed on the secured party to file a termination statement unless demanded by the debtor, except in the case of consumer goods. Because many consumers will not realize the importance of clearing the situation as it appears on file, an affirmative duty is put on the secured party in that case. But many purchase money security interests in consumer goods will not be filed, except for motor vehicles (Section 9–302(1)(d); and in the case of motor vehicles a certificate of title law may control instead of the provisions of Article 9.

2. This section adds to the usual provisions one covering the problem which arises because a secured party under a notice filing system may file notice of an intention to make advances which may never be made. Under this section a debtor may require a secured party to send a termination statement when there is no outstanding obligation and no commitment to make future advances.

Cross Reference:

Point 2: Section 9–402(1).

Definitional Cross References:

"Consumer goods." Section 9–109.
"Debtor." Section 9–105.
"Financing statement." Section 9–402.
"Person." Section 1–201.
"Secured party." Section 9–105.
"Security interest." Section 1–201.
"Send." Section 1–201.
"Value." Section 1–201.
"Written." Section 1–201.

Section 9–405. Assignment of Security Interest; Duties of Filing Officer; Fees.

(1) A financing statement may disclose an assignment of a security interest in the collateral described in the statement by indication in the statement of the name and address of the assignee or by an assignment itself or a copy thereof on the face or back of the statement. Either the original secured party or the assignee may sign this statement as the secured party. On presentation to the filing officer of such a financing statement the filing officer shall mark the financing statement or assign a consecutive file number to the computerized record of the financing statement as provided in Section 9-403 (4). The secretary of state pursuant to the provisions of section ninety-six-a of the executive law shall prescribe the uniform fee for filing, indexing and furnishing filing data for a financing statement so indicating an assignment on a form conforming to standards prescribed by the secretary of state, and the fee if such a statement otherwise conforms to the requirements of this section, plus an additional fee for each name more than one against which the financing statement is required to be indexed.

(2) A secured party may assign of record all or a part of his/her rights under a financing statement by the filing in the place where the original financing statement was filed of a separate written statement of assignment signed by the secured party of record and setting forth the name of the secured party of record, the debtor, the file number and the date of filing of the financing statement and the name and address of the assignee and containing a description of the collateral assigned. A copy of the assignment is sufficient as a separate statement if it complies with the preceding sentence. On presentation to the filing officer of such a separate statement, the filing officer shall mark such separate statement with the date of the filing or enter into a computerized filing system the date of filing of such statement in the record maintained for such statement. He or she shall note the assignment on the indices of the financing statement or enter the assignment information into the computerized system for the financing statement, if a computerized index is in use. The secretary of state shall prescribe

pursuant to the provisions of section ninety-six-a of the executive law the uniform fee for filing, indexing and furnishing filing data about such a separate statement of assignment on a form conforming to standards prescribed by the secretary of state, and the fee if such a statement otherwise conforms to the requirements of this section, plus, in either case, for each additional person, firm or organization, beyond the first, named as a debtor in the statement, an additional fee. Notwithstanding the provisions of this subsection, an assignment of record of a security interest in a fixture contained in a mortgage effective as a fixture filing (subsection (6) of Section 9–402) may be made only by an assignment of the mortgage in the manner provided by the law of the state other than this Act.

(3) After the disclosure or filing of an assignment under this section, the assignee is the secured party of record.

Amended by Laws 1977, Ch. 866, eff. July 2, 1978; Laws 1982, Ch. 692, eff. Aug. 21, 1982; Laws 1986, Ch. 453, eff. July 21, 1986; Laws 1990, Ch. 561, eff. July 18, 1990; Laws 1996, Ch. 309, eff. July 13, 1996.

New York Annotations

Presently Lien Law, § 232–a, provides for an assignment of a chattel mortgaged and the filing of such an assignment prior to satisfaction of the mortgage. Special provision is made for agricultural mortgages under McKinney's Unconsolidated Laws of New York, § 8, making assignment effective against others only from the time of filing. No specific provision is made for filing assignments of conditional sales contracts, but the practice if is recognized in Personal Property Law, § 72. In Personal Property Law, §§ 302(10) and 411, the transfer of motor vehicle and retail instalment contracts is effective against the seller's creditors without filing.

Historical Note: This section was added in 1956 to provide additional flexibility. Note that it permits but does not require filing in respect of an assignment of a security interest perfected by filing. Compare Section 9–302(2) and Section 9–404(4). (1956 Recommendations, p. 304.)

In 1958 the section was further revised to separate, for clarification, the provisions for an assignment indicated in the financing statement from the provisions for a separate statement of assignment, and to provide that only one filing fee is payable when the assignment is indicated on the financing statement. (1958 Supplement, p. 19.)

Official Uniform Comment

Prior Uniform Statutory Provision: None.

Purposes:

This section provides a permissive device whereby a secured party who has assigned all or part of his interest may have the assignment noted of record. Note that under Section 9–302(2) no filing of such an assignment is required as a condition of continuing the perfected status of the security interest against creditors and transferees of the original debtor. A secured party who has assigned his interest might wish to have the fact noted of record, so that inquiries concerning the transaction would be addressed not to him but to the assignee (see Point 2 of Comment to Section 9–402).

After a secured party has assigned the rights of record, the assignee becomes the "secured party of record" and may file a continuation statement under Section 9–403, a termination statement under Section 9–404, or a statement of release under Section 9–406.

Where a mortgage of real estate is effective as a financing statement filed as a fixture filing (Section 9–402(6)), then assignment of record of the security interest may be made only in the manner in which an assignment of the mortgage may be made under the local state law.

Cross References:

Sections 9–302(2) and 9–402 through 9–406.

Definitional Cross References:

"Collateral." Sections 9–105.
"Debtor." Section 9–105.
"Financing statement." Section 9–402.
"Rights." Section 1–201.
"Secured party." Section 9–105.
"Signed." Section 1–201.
"Written." Section 1–201.

Section 9–406. Release of Collateral; Duties of Filing Officer; Fees.

A secured party of record may by his signed statement release all or a part of any collateral described in a filed financing statement. The statement of release is sufficient if it contains a description of the collateral being released, the name and address of the debtor, the name and address of the secured party, and the file number of the financing statement. A statement of release signed by a person other than the secured party of record must be accompanied by a separate written statement of assignment signed by the secured party of record and complying with subsection (2) of Section 9-405, including payment of the required fee. Upon presentation of such a statement of release to the filing officer he or she shall mark the statement with the date of filing and shall note the same upon the margins of the indices of the filing of the financing statement or, in the case of a computerized filing system he or she shall enter the release information and the date of filing into the computerized system. The secretary of state shall prescribe pursuant to the provisions of section ninety-six-a of the executive law the uniform fee for filing and noting such a statement of release on a form conforming to standards prescribed by the secretary of state, and the fee if such a statement otherwise conforms to the requirements of this section, plus, in either case, for each additional person, firm or organization, beyond the first, named as a debtor in the statement, an additional fee.

Amended by Laws, 1977, Ch. 866, eff. July 2, 1978; Laws 1982, Ch. 692, eff. Aug. 21, 1982; Laws 1986, Ch. 453, eff. July 17, 1986; Laws 1990, Ch. 561, eff. July 18, 1990; Laws 1996, Ch. 309, eff. July 13, 1996.

New York Annotations

This provision, like Section 9-405, is a permissive method of clearing the record. Note that Section 9-404 is a compulsory method, and see the annotation to that section for the present law. Debtor and Creditor Law, § 243, now permits release of collateral without consideration.

Historical Note: This new section has been added to provide additional flexibility. (1956 Recommendations, p. 304.)

Official Uniform Comment

Prior Uniform Statutory Provision: None.

Purposes:

Like the preceding section, this section provides a permissive device for noting of record any release of collateral. There is no requirement that such a statement be filed when collateral is released (cf. Section 9–404 on Termination Statements). It is merely a method of making the record reflect the true state of affairs so that fewer inquiries will have to be made by persons who consult the files.

If the statement of release is not signed by the secured party of record, the assignment procedure of Section 9–405(2) must be followed.

Cross Reference:

Section 9–404.

Definitional Cross References:

"Collateral." Section 9–105.
"Debtor." Section 9–105.
"Financing statement." Section 9–402.
"Secured party." Section 9–105.
"Signed." Section 1–201.

Section 9–407. Information From Filing Officer.

(1) If the person filing any financing statement, termination statement, statement of assignment, or statement of release, furnishes the filing officer a copy thereof, the filing officer, other than the secretary of state, shall upon request note upon the copy the file number and date of the filing of the original and deliver or send the copy to such person or shall deliver or send a computerized image of the first page of the filing setting forth the file number and date of the filing to such person or to such person as the secured party filing such statement may direct. The secretary of state shall, except as provided in section 9-404, deliver or send a computerized image of the first page of the filing of a financing statement, termination statement, statement of assignment, or statement of release to the secured party filing such statement or to such other person as the secured party filing such statement may direct. The computerized image of the first page of the filing shall show the file number and date of the filing of such statement. The secretary of state shall provide pursuant to the provisions of section ninety-six-a of the executive law, the uniform fee for the services of a filing officer under this subsection.

(2) Upon request of any person, the filing officer shall issue his certificate showing whether there is on file on the date and hour stated therein, any presently effective financing statement naming a particular debtor or naming a particular

debtor at an address supplied by the person making such request and any statement of assignment thereof and if there is, giving the date and hour of filing of each such statement and the names and addresses of each secured party therein. Such certificates shall also show whether there is on file on the date and hour stated therein, any notice of federal tax lien or certificate or notice affecting such lien, filed on or after July third, nineteen hundred sixty-six, naming the debtor and if there is, giving the date and hour of filing of each such notice or certificate. The secretary of state shall prescribe pursuant to the provisions of section ninety-six-a of the executive law the uniform fee for such a certificate if the request for the certificate is on a form conforming to standards prescribed by the secretary of state and other fees. Upon request the filing officer shall furnish a copy of any filed financing statement, notice of federal tax lien or notice or certificate affecting such lien, if filed on or after July third, nineteen hundred sixty-five, continuation statement, termination statement, statement of assignment or statement of release for a uniform fee prescribed by the secretary of state pursuant to section ninety-six-a of the executive law.

Amended by Laws 1963, Ch. 1003, Laws 1964, Ch. 476, eff. Sept. 27, 1964; Laws 1966, Ch. 608, eff. July 3, 1966; Laws 1982, Ch. 692, eff. Aug. 21, 1982; Laws 1986, Ch. 453, eff. July 17, 1986; Laws 1990, Ch. 561, eff. July 18, 1990; Laws 1996, Ch. 309, eff. July 13, 1996.

New York Annotations

This is an optional section and is similar to Lien Law, § 233, and Personal Property Law, § 70, which provide for the issuance of a receipt upon request by all filing officers outside of New York City. Personal Property Law, § 45 (factor's liens), provides for such receipts generally.

Official Uniform Comment

Prior Uniform Statutory Provision: None.

Purposes:

1. Subsection (1) requires the filing officer upon request to return to the secured party a copy of the financing statement on which the material data concerning the filing are noted. Receipt of such a copy will assure the secured party that the mechanics of filing have been complied with. Note, however, that under Section 9–403(1) the secured party does not bear the risk that the filing officer will not properly perform his duties; under that section the secured party has complied with the filing requirements when he presents his financing statement for filing and the filing fee has been tendered or the statement accepted by the filing officer.

2. Subsection (2) requires the filing officer on request to issue to any person who has tendered the proper fee his certificate as to what filings have been made against any particular debtor and to furnish copies of such filed financing statement. In view of the centralized filing system adopted by this Article (see Section 9–401 and Comment thereto), this provision is of obvious convenience to a person who wishes to know what the files contain but who cannot conveniently consult files located in the state capital.

Cross References:

Point 1: Section 9–403(1).
Point 2: Section 9–401.

Definitional Cross References:

"Debtor." Section 9–105.
"Financing statement." Section 9–402.
"Person." Section 1–201.
"Secured party." Section 9–105.
"Send." Section 1–201.

Section 9–408. Financing Statements Covering Consigned or Leased Goods.

A consignor or lessor of goods may file a financing statement using the terms "consignor," "consignee," "lessor," "lessee" or the like instead of the terms specified in Section 9-402. The provisions of this Part shall apply as appropriate to such a financing statement but its filing shall not of itself be a factor in determining whether or not the consignment or lease is intended as security (subsection (37) of Section 1-201). However, if it is determined for other reasons that the consignment or lease is so intended, a security interest of the consignor or lessor which attaches to the consigned or leased goods is perfected by such filing.

Added by L. 1977, Ch. 866, eff. July 2, 1978.

Official Uniform Comment

Prior Uniform Statutory Provisions: None.

Purposes:

1. Where filing is required under Sections 2–326(3) and 9–114 for a consignment which is not a security interest (Section 1–201(37)), this section authorizes the appropriate adaptations of terminology.

Apart from the rules in Part 4, the rules of this article using the terms "debtor" and "secured party" will not apply to consignments if they are not security interests. Section 9–114 on consignments essentially parallels Section 9–312(3) on inventory priorities, and the latter rule therefore does not apply to consignments. Section 2–326 states the rights of creditors of a consignee who has not filed or otherwise complied with subsection (3), and Section 9–301 on unperfected security interests is therefore not applicable. Section 2–326 and the law of consignments supply rules which are provided by Section 9–311 for security interest and that section is therefore not applicable to consignments. For reasons indicated in the Comment to Section 9–114, Section 9–306 on proceeds is inapplicable to consignments. An equivalent to the protection of a buyer in ordinary course of business against a security interest under Section 9–307(1) is provided against consignments by Section 2–403(2) and (3).

2. If a lease is actually intended as a security (Section 1–201(37)), this Article applies in full. But this question of intention is a doubtful one, and the lessor may choose to file for safety even while contending that the lease is a true lease for which no filing is required. This section authorizes filing with appropriate changes of terminology, and without affecting the substantive question of classification of the

lease. If the lease is a true lease, none of the provisions of the Article is applicable to the lease as an interest in chattel. Note, however, that the Article may be applicable to the lease in its aspect as a chattel paper. See Section 9–105(b).

Section 9–409. Destruction of Old Records.

Unless a filing officer has notice of an action pending relative thereto, he may remove from the files and destroy

(a) a lapsed financing statement, a lapsed continuation statement, a statement of assignment or release relating to either, and any index of any of them, one year or more after lapse; and

(b) a termination statement, the index on which it is noted and the related financing statement and any continuation statement, statement of assignment or statement of release pertaining thereto, one year or more after the filing of the termination statement.

Amended by 1965, Ch. 959, eff. July 19, 1965.

1977 Amendment

Section 9–409 was renumbered by L. 1977, ch. 866, effective July 2, 1978 from Section 9–408. A new Section 9-408 was inserted as above.

Section 9–410. Pre-Signing of Security Agreements and Financing Statements; Pre-filing of Financing Statements.

(1) Although signed prior to the effective date of this Act, a security agreement and a financing statement shall have the same effect on and after the effective date as if signed after this Act takes effect.

(2) Unless a filing officer other than the secretary of state files with the department of state on or before July thirty-first, nineteen hundred sixty-four, his certificate that financing statement swill not be accepted by him for filing prior to the effective date of this Act, a filing officer shall accept financing statements for filing on and after September eighth, nineteen hundred sixty-four; the provisions of this Act and of all other laws relating to financing statements and the filing of financing statements apply to the financing statements so filed notwithstanding that this Act or such other laws have not then taken effect; notwithstanding the date and hour of filing marked on the statement each financing statement so filed shall be deemed to have been filed on the date and at the hour when the office of the filing officer is first open for the transaction of business on or after the effective date of this Act.

Added by Laws 1964, Ch. 476, eff. April 10,1964.

1977 Amendment

Section 9–410 was renumbered Section 9–410 by L.1977, ch. 866, effective July 2, 1978, from Former Section 9–409.

UCC

PART 5

DEFAULT

Section 9–501. Default; Procedure When Security Agreement Covers Both Real and Personal Property.

(1) When a debtor is in default under a security agreement, a secured party has the right sand remedies provided in this Part and except as limited by subsection (3) those provided in the security agreement. He may reduce his claim to judgment, foreclose or otherwise enforce the security interest by any available judicial procedure. If the collateral is documents the secured party may proceed either as to the documents or as to the goods covered thereby. A secured party in possession has the rights, remedies and duties provided in Section 9–207. The rights and remedies referred to in this subsection are cumulative.

(2) After default, the debtor has the rights and remedies provided in this Part, those provided in the security agreement and those provided in Section 9–207.

(3) To the extent that they give rights to the debtor and impose duties on the secured party, the rules stated in the sections and subsections referred to below may not be waived or varied except as provided with respect to compulsory disposition of collateral (sub-section (3) of Section 9-504 and subsections (1) and (2) of Section 9-505) and with respect to redemption of collateral (Section 9-506) but the parties may by agreement determine the standards by which the fulfillment of these rights and duties is to be measured if such standards are not manifestly unreasonable:

(a) subsection (2) of Section 9–502 and subsection (2) of Section 9–504 insofar as they require accounting for surplus proceeds of collateral;

(b) subsection (3) of Section 9–504 and subsection (1) of Section 9–505 which deal with disposition of collateral;

(c) subsection (2) of Section 9–505 which deals with acceptance of collateral as discharge of obligation;

(d) Section 9–506 which deals with redemption of collateral; and

(e) subsection (1) of Section 9–507 which deals with the secured party's liability for failure to comply with this Part.

(4) If the security agreement covers both real and personal property, the secured party may proceed under this Part as to the personal property or he may proceed as to both the real and the personal property in accordance with his rights and remedies in respect of the real property in which case the provisions of this Part do not apply.

(5) When a secured party has reduced his claim to judgment the lien of any levy which maybe made upon his collateral by virtue of any execution based upon the judgment shall relate back to the date of the perfection of the security interest in such collateral. A judicial sale, pursuant to such execution, is a

foreclosure of the security interest by judicial procedure within the meaning of this section, and the secured party may purchase at the sale thereafter hold the collateral free of any other requirements of this Article.

Amended by Laws 1977, Ch. 866, eff. July 2, 1978.

New York Annotations

The overall scheme of this section is one that provides for rights on default depending upon the type of collateral involved, rather than a distinct set of enforcement rules for each security device as under present law.

The Code subjects realization on all security interests to statutory control even though other remedies by agreement are permitted. In New York today, rights upon default of chattel mortgages for more than $3,000 or for a commercial or business use are not regulated by statute, and enforcement procedure generally depends upon the contractual agreement of the parties. See Sheeley v. Holmes Music Co., 189 App.Div. 756, 179 N.Y.S. 202 (1919). Although it is not completely clear, the agreement between pledgor and pledgee apparently does not need to make an enforcement sale subject to statutory restrictions such as the notice required under Lien Law, § 201. Matter of Kiamie, 309 N.Y. 325, 130 N.E.2d 745 (1955); Fullerton v. Northern Bank of N.Y., 184 App.Div. 37 171 N.Y.S. 547 (1918). Compare Lien Law, § 202–a,and the definition of "lienor" in Lien Law, § 2. Under the Code, this doctrine, making the contractual agreement controlling, would be subject to the limitation of subsection (3) of Section 9–501 which specifically enumerates the provisions which may not be varied by agreement.

The following summary of relevant law and statutes for enforcement upon default of the various types of existing security devices will help to indicate some differences between the Code and present law:

Chattel mortgages may now be enforced by:

(i) An action to recover a money judgment for the mortgage debt. Ziepke v. Cusimano, 222 App.Div. 827, 226 N.Y.S. 254 (1928); Emerson v. Knapp, 129 App.Div. 827, 114 N.Y.S. 794 (1909). This is, of course, entirely consistent with the second sentence of subsection (1).

(ii) Holding possession of the property after default, extinguishing the debt only up to the value of the property. Strong v. Dahm, 39 N.Y.S.2d 666 (1942). This appears to be contrary to Code Section 9–505(2) which calls for "satisfaction of the obligation." Under present law the mortgage is deemed paid to the extent of the value of the property. Harrison v. Hall, 239 N.Y. 51,145 N.E. 737 (1924).

(iii) Seizure and sale of the property pursuant to a power granted in the mortgage. Briggs v. Oliver, 68 N.Y. 336 (1877). Under the Code this procedure is recognized, but also limited by Sections 9–501, 9–503, and 9–504.

(iv) Bringing an action of foreclosure pursuant to the provisions of Lien Law, §§ 206–210. This is in *accord* with Code Section 9–501. It should be noted that Lien Law, § 206, defines a lien upon a chattel as "a chattel mortgage to secure the payment of a loan of money or other debt, or the purchase price of chattels, a contract of conditional sale of personal property, and a hiring of personal property whose title is not to vest in the person hiring until payment of a certain sum . . ."

Where there is a chattel mortgage given to secure the purchase price of goods, wares, or merchandise amounting to $3,000 or less, sold for any use other than a commercial or business use, the enforcement upon default is regulated by Lien Law, §§ 239–a and 239–f. See Lien Law, § 239.

Other than this limited area, it is clear that chattel mortgage enforcement is pretty much a matter of common law interpretation. For complete coverage see Eager, Chattel Mortgages and Conditional Sales, §§ 223–256.

On the other hand, provisions for enforcement upon default on a conditional sales contract are stated in Personal Property Law, §§ 76-80. In addition, the seller, if he wishes, can also reduce his claim to a money judgment. Personal Property Law, § 63; Thomas Nelson & Sons Publishing Co. v. Bonner, 200 N.Y.S. 341 (1923). As noted above, (iv), he can bring an action to foreclose under Lien Law, 1 206-210. See Personal Property Law, § 80–d,as to election of remedies.

Personal property Law, § 56, provides for the entruster's rights on default in a trust receipt transaction.

A pledgee may: (1) bring an action to enforce the debt; (2) obtain a judicial sale; or (3) exercise any power of sale pursuant to the pledge agreement. Restatement, Security, § 48.Compare generally on enforcement: Restatement, Security, §§ 47-48. See restriction imposed by Code Section 9–504.

The reference in subsection (2) to Code Section 9–207, providing that a secured party must use reasonable care in the custody and preservation of collateral in his possession, is in *accord* with present New York law. Coe v. Cassidy, 72 N.Y. 133, 139 (1878). See Historical Note to Section 9–207.

The provision in subsection (4) permitting, where the collateral consists of both real and personal property, a foreclosure under real property law, is probably new to New York law. Where an instrument mortgaging real property also transfers personal property as security, the instrument is considered a chattel mortgage insofar as it relates to personal property and is to such extent subject to the rules governing chattel mortgages. Zartman v. First National Bank, 189 N.Y.267, 269, 82 N.E. 127 (1907); Prudential Insurance Co. v. McGoldrick, 256 App.Div. 205, 9 N.Y.S.2d 515, aff'd 281 N.Y. 595, 22 N.E.2d 166 (1939).

Historical Note: Various changes were made in this section in 1956 and 1958.The changes in subsection (1) and (2) were for clarification and made it clear that the statement of rights and remedies in Part 5 does not exclude other remedies provided by agreement or by law, and that the remedies are cumulative. Subsection (3) was entirely rewritten to specify clearly which provisions of Part 5 are not subject to variation by agreement. Compare the 1958 changes in Section 9–207. Provisions not specified in the revised subsection (3) are subject to the general rules stated in Section 1–102(3). This follows a suggestion of the Law Revision Commission. The change in subsection (4) made it clear that all rights and remedies provided by the law of real property are made applicable to personal property by this Act if the security agreement covers both real and personal property. Subsection (5) was added in Supp. No. 1 to make it clear that a judicial sale on a judgment is a foreclosure of a security interest to which the requirements of Part 5 are not applicable. (1958 Supplement, p. 21; 1956 Recommendations, p.307; Excerpts, pp. 482-483.)

Official Uniform Comment

Prior Uniform Statutory Provision: Section 6, Uniform Trust Receipts Act; Sections 16 through 26, Uniform Conditional Sales Act.

Purposes:

1. The rights of the secured party in the collateral after the debtor's default are of the essence of a security transaction. These are the rights which distinguish the secured from the unsecured lender. This section and the following six sections state those rights as well as the limitations on their free exercise which legislative policy requires for the protection not only of the defaulting debtor but of other creditors. But subsections (1) and (2) make it clear that the statement of rights and remedies in this Part does not exclude other remedies provided by agreement.

2. Following default and the taking possession of the collateral by the secured party, there is no longer any distinction between the security interest which before default

was non-possessory and that which was possessory under a pledge. Therefore no general distinction is taken in this Part between the rights of a non-possessory secured party and those of a pledgee; the latter, being in possession of the collateral at default, will of course not have to avail himself of the right to take possession under Section 9–503.

3. Section 9–207 states rights, remedies and duties with respect to collateral in the secured party's possession. That section applies not only to the situation where he is in possession before default, as a pledgee, but also, by subsections (1) and (2) of this section, to the secured party in possession after default. Nevertheless the relations of the parties have been changed by default, and Section 9–207 as it applies after default must be read together with this Part. In particular, agreements permitted under Section 9–207 cannot waive or modify the rights of the debtor contrary to subsection (3) of this section.

4. Section 1–102(3) states rules to determine which provisions of this Act are mandatory and which may be varied by agreement. In general, provisions which relate to matters which come up between immediate parties may be varied by agreement. In the area of rights after default our legal system has traditionally looked with suspicion on agreements designed to cut down the debtor's rights and free the secured party of his duties; no mortgage clause has ever been allowed to clog the equity of redemption. The default situation offers great scope for overreaching; the suspicious attitude of the courts has been grounded in common sense.

Subsection (3) of this section contains a codification of this long standing and deeply rooted attitude: the specified rights of the debtor and duties of the secured party may not be waived or varied except as stated. Provisions not specified in subsection (3) are subject to the general rules stated in Section 1–102(3).

5. The collateral for many corporate security issues consists of both real and personal property. In the interest of simplicity and speed subsection (4) permits, although it does not require, the secured party to proceed as to both real and personal property in accordance with his rights and remedies in respect of the real property. Except for the permission so granted, this Act leaves to other state law all questions of procedure with respect to real property. For example, this Act does not determine whether the secured party can proceed against the real estate alone and later proceed in a separate action against the personal property in accordance with his right sand remedies against the real estate. By such separate actions the secured party "proceeds as to both," and this Part does not apply in either action. But subsection (4) does give him an option to proceed under this Part as to the personal property.

6. Under subsection (1) a secured party is entitled to reduce his claim to judgment or to foreclose his interest by any available procedure, outside this Article, which state law may provide. The first sentence of subsection (5) makes clear that any judgment lien which the secured party may acquire against the collateral is, so to say, a continuation of his original interest (if perfected) and not the acquisition of a new interest or a transfer of property to satisfy an antecedent debt. The judgment lien is therefore stated to relate back to the date of perfection of the security interest. The second sentence of the subsection makes clear that a judicial sale following judgment, execution and levy is one of the methods of foreclosure contemplated by subsection (1); such a sale is governed by other law and not by this Article and the restrictions which this Article imposes on the right of a secured party to buy in the collateral at a sale under Section 9–504 do not apply.

Cross References:

Point 2: Section 9–503.
Point 3: Section 9–207.
Point 4: Section 1–102(3).
Point 5: Sections 9–102(1) and 9–104(j).

UCC

Point 6: Section 9–504.

Definitional Cross References:

"Agreement." Section 1–201.
"Collateral." Section 9–105.
"Debtor." Section 9–105.
"Documents." Section 9–105.
"Goods." Section 9–105.
"Remedy." Section 1–201.
"Rights." Section 1–201.
"Secured party." Section 9–105.
"Security agreement." Section 9–105.
"Security interest." Section 1–201.

Section 9–502. Collection Rights of Secured Party.

(1) When so agreed and in any event on default the secured party is entitled to notify an account debtor or the obligor on an instrument to make payment to him whether or not the assignor was theretofore making collections on the collateral, and also to take control or any proceeds to which he is entitled under Section 9–306.

(2) A secured party who by agreement is entitled to charge back uncollected collateral or otherwise to full or limited recourse against the debtor and who undertakes to collect from the account debtors or obligors must proceed in a commercially reasonable manner and may deduct his reasonable expenses of realization from the collections. If the security agreement secures an indebtedness, the secured party must account to the debtor for any surplus, and unless otherwise agreed, the debtor is liable for any deficiency. But, if the underlying transactions was a sale of accounts or chattel paper, the debtor is entitled to any surplus or is liable for any deficiency only if the security agreement so provides.

Amended by Laws 1977, Ch. 866, eff. July 2, 1978.

New York Annotations

This section is completely new, and there are no directly relevant New York decisions or statutory provisions. See Flynn v. Dick, 13 A.D.2d 756, 215 N.Y.S.2d 382 (1961). The section, generally, is a recognition of accepted accounts receivable financing practices with the introduction of a new legal concept, "commercially reasonable manner." The difference between an assignment of accounts receivable and the factoring sale of accounts, as discussed in Comment 2, is well established, as is the difference between "notification" financing and "non-notification" financing, mentioned in Comment 1. For judicial recognition of the practice of factoring in respect of accounts, see Irving Trust Co. v. B. Lindner & Bros., 264 N.Y. 165, 190 N.E. 332 (1934).

Historical Note: Changes were made in the caption and in the statement of subsection (2) for clarification. The last two sentences were added to subsection (2) for the same reason. (1956 Recommendations, p. 308; Excerpts, p. 483.)

Official Uniform Comment

Prior Uniform Statutory Provision: None.

Purposes:

1. The assignee of accounts, chattel paper, or instruments holds as collateral property which is not only the most liquid asset of the debtor's business but also property which may be collected without any interruption of the business, assuming it to continue after default. The situation is far different from that where the collateral is inventory or equipment, whose removal may bring the business to halt. Furthermore the problems of valuation and identification, present where the collateral is tangible chattels, do not arise so sharply on the assignment of intangibles. Considerations, similar although not identical, apply to assignments of general intangibles, which are also covered by the rule of the section. Consequently, this section recognizes the fact that financing by assignment of intangibles lacks many of the complexities which arise after default in other types of financing, and allows the assignee to liquidate in the regular course of business by collecting whatever may become due on the collateral, whether or not the method of collection contemplated by the security arrangement before default was direct (i.e., payment by the account debtor to the assignees, "notification" financing) or indirect (i.e., payment by the account debtor to the assignor, "non-notification" financing). By agreement, of course, the secured party may have the right to give notice and to make collections before default.

2. In one form of accounts receivable financing, which is found in the "factoring" arrangements which are common in the textile industry, the assignee assumes the credit risk—that is, he buys the account under an agreement which does not provide for recourse or charge back against the assignor in the event the account proves uncollectible. Under such an arrangement, neither the debtor nor his creditors have any legitimate concern with the disposition which the assignee makes of the accounts. Under another form of accounts receivable financing, however, the assignee does not assume the credit risk and retains a right of full or limited recourse or charge back for uncollectible accounts. In such a case both debtor and creditors have a right that the assignee not dump the accounts, if the result will be to increase a possible deficiency claim or to reduce a possible surplus.

3. Where an assignee has a right of charge-back or a right of recourse, subsection (2) provides that liquidation must be made with due regard to the interest of the assignor and of his other creditor–"in a commercially reasonable manner" (compare Section 9–504 and see Section 9–507(2))—and the proceeds allocated to the expenses of realization and to the indebtedness. If the "charge-back" provisions of he assignment arrangement provide only for "charge-back" of bad accounts against a reserve, the debtor's claim to surplus and his liability for a deficiency are limited to the amount of the reserve.

4. Financing arrangements of the type dealt with by this section are between business men. The last sentence of subsection (2) therefore preserves freedom of contract, and the subsection recognizes that there may be a true sale of accounts or chattel paper although recourse exists. The determination whether a particular assignment constitutes a sale or a transfer for security is left to the courts. Note that, under Section 9–102, this Article applies both to sales and to security transfers of such intangibles.

Cross References:

Sections 9–205 and 9–306.
Point 3: Sections 9–504 and 9–507(2).
Point 4: Sections 9–102(1)(b) and 9–104(f).

Definitional Cross References:

"Account." Section 9–106.
"Account debtor." Section 9–105.
"Agreement." Section 1–201.
"Chattel paper." Section 9–105.
"Collateral." Section 9–105.
"Debtor." Section 9–105.
"Instrument." Section 9–105.
"Notify." Section 1–201.
"Proceeds." Section 9–306.
"Secured party." Section 9–105.
"Security agreement." Section 9–105.

Section 9–503. Secured Party's Right to Take Possession After Default.

Unless otherwise agreed a secured party has on default the right to take possession of the collateral. In taking possession a secured party may proceed without judicial process if this can bed one without breach of the peace or may proceed by action. If the security agreement so provides the secured party may require the debtor to assemble the collateral and make it available to the secured party at a place to be designated by the secured party which is reasonably convenient to both parties. Without removal a secured party may render equipment unusable, and may dispose of collateral on the debtor's premises under Section 9–504.

New York Annotations

Substantially similar provisions for taking possession of the collateral now exist in Personal property Law, §§ 76, 77 (conditional sales); Personal Property Law, § 56(2) (trust receipts); Lien Law, §§ 239–a, 239–b (chattel mortgages given to secure a purchase price of $3,000 or less in a non-commercial transaction). The right also is recognized in case law for chattel mortgages not covered by statute: Lewis v. Palmer, 28 N.Y. 271, 276 (1863). No specific provision for taking possession exists under Personal Property Law, §45 (factor's lien).

Under Personal Property Law, § 76, and Lien Law, § 239–a, there is aright of repossession only where the contract so provides, whereas, under the Code, repossession is a right of the secured party unless otherwise agreed.

The provision in this section that in lieu of removal the lender may render equipment unusable or dispose of collateral on the debtor's premises, has no counterpart in present law.

Personal Property Law, § 77, and Lien Law, § 239–b, allow a creditor to give 20 to 40 days' notice of intention to retake, which will cut off the debtor's redemption rights in the event he does not perform the obligations in which he has made default before the day set for retaking. No such provision is included in the Code.

Historical Note: The language following "breach of the peace" and between "place" and "reasonably convenient" was added for clarification. (1956 Recommendations, p. 308; Excerpts, p. 483.)

Official Uniform Comment

Prior Uniform Statutory Provision: Section 6, Uniform Trust Receipts Act; Sections 16 and 17, Uniform Conditional Sales Act.

Purposes:

Under this Article the secured party's right to possession of the collateral (if he is not already in possession as pledgee) accrues on default unless otherwise agreed in the security agreed in the security agreement. This Article follows the provisions of the earlier uniform legislation in allowing the secured party in most cases to take possession without the issuance of judicial process. In the case of collateral such as heavy equipment, the physical removal from the debtor's plant and the storage of the equipment pending resale may be exceedingly expensive and in some cases impractical. The section therefore provides that in lieu of removal the lender may render equipment unusable or dispose of collateral on the debtor's premises. The authorization to render equipment unusable or to dispose of collateral without removal would not justify unreasonable action by the secured party, since, under Section 9–504(3), all his actions in connection with disposition must be taken in a "commercially reasonable manner."

Cross Reference:

Section 9–504.

Definitional Cross References:

"Action." Section 1–201.
"Collateral." Section 9–105.
"Debtor." Section 9–105.
"Equipment." Section 9–109.
"Rights." Section 1–201.
"Secured party." Section 9–105.
"Security agreement." Section 9–105.

Section 9–504. Secured Party's Right to Dispose of Collateral After Default; Effect of Disposition.

(1) A secured party after default may sell, lease or otherwise dispose of any or all of the collateral in its then condition or following any commercially reasonable preparation or processing. Any sale of goods is subject to the Article on Sales (Article 2). The proceeds of disposition shall be applied in the order following to

(a) the reasonable expenses of retaking, holding, preparing for sale or lease, selling, leasing and the like and, to the extent provided for in the agreement and not prohibited by law, the reasonable attorneys' fees and legal expenses incurred by the secured party;

(b) the satisfaction of indebtedness secured by the security interest under which the disposition is made;

(c) the satisfaction of indebtedness secured by any subordinate security interest in the collateral if written notification of demand therefor is received before distribution of the proceeds is completed, but only to the extent of the proceeds undistributed when such notification is received. If requested by the secured party, the holder of a subordinate security interest must seasonably furnish reasonable proof of his interest, file with the secured party a sufficient indemnity bond, and satisfy any other reasonable requirements imposed by the

UCC

secured party, and unless he does so, the secured party need not comply with his demand.

(2) If the interest secures an indebtedness, the secured party must account to the debtor for any surplus, and, unless otherwise agreed, the debtor is liable for any deficiency. But if the underlying transaction was a sale of accounts, or chattel paper, the debtor is entitled to any surplus or is liable for any deficiency only if the security agreement so provides.

(3) Disposition of the collateral may be by public or private proceedings and may be made by way of one or more contracts. Sale or other disposition may be as a unit or in parcels and at any time and place and on any terms but every aspect of the disposition including the method, manner, time, place and terms must be commercially reasonable. Unless collateral is perishable or threatens to decline speedily in value or is of a type customarily sold on a recognized market, reasonable notification of the time and place of any public sale or reasonable notification of the time after which any private sale or other intended disposition is to be made shall be sent by the secured party to the debtor, if he has not signed after default a statement renouncing or modifying his right to notification of sale. In the case of consumer goods no other notification need be sent. In other cases notification shall be sent to any other secured party from whom the secured party has received (before sending his notification to the debtor or before the debtor's renunciation of his rights) written notice of a claim of an interest in the collateral. The secured party may buy at any public sale and if the collateral is of a type customarily sold in a recognized market or is of a type which is the subject of widely distributed standard price quotations he may buy at private sale.

(4) When collateral is disposed of by a secured party after default, the disposition transfers to a purchaser for value all of the debtor's rights therein, discharges the security interest under which it is made and any security interest or lien subordinate thereto. The purchaser takes free of all such rights and interests even though the secured party fails to comply with the requirements of this Part or of any judicial proceedings

(a) in the case of a public sale, if the purchaser has no knowledge of any defects in the sale and if he does not buy in collusion with the secured party, other bidders or the person conducting the sale; or

(b) in any other case, if the purchaser acts in good faith.

(5) A person who is liable to a secured party under a guaranty, indorsement, repurchase agreement or the like and who receives a transfer of collateral from the secured party or is subrogated to his rights has thereafter the rights and duties of the secured party. Such a transfer of collateral is not a sale or disposition of the collateral under this Article.

Amended by Laws 1977, Ch. 866, eff. July 2, 1978.

New York Annotations

Although it differs as to details, this section is substantially in *accord* with present New York law. The following is a summary of the present law:

After repossession under a conditional sales contract, the seller must sell the goods at a public sale within 30 days after the retaking, if the buyer has paid 50 percent of the purchase price. The seller must give the buyer not less than 10 days' notice. Exacting public notice requirements are stated. Personal Property Law, § 80. The Code permits a private sale.

An action may be maintained to foreclose a "lien" upon a chattel under Lien Law, §§ 206–210. "Lien" is defined as follows: ". . . a chattel mortgage to secure the payment of a loan of money or other debt, or the purchase price of chattels, a contract of conditional sale of personal property, and a hiring of personal property where title is not to vest in the person until payment of a certain sum, shall be deemed a lien upon a chattel." Lien Law, § 206.

Where the mortgage merely states in effect that the mortgagee, upon default, may sell the property at public or private sale, the only general requirement is that the sale be fairly and honestly made within a reasonable time. McKinney v. Donahue, 59 N.Y.S. 2d 726 (1946), and cases cited. However, where the mortgage is one to secure the unpaid price of goods amounting to $3,000 or less, sold for other than a commercial or business use, it is provided that the mortgagee, after retaking the goods, shall hold them for ten days for the purpose of allowing redemption by the mortgagor, unless the mortgagee has served a formal notice of intention to retake the goods as provided by statute. Lien Law, §§ 239–b, 239–c.

(1) As the comment indicates, this subsection follows the more liberal provision of Personal property Law, § 56(3)(b) (but requiring five days' notice before the sale, which may be public or private).

Pledges are apparently not regulated exclusively by statute. Upon default the pledgee may, after giving notice to the debtor (which may be waived), sell at a public or private sale. The sale must be made in good faith. Matter of Kiamie, 309 N.Y. 325, 130 N.E.2d 745 (1955); General Phoenix Corp. v. Cabot, 300 N.Y. 87, 89 N.E.2d 238 (1949), First Trust & Deposit Co. v. Potter, 155 Misc. 106, 278 N.Y.S. 847 (1935). Restatement, Security, § 48, but compare Restatement, Security, § 49, Comment b. The pledge may also sell under Lien Law, §§ 200–205, and in any event may himself purchase at a public sale under Lien Law, § 202–b.

(2) The Code follows present law, in general, in respect of the application of proceeds and the debtor's right to surplus and liability for deficiency. Personal Law, §§ 56(3)(b),80 a, 80–b; Lien Law, § 239–d; Coe v. Cassidy, 72 N.Y. 133 (1878) (chattel mortgages); Keshishian Bros., Inc. v. Deverian, 279 App.Div. 324, 109 N.Y.S.2d 378, amended, 280 App.Div. 910, 116 N.Y.S.2d 925 (1952) (pledges).

The provision for distribution of surplus proceeds to holders of junior security interests making a written demand therefor is new. Under present law such surplus proceeds go to the debtor. Personal Property Law, §§ 56, 80–a.

(3) The requirements in this subsection for notice to the debtor are substantially the same as those in Personal Property Law, § 79, although no particular public posting or newspaper notice is required by the Code. Notice of sale pursuant to a chattel mortgage is not now required, Chamberlain v. Martin, 43 Barb. 607 (1865), unless provided for in the contract. Sales by pledges usually require notice to the pledgor, but such requirement may be waived. Phillips v. Bank of Athens Trust Co., 202 Misc. 698, 119 N.Y.S.2d 47 (1952). See Restatement, Security, § 48(a) and Comment b.

The provision for notice to junior secured holders in non-consumer goods cases appears to be a new feature.

The exception to the notice requirement, where the goods are perishable, is similar to the provisions in Personal Property Law, § 78, and Lien Law, § 239–c.

The provision in Section 9–504 (3), allowing the secured party to buy at any public sale but at a private sale only under certain conditions, would change present law. Under Personal property Law, § 79 (conditional sales), the sale can only be public, but "the seller may bid for the goods . . . ." Under Personal Property Law, § 56(3)(b) (trust receipts), the sale may be public or private but the entruster can purchase only at a public sale. In chattel mortgage foreclosure sales, the sale can be public or private and the mortgagee can be a purchaser at either, Casserly v. Wither bee, 119 N.Y. 522, 23 N.E. 1000 (1890), but where a mortgagee, upon a seizure of the mortgaged chattels, sells them to himself at a private sale, the sale will generally be considered an irregular one requiring the mortgagee to give the mortgagor a fair credit for the chattels, the amount of which is to be determined on a trial. Strong v. Dahm, 39 N.Y.S.2d 266 (1942). Generally, a pledgee may not purchase the pledged property upon the sale after default unless there be express authorization to do so in the contract or unless the sale is conducted by of equity. Restatement, Security, § 51. Under Lien Law, § 202–b, the pledgee is now specifically permitted to buy at a public sale.

(4) This subsection is in *accord* with Personal Property Law, 56(3)(c), which provides that "A purchaser in good faith and for value from an entruster in possession takes free of the trustee's interest, even in a case in which the entruster is liable to the trustee for conversion." Compare Civil Practice Act, § 109–a [now CPLR 2003].

(5) This result would seem to follow from the definition of "seller" in Personal Property Law, § 61 (conditional sales). Manhattan Taxi Service Corp. v. Checker Cab Mfg. Corp., 253 N.Y. 455, 171 N.E. 705 (1930).

Historical Note: Subsection (1) was changed to broaden the scope of expenses that can be charged to proceeds on disposition of collateral, and to require a subordinate secured party to furnish proof of his interest.

In addition to clarifying changes in subsection (3), the requirement of notice of time and place is limited to public sales. Since the exact time and place of private sale may not be known, the notice need only state the time after which private sale may be made. The changes also eliminate notification to any other secured party when consumer goods are sold because there normally is no such other secured party. Finally, notification to another secured party is required only in respect of one who has filed a financing statement indexed in the name of the debtor in this state.

The changes in subsection (4) are clarifying, and the reference to collusion by the persons conducting the sale meets a suggestion of the Law Revision Commission. New subsection (5) was added to state definitely the status of a third party stepping into the shoes of the secured party. (1956 Recommendations, p. 310; Excerpts, p. 483.)

Official Uniform Comment

Prior Uniform Statutory Provision: Section 6, Uniform Trust Receipts Act; Sections 19, 20, 21, and 22, Uniform Conditional Sales Act.

Purposes:

1. The Uniform Trust Receipts Act provides that an entruster in possession after default holds the collateral with the rights and duties of a pledgee, and, in particular, that he may sell such collateral at public or private sale with a right to claim deficiency and a duty to account for any surplus. The Uniform Conditional Sales Act insisted on a sale at public auction with elaborate provisions for the giving of notice of sale. This section follows the more liberal provisions of the Trust Receipts Act. Although public sale is recognized, it is hoped that private sale will been couraged where, as

is frequently the case, private sale through commercial channels will result in higher realization on collateral for the benefit of all parties. The only restriction placed on the secured party's method of disposition is that it must be commercially reasonable. In this respect this section follows the provisions of the section on resale by a seller following a buyer's rejection of goods (Section 2–706). Subsection (1) does not restrict disposition to sale: the collateral may be sold, leased, or otherwise disposed of–subject of course to the general requirement of subsection (2) that all aspects of the disposition be "commercially reasonable." Section 9–507(2) states some tests as to what is "commercially reasonable."

2. Subsection (1) in general follows prior law in its provisions for the application of proceeds and for the debtor's right to surplus and liability for deficiency. Under paragraph (1)(c) the secured party, after paying expenses of retaking and disposition and his own debt, is required to pay over remaining proceeds to the extent necessary to satisfy the holder of any junior security interest in the same collateral if the holder of the junior interest has made a written demand and furnished on request reasonable proof of his interest: this provision is necessary in view of the fact that under subsection (4) the junior interest is discharged by the disposition. Since the requirement is conditioned on written demand, it should not result in undue burden on the secured party making the disposition. It should be noted also that under Section 9–112 where the secured party knows that the collateral is owned by a person who is not the debtor, the owner of the collateral and not the debtor is entitled to any surplus.

3. In any security transaction the debtor (or the owner of the collateral if other than the debtor: see Section 9–112) is entitled to any surplus which results from realization on the collateral; the debtor will also, unless otherwise agreed, be liable for any deficiency. Subsection (2) so provides. Since this Article covers sales of certain intangibles as well as transfers for security, the subsection also provides that apart from agreement the right to surplus or liability for deficiency does not accrue where the transaction between debtor and secured party was a sale and not a security transaction.

4. Subsection (4) provides that a purchaser for value from a secured party after default takes free of any rights of the debtor and of the holders of junior security interests and liens, even though the secured party has not complied with the requirement of this Part or of any judicial proceedings. This subsection follows a similar provision in the Uniform Trust Receipts Act and in the section of this Act on resale by a seller (Section 2–706). Where the purchaser for value has bought at a public sale he is protected under paragraph (a) if he has no knowledge of any defects in the sale and was not guilty of collusive practices. Where the purchaser for value has bought at a private sale he must, to receive the protection of paragraph (b), qualify in all respects as a purchaser in good faith. Thus while the purchaser at a private sale is required to proceed in the exercise of good faith, the purchaser at public sale is protected so long as he is not actively in bad faith, and is put under no duty to inquire into the circumstances of the sale.

5. Both the Uniform Trust Receipts Act and the Uniform Conditional Sales Act required awaiting period after repossession and before sale (five days in the Trust Receipts Act, ten days in the Conditional Sales Act). Under subsection (3), the secured party in most cases is required to give reasonable notification of disposition to the debtor unless the debtor has after default signed a statement renouncing or modifying his right to notification of sale.

The secured party must also (except for consumer goods) give notice to any other secured parties who have in writing given notice of a claim of an interest in the collateral. This latter notice must be given before the debtor renounces his rights or before the secured party gives his notification to the debtor. Compare Section 9–505(2). Except for the requirement of notification there is no statutory period during which the collateral must be held before disposition. "Reasonable notification" is not defined in this Article; at a minimum it must be sent in such time that persons entitled to receive it will have sufficient time to take appropriate steps to protect their interests by taking part in the sale or other disposition if they so desire.

6. Section 19 of the Uniform Conditional Sales Act required that sale be made not more than thirty days after possession taken by the conditional vendor. The Uniform Trust Receipts Act contained no comparable provision. Here again this Article follows the Trust Receipts Act, and no period is set within which the disposition must be made, except in the case of consumer goods which under Section 9–505(1) must in certain instances be sold within ninety days after the secured party has taken possession. The failure to prescribe a statutory period during which disposition must be made is in line with the policy adopted in this Article to encourage disposition by private sale through regular commercial channels. It may, for example, be wise not to dispose of goods when the market has collapsed, or to sell a large inventory in parcels over a period of time instead of in bulk. Note, however, that under subsection (3) every aspect of the sale or other disposition of the collateral must be commercially reasonable; this specifically includes method, manner, time, place and terms. See Section 9–507(2). Under that provision a secured party who without proceeding under Section 9–505(2) held collateral a long time without disposing of it, thus running up large storage charges against the debtor, where no reason existed for not making a prompt sale, might well be found not to have acted in a "commercially reasonable" manner. See also Section 1–203 on the general obligation of good faith.

Cross References:

Point 1: Sections 2–706 and 9–507(2).
Point 2: Section 9–112.
Point 3: Sections 9–102(1)(b) and 9–112.
Point 4: Section 2–706.
Point 6: Sections 9–505 and 9–507(2).

Definitional Cross References:

"Account." Section 9–106.
"Agreement." Section 1–201.
"Chattel paper." Section 9–105.
"Collateral." Section 9–105.
"Consumer goods." Section 9–109.
"Contract." Section 1–201.
"Debtor." Section 9–105.
"Financing statement." Section 9–402.
"Gives notification." Section 1–201.
"Good faith." Section 1–201.
"Goods." Section 9–105.
"Knowledge." Section 1–201.
"Person." Section 1–201.
"Proceeds." Section 9–306.
"Purchaser." Section 1–201.
"Receives notification." Section 1–201.
"Rights." Section 1–201.
"Sale." Sections 2–106 and 9–105.
"Secured party." Section 9–105.
"Security agreement." Section 9–105.
"Security interest." Section 1–201.

"Send." Section 1–201.
"Term." Section 1–201.
"Value." Section 1–201.
"Written." Section 1–201.

Section 9–505. Compulsory Disposition of Collateral; Acceptance of the Collateral as Discharge of Obligation.

(1) If the debtor has paid sixty per cent of the cash price in the case of a purchase money security interest in consumer goods or sixty per cent of the loan in the case of another security interest in consumer goods, and has not signed after default a statement renouncing or modifying his rights under this Part a secured party who has taken possession of collateral must dispose of it under Section 9–504 and if he fails to do so within ninety days after he takes possession the debtor at his option may recover in conversion or under Section 9–507(1) on secured party's liability.

(2) In any other case involving consumer goods or any other collateral a secured party in possession may, after default, propose to retain the collateral in satisfaction of the obligation. Written notice of such proposal shall be sent to the debtor if he has not signed after default a statement renouncing or modifying his rights under this subsection. In the case of consumer goods no other notice need be given. In other cases notice shall be sent to any other secured party from whom the secured party has received (before sending his notice to the debtor or before the debtor's renunciation of his rights) written notice of a claim of an interest in the collateral. If the secured party receives objection in writing from a person entitled to receive notification within twenty one days after the notice was sent, the secured party must dispose of the collateral under Section 9-504. In the absence of such written objection the secured party may retain the collateral in satisfaction of the debtor's obligation.

Amended by Laws 1977, Ch. 866, eff. July 2, 1978.

New York Annotations

The policy of this section is in substantial *accord* with the New York law, although there are distinct procedural changes.

Compulsory resale within 30 days is provided for in Personal Property Law, § 79, where the buyer has paid at least 50 per cent of the purchase price in a conditional sales contract. If the buyer has not paid 50 per cent, the seller is not under a duty to resell, "unless the buyer serves upon the seller, within ten days after the retaking, a written notice demanding a resale . . .." Personal Property Law, § 80. Note that the Code places the burden upon the secured party to notify the debtor and other secured parties, of his proposal to retain the collateral. This is new—particularly in respect of the protection given to these other secured parties.

A provision analogous to compulsory resale is found in Personal Property Law, § 56(5); under that section, upon forfeiture, the entruster must cancel stipulated percentages of the purchase price (or original indebtedness, whichever is greater).

While in the case of ordinary chattel mortgages and in the pledge situation there are no provisions for compulsory resale, the secured party will usually wish to sell in order to cut off the equity of redemption. Such a sale must be fairly and honestly made. Strong v. Dahm, 39 N.Y.S.2d 266 (1942) (chattel mortgage); Matter of Kiamie, 309 N.Y. 325, 130 N.E.2d 745 (1955) (pledge); General Phoenix Corp. v. Cabot, 300 N.Y. 87, 89 N.E.2d 238 (1949) (pledges).

The special protection given to purchasers of consumer goods in subsection (1) of Section 9–505 has an existing and more demanding counterpart in Personal Property Law § 80–b (conditional sales), and Lien Law, § 329–d (chattel mortgages) where there is a purchase or contract price of $3,000 ($5,000 under Personal Property Law, § 80–b, L.1961, c. 608, eff. Oct. 1, 1961) or less for goods, wares, or merchandise sold for any use other than a commercial or business use, and the buyer has paid an amount equal to 80 per cent or more of the purchase price at the time of default. Under these sections, the seller has five days to elect (1) to retain the goods and release the debtor from further obligation under the contract, or (2) to return the goods to the buyer at his own expense and be limited to an action to recover the balance of the indebtedness. Personal Property Law, § 80–c, also allows recovery of damages, as under the Code, for failure to comply with the compulsory resale provision.

The provision that after default a consumer-debtor may renounce his rights to require resale of the collateral is similar to a provision for waiver in Personal Property Law, § 80–b.

Allowing the secured party to retain the collateral in satisfaction of the debt where all statutory requirements have been met or the debtor has agreed, is not new. See Personal Property Law, § 80–c.

Historical Note: The changes were all for purposes of clarity and for the most part result from Law Revision Commission suggestions. (1956 Recommendations, p. 312; Excerpts, p. 484.)

Official Uniform Comment

Prior Uniform Statutory Provision: Section 23, Uniform Conditional Sales Act.

Purposes:

1. Experience has shown that the parties are frequently better off without a resale of the collateral; hence this section sanctions an alternative arrangement. In lieu of resale or other disposition, the secured party may propose under subsection (2) that he keep the collateral as his own, thus discharging the obligation and abandoning any claim for a deficiency. This right may not be exercised in the case of consumer goods where the debtor has paid 60% of the price or obligation and thus has a substantial equity, and may be exercised in other cases only on notification to the debtor, unless the debtor has signed after default a statement renouncing or modifying his rights under this section, and (except in the case of consumer goods) to any other secured party who has given written notice of a claim of an interest in the collateral. In the latter case, notice must be given before the secured party receives the debtor's renunciation or before he sends his notice to the debtor. The secured party may keep the goods in lieu of sale on failure of anyone receiving notification to object within twenty-one days.

2. When an objection is received by the secured party he must then proceed to dispose of the collateral in accordance with Section 9–504, and on failure to do so would incur the liabilities set out in Section 9–507. In the case of consumer goods where 60% of the price or obligation has been paid the disposition must be made within 90 days after possession taken. For failure to make the sale within the 90-day period the secured party is liable in conversion or alternatively may incur the liabilities set out in Section 9–507.

In the absence of objection the secured party is bound by his notice.

3. After default (but not before) a consumer-debtor who has paid 60% of the cash price may sign a written renunciation of his rights to require resale of the collateral.

Cross References:

Sections 9–504 and 9–507(1).

Definitional Cross References:

"Collateral." Section 9–105.
"Consumer goods." Section 9–109.
"Debtor." Section 9–105.
"Knows." Section 1–201.
"Notice." Section 1–201.
"Person." Section 1–201.
"Purchase money security interest." Section 9–107.
"Receives notification." Section 1–201.
"Rights." Section 1–201.
"Secured party." Section 9–105.
"Security interest." Section 1–201.
"Send." Section 1–201.
"Signed." Section 1–201.
"Written." Section 1–201.

Section 9–506. Debtor's Right to Redeem Collateral.

At any time before the secured party has disposed of collateral or entered into a contract for its disposition under Section 9–504 or before the obligation has been discharged under Section 9–505(2) the debtor or any other secured party may unless otherwise agreed in writing after default redeem the collateral by tendering fulfillment of all obligations secured by the collateral as well as the expenses reasonably incurred by the secured party in retaking, holding and preparing the collateral for disposition, in arranging for the sale, and to the extent provided in the agreement and not prohibited by law, his reasonable attorneys' fees and legal expenses.

New York Annotations

This section is in substantial *accord* with present New York law. Both Personal property Law, § 78 (conditional sales), and Lien Law, § 239–c (chattel mortgages given to secure the unpaid purchase price of goods, wares, or merchandise, amounting to $3,000 or less, sold for any use other than a commercial or business use) provide for a ten-day period after retaking in which the debtor may redeem. It appears that a buyer may redeem after these ten days but before resale. Schnitzer v. Fruehauf Trailer Co., 283 App. Div. 421, 128 N.Y.S.2d 242, aff'd, 307 N.Y. 876, 122 N.E.2d 754 (1954). Cf. Fisk Discount Corp. v. Brooklyn Taxicab Trans. Co., 270 App. Div. 491, 60 N.Y.S.2d 453 (1946); Eisenberg v. Commercial Credit Corp., 267 N.Y. 80, 195 N.E. 691 (1935). Resale is required only when either the 50 percent requirement of Personal Property Law, § 79, is met, or when the buyer's demand requirements of Personal Property Law, § 80, are met.

The common law rule permits a chattel mortgagor to redeem after default if the redemption right has not been cut off by an appropriate proceeding. King v. Van Vleck, 109 N.Y. 363, 16N.E. 547 (1888); Waitt Operating Co. v. N.Y. Life Ins. Co.,

29 N.Y.S.2d 705, aff'd 263 App.Div. 936, 33 N.Y.S.2d 110 (1942). Redemption must be within a reasonable time. Pratt v. Stiles, 17 How.Pr. 211, 9 Abb.Prac. 150 (1859). It is not clear whether this common law right of redemption is available to a purchase money mortgagor under Lien Law, § 239–c. The Code Provision solves these problems by providing that the right of redemption continues unless there has been (1) a disposition under Section 9–504, or (2) a discharge under Section 9–505.

Three other important changes in existing law would be made by Section 9–506:

(i) Under Personal Property Law, § 77, and Lien Law, § 239–b, the secured party may cut off the debtor's right of redemption by serving a notice of intention to retake. No such provision exists in the Code.

(ii) Under Personal Property Law, § 78, and Lien Law, § 239–b, where the debtor redeems, ". . . the seller shall not be entitled to the expenses of retaking, keeping and storage, unless at least five days before the retaking the seller shall have mailed to the last known address of the buyer as shown by the seller's records, a notice stating the buyer's default." The provision of Personal Property Law, § 78, does not appear in the Uniform Conditional Sales Act, and there is no corresponding provision in the Code. These sections of the present law also have provisions under which the debtor may demand a statement of the sum due under the contract and the expense of retaking, keeping, and storage, with an ensuing penalty and liability for damages in the event the secured party does not comply. Section 9–208 does not explicitly cover this kind of a demand as to default expenses.

(iii) Under Personal Property Law, § 78, as interpreted by the Supreme Court, Appellate Term, Second Department, in Clark v. Tri-State Discount Co., Inc., 151 Misc. 679, 271 N.Y.S. 779 (1934) and Supreme Court, Special Term, New York County, in Manufacturers Hanover Trust Co. v. Nascarella, 39 Misc.2d 971, 242 N.Y.S.2d 326 (1963), it has been held that a buyer under a conditional sale contract, maturity of which has been accelerated for non-payment of an installment, may redeem the property sold, if repossessed, upon payment of only the amount unpaid instalments and expenses of repossession. Section 9–506 requires for the redemption of the collateral fulfillment of all obligations secured by the collateral as well as the secured party's expenses reasonably incurred. Personal Property Law, §§ 302 and 403, as enacted by L.1964, c. 504, effective September 27, 1964, appear to reenact the rule of Personal Property Law, § 78, as so interpreted, but only with respect to retail instalment contracts subject to the Motor Vehicle Retail Instalment Sales Act or the Retail Instalment Sales Act, Personal property Law, Articles 9 and 10.

It should be noted that in a pledge there is also a right of redemption. Keshishian Bros. Inc.v. Deverian, 279 App.Div. 324, 109 N.Y.S.2d 378, amended, 280 App.Div. 910, 116 N.Y.S.2d 925 (1952); Vickers v. Batter shall, 32 N.Y.S. 314 (1895); Restatement, Security, § 54.

Historical Note: Minor changes were made for clarification and to conform to Section 9–504(1). (1956 Recommendations, p. 312; Excerpts, p. 485.)

Official Uniform Comment

Prior Uniform Statutory Provision: Section 18, Uniform Conditional Sales Act.

Purposes:

Except in the case stated in Section 9–501(1) (consumer goods) the secured party is not required to dispose of collateral within any stated period of time. Under this section so long as the secured party has not disposed of collateral in his possession or contracted for its disposition, and so long as his right to retain it has not become fixed under Section 9–505(2), the debtor or another secured party may redeem. The debtor must tender fulfillment of all obligations secured, plus certain expenses: if due on default in one installment, the entire balance would have to be tendered. "Tendering fulfillment" obviously means more than a new promise to perform the existing promise; it requires payment in full of all monetary obligations then due and performance in full of all other obligations then matured. If unmatured obligations remain, the security interest continues to secure them as if there had been no default.

Under Section 9–504 the secured party may make successive sales of parts of the collateral in his possession. The fact that he may have sold or contracted to sell part of the collateral would not affect the debtor's right under this section to redeem what was left. In such a case, of course, in calculating the amount required to be tendered the debtor would receive credit for net proceeds of the collateral sold.

Cross References:

Sections 9–504 and 9–505.

Definitional Cross References:

"Agreement." Section 1–201.
"Collateral." Section 9–105.
"Contract." Section 1–201.
"Debtor." Section 9–105.
"Secured party." Section 9–105.
"Writing." Section 1–201.

Section 9–507. Secured Party's Liability for Failure to Comply With This Part.

(1) If it is established that the secured party is not proceeding in accordance with the provisions of this Part disposition may be ordered or restrained on appropriate terms and conditions. If the disposition has occurred the debtor or any person entitled to notification or whose security interest has been made known to the secured party prior to the disposition has aright to recover from the secured party any loss caused by a failure to comply with the provisions of this Part. If the collateral is consumer goods, the debtor has a right to recover in any event an amount not less than the credit service charge plus ten per cent of the principal amount of the debtor the time price differential plus ten per cent of the cash price.

(2) The fact that a better price could have been obtained by a sale at a different time or in a different method from that selected by the secured party is not of itself sufficient to establish that the sale was not made in a commercially reasonable manner. If the secured party either sells the collateral in the usual manner in any recognized market therefor or if he sells at the price current in such market at the time of his sale of if he has otherwise sold in conformity with reasonable commercial practices among dealers in the type of property sold he has sold in a commercially reasonable manner. The principles stated in the two preceding sentences with respect to sales also apply as may be appropriate to other types of disposition. A disposition which has been approved in any judicial proceeding or by any bona fide creditors' committee or representative of creditors shall conclusively be deemed to be commercially reasonable, but this sentence does not indicate that any such approval must be obtained in any case nor does it indicate that any disposition not so approved is not commercially reasonable.

New York Annotations

This section is in general *accord* with present New York law.

Reference should be made to Rule 267 of the New York Rules of Civil Practice (now line Law, § 206) which makes Title 31–"Action for Foreclosure" of those Rules applicable to actions to foreclose a mortgage or other lien on chattels or other personal property. Secured parties enforcing their interests by judicial action will be bound by this Title insofar as it may be applicable.

Under present law a court can grant an injunction pendente lite restraining disposition of property. See Fleischmann v. Clausen, 222 App.Div. 7, 225 N.Y.S. 288 (1927).

Provisions for minimum recovery or damages where there is a failure to comply with statutory requirements are found in Personal Property Law, § 80–e, and in Lien Law, § 239–e (chattel mortgage to secure purchase price of $3,000 or less, where purchase not for commercial or business use). See also Personal Property Law, § 64–a, and Lien Law, § 239–i (statutory recovery for non-compliance with requirements for contents of chattel mortgage and conditional sales contracts for $3,000 or less not for commercial or businessuse); Personal Property Law, § 78, and Lien Law, § 239–c (statutory liability for $10 plus damages where secured party fails to furnish the debtor a statement of the sum due under mortgage and the expense of retaking, keeping, and storage); and Personal Property Law, §§ 307 and 414 (recovery of credit service charge and like charges where instalment sales provisions violated; but correction is allowed).

No statutory penalty for noncompliance with enforcement provisions exists in the Trust Receipts Act, but Personal Property Law, § 56(3)(c), indicates that the entruster may be liable for conversion.

For the remedies of a pledgor for breach of duty by the pledgee in the sale of pledged chattels, see Restatement, Security, § 50, and Matter of Kiamie, 309 N.Y. 325, 130N.E.2d 745 (1955).

There are no mandatory statutory requirements for enforcement of chattel mortgages (except for the consumer-purchaser chattel mortgage under Lien Law, § 239), and hence no statutory provisions for non-compliance.

Where the chattel mortgage is in default, an irregular or unfair sale ordinarily furnished the mortgagor or his assignee with the following remedies: (i) the equitable right of redemption, McKinney v. Donahue, 59 N.Y.S.2d 726 (1946), Fleischmann v. Clausen, *supra;* or (ii) an accounting, Ever-Ready Label Corp. v. Stuyvesant Photo Engraving Corp., 36 N.Y.S.2d 468 (1942).

Historical Note: Language changes were made for clarification. (1956 Recommendations, p. 313; Excerpts, p. 485.)

Official Uniform Comment

Prior Uniform Statutory Provision: None.

Purposes:

1. The principal limitation on the secured party's right to dispose of collateral is the requirement that he proceed in good faith (Section 1–203) and in a commercially reasonable manner. See Section 9–504. In the case where he proceeds, or is about to proceed, in a contrary manner, it is vital both to the debtor and other creditors to provide a remedy for the failure to comply with the statutory duty. This remedy will be of particular importance when it is applied prospectively before the unreasonable disposition has been concluded. This section therefore provides that a secured party proposing to dispose of collateral in an unreasonable manner, may, by

court order, be restrained from doing so, and such an order might appropriately provide either that he proceed with the sale or other disposition under specified terms and conditions, or that the sale be made by a representative of creditors where insolvency proceeding shave been instituted. The section further provides for damages where the unreasonable disposition has been concluded, and, in the case of consumer goods, states a minimum recovery.

A case may be put in which the liquidation value of an insolvent estate would be enhanced by disposing of all the debtor's property (including that subject to a security interest) in the liquidation proceeding and in which, if a secured party repossesses and sells that part of the property which he holds as collateral, the remainder will have little or no resale value. In such a case the question may arise whether a particular court has the power to control the manner of disposition, although reasonable in other respects, in order to preserve the estate for the benefit of creditors. Such a power is no doubt inherent in a Federal bankruptcy court, and perhaps also in other courts of equity administering insolvent estates. Traditionally it was not exercised where the secured party claimed under a title retention device, such as a conditional sale or trust receipt. See In re Lake's Laundry, Inc., 79 F.2d 326 (2d Cir. 1935) and the remarks of Clark, J., concurring, in In re White Plains Ice Service, Inc., 109 F.2d 913 (2d Cir. 1940). It has been held that distinctions in results based on these distinctions in form have been made obsolete by this Article. In re Yale Express System, Inc., 370 F.2d 433 (2d Cir. 1966), 384 F.2d 990 (2d Cir. 1967).

2. In view of the remedies provided the debtor and other creditors in subsection (1) when a secured party does not dispose of collateral in a commercially reasonable manner, it is of great importance to make clear what types of disposition are to be considered commercially reasonable, and in an appropriate case to give the secured party means of getting, by court order or negotiation with a creditors' committee or a representative of creditors, approval of a proposed method of disposition as a commercially reasonable one. Subsection (2) states rules to assist in the determination, and provides for such advance approval in appropriate situations. One recognized method of disposing of repossessed collateral is for the secured party to sell the collateral to or through a dealer– a method which in the long run may realize better average returns since the secured party does not usually maintain his own facilities for making of such sales. Such a method of sale, fairly conducted, is recognized as commercially reasonable under the second sentence of subsection (2). However, none of the specific methods of disposition set forth in subsection (2) is to be regarded as either required or exclusive, provided only that the disposition made or about to be made by the secured party is commercially reasonable.

Cross References:

Point 1: Sections 1–203, 9–202 and 9–504.

Definitional Cross References:

"Collateral." Section 9–105.
"Consumer goods." Section 9–109.
"Creditor." Section 1–201.
"Debtor." Section 9–105.
"Knows." Section 1–201.
"Notification." Section 1–201.
"Person." Section 1–201.
"Representative." Section 1–201.
"Rights." Section 1–201.
"Secured party." Section 9–105.
"Security interest." Section 1–201.

court order restraining him from disposing, and such an order might appropriately provide either that he proceed with the sale or other disposition under specified terms and conditions or that the sale be made by a representative of creditors. Where no such proceedings have been instituted, this section further provides for damages where the disposition has been concluded and, in the case of consumer goods, sets a minimum recovery.

A case may be put in which the liquidation value of an insolvent estate would be enhanced by disposing of all the debtor's property (including that subject to a security interest) in the liquidation proceeding and in which, if a secured party repossesses and sells that part of the property which he holds as collateral, the remainder will have little or no resale value. In such a case the question may arise whether a bankruptcy court has the power to control the manner of disposition, although proceeding in other respects in order to preserve the estate for the benefit of creditors. Such a power is no doubt inherent in a Federal bankruptcy court, and perhaps also in other courts of equity administering insolvent estates. Traditionally it was not exercised where the secured party claimed under a title retention device, such as a conditional sale or trust receipt. See In re Lee Cadillac Company, Inc., 70 F. Supp. 36 (D.C.N.J. 1939) and the remarks of Clark, J., concurring, in In re White Plains Ice Service, Inc., 109 F.2d 913 (2 Cir. 1940). It has been held that distinctions drawn on such uses of security have been made obsolete by this Article. In re Yale Express System, Inc., 370 F.2d 433 (2d Cir. 1966), 384 F.2d 990 (2d Cir. 1967).

2. One of the remedies provided the debtor and other creditors in subsection (1) when a secured party does not dispose of collateral in a commercially reasonable manner. It is of great importance to make clear what types of disposition are to be considered commercially reasonable, and in an appropriate case require the secured party to obtain, in advance, by court order or agreement with a creditors' committee or a representative of creditors, approval of a proposed method of disposition as a commercially reasonable one. Subsection (2) states rules to assist in the determination and provides for such advance approval in appropriate situations. One recognized method of disposing of repossessed collateral is for the secured party to sell the collateral to or through a dealer—a method which in the long run may realize better average returns since the secured party does not usually maintain his own facilities for making such sales. Such a method of sale, fairly conducted, is recognized as commercially reasonable under the second sentence of subsection (2). However, none of the specific methods of disposition set forth in subsection (2) is to be regarded as either required or exclusive, provided only that the disposition ultimately made by the secured party is commercially reasonable.

Cross References:

Point 1: Sections 1-203, 9-[illegible] and 9-[illegible].

Definitional Cross References:

"Collateral". Section 9-105.
"Consumer goods". Section 9-109.
"Creditor". Section 1-201.
"Debtor". Section 9-105.
"Knows". Section 1-201.
"Notification". Section 1-201.
"Party". Section 1-201.
"Representative". Section 1-201.
"Rights". Section 1-201.
"Secured party". Section 9-105.
"Security interest". Section 1-201.

ARTICLE 11

PROVISIONS FOR TRANSITION FROM ORIGINAL ARTICLE 9 TO REVISED ARTICLE 9.

Section 11–101. Definitions.

As used in this Article 11:

(a) The term "Original Article 9" means Article 9 of the uniform commercial code as enacted by chapter five hundred fifty-three of the laws of nineteen hundred sixty-two and as amended by chapter eight hundred ninety-nine of the laws of nineteen hundred seventy.

(b) The term "Revised Article 9" means Article 9 of the uniform commercial code as amended by the act enacting this Article.

Section 11–102. Preservation of Old Transition Provision.

The provisions of Article 10 of the uniform commercial code as enacted by chapter five hundred fifty-three of the laws of nineteen hundred sixty-two and at last amended by chapter eight hundred sixty-eight of the laws of nineteen hundred sixty-five shall continue to apply to Revised Article 9 and for this purpose Original Article 9 and Revised Article 9 shall be considered one continuous statute.

Section 11–103. Transition to Revised Article 9–General Rule.

Transactions validly entered into after September twenty-seventh, nineteen hundred sixty-four and before the effective date of Revised Article 9, and which were subject to the provisions of Original Article 9 and which would be subject to Revised Article 9 if they had been entered into on or after the effective date of Revised Article 9 and the rights, duties and interests flowing from such transactions remain valid after the latter date and may be terminated, completed, consummated or enforced as required or permitted by Revised Article 9. Security interests arising out of such transactions which are perfected when Revised Article 9 becomes effective shall remain perfected until they lapse as provided in Revised Article 9, and may be continued as permitted by the Revised Article 9, except as provided in Section 11-105.

Section 11–104. Transition Provision on Change of Requirement of Filing.

A security interest for the perfection of which filing or the taking of possession was required under Original article 9 and which attached prior to the effective date of Revised Article 9 but was not perfected shall be deemed perfected on the effective date of Revised Article 9 if Revised Article 9 permits perfection without filing or authorizes filing in the office or offices where a prior ineffective filing was made.

Section 11–105. Transition Provision on Change of Place of Filing.

(1) A financing statement or continuation statement filed prior to the effective date of Revised Article 9 which shall not have lapsed prior to the effective date of Revised Article 9 shall remain effective for the period provided in Original Article 9, but not less than five years after the filing.

(2) With respect to any collateral acquired by the debtor subsequent to the effective date of Revised Article 9, any effective financing statement or continuation statement described in this section shall apply only if the filing or filings are in the office or offices that would be appropriate to perfect the security interests in the new collateral under Revised Article 9.

(3) The effectiveness of any financing statement or continuation statement filed prior to the effective date of Revised Article 9 may be continued by a continuation statement as permitted by Revised Article 9, except that if Revised Article 9 requires a filing in an office where there was no previous financing statement, a new financing statement conforming to Section 11-106 shall be filed in that office.

(4) If the record of a mortgage of real estate would have been effective as a fixture filing of goods described therein if Revised Article 9 have been in effect on that date of recording the mortgage, the mortgage shall be deemed effective as a fixture filing as to such goods under subsection (6) of Section 9-402 of Revised Article 9 on the effective date of Revised Article 9.

Section 11–106. Required Refilings.

(1) If a security interest is perfected or has a priority when the act enacting this Article takes effect as to all persons or as to certain persons without any filing or recording, and if the filing of a financing statement would be required for the perfection or priority of the security interest against those persons under

Revised Article 9, the perfection and priority rights of the security interest continue until three years after the effective date of Revised Article 9. The perfection will then lapse unless a financing statement is filed as provided in subsection (2) or unless the security interest is perfected otherwise than by filing.

(2) A financing statement may be filed within six months before the perfection of a security interest would otherwise lapse. Any such financing statement may be signed by either the debtor or the secured party. It must identify the security agreement, statement or notice (however denominated in any statute or other law repealed or modified by the act enacting this Article, state the office where and the date when the last filing, refiling or recording, if any, was made with respect thereto, and the filing number, if any, or book and page, if any, of recording and further state that the security agreement, statement or notice, however denominated, in another filing office under the uniform commercial code or under any statute or other law repealed or modified by the act enacting this Article is still effective. Section 9-401 and Section 9-103 determine the proper place to file such a financing statement. Except as specified in this subsection, the provisions of subsection (3) of Section 9-403 for continuation statements apply to such a financing statement.

Section 11–107. Transition Provisions as to Priorities.

Except as otherwise provided in this Article, Original Article 9 shall apply to any questions of priority if the positions of the parties were fixed prior to the effective date of Revised Article 9. In other cases questions of priority shall be determined by Revised Article 9.

Section 11–108. Presumption that Rule of Law Continues Unchanged.

Unless a change in law has clearly been made, the provisions of Revised Article 9 shall be deemed declaratory of the meaning of Original Article 9.

1977 Amendment

A new Article 11 was added by L. 1977, Ch. 866, effective July 2, 1978. Article 11 governs the transition from Original Article 9 to Revised Article 9.

ARTICLE 13

EFFECTIVE DATE AND REPEALER

Section 13–101. Application of Act.

This Act applies to transactions entered into and events occurring on and after the effective date specified in Section 13–105 of this Act.

Official Uniform Comment

This effective date is suggested so that there may be ample time for all those who will be affected by the provisions of the Code to become familiar with them.

Section 13–102. Laws Repealed; Provision for Transition.

(1) Of the laws enumerated in the schedule hereto annexed following Section 13–105 of this Act and subject to the provisions of this Article, that portion specified in the last column is hereby repealed.

(2) Transactions validly entered into before the effective date specified in Section13–105 of this Act and the rights, duties and interests flowing from them remain valid thereafter and may be terminated, completed, consummated or enforced as required or permitted by any statute or other law repealed or modified by this Act as though such repeal or modification had not occurred; provided, however, that the perfection of a security interest, as defined in this Act (Section 1–201) and however denominated in any law repealed or modified by this Act,

(a) which was perfected when this Act takes effect by a filing, re-filing or recording under a law repealed by this Act and requiring a further filing, refiling or recording to continue its perfection, continues until and will lapse on the date provided by the law so repealed for such further filing, refiling or recording;

(b) which was perfected when this Act takes effect by a filing, refiling or recording under a law repealed by this Act and requiring no further filing, refiling or recording to continue its perfection, continues until and will lapse twelve months after the date this Act takes effect;

(c) which was perfected when this Act takes effect without any filing, refiling or recording, and for the perfection of which the filing of a financing statement would be required if this Act applied, continues until and will lapse twelve months after this Act takes effect if the security interest is in accounts or, otherwise, thirty-six months after this Act takes effect; unless, in each case, a continuation statement is filed by the secured party before the perfection of the security interest would otherwise lapse. Any such continuation statement must be signed by the secured party, identify the security agreement, statement or notice, however denominated in any statute or other law repealed or modified by this Act, state the office where and the date when the last filing, refiling or recording, if any, was made with respect thereto, and the filing number, if any, or book and page, if any, of recording and further state that the security agreement, statement or notice, however, denominated in any statute or other law repealed or modified by this Act, is still effective. Section 9–401(1) determines the proper place to file such a continuation statement. Except as specified in this subsection and except that the perfection of the security interest will lapse five years after the filing of a continuation statement in accordance with this subsection unless another continuation statement is filed within six months prior to such lapse, the provisions of Section 9–403(3) apply to such a continuation statement.

(3) Notwithstanding subsection (2):

(a) The perfection of a security interest, however denominated in any law repealed by this Act, which was perfected when this Act takes effect by a filing, refiling or recording under a law repealed by this Act, and for the perfection of which, if this Act applied, no filing of a financing statement would be required, continues under this Act.

(b) A security interest, however denominated in any law repealed by this Act, which was not perfected when this Act takes effect but which could have been perfected before this Act takes effect by a filing, refiling or recording under a law repealed by this Act, and which, if this Act applied, could be perfected by the filing of a financing statement under this Act, may be perfected by the filing of a financing statement in accordance with this Act.

(c) A security interest, however denominated in any law repealed or modified by this Act, which was not perfected when this Act takes effect but which could have been perfected before this Act takes effect by the secured party's taking possession of the collateral under a law repealed or modified by this Act, and which, if this Act applied, could be perfected by the secured party's taking possession of the collateral, may be perfected by the secured party's taking possession of the collateral in accordance with this Act.

(d) A continuation statement heretofore filed in accordance with subsection (2) except for having been filed more than twelve months before the perfection of the security interest would otherwise lapse shall be deemed to have been filed in accordance with subsection (2).

(e) A security interest which was perfected when this Act took effect and the perfection of which was or is continued by the filing of a continuation statement in accordance with subsection(2) is a perfected security interest for the purposes of subsection (2) of Section 9–302.

(f) After September first, nineteen hundred sixty-five, no further filing shall be made in accordance with any statute repealed by this Act with respect to a security interest perfected when this Act takes effect, except that a certificate of payment or other satisfaction or discharge of a conditional sale contract or a certificate of payment or satisfaction of a chattel mortgage may be filed in accordance with section seventy-two of the personal property law or section two hundred thirty-eight of the lien law, respectively, both repealed by this Act.

Amended by Laws 1964, Ch. 476, eff. Sept. 27, 1964; Laws 1965, Ch. 868, eff. July 16, 1965.

N.Y. Commission Comments

Subsection (1) has been revised to conform to New York practice. The addition to subsection (2) [proviso clause and all text following] and the addition of subsection (3)provide a method for the continued perfection of security interests created before the Act takes effect.

Official Uniform Comment

Subsection (1) provides for the repeal of present uniform and other acts superseded by this Act. Subsection (2) provides for the transition to the Code.

Section 13–103. Inconsistent Laws; Which Law Governs.

If any other provision of law is inconsistent with this Act, this Act shall govern unless this Act or such inconsistent provision of law specifically provides otherwise.

N.Y. Commission Comments

New York practice does not permit a general, as distinguished from a specific, repealer.

Official Uniform Comment

This section provides for the repeal of all other legislation inconsistent with this Act.

Section 13–104. Laws Not Repealed.

(1) The Article on Documents of Title (Article 7) does not repeal or modify any laws prescribing the form or contents of documents of title or the services or facilities to be afforded by bailees, or otherwise regulating bailees' businesses in respects not specifically dealt with herein; but the fact that such laws are violated does not affect the status of a document of title which otherwise complies with the definition of a document of title (Section 1–201).

(2) This act does not repeal Article 23-C of the general business law, cited as the Uniform Act of Simplification of Fiduciary Security Transfers, and if in any respect there is any inconsistency between that Act and the Article of this Act on investment securities (Article 8) the provisions of the Former Act shall control.

Official Uniform Comment

This Section subordinates the Article of this Act on Documents of Title (Article 7) to the more specialized regulations of particular classes of bailees under other legislation and international treaties. Particularly, the provisions of that Article are superseded by applicable inconsistent provisions regarding the obligation of carriers and the limitation of their liability found in federal legislation dealing with transportation by water (including the Harare Act, Act of February 13, 1893, 27 Stat. 445, and the Carriage of Goods by Sea Act, Act of April 16, 1936, 49 Stat. 1207); the Warsaw Convention on International Air Transportation, 49 Stat. 3000, and Section 20(11) of the Interstate Commerce Act, Act of February 20, 1887, 24 Stat. 386, as amended. The Documents of Title provisions of this Act supplement such legislation largely in matters other than obligation of the bailee, e.g., form and effects of negotiation, procedure in the case of lost documents, effect of over-issue, possibility of rapid transmission.

Doubts have been expressed whether Article 8 provides as complete protection on transfers of securities by fiduciaries as the Uniform Act for the Simplification of Fiduciary Security Transfers. The Editorial Board entirely favors the policy of simplifying fiduciary security transfers and believes that Article 8 soundly implements this policy. However, since the shorter Simplification Act has been so widely enacted and has been working satisfactorily, the Editorial Board recommends that it be retained [As amended in 1962].

Cross Reference:

Section 7–103.

Section 13–105. Effective Date.

This Act shall take effect September twenty seventh, nineteen hundred sixty-four.

1977 Amendment

Article 13 was renumbered From Former Article 10 and Sections 10–101 through10–105 were renumbered 13–101 through 13–105, by L.1977, ch. 866, effective July 2, 1978.

GENERAL OBLIGATIONS LAW

(Enacted by Laws of 1963, Ch. 576, eff. Sept. 27, 1964, as amended by the 2000 Regular Legislative Session through June 23, 2000. Note that omitted section numbers have been reserved for future use by the Legislature.)

GOL

TABLE OF CONTENTS

ARTICLE 1

SHORT TITLE; CONSTRUCTION; APPLICABILITY OF CERTAIN SECTIONS

1 SHORT TITLE

2 CONSTRUCTION; APPLICABILITY OF CERTAIN SECTIONS

ARTICLE 3

CAPACITY; EFFECT OF STATUS OR OF CERTAIN RELATIONSHIPS OR OCCUPATIONS UPON THE CREATION, DEFINITION OR ENFORCEMENT OF OBLIGATIONS

TITLE 1

INFANCY

TITLE 3

HUSBAND AND WIFE

TITLE 5

CERTAIN OCCUPATIONS

ARTICLE 5

CREATION, DEFINITION AND ENFORCEMENT OF CONTRACTUAL OBLIGATIONS

TITLE 1

DEFINITIONS OF TERMS

TITLE 3

CERTAIN PROHIBITED CONTRACTS AND PROVISIONS OF CONTRACTS

GOL

TITLE 4

CONTRACTS RELATING TO WAGERING; FORFEITURE AND RECOVERY OF CERTAIN PROPERTY

TITLE 5

INTEREST AND USURY, BROKERAGE ON LOANS

TITLE 6

INTEREST ON CERTAIN DEPOSITS

TITLE 7

REQUIREMENTS OF WRITING, EXECUTION OR ACKNOWLEDGMENT FOR EFFECTIVENESS OR ENFORCEABILITY

TITLE 9

REQUIREMENTS OF NOTICE FOR EFFECTIVENESS OR ENFORCEABILITY

TITLE 11

CONSIDERATION; EFFECT OF WRITING ON REQUIREMENT OF CONSIDERATION

GOL

TITLE 13

CONSTRUCTION OF PARTICULAR TERMS IN CONTRACTUAL TRANSACTIONS

TITLE 14

ENFORCEABILITY OF CLAUSES RESPECTING CHOICE OF LAW AND CHOICE OF FORUM IN CERTAIN TRANSACTIONS

TITLE 15

STATUTORY SHORT FORM POWER OF ATTORNEY

TITLE 16

CONTINUITY OF CONTRACT

ARTICLE 6

DISCLOSURE

(*NEW YORK STATE TRUTH–IN–LENDING ACT*)

(*Repealed by Laws of 1969, Ch. 1141, eff. July 1, 1969. Superseded by the Federal Truth–in–Lending Act (15 U.S.C.A. § 1601 et seq.) and Federal Reserve Board regulations thereunder.*)

ARTICLE 7

OBLIGATIONS RELATING TO PROPETY RECEIVED AS SECURITY

TITLE 1

MONEY DEPOSITED AS SECURITY TO BE HELD IN TRUST IN CERTAIN CASES

TITLE 2

SALE OF CERTAIN LICENSED TAXICABS

TITLE 3

BONDS AND UNDERTAKINGS

GOL

TITLE 4

ARTICLE 9

OBLIGATIONS OF CARE

TITLE 1

CONDITIONS ON REAL PROPERTY

ARTICLE 11

OBLIGATIONS TO MAKE COMPENSATION OR RESTITUTION

TITLE 1

COMPENSATION

ARTICLE 12

DRUG DEALER LIABILITY ACT

ARTICLE 13

TRANSFER OF OBLIGATIONS AND RIGHTS

TITLE 1

TRANSFERABILITY; EFFECT OF TRANSFER

ARTICLE 15

MODIFICATION AND DISCHARGE OF OBLIGATIONS

TITLE 1

DISCHARGE OF JOINT OBLIGORS

TITLE 3

REQUIREMENTS FOR EFFECTIVENESS OR ENFORCEABILITY OF MODIFICATION OR DISCHARGE

GOL

TITLE 5

ACCORD AND SATISFACTION

TITLE 7

DISCHARGE OF SURETY

ARTICLE 17

REVIVAL OR EXTENSION; WAIVER OF DEFENSE OR BAR

TITLE 1

OBLIGATIONS BARRED BY STATUTES OF LIMITATION

ARTICLE 18

SAFETY IN SKIING CODE

ARTICLE 18-A

SPECIFICATIONS OF LIABILITY FOR EMPLOYERS AND EMPLOYEES

ARTICLE 19

LAWS REPEALED; EFFECTIVE DATE

ARTICLE 1

SHORT TITLE; CONSTRUCTION; APPLICABILITY OF CERTAIN SECTIONS

TITLE 1

SHORT TITLE

Section 1-101. Short title

This chapter shall be known and may be cited as the "General Obligations Law."

TITLE 2

CONSTRUCTION; APPLICABILITY OF CERTAIN SECTIONS

Section 1–201. Construction of act of reconsolidation

1. This chapter shall be construed as a continuation and re–enactment of the provisions repealed by article nineteen hereof as such provisions existed on December thirty–first, nineteen hundred sixty–two.

2. The repeal by this chapter of provisions specified in article nineteen hereof and the enactment of this chapter shall not affect any action or proceeding pending under any such provision at the time this chapter shall take effect.

3. Any act of the legislature of the year nineteen hundred sixty–three or nineteen hundred sixty–four which in form amends or repeals or purports to amend or repeal any provision or provisions repealed by article nineteen of this chapter shall be legally effective notwithstanding the repeal of such provision or provisions and shall be construed as an amendment or repeal, as the case may be, of the corresponding provision or provisions of this chapter, and such corresponding provisions shall be construed to be amended, modified, changed or repealed as though they had been expressly and in terms so amended or repealed.

4. Reference by any law, general or special, in force on December thirty–first, nineteen hundred sixty–two, or in any act of the legislature of the year nineteen hundred sixty–three or nineteen hundred sixty–four, to a provision repealed by article nineteen of this chapter, as in force immediately before the time this chapter shall take effect, shall be construed to refer to the corresponding provision of this chapter.

Section 1–202. Definition

As used in this chapter, the term "infant" or "minor" means a person who has not attained the age of eighteen years.

Added by Laws 1974, Ch. 898, eff. Sept. 1, 1974.

Section 1–203. Provisions excluding application of certain sections to matters previous to dates of their original enactment

1. Section 1–202 applies to all obligations arising on or after September first, nineteen hundred seventy–four.

2. Section 3–101 applies to contracts made on or after April thirteenth, nineteen hundred forty–one.

3. Section 3–107 applies to contracts made on or after September first, nineteen hundred sixty–one.

5. Section 3–311 does not affect any interest or right of survivorship existing prior to April twentieth, nineteen hundred forty–nine.

7. Subdivision two of section 3–313 does not affect any right, cause of action or defense existing prior to September first, nineteen hundred thirty–seven.

9. Section 5–301 applies to undertakings or promises made on or after January twenty–fifth, nineteen hundred thirty–five.

11. Section 5–903 applies to contracts executed or renewed after October first, nineteen hundred sixty–one.

13. Section 5–1103 applies to agreements made on or after April sixth, nineteen hundred thirty–six; sections 5–1105, 5–1107 and 5–1109 apply to assignments, promises or offers made on or after September first, nineteen hundred forty–one.

14. Section 5–1115 applies to deeds or conveyances delivered on or after September first, nineteen hundred forty–four.

17. Section 5–1311 applies to contracts made after May twenty–sixth, nineteen hundred thirty–six.

19. Section 9–101 applies to injuries sustained after September first, nineteen hundred forty–six.

21. Section 13–107 applies to transfers made after September first, nineteen hundred fifty.

23. Title 1 of Article 15 applies to obligations arising on or after April sixth, nineteen hundred twenty–eight.

25.a. Subdivision one of section 15–301 applies to agreements or instruments executed on or after September first, nineteen hundred forty–one.

b. Subdivisions two, three and four of section 15–301 apply to agreements or instruments executed on or after September first, nineteen hundred fifty–two.

c. Subdivision five of section 15–301 applies to agreements, evidences of termination, notices of termination or waivers with respect to agreements or other instruments executed on or after April fifth, nineteen hundred forty–four.

27. Section 15–303 applies to written instruments executed on or after April third, nineteen hundred thirty–six.

29. Section 15–501 applies to executory accords made on or after March eighteenth, nineteen hundred thirty–seven.

31. Subdivision one of section 15–503 applies to offers made on or after March eighteenth, nineteen hundred thirty–seven.

33. Section 17–103 applies to promises made on or after September first, nineteen hundred sixty–one.

35. Section 17–105 applies to waivers, promises, agreements, recitals and acknowledgments made on or after September first, nineteen hundred sixty–one.

37. Section 17–107 applies to payments made on or after September first, nineteen hundred sixty–one.

Amended by Laws 1974, Ch. 898, eff. Sept. 1, 1974.

ARTICLE 3

CAPACITY; EFFECT OF STATUS OR OF CERTAIN RELATIONSHIPS OR OCCUPATIONS UPON THE CREATION, DEFINITION OR ENFORCEMENT OF OBLIGATIONS

TITLE 1

INFANCY

Section 3–101. When contracts may not be disaffirmed on ground of infancy

1. A contract made on or after September first, nineteen hundred seventy–four by a person after he has attained the age of eighteen years may not be disaffirmed by him on the ground of infancy.

2. A contract made on or after April thirteenth, nineteen hundred forty–one, and before September first, nineteen hundred seventy–four, by a person after

he has attained the age of eighteen years, may not be disaffirmed by him on the ground of infancy, where the contract was made in connection with a business in which the infant was engaged and was reasonable and provident when made.

In any action or proceeding in which the right to disaffirm on the ground of infancy a contract made by an infant after he has attained the age of eighteen years is in issue, the burden of proof on the question whether the contract was made in connection with a business in which the infant was engaged, and also on the question whether the contract was reasonable and provident when made, shall be upon the person seeking to deny or defeat such disaffirmance or to enforce the contract.

3. A husband and wife, with respect only to real property they occupy or which they affirm they are about to occupy as a home, regardless of the minority of either or both and without limitation of the powers of any such person who is of full age, shall each have power (a) to enter into and contract for a loan or loans with a bank, trust company, private banker, national bank, branch or agency of a foreign banking corporation licensed pursuant to article two, or branch of an out–of–state depository institution authorized pursuant to article five–C of the banking law, savings bank or savings and loan association whose home office is located in this state, with any insurance company authorized to do business in this state, with the United States government and its agencies, with respect to such real property and take any other action and execute any other document or instrument to the extent necessary or appropriate to effect any such loan, provide security therefor, carry out or modify the terms thereof, and effect any compromise or settlement of any such loan or of any claim with respect thereto; (b) to receive, hold and dispose of such real property, make and execute contracts, notes, deeds, mortgages, agreements and other instruments necessary and appropriate to acquire such property, and (c) to dispose of such real property so acquired, and make and execute contracts, deeds, agreements and other instruments necessary and appropriate to dispose of such property.

Notwithstanding any contrary provision or rule of law, no such husband or wife shall have the power to disaffirm, because of minority, any act or transaction which he or she is herein above empowered to perform or engage in, nor shall any defense based upon minority be interposed in any action or proceeding arising out of any such act or transaction.

The above provision, however shall affect only transactions entered into subsequent to September first, nineteen hundred sixty–five.

4. A person who has attained the age of eighteen years shall have the power, regardless of his or her minority to enter into a binding and enforceable contract for a loan or loans with a bank, trust company, private banker, national bank, branch or agency of a foreign banking corporation licensed pursuant to article two, or branch of an out–of–state depository institution authorized pursuant to article five–C of the banking law or savings bank, or with a saving and loan association or credit union which is chartered under the laws of this state or

under the provisions of federal law and is authorized to do business in this state and, in the case of a credit union, if said person is within the field of membership of the credit union, and to take any other action and execute any other document or instrument to the extent necessary or appropriate to effect any such loan, provide security therefor, carry out or modify the terms thereof, and effect any compromise or settlement of any loan or of any claim with respect thereto.

Notwithstanding any contrary provision or rule of law, no such person who has attained the age of eighteen years shall have the power to disaffirm or renounce solely because of his minority any act or transaction which he or she is hereinabove empowered to perform or engage in, nor shall any defense based upon minority be interposed in any action or proceeding arising out of such act or transaction.

The above provision shall affect only transactions entered into on or after June twenty–third, nineteen hundred seventy–three and before September first, nineteen hundred seventy–four.

Amended by Laws 1965, Ch. 226, eff. Sept. 1, 1965; Laws 1966, Ch. 340, eff. May 10, 1966; Laws 1971, Ch. 1019, eff. July 2, 1971; Laws 1973, Ch. 1027, eff. June 23, 1973; Laws 1974, Ch. 898, eff. Sept. 1, 1974; Laws 1977, Ch. 877, eff. Aug. 11, 1977; Laws 1992, Ch. 222, eff. June 23, 1992.

Section 3–102. Obligations of certain minors for hospital, medical and surgical treatment and care

1. An obligation incurred by a married minor for hospital, medical and surgical treatment and care for such minor or such minor's children shall not be voidable because of minority. For the purpose of this section only, subsequent judgment of divorce or annulment shall not alter the obligation previously incurred.

Added by Laws 1968, Ch. 697, eff. Sept. 1, 1968.

Section 3–103. Contracts pursuant to the "Servicemen's Readjustment Act of 1944" as amended; when they may not be disaffirmed

1. A veteran, eligible for the benefits provided for in Section 1801 and following of Title 38 of the United States Code, and the spouse of such veteran, regardless of the minority of either or both and without limitation of the powers of any such person who is of full age, shall each have power (a) to enter into and contract for a loan or loans to such veteran pursuant to such title; (b) to receive, hold and dispose of real or personal property, make and execute contracts, notes, deeds, mortgages, agreements and other instruments, and take any other action, to the extent necessary or appropriate to effect any such loan, provide security therefor, carry out or modify the terms thereof, and effect any compromise or settlement of any such loan or of any claim with respect thereto; and (c) to dispose of real or personal property so acquired and make and execute

contracts, deeds, agreements and other instruments necessary or appropriate for such purpose.

2. Notwithstanding any contrary provision or rule of law, no such veteran or spouse shall have the power to disaffirm, because of minority, any act or transaction which he or she is hereinabove empowered to perform or engage in, nor shall any defense based upon minority be interposed in any action or proceeding arising out of any such act or transaction.

Amended by Laws 1972, Ch. 670, eff. June 29, 1972.

Section 3–105. [Repealed.] [Laws 1983, Ch. 876, eff. Dec. 31, 1983.]

Section 3–107. Certain contracts of parents or guardians respecting employment of infants not enforceable unless approved

Where a contract providing for performance or rendering of services by an infant is one which the supreme court or surrogate's court has jurisdiction to approve as provided in section 3–105 of this chapter, no parent or guardian of the infant with respect to whose services the contract is made shall, unless the contract is so approved, be liable on the contract either as a party or as a guarantor of its performance:

1. If the infant was a resident of the state at the time the contract was made or at the time of the event by reason of which liability is sought to be imposed, by reason of any disaffirmance, repudiation or breach of the contract or any term thereof, or any failure or refusal of the infant to perform, or

2. In any other case, by reason of any failure or refusal of the infant to perform or render services required or permitted by the contract to be performed or rendered in this state or any failure or refusal of the parent or guardian to cause such services to be rendered or performed.

Section 3–109. Payment of wages to minor; when valid

Where a minor is in the employment of a person other than his parent or guardian, payment to such minor of his wages is valid, unless such parent or guardian notify the employer in writing, within thirty days after the commencement of such service, that such wages are claimed by such parent or guardian, but whenever such notice is given at any time payments to the minor shall not be valid for services rendered thereafter.

Section 3–111. Negligence of parent or other custodian not imputed to infant

In an action brought by an infant to recover damages for personal injury the contributory negligence of the infant's parent or other custodian shall not be imputed to the infant.

Section 3–112. Liability of parents and legal guardians having custody of an infant for certain damages caused by such infant

1. The parent or legal guardian, other than the state, a local social services department or a foster parent, of an infant over ten and less than eighteen years of age, shall be liable to any public officer, organization or authority, having by law the care and/or custody of any public property of the state or of any political subdivision thereof, or to any private individual or organization having by law the care, custody and/or ownership of any private property, for damages caused by such infant, where such infant has willfully, maliciously, or unlawfully damaged, defaced or destroyed such public or private property, whether real or personal, or, where such infant, with intent to deprive the owner and/or custodian of such property or to appropriate the same to himself or herself or to a third person, has knowingly entered or remained in a building and has wrongfully taken, obtained or withheld such public or private personal property from such building which personal property is owned or maintained by the state or any political subdivision thereof or which is owned or maintained by any individual, organization or authority, or where such infant has falsely reported an incident or placed a false bomb as defined in section 240.50, subdivision one or two of section 240.55, section 240.60 or section 240.61 of the penal law. Such public officer, organization or authority, or private individual or organization, as the case may be, may bring an action for civil damages in a court of competent jurisdiction for a judgment to recover such damages from such parent or legal guardian other than the state or a local social services department or a foster parent. For the purposes of this subdivision, damages for falsely reporting an incident or placing a false bomb shall mean the funds reasonably expended by a victim in responding to such false report, as set forth in subdivision eleven of section 60.27 of the penal law. In no event shall such damages portion of a judgment authorized by this section, as described in this subdivision, exceed the sum of five thousand dollars.

2. Notwithstanding the provisions of subdivision one of this section, prior to the entering of a judgment under this section in the sum total of five hundred dollars or more, the court shall provide such parent or legal guardian of such infant with an opportunity to make an application to the court based upon such parent's or legal guardian's financial inability to pay any portion or all of the amount of such sum total which is in excess of five hundred dollars, and upon the return date of such application, or any adjournment thereof, the court shall, in summary fashion, hear and consider all evidence of financial hardship presented tending to establish the inability of such parent or legal guardian to pay any or all of the amount of the sum total in excess of five hundred dollars, and the court shall render its decision as to such party's inability to make such payment based upon a preponderance of the evidence presented. Upon a decision that such party has established his or her inability to make such payment, the court shall enter the judgment authorized by this section but in an amount within

the financial capacity of such parent or legal guardian, provided, however, that since the original of the sum total exceeded five hundred dollars, no such judgment shall be entered for an amount which is less than five hundred dollars.

3. It shall be a defense to an action brought under this section that restitution has been paid pursuant to section seven hundred fifty–eight–a or 353.6 of the family court act, or paragraph (g) of subdivision two of section 65.10 of the penal law. It shall also be a defense to an action brought under this section that such infant had voluntarily and without good cause abandoned the home of the parent or guardian and without good cause refused to submit to the guidance and control of the parent or guardian prior to and at the time of the occurrence of such damages or destruction. In no event shall it be a defense that the parent or legal guardian has exercised due diligent supervision over the activities of such infant, provided, however, that in the interests of justice, the court may consider mitigating circumstances that bear directly upon the actions of the parent or legal guardian in supervising such unemancipated infant.

4. For the purposes of this section the following definitions shall apply:

a. The terms "enters or remains unlawfully" and "building" shall have the same meaning as ascribed to such terms in section 140.00 of the penal law.

b. "Public officer, organization or authority" shall include but not be limited to: those having by law the care and custody of a municipal district or corporation; those having by law the care and custody of the public property of the state or of any agency, department, board, bureau, commission, division, office, council, committee of the state, or of a public benefit corporation or public authority; and the board of education or trustees of any city, union free or common school district or the city board of any New York City community school district.

c. "Private individual or organization" shall include, but not be limited to: any individual, private or public corporation or partnership or sole proprietorship, organized church, synagogue or temple, not–for profit organization or corporation, cemetery corporation, or, if such liability is as a result of damage upon any cemetery plot or mausoleum, the next of kin of a person upon whose gravesite such damage or destruction occurred.

Amended by Laws 1995, Ch. 398, eff. Oct. 31, 1995; **amended** by Laws 1999, Ch. 207, eff. July 6, 1999.

Section 3–113. [Repealed.] [Laws 1995, Ch. 398, eff. Oct. 31, 1995.]

TITLE 3

HUSBAND AND WIFE

GOL

Section 3–301. Powers of married woman

1. A married woman has all the rights in respect to property, real or personal, and the acquisition, use, enjoyment and disposition thereof, and to make contracts in respect thereto with any person, including her husband, and to carry on any business, trade or occupation, and to exercise all powers and enjoy all rights in respect thereto and in respect to her contracts, and be liable on such contracts, as if she were unmarried.

2. All sums that may be recovered in actions or special proceedings by a married woman to recover damages to her person, estate or character shall be the separate property of the wife.

3. Judgment for or against a married woman, may be rendered and enforced, in a court of record, or not of record, as if she was single. A married woman may confess a judgment.

Section 3–303. Contracts in contemplation of marriage

A contract made between persons in contemplation of marriage, remains in full force after the marriage takes place.

Section 3–305. Contract of married woman not to bind husband

A contract made by a married woman does not bind her husband or his property.

Section 3–307. Liability of husband for antenuptial debts

A husband who acquires property of his wife by antenuptial contract or otherwise, is liable for her debts contracted before marriage, but only to the extent of the property so acquired.

Section 3–309. Husband and wife may convey to each other or make partition

Husband and wife may convey or transfer real or personal property directly, the one to the other, without the intervention of a third person; and may make partition or division of any real property held by them as tenants in common, joint tenants or tenants by the entireties. If so expressed in the instrument of partition or division, such instrument bars the wife's right to dower in such property, and also, if so expressed, the husband's tenancy by curtesy.

Section 3–311. Marriage relationship not to affect construction of instruments and transactions involving personal property

1. Where an instrument or transaction creating or transferring an interest in personal property would create a joint tenancy or a tenancy in common in persons not husband and wife, it shall create a joint tenancy or a tenancy in common, as the case may be, in persons who are husband and wife.

2. An instrument or transaction which does not create a right of survivorship in personal property between persons who are not husband and wife shall not create a right of survivorship in personal property between persons who are husband and wife.

3. This section applies without regard to the identity of the person who makes the transfer or at whose instance it is had, or from whom the consideration for the instrument or transaction proceeds.

Section 3–313. Right of action by or against married woman, and by husband or wife against the other, for torts

1. A married woman has a right of action for an injury to her person, property or character or for an injury arising out of the marital relation, as if unmarried. She is liable for her wrongful or tortious acts; her husband is not liable for such acts unless they were done by his actual coercion or instigation; and such coercion or instigation shall not be presumed, but must be proved.

2. A married woman has a right of action against her husband for his wrongful or tortious acts resulting to her in any personal injury as defined in section thirty–seven–a of the general construction law, or resulting in injury to her property, as if they were unmarried, and she is liable to her husband for her wrongful or tortious acts resulting in any such personal injury to her husband or to his property, as if they were unmarried.

Section 3–315. Married woman's right of action for wages

1. A married woman shall have a cause of action in her own sole and separate right for all wages, salary, profits, compensation or other remuneration for which she may render work, labor or services or which may be derived from any trade, business or occupation carried on by her, and her husband shall have no right of action therefor unless she or he with her knowledge and consent has otherwise expressly agreed with the person obligated to pay such wages, salary, profits, compensation or other remuneration.

2. In any action or proceeding in which a married woman or her husband shall seek to recover wages, salary, profits, compensation or other remuneration for which such married woman has rendered work, labor or services or which

GOL

was derived from any trade, business or occupation carried on by her or in which the loss of such wages, salary, profits, compensation or other remuneration shall be an item of damage claimed by a married woman or her husband, the presumption of law in all such cases shall be that such married woman is alone entitled thereto, unless the contrary expressly appears.

TITLE 5

CERTAIN OCCUPATIONS

Section 3–501. Effect of death upon power of attorney given by persons engaged in certain occupations

1. No agency created by a power of attorney in writing given by a principal who is at the time of execution, or who, after executing such power of attorney, becomes, either

a. a person serving in the armed forces of the United States; or

b. a person serving as a merchant seaman outside the continental limits of the United States; or

c. a person outside such continental limits by permission, assignment or direction of any department or official of the United States government, in connection with any activity pertaining to or connected with the prosecution of any war or any campaign of a military nature in which the armed forces of the United States are participating or have been ordered to participate;

shall be revoked or terminated by the death of the principal as to the attorney–in–fact, agent or other person who, without actual knowledge or actual notice of the death of the principal shall have acted or shall act, in good faith, under or in reliance upon such power of attorney or agency, and any action so taken, unless otherwise invalid or unenforceable, shall be binding on the heirs, devisees, legatees or personal representatives of the principal.

2. An affidavit, executed by the attorney–in–fact or agent, setting forth that he has not or had not, at the time of doing any act pursuant to the power of attorney, received actual knowledge or actual notice of revocation or termination of the power of attorney, by death or otherwise, or notice of any facts indicating the same, shall, in the absence of fraud, be conclusive proof of the nonrevocation or nontermination of the power at such time. If the exercise of the power requires execution and delivery of any instrument which is recordable under the laws

of this state, such affidavit when authenticated for record in the manner prescribed by law shall likewise be recordable.

3. No report or listing, either official or otherwise, of "missing" or "missing in action", as such words are used in military parlance, shall constitute or be interpreted as constituting actual knowledge or actual notice of the death of such principal or notice of any facts indicating the same, or shall operate to revoke the agency.

4. This section shall not be construed so as to alter or affect any provision for revocation or termination contained in such power of attorney.

5. If any provision of this section or the application thereof to any person or circumstance be held invalid, such invalidity shall not affect any other provision or application of the section which can be given effect without the invalid provision or application, and to this end the provisions of this section are declared to be severable.

Section 3–503. Required information and statement in applications for licenses to conduct occupations; fulfillment of child support obligations

1. As used in this section:

a. "Agency" means the legal authority or entity responsible for determining whether or not a license shall be issued or renewed.

b. "Application" means the form or statements required to be completed or supplied in order to obtain a license.

c. "License" means any certificate, license, permit or grant of permission required by the laws of this state, its political subdivisions or instrumentalities as a condition for the lawful practice of any occupation, employment, trade, vocation, business, or profession, and shall also include any registration required by law or agency regulation as a condition for such lawful practice.

2. Every applicant for a license or renewal thereof shall provide his or her social security number on the application. Additionally, every applicant for a license or renewal thereof shall certify in the application in a written statement under oath, duly sworn and subscribed, that as of the date the application is filed he or she is (or is not) under obligation to pay child support and that if he or she is under such an obligation, that he or she does (or does not) meet one of the following requirements:

a. He or she is not four months or more in arrears in the payment of child support; or

b. He or she is making payments by income execution or by court agreed payment or repayment plan or by plan agreed to by the parties; or

c. The child support obligation is the subject of a pending court proceeding; or

d. He or she is receiving public assistance or supplemental security income.

3. If the applicant is not under an obligation to pay child support, the agency may issue or renew such license. If the applicant is under an obligation to pay child support and is not four months or more in arrears in the payment of child support, or meets the conditions of paragraphs b, c and d of this subdivision, the agency may issue or renew such license. If the applicant does not meet one of the above requirements, the agency may issue or renew such license but such license shall expire in six months unless before that time the applicant submits a written certification under oath, duly sworn and subscribed that he or she:

a. Is no longer in arrears in the payment of child support; or

b. Is making payments by income execution or by court agreed payment or repayment plan or by plan agreed to by the parties or repayment plan with the appropriate support collection unit; or

c. The child support obligation is the subject of a pending court proceeding; or

d. He or she is receiving public assistance or supplemental security income.

Upon the submission of such certification, the expiration date of such license shall be governed by the agency's customary practice and no fee, in addition to the initial license application fee, shall be charged unless the six month period has expired.

4. Every application shall state in bold face that persons who are four months or more in arrears in child support or who have failed to comply with a summons, subpoena or warrant relating to a paternity or child support proceeding may be subject to suspension of their business, professional, drivers and/or recreational licenses and permits including, but not limited to, licences issued pursuant to section 11–0713 of the environmental conservation law.

5. Every application shall state that the intentional submission of false written statements for the purpose of frustrating or defeating the lawful enforcement of support obligations is punishable pursuant to section 175.35 of the penal law.

Added by Laws 1995, Ch. 81, eff. July 1, 1995; **amended** by Laws 1997, Ch. 398, eff. Jan. 1, 1998.

ARTICLE 5

CREATION, DEFINITION AND ENFORCEMENT OF CONTRACTUAL OBLIGATIONS

TITLE 1

DEFINITIONS OF TERMS

Section 5–101. Definitions of terms as used in certain sections

1. As used in sections 5–331, 5–703, 5–1115, the term "conveyance" includes every instrument, in writing, except a will, by which any estate or interest in real property is created, transferred, assigned or surrendered.

2. As used in sections 5–703, 5–1111 and 5–1115, the terms "estate" and "interest in real property" include every such estate and interest, freehold or chattel, legal or equitable, present or future, vested or contingent.

3. As used in section 5–321, 5–323, 5–331, 5–703 and 5–1115, the term "real property" is co–extensive in meaning with lands, tenements and hereditaments.

TITLE 3

CERTAIN PROHIBITED CONTRACTS AND PROVISIONS OF CONTRACTS

Section 5–301. Certain employment contracts void

Every undertaking or promise, whether written or oral, express or implied, constituting or contained, in any contract or agreement of hiring or employment between any individual, firm, company, association or corporation and any employee or prospective employee of the same, whereby (a) any employee or prospective employee undertakes or promises to join, become or remain a member of a company union; or (b) either party to such contract or agreement undertakes or promises not to join, become, or remain a member of any organization or any organization of employers; or (c) either party to such contract or agreement undertakes or promises that he will withdraw from the employment relation in the event that he joins, becomes or remains a member of any labor organization or of any organization of employers, is hereby declared to be contrary to public policy and wholly void and shall not afford any basis for the granting of legal or equitable relief by any court against a party to such undertaking or promise, or against any other persons who may advise, urge or induce, without fraud, violence, or threat thereof, either party thereto to act in disregard of such undertaking or promise.

Section 5–311. Certain agreements between husband and wife void

Except as provided in section two hundred thirty–six of the domestic relations law, a husband and wife cannot contract to alter or dissolve the marriage or to relieve either of his or her liability to support the other in such a manner that he or she will become incapable of self–support and therefore is likely to become a public charge. An agreement, heretofore or hereafter made between a husband and wife, shall not be considered a contract to alter or dissolve the marriage unless it contains an express provision requiring the dissolution of the marriage or provides for the procurement of grounds of divorce.

Added by Laws 1980, Ch. 281, eff. July 19, 1980 (repealed former Section 5–311).

Section 5–321. Agreements exempting lessors from liability for negligence void and unenforceable

Every covenant, agreement or understanding in or in connection with or collateral to any lease of real property exempting the lessor from liability for damages for injuries to person or property caused by or resulting from the negligence of the lessor, his agents, servants or employees, in the operation or maintenance of the demised premises or the real property containing the demised premises shall be deemed to be void as against public policy and wholly unenforceable.

Section 5–322. Agreements exempting caterers and catering establishment from liability for negligence void and unenforceable

Every covenant, agreement or understanding in or in connection with or collateral to any contract entered into with any caterer or catering establishment exempting the said caterer or catering establishment from liability for damages caused by or resulting from the negligence of the caterer or catering establishment, his agents, servants, employees or patrons at the affair contracted therefor, shall be deemed to be void as against public policy and wholly unenforceable.

Added by Laws 1966, Ch. 586, ef. June 14, 1966.

Section 5–322.1. Agreements exempting owners and contractors from liability for negligence void and unenforceable; certain cases

1. A covenant, promise, agreement or understanding in, or in connection with or collateral to a contract or agreement relative to the construction, alteration, repair or maintenance of a building, structure, appurtenances and appliances including moving, demolition and excavating connected therewith, purporting to indemnify or hold harmless the promisee against liability for damage arising out of bodily injury to persons or damage to property contributed to, caused by or resulting from the negligence of the promisee, his agents or employees, or indemnitee, whether such negligence be in whole or in part, is against public policy and is void and unenforceable; provided that this section shall not affect the validity of any insurance contract, workers' compensation agreement or other agreement issued by an admitted insurer. This subdivision shall not preclude a promisee requiring indemnification for damages arising out of bodily injury to persons or damage to property caused by or resulting from the negligence of a party other than the promisee, whether or not the promisor is partially negligent.

2. The provisions of this section shall only apply to covenants, promises, agreements or understandings in, or in connection with or collateral to a contract or agreement, as enumerated in subdivision one hereof, entered into on or after the thirtieth day next succeeding the date on which it shall become a law.

Added by Laws 1975, Ch. 408, eff. Aug. 7, 1975; **amended** by Laws 1981, Ch. 964, eff. Aug. 30, 1981; Laws 1993, Ch. 67, eff. May 21, 1993.

Section 5–322.2. Contents of certain construction contracts

1. Every written contract or agreement executed by an owner providing for the building, construction, repair or renovation of buildings, structures, or improvements upon real property owned by him other than contracts involving public improvements as defined in the lien law and contracts involving residential property with housing accommodations for less than five families, shall contain a clause requiring such owner to set forth in said contract the following information:

(a) the full name and address of the owner or owners;

(b) the full name and address of the owner of the land and the owner of the building or improvements if the owner of the land and the owner of the building or improvements shall be different persons or entities; and

(c) a description by street address; or section, block, and lot numbers; or reference to a deed book and page number;

In the event the names required to be set forth as hereinabove provided shall be changed after the execution of any such contract or agreement and during the period of such construction, the owner shall within five days notify the contractor of such change in writing sent to the contractor by certified mail to the address of the contractor as set forth in said contract.

2. Every written subcontract or agreement executed by a contractor for performance of any portion of the said construction, shall contain the same information required to be provided to the contractor by the owner described in subdivision one of this section.

3. The provisions of this section shall apply only to contracts or agreements as enumerated in subdivision one of this section, entered into on or after the date on which the provisions of this section become effective.

4. Any failure to comply with the provisions of this section shall not render any agreement or contract hereof, enumerated in subdivision one hereof, void or voidable nor shall it otherwise impair any obligations or rights under any such agreement or contract.

Added by Laws 1978, Ch. 535, eff. Sept. 22, 1978; **amended** by Laws 1981, Ch. 497, eff. July 15, 1981.

Section 5–322.3. Payment bonds to be filed

A copy of any payment bond executed in connection with a contract for the improvement of real property other than a contract for a public improvement, shall be filed within thirty days of such execution by the owner of the improvement in the office of the county clerk in the county in which the improvement is to be undertaken; provided, however, that such filing shall be required only where the contract for the improvement of real property is for an amount in excess of one hundred thousand dollars. Any owner failing to file such payment bond as provided herein shall be liable for the reasonable attorney's fees, as determined by the court, of any claimant successfully bringing an action or proceeding on the bond.

Added by Laws 1981, Ch. 192, eff. July 9, 1981.

Section 5–323. Agreements exempting building service or maintenance contractors from liability for negligence void and unenforceable

Every covenant, agreement or understanding in or in connection with or collateral to any contract or agreement affecting real property made or entered into, whereby or whereunder a contractor exempts himself from liability for injuries to person or property caused by or resulting from the negligence of such contract or, his agent, servants or employees, as a result of work performed or services rendered in connection with the construction, maintenance and repair of real property or its appurtenances, shall be deemed to be void as against public policy and wholly unenforceable.

Section 5–324. Agreements by owners, contractors, subcontractors or suppliers to indemnify architects, engineers and surveyors from liability caused by or arising out of defects in maps, plans, designs and specifications void and unenforceable

Every covenant, agreement or understanding in, or in connection with any contract or agreement made and entered into by owners, contractors, subcontractors or suppliers whereby an architect, engineer, surveyor or their agents, servants or employees are indemnified for damages arising from liability for bodily injury to persons or damage to property caused by or arising out of defects in maps, plans, designs or specifications, prepared, acquired or used by such architect, engineer, surveyor or their agents, servants or employees shall be deemed void as against public policy and wholly unenforceable.

Added by Laws 1965, Ch. 375, eff. Sept. 1, 1965.

Section 5–325. Garages and parking places

1. No person who conducts or maintains for hire or other consideration a garage, parking lot or other similar place which has the capacity for the housing, storage, parking, repair or servicing of four or more motor vehicles, as defined by the vehicle and traffic law, may exempt himself from liability for damages for injury to person or property resulting from the negligence of such person, his agents or employees, in the operation of any such vehicle, or in its housing, storage, parking, repair or servicing, or in the conduct or maintenance of such garage, parking lot or other similar place, and, except as hereinafter provided, any agreement so exempting such person shall be void.

2. Damages for loss or injury to property may be limited by a provision in the storage agreement limiting the liability in case of loss or damage by theft, fire or explosion and setting forth a specific liability per vehicle, which shall in no event be less than twenty–five thousand dollars, beyond which the person owning or operating such garage or lot shall not be liable; provided, however, that such liability may on request of the person delivering such vehicle be increased, in which event increased rates may be charged based on such increased liability.

Amended by Laws 1983, Ch. 957, eff. Oct. 7, 1983.

Section 5–326. Agreements exempting pools, gymnasiums, places of public amusement or recreation and similar establishments from liability for negligence void and unenforceable

Every covenant, agreement or understanding in or in connection with, or collateral to, any contract, membership application, ticket of admission or similar writing, entered into between the owner or operator of any pool, gymnasium, place of amusement or recreation, or similar establishment and the user of such facilities, pursuant to which such owner or operator receives a fee or other compensation for the use of such facilities, which exempts the said owner or operator from liability for damages caused by or resulting from the negligence of the owner, operator or person in charge of such establishment, or their agents, servants or employees, shall be deemed to be void as against public policy and wholly unenforceable.

Added by Laws 1976, Ch. 414, eff. Sept. 1, 1976.

Section 5–327. Consumers' right to recover attorney's fees in actions arising out of consumer contracts

1. As used in this section, the following terms shall have the following meanings:

(a) "Consumer contract" means a written agreement entered into between a creditor, seller or lessor as one party with a natural person who is the debtor, buyer, or lessee as the second party, and the money, other personal property or services which are the subject of the transaction are primarily for personal, family or household purposes;

(b) "Creditor" means a person who regularly extends, or arranges for the extension of, credit which is payable by agreement in more than four installments or for which the payment of a finance charge is or may be required;

(c) "Seller" means a person who sells or provides or agrees to sell or provide the subject of a consumer transaction.

(d) "Lessor" means a person who regularly leases, or arranges for the lease of, personal property which is the subject of a consumer contract.

2. Whenever a consumer contract provides that the creditor, seller or lessor may recover attorney's fees and expenses incurred as the result of a breach of any contractual obligation by the debtor, buyer or lessee, it shall be implied that the creditor, seller or lessor shall pay the attorney's fees and expenses of the debtor, buyer or lessee incurred as the result of a breach of any contractual obligation by the creditor, seller or lessor, or in the successful defense of any action arising out of the contract commenced by the creditor, seller or lessor. Any limitations on attorney's fees recoverable by the creditor, seller or lessor shall also be applicable to attorney's fees recoverable by the debtor, buyer or lessee under this section. Any waiver of this section shall be void as against public policy.

Added by Laws of 1983, Ch. 294, eff. June 13, 1983; **amended** by Laws 1994, Ch. 1, eff. Jan. 1, 1994.

Section 5–328. Processing fee by holder of dishonored check

1. As used in this section the following terms shall have the following meanings:

(a) "Holder of a check" means the holder or its assignee, representative or any other person retained by the holder to seek collection of the face value of a dishonored check.

(b) "Dishonored check" means a check, draft or like instrument, drawn on a bank or depository institution as full or partial payment for an unpaid balance on an account, or for other extensions of credit or payments of money in connection with a consumer transaction, which is not paid or is dishonored or is returned by such institution due to insufficient funds or other cause not attributable to the holder.

(c) "Consumer transaction" means a transaction in which a natural person is extended credit for, or purchases or leases, personal property, money or services primarily for personal, family or household purposes.

(d) "Account" means a loan account, a retail credit account or an obligation under a retail lease agreement, retail instalment contract or retail instalment obligation or a retail instalment credit agreement, as defined in sections three hundred one, three hundred thirty–one and four hundred one of the personal property law.

2. Notwithstanding the provisions of any law:

(a) The holder of a dishonored check given in payment for a consumer transaction or an account may collect from, charge, or add to the outstanding balance of the account of, the person from whom such check was received or to whom such credit was extended, a dishonored check charge of not more than the lesser of the amount agreed upon, if contracted for, or twenty dollars.

(b) A dishonored check charge shall not be deemed a credit service charge, interest or an incident to or a condition to the extension of credit, for any purpose of law.

3. Notwithstanding any other provision of law, any person to whom a check, draft or like instrument, other than a money order, bank cashier's check or certified check, is tendered for any transaction, other than a consumer transaction, may, if such instrument is dishonored charge or collect from the maker or drawer the amount of twenty dollars for the return of such unpaid or dishonored instrument.

Added by Laws 1985, Ch. 708, eff. Aug. 1, 1985; **amended** by Laws 1989, Ch. 60, eff. April 17, 1989; Laws 1991, Ch. 15, eff. April 6, 1991. The 1989 amendment to the opening paragraph of subdivision 2 deleted the following language: "the provisions of subdivision five of section four hundred thirteen and subdivision four of section four hundred four of the personal property law, and notwithstanding" after "Notwithstanding"; and "other" after "any". This amendment remains in effect until June 30, 1993, at which time the language deleted by the 1989 amendment will be reinstated; **amended** by Laws 1994, Ch. 1, eff. Jan. 1, 1994; Laws 1995, Ch. 529, eff. Oct. 31, 1995.

Section 5–331. Certain covenants and restrictions in conveyances and other agreements affecting real property void as against public policy

Any promise, covenant or restriction in a contract, mortgage, lease, deed or conveyance or in any other agreement affecting real property, heretofore or hereafter made or entered into, which limits, restrains, prohibits or otherwise provides against the sale, grant, gift, transfer, assignment, conveyance, ownership, lease, rental, use or occupancy of real property to or by any person because of race, creed, color, national origin, or ancestry, is hereby declared to be void as against public policy, wholly unenforceable, and shall not constitute a defense in any action, suit or proceeding. No such promise, covenant or restriction shall be listed as a valid provision affecting such property in public notices concerning such property. The invalidity of any such promise, covenant or restriction in any such instrument or agreement shall not affect the validity of any other provision therein, but no reverter shall occur, no possessory estate shall result, nor any right of entry or right to a penalty or forfeiture shall accrue by reason of the disregard of such promise, covenant or restriction. This section shall not apply to conveyances or devises to religious associations or corporations for religious purposes, but, such promise, covenant or restriction shall cease to be enforceable and shall otherwise become subject to the provisions of this section when the real property affected shall cease to be used for such purpose.

Amended by Laws 1964, Ch. 196, eff. Sept. 27, 1964.

Section 5–332. Unsolicited and voluntarily sent merchandise deemed unconditional gift

1. No person, firm, partnership, association or corporation, or agent or employee thereof, shall, in any manner, or by any means, offer for sale goods, wares, or merchandise, where the offer includes the voluntary and unsolicited sending of such goods, wares, or merchandise not actually ordered or requested by the recipient, either orally or in writing. The receipt of any such goods, wares, or merchandise shall for all purposes be deemed an unconditional gift to the recipient who may use or dispose of such goods, wares, or merchandise in any manner he sees fit without any obligation on his part to the sender.

If after any such receipt deemed to be an unconditional gift under this section, the sender continues to send bill statements or requests for payment with respect thereto, an action may be brought by the recipient to enjoin such conduct in which action there may also be awarded reasonable attorney's fees and costs to the prevailing party.

2. If a person is a member of an organization which makes retail sales of any goods, wares, or merchandise to its members, and the person notifies the organization of his termination of membership by certified mail, return receipt requested, any unordered goods, wares or merchandise which are sent to the person after thirty days following execution of the return receipt for the certified

letter by the organization, shall for all purposes be deemed unconditional gifts to the person, who may use or dispose of the goods, wares, or merchandise in any manner he sees fit without any obligation on his part to the organization.

If the termination of a person's membership in such organization breaches any agreement with the organization, nothing in this section shall relieve the person from liability for damages to which he might be otherwise subjected to pursuant to law, but he shall not be subject to any damages with respect to any goods, wares, or merchandise which are deemed unconditional gifts to him under this section.

If after any receipt deemed to be an unconditional gift under this section, the sender continues to send bill statements or requests for payment with respect thereto, an action may be brought by the recipient to enjoin such conduct, in which action there may also be awarded reasonable attorneys' fees and costs to the prevailing party.

Added by Laws 1970, Ch. 853, eff. July 1, 1970.

Section 5–333. Validity of oil, gas or mineral land lease

1. Any oil, gas or mineral land lease given on land situated in this state shall be deemed to incorporate subdivisions two and three of this section and any provisions to the contrary shall be void and unenforceable.

2. Any oil, gas or mineral land lease which provides for delay rental payments, such payments being periodic payments to the lessor for the right to delay drilling or excavation upon the leased property, shall provide that the first such payment shall be due and payable no later than one hundred eighty days after the effective date of the lease. Any bonus or up front payment made by the lessee equal to or greater than the first delayed rental payment shall constitute compliance with this subdivision.

3. Any oil, gas or mineral land lease shall contain a statement advising the lessor of the provisions of section 15–304 of this chapter. Such statement shall be printed in at least ten point bold type and shall read as follows:

IF THIS LEASE BECOMES FORFEITED, TERMINATED OR EXPIRES, THE LESSEE, OR IF THE LEASE HAS BEEN ASSIGNED, THE ASSIGNEE IS REQUIRED TO PROVIDE A DOCUMENT CANCELLING THE LEASE AS OF RECORD, AT NO COST TO THE CURRENT LANDOWNER. IF THE LESSEE OR ASSIGNEE FAILS TO CANCEL THE LEASE, THE CURRENT LANDOWNER MAY COMPEL A CANCELLATION PURSUANT TO SECTION 15–304 OF THE GENERAL OBLIGATIONS LAW.

4. For the purposes of this section, the term "mineral" shall not include salt, as defined by subdivision eighteen of section 23–0101 of the environmental conservation law.

5. This section shall apply to leases entered into on or after January first, nineteen hundred eighty–five.

Added by Laws 1984, Ch. 565, eff. Sept. 1, 1984 (applies to all oil, gas or mineral land leases entered into on or after Jan. 1, 1985); amended by Laws 1984, Ch. 566, eff. Sept. 1, 1984. § 3, Ch. 565, as amended by § 2, Ch. 566, provides that nothing contained in this section shall diminish the legal remedies any party may have under Article 15 of the Real Property Actions and Proceedings Law.

Section 5–334. Option or right to acquire interest in property

1. An option or right to acquire an equity or other ownership interest in property or in a partnership, corporation, trust or other entity that owns property shall not be unenforceable because the owner of such interest grants such option or right to the holder of a mortgage which is a lien on such property or to the holder of a security interest in such property, simultaneously with or in connection with any loan or forbearance of money secured by such mortgage or security interest, if (a) the power to exercise such option or right is not dependent upon the occurrence of a default with respect to such loan, forbearance, mortgage or security interest, and (b) such loan or forbearance is for the principal sum of two million five hundred thousand dollars or more when the option or right is granted. Loans or forbearances aggregating two million five hundred thousand dollars or more which are to be made or advanced to any one borrower in one or more installments pursuant to a written agreement by one or more lenders shall be deemed a single loan or forbearance for the total amount which the lender or lenders have agreed to make or advance pursuant to such agreement.

2. This section shall not be construed to limit, impair or otherwise affect the power of the holder of any option or right to acquire an equity or other ownership interest in property or in a partnership, corporation, trust or other entity that owns property, if such option or right is or would be enforceable without reference to this section.

3. This section shall apply to all options or rights which are exercised on or after the effective date of this section, notwithstanding the date when such options or rights were granted.

Added by Laws 1985, Ch. 177, eff. June 11, 1985.

TITLE 4

CONTRACTS RELATING TO WAGERING; FORFEITURE AND RECOVERY OF CERTAIN PROPERTY

GOL

Section 5–401. Illegal wagers, bets and stakes

All wagers, bets or stakes, made to depend upon any race, or upon any gaming by lot or chance, or upon any lot, chance, casualty, or unknown or contingent event whatever, shall be unlawful.

Added by Laws 1965, Ch. 1031, eff. Sept. 1, 1967.

Section 5–411. Contracts on account of money or property wagered, bet or staked are void

All contracts for or on account of any money or property, or thing in action wagered, bet or staked, as provided in section 5–401, shall be void.

Added by Laws 1965, Ch. 1031, eff. Sept. 1, 1967.

Section 5–413. Securities for money lost at gaming, void

All things in action, judgments, mortgages, conveyances, and every other security whatsoever, given or executed, by any person, where the whole or any part of the consideration of the same shall be for any money or other valuable thing won by playing at any game whatsoever, or won by betting on the hands or sides of such as do play at any game, or where the same shall be made for the repaying any money knowingly lent or advanced for the purpose of such gaming or betting aforesaid, or lent or advanced at the time and place of such play, to any person so gaming or betting aforesaid, or to any person who during such play, shall play or bet, shall be utterly void, except where such securities, conveyances or mortgages shall affect any real estate, when the same shall be void as to the grantee therein, so far only as hereinafter declared.

When any securities, mortgages or other conveyances, executed for the whole or part of any consideration specified in the preceding paragraph shall affect any real estate, they shall inure for the sole benefit of such person as would be entitled to the said real estate, if the grantor or person incumbering the same, had died, immediately upon the execution of such instrument, and shall be deemed to be taken and held to and for the use of the person who would be so entitled. All grants, convenants and conveyances, for preventing such real estate from coming to, or devolving upon, the person hereby intended to enjoy the same as aforesaid, or in any way incumbering or charging the same, so as to prevent such person from enjoying the same fully and entirely, shall be deemed fraudulent and void.

Added by Laws 1965, Ch. 1031, eff. Sept. 1, 1967.

Section 5–415. Certain transfers of property in pursuance of lottery, void

Every grant, bargain, sale, conveyance, or transfer of any real estate, or of any goods, chattels, things in action, or any personal property, which shall hereinafter be made in pursuance of any lottery, or for the purpose of aiding and assisting in such lottery, game or other device, to be determined by lot or chance is hereby declared void and of no effect.

Added by Laws 1965, Ch. 1031, eff. Sept. 1, 1967.

Section 5–417. Contracts, agreements and securities on account of raffling, void

All contracts, agreements and securities given made or executed, for or on account of any raffle, or distribution of money, goods or things in action, for the payment of any money, or other valuable thing, in consideration of a chance in such raffle or distribution, or for the delivery of any money, goods or things in action, so raffled for, or agreed to be distributed as aforesaid, shall be utterly void.

Added by Laws 1965, Ch. 1031, eff. Sept. 1, 1967.

Section 5–419. Property staked may be recovered

Any person who shall pay, deliver or deposit any money, property or thing in action, upon the event of any wager or bet prohibited, may sue for and recover the same of the winner or person to whom the same shall be paid or delivered, and of the stakeholder or other person in whose hands shall be deposited any such wager, bet or stake, or any part thereof, whether the same shall have been paid over by such stakeholder or not, and whether any such wager be lost or not.

Added by Laws 1965, Ch. 1031, eff. Sept. 1, 1967.

Section 5–421. Losers of certain sums may recover them

Every person who shall, by playing at any game, or by betting on the sides or hands of such as do play, lose at any time or sitting, the sum or value of twenty–five dollars or upwards, and shall pay or deliver the same or any part thereof, may, within three calendar months after such payment or delivery, sue and recover the money or value of the things so lost and paid or delivered from the winner thereof.

Added by Laws 1965, Ch. 1031, eff. Sept. 1, 1967.

Section 5–423. Money paid for lottery tickets may be recovered by action

Any person who shall purchase any share, interest, ticket, certificate of any share or interest, or part of a ticket, or any paper or instrument purporting to be a ticket or share or interest in any ticket, or purporting to be a certificate of any share or interest in any ticket, or in any portion of any lottery, may sue for and recover double the sum of money, and double the value of goods or things in action, which he may have paid or delivered in consideration of such purchase, with double costs of suit.

Any person who shall have paid any money, or valuable thing, for a chance or interest in any lottery or distribution, prohibited by the penal law, may sue for and recover the same of the person to whom such payment or delivery was made.

Added by Laws 1965, Ch. 1031, eff. Sept. 1, 1967.

TITLE 5

INTEREST AND USURY; BROKERAGE ON LOANS

Section 5–501. Rate of interest; usury forbidden

1. The rate of interest, as computed pursuant to this title, upon the loan or forbearance of any money, goods, or things in action, except as provided in subdivisions five and six of this section or as otherwise provided by law, shall be six per centum per annum unless a different rate is prescribed in section fourteen–a of the banking law.

2. No person or corporation shall, directly or indirectly, charge, take or receive any money, goods or things in action as interest on the loan or forbearance of any money, goods or things in action at a rate exceeding the rate above prescribed. The amount charged, taken or received as interest shall include any and all amounts paid or payable, directly or indirectly, by any person, to or for the account of the lender in consideration for making the loan or forbearance as defined by the banking board pursuant to subdivision three of section fourteen–a of the banking law except such fee as may be fixed by the

commissioner of taxation and finance as the cost of servicing loans made by the property and liability insurance security fund.

3. If the rate of interest charged, taken or received on any loan or forbearance secured primarily by either (i) an interest in real property improved by a one to six family residence occupied by the owner or (ii) certificates of stock or other evidence of an ownership interest in a corporation or partnership formed for the purpose of the cooperative ownership of real estate taken as security for a loan under subdivision five of section one hundred three of the banking law, subdivision eight–a of section two hundred thirty–five of such law or subdivision two–a of section three hundred eighty of such law, exceeds six per centum per annum,

a. in the case of a loan referred to by clause (i) of this subdivision, the term of such loan or forbearance may extend five years beyond the maximum maturity of such loan otherwise prescribed by law, and

b. notwithstanding any other provision of law, the unpaid balance of the loan or forbearance may be prepaid, in whole or in part, at any time. If prepayment is made on or after one year from the date the loan or forbearance is made, no penalty may be imposed. If prepayment is made prior to such time, no penalty may be imposed unless provision therefor is expressly made in the loan contract. In all cases, the right of prepayment shall be stated in the instrument evidencing the loan or forbearance, provided, however, that the provisions of this subdivision shall not apply to the extent such provisions are inconsistent with any federal law or regulation.

4. Except as otherwise provided by law, interest shall not be charged, taken or received on any loan or forbearance at a rate exceeding such rate of interest as may be authorized by law at the time the loan or forbearance is made, whether or not the loan or forbearance is made pursuant to a prior contract or commitment providing for a greater rate of interest, provided, however, that no change in the rate of interest prescribed in section fourteen–a of the banking law shall affect (a) the validity of a loan or forbearance made before the date such rate becomes effective, or (b) the enforceability of such loan or forbearance in accordance with its terms, except that if any loan or forbearance provides for an increase in the rate of interest during the term of such loan or forbearance, the increased rate shall not exceed such rate of interest as may have been authorized by law at the time such loan or forbearance was made.

4–a. Notwithstanding the provisions of subdivision four of this section, a loan or forbearance repayable on demand may provide for changes, reflecting variations in lending rates, from time to time in the rate of interest payable on such loan or forbearance up to the rate of interest authorized by law at the time of such change and in such case the rate of interest may be so changed in accordance with the terms of the contract or loan commitment relating thereto; provided, however, that the rate of interest charged, taken or received on such a loan or forbearance shall not exceed the rate of interest authorized by law as it may subsequently be reduced from time to time; and further provided, however, that in no event shall such a loan or forbearance be subject to an authorized rate of interest less than that applicable at the time such loan or forbearance was made. The provisions of this subdivision shall apply only to a loan or forbearance repayable on demand which has an initial principal of more than five thousand dollars and which the borrower has the right to repay at any time in whole or in part, together with accrued interest on the principal so repaid, without any penalty. With respect to a loan or forbearance covered by this subdivision, the lender shall disclose to the borrower in writing not less often than annually the amount of interest accrued or payable as of the date of such disclosure and the manner by which such amount was computed.

5. No law regulating the maximum rate of interest which may be charged, taken or received shall apply to any loan or forbearance insured by the federal housing commissioner or for which a commitment to insure has been made by the federal housing commissioner or to any loan or forbearance insured or guaranteed pursuant to the provisions of an act of congress entitled "Servicemen's Readjustment Act of 1944."

6. a. No law regulating the maximum rate of interest which may be charged, taken or received, except section 190.40 and section 190.42 of the penal law, shall apply to any loan or forbearance in the amount of two hundred fifty thousand dollars or more, other than a loan or a forbearance secured primarily by an interest in real property improved by a one or two family residence. A loan of two hundred fifty thousand dollars or more which is to be advanced in installments pursuant to a written agreement by a lender shall be deemed to be a single loan for the total amount which the lender has agreed to advance pursuant to such agreement on the terms and conditions provided therein.

b. No law regulating the maximum rate of interest which may be charged, taken or received, including section 190.40 and section 190.42 of the penal law, shall apply to any loan or forbearance in the amount of two million five hundred thousand dollars or more. Loans or forbearances aggregating two million five hundred thousand dollars or more which are to be made or advanced to any one borrower in one or more installments pursuant to a written agreement by one or more lenders shall be deemed to be a single loan or forbearance for the total amount which the lender or lenders have agreed to advance or make pursuant to such agreement on the terms and conditions provided therein.

7. Except as otherwise expressly provided by law, in the event of prepayment in full of a loan, any refund of unearned interest to which the borrower may be entitled may not be computed by a sum of the balances or similar method but must be determined according to a generally accepted actuarial method.

Amended by Laws 1968, Ch. 349, eff. May 15, 1968, Ch. 944, eff. June 22, 1968, and Ch. 1072, eff. July 1, 1969; Laws 1970, Ch. 611, eff. May 12, 1970; Laws 1974, Ch. 119, eff. April 1, 1974, and Ch. 770, eff. June 7, 1974; Laws 1976, Ch. 721, eff. July 24, 1976; Laws 1980, Ch. 369, eff. June 23, 1980, and Ch. 883, eff. Dec. 1, 1980; Laws 1983, Ch. 296, eff. June 13, 1984.

Section 5–511. Usurious contracts void

1. All bonds, bills, notes, assurances, conveyances, all other contracts or securities whatsoever, except bottomry and respondentia bonds and contracts, and all deposits of goods or other things whatsoever, whereupon or whereby there shall be reserved or taken, or secured or agreed to be reserved or taken, any greater sum, or greater value, for the loan or forbearance of any money, goods or other things in action, than is prescribed in section 5–501, shall be void, except that the knowingly taking, receiving, reserving or charging such a greater sum or greater value by a savings bank, a savings and loan association or a federal savings and loan association shall only be held and adjudged a forfeiture of the entire interest which the loan or obligation carries with it or which has been agreed to be paid thereon. If a greater sum or greater value has been paid, the person paying the same or his legal representative may recover from the savings bank, the savings and loan association or a federal savings and loan association twice the entire amount of the interest thus paid.

2. Except as provided in subdivision one, whenever it shall satisfactorily appear by the admissions of the defendant, or by proof, that any bond, bill, note, assurance, pledge, conveyance, contract, security or any evidence of debt, has been taken or received in violation of the foregoing provisions, the court shall declare the same to be void, and enjoin any prosecution thereon, and order the same to be surrendered and cancelled.

Amended by Laws 1968, Ch. 1072, eff. July 1, 1969.

Section 5–513. Recovery of excess

Every person who, for any such loan or forbearance, shall pay or deliver any greater sum or value than is allowed to be received pursuant to section 5–501, and his personal representatives, may recover in an action against the person who shall have taken or received the same, and his personal representatives, the amount of the money so paid or value delivered, above the rate aforesaid.

Amended by Laws 1964, Ch. 196, eff. Sept. 27, 1964; Laws 1968, Ch. 1072, eff. July 1, 1969.

Section 5–515. Borrower bringing an action need not offer to repay

Whenever any borrower of money, goods or things in action, shall begin an action for the recovery of the money, goods or things in action taken in violation of the foregoing provisions of this title, it shall not be necessary for him to pay or offer to pay any interest or principal on the sum or thing loaned; nor shall any court require or compel the payment or deposit of the principal sum or interest, or any portion thereof, as a condition of granting relief to the borrower in any case of usurious loans forbidden by the foregoing provisions of this title.

Section 5–517. Transfer of cause of action for usury

A cause of action to cancel, or otherwise affect, an instrument executed, or an act done, as security for a usurious loan or forbearance, can be transferred, where the instrument or act creates a specific charge upon property, which is also transferred in disaffirmance thereof, and not otherwise; but, in that case, the transferee does not succeed to the right, conferred by statute upon the borrower, to procure relief, without paying, or offering to pay, any part of the sum or thing loaned.

Section 5–519. Return of excess a bar to further penalties

Every person who shall repay or return the money, goods or other things so taken accepted or received, or the value thereof, shall be discharged from any other or further forfeiture or penalty which he may have incurred, under sections 5–511 or 5–513, by taking or receiving the money, goods or other thing so repaid, or returned, as aforesaid.

Amended by Laws, 1965, Ch. 328, eff. July 1, 1965.

Section 5–521. Corporations prohibited from interposing defense of usury

1. No corporation shall hereafter interpose the defense of usury in any action. The term corporation, as used in this section, shall be construed to include all associations, and joint–stock companies having any of the powers and privileges of corporations not possessed by individuals or partnerships.

2. The provisions of subdivision one of this section shall not apply to a corporation, the principal asset of which shall be the ownership of a one or two family dwelling, where it appears either that the said corporation was organized and created, or that the controlling interest therein was acquired within a period of six months prior to the execution, by said corporation of a bond or note evidencing indebtedness, and a mortgage creating a lien for said indebtedness on the said one or two family dwelling; provided, that as to any such bond, note or mortgage executed by such corporation and effective prior to April sixth, nineteen hundred fifty–six, the defense of usury may be interposed only in an action or proceeding instituted for the collection, enforcement or foreclosure of such note, bond or mortgage.

Any provision of any contract, or any separate written instrument executed prior to, simultaneously with or within sixty days after the delivery of any moneys to any borrower in connection with such indebtedness, whereby the defense of usury is waived or any such corporation is estopped from asserting it, is hereby declared to be contrary to public policy and absolutely void.

3. The provisions of subdivision one of this section shall not apply to any action in which a corporation interposes a defense of criminal usuary as described in section 190.40 of the penal law.

Amended by Laws 1965, Ch. 328, eff. July 1, 1965; Laws 1974, Ch. 768, eff. June 7, 1974.

Section 5–523. Interest permitted on advances on collateral security

In any case in which advances of money, repayable on demand, to an amount not less than five thousand dollars, are made upon documents of title within article seven of the uniform commercial code or negotiable instruments within article three or article eight of the uniform commercial code pledged as collateral security for such repayment, it shall be lawful to receive or to contract to receive and collect, as compensation for making such advances, any sum to be agreed upon in writing, by the parties to such transaction, provided that there shall not be received or contracted to be received and collected on such advances any amount which would be in violation of section 190.40 of the penal law.

Amended by Laws 1965, Ch. 328, eff. July 1, 1965 and Ch. 843, eff. July 16, 1965; Laws 1974, Ch. 768, eff. June 7, 1974.

Section 5–524. Taking security upon certain property for usurious loans

A person who takes security, upon any household furniture, sewing machines, plate or silverware in actual use, tools or implements of trade, wearing apparel or jewelry, for a loan or forbearance of money, or for the use or sale of his personal credit, conditioned upon the payment of a greater rate than the rate prescribed by the banking board pursuant to section fourteen–a of the banking law, or, if no rate has been so prescribed, six per centum per annum, or who as security for such loan, use or sale of personal credit as aforesaid, makes a pretended purchase of such property from any person, upon the like condition, and permits the pledgor to retain the possession thereof is guilty of a misdemeanor.

Added by Laws 1965, Ch. 1031, eff. Sept. 1, 1967; **amended** by Laws 1968, Ch. 349, eff. May 15, 1968.

Section 5–525. Interest charged by a registered broker or dealer for carrying debit balances

Interest charged by a broker or dealer registered under the securities exchange act of nineteen hundred thirty–four, as amended, for carrying a debit balance including a debit balance arising out of a non–purpose loan, in an account for a customer shall not be subject to the limitations of this title, including the limitations contained in subdivision two of section 5–527 of this title, if such debit balance is payable on demand and secured by securities or commodities upon which credit can be extended by a broker or dealer, and if, on the date when the interest is charged or accrued, such interest is not greater than eight percentage points above the prime rate. For the purposes of this section, the prime rate shall equal the average prime rate on short term business loans which is published by the board of governors of the federal reserve system for the most recent week which was publicly available from the board of governors of the federal reserve system on the previous business day.

Amended by Laws 1965, Ch. 328, eff. July 1, 1965; Laws 1967, Ch. 777, eff. May 2, 1967; Laws 1980, Ch. 883, eff. March 1, 1981; Laws 1982, Ch. 145, eff. June 1, 1982; Laws 1991, Ch. 312, eff. July 15, 1991.

Section 5–526. Interest on secured loans or forbearances

1. Interest charged on loans or forbearances made to corporations for business or commercial purposes in the amount of one hundred thousand dollars or more and secured in compliance with the uniform commercial code shall not be subject to the limitations of this title or sections 190.40 and 190.42 of the penal law, if on the date when the interest is charged or accrued, such interest is not greater than eight percentage points above the prime rate.

2. Such secured loans or forbearances which are made or advanced to any one corporate borrower in one or more installments pursuant to a written agreement which provides for either discretionary or mandatory advances by one or more lenders shall be deemed to be a single loan or forbearance for the total amount which the lender or lenders have advanced, if such advances are discretionary, or have agreed to advance, if such advances are mandatory, pursuant to such agreement on the terms and conditions provided therein.

3. For purposes of this section, the loan or forbearance transaction must either (a) create a security interest as set forth in section 9–102 of the uniform commercial code and must be filed pursuant to article nine of such code unless filing is not required pursuant to section 9–302 of such code, or (b) must create a security interest set forth in subdivision (a) of section 9–104 of such code.

4. For purposes of this section, the prime rate shall equal the average prime rate on short term business loans which is published by the board of governors of the federal reserve system for the most recent week which was publicly available from the board of governors of the federal reserve system on the previous business day.

Added by Laws 1984, Ch. 844, eff. Sept. 4, 1984; **amended** by Laws 1985, Ch. 388, eff. July 19, 1985.

Section 5–527. Enforceability of compound interest

1. A loan or other agreement providing for compound interest shall be enforceable notwithstanding the date that such loan or other agreement providing for such compound interest shall have been executed; provided, however, that such compound interest shall begin to accrue and become due and payable on the later to occur of (a) June twenty-fourth, nineteen hundred eighty-nine or (b) the date that any obligation to pay such compound interest may have arisen, including, but not limited to, the date of any default or event of default under such loan or other agreement. For purposes of this subdivision, the term "compound interest" shall mean the accruing of interest upon unpaid interest irrespective of whether such unpaid interest is added to the principal debt.

2. The provisions of this section shall not be applicable to any loan or other financing agreement where the original principal debt is in an amount of two

hundred fifty thousand dollars or less, or to any loan or other financing agreement secured primarily by a one or two family owner–occupied residence. For purposes of this subdivision the term "residence" shall include a lessees interest in a proprietary lease granted by a cooperative housing corporation.

3. Notwithstanding the provisions of subdivision two of this section, nothing in this section shall affect the maximum rate of interest which may be charged, taken or received as provided by law, or be construed to limit, impair or otherwise affect any loan or other agreement which is, or would be, enforceable without reference to this section, including but not limited to an agreement made pursuant to section six–f of the banking law.

Added by Laws 1989, Ch. 202, eff. June 24, 1989; **amended** by Laws 1997, Ch. 308, eff. July 29, 1997.

Section 5–531. Brokerage on loans; recovery of excess; effect of restitution

1. No person shall, directly or indirectly, take or receive more than fifty cents for a brokerage, soliciting, driving or procuring the loan or forbearance of one hundred dollars, and in that proportion for a greater or less sum, except loans on real estate security; nor more than thirty–eight cents for making or renewing any bond, bill, note or other security given for such loan or forbearance, or for any counter bond, bill, note or other security concerning the same.

2. For the purposes of this section:

a. "Consumer" means a natural person.

b. "Loan broker" means any individual, firm, corporation, or partnership who agrees for a fee to obtain a loan or credit for a consumer or to assist a consumer in obtaining a loan or credit, other than a loan or credit on real estate security.

c. No loan broker shall solicit, receive or collect from a consumer the fee authorized by subdivision one of this section in advance of the disbursement of loan proceeds or the extension of credit to a consumer.

d. No loan broker shall solicit, receive or collect from a consumer any fee, advance payment or compensation of any nature other than the fee authorized by subdivision one of this section.

3. a. Every person who shall pay, deliver or deposit any money, property or thing in action, over and above the rate aforesaid, and his personal representatives may, within three years after such payment, delivery or deposit, sue for and recover the same of the person so taking or receiving such money, property or thing in action, or of his personal representatives. Judgment may be entered in favor of a consumer in an amount not to exceed three times the actual damages plus reasonable attorneys' fees.

b. In case such suit shall not be brought within the time above prescribed, in good faith, or in case it shall be discontinued, or willfully delayed, then the public welfare officials of the city or town where the offense was committed, may, within one year after such neglect, discontinuance or delay, sue for and recover the money, property or thing in action, so received, delivered or deposited, from the person receiving the same, or his personal representatives, for the use of the poor of the county.

c. In addition to the other remedies provided, whenever there shall be a violation of subdivision two of this section, application may be made by the attorney general in the name of the people of the state of New York to a court or justice having jurisdiction by a special proceeding to issue an injunction, and upon notice to the defendant of not less than five days, to enjoin and restrain the continuance of such violations; and if it shall appear to the satisfaction of the court or justice that the defendant has, in fact, violated this article, an injunction may be issued by such court or justice, enjoining and restraining any further violation, without requiring proof that any person has in fact, been injured or damaged thereby. In any such proceeding, the court may make allowances to the attorney general as provided in paragraph six of subdivision (a) of section eighty–three hundred three of the civil practice law and rules, and direct restitution. Whenever the court shall determine that a violation of this article has occurred, the court may impose a civil penalty of not more than one thousand dollars for each violation. In connection with any such proposed application, the attorney general is authorized to take proof and make a determination of the relevant facts and to issue subpoenas in accordance with the civil practice law and rules.

Amended by Laws 1984, Ch. 799, eff. Aug. 5, 1984.

TITLE 6

INTEREST ON CERTAIN DEPOSITS

Section 5–601. Interest on deposits in escrow with mortgage investing institutions

Any mortgage investing institution which maintains an escrow account pursuant to any agreement executed in connection with a mortgage on any one to six family residence occupied by the owner or on any property owned by a cooperative apartment corporation, as defined in subdivision twelve of section three hundred sixty of the tax law, (as such subdivision was in effect on December thirtieth, nineteen hundred sixty), and located in this state shall, for each quarterly period in which such escrow account is established, credit the same with dividends or interest at a rate of not less than two per centum per year based on the average of the sums so paid for the average length of time on deposit or a rate prescribed by the banking board pursuant to section fourteen–b of the banking law and pursuant to the terms and conditions set forth in that section whichever is higher. The banking board shall prescribe by regulation the method or basis of computing any minimum rate of interest required by this section and any such minimum rate shall be a net rate over and above any service charge that may be imposed by any mortgage lending institution for maintaining an escrow account. No mortgage investing institution shall impose a service charge in connection with the maintenance of an escrow account unless provision therefor was expressly made in a loan contract executed prior to the effective date of this section.

Added by Laws 1974, Ch. 119, eff. July 1, 1974; **amended** by Laws 1979, Ch. 32, eff. March 30, 1979; Laws 1987, Ch. 267, eff. July 20, 1987.

Section 5–602. Interest on insurance draft deposits in escrow with mortgage investing institutions

Any mortgage investing institution which maintains an escrow account pursuant to any agreement executed in connection with a mortgage or any loan, secured by a lien on any one to six family residence occupied by the owner or on any property owned by a cooperative apartment corporation as defined in subdivision twelve of section three hundred sixty of the tax law and located in this state and which residence or cooperative apartment corporation received from an insurance carrier a draft, forwarded to a mortgage investing institution, as compensation for damage done to a residence shall, for each quarterly period in which such escrow account is established, credit the same with dividends or interest at a rate of not less than two per centum per year based on the average of the sums so paid for the average length of time on deposit or a rate prescribed by the banking board pursuant to section fourteen–b of the banking law and pursuant to the terms and conditions set forth in that section whichever is higher. The banking board shall prescribe by regulation the method or basis of computing any minimum rate of interest required by this section and any such minimum rate shall be a net rate over and above any service charge that may be imposed by any mortgage lending institution for maintaining an escrow account. No mortgage investing institution shall impose a service charge in connection with the maintenance of an escrow account unless provision therefor was expressly made in a loan contract executed prior to the effective date of this section.

Added by Laws 1986, Ch. 342, eff. Nov. 14, 1986, provided however, that effective immediately, the addition, amendment and/or repeal of any rule or regulation necessary for the implementation of this chapter on such effective date are authorized and directed to be made and completed on or before such effective date; **amended** by Laws 1987, Ch. 267, eff. July 20, 1987.

TITLE 7

REQUIREMENTS OF WRITING, EXECUTION OR ACKNOWLEDGMENT FOR EFFECTIVENESS OR ENFORCEABILITY

Section 5–701. Agreements required to be in writing

a. Every agreement, promise or undertaking is void, unless it or some note or memorandum thereof be in writing, and subscribed by the party to be charged therewith, or by his lawful agent, if such agreement, promise or undertaking:

1. By its terms is not to be performed within one year from the making thereof or the performance of which is not to be completed before the end of a lifetime;

2. Is a special promise to answer for the debt, default or miscarriage of another person;

3. Is made in consideration of marriage, except mutual promises to marry;

4. [*Repealed*]

5. Is a subsequent or new promise to pay a debt discharged in bankruptcy;

6. Notwithstanding section 2–201 of the uniform commercial code, if the goods be sold at public auction, and the auctioneer at the time of the sale, enters in a sale book, a memorandum specifying the nature and price of the property sold, the terms of the sale, the name of the purchaser, and the name of the person on whose account the sale was made, such memorandum is equivalent in effect to a note of the contract or sale, subscribed by the party to be charged therewith;

7, 8. [*Repealed*]

9. Is a contract to assign or an assignment, with or without consideration to the promisor, of a life or health or accident insurance policy, or a promise, with or without consideration to the promisor, to name a beneficiary of any such policy. This provision shall not apply to a policy of industrial life or health or accident insurance.

10. Is a contract to pay compensation for services rendered in negotiating a loan, or in negotiating the purchase, sale, exchange, renting or leasing of any real estate or interest therein, or of a business opportunity, business, its good will, inventory, fixtures or an interest therein, including a majority of the voting

stock interest in a corporation and including the creating of a partnership interest. "Negotiating" includes procuring an introduction to a party to the transaction or assisting in the negotiation or consummation of the transaction. This provision shall apply to a contract implied in fact or in law to pay reasonable compensation but shall not apply to a contract to pay compensation to an auctioneer, an attorney at law, or a duly licensed real estate broker or real estate salesman.

b. Notwithstanding paragraph one of subdivision a of this section:

1. An agreement, promise, undertaking or contract, which is valid in other respects and is otherwise enforceable, is not void for lack of a note, memorandum or other writing and is enforceable by way of action or defense provided that such agreement, promise, undertaking or contract is a qualified financial contract as defined in paragraph two of this subdivision and (a) there is, as provided in paragraph three of this subdivision, sufficient evidence to indicate that a contract has been made, or (b) the parties thereto, by means of a prior or subsequent written contract, have agreed to be bound by the terms of such qualified financial contract from the time they reach agreement (by telephone, by exchange of electronic messages, or otherwise) on those terms.

2. For purposes of this subdivision, a "qualified financial contract" means an agreement as to which each party thereto is other than a natural person and which is:

(a) for the purchase and sale of foreign exchange, foreign currency, bullion, coin or precious metals on a forward, spot, next–day value or other basis;

(b) a contract (other than a contract for the purchase and sale of a commodity for future deliver on, or subject to the rules of, a contract market or board of trade) for the purchase, sale or transfer of any commodity or any similar good, article, service, right, or interest which is presently or in the future becomes the subject of dealing in the forward contract trade, or any product or by product thereof, with a maturity date more than two days after the date the contract is entered into;

(c) for the purchase and sale of currency, or interbank deposits denominated in United States dollars;

(d) for a currency option, currency swap or cross–currency rate swap;

(e) for a commodity swap or a commodity option (other than an option contract traded on, or subject to the rules of a contract market or board of trade);

(f) for a rate swap, basis swap, forward rate transaction, or an interest rate option;

(g) for a security–index swap or option or a security (or securities) price swap or option;

(h) an agreement which involves any other similar transaction relating to a price or index (including, without limitation, any transaction or agreement involving any combination of the foregoing, any cap, floor, collar or similar transaction with respect to a rate, commodity price, commodity index, security (or securities) price, security–index or other price index); or

(i) an option with respect to any of the foregoing.

3. There is sufficient evidence that a contract has been made if:

(a) There is evidence of electronic communication (including, without limitation, the recording of a telephone call or the tangible written text produced by computer retrieval), admissible in evidence under the laws of this state, sufficient to indicate that in such communication a contract was made between the parties;

(b) A confirmation in writing sufficient to indicate that a contract has been made between the parties and sufficient against the sender is received by the party against whom enforcement is sought no later than the fifth business day after such contract is made (or such other period of time as the parties may agree in writing) and the sender does not receive, on or before the third business day after such receipt (or such other period of time as the parties may agree in writing), written objection to a material term of the confirmation; for purposes of this subparagraph, a confirmation or an objection thereto is received at the time there has been actual receipt by an individual responsible for the transaction or, if earlier, at the time there has been constructive receipt which is the time actual receipt by such an individual would have occurred if the receiving party, as an organization, has exercised reasonable diligence; and a "business day" for the purposes of this subparagraph is a day on which both parties are open and transacting business of the kind involved in that qualified financial contract which is the subject of the confirmation;

(c) The party against whom enforcement is sought admits in its pleading, testimony or otherwise in court that a contract was made; or

(d) There is a note, memorandum or other writing sufficient to indicate that a contract has been made, signed by the party against whom enforcement is sought or by its authorized agent or broker.

For purposes of this paragraph evidence of an electronic communication indicating the making therein of a contract or a confirmation, admission, note, memorandum or writing is not insufficient because it omits or incorrectly states one or more material terms agreed upon, so long as such evidence provides a reasonable basis for concluding that a contract was made.

4. For purposes of this subdivision, the tangible written text produced by telex, telefacsimile, computer retrieval or other process by which electronic signals are transmitted by telephone or otherwise shall constitute a writing and any symbol executed or adopted by a party with the present intention to authenticate a writing shall constitute a signing. The confirmation and notice of objection referred to in subparagraph (b) of paragraph three of this subdivision may be communicated by means of telex, telefacsimile, computer or other similar process by which electronic signals are transmitted by telephone or otherwise,

provided that a party claiming to have communicated in such a manner shall, unless the parties have otherwise agreed in writing, have the burden of establishing actual or constructive receipt by the other party as set forth in subparagraph (b) of paragraph three of this subdivision.

Amended by Laws 1964, Ch. 561, eff. Sept. 27, 1964; Laws 1977, Ch. 747, eff. June 1, 1978; Laws 1978, Ch. 199, eff. May 31, 1978; Laws 1994, Ch. 467, eff. Sept. 18, 1994.

Section 5–702. Requirements for use of plain language in consumer transactions

a. Every written agreement entered into after November first, nineteen hundred seventy–eight, for the lease of space to be occupied for residential purposes, for the lease of personal property to be used primarily for personal, family or household purposes or to which a consumer is a party and the money, property or service which is the subject of the transaction is primarily for personal, family or household purposes must be:

1. Written in a clear and coherent manner using words with common and every day meanings;

2. Appropriately divided and captioned by its various sections. Any creditor, seller or lessor who fails to comply with this subdivision shall be liable to a consumer who is a party to a written agreement governed by this subdivision in an amount equal to any actual damages sustained plus a penalty of fifty dollars. The total class action penalty against any such creditor, seller or lessor shall not exceed ten thousand dollars in any class action or series of class actions arising out of the use by a creditor, seller or lessor of an agreement which fails to comply with this subdivision. No action under this subdivision may be brought after both parties to the agreement have fully performed their obligation under such agreement, nor shall any creditor, seller or lessor who attempts in good faith to comply with this subdivision be liable for such penalties. This subdivision shall not apply to a good faith attempt to describe the constant yield or other method of determining the lease charge and depreciation portions of each base rental payment under a lease of personal property. It also shall not apply to agreements involving amounts in excess of fifty thousand dollars nor prohibit the use of words or phrases or forms of agreement required by state or federal law, rule or regulation or by a governmental instrumentality.

Amended by Laws 1978, Ch. 199, effective May 31, 1978; **amended** by Laws 1994, Ch. 1, eff. June 30, 1995.

Section 5–703. Conveyances and contracts concerning real property required to be in writing

1. An estate or interest in real property, other than a lease for a term not exceeding one year, or any trust or power, over or concerning real property, or in any manner relating thereto, cannot be created, granted, assigned,

surrendered or declared, unless by act or operation of law, or by a deed or conveyance in writing, subscribed by the person creating, granting, assigning, surrendering or declaring the same, or by his lawful agent, thereunto authorized by writing. But this subdivision does not affect the power of a testator in the disposition of his real property by will; nor prevent any trust from arising or being extinguished by implication or operation law, nor any declaration of trust from being proved by a writing subscribed by the person declaring the same.

2. A contract for the leasing for a longer period than one year, or for the sale, of any real property, or an interest therein, is void unless the contract or some note or memorandum thereof, expressing the consideration, is in writing, subscribed by the party to be charged, or by his lawful agent thereunto authorized by writing.

3. A contract to devise real property or establish a trust of real property, or any interest therein or right with reference thereto, is void unless the contract or some note or memorandum thereof is in writing and subscribed by the party to be charged therewith, or by his lawfully authorized agent.

4. Nothing contained in this section abridges the powers of courts of equity to compel the specific performance of agreements in cases of part performance.

Section 5–705. Execution and acknowledgment of assumption of mortgage debt by grantee of mortgaged real property

No grantee of real property shall be liable upon any indebtedness secured by a mortgage thereon executed prior to the time of the conveyance of the real property to the grantee, nor shall he be liable for any deficiency that may remain upon the foreclosure and sale of real property covered by such a mortgage, after application of the proceeds of sale, unless such grantee shall simultaneously with the conveyance to him of such real property execute and acknowledge, before an officer authorized to take acknowledgments of deeds, a statement in writing stating in substance that such grantee assumes and agrees to pay such mortgage debt and giving the specific amount of the debt assumed. The execution and acknowledgment by a grantee of the deed of conveyance to him containing such written statement shall be sufficient compliance with the provisions of this section. This section shall not apply, however, where, subsequent to the conveyance and upon an extension or modification of the indebtedness secured by the mortgage, the grantee shall execute and acknowledge, before an officer authorized to take acknowledgments of deeds, a statement in writing stating that such grantee assumes and agrees to pay such mortgage debt, and giving the specific amount of the debt assumed.

TITLE 9

REQUIREMENTS OF NOTICE FOR EFFECTIVENESS OR ENFORCEABILITY

Section 5–901. Certain provisions of leases of personal property inoperative unless notice thereof given to lessee

Certain provisions of leases of personal property inoperative unless notice thereof given to lessee. No provision of a lease of any personal property which states that the term thereof shall be deemed renewed for a specified additional period unless the lessee gives notice to the lessor of his intention to release the property at the expiration of such term, shall be operative unless the lessor, at least fifteen days and not more than thirty days previous to the time specified for the furnishing of such notice to him, shall give to the lessee written notice, served personally or by mail, calling the attention of the lessee to the existence of such provision in the lease. Nothing herein contained shall be construed to apply to a contract in which the automatic renewal period specified is one month or less.

Amended by Laws 1999, Ch. 271, eff. July 20, 1999.

Section 5–903. Automatic renewal provision of contract for service, maintenance or repair unenforceable by contractor unless notice thereof given to recipient of services

1. As used in this section, "person" means an individual, firm, company, partnership or corporation.

2. No provision of a contract for service, maintenance or repair to or for any real or personal property which states that the term of the contract shall be deemed renewed for a specified additional period unless the person receiving the service, maintenance or repair gives notice to the person furnishing such contract service, maintenance or repair of his intention to terminate the contract at the expiration of such term, shall be enforceable against the person receiving the service, maintenance or repair, unless the person furnishing the service, maintenance or repair, at least fifteen days and not more than thirty days previous to the time specified for serving such notice upon him, shall give to the person receiving the service, maintenance or repair written notice, served personally

GOL

or by certified mail, calling the attention of that person to the existence of such provision in the contract.

3. Nothing herein contained shall be construed to apply to a contract in which the automatic renewal period specified is one month or less.

Section 5–905. Certain provisions of leases to be inoperative unless express notice thereof is given to tenant

No provision of a lease of any real property or premises which states that the term thereof shall be deemed renewed for a specified additional period of time unless the tenant gives notice to the lessor of his intention to quit the premises at the expiration of such term shall be operative unless the lessor, at least fifteen days and not more than thirty days previous to the time specified for the furnishing of such notice to him, shall give to the tenant written notice, served personally or by registered or certified mail, calling the attention of the tenant to the existence of such provision in the lease.

TITLE 11

CONSIDERATION; EFFECT OF WRITING ON REQUIREMENT OF CONSIDERATION

Section 5–1101. Agreements relating to securities

An agreement, promise or undertaking for the purchase, sale, transfer, assignment or delivery of a certificate or other evidence of debt, issued by the United States or by any state, or a municipal or other corporation, or of any share or interest in the stock of any bank corporation or joint stock association, incorporated or organized under the laws of the United States or of any state, is not void or voidable, for want of consideration, or because of the nonpayment of consideration, or because the vendor, at the time of making such contract, is not the owner or possessor of the certificate or certificates or other evidence of debt, share or interest.

Section 5–1103. Written agreement for modification or discharge

An agreement, promise or undertaking to change or modify, or to discharge in whole or in part, any contract, obligation, or lease, or any mortgage or other security interest in personal or real property, shall not be invalid because of the absence of consideration, provided that the agreement, promise or undertaking changing, modifying, or discharging such contract, obligation, lease, mortgage or security interest, shall be in writing and signed by the party against whom it is sought to enforce the change, modification or discharge, or by his agent.

Section 5–1105. Written promise expressing past consideration

A promise in writing and signed by the promisor or by his agent shall not be denied effect as a valid contractual obligation on the ground that consideration for the promise is past or executed, if the consideration is expressed in the writing and is proved to have been given or performed and would be a valid consideration but for the time when it was given or performed.

Section 5–1107. Written assignment

An assignment shall not be denied the effect of irrevocably transferring the assignor's rights because of the absence of consideration, if such assignment is in writing and signed by the assignor, or by his agent.

Section 5–1109. Written irrevocable offer

Except as otherwise provided in section 2–205 of the uniform commercial code with respect to an offer by a merchant to buy or sell goods, when an offer to enter into a contract is made in a writing signed by the offeror, or by his agent, which states that the offer is irrevocable during a period set forth or until a time fixed, the offer shall not be revocable during such period or until such time because of the absence of consideration for the assurance of irrevocability. When such a writing states that the offer is irrevocable but does not state any period or time of irrevocability, it shall be construed to state that the offer is irrevocable for a reasonable time.

Amended by Laws 1964, Ch. 196, eff. Sept. 27, 1964.

Section 5–1111. Execution by agent in real property transactions; written authorization required

If executed by an agent, any agreement, promise, undertaking, assignment or offer required by Sections 5–1103, 5–1105, 5–1107 or 5–1109 to be in writing, which affects or relates to real property or an interest therein in any manner stated in subdivisions one or two of section 5–703 of this chapter, shall be void unless such agent was thereunto authorized in writing.

Section 5–1113. Written or published promise of reward

A promise to pay a reward for return of lost or mislaid property is not unenforceable because of absence of consideration if the promise was made in writing or the promisor caused it to be published.

Section 5–1115. Promises and warranties in conveyances made without consideration

A promise or warranty by the grantor in a deed or conveyance of an estate or interest in real property and acknowledged or proved in the manner prescribed by law to entitle it to be recorded shall not be denied effect because of the absence of consideration, if no consideration was intended.

TITLE 13

CONSTRUCTION OF PARTICULAR TERMS IN CONTRACTUAL TRANSACTIONS

Section 5–1301. How interest calculated

Whenever, in any statute, act, deed, written or verbal contract, or in any public or private instrument whatever, any certain rate of interest is or shall be mentioned, and no period of time is stated for which such rate is to be calculated, interest shall be calculated at the rate mentioned, by the year, in the same manner as if the words "per annum" or "by the year" had been added to such rate.

Section 5–1311. Uniform vendor and purchaser risk act

1. Any contract for the purchase and sale or exchange of realty shall be interpreted, unless the contract expressly provides otherwise, as including an agreement that the parties shall have the following rights and duties:

a. When neither the legal title nor the possession of the subject matter of the contract has been transferred to the purchaser: (1) if all or a material part thereof is destroyed without fault of the purchaser or is taken by eminent domain, the vendor cannot enforce the contract, and the purchaser is entitled to recover any portion of the price that he has paid; but nothing herein contained shall be deemed to deprive the vendor of any right to recover damages against the purchaser for any breach of contract by the purchaser prior to the destruction or taking; (2) if an immaterial part thereof is destroyed without fault of the purchaser or is taken by eminent domain, neither the vendor nor the purchaser is thereby deprived of the right to enforce the contract; but there shall be, to the extent of the destruction or taking, an abatement of the purchase price.

b. When either the legal title or the possession of the subject matter of the contract has been transferred to the purchaser, if all or any part thereof is destroyed without fault of the vendor or is taken by eminent domain, the purchaser is not thereby relieved from a duty to pay the price, nor is he thereby entitled to recover any portion thereof that he has paid; but nothing herein contained shall be deemed to deprive the purchaser of any right to recover damages against the vendor for any breach of contract by the vendor prior to the destruction or taking.

2. This section shall be so interpreted and construed as to effectuate its general purpose to make uniform the law of those states which enact it.

3. This section may be cited as the uniform vendor and purchaser risk act.

TITLE 14

ENFORCEABILITY OF CLAUSES RESPECTING CHOICE OF LAW AND CHOICE OF FORUM IN CERTAIN TRANSACTIONS

Section 5–1401. Choice of law

1. The parties to any contract, agreement or undertaking, contingent or otherwise, in consideration of, or relating to any obligation arising out of a transaction covering in the aggregate not less than two hundred fifty thousand dollars, including a transaction otherwise covered by subsection one of section 1–105 of the uniform commercial code, may agree that the law of this state shall govern their rights and duties in whole or in part, whether or not such contract, agreement or undertaking bears a reasonable relation to this state. This section shall not apply to any contract, agreement or undertaking (a) for labor or personal services, (b) relating to any transaction for personal, family or household services, or (c) to the extent provided to the contrary in subsection two of section 1–105 of the uniform commercial code.

2. Nothing contained in this section shall be construed to limit or deny the enforcement of any provision respecting choice of law in any other contract, agreement or undertaking.

Added by Laws 1984, Ch. 421, eff. July 19, 1984.

Section 5–1402. Choice of forum

1. Notwithstanding any act which limits or affects the right of a person to maintain an action or proceeding, including, but not limited to, paragraph (b) of section thirteen hundred fourteen of the business corporation law and subdivision two of section two hundred–b of the banking law, any person may

maintain an action or proceeding against a foreign corporation, non–resident, or foreign state where the action or proceeding arises out of or relates to any contract, agreement or undertaking for which a choice of New York law has been made in whole or in part pursuant to section 5–1401 and which (a) is a contract, agreement or undertaking, contingent or otherwise, in consideration of, or relating to any obligation arising out of a transaction covering in the aggregate, not less than one million dollars, and (b) which contains a provision or provisions whereby such foreign corporation or non–resident agrees to submit to the jurisdiction of the courts of this state.

2. Nothing contained in this section shall be construed to affect the enforcement of any provision respecting choice of forum in any other contract, agreement or undertaking.

Added by Laws 1984, Ch. 421, eff. July 19, 1984.

TITLE 15

STATUTORY SHORT FORM POWER OF ATTORNEY

Section 5–1501. Statutory short form of general power of attorney; durable and nondurable; formal requirements; joint agents

1. The use of the following form in the creation of a durable power of attorney is lawful, and, when used, it shall be construed as a statutory short form power of attorney in accordance with the provisions of this title:

"DURABLE GENERAL POWER OF ATTORNEY NEW YORK STATUTORY SHORT FORM

THE POWERS YOU GRANT BELOW CONTINUE TO BE EFFECTIVESHOULD YOU BECOME DISABLED OR INCOMPETENT

(CAUTION: THIS IS AN IMPORTANT DOCUMENT. IT GIVES THE PERSON WHOM YOU DESIGNATE (YOUR "AGENT") BROAD POWERS TO HANDLE YOUR PROPERTY DURING YOUR LFETIME, WHICH MAY INCLUDE POWERS TO MORTGAGE, SELL, OR OTHERWISE DISPOSE OF ANY REAL OR PERSONAL PROPERTY WITHOUT ADVANCE NOTICE TO YOU OR APPROVAL BY YOU. THESE POWERS WILL CONTINUE TO EXIST EVEN AFTER YOU BECOME DISABLED OR INCOMPETENT.

THESE POWERS ARE EXPLAINED MORE FULLY IN NEW YORK GENERAL OBLIGATIONS LAW, ARTICLE 5, TITLE 15, SECTIONS 5–1502A THROUGH 5–1503, WHICH EXPRESSLY PERMIT THE USE OF ANY OTHER OR DIFFERENT FORM OF POWER OF ATTORNEY.

THIS DOCUMENT DOES NOT AUTHORIZE ANYONE TO MAKE MEDICAL OR OTHER HEALTH CARE DECISIONS. YOU MAY EXECUTE A HEALTH CARE PROXY TO DO THIS.

IF THERE IS ANYTHING ABOUT THIS FORM THAT YOU DO NOT UNDERSTAND, YOU SHOULD ASK A LAWYER TO EXPLAIN IT TO YOU.)

THIS is intended to constitute a DURABLE GENERAL POWER OF ATTORNEY pursuant to Article 5, Title 15 of the New York General Obligations Law:

I, ...

(insert your name and address)

do hereby appoint: . . . .
. . . .
. . . .
. . . .

(If 1 person is to be appointed agent, insert the name and address of your agent above) . . . .

GOL

(If 2 or more persons are to be appointed agents by you insert theirnames and addresses above) my attorney(s)–in–fact TO ACT

(If more than one agent is designated, CHOOSE ONE of the following two choices by putting your initials in ONE of the blank spaces to the to the left of your choice:)

( ) Each Agent may SEPARATELY act.

( ) All agents must act to TOGETHER.

(If neither blank space is initialed, the agents will be required to act TOGETHER) IN MY NAME, PLACE AND STEAD in any way which I myself could do, if I were personally present, with respect to the following matters as each of them is defined in Title 15 of Article 5 of the New York General Obligations Law to the extent that I am permitted by law to act through an agent:

(DIRECTIONS: initial in the blank space to the left of your choice any one or more of the following lettered subdivisions as to which you WANT to give your agent authority. If the blank space to the left of any particular lettered subdivision is NOT initialed, NO AUTHORITY WILL BE GRANTED for matters that are included in that subdivision. Alternatively, the letter corresponding to each power you wish to grant may be written or typed on the blank line in subdivision "(Q)", and you may then put your initials in the blank space to the left of subdivision "(Q)"in order to grant each of the powers so indicated)

( ) (A) real estate transactions;

( ) (B) chattel and goods transactions;

( ) (C) bond, share and commodity transactions;

( ) (D) banking transactions;

( ) (E) business operating transactions;

( ) (F) insurance transactions;

( ) (G) estate transactions;

( ) (H) claims and litigation;

( ) (I) personal relationships and affairs;

( ) (J) benefits from military service;

( ) (K) records, reports and statements;

( ) (L) retirement benefit transactions;

( ) (M) making gifts to my spouse, children and more remote descendants, and parents, not to exceed in the aggregate $10,000 to each of such persons in any year;

( ) (N) tax matters;

( ) (O) all other matters;

( ) (P) full and unqualified authority to my attorney(s)–in–fact to delegate any or all of the foregoing powers to any person or persons whom my attorney(s)–in–fact shall select;

( ) (Q) each of the above matters identified by the following letters: . . . .
. . . .

(special provisions and limitations may be included in the statutory short form durable power of attorney only if they conform to the requirements of section 5–1503 of the New York General Obligations Law.)

This durable Power of Attorney shall not be affected by my subsequentdisability or incompetence.

If every agent named above is unable or unwilling to serve, I appoint
. . . .

(Insert name and address of successor)

to be my agent for all purposes hereunder.

TO INDUCE ANY THIRD PARTY TO ACT HEREUNDER, I HEREBY AGREE THAT ANY THIRD PARTY RECEIVING A DULY EXECUTED COPY OR FACSIMILE OF THIS INSTRUMENT MAY ACT HEREUNDER, AND THAT REVOCATION OR TERMINATION HEREOF SHALL BE INEFFECTIVE AS TO SUCH THIRD PARTY UNLESS AND UNTIL ACTUAL NOTICE OR KNOWLEDGE OF SUCH REVOCATION OR TERMINATION SHALL HAVE BEEN RECEIVED BY SUCH THIRD PARTY, AND I FOR MYSELF AND FOR MY HEIRS, EXECUTORS, LEGAL REPRESENTATIVES AND ASSIGNS, HEREBY AGREE TO INDEMNIFY AND HOLD HARMLESS ANY SUCH THIRD PARTY FROM AND AGAINST ANY AND ALL CLAIMS THAT MAY ARISE AGAINST SUCH THIRD PARTY BY REASON OF SUCH THIRD PARTY HAVING RELIED ON THE PROVISIONS OF THIS INSTRUMENT.

THIS DURABLE GENERAL POWER OF ATTORNEY MAY BE REVOKED BY ME AT ANY TIME.

In Witness Whereof I have hereunto signed my name this . . . . .day of . . . . .19 . . . .

(YOU SIGN HERE:) . . . .

(Signature of principal)

(ACKNOWLEDGEMENT)"

The execution of this statutory short form durable power of attorney shall be duly acknowledged by the principal in the manner prescribed for the acknowledgement of a conveyance of real property.

No provision of this article shall be construed to bar the use of any other or different form of power of attorney desired by the parties concerned.

Every statutory short form durable power of attorney, to be valid, must be written, typed or printed using letters which are in legible writing of or clear type of no less than twelve–point in size or if in writing a reasonable equivalent thereof and must contain, in bold face upper case or upper and lower case type or a reasonable equivalent thereof the "CAUTION" which is printed in bold face type at the beginning of the statutory form printed above and the "DIRECTIONS" which are printed in bold face type immediately before subdivisions (a) through (q) of the statutory form printed above.

1–a. The use of the following form in the creation of a nondurable power of attorney is lawful, and, when used, it shall be construed as a statutory short form power of attorney in accordance with the provisions Of this title:

"NONDURABLE GENERAL POWER OF ATTORNEY NEW YORK STATUTORY SHORT FORM.

THE POWERS YOU GRANT BELOW CEASE TO BE EFFECTIVE SHOULD YOU BECOME DISABLED OR INCOMPETENT (CAUTION: THIS IS AN IMPORTANT DOCUMENT. IT GIVES THE PERSON WHOM YOU DESIGNATE (YOUR "AGENT") BROAD POWERS TO HANDLE YOUR PROPERTY DURING YOUR LIFETIME, WHICH MAY INCLUDE POWERS TO MORTGAGE, SELL, OR OTHERWISE DISPOSE OF ANY REAL OR PERSONAL PROPERTY WITHOUT ADVANCE NOTICE TO YOU OR APPROVAL BY YOU. THESE POWERS WILL TERMINATE IF YOU BECOME DISABLED OR INCOMPETENT. THESE POWERS ARE EXPLAINED MORE FULLY IN NEW YORK GENERAL OBLIGATIONS LAW, ARTICLE 5, TITLE 15, SECTIONS 5–1502A THROUGH 5–1503, WHICH EXPRESSLY PERMIT THE USE OF ANY OTHER OR DIFFERENT FORM OF POWER OF ATTORNEY.

THIS DOCUMENT DOES NOT AUTHORIZE ANYONE TO MAKE MEDICAL OR OTHER HEALTH CARE DECISIONS. YOU MAY EXECUTE A HEALTH CARE PROXY TO DO THIS. IF THERE IS ANYTHING ABOUT THIS FORM THAT YOU DO NOT UNDERSTAND, YOU SHOULD ASK A LAWYER TO EXPLAIN IT TO YOU.)

THIS is intended to constitute a NONDURABLE GENERAL POWER OF ATTORNEY Pursuant to article 5, title 15 of the New York General Obligations law:

I, ...

(Insert your name and address)

do hereby appoint: . . . .

(If 1 person is to be appointed agent, insert the name and address of your agent above) . . . .

. . . .

....

....

(If 2 or more persons are to be appointed agents by you, insert Their names and addresses above)

my attorney(s)–in–fact TO ACT

(If more than one agent is designated, CHOOSE ONE of the following Two choices by putting your initials in ONE of the blank spaces

( ) to the left of your choice:)

( ) each agent may SEPARATELY act.

( ) ALL agents must act TOGETHER.

(If neither blank space is initialed, the agents will be required to Act TOGETHER)

IN MY NAME, PLACE AND STEAD in any way which I myself could do, if I were personally present, with respect to the following matters as each of them is defined in title 15 of article 5 of the New York General Obligations law to the extent that I am permitted by law to act throughan agent:

(DIRECTIONS: Initial in the blank space to the left of your choice any one or more of the following lettered subdivisions as to which you want to give your agent authority. If the blank space to the left of any particular lettered subdivision is not initialed, no authority will be GRANTED for matters that are included in that subdivision. ALTERNATIVELY, the letter corresponding to each power you wish to grant may be written or typed on the blank line in Subdivision "(Q)", and you may then put your initials in the blank space to the left of subdivision "(Q)" in order to grant each of the powers so indicated)

( ) (A) real estate transactions;

( ) (B) chattel and goods transactions;

( ) (C) bond, share and commodity transactions;

( ) (D) banking transactions;

( ) (E) business operating transactions;

( ) (F) insurance transactions;

( ) (G) estate transactions;

( ) (H) claims and litigation;

( ) (I) personal relationships and affairs;

( ) (J) benefits from military service;

( ) (K) records, reports and statements;

( ) (L) retirement benefit transactions;

( ) (M) making gifts to my spouse, children and more remote descendants, and parents, not to exceed in the aggregate $10,000 to each of such persons in any year;

( ) (N) tax matters;

( ) (O) all other matters;

( ) (P) full and unqualified authority to my attorney(s)–in–fact to delegate any or all of the foregoing powers to any person or persons whom my attorney(s)–in–fact shall Select;

( ) (Q) each of the above matters identified by the following letters: . . . .

. . . .

(Special provisions and limitations may be included in the statutory short form nondurable power of attorney only if they conform to the requirements of section 5–1503 of the New York General Obligations Law.)

. . . .

. . . .

. . . .

. . . .

If every agent named above is unable or unwilling to serve, I appoint . . . .

(Insert name and address of successor)

. . . .

To be my agent for all purposes hereunder.

TO INDUCE ANY THIRD PARTY TO ACT HEREUNDER, I HEREBY AGREE THAT ANY THIRD PARTY RECEIVING A DULY EXECUTED COPY OR FACSIMILE OF THIS INSTRUMENT MAY ACT HEREUNDER, AND THAT REVOCATION OR TERMINATION HEREOF SHALL BE INEFFECTIVE AS TO SUCH THIRD PARTY UNLESS AND UNTIL ACTUAL NOTICE OR KNOWLEDGE OF SUCH REVOCATION OR TERMINATION SHALL HAVE BEEN RECEIVED BY SUCH THIRD PARTY, AND I FOR MYSELF AND FOR MY HEIRS, EXECUTORS, LEGAL REPRESENTATIVES AND ASSIGNS, HEREBY AGREE TO INDEMNIFY AND HOLD HARMLESS ANY SUCH THIRD PARTY FROM AND AGAINST ANY AND ALL CLAIMS THAT MAY ARISE AGAINST SUCH THIRD PARTY BY REASON OF SUCH THIRD PARTY HAVING RELIED ON THE PROVISIONS OF THIS INSTRUMENT.

THIS NONDURABLE GENERAL POWER OF ATTORNEY MAY BE REVOKED BY ME AT ANY TIME.

In witness whereof I have hereunto signed my name this . . . . .day of. . . . ., 19 . . . .

(YOU SIGN HERE:) . . . .

(Signature of principal)

(ACKNOWLEDGEMENT)"

The execution of this statutory short form nondurable power of attorney shall be duly acknowledged by the principal in the manner prescribed for the acknowledgement of a conveyance of real property.

No provision of this article shall be construed to bar the use of any other or different form of power of attorney desired by the parties concerned.

Every statutory short form nondurable power of attorney, to be valid, must be written, typed or printed using letters which are in legible writing of or clear type of no less than twelve–point in size or if in writing a reasonable equivalent thereof and must contain, in bold face upper case or upper and lower case type or a reasonable equivalent thereof the "caution" which is printed in bold face type at the beginning of the statutory form printed above and the "DIRECTIONS" which are printed in bold face type immediately before subdivisions (A) through (Q) of the statutory form printed above.

2. A power of attorney is a "statutory short form power of attorney", as this phrase is used in the following sections of this title, when, but only when, it meets the requirements of the closing paragraph of subdivision one or subdivision one–a of this section and has been duly acknowledged by the principal in the manner prescribed for the acknowledgement of a conveyance of real property and it contains the exact wording of the form set forth in subdivision one or subdivision one–a of this section, except that any blank space to the left of any one or more of lettered subdivisions (A) through (Q) may be initialed by the principal, in which case the corresponding subdivisions to the right of the blank spaces so initialed shall be deemed chosen by the principal and effective with respect to the powers conferred in the particular sections of this title which are represented by the subdivisions so chosen. Notwithstanding the foregoing, a "statutory short form power of attorney" may contain modifications or additions of the types described in section 5–1503 of this chapter.

3. If more than one agent is designated by the principal, such agents, in the exercise of the powers conferred, must act jointly or separately consistent with the interpretive instructions contained in such statutory short form power of attorney.

4. Notwithstanding subdivisions one, one–a and two of this section, a power of attorney executed either before, on, or after september twenty–seventh, nineteen hundred sixty–four and before october first, nineteen hundred ninety–four is a "statutory short form power of attorney" as this phrase is used in the following sections of this title when it uses the words "New York General Business law, article 13, sections 222–234" and the words "article 13 of the New York General Business Law" in lieu of the words "New York General

Obligations Law, Article 5, title 5, sections 5–1502a through 5–1503" and "Article 5, Title 15 of the New York General Obligations Law" and in other respects complies with subdivision two of this section as such subdivision two existed before its amendment effective October first, nineteen hundred ninety–four.

4–a. Notwithstanding subdivisions one, one–a and two of this section, a power of attorney executed either on or after october first, nineteen hundred ninety–four and before the effective date of subdivision five–a of this section is a "statutory short form power of attorney" as this phrase is used in the following sections of this title when it uses the words "New York General Obligations Law, Article 5, Title 15, sections 5–1502a through 5–1503" and "Article 5, Title 15 of the New York General Obligations Law" and in other respects complies with subdivision two of this section as such subdivision two existed before its amendment effective on the same date as the effective date of subdivision five–a of this section.

5. Every "statutory short form power of attorney", as this phrase is used in the following sections of this title, which was executed before October first, nineteen hundred ninety–four in accordance with provisions of law effective at the time of such execution, shall continue to remain effective and be governed by the requirements of such prior law, on and after October first, nineteen hundred ninety–four; provided, however, that every "statutory short form power of attorney" executed on and after October first, nineteen hundred ninety–four shall be subject to the provisions of this section as amended by chapter six hundred ninety–four of the laws of nineteen hundred ninety–four.

5–a. Every "statutory short form power of attorney", as this phrase is used in the following sections of this title, which was executed before the effective date of this subdivision in accordance with provisions of law effective at the time of such execution, shall continue to remain effective and be governed by the requirements of such prior law, on and after the effective date of this subdivision; provided, however, that every "statutory short form power of attorney" executed on and after the effective date of this subdivision shall be subject to the provisions of this section as amended by the same chapter of the laws as the one which added this subdivision to this section.

Amended by Laws 1967, ch. 197, eff. April 10, 1967; Laws 1980, Ch. 140, eff. Jan. 1, 1981; Laws 1981, Ch. 458, eff. July 7, 1981; Laws 1986, Ch. 215, eff. Sept. 21, 1986.; Laws 1994, Ch. 694, eff. Oct. 1, 1994, Laws 1996 Ch. 499, eff. Jan. 1, 1997

Section 5–1502A. Construction—real estate transactions

In a statutory short form power of attorney, the language conferring general authority with respect to "real estate transactions," must be construed to mean that the principal authorizes the agent:

1. To accept as a gift, or as security for a loan, to reject, to demand, to buy, to lease, to receive, or otherwise to acquire either ownership or possession of any estate or interest in land;

2. To sell, to exchange, to convey either with or without covenants, to quitclaim, to release, to surrender, to mortgage, to incumber, to partition or to consent to the partitioning, to revoke, create or modify a trust, to grant options concerning, to lease or to sublet, or otherwise to dispose of, any estate or interest in land;

3. To release in whole or in part, to assign the whole or a part of, to satisfy in whole or in part, and to enforce by action, proceeding or otherwise, any mortgage, incumbrance, lien or other claim to land which exists, or is claimed to exist, in favor of the principal;

4. To do any act of management or of conservation with respect to any estate or interest in land owned, or claimed to be owned, by the principal, including by way of illustration, but not of restriction, power to insure against any casualty, liability or loss, to obtain or to regain possession or to protect such estate or interest by action, proceeding or otherwise, to pay, to compromise or to contest taxes or assessments, to apply for refunds in connection therewith, to purchase supplies, to hire assistance or labor and to make repairs or alterations in the structures or lands;

5. To utilize in any way, to develop, to modify, to alter, to replace, to remove, to erect or to install structures or other improvements upon any land in which the principal has, or claims to have, any estate or interest;

6. To demand, to receive, to obtain by action, proceeding or otherwise, any money, or other thing of value to which the principal is, or may become, or may claim to be entitled as the proceeds of an interest in land or of one or more of the transactions enumerated in this section, to conserve, to invest, to disburse or to utilize anything so received for purposes enumerated in this section, and to reimburse the agent for any expenditures properly made by him in the execution of the powers conferred on him by the statutory short form power of attorney;

7. To participate in any reorganization with respect to real property and to receive and to hold any shares of stock or instrument of similar character received in accordance with such plan or reorganization, and to act with respect thereto, including by way of illustration, but not of restriction, power to sell or otherwise to dispose of such shares, or any of them, to exercise or to sell any option, conversion or similar right with respect thereto, and to vote thereon in person or by the granting of a proxy;

8. To agree and to contract, in any manner, and with any person and on any terms, which the agent may select, for the accomplishment of any of the purposes enumerated in this section, and to perform, to rescind, to reform, to release or to modify any such agreement or contract or any other similar agreement or contract made by or on behalf of the principal;

9. To execute, to acknowledge, to seal and to deliver any deed, revocation, declaration or modification of trust, mortgage, lease, notice, check or other

instrument which the agent may think useful for the accomplishment of any of the purposes enumerated in this section;

10. To prosecute, to defend, to submit to arbitration, to settle, and to propose or to accept a compromise with respect to, any claim existing in favor of, or against, the principal based on or involving any real estate transaction or to intervene in any action or proceeding relating thereto;

11. To hire, to discharge, and to compensate any attorney, accountant, expert witness or other assistant or assistants when the agent shall think such action to be desirable for the proper execution by him of any of the powers described in this section, and for the keeping of needed records thereof; and

12. In general, and in addition to all the specific acts in this section enumerated, to do any other act or acts, which the principal can do through an agent, with respect to any estate or interest in land.

All powers described in this section 5–1502A of the general obligations law shall be exercisable equally with respect to any estate or interest in land owned by the principal at the giving of the power of attorney or thereafter acquired, and whether located in the state of New York or elsewhere.

Section 5–1502B. Construction—chattel and goods transactions

In a statutory short form power of attorney, the language conferring general authority with respect to "chattel and goods transactions," must be construed to mean that the principal authorizes the agent:

1. To accept as a gift, or as security for a loan, to reject, to demand, to buy, to receive, or otherwise to acquire either ownership or possession of, any chattel or goods or any interest in any chattel or goods;

2. To sell, to exchange, to convey either with or without covenants, to release, to surrender, to mortgage, to incumber, to pledge, to hypothecate, to pawn, to revoke, create or modify a trust, to grant options concerning, to lease or to sublet to others, or otherwise to dispose of any chattel or goods or any interest in any chattel or goods;

3. To release in whole or in part, to assign the whole or a part of, to satisfy in whole or in part, and to enforce by action, proceeding or otherwise, any mortgage, incumbrance, lien or other claim, which exists, or is claimed to exist, in favor of the principal, with respect to any chattel or goods or any interest in any chattel or goods;

4. To do any act of management or of conservation, with respect to any chattel or goods or to any interest in any chattel or goods owned, or claimed to be owned, by the principal, including by way of illustration, but not of restriction, power to insure against any casualty, liability or loss, to obtain or to regain possession, or to protect such chattel or goods or interest in any chattel or goods, by action, proceeding or otherwise, to pay, to compromise or to contest taxes or assessments, to apply for refunds in connection therewith, to move from place

to place, to store for hire or on a gratuitous bailment, to use, to alter, and to make repairs or alterations of any such chattel or goods, or interest in any chattel or goods;

5. To demand, to receive, to obtain by action, proceeding or otherwise, any money or other thing of value to which the principal is, or may become, or may claim to be entitled as the proceeds of a chattel or goods or of any interest in any chattel or goods, or of one or more of the transactions enumerated in this section, to conserve, to invest, to disburse or to utilize anything so received for purposes enumerated in this section, and to reimburse the agent for any expenditures properly made by him in the execution of the powers conferred on him by the statutory short form power of attorney;

6. To agree and to contract, in any manner, and with any person and on any terms, which the agent may select, for the accomplishment of any of the purposes enumerated in this section, and to perform, to rescind, to reform, to release or to modify any such agreement or contract or any other similar agreement or contract made by or on behalf of the principal;

7. To execute, to acknowledge, to seal and to deliver any conveyance, revocation, declaration or modification of trust, mortgage, lease, notice, check or other instrument which the agent may think useful for the accomplishment of any of the purposes enumerated in this section;

8. To prosecute, to defend, to submit to arbitration, to settle, and to propose or to accept a compromise with respect to, any claim existing in favor of, or against, the principal based on or involving any chattel or goods transaction or to intervene in any action or proceeding relating thereto;

9. To hire, to discharge, and to compensate any attorney, accountant, expert witness or other assistant or assistants when the agent shall think such action to be desirable for the proper execution by him of any of the powers described in this section, and for the keeping of needed records thereof; and

10. In general, and in addition to all the specific acts in this section enumerated, to do any other act or acts, which the principal can do through an agent, with respect to any chattel or goods or interest in any chattel or goods.

All powers described in this section 5–1502B of the general obligations law shall be exercisable equally with respect to any chattel or goods or interest in any chattel or goods owned by the principal at the giving of the power of attorney or thereafter acquired, and whether located in the state of New York or elsewhere.

Section 5–1502C. Construction—bond, share and commodity transactions

In a statutory short form power of attorney, the language conferring general authority with respect to "bond, share and commodity transactions," must be construed to mean that the principal authorizes the agent:

1. To accept as a gift, or as security for a loan, to reject, to demand, to buy, to receive, or otherwise to acquire either ownership or possession of, any bond, share, instrument of similar character, commodity interest or any instrument with respect thereto, together with the interest, dividends, proceeds or other distributions connected therewith;

2. To sell (including short sales), to exchange, to transfer either with or without a guaranty, to release, to surrender, to hypothecate, to pledge, to revoke, create or modify a trust, to grant options concerning, to loan, to trade in, or otherwise to dispose of any bond, share, instrument of similar character, commodity interest or any instrument with respect thereto;

3. To release in whole or in part, to assign the whole or a part of, to satisfy in whole or in part, and to enforce by action, proceeding or otherwise, any pledge, incumbrance, lien or other claim as to any bond, share, instrument of similar character, commodity interest or any interest with respect thereto, when such pledge, incumbrance, lien or other claim is owned, or claimed to be owned, by the principal;

4. To do any act of management or of conservation with respect to any bond, share, instrument of similar character, commodity interest or any instrument with respect thereto, owned or claimed to be owned by the principal or in which the principal has or claims to have an interest, including by way of illustration, but not of restriction, power to insure against any casualty, liability or loss, to obtain or to regain possession or to protect the principal's interest therein by action, proceeding or otherwise, to pay, to compromise or to contest taxes or assessments, to apply for refunds in connection therewith, to consent to and to participate in any reorganization, recapitalization, liquidation, merger, consolidation, sale or lease, or other change in or revival of a corporation or other association, or in the financial structure of any corporation or other association, or in the priorities, voting rights or other special rights with respect thereto, to become a depositor with any protective, reorganization or similar committee of the bond, share, other instrument of similar character, commodity interest or any instrument with respect thereto, belonging to the foregoing, to exercise or to sell any option, conversion or similar right, to vote in person or by the granting of a proxy (with or without the power of substitution), either discretionary, general or otherwise, for the accomplishment of any of the purposes enumerated in this section;

5. To carry in the name of a nominee selected by the agent any evidence of the ownership of any bond, share, other instrument of similar character, commodity interest or instrument with respect thereto, belonging to the principal;

6. To employ, in any way believed to be desirable by the agent, any bond, share, other instrument of similar character, commodity interest or any instrument with respect thereto, in which the principal has or claims to have any interest, for the protection or continued operation of any speculative or margin transaction personally begun or personally guaranteed, in whole or in part, by the principal;

7. To demand, to receive, to obtain by action, proceeding or otherwise, any money or other thing of value to which the principal is, or may become, or may claim to be entitled as the proceeds of any interest in a bond, share, other instrument of similar character, commodity interest or any instrument with respect thereto, or of one or more of the transactions enumerated in this section, to conserve, to invest, to disburse or to utilize anything so received for purposes enumerated in this section, and to reimburse the agent for any expenditures properly made by him in the execution of the powers conferred on him by the statutory short form power of attorney;

8. To agree and to contract, in any manner, and with any broker or other person, and on any terms, which the agent may select, for the accomplishment of any of the purposes enumerated in this section, and to perform, to rescind, to reform, to release or to modify any such agreement or contract or any other similar agreement made by or on behalf of the principal;

9. To execute, to acknowledge, to seal and to deliver any consent, agreement, authorization, assignment, revocation, declaration or modification of trust notice, waiver of notice, check, or other instrument which the agent may think useful for the accomplishment of any of the purposes enumerated in this section;

10. To execute, to acknowledge and to file any report or certificate required by law or governmental regulation;

11. To prosecute, to defend, to submit to arbitration, to settle and to propose or to accept a compromise with respect to, any claim existing in favor of, or against, the principal based on or involving any bond, share or commodity transaction or to intervene in any action or proceeding relating thereto;

12. To hire, to discharge, and to compensate any attorney, accountant, expert witness or other assistant or assistants when the agent shall think such action to be desirable for the proper execution by him of any of the powers described in this section, and for the keeping of needed records thereof; and

13. In general, and in addition to all the specific acts in this section enumerated, to do any other act or acts, which the principal can do through an agent, with respect to any interest in any bond, share or other instrument of similar character, commodity, or instrument with respect to a commodity.

All powers described in this section 5–1502C of the general obligations law shall be exercisable equally with respect to any interest in any bond, share or other instrument of similar character, commodity, or instrument with respect to a commodity owned by the principal at the giving of the power of attorney or thereafter acquired, whether located in the state of New York or elsewhere.

Section 5–1502D. Construction—banking transactions

In a statutory short form power of attorney, the language conferring general authority with respect to "banking transactions," must be construed to mean that the principal authorizes the agent:

GOL

1. To continue, to modify and to terminate any deposit account, or other banking arrangement made by or on behalf of the principal prior to the creation of the agency;

2. To open either in the name of the agent alone, or in the name of the principal alone, or in both their names jointly or otherwise, a deposit account of any type with any banker or in any banking institution selected by the agent, to hire such safe deposit box or vault space and to make such other contracts for the procuring of other services made available by any such banker or banking institution as the agent shall think to be desirable;

3. To make, to sign and to deliver checks or drafts for any purpose, to withdraw by check, order or otherwise any funds or property of the principal deposited with, or left in the custody of, any banker or banking institution, wherever located, either before or after the creation of the agency;

4. To prepare from time to time financial statements concerning the assets and liabilities or income and expenses of the principal, and to deliver statements so prepared to any banker, banking institution or other person, whom the agent believes to be reasonably entitled thereto;

5. To receive statements, vouchers, notices or other documents from any banker or banking institution and to act with respect thereto;

6. To have free access at any time or times to any safe deposit box or vault to which the principal might have access, if personally present;

7. To borrow money by bank overdraft, or by promissory note of the principal given for such period and at such interest rate as the agent shall select, to give such security out of the assets of the principal as the agent shall think to be desirable or necessary for any such borrowing, to pay, to renew or to extend the time of payment of any note so given or given by or on behalf of the principal, and to procure for the principal a loan from any banker or banking institution by any other procedure made available by such banker or institution;

8. To make, to assign, to indorse, to discount, to guarantee, and to negotiate, for any and all purposes, all promissory notes, bills of exchange, checks, drafts or other negotiable or non-negotiable paper of the principal, or payable to the principal or to his order, to receive the cash or other proceeds of any such transactions, to accept any bill of exchange or draft drawn by any person upon the principal, and to pay it when due;

9. To receive for the principal and to deal in and to deal with any trust receipt, warehouse receipt or other negotiable or non-negotiable instrument, in which the principal has or claims to have an interest;

10. To apply for and to receive letters of credit or travelers checks from any banker or banking institution selected by the agent, giving such indemnity or other agreements in connection therewith as the agent shall think to be desirable or necessary;

11. To consent to an extension in the time of payment with respect to any commercial paper or any banking transaction in which the principal has an interest or by which the principal is, or might be, affected in any way;

12. To pay, to compromise or to contest taxes or assessments and to apply for refunds in connection therewith;

13. To demand, to receive, to obtain by action, proceeding, or otherwise any money or other thing of value to which the principal is, or may become, or may claim to be entitled as the proceeds of any banking transaction conducted by the principal himself, or by the agent in the execution of any of the powers described in this section, or partly by the principal and partly by the agent so acting, to conserve, to invest, to disburse or to utilize anything so received for purposes enumerated in this section, and to reimburse the agent for any expenditures properly made by him in the execution of the powers conferred upon him by the statutory short form power of attorney;

14. To execute, to acknowledge, to seal and to deliver any instrument of any kind, in the name of the principal or otherwise, which the agent may think useful for the accomplishment of any of the purposes enumerated in this section;

15. To prosecute, to defend, to submit to arbitration, to settle, and to propose or to accept a compromise with respect to, any claim existing in favor of, or against, the principal based on or involving any banking transaction or to intervene in any action or proceeding relating thereto;

16. To hire, to discharge, and to compensate any attorney, accountant, expert witness or other assistant or assistants when the agent shall think such action to be desirable for the proper execution by him of any of the powers described in this section, and for the keeping of needed records thereof; and

17. In general, and in addition to all the specific acts in this section enumerated, to do any other act or acts, which the principal can do through an agent, in connection with any banking transaction which does or might in any way affect the financial or other interests of the principal.

All powers described in this section 5–1502D of the general obligations law shall be exercisable equally with respect to any banking transaction engaged in by the principal at the giving of the power of attorney or thereafter engaged in, and whether conducted in the state of New York or elsewhere.

GOL

Section 5–1502E. Construction—business operating transactions

In a statutory short form power of attorney, the language conferring general authority with respect to "business operating transactions," must be construed to mean that the principal authorizes the agent:

1. To the extent that an agent is permitted by law thus to act for a principal, to discharge and to perform any duty or liability and also to exercise any right, power, privilege or option which the principal has, or claims to have, under any contract of partnership whether the principal is a general or special partner

thereunder, to enforce the terms of any such partnership agreement for the protection of the principal, by action, proceeding or otherwise, as the agent shall think to be desirable or necessary, and to defend, submit to arbitration, settle or compromise any action or other legal proceeding to which the principal is a party because of his membership in said partnership;

2. To exercise in person or by proxy or to enforce by action, proceeding or otherwise, any right, power, privilege or option which the principal has as the holder of any bond, share, or other instrument of similar character and to defend, submit to arbitration, settle or compromise any action or other legal proceeding to which the principal is a party because of any such bond, share, or other instrument of similar character;

3. With respect to any business enterprise which is owned solely by the principal;

a. to continue, to modify, to renegotiate, to extend and to terminate any contractual arrangements made with any person, firm, association or corporation whatsoever by or on behalf of the principal with respect thereto prior to the creation of the agency;

b. to determine the policy of such enterprise as to the location of the site or sites to be utilized for its operation, as to the nature and extent of the business to be undertaken by it, as to methods of manufacturing, selling, merchandising, financing, accounting and advertising to be employed in its operation, as to the amount and types of insurance to be carried, as to the mode of securing, compensating and dealing with accountants, attorneys, servants and other agents and employees required for its operation, to agree and to contract, in any manner, and with any person and on any terms, which the agent thinks to be desirable or necessary for effectuating any or all of such decisions of the agent as to policy, and to perform, to rescind, to reform, to release or to modify any such agreement or contract or any other similar agreement or contract made by or on behalf of the principal;

c. to change the name or form of organization under which such business is operated and to enter into such partnership agreement with other persons or to organize such corporation to take over the operation of such business, or any part thereof, as the agent shall think to be desirable or necessary;

d. to demand and to receive all moneys which are, or may become, due to the principal, or which may be claimed by the principal or on his behalf in the operation of such enterprise, and to control and to disburse such funds in the operation of such enterprise in any way which the agent shall think to be desirable or necessary, to engage in any banking transactions which the agent shall think to be desirable or necessary for effectuating the execution of any of the powers of the agent described in this subdivision;

4. To prepare, to sign, to file and to deliver all reports, compilations of information, returns or other papers with respect to any business operating transaction of the principal, which are required by any governmental agency,

department or instrumentality or which the agent shall think to be desirable or necessary for any purpose, and to make any payments with respect thereto;

5. To pay, to compromise or to contest taxes or assessments and to do any act or acts which the agent shall think to be desirable or necessary to protect the principal from illegal or unnecessary taxation, fines, penalties or assessments in connection with his business operations, including power to attempt to recover, in any manner permitted by law, sums paid before or after the creation of the agency as taxes, fines, penalties or assessments;

6. To demand, to receive, to obtain by action, proceeding or otherwise, any money, or other thing of value to which the principal is, or may become, or may claim to be entitled as the proceeds of any business operation of such principal, to conserve, to invest, to disburse or to utilize anything so received for purposes enumerated in this section, and to reimburse the agent for any expenditures properly made by him in the execution of the powers conferred upon him by the statutory short form power of attorney;

7. To execute, to acknowledge, to seal and to deliver any deed, assignment, mortgage, lease, notice, consent, agreement, authorization, check or other instrument which the agent may think useful for the accomplishment of any of the purposes enumerated in this section;

8. To prosecute, to defend, to submit to arbitration, to settle, and to propose or to accept a compromise with respect to, any claim existing in favor of, or against, the principal based on or involving any business operating transaction or to intervene in any action or proceeding relating thereto;

9. To hire, to discharge, and to compensate any attorney, accountant, expert witness or other assistant or assistants when the agent shall think such action to be desirable for proper execution by him of any of the powers described in this section, and for the keeping of needed records thereof; and

10. In general, and in addition to all the specific acts in this section enumerated, to do any other act or acts, which the principal can do through an agent, in connection with any business operated by the principal, which the agent shall think to be desirable or necessary for the furtherance or protection of the interests of the principal.

All powers described in this section 5–1502E of the general obligations law shall be exercisable equally with respect to any business in which the principal is interested at the creation of the agency or in which the principal shall thereafter become interested, and whether operated in the state of New York or elsewhere.

Section 5–1502F. Construction—insurance transactions

In a statutory short form power of attorney, the language conferring general authority with respect to "insurance transactions," must be construed to mean that the principal authorizes the agent:

1. To continue, to pay the premium or assessment on, to modify, to rescind, to release or to terminate any contract of life, accident, health, disability or

liability insurance or any combination of such insurance procured by or on behalf of the principal prior to the creation of the agency which insures either the principal or any other person, without regard to whether the principal is or is not a beneficiary thereunder;

2. To procure new, different or additional contracts of insurance on the life of the principal or protecting the principal with respect to ill-health, disability, accident or liability of any sort, to select the amount, the type of insurance contract and the mode of payment under each such policy, to pay the premium or assessment on, to modify, to rescind, to release or to terminate, any contract so procured by the agent and to designate the beneficiary of any such contract of insurance, provided, however, that the agent himself cannot be such beneficiary unless the agent is spouse, child, grandchild, parent, brother or sister of the principal;

3. To apply for and to receive any available loan on the security of the contract of insurance, whether for the payment of a premium or for the procuring of cash, to surrender and thereupon to receive the cash surrender value, to exercise any election as to beneficiary or mode of payment, to change the manner of paying premiums, to change or to convert the type of insurance contract, with respect to any contract of life, accident, health, disability or liability insurance as to which the principal has, or claims to have, any one or more of the powers described in this section and to change the beneficiary of any such contract of insurance, provided, however, that the agent himself cannot be such new beneficiary unless the agent is spouse, child, grandchild, parent, brother or sister of the principal;

4. To demand, to receive, to obtain by action, proceeding or otherwise, any money, dividend, or other thing of value to which the principal is, or may become, or may claim to be entitled as the proceeds of any contract of insurance or of one or more of the transactions enumerated in this section, to conserve, to invest, to disburse or to utilize anything so received for purposes enumerated in this section, and to reimburse the agent for any expenditures properly made by him in the execution of the powers conferred on him by the statutory short form power of attorney;

5. To apply for and to procure any available governmental aid in the guaranteeing or paying of premiums of any contract of insurance on the life of the principal;

6. To sell, to assign, to hypothecate, to borrow upon, or to pledge the interest of the principal in any contract of insurance;

7. To pay, from such proceeds or otherwise, to compromise or to contest, and to apply for refunds in connection with, any tax or assessment levied by a taxing authority with respect to any contract of insurance or the proceeds thereof or liability accruing by reason of such tax or assessment;

8. To agree and to contract, in any manner, and with any person and on any terms, which the agent may select for the accomplishment of any of the purposes

enumerated in this section, and to perform, to rescind, to reform, to release or to modify any such agreement or contract;

9. To execute, to acknowledge, to seal and to deliver any consent, demand, request, application, agreement, indemnity, authorization, assignment, pledge, notice, check, receipt, waiver or other instrument which the agent may think useful for the accomplishment of any of the purposes enumerated in this section;

10. To continue, to procure, to pay the premium or assessment on, to modify, to rescind, to release, to terminate or otherwise to deal with any contract of insurance, other than those enumerated in subdivisions one or two of this section, whether fire, marine, burglary, compensation, disability, liability, hurricane, casualty, or other type, or any combination of insurance, to do any act or acts with respect to any such contract or with respect to its proceeds or enforcement which the agent thinks to be desirable or necessary for the promotion or protection of the interests of the principal;

11. To prosecute, to defend, to submit to arbitration, to settle, and to propose or to accept a compromise with respect to any claim existing in favor of, or against, the principal based on or involving any insurance transaction or to intervene in any action or proceeding relating thereto;

12. To hire, to discharge, and to compensate any attorney, accountant, expert witness or other assistant or assistants when the agent shall think such action to be desirable for the proper execution by him of any of the powers described in this section and for the keeping of needed records thereof; and

13. In general, and in addition to all the specific acts in this section enumerated, to do any other act or acts, which the principal can do through an agent, in connection with procuring, supervising, managing, modifying, enforcing and terminating contracts of insurance in which the principal is the insured or is otherwise in any way interested.

All powers described in this section 5–1502F of the general obligations law shall be exercisable with respect to any contract of insurance in which the principal is in any way interested, whether made in the state of New York or elsewhere.

Section 5–1502G. Construction—estate transactions

In a statutory short form power of attorney, the language conferring general authority with respect to "estate transactions," must be construed to mean that the principal authorizes the agent:

1. To the extent that an agent is permitted by law thus to act for a principal, to apply for and to procure, in the name of the principal, letters of administration, letters testamentary, letters of trusteeship, or any other type of authority, either judicial or administrative, to act as a fiduciary of any sort;

2. To the extent that an agent is permitted by law thus to act for a principal, to represent and to act for the principal in all ways and in all matters affecting

any estate of a decedent, absentee, infant or incompetent, or any trust or other fund, out of which the principal is entitled, or claims to be entitled, to some share or payment, or with respect to which the principal is a fiduciary;

3. To accept, to reject, to receive, to receipt for, to sell, to assign, to release, to pledge, to exchange, or to consent to a reduction in or modification of, any share in or payment from any estate, trust or other fund;

4. To demand, to obtain by action, proceeding or otherwise any money, or other thing of value to which the principal is, or may become, or may claim to be entitled by reason of the death testate or intestate of any person or of any testamentary disposition or of any trust or by reason of the administration of the estate of a decedent or absentee or of the guardianship of an infant or incompetent or the administration of any trust or other fund, to initiate, to participate in and to oppose any proceeding, judicial or otherwise, for the ascertainment of the meaning, validity or effect of any deed, will, declaration of trust, or other transaction affecting in any way the interest of the principal, to initiate, to participate in and to oppose any proceeding, judicial or otherwise, for the removal, substitution or surcharge of a fiduciary, to conserve, to invest, to disburse or to utilize anything so received for purposes enumerated in this section, and to reimburse the agent for any expenditures properly made by him in the execution of the powers conferred on him by the statutory short form power of attorney;

5. To prepare, to sign, to file and to deliver all reports, compilations of information, returns or papers with respect to any interest had or claimed by or on behalf of the principal in any estate, trust, or other fund, to pay, to compromise or to contest, and to apply for refunds in connection with, any tax or assessment, with respect to any interest had or claimed by or on behalf of the principal in any estate, trust or other fund or by reason of the death of any person, or with respect to any property in which such interest is had or claimed;

6. To agree and to contract, in any manner and with any person and on any terms, which the agent may select, for the accomplishment of the purposes enumerated in this section, and to perform, to rescind, to reform, to release, or to modify any such agreement or contract or any other similar agreement or contract made by or on behalf of the principal;

7. To execute, to acknowledge, to verify, to seal, to file and to deliver any consent, designation, pleading, notice, demand, election, conveyance, release, assignment, check, pledge, waiver, admission of service, notice of appearance or other instrument which the agent may think useful for the accomplishment of any of the purposes enumerated in this section;

8. To submit to arbitration or to settle, and to propose or to accept a compromise with respect to any controversy or claim which affects the estate of a decedent, absentee, infant or incompetent, or the administration of a trust or other fund, in any one of which the principal has, or claims to have, an interest, and to do any and all acts which the agent shall think to be desirable or necessary in effectuating such compromise;

9. To hire, to discharge, and to compensate any attorney, accountant, expert witness or other assistant or assistants, when the agent shall think such action to be desirable for the proper execution by him of any of the powers described in this section, and for the keeping of needed records thereof; and

10. In general, and in addition to all the specific acts in this section enumerated, to do any other act or acts, which the principal can do through an agent, with respect to the estate of a decedent, absentee, infant or incompetent, or the administration of a trust or other fund, in any one of which the principal has, or claims to have, an interest, or with respect to which the principal is a fiduciary.

All powers described in this section 5–1502G of the general obligations law shall be exercisable equally with respect to any estate of a decedent, absentee, infant or incompetent, or the administration of any trust or other fund, in which the principal is interested at the giving of the power of attorney or may thereafter become interested and whether located in the state of New York or elsewhere.

Section 5–1502H. Construction—claims and litigation

In a statutory short form power of attorney, the language conferring general authority with respect to "claims and litigation," must be construed to mean that the principal authorizes the agent:

1. To assert and to prosecute before any court, administrative board, department, commissioner or other tribunal, any cause of action, claim, counter-claim, offset or defense, which the principal has, or claims to have, against any individual, partnership, association, corporation, government, or other person or instrumentality, including by way of illustration and not of restriction, power to sue for the recovery of land or of any other thing of value, for the recovery of damages sustained by the principal in any manner, for the elimination or modification of tax liability, for an injunction, for specific performance, or for any other relief;

2. To bring an action of interpleader or other action to determine adverse claims, to intervene or to interplead in any action or proceeding, and to act in any litigation as amicus curiae;

3. In connection with any action or proceeding or controversy, at law or otherwise, to apply for and, if possible, to procure a libel, an attachment, a garnishment, an order of arrest or other preliminary, provisional or intermediate relief and to resort to and to utilize in all ways permitted by law any available procedure for the effectuation or satisfaction of the judgment, order or decree obtained;

4. In connection with any action or proceeding, at law or otherwise, to perform any act which the principal might perform, including by way of illustration and not of restriction, acceptance of tender, offer of judgment, admission of any facts, submission of any controversy on an agreed statement of facts, consent to

examination before trial, and generally to bind the principal in the conduit of any litigation or controversy as seems desirable to the agent;

5. To submit to arbitration, to settle, and to propose or to accept a compromise with respect to, any claim existing in favor of or against the principal, or any litigation to which the principal is, or may become or be designated a party;

6. To waive the issuance and service of a summons, citation or other process upon the principal, to accept service of process, to appear for the principal, to designate persons upon whom process directed to the principal may be served, to execute and to file or deliver stipulations on the principal's behalf, to verify pleadings, to appeal to appellate tribunals, to procure and to give surety and indemnity bonds at such times and to such extent as the agent shall think to be desirable or necessary, to contract and pay for the preparation and printing of records and briefs, to receive and to execute and to file or deliver any consent, waiver, release, confession of judgment, satisfaction of judgment, notice, agreement, or other instrument which the agent shall think to be desirable or necessary in connection with the prosecution, settlement or defense of any claim by or against the principal or of any litigation to which the principal is or may become or be designated a party;

7. To appear for, to represent and to act for the principal with respect to bankruptcy or insolvency proceedings, whether voluntary or involuntary, whether of the principal or of some other person, with respect to any reorganization proceeding, or with respect to any receivership or application for the appointment of a receiver or trustee which, in any way, affects any interest of the principal in any land, chattel, bond, share, commodity interest, chose in action or other thing of value;

8. To hire, to discharge, and to compensate any attorney, accountant, expert witness or other assistant or assistants when the agent shall think such action to be desirable for the proper execution by him of any of the powers described in this section;

9. To pay, from funds in his control or for the account of the principal, any judgment against the principal or any settlement which may be made in connection with any transaction enumerated in this section, and to receive and conserve any moneys or other things of value paid in settlement of or as proceeds of one or more of the transactions enumerated in this section, and to receive and endorse checks and to deposit the same; and

10. In general, and in addition to all the specific acts in this section enumerated, to do any other act or acts, which the principal can do through an agent, in connection with any claim by or against the principal or with litigation to which the principal is or may become or be designated a party.

All powers described in this section 5–1502H of the general obligations law shall be exercisable equally with respect to any claim or litigation existing at the giving of the power of attorney or thereafter arising, and whether arising in the state of New York or elsewhere.

Section 5–1502I. Construction—personal relationships and affairs

In a statutory short form power of attorney, the language conferring general authority with respect to "personal relationships," must be construed to mean that the principal authorizes the agent:

1. To do all acts necessary for maintaining the customary standard of living of the spouse and children and other dependents of the principal, including by way of illustration and not by way of restriction, power to provide living quarters by purchase, lease or by other contract, or by payment of the operating costs, including interest, amortization payments, repairs and taxes, of premises owned by the principal and occupied by his family or dependents, to provide normal domestic help for the operation of the household, to provide usual vacations and usual travel expenses, to provide usual educational facilities, and to provide funds for all the current living costs of such spouse, children and other dependents, including, among other things, shelter, clothing, food and incidentals;

2. To provide, whenever necessary, medical, dental and surgical care, hospitalization and custodial care for the spouse, children and other dependents of the principal;

3. To continue whatever provision has been made by the principal, prior to the creation of the agency or thereafter, for his spouse, children and other dependents, with respect to automobiles, or other means of transportation, including by way of illustration but not by way of restriction, power to license, to insure and to replace any automobiles owned by the principal and customarily used by the spouse, children or other dependents of the principal;

4. To continue whatever charge accounts have been operated by the principal prior to the creation of the agency or thereafter, for the convenience of his spouse, children, or other dependents, to open such new accounts as the agent shall think to be desirable for the accomplishment of any of the purposes enumerated in this section, and to pay the items charged on such accounts by any person authorized or permitted by the principal to make such charges prior to the creation of the agency;

5. To continue the discharge of any services or duties assumed by the principal, prior to the creation of the agency or thereafter, to any parent, relative or friend of the principal;

6. To supervise and to enforce, to defend or to settle any claim by or against the principal arising out of property damages or personal injuries suffered by or caused by the principal, or under such circumstances that the loss resulting therefrom will, or may fall on the principal;

7. To continue payments incidental to the membership or affiliation of the principal in any church, club, society, order or other organization or to continue contributions thereto;

8. To demand, to receive, to obtain by action, proceeding or otherwise any money or other thing of value to which the principal is or may become or may claim to be entitled as salary, wages, commission or other remuneration for services performed, or as a dividend or distribution upon any stock, or as interest or principal upon any indebtedness, or any periodic distribution of profits from any partnership or business in which the principal has or claims an interest, and to indorse, collect or otherwise realize upon any instrument for the payment so received;

9. To prepare, to execute and to file all tax, social security, unemployment insurance and information returns required by the laws of the United States, or of any state or subdivision thereof, or of any foreign government, to prepare, to execute and to file all other papers and instruments which the agent shall think to be desirable or necessary for the safeguarding of the principal against excess or illegal taxation or against penalties imposed for claimed violation of any law or other governmental regulation, and to pay, to compromise, or to contest or to apply for refunds in connection with any taxes or assessments for which the principal is or may be liable;

10. To utilize any asset of the principal for the performance of the powers enumerated in this section, including by way of illustration and not by way of restriction, power to draw money by check or otherwise from any bank deposit of the principal, to sell any land, chattel, bond, share, commodity interest, chose in action or other asset of the principal, to borrow money and to pledge as security for such loan, any asset, including insurance, which belongs to the principal;

11. To execute, to acknowledge, to verify, to seal, to file and to deliver any application, consent, petition, notice, release, waiver, agreement or other instrument which the agent may think useful for the accomplishment of any of the purposes enumerated in this section;

12. To prosecute, to defend, to submit to arbitration, to settle, and to propose or to accept a compromise with respect to, any claim existing in favor of, or against, the principal based on or involving any transaction enumerated in this section or to intervene in any action or proceeding relating thereto;

13. To hire, to discharge, and to compensate any attorney, accountant, expert witness or other assistant or assistants when the agent shall think such action to be desirable for the proper execution by him of any of the powers described in this section, and for the keeping of needed records thereof; and

14. In general, and in addition to all the specific acts in this section enumerated, to do any other act or acts, which the principal can do through an agent, for the welfare of the spouse, children or dependents of the principal or for the preservation and maintenance of the other personal relationships of the principal to parents, relatives, friends and organizations.

All powers described in this section 5–1502I of the general obligations law shall be exercisable equally whether the acts required for their execution shall relate to real or personal property owned by the principal at the giving of the power of attorney or thereafter acquired and whether such acts shall be performable in the state of New York or elsewhere.

Section 5–1502J. Construction—benefits from military service

In a statutory short form power of attorney, the language conferring general authority with respect to "benefits from military service," must be construed to mean that the principal authorizes the agent:

1. To execute vouchers in the name of the principal for any and all allowances and reimbursements payable by the United States, or by any state or subdivision thereof, to the principal, including by way of illustration and not of restriction, all allowances and reimbursements for transportation of the principal and of his dependents, and for shipment of household effects, to receive, to indorse and to collect the proceeds of any check payable to the order of the principal drawn on the treasurer or other fiscal officer or depositary of the United States or of any state of subdivision thereof;

2. To take possession and to order the removal and shipment, of any property of the principal from any post, warehouse, depot, dock or other place of storage, safekeeping, either governmental or private, to execute and to deliver any release, voucher, receipt, bill of lading, shipping ticket, certificate or other instrument which the agent shall think to be desirable or necessary for such purpose;

3. To prepare, to file and to prosecute the claim of the principal to any benefit or assistance, financial or otherwise, to which the principal is, or claims to be, entitled, under the provisions of any statute or regulation existing at the creation of the agency or thereafter enacted by the United States or by any state or by any subdivision thereof, or by any foreign government, which benefit or assistance arises from or is based upon military service performed prior to or after the creation of the agency by the principal or by any person related by blood or by marriage to the principal, to execute any receipt or other instrument which the agent shall think to be desirable or necessary for the enforcement or for the collection of such claim;

4. To receive the financial proceeds of any claim of the type described in this section, to conserve, to invest, to disburse or to utilize anything so received for purposes enumerated in this section, and to reimburse the agent for any expenditures properly made by him in the execution of the powers conferred on him by the statutory short form power of attorney;

5. To prosecute, to defend, to submit to arbitration, to settle, and to propose or to accept a compromise with respect to, any claim existing in favor of, or against, the principal based on or involving any benefits from military service or to intervene in any action or proceeding relating thereto;

6. To hire, to discharge, and to compensate any attorney, accountant, expert witness, or other assistant or assistants when the agent shall think such action

to be desirable for the proper execution by him of any of the powers described in this section; and

7. In general, and in addition to all the specific acts in this section enumerated, to do any other act or acts, which the principal can do through an agent, and which the agent shall think to be desirable or necessary, to assure to the principal, and to the dependents of the principal, the maximum possible benefit from the military service performed prior to or after the creation of the agency by the principal or by any person related by blood or marriage to the principal.

All powers described in this section 5–1502J of the general obligations law shall be exercisable equally with respect to any benefit from military service existing at the giving of the power of attorney or thereafter accruing, and whether accruing in the state of New York or elsewhere.

Section 5–1502K. Construction—records, reports and statements

In a statutory short form power of attorney, the language conferring general authority with respect to "records, reports and statements," must be construed to mean that the principal authorizes the agent:

1. To keep records of all cash received and disbursed for or on account of the principal, of all credits and debits to the account of the principal, and of all transactions affecting in any way the assets and liabilities of the principal;

2. To prepare, to execute and to file all tax, social security, unemployment insurance and information returns, required by the laws of the United States, of any state or of any subdivision thereof or any foreign government, to prepare, to execute and to file all other papers and instruments which the agent shall think to be desirable or necessary for the safeguarding of the principal against excess or illegal taxation or against penalties imposed for claimed violation of any law or other governmental regulation;

3. To prepare, to execute and to file any record, report or statement which the agent shall think to be desirable or necessary for the safeguarding or maintenance of the principal's interest, with respect to price, rent, wage or rationing control, or other governmental activity;

4. To hire, to discharge, and to compensate any attorney, accountant, or other assistant or assistants when the agent shall think such action to be desirable for the proper execution by him of any of the powers described in this section; and

5. In general, and in addition to all the specific acts in this section enumerated, to do any other act or acts, which the principal can do through an agent, in connection with the preparation, execution, filing, storage or other utilization of any records, reports or statements of or concerning the principal's affairs.

All powers described in this section 5–1502K of the general obligations law shall be exercisable with respect to any records, reports or statements of or concerning the affairs of the principal existing at the giving of the power of attorney or thereafter arising, and whether arising in the state of New York or elsewhere.

Section 5-1502L. Construction—retirement benefit transactions

In a statutory short form power of attorney, the language conferring general authority with respect to "retirement benefit transactions" must be construed to mean that the principal authorizes the agent:

1. To contribute to, withdraw from and deposit funds in any type of retirement benefit or plan (including, but not limited to, any tax qualified or nonqualified pension, profit sharing, stock bonus, employee savings and retirement plan, deferred compensation plan, individual retirement account, or any public pension fund or retirement system);

2. To make investment directions, to select and change payment options, to designate a beneficiary or beneficiaries, provided, however, that the agent may not designate herself or himself as a beneficiary unless the agent is a spouse, child, grandchild, parent, brother or sister of the beneficiary, or unless the short form power of attorney permits the agent to designate himself or herself, and to exercise any other election for the principal with regard to any retirement benefit or plan in which the principal has an interest;

3. To make rollover contributions from any retirement benefit or plan to other retirement benefits or plans;

4. To prepare, execute and deliver any application, agreement, trust agreement, authorization, check or other instrument or document which may be required under the terms of any retirement benefit or plan in which the principal has an interest or by the administrator thereof, or which the agent deems useful for the accomplishment of any of the purposes enumerated in this section;

5. To represent the principal in any matter or thing relating to any interest that the principal has or may become entitled to under any retirement benefit or plan;

6. To prosecute, defend, submit to arbitration, settle, and propose or accept a compromise with respect to any claim existing in favor of, or against, the principal based upon or involving any retirement benefit or plan and to intervene in any action or proceeding relating thereto;

7. To hire, discharge, and compensate any attorney, accountant, expert witness or other assistant or assistants when the agent deems such action to be desirable for the proper execution by the agent of the powers described in this section or for the keeping of required records thereof; and

8. In general, and in addition to all the specific acts in this section enumerated, to do any other act or acts, which the principal can do through an agent, with respect to any retirement benefit or plan maintained by the principal or in which the principal has an interest or may thereafter have an interest.

All powers described in this section 5-1502L of the general obligations law shall be exercisable with respect to any retirement benefit or plan in which the principal has any interest, whether in the state of New York or elsewhere.

The powers explicitly authorized in the provisions of this section 5–1502L of the general obligations law shall not be construed to diminish any like powers authorized in any other section of title 15 of article5 of the general obligations law. Accordingly, such powers as are authorized in any other section of title 15 of article 5 of the general obligations law shall be construed as if the provisions of this section do not exist.

Section 5–1502M. Construction–certain gift transactions

In a statutory short form power of attorney, the language conferring general authority with respect to "making gifts to my spouse, children and more remote descendants, and parents, not to exceed in the aggregate $10,000 to any person in any year" must be construed to mean that the principal authorizes the agent:

1. To make gifts on behalf of the principal to the principal's spouse, children and other descendants, and parents, including the agent, either outright or to a trust for the sole benefit of one or more of said persons, whether an existing trust or a trust which the agent is hereby authorized to create, only for purposes which the agent reasonably deems to be in the best interest of the principal, specifically including minimization of income, estate, inheritance, generation–skipping transfer or gift taxes, provided that no person may be the recipient of gifts in any one calendar year which, in the aggregate, exceed $10,000, unless the statutory short form power of attorney contains additional language pursuant to section 5–1503 of the general obligations law authorizing gifts in excess of said amount or gifts to other beneficiaries;

2. To consent, pursuant to section 2513(a) of the United States Internal Revenue Code, to the splitting of gifts made by the principal's spouse to the principal's children and other descendants in any amount, and to the splitting of gifts made by the principal's spouse to any other persons in amounts not exceeding the aggregate annual gift tax exclusions for both spouses under section 2503(b) of said code (or cognate provisions of any successor statute);

3. To satisfy pledges made to organizations, whether charitable or otherwise, by the principal;

4. To prepare, execute, consent to on behalf of the principal, and file any return, report, declaration, or other document required by the laws of the united states, or by any state or political subdivision thereof, or by any foreign country or political subdivision thereof, which the agent deems to be desirable or necessary with respect to any gift made under the authority of this section;

5. To execute, acknowledge, seal, and deliver any deed, assignment, agreement, trust agreement, authorization, check, or other instrument which the agent deems useful for the accomplishment of any of the purposes enumerated in this section;

6. To prosecute, defend, submit to arbitration, settle and propose or accept a compromise with respect to any claim existing in favor of or against the

principal based on or involving any gift transaction or to intervene in any related action or proceeding;

7. To hire, discharge and compensate any attorney, accountant, expert witness, or other assistant or assistants when the agent deems that action to be desirable for the proper execution by the agent of any of the powers described in this section, and for the keeping of needed records thereof; and

8. In general, and in addition to but not in contravention of all the specific acts listed in this section, to do any other act or acts which the agent deems desirable or necessary to complete any such gift on behalf of the principal.

All powers described in this section 5–1502M of the general obligations law shall be exercisable equally with respect to a gift of any property in which the principal is interested at the time the power of attorney is given or in which the principal becomes interested after that time, and whether located in the state of New York or elsewhere.

The powers explicitly authorized in the provisions of this section 5–1502M of the general obligations law shall not be construed to diminish any like powers authorized in any other section of title 15 of article 5 of the general obligations law. Accordingly, such powers as are authorized in any other section of title 15 of article 5 of the general obligations law shall be construed as if the provisions of this section do not exist.

Section 5–1502N. Construction–tax matters

In a statutory short form power of attorney, the language conferring general authority with respect to "tax matters", must be construed to mean that the principal authorizes the agent:

1. To prepare, sign, and file federal, state, local, and foreign income, gift, payroll, federal insurance contributions act returns, and other tax returns, claims for refunds, requests for extension of time, petitions regarding tax matters, and any other tax–related documents, including receipts, offers, waivers, consents (including consents and agreements under united states internal revenue code section 2032A or cognate provisions of any successor statute), closing agreements, and any power of attorney required by the federal internal revenue service or other taxing authority with respect to a tax year upon which the statute of limitations has not run and with respect to the tax year in which the power of attorney was executed and with respect to any subsequent tax year;

2. To pay taxes due, collect refunds, post bonds, receive confidential information, and contest deficiencies determined by the united states Internal Revenue Service or other taxing authority;

3. To exercise any election available to the principal under federal, state, local, or foreign tax law; and

4. To represent the principal, or to designate another person to represent the principal, in all tax matters for all tax periods before the united states internal revenue service and any other taxing authority.

The powers explicitly authorized in the provisions of this section 5–1502N of the general obligations law shall not be construed to diminish any like powers authorized in any other section of title 15 of article 5 of the general obligations law, such as, but not limited to, those authorized in subdivision 9 of section 5–1502I of this title. Accordingly, such powers as are authorized in any other section of title 15 of article 5 of the general obligations law shall be construed as if the provisions of this section do not exist.

Section 5–1502O. Construction–all other matters

In a statutory short form power of attorney, the language conferring general authority with respect to "all other matters" must be construed to mean that the principal authorizes the agent to act as an alter ego of the principal with respect to any and all possible matters and affairs which are not enumerated in sections 5–1502A to 5–1502N, inclusive, of this chapter, and which the principal can do through an agent, except that such authority shall not include authorization for the agent to make medical or other health care decisions for the principal.

Amended by Laws 1994, Ch. 419, eff. Oct. 1, 1994; Laws 1994, Ch. 694, eff. Oct. 1, 1994, Laws 1996 Ch. 499, eff. Jan. 1, 1997 to designate section 5–1502L as 1502O and add sections 5–1502L, 5–1502M and 5–1502N.

Section 5–1503. Modifications of the statutory short form power of attorney

A power of attorney which satisfies the requirements of subdivision two of section 5–1501 of this chapter or of subdivision six of section 5–1506 of this chapter is not prevented from being a "statutory short form power of attorney", or a "statutory short form power of attorney effective at a future time", as either of these phrases is used in the sections of this title, by the fact that it also contains additional language which:

1. Eliminates from the power of attorney one or more of the powers enumerated in one or more of the constructional sections of this title with respect to a subdivision of the statutory short form power of attorney, or of the statutory short form power of attorney effective at a future time, affirmatively chosen by the principal; or

2. Supplements one or more of the powers enumerated in one or more of the constructional sections in this title with respect to a subdivision of the statutory short form power of attorney, or of the statutory short form power of attorney effective at a future time, affirmatively chosen by the principal, by specifically listing additional powers of the agent; or

3. Makes some additional provision which is not inconsistent with the other provisions of the statutory short form power of attorney or of the statutory short form power of attorney effective at a future time.

Amended by Laws 1994, Ch. 419, eff. Oct. 1, 1994; Laws 1994, Ch. 694, eff. Oct. 1, 1994, Laws 1996 Ch. 499, eff. Jan 1, 1997.

Section 5–1504. Acceptance of statutory short form power of attorney

1. As used in this section, the term "financial institution" means each of the following: a bank, trust company, national bank, savings bank, federal mutual savings bank, savings and loan association, federal savings and loan association, federal mutual savings and loan association, credit union, federal credit union, branch of a foreign banking corporation, public pension fund, retirement system.

2. No financial institution located in this state shall refuse to honor a statutory short form power of attorney properly executed in accordance with section 5–1501 OR 5–1506 of this title.

3. The failure of a financial institution to honor a properly executed statutory short form power of attorney shall be deemed unlawful.

4. No financial institution receiving and retaining a statutory short form power of attorney properly executed in accordance with section 5–1501 or 5–1506 of this title or a complete photostatic copy of the properly executed original thereof nor any officer, agent or employee of such financial institution shall incur any liability by reason of acting upon the authority thereof unless the financial institution shall have actually received, at the office where the account is located, written notice of the revocation or termination of such power of attorney.

5. If the application of the provisions of subdivision two or three of this section shall be held invalid to any financial institution the application of such provisions to any other financial institution other than those to which it is held invalid, shall not be affected thereby.

Added by Laws 1986, Ch. 215, eff. Sept. 21, 1986; **amended** by Laws 1991, Ch. 89, eff. Aug. 1, 1991, Laws 1996 Ch. 499, eff. Jan. 1, 1997.

Section 5–1505. Powers of attorney which survive disability or incompetence: durable powers of attorney

1. The subsequent disability or incompetence of a principal shall not revoke or terminate the authority of an attorney–in–fact who acts under a power of attorney in a writing executed by such principal which contains the words "This power of attorney shall not be affected by my subsequent disability or incompetence", or words of similar import showing the intent of such principal that the authority conferred shall be exercisable notwithstanding his or her subsequent disability or incompetence.

2. All acts done by an attorney–in–fact pursuant to a power granted pursuant to subdivision one of this section during any period of disability or incompetence shall have the same effect and inure to the benefit of and bind a principal and his or her distributees, devisees, legatees and personal representatives as if such principal were competent and not disabled. If a committee or guardian thereafter is appointed for such principal, such attorney–in–fact, during the continuance of the appointment, shall account to the committee or guardian rather than to such principal. The committee or guardian shall have the same power such

principal would have had if he or she were not disabled or incompetent to revoke, suspend or terminate all or any part of such power of attorney.

Added by Laws 1975, Ch. 195, eff. June 10, 1975; **amended** by Laws 1994, Ch. 419, eff. Oct. 1, 1994, Laws 1996, Ch. 499, eff. Jan. 1, 1997.

Section 5–1506. Powers of attorney effective at a future time or upon the occurrence of a contingency specified in the instrument; statutory short form; formal requirements; joint agents

1. An instrument granting a power of attorney may limit such power to take effect at a specified future time.

2. An instrument granting a power of attorney may limit such power to take effect upon the occurrence of a specified contingency, including but not limited to the incapacity of the principal, provided that the instrument requires that a person or persons named in the instrument declare, in writing, that such contingency has occurred. A power limited as provided in the preceding sentence shall take effect upon the written declaration of the person or persons named in the instrument that the specified contingency has occurred, without regard to whether the specified contingency has occurred.

3. The disability or incompetence of a principal shall not revoke or terminate the authority of an attorney–in–fact who acts under a power of attorney executed in writing by the principal in accordance with subdivision one or two of this section if the instrument contains the words "This power of attorney shall not be affected by my disability or incompetence", or words of similar import showing the intent of the principal that the authority conferred shall be exercisable notwithstanding the principal's disability or incompetence.

4. The powers delegable to an attorney–in–fact under this section shall be the same as those delegable under sections 5–1501, 5–1502A through 5–1502O and 5–1503 through 5–1505 of this title.

The use of the following form in the creation of a power of attorney effective at a future time is lawful, and, when used, it shall be construed as a statutory short form power of attorney effective at a future time in accordance with the provisions of this title:

"DURABLE GENERAL POWER OF ATTORNEY EFFECTIVE AT A FUTURE TIME NEW YORK STATUTORY SHORT FORM

(CAUTION: THIS IS AN IMPORTANT DOCUMENT. IT GIVES THE PERSON WHOM YOU DESIGNATE (YOUR "AGENT") BROAD POWERS TO HANDLE YOUR PROPERTY DURING YOUR LIFETIME, WHICH MAY INCLUDE POWERS TO MORTGAGE, SELL, OR OTHERWISE DISPOSE OF ANY REAL OR PERSONAL PROPERTY WITHOUT ADVANCE NOTICE TO YOU OR APPROVAL BY YOU. THESE POWERS MAY ONLY BE USED AFTER A CERTIFICATION THAT

YOU HAVE BECOME DISABLED, INCAPACITATED, OR INCOMPETENT OR THAT SOME OTHER EVENT HAS OCCURRED. THESE POWERS ARE EXPLAINED MORE FULLY IN NEW YORK GENERAL OBLIGATIONS LAW, ARTICLE 5, TITLE 15, SECTIONS 5–1502A THROUGH 5–1506, WHICH EXPRESSLY PERMITS THE USE OF ANY OTHER OR DIFFERENT FORM OF POWER OF ATTORNEY.

THIS DOCUMENT DOES NOT AUTHORIZE ANYONE TO MAKE MEDICAL OR OTHER HEALTH CARE DECISIONS. YOU MAY EXECUTE A HEALTH CARE PROXY TO DO THIS.

IF THERE IS ANYTHING ABOUT THIS FORM THAT YOU DO NOT UNDERSTAND, YOU SHOULD ASK A LAWYER TO EXPLAIN IT TO YOU.)

THIS IS intended to constitute a POWER OF ATTORNEY EFFECTIVE AT A FUTURE TIME pursuant to Article 5, Title 15 of the New York General Obligations Law:

I, ...

(insert your name and address)

. . . .

do hereby appoint: . . . .

(If 1 person is to be appointed agent, insert the name and address of your agent above) . . . .

. . . .

. . . .

. . . .

(If 2 or more persons are to be appointed agents by you, insert their ames and addresses above)

my attorney(s)–in–fact to act

(If more than one agent is designated, choose one of the following two choices by putting your initials in one of the blank spaces

( ) to the left of your choice:)

( ) Each agent may SEPARATELY act.

( ) all agents must act TOGETHER.

(If neither blank space is intialed, the agents will be required to act TOGETHER)

TO TAKE EFFECT upon the occasion of the signing of a written statement EITHER:

(INSTRUCTIONS: COMPLETE OR OMIT SECTION (I) –OR– SECTION (II) BELOW BUT NEVER COMPLETE BOTH SECTIONS (I) AND (II) BELOW.

IF YOU DO NOT COMPLETE EITHER SECTION (I) OR SECTION (II) BELOW, IT SHALLBE PRESUMED THAT YOU WANT THE PROVISIONS OF SECTION (I) BELOW TOAPPLY)

(I) by a physician or physicians named herein by me at this point:

Dr. . . . .

. . . .

. . . .

. . . .

(Insert Full Name(s) and Address(es) of Certifying Physician(s) Chosen by you)

or if no physician or physicians are named hereinabove, or if the physician or physicians named hereinabove are unable to act, by my regular physician, or by a physician who has treated me within one year preceding the date of such signing, or by a licensed psychologist or psychiatrist, certifying that I am suffering from diminished capacity that would preclude me from conducting my affairs in a competent manner;

–OR–

. . . .

. . . .

(II) by a person or persons named herein by me at this point: . . . . . .

. . . .

. . . .

(Insert Full Name(s) and Address(es) of Certifying Person(s) Chosen by you) CERTIFYING that the following specified event has occurred:

. . . .

. . . .

(Insert hereinabove the specified event the certification of which will cause THIS POWER OF ATTORNEY to take effect)

IN MY NAME, PLACE AND STEAD in any way which I myself could do, if I were personally present, with respect to the following matters as each of them is defined in Title 15 of Article 5 of the New York General Obligations Law to the extent that I am permitted by law to act through an agent:

(DIRECTIONS: Initial in the blank space to the left of your choice any one or more of the following lettered subdivisions as to which you WANT to give your agent authority. If the blank space to the left of any particular lettered subdivision is NOT initialed, NO AUTHORITY WILL BE GRANTED for matters that are included in that subdivision. Alternatively, the letter corresponding to each power you wish to grant may be written or typed on the blank line in subdivision "(Q)", and you may then put your initials in the blank space to the left of subdivision "(Q)" in order to grant each of the powers so indicated)

( ) (A) real estate transactions;

( ) (B) chattel and goods transactions;

( ) (C) bond, share and commodity transactions;

( ) (D) banking transactions;

( ) (E) business operating transactions;

( ) (F) insurance transactions;

( ) (G) estate transactions;

( ) (H) claims and litigation;

( ) (I) personal relationships and affairs;

( ) (J) benefits from military service;

( ) (K) records, reports and statements;

( ) (L) retirement benefit transactions;

( ) (M) making gifts to my spouse, children and more remote descendants, and parents, not to exceed in the aggregate $10,000 to each of such persons in any year;

( ) (N) tax matters;

( ) (O) all other matters;

( ) (P) full and unqualified authority to my attorney(s)–in–fact to delegate any or all of the foregoing powers to any person or persons whom my attorney(s)–in–fact shall select;

( ) (Q) each of the above matters identified by the following letters:

. . . .

. . . .

This durable Power of Attorney shall not be affected by my subsequent disability or incompetence.

(Special provisions and limitations may be included in the statutory short form power of attorney effective at a future time only if they conform to the requirements of section 5–1503 of the New York General Obligations Law.) . . . .

. . . .

. . . .

. . . .

If every agent named above is unable or unwilling to serve, I appoint . . .

(insert name and address of successor)

to be my agent for all purposes hereunder.

INDUCE ANY THIRD PARTY TO ACT HEREUNDER, I HEREBY AGREE THAT ANY THIRD PARTY RECEIVING A DULY EXECUTED COPY OR FACSIMILE OF THIS INSTRUMENT TOGETHER WITH A DULY EXECUTED COPY OR FACSIMILE OF THE WRITTEN STATEMENT OR STATEMENTS OF CERTIFICATION REQUIRED FOR THIS INSTRUMENT TO BE EFFECTIVE MAY ACT HEREUNDER, AND THAT THE SUSPENSION, REVOCATION OR TERMINATION HEREOF SHALL BE INEFFECTIVE AS TO SUCH THIRD PARTY UNLESS AND UNTIL ACTUAL NOTICE OR KNOWLEDGE OF SUCH SUSPENSION, REVOCATION OR TERMINATION SHALL HAVE BEEN RECEIVED BY SUCH THIRD PARTY, AND I FOR MYSELF AND FOR MY HEIRS, EXECUTORS, LEGAL REPRESENTATIVES AND ASSIGNS, HEREBY AGREE TO INDEMNIFY AND HOLD HARMLESS ANY SUCH THIRD PARTY FROM AND AGAINST ANY AND ALL CLAIMS THAT MAY ARISE AGAINST SUCH THIRD PARTY BY REASON OF SUCH THIRD PARTY HAVING RELIED ON THE PROVISIONS OF THIS INSTRUMENT.

THIS GENERAL POWER OF ATTORNEY EFFECTIVE AT A FUTURE TIME MAY BE REVOKED BY ME AT ANY TIME.

In Witness Whereof I have hereunto signed my name this . . . . .day of . . . ., 19 . . . .

. . . .

(Signature of Principal)

(ACKNOWLEDGEMENT)"

The execution of this statutory short form power of attorney effective at a future time shall be duly acknowledged by the principal in the manner prescribed for the acknowledgement of a conveyance of real property.

No provision of this article shall be construed to bar the use of any other or different form of power of attorney effective at a future time desired by the parties concerned. Every statutory short form power of attorney effective at a future time, to be valid, must be written, typed or printed using letters which are in legible writing of or clear type of no less than twelve–point in size or if in writing a reasonable equivalent thereof and must contain, in bold face upper case or upper and lower case type or a reasonable equivalent thereof the "CAUTION" which is printed in boldface type at the beginning of the statutory form printed above and the "DIRECTIONS" which are printed in bold face type immediately before subdivisions (A) through (Q) of the statutory form printed above.

6. A power of attorney is a "statutory short form power of attorney effective at a future time", as this phrase is used in this title, when, but only when, it meets the requirements of the closing paragraph of subdivision five of this section and has been duly acknowledged by the principal in the manner prescribed for the acknowledgement of a conveyance of real property and it contains the exact wording of the form set forth in subdivision five of this section, except that any blank space to the left of any one or more of lettered subdivisions (A) through (Q) may be initialed by the principal, in which case the corresponding subdivisions to the right of the blank spaces so initialed shall be deemed chosen by the principal and effective with respect to the powers conferred in the particular sections of this title which are represented by the subdivisions so chosen. Notwithstanding the foregoing, a "statutory short form power of attorney effective at a future time" may contain modifications or additions of the types described in section 5–1503 of this chapter.

7. If more than one agent is designated by the principal, such agents, in the exercise of the powers conferred, must act jointly or separately consistent with the interpretive instructions contained in such statutory short form power of attorney effective at a future time.

Added by Laws 188, Ch. 210, eff. July 31, 1988, applicable to all powers of attorney created on or after such effective date; **amended** by Laws 1994, Ch. 419, eff. Oct. 1, 1994, Laws 1996, Ch. 499, eff. Jan. 1, 1997.

GOL

TITLE 16

CONTINUITY OF CONTRACT

Section 5–1601. Definitions

As used in this title the following terms shall have the following meanings:

1. "Euro" shall mean the currency of participating member states of the European Union that adopt a single currency in accordance with the treaty on European Union signed February seventh, nineteen hundred ninety-two.

2. "Introduction of the euro" shall mean and include the implementation from time to time of economic and monetary union in member states of the European Union in accordance with the Treaty on European Union signed February seventh, nineteen hundred ninety-two.

3. "ECU" or "European Currency Unit" shall mean the currency basket that is from time to time used as the unit of account of the European community

as defined in European Council regulation no. 3320/94. When the euro first becomes the monetary unit of participating member states of the European Union, references to the ECU in a contract, security or instrument that also refers to such definition of the ECU shall be replaced by references to the euro at a rate of one euro to one ECU. References to the ECU in a contract, security or instrument without such a definition of the ECU shall be presumed, unless either demonstrated or proven to the contrary by the intention of the parties, to be references to the currency basket that is from time to time used as the unit of account of the European community.

Added by Laws 1997, Ch. 311, eff. July 29, 1997.

Section 5–1602. Continuity of contract

1.(a) If a subject or medium of payment of a contract, security or instrument is a currency that has been substituted or replaced by the euro, the euro will be a commercially reasonable substitute and substantial equivalent that may be either: (i) used in determining the value of such currency; or (ii) tendered, in each case at the conversion rate specified in, and otherwise calculated in accordance with, the regulations adopted by the council of the European Union.

(b) If a subject or medium of payment of a contract, security or instrument is the ECU, the euro will be a commercially reasonable substitute and substantial equivalent that may be either: (i) used in determining the value of the ECU; or (ii) tendered, in each case at the conversion rate specified in, and otherwise calculated in accordance with, the regulations adopted by the council of the European Union.

(c) Performance of any of the obligations described in paragraph (a) or (b) of this subdivision may be made in the currency or currencies originally designated in such contract, security or instrument (so long as such currency or currencies remain legal tender) or in euro, but not in any other currency, whether or not such other currency (i) has been substituted or replaced by the euro or (ii) is a currency that is considered a denomination of the euro and has a fixed conversion rate with respect to the euro.

2. None of: (a) the introduction of the euro; (b) the tendering of euros in connection with any obligation in compliance with paragraph (a) or (b) of subdivision one of this section; (c) the determining of the value of any obligation in compliance with paragraph (a) or (b) of subdivision one of this section; or (d) the calculating or determining of the subject or medium of payment of a contract, security or instrument with reference to interest rate or other basis has been substituted or replaced due to the introduction of the euro and that is a commercially reasonable substitute and substantial equivalent, shall either have the effect of discharging or excusing performance under any contract, security or instrument, or give a party the right to unilaterally alter or terminate any contract, security or instrument.

Added by Laws 1997, Ch. 311, eff. July 29, 1997.

Section 5–1603. Effect of agreements

The provisions of this title shall not alter or impair and shall be subject to any agreements between parties with specific reference to or agreement regarding the introduction of the euro.

Added by Laws 1997, Ch. 311, eff. July 29, 1997.

Section 5–1604. Application

1. Notwithstanding the Uniform Commercial Code or any other law of this state, this title shall apply to all contracts, securities and instruments, including contracts with respect to commercial transactions, and shall not be deemed to be displaced by any other law of this state.

2. In circumstances of currency alteration, other than the introduction of the euro, the provisions of this title shall not be interpreted as creating any negative inference or negative presumption regarding the validity or enforceability of contracts, securities or instruments denominated in whole or in part in a currency affected by such alteration.

Added by Laws 1997, Ch. 311, eff. July 29, 1997.

ARTICLE 6

DISCLOSURE
(*NEW YORK STATE TRUTH–IN–LENDING ACT*)

(*Repealed by Laws of 1969, Ch. 1141, eff. July 1, 1969. Superseded by the Federal Truth–in–Lending Act (15 U.S.C.A. § 1601 et seq.) and Federal Reserve Board regulations thereunder.*)

ARTICLE 7

OBLIGATIONS RELATING TO PROPERTY RECEIVED AS SECURITY

TITLE 1

MONEY DEPOSITED AS SECURITY TO BE HELD IN TRUST IN CERTAIN CASES

Section 7–101. Money deposited or advanced for use or rental of personal property; waiver void.

1. Whenever money shall be deposited or advanced on a contract for the use or rental of personal property as security for performance of the contract or to be applied to payments upon such contract when due, such money, with interest accruing thereon, if any, until repaid or so applied, shall continue to be the money of the person making such deposit or advance and shall be a trust fund in the

GOL

possession of the person with whom such deposit or advance shall be made and shall be deposited in a bank or trust company and shall not be mingled with other funds or become an asset of such trustee, excepting, however, that such trust funds may be deposited with other funds that have been deposited or advanced to the trustee as security for performance of a contract for the use or rental of personal property or be applied to payments upon such contract when due. If the money being deposited or advanced is for the use or rental of personal property and the money deposited or advanced is seven hundred fifty dollars or more and is for the use or rental of personal property for a period equal to or greater than one hundred twenty days, the person receiving such money shall deposit it pursuant to the provisions of subdivision one-a of this section.

1–a. Whenever the money so deposited or advanced is seven hundred fifty dollars or more and is for the use or rental of personal property for a period equal to or greater than one hundred twenty days, the person receiving such money shall, subject to the provisions of this section, deposit it in an interest bearing account in a banking organization within the state which account shall earn interest at a rate which shall be the prevailing rate earned by other such deposits made with banking organizations in such area. Such person shall not be required to keep the funds of the separate persons from whom security deposits or advances have been received in separate depository accounts, provided his books of account shall clearly show the allocation of the funds deposited in his general or special depository account. The person depositing such security money shall be entitled to receive, as administration expenses, a sum equivalent to one per cent per annum upon the security money so deposited, which shall be deducted from the interest earned on such security money from the banking organization and shall be in lieu of all other administrative and custodial expenses relating to the security deposit or advance. The balance of the interest paid by the banking organization shall be the money of the lessee making the deposit or advance and shall either be held in trust by the person with whom such deposit or advance shall be made, until repaid or applied for the use or rental of the personal property, or annually paid to the lessee making the deposit of security money.

1-b. This section shall not be applicable to any advance payment of money under or with respect to any contract for the use or rental of personal property that, in accordance with the terms applicable to such payment, either (a) is not revocable by the person making such payment and is not otherwise subject to being returned or refunded to such person, or (b) otherwise satisfies or discharges an equivalent liability under such contract when such payment is made, whether or not such liability is otherwise then due and payable under the terms of such contract.

1-c. This section shall apply to money deposited or advanced on contracts for the use or rental of personal property as security for performance of the contract or to be applied to payments upon such contract when due, only if (a) such contract is governed by the laws of this state as the result of a choice of law provision in such contract, in accordance with section 1-105 of the uniform commercial code (subject to the limitations on choice of law by the parties to a consumer lease under section 2A-106 of the uniform commercial code), or such contract is otherwise governed by the laws of this state in accordance with applicable conflict of laws rules, and (b) the lessee under such contract is located within this state, within the meaning of paragraph (d) of subdivision three of section 9-103 of the uniform commercial code (with respect to the location of debtors), except that a foreign air carrier under the federal aviation act of 1958, as amended, shall not be deemed located in this state solely as a result of having a designated office of an agent upon whom service of process may be made located in this state.

2. Any provision of a contract whereby a person who has deposited or advanced money on a contract for the use or rental of personal property as security for the performance of the contract waives any provision of this section is absolutely void.

3. This section shall not be applicable to any deposit or advance of money made in connection with the borrowing of securities for any lawful purpose.

Amended by Laws 1977, Ch. 749, eff. Aug. 5, 1977; Laws 1997, Ch. 107, eff. Jan. 1, 1998 and applicable only to monies deposited after Jan. 1, 1998; Laws 1998, Ch. 451, §1, added subds. 1-b and 1-c, eff. July 22, 1998 and deemed to be in full force and effect Jan. 1, 1998, irrespective of when any such monies were deposited or advanced.

Section 7–103. Money deposited or advanced for use or rental of real property; waiver void; administration expenses.

1. Whenever money shall be deposited or advanced on a contract or license agreement for the use or rental of real property as security for performance of the contract or agreement or to be applied to payments upon such contract or agreement when due, such money, with interest accruing thereon, if any, until repaid or so applied, shall continue to be the money of the person making such deposit or advance and shall be held in trust by the person with whom such deposit or advance shall be made and shall not be mingled with the personal moneys or become an asset of the person receiving the same, but may be disposed of as provided in section 7–105 of this chapter.

2. Whenever the person receiving money so deposited or advanced shall deposit such money in a banking organization, such person shall thereupon notify in writing each of the persons making such security deposit or advance, giving the name and address of the banking organization in which the deposit of security money is made, and the amount of such deposit. Deposits in a banking organization pursuant to the provision of this subdivision shall be made in a banking organization having a place of business within the state. If the person depositing such security money in a banking organization shall deposit same in an interest bearing account, he shall be entitled to receive, as administration expenses, a sum equivalent to one per cent per annum upon the security money so deposited, which shall be in lieu of all other administrative and custodial

expenses. The balance of the interest paid by the banking organization shall be the money of the person making the deposit or advance and shall either be held in trust by the person with whom such deposit or advance shall be made, until repaid or applied for the use or rental of the leased premises, or annually paid to the person making the deposit of security money.

2–a. Whenever the money so deposited or advanced is for the rental of property containing six or more family dwelling units, the person receiving such money, shall, subject to the provisions of this section, deposit it in an interest bearing account in a banking organization within the state which account shall earn interest at a rate which shall be the prevailing rate earned by other such deposits made with banking organizations in such area.

2–b. In the event that a lease terminates other than at the time that a banking organization in such area regularly pays interest, the person depositing such security money shall pay over to his tenant such interest as he is able to collect at the date of such lease termination.

3. Any provision of such a contract or agreement whereby a person who so deposits or advances money waives any provision of this section is absolutely void.

4. The term "real property" as used in this section is co–extensive in meaning with lands, tenements and hereditaments.

Amended by Laws 1967, Ch. 680, eff. Sept. 1, 1967; Laws 1970, Ch. 1009, eff. Sept. 1, 1970; Laws 1979, Ch. 402, eff. Sept. 1, 1979.

Section 7–105. Landlord failing to turn over deposits made by tenants or licensees and to notify tenants or licensees thereof in certain cases.

1. Any person, firm or corporation and the employers, officers or agents thereof, whether the owner or lessee of the property leased, who or which has or hereafter shall have received from a tenant or licensee a sum of money or any other thing of value as a deposit or advance of rental as security for the full performance by such tenant or licensee of the terms of his lease or license agreement, or who or which has or shall have received the same from a former owner or lessee, shall, upon conveying such property or assigning his or its lease to another, or upon the judicial appointment and qualifying of a receiver in an action to foreclose a mortgage or other lien of record affecting the property leased, or upon the conveyance of such property to another person, firm or corporation by a referee in an action to foreclose a mortgage or other lien of record affecting the property leased if a receiver shall not have been appointed and qualified in such action, at the time of the delivery of the deed or instrument or assignment or within five days thereafter, or within five days after the receiver shall have qualified, deal with the security deposit as follows:

Turn over to his or its grantee or assignee, or to the receiver in the foreclosure action, or to the purchaser at the foreclosure sale if a receiver shall not have been appointed and qualified the sum so deposited, and notify the tenant or licensee by registered or certified mail of such turning over and the name and address of such grantee, assignee, purchaser or receiver.

2. Any owner or lessee turning over to his or its grantee, assignee, to a purchaser of the leased premises at a foreclosure sale, or to the receiver in the foreclosure action the amount of such security deposit is hereby relieved of and from liability to the tenant or licensee for the repayment thereof; and the transferee of such security deposit is hereby made responsible for the return thereof to the tenant and or licensee, unless he or it shall thereafter and before the expiration of the term of the tenant's lease or licensee's agreement, transfer such security deposit to another, pursuant to subdivision one hereof and give the requisite notice in connection therewith as provided thereby. A receiver shall hold the security subject to such disposition thereof as shall be provided in an order of the court to be made and entered in the foreclosure action. The provisions of this section shall not apply if the agreement between the landlord and tenant or licensee is inconsistent herewith.

3. Any failure to comply with this section is a misdemeanor.

Added by Laws, 1965, Ch. 1031, eff. Sept. 1, 1967; **amended** by Laws 1974, Ch. 209, eff. Sept. 1, 1974.

GOL

Section 7–106. Money deposited or advanced for certain installations; waiver void.

1. Whenever any non–public moneys shall be deposited or advanced by the owner of an occupied residential dwelling on a contract for the installation of a private connection to a public sewer line as security for payments or to be applied to payments upon such contract when due, such money, with interest accruing thereon, if any, until repaid or so applied, shall continue to be the money of the person making such deposit or advance and shall be a trust fund in the possession of the person with whom such deposit or advance shall be made and shall be deposited in a bank, trust company, savings bank, savings and loan association, federal savings and loan association or federal mutual savings bank and shall not be mingled with other funds or become an asset of such trustee.

2. Any provision of a contract whereby a person who has deposited or advanced money on a contract for the installation of a private connection to a public sewer line as security for payments or to be applied to payments upon such contract when due waives any provision of this section is absolutely void.

Added by Laws 1982, Ch. 221, eff. July 1, 1982.

Section 7–107. Liability of a grantee or assignee for deposits made by tenants upon conveyance of rent–stabilized dwelling units.

1. This section shall apply only to dwelling units subject to the New York city rent stabilization law of nineteen hundred sixty–nine or the emergency tenant protection act of nineteen seventy–four.

2.(a) Any grantee or assignee of any dwelling unit referred to in subdivision one of this section shall be liable to a tenant for any sum of money or any other thing of value deposited as security for the full performance by such tenant of the terms of his lease, plus any accrued interest, if his or its predecessor in interest was liable for such funds. Such liability shall attach whether or not the successor in interest has, upon the conveyance of such dwelling unit, received the sum as deposited.

(b) The liability of a receiver for payment of any security deposit plus accrued interest pursuant to this subdivision shall be limited to the amount of such deposit actually turned over to him or it pursuant to subdivision one of section 7–105 of this chapter and to the operating income in excess of expenses generated during his or its period of receivership.

3. Any agreement by a lessee or tenant of a dwelling unit waiving or modifying his rights as set forth in this section shall be void.

Added by Laws 1984, Ch. 917, eff. Sept. 30, 1984.

Section 7–108. Liability of a grantee or assignee for deposits made by tenants upon conveyance of non–rent–stabilized dwelling units.

1. This section shall apply to all dwelling units with written leases in residential premises containing six or more dwelling units and to all dwelling units subject to the city rent and rehabilitation law or the emergency housing rent control law, unless such dwelling unit is specifically referred to in section 7–107 of this chapter.

2. (a) In circumstances where any sum of money or any other thing of value deposited as security for the full performance by a tenant of the terms of his lease is not turned over to a successor in interest pursuant to section 7–105 of this chapter, the grantee or assignee of the leased premises shall also be liable to such tenant, upon conveyance of such leased premises, for the repayment of any such security deposit, plus accrued interest, as to which such grantee or assignee has actual knowledge.

(b) For purposes of this section, a grantee or assignee of the leased premises shall be deemed to have actual knowledge of any security deposit which is (i) deposited at any time during the six months immediately prior to closing or other transfer of title in any banking organization pursuant to subdivision two–a of section 7–103 of this chapter, or (ii) acknowledged in any lease in effect at the time of closing or other transfer of title, or (iii) supported by documentary evidence provided by the tenant or lessee as set forth in paragraph (c) of this subdivision.

(c) With respect to any leased premises for which there is no record of security deposit pursuant to subparagraph (i) or (ii) of paragraph (b) of this subdivision, the grantee or assignee of the leased premises shall be obligated to notify the tenant thereof in writing no later than thirty days following the closing or other transfer of title to the fact that there is no record of a security deposit for said leased premises and that unless the tenant within thirty days after receiving notice provides him or it with documentary evidence of deposit, the tenant shall have no further recourse against him or it for said security deposit. For purposes of this subdivision, "documentary evidence" shall be limited to any cancelled check drawn to the order of, a receipt from, or a lease signed by any predecessor in interest, if such predecessor's interest in the leased premises existed on or after the effective date of this section. Except as otherwise provided by subparagraphs (i) and (ii) of paragraph (b) of this subdivision the grantee or assignee of the leased premises shall not be charged with actual knowledge of the security deposit where the tenant fails within the thirty–day period to provide said documentary evidence. Where the grantee or assignee of the leased premises fails to notify the tenant as specified in this paragraph within thirty days following the closing or other transfer of title, the tenant shall be entitled to produce documentary evidence at any time.

(d) The grantee or assignee of the leased premises shall have the right to demand that the grantor or assignor thereof establish an escrow account equal to one month's rent for any leased premises for which there is no record of a security deposit pursuant to paragraph (b) of this subdivision to be used for the purpose of holding harmless the grantee or assignee in any case where, at a date subsequent to the closing or other transfer of title, the tenant gives notice pursuant to paragraph (c) of this subdivision.

(e) The liability of a receiver for payment of any security deposit plus accrued interest pursuant to this subdivision shall be limited to the amount of such deposit actually turned over to him or it pursuant to subdivision one of section 7–105 of this chapter and to the operating income in excess of expenses generated during his or its period of receivership.

3. Any agreement by a lessee or tenant of a dwelling waiving or modifying his rights as set forth in this section shall be absolutely void.

Added by Laws 1984, Ch. 917, eff. Sept. 30, 1984 (applicable to all written contracts for the transfer of real property entered into on or after effective date).

Section 7–109. Commencement of a proceeding or action by the attorney general to compel compliance.

If it appears to the attorney general that any person, association, or corporation has violated or is violating any of the provisions of title one of this article, an action or proceeding may be instituted by the attorney general in the name of the people of the state of New York to compel compliance with such provisions and enjoin any violation or threatened violation thereof.

Added by Laws 1973, Ch. 341, eff. July 1, 1973; **amended** by Laws 1984, Ch. 917, eff. Sept. 30, 1984 (renumbered from Section 7–107 to Section 7–109).

TITLE 2

SALE OF CERTAIN LICENSED TAXICABS

Section 7–201. Sale of certain licensed taxicabs.

Notwithstanding any other law a bank, trust company, national bank, licensed lender or credit union which has made a loan to the owner of a licensed taxicab, and has taken as collateral a security agreement wherein the debtor pledges the licensed taxicab as security for the repayment of the loan as prescribed by the uniform commercial code, and in turn the secured party has filed a financing statement in the proper filing offices, and default has occurred in payment of the debt by the debtor, the secured party, if possession has been had of the licensed taxicab must dispose of said licensed taxicab for use and operation as a licensed taxicab pursuant to law. When the secured party takes possession of such licensed taxicab it shall immediately notify the licensing agency.

The purchaser of such licensed taxicab at sale hereunder, or his vendee shall have the same rights in respect of the use and operation thereof as a licensed taxicab as he would be entitled to under the law pursuant to which such taxicab was licensed if he were the purchaser thereof at a voluntary sale. Said sale shall be conditioned upon the approval by the licensing or supervisory agency of the purchaser as an owner of such taxicab. In making such determination, the licensing or supervisory agency shall use the same procedure and standards as if the purchaser thereof was a purchaser at a voluntary sale and such approval shall not be arbitrarily withheld by the licensing or supervisory agency. In the event such approval is not granted by the licensing or supervisory agency, said sale shall be declared a nullity, all monies paid hereunder, shall be returned to the purchaser at said sale. Such sale shall continue until a purchaser acceptable to the licensing or supervisory agency is obtained or the vehicle is otherwise disposed of according to law.

As used herein the term licensed taxicab shall mean a vehicle carrying passengers for hire and licensed by any county, city, town, village or any other such licensing agency, to operate as a taxicab within any such jurisdiction.

Added by Laws 1969, Ch. 722, eff. May 22, 1969; **amended** by Laws 1977, Ch. 107, eff. May 10, 1977; Laws 1980, Ch. 687, eff. June 26, 1980.

TITLE 3

BONDS AND UNDERTAKINGS

Section 7–301. Liability of surety on an undertaking.

When any undertaking executed within or without the state specifies that it is to be void upon payment of an amount or performance of an act, the undertaking shall be deemed to contain a covenant either to pay the amount or to perform the act specified. In the event of payment, the amount recoverable from a surety shall not exceed the amount specified in the undertaking except that interest in addition to this amount shall be awarded from the time of default by the surety.

Added by Laws 1970, Ch. 848, eff. Sept. 1, 1970.

TITLE 4

BUYER'S RIGHT OF REDEMPTION

Section 7–401. Buyer's right of redemption.

1. No note or security agreement used in connection with a loan for the purpose of financing the purchase of a motor vehicle, used primarily for personal or household purposes, shall contain any provision for acceleration of payment which would prevent the buyer's right of redemption pursuant to section three hundred two of the personal property law. Any such provision shall be void but shall not otherwise affect the validity of the note or security agreement.

2. Within seventy–two hours after the repossession or surrender of such motor vehicle the holder shall personally deliver or mail to the borrower at his last known address a written notice setting forth the right granted to redeem the vehicle, the dollar amount necessary to redeem, and the name, address and telephone number of the holder where information may be obtained regarding redemption of the vehicle.

Added by Laws 1986, Ch. 592, eff. Jan. 1, 1987; **amended** by Laws 1987, Ch. 80, eff. June 21, 1987.

GOL

ARTICLE 9
OBLIGATIONS OF CARE

TITLE 1
CONDITIONS ON REAL PROPERTY

Section 9–101. Liability of receiver of rents and profits appointed in mortgage foreclosure.

A receiver of rents and profits appointed in an action to foreclose a mortgage upon real property shall be liable, in his official capacity, for injury to person or property sustained by reason of conditions on the premises, in a case where an owner would have been liable. Nothing herein contained shall be construed to enlarge the liability of the receiver in his personal capacity.

Section 9–103. No duty to keep premises safe for certain uses; responsibility for acts of such users.

1. Except as provided in subdivision two,

a. an owner, lessee or occupant of premises, whether or not posted as provided in section 11–2111 of the environmental conservation law, owes no duty to keep the premises safe for entry or use by others for hunting, fishing, organized gleaning as defined in section seventy–one–y of the agriculture and markets law, canoeing, boating, trapping, hiking, cross–country skiing, speleological activities, horseback riding, bicycle riding, hang gliding, motorized vehicle operation for recreational purposes, snowmobile operation, cutting or gathering of wood for non–commercial purposes or training of dogs, or to give warning of any hazardous condition or use of or structure or activity on such premises to persons entering for such purposes; (L. 1984, Ch. 286, eff. Oct. 24, 1984).

b. an owner, lessee or occupant of premises who gives permission to another to pursue any such activities upon such premises does not thereby (1) extend any assurance that the premises are safe for such purpose, or (2) constitute the person to whom permission is granted an invitee to whom a duty of care is owed, or (3) assume responsibility for or incur liability for any injury to persons or property caused by any act of persons to whom the permission is granted.

c. an owner, lessee or occupant of a farm, as defined in section six hundred seventy–one of the labor law, whether or not posted as provided in section 11–2111 of the environmental conservation law, owes no duty to keep such farm safe for entry or use by a person who enters or remains in or upon such farm without consent or privilege, or to give warning of any hazardous condition or use of or structure or activity on such farm to persons so entering or remaining. This shall not be interpreted, or construed, as a limit on liability for acts of gross negligence in addition to those other acts referred to in subdivision two of this section.

2. This section does not limit the liability which would otherwise exist

a. for willful or malicious failure to guard, or to warn against, a dangerous condition, use, structure or activity; or

b. for injury suffered in any case where permission to pursue any of the activities enumerated in this section was granted for a consideration other than the consideration, if any, paid to said landowner by the state or federal government, or permission to train dogs was granted for a consideration other than that provided for in section 11–0925 of the environmental conservation law; or

c. for injury caused, by acts of persons to whom permission to pursue any of the activities enumerated in this section was granted, to other persons as to whom the person granting permission, or the owner, lessee or occupant of the premises, owed a duty to keep the premises safe or to warn of danger.

3. Nothing in this section creates a duty of care or ground of liability for injury to person or property.

Amended by Laws 1965, Ch. 367, eff. July 1, 1965; Laws 1966, Ch. 886, eff. July 1, 1966; Laws 1968, Ch. 7, eff. Sept. 1, 1968; Laws 1971, Ch. 343, eff. Sept. 1, 1971; Laws 1972, Ch. 106, eff. Sept. 1, 1972; Laws 1977, Ch. 91, eff. Sept. 1, 1977; Laws 1978, Ch. 147, eff. June 15, 1978, Ch. 187, eff. Sept. 1, 1978, Ch. 195, eff. May 23, 1978; Laws 1979, Ch. 336, eff. Sept. 1, 1979, Ch. 408, eff. Sept. 1, 1979; Law 1980, Ch. 174, eff. June 2, 1980; Laws 1984, Ch. 141, eff. Sept. 1, 1984; Ch. 286, eff. Oct. 24, 1984 (this amendment did not include amendment contained in Ch. 141).

ARTICLE 11

OBLIGATIONS TO MAKE COMPENSATION OR RESTITUTION

TITLE 1

COMPENSATION

Section 11-100. Compensation for injury or damage caused by the intoxication of a person under the age of twenty-one years.

1. Any person who shall be injured in person, property, means of support or otherwise, by reason of the intoxication or impairment of ability of any person under the age of twenty-one years, whether resulting in his death or not, shall have a right of action to recover actual damages against any person who knowingly causes such intoxication or impairment of ability by unlawfully furnishing to or unlawfully assisting in procuring alcoholic beverages for such person with knowledge or reasonable cause to believe that such person was under the age of twenty-one years.

2. In case of the death of either party, the action or right of action established by the provisions of this section shall survive to or against his or her executor

or administrator, and the amount so recovered by either a husband, wife or child shall be his or her sole and separate property.

3. Such action may be brought in any court of competent jurisdiction.

4. In any case where parents shall be entitled to such damages, either of such parents may bring an action therefor; but that recovery by either one of such parties shall constitute a bar to suit brought by the other.

Added by Laws 1983, Ch. 641, eff. Oct. 23, 1983; **amended** by Laws 1985, Ch. 277, eff. Dec. 1, 1985.

Section 11–101. Compensation for injury caused by the illegal sale of intoxicating liquor.

1. Any person who shall be injured in person, property, means of support, or otherwise by any intoxicated person, or by reason of the intoxication of any person, whether resulting in his death or not, shall have a right of action against any person who shall, by unlawful selling to or unlawfully assisting in procuring liquor for such intoxicated person, have caused or contributed to such intoxication; and in any such action such person shall have a right to recover actual and exemplary damages.

2. In case of the death of either party, the action or right of action given by this section shall survive to or against his or her executor or administrator, and the amount so recovered by either a husband, wife or child shall be his or her sole and separate property.

3. Such action may be brought in any court of competent jurisdiction.

4. In any case where parents shall be entitled to such damages, either the father or mother may sue alone therefor, but recovery by one of such parties shall be a bar to suit brought by the other.

Amended by Laws 1980, Ch. 281, eff. July 19, 1980.

Section 11–102. Liability of utilities for compensation for damages caused by interfering with, or delaying the progress of work under state public construction contracts.

1. No utility shall interfere with, or delay the progress of work under any contract with the state department, agency, division or board, for the construction, reconstruction or improvement of any highway, street, road, railroad grade crossing, bridge, tunnel, underpass, overpass or other state contract work, by failing to remove or relocate its poles, wires, cables, conduits, pipes or any other facilities or structures within the time schedule therefor by an agreement or under the terms of an agreement between the department, agency, division or board and the utility, or if no time is fixed by such an agreement or under the terms of such an agreement, within the time fixed by the department, agency, division or board, by notice served upon such utility by such state department, agency, division or board.

GOL

2. If such notice is utilized, it shall describe the public improvement and the geographical location thereof, the date of commencement and the date of completion, if any, provided for by the contract, the contractor's name and address, the manner in which and the extent to which the facilities and structures of the utility obstruct or prevent the contractor from progressing or performing the work comprehended by the contract, and shall fix the date or time within such utility is required to remove or relocate its facilities or structures, specifying the same, in order to provide the contractor with the site when required by the contractor for progressing or performing the work pursuant to such state contract. Such notice shall be in writing and shall be served upon such utility either personally or by certified mail at its principal office or place of business in the county where the work under such contract is to be performed, or, if there be no such principal office or place of business in such county, at the nearest principal office or place of business of such utility, outside of such county. In the event the utility to whom the aforesaid notice was directed is for any reason unable, within the prescribed period, to remove or relocate said facilities or structures specified in the notice, said utility shall immediately advise said department, agency, division or board and the contractor, in writing, of such inability, and in the same communication so advise said department, agency, division or board, and the contractor of the approximate date that such removal or relocation of facilities or structures could be effected; and shall further state the basis for the inability of said utility to remove or relocate said facilities or structures within the time specified by the notice served thereon by said department, agency, division or board. The department, agency, division or board, after examining and considering the utility's basis for establishing a different schedule for such removal or relocation, shall if such basis is reasonable, establish and notify the utility of a revised schedule for completing such removal or relocation.

3. In cases where the utility has been reimbursed for removal, relocation, replacement or reconstruction pursuant to subdivision twenty–four–b of section ten of the highway law, a utility failing to complete the removal or relocation of such structures or facilities within a period of thirty days beyond the time fixed therefor by the latest time schedule established in accordance with this section, shall be liable and responsible to any such contractor for any damages, direct or consequential, sustained by any such contractor as the result thereof, in an action to be brought by such contractor against such utility in a court of competent jurisdiction within two years from the time fixed for the removal or relocation of such structures or facilities. If an action is commenced against a utility, as heretofore provided, said utility may interpose in its answer in such action any defense available under the provisions of the civil practice law and rules. The unreasonableness of the time schedule imposed by the state department, agency, division or board shall be an absolute defense by the utility to any such action by the contractor. If, in any such action, the utility is found to owe nothing to the contractor, or if an offer of settlement is made by the utility which is not accepted by the contractor and the resulting verdict against the utility is less than the offer of settlement, then in either such event the total

cost of the utility of litigation, including reasonable attorney's fees, shall be paid to the utility by the contractor.

Added by Laws 1979, Ch. 717, eff. Sept. 1, 1979.

Section 11–103. Compensation for injury caused by the illegal sale of controlled substances.

1. (a) Any person who is injured in person, property, means of support or otherwise by a person whose abilities are impaired by the use of a controlled substance, or by reason of such person's impairment, shall have a right of action against any person who caused or contributed to such impairment by unlawfully selling to or unlawfully assisting in procuring a controlled substance for such person.

(b) In any such action, the injured person shall have a right to recover actual and exemplary damages.

2. In case of the death of either party, the action or right of action given by this section shall survive to or against his or her executor or administrator, and the amount so recovered by either a husband, wife or child shall be his or her sole and separate property.

3. Such action may be brought in any court of competent jurisdiction.

4. In any case where parents shall be entitled to such damages, either the father or mother may sue alone therefor, but recovery by one of such parties shall be a bar to suit brought by the other.

5. The term "controlled substance" when used in this section, means and includes any substance listed in section thirty–three hundred six of the public health law.

Added by Laws 1983, Ch. 222, eff. August 2, 1983.

Section 11–104. Additional liability of drawer.

1. Notwithstanding any contrary provision of law, a drawer negotiating a check who knows or should know the payment of such check will be refused by the drawee bank either because the drawer has no account with such bank or because the drawer has insufficient funds on deposit with such bank shall be liable, except as provided in subdivision four of this section, to the payee who has presented such check for payment not only for the face amount of the check but also for additional, liquidated damages, where the check is dishonored and the drawer fails to pay the face amount of such check within thirty days following the date of mailing by the payee of the second written demand for payment as provided in this section.

2. In the case of a drawer negotiating a check who knows or should know that payment of such check will be refused by the drawee bank because the drawer has no account with such bank, such additional, liquidated damages shall be in an amount to be determined by the court in light of the circumstances,

but in no event shall such amount be greater than twice the face amount of the check or seven hundred fifty dollars, whichever is less.

3. In the case of a drawer negotiating a check who knows or should know that payment of such check will be refused by the drawee bank because the drawer has insufficient funds on deposit with such bank, such additional, liquidated damages shall be in amount to be determined by the court in light of the circumstances, but in no event shall such amount be greater than twice the face amount of the check or four hundred dollars, whichever is less.

4. The drawer shall not be liable to the payee for the additional, liquidated damages provided for this section if:

(a) The drawer gave such check as payment for the rental of residential premises; or

(b) The drawer gave such check as payment for residential service supplied by a gas, electric, steam, telephone or water corporation; or

(c) The drawer gave such check as repayment of all, or a portion of, a debt secured by collateral which the payee has repossessed.

5. Defenses which may be asserted against any person not having the rights of a holder in due course, as specified in sections 3–306 and 3–408 of the uniform commercial code, shall be available to a defendant in any action or proceeding in which additional liability is claimed under this section.

6. The additional liquidated damages provided for in this section shall be available only to those persons or entities which post or otherwise give conspicuous notice to the public of the additional, liquidated damages which may be imposed pursuant to this section. Such notice shall set forth the additional liquidated damages that may be imposed if a check is dishonored and the section of law authorizing imposition of such damages, and provide notice that criminal penalties also may apply.

7. The first written demand for payment of the dishonored check shall be in the form prescribed by subdivision eight of this section and shall be sent to the drawer's last known residence address or last known place of business by first class mail and by certified mail return receipt requested with delivery restricted to the drawer, on or after the date the payee received notice that such check had been dishonored. The second written demand for payment on the dishonored check shall be in the form provided in subdivision eight of this section and shall be sent to the drawer at the drawer's last known residence address or last known place of business by first class mail on or after the fifteenth day following the date of receipt of the first written demand for payment.

8. The written demands for payment required by subdivision seven of this section, shall be in the following form and shall be printed in at least ten point type in both the English and Spanish languages:

DEMAND FOR PAYMENT OF DISHONORED CHECK

DATE:

TO: ______________________

NAME OF DRAWER

____

____

____

LAST KNOWN RESIDENCE ADDRESS OR PLACE OF BUSINESS

1ST NOTICE
2ND AND FINAL NOTICE
WARNING: YOU MAY BE SUED 30 DAYS AFTER THE DATE OF THIS NOTICE IF YOU DO NOT MAKE PAYMENT

YOUR CHECK IN THE AMOUNT OF $______DATED ________PAYABLE TO THE ORDER OF ______HAS BEEN DISHONORED BY THE BANK UPON WHICH IT WAS DRAWN BECAUSE:

—YOU HAD NO ACCOUNT WITH THAT BANK

—YOU HAD INSUFFICIENT FUNDS ON DEPOSIT WITH THAT BANK

IF YOU DO NOT MAKE PAYMENT, YOU MAY BE SUED UNDER SECTION 11–104 OF THE GENERAL OBLIGATIONS LAW TO RECOVER PAYMENT. IF A JUDGMENT IS RENDERED AGAINST YOU IN COURT, IT MAY INCLUDE NOT ONLY THE ORIGINAL FACE AMOUNT OF THE CHECK, BUT ALSO LIQUIDATED DAMAGES, AS FOLLOWS:

—IF YOU HAD NO ACCOUNT WITH THE BANK UPON WHICH THE CHECK WAS DRAWN, AN ADDITIONAL SUM WHICH MAY BE EQUIVALENT TO TWICE THE FACE AMOUNT OF THE CHECK OR SEVEN HUNDRED FIFTY DOLLARS, WHICHEVER IS LESS; OR

—IF YOU HAD INSUFFICIENT FUNDS ON DEPOSIT WITH THE BANK UPON WHICH THE CHECK WAS DRAWN, AN ADDITIONAL SUM WHICH MAY BE EQUIVALENT TO TWICE THE FACE AMOUNT OF THE CHECK OR FOUR HUNDRED DOLLARS, WHICHEVER IS LESS.

PLEASE MAKE PAYMENT IN THE AMOUNT OF ________TO:

____

NAME OF PAYEE

____

____

____

ADDRESS TO WHICH PAYMENT SHOULD BE DELIVERED

IF YOU DISPUTE ANY OF THE FACTS LISTED ABOVE, CONTACT THE PAYEE IMMEDIATELY.

GOL

9. The public service commission shall study the extent to which checks given in payment for residential service supplied by a gas, electric, steam, telephone or water corporation are dishonored either because the drawer had no account with the bank on which the check was written or because the drawer had insufficient funds on deposit with such bank, including the extend of chronic payment with checks that are dishonored and the impact of such dishonored checks on the operating costs of these corporations and the requests for rate increases, and whether any penalty for dishonored checks, in addition to recovery of the utilities' administrative costs, is necessary. The commission shall report to the governor and the legislature no later than one year after the effective date of this section.

Added by Laws 1985, Ch. 921, eff. Feb. 18, 1986 and applies to checks drawn after that date.

Section 11–105. Larceny in mercantile establishments.

1. When used in this section, the term "mercantile establishment" shall mean a place or vehicle where goods, wares or merchandise are offered for sale or a place or vehicle from which deliveries of goods, wares or merchandise are made.

2. When used in this section, the term "larceny" is an act heretofore defined or known as common law larceny by trespassory taking as defined in paragraph (a) of subdivision two of section 155.05 of the penal law committed against the property of a mercantile establishment.

3. When used in this section, the term "emancipated minor" shall mean a person who was over the age of sixteen at the time of the alleged larceny and who was no longer a dependent of or in the custody of a parent or legal guardian.

4. In any proceeding brought under this section the burden of proof shall be by a preponderance of the evidence.

5. An adult or emancipated minor who commits larceny against the property of a mercantile establishment shall be civilly liable to the operator of such establishment in an amount consisting of:

(a) the retail price of the merchandise if not recovered in merchantable condition up to an amount not to exceed fifteen hundred dollars; plus

(b) a penalty not to exceed the greater of five times the retail price of the merchandise or seventy–five dollars; provided, however, that in no event shall such penalty exceed five hundred dollars.

6. Parents or legal guardians of an unemancipated minor shall be civilly liable for said minor who commits larceny against the property of a mercantile establishment to the operator of such establishment in an amount consisting of:

(a) the retail price of the merchandise if not recovered in merchantable condition up to an amount not to exceed fifteen hundred dollars; plus

(b) a penalty not to exceed the greater of five times the retail price of the merchandise or seventy–five dollars; provided, however, that in no event shall such penalty exceed five hundred dollars.

7. A conviction or a plea of guilty for committing larceny is not a prerequisite to the bringing of a civil suit, obtaining a judgment, or collecting that judgment under this section.

8. The fact that an operator of a mercantile establishment may bring an action against an individual as provided in this section shall not limit the right of such merchant to demand, orally or in writing, that a person who is liable for damages and penalties under this section remit the damages and penalties prior to the commencement of any legal action.

9. In any action brought under subdivision six of this section, the court shall consider in the interest of justice mitigating circumstances that bear directly upon the actions of the parent or legal guardian in supervising the unemancipated minor who committed the larceny.

10. An action for recovery of damages and penalties under this section may be brought in any court of competent jurisdiction.

11. The provisions of this section shall not be construed to prohibit or limit any other cause of action which an operator of a mercantile establishment may have against a person who unlawfully takes merchandise from the mercantile establishment.

12. Any testimony or statements of the defendant or unemancipated minor child of the defendant or any evidence derived from an attempt to reach a civil settlement or from a civil proceeding brought under this section shall be inadmissible in any other court proceeding relating to such larceny.

Added by Laws 1991, Ch. 724, eff. Nov. 1, 1991, applicable only to acts committed on or after that date.

Section 11–106. Compensation for injury or death to police officers and firefighters or their estates.

1. In addition to any other right of action or recovery otherwise available under law, whenever any police officer or firefighter suffers any injury, disease or death while in the lawful discharge of his official duties and that injury, disease or death is proximately caused by the neglect, willful omission, or intentional or culpable conduct of any person or entity, other than that police officer's or firefighter's employer or co-employee, the police officer or firefighter suffering that injury or disease, or, in the case of death, a representative of that police officer or firefighter may seek recovery and damages from the person or entity whose neglect, willful omission, or intentional, willful or culpable conduct resulted in that injury, disease or death.

2. Nothing in this section shall be deemed to expand or restrict the existing liability of an employer or co-employee at common-law or under sections two

hundred five-a and two hundred five-e of the general municipal law for injuries or death sustained in the line-of-duty by any police officer or firefighter.

Added by Laws 1996, Ch. 703, eff. Oct. 9, 1996, and shall apply to all actions commenced or pending on and after such date.

Section 11–107. Compensation for harm to a guide, hearing or service dog.

In addition to any other right of action or recovery otherwise available under law, a disabled person whose guide, hearing or service dog is injured due to the negligence of the owner of another dog in handling that other dog may recover damages from the owner or custodian of the non-guide, hearing or service dog that causes injury to the guide, hearing or service dog. Such damages may include, but are not limited to veterinarian fees, the cost of retraining or replacing the guide, hearing or service dog, and lost wages or damages due to loss of mobility incurred while retraining or replacement is taking place.

Added by Laws 2000, Ch. 263, eff. Nov. 1, 2000.

ARTICLE 12
DRUG DEALER LIABILITY ACT

Section 12–101. Short title.

This article shall be known and may be cited as "the drug dealer liability act".

Added by Laws 2000, Ch. 406, eff. Sept. 30, 2000.

Section 12–102. Definitions.

As used in this article:

1. "Illegal drug" means any controlled substance or marijuana the possession of which is an offense under the public health law or the penal law.

2. "Drug market" means the support system of illegal drug–related operations, from production to retail sales, through which an illegal drug reaches a drug user.

3. "Drug user" means the individual whose illegal drug use is the basis of an action brought pursuant to this article.

4. "Grade one violation" means possession of one–quarter ounce or more, but less than four ounces, or distribution of less than one ounce of an illegal drug other than marijuana, or possession of one pound or twenty–five plants or more, but less than four pounds or fifty plants, or distribution of less than one pound of marijuana.

5. "Grade two violation" means possession of four ounces or more, but less than eight ounces, or distribution of one ounce or more, but less than two ounces, of an illegal drug other than marijuana, or possession of four pounds or more or fifty plants or distribution of more than one pound but less than ten pounds of marijuana.

6. "Grade three violation" means possession of eight ounces or more, but less than sixteen ounces, or distribution of two ounces or more, but less than four ounces, of a specified illegal drug or possession of eight pounds or more or seventy–five plants or more, but less than sixteen pounds or one hundred plants, or distribution of more than five pounds but less than ten pounds of marijuana.

7. "Grade four violation" means possession of sixteen ounces or more or distribution of four ounces or more of a specified illegal drug or possession of sixteen pounds or more or one hundred plants or more or distribution of ten pounds or more of marijuana.

8. "Participate in a drug market" means to distribute, possess with intent to distribute, commit an act intended to facilitate or in furtherance of the marketing or distribution of, or agree to distribute, possess with an intent to distribute, or commit an act intended to facilitate or in furtherance of the marketing and distribution of an illegal drug. "Participate in a drug market" does not include the purchase, receipt or possession of an illegal drug for personal use only.

9. "Person" means an individual, a governmental entity, corporation, firm, trust, partnership, or incorporated or unincorporated association, existing under or authorized by the laws of this state, another state, or a foreign country.

10. "Period of drug use" means, in relation to an individual drug user, the time of first use by an individual of an illegal drug to the accrual of the cause of action.

11. "Place of drug activity" means, in relation to an individual drug user, each county in which the individual purchases, receives, possesses or uses an illegal drug or in which the individual resides, attends school, or is employed during the period of the illegal drug use of the individual, unless the defendant proves otherwise by clear and convincing evidence.

12. "Place of participation" means, in relation to a defendant in an action brought under this article, each county in which such defendant is alleged to have participated in a drug market or in which such defendant resides, attends school, or is employed during the period of the participation in a drug market by such defendant.

13. "Drug trafficker" means a person convicted of a class A or class B felony controlled substance or marijuana offense who, in connection with the criminal conduct for which he or she stands convicted, possessed, distributed, sold or conspired to sell a controlled substance or marijuana which, by virtue of its quantity, the person's prominent role in the enterprise responsible for the sale or distribution of such controlled substance and other circumstances related to such criminal conduct indicate that such person's criminal possession, sale or conspiracy to sell such substance was not an isolated occurrence and was part of an ongoing pattern of criminal activity from which such person derived substantial income or resources and in which such person played a leadership role.

Added by Laws 2000, Ch. 406, eff. Sept. 30, 2000.

Section 12–103. Liability established.

A person who knowingly participates in a drug market within this state and has been convicted of a crime for such participation in a drug market and is a drug trafficker shall be liable for civil damages as provided in this article.

Added by Laws 2000, Ch. 406, eff. Sept. 30, 2000.

Section 12–104. Recovery by persons other than illegal drug users.

1. One or more of the following persons may bring an action for and recover damages caused by use of an illegal drug by an individual:

(a) A parent, legal guardian, child, or spouse of an individual drug user;

(b) An employer of an individual drug user; and

(c) A medical facility, insurer, governmental entity, employer, or other entity that funds a drug treatment program or employee assistance program for the individual drug user.

2. A person entitled to bring an action pursuant to subdivision one of this section may be awarded damages from a person who knowingly participated in the chain of distribution of an illegal drug actually used by the individual drug user.

3. A person knowingly participates in a drug market if:

(a) The place of the illegal drug use by the individual drug user is within a drug market target community of the defendant;

(b) The participation of the defendant in such drug market was connected with the same type of illegal drug used by the individual user; and

(c) The defendant participated in such drug market at any time during the illegal drug use by the individual user.

4. A person entitled to bring an action under this section may recover the following damages:

(a) Economic damages including, but not limited to, the cost of treatment and rehabilitation, medical expenses, loss of economic potential, loss of productivity, and support expenses;

(b) Non–economic damages, including, but not limited to, physical and emotional pain and suffering, disfigurement, loss of companionship and consortium;

(c) Reasonable attorney fees;

(d) Reasonable expert consultant and expert witness fees; and

(e) Costs and disbursements as provided for in the civil practice law and rules.

Added by Laws 2000, Ch. 406, eff. Sept. 30, 2000.

GOL

Section 12–105. Recovery by illegal drug users.

1. An individual drug user may not bring an action for damages caused by the use of an illegal drug, unless all of the following conditions are met:

(a) The individual discloses to law enforcement authorities, more than six months before filing the action, information known to the individual regarding their source of illegal drugs;

(b) The individual has not used an illegal drug within the six month period preceding filing the action.

2. A person entitled to bring an action under this section may be awarded damages only from a person who knowingly participated in the chain of distribution of an illegal drug that was actually used by the individual drug user.

3. A person entitled to bring an action under this section may recover economic damages, including but not limited to the cost of treatment, rehabilitation, and medical expenses, loss of economic potential, and loss of productivity.

Added by Laws 2000, Ch. 406, eff. Sept. 30, 2000.

Section 12–106. Scope of defendant's liability established.

A person shall be deemed to have affected a target community based upon the following grades of offenses:

1. For a grade one violation, the county in which the place of participation by the defendant is situated;

2. For a grade two violation, the community described in subdivision one of this section along with all counties with a border contiguous to such community;

3. For a grade three violation, the community described in subdivision two of this section plus all counties with a border contiguous to such community; and

4. For a level four offense, the entire state.

Added by Laws 2000, Ch. 406, eff. Sept. 30, 2000.

Section 12–107. Joinder.

Two or more persons may join in one cause of action under this article as plaintiffs if each action has at least one place of illegal drug activity in common and if any portion of the period of illegal drug use overlaps with the period of illegal drug use for every other plaintiff.

Added by Laws 2000, Ch. 406, eff. Sept. 30, 2000.

Section 12–108. Culpable conduct; contribution.

1. An action by an individual drug user shall be governed by the provisions of article fourteen-a of the civil practice law and rules. An action by a person

other than an individual drug user shall not be governed by the provisions of article fourteen–A of the civil practice law and rules.

2. The defendant shall bear the burden of proving the comparative culpable conduct of the plaintiff.

3. Comparative culpable conduct shall not be attributed to a plaintiff who is not an individual drug user.

4. A person subject to liability under this article shall have a right of action for contribution against another person subject to liability under this article pursuant to article fourteen of the civil practice law and rules. A plaintiff may seek recovery in accordance with this article and any other appropriate provision of law from a person against whom a defendant has asserted a right of contribution.

Added by Laws 2000, Ch. 406, eff. Sept. 30, 2000.

Section 12–109. Judgments; execution and enforcement.

1. The provisions of the civil practice law and rules relating to the exemption of certain real and personal property from execution and enforcement of civil judgments shall not apply to judgment rendered in favor of the plaintiff under this article.

2. Any assets subject to an administrative, civil or criminal forfeiture proceeding under state or federal law or which have been seized for forfeiture by any state or federal agency may not be used to satisfy a judgment under this article unless and until such assets have been released following the conclusion of the forfeiture action or released by the agency that seized such assets.

Added by Laws 2000, Ch. 406, eff. Sept. 30, 2000.

Section 12–110. Periods of limitation.

1. Notwithstanding any provision of law to the contrary, a claim under this article may not be brought more than two years after the cause of action accrues. A cause of action accrues under this article when a person who may recover has reason to know of the harm from illegal drug use that is the basis for the cause of action and has reason to know that the illegal drug use is the cause of such harm.

2. Notwithstanding any other provision of law to the contrary for a plaintiff, the statute of limitations under this section shall be tolled when an individual potential plaintiff is incapacitated by the use of an illegal drug to the extent that such individual cannot reasonably be expected to seek recovery under this article or as otherwise provided for by law. For a defendant, the statute of limitations under this section shall be tolled until six months after the individual potential defendant is convicted of a crime involving participation in a drug market.

Added by Laws 2000, Ch. 406, eff. Sept. 30, 2000.

ARTICLE 13

TRANSFER OF OBLIGATIONS AND RIGHTS

TITLE 1

TRANSFERABILITY; EFFECT OF TRANSFER

Section 13–101. Transfer of claims.

Any claim or demand can be transferred, except in one of the following cases:

1. Where it is to recover damages for a personal injury.

2. Where it is founded upon a grant, which is made void by a statute of the state or upon a claim to or interest in real property, a grant of which, by the transferrer, would be void by such a statute;

3. Where a transfer thereof is expressly forbidden by a statute of the state, or of the United States, or would contravene public policy.

Section 13–103. Transfer of judgment for sum of money.

A judgment for a sum of money, or directing the payment of a sum of money, recovered upon any cause of action, may be transferred; but if it is vacated or reversed, the transfer thereof does not transfer the cause of action unless the latter was transferable before the judgment was recovered. A person who executes such a transfer without acknowledging his signature before an officer authorized to take the acknowledgment of a deed must so acknowledge it at the request of his assignee or of a subsequent assignee or of the judgment debtor upon payment of the officer's fees.

Section 13–105. Effect of transfer of claim or demand.

Where a claim or demand can be transferred, the transfer thereof passes an interest, which the transferee may enforce by an action or special proceeding, or interpose as a defense or counter–claim, in his own name, as the transferrer might have done; subject to any defense or counter–claim, existing against the transferrer, before notice of the transfer, or against the transferee. But this section does not apply, where the rights or liabilities of a party to a claim or demand, which is transferred, are regulated by special provision of law; nor does it vary the rights or liabilities of a party to a negotiable instrument, which is transferred.

Section 13–107. Claims or demands transferred with bond unless reserved.

1. Unless expressly reserved in writing, a transfer of any bond shall vest in the transferee all claims or demands of the transferrer, whether or not such claims or demands are known to exist, (a) for damages or rescission against the obligor on such bond, (b) for damages against the trustee or depositary under any indenture under which such bond was issued or outstanding, and (c) for damages against any guarantor of the obligation of such obligor, trustee or depositary.

2. As used in this section, "bond" shall mean and include any and all shares and interests in an issue of bonds, notes, debentures or other evidences of indebtedness of individuals, partnerships, associations or corporations, whether or not secured.

3. As used in this section, "indenture" means any mortgage, deed of trust, trust or other indenture, or similar instrument or agreement (including any supplement or amendment to any of the foregoing), under which bonds as herein defined are issued or outstanding, whether or not any property, real or personal, is, or is to be, pledged, mortgaged, assigned, or conveyed thereunder.

Section 13–109. Definition of "transfer."

As used in sections 13–101, 13–103, 13–105 and 13–107, the term "transfer" includes sale, assignment, conveyance, deed and gift.

ARTICLE 15

MODIFICATION AND DISCHARGE OF OBLIGATIONS

TITLE 1

DISCHARGE OF JOINT OBLIGORS

Section 15–101. Definitions.

In this title, unless otherwise expressly stated, "obligation" does not include a liability in tort; "obligor" does not include a person liable for a tort; "obligee" does not include a person having a right based on a tort. "Several obligors" means obligors severally bound for the same performance.

Amended by Laws 1972, Ch. 830, eff. Sept. 1, 1972.

Section 15–102. Co–obligor not a party.

A judgment against one or more of several obligors, or against one or more of joint, or of joint and several obligors shall not discharge a co–obligor who was not a party to the proceeding wherein the judgment was rendered.

Section 15–103. Consideration to be credited to co–obligor.

The amount or value of any consideration received by the obligee from one or more of several obligors, or from one or more of joint, or of joint and several obligors, in whole or in partial satisfaction of their obligations, shall be credited to the extent of the amount received on the obligations of all co–obligors to whom the obligor or obligors giving the consideration did not stand in the relation of a surety.

Section 15–104. Discharge of one obligor, with reservations.

Subject to the provisions of section 15–103, the obligee's release or discharge of one or more of several obligors, or of one or more of joint, or of joint and several obligors shall not discharge co–obligors, against whom the obligee in writing and as part of the same transaction as the release or discharge, expressly reserves his rights; and in the absence of such a reservation of rights shall discharge co–obligors only to the extent provided in section 15–105.

Section 15–105. Discharge of one obligor, without reservation.

1. If an obligee releasing or discharging an obligor without express reservation of rights against a co–obligor, then knows or has reason to know that the obligor released or discharged did not pay so much of the claim as he was bound by his contract or relation with that co–obligor to pay, the obligee's claim against that co–obligor shall be satisfied to the amount which the obligee knew or had reason to know that the released or discharged obligor was bound to such co–obligor to pay.

2. If an obligee so releasing or discharging an obligor has not then such knowledge or reason to know, the obligee's claim against the co–obligor shall be satisfied to the extent of the lesser of two amounts, namely (a) the amount of the fractional share of the obligor released or discharged, or (b) the amount that such obligor was bound by his contract or relation with the co–obligor to pay.

Section 15–106. Death of joint obligor.

On the death of a joint obligor in contract, his estate shall be bound as such jointly and severally with the surviving obligor or obligors.

Section 15–107. Release of partner.

A release of a partner from a partnership liability shall release his co–partners from the same liability to the creditor giving the release, but after a partnership has been dissolved, by consent or otherwise, any partner may make a separate composition or compromise with any partnership creditor, and such composition or compromise shall discharge from such liability the partner making it, and him only.

Section 15–108. Release or covenant not to sue.

(a) Effect of release of or covenant not to sue tortfeasors. When a release or a covenant not to sue or not to enforce a judgment is given to one of two or more persons liable or claimed to be liable in tort for the same injury, or the same wrongful death, it does not discharge any of the other tortfeasors from liability for the injury or wrongful death unless its terms expressly so provide, but it reduces the claim of the releasor against the other tortfeasors to the extent of any amount stipulated by the release or the covenant, or in the amount of the consideration paid for it or in the amount of the released tortfeasor's equitable share of the damages under article fourteen of the civil practice law and rules, whichever is the greatest.

(b) Release of tortfeasor. A release given in good faith by the injured person to one tortfeasor as provided in subdivision (a) relieves him from liability to any other person for contribution as provided in article fourteen of the civil practice law and rules.

(c) Waiver of contribution. A tortfeasor who has obtained his own release from liability shall not be entitled to contribution from any other person.

Added by Laws 1972, Ch. 830, eff. Sept. 1, 1972; **amended** by Laws 1974, Ch. 742, eff. Sept. 1, 1974.

Section 15–109. Uniformity of interpretation.

This title shall be so interpreted and construed as to effectuate its general purpose to make uniform the law of those states which enact it.

Amended by Laws 1972, Ch. 830, eff. Sept. 1, 1972 (formerly § 15–108).

Section 15–110. Inconsistent laws repealed.

All acts or parts of acts inconsistent with this title are hereby repealed; but nothing in this title shall be construed as repealing any of the provisions of the civil practice law and rules or the partnership law.

Amended by Laws 1972, Ch. 830, eff. Sept. 1, 1972 (formerly § 15–109).

TITLE 3

REQUIREMENTS FOR EFFECTIVENESS OR ENFORCEABILITY OF MODIFICATION OR DISCHARGE

Section 15–301. When written agreement or other instrument cannot be changed by oral executory agreement, or discharged or terminated by oral executory agreement or oral consent or by oral notice.

1. A written agreement or other written instrument which contains a provision to the effect that it cannot be changed orally, cannot be changed by an executory agreement unless such executory agreement is in writing and signed by the party against whom enforcement of the change is sought or by his agent.

2. A written agreement or other written instrument which contains a provision to the effect that it cannot be terminated orally, cannot be discharged by an executory agreement unless such executory agreement is in writing and signed by the party against whom enforcement of the discharge is sought, or by his agent, and cannot be terminated by mutual consent unless such termination is effected by an executed accord and satisfaction other than the substitution of one executory contract for another, or is evidenced by a writing signed by the party against whom it is sought to enforce the termination, or by his agent.

3.a. A discharge or partial discharge of obligations under a written agreement or other written instrument is a change of the agreement or instrument for the purpose of subdivision one of this section and is not a discharge or termination for the purpose of subdivision two, unless all executory obligations under the agreement or instrument are discharged or terminated.

b. A discharge or termination of all executory obligations under a written agreement or other written instrument is a discharge or termination for the purpose of subdivision two even though accrued obligations remaining unperformed at the date of the discharge or termination are not affected by it.

c. If a written agreement or other written instrument containing a provision that it cannot be terminated orally also provides for termination or discharge on notice by one or either party, both subdivision two and subdivision four of this section apply whether or not the agreement or other instrument states specifically that the notice must be in writing.

4. If a written agreement or other written instrument contains a provision for termination or discharge on written notice by one or either party, the requirement that such notice be in writing cannot be waived except by a writing signed by the party against whom enforcement of the waiver is sought or by his agent.

5. If executed by an agent, any agreement, evidence of termination, notice of termination or waiver, required by this section to be in writing, which affects or relates to real property or an interest therein as defined in section 5–101 in any manner stated in subdivisions one or two of section 5–703 of this chapter shall be void unless such agent was thereunto authorized in writing.

6. As used in this section the term "agreement" includes promise and undertaking.

Section 15–303. Release in writing without consideration or seal.

A written instrument which purports to be a total or partial release of all claims, debts, demands or obligations, or a total or partial release of any particular claim, debt, demand or obligation, or a release or discharge in whole or in part of a mortgage, lien, security interest or charge upon personal or real property, shall not be invalid because of the absence of consideration or of a seal.

Section 15–304. Forfeiture and cancellation of oil, gas or mineral land leases.

1. When any oil, gas or mineral land lease given on land situated in any county of New York state and recorded therein becomes forfeited, terminates or expires by its own terms, the lessee, or where the lessee has assigned its interest, the assignee, within thirty days after the date of the forfeiture, termination or expiration, shall provide to the current owner of the land which is subject to the lease, without cost to such owner, a document in recordable form cancelling the lease as of record in the county where the leased land is situated.

2. If any lessee, or its assignee fails to cancel a lease, as provided for in subdivision one of this section, the current owner of the land which is subject to the lease may:

(a) serve notice upon the lessee, and if actual or record notice of their identity exists, to its assignee, that such lease be cancelled as of record, and stating that if such release is not executed within thirty days of the service of such notice, the lease will be terminated and no longer of any effect. Such notice shall also state;

(i) the names and addresses of the lessor and lessee if contained in the lease;

(ii) the name and address of the person giving notice and a statement as to his interest;

(iii) the state, county and city or town where the leased premises is located along with the location and a general description of the property as contained in the lease;

(iv) if located in a unit, the name or description of the unit if known;

(v) if there is a well on the leased land, the name or number of the well if known;

(vi) the date of the execution of the lease; and

(vii) the date of termination of the lease and the basis of such termination.

(b) service of such notice demanding a release shall be effected either personally, by certified mail to the lessee's, and where the lease has been assigned, the assignee's, last known business address, or, if service cannot be made with due diligence by the prior two methods, by publication once a week for three weeks in a newspaper of general circulation in the county where the leased land is situated;

(c) If the lessee or its assignee claims that the lease is still in full force and effect, either of these parties shall, within thirty days of the service of such notice of demand to cancel the lease, file an affidavit with the recording offices of the county wherein the land is situated. Such affidavit shall state that the lease is in full force and affect and a copy of such affidavit shall be delivered to the person serving the demand within ten days of the filing of the affidavit;

(d) If such affidavit is not filed within the required time, the current landowner may file a copy of the original notice to the lessee or assignee and an affidavit of service thereof with the recording officer of the county in which the leased land is situated, and by such filing the lease shall be cancelled and of no further effect.

3. Repealed (L. 1984, Ch. 566, eff. Sept. 1, 1984).

4. For purposes of this section, the term "mineral" shall not include salt, as defined by subdivision eighteen of section 23–0101 of the environmental conservation law.

5. For the purposes of this section, where the landowner is not the owner of the oil, gas or mineral rights, the reference to "landowner" shall be deemed to mean the owner of such oil, gas or mineral rights.

6. This section shall apply to all leases entered into before, on or after the effective date of this section.

Added by Laws 1984, Ch. 565, eff. Sept. 1, 1984 (applies to all oil, gas or mineral land leases entered into before, on or after Sept. 1, 1984); **amended** by Laws 1984, Ch. 566, eff. Sept. 1, 1984.

TITLE 5

ACCORD AND SATISFACTION

Section 15–501. Executory accord.

1. Executory accord as used in this section means an agreement embodying a promise express or implied to accept at some future time a stipulated performance in satisfaction or discharge in whole or in part of any present claim, cause of action, contract, obligation, or lease, or any mortgage or other security interest in personal or real property, and a promise express or implied to render such performance in satisfaction or in discharge of such claim, cause of action, contract, obligation, lease, mortgage or security interest.

2. An executory accord shall not be denied effect as a defense or as the basis of an action or counterclaim by reason of the fact that the satisfaction or discharge of the claim, cause of action, contract, obligation, lease, mortgage or other

security interest which is the subject of the accord was to occur at a time after the making of the accord, provided the promise of the party against whom it is sought to enforce the accord is in writing and signed by such party or by his agent. If executed by an agent, any promise required by this section to be in writing which, affects or relates to real property or an interest therein as defined in section 5–101 in any manner stated in subdivisions one or two of section 5–703 of this chapter shall be void unless such agent was thereunto authorized in writing.

3. If an executory accord is not performed according to its terms by one party, the other party shall be entitled either to assert his rights under the claim, cause of action, contract, obligation, lease, mortgage or other security interest which is the subject of the accord, or to assert his right under the accord.

Section 15–503. Offer of accord followed by tender.

1. An offer in writing, signed by the offeror or by his agent, to accept a performance therein designated in satisfaction or discharge in whole or in part of any claim, cause of action, contract, obligation, or lease, or any mortgage or other security interest in personal or real property, followed by tender of such performance by the offeree or by his agent before revocation of the offer, shall not be denied effect as a defense or as the basis of an action or counterclaim by reason of the fact that such tender was not accepted by the offeror or by his agent.

2. If executed by an agent, any offer required by this section to be in writing which affects or relates to real property or an interest therein as defined in section 5–101 in any manner stated in subdivisions one or two of section 5–703 of this chapter shall be void unless such agent was thereunto authorized in writing.

TITLE 7

DISCHARGE OF SURETY

Section 15–701. Surety not discharged by failure or refusal by creditor to sue principal debtor.

Unless otherwise agreed between the parties in writing, the failure or refusal by a creditor, after a demand by a person bound as surety, to bring an action against a principal debtor upon a contract hereafter made or an obligation hereafter created for the payment of money or the performance of any act shall not discharge such surety.

Added by Laws 1968, Ch. 419, eff. Sept. 1, 1968.

Section 15–702. Surety disclosure.

1. As used in this section:

a. "Consumer" means a natural person.

b. "Consumer credit transaction" or "transaction" means a loan or sale pursuant to which credit is extended to a consumer, primarily for personal, family, or household purposes. The term does not include transactions pursuant to a consumer credit account.

c. "Consumer credit account" means an account established pursuant to an agreement under which the creditor may permit the consumer to make purchases or obtain loans, for personal, family or household purposes, from time to time, directly from the creditor or indirectly by use of a credit card, check, or other device as the agreement may provide.

d. "Creditor" means a person, partnership, corporation, association, or other entity who, in the ordinary course of business, regularly enters into or acquires evidences of, consumer credit transactions or extends credit pursuant to consumer credit accounts.

e. "Co–signer" means a natural person who (i) in the case of a consumer credit transaction becomes obligated on the transaction as a cosigner, co–maker, guarantor, endorser or surety, but who does not receive the property, services, or money that is the subject of the transaction. The term does not include a seller, holder or lender who becomes obligated to an assignee of such party's rights; or (ii) in the case of a consumer credit account becomes obligated under the agreement as a co–signer, co–maker, guarantor, endorser or surety with respect either to all purchases and loans, or a specified maximum dollar amount of purchases and loans that will be obtained from time to time pursuant to the agreement whether or not it is contemplated that the co–signer may receive any of the property, services or money to be obtained. The term does not include a seller, holder or lender who becomes obligated to an assignee of such party's rights or a joint applicant for credit who is intended to be primarily liable under the agreement.

2. The creditor shall:

a. before a co–signer becomes obligated on a consumer credit transaction, deliver to the co–signer a completed copy of each note, contract, or other writing evidencing the obligation of the consumer or of the co–signer on the transaction, and a written notice that identifies the debt the co–signer may have to pay and reasonably informs the co–signer of his or her obligation with respect to it;

b. before a cosigner becomes obligated on a consumer credit account, deliver to the co–signer a completed copy of the agreement establishing the account, any other writing evidencing the co–signer's obligation and a written notice that identifies the account the co–signer may have to pay and reasonably informs the co–signer of his or her obligation with respect to it.

If the creditor does not comply with the provisions of this section the co–signer shall not be obligated as a guarantor of payment as described in subdivision one of section 3–416 of the uniform commercial code.

3. The notice must be in at least ten point type and may be on a separate sheet, attached to a guarantee or similar instrument, or part of the note, contract, or other writing evidencing the consumer credit transaction, or agreement establishing the consumer credit account. A separately signed written acknowledgment of receipt in substantially the form below is prima facie proof of such receipt in any action by or against the co–signer. A notice substantially similar to the following complies with this section:

(a) as to a consumer credit transaction:

NOTICE

You agree to pay the debt identified below although you may not personally receive any property, services, or money. You may be sued for payment although the person who receives the property, services, or money is able to pay. You should know that the Total of Payments listed below does not include finance charges resulting from delinquency, late charges, repossession or foreclosure costs, court costs or attorney's fees, or other charges that may be stated in the note or contract. You will also have to pay some or all of these costs and charges if the note or contract, the payment of which you are guaranteeing, requires the borrower to pay such costs and charges.

This notice is not the note, contract, or other writing that obligates you to pay the debt. Read that writing for the exact terms of your obligation.

____

(Name of Debtor)

____

(Name of Creditor)

____

(Date)

________________ $ ________________

(Kind of Debt) (Total of Payments)

I have been given a completed copy of this notice and of each writing that obligates me or the Debtor on this debt.

________________ ________________

(Date) (Signed)

(b) as to a consumer credit account:

NOTICE

You agree to pay the debts incurred from time to time on the account identified below although you may not personally receive any property, services, or money.

You may be sued for payment although the person opening the account is able to pay. You should know that the Limit of Liability listed below does not include court costs or attorney's fees, or other costs or charges that may be stated in the agreement. You will also have to pay some or all of these costs and charges if the agreement for the consumer credit account, payment of which you are guaranteeing, requires the borrower to pay such costs and charges.

This notice is not the agreement, or other writing that obligates you to pay. Read that writing for the exact terms of your obligations and of your rights to limit or end your obligations.

IDENTIFICATION OF ACCOUNT(S) YOU MAY HAVE TO PAY

____

(Name of Debtor)

____

(Name of Creditor)

____

(Date)

________________ $ ________________

(Kind of Account) (Limit of Liability)

I have been given a completed copy of this notice and of each writing that obligates me or the Debtor on this account.

________________ ________________

(Date) (Signed)

Added by Laws 1983, Ch. 293, eff. June 13, 1984; **amended** by Laws 1989, Ch. 624: changes in paragraphs (b) and (c) of subdivision 1 eff. Jan. 1, 1990; changes in paragraphs (a) and (b) of subdivision 3 eff. July 1, 1990.

ARTICLE 17

REVIVAL OR EXTENSION; WAIVER OF DEFENSE OR BAR

TITLE 1

OBLIGATIONS BARRED BY STATUTES OF LIMITATION

Section 17–101. Acknowledgment or new promise must be in writing.

An acknowledgment or promise contained in a writing signed by the party to be charged thereby is the only competent evidence of a new or continuing contract whereby to take an action out of the operation of the provisions of limitations of time for commencing actions under the civil practice law and rules other than an action for the recovery of real property. This section does not alter the effect of a payment of principal or interest.

Section 17–103. Agreements waiving the statute of limitation.

1. A promise to waive, to extend, or not to plead the statute of limitation applicable to an action arising out of a contract express or implied in fact or in law, if made after the accrual of the cause of action and made, either with or without consideration, in a writing signed by the promisor or his agent is effective, according to its terms, to prevent interposition of the defense of the statue of limitation in an action or proceeding commenced within the time that would be applicable if the cause of action had arisen at the date of the promise, or within such shorter time as may be provided in the promise.

2. A promise to waive, to extend, or not to plead the statute of limitation may be enforced as provided in this section by the person to whom the promise is made or for whose benefit it is expressed to be made or by any person who,

after the making of the promise, succeeds or is subrogated to the interest of either of them.

3. A promise to waive, to extend, or not to plead the statute of limitation has no effect to extend the time limited by statute for commencement of an action or proceeding for any greater time or in any other manner than that provided in this section, or unless made as provided in this section.

4. This section

a. does not change the requirements or the effect with respect to the statute of limitation, of an acknowledgment or promise to pay, or a payment or part payment of principal or interest, or a stipulation made in an action or proceeding.

b. does not affect the power of the court to find that by reason of conduct of the party to be charged it is inequitable to permit him to interpose the defense of the statute of limitation; and

c. does not apply in any respect to a cause of action to foreclose a mortgage of real property or a mortgage of a lease of real property, or to a cause of action to recover a judgment affecting the title to or the possession, use or enjoyment of real property, or a promise or waiver with respect to any statute of limitation applicable thereto.

Section 17–105. Promises and waivers affecting the time limited for action to foreclose a mortgage.

1. A waiver of the expiration of the time limited for commencement of an action to foreclose a mortgage of real property or a mortgage of a lease of real property, or a waiver of the time that has expired, or a promise not to plead the expiration of the time limited, or not to plead the time that has expired, or a promise to pay the mortgage debt, if made after the accrual of a right of action to foreclose the mortgage and made, either with or without consideration, by the express terms of a writing signed by the party to be charged is effective, subject to any conditions expressed in the writing, to make the time limited for commencement of the action run from the date of the waiver or promise. If the waiver or promise specifies a shorter period of limitation than that otherwise applicable, the time limited shall be the period specified.

2.a. A statement by a grantee of real property or assignee of a lease of real property, effective under section 5–705 of this chapter as an assumption of or agreement to pay an indebtedness or other sum secured by a mortgage of such property or lease has also, to the extent of the amount specified therein, the same effect as provided in this section with respect to a waiver or promise described in subdivision one, unless it contains language disclaiming an intention to affect the statute of limitation.

b. A recital, in an instrument in which real property is conveyed or a lease is assigned, that the conveyance or assignment is made subject to a mortgage, or provision to that effect in a contract for purchase of real property or purchase of a lease, or an agreement or instrument by which another encumbrance or interest is subordinated to the lien of a mortgage, does have the effect provided in this section with respect to a waiver or promise described in subdivision one.

3. A waiver or promise made as provided in this section is effective

a. against (1) the person who made it, to the extent of any interest held by him at the date thereof and (2) any person subsequently acquiring from him any such interest, without giving value or with actual notice of the making of the waiver or promise, to the extent of the interest so acquired; and

b. in favor of (1) the mortgagee or his assignee, (2) any other person to whom or for whose benefit it is expressed to be made, and (3) any person who, after the making of the waiver or promise, succeeds or is subrogated to the interest of either of them in the mortgage or otherwise acquires an interest in the enforcement of the mortgage.

4. Except as provided in subdivision five, no acknowledgment, waiver or promise has any effect to extend the time limited for commencement of an action to foreclose or mortgage for any greater time or in any other manner than that provided in this section, nor unless it is made as provided in this section.

5. This section does not change the requirements, or the effect with respect to the time limited for commencement of an action, of

a. a payment or part payment of the principal or interest secured by the mortgage, or

b. a stipulation made in an action or proceeding.

6. The term "real property" as used in this section is co–extensive in meaning with lands, tenements and hereditaments.

Section 17–107. Effect of part payment on time limited for foreclosure of a mortgage.

1. A payment on account of a mortgage indebtedness, or instalment thereof or interest thereon, which is effective to revive an action to recover such indebtedness, instalment or interest or to extend the time limited for such action, is also effective, between persons described in subdivision two of this section, to make the time limited for commencement of an action to foreclose the mortgage run from the date of payment, unless the payment is accompanied by written disclaimer of intention to affect the time limited for foreclosure of the mortgage.

2. A payment on account of the indebtedness secured by a mortgage of real property as defined in section 17–105, or a mortgage of a lease of real property, or on account of an instalment thereof or interest thereon, is effective as provided in this section:

a. as against (1) the person who made it, to the extent of any interest held by him at the date thereof, and (2) any person subsequently acquiring from him any such interest, without giving value or with actual notice of the making of the payment, to the extent of the interest so acquired; and

b. in favor of (1) the mortgagee or his assignee, and (2) any person who, after the date of the payment, succeeds or is subrogated to the interest of either of them in the mortgage or otherwise acquires an interest in the enforcement of the mortgage.

If the payment is made before expiration of the time limited for the commencement of the action, it is also effective against any subsequent purchaser of the interest of the person who made the payment, to the extent of the interest that the person who made the payment had at the time thereof.

3. No payment described in subdivision one of this section has any greater effect, with respect to the time limited for foreclosure of the mortgage, than that provided in this section.

ARTICLE 18

SAFETY IN SKIING CODE

Section 18–101. Legislative purpose.

The legislature hereby finds that alpine or downhill skiing is both a major recreational sport and a major industry within the state of New York. The legislature further finds: (1) that downhill skiing, like many other sports, contains inherent risks including, but not limited to, the risks of personal injury or death or property damage, which may be caused by variations in terrain or weather conditions; surface or subsurface snow, ice, bare spots or areas of thin cover, moguls, ruts, bumps; other persons using the facilities; and rocks, forest growth, debris, branches, trees, roots, stumps or other natural objects or man–made objects that are incidental to the provision or maintenance of a ski facility in New York state; (2) that downhill skiing, without established rules of conduct and care, may result in injuries to persons and property; (3) that it is appropriate, as well as in the public interest, to take such steps as are necessary to help reduce the risk of injury to downhill skiers from undue, unnecessary and unreasonable hazards; and (4) that it is also necessary and appropriate that skiers become apprised of, and understand, the risks inherent in the sport of skiing so that they may make an informed decision of whether or not to participate in skiing notwithstanding the risks. Therefore, the purpose and intent of this article is to establish a code of conduct for downhill skiers and ski area operators to minimize the risk of injury to persons engaged in the sport of downhill skiing and to promote safety in the downhill ski industry.

Added by Laws 1988, Ch. 711, eff. Nov. 1, 1988.

Section 18–102. Definitions.

The following words and phrases when used in this article shall have, unless the context clearly indicates otherwise, the meanings given to them in this section:

1. "Lift ticket" means any item issued by a ski area operator to any skier that is intended to be affixed to the outerwear of the skier, or otherwise displayed by a skier, to signify lawful entry upon and use of the passenger tramways or ski slopes or trails maintained by the ski area operator.

2. "Passenger tramway" means a mechanical device intended to transport skiers for the purpose of providing access to ski slopes and trails as defined by the commissioner of labor pursuant to section two hundred two–c or eight hundred sixty–seven of the labor law.

3. "Passenger" means a person in or on or being transported by a tramway.

4. "Ski area" means all ski slopes, ski trails and passenger tramways administered as a single enterprise within this state.

5. "Ski area operator" means a person, firm or corporation, and its agents and employees, having operational and administrative responsibility for any ski area, including any agency of the state, any political subdivision thereof, and any other governmental agency or instrumentality.

6. "Skier" means any person wearing a ski or skis and any person actually on a ski slope or trail located at a ski area, for the purpose of skiing.

7. "Ski slopes and trails" mean those areas designated by the ski area operator for skiing.

Added by Laws 1988, Ch. 711, eff. Nov. 1, 1988.

Section 18–103. Duties of ski area operators.

Every ski area operator shall have the following duties:

1. To equip all trail maintenance vehicles with such warning implements or devices as shall be specified by the commissioner of labor pursuant to section eight hundred sixty–seven of the labor law. Such implements or devices shall be present and operating whenever the vehicle is within the borders of any slope or trail.

2. To post in a location likely to be seen by all skiers signs of such size and color as will enable skiers to have knowledge of their responsibilities under this article.

3. To hold employee training sessions at least once before the beginning of each season, the contents of which shall be specified by the commissioner of labor upon the recommendation of the passenger tramway advisory council, as follows:

a. for operators of trail maintenance equipment concerning the safe operation of such vehicles in the ski area;

b. for passenger tramway attendants concerning the safe operation of passenger tramways;

c. for ski personnel charged with the responsibility of evacuating passengers from passenger tramways concerning proper evacuation techniques; and

d. for all other personnel charged with on–mountain maintenance, inspection or patrol duties as to methods to be used for summoning aid in emergencies.

4. To conspicuously mark with such implements as may be specified by the commissioner of labor pursuant to section eight hundred sixty–seven of the labor law, the location of such man–made obstructions as, but not limited to, snow–making equipment, electrical outlets, timing equipment, stanchions, pipes, or storage areas that are within the borders of the designated slope or trail, when the top of such obstruction is less than six feet above snow level.

5. To maintain in a central location at the ski area an information board or boards showing at a minimum the following:

a. the location of tramways, slopes or trails;

b. the status of each trail–open or closed;

c. the location of emergency communications or medical equipment and sites designated by the ski area operator for receipt of notice from skiers pursuant to subdivision thirteen of this section;

d. the relative degree of difficulty of each slope or trail (at a minimum easier, more difficult, most difficult); and

e. the general surface condition of each slope and trail as most recently recorded in the log required to be maintained by subdivision six of this section.

6. To inspect each open slope or trail that is open to the public within the ski area at least twice a day, and enter the results of such inspection in a log which shall be available for examination by the commissioner of labor. The log shall note:

a. the general surface conditions of such trail at the time of inspection (powder, packed powder, frozen granular, icy patches or icy surface, bare spots or other surface conditions);

b. the time of inspection and the name of the inspector;

c. the existence of any obstacles or hazards other than those which may arise from:

(i) skier use;

(ii) weather variations including freezing and thawing; or

(iii) mechanical failure of snow grooming or emergency equipment which may position such equipment within the borders of a slope or trail.

7. To develop and maintain a written policy consistent with the regulations of the commissioner of labor upon the advice of the passenger tramway advisory

council for situations involving the reckless conduct of skiers, which shall include, but not be limited to:

a. a definition of reckless conduct; and

b. procedures for approaching and warning skiers of reckless conduct and procedures for dealing with such skiers which may include the revocation of the lift tickets of such skiers.

8. To designate personnel to implement the ski area's policy on reckless conduct.

9. To report to the commissioner of labor by telephone within twenty–four hours any fatality or injury resulting in a fatality at the ski area.

10. To conspicuously post and maintain such ski area signage, including appropriate signage at the top of affected ski slopes and trails, notice of maintenance activities and for passenger tramways as shall be specified by the commissioner of labor pursuant to section two hundred two–c or eight hundred sixty–seven of the labor law.

11. To post in a conspicuous location at each lift line a sign, which shall indicate the degree of difficulty of trails served by that lift with signs as shall be specified by the commissioner of labor pursuant to section two hundred two–c or eight hundred sixty–seven of the labor law.

12. To ensure that lift towers located within the boundaries of any ski slope or trail are padded or otherwise protected and that no protruding metal or wood objects, such as ladders or steps, shall be installed on the uphill or side portion of lift towers within the borders of a ski slope or trail, unless such objects are below the snow line, at least six feet above it, or padded or otherwise protected with such devices as, but not limited to, the following:

a. commercially available tower padding;

b. air or foam filled bags;

c. hay bales encased in a waterproof cover; or

d. soft rope nets properly spaced from the tower.

13. To, within a reasonable amount of time after the inspection required by subdivision six of this section, conspicuously mark with such implements as may be specified by the commissioner of labor pursuant to section eight hundred sixty–seven of the labor law and to provide sufficient warning to skiers by such marking or remove such obstacles or hazards which are located within the boundaries of any ski slope or trail and were noted pursuant to paragraph c of subdivision six of this section; and to also conspicuously mark with such implements and provide such warning or remove such obstacles or hazards within a reasonable amount of time after receipt of notice by the ski area operator from any skier as to the presence of such obstacles or hazards when notice is given at sites designated by the ski area operator for such receipt and the locations of which are made known to skiers pursuant to paragraph c of subdivision five of this section.

14. To have present at all times when skiing activity is in progress, individuals properly and appropriately trained for the safe operation of on–slope vehicles; trail maintenance equipment; tramways; tramway evacuations; implementation of the reckless skier policy; first aid and outdoor rescue; and, to have present according to a schedule posted for access by skiers, by the ski area operator, personnel appropriately trained in the instruction of skiers and passengers in methods of risk reduction while using ski slopes and passenger tramways and the instruction of skiers with respect to the risks inherent in the sport.

Added by Laws 1988, Ch. 711, eff. Nov. 1, 1988; **amended** by Laws 1989, Ch. 322, eff. July 10, 1989.

Section 18–104. Duties of passengers.

All passengers shall have the following duties:

1. To familiarize themselves with the safe use of any tramway prior to its use;

2. To remain in the tramway if the operation of a passenger tramway, as defined pursuant to section two hundred two–c of the labor law, is interrupted for any reason, until instructions or aid are provided by the ski area operator;

3. To board or disembark from passenger tramways only at points or areas designated by the ski area operator;

4. Not to eject any objects or material from a passenger tramway;

5. To use restraint devices in accordance with posted instructions;

6. To wear retention straps or other devices to prevent runaway skis;

7. Not to interfere with the operation of a passenger tramway;

8. Not to place or caused to be placed on the uphill track of a surface lift any object which may interfere with its normal operation; and

9. Not to wear loose scarves, clothing or accessories or expose long hair which may become entangled with any part of the device.

Added by Laws 1988, Ch. 711, eff. Nov. 1, 1988.

Section 18–105. Duties of skiers.

All skiers shall have the following duties:

1. Not to ski in any area not designated for skiing;

2. Not to ski beyond their limits or ability to overcome variations in slope, trail configuration and surface or subsurface conditions which may be caused or altered by weather, slope or trail maintenance work by the ski area operator, or skier use;

3. To abide by the directions of the ski area operator;

4. To remain in constant control of speed and course at all times while skiing so as to avoid contact with plainly visible or clearly marked obstacles and with other skiers and passengers on surface operating tramways;

5. To familiarize themselves with posted information before skiing any slope or trail, including all information posted pursuant to subdivision five of section 18–103 of this article;

6. Not to cross the uphill track of any surface lift, except at points clearly designated by the ski area operator;

7. Not to ski on a slope or trail or portion thereof that has been designated as "closed" by the ski area operator;

8. Not to leave the scene of any accident resulting in personal injury to another party until such times as the ski area operator arrives, except for the purpose of summoning aid;

9. Not to overtake another skier in such a manner as to cause contact with the skier being overtaken and to yield the right–of–way to the skier being overtaken;

10. Not to willfully stop on any slope or trail where such stopping is likely to cause a collision with other skiers or vehicles;

11. To yield to other skiers when entering a trail or starting downhill;

12. To wear retention straps or other devices to prevent runaway skis;

13. To report any personal injury to the ski area operator before leaving the ski area; and

14. Not to willfully remove, deface, alter or otherwise damage signage, warning devices or implements, or other safety devices placed and maintained by the ski area operator pursuant to the requirements of section 18–103 of this article.

Added by Laws 1988, Ch. 711, eff. Nov. 1, 1988.

Section 18–106. Duties of skiers and ski area operators with respect to inherent risks.

It is recognized that skiing is a voluntary activity that may be hazardous regardless of all feasible safety measures that can be undertaken by ski area operators. Accordingly:

1. Ski area operators shall have the following additional duties:

a. To post at every point of sale or distribution of lift tickets, whether on or off the premises of the ski area operator, a conspicuous "Warning to Skiers" relative to the inherent risks of skiing in accordance with regulations promulgated by the commissioner of labor pursuant to subdivision four of section eight hundred sixty–seven of the labor law, and to imprint upon all lift tickets sold or distributed, such text and graphics as the commissioner of labor shall similarly specify, which shall conspicuously direct the attention of all skiers to the required "Warning to Skiers";

b. To post at every point of sale or distribution of lift tickets at a ski area notice to skiers and passengers that this article prescribes certain duties for skiers, passengers and ski area operators, and to make copies of this article in its entirety available without charge upon request to skiers and passengers in a central location at the ski area;

c. To make available at reasonable fees, as required by subdivision thirteen of section 18–103 of this article, instruction and education for skiers relative to the risks inherent in the sport and the duties prescribed for skiers by this article, and to conspicuously post notice of the times and places of availability of such instruction and education in locations where it is likely to be seen by skiers; and

d. To post notice to skiers of the right to a refund to the purchaser in the form and amount paid in the initial sale of any lift ticket returned to the ski area operator, intact and unused, upon declaration by such purchaser that he or she is unprepared or unwilling to ski due to the risks inherent in the sport or the duties imposed upon him or her by this article.

2. Skiers shall have the following additional duties to enable them to make informed decisions as to the advisability of their participation in the sport:

a. To seek out, read, review and understand, in advance of skiing, a "Warning to Skiers" as shall be defined pursuant to subdivision five of section eight hundred sixty–seven of the labor law, which shall be displayed and provided pursuant to paragraph a of subdivision one of this section; and

b. To obtain such education in the sport of skiing as the individual skier shall deem appropriate to his or her level of ability, including the familiarization with skills and duties necessary to reduce the risk of injury in such sport.

Added by Laws 1988, Ch. 711, eff. Oct. 1, 1988; **amended** by Laws 1989, Ch. 322, eff. Oct. 1, 1989.

Section 18–107. Construction.

Unless otherwise specifically provided in this article, the duties of skiers, passengers, and ski area operators shall be governed by common law.

Added by Laws 1988, Ch. 711, eff. Nov. 1, 1988.

Section 18–108. Severability.

If any provision of this article or the application thereof to any person or circumstances is held invalid, such invalidity shall not affect other provisions or applications of this article that can be given effect without the invalid provision or application, and to this end the provisions of this article are declared to be severable.

Added by Laws 1988, Ch. 711, eff. Nov. 1, 1988.

ARTICLE 18–A

SPECIFICATIONS OF LIABILITY FOR EMPLOYERS AND EMPLOYEES

Section 18–201. Specifications of liability for employers and employees.

1. As used in this section:

(A) "Person" means any individual, firm, company, partnership, joint venture, joint-stock association, corporation, association, trust or other legal entity.

(B) The words "employer", "employee", "employment", "compensation", "injury" and "death" shall have the same meaning as set forth in section two of the workers' compensation law.

(C) The terms "indemnity" and "contribution" shall not include a claim or cause of action for contribution or indemnification based upon a provision in a written contract entered into prior to the accident or occurrence by which the employer had expressly agreed to contribution to or indemnification of the claimant or person asserting the cause of action for the type of loss suffered.

2. The liability of an employer and his or her employees set forth in sections ten, eleven and twenty-nine of the workers' compensation law shall be exclusive and in place of any other liability whatsoever, to employees, their personal representatives, spouses, parents, dependents,distributees or any person otherwise entitled to recover damages, contribution or indemnity, at common law or otherwise, on account of injury or death or liability arising therefrom, except that if as employer fails to secure the payment of compensation for its injured employees and their dedendents as provided in section fifty of the workers' compensation law, an injured employee, or his or her legal representative in case death results from the injury, may, at his or her option, elect to claim compensation under the workers' compensation law, or to maintain an action in the courts for damages against the employer on account of such injury and in such an action it shall not be necessary to plead or prove freedom from contributory negligence nor may the defendant plead as a defense that the injury was caused by the negligence of a fellow servant nor that the employee assumed the risk of his or her employment, nor that the injury was due to the contributory negligence of the employee.

Added by Laws 1996, Ch. 635, effective September 10, 1996.

GOL

ARTICLE 19

LAWS REPEALED; EFFECTIVE DATE

Section 19–101. Laws repealed.

1. The following sections of the civil rights law are hereby repealed:

Section sixteen, as added by chapter one hundred fifty–seven of the laws of nineteen hundred twenty–one.

Section seventeen, as added by chapter eleven of the laws of nineteen hundred thirty–five.

2. The following section of the conservation law is hereby repealed:

Section three hundred seventy, as added by chapter eight hundred forty–two of the laws of nineteen hundred fifty–six.

3. The following sections of the debtor and creditor law are hereby repealed:

Sections two hundred thirty–one, two hundred thirty–two, two hundred thirty-three, two hundred thirty–four, two hundred thirty–five, two hundred thirty–six, two hundred thirty–seven, two hundred thirty–eight, and two hundred thirty-nine, as added by chapter eight hundred thirty–three of the laws of nineteen hundred twenty–eight;

Section two hundred forty, as amended by chapter three hundred ten of the laws of nineteen hundred sixty–two;

Section two hundred forty–three, as amended by chapter five hundred fifty-two of the laws of nineteen hundred sixty–two;

Section two hundred sixty, as added by chapter three hundred twenty–seven of the laws of nineteen hundred forty–one;

Section two hundred sixty–one, as amended by chapter four hundred five of the laws of nineteen hundred fifty–three.

4. The following sections of the domestic relations law are hereby repealed:

Section fifty–one, as last amended by chapter three hundred thirteen of the laws of nineteen hundred sixty–two;

Sections fifty–three, fifty–four, fifty–five, and fifty–six;

Section fifty–six–a, as added by chapter five hundred eighty of the laws of nineteen hundred fifty–nine;

Section fifty–seven, as amended by chapter six hundred sixty–nine of the laws of nineteen hundred thirty–seven;

Section sixty, as amended by chapter thirteen of the laws of nineteen hundred forty–one;

Section seventy–two;

Section seventy–three, as added by chapter seven hundred ninety–six of the laws of nineteen hundred thirty–five;

Section seventy–four, as added by chapter one hundred thirty–seven of the laws of nineteen hundred sixty–one.

Section seventy four–a, as added by chapter one hundred thirty–six of the laws of nineteen hundred sixty–one

5. The following sections of the general business law are hereby repealed:

Section eighty–nine–b, as added by chapter three hundred thirty–two of the laws of nineteen hundred forty–nine;

Sections two hundred twenty, two hundred twenty–one, two hundred twenty–two, two hundred twenty–three, two hundred twenty–four, two hundred twenty–five, two hundred twenty–six, two hundred twenty–seven, two hundred twenty–eight, two hundred twenty–nine, two hundred thirty, two hundred thirty–one, two hundred thirty–two, two hundred thirty–three, and two hundred thirty–four, as added by chapter four hundred twenty–two of the laws of nineteen hundred forty–eight;

Section two hundred thirty–five, as added by chapter seven hundred fifty–seven of the laws of nineteen hundred fifty–four;

Sections three hundred seventy and three hundred seventy–one;

Section three hundred seventy–two, as amended by chapter thirty–nine of the laws of nineteen hundred forty–one;

Section three hundred seventy–three, as amended by chapter nine hundred sixty of the laws of nineteen hundred sixty;

Section three hundred seventy–four, as last amended by chapter nine hundred sixty–eight of the laws of nineteen hundred fifty–seven;

Sections three hundred seventy–five, three hundred seventy–six, three hundred seventy–seven, and three hundred seventy–eight;

Section three hundred seventy–nine, as last amended by chapter five hundred fifty–two of the laws of nineteen hundred sixty–two;

Section three hundred seventy–nine–a, as added by chapter nine hundred seventy–four of the laws of nineteen hundred sixty;

Section three hundred eighty;

Section three hundred eighty–one, as amended by chapter thirty–nine of the laws of nineteen hundred forty–one;

Section three hundred eighty–two;

Section three hundred eighty–two–a, as added by chapter nine hundred thirty–nine of the laws of nineteen hundred twenty;

Section three hundred eighty–two–b, as added by chapter nine hundred forty of the laws of nineteen hundred twenty;

Section three hundred ninety–nine, as added by chapter seven hundred one of the laws of nineteen hundred fifty–three;

Section three hundred ninety–nine–a, as added by chapter five hundred seven of the laws of nineteen hundred sixty–one.

6. The following sections of the personal property law are hereby repealed:

Sections thirty–one and thirty–three, as amended;

Sections thirty–three–a and thirty–three–b, as amended by chapter five hundred eighty–eight of the laws of nineteen hundred forty–four;

Section thirty–three–c, as last amended by chapter eight hundred thirty–one of the laws of nineteen hundred fifty–two;

Section thirty–three–d, as added by chapter three hundred ten of the laws of nineteen hundred sixty–two;

Section thirty–four, as added by chapter nine hundred twenty–five of the laws of nineteen hundred sixty–one;

Section forty–one, as amended.

7. The following sections of the real property law are hereby repealed;

Section two hundred thirty, as last amended by chapter five hundred sixty–four of the laws of nineteen hundred sixty–one;

Section two hundred thirty–three, as last amended by chapter seventy–four of the laws of nineteen hundred sixty–one;

Section two hundred thirty–four, as added by chapter nine hundred seven of the laws of nineteen hundred thirty–seven;

Section two hundred thirty–five, as added by chapter seven hundred sixteen of the laws of nineteen hundred fifty–three;

Section two hundred forty–a, as added by chapter seven hundred thirty–one of the laws of nineteen hundred thirty–six;

Section two hundred forty–two;

Section two hundred fifty–one–a, as amended by chapter three hundred twelve of the laws of nineteen hundred sixty–two;

Section two hundred fifty–one–b, as added by chapter five hundred eighty–one of the laws of nineteen hundred sixty–one;

Section two hundred fifty–nine, as last amended by chapter one hundred ninety–eight of the laws of nineteen hundred forty–four;

Section two hundred fifty–nine–a, as added by chapter five hundred seventy–four of the laws of nineteen hundred thirty–three;

Section two hundred fifty–nine–b, as added by chapter six hundred forty–six of the laws of nineteen hundred sixty–two;

Section two hundred seventy–nine, as last amended by chapter five hundred eighty–eight of the laws of nineteen hundred forty–four;

Sections two hundred eighty and two hundred eighty–one, as amended by chapter five hundred eighty–eight of the laws of nineteen hundred forty–four;

Section two hundred eighty–two, as last amended by chapter eight hundred thirty–one of the laws of nineteen hundred fifty–two;

Section two hundred eighty–three, as added by chapter two hundred fifty of the laws of nineteen hundred forty–four.

8. The following sections of the real property actions and proceedings law are hereby repealed:

Subdivision three of section thirteen hundred twenty–five, as added by chapter three hundred twelve of the laws of nineteen hundred sixty–two;

Section thirteen hundred eighty–one, as added by chapter three hundred twelve of the laws of nineteen hundred sixty–two.

Amended by Laws 1963, Ch. 664, eff. Sept. 27, 1964.

Section 19–103. Effective date.

This act shall take effect September twenty–seventh, nineteen hundred sixty–four.

LOCATIONS FOR LOCAL FILINGS

COUNTY CLERK	ADDRESS AND TELEPHONE NUMBER
Albany County Clerk	Court House, Rm. 128, 16 Eagle Street, Albany, New York 12207 (518) 487-5100
Allegany County Clerk	7 Court Street, Belmont, New York 14813 (716) 268-9270
Broome County Clerk	P.O. Box 2062, Binghamton, New York 13902-2062 (607) 778-2451
Cattaraugus County Clerk	County Office Building, 303 Court Street, Little Valley, New York 14755 (716) 938-9111
Cayuga County Clerk	160 Genesee Street, Auburn, New York 13021 (315) 253-1271
Chautauqua County Clerk	P.O. Box 170, Mayville, New York 14757 (716) 753-4331
Chemung County Clerk	210 Lake Street, P.O. Box 588, Elmira, New York 14902-0588 (607) 737-2920
Chenango County Clerk	5 Court Street, Norwich, New York 13815 (607) 337-1451
Clinton County Clerk	County Government Center, 137 Margaret Street, Plattsburgh, New York 12901 (518) 565-4700
Columbia County Clerk	560 Warrant St., Hudson, New York 12534 (518) 828-3339
Cortland County Clerk	46 Greenbush Street, Suite 101, Cortland, New York 13045-3702 (607) 753-5021
Delaware County Clerk	P.O. Box 426, Delhi, New York 13753 (607) 746-2123

Local Filings

COUNTY CLERK	ADDRESS AND TELEPHONE NUMBER
Dutchess County Clerk	22 Market Street, Poughkeepsie, New York 12601 (914) 486-2120
Erie County Clerk	25 Delaware Ave., Buffalo, New York 14202 (716) 858-8785
Essex County Clerk	100 Court Street, P.O. Box 247, Elizabethtown, New York 12932 (518) 873-3600
Franklin County Clerk	63 W. Main St., P.O. Box 70, Malone, New York 12953 (518) 481-1681
Fulton County Clerk	223 W. Main St., P.O. Box 485, Johnstown, New York 12095 (518) 736-5555
Genesee County Clerk	P.O. Box 379, Batavia, New York 14021-0379 (716) 344-2550
Greene County Clerk	P.O. Box 446, Catskill, New York 12414 (518) 943-2050
Hamilton County Clerk	P.O. Box 204, Route 8, Lake Pleasant, New York 12108 (518) 548-7111
Herkimer County Clerk	County Office Building, 109 Mary Street, Suite 1111, Herkimer, New York 13350 (315) 867-1133
Jefferson County Clerk	175 Arsenal St., Watertown, New York 13601 (315) 785-3081
Lewis County Clerk	P.O. Box 232, Lowville, New York 13367 (315) 376-5333
Livingston County Clerk	Livingston County Government Center, Room 201, 6 Court St., Geneseo, New York 14454 (716) 243-7010
Madison County Clerk	P.O. Box 668, Wampsville, New York 13163 (315) 366-2261

COUNTY CLERK	ADDRESS AND TELEPHONE NUMBER
Monroe County Clerk	39 W. Main St., County Office Building, Room 101, Rochester, New York 14614 (716) 428-5151
Montgomery County Clerk	P.O. Box 1500, County Office Building, Fonda, New York 12068 (518) 853-8115
Nassau County Clerk	240 Old Country Rd., Mineola, New York 11501 (516) 571-2663
Niagara County Clerk	P.O. Box 461, Lockport, New York 14095-0461 (716) 439 7022
Oneida County Clerk	800 Park Ave., Utica, New York 13501 (315) 798-5775
Onondaga County Clerk	Room 200 Court House, 401 Montgomery St., Syracuse, New York 13202 (315) 435-2226
Ontario County Clerk	20 Ontario St., Canandaigua, New York 14424 (716) 396-4200
Orange County Clerk	255-275 Main St., Government Center, Goshen, New York 10924 (914) 294-5151
Orleans County Clerk	Court House Square, 3 S. Main St., Albion, New York 14411-1498 (716) 589-5334
Oswego County Clerk	46 E. Bridge St., Oswego, New York 13126 (315) 349-8385
Otsego County Clerk	P.O. Box 710, Cooperstown, New York 13326 (607) 547-4276
Putnam County Clerk	40 Gleneida Ave., Carmel, New York 10512 (914) 225-3641 ext. 307
Rensselaer County Clerk	Court House, 105 3rd Street, Troy, New York 12180 (518) 270-4090
Richmond County Clerk	130 Stuiveysant Place, Staten Island, New York 10301 (718) 390-5386

Local Filings

COUNTY CLERK	ADDRESS AND TELEPHONE NUMBER
Rockland County Clerk	27 New Hempstead Rd., New City, New York 10956 (914) 638-5070
St. Lawrence County Clerk	48 Court St., Canton, New York 13617 (315) 379-2237
Saratoga County Clerk	40 McMaster St., Ballston Spa, New York 12020 (518) 885-2213
Schenectady County Clerk	Third Floor, 620 State St., Schenectady, New York 12305 (518) 388-4220
Schoharie County Clerk	P.O. Box 549, Schoharie, New York 12157 (518) 295-8316
Schuyler County Clerk	105 9th St., Unit 8, Watkins Glen, New York 14891 (607) 535-8133
Seneca County Clerk	County Office Building, 1 DiPronio Dr., Waterloo, New York 13165 (315) 539-5655 ext. 2044
Steuben County Clerk	County Office Building, 3 E. Pullteney Square, Bath, New York 14810 (607) 776-9631 ext. 3210
Suffolk County Clerk	310 Center Dr., Riverhead, New York 11901 (516) 852-2000
Sullivan County Clerk	Sullivan Government Center, County Clerk Office, 100 North St., Monticello, New York 12701 (914) 794-3000, ext. 5012
Tioga County Clerk	P.O. Box 307, 16 Court St., Owego, New York 13827 (607) 687-8660
Tompkins County Clerk	320 N. Tioga St., Ithaca, New York 14850 (607) 274-5431
Ulster County Clerk	P.O. Box 1800, Kingston, New York 12402 (914) 340-3000 ext. 3288
Warren County Clerk	Warren County Municipal Center, 1340 State Route 9, Lake George, New York 12845 (518) 761-6429

COUNTY CLERK	ADDRESS AND TELEPHONE NUMBER
Washington County Clerk	383 Broadway, Building A, Fort Edward, New York 12828 (518) 746-2170
Wayne County Clerk	9 Pearl St., P.O. Box 608, Lyons, New York 14489-0608 (315) 946-5870
Westchester County Clerk	110 Dr. Martin Luther King Blvd., White Plains, New York 10601 (914) 285-3098
Wyoming County Clerk	143 N. Main St., Warsaw, New York 14569 (716) 786-8810
Yates County Clerk	110 Court St., Penn Yan, New York 14527 (315) 536-5120

NEW YORK CITY REGISTERS

Bronx County Office	851 Grand Concourse, Rm 118, Bronx, New York 10451 (718) 590-3646
Kings County Office	360 Adams St., Brooklyn, New York 11201 (718) 643-5897
New York County Office	60 Centre St., New York, New York 10007 (212) 374-8361
Queens County Office	88-11 Sutphin Blvd., Jamaica, New York 11435 (718) 520-3137
Richmond County Office	(See Richmond County Clerk)

INDEX

[References are to Uniform Commercial Code sections and General Obligations Law sections (designated by GOL).]

Index

[References are to Uniform Commercial Code sections and General Obligations Law sections (designated by GOL).]

B

[References are to Uniform Commercial Code sections and General Obligations Law sections (designated by GOL).]

[References are to Uniform Commercial Code sections and General Obligations Law sections (designated by GOL).]

[References are to Uniform Commercial Code sections and General Obligations Law sections (designated by GOL).]

Index

[References are to Uniform Commercial Code sections and General Obligations Law sections (designated by GOL).]

[References are to Uniform Commercial Code sections and General Obligations Law sections (designated by GOL).]

Index

[References are to Uniform Commercial Code sections and General Obligations Law sections (designated by GOL).]

[References are to Uniform Commercial Code sections and General Obligations Law sections (designated by GOL).]

[References are to Uniform Commercial Code sections and General Obligations Law sections (designated by GOL).]

[References are to Uniform Commercial Code sections and General Obligations Law sections (designated by GOL).]

Index

[References are to Uniform Commercial Code sections and General Obligations Law sections (designated by GOL).]

[References are to Uniform Commercial Code sections and General Obligations Law sections (designated by GOL).]

[References are to Uniform Commercial Code sections and General Obligations Law sections (designated by GOL).]

[References are to Uniform Commercial Code sections and General Obligations Law sections (designated by GOL).]

Index

[References are to Uniform Commercial Code sections and General Obligations Law sections (designated by GOL).]

[References are to Uniform Commercial Code sections and General Obligations Law sections (designated by GOL).]

Index

[References are to Uniform Commercial Code sections and General Obligations Law sections (designated by GOL).]

L

[References are to Uniform Commercial Code sections and General Obligations Law sections (designated by GOL).]

Index

[References are to Uniform Commercial Code sections and General Obligations Law sections (designated by GOL).]

[References are to Uniform Commercial Code sections and General Obligations Law sections (designated by GOL).]

[References are to Uniform Commercial Code sections and General Obligations Law sections (designated by GOL).]

[References are to Uniform Commercial Code sections and General Obligations Law sections (designated by GOL).]

[References are to Uniform Commercial Code sections and General Obligations Law sections (designated by GOL).]

[References are to Uniform Commercial Code sections and General Obligations Law sections (designated by GOL).]

[References are to Uniform Commercial Code sections and General Obligations Law sections (designated by GOL).]

[References are to Uniform Commercial Code sections and General Obligations Law sections (designated by GOL).]

[References are to Uniform Commercial Code sections and General Obligations Law sections (designated by GOL).]

[References are to Uniform Commercial Code sections and General Obligations Law sections (designated by GOL).]

R

Index

[References are to Uniform Commercial Code sections and General Obligations Law sections (designated by GOL).]

S

[References are to Uniform Commercial Code sections and General Obligations Law sections (designated by GOL).]

[References are to Uniform Commercial Code sections and General Obligations Law sections (designated by GOL).]

[References are to Uniform Commercial Code sections and General Obligations Law sections (designated by GOL).]

[References are to Uniform Commercial Code sections and General Obligations Law sections (designated by GOL).]

[References are to Uniform Commercial Code sections and General Obligations Law sections (designated by GOL).]

[References are to Uniform Commercial Code sections and General Obligations Law sections (designated by GOL).]

U

[References are to Uniform Commercial Code sections and General Obligations Law sections (designated by GOL).]

V

W

[References are to Uniform Commercial Code sections and General Obligations Law sections (designated by GOL).]